Fifteenth Edition

The LAW and BUSINESS ADMINISTRATION in CANADA

J. E. SMYTH
LATE PROFESSOR OF COMMERCE,
FACULTY OF MANAGEMENT STUDIES,
UNIVERSITY OF TORONTO

D. A. SOBERMAN
LATE PROFESSOR OF LAW,
FACULTY OF LAW,
QUEEN'S UNIVERSITY

A. J. EASSON
LATE PROFESSOR OF LAW,
FACULTY OF LAW,
QUEEN'S UNIVERSITY

S. A. McGILL
PROFESSOR OF BUSINESS LAW,
LAZARIDIS SCHOOL OF BUSINESS & ECONOMICS,
WILFRID LAURIER UNIVERSITY

Pearson Canada Inc., 26 Prince Andrew Place, North York, Ontario M3C 2H4.

Copyright © 2020, 2016, 2013 Pearson Canada Inc. All rights reserved.

Printed in the United States of America. This publication is protected by copyright, and permission should be obtained from the publisher prior to any prohibited reproduction, storage in a retrieval system, or transmission in any form or by any means, electronic, mechanical, photocopying, recording, or otherwise. For information regarding permissions, request forms, and the appropriate contacts, please contact Pearson Canada's Rights and Permissions Department by visiting www.pearson.com/ca/en/contact-us/permissions.html.

Attributions of third-party content appear on the appropriate page within the text. Cover image: © Billion Photos/Shutterstock and © Mega Pixel/Shutterstock

PEARSON, ALWAYS LEARNING, and MyLab are exclusive trademarks owned by Pearson Canada Inc. or its affiliates in Canada and/or other countries.

Unless otherwise indicated herein, any third party trademarks that may appear in this work are the property of their respective owners and any references to third party trademarks, logos, or other trade dress are for demonstrative or descriptive purposes only. Such references are not intended to imply any sponsorship, endorsement, authorization, or promotion of Pearson Canada products by the owners of such marks, or any relationship between the owner and Pearson Canada or its affiliates, authors, licensees, or distributors.

If you purchased this book outside the United States or Canada, you should be aware that it has been imported without the approval of the publisher or the author.

9780134841298

9 2023

Library and Archives Canada Cataloguing in Publication

Smyth, J. E. (James Everil), 1920-1983, author
   The law and business administration in Canada / J.E. Smyth, Late Professor of Commerce, Faculty of Management Studies, University of Toronto, D.A. Soberman, Late Professor of Law, Faculty of Law, Queen's University, A.J. Easson, Late Professor of Law, Faculty of Law, Queen's University, S.A. McGill, (School of Business & Economics, Wilfrid Laurier University. -- Fifteen edition.

ISBN 978-0-13-484129-8 (hardcover)

   1. Commercial law--Canada--Textbooks. 2. Commercial law--Canada--Cases. 3. Textbooks. I. Soberman, D. A., author II. Easson, A. J., author III. McGill, S. A. (Shelley A.), author IV. Title.

KE919.S69 2019   346.7107   C2018-906227-4
KF889.S69 2019

Brief Table of Contents

Part 1 The Law in Its Social and Business Context 1
- Chapter 1   Law, Society, and Business 1
- Chapter 2   The Machinery of Justice 21
- Chapter 3   Government Regulation of Business 47

Part 2 Torts 75
- Chapter 4   The Law of Torts 75
- Chapter 5   Professional Liability: The Legal Challenges 101

Part 3 Contracts 124
- Chapter 6   Formation of a Contract: Offer and Acceptance 124
- Chapter 7   Formation of a Contract: Consideration and Intention 145
- Chapter 8   Formation of a Contract: Capacity to Contract and Legality of Object 163
- Chapter 9   Contract Issues: Mistake and Misrepresentation 188
- Chapter 10   Writing and Interpretation 207
- Chapter 11   Privity of Contract and the Assignment of Contractual Rights 232
- Chapter 12   The Discharge of Contracts 254
- Chapter 13   Breach of Contract and Remedies 274

Part 4 Special Types of Contracts 298
- Chapter 14   Sale of Goods and Consumer Contracts 298
- Chapter 15   Bailment and Leasing 327
- Chapter 16   Insurance and Guarantee 348
- Chapter 17   Agency and Franchising 368
- Chapter 18   The Contract of Employment 393
- Chapter 19   Banking and Negotiable Instruments 422

Part 5 Property 447
- Chapter 20   Intellectual Property 447
- Chapter 21   Interests in Land and Their Transfer 483
- Chapter 22   Landlord and Tenant 508
- Chapter 23   Mortgages of Land and Real Estate Transactions 536

Part 6 Business Organizations: Their Forms, Operation, and Management 563
- Chapter 24   Sole Proprietorships and Partnerships 563
- Chapter 25   The Nature of a Corporation and Its Formation 588
- Chapter 26   Corporate Governance: The Internal Affairs of Corporations 611
- Chapter 27   Corporate Governance: External Responsibilities 645

Part 7 Creditors and Debtors 670
- Chapter 28   Secured Transactions 670
- Chapter 29   Creditors' Rights 692

Part 8 The Modern Legal Environment for Business 718
- Chapter 30   International Business Transactions 718
- Chapter 31   Electronic Commerce 749
- Chapter 32   Privacy 776

Detailed Table of Contents

About the Authors   xvii
Preface   xviii
Authors' Acknowledgments   xxiv
Table of Statutes   xxv
Table of Cases   xxx

Part 1 The Law in Its Social and Business Context   1

1 Law, Society, and Business   1
The Role of Law   2
How Is Law Defined?   2
How Is Law Linked to Morals and Ethics?   2
Is It Ever Right to Break the Law?   3
How Does Law Influence Behaviour?   4
Law and Business   5
The Significance of Law for the Business Environment   5
Law and International Business   5
Legal Risk Management   6
Developing a Legal Risk Management Plan   6
Strategies to Manage Legal Risks   7
The Legal Profession   7
Business and the Legal Profession   9
Law and Business Ethics   10
Business Ethics   10
Codes of Conduct   11
Who Makes Law?   11
The Courts and Legislation   12
Federalism and the Constitution   12
The *Charter of Rights and Freedoms*   14
The Rights and Freedoms Protected by the *Charter*   16
The Significance of the *Charter* for Business   16
Challenging the Application of a Statute   18
Questions for Review   20

2 The Machinery of Justice   21
Classifying Law   22
Who Makes Law?   22
Two Legal Systems: Civil Law and Common Law   22
Regions of the World under Each System   22
The Need for Consistency and Predictability   23
Common Law: The Theory of Precedent   24
Certainty Versus Flexibility   24
Accommodating Change   24
The Sources of Law   25
Legislation: Government Made Law   25
Case Law: Judge-Made Law   27
The System of Courts   29
The Courts of First Instance—Trial Courts   29
The Court of Appeal   29
Final Court of Appeal—The Supreme Court   30
The System of Courts in Canada   30
The Provincial Court System   31
The Federal Court System   32
The Supreme Court of Canada   32
Procedural Law: Using the Courts   33
Who May Sue?   34
Standing to Sue   34
Class Actions   34
Procedure before Trial   35
The Trial   36
Judgment   37
Appeals   37
Costs   37
The Economics of Civil Litigation   38
Contingent Fees   39
Settlement Out of Court   40
Alternative Dispute Resolution   41
Strategies to Manage the Legal Risks   45
Questions for Review   45
Cases and Problems   46

3 Government Regulation of Business   47
The Legal Framework for Doing Business in Canada   48
Challenging Government Regulation of Business   48
Jurisdiction over "Business Activities" under the Constitution   48
Business Regulations that Offend the *Charter*   51
Regulation Improperly Applied in the Circumstances   52
Competition   54
The *Competition Act*   54
Conspiracies   55
Monopolizing   57
Mergers   60
Consumer Protection   61
Why Is Consumer Protection Legislation Necessary?   61
Principal Types of Consumer Legislation   62
Environmental Protection   68
The Legislative Framework   68
Environmental Impact Assessment Review   70
Enforcement and Liability   70

v

Strategies to Manage the Legal Risks 71
Questions for Review 72
Cases and Problems 72

Part 2 Torts 75

4 The Law of Torts 75
The Development of Tort Law 76
The Basis for Liability 76
Fault 76
Strict Liability 77
Public Policy 77
Vicarious Liability 78
Intentional Torts 79
Assault and Battery 79
Nuisance 79
False Imprisonment and Malicious Prosecution 80
Defamation 81
Other Intentional Torts Related to Business 82
Unintentional Torts 84
Negligence 84
Elements of Negligence 84
Defences to Negligence: The Plaintiff's Own Conduct 89
The Relevance of Insurance 90
Product Liability 90
Inherently Dangerous Products 92
Occupier's Liability 94
Remedies 96
Strategies to Manage the Legal Risks 98
Questions for Review 98
Cases and Problems 99

5 Professional Liability: The Legal Challenges 101
Professional Liability: The Challenge 102
Liability of Professionals 102
Contracts 102
Fiduciary Duty 103
Tort Liability 105
Statutory Liability 106
Choosing a Cause of Action 107
Tort Liability for Inaccurate Statements 108
Fraudulent Misrepresentation 108
Negligent Misrepresentation 108
Proving Negligent Misrepresentation 109
The Duty of Care—Special Relationship 109
Accuracy of the Statement 112
The Standard of Care for Professionals 112
Reliance and Detriment 114
The Role of Professional Organizations 115
Responsibilities and Powers 115
Codes of Conduct 116
Discipline 117
Conflict of Duty toward Clients, the Profession, and the Courts 117

Multi-Disciplinary Partnerships 118
Strategies to Manage the Legal Risks 119
Questions for Review 120
Cases and Problems 120

Part 3 Contracts 124

6 Formation of a Contract: Offer and Acceptance 124
The Role of Contract Law 125
The Nature of a Contract 125
The Nature of an Offer 125
The Communication of an Offer 126
Written Offers 127
Standard Form Contracts: Their Risks and Benefits 127
Notice of Terms 128
The Lapse and Revocation of an Offer 129
Lapse 129
Revocation 130
Options 130
Rejection and Counter-offer by the Offeree 131
The Elements of Acceptance 132
Positive and Unconditional 132
Communication to the Offeror 132
The Moment of Formation 133
Transactions Between Parties at a Distance from Each Other 135
Method of Acceptance 135
Methods of Revocation 136
Determining the Jurisdiction Where a Contract Is Made 136
Unilateral and Bilateral Contracts 137
Bilateral: Offer of a Promise for a Promise 137
Unilateral: Offer of a Promise for an Act 137
Formation of Internet Contracts 138
Uncertainty in the Wording of an Offer 139
Strategies to Manage the Legal Risks 140
Questions for Review 141
Cases and Problems 141

7 Formation of a Contract: Consideration and Intention 145
The Meaning of Consideration 146
Gratuitous Promises 146
Adequacy of Consideration 147
Motive Contrasted with Consideration: Past Consideration 148
Relation Between Existing Legal Duty and Consideration 148
Gratuitous Reduction of a Debt 150
Equitable Estoppel 151
Estoppel Based on Fact 152
Injurious Reliance 153

The Effect of a Request for Goods or Services 155
The Use of a Seal 155
Intention to Create Legal Relations 157
Strategies to Manage the Legal Risks 158
Questions for Review 159
Cases and Problems 160

8 Formation of a Contract: Capacity to Contract and Legality of Object 163

The Burden of Proving Essential Elements of a Contract 164
The Meaning of Capacity to Contract 164
Limited Capacity 164
Minors (or Infants) 164
Other Persons of Diminished Contractual Capacity 167
Corporations 167
Labour Unions, Associations, and Other Organizations 168
Aboriginal Peoples 169
The Role of Legality in the Formation of a Contract 170
The Difference Between Void and Illegal Contracts 170
Contracts Affected by Statute 171
Significance of the Wording of a Statute 171
Examples of Contracts Void by Statute 171
Examples of Statutes Affecting Public Policy 172
Examples of Agreements Illegal by Statute 174
Examples of Agreements Made Legal by Statute 175
Contracts Illegal by the Common Law and Public Policy 176
The Common Law 176
Public Policy 177
Agreements in Restraint of Trade 178
Strategies to Manage the Legal Risks 182
Questions for Review 183
Cases and Problems 184

9 Contract Issues: Mistake and Misrepresentation 188

Setting Aside a Contract 189
The Narrow Meaning of Mistake 189
Void and Voidable Contracts 189
Mistakes About the Terms 191
Words Used Inadvertently 191
Errors in Recording an Agreement 191
Misunderstandings About the Meanings of Words 192
Mistakes About the Subject Matter 193
Mistake About the Existence of the Subject Matter of a Contract 193
Mistake About the Value of the Subject Matter 193
Mistakes About the Identity of a Party to a Contract 194
Mistakes About the Nature of a Signed Document 196
Non Est Factum 196
Misrepresentation 196
Contract Versus Tort 196
Consequences of Misrepresentation in Contracts 197
Misrepresentation by Silence or Omission 198
Undue Influence 199
Burden of Proof 200
Arrangements Involving Spouses 200
Importance of Independent Legal Advice 201
Consumer Protection 201
Duress 202
Strategies to Manage the Legal Risks 203
Questions for Review 203
Cases and Problems 204

10 Writing and Interpretation 207

The Distinction Between Substance and Form 208
The Benefits of a Written Record 208
Legislation Dealing with Writing 208
The *Statute of Frauds* 209
The Types of Contracts Covered by the *Statute of Frauds* 209
Requirements for a Written Memorandum 212
Consequences for Contracts Within Its Scope 213
What Constitutes a Sale of Goods for the Purposes of the Writing Requirement? 215
Evidence That Satisfies the Act 216
When Both Acts Apply 216
Consumer Protection Legislation 217
The Interpretation of Express Terms 219
The Goal of the Courts: To Give Validity to Contracts 219
Legal Principles of Interpretation 219
General Approach to Interpretation 220
Special Usage of Words 220
Conflicting Testimony and Credibility 220
Special Contracts or Clauses 221
The Parol Evidence Rule 221
The Meaning of Parol Evidence 221
The Meaning of the Parol Evidence Rule 222
Exceptions to the Parol Evidence Rule 222
Implied Terms as a Method of Interpretation 224
Terms Established by Custom or Statute 225
Reasonable Expectation of the Parties 226
Strategies to Manage the Legal Risks 227
Questions for Review 228
Cases and Problems 228

11 Privity of Contract and the Assignment of Contractual Rights 232

Privity of Contract 233
Scope of Contractual Rights and Duties 233
Comparison with Rights and Duties in Tort 234
Tort Liability and Vicarious Performance 234
Exceptions to the Privity of Contract Rule 236
Trusts 236
Insurance 237
The Undisclosed Principal 237
Contracts Concerning Land 237
Express Language in the Contract 237
Assignment of Rights 239
The Nature of an Assignment 239
The Importance of Assignments 240
The Role of Equity 241
Equitable Assignments 241
Assignment of Part of a Debt 241
Statutory Assignments 243
Reform 243
The Requirements of the Statute 243
Notice to the Promisor 243
The Effect of Notice on the Promisor 243
The Effect of Notice from Multiple Assignees 244
The Assignee's Title 244
An Assignee "Takes Subject to the Equities" 244
The Right to Set Off 245
Assignments by Operation of Law 247
Death 247
Bankruptcy 247
Negotiable Instruments 247
Their Nature and Uses 247
Negotiability Compared with Assignability 248
Commercial Importance of Negotiability 249
Currency 250
Strategies to Manage the Legal Risks 251
Questions for Review 251
Cases and Problems 252

12 The Discharge of Contracts 254

The Ways in Which a Contract May Be Discharged 255
Discharge by Performance 255
The Nature of Discharge by Performance 255
Tender of Performance 255
Discharge by Agreement 255
Waiver 255
Substituted Agreement 256
A Contract Provides for Its Own Dissolution 257
Discharge by Frustration 260
Doctrine of Frustration 260
Self-Induced Frustration 263
The Effect of Frustration 264
Discharge by Operation of Law 267

Strategies to Manage the Legal Risks 268
Questions for Review 269
Cases and Problems 269

13 Breach of Contract and Remedies 274

Implications of Breach 275
How Breach May Occur 276
Express Repudiation 276
One Party Renders Performance Impossible 278
Failure of Performance 279
Degree of Failure 279
Doctrine of Substantial Performance 280
Duty of Honesty in Performance 280
Overperformance 280
Exemption Clauses 281
Purpose 281
Analytical Approach 281
Types of Remedies 283
Damages 283
The Purpose of an Award of Damages 283
Prerequisites for an Award of Damages 284
The Measurement of Damages 285
Liquidated Damages 285
Nominal Damages 286
Types of Damages 286
Expectation Damages 286
Consequential Damages 287
General Damages 288
Reliance Damages 288
Punitive Damages 288
Challenges in Measuring Damages 289
Mental Anguish 289
Cost of Performance Versus Economic Loss 290
Equitable Remedies 291
Reasons for the Intervention of Equity 291
Prerequisites for an Equitable Remedy 291
Specific Performance 291
Injunction 292
Rescission 292
Quantum Meruit 293
Methods of Enforcing Judgments 293
Strategies to Manage the Legal Risks 295
Questions for Review 295
Cases and Problems 296

Part 4 Special Types of Contracts 298

14 Sale of Goods and Consumer Contracts 298

The *Sale of Goods Act* 299
History of the *Sale of Goods Act* 299
Contracts of Sale 299

Goods   300
Ownership and Possession   301
Terms in a Contract of Sale   302
The *Caveat Emptor* Principle   302
Statutory Protection for the Buyer:
Implied Terms   302
Exemption Clauses   307
Payment   309
Delivery   309
Risk of Loss before Delivery   309
Title to Goods   310
Who May Pass Title?   310
When Does Title Pass?   311
Bills of Lading   311
Remedies of the Seller   311
Lien   311
Repossession   312
Resale   312
Damages for Non-Acceptance   312
Action for the Price   313
Retention of Deposit   313
The Seller's Liability   314
Breach of a Term   314
Wrongful Withholding or Disposition by the
Seller   314
Remedies of the Buyer   315
Consumer Contracts   316
Consumer Protection   316
**Business Sales Tactics Targeting
Consumers   316**
Pressure Selling   316
Unsolicited Goods   317
Telemarketing   317
Terms in Consumer Contracts   318
Legislated Terms   318
Exemption Clauses   319
Repossession   319
Arbitration and Class Actions   319
Severance   320
Financing Arrangements and Disclosure of the True
Cost of Credit   320
Consumer Remedies   321
Strategies to Manage the Legal Risks   322
Questions for Review   323
Cases and Problems   323

15 Bailment and Leasing   327
Bailment   328
Definition   328
Nature of Bailment   328
Sub-Bailment   329
Rights and Duties of a Bailee   330
Liability under Contract and Tort   330
The Standard of Care   331
Rights and Remedies   332

Lien   332
The Right of Sale   333
Special Types of Bailment   333
Storage and Safekeeping   333
Repairs and Work on a Chattel   334
Transportation   334
Innkeepers   336
Pledge or Pawn   337
Leasing   337
Types of Chattel Lease   338
Operating Leases   338
Purchase Leases   338
Security and Finance Leases   339
Sale-and-Leaseback   340
Reasons for Chattel Leasing   340
Common Terms in Chattel Leases   340
Duration   341
Rent   341
Insurance and Other Costs Payable by the Lessee   341
Purchase Option   341
Consent to Assignment (Sub-Bailment)   341
Early Termination—Minimum Payment   342
Implied Terms   342
Rights of the Parties   343
The Lessor   343
The Lessee   343
Strategies to Manage the Legal Risks   344
Questions for Review   345
Cases and Problems   345

16 Insurance and Guarantee   348
**Insurance and the Management of Legal
Risk   349**
Insurance Terminology   349
Regulation of Insurance Business   350
Types of Insurance   351
Insurance against Loss or Damage   351
Insurance against Liability   352
Comprehensive Insurance   352
Special Aspects of Insurance Contracts   353
Legality of Objects—Wrongful Act of the
Insured   353
Insurable Interest   354
Formation of the Contract   355
Renewal   355
Interpreting Terms of the Contract   356
Good Faith, Fairness, and Disclosure   357
Subrogation   359
Recovery   359
Assignment   360
Guarantee   360
The Nature of a Guarantee   360
Continuing Guarantee   362
Consideration   362
Discharge of Guarantee   363

Rights of the Guarantor on Default 363
Requirement of Writing 364
Strategies to Manage the Legal Risks 364
Questions for Review 365
Cases and Problems 365

17 Agency and Franchising 368
Defining Agency 369
Creation of an Agency Relationship 369
By Agreement 370
Other Ways to Create an Agency Relationship 370
Duties Owed by an Agent to the Principal 371
Duty to Comply with the Agency Agreement 371
Duty of Care 371
Personal Performance 371
Good Faith 371
Duties Owed by the Principal to the Agent 372
The Authority of the Agent 373
Actual Authority 373
Apparent Authority 374
Ratification 375
Rights and Liability of Principal and Agent 377
The Principal Alone Is Liable on the Contract 377
The Agent Alone Is Liable on the Contract 378
Either the Principal or the Agent May Be Held Liable on the Contract 378
Rights of the Undisclosed Principal 378
Liability for Torts 379
Breach of Warranty of Authority 380
Terminating an Agency Relationship 381
Franchising 381
The Nature of Franchising 381
Contents of a Typical Franchising Agreement 382
Legal Relationships Created by Franchising 385
Various Franchise Models 386
Franchise Legislation 386
Strategies to Manage the Legal Risks 388
Questions for Review 389
Cases and Problems 390

18 The Contract of Employment 393
Development of Employment Law 394
Relationship of Employer and Employee 394
Compared with Agency 394
Compared with Contractors 395
Employment Relationship at Common Law 396
The Employer's Liability to Third Persons 396
Liability in Contract 396
Liability in Tort 396
Notice of Termination of Individual Employment Contracts 398
Express Term in the Contract 398
Implied Term of Reasonable Notice 398
Length of Reasonable Notice 399

Dismissal without Notice 400
Misconduct 400
Disobedience 401
Incompetence 401
Illness 401
Discovery of Cause 402
Progressive Discipline 402
Adverse Economic Conditions 403
Wrongful Dismissal 403
Damages 403
Mitigation 404
Reinstatement 404
Employee Welfare Legislation 406
Background 406
Federal and Provincial Jurisdiction 406
Employee Rights 407
Regulation of Working Conditions 410
Employment Insurance 411
Workers' Compensation 411
Collective Bargaining 413
The Process 413
Content of a Collective Agreement 413
Labour Disputes 414
Types of Disputes 414
Legislative Regulation of Dispute Resolution 414
Implications of the Collective Agreement for the Individual Employee 415
The Legal Status of Trade Unions 416
Strategies to Manage the Legal Risks 417
Questions for Review 418
Cases and Problems 418

19 Banking and Negotiable Instruments 422
What Is a Bank? 423
Regulation of Banks 423
Regulation of Non-Bank Financial Institutions 424
What Is a Negotiable Instrument? 425
Nature and Uses of Negotiable Instruments 426
Personal Property 426
Types of Instruments 426
Bills of Exchange (Drafts) 426
Promissory Notes 427
Cheques 428
Prerequisites for Payment 430
Negotiability 430
Meaning of Negotiability 430
Consequences When a Document Is Not Negotiable 432
Methods of Negotiation 432
Purposes of Endorsement 433
Liability of Parties 434
A Drawer or Maker 435

A Drawee or Acceptor 435
An Endorser 435
Proving Liability 436
Presented for Payment 436
Notice of Dishonour 437
Limitation Periods 437
Holder in Due Course 437
Requirements to Become a Holder in Due Course 437
Defences 438
Personal Defences 438
Defect of Title Defences 439
Real Defences 439
Consumer Bills and Notes 440
Modern Alternatives to Cash 440
Regulation of the Electronic Transfer of Funds 441
Strategies to Manage the Legal Risks 443
Questions for Review 443
Cases and Problems 444

Part 5 Property 447

20 Intellectual Property 447
The Nature of Intellectual Property 448
Forms of Intellectual Property 448
Should Intellectual Property Be Protected? 448
Trademarks 449
Nature of Trademarks 449
Business Names 450
Protection of Trademarks 450
Section 7 of the *Trade-marks Act* 452
Registered Trademarks 452
Requirements for Registration 453
Opposition Proceedings 455
Actions for Infringement 456
Assignment, Licensing, and Franchising 457
Copyright 458
Statutory Origin 458
International Treaties 458
Reform—2012 459
Nature of Copyright 459
Limits to Copyright 462
Works in Which Copyright Exists 462
The Protection of Copyright 464
Infringement of Copyright 466
Patents 469
International Treaties 469
The Nature of Patents 470
Patentable Inventions 470
Obtaining a Patent 473
Enforcing Patent Rights 473
Patents and the Public Interest 474
Industrial Designs 476
Meaning of "Industrial Design" 476
Protection by Registration 476
Overlap 477
Confidential Information, Trade Secrets, and Know-How 477
Technological Change and Intellectual Property Law 478
Strategies to Manage the Legal Risks 479
Questions for Review 480
Cases and Problems 480

21 Interests in Land and Their Transfer 483
The Nature of Interests in Land 484
The Definition of Land 484
Real Property or Real Estate 484
Crown Grant 484
Aboriginal Title and Rights 485
Estates in Time 489
Freehold Estates 489
Leasehold Estates 490
Sharing Title: Co-Ownership 491
Interests Less Than Estates 491
Easements 491
Covenants 493
Other Interests 494
Government Regulation of Land 495
Use and Development 495
Rights in the Matrimonial Home 497
Condominiums 497
Cooperative Housing 498
Transferring Interests in Land 499
By a Sale or Gift 499
Adverse Possession 500
Registration of Interests in Land 501
First in Time 501
Registry System 501
Land Titles System 501
Claims That Are Not Registered on Title 502
Title Insurance 503
Strategies to Manage the Legal Risks 504
Questions for Review 504
Cases and Problems 505

22 Landlord and Tenant 508
The Nature of the Relationship 509
Definition of a Tenancy 509
Exclusive Possession 509
Leasing Compared to Condominium Ownership 510
Classes of Tenancies 511
Term Certain 511
Periodic Tenancy 511
Tenancy at Will 511
Tenancy at Sufferance 511
Covenants 512
To Pay Rent 512
Assignment and Subletting 513
The Landlord's Consent to Assignment 513

Subletting 513
Restrictions on Use of Premises 514
Fitness for Occupancy 514
Repairs 515
Usual Covenants in the Lease of a Building 515
Quiet Enjoyment 515
Insurance 516
Provision of Services and Payment of Taxes 517
Remedies of the Landlord 518
Damages and Recovery of Rent 518
Eviction 519
Distress 519
Injunction 520
Bankruptcy of the Tenant 520
Remedies of the Tenant 521
Damages 521
Injunction 521
Termination of the Lease 521
Termination and Renewal of a Tenancy 522
Surrender 522
Forfeiture 522
Termination by Notice to Quit 522
Parties May Set Their Own Terms for Notice 523
Renewal 523
Fixtures 524
General Rules for Ownership of Fixtures 524
Fixture or Not? 524
Tenant's Fixtures 525
Oral Leases 525
Sale of the Landlord's Interest 526
Relationship Between a Tenant and a Purchaser of the Landlord's Interest 526
Privity of Contract with the Former Landlord 526
Relationship Between a Tenant and the Landlord's Mortgagee 526
The Need to Register a Long-Term Lease 527
Leasebacks 527
Residential Tenancies 528
Changing Needs of Residential Tenants 528
Legislative Protection for Tenants 528
Strategies to Manage the Legal Risks 530
Questions for Review 531
Cases and Problems 532

23 Mortgages of Land and Real Estate Transactions 536

The Essence of Mortgage Law 537
The Mortgage as a Contract 537
The Mortgage as an Interest in Land 538
The Mortgagor's Right to Redeem 538
The Mortgagee's Right to Foreclose 538
Land Titles System 539
Registration 539
Rights of the Mortgagee and Mortgagor 539
The Mortgagee 539
The Mortgagor 540

The Mortgagee's Remedies upon Default 540
Foreclosure 540
Sale by the Court 541
Sale by the Mortgagee 541
Sale by a Mortgagor of His Interest 543
Financial Arrangements 543
Second Mortgages 544
Uses of a Second Mortgage 544
Rights of a Second Mortgagee 544
Risks for a Second Mortgagee When the Mortgagor Defaults 545
Subsequent Mortgages after a Second Mortgage 545
Mortgagee's Rights Compared with Rights of Other Creditors 546
Transferring a Mortgagee's Interest in Land 547
Assignment 547
Discharge of Mortgages 547
Provincial Variations 549
The Mortgagee's Rights 549
The Mortgagor's Rights 549
Reverse Mortgages 549
Mortgage Fraud 550
A Typical Real Estate Transaction 551
The Circumstances 551
Vendor Lists the Property for Sale 552
The Offer to Purchase 552
Accepting the Offer and Waiver of Conditions 553
Preparations for Completing the Transaction 554
The Closing 556
Strategies to Manage the Legal Risks 557
Questions for Review 558
Cases and Problems 559

Part 6 Business Organizations: Their Forms, Operation, and Management 563

24 Sole Proprietorships and Partnerships 563

Choosing the Appropriate Form of Business Organization 564
Sole Proprietorships 564
Partnerships 565
Advantages and Disadvantages 565
The *Partnership Act* 565
The Nature of Partnership 565
The Definition of Partnership 565
The Legal Nature of Partnership 568
The Creation of a Partnership 569
The Partnership Agreement 569
Registration 570
The Liability of a Partner 570
Contractual Liability 570
Tort and Breach of Trust 573

The Relationship Between Partners 573
Implied Terms 574
Fiduciary Duties 576
Termination of Partnership 578
Express Provision 578
Implied Statutory Rules 578
Dissolution by Law 579
Effects of Dissolution 579
Limited Partnerships 580
Limited Liability Partnerships 581
Joint Ventures 583
Income Trusts 584
Strategies to Manage the Legal Risks 584
Questions for Review 585
Cases and Problems 586

25 The Nature of a Corporation and Its Formation 588

The Nature of a Corporation 589
The Corporation as a Legal Person 589
Characteristics of Corporations vs. Partnerships 589
Consequences of Separate Corporate Personality 591
Limitations on the Principle of Separate Corporate Existence 593
Lifting the Corporate Veil 594
Methods of Incorporation 595
Early Methods of Incorporation 595
General Incorporation Statutes 595
The Choice of Jurisdiction 596
The Constitution of a Corporation 597
Articles of Incorporation 597
The Corporate Name 598
Bylaws 598
Types of Business Corporations 600
Public and Private Corporations 600
Corporate Groups 601
Cooperatives 601
Professional Corporations 602
Corporate Capital 603
Equity and Debt 603
Share Capital 603
Par Values 603
Corporate Securities 604
The Distinction Between Shares and Bonds 604
Rights of Security Holders 605
The Transfer of Corporate Securities 606
Strategies to Manage the Legal Risks 607
Questions for Review 608
Cases and Problems 608

26 Corporate Governance: The Internal Affairs of Corporations 611

What Is Corporate Governance? 612
Corporate Governance of Publicly Traded Corporations 612
The Structure of the Modern Business Corporation 613
Directors 615
The Role of the Directors 615
Appointment and Removal of Directors 616
Officers 617
Duties of Directors and Officers 618
What Duties Are Owed? 618
To Whom Are Directors' and Officers' Duties Owed? 619
Defences to Breach of Duty 621
Strict Liability 622
Specific Conduct Involving Conflicts of Interest 622
Insider Trading 625
Shareholders 626
The Role of Shareholders 626
Rights Attached to Shares 627
Meetings and Voting 628
Financial Rights 629
The Right to Information 631
Duties of Shareholders 633
The Protection of Minority Shareholders 634
Majority Rule 634
The Appraisal Remedy 635
The Derivative Action 635
Winding Up 636
Oppression Remedy 636
Shareholder Agreements 638
Advantages 638
Unanimous Shareholder Agreements 639
Strategies to Manage the Legal Risks 640
Questions for Review 640
Cases and Problems 641

27 Corporate Governance: External Responsibilities 645

Liability Arising from Business Responsibilities 646
Types of Liability 646
The Requirement of *Mens Rea* 646
Protection of Creditors 647
Implications of Limited Liability 647
Preservation of Capital 648
Protection of Employees 650
Protection of Consumers and Competitors 650
Protection of Investors 650
Securities Legislation 650
The Securities Industry 651
The Public Corporation: Public Offering 652
Protection of the Public Interest 655
Civil Liability of Corporations 656
Tort Liability 656
Contractual Liability 656
Pre-Incorporation Contracts 657

Criminal Liability of Corporations 658
The Nature of Corporate Criminal Liability 658
Criminal Code Offences 660
Sentencing 660
Criminal Liability of Directors and Officers 661
Liability for Environmental Offences 662
What Standard of Skill and Care Must Be Met? 662
Who Should Be Found Liable? 663
What Should the Punishment Be? 665
The Business Consequences 665
Strategies to Manage the Legal Risks 666
Questions for Review 667
Cases and Problems 667

Part 7 Creditors and Debtors 670

28 Secured Transactions 670
The Meaning of "Security" 671
Security Practices 671
Rights of a Secured Creditor 671
Creating a Security Interest in Personal Property 672
Familiar Security Agreements 673
Additional Security Agreements 673
Personal Property Security Legislation 676
Jurisdiction and Application 676
Purpose of PPSA Legislation 677
Key Components of the *Personal Property Security Act* 678
Registration 679
Priority and Competing Interests 680
Effect of Security Interests on Purchasers 681
Separation of Possession and Ownership 681
Effect of Registration 681
Exceptions for Good Faith Buyers 682
Registration Practice 682
Maintaining Perfection 683
Security Interests in Intangible Property 683
Assignment of Book Debts 683
Investment Property 683
Effect of Security Interests on Other Creditors 684
Conflicting Priorities 684
Security for Bank Loans 685
Loans under the *Bank Act* 685
Rights of a Lending Bank 686
Other Forms of Collateral Security for Bank Loans 687
Conflicts Between the *Bank Act* and *Personal Property Security Acts* 687
Strategies to Manage the Legal Risks 688
Questions for Review 689
Cases and Problems 689

29 Creditors' Rights 692
Statutory Arrangements for the Protection of Creditors 693
The *Bankruptcy and Insolvency Act* 693
Competing Policy Issues 693
Government Supervision 695
Persons to Whom the Act Applies 695
Procedures under the Act 696
Acts of Bankruptcy 699
Administration of a Bankrupt's Affairs 700
Powers and Duties of the Trustee 700
Payment of Claims 703
Duties of the Bankrupt Debtor 706
Bankruptcy Offences 706
Discharge of the Bankrupt Debtor 706
Automatic Discharge Availability 707
Other Methods of Liquidation and Reorganization 707
Corporate Winding Up 707
The *Companies' Creditors Arrangement Act* 708
Builders' Liens 709
Who Is Protected? 710
Procedures under Builders' Lien Legislation 711
Practical Application of Builders' Liens 712
Other Statutory Protection of Creditors 713
Business Corporations Acts 713
Limitations Statutes 714
Strategies to Manage the Legal Risks 715
Questions for Review 715
Cases and Problems 716

Part 8 The Modern Legal Environment for Business 718

30 International Business Transactions 718
Canadian Business in a Global Economy 719
Law and International Business 719
Foreign Trade 721
Export/Import Contracts 721
Government Regulation of International Trade 726
The International Law of Trade 728
The GATT and the World Trade Organization (WTO) 728
North American Free Trade 730
Trans-Pacific Partnership 732
Foreign Investment 732
Forms of Foreign Investment 732
Government Regulation of Foreign Investment 733
Foreign Investment and International Law 734
The Resolution of International Business Disputes 736
Courts 736

Commercial Arbitration   740
Disputes Involving Governments   741
Strategies to Manage the Legal Risks   745
Questions for Review   746
Cases and Problems   747

31   Electronic Commerce   749
Ecommerce   750
What Is Ecommerce?   750
Increasing Impact of Ecommerce on Business   750
The Impact of Ecommerce on the Law   753
Ecommerce and the Law   753
Contract Law   753
Torts   756
Intellectual Property   758
Trademarks   758
Privacy   766
Other Illegal Activities   768
International Aspects of Ecommerce   769
Jurisdiction   769
Non-Governmental Organizations   772
Strategies to Manage the Legal Risks   773
Questions for Review   773
Cases and Problems   774

32   Privacy   776
Privacy   777
What Is Privacy?   777
Privacy as a Human Right   777
Privacy and Technology   778
Privacy and Business   779
Government Regulation of Privacy   780
Regulation of Privacy in the Public Sector   781
Government Transparency and Accountability   782
Provincial Variation   784
Regulation of Privacy in the Private Sector   786
Specific Stakeholders   792
Civil Liability   795
Tort Liability   795
Tort: Negligence   796
Criminal Liability   797
Codes of Conduct   797
Strategies to Manage the Legal Risks   798
Questions for Review   799
Cases and Problems   799

Glossary   801
Index   818

About the Authors

J. E. Smyth

James Everil (Ev) Smyth (1920–1983) studied commerce at the University of Toronto, where he earned a BA and an MA. He also became a Chartered Accountant and a Fellow of the Institute of Chartered Accountants. He taught at Queen's University from 1946 to 1963 and then returned to the University of Toronto, where he taught until 1983. He was an outstanding teacher and also served a term as head of the Department of Political Economy and then as head of the School of Business at the University of Toronto. He was the author of *Introduction to Accounting Methods* (Kingston: Jackson Press, 1951) and *The Basis of Accounting* (Toronto: Ryerson Press, 1954). In 1983, he was posthumously given the L.S. Rosen Award for Outstanding Contribution to Canadian Accounting Education by the Canadian Academic Accounting Association.

Dan Soberman

Dan Soberman (1929–2010) studied law at Dalhousie University and Harvard University. He began teaching at Dalhousie in 1955, and in 1957 he moved to Queen's University to help start the law faculty. He was dean of the faculty from 1968 to 1977, taught full-time until retirement in 1993, and continued to teach part-time there and in the School of Business until 1999. In the late 1960s, he was a member of the federal Business Corporations Task Force that drafted the *Canada Business Corporations Act*. In the autumn term of 2000, he was visiting professor at Kwansai Gakuin University in Japan. From 1977 until 2000, he was an adjudicator on human rights tribunals in Ontario and federally, and also acted as an arbitrator in labour disputes. He authored, or co-authored, chapters in various legal books and articles in law journals.

Alex Easson

Alex Easson (1936–2007) studied law in England, at Oxford University and the London School of Economics. Prior to coming to Canada, he practised law as a solicitor in London and taught at the University of Southampton. He was appointed professor of law at Queen's University in 1976 and remained at Queen's until he retired from full-time teaching in 2000. He then concentrated on his consulting practice, working principally for international organizations such as the IMF and the OECD, and specializing in international taxation, foreign investment, and economic reform. His work took him to more than 40 countries on five continents. He authored, or co-authored, more than a dozen books, the most recent being *Tax Incentives for Foreign Direct Investment* (The Hague: Kluwer Law International, 2004). We at Pearson Canada appreciate his contributions to several editions of this highly acclaimed text.

Shelley McGill

Shelley McGill holds an LLB from the University of Western Ontario and an LLM from Osgoode Hall Law School at York University. She is a full professor of business law and Director of Undergraduate Business Programs in the Lazaridis School of Business and Economics at Wilfrid Laurier University. Professor McGill teaches law to graduate and undergraduate business students. She is also a deputy judge of the Ontario Small Claims Court, where she presides on a part-time basis. Prior to joining Laurier, Professor McGill was a partner in the Ontario law firm of Sims Clement Eastman. Her research focuses on consumer protection issues and is published in a variety of Canadian and international law journals, including the *Canadian Business Law Journal* and the *American Business Law Journal*.

Preface

We are excited to introduce the 15th edition of *The Law and Business Administration in Canada*! Over the past five decades, this text has been studied by thousands of business students. It has shaped today's business leaders and given them an introduction to the integral relationship between law and business. More today than ever before, law plays a part in every facet of day-to-day business activities.

The 15th edition takes a multi-stakeholder perspective for businesses operating in the common law jurisdictions of Canada. Contractual relationships are the foundation of most business dealings. It devotes eight chapters to the study of contractual principles. In addition, the process of government regulation of business is introduced early in the text before specific regulatory regimes such as corporate governance, environmental protection, privacy, and globalization are studied. Each chapter integrates the study of case law with relevant legislation so students understand the varied sources of law.

The Law and Business Administration in Canada is a multipurpose text that meets the needs and priorities of different types of courses. The comprehensive coverage of a wide variety of relevant legal topics makes this text perfect for the business law survey course offered in most business schools. As well, the stand-alone format of each chapter allows instructors to mix and match chapters to suit the needs of even the most specialized electives. Some specialty topics, such as intellectual property, privacy, and negotiable instruments, are addressed in multiple formats; instructors may choose between an overview of the topic or an in-depth discussion depending on the chapter selected. Real case examples support the legal principles described in each chapter, and students may examine the legal issues facing a single fictional business as it evolves through every chapter's Cases and Problems section. Finally, each chapter concludes by offering practical strategies to manage businesses' legal risks.

Many Canadian business schools seek accreditation of their programs from external professional organizations, including Chartered Professional Accountants (CPA) and AACSB. This 15th edition facilitates these efforts by placing new emphasis on topics required for CPA recognition. Franchising and banking are among the expanded CPA topics. AACSB accreditation prioritizes ethical and global perspectives, so each chapter contains international and ethical issue boxes to integrate these priorities into each legal topic. Finally, the 15th edition expands Indigenous content with added detail on Aboriginal rights, title, and the duty to consult.

As in previous editions, this edition combines an unsurpassed commitment to in-depth legal content with an integrated practical approach to legal risk management. It is a perfect fit for the current business education environment, maximizing both print and online resources. It retains the online resources students have come to rely on. In addition to legal content available in print, each chapter has supplemental detail or topics available on the MyLab Business Law, giving instructors greater flexibility in the depth to which they cover certain topics.

As always, the new edition incorporates recent developments in the law. Significant changes to legislation and landmark Supreme Court judgments are added with an increased emphasis on case examples originating in Alberta and British Columbia. We completed the research supporting the revisions in spring 2018, so subsequent changes in the law will be reflected in the next edition. In particular, NAFTA renegotiations were incomplete at the time of writing. The next edition will capture this content.

In sum, the 15th edition presents a comprehensive overview of traditional and current business law topics in a readable, practical, multiplatform format with online content and resources.

Shelley McGill
September 2018

WHAT'S NEW

We set general goals for this edition:

- Emphasize and expand topics important for CPA recognition and AASCB accreditation.
- Emphasize case examples from British Columbia and Alberta.
- Expand Indigenous content.
- Add titles for all cases and illustrations to help readers identify their purpose.

Accreditation from AASCB does not involve a list of substantive legal topics to be taught but does include "ethical understanding and reasoning" and legal principles for a "global society." The 15th edition embraces the existing format of not only including a stand-alone chapter on international law but also embedding an international issue box into each chapter so instructors can ensure students receive the required AACSB global perspective even if the international chapter is not taught. The similarly placed ethical issue boxes reinforce the content in Chapters 1 and 2 on law, ethics, and corporate social responsibility. The 15th edition also facilitates coverage of CPA content following the development of a revised list of topics after the merger of various accounting designations. Franchising and banking are among the new CPA topics, and somewhat surprisingly, negotiable instruments remain. Therefore, this edition expands its franchise content, and Chapter 19 is revised and renamed to reflect its new content on "Banking and Negotiable Instruments."

Alberta and British Columbia case examples are added to most chapters of the text so users from across the county can draw province-specific content for their students. The 15th edition retains its Canada-wide perspective, but at reviewers' request this edition attempts to balance the Ontario examples with new cases from western provinces.

Indigenous content remains topic specific, but the 15th edition significantly expands the detail in the constitutional discussion of division of powers in Chapters 1 and 2 and in the Aboriginal rights and land claims discussion in Chapter 21. It incorporates several landmark Supreme Court of Canada decisions issued in 2014, 2015, and 2017.

Specific revisions to particular chapters are summarized below.

Part 1: The Law in Its Social and Business Context

Part 1 provides the foundation ethical content that connects law and ethics with corporate social responsibility.

Chapter 1: Law, Society, and Business

- **Updated** content to include discussion of Uber and legal treatment of marijuana
- **Added** references and examples from multiple cases from Manitoba, Alberta, and British Columbia

Chapter 2: The Machinery of Justice

- **Added** banking content
- **Added** two western province case references
- **Added** a checklist for dispute resolution

Chapter 3: Government Regulation of Business

- **Added** new case on banking and consumer protection
- **Added** new text and case examples on Aboriginal duty to consult
- **Added** new references to cases from western provinces

Part 2: Torts

Significant changes in the law impacted the chapters in Part 2.

Chapter 4: The Law of Torts

- **Added** content on duty of care with the new Supreme Court of Canada cases
- **Revised** content on defamation torts
- **Revised** the causation discussion of negligence to consider material contribution
- **Revised** content on mental health damages
- **Expanded** occupier's liability content
- **Added** new references to cases from western provinces

Chapter 5: Professional Liability: The Legal Challenges

- **Revised** the content on fiduciary duty to incorporate the new criteria set by the Supreme Court in 2013
- **Reordered** content to highlight fraudulent misrepresentation
- **Added** new references to cases from western provinces specifically related to professional organizations

Part 3: Contracts

All contract chapters were revised to streamline and update content and remove duplication. We added case references and examples from western provinces to all chapters. Major changes are noted here.

Chapter 8: Formation of a Contract: Capacity to Contract and Legality of Object

- **Revised** Indigenous content, including reference to guiding principles
- **Revised** content on agreements in restraint of trade

Chapter 9: Title Changed to "Contract Issues: Mistake and Misrepresentation"

- **Changed** title to better connect with CPA topics
- **Revised** undue influence

Chapter 10: Writing and Interpretation

- **Revised** interpretation of express terms with reference to several Supreme Court decisions
- **Added** reference to good faith in implied terms

Chapter 12: The Discharge of Contracts

- **Revised** discharge by frustration with new text and checklist
- **Merged** sections on harshness of common law into one section on release of performance

Chapter 13: Breach of Contract and Remedies

- **Revised** content on "Duty of Honest Performance" referencing two Supreme Court of Canada decisions from 2014
- **Added** content on injunctions to reference 2017 Supreme Court of Canada decision

Part 4: Special Types of Contracts

Chapters 17 and 19 were targets of major revision for CPA purposes. Chapter 18 was also significantly amended to emphasize greater human rights content and reflect changes in the law.

Chapter 17: Agency and Franchising

- **Amended** to reference new BC franchise legislation throughout
- **Added** new illustration box and checklists
- **Added** new section on various franchise models and intermediaries
- **Expanded** existing franchise legislation section to include purpose, disclosure, and new case
- **Added new** section on non-waiver
- **Changed** international box from dispute resolution to foreign franchisors
- **Added** new references to cases from western provinces

Chapter 18: The Contract of Employment

- **Added** new content on independent contractors
- **Added** new case on liability in tort
- **Expanded** reference to progressive discipline in text and glossary
- **Expanded** human rights content with four specific sections on disability, sexual harassment, hostile workplaces, and constructive discrimination, complete with new case examples
- **Revised** content on legal status of trade unions
- **Added** new references to cases from western provinces

Chapter 19: Title changed to "Negotiable Instruments and Banking"

The new chapter divides content into three parts: a new banking section, a reduced negotiable instruments section, and an expanded modern alternatives section.

- **Added** new banking content defining banks and how they are regulated as distinct from non-bank financial institutions
- **Added** new international issue about money laundering and terrorism
- **Reduced** negotiable instruments content on bills of exchange
- **Added** defences checklist
- **Expanded** modern alternatives to cash with new section on regulation of the electronic transfer of funds
- **Changed** ethical issue to the digital future of money
- **Added** new references to cases from western provinces

Part 5: Property

Chapters 20 and 21 required significant revisions.

Chapter 20: Intellectual Property

- **Revised** throughout to reference pending legislations that significantly revise trademark legislation; some copyright and industrial design, current and pending, are noted
- **Added** several new Supreme Court of Canada intellectual property cases
- **Added** new references to cases from western provinces

Chapter 21: Interests in Land and Their Transfer

- **Revised** content under Crown grant to reflect Indigenous issues
- **Added** new sections, content, and cases under Aboriginal land rights and title, including content on infringement and duty to consult
- **Added** references to Truth and Reconciliation Commission of Canada report and several Supreme Court of Canada decisions
- **Added** new international issue box on the United Nations Declaration on the Rights of Indigenous Peoples
- **Expanded** content on oil, gas, and mineral leases
- **Reduced** content on electronic registration
- **Added** new references to cases from western provinces

Part 8: The Modern Legal Environment for Business

Chapter 31: Electronic Commerce

- **Updated** the discussion of Canadian anti-spam legislation
- **Added** content on patents in the intellectual property section
- **Updated** content on breach notification in the privacy section
- **Expanded** discussion of forum selection clauses with new case contracts

Chapter 32: Privacy

- **Added** discussion of new invasion of privacy torts and legislative causes of action
- **Added** new content on Supreme Court of Canada decisions on privacy

FEATURES

A careful effort has been made to standardize features in each chapter that will facilitate learning and enhance an understanding of business applications.

- A Table of Statutes and a Table of Cases are provided on pages xxv and xxx, respectively.
- Case and illustration boxes throughout each chapter in the text and on the MyLab Business Law provide examples based on actual cases and have new titles for easy reading.
- The opening section of each chapter summarizes the focus of the material to follow and lists some of the questions that will be considered.
- Definitions of key terms are included in the margins of each page.
- A continuing scenario involving the same business is included in the Cases and Problems section of each chapter.
- For convenience, an explanation of How to Read a Citation is printed on the inside back cover.

FEATURES

The text contains many features aimed at helping students understand, apply, and retain important concepts.

Cases: Real court decisions that demonstrate how judges create or apply a legal principle.

Illustrations: Simple factual scenarios that allow students to see a simple example of the legal principle in action.

Checklists: Summaries that condense the text into a simple list of steps to follow when defining the law or applying a legal principle.

Ethical Issues: Descriptions of real events that present an ethical dilemma or demonstrate the link between law and ethics.

International Issues: Descriptions of real events that present an example of conflict of laws between jurisdictions.

Strategies to Manage the Risk: A practical look at proactive ways a manager can address the legal issues presented in the chapter.

Authors' Acknowledgments

Over the years we have been fortunate to receive helpful advice and encouragement from many of our colleagues. In particular, our thanks are due to Stuart Ryan, Hugh Lawford, Richard Gosse, Donald Wood, David Bonham, Bruce McDonald, Gordon Simmons, Marvin Baer, David Mullan, Kenneth Swan, William Lederman, Robert Land, Nicholas Bala, Stanley Sadinsky, and Donald Stuart. We have also had the assistance of a number of excellent student researchers, notably Ib Petersen, Don Luck, Darryl Aarbo, Colleen Dempsey, Rebecca Lovelace, Grace Pereira, Ryan Mills, Samia Alam, Allison Ostafew McLure, Michelle Frigon, Brendan McGill, Scott Buchanan, Scott Lin and Madison Derraugh. Additionally, we have had the benefit of the many helpful and constructive suggestions that have been passed on to us by our publishers from the reviewers of each new edition. To all of these people we express our thanks.

We appreciate the insights and suggestions of the following individuals—as well as others who choose to remain anonymous—who provided feedback on the 14th edition or reviewed the manuscript for the 15th edition:

    Daniel Dylan, Lakehead University
    Scott Harling, University of Lethbridge
    Werner Keller, University of Windsor
    Laurie Marshall (Priske), Durham College
    Gerald Palmer, University of the Fraser Valley

We would also like to thank everyone at Pearson Education Canada who worked so diligently to bring this text into print. Among others, thanks go to Karen Townsend, Portfolio Manager; Madhu Ranadive, Content Manager; Cheryl Finch, Content Developer; Lisa Gillis, Marketing Manager; Susan Johnson, Project Manager; and Sally Glover, Copy Editor.

Table of Statutes

A

Abolition of Compulsory Retirement Act, SQ 1982, c 12, 410n

Access to Information Act, RSC 1985, c A-1, 781n

Access to Information and Protection of Privacy Act, SNL 2002, c A-1.1, 784n

Act Respecting Labour Standards, RSQ, c N-1.1, 405n

Act Respecting the Protection of Personal Information in the Private Sector, RSQ, c P-39.1, 766n, 792n

Act to Repeal the Statute of Frauds, RSM 1987, c F-158, 364n

Aeronautics Act, RSC 1985, c A-2, 484n, 794n

Age of Majority Act, CCSM c A-7, 164n

Age of Majority Act, RSBC 1996, c 7, 164n

Age of Majority Act, RSNS 1989, c 4, 164n

Age of Majority and Accountability Act, RSO 1990, c A.7, 164n

Aggregate Resources Act, RSO 1990, c A.8, 27

Anticybersquatting Consumer Protection Act, 15 USC § 1125, 761n

Arbitration Act, 1992, SS 1992, c A-24.1, 43n

Arbitration Act, CCSM c A120, 43n

Arbitration Act, RSA 1991, c A-43, 176n

Arbitration Act, RSA 2000, c A-43, 43n

Arbitration Act, RSBC 1996, c 55, 43n

Arbitration Act, RSNL 1990, c A-14, 43n

Arbitration Act, RSNS 1989, c 19, 43n

Arbitration Act, RSNWT 1988, c A-5, 43n

Arbitration Act, RSPEI 1988, c A-16, 43n

Arbitration Act, RSY 2002, c 8, 43n

Arbitration Act, SNB 1992, c A-10.1, 43n

Arthur Wishart Act (Franchise Disclosure), 2000, SO 2000, c 3, 386n

Assignment of Wages Act, RSS 1978, c A-30, 245n

Assignments and Preferences Act, RSO 1990, c A.33, 693n, 713n

B

Bank Act, SC 1991, c 46, 26n, 423n, 648n, 685n, 752n

Bank of Canada Act, RSC 1985, c B-2, 250n, 423n

Bankruptcy and Insolvency Act, RSC 1985, c B-3, 171n, 247n, 267, 311n, 312n, 510n, 520, 568, 593, 648n, 690, 693–700, 702, 703, 706, 708

Bankruptcy Code (US), 708

Bill C-11, see *Copyright Modernization Act*

Bill C-12, *An Act to amend the Bankruptcy and Insolvency Act, the Companies' Creditors Arrangement Act, the Wage Earner Protection Program Act, and chapter 47 of the Statutes of Canada, 2005*, 694n

Bill C-58, 1st Sess., 42nd Parl., 2015–2016–2017, *An Act to Amend the Access to Information Act and the Privacy Act and to make consequential amendments to other Acts*, 782n, 786n

Bill S-4, see *Digital Privacy Act*, 2nd Sess, 41st Parl, 2014

Bill S-11, *An Act to Amend the Canada Business Corporations Act and the Canada Cooperatives Act and to Amend Other Acts*, SC 2001, 612n

Bills of Exchange Act, RSC 1985, c B-4, 248n, 249n, 250, 321, 322, 370n, 425n, 428, 429, 430, 432, 752

British North America Act, 1867, 30 & 31 Vict, c 3, 13n

Broadcasting Act, SC 1991, c 11, 26n, 753

Builders' Lien Act, SBC 1997, c 45, 693, 710n

Business Corporations Act, RSA 2000, c B-9, 594n, 596n, 612n, 616n, 620n

Business Corporations Act, RSNB c 9.1, 616n

Business Corporations Act, RSO 1990, c B-16, 594n, 596n, 612n, 621n, 648n, 708

Business Corporations Act, SNB 1981, c B-9.1, 596n

Business Corporations Act, RSS 1978, c B-10, 594n, 596n, 612n, 616n

Business Corporations Act, SBC 2002, c 57, 595n, 612n

Business Names Act, RSO 1990, c B.17, 174n, 565n, 570n

Business Names Registration Act, RSS 1978, B-11, 565n

Business Practices and Consumer Protection Act, SBC 2004, c 2, 34n, 126, 132n, 199n, 217n, 218n, 249n, 316n, 741n, 794n

C

Canada Business Corporations Act, RSC 1985, c C-44, 426, 427, 591n, 592n, 592, 596n, 598n, 599n, 600n, 603n, 606n, 607n, 612n, 614n, , 618–619, 621–622, 622n, 625, 627–628, 632n, 633, 636, 639–640, 648, 649, 648n, 657n, 696n, 708n, 713n, 733n

Canada Consumer Product Safety Act, SC 2010, c 21, 62, 64, 68

Canada Cooperatives Act, SC 1998, c 1, 601n

Canada Deposit Insurance Corporation Act, RSC 1985, c C-3, 424

Canada–European Union Comprehensive Economic and Trade Agreement Implementation Act, SC 2017, c 6, 475n

Canada Labour Code, RSC 1985, c L-2, 403n, 405

Canada Labour Standards Regulations,CRC 1978, c 986, 403n

Canada Oil and Gas Operations Act, RSC 1985, c O-7, 494n

Canada Student Loans Act, RSC 1985, c S-23, 166n

Canadian Charter of Rights and Freedoms, 13n, 15n, 745

Canadian Environmental Assessment Act, 2012, SC 2012, c 19, 70, 662n

Canadian Environmental Protection Act, SC 1999, c 33, 68, 662n, 666

Canadian Human Rights Act, RSC 1985, c H-6, 407n, 778n

Canadian Payments Act, RSC 1985, c C-21, 426, 429, 441n

Canadian Wheat Board Act, RSC 1985, c C-24, 51n

Choses in Action Act, RSS 1978, c C-11, 243n

City of Toronto Act, 2006, SO 2006, c 11, Sch A, 50

Civil Code of Quebec, SQ 1991, c 64, 44n, 278

Civil Enforcement Act, RSA 2000, c C-15, 703n

Class Proceedings Act, 1992, SO 1992, c 6, 34n

Class Proceedings Act, CCSM c C30, 35n

Class Proceedings Act, RSBC 1996, c 50, 35n

Class Proceedings Act, SS 2001, c 12.01, 35n

Clean Air Act, SS 1986–87–88, c 12.1, 68n

Climate Change and Emissions Management Act, SA 2003, c C-16.7, 662n

Code Napoléon of 1804, 22

Code of Civil Procedure, RSQ, c C-25, 43n

Collective Agreement Decrees Act, RSQ, c D-2, 415n

Combating Counterfeit Products Act, 459n, 765 – see also Bill C-8

Commercial Arbitration Act, RSC 1985, c 17, 741n

Commercial Tenancies Act, RSO 1990, c L-7, 491n, 509n, 513n, 519n, 521n

Commercial Tenancy Act, RSBC 1996, c 57, 509n, 512n, 521n, 523n

Companies Act, RSNB 1973, c C-13, 612n

Companies Act, RSNS 1989, c 81, 595n, 612n

Companies Act, RSPEI 1988, c C-14, 596n, 612n

Companies' Creditors Arrangement Act, RSC 1985, c C-36, 693n, 697, 708, 709

Companies Winding-up Act, RSNS 1989, c 82, 708n

Competition Act, RSC 1985, c C-34, 54, 55, 56n, 57, 60, 63n, 64n, 68, 82n, 174, 178, 317n, 475, 650, 767n, 768

Condominium Act, SO 1998, c 19, 497n

Condominium Act, RSNS 1989, c 85, 497n

Conservation Easements Act, SS 1996, c C-27.01, 492

Conservation Land Act, RSO 1990, c C.28, 492

Constitution Act, 1867, 30 & 31 Vict, c 3, 13, 16, 30n, 48, 49, 406n, 448n, 753n

Constitution Act, 1982, Schedule B to the Canada Act 1982 (UK), 1982, c 11, 13n, 169n, 485n

Consumer Packaging and Labelling Act, RSC 1985, c C-38, 65n

Consumer Product Safety Act, SC 2010, c 21, 234, 234n

Consumer Product Warranty and Liability Act, SNB 1978, c C-18.1, 91n, 234, 234n, 239, 302n, 316n, 318n

Consumer Products Warranties Act, RSS 1978, c C-30, 302n

Consumer Protection Act, 2002, SO 2002, c 30, Sch A, 44n, 64n, 127, 132n, 138n, 147n, 176n, 199n, 217n, 308n, 316n, 341n, 674n, 741n, 755n, 756n,

Consumer Protection Act, CCSM c 200, 343n

Consumer Protection Act, RSA 2000, c 26.3, 317n

xxv

Consumer Protection Act, RSM 1987, c 200, 316n

Consumer Protection Act, RSNS 1989, c 92, 217n, 317n, 318n

Consumer Protection Act, RSQ, c P-40.1, 44n, 320n

Consumer Protection Act, SS 1996, c C-30.1, 218n, 302, 318n, 756n

Consumer Protection and Business Practices Act, SNL 2009, c C-31.1, 756n

Contingency Fee Agreements, O Reg 195/04, 40n

Contracts (Rights of Third Parties) Act 1999, c 31 (Eng), 239n

Conveyancing and Law of Property Act, RSO 1990, c C-34, 243n, 493n

Cooperative Association Act, SBC 1999, c 28, 601n

Co-operative Corporations Act, RSO 1990, c C.35, 601n

Cooperatives Act, 2001, SA 2001, c C-28.1, 601n

Copyright Act, RSC 1985, c C-42, 458, 461, 462, 467, 477n, 762, 763n, 764n

Copyright Modernization Act, SC 2012, c 20, 459n, 460, 731n

Corporations Act, CCSM c C225, 594n, 612n, 708n

Corporations Act, RSNL 1990, c C-36, 596n, 612n

Corporations Information Act, RSO 1990, c C-39, 596n, 733n

Corruption of Foreign Public Officials Act, SC 1998, c 34, 71, 720n

Court Jurisdiction and Proceedings Transfer Act, SBC 2003, c 28, 737n, 771n

Court Jurisdiction and Proceedings Transfer Act, SNS 2003, c 2, 737n

Court Jurisdiction and Proceedings Transfer Act, SS 1997, c C-41.1, 737n

Court Order Enforcement Act, RSBC 1996, c 78, 294n

Courts of Justice Act, RSO 1990, c C.43, 519n

Creditors Relief Act, 2010, SO 2010, c C.16, 699n

Credit Union Incorporation Act, RSBC 1996, c 82, 424

Criminal Code, RSC 1985, c C-46, 67n, 80n, 166n, 172n, 174, 177n, 201n, 372n, 432n, 625n, 646n, 653n, 659–660, 797

Cuban Liberty and Democratic Solidarity Act of 1996, 22 U.S.C., 727n

Currency Act, RSC 1985, c C-52, 250n, 423n

Customs Act, RSC 1985, c 1 (2nd Supp), 727n

Customs Act, RSC 1985, c C-1, 174n

Customs Tariff, SC 1997, c 36, 727n

Cutting Unnecessary Red Tape Act, 2017, SO 2017, c 20, Sch 9, 386n

D

Dangerous Goods Handling and Transportation Act, CCSM c D-12, 69n

Dangerous Goods Transportation Act, RSO 1990, c D.1, 69n

Defamation Act, RSA 2000, c D-7, 81n

Department of Industry Act, SC 1995 C. 1, 65n

Digital Millennium Copyright Act, 112 Stat. 2860 (1998) (US), 459n, 765n

Digital Privacy Act, SC 2015, c 32, 766n, 791n

Dower Act, RSA 2000, c D-15, 497n

Drug and Pharmacies Regulation Act, RSO 1990, c H.4, 174n

E

Education Act, RSO 1990, c E-2, 785n

Electronic Commerce Act, 2000, SO 2000, c 17, 136n, 138n, 208n, 215, 755n

Electronic Commerce Act, RSPEI 1988, c E-4.1, 755n

Electronic Commerce Act, SNL 2001, c E-5.2, 755n

Electronic Commerce Act, SNS 2000, c 26, 755n

Electronic Commerce and Information Act, CCSM c E-55, 755n

Electronic Information and Documents Act, SS 2000, c E-7.22, 755n

Electronic Transactions Act, SA 2001, c E-5.5, 208n, 755n

Electronic Transactions Act, SBC 2001, c 10, 755n

Electronic Transactions Act, SNB 2001, c E-5.5, 755n

Employment Equity Act, SC 1995, c 44, 409n

Employment Equity Act, SO 1993, c 35, 409n

Employment Insurance Act, SC 1996, c 23 E-5, 411

Employment Standards Act, 2000, SO 2000, c 41, 398n, 400n, 403n, 411n, 594n, 708

Energy Consumer Protection Act, 2010, SO 2010, c 8, 316n, 317n

Environment Act, SNS 1994–95, c 1, 69n

Environmental Assessment Act, RSO 1990, c E.18, 662n

Environmental Assessment Act, SBC 2002, c 43, 662n

Environmental Bill of Rights, 1993, SO 1993, c 28, 662n

Environmental Management Act, SBC 2003, c 53, 69n, 662n

Environmental Management and Protection Act, 2010, SS 2010, c E-10.22, 69n

Environmental Protection Act, RSO 1990, c E-19, 69n, 662n

Environmental Protection and Enhancement Act, RSA 2000, c E-12, 69n, 662n

Estate Administration Act, RSBC 1996, c 122, Part 7, 247n

Estates Administration Act, RSO 1990, c E.22, 247n

Execution Act, RSO 1990, c E.24, 294n, 693n, 703n

Export Act, RSC 1985, c E-18, 726n

Export Act of 1897, SC 1897, c 17, 726

Export and Import Permits Act, RSC 1985, c E-19, 726, 727n

Export and Imports Permit Act, SC 1947, c 17, 726

Export Development Act, RSC 1985, c E-20, 726n

Expropriation Act, RSA 2000, c E-13, 144, 500

Extra-Provincial Corporations Act, RSO 1990, c E.27, 596n, 733n

F

Factors Act, RSA 2000, c F-1, 310n

Factors Act, RSO 1990, c F.1, 310n

Fair Trading Act, RSA 2000, c F-2, 44n, 65n, 316n, 741n, 756n

Family Law Act, RSO 1990, c F.3, 166n, 209n, 497n

Family Law Act, SBC 2011, c 25, 209n

Family Statute Law Amendment Act, 2006, SO 2006, c 1, 44n

Federal Court Act, RSC 1985, c F-7, 53n

Financial Consumer Agency of Canada Act, SC 2001, c 9, 424n

Financial Institutions Act, RSBC 1996, c 141, 414

Financial System Review Act, SC 2012, c 5, 688n

Fisheries Act, RSC 1985, c F-14, 68n, 663n

Food and Drugs Act, RSC 1985, c F-27, 63, 66n, 68, 186, 475

Foreign Corrupt Practices Act, 91 Stat. 1494, 71

Foreign Extra-Territorial Measures Act, RSC 1985, c F-29, 727n

Franchise Act, CCSM c F156, 386n

Franchises Act, RSA 2000, c F-23, 386n, 387

Franchises Act, RSPEI 1998, c F-14.1, 386n, 387

Franchises Act, SBC 2015 c 35, 386n

Franchises Act, SNB 2007, c F-23.5, 386n

Fraudulent Conveyances Act, RSA 2000, c F-24, 701n

Fraudulent Conveyances Act, RSBC 1996, c 163, 701n, 702

Fraudulent Conveyances Act, RSNL 1990, c F-24, 701n

Fraudulent Conveyances Act, RSO 1990, c F.29, 703n, 713n

Fraudulent Conveyances Act, RSS 1978, c F-21, 703n

Freedom of Information and Protection of Privacy Act, CCSM c F175, 784n

Freedom of Information and Protection of Privacy Act, RSA 2000, c F-25, 780n, 784n

Freedom of Information and Protection of Privacy Act, RSBC 1996, c 165, 780n, 784n

Freedom of Information and Protection of Privacy Act, RSO 1990, c F-31, 778n, 784n

Freedom of Information and Protection of Privacy Act, RSPEI 1988, c F-15.01, 784n

Freedom of Information and Protection of Privacy Act, SNS 1993, c 5, 784n

Freedom of Information and Protection of Privacy Act, SS 1990–1, c F-22.01, 784n

Frustrated Contract Act, RSBC 1996, c 166. Section 5(2), 265n

Frustrated Contracts Act, CCSM, c F-190, 265n

Frustrated Contracts Act, RSA 2000, c F-27, 265n

Frustrated Contracts Act, RSBC 1996, c 166, 265

Frustrated Contracts Act, RSNB 2011, c 164, 265n

Frustrated Contracts Act, RSNL 1990, c F-26, 265n

Frustrated Contracts Act, RSNWT 1988, c F-12, 265n

Frustrated Contracts Act, RSO 1990, c F-34, 265n

Frustrated Contracts Act, RSPEI 1988, c F-16, 265n

Frustrated Contracts Act, RSY 2002, c 96, 265n

Frustrated Contracts Act, SS 1994, c F-22.2, 265n

G

Gaming Control Act, SBC 2002, c 14, 172n

Gaming Control Act, SNS 1994–95, c 4, 172n

Gaming Control Act, SO 1992, c 24, 172n

Goods Transportation Act, RSO 1990, c D.1, 69n

General, O Reg 98/09, 67n, 321n

Guarantees Acknowledgement Act, RSA 2000, c G-11, 364n

H

Hazardous Products Act, RSC 1985, c H-3, 65, 68
Health Information Act, RSA 2000, c H-5, 784n, 785
Health Information Protection Act, SS 1999, c H-0.021, 784n
Helms-Burton law – see *Cuban Liberty and Democratic Solidarity Act of 1996*
Homestead Act, CCSM c H80, 497n
Homestead Act, SS 1989–90, c H-5.1, 497n
Homesteads Act, CCSM, 497n
Hotel Keepers Act, RSBC 1996, c 206, 337n
Human Rights Act, RSA 2000, c A-25.5, 778n
Human Rights Act, RSC 1985, c H-6, 407n, 778n
Human Rights Act, RSNB 2011, c 171, 410n, 778n
Human Rights Act, RSNS 1989, c 214, 778n
Human Rights Act, RSPEI 1988, c H-12, 778n
Human Rights Code, CCSM c H-175, 407n, 778n
Human Rights Code, RSBC 1996, c 210, 407n, 410n, 528, 778n
Human Rights Code, RSO 1990, c H-19, 407n, 408n, 528, 778n
Human Rights Code, SM 1974, c 65, 410n
Human Rights Code, SNL 2010, c H-13.1, 778n
Human Rights Code, SS 1979, c S-24.1, 407n
Hydro and Electric Energy Act, RSA 2000, c H-16, 484n

I

Income Tax Act, RSC 1985, c 1, 71, 174, 567n, 593n, 622n, 649n, 684n, 705
Indian Act, RSC 1985, c I-5, 485
Indian Oil and Gas Act, RSC 1985, c I-7, 494n
Industrial Design Act, RSC 1985, c I-9, 476, 477
Industrial Relations Act, RSNB 1973, c I-4, 416n
Infants Act, RSBC 1996, c 223, 167n
Innkeepers Act, RSBC 1996, c 206, 337n
Innkeepers Act, RSNL 1990, c I-7, 337n
Innkeepers Act, RSO 1990, c I-7, 337n
Innkeepers Act, RSPEI 1988, c T-3.3, 337n
Innkeepers Act, SNS 1994–5, c 9, 337n
Insurance (Vehicle) Act, RSBC 2012, c 1, 237n
Insurance Act, RSA 2000, c I-3, 198n
Insurance Act, RSBC 1996, c 206, 237n
Insurance Act, RSBC 2012, c 1, 173n, 198n, 355n
Insurance Act, RSNS 1989, c 231, 173n, 198n, 237n
Insurance Act, RSO 1990, c I.8, 173n, 198n, 237n
Insurance Companies Act, SC 1991, c. 47, 351, 424
Integrated Circuit Topography Act, SC 1990, c 37, 479
Interest Act, RSC 1985, c I-15, 320, 322
International Commercial Arbitration Act, RSBC 1996, c 233, 741n
International Commercial Arbitration Act, RSO 1990, c I.9, 741n
International Conventions Implementation Act, RSA 2000, c I-6, 315n
International Interests in Mobile Equipment (Aircraft Equipment) Act, SC 2005, c 3, 685n
International Sale of Goods Act, RSBC 1996, c 236, 315n
International Sale of Goods Act, RSNL 1990, c I-16, 315n
International Sale of Goods Act, RSO 1990, c I.10, 315n, 722n
International Sale of Goods Act, SNS 1988, c 13, 722n
International Sale of Goods Contracts Convention Act, SC 1991, c 13, 315n, 722n
Interpretation Act, RSC 1985, c I-21, 27n, 208n
Intestate Succession Act, RSNS 1989, c 236, 247n
Intimate Image Protection Act, CCSM c I87, 82n, 796n
Investment Canada Act, RSC 1985, c 28 (1st Supp), 60n, 594, 733n, 734, 735

J

Job Quotas Repeal Act, SO 1995, c 4, 409n
Judicature Act, RSA 2000, c J-1, 151n
Judicature Act, RSA 2000, c J-2, 243n
Judicature Act, RSNS 1989, c 240, 243n
Judicial Review Procedure Act, RSBC 1996, c 241, 53n
Judicial Review Procedure Act, RSO 1990, c J.1, 53n
Justice Statute Law Amendment Act, 2002, SO 2002, c 24, 40n

L

Labour Code, RSQ, c C-27, 414n
Labour Relations Act, 1995, SO 1995, c 1, Sch A, 168n, 413n, 414n
Labour Relations Code, RSBC 1996, c 244, 168n, 413n, 414n, 416n
Labour Relations Code, RSM 1987, c L-10, 414n
Labour Relations Code, RSQ, c C-27, 414n
Labour Standards Act, RSS 1978, c L-1, 398n
Labour Standards Code, RSNS 1989, c 246, 245n, 398n, 405n
Land Contracts (Actions) Act, RSS 1978, c L-3, 549n
Land Registration Act, SNS 2001, c 6, 500n, 502n
Land Registration Reform Act, RSO 1990, c L-4, 502n, 539n
Land Stewardship Act, SA 2009, c A-26.8, 492
Land Title Act, RSBC 1996, c 250, 501n, 502n, 527n
Land Titles Act, RSA 2000, c L-4, 493n, 500n, 539n, 551n
Land Titles Act, RSO 1990, c L.5, 493n, 500n, 502n, 551n
Land Titles Act, SNB 1981, c L-1.1, 527n
Landlord and Tenant Act, CCSM c L-70, 521n
Landlord's Rights on Bankruptcy Act, RSA 2000, c L-5, 510n, 521n
Law and Equity Act, RSBC 1996, c 253, 151n, 209n, 210n, 211n, 243n, 519n, 540n, 541n
Law of Property Act, 1925, 15 & 16 Geo. 5, c 20, 211n
Law of Property Act, CCSM c L90, 243n
Law of Property Act, RSA 2000, c L-7, 540n, 541n, 549n
Law Reform Act, RSNB 2011, c 184, 239n
Law Reform Amendment Act, SBC 1985, c 10, 209n
Law Reform (Enforcement of Contracts) Act, 1954, 2 & 3 Eliz. 2, c 34, 210n, 215n
Law Society Act, RSO 1990, c L-8, 9n
Legal Profession Act, SBC 1998, c 9, 119n
Libel and Slander Act, RSBC 1996, c 263, 81n
Libel and Slander Act, RSO 1990, c L-12, 81n
Limitation Act, RSBC 1996, c 266, 500n, 714n
Limitation of Actions Act, RSNS 1989, c 258, 500n, 501n, 714n
Limitation of Civil Rights Act, RSS 1978, c L-16, 540n, 549n
Limitations Act, RSA 2000, c L-12, 714n
Limitations Act, SO 2002 c 24, 714n
Limited Partnerships Act, RSNS 1989, c 259, 580n
Limited Partnerships Act, RSO 1990, c L.16, 580n
Liquor Licence Act, RSO 1990, c L.19, 26
Loans and Trust Companies Act, SC 1991, c 45, 752n
Local Authority Freedom of Information and Protection of Privacy Act, SS 1990–91, c L-27.1, 784n
Lord's Day Act, RSC 1970, c.L-13, 14, 17

M

Matrimonial Property Act, RSNS 1989, c 275, 209n, 497n
Mercantile Law Amendment Act, CCSM c M-129, 151n
Mercantile Law Amendment Act, RSO 1990, c M.10, 151n
Mortgage Act, CCSM c M200, 540n, 550n
Mortgages Act, RSO 1990, c M.40, 540n
Motor Vehicle Safety Act, SC 1993, c 16, 66
Municipal Freedom of Information and Protection of Privacy Act, RSO 1990, c M-56, 784n
Mutual Legal Assistance in Criminal Matters Act, RSC 1985 (4th Supp), c 30, 783n

N

National Energy Board Act, RSC 1985, c N-7, 495
Natural Resources Conservation Board Act, RSA 2000, c N-3, 662n
Negligence Act, RSBC 1996, c 333, 87n
Negligence Act, RSO 1990, c N-1, 87n, 89n
Negligence Act, SO 1924, c 32, 89n
North American Free Trade Agreement Implementation Act, SC 1993, c 44, 730n
Northern Pipeline Act, RSC 1985, c N-26, 495n
Nova Scotia Civil Procedure Rules, Royal Gaz Nov 19, 2008, 41n
Nova Scotia Rules of Court – see *Nova Scotia Civil Procedure Rules*
Nuclear Energy Act, RSC 1985, c A-16, 68n

O

Occupational Health and Safety Act, RSO 1990, c O.1, 412n
Occupiers' Liability Act, CCSM c O8, 94n, 95n, 514n
Occupiers' Liability Act, RSA 2000, c O-4, 95n
Occupiers' Liability Act, RSBC 1996, c 337, 95n, 514n
Occupiers' Liability Act, RSM 1987, c O-8; SNS 1996, c 27, 95n
Occupiers' Liability Act, RSO 1990, c O-2, 94n, 95, 514n
Occupiers' Liability Act, SNS 1996, c 27, 95n, 514n
Office of the Superintendent of Financial Institutions Act, RSC 1985, c 18, 26n, 423n
Ontario Payday Loans Regulation – see *General*, O Reg 98/09

P

Partnership Act, 1890, 53 and 54 Vict., c 39 (UK), 565n
Partnership Act, CCSM c P30, 581n
Partnership Act, RSA 2000, c P-3, 581n, 582n
Partnership Act, RSBC 1996, c 348, 565n, 567, 568, 570, 570n, 571, 572, 574, 575, 576, 577, 578, 579, 580n, 581n
Partnership Act, RSNB 1973, c P-4, 581n
Partnership Act, RSNS 1989, c 334, 565n, 567, 568, 570, 571, 572, 574, 575, 576, 577, 578, 579, 581n
Partnership Act, RSS 1978, c P-3, 581n, 582n
Partnerships Act, RSO 1990, c P.5, 565n, 566, 567, 568, 570, 571, 572, 574, 575, 576, 577, 578, 579, 581n
Partnerships Statute Law Amendment Act, 1998, SO 1998, c 2, 581n
Patent Act, RSC 1985, c P-4., 458, 469, 475n
Patriot Act, 115 Stat. 272, 780
Pawnbrokers Act, RSO 1990, c P. 6, 337n
Pay Equity Act, RSO 1990, c P-7, 409n
Payday Loans Act, 2008, SO 2008, c 9, 67n, 202n, 321n
Payday Loans Regulation, 2008, Alta Reg 157/2009, 321n
Payday Loans Regulation, 2008, BC Reg 57/2009, 321n
Payment Card Networks Act, SC 2010, c 12, 441, 752n, 752
Payment Clearing and Settlements Act, SC 1996, c C-21, 429n, 441n
Personal Health Information Act, CCSM c P-33.5, 784n, 785n
Personal Health Information Privacy and Access Act, SNB 2009, c P-7.05, 784n
Personal Health Information Protection Act, SO 2004, c 3, 784n
Personal Information International Disclosure Act, SNS 2006, c 3, 780n
Personal Information Protection Act, SA 2003, c P-6.5, 766n, 792n
Personal Information Protection Act, SBC 2003, c 63, 792n
Personal Information Protection and Electronic Documents Act, SC 2000, c 5, 208n, 405, 755, 767n, 779, 791
Personal Information Protection and Identity Theft Prevention Act, CCSM c P33.7, 792n
Personal Property Security Act, CCSM c P35, 672n
Personal Property Security Act, RSBC 1996, c 359, 673n
Personal Property Security Act, RSO 1990, c P.10, 319n, 672n, 674n, 676–681, 678n, 681n, 682n, 683n, 766
Personal Property Security Act, SNS 1995-6, c 13, 674n
Personal Property Security Act, SS 1993, c P-6.2, 672n, 682n
Pest Control Products Act, SC 2002, c 28, 68n
Petroleum and Natural Gas Act, RSBC 1996, c 361, 494n
Plant Breeders' Rights Act, SC 1990, c 20, 471n, 478
Power of Attorney Act, RSBC 1996, c 370, 370n
Power of Attorney and Mental Health Amendment Act, CCSM c P97, 370n
Powers of Attorney Act, 2002, SS 2002, c P20.3, 370n
Privacy Act, CCSM c P125, 796n
Privacy Act, RSBC 1996, c 373, 796n
Privacy Act, RSC 1985, c P-21, 778n, 781–783, 786
Privacy Act, RSNL 1990, c P-22, 796n
Privacy Act, RSS 1978, c P-24, 796n
Private Security and Investigative Services Act, 2005, SO 2005, c 34, 794n
Proceeds of Crime (Money Laundering) and Terrorist Financing Act, SC 2000, c 17, 551
Professional Corporations Act, SS 2001, c P-27.1, 602n
Property Law Act, RSBC 1996, c 377, 494n, 540n, 549n
Property Rights Advocate Act, SA 2012, c P-26.5, 500
Public Accounting Act, 2004, SO 2004, c 8, 174n
Public Servants Disclosure Protection Act, SC 2005, c 46, 782

Q

Queen's Bench Act, 1998, SS 1998, c Q-1.01, 44n, 151n

R

Real Estate Act, RSA 2000, c R-5, 373n
Real Estate Amendment Act, 2006, SA 2006, c 29, 551n
Real Estate and Business Brokers Act, S.O 2002, c 30, Sch C, 174n, 373n
Real Estate Trading Act, SNS 1996, c 28, 373n
Real Property Act, CCSM c R-30, 500n, 541n, 543n
Real Property Act, RSPEI 1988, c R-3, 540n, 541n, 543n
Real Property Limitations Act, RSO 1990, c L.15, 500n
Reciprocal Enforcement of Judgments (UK) Act, RSO 1990, c R.6, 739n
Registry Act, RSO 1990, c R-20, 501n
Regulated Health Professions Act, 1991, SO 1991, c 18, 116n
Religious Organization's Lands Act, RSO 1990, c R-23, 168n
Rent Controls Act, 1992, SO c 11, 530n
Repair and Storage Liens Act, RSO 1990, c R-25, 333n
Residential Tenancies Act, 2006, SO 2006, c 17, 260n, 491n, 509n, 519n, 528n, 529n, 530n
Residential Tenancies Act, 2006, SS 2006, c R-22.0001, 260n
Residential Tenancies Act, CCSM c R119, 519n, 528n, 529n
Residential Tenancy Act, SBC 2002, c 78, 52, 319n, 509n, 519n, 528n, 529n
Restatement of Contracts (US), 278n
Restatement of Torts (US), 278n
Right to Information and Protection of Privacy Act, SNB 2009, c R-10.6, 784n
Rights of Labour Act, RSO 1990, c R.33, 416n
Rules of Civil Procedure, RRO 1990, Reg 194, 41n, 44n
Rules of the Small Claims Court, O Reg 258/98, 256n

S

Sale of Goods Act, 25, 139, 165, 193, 199, 209, 215–217, 224, 299–302, 308, 311, 313–314, 316, 319, 321, 322–323
Sale of Goods Act, RSA 2000, c S-2, 225n, 303n, 304n, 305n, 306n, 310n, 314n
Sale of Goods Act, RSBC 1996, c 410, 139n, 165n, 193n, 216n, 265n, 302, 303n, 304n, 305n, 306n, 310n, 312n, 314n, 342n, 343n
Sale of Goods Act, RSNL 1990, c S-6, 303n, 304n, 305n, 303n, 310n, 315n
Sale of Goods Act, RSNS 1989, c 408, 139n, 165n, 193n, 216n, 265n
Sale of Goods Act, RSO 1990, c S-1, 159n, 164n, 193n, 216n, 265n, 303n, 304n, 305n, 306n, 310n, 315n, 318n
Sarbanes-Oxley Act of 2002, 116 Stat. 745, 118, 612
Saskatchewan Human Rights Code, SS 1979, c S-24.1, 778n
Securities Act, RSA 2000, c P-7, 678n
Securities Act, RSA 2000, c S-4, 107n, 651n
Securities Act, RSBC 1996, c 418, 107n, 651n
Securities Act, RSO 1990, c S-5, 107n, 174n, 199n, 617n, 625n, 651n, 653n, 654n
Securities Act, RSQ, c V-1.1, 651n
Securities Transfer Act, SO 2006, c 8, 607n, 679n
Settled Estates Act, RSO 1990, c S.7, 490n
Settlement of International Investment Disputes Act, SC 2008, c 8, 741n
Solicitors Act, RSO 1990, c S-15, 40n
Sonny Bono Copyright Extension Act of 1998, 112 Stat. 2827, 449n, 460
Special Economic Measures Act, SC 1992, c 17, 726
Special Import Measures Act, RSC 1985, c S-15, 727n, 728
Specific Claims Tribunal Act, SC 2008, c 22, 485n
Statute Law Amendment Act, 1958, SBC 1958, c 52, 215n
Statute Law Amendment (Government Management and Services) Act, 1994, SO 1994, c 27, 215n
Statute of Frauds, 207, 209–217, 224, 227, 242, 364, 569n
Statute of Frauds: An Act for the prevention of frauds and perjuries, 29 Charles II, c 3 (1677, UK), 209n
Statute of Frauds, RSM 1987, c F-158, 209n
Statute of Frauds, RSNS 1989, c 442, 167n, 212n, 525n
Statute of Frauds, RSO 1990, c S. 19, 212n, 525n
Statute of Frauds, RSPEI 1988, c S-6, 212n
Strata Property Act, SBC 1998, c 43, 497n
Substitute Decisions Act, 1992, SO 1992, c 30, 370n
Supreme Court Act, RSC 1985, c S-26, 32
Supreme Court of Judicature Act, 1873, 36 & 37 Vict, c 66, 28n
Supreme Court of Judicature Act, 1875, 38 & 39 Vict, c 77, 28n
Supreme Court Rules, BC Reg 221/90, 41n
Surface Rights Acquisition and Compensation Act, RSS 1978, c S-65, 494n
Surface Rights Act, CCSM c 5235, 494n
Surface Rights Act, RSA 2000, c S-24T, 494n

T

Telecommunications Act, SC 1993, c 38, 318n, 752, 767n, 786, 794, 795
Tenant Protection Act, SO 1997, c 24, 530n
Textile Labelling Act, RSC 1985, c T-10, 65, 68
Ticket Sales Act, 2017, SO 2017, c 33, Sched. 3, 316n
Title 17, Code of Federal Regulations, Part 205, 118n
Tobacco Act, SC 1997, c 13, 52n
Tobacco Damages and Health Care Costs Recovery Act, SBC 1998, c 45, 93n
Tobacco Damages and Health Care Costs Recovery Act, SBC 2000, c 30, 94n

Tobacco Health Care Costs Recovery Act, SNL 2001, c T-4.2, 94n

Tourism Industry Act, RSPEI 1988, c T-3.3, 337n

Tourist Accommodation Act, SNS 1994–5, c 9, 337n

Trade Practice Act, RSBC 1996, c 457, 65n

Trade Union Act, RSNS 1989, c 475, 168n, 413n

Trade Union Act, RSS 1978, c T-17, 416n

Trademark Dilution Revision Act of 2006, 15 U.S.C § 114, 761n

Trade-marks Act, RSC 1985, c T-13, 449n, 450, 452, 453, 454n, 455n, 456–458, 761

Transportation of Dangerous Goods Act, SC 1992, c 34, 68n

Trust and Loan Companies Act, SC 1991, c 45, 26, 424

Tsawwassen First Nation Final Agreement Act, SC 2008, c 32, 169

U

Unconscionable Transactions Act, RSA 2000, c U-2, 201n

Unconscionable Transactions Act, RSNB 2011, c 233, 201n

Unconscionable Transactions Relief Act, CCSM c U20, 201n

Unconscionable Transactions Relief Act, RSPEI 1988, c U-2, 201n

United Nations Commission on International Trade Law (UNCITRAL) Model Law on Electronic Signatures (2001), 139

UNCITRAL Model Law on Electronic Commerce (1996), 139

United Nations Convention on Contracts for the International Sale of Goods, 215, 315

United Nations Convention on the Use of Electronic Communications in International Contracts (2005), 139

United Nations Foreign Arbitral Awards Convention Act, RSC 1985, c 16, 741n

W

Wage Earner Protection Program Act, SC 2005, c 47, 694n, 704n

Wages Act, RSO 1990, c W.1, 245n

War Measures Act, 1914, 5 George V, c 2, 500

Warehouse Lien Act, RSBC 1996, c 480, 333n, 334n

Warehousemen's Lien Act, RSNS 1989, c 499, 334n

Waste Diversion Act, 2002, SO 2002, c 6, 662n

Waste Management Act, RSBC 1996, c 482, 662n

Water Act, RSA 2000, c W-3, 662n

Water Act, RSBC 1996, c 483, 662n

Water Resources Act, RSO 1990, c. O.40, 662n

Weights and Measures Act, RSC 1985, c W-6, 63n

Westbank First Nation Self-Government Act, SC 2004, c 17, 169n

Winding-Up and Restructuring Act, RSC 1985, c W-11, 693n, 708

Wireless Service Agreement Act, SO 2013, c 8, 127n

Workers' Compensation Act, RSBC 1996, c 492, 171n, 411n

Workers' Compensation Act, SNS 1994–95, c 10, 171n, 411n

Workplace Safety and Insurance Act, SO 1997, c 16, 171n, 411n

Table of Cases

Numbers

394 Lakeshore Oakville Holdings Inc v Misek (2010), OJ No 4659, 492n

1017933 Ontario Ltd v Robin's Foods Inc (1998), OJ No 1110, 383n

1028840 BC Ltd v The Heritage Dispensary Clinic Society (2018), BCSC 82, 518n

1146845 Ontario Inc v Pillar to Post Inc (2014), ONSC 7400, 387n

1267623 Ontario Inc v Nexx Online Inc (1999), 45 OR (3d) 40, 767n

1394918 Ontario Ltd v 1310210 Ontario Inc (2002), 57 OR (3d) 607, 658n

175777 Ontario Ltd v Magna International Inc (2001), 200 DLR (4th) 521, 83n

2105582 Ontario Ltd (Performance Plus Golf Academy) v 375445 Ontario Limited (Hydeaway Golf Club) (2017), ONCA 980, 519n

32262 BC Ltd v 411676 Alberta Ltd (1995), 29 Alta LR (3d) 415 (Alta QB), 374n

347671 BC Ltd v Heenan Blaikie (2002), BCJ No 347, 111n

405341 Ontario Ltd v Midas Canada Inc (2010), ONCA 478, 386n

671122 Ontario Ltd v Sagaz Industries Canada Inc (2001), SCC 59, 83n, 395n

6792341 Canada Inc v Dollar IT Limited (2009) ONCA385, 386n

859587 Ontario Ltd v Starmark Property Management Ltd (1999), 42 BLR (2d) 16, 684n

978011 Ontario Ltd v Cornell Engineering Co (2001), 12 BLR (3d) 240 (Ont CC), 129n

A

AE Le Page Ltd v Kamex Developments Ltd (1977), 78 DLR (3d) 223, 566n

AG of Canada v Laminated Structures & Holdings Ltd (1961), 28 DLR (2d) 92, 301n

AG of Quebec v Quebec Association of Protestant School Boards et al (1984), 10 DLR (4th) 321, 14n

AMS Equipment Inc v Case (1999), BCJ No 124, 310n

A T v Globe24h.com, 2017 FC 114, 778n

Abraham v Canadian Admiral Corp (1998), 39 OR (3d) 176, 703n

Adams-Eden Furniture Ltd v Kansa General Insurance Co (1996), 141 DLR (4th) 288, 350n

Adelaide Capital Corp v Integrated Transportation Finance Inc (1994), 111 DLR (4th) 493, 338n, 339n

Addison Chevrolet Buick v General Motors of Canada (2016), ONCA 324, 386n

ADGA Systems International Ltd v Valcom Ltd (1999), 43 OR (3d) 101, 661n

AGC Flat Glass North America Ltd v CCP Atlantic Specialty Products Inc (2010), NSJ No 140, 518n

Agrifoods International Corp v Beatrice Foods Inc (1997), BCJ No 393, 280n

AI Enterprises v Bram (2014), SCC 12, 82n, 83n

Air Canada Pilots Assn v Kelly (2011), FCJ No 152, 410n

Air Canada v M & L Travel Ltd (1993), 108 DLR (4th) 592, 620n

Air France v Virtual Dates, Inc, 761n

Alberta (Attorney General) v Moloney (2015), SCC 51, 693n

Alberta (Education) v Canadian Copyright Licensing Agency (Access Copyright) (2012), SCC 37, 459n, 468n

Alberta (Information and Privacy Commissioner) v United Food and Commercial Workers, Local 401 (2013), SCC 62, 777n

Alberta (Information and Privacy Commissioner) v University of Calgary (2016), SCC 53, 27n

Alberta (Minister of Education) v Canadian Copyright Licensing Agency (2012), 2 SCR 345, 449n

Alberta (Privacy Commissioner) v University of Calgary (2016), SCC 53, 786

Alberta v Elder Advocates of Alberta Society (2011), SCC 24, 103n

Albo v Concorde Group Corp (2004), 235 DLR (4th) 465, 519n

Allen v Hearn (1875), 1 TR 56, 172n

Allen v Taku Safari Inc (2003), BCSC 516, 262n

Alleslev–Krofchak v Vlacom Limited (2010), ONCA 557, 82n

Allied Domecq Retailing International Canada Ltd v Bertico Inc (2015), QCCA 624, 385n

Alvin's Auto Service Ltd v Clew Holdings Ltd (1997), SJ No 387, 380n

Amazon.com, Inc v Canada (Attorney General) (2010), FCJ No 1209, reversed (2012) 2 FCR 459, 472n, 765n

Amberwood Investments Ltd v Durham Condominium Corp No 123 (2002), 211 DLR (4th) 1, 493n

American International Assurance Life Company Ltd v Martin (2003), 223 DLR (4th) 1, 354n

Amex Bank v Adams (2014), SCC 56, 62n

Amexon Realty Inc v Comcheq Services Ltd (1998), 155 DLR (4th) 661, 359n

Amirault v MNR (1990), 90 DTC 1330, 257n

Andrews Bros Ltd v Singer & Co Ltd (1934), 1 KB 17, 308n

Andrews v Grand & Toy Alberta Ltd (1978), 2 SCR 229, 97n

Andrews v Law Society British Columbia (1989), 1 SCR 143, 16n

Andrews v Ramsay (1903), 2 KB 635, 372n

Angevaare v McKay (1960), 25 DLR (2d) 521, 193n

Ann of Green Gables Licensing Authority Inc v Avonlea Traditions Inc (2000), OJ No 740, 725n

Anns v Merton London Borough Council (1978), AC 728 (HL), 85n, 110n

Anton Piller KG v Manufacturing Processing Ltd (1976), Ch 55, 457n

Antrim Centre Ltd v Ontario Transport (2011), ONCA 419, aff'd 2013 SCC 13, 80n

Apeco of Canada Ltd v Windmill Place (1978), 82 DLR (3d) 1, 287n

Apotex Fermentation Inc v Novopharm Ltd (1998), 162 DLR (4th) 111, 478n

Apotex Inc v Sanofi-Synthelabo Canada Inc (2008), SCC 61 471

Apotex Inc v Wellcome Foundation Ltd (2002), 219 DLR (4th) 660, 472n

Apple Canada Inc v Canadian Private Copying Collective (2008), FCJ No 5 (FCA), 764n

Appleby v Myers (1867), LR 2 CP 651, 265n

Archibald v Canada (2000), 188 DLR (4th) 538, 51n

Armstrong v Northwest Life Insurance Co of Canada (1990), 72 DLR (4th) 410, 414, 198n

Arndt v Smith (1997), 148 DLR (4th) 48 (SCC), 93n

Arnold v Teno (1978), 2 SCR 287, 97n

Aros Investments Ltd v Picchi (2003), BCSC 78 (CanLII), 541n

Assaad v Economic Mutual Insurance Group (2002), 214 DLR (4th) 655, 354n

Assn of Justices of the Peace of Ontario v Ontario (Attorney General) (2008), 92 OR (3d) 16, 410n

Astley Industrial Trust Ltd v Grimley (1963), 1 WLR 584, 342n

Astley v Verdun (2011 ONSC 3651; 2013 ONSC 2998; 2013 ONSC 6734), 97n

Astra Zeneca v Apotex (2017), SCC 36, 472

Atcor Ltd v Continental Energy Marketing Ltd (1996), 6 WWR 274, 263n

Attis v Ontario (2011), ONCA 675, 380n

Attorney General v Walsh (2002), SCC 83, 497n

Attwood v Lamont (1920), 3 KB 571, 180n

Austie v Aksnowicz (1999), 10 WWR 713, 70 Alta LR (3d) 154 (CA), 215

Australian Knitting Mills Ltd v Grant (1933), 50 CLR 387, 306n

Automatic Self-Cleansing Filter Syndicate Co Ltd v Cuninghame (1906), 2 Ch 34 (UKCA), 616

Avco Financial Services Realty Ltd v Norman (2003), 226 DLR (4th) 175, 114n

Avery v Salie (1972), 25 DLR (3d) 495, 379n

Awan v Levant (2016), ONCA 970, 82n

B

B & R Development Corp (cob Abbey Lane Homes) v Trail South Developments Inc (2012), AJ No 1171, 211n

BC Saw Mill Co v Nettleship (1868), LR 3 CP 499, 284n

BCGEU v British Columbia (Minister of Health Services) (2005), BCSC 446, 780n

BG Preeco 3 Ltd v Universal Exploration (1987), 6 WWR 127, 518n

Backman v Canada (2001), 196 DLR (4th) 193 (SCC), 567n

Bahlieda v Santa (2003), 233 DLR (4th) 382 (ONCA), 757n

Baldry v Marshall (1925), 1 KB 260, 305n

Bangoura v Washington Post (2004), 235 DLR (4th) 564, 771n

Bank Leu AG v Gaming Lottery Corp (2003), 231 DLR (4th) 251, 607n
Bank of British Columbia v Turbo Resources Ltd (1983), 23 BLR 152, 363n
Bank of Montreal v Bray (1997), 36 OR (3d) 99, 701n
Bank of Montreal v Cochrane (2010), AJ No 1210, 796n
Bank of Montreal v Duguid (2000), 185 DLR (4th) 458, 200n
Bank of Montreal v Dynex Petroleum (2002), 1 SCR 146, 494n
Bank of Montreal v Giannotti (2000), 197 DLR (4th) 266, 707n
Bank of Montreal v Hall (1990), 1 SCR 121, 14n
Bank of Montreal v Innovation Credit Union (2010) SCC 47 2010, 3 SCR 3, 672n, 676n, 684n, 687n
Bank of Montreal v Javed (2016), ONCA 49, 201n, 361n
Bank of Montreal v Korico Enterprises Limited (2000), 50 OR (3d) 520, 363n
Bank of Montreal v Marcotte (2014), SCC 55, 62n
Bank of Montreal v Wilder (1986), 32 DLR (4th) 9 (SCC), 363n
Bannister v General Motors of Canada Limited (1998), 40 OR (3d) 577, 402n
Barafield Realty Ltd v Just Energy (BC) Limited Partnership (2017), BCCA 307, 281n
Barclays Bank plc v O'Brien (1993), 4 All ER 417, 200n
Bardal v The Globe and Mail Ltd (1960), 24 DLR (2d) 140, 399n
Barrick Gold Corporation v Lopehandia (2004), 71 OR (3d) 416 (Ont CA), 757n
Barrick v Clark (1950), 4 DLR 529, 130n
Bartin Pipe & Piling Supply Ltd v Epscan Industries Ltd (2004), 236 DLR (4th) 75, 310n
Bassie v Melnychuk (1993), 14 Alta LR (3d) 31, 210n
Bata v City Parking Canada Ltd (1973), 2 OR (2d) 446, 328n
Bayliner Marine Corp v Doral Boats Ltd (1986), 10 CPR (3d) 289, 477n
Bazley v Curry (1999), 2 SCR 534, 78n, 397n
BCE Inc v 1976 Bondholders (2008), SCC 69, 713, 714
Beals v Saldanha (2003), 3 SCR 416, 294, 740n
Beecham Canada Ltd v Proctor & Gamble Co (1982), 61 CPR (2d) 1, 472n
Beheyt v Chrupalo (2004), 244 DLR (4th) 688, 94n
Belknap v Meekes (1989), 64 DLR (4th) 452, 113n
Bell Actimedia Inc v Puzo (1999), 166 FTR 202, 759n
Bell Canada v SOCAN (2012), 2 SCR 326, 449n
Bell v City of Sarnia (1987), 37 DLR (4th) 438, 111n
Benavides v Insurance Corporation of British Columbia (2017), BCCA 15, 84n
Benham v St Germain (2016), SCC 48, 87n
Beresford v Royal Insurance Co (1938), AC 586, 353n
Berger v Willowdale (1983), 41 OR (2d) 89, 593n
Bernard v Canada (Attorney General) (2014), SCC 13, 781n
Berry v Pulley (2002), SCC 40, 417n
Bertalan Estate v American Home Assurance Co (2001), 196 DLR (4th) 445, 354n
Beswick v Beswick (1968), AC 58, 236n
Bet-Mur Investments Ltd v Spring (1994), 17 BLR (2d) 55, aff'd (1999) OJ No 342 (Ont CA), 572n
Bhamre Employment Insurance Claim Appeal (September 23, 1998), CUB42012A, 793n
Bhasin v Hrynew (2014), SCC 71, 219n, 226n, 279
Bilski v Kappos 561 US (2010), 472n
Birch v Brenner (2017), BCCA 22, 492n
Bisaillon v Concordia University (2006), 1 SCR 666, 741n
Black v Law Society of Alberta (1989), 1 SCR 591, 119n
Black v Owen (2017), ONCA 397, 493n
Blacklaws v 470433 Alberta Ltd (2000), 187 DLR (4th) 614, 590n
Blackpool and Fylde Aero Club Ltd v Blackpool Borough Council (1990), 1 WLR 1195, 134n
Blue Line Hockey Acquisition Co v Orca Bay Hockey Limited Partnership (2008), BCJ No 24, 583n
BMG Canada Inc v John Doe (2004), 239 DLR (4th) 726, 460n
BMP & Daughters Investment Corp v 941242 Ontario Ltd (1993), 7 BLR (2d) 270, 680n
Bomford v Wayden Transportation Systems Inc (2010), BCJ No 2080 (BCSC), 402n
Bon Malhab v Diffusion Métroméda CMR Inc (2011), SCC 9, 81n
Bonazza v Forensic Investigations Canada Inc (2009), OJ No 2626, 180n
Bonisteel v Collis Leather Co Ltd (1919), 45 OR 195, 630n
Bonsor v Musicians' Union (1954), Ch 479, overturned on appeal (1956) AC 105, 416
Border Enterprises Ltd v Beazer East Inc (2002), 216 DLR (4th) 107, 111n
Borgo Upholstery Ltd v Canada (2004), NSJ No 7 (NSCA), 305n
Bow Valley Husky (Bermuda) Ltd v Saint John Shipbuilding Ltd (1997), 153 DLR (4th) 385, 92n
Brackenbury v Hodgkin, 102 A 106, 116 Me 399 (1917), 138n
Braintech Inc v Kostiuk (1999), 171 DLR (4th) 46, 770n
Bramble v Medis Health & Pharmaceutical Services Inc (1999), 175 DLR (4th) 385 (NBCA), 399n
Brandt's Sons & Co v Dunlop Rubber Co Ltd (1905), AC 454, 244n
Brant Investments Ltd v Keeprite Inc (1991), 3 OR (3d) 289, 633n, 637n
Brantford General Hospital Foundation v Marquis Estate (2003), 67 OR (3d) 432 (SCJ), 147n
Breedan v Black (2012), SCC 19, 757n, 771n
Briar et al v Treasury Board (2003), PSSRB 3, 793n
Brinkibon Ltd v Stahag Stahl Und Stahlwarenhandelsgesellschaft mbH (1983), 2 AC 34 (HL), 136n
Brisebois v Chamberland et al (1991), 77 DLR (4th) 583, 192n
Brisette Estate v Westbury Life Insurance Co (1992), 3 SCR 87, 353n
Bristol Tramways v Fiat Motors (1910), 2 KB 831, 306n
British Columbia Automobile Assn v Office and Professional Employees' International Union, Local 378 (2001), BCJ No 151, 761n
British Columbia Ferry Corp v Commonwealth Insurance Co (1985), 40 DLR (4th) 766, 356n
British Columbia Ferry Corp v Invicta Security Service Corp (1998), 167 DLR (4th) 193, 78n
British Columbia Human Rights Tribunal v Schrenk (2017), SCC 62, 408n
British Columbia Insurance Corp v Kraiger (2002), 219 DLR (4th) 49, 354n
British Columbia (Public Service Employee Relations Commission) v British Columbia Government and Service Employees' Union (1999), 3 SCR 3, 410n
British Columbia Teachers' Federation v British Columbia (2016), SCC 49, 413n
British Columbia v Henfrey Samson Belair Ltd (1989), 59 DLR (4th) 726 (SCC), 693n
British Columbia v Imperial Tobacco Canada Ltd (2005), 2 SCR 473, 2005 SCC 49, 94n
British Telecommunications, plc v One in a Million Ltd (1998), EWJ No 954 (CA), 761n
Brixham Investments Ltd v Hansink, (1971), 18 DLR (3d) 533, 140n
Brown Economic Assessments Inc v Stevenson (2003), SJ No 295, aff'd (2004) SJ No 377 (Sask CA), 572n
Brown v Belleville (City) (2013), ONCA 148, 237n, 239, 277n
Brown v Pronghorn Controls Ltd (2011), ABCA 328, 400n
Brown v Toronto Auto Parks Ltd (1954), OWN 869, 129n
Bruno Appliance and Furniture, Inc v Hryniak (2014), SCC 8, 108n
Buchan v Ortho Pharmaceutical (Canada) Ltd (1984), 28 CCLT 233 (Ont HCJ), 92n
Buck Bros Ltd v Frontenac Builders (1994), OJ No 37, 43n
Budget Rent-A-Car of Edmonton Ltd v University of Toronto (1995), ABCA 52, (1995), 165 AR 236 (Alta CA), 129n
Budgett & Co v Binnington & Co (1891), 1 QB 35, 260n
Bulut v Carter (2014), ONCA 424, 196n
Burke v John Doe (2013), BCSC 964, 757n
Burke v NYP Holdings Inc (2005), 48 BCLR (4th) 363 (BCSC), 771n
Butwick v Grant (1924), 2 KB 483, 375n

C

CC Petroleum Ltd v Allen (2003), 36 BLR (3d) 244, 714n
Cadbury Schweppes Inc v FBI Foods Ltd (1999), 167 DLR (4th) 577, 477n
CadburySchweppes Inc v FBI Foods Ltd (1999), 1 SCR 142, 583n
Calder et al v Attorney-General of British Columbia (1973) SCR 313, 485n
Caldwell v Valiant Property Management (1997), 145 DLR (4th) 559, 516n
Camosun College v CUPE (1999), BCCAAA No 490, 793n
Campanaro v Kim (1998), 112 OAC 171, 198n
Campeau v Desjardins Financial Security Life Assurance Co (2005), MJ No 448 (Man CA), 222n

Canada (Attorney General) v Amazon.com, Inc (2011), FCA 328, 765n
Canada (Attorney General) v Bedford (2013), SCC 72, 20n
Canada (Attorney General) v Downtown Eastside Sex Workers United Against Violence (2012), SCC 46, 20n
Canada (Attorney General) v Fairmont Hotels Inc (2016), SCC 56, 192n
Canada (Attorney General) v Federation of Law Societies of Canada (2015), SCC 7, 551n
Canada (Attorney General) v Lamerman (2008), SCC 14, 268n
Canada (Commissioner of Competition) v Canada Pipe Co (2006), FCA 233, 59n
Canada (Competition Bureau) v Chatr Wireless Inc (2013), ONSC 5315 (CanLII), 63n
Canada (Competition Bureau) v Yellow Pages Marketing BV (2013), ONCA 71, 64n
Canada (Director of Investigation and Research, Competition Act) v Southam Inc (1997), 1 SCR 748, 59n
Canada (Information Commissioner) v Canada (Transportation Accident Investigation & Safety Board) (2006), FCA 157 (CA), 777n
Canada Post v Hamilton (2016), ONCA 767, 50n
Canada (Privacy Commissioner) v Blood Tribe Department of Health (2008), SCC 44, 118n, 786n
(Canada) Commissioner of Competition v Toronto Real Estate Board (2014), FCA 29, 59n
Canada Safeway Ltd v Thompson (1951), 3 DLR 295, 623n
Canada Safeway v Thompson (City) (1997), 7 WWR 565, 493n
Canada Trustco Mortgage Co v Canada (2011), SCC 36 (2011) 2 SCR 635, 248n, 433n, 435n
Canada v Lameman (2008), SCC 14, 488n
Canadian Aero Service Ltd v O'Malley (1973), 40 DLR (3d) 371 (SCC), 624n
Canadian American Financial Corp v King (1989), 60 DLR (4th) 293, 180n
Canadian Association of Internet Providers v SOCAN, (2004), 240 DLR (4th) 193, 466n, 758n, 763n, 764n
Canadian Copyright Licensing Agency v York University (2017), FC 669, 468n
Canadian Council of Churches v Canada (1992), 1 SCR 236, 34n
Canadian Egg Marketing Agency v Richardson (1998), 3 SCR 157, 51n
Canadian Imperial Bank of Commerce v Dene Mat Construction Ltd and others (1988), 4 WWR 344 (NWTSC), 156n
Canadian Imperial Bank of Commerce v Kawartha Feed Mills Inc (1998), 41 OR (3d) 124, 684n
Canadian Imperial Bank of Commerce v Melnitzer (Trustee) (1993), OJ No 3021, aff'd (1997) OJ No 3021, 606n
Canadian Imperial Bank of Commerce v Otto Timm Enterprises Ltd (1995), 130 DLR (4th) 91, 681n
Canadian Indemnity Co v Canadian Johns Mansville Co (1990), 2 SCR 549, 357n
Canadian National Railway Co v Harris (1946), SCR 352, 335n
Canadian National Railway Co v Lovat Tunnel Equipment Inc (1999), 174 DLR (4th) 385, 43n

Canadian Western Bank v 702348 Alberta Ltd (2009), AJ No 481, 512n
Canadian Wireless Telecommunications Association, Bell Mobility Inc, and Telus Communications Company v SOCAN (2008) FCJ No 21, 764n
Canadian-Dominion Leasing Corp Ltd v Suburban Superdrug Ltd (1966), 56 DLR (2d) 43, 308n
Candrug Health Solutions Inc v Thorkelson (2007), FCJ No 586, 760n
Caners v Eli Lilly Canada Inc (1996), 134 DLR (4th) 730, 107n, 305n
Canlan Investment Corp v Gettling (1997), 37 BCLR (3d) 140 (BCCA), 583n
Capital Community Credit Union Ltd v BDO Dunwoody (2001), OJ No 4249, 105n
Capital Pontiac Buick Cadillac GMC Ltd v Coppolla (2013), SKCA 80, 403n
Capital Quality Homes Ltd v Colwyn Construction Ltd (1975), 9 OR (2d) 617, 260n
Caputo v Imperial Tobacco Limited (2004), 236 DLR (4th) 348, 93n
Carlill v Carbolic Smoke Ball Co (1892), 2 QB 484, 133n
Carlill v The Carbolic Smoke Ball Company (1892), 2 QB 484, 158
Carmichael v Provincial Dental Board of Nova Scotia (1998), 169 NSR (2d) 294, 51n
Carter v Irving Oil Co (1952), 4 DLR 128, 525n
Carttera Management Inc, v Palm Holdings Canada Inc (2011), ONSC 2573, 291n
Cash Converters Pty Ltd v Armstrong (1997), OJ No 2659, 384n
Castonguay Blasting Ltd v Ontario (Environment) (2013), SCC 52, 69n
Catalyst Fund General Partner 1 Inc v Hollinger Inc (2006), 79 OR (3d) 288 (Ont CA), 638n
Catalyst Fund General Partner I Inc v Hollinger Inc (2004), OJ No 4722, 601n, 624n
Cathcart Inspection Services Ltd v Purolator Courier Ltd (1982), 34 OR (2d) 187, 282n
CBS Songs Ltd v Amstrad Consumer Electronics (1988), 2 All ER 484, 467n
CCH Canadian Ltd v Law Society of Upper Canada (2004), 1 SCR 339, 449n, 468n
Celestica Inc v ACE INA Insurance (2003), 229 DLR (4th) 392, 351n
Central London Property Trust, Ltd v High Trees House, Ltd (1947), KB 130, 153n
Central Mortgage and Housing Corp v Graham (1973), 43 DLR (3d) 686, 584n
Central Trust Co v Rafuse (1986), 31 DLR (4th) 481, 105n, 107n
Centrale des syndicats du Québec v Quebec (Attorney General) (2018), SCC 18, 409n
Century 21 Canada Limited Partnership v Rogers Communications Inc (2011), BCSC 1196, 754n
Century Services Inc v Canada (Attorney General) (2010), SCC 60 (2010) 3 SCR 379, 709n
Chan v Stanwood (2002), 216 DLR (4th) 625, 701n
Chandler v Webster (1904), 1 KB 493, 264n
Chanore Property Inc v ING Insurance Co of Canada (2010), 94 CLR (3d) 223, 351n
Chaouilli v Quebec (Attorney General) (2005), SCC 35, 20
Chappell's Ltd v Municipality of County of Cape Breton (1963), SCR 340, 396n

Chapronière v Mason (1905), 21 TLR 633, 305n
Chapters Inc v Davies, Ward & Beck LLP (2000), OJ No 4973, aff'd (2001) OJ No 206, 104n
Charlebois v Baril (1928), SCR 88, 135n
Charron Estate v Bel Air Travel Group Ltd (2010), SCCA 114, 770n
Chaston Construction Corp v Henderson Land Holdings (Canada) Ltd (2002), 214 DLR (4th) 405, 711n
Chenier v Canada (Attorney General) (2005), CanLII 23125 (Ont Sup Ct), 706n
Chevalier v Active Tire & Auto Centre Inc (2013), ONCA 548, 404n
Childs v Desormeaux (2006), SCC 18, 84n, 87n, 110n
Chippewas of the Thames First Nations v Enbridge Pipelines Inc (2017), SCC 41, 70n, 488n
Chitel v Bank of Montreal (2002), OJ No 2170, 583n, 584n
Chung v Idan (2006), OJ No 299, aff'd 2007 ONCA 544, 175n
CIA Inspection Inc v Dan Lawrie Insurance Brokers (2010), OJ No 3313, 113n
Ciba-Geigy Canada Ltd v Apotex Inc (1992), 44 CPR (3d) 289 (SCC), 451n
CIBC v Green (2015), SCC 60, 654n
Cinar v Robinson Corporation (2013), SCC 73, 466n, 469n
Citizen's Insurance Co v Parsons (1881), 7 App Cas 96, 49n
City National Leasing Ltd v General Motors of Canada (1989), 1 SCR 641, 55n
City of Kamloops v Nielsen (1984), 2 SCR 2, 85n
Clements v Clements (2012), SCC 32, 87n
Club Resorts Ltd v Van Breda (2012), SCC 17, 294n, 736n, 737n, 740n
Clyde River (Hamlet) v Petroleum Geo Services Inc (2017), SCC 40, 488n
Coast Hotels Ltd v Royal Doulton Canada Ltd (2000), BCJ 2115, 2000 BCSC 1545, 301n
Coca-Cola Ltd Pardhan (2003), FCJ No 22, 457n
Coca-Cola Ltd v Pardhan (1999), 85 CPR (3d) 489, 456
Cojocaru v British Columbia Women's Hospital and Health Centre (2013), SCC 30, 87n
Collins v Associated Greyhound Racecourses (1930), 1 Ch 1, 378n
Collins Barrow Vancouver v Collins Barrow National Cooperative Inc (2016), BCCA 60, affirming 2015 BCSC 510, 601n
Columbia Caterers & Sherlock Co v Famous Restaurants Ltd (1956), 4 DLR (2d) 601, 373n
Commissioner of Competition v BCE Inc, CT 2013-002 (Consent Agreement March 4, 2013), 61n
Commissioner of Competition v F Hoffman La-Roche Ltd (1999), 55n
Commissioner of Competition v Superior Propane Inc (2002), 18 CPR (4th) 417, aff'd (2003) DLR (4th) 55 (FCA), 60n
Communities Economic Development Fund v Maxwell (1991), 3 SCR 388, 364n
Community Savings Credit Union v United Assn of Journeymen and Apprentices of the Plumbing and Pipefitting Industry (2002), BCJ No 654, 376n
Condon v Canada (2014), FC 250, 795n

Consolidated Bathurst Export Limited v Mutual Boiler and Machinery Insurance Company (1980), 1 SCR 888, 722n

Consolidated Exploration and Finance Co v Musgrave (1900), 1 Ch 37, 177n

Conwest Exploration Co v Letain (1964), SCR 20, 41 DLR (2d) 198, 153, 154n

Cook v Deeks (1916), AC 554, 624n

Cooke v CKOY Ltd (1963), 39 DLR (2d) 209, 226n

Co-operators Life Insurance Co v Gibbens (2009), 3 SCR 605, 354n

Cooper v Hobart (2001), SCC 79, (2001) 3 SCR 537, 206 DLR (4th) 193, 85n, 109n, 110n, 116n

Corey Developments Inc v Eastbridge Developments (Waterloo) Ltd (1997), 34 OR (3d) 73, aff'd (1999) 44 OR (3d) 95, 223n

Cornwall Gravel Co Ltd v Purolator Courier Ltd (1978), 18 OR (2d) 551, 284n

Coronation Insurance Co v Taku Air Transport (1991), 85 DLR (4th) 609, 198n

Coronation Insurance Company v Taku Air Transport Ltd (1991), 3 SCR 622, 357

Costco Wholesale Canada Ltd v British Columbia (1998), 157 DLR (4th) 725, 117n

Council of Canadians v Canada (Attorney General) (2006), 277 DLR (4th) 527 (OAC), 745n

Country Style Food Services Inc v Hotoyan (2001), OJ No 2889, 382n

Crabb v Arun District Council (1976), Ch 179, 153n

Cricklewood Property & Investment Trust, Ltd v Leighton's Investment Trust, Ltd (1945) AC 221, 260n

Cronk v Canadian General Insurance Co (1995), 128 DLR (4th) 147 (Ont CA), 399n

Crookes v Multimedia Foundation Inc (2011), SCC 47, 81n

Crookes v Newton (2011), SCC 47, 758n

Crookes v Wikimedia Foundation Inc (2008), BCSC 1424, aff'd (2009) BCJ No 1832, 758n

Crookes v Yahoo (2007), BCSC 1325, aff'd (2008) BCJ No 834, 771n

Cross v Piggott (1922), 2 WWR 662, 512n

Crowell Bro v Maritime Minerals Ltd (1940), 2 DLR 472, 711n

Crown West Steel Fabricators v Capri Insurance Services Ltd (2002), 214 DLR (4th) 577, 107n

Crystalline Investments Ltd v Domgroup Ltd (2004), 234 DLR (4th) 513 (2004) SCJ No 3, 513n, 520n

Culhane v ATP Aero Training Products Inc (2004), 238 DLR (4th) 112, 55n

Cummings v Ford Motor Co of Canada (1984), OJ No 43, 234n

Cundy v Lindsay (1878), 3 App Cas 459, 194, 195

Cunningham v Wheeler (1994), 1 SCR 359, 360n

Cunningham v Whitby Christian Non-Profit Housing Corp (1997), 33 OR (3d) 171, 516n

Cuthing v Lynn (1831), 109 ER 1130, 139n

Cutter v Powell, (1795), 101 ER 573, 264

Cuvelier v Bank of Montreal (2002), 212 NSR (2d) 17, 328n

Cybersell Inc (Arizona) v Cybersell Inc (Florida) (1997), US App LEXIS 33871, 770n

D

D Karrasch Construction Ltd v Telosky (2010), BCSC 423, 290n

DJ Provencher Ltd v Tyco Investments of Canada Ltd (1997), 42 BLR (2d) 45, 129n

Dakin & Co Ltd v Lee (1916), 1 KB 566, 280n

Dale v Manitoba (1997), 147 DLR (4th) 605, 133n

Daniels v Fielder (1989), 52 DLR (4th) 424, 636n

Davies v Collins (1945), 1 All ER 247, 330n

Davis Contractors Ltd v Fareham (1956), AC 696, 261n

Davis v Ouellette (1981), 27 BCLR 162, 577n

Dawson v Helicopter Exploration (1955), SCR 868, 143n

Desjardins Financial Security Life Assurance Company v Emond (2017), SCC 19, 354n

Delane Industry Co Ltd v PCI Properties Corp (2014), BCCA 285, 519n

Delgamuuk v BC (1997), 3 SCR 1010, 170n

Delgamuukw et al v The Queen (1997), 153 DLR (4th) 193, 486n, 487n

Dell Computer Corp v Union des consommateurs (2007), SCC 34, 44n, 741n, 754n

Delrina Corp v Triolet Systems Inc (2002), OJ No 3729, 463n

Delta Construction Co Ltd v Lidstone (1979), 96 DLR (3d) 457, 380n, 657n

Deluce Holdings Inc v Air Canada (1992), OJ No 2382, 43n

Demeter v Dominion Life Assurance Co (1982), 132 DLR (3d) 248, 353n

Design Services Ltd v Canada (2008), SCC 22, 134n

Desjean v Intermix Media, Inc (2006), 57 CPR (4th) 314, aff'd (2007) FCJ No 1523 (FCA), 770n

Diageo Canada Inc v Heaven Hill Distilleries Inc et al (2017), FC 571, 451n

Diamond & Diamond v Srebrolow (2003), OJ No 4004, 43n

Dick Bentley Productions Ltd v Harold Smith Motors Ltd (1965), 2 All ER 65, 197n

Dicker v Angerstein (1876), 3 Ch D 395, 548n

Dickerson v 1610396 Ontario Inc (2013), ONCA 653, 706n

Dickinson v Dodds (1876), 2 Ch D 463, 130n

Dionne v Commission scolaire des Patriotes (2014), SCC 33 (2014) 1 SCR 765, 412n

Director of Investigation and Research v NutraSweet Co (1990), 32 CPR (3d) 1, 59n

Dockrill v Coopers & Lybrand (1994), 111 DLR (4th) 62, 576n

Doe 464533 v ND (2016), ONSC 54, 82n

Doef's Iron Works Ltd v MCCI (2004), OJ No 4358, 154n

Doiron v Devon Capital Corp (2003), 232 DLR (4th) 732 (Alta CA), 375n

Donoghue v Stevenson (1932), AC 562, 91, 234n

Dore v Barreau du Quebec (2012), SCC 12, 53n

Douez v Facebook (2017), SCC 33, 128n

Douglas v Kinger (2008), ONCA 452, 397n

Douglas/Kwantlen Faculty Association v Douglas College (1990), 3 SCR 570, 410n

Dovey v Corey (1901), AC 477, 619n

Dow Chemical Company v Nova Chemicals Corporation (2017), FC 350, 474n

Doyle v Zochem Inc (2017), ONCA 130, 404n

Dube v Canada (2011), SCC 39, 170n

Duckworth v Armstrong (1996), 29 CCLT (2d) 239, 331n

Duncan v Cockshutt Farm Equipment Ltd (1956), 19 WWR 554, 401n

Dunsmuir v New Brunswick (2008), 1 SCR 190, 2008 SCC 9, 53n

Dylex Ltd v Anderson (2003), 63 OR (3d) 659, 637n

E

Eastern Power Ltd v Azienda Communale Energia & Ambiente (1999), 178 DLR (4th) 409 (Ont CA), 136n

Eastern Power Ltd v Ontario Electric Financial Corporation (2010), ONCA 467, 101 OR (3d) 81, 104n

Easthaven Ltd v Nutrisystem.com Inc (2001), 202 DLR (4th) 560, 770n

Eastmond v Canadian Pacific Railway (2004), FC 852 (2004) FCJ No 1043, 406, 788n

Eastwood v Kenyon, (1840), 113 ER 482, 148n

eBay Canada Ltd v MNR (2008), FCA 348, 779n

Economy Foods & Hardware Ltd v Klassen (2001), 196 DLR (4th) 413, 87n

Edgeworth Constructions Ltd v ND Lea & Associates Ltd (1993), 107 DLR (4th) 169, 78n, 111n, 656n

Ediger v Johnston (2013), SCC 18, 86n, 87n

Edmonton (City) v Edmonton East (Capilano) Shopping Centres Ltd (2016), SCC 47, 53n

Edmonton (City) v Uber Canada Inc (2015), ABQB 214, 3, 67n

Edutile Inc v Automobile Protection Association (2000), 188 DLR (4th) 132, 462n

Edwards v Law Society of Upper Canada (2001), 206 DLR (4th) 211, 116n

Eiserman v Ara Farms (1989), 52 DLR (4th) 498, 637n

El Dali v Panjalingham (2013), ONCA 24, 86n

Elder v Koppe (1974), 53 DLR (3d) 705, 290n

Elgert v Home Hardware Stores Ltd (2010), ABQB 65, 402n

Eli Lilly and Co v Novopharm Ltd (2000), 195 DLR (4th) 547, 451n, 470n, 475n

Eli Lilly Canada Inc v Novopharm Limited (2011), FC 1288, aff'd 2012 FCA 232 (CanlII), 744n

Ellesmere v Wallace (1929) 2 Ch 1, 172n

Ellis v Subway Franchise Systems of Canada Ltd (2000), OJ No 3849, 384n

Emcan Bakey Equipment & Supply Ltd v DMI Property Management Inc (2010), OJ No 2315, 520n

Empress Towers Ltd v Bank of Nova Scotia (1990), 73 DLR (4th) 400 (BCCA), 134n

Eng v Toronto (2012), ONSC 6818, 50n

Ennis v Klassen (1990), 4 WWR 609 (Man CA), 194n

Entertainment Software Association v SOCAN (2012), SCC 34, 460n, 461n, 763n

Entertainment Software Association v Society of Composers, Authors and Music Publishers of Canada (2012), SCC 34 (2012) 2 SCR 231, 459n

Entertainment Software Associations v SOCAN (2012), SCC 34 (2012) 2 SCR 231, 764n

Entores, Ltd v Miles Far East Corporation (1955), 2 QB 327, 136n

Envoy Relocation Services Inc v Canada (2013), ONSC 2034, 134n

Equustek Solutions Inc v Jack (2018), BCSC 610, 740n

Erie Sand and Gravel Ltd v Seres' Farms Ltd (2009), 97 OR (3d) 241, 211n

Ernst & Young v Stuart (1997), 144 DLR (4th) 328, 82n, 574n
Errington v Errington (1952), 1 All ER 149, 138n
Esso Petroleum Co Ltd v Mardon (1976), 2 All ER 5 (CA), 197n
Estate of Lynn Louise Hawkins (2006), BCSC 1374, 490n
Evans v Teamsters Local Union No 31 (2008), SCC 20 (2008) 1 SCR 661, 404n
Evergreen Manufacturing Corp v Dominion of Canada General Insurance Co (1999), 170 DLR (4th) 240, 354n
Existological Laboratories Ltd v Century Insurance Co (1982), 133 DLR (3d) 727, aff'd (1983) SCJ No 61, 357n
Eye Masters Ltd v Ross King Holdings Ltd (1992), 44 CPR (3d) 459, 456n

F

Fabbi et al v Jones (1972), 28 DLR (3d) 224, 176n
Fairgrief v Ellis (1935), 2 DLR 806, 147n
Fairview Donut Inc v The TDL Grp Corp (2012), ONCA 867, 384n
Fallowfield v Bourgault (2003), 235 DLR (4th) 263, 492n
Family Insurance Corp v Lombard Canada Ltd (2002), 212 DLR (4th) 193, 359n
Famous Foods Ltd v Liddle (1941), 3 DLR 525, 147n
Far East Food Products Ltd v 1104742 Ontario Ltd (2009), OJ No 1153 (Ont SC), 713n
Farber v Royal Trust Co (1997), 1 SCR 845, 400n
Fast Labour Solutions (Edmonton) Limited v Kramer's Technical Services Inc (2016), ABCA 266, 678n, 700n, 703n
Fernandes v Peel Educational & Tutorial Services Limited (Mississauga Private School) (2016), ONCA 468, 401
Ferrar v Lorenzetti, Wolfe (2012), ONCA 851, 107n
Fibrosa Spolka Akcyjna v Fairbairn Lawson Combe Barbour, Ltd (1943), AC 32, 265n, 266
Fidler v Sun Life Assurance Co (2006), 2 SCR 3, 289, 289n, 358n, 404n
Financial Management Inc v Associated Financial Planners Ltd (2006), 56 Alta LR (4th) 207 (Alta CA), 374n
Fine's Flowers Ltd v General Accident Assurance Co et al (1974), 49 DLR (3d) 641, aff'd (1977), 81 DLR (3d) 139, 113n, 350n
Finlay v Minister of Finance (1986), 2 SCR 607, 34n
First Charter Financial Corp v Musclow (1974), 49 DLR (3d) 138 (BCSC), 165n
First Edmonton Place Ltd v 315888 Alberta Ltd (1988), AJ No 511 (Alta QB), aff'd (1989) AJ No 1021 (Alta CA), 713n
First Real Properties Ltd v Biogen Idec Canada Inc (2013), ONSC 6281, 260n
Fitzgerald v Grand Trunk Railway (1880), 4 OAR 601, 331n
Fletcher v Manitoba Insurance Co (1990), 3 SCR 191, 113n
Flightcraft Inc v Parsons (1999), 175 DLR (4th) 642, 702n
Fluor Corporations v Fluor Curling, CDRP Dispute No 0281, 761n
Foakes v Beer, (1884), 9 App Cas 605, 150n, 151
Focal Properties Ltd v George Wimpey (Canada) Ltd (1975), 14 OR (2d) 295 (ONCA), aff'd (1978) 1 SCR 2, 261n
Fording Coal Ltd v Harnischfeger Corp of Canada (1991), 6 BLR (2d) 157, 307n
Forty Ninth Ventures Ltd v British Columbia (2005), BCCA 213, 494n
Foster v Caldwell (1948), 4 DLR 70, 260n
Fraser River Pile & Dredge Ltd v Can-Dive Services Ltd (1999), 176 DLR (4th) 257, 238n
Free Trade Medical Network Inc v RBC Travel Insurance Co (2006), 215 OAC 230 (OCA), 478n
Friedmann Equity Developments Inc v Final Note Ltd (2000), 1 SCR 842, 156n
Friends of Landsdowne Inc Ottawa (City) (2012), ONCA 273, 50n
Fullowka v Pinkerton's of Canada (2010), SCC 5, 84n
Future Shop Ltd v A & B Sound Ltd (1994), 55 CPR (3d) 182, 456n

G

Gainers Inc v Pocklington Holdings Inc (2000), 194 DLR (4th) 109, 82n
Galambos v Perez (2009), SCC 48 (2009), 2 SCR 678, 104n
Galaske v O'Donnell (1994), 112 DLR (4th) 109 (SCC), 89n
Galerie d'Art du Petit Champlain Inc v Theberge (2002), SCC 34, 458n
Gallant v Roman Catholic Episcopal Corp for Labrador (2001), 200 DLR (4th) 643, 95n
Gallen v Allstate Grain Co (1984), 9 DLR (4th) 496, 222n
Gari Holdings Ltd v Lanham Credit Union (2005), DLR (4th) 74, 512n
Garland v Consumer's Gas Co (1998), 3 SCR 112, 201n
Garner v Murray (1904), 1 Ch 57, 580n
Garratt et al v Orillia Power Distribution Corporation (2008), 90 OR (3d) 161, 171, 86n
Gee v White Spot Ltd (1986), 32 DLR (4th) 238, 301n
Geffen v Goodman Estate (1991), 2 SCR 353, 200
General Billposting Co v Atkinson (1909), AC 118, 277n
General Dry Batteries of Canada Ltd v Brigenshaw (1951), OR 522, 415n
General Electric Capital Canada Inc v Interlink Freight Systems Inc (1998), 42 OR (3d) 348, 684n
General Motors Acceptance Corp of Canada v Cardinali (2000), 185 DLR (4th) 141, 678n
General Motors of Canada Ltd v City National Leasing (1989), 58 DLR (4th) 255 (SCC), 786n
George Mitchell (Chesterhall) Ltd v Finney Lock Seeds Ltd (1983), 1 All ER 108, 61
Gerhard Horn Investments Ltd v Registrar of Trade Marks (1983), 2 FC 878, 454n
Gilbert Steel Ltd v University Construction Ltd (1976), 67 DLR (3d) 606, 149n
Gilbert v Sykes (1812), 16 East 150, 172n
Gilford Motor Company v Horne (1933), Ch 935 (CA), 594n
Gimli Auto Ltd v BDO Dunwoody Ltd (1998), 160 DLR (4th) 373, 676n
Glasbrook Brothers v Glamorgan County Council (1925), AC 270, 150n
Globe Convestra Ltd v Vucetic (1990), 15 RPR (2d) 220 (Ont Gen Div), 518n
GMAC Commercial Credit Corp v TCT Logistics Inc (2004), 238 DLR (4th) 487, 676n
GMS Securities & Appraisals Ltd v Rich-Wood Kitchens Ltd (1995), 121 DLR (4th) 278, 684n
Goderich Elevators Ltd v Royal Insurance Co (1999), 169 DLR (4th) 763, 352n
Gold v Rosenberg (1997), 3 SCR 767, 200n
Goldsoll v Goldman (1915), 1 Ch 292, 180n
Goldthorpe v Logan (1943), 2 DLR 519, 197n
Google Inc v Equustek Solutions Inc (2017), SCC 34, 292n
Google LLC v Equustek Solutions Inc et al, USDC, Northern District of California, San Jose Division, Case No 5:17-cv-04207-EJD, 772n
Gould Estate v Stoddart Publishing (1998), 161 DLR (4th) 321, 463n
Governors of Dalhousie College v Boutilier (1934), 3 DLR 593, 146n
Graham v Wagman (1976), 14 OR (2d) 349, 262n
Grant v Australian Knitting Mills (1936) AC 85, 91n
Grant v Commissioner of Patents (2006), FCAFC 120, 472n
Grant v Prov of New Brunswick (1973), 35 DLR (3d) 141, 133n
Grant v Torstar Corp (2009), SCC 61, 82n
Grant Forest Products Inc v The Toronto-Dominion Bank (2015), ONCA 570, 684n, 709n
Great Lakes Brick and Stone Ltd v Vanderlinder (1993), OJ No 2763, 512n
Greater Fredericton Airport Authority Inc v NAV Canada, (2008), 290 DLR (4th) 405, 149n
Greater Toronto Airports Authority v City of Mississauga (2000), 192 DLR (4th) 443, 14n
Greater Vancouver Regional District Employees' Union v Greater Vancouver Regional District, (2001), BCCA 435, 410n
Green v Law Society of Manitoba (2017), SCC 20, 8n, 117n
Greenman v Yuba Power Products, 59 Cal 2d 57 (1963), 97
Greenwood Shopping Plaza Ltd v Beattie (1980), 2 SCR 228, 516n
Gregorio v Intrans-Corp (1994), 115 DLR (4th) 200 (Ont CA), 308n
Griffin v College of Dental Surgeons of British Columbia (1989), 64 DLR (4th) 652, 51n
Griffith SS Co v Western Plywood Co (1953), 3 DLR 29, 342n
Guerin v The Queen (1984), 2 SCR 335, 487n

H

HJ Heinz Co of Canada Ltd v Canada (Attorney General) (2006), 1 SCR 441, 781n
Hadley v Baxendale (1854), 156 ER 145, 284n
Hager v ECW Press Ltd (1999), 2 FC 287, 463n, 467n
Haida Nation v British Columbia (2004), SCC 73, 487n
Haig v Bamford (1976), 72 DLR (2d) 68, 111n
Haigh v Brooks (1839), 113 ER 119, 147n

Hall v Halifax Transfer Co Ltd (1959), 18 DLR (2d) 115, 397n

Hallmark Pool Corp v Storey (1983), 144 DLR (3d) 56, 344n

Halpern v Attorney General of Ontario et al (2003), 65 OR (3d) 161 (CA), 19n

Hamilton-Wentworth District School Board v Fair (2016), ONCA 421, 405n, 408n

Hamlyn & Co v Talisker Distillery (1894), AC 202, 722n

Hamm v Metz (2002), 209 DLR (4th) 385, 702n

Hanis v Teevan (1998), 162 DLR (4th) 414, 465n

Haraba v Wawanesa Mutual Insurance Company (2017), ABQB 190, 357n

Harbord Insurance Services Ltd v Insurance Corp of British Columbia (1993), 9 BLR (2d) 81, 82n

Harmony Consulting Ltd v GA Foss Transport Ltd (2011), FCJ No 451, 463n

Harrison v University of British Columbia (1990), 3 SCR 451, 410n

Harvard College v Canada (Commissioner of Patents) (2002), 219 DLR (4th) 577, 471

Harvie and Hawryluk v Gibbons (1980), 12 Alta LR (2d) 72, 212n

Hawrish v Bank of Montreal (1969), SCR 515, 223n

Hayter v Canada (2010), TCJ No 175, 567n

Healey v Lakeridge Health Corporation (2010), OJ No 417, 289n

Health Services and Support - Facilities Subsector Bargaining Assn v British Columbia (2007), SCC 27, 17n

Healy v Canadian Tire Corp (2012), ONSC 77, 385n

Hedley Byrne & Co Ltd v Heller & Partners Ltd (1964), AC 465, 96n, 103n, 108n

Hefferon v Imperial Parking Co Ltd (1973), 46 DLR (3d) 642, 129n

Heffron v Imperial Parking Co et al (1974), 3 OR (2d) 722, 328n

Helby v Matthews (1895), AC 471, 338n

Heller v Martens (2002), 213 DLR (4th) 124, 89n

Helps v Clayton (1864), 144 ER 222, 165n

Henco Industries Limited v Haudenosaunee Six Nations Confederacy Council (2006), OR (3d) 721, 497n

Henthorn v Fraser (1892), 2 Ch 27, 135n

Hepburn v Jannock Limited, (2008), 63 CCEL (3d) 101, 154, 192n

Her Majesty the Queen v Pamajewon (1996), 2 SCR 821, 174

Herbison v Canada (Attorney General) (2013), BCSC 2020, 485n

Hercules Managements Ltd v Ernst & Young (1997), 146 DLR (4th) 577, 102n, 110n, 632n

Hercules Management v Ernst Young (1997), 2 SCR 165, 592n

Heritage Capital Corp v Equitable Trust Co (2016), SCC 19, 493n

Herman v Alberta (Public Trustee) (2002), ABQB 255, 722n

Herman v Jeuchner (1885), 15 QBD 561, 177n

Hertz Canada Ltd v Suburban Motors Ltd (2000), BCJ No 830, 328n, 331n

Highway Properties Ltd v Kelly, Douglas & Co Ltd (1971), 17 DLR (3d) 710, 518n

Hill v Hamilton- Wentworth Regional Police Services Board (2007), SCC 41, 110n

Hill v Hamilton-Wentworth Regional Police (2007), SCC 47, 84n

Hill v Nova Scotia (Attorney General) (1997), 1 SCR 69, 211n

Hillis Oil and Sales Ltd v Wynn's Canada, Ltd (1986), 1 SCR 57, 221n, 282n

Hills v Sughrue (1846), 153 ER 844, 260n

Hinz v Berry (1970), 1 All ER 1074, 85n

Hirachand Punamchand v Temple (1911), 2 KB 330, 151n

Hoare v Rennie (1859), 157 ER 1083, 279n

Hodgins v Hydro-Electric Commission of the Township of Nepean (1975), 60 DLR (3d) 1, 112n

Hodgkinson v Economic Mutual Insurance Co (2003), 235 DLR (4th) 1, 354n

Hodgkinson v Hitch House Ltd (1985), 60 OR (2d) 793, aff'd (1987), 60 OR (2d) 797, 301n

Hodgkinson v Simms (1994), 3 SCR 377, 103n, 104n, 107

Hoffer v School Division of Assiniboine South (1973), WWR 765 (SCC), 88n, 89n

Hogarth v Archibald Moving & Storage Ltd (1991), 57 BCLR (2d) 319, 333n

Holland v Hostopia.com Inc (2015), ONCA 762, 398n

Hollis v Dow Corning Corp (1995), 129 DLR (4th) 609, 93n

Honda Canada Inc v Keays (2008), SCC 39 (2008) 2 SCR 362, 279n, 290n, 399n, 402n, 404n

Hongkong Bank of Canada v New Age Graphic Design Inc (1996), CanLII 1898 (BCSC), 156n

Hooper v College of Nurses of Ontario (2006), CanLII 22656 (ON SCDC), 785n

Hopkins v Kay (2014), ONSC 321, 795n

Hopp v Lepp (1980), 112 DLR (3d) 67, 114n

Household Realty Corp Ltd v Liu (2005), 261 DLR (4th) 679 (CA), 24n, 550

Housen v Nikolaisen (2002), 211 DLR (4th) 577, 89n

House v Baird (2017), ONCA 885, 85n, 86n, 95n

Howard v Benson Group Inc (2016), ONCA 256, 398n

Hughes v Gyratron Developments Ltd (1988), BCJ No 1598, 130n

Hughes v Lord Advocate (1963), AC 837, 88n

Hughes v Metropolitan Railway Co, (1877), 2 App Cas 439, 152

Hughes v Sunbeam Corp (Canada) Ltd (2003), 219 DLR (4th) 467, 112n

Hunt v TD Securities Inc (2003), 229 DLR (4th) 609 (Ont CA), 103n

Hunter Engineering Co v Syncrude Canada Ltd (1989), 57 DLR (4th) 321 (SCC), 307n

Hunter Engineering v Syncrude (1989), 1 SCR 426 (SCC), 282n

Hunter v Baluke (1998), 42 OR (3d) 553 (Ont SCJ), 212n

Hunter v Southam Inc (1984), 2 SCR 145, 777n

Hydraulic Engineering Co v McHaffie Goslett (1878), 4 QBD 670, 284n

Hyrsky et al v Smith, (1969), 5 DLR (3d) 385, 194

I

Icahn Partners LP v Lionsgate Entertainment Corp (2010), BCJ No 2130, 631n

IMAX Corp v Showmax Inc (2000), 5 CPR (4th) 81 (FCTD), 759n

Imperial Life Assurance Co of Canada v Colmenares (1967), SCR 443, 722n

International Association of Bridge, Structural, Ornamental and Reinforcing Iron Workers and Its Local 736 v ES Fox Ltd (2006), CanLII 468 (ON LRB), 792n

International Brotherhood of Teamsters v Thérien, (1960), 22 DLR (2d) 1, 416n

Interprovincial Corp Ltd v R (1976), SCR 477, 68n

Investors Compensation Scheme Ltd v West Bromwich Building Society (1998), 1 All ER 98, 219n

IPC Investment Corporation v Sawaged (2011), ONCA 827, 134n

IPSCO Inc & IPSCO Steel Inc v United States & Lone Star Steel Co (1990), 899 F2d 1192 (US Court of Appeals), 728n

IRIS The Visual Group Western Canada Inc v Park (2017), BCCA 301, 181n

Irwin Toy Ltd v Quebec (Attorney-General) (1989), 1 SCR 927, 58 DLR (4th) 577, 13n, 51n

iTrade Finance Inc v Bank of Montreal (2011), SCC 26, 337n, 672n

itravel2000.com Inc v Fagan (2001), 197 DLR (4th) 760, 762n

ITV Technologies, Inc v WIC Television Ltd (2003), 239 FTR 203, aff'd (2005) FCJ No 438 (FCA), 760n

Ivic v Lakovic (2017), ONCA 446, 398n

J

JG Collins Insurance Agencies Ltd v Elsley (1978), 2 SCR 916, 181n

JJ Barnicke Ltd v Commercial Union Assurance Co of Canada (2000), 5 BLR (3d) 199, 357n

JTI MacDonald Corp v Canada (2002), 102 CRR (2d) 189, 52n

Jade Agencies Ltd v Meadow's Management Ltd (1999), BCJ No 214, 518n

Jade West Holdings Ltd v Canada Zau Fu Trade Ltd (2002), BCSC 420, 378n

James v Hutton & J Cool & Sons Ltd (1950), 1 KB 9, 290n

Jane Doe 464533 v ND (2016), ONSC 541, 795

Janiak v Ippolito (1985), 16 DLR (4th) 1 (SCC), 89n

Janssen-Ortho Inc v Amgen Canada Inc (2005), OJ No 2265, 757n

Jarvis v Swan Tours Ltd (1973), QB 233, 290n

JB Printing Ltd v 829085 Ontario Ltd (2003), OJ No 1230, aff'd (2004) 192 OAC 313 (Ont CA), 111n

Jedfro Investments (USA) Ltd v Jacyk (2007), SCC 55, 257n

Jer-Mar Foods Ltd v Arrand Refrigeration Inc (2010), OJ No 1119 (Ont SC) (QL), 364n

Jirna Ltd v Mister Donut of Canada Ltd (1973), 40 DLR (3d) 303, 385n

Johansson v General Motors of Canada Ltd (2012), NSCA 120, 92n

John Campbell Law Corporation v Owners, Strata Plan 1350 (2001), BCSC 1342, 77n

John Labatt Ltd v Molson Cos (1987), 19 CPR (3d) 88 (Fed CA), 454n

Johnson Investments v Pagritide (1923), 2 DLR 985, 223n

Johnson v Bell Canada (2008), FC 1086, supp'l reasons (2009) FCJ No 1066, 793n

Johnson v BFI Canada Inc (2010), MBCA 101, 82n
Jones v Tsige (2012), ONCA 32, 82n, 795n
Jordan & Ste Michelle Cellars Ltd v Gillespies & Co (1985), 6 CPR (3d) 377, 454n
Joseph Constantine Steamship Line Ltd v Imperial Smelting Corp Ltd (1942), AC 154, 263n
Journet v Superchef Food Industries Ltd (1984), 29 BLR 206, 637n
JTI-Macdonald Corp v British Columbia (2000), 184 DLR (4th) 335, 94n
Jurak Holdings Ltd v Matol Biotech Laboratories Ltd (2006), TMOB No 36, 454n

K

Kanitz v Rogers Cable Inc (2002), 58 OR (3d) 299, 44n, 754n
Kardish Food Franchising Corp v 874073 Ontario Inc (1995), OJ No 2849, 384n
Karsales (Harrow) Ltd v Wallis (1956), 2 All ER 866, 308n
Kauffman v Toronto Transit Commission (1960), SCR 251, 335n
Kavanagh v Lajoie (2014), ONCA 187, 200n
KBK No 138 Ventures Ltd v Canada Safeway Ltd (2000), 185 DLR (4th) 650 (BCCA), 265n
KBK No 138 Ventures Ltd v Canada Safeway Ltd (2000), 185 DLR (4th) 651, 265n
Keenan v Canac Kitchens (2016), ONCA 79, 396n, 399n
Keks v Esquire Pleasure Tours Ltd (1974), 3 WWR 406, 290n
Kelly v Cooper (1993), AC 205, 371n
Kelner v Baxter (1866), LR 2 CP 174, 657n
Kendall v Hamilton (1879), 4 App Cas 504, 378n
Kendall v Ivanhoe Insurance Managers Ltd (1985), OJ No 1725, 263n
Keneric Tractor Sales Ltd v Langille (1987), 43 DLR (4th) 171 (SCC), 343n
Kentucky Fried Chicken Canada v Scott's Food Services Inc (1998), 41 BLR (2d) 42, 383n
Kerr v Baranow (2011), SCC 10, 236n, 497n
Kerr v Danier Leather Inc (2007), SCC 44, 107n, 622n, 653n
Kettle v Borris (2000), 10 BLR (3d) 122, 657n
Killoran v RMO Site Management Inc (1997), 33 BLR (2d) 240, 372n
King v Operating Engineers Training Institute of Manitoba Inc (2011), MBCA 80, 222n
King's Norton Metal Co v Edridge (1879), 14 TLR 98, 195, 245n
Kirby v Amalgamated Income Limited Partnership (2009), BCJ No 1555, 235n
Kirkbi AG v Ritvik Holdings Inc (2003), 228 DLR (4th) 297, aff'd (2005) 3 SCR 302, 449n, 470n
Kirkham v Marter (1819), 106 ER 490, 210n
Kitchen v McMullen (1989), 62 DLR (4th) 481, 114n
KKBL No 297 Ventures Ltd v IKON Office Solutions Inc (2004), 243 DLR (4th) 602, 520n
Knoch Estate v Jon Picken Ltd (1991), OJ No 1394 (Ont CA), 371n
Kocotis v D'Angelo (1957), 13 DLR (2d) 69 (ONCA), 175n
Konjevic v Uber Technologies Inc (2016), ONSC 7804, 4n, 67n
Koo v 5220459 Manitoba Inc (2010), 254 Man R (2d) 62, 175n
Korz v St Pierre (1987), 61 OR (2d) 609, 104n
Korz v St Pierre (1988), 43 DLR (4th) 528, 573n
Kosmopoulos v Constitution Insurance Co of Canada (1987), 34 DLR (4th) 208, 354n, 592n, 594
Kotai v Queen of the North (2009), BCJ No 2022, 289n
Koufos v C Czarnikow, The Heron II (1969), 1 AC 350, 284n
Krawchuk v Scherbak (2011), ONCA 352, 360n, 379n
Kreuchen v Park Savannah Development Ltd (1999), 171 DLR (4th) 377, 710n
Ktunaxa Nation v British Columbia (Forests, Lands and Natural Resource Operations) (2017), SCC 54, 70n, 488n, 496n

L

Labatt Breweries v Attorney General of Canada (1980), 1 SCR 914, 51n
Lac Minerals Ltd v International Corona Resources Ltd (1989), 2 SCR 574, 61 DLR (4th) 14, 103n, 478n, 583n, 584n
Lachman Estate v Norwich Union Life Insurance Co (1998), 40 OR (3d) 393, 353n, 357n
Laing Property Corp v All Seasons Display Inc (1998), 53 BCLR (3d) 142, aff'd (2000) 6 BLR (3d) 206 (BCCA), 516n
Lake Ontario Portland Cement v Groner (1961), 28 DLR (2d) 589, 402n
Lakelse Dairy Products Ltd v General Dairy Machinery & Supply Ltd (1970), 10 DLR (3d) 277, 287n
Lambert v Lastoplex Chemical Co Ltd (1972), SCR 569, 92n
Laminated Structures & Holdings Ltd v Easter Woodworkers Ltd (1962), SCR 160, 301n
Lampleigh v Braithwait (1615), 80 ER 255, 155n
Lang Transport Ltd v Plus Factor International Trucking Ltd (1997), 143 DLR (4th) 672, 378n
Langille v Keneric Tractor Sales Ltd (1985), NSJ No 118, 338n
Langley Crossing Shopping Centre v North-West Produce Ltd (2000), BCCA 107, 518n
Lansing Building Supply (Ontario) Ltd v Ierullo (1990), 71 OR (2d) 173, 566n, 584n
Lau v Royal Bank of Canada (2017), BCCA 253, 402n
Laurwen Investments Inc v 814693 NWT Ltd (1990), 48 BLR 100, 261n
Law Society of British Columbia v Canada Domain Name Exchange Corp (2004), 243 DLR (4th) 746, aff'd (2005) 259 DLR (4th) 171 (BCCA), 761n
Law Society of Upper Canada v CCH Canadian Ltd (2004), 236 DLR (4th) 395, 468n
Lawrence v Fox, 20 NY 268 (1859), 239
Lawrence v Maple Trust Co (2007), 84 OR (3d) 94 (Ont CA), 551n
Lawrence v Maple Trust Co et al (2007), 84 OR (3d) 94, 24n
Lawson v Accusearch Inc (2007), FC 125 (FC), 779n
LBP Holdings Ltd v Hycroft Mining Corporation (2017), ONSC 6342, 107n
Leaf v International Galleries (1950), 1 All ER 693 (1950), 2 KB 86 (CA), 194n, 314n
Learmonth v Letroy Holdings Ltd (2011), BCSC 143, 518n
Leatherman v 0969708 BC Ltd (2018), BCCA 33, 537n
Ledcor Construction Ltd v Northbridge Indemnity Insurance Co (2016), SCC 37, 221n
Leese v Martin (1873), LR 17 Eq 224, 687n
Lefebvre (Trustee) v Tremblay (2004), 3 SCR 326, 700n
Lennard's Carrying Co Ltd v Asiatic Petroleum Co Ltd (1915), AC 705, 659n
Leonard v PepsiCo, Inc, 88 F Supp 2d 116 (SDNY 1999), aff'd 210 F 3d 88 (2d Cir 2000), 158n
Leoppky v Meston (2008), ABQB 45, 208n, 212n, 213n
Letourneau v Otto Mobiles Edmonton (1984) Ltd (2002), AJ No 825, 334n
Levy-Russell Ltd v Shieldings Inc (1998), OJ No 3932, 713n
Lewis v Averay (1971), 3 All ER 907, 245n
Lilydale Cooperative Limited v Meyn Canada Inc (2015), ONCA 281, 722n
Lindal v Lindal (1981), 129 DLR (3d) 263, 289n
Lindsey v Heron & Co (1921), 64 DLR 92, 50 OLR 1, 157n, 192n
Livent v Deloitte & Touche (2017), SCC 63, 84n, 87n, 109n, 111, 353n
L-Jalco Holdings Inc v Marino (2011), OJ No 419, 540n
Lloyd v Grace, Smith & Co Ltd (1912), AC 716, 379n
Loft v Physicians' Services Inc (1966), 56 DLR (2d) 481, 135n
London Drugs Ltd v Kuehne & Nagel International Ltd (1992), 97 DLR (4th) 261, 107n, 235n, 238, 238n, 329n, 516n
Louden Manufacturing Co v Milmine (1908), 15 OLR 53, 165n
Love v Acuity Investment Management Inc (2011), ONCA 130, 399n
Low v Pfizer Canada Inc (2015), BCCA 506, 475n
Lyons v Multari (2000), 50 OR (3d) 526 (CA), 180n, 181n
Lysko v Braley (2006), 79 OR (3d) 721 (OCA), 478n

M

M Tucci Construction Ltd v Lockwood (2000), OJ No 3192, 98n, 115n, 566n
MAA Diners Inc v 3 for 1 Pizza & Wings (Canada) Inc (2003), OJ No 430, aff'd (2004) OJ No 297 (QL), 386n
MANB & W Diesel v Kingsway Transports Ltd (1997), 33 OR (3d) 355, 235n
MJB Enterprises Ltd v Defence Construction (1951) Ltd et al (1999), 1 SCR 619, 134n
MacDonald v Vapor Canada (1977), 2 SCR 134, 49n
Machias v Mr Submarine Ltd (2002), OJ No 1261, 385n, 387n
Machtinger v HOJ Industries Ltd (1992), 1 SCR 986, 403n
Machtinger v HOJ Industries Ltd (1992), 91 DLR (4th) 491 (SCC), 398n
MacKay v Starbucks Corporation (2017), ONCA 350, 94n, 95n
MacLeod Savings & Credit Union Ltd v Perrett (1981), 1 SCR 78, 431n
MacMillan-Bloedel Ltd v Binstead (1983), 22 BLR 255, 618n
MacNeil (Litigation Guardian of) v Bryan, (2009), CCLI (4th) 96 (Ont SC), 357n

MacPherson v Buick Motor Co, 111 NE 1050 (1916), 91
Maison Development & Construction Ltd v Jefferson (2015), BCSC 1329, 260n
Mallais v DA Campbell Amusements Ltd (2007), 84 OR (3d) 687 (CA), 335n
Manitoba Metis Federation Inc v Canada (Attorney General) (2013), SCC 14, 104n, 487n
Manufacturers Life Insurance Co v Executive Centre at Manulife Place Inc (2011), AJ No 320, 518n
Manufacturer's Life Insurance Co v Pitblado & Hoskins (2009), MBCA 83, 113n
Manulife Bank of Canada v Conlin (1996), 3 SCR 415, 139 DLR (4th) 426 (SCC), 220n, 363n
Maracle v Travellers Indemnity Co of Canada, (1991), 2 SCR 50, 154
Maritime National Fish Ltd v Ocean Trawlers Ltd (1935), 3 DLR 12, 263n
Mars Canada Inc v Bemco Cash & Carry Inc (2018), ONCA 239, 456n
Marsh v Stacey (1963), 103 Sol J 512 (UK), 575n
Martel Building Ltd v Canada (2000), 2 SCR 860, 134n
Martin v General Teamsters (2011), ABQB 412, 796n
Martin v Goldfarb (1998), 163 DLR (4th) 639, 104n, 107n, 113n, 114n, 592n
Marvco Color Research Ltd v Harris (1982), 2 SCR 744, 196n
Mason v Westside Cemeteries Ltd (1996), CanLII 9113, 135 DLR (4th) 361 (Ont SC), 329n
Massey-Ferguson Industries Ltd v Bank of Montreal (1983), 4 DLR (4th) 96, 678n
Masterpiece Inc v Alavida Lifestyles Inc (2011), SCC 27 (2011) 2 SCR 387 (2011) SCJ No 27, 453n, 454n, 455n
Mattel, Inc v 3894207 Canada Inc (2006), 1 SCR 772, 454n, 456n
Mayfield Investments Ltd v Stewart (1995), 121 DLR (4th) 222, 87n
McCann v Sears Canada Ltd (1998), 43 BLR (2d) 217, aff'd (1999), 122 OCC 91, 306n
McCormick v Fasken, Martineau, DuMoulin, LLP (2014), SCC 39, 395n, 407n
McCready Products Ltd v Sherwin Williams Co of Canada Ltd (1985), 61 AR 234, 305n
McCuaig v Lalonde (1911), 23 OLR 312, 520n
McCullough v Teniglia (1999), 40 BLR (2d) 222, aff'd (1999) OJ No 4401 (QL), 372n
McDiarmid Lumber Ltd v God's Lake First Nation (2006), 2 SCR 846, 170n
McDonic v Hetherington (1997), 142 DLR (4th) 648, 573n
McDonnell v Richter (2010), AJ No 794, 107n
McGaw v Fisk (1908), 38 NBR 354, 165n
McIntire v University of Manitoba (1981), 119 DLR (3d) 352, 410n
McIntyre Estate v Ontario (2003), 218 DLR (4th) 193, 93n
McKee v Reid's Heritage Homes Ltd (2009), ONCA 916, 396n
McKesson Canada v Teamsters Chemical Energy and Allied Workers Union, Local 424, 136 LAC (4th) 102, 792n
McKinley v BC Tel (2001), 2 SCR 161, 400n
McKinney v University of Guelph (1990), 3 SCR 229, 15n, 410n
McKnight v Hutchison (2002), 28 BLR (3d) 269, 577n

McLean v McLean (2013), ONCA 788, 192n
McLintock v Alidina (2010), OJ No 49, 113n
McPherson v Gedge (1883–4), 4 OR 246, 710n
McRae Management Ltd v Breezy Properties Ltd (2008), 74 RPR (4th) 50 (BCSC), 375n
MDG Kingston Inc et al v MDG Computers Canada Inc et al (2008), 92 OR (3d) 4 (Ont CA), 386n, 387n
Mechanical Services Inc v Flesch (2011), ONCA 764, 492n
Mediatube Corp v Bell Canada (2017), FC 6, 474n
Meditrust Healthcare Inc v Shoppers Drug Mart (2002), 220 DLR (4th) 611, 592n
Mellco Developments Ltd v Portage Le Prairie (City) (2002), 222 DLR (4th) 67 (Man CA), 134n
Mendoza v Active Tire & Auto Centre Inc (2017), ONCA 471, 386n
Mennillo v Intramodal Inc (2016), SCC 51, 637n
Menow v Honsberger and Jordan House Ltd (1974), SCR 239, 87n
Mercantile Credit Co Ltd v Garrod (1962), 3 All ER 1103, 374n, 571n
Mercantile Union Guarantee Corp v Ball (1937), 2 KB 498, 165n
Merchants Bank v Thompson (1912), 26 OLR 183, 687n
Merck Frosst Canada Inc v Canada (1998), 161 DLR (4th) 47, 475n
Merck Frosst Canada Ltd v Canada (Health) (2012), SCC 3, 781n
Methanex Corporation v United States of America, 744n
Metropolitan Asylums Board Managers v Kingham & Sons (1890), 6 TLR 217, 376n
Metropolitan Water Board v Dick, Kerr & Co (1918), AC 119, 262n
Miazga v Kevello Estate (2009), SCC 51, 81n
Microsoft v Rudder, (1999), 2 CPR (4th) 474, 282
Miller v Advanced Farming Systems Ltd (1969), SCR 845, 280n
Miller v Guardian Insurance Co of Canada (1997), 149 DLR (4th) 375, leave denied (1997) SCCA No 480, 350n
Miller v Smith & Co (1925), 2 WWR 360 (Sask CA), 165n
Millstone Consulting Services Inc v Cleary (2008), OJ No 3106, aff'd (2009) OJ No 4510 (Ont CA), 493n
Milna v Bartsch (1985), BC No 2762, 97n
Milson v Corporate Computers Inc (2003), WWR 250, 793n
Minister of Justice of Canada v Borowski (1981), 130 DLR (3d) 588, 34n
Mira Design v Seascape Holdings (1982), 1 WWR 744 (BCSC), 201n
Mississauga (City) v Uber Canada Inc (2016), ONCJ 461, 3n, 67n
Mitsubishi Heavy Industries Ltd v Canadian National Railway Co (2012), BCSC 1415, 335n
Mitsui & Co (Canada) Ltd v Royal Bank of Canada (1995), 123 DLR (4th) 449, 339n
MNR v Corsano (1999), FCJ No 401 (FCCA), 622n
Mohl v University of British Columbia (2009), BCCA 249, 796n
Molson Breweries v Kuettner (1999), 94 ACWS (3d) 550, 761n

Molson Canada v Oland Brewery Ltd (2002), 214 DLR (4th) 473, 453n
Molson Canada 2005 v Miller Brewing Company (2013), ONSC 2758, 134n
Molson Cos v Moosehead Breweries Ltd et al (1990), 32 CPR (3d) 363, 456n
Momentous.ca Corp v Canadian American Association of Professional Baseball Ltd (2012), SCJ No 9, 737n
Mondesir v Manitoba Assn of Optometrists (1998), 163 DLR (4th) 703, 117n
Monenco Ltd v Commonwealth Insurance Co (2001), 2 SCR 699, 352n
Monta Arbre Inc v Inter-Traffic (1983) Ltd (1989), 71 OR (2d) 182, 282n
Monticchio v Torcema Construction Ltd (1979), 26 OR (2d) 305, 175n
Montreal Gas Co v Vasey (1900), AC 595, 139n
Moore v Bertuzzi (2012), ONSC 3497 (CanLII), 79n
Moreau v St Vincent (1950), Ex CR 198, 462n
Morguard Investments Ltd v de Savoye (1990), 76 DLR (4th) 256, 740n
Morguard Investments v De Savoye (1990), 3 SCR 1077, 294n
Morris Products SA v Marlboro Canada Ltd (2010), FCJ No 1385, 453n
Morris v Baron (1918), AC 1, 214n, 223n
Motherwell v Motherwell (1976), 73 DLR (3d) 62 (Alta CA), 795n
Motherwell v Schoof (1949), 4 DLR 812, 639n
Multiple Access v McCutcheon (1982), 2 SCR 161, 14n
Mundell v 796586 Ontario Ltd (1996), 3 RPR (3d) 277, 519n
Murano v Bank of Montreal (1998), 163 DLR (4th) 21, 672n
Murphy v Little Memphis Cabaret Inc (1998), 167 DLR (4th) 190, 87n
Murray v Sperry Rand Corp et al (1979), 23 OR (2d) 456, 96 DLR (3d) 113, 197n, 234n
Muscutt v Courcelles (2002), 60 OR (3d) 20 (Ont CA), 770n
Mustapha v Culligan of Canada Ltd (2008), SCC 27, 84n, 85n, 88n, 91n, 110n, 234n

N

NM v ATA (2003), BCCA 297, 154n
Nadherny v 880474 Ontario Inc (2010), OJ No 2263, 500n
Naken v General Motors of Canada Ltd (1983), 144 DLR (3d) 385, 35n
National Carriers v Panalpina (Northern) Ltd (1981), AC 675, 512n
National Federation of Independent Business v Sebelius (2012), 567 US 519, 49n
National Hockey League v Pepsi-Cola Canada Ltd (1995), 122 DLR (4th) 412, 451n
National Trust Co v Mead (1990), 2 SCR 410, 549n
Naylor Group v Ellis-Don Construction (2001), SCC 58, 260n
NBD Bank of Canada v Dofasco Inc (1999), 181 DLR (4th) 37, 593n
Neff v St Catharines Marina Ltd (1998), 155 DLR (4th) 647, 333n
Neish v Melenchuk (1993), 120 NSR (2d) 239, 385n
Nelson (City of) v Mowatt (2017), SCC 8, 500n

New Brunswick (Human Rights Commission) v Potash Corporation of Saskatchewan Inc (2008), SCC 45, 410n

New York State Board of Elections v Lopez Torres, 552 US 196 (2008), 33

Newell v CP Air (1976), 74 DLR (3d) 574, 289n

Newfoundland (Treasury Board) v NAPE (2004), 244 DLR (4th) 294, 19n

Newfoundland and Labrador (Human Rights Commission) v Newfoundland Liquor Corp (2004), NLCA 5, 258n

Newfoundland and Labrador v AbitibiBowater Inc (2012) 3 SCR 443, 2012 SCC 67, 703n

Newman v Halstead, (2006), BCJ No 59, 757n

Newport v Government of Manitoba (1982), 131 DLR (3d) 564, 410n

Nicholson v John Deere Ltd (1989), 57 DLR (4th) 639, 93n

Nickel Developments Ltd v Canada Safeway Ltd (2001), 199 DLR (4th) 629, 226n

Nikka Traders, Inc v Gizella Pastry Ltd (2012), BCSC 1412, 306n

Nixon v MacIver (2016), BCCA 8, 554n

Nocton v Lord Ashburton (1914), AC 932, 103n

Nordenfelt v Maxim Nordenfelt Guns and Ammunition Co Ltd (1894), AC 535, 180n

Norman Estate v Norman (1990), BCJ No 199 (BCSC), 222n

Northern Cartage Ltd v Motorway (1980) Ltd (1999), MJ No 323, 512n

Northwest Territories (Commissioner) v Portz, 27 CCLT (2d) 241 (1996), 3 WWR 94, 107n

North-West Transportation v Beatty (1887), 12 App Cas 589, 634n

Nova Scotia (Attorney General v Walsh) (2002), SCC 83, 497n

Nova Scotia Board of Censors v MacNeil (1975), 55 DLR (3d) 632, 34n

Novopharm Ltd v AstraZeneca AB (2003), 233 DLR (4th) 150, supp'l reasons (2006) FCJ No 854, 451n

NPV Management Ltd v Anthony (2003), 231 DLR (4th) 681, 637n

NTP, Inc v Research in Motion Ltd, (2005), 418 F 3d 1282 (US App); (2006) 546 US 1157, 474n

Nutrilawn International Inc v Stewart (1999), OJ No 643, 384n, 385n

O

OK Economy Stores v RWDSU, Local 454 (1994), 118 DLR (4th) 345, 415n

OMBD (2010), No PL050611, 496n

OBG Ltd v Allan (2007), UKHL 21, 82n

Olar v Laurentian University (2007), CarswellOnt 3595, aff'd (2008) OJ No 4623, 758n

Oldfield v Transamerica Life Insurance Co of Canada (1998), 43 OR (3d) 114, aff'd (2002), 210 DLR (4th) 1, 354n

Olivieri v Sherman (2007), 284 DLR (4th) 516, 86 OR (3d) 778 (Ont CA), 139n, 157n

Olley v Marlborough Court Ltd (1949), 1 All ER 127, 129n

Olsen v Behr Process Corporation (2003), BCJ No 627, 234n

Olson v Gullo (1994), 113 DLR (4th) 42, 577n

Onex Corp v Ball Corp (1994), 12 BLR (2d) 151, 43n

Ontario (Alcohol and Gaming Commission of Ontario) v 751809 Ontario Inc (2013), ONCA 157, 26n

Ontario Hydro v Denison Mines Ltd (1992), OJ No 2948, 43n

Orion Industries Ltd v Neil's General Contracting Ltd (2013), ABCA 330, 702n

Orion Interiors Inc v State Farm Fire and Casualty Co (2016), ONCA 164, 359n

Orr v Alook (2013), ABQB 86, 169n

Overseas Tankship (UK) Ltd v Miller Steamship Co Pty Ltd (The Wagon Mound No 2) (1967), AC 617, 88n

Oz Optics Ltd v Timbercon, Inc (2010), OJ No 1963, 6, 105n

P

Pacific Wash-A-Matic Ltd v RO Booth Holdings Ltd (1979), 105 DLR (3d) 323, 257n

Pakozdi v B & B Heavy Civil Construction Ltd (2018), BCCA 23, 399n

Palachik v Kiss (1983), 1 SCR 623, 265n

Panavision International Inc v Toeppen (1996), US Dist LEXIS 19698, 761n

Panorama Developments (Guildford) Ltd v Fidelis Furnishing Fabrics Ltd (1971), 2 QB 711, 374n

Pao On v Lau Yiu Long (1979), 3 WLR 435 (1980), AC 614 (PC), 150n, 202n

Paquette v TeraGo Networks Inc (2016), ONCA 618, 403n

Paradine v Jane (1647), 82 ER 897, 260n

Paramount Pictures Corp v Howley (1992), OJ No 1921, 451n

Parker v South Eastern Railway Co (1877), 2 CPD 416, 128n

Parrish & Heimbecker Ltd v Gooding Lumber Ltd (1968), 1 OR 716, 262n

Pasnak v Chura (2004), BCJ No 790, 637n

Patheon Inc v Global Pharm Inc (2000), OJ No 2532, 636n

Paterson v Burgess (2017), BCCA 298, 494n

Patterson v Gallant (1994), 120 DLR (4th) 1, 356n

Paul v Lam (2011), BCSC 980, 153n

Pax Management Ltd v Canadian Imperial Bank of Commerce (1992), 2 SCR 998, 363n

Payette v Guay Inc (2013), SCC 45, 179n, 181n

Pearce v Gardner (1897), 1 QB 688, 212n

Pearlman v Manitoba Law Society Judicial Committee (1991), 2 SCR 869, 8n

Peevyhouse v Garland Coal & Mining Company, 382 P2d 109 (Okla 1963), 290n

Peinet Inc v O'Brien (1995), 61 CPR (3d) 334, 761n

Peoples Department Stores Inc v Wise (2004), 244 DLR (4th) 564620n, 622n, 648n

Peso Silver Mines Ltd v Cropper (1966), 56 DLR (2d) 117 (SCC), 624n

Peter Kiewit Sons' Co v Eakins Construction Ltd (1960), SCR 361, 260n

Pharmaceutical Society of Great Britain v Boots Cash Chemists (Southern) Ltd (1952), 2 All ER 456, 126n

Phillips v Brooks (1918–19), All ER 246, 195

Pilato v Hamilton Place Convention Centre (1984), 45 OR (2d) 652, 402n

Piller Sausages & Delicatessen Ltd v Cobb International Corp (2003), OJ No 2647, 637n

Pink Panther Beauty Corp v United Artists Corp (1998), 80 CPR (3d) 247 (FCA), 456n

Pinnock Brothers v Lewis and Peat Ltd (1923), 1 KB 690, 308n

Pinteric v People's Bar and Eatery Ltd (2001), OJ No 499, 566n

Pioneer Container (1994), 2 AC 324 (PC), 330n

Pioneer Hi-Bred Ltd v Canada (Commissioner of Patents) (1987), 14 CPR (3d) 491 (FCA), aff'd (1989), 25 CPR (3d) 257 (SCC), 471n

Pittman Estate v Bain (1994), 19 CCLT (2d) 1 (Ont Gen Div), 301n

Planidin v Insurance Corporation of British Columbia (2004), 245 DLR (4th) 511, 350n

Planned Parenthood v Bucci (1997), US Dist LEXIS 3338, 761n

Plas-Tex Canada Ltd v Dow Chemical of Canada Ltd (2004), ABCA 309, 92n, 283n

Playboy Enterprises Inc v Germain (1978), 39 CPR (2d) 32, aff'd (1979), 43 CPR (2d) 271 (Fed CA), 452n

Pliniussen v University of Western Ontario (1983), 2 CCEL 1, 400n

Poliquin v Devon Canada Corporation (2009), ABCA 216, 793n

Portavon Cinema Co Ltd v Price and Century Insurance Co Ltd (1939), 4 All ER 601, 376n

Potter v New Brunswick Legal Aid Services Commission (2015), SCC 10, 276n

Powder Mountain Resorts Ltd v British Columbia (2001), 11 WWR 488 (BCCA), 134n

Practicar Systems Inc v 696373 Alberta Ltd (2007), ABQB 143, 74 Alta LR (4th) 59, 431n

Prebushewski v Dodge City Auto (1984) Ltd (2005), SCC 28, 321n

PreMD Inc v Ogilvy Renault LLP (2013), ONCA 412, 288n

Premium Properties Limited v Subway Franchise Restaurants of Canada, Ltd (2014), ONSC 3150, 135n

Price v Easton (1883), 110 ER 518, 233n

Price v Letros (1973), OJ No 2260, 540n

Privacy Commissioner of Alberta v University of Calgary (2016), SCC 53, 8n

Pro-C Ltd v Computer City Inc (2000), 7 CPR (4th) 193, rev'd (2001), 205 DLR (4th) 568 (2001) OJ No 3600, 456n, 770n

Process Automation Inc v Norsteam Intertec Inc & Arroyave (2010), ONSC 3987, 150n, 151n

Progressive Homes Ltd v Lombard General Insurance Co of Canada (2010), SCC 33, 221n, 352n

Proulx v Sahelian Goldfields Inc (2001), 204 DLR (4th) 670, 622n

PS International Canada Corp (Seaboard Specialty Grains and Foods) v Palimar Farms Inc (2017), SKCA 78, 258n

Public Trustee v Mortimer (1985), 16 DLR (4th) 404, 573n

Pulsifer v GTE Sylvania Canada Ltd (1983), 56 NSR (2d) 424, 402n

Punch v Savoy Jewellers, (1986), 26 DLR (4th) 546, 329n

Pure Energy Marketing Ltd v Ramarro Resources Inc (2003), AJ No 1105, 372n

Q

QNS Paper Co v Chartwell Shipping Ltd (1989), 62 DLR (4th) 36, 378n

Quebec (Procureure generale) v Canada (Procureure general) (2011), QCCA 591, 651n

Queen v Cognos Ltd (1993), 1 SCR 87, 105n, 109, 112n

R

R v 311578 Ontario Corp (2012), ONCA 604, 27n
R v Adams (1996), 3 SCR 101, 487n
R v Armco Canada Ltd (1976), 70 DLR (3d) 287, 56n
R v Armour Pharmaceutical Company (2006), 205 CCC (3d) 97, 658n
R v Badger (1996), 1 SCR 771, 485n
R v Bata Industries Ltd (1995), OJ No 2691, 664n
R v Bata Industries Ltd (1992), 9 OR (3d) 329, 664n
R v Benlolo (2006), 81 OR (3d) 440 (Ont CA), 64n
R v Benson (2009), OJ No 239 (OSC), 477n
R v Bertuzzi (2004), BCJ No 2692, 79n
R v Big M Drug Mart (1985), 1 SCR 295, 14n
R v Big M Drug Mart Ltd (1985), 18 DLR (4th) 321, 14n, 17n
R v Binus (1968), 1 CCC 227, 24n
R v Canadian Dredge & Dock Co Ltd (1985), 19 DLR (4th) 314 (SCC), 658n
R v City of Sault Ste Marie (1978), 85 DLR (3d) 161 (SCC), 647n
R v Cole (2012), SCC 53, 777n, 793n
R v Côté (1996), 3 SCR 139, 486n, 487n
R v Curragh Inc (1997), 1 SCR 537, 658n
R v Drabinsky (2011), ONCA 582, 661n
R v Dyment (1988), 2 SCR 417, 777n, 778nR v Gamboc (2010) SCJ No 55, 777n
R v Gladstone (1997), 2 SCR 723, 487n
R v Guignard (2002), 209 DLR (4th) 549, 51n
R v Harper (2003), 232 DLR (4th) 738, 625n
R v Hoffmann-LaRoche Ltd (1980), 28 OR (2d) 151, aff'd (1981) OJ No 3075, 58n
R v Imperial Tobacco Canada Ltd (2011), SCC 42, 85n, 94n, 109n, 111n
R v Jones (2017), SCC 60, 778n
R v Kanda (2008), 88 OR (3d) 732, ONCA 22 (CanLII), 647n
R v Karigar (2013), ONSC 5199; 71n
R v Kelly (1992), SCJ No 53, 369n, 371n, 372n
R v MacMillan Bloedel Ltd (2002), 220 DLR (4th) 173, 662n
R v Marakah (2017), SCC 59, 778n
R v Marshall (1999), 3 SCR 456, 486n
R v Melnitzer (1992), OJ No 1363, 606n
R v Metron Construction Corporation (2013), ONCA 541, 660n
R v Oakes (1986), 1 SCR 103, 52n
R v Placer Developments Ltd, (1983), 13 CELR 42 (YT Terr Ct), 662n
R v Romaniuk (1993), 112 Sask R 129 (QB), 665n
R v Safety-Kleen Canada Inc (1997), 145 DLR (4th) 276, 659n
R v Sappier/R v Gray (2006), SCC 54, 486n
R v Saskatchewan Wheat Pool (1983), 1 SCR 205, 86n
R v Sim (2017), ONCA 856, 797n
R v Sparrow (1990), 1 SCR 1075, 487n
R v Spencer (2014), SCC 43, 777n, 778n
R v Starnet Communications International Inc (August 17, 2001), Vancouver 125795-1 (BCSC), 173n
R v Stewart (1988), 1 SCR 963, 477n
R v Tessling (2004), 3 SCR 432, 777n
R v Transport Robert (1973) Ltée (2003), 234 DLR (4th) 546, 647n
R v Van der Peet (1996), 2 SCR 507, 486n, 487n
R v Van Kessel Estate (2013), BCCA 221, 13n
R v Varnicolor Chemical Ltd (1992), OJ No 1978, 665n
R v Waterloo Mercury Sales Ltd (1974), 49 DLR (3d) 131, 659n
R v Watts (2005), AJ No 568, 71
R v Weymouth Sea Products Ltd, (1983), 149 DLR (3d) 637, 135n
R v Wilson (2014), ONCA 212, 647n
RLTV Investments Inc v Saskatchewan Telecommunications (2009), 9 WWR 15 (Sask CA), 592n
Raffles v Wichelhaus, (1864), 159 ER 375, 193
Raibex Canada Ltd v ASWR Franchising Corp (2018), ONCA 62, 387n
Rajakaruna v Peel (Regional Municipality) (1981), 10 ACWS (2d) 522 (Ont Co Ct), 402n
Rankin (Rankin's Garage & Sales) v JJ (2018), SCC 19, 85n, 234n
Rausch v Pickering (City) (2013), ONCA 740, 85n
Ray Plastics Ltd v Dustbane Products Ltd (1994), 57 CPR (3d) 474, 451n
RBC Dominion Securities Inc v Merrill Lynch Canada Inc (2008), SCC 54, 399n
Re Application of Abitibi Co (1982), 62 CPR (2d) 81, 471n
Re Assisted Human Reproduction Act (2010), SCJ No 61, 13n
Re BC Motor Vehicle Act (1985), 2 SCR 486, 647n
Re BCE Inc (2008), SCC 69, 620n, 621n, 637n
Re Broadcasting Act (2012), SCC 4, 758n
Re Broadcasting Act (Can) (2011), FCJ No 197, 464n
Re Dowswell (1999), 178 DLR (4th) 193, 701n
Re Estate of Johnson, Rick (2017), ABQB 309, 497n
Re Ferguson and Imax Systems Corp (1983), 150 DLR (3d) 718, 636n
Re Flavell, (1883), 25 Ch D 89, 236n
Re Giffen (1998), 1 SCR 91, 340n, 678n, 700n, 703n
Re Gray (2014), ONCA 236, 706n
Re Green Gables Manor Inc (1998), 41 BLR (2d) 299, 702n
Re Lambert (1994), 119 DLR (4th) 93, 679n
Re McDonic Estate (1997), 31 OR (3d) 577 (OCA), 573n
Re Michael Katz (2013), ONSC 7426, 707n
Re Noel Tedman Holdings Pty Ltd (1967), Qd R 561 (Queensland SC), 590n
Re Olympia & York Enterprises Ltd and Hiram Walker Resources Ltd (1986), 59 OR (2d) 254, 621n
Re Ouellet (2004), 3 SCR 348, 700n
Re Pope & Talbot Ltd (2009), BCJ No 2248, 722n
Re Public Service Employee Relations Act (Alta) (1987), 1 SCR 313, 402n
Re Rizzo & Rizzo Shoes Ltd (1998), 1 SCR 26, 398n
Re Same-Sex Marriage (2004), 246 DLR (4th) 193, 19n
Re Securities Act (2011), SCC 66, 651n
Re Securities Act (Canada) (2011), ABCA 77, 651n
Re Sekretov and City of Toronto (1973), 33 DLR (3d) 257, 493n
Re Sound v Motion Picture Theatre Associations of Canada (2012), SCC 38 (2012) 2 SCR 376, 459n
Re Speedrack Ltd (1980), 1 PPSAC 109, 338n
Re Star Flooring Co Ltd (1924), 3 DLR 269, 257n
Re Still and Minister of National Revenue (1997), 154 DLR (4th) 229, 175n
Re Surrey Creep Catcher (2017), BCIPC 38, 792n
Re Tudale Exploration Ltd and Bruce et al (1978), 20 OR (2d) 593, 153n
Re Williams (1903), 7 OLR 156, 687n
Read v Nash (1751), 95 ER 632, 210n
Reclamation Systems Inc v The Honourable Bob Rae (1996), CanLII 7950 (ON SC), (1996), 27 OR (3d) 419, 154n
Red Label Vacations Inc (Redtag.ca) v 411 Travel Buys Ltd (411 Travel Buys Ltd)(2015), FCA 290, 761n
Redmond v Dainton (1920), 2 KB 256, 260n
Registrar of Trade Marks v Provenzano (1978), 40 CPR (2d) 288, 454n
Reibl v Hughes (1980), 114 DLR (3d) 1, 114n
Reilly v Steelcase Canada Ltd (1979), 26 OR (2d) 725, 402n
Reimer v Friesen (2012), MBQB 32, 174n
Reisman v Reisman (2014), ONCA 109, 702n
Remedy Drug Store Co Inc v Farnham (2015), ONCA 576, 277n
Renaissance Leisure Group Inc v Frazer (2004), 242 DLR (4th) 229, 87n
Renard v Facet Decision Systems Inc (2010), BCJ No 2694, 404n
Resurfice Corp v Hanke (2007), SCC 7, 87n
Reviczky v Melekina (2008), 88 OR (3d) 699, 551n
Reynolds v Clarke (1726), 93 ER 747, 76n
Reynolds v Roxburgh (1886), 10 OR 649, at 655, 343n
Ribeiro v CIBC (1992), 13 OR(3d) 278, 288n
Richcraft Homes Ltd v Urbandale Corp (2016), ONCA 622, 149n
Ricketts v Scothorn, 77 NW 365 (1898), 153n
Riddell v Bank of Upper Canada (1859), 18 UCQB 139, 687n
Rio Tinto Alcan Inc v Carrier Sekani Tribal Council (2010), SCC 43, 70n
Riordan Leasing Inc v Veer Transportation Services Inc (2002), 61 OR (3d) 536, 684n
River Wind Ventures Ltd v British Columbia (2011), BCCA 79, 223n
RJR-MacDonald Inc v Canada (1995), 127 DLR (4th) 1, 52n
Roberge v Bolduc (1991), 1 SCR 374, 113n
Robert v Brokerage Services Inc (2001), 104 ACWS (3d) 988, 758n
Roberts v Canada (1989) 57 DLR 4th 197, 485n
Robertson v Thomson Corp (2006), 2 SCR 363, 460n, 465n
Robinson v Davison (1871), LR 6 Ex 269, 261n
Robinson v Mann (1901), 331 SCR 484, 433n
Rochwerg v Truster (2002), 212 DLR (4th) 498 (Ont CA), 577n
Rocket v Royal College of Dental Surgeons of Ontario (1990), 71 DLR (4th) 68, 51n
Rockwell Developments Ltd v Newtonbrook Plaza Ltd (1972), 27 DLR (3d) 651, 593n
Rodgers v Calvert (2004), 49 BLR (3d) 53, 792n
Rogers Communications Inc v Chateauguay (Ville) (2016), SCC 23, 51n

Rogers Communications Inc v SOCAN – See Rogers Communications Inc v Society of Composers, Authors and Music Publishers of Canada
Rogers Communications Inc v Society of Composers, Authors and Music Publishers of Canada (2012), SCC 35 (2012) 2 SCR 283, 459n, 466n
Rogers v Faught (2002), 212 DLR (4th) 366, 116n
Rogers Wireless Inc v Muroff (2007), SCC 35, 754n
Rolling v William Investments (1989), 63 DLR (4th) 760, 212n
Rollins v Niagara Regional Police Service (2016), ONSC 7735, 96n
Romaine v Romaine (2001), BCCA 509, 156n
Roman Corp v Peat Marwick Thorne (1992), 8 BLR (2d) 43, 632n
Ron Engineering & Construction Eastern Ltd v Ontario (1981), 1 SCR 111, 134n
Ron Ghitter Property Consultants Ltd v Beaver Lumber Co (2003), ABCA 221, 157n
Ronald Elwyn Lister Ltd v Dunlop Canada Ltd (1982), 135 DLR (3d) 1, 672n
Rose and Frank v Crompton (1925), AC 445, 159n
Rose v Aftenberger (1969), 9 DLR (3d) 42, 363n, 492n
Rose v Krieser (2002), 212 DLR (4th) 123, 492n
Rose v Pim (1953), 2 All ER 739, 192n
Ross v Holley (2004), OJ No 4643, 757n
Rothfield v Manolakos (1989), 63 DLR (4th) 449, 85n
Rothmans, Benson & Hedges Inc v Saskatchewan (2005), 1 SCR 188, 14n, 52n
Rouge Valley Health System v TD Canada Trust (2010), OJ No 5302 (Ont SC), 432n
Roy v 1216393 Ontario Inc (2011), BCCA 500, 281n
Royal Bank of Canada v Bruce Industrial Sales Ltd (1998), 40 OR (3d) 307, 363n
Royal Bank of Canada v Kiska, (1967), 63 DLR (2d) 582, 156, 156n
Royal Bank of Canada v Lions Gate Fisheries Ltd (1991), 76 DLR (4th) 289, 686n
Royal Bank of Canada v Nobes (1982), 49 NSR (2d) 634, 363n
Royal Bank of Canada v North American Life Assurance Co (1996), 132 DLR (4th) 193 (SCC), 701n
Royal Bank of Canada v Radius Credit Union Ltd (2010), SCC 28, 684n
Royal Bank of Canada v Reddy (2007), ABQB 613, 215n
Royal Bank of Canada v Reynolds (1976), 66 DLR (3d) 88, 328n
Royal Bank of Canada v Sparrow Electric Corp (1997), 1 SCR 411, 143 DLR (4th) 385, 684n, 703n
Royal Bank of Canada v Trang (2016), SCC 50, 789n
Royal Bank of Canada v W Got & Associates Electric Ltd (1999), 178 DLR (4th) 385, 672n
Royal British Bank v Turquand (1856), 119 ER 886, 656n
Royal Trust Corp of Canada v Hordo (1993), 10 BLR (2d) 86, 714n
Rudco Insulation Ltd v Toronto Sanitary Inc (1998), 42 OR (3d) 292, 710n

Rudder v Microsoft Corp (1999), OJ No 3778, 754n
Ryan v Victoria (City) (1999), 1 SCR 201, 80n
Rylands v Fletcher (1868), LR 3 HL 330, 77n

S

Saadati v Moorehead (2017), SCC 28, 84n, 87n
Sabre Inc v International Air Transport Assn (2011), OJ No 95, aff'd 2011 ONCA 747, 478n
Sail Labrador Ltd v Challenge One (1999), 1 SCR 265, 131n, 280n
Salomon v Salomon & Co Ltd (1897), AC 22, 591
Salomons v Pender, (1865), 195 ER 682, 372n
Salter v Cormie (1993), 108 DLR (4th) 372 (Alta CA), 380n
Samuel Smith & Sons Ltd v Silverman (1961), 29 DLR (2d) 98, 129n
Sanitary Refuse Collectors Inc v City of Ottawa (1972), 1 OR 296, 156n
Sanofi-Aventis Canada Inc v Hospira Healthcare Corp (2009), FCJ No 1380, 475n
Saskatchewan River Bungalows Ltd v Maritime Life Assurance Co (1994), 115 DLR (4th) 478, 356n
Saskatchewan Star Phoenix Group Inc v Noton (2001), SJ No 275, 761n
Sattva Capital Corp v Creston Moly Corp (2014), SCC 53, 42n, 219n
Saunders v Anglia Building Society (1971), AC 1004, 196
Savage v Wilby (1954), SCR 376, 396n
Scammell v Ouston (1941), 1 All ER 14, 222n
Schachter v Canada (1992), 2 SCR 679, 17n
Schilling v Certified General Accountants Assn of British Columbia (1996), 135 DLR (4th) 669, 116n
Schlink v Blackburn (1993), 18 CCLT (2d) 173, 85n
Schlumberger Canada Ltd v Commissioner of Patents (1982), 1 FC 845, 471n
Schmeiser v Monsanto Canada Inc (2004), 239 DLR (4th) 271, 478n
Schneider v St Clair Region Conservation Authority (2008), 89 OR (3d) 150, rev'd 2009 ONCA 640, 95n
Schoff v Royal Insurance Company of Canada (2004), 10 WWR 32 (Alta CA), 198n
SCI Systems, Inc v Gornitzki Thompson & Little Co (1997), 147 DLR (4th) 300, 713n
Scotia McLeod Inc v Peoples Jewellers Limited et al (1995), 26 OR (3d) 481, 593n
Scotson v Pegg (1861), 158 ER 121, 150n
Scott v Wawanesa Mutual Insurance Co (1989), 59 DLR (4th) 660, 353n
Sears Canada Inc v Bartram (2004), BCSC 509, 95n
Sears Canada Inc v C&S Interior Designs Ltd (2012), ABQB 573, 737n
Seidel v TELUS (2011), SCC 15, 34n, 44n, 128n, 218, 319n, 741n
Semchyshen v Semchyshen (2013), SJ No 342, 213n
Semelhago v Paramadevan (1996), 2 SCR 415, 291n
Seney v Crooks (1998), 166 DLR (4th) 337, 114n
Sevidal v Chopra (1987), 64 OR (2d) 169, 199n
Shadwell v Shadwell (1860), 142 ER 62, 150n
Shafron v KRG Insurance Brokers (2009), SCC 6, 179n

Shanahan v Turning Point Restaurant Ltd (2012), BCCA 411, 192n
Shanklin Pier Ltd v Detel Products Ltd (1951), 2 KB 854, 234n, 344n
Sharbern Holding Inc, v Vancouver Airport Centre Ltd (2011), SCC 23, 106n
Shaw Cablesystems (Manitoba) Ltd v Canadian Legion Memorial Housing Foundation (Manitoba) (1997), 143 DLR (4th) 193, 226n
Shelanu Inc v Print Three Franchising Corp (2003), 226 DLR (4th) 577, 385n
Shennan v Szewczyk (2010), ONCA 679, 500n
Sheraton Desert Inn Corp v Yung (1998), 168 DLR (4th) 126, 689n
Sherman v American Institute Co (1937), 4 DLR 723, 198n
Sibtac Corporation Ltd v Soo; Lienster Investments Ltd, Third Party (1978), 18 OR (2d) 395, 135n
Sickel v Gordy (2008), SKCA 100, 396n
Sidmay Ltd et al v Wehttam Investments Ltd (1967), 61 DLR (2d) 358, aff'd (1968), 69 DLR (2d) 336, 175n
Sign-O-Lite Plastics Ltd v Metropolitan Life Insurance Co (1990), 49 BCLR (2d) 183, 379n
Silver v IMAX Corporation et al (2009), CanLII 72334 (2012) ONSC 4881, 107n
Simpson v Crippin (1872), LR 8 QB 14, 279n
Simpson v Mair (2008), SCC 40, 82n
Sincies Chiementin SpA (Trustee) v King (2010), OJ No 5124, aff'd (2012) OJ No 4562 (OAC), 740n
Slate Ventures Inc v Hurley (1998), 37 BLR (2d) 138, 623n
Smith & Nephew Inc v Glen Oak Inc et al (1996), 68 CPR (3d) 153, 456n
Smith v Busler (1988), BCJ No 2739 (SC), 518n
Smith v Clinton (1908), 99 LT 840, 176n
Smith v Inco Ltd (2011), OJ No 4386, 80n
Smith v Inco Ltd (2011), ONCA 628, 107 OR (3d) 321, 77n
Smith v Jones (1999), 169 DLR (4th) 385 (SCC), 118n
Smith v National Money Mart (2011), OJ No 1321 (Ont CA), 40n
Smith v National Money Mart (2010), ONSC 1334 (CanLII), 40n
SNC-Lavalin International Inc v Liquid Carbonic Inc (1996), 28 BLR (2d) 1, 305n
Snow v Eaton Centre Ltd (1982), 70 CPR (2d) 105, 462n
Sobeys West Inc v College of Pharmacists of British Columbia (2016), BCCA 41, 116n
SOCAN v Bell Canada (2012), SCC 366, 764n
Sociedad Agricola Santa Teresa Ltda v VinaLeyda Limitada (2007), FCJ No 1681, 454n
Society of Composers, Authors and Music Publishers of Canada v Bell Canada (2012), SCC 36, 459n, 469n
Software Guy Brokers Ltd v Hardy (2004), BCJ No 95, 759n
Solway v Davis Moving & Storage Inc (2002), 62 OR (3d) 522, leave dismissed (2003) SCCA No 57, 330n, 331n
Somersall v Friedman (2002), 215 DLR (4th) 577 (SCC), 356n
Sotramex Inc v Sorenviq Inc (1998), AQ No 2241, 763n

Source Perrier SA v Fira-Less Marketing Co Ltd (1983), 70 CPR (2d) 61, 456n
Spanos v Dufferin Tile & Marble Inc (2007), CarswellOnt 8625, 301n
Spire Freezers Ltd v Canada (2001), 196 DLR (4th) 211 (SCC), 567n
Sproule v Nortel Networks Corp (2009), ONCA 833, 708n
Stabilisierungsfonds fur Wein v TG Bright & Co Ltd (1985), 4 CPR (3d) 526, 454n
Staiman Steel Ltd v Commercial & Home Builders Ltd (1976), 71 DLR (3d) 17, 193n
State Farm Mutual Automobile Insurance Co v General Accident Assurance Co of Canada (1995), NBJ No 405 (CA), 198n
Stearman v Powers (2014), BCCA 206, 516n
Stevens v Globe and Mail et al (1992), 86 DLR (4th) 204, 399n
Stevenson v Colonial Homes Ltd (1961), 27 DLR (2d) 698, 314n
Stewart v Elk Valley Corp (2017), SCC 30, 407n
Stilk v Myrick (1809), 70 ER 1168, 149n
Stockloser v Johnson (1954), 1 QB 476, 313n
Stoffman v Vancouver General Hospital (1990), 3 SCR 483, 410n
Stone v Stone (2001), 55 OR (3d) 491, 701n
Stott v Merit Investment Corp (1988), 63 OR (2d) 545 (Cont CA), 202n
Stow v Canada (2010), TCJ No 322, 567n
Strategic Acquisition Corp v Starke Capital Corp (2017), ABCA 250, 292n
Straus Estate v Decaire (2011), OJ No 737, 380n
Strother v 3464920 Canada Inc (2007), 2 SCR 177, 104n, 573n
Strudwick v Applied Consumer & Clinical Evaluations Inc (2016), ONCA 520, 404n
Sugar v Peat Marwick Ltd (1988), 55 DLR (4th) 230, 108n
Suhaag Jewellers Ltd v Alarm Factory Inc (2016), ONCA 33, 128n
Sullivan v O'Connor, 296 NE 2d 183 (1973), 288n
Sun Toyota Ltd v Granville Toyota Ltd (2002), BCJ No 847 (QL), 311n
Sutton & Co v Grey (1894), 1 QB 285, 210n
Sylvan Lake Golf & Tennis Club Ltd v Performance Industries Ltd (2002), 209 DLR (4th) 318 (SCC), 192n
Symington v Vancouver Breweries and Riefel (1931), 1 DLR 935, 177n
Szecket v Huang (1998), 168 DLR (4th) 402, 644n
Szilvasy v Reliance Home Comfort (2012), ONCA 821, 225n, 318n

T

Taff Vale Railway Co v Amalgamated Society of Railway Servants (1901), AC 426, 416n
Taylor v Caldwell (1863), 122 ER 309, 261n
Taylor-Baptiste v Ontario Public Service Employees Union (2015), ONCA 495, 408n
TCF Ventures Corp v The Cambie Malone's Corporation (2017), BCCA 129, 396n
Teal Cedar Products Ltd v British Columbia (2017), SCC 32, 176n
Techform v Wolda (2001), 206 DLR (4th) 171, 473n
Teck Cominco Metals Ltd v Lloyd's Underwriters (2009), SCC 11, 737n
Teck Corp v Millar (1973), 33 DLR (3d) 288, 631n

Telecommander Corp v United Parcel Service Canada Ltd (1996), OJ No 4664, 284n
Tele-Direct (Publications) Inc v American Business Information, Inc (1998), 2 FC 22, 462n
Tele-Direct (Publications) Inc v Canadian Business Online Inc (1998), 85 CPR (3d) 332, 759n
Teleflex Inc v IMP Group Ltd (1996), 149 NSR (2d) 355, 261n
Telex (Austral/Asia) Proprietary Ltd v Thomas Cook & Sons (Austral/Asia) Proprietary Ltd (1970), 2 NSWR 257 (CA), 514n
Ter Neuzen v Korn (1995), 3 SCR 674, 127 DLR (4th) 577, 113n, 301n
Tercon Contractors Ltd v British Columbia (Transportation and Highways) (2010), SCC 4, 281n, 308n
Terry v Vancouver Motors U-Drive Ltd and Walker (1942), SCR 391, 195n
Teva Canada Ltd v Pfizer Canada Inc (2012), SCC 60, 470n
Theberge v Galerie d'Art du Petit Champlain (2002), 2 SCR 336, 210 DLR (4th) 385, 449n, 458n, 462n
The Los Angeles Salad Company Inc v Canadian Food Inspection Agency (2013), BCCA 34, 110n
Thiessen v Mutual Life Assurance Co of Canada (2002), 219 DLR (4th) 98, 380n
Thomas & Betts Ltd v Panduit Corp (2000), 185 DLR (4th) 150, 470n
Thomas v Rio Tinto Alcan (2013), BCSC 2303, 170n
Thomson Consumer Electronics Canada, Inc v Consumers Distributing Inc (1999), 170 DLR (4th) 115, 704n
Thornhill v Neats (1860), 141 ER 1392, 257n
Thornton v Prince George School District No 57 (1978), 2 SCR 267, 97n
Tilden Rent-A-Car Co v Clemdenning (1978), 18 OR (2d) 601, 129n, 199
Tilley v Hailes (1992), 7 OR (3d) 257, 637n, 638n
TMS Lighting Ltd v KJS Transport Inc (2014), ONCA 1, 80n
Toromont Industrial Holdings v Thorne, Gunn, Helliwell & Christenson (1977), 14 OR (2d) 87, 114n
Toronto Marlboro Major Junior "A" Hockey Club et al v Tonelli et al (1979), 23 OR (2d) 193, 165n
Toronto Star v Aiken (1955), OWN 613, 257n
Toronto Truck Centre Ltd v Volvo Trucks Canada Inc (1998), 163 DLR (4th) 740, 384n
Tote Investors Ltd v Smoker (1968), 1 QB 509, 172n
Townsend v Sun Life Financial (2012), FC 550, 789n
Toyota Jidosha Kabushiki Kaisha v Lexus Foods Inc (2000), 194 DLR (4th) 491, 452n
Tran v Canada Public Safety (2017), SCC 50, 27n
Transamerica Life Canada Inc v ING Canada Inc (2003), 68 OR (3d) 457 (CA), 279n
Transco Mills Ltd v Percan Enterprises Ltd (1993), 83 BCLR (2d) 254 (CA), 518n
Transport North American Express Inc v New Solutions Financial Corp (2004), 1 SCR 249, 174n
TREB v Commission (2017), FCA 236, 552n
Trillium v General Motors (2013), ONSC 2289, 737n

Trout Point Lodge Ltd Handshoe (2012), NSSC 245, 795n
Tsilhqot'in Nation v British Columbia (2014), SCC 44, 485n, 486n
Turner v Indirect Enterprises Inc (2009), OJ No 6345, 404n
Turner v Owen (1862), 6 ER 79, 149n
Turner v Visscher Holdings Inc (1996), 23 BCLR (3d) 303 (CA), 227n
Twentsche Overseas Trading Co v Uganda Sugar Factory Ltd (1945), 114 LJPC 25, 262n

U

UL Canada Inc v Attorney General of Quebec (2003), 234 DLR (4th) 398, aff'd (2005) SCJ No 11, 51n
UNA v Alberta (Attorney-General) (1990), 89 DLR (4th) 609, 416n
Unger v Unger (2003), 234 DLR (4th) 119, 359n
Unifor Local 2301 v Rio Tinto Alcan Inc (2017), BCCA 300, 53n
United Airlines Inc v Cooperstock (2017), FC 616, 456n
United Parcel Service of America, Inc ("UPS") v Government of Canada, 744n
United States v Arnold, Schwinn & Co, 388 US 365, 382n
United States v Microsoft, 87 F Supp 2d 30 (DDC 2000), aff'd in part 253 F 3d 34 (DC Cir 2001), 58n
UPM-Kymmene Corp v UPM-Kymmene Miramichi Inc (2002), 214 DLR (4th) 496, 623n
Urban Communications Inc v BCNET Networking Society (2015), BCCA 297 (appeal dismissed 2016 SCC 45), 42n
Urban Outdoor Trans Ad v City of Scarborough (2001), 196 DLR (4th) 304, 51n

V

Valenti v Canali (1889), 24 QBD 166, 166n
Van Breda v Club Resorts (2012), SCC 17, 769n
Van Breda v Village Resorts Ltd, (2010), OJ No 402, aff'd 2012 SCC 17, 770n
Vancouver Community College v Vancouver Career College (Burnaby) Inc (2017) BCCA 41, 451n, 761n
Vann Media Ltd v Oakville (Town) (2008), ONCA 752, 51n
Vann Niagara Ltd v Town of Oakville (2004), 234 DLR (4th) 118 (SCC), 51n
Vanvic Enterprises Ltd v Mark (1985), 3 WWR 644, 313n
Varsity Plymouth Chrysler (1994) Ltd v Pomerleau (2002), 23 CCEL (3d) 148 (Alta QB), 402n
Veuve Clicquot Ponsardin v Boutiques Cliquot Ltee (2006), 1 SCR 824, 454n, 455n
Veuve Clicquot Ponsardin v Boutiques Cliquot Ltee (2006), SCC 23, (2006) 1 SCR 824, 450n, 454n, 455n
Vic Priestly Landscaping Contracting Ltd v Elder (1978), 19 OR (2d) 591, 395n
Victoria Wood Development Corp Inc v Ondrey (1977), 14 OR (2d) 723, aff'd (1978), 92 DLR (3d) 229 (Ont CA), 260n
Vista Sudbury Hotel Inc v The Oshawa Group Limited (2018), ONSC 1164, 261n
Vita Food Products Inc v Unus Shipping Co Ltd (1939), AC 277, 721n

Vlastiak v Valastiak (2010), BCJ No 233 (BCAA), 620n
Von Hatzfeldt-Wildenburg v Alexander (1912), 1 Ch 284, 140n
Vorvis v Insurance Corporation of BC (1989), 1 SCR 1085, 290n
Vriend et al v The Queen in the Right of Alberta et al (1998), 156 DLR (4th) 385, 15n, 19n

W

WD Latimer Co Ltd v Dijon Investments Ltd (1992), 12 OR (3d) 415, 594n
Waldick v Malcolm (1991), 2 SCR 456, 95n
Wallace Sign Crafters West Ltd v Delta Hotels Ltd (1994), CanLII 1510 (BCSC), 342n
Wallace v Allen (2007), 85 OR (3d) 88, appeal allowed (2009), 93 OR (3d) 723 (Ont CA), 157n
Wallace v United Grain Growers Ltd (1997), 3 SCR 701, 152 DLR (4th) 1 (SCC), 279n, 288n, 290n, 404n
Wal-Mart Stores, Inc v wallmartcanadasucks.com and Kenneth J Harvey, WIPO Decision No D2000-1104, 761n
Walt Disney Productions v Fantasyland Hotel Inc (1998), 85 CPR (3d) 36, aff'd (2000), 4 CPR (4th) 370, 452n
Walt Disney Productions v Triple Five Corp (1992) AJ No 571, aff'd (1994) AJ No 196, 452n, 456n
Walton v General Accident Assurance Co of Canada (2000), 194 DLR (4th) 315, 355n
Wanderers Hockey Club v Johnson (1913), 14 DLR 42, 176n
Wang v Lin, 2013 ONCA 33, 737n
Wardle v Manitoba Farm Loan Association (1956), SCR 3, 485n
Warman v Fromm (2007), OJ No 4754, aff'd (2008) OJ No 5043, 757n
Warman v Grosvenor (2008) OJ No 4462, 757n
Watkins v Rymill (1883), 10 QBD 178, 129n
Waxman v Waxman (2004) OJ No 1765, 637n
Webster v Cecil (1861), 54 ER 812, 191

Wells v Newfoundland (1999), 3 SCR 199, 263n
Wembley Marketing Ltd v ITEX Corp (2008), OJ No 5194, 754n
Werle v Saskenergy Inc (1992), 103 Sask R 241, 400n
Westboro Flooring & Decor Inc v Bank of Nova Scotia (2004), 241 DLR (4th) 257 (Ont CA), 432n
Westcom TV Group Ltd v CanWest Global Broadcasting Inc (1997), 1 WWR 761 (BCSC), 134n
Western Canadian Shopping Centres v Dutton (2001), 2 SCR 534, 35n
Western Surety Co v Brakop (1994), 47 ACWS (3d) 589, 210n
Westfair Food Ltd v Watt (1991), 79 DLR (4th) 48, 637n
Wharton v Tom Harris Chevrolet Oldsmobile Cadillac Ltd (2002), BCJ No 233, 306n
Whiten v Pilot Insurance (2002), SCC 18, 288, 289n, 358
Whittington v Seale-Hayne (1900), 82 LT 49, 197n
Wiebe v Bouchard (2005), BCJ No 73, 770n
Wightman Estate v 2774046 Canada Inc (2006) BCCA 424, 260n
Wilfred v Dare (2017), ONSC 1633, 635n
Wilkie v Jeong (2017), BCSC 2131, 262n
Wilkinson Sword (Canada) Ltd v Juda (1968), 2 Ex CR 137, 457n
William E Thompson Associates Inc v Carpenter (1989), 61 DLR (4th) 1, 364n
William H Cosby, Jr v Sterling Davenport, WIPO Decision No D2005-076, 762n
Williams v Roffey Brothers & Nicholls (Contractors) Ltd (1990), 1 All ER 512, 149n
Wilson v Alharayeri (2017), SCC 39, 638n
Wilson v British Columbia (2007), BCSC 1324, 169n
Wilson v Clarica Life Insurance Co (2002), BCJ No 292, 380n
Wilson v Saskatchewan Government Insurance (2011), 2 WWR 154 (Sask QB), 358n

Win Sun Produce Co v Albert Fisher Canada Ltd (1998), 111 BCAC 295 (BCCA), 300n
Winnipeg Condominium Corp No 36 v Bird Construction Co (1995), 1 SCR 85, 96n, 234n
Winnipeg Condominium Corp No 36 v Bird Construction Co (1995), 121 DLR (4th) 19, 96n
Winnipeg Condominium Corporation No 36 v Bird Construction Co Ltd (1995), 1 SCR 85, 234n
Wood v Fred Deeley Imports Ltd (2017), ONCA 158, 398n
Wolf v Advance Fur Dressers Ltd (2005), BCSC 1097, 290n
Wren v Holt (1903), 1 KB 610, 306n

X

XLO Investments Ltd v Hurontario Management Services (1999), 170 DLR (4th) 381 (Ont CA), 701n

Y

Yesac Creative Foods Inc v Hohnjec (1985), 6 CPR (3d) 398, 384n
Young v Kitchen (1878), 3 Ex D 127, 246n

Z

ZI Pompey Industrie v ECU-Line NV (2003), 1 SCR 450, 737n, 738n
Zawadzki v Matthews Group Ltd (1999), OJ No 2012, 576n
Zippo Manufacturing Co v Zippo Dot Com, Inc (1997), 952 F Supp 1119 (WD Pa), 770n
Zurich Canadian Holdings v Questar Exploration Inc (1999), 171 DLR (4th) 457 (Alta CA), 514n
Zurich Insurance Co v 686234 Ontario Ltd (2002), 222 DLR (4th) 655, leave denied (2003) SCCA No 33, 356n
Zurich Insurance Co v Ison TH Auto Sales Inc (2011), OJ No 1487, 358n

Part 1 The Law in Its Social and Business Context

Chapter 1
Law, Society, and Business

- THE ROLE OF LAW
- LAW AND BUSINESS
- LEGAL RISK MANAGEMENT
- LAW AND BUSINESS ETHICS
- WHO MAKES LAW?
- THE COURTS AND LEGISLATION
- THE *CHARTER OF RIGHTS AND FREEDOMS*
- CHALLENGING THE APPLICATION OF A STATUTE

What do we mean by "law"? Simple definitions require explanation. We begin by examining the role of law in society, how law relates to morals and ethics, and how it applies to the business environment.

In this chapter we examine such issues as:

- How does law reflect society's attitudes?
- What is the significance of the law to the business environment?
- How should business approach the management of legal risks?
- What is the relationship between the law and business ethics?
- Who makes law?
- How do courts decide whether the legislation is valid under the Constitution?
- What else do courts do?
- How does the *Charter of Rights and Freedoms* protect our human rights?
- Why is the *Charter* relevant for business?
- What is the purpose of a code of conduct?
- How does law impact international business activities?

THE ROLE OF LAW

How Is Law Defined?

Law is diverse and complex, so it is helpful to begin with a brief description of what law does: The law sets basic standards of behaviour that are enforced by government and also by individuals and groups with the help of government. Law applies to all of us; we cannot opt out of the legal system as we may from a club's rules (by simply resigning).

Why do we have—and need—law? First, law is needed to protect people, property, and society as a whole; it prohibits conduct that society believes could be harmful to others, such as assaulting another person or stealing that person's property. The law punishes someone who commits illegal conduct. However, it does much more than forbid harmful conduct. It also prescribes simple but vital rules that allow us to get on with everyday life—for example, requiring motor vehicles to drive on the right-hand side of the road. There is no moral reason to drive on the right side rather than on the left, as a number of countries require. But clearly, we must have one rule that all drivers follow.

Second, law gives government the power to act for the benefit of society as a whole. It authorizes government to provide policing, firefighting, education, and healthcare—and to raise taxes to pay for those activities. We expect our government to operate in accordance with the **rule of law**. Law involving the government is labelled **public law**.

Third, law regulates the interaction and relationships between individuals; for example, it enables us to make legally binding agreements enforceable in the courts. This is known as **private law**, also sometimes referred to as civil law. It allows us to plan and organize our affairs, and we can make deals with others for mutual benefit. The important legal feature is that we can rely on such arrangements because they are enforceable. We can book a flight, accept an employment contract, lease business offices, or buy an interest in a partnership or a corporation. The law provides certainty in determining contractual and property rights—something that is essential for business to carry on efficiently.

rule of law established legal principles that treat all persons equally and that government itself obeys

public law law that regulates the conduct of government and the relations between government and private persons

private law law that regulates the relations between private persons and groups of private persons

CHECKLIST
What Does Law Do?

- It influences and controls the behaviour of individuals in society.
- It empowers, influences, and controls the actions of government.
- It influences and controls interaction between individuals.

How Is Law Linked to Morals and Ethics?

Law, morals, and ethics are interrelated but distinct concepts. Individuals "must" comply with the law—doing so is not optional. Therefore, laws must be fair so that most of society views them as acceptable and therefore voluntarily complies. Most laws naturally evolve from basic moral principles that most people accept. Still, law often reflects only a minimum standard acceptable to the majority of people.

Morals and ethics, on the other hand, are optional standards of behaviour that people "ought" to observe even though doing so is not compulsory. They are considered to be a higher standard than the law, involving concepts of integrity, trust, and honour. Although legal philosophers try to create clear distinctions, the categories overlap. For example, lying is always unethical and immoral, and sometimes against the law. The law imposes ethical obligations of trust and integrity on some positions, such as directors of corporations, lawyers, and doctors. Once unethical and immoral behaviour is recognized by most of society as unacceptable, it is likely that a law will be introduced to regulate the unethical conduct. Therefore, the moral and ethical values of society as a whole shape the development and direction of new law. An ethical issue is highlighted in each chapter of this text.

Is It Ever Right to Break the Law?

Even a well-developed legal system leaves a number of difficult questions. Is it ever right to break the law? Is "law" the same thing as "justice"? What if a law is unjust? Intelligent, moderate people generally agree that the law should be obeyed, but there will be times when an individual is justified in breaking the law. They would also agree that there are unjust laws, but even these ought to be obeyed because of the chaotic consequences for society if many people fail to obey them. Even while trying to get unjust laws changed by normal, lawful means, we should still comply with them.

ILLUSTRATION 1.1 Exceptional Circumstances

Mary Brown was at home tending her sick 18-month-old baby. The baby had a high temperature and suddenly lapsed into a coma. Fearing that he might die, she drove him to the nearest hospital, driving at 110 km/h in a 50 km/h zone. On arrival at the hospital, the child was placed in emergency care, and the doctor commended her for having saved the life of her child. A police officer arrived on the scene and presented her with a summons for dangerous driving.

Mary exceeded the speed limit—a speed limit designed to promote safety. She endangered the lives of other users of the streets, but only because her child's life was in danger. She would admit that she broke the law, and she would not say that the 50 km/h speed limit was unreasonable or unjust. She would say that, in the circumstances, she was justified in breaking the law or, possibly, that the law should not apply to her particular situation.

Law and justice may not always coincide. Most people recognize that exceptions should be made in extreme situations, and this is what judges decide: how (or if) the law should be applied in the circumstances of a particular situation.

But what about a planned decision to stop following the law because you dislike the law? What if it is too expensive to comply with, or no one will catch the violator? Is there any point in having a law that most people will not obey? Consider unauthorized music downloading.

ILLUSTRATION 1.2 Ignoring the Law

Uber launched a mobile driving service app without complying with the existing laws applicable to taxi services (such as the obligations to obtain a permit, carry special insurance, and bond drivers). Uber did this because it was too difficult and expensive to obtain permits. Municipal regulators prosecuted Uber[1], but the app remained popular with passengers.

---

[1] See e.g. *Mississauga (City) v Uber Canada Inc*, 2016 ONCJ 461; *Edmonton (City) v Uber Canada Inc*, 2015 ABQB 214.

Uber's disregard for the law forced some municipalities to change their laws, but is this fair to the taxi drivers who had complied with the law all along?[2] These perplexing questions demonstrate the challenge of setting a fair law that society will voluntarily respect.

How Does Law Influence Behaviour?

The vast majority of individuals instinctively understand the need to obey the rules and follow the law simply because it is the law. However, to further encourage compliance, most laws, if broken, trigger penalties or consequences. When a person breaks the law, he or she is held responsible for the consequences; this is often described as **legal liability**. How offensive society finds the misconduct determines how severe the consequence of misconduct will be.

If lawmakers view the misconduct as extremely offensive to society as a whole, as with murder, they will consider it a matter of public law, require the government to enforce the law, and impose the most serious consequence, that of **criminal liability**. If society views the misconduct as less offensive but still necessary for an orderly society, as with proper driving habits, then the misconduct might trigger only **regulatory or quasi-criminal liability**, and the government will generally ticket or fine offenders. Alternatively, if lawmakers designate the misconduct as primarily a private matter affecting only the parties involved, such as when a tenant fails to pay rent, it will be a matter of private law, and persons harmed by the conduct will be responsible for enforcing the law through private or civil lawsuits. This type of liability is known as **civil liability**. These three forms of legal liability are the tools used by lawmakers to encourage people to comply with the law. As societal views change, the type of liability may also change.

legal liability responsibility for the consequences of breaking the law

criminal liability responsibility arising from commission of an offence against the government or society as a whole

regulatory or quasi-criminal liability responsibility arising from breaches of less serious rules of public law, often enforced through specialized regulatory tribunals set up by the government for specific purposes

civil liability responsibility arising from a breach of a private law, enforced through a lawsuit initiated by the injured victim

CHECKLIST
Forms of Legal Liability

Lawmakers use three forms of liability to influence individual behaviour:
- Criminal liability
- Regulatory or quasi-criminal liability
- Civil liability

ILLUSTRATION 1.3 Society's Attitude

Prior to 2004, possession of marijuana was a criminal offence triggering a criminal record and possible jail time. When the federal government announced plans to decriminalize possession of recreational-use marijuana in 2004, it sparked a debate about whether society's attitude toward marijuana use had changed. Some people misunderstood the plan as one that would legalize marijuana use when, in fact, the conduct would remain illegal as a regulatory offence, but jail would no longer be a penalty until 2018, when recreational-use of marijuana was "legalized." Civil liability remains applicable to situations where an "impaired" marijuana user injures another person, for example, in a car accident.

It is possible for one event to attract all three types of liability.

---

[2] Taxi drivers sued Uber in class actions: *Konjevic v Uber Technologies Inc*, 2016 ONSC 7804.

> **ILLUSTRATION 1.4 Multiple Types of Liability**
>
> A business releases chemicals into the groundwater, contrary to the environmental emissions standards. Local residents drink the contaminated water and die. The company would face criminal liability if charged by the government with the offence of criminal negligence causing death. It could also face regulatory liability if fined for breach of the particular environmental regulations, and it would also face civil liability when sued by the victims' families for the losses associated with the deaths of their loved ones.

LAW AND BUSINESS

The Significance of Law for the Business Environment

Law is part of every facet of doing business and is central to a business's interaction with its customers, suppliers, competitors, and government. Law outlines what to do, how to do it, and what not to do. Businesses could face criminal, regulatory, and/or civil liability if they do not comply. Some say that there are too many laws—that business is overregulated. Laws may be resented because they add to the cost of doing business. Too much regulation can restrict economic freedom and make a country's businesses less competitive globally.

There is no doubt, however, that society cannot function without laws, and businesses cannot succeed without understanding those laws. Business executives identify legal certainty as one of the key factors that determine whether or not to invest in a particular country. For a welcoming business environment, a country must provide a dependable legal infrastructure that clearly defines rights and responsibilities and properly enforces them. Overregulation may be a severe inconvenience—but the complete absence of regulation may be worse.

Law and International Business

Generally, law regulates conduct within a country's jurisdictional boundaries, but business is not restricted to the borders of a single country. Increasingly, the world is becoming a single giant marketplace in which firms from different countries carry on business; they make agreements, and they compete against and sometimes cooperate with each other. For Canada, more than for most countries, the international dimension of business is especially important; foreign trade and foreign investment result in a wide variety of legal relationships between parties in two or more countries. Accordingly, the law is a significant element in the international business environment.

Businesses are subject to different laws for each country in which they operate. Determining which laws apply to any given situation can lead to a conflict of laws. As will be discussed in later chapters, governments and non-governmental organizations are trying to harmonize laws in order to address these conflicts through the use of treaties, conventions, and **model laws**. Model laws are recommended templates for domestic laws that are developed by advisory organizations such as law reform commissions. Treaties and conventions are international agreements between governments in which countries agree to pass similar laws. These agreements are often brokered through **super-governmental organizations** such as the United Nations. The success of these initiatives depends on the willingness of countries to implement the agreed-upon treaty rules. Each chapter of this text identifies an international issue where countries take differing legal positions or are working to harmonize conflicting laws.

model laws recommended templates for domestic laws that are developed by advisory organizations such as law reform commissions

super-governmental organizations non-profit associations of governments from around the world working to find common approaches to international issues, such as the World Trade Organization or the United Nations

LEGAL RISK MANAGEMENT

Businesses must understand the laws that affect them, the relevant compliance requirements, and the risks of legal liability associated with their activities. Some may question why business managers need to familiarize themselves with the law, correctly suggesting that lawyers are the experts in this field. However, business managers are the experts in the activities of their businesses, and they must understand the **legal risk** associated with the everyday choices they make. Business managers cannot effectively use lawyers unless the managers know what to ask and when to ask it—and then understand the advice they receive.

Early identification of a legal risk is vital to effective management. Businesses must develop a **legal risk management plan** that anticipates possible legal liability and provides preventive and remedial strategies. The involvement of lawyers is only part of the overall plan.

> **legal risk** business activities, conduct, events, or scenarios that could expose a business to some type of legal liability
>
> **legal risk management plan** a plan developed by a business that identifies potential legal liability and provides preventive and remedial strategies
>
> **legal audit** a review of each area, action, and interaction of the business to identify potential legal liability and legal compliance risks

Developing a Legal Risk Management Plan

Developing a legal risk management plan requires five distinct steps involving every facet of the organization, as well as experts in law, finance, and insurance. The process is continuous and includes ongoing revision as law evolves, business expands and diversifies, and personnel changes.

First, managers must undertake a **legal audit** of the operation, which involves an examination of every area, action, and interaction of the business in order to identify potential legal liability and legal compliance risks. This audit requires the participation of those most familiar with the functional areas of the business, and these managers must be conversant in the principles of legal liability. This text focuses on the important business law principles of legal liability.

Second, after a comprehensive list of legal risks is developed, the risks must be prioritized. What is the most serious legal risk facing the business? Prioritization involves assessing the likelihood or frequency of the event occurring and the magnitude of the consequences if the event occurs. Risks should be addressed in order of their priority. This text reviews important business law cases that will help quantify risks.

Third, managers must develop effective strategies to deal with each risk. The strategy must have proactive and reactive elements; in other words, there must be a plan to prevent the risk from occurring and also a plan to deal with the risk in a way that minimizes its consequences if it does occur. Prevention is important because even a successful legal dispute is undesirable. A legal dispute is expensive and time-consuming to process; it drains energy, focus, and resources from other areas of the business; and it attracts negative publicity. Reaction is important because you cannot prevent every eventuality. For example, a nuclear power plant puts safety measures in place to prevent an accident but must still have an evacuation plan in case an accident occurs.

Fourth, the business must implement the plan. Implementation involves more than just announcing the plan. There must be education, training, testing, and monitoring. Employees must be aware of the plan and capable of complying with it. Management must undertake regular monitoring to ensure that the plan is followed. Having a plan and not following it is worse for a business than having no plan at all.

Fifth and finally, the plan must be revised regularly. New legal risks must be added to the plan. Legal risks change every day as new laws are introduced and cases are decided. As businesses expand to new jurisdictions, different laws apply. New products and processes bring new risks. Personnel restructuring means responsibilities may shift. A legal risk management plan must reflect current organizational structures so that everyone performs appropriately.

> **CHECKLIST**
>
> ## Steps in the Development of a Legal Risk Management Plan
>
> - Identify potential legal risks.
> - Assess and prioritize each legal risk based on likelihood and magnitude.
> - Develop a strategy to address each risk from both proactive and reactive perspectives.
> - Implement the plan.
> - Regularly review and update the plan.

Strategies to Manage Legal Risks

As noted, every legal risk management plan involves preventive and reactive strategies. Four general strategies exist for managing legal risk:

- Avoid the risk: This strategy involves discontinuing the conduct or finding another way to achieve the result.
- Reduce the risk: This strategy includes quality control initiatives that decrease the likelihood of the risk or minimize its damage.
- Transfer the risk: This strategy accepts that the risk may occur and shifts the consequences to someone else—an insurance company or a consumer who, through contracts, assumes responsibility.
- Absorb the risk: This strategy accepts that the risk may occur and budgets for the expenses. This strategy is used with remote risks or small-valued risks. The potential cost is factored into the price of the product, and the strategy is known as "self-insuring."

A business will use a combination of all of these strategies.

Subsequent chapters conclude with suggested strategies to manage the legal risks discussed in that chapter.

> **ILLUSTRATION 1.5   Applying Legal Risk Management Strategies**
>
> Illustration 1.4 described the legal liability risks associated with water contamination. A manufacturing business can avoid the most serious risks by selecting the safest chemicals for its manufacturing process. It will further reduce the likelihood of the risk by implementing strong quality control measures and warning those nearby of the use of chemicals. Naturally, it will also carry insurance to transfer the costs of an environmental clean-up. However, this insurance is very expensive, so the business may absorb some of the risk by choosing a high deductible.

The Legal Profession

Every legal risk management plan involves the use of legal experts. In England, the legal profession is divided into two separate groups: solicitors and barristers. A **solicitor** is an "office" lawyer whose time is mostly spent interviewing clients and carrying on the legal aspects of business and family affairs. Solicitors also prepare cases for trial. A **barrister** takes cases assigned by solicitors—and presents them in court. Barristers also give opinions with respect to potential litigation and are consulted by

solicitor   an "office" lawyer in England who interviews clients, carries on legal aspects of business and family affairs, and prepares cases for trial

barrister   a lawyer in England who accepts cases from solicitors and presents them in court and also acts as consultant in complex legal issues

solicitors on a wide variety of more complex legal issues such as corporate mergers and tax planning.

Under the civil law of Quebec, the profession is divided in approximately the same way as in England. Quebec recognizes the designations of **notary**[3] (solicitor) and **advocate** (barrister). In the other Canadian provinces, all lawyers are qualified as both barristers and solicitors; they may carry out the duties of both professions and often do so, especially in smaller cities and towns. In larger cities, lawyers tend to specialize in particular areas of the law; lawyers who specialize in private (civil) trials are known as "litigation" lawyers. In the United States the distinction has disappeared. A lawyer is not even called "barrister and solicitor" as in Canada but is simply an **attorney**.

notary a solicitor in Quebec

advocate a barrister in Quebec

attorney a lawyer in the United States, encompassing the roles of both barrister and solicitor

The Canadian legal profession is regulated on a provincial basis. Each province has its own "bar" (barristers' society or law society), and an individual must qualify and be licensed as a member in order to practise law. Law societies set professional standards of behaviour for all their members and discipline lawyers who violate the standards. The standards—including honesty, integrity, confidentiality, and competency—govern the lawyer's relationship with clients, the courts, the administration of justice, and the public. The most serious violations result in a lawyer's being **disbarred**—expelled from the law society and losing the privilege of practising law.

disbarred expelled from the law society and deprived of the privilege of practising law

CASE 1.1 The Power of the Law Society

A lawyer was suspended by the Law Society of Manitoba for failing to complete the mandatory continuing education requirement. The Supreme Court of Canada upheld the suspension, saying the rule requiring continuous education was reasonable, and the Law Society had complete control over who can practise law in the province, over the conditions or requirements placed upon those who practise and over enforcement of those conditions or requirements.[4]

The National Mobility Agreement (signed by all provincial law societies) sets the rules for temporary and permanent movement of lawyers between provinces.[5] A member in one province must meet the standards and pay the fees of the provincial bar in another province before practising in that province permanently. Out-of-province lawyers may carry on some minor (temporary) activity within another province without fees or licensing. A member of any provincial bar, however, may appear before the Supreme Court of Canada.

When a client hires a lawyer, the relationship is governed by the professional standards of his or her law society as well as the historic protection of **solicitor–client privilege**. This privilege requires the lawyer to keep confidential all communications between the lawyer and the client. The lawyer cannot be forced to reveal such communication to a court unless the client approves. This privilege protects the client and allows the client to speak candidly to the lawyer, ultimately ensuring the best possible legal advice. Without it, the legal system would not function properly.[6]

solicitor–client privilege a client's right to have all communications with his or her lawyer kept confidential

A recent development affecting the legal profession is the emergence of the **paralegal**—a non-lawyer who provides some form of legal service. For many years, lawyers have hired non-lawyers, trained them in a specific area, and then delegated

paralegal a non-lawyer who provides some form of legal service to the public

---

[3] In the rest of Canada, notary stands for notary public, and they certify the authenticity of documents. They need not be lawyers at all.

[4] *Green v Law Society of Manitoba*, 2017 SCC 20 (citing *Pearlman v Manitoba Law Society Judicial Committee*, [1991] 2 SCR 869 at 886).

[5] National Mobility Agreement, 2013, Federation of Law Societies of Canada, www.flsc.ca.

[6] *Privacy Commissioner of Alberta v University of Calgary*, 2016 SCC 53.

clerical responsibilities to the paralegal. In this model, they work under the supervision of a lawyer, and the lawyer is responsible to the client for the work. Most provinces such as British Columbia and Alberta follow this model and regulate the lawyer responsible for the supervision arrangement.[7] Ontario took a different path and introduced a regulatory model that allows paralegals to offer services directly to the public, without supervision, in limited areas, including incorporations, uncontested divorces, and minor contested court matters such as highway traffic tickets, landlord and tenant disputes, and Small Claims Court matters.

Although some paralegals offer exceptional service, unregulated paralegals present risks to the public. The quality of service varies widely; they are not subject to educational requirements, licensing, professional standards, or discipline; and they do not have to carry liability insurance. Ontario was the first jurisdiction in North America to regulate paralegals. In order to offer services directly to the public, Ontario requires paralegals to be licensed by the law society, carry insurance, meet competency standards, and be subject to discipline.[8]

Business and the Legal Profession

The development of a legal risk management plan, as discussed, will help a business to identify its legal needs and choose the best type of legal representation. Should a business hire a lawyer to deal with a problem when it arises, or should it reserve the services of a lawyer by paying a **retainer** in advance of any particular need? Should a business hire or retain one lawyer or law firm to handle all its needs? Should the business retain multiple lawyers with specific specialties? Is the best solution an **in-house counsel**? Are paralegals best for some problems? These are difficult questions that every business must answer. The answer depends on the size of the business, the types of legal risks, and the resources available.

Most businesses use some **outside counsel**—self-employed lawyers who work alone, in small partnerships, or in large national firms, and bill the business for services rendered. Using this type of lawyer allows a business to select the specific specialty needed for the job. However, it is also valuable for a business to have a long-term relationship with one lawyer or firm that becomes familiar with its business and legal needs. Sometimes this is accomplished by hiring a large firm, building a relationship with one contact lawyer, and referring work as needed to various lawyers within the firm.

Businesses with regular legal needs sometimes hire a lawyer, known as in-house counsel, as a full-time employee of the business. The in-house counsel might need to hire outside counsel for matters beyond his or her capabilities, but in such circumstances the in-house counsel can communicate with and supervise the outside counsel in a way that minimizes the cost. In addition, the in-house counsel often supervises a team of paralegals working as compliance officers in various areas of the business. A **compliance officer** monitors regulatory and legislative requirements applicable to the business and ensures that the business complies. The role of in-house counsel is expanding to include a proactive role in the management and strategy of the business. An in-house counsel can be a valuable member of the management team, and the decision to hire such a lawyer should not be undertaken as a purely mathematical calculation of saved legal fees.

retainer the contract between a lawyer and client that describes the work that will be done and the fee that will be charged

in-house counsel a lawyer who provides legal services to a business as a full-time employee of the business

outside counsel self-employed lawyers who work alone, in small partnerships, or in large national firms, and bill the business for services rendered

compliance officer an employee who monitors regulatory and legislative requirements applicable to the business and ensures that the business complies

---

[7] The Law Society of British Columbia, www.lawsociety.bc.ca/support-and-resources-for-lawyers/law-office-administration/paralegals.

[8] *Law Society Act*, RSO 1990, c L-8 as amen. See also the criticism of the Ontario model contained in Chapter 4 of the Federal Competition Bureau Report Self-Regulated Professions Balancing Competition and Regulation, December 2007, www.competitionbureau.gc.ca/epic/site/cb-bc.nsf/en/02523e.html.

LAW AND BUSINESS ETHICS

Business Ethics

Earlier we discussed whether breaking the law can ever be right. We should also consider whether merely abiding by the law is sufficient. Are there occasions when a higher standard of behaviour is required? This question raises issues of business ethics and **corporate social responsibility**. As shown in Figure 1.1, corporate social responsibility expands the factors involved in business decision making to include three criteria: ethical, legal, and economic. In the wake of recent corporate scandals, businesses are encouraged to live up to a higher ethical standard than is imposed on them by law. One way to promote an ethical climate in a business is to introduce a **code of conduct** that requires behaviour in line with ethical values such as honesty, trust, loyalty, and responsibility.[9]

Why should a firm commit itself to observing a higher ethical standard than the law requires? The answer may be quite straightforward: A firm behaves ethically because that is how its owners or managers believe it should behave. More often, however, ethical behaviour is a matter of enlightened self-interest. A firm that respects its employees is more likely to have a stable, contented, and productive work force; a firm that operates a liberal "returns" policy is more likely to create consumer loyalty; a firm that shows concern for the environment and the community in which it is located will benefit from an improved public image; and a firm with transparent and independent leadership will benefit from the trust and confidence of the public investor. Finally, as we have noted, the ethical values of society shape the development of the law; proactive legal risk management anticipates where the law may go in the future and prepares for it now. Today's voluntary ethical standard may be tomorrow's mandatory obligation. Most chapters of this text identify a relevant ethical issue.

> **corporate social responsibility** a concept that suggests business decision makers consider ethical issues—including the interests of customers, employees, creditors, the public, and other stakeholders—in addition to legal and financial concerns
>
> **code of conduct** a common standard of behaviour that may take the form of a values statement or a prescribed set of rules often used by a professional organization setting out the duties and appropriate standards of behaviour to be observed by its members

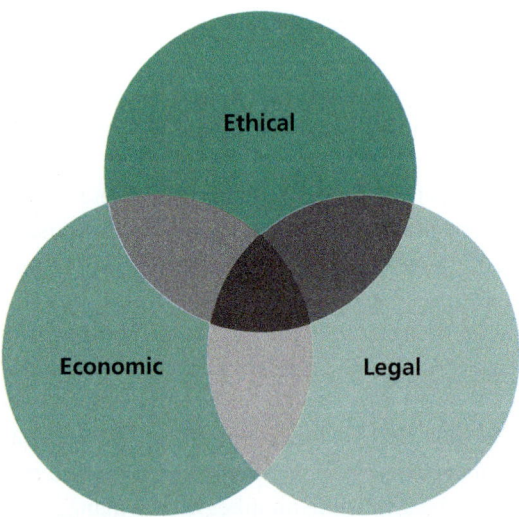

Figure 1.1 Corporate Social Responsibility: A Three Domain Approach

Source: Based on Mark S. Schwartz and Archie B. Carroll, "Corporate Social Responsibility: A Three Domain Approach" (2003), 13(4) Business Ethics Quarterly 509. Cambridge University Press.

---

[9] Mark S. Schwartz, "A Code of Ethics for Corporate Codes of Ethics" (2002), 41 *Journal of Business Ethics* 27–43; Mark S. Schwartz and Archie B. Carroll, "Corporate Social Responsibility: A Three Domain Approach" (2003), 13(4) *Business Ethics Quarterly* 503–30.

Codes of Conduct

Codes of conduct take a variety of forms and can fill gaps that law cannot reach:

Binding Codes Some activities, particularly of professionals, are regulated by a code of conduct or a similar set of rules laid down by a governing body or trade association. Professional codes of conduct are considered further in Chapter 5.

Although these rules are not law, their effect is often similar. A member of a profession or trade association who breaches the code of conduct may face disciplinary proceedings and may even be expelled from that body—a very severe sanction, since often expulsion will deprive the offender of the right to work in the profession. These bodies can cross jurisdictional boundaries that the law does not.

Voluntary Codes Some industries have established voluntary codes of conduct for their activities. Although voluntary, these codes often have a strong persuasive effect. A voluntary code may even be used as a substitute for government regulation, the implicit threat being that, if an industry—for example, the advertising industry—does not regulate itself satisfactorily, the government will step in and legislate standards. In other cases, voluntary codes are adopted where no effective power to legislate exists. A well-known example is the United Nations Code of Conduct on Transnational Corporations. Multinational enterprises are urged to observe certain minimum standards—for example, on employment of child labour—even though there are no legal restrictions in countries in which they operate.

Self-Imposed Codes Some firms have adopted and published their own codes of conduct, especially in relation to employment conditions and environmental protection. Codes may be a response to public criticism—for example, to criticism of working conditions in overseas factories of manufacturers of clothing and sporting goods. Sometimes they may be used to impress and attract particular groups of consumers. In other cases, they simply reflect the philosophy of the owners or managers of the firm. The contents of the code may form part of employment contracts, and employees may be disciplined for violations.

ILLUSTRATION 1.6 Binding Code of Conduct

Students attending a university are governed by an academic code of conduct that forbids cheating. Cheating is unethical. The code allows the university to expel or suspend a student for cheating. The university does not have to establish that the student broke the law, only that he or she violated the academic code of conduct that forms part of the contractual relationship between the university and the student.

WHO MAKES LAW?

Law comes from a variety of sources:

(a) The constitution—the **basic law** from which all other laws draw their power. This law might be created by a sovereign, such as a monarch, or by a government.

   A constitution is a "higher" law by which all other laws are judged; other laws must comply with the constitution in order to be valid and enforceable.

basic law a constitution that lists the founding legal principles accepted by the citizens of a country and that they regard as legitimate and binding

(b) Legislation—also known as statute law, **statutes**, or acts—is passed by Parliament and by provincial legislatures under the authority of and in compliance with Canada's Constitution.

   (i) Subordinate legislation—rules passed under authorization of a statute by a body designated in the statute, such as the federal or a provincial cabinet,

statutes pieces of legislation passed by government

regulations administrative rules implemented by government as a result of authorization given in a statute

or by a cabinet minister, or by an administrative body such as the Canadian Radio-television and Telecommunications Commission. These rules are referred to as **regulations**.

(ii) Administrative rulings—rulings handed down by administrative regulatory bodies created by the legislation to hear complaints and applications by individuals and groups, according to the terms of the legislation. We will discuss regulatory law in Chapter 3.

case law a collection of individual cases decided by the courts that develop and shape legal principles

(c) Court decisions—judgments handed down by single judges or a panel of judges after hearing a case before the court. These decisions are collectively referred to as **case law**. Sometimes a decision impacts only the parties involved, but other times the decision includes explanations and opinions that shape the law and have relevance beyond the specific parties. We will deal with this type of law in more detail in Chapter 2.

Courts play a very special role in our society. Whenever the government itself or any private citizen or group believes another person has broken the law, the complaining party may resort to the courts. Courts are central to law enforcement. Under a legal system such as ours, derived from the English system, legislation has historically played only a small part in resolving legal disputes between private parties—individuals, corporations, or other organized groups not connected with the government. Large areas of the law are unaffected by legislation. In these areas, the courts apply principles from case law that they themselves have developed in their long history of delivering written decisions and in novel situations of developing new principles. These activities of the courts are important and complex. We will discuss the evolution and continuing importance of court decisions based on principles developed by the courts themselves in Chapter 2. This chapter continues with the relationship between legislation and the courts.

CHECKLIST
What Do Courts Do?

- They determine the validity of legislation.
- They interpret legislation.
- They protect human rights.
- They develop case law, creating new principles to be applied to resolve disputes without court intervention.
- They determine disputes for the parties before the courts.

THE COURTS AND LEGISLATION

Even in areas where there is legislation, courts play an important role. It will be the court that decides if a statute is valid and enforceable. In Canada, validity depends on compliance with the Constitution. If it is valid, the court must decide what the words of the statute mean and whether that interpretation covers the subject of the dispute.

Federalism and the Constitution

In a federal country such as Canada (and also the United States), there are two distinct levels of government: federal and provincial (or state in the United States). Under the

Constitution Act, 1867,[10] each level has its own sphere of authority. Our national Parliament cannot alter the structure of provincial governments.[11] The division of legislative power, mainly under sections 91 and 92 of the Constitution, allocates certain areas to the federal Parliament and others (including power over municipalities) to the provincial legislatures. When conflict arises, the courts determine if legislation is within the jurisdiction of the enacting government. Whenever an act—or any provision in an act—is found by the court to be outside the legislature's jurisdiction and therefore beyond its powers (**ultra vires**), that act or provision is invalid. The Constitution gives **residual powers** to the federal government, so that topics not expressly allocated to the provinces are within federal jurisdiction. Examples are new activities developed after 1867, such as air traffic and radio and television broadcasting. This means that the federal government's powers will grow over time.

Sometimes practical problems do not fit neatly into well-defined subjects that fall clearly within either federal or provincial jurisdiction. The courts must resolve these jurisdictional disputes. The Canadian Supreme Court has become the constitution's jurisdiction umpire.

Courts follow a two-step process when deciding jurisdictional disputes between federal and provincial powers. First, they look at the law itself—what does the law do and why? The primary topic or dominant feature known as the "pith and substance" of the law is identified. Second, the court decides under which delegated power the identified topic falls—where does this *primary* subject matter fit?

If the court places the topic under a power of the other government, the law will be found invalid.[12] Minor infringements for incidental matters will not defeat a law whose primary purpose falls within the power of the enacting government.

ultra vires beyond the powers and therefore void

residual powers powers that fall within federal jurisdiction because they are not expressly allocated to the provinces by the Constitution

CASE 1.2 Primary Purpose

The Quebec *Consumer Protection Act* prohibits advertising directed at persons under the age of 13. The provisions of the Act apply to all forms of advertising—including newspapers, magazines, and television. After receiving warnings from the Quebec government about its television advertising for children, Irwin Toys Limited asked that the court declare the provisions in the provincial act invalid because they interfered with the federal government's jurisdiction to regulate television. The court refused; it found that the primary purpose of the Act was to protect children, "a valid provincial objective," and while it did have an "incidental" effect on television advertising, it did not conflict with existing federal regulations. "Neither television broadcasters nor advertisers are put into a position of defying one set of standards by complying with the other."[13] Consequently, the court held that the provisions of the Quebec *Consumer Protection Act* were valid and Irwin Toys had to comply with them.

Usually, the court will not strike down legislation unless the legislation is clearly inconsistent with the constitutional division of powers.

Sometimes power is shared by both levels of government, and they are given **concurrent powers** to regulate an activity. Section 95 is an example where the Constitution actually grants shared jurisdiction over agriculture and immigration.

concurrent powers overlapping powers of both levels of government to regulate the same activities

---

[10] This Act was formerly known as the *British North America Act* but was officially renamed the *Constitution Act, 1867* by the *Constitution Act, 1982*. Both of these Acts and all intervening amendments are now referred to as the Constitution.

[11] Such changes may be done only by amending the Constitution, a difficult task that requires approval of the provinces themselves.

[12] *Reference Re Assisted Human Reproduction Act*, [2010] SCJ.No 61 at para 19; *R v Van Kessel Estate*, 2013 BCCA 221.

[13] *Irwin Toy Ltd v Quebec (Attorney-General)*, [1989] 1 SCR 927 at 964. *Canadian Charter of Rights and Freedoms* issues were also raised, noted later in this chapter.

More often a problem overlaps jurisdictions, and each government will have passed laws in the same area, relying on their own respective powers in section 91 and section 92. The court may find that the subject matter has a "double aspect"—that is, it clearly falls within both a federal and a provincial head of power. If there is no conflict between the federal and provincial laws, then both are valid.[14]

But what if there is a conflict? In that event, the principle of **federal paramountcy** applies. In order to preserve the same law across the country in an area of federal jurisdiction, the federal law prevails over a conflicting provincial law.[15]

federal paramountcy the principle that a federal law prevails over a conflicting provincial law

THE *CHARTER OF RIGHTS AND FREEDOMS*

The Constitution does more than allocate jurisdiction between levels of government; it also limits government interference or behaviour in certain areas. The *Charter of Rights and Freedoms* forms part of the Constitution and places limits on many aspects of government action in order to protect **human rights**.[16]

human rights recognized entitlements encompassing traditional freedoms associated with civil liberty and basic human necessities

The *Charter* lists a variety of "rights and freedoms" that the government may not unreasonably eliminate, restrict, or ignore. We will collectively refer to this list as "human rights," and even though the *Charter* controls only government behaviour, it has important ramifications for businesses as well as individuals. First, the *Charter* is entrenched in the Constitution. It cannot be repealed by an ordinary act of Parliament or of provincial legislatures. Section 52(1) states:

> The Constitution of Canada is the supreme law of Canada, and any law that is inconsistent with the provisions of the Constitution is, to the extent of the inconsistency, of no force or effect.[17]

The *Charter* can only be changed by amending the *Constitution Act*—that is, by consent of the Parliament of Canada and the legislatures of at least two-thirds of the provinces containing at least 50 percent of the population of all the provinces. Obviously, the *Charter* is much more difficult to change than is an ordinary statute.

Second, subject to the important qualifications in the following paragraphs, rights entrenched in the *Charter* cannot be infringed upon by ordinary legislation. To the extent that a statute offends a right in the *Charter*, the statute will be declared invalid. The legislature cannot interfere with those rights that are founded on the "higher law" of the Constitution. Therefore, every law passed by a government must comply with the *Charter*.

Courts determine if a law violates the *Charter* and the Supreme Court of Canada has shown that it is prepared to strike down those provisions in statutes that offend the rights and freedoms guaranteed in the *Charter*.[18] Alternatively, the Supreme Court

---

[14] See e.g. *Multiple Access v McCutcheon*, [1982] 2 SCR 161. The court found no conflict between federal and provincial laws concerning insider trading in corporate securities, and both laws could coexist. See also *Rothmans, Benson & Hedges Inc v Saskatchewan*, [2005] 1 SCR 188.

[15] See e.g. *Bank of Montreal v Hall*, [1990] 1 SCR 121, which considered the interaction between the federal *Bank Act* and the provincial PPSA legislation as discussed in Chapter 28. Both were jurisdictionally valid, but if there was a conflict, the federal legislation prevailed. In another case, provincial building code legislation and municipal zoning bylaws were not applicable to the construction of airport buildings because airports are federal: *Greater Toronto Airports Authority v City of Mississauga* (2000), 192 DLR (4th) 443.

[16] The terms "human rights," "civil liberties," and "civil rights" are synonyms.

[17] Section 52(1), *Constitution Act, 1982*.

[18] See e.g. *R v Big M Drug Mart Ltd* (1985), 18 DLR (4th) 321, striking down the *Lord's Day Act* of Canada as a form of compulsory religious practice; and *AG of Quebec v Quebec Association of Protestant School Boards et al* (1984), 10 DLR (4th) 321, nullifying parts of Quebec's *Charter of the French Language* as violating minority language rights under the *Charter of Rights and Freedoms*.

has sometimes added words to a statute to make the law compliant with the *Charter*; for example it "read into" a human rights act (rather than striking down a part of the act) words prohibiting discrimination on the basis of sexual orientation, words that the legislature had not chosen to include as part of the act.[19]

Third, there are some exceptions to compliance. The *Charter* includes section 33, which permits a legislature to override certain other sections. That is, if a statute states expressly that it "shall operate notwithstanding" those specified sections, a legislature may infringe some of the most important rights guaranteed by the *Charter*. Section 33 also contains a so-called sunset clause. The overriding section of the statute expires five years after it comes into force unless it is re-enacted by the legislature—and continues to expire after each further five years. The reasoning behind these provisions seems to be as follows: The declaration of certain rights in our Constitution gives them great moral and political force. Governments will rarely dare to pass legislation expressly overriding the *Charter*, and very likely for only limited purposes—and they will have to produce strong reasons for continuing the override beyond the first five years. In the years since the *Charter*, legislatures have operated within these constraints; in general, they have not found it politically easy to avoid the *Charter* and to use the override section.

Fourth, none of the rights set out in the *Charter* is absolute. Section 1 states that they are all subject "to such reasonable limits prescribed by law as can be demonstrably justified in a free and democratic society." The problem of what amounts to "reasonable limits" arises whenever a complainant claims that a right entrenched in the *Charter*, such as the freedom of expression, has been infringed.

In general, a statute is presumed to be valid (that is, to be within the power of a legislature passing it). A person attacking it must show why it is invalid. However, a person need show only that one of his constitutionally guaranteed rights has been infringed by a provision in a statute; the provision would then be presumed invalid unless the government could persuade the court that the infringement was "demonstrably justified." So the **burden** shifts to the government to show that the section of a statute that interferes with constitutional rights is justified. It is difficult to predict in a general way how deferential the courts will be to the legislatures, but judges making these decisions have great power.

Fifth, the *Charter* applies to governments and governmental activities; it has limited application between private persons. In the private sector, the protection of human rights has been a matter for human rights codes passed by each of the provinces and by Parliament (to cover those activities that are under federal jurisdiction). These codes are not entrenched and may be amended from time to time by the legislature, or even repealed entirely, although complete repeal is highly unlikely. The *Charter* itself states that it applies "in respect of all matters within the authority of Parliament . . . [and] . . . of the legislature of each province."[20] These words make the *Charter* applicable to all statutes, to regulations under statute law, to municipal laws, and to Crown corporations. However, the Supreme Court of Canada has refused to extend *Charter* requirements to corporations and even to our publicly funded universities because they are considered to be independent of the government.[21] This matter has been left to provincial human rights codes.

burden the requirement that, unless a party can establish facts and law to prove its case, it will lose

---

[19] *Vriend et al v The Queen in the Right of Alberta et al* (1998), 156 DLR (4th) 385.

[20] Section 32, *Canadian Charter of Rights and Freedoms*.

[21] *McKinney v University of Guelph*, [1990] 3 SCR 229 at 266, "the mere fact that an entity is a creature of statute . . . is in no way sufficient to make its actions subject to the *Charter*."

> **CHECKLIST**
>
> ## Key Features of the *Charter*
>
> - Embedded in the Constitution
> - Limited ability to change
> - Overrides other legislation except when notwithstanding clause invoked
> - Reasonable not absolute protection of individual rights and freedoms
> - Application limited to governments and governmental activities

The Rights and Freedoms Protected by the *Charter*

The important protections listed in the *Charter* are set out in the chart below.

Freedoms[22]	Legal Rights[23]	Equality Rights[24]
Conscience and religion	Life, liberty, and security	Age, religion
Opinion and expression	No Unreasonable search or seizure	Race, colour
Assembly	To Counsel	Nationality or ethnicity
Association	No Arbitrary detention	Sex
		Mental or physical disability

The list of equality rights is not exhaustive and may be expanded on analogy grounds by the courts as necessary; sexual orientation was recognized as analogous.[25] Note that religion is both a freedom and an equality right. This means individuals are free to practice the religion of their choice, and others may not discriminate against said individuals based on religion. "Affirmative action" (or "reverse discrimination") programs—that is, programs aimed at assisting disadvantaged people such as older adults or individuals who have disabilities—do not violate the *Charter*'s ban on discrimination.

Courts follow a two-step analysis to determine whether a law violates the *Charter*. First, the court assesses whether or not an infringement of a guaranteed right has occurred. Second, it looks at whether the discrimination can be justified in a "free and democratic society."[26]

The Significance of the *Charter* for Business

As noted, the *Charter of Rights and Freedoms* applies to government behaviour and not the private sector, so why is it relevant to business? The answer lies in the fact that government regulates and controls the business environment through legislation. If that legislation violates the *Charter of Rights and Freedoms*, it can be declared invalid, and business will be free of the regulation. This is the strategy unsuccessfully

---

[22] Section 2, *Charter of Rights and Freedoms*, Constitution Act, 1982.

[23] Sections 7, 8, 9, 10, *Charter of Rights and Freedoms*, Constitution Act, 1982.

[24] Sections 15, 28, *Charter of Rights and Freedoms*, Constitution Act, 1982.

[25] *Andrews v Law Society British Columbia* [1989] 1 SCR 143, holding that discrimination may be on an enumerated or analogous ground; *Vriend v Alberta*, *supra* note 19 (sexual orientation).

[26] Section 1, *Charter of Rights and Freedoms*, Constitution Act, 1982.

attempted by Irwin Toys in Case 1.2. Here are some examples of *Charter* cases with key business significance.

> ### CASE 1.3 Sunday Shopping and Religion
>
> The *Lord's Day Act* was a federal statute dating back to 1906 that required businesses to remain closed on Sundays. In 1982, an Alberta-based pharmacy, Big M Drug Mart Ltd., remained open on a Sunday and was charged with a violation of the Act. In defence, the company claimed that the law was invalid because it violated the *Charter of Rights and Freedoms*, specifically freedom of religion. They felt the *Lord's Day Act* forced non-Christians to honour the Christian religious practice of not working on Sunday. The Supreme Court agreed, held the *Lord's Day Act* invalid for offending the *Charter*, and found Big M Drug Mart Ltd. not guilty because no one can be convicted of an offence under an unconstitutional law.[27]

Sunday shopping became the norm, and the retail industry was forever changed. Employment in the retail industry rose between 5 and 12 percent, depending upon the province, because of the increased hours of operation.[28]

The *Charter* expanded the availability of employment leaves and benefits to a larger number of employees.

> ### CASE 1.4 Unemployment Benefits
>
> An adoptive parent took a parental leave from his employment but was denied unemployment insurance benefits. He challenged the law saying it discriminated against adoptive parents because natural parents received more generous benefits. The Federal Court agreed that the law was discriminatory and ordered the benefits to be given. The Supreme Court of Canada agreed with the remedy and said a court may give the legislature time to amend an offending law before it strikes it down.[29]

Collective bargaining between union employees and their employers has been influenced and protected by multiple *Charter* decisions.

> ### CASE 1.5 Unions
>
> The British Columbia legislature passed legislation that took away some collective agreement protections for employees in the healthcare sector, including rules related to layoffs, seniority, and contracting out. The Union challenged the law because the removal of these protections undermined their collective bargaining right and therefore violated the *Charter*. The Supreme Court decided that governments should not "substantially" interfere with the collective bargaining process as "freedom of association" gives workers the freedom to unite and present demands to government employers collectively. This law violated the freedom of association and was declared invalid.[30]

Access to the professions was expanded by the *Charter*.

---

[27] *R v Big M Drug Mart Ltd*, *supra* note 18.

[28] Mikal Skuterud, "The Impact of Sunday Shopping on Employment and Hours of Work in the Retail Industry: The Canadian Experience" (2005) 49 (8) *European Economic Rev.* 1953, available at http://economics.-uwaterloo.-ca/-~skuterud/-eer.-pdf.

[29] *Schachter v Canada*, [1992] 2 SCR 679.

[30] *Health Services and Support - Facilities Subsector Bargaining Assn v British Columbia*, 2007 SCC 27.

CASE 1.6 Membership in a Profession

The *Barristers and Solicitors Act* of British Columbia set Canadian citizenship as a prerequisite for issuing a licence to practice law in that province. When a British citizen who was also Canadian permanent resident was denied a law licence, he challenged the law. The Supreme Court of Canada held that the Act violated the equality rights of the *Charter*. Even though citizenship is not expressly listed in the *Charter*, citizenship was considered analogous to other minority personal characteristics listed. The Court held that "a rule which bars an entire class of persons from certain forms of employment solely on the ground that they are not Canadian citizens violates the equality rights."[31]

CHALLENGING THE APPLICATION OF A STATUTE

As we have seen, a business may ask a court to declare a statute invalid if

- the subject matter is outside the constitutional jurisdiction of the government, or
- the statute violates the *Charter of Rights and Freedoms*.

Alternatively, the business may accept the validity of the statute but still argue that the reasonable meaning of the words in the statute does not cover the specific business activity.

ILLUSTRATION 1.7 Multiple Ways to Challenge Application of a Statute

The Canadian Parliament receives a report about abuses in the stock market that cause investors to lose their savings. In response, it passes a statute prohibiting as misleading certain kinds of advertising of securities and making them criminal offences. A broker who specializes in these transactions claims that his activity is lawful and carries on in defiance of the statute. He is charged with an offence and raises the following arguments in defence: (a) that the law is unconstitutional because it purports to make changes in an area that is exclusively within the jurisdiction of the provinces under the *Constitution Act, 1867*; and (b) that even if his first argument is wrong, the government as prosecuting authority has placed an unreasonable interpretation upon the statute and has applied it too broadly in charging him with an offence. He argues, in other words, that under any reasonable interpretation of the statute, his activity would remain lawful.

The court must interpret the meaning of the statute to decide both (a) and (b) in Illustration 1.7. If the words are given a very broad meaning, it is more likely that the statute will go beyond the powers of the federal Parliament. However, if their meaning is narrowly restricted, the regulation will be within federal jurisdiction and valid but may not catch the specific behaviour of the broker in question.

It is obvious that a constitutional defeat on jurisdictional grounds is more serious for the government than a narrow interpretation that allows some brokers to escape regulation. When the Supreme Court nullifies legislation on constitutional grounds, it can arouse strong feelings and sometimes vehement attacks, both for and against the judges as individuals and the idea that a court can have so much authority. Judges of the Supreme Court cannot escape making decisions that play a critical role in political, social, and economic change. As a result, the role and the personality of Supreme Court judges in particular, and of judges generally, have become subjects of great interest to legal theorists, sociologists, psychologists, and the media, as well as to the practising lawyers who appear before them.

---

[31] *Andrews v Law Society of British Columbia*, *supra* note 25.

CHECKLIST
Three Ways to Challenge a Statute

- Argue that the statute is invalid because the subject matter of the legislation is not within the jurisdiction of the relevant government.
- Argue that the statute is invalid because the legislation violates the *Charter of Rights and Freedoms*.
- Argue that the interpretation of the legislation is wrong, and the statute does not apply to the particular conduct.

CONTEMPORARY ISSUE
The Role of Judges

Have judges become too "political"? Are they "usurping" the powers of Parliament and the provincial legislatures? Should the political views of judges be explored during appointment? The very public and politicized confirmation process for United States Supreme Court judges is a stark contrast to the private appointment of Canadian Supreme Court judges.

Earlier in this chapter, we discussed the role of our courts in interpreting the Constitution. The traditional role of the courts in a federation has been to act as umpire in jurisdictional disputes involving legislation affecting levels of government. However, since the *Charter of Rights and Freedoms* became part of our Constitution in 1982, increasingly the courts have been asked to interpret and strike down legislation of both levels as being inconsistent with rights entrenched in the *Charter*. There are decisions that place the courts in position of policy makers or "activists."

In *Vriend v Alberta*,[32] the Supreme Court of Canada went further than simply striking down a provision in a statute; it in effect ordered the legislature of Alberta to amend its human rights legislation to prohibit discrimination based on a person's sexual orientation. In another case, the court upheld the decision of a federal Human Rights Tribunal[33] requiring the federal government to pay several billion dollars in compensation to current federal employees and to former employees—almost entirely women—who were discriminated against because they were not paid fairly for work of equal value usually performed by male counterparts.

Some critics complained that such court activism is depriving elected legislators of the power to make policy decisions and to enact legislation based on their value judgments and what they believe their constituents want. Others defended the courts on the basis that our federal and provincial governments together made the decision to entrench *Charter* rights. Ever since, legislatures must abide by the consequences because the courts have no alternative but to interpret statutes in the light of the *Charter*.

In 2004, the Supreme Court handed down two decisions that appeared to recognize the central role of legislatures.[34] In October 2004, the Court deferred to a decision by the government of Newfoundland and Labrador not to honour a deal reached in 1988 with its public sector workers to end pay discrimination against female hospital workers. By 1991, the government claimed it could not deliver on the deal because of the "severe" fiscal crisis hitting the province. The Court agreed that such a denial of *Charter* rights could only be justified by "extraordinary" circumstances, but it accepted the position taken by the province. This decision has generated criticism that the Supreme Court has become too deferential to government decisions.

In December 2004, the Supreme Court gave its opinion in the reference on the controversial subject of same-sex marriages,[35] in which it stated that the power to change the definition of marriage lies exclusively with the federal government. Although it appeared that the Court was showing deference to the legislature, it did declare that churches could not be forced to perform same-sex marriages. This was after the Ontario Court of Appeal had already effectively legalized same-sex marriage by striking down the marriage licence rules that prevented same-sex couples from obtaining a licence.[36] The Court refused to state whether it agreed with lower courts that the traditional man–woman definition of marriage offends the *Charter* rights of same-sex couples because the judgment was not appealed by the government.

---

[32] *Vriend v Alberta*, *supra* note 19.

[33] *Canada (Attorney General) v Public Service Alliance of Canada*, [2000] 1 FC 146.

[34] *Newfoundland (Treasury Board) v NAPE* (2004), 244 DLR (4th) 294.

[35] *Reference re: Same-Sex Marriage* (2004), 246 DLR (4th) 193.

[36] *Halpern v Attorney General of Ontario et al* (2003), 65 OR (3d) 161.

In 2013, the Court made another decision that could transform Canadian society, by striking down the laws against prostitution. The laws against bawdy houses, soliciting on city streets, and living off avails of prostitution were held to violate the *Charter* because they disproportionately endangered vulnerable women, actually making them less safe. The ruling was suspended for one year for the federal government to decide on a new strategy to regulate the sex worker industry.[37]

In response, the critics claim that the courts have not shown enough deference to legislatures and to their values as implemented in statutes; instead the courts are imposing their own values. This has led to calls for the reform of the judicial appointment process. In 2016, a new, more transparent process for appointment of Supreme Court judges was announced by the federal government.

Questions to Consider

1. When a court determines that a particular provision in a statute is contrary to the *Charter of Rights and Freedoms*, what alternative does it have, apart from striking down the provision?
2. What option may legislatures use to overcome the power of the courts? Why do they not utilize this option frequently?
3. Assuming that a sufficient majority of provincial legislatures along with the federal Parliament could be formed to amend the Constitution, what form of amendment would you suggest to limit the powers of the judges?
4. Should Canada adopt a more American-style appointment process for new Supreme Court judges where political views are publicly examined?
5. Is suspending the ruling to give the government time to pass new laws a compromise that shows deference to the legislature?

Sources: Roger Kerans, "Don't Blame the Judges," *Globe and Mail*, March 22, 2000; Raj Anand, "Vriend Will Affect Charter Equality Rights and Remedies" (June 1988), 18(7) *Lawyers Weekly*; see also Craig Bavis, "The Latest Steps on the Winding Path to Substantive Equality" (August 1999), 37 Alberta Law Review 683; Tonda MacCharles, "Same-Sex Marriage Is Upheld," *Globe and Mail*, December 10, 2004; Campbell Clark and Kirk Makin, *Chaouilli v Quebec (Attorney General)*, 2005 SCC 35; New process for judicial appointments to the Supreme Court of Canada, http://pm.gc.ca/eng/news/2016/08/02/new-process-judicial-appointments-supreme-court-canada

QUESTIONS FOR REVIEW

1. Describe the three main roles of law in our society.
2. How is the legal infrastructure of a country significant for business?
3. What is legal liability?
4. Distinguish between criminal liability and civil liability.
5. Are law and ethics the same thing?
6. What are the features of a legal risk management plan?
7. Why have business organizations adopted codes of conduct?
8. What is the special role of the courts in a federal country?
9. What are residual powers? Concurrent powers?
10. How does the Constitution give the courts power over the legislature?
11. What strategies does business use to manage legal risk?
12. What is the special meaning of "public law" as distinct from "private law"?
13. Describe the special significance of sections 91 and 92 of the *Constitution Act*. What happens if the topic is not listed in either section 91 or 92?
14. If a citizen proves that a provision in a statute is contrary to the *Canadian Charter of Rights and Freedoms*, how will the government respond? Explain.
15. Which activities are governed by the *Charter*, and which are not? Describe the distinction.
16. "We have a parliament to pass laws, a government to administer laws, and a police department to enforce laws. Ironically, these potent instruments for the restriction of liberty are necessary for the enjoyment of liberty." (A. A. Borovoy, *The Fundamentals of Our Fundamental Freedoms* [Toronto: The Canadian Civil Liberties Education Trust, 1974] at 5.) Comment on the meaning of this quotation.

---

[37] *Canada (Attorney General) v Bedford*, 2013 SCC 72; See also *Canada (Attorney General) v Downtown Eastside Sex Workers United Against Violence*, 2012 SCC 46.

Chapter 2
The Machinery of Justice

- **CLASSIFYING LAW**
- **WHO MAKES LAW?**
- **TWO LEGAL SYSTEMS: CIVIL LAW AND COMMON LAW**
- **COMMON LAW: THE THEORY OF PRECEDENT**
- **THE SOURCES OF LAW**
- **THE SYSTEM OF COURTS**
- **THE SYSTEM OF COURTS IN CANADA**
- **PROCEDURAL LAW: USING THE COURTS**
- **STRATEGIES TO MANAGE THE LEGAL RISKS**

This chapter provides the basic information needed to use the legal system and to develop risk management strategies. Chapter 1 introduced the sources of law and considered the key role of the Constitution. In this chapter, we identify the various ways in which law is classified. We revisit the sources of law—judge-made law, legislation, and administrative rulings—and examine how each type develops and evolves.

In this chapter we examine such questions as:

- What is the difference between substantive and procedural law? Public and private law? The civil and common law legal systems?
- How does the theory of precedent balance the need for both certainty and flexibility?
- How are the systems of courts organized?
- What are the procedures for using the courts and making out-of-court settlements?
- What costs are associated with going to court, and who pays them?
- What alternative methods of resolving disputes are available?
- What is a class action?
- How is legislative policy implemented?

CLASSIFYING LAW

Dividing law into broad categories helps us understand and organize the many laws that govern us. In Chapter 1, we explained that laws fall into two basic categories: public law (dealing with government actions) and private law (dealing with non-government relationships). Each of these categories is subdivided into more specific topics. Subcategories of public law include constitutional law, criminal law, and taxation. Private law covers topics such as contracts, torts, and property law. Business law draws on topics from both public and private law. This text emphasizes contract law, as it is the foundation of most business transactions.

Laws are also divided into two other categories: **substantive law** and **procedural law**. When lawmakers decide to address particular conduct, they define acceptable conduct and then identify a process to enforce it. The rules that define the acceptable conduct or the rights and duties of each person are substantive laws. Some examples are the right to own property, to vote, to enter into contracts, and to sell or give away property; and the duty to avoid injuring others and to perform contractual obligations. Rules that deal with how the rights and duties may be protected and enforced are procedural laws. Put more simply, substantive law is "what" the law is, and procedural law deals with "how" the law is enforced.

substantive law the rights and duties that each person has in society

procedural law rules that deal with how substantive rights and duties may be enforced

WHO MAKES LAW?

Chapter 1 identified two key sources of law:

- the courts through case decisions; and
- the government through legislation.

The Constitution is the foundation of all legislation, and its role in establishing and enforcing the law was discussed in Chapter 1. Depending upon the Constitution's classification of a topic, legislation is passed by federal, provincial, and even local governments and includes, for instance, regulations passed by a licence committee of a town council. The committee's authority can be traced to provincial legislation, but as a practical matter, the committee is creating new law. This chapter will examine the development of both legislation and case law. Chapter 3 will look at how government uses legislation to regulate business behaviour. The relative importance of case law and legislation varies from country to country depending on the type of legal system adopted by the jurisdiction.

TWO LEGAL SYSTEMS: CIVIL LAW AND COMMON LAW

Regions of the World under Each System

Two European systems of law developed and spread through the parts of the world colonized by European nations. The older of the two systems is the **civil law** system. It covers continental Europe, Scotland, much of Africa, and the whole of South and Central America. In North America, it applies in Quebec, Mexico, and, to some degree, a few southern United States such as Louisiana. When the English conquered French Canada, they guaranteed the people of Quebec the continued use of French civil law in most areas of private law. To this day, most of the private law of the province of Quebec operates under the civil law system.

Civil law is derived from **Roman law**, and it prioritizes legislation. A civil law system requires that all law be collected into a consolidated body of legislation known

civil law the system of law involving a comprehensive legislated code, derived from Roman law that developed in continental Europe and greatly influenced by the Code Napoléon of 1804

Roman law the system of law codified by the Eastern Roman Emperor Justinian in the 6th century as the civil code, and this code is far more important than any case decision. The civil law court always refers to the code to settle a dispute. If the code does not seem to cover a new problem, then the court is free to reason by analogy to settle the problem from general principles in the code. In theory, a later court need not follow the earlier reasoning in a similar case; the second court may decide that, in its view of the code, a just result of the law ought to be the reverse of the earlier decision.

The other legal system is the **common law** system, and it originated in England. The common law system is followed in most of the English-speaking world (including Canada, the United States, and Australia), and it is a significant part of the law of many non-English–speaking countries that were part of the British Empire (notably India, Pakistan, Bangladesh, and the former colonies in Africa and the Caribbean). The common law system favours case law—the recorded reasons given by courts (and judges) for their decisions and applied by judges in later cases. This text focuses on common law systems, and we describe the basis of common law in the following sections entitled "The Theory of Precedent" and "The Sources of Law."

common law the case-based system of law originating in England and covering most of the English-speaking world—based on the recorded reasons given by courts for their decisions

Simply put, civil law values legislation over case law, and common law gives case law the same or sometimes greater value than legislation. Although civil and common law courts often reach similar conclusions, there are some important differences. Here, we deal only with principles of the common law. Much of what is written in this text does not apply to the civil law jurisdiction of Quebec.

The Need for Consistency and Predictability

For consistency and fairness, we need like cases to be treated alike. This also reduces the number of disputes that go to court because parties can anticipate how a case will turn out based on prior outcomes.

ILLUSTRATION 2.1   Consistency

A contracts to build a house for B but does not carry out the agreement. Their contract specifies that B is entitled to only $50 if A defaults. B sues A and collects only $50 for the breach. X makes a similar contract with Y and fails to carry out the contract. Y sues X for damages, but the court awards Y $10 000 in the suit, refusing to enforce the $50 cap on damages.

Either decision, examined entirely separately, might seem reasonable enough. Some people might well believe that the builder should pay only $50; others might favour the owner's true losses. But if we place the two decisions side by side, for example, in adjoining courtrooms on the same day, there would be two very unhappy litigants. X would complain because A, in a similar situation, escaped without paying any real damages; B would be angry because she obtained virtually nothing while Y got substantial damages for breach of a similar contract. X and B would both feel unjustly treated, and most people would agree with them—the law should be either one way or the other.

Equal and consistent treatment in like situations is an important part of justice. Therefore, judges must be interested in, and influenced by, what other judges have decided in similar cases.

A second major element of law is predictability. Suppose, after the conflicting decisions just discussed, P wishes to make a similar contract with Q. Q asks a lawyer whether the contractual limit on damages is a binding one. If P backs out, will he be liable to pay damages to Q for any loss caused by failing to carry out the bargain, or will he only need to pay $50? Q's lawyer would have to say, "Maybe yes, maybe no; it depends on whether the court prefers the result in the case of A against B or that in X against Y." You can imagine the state of confusion if this were the normal advice a client was to receive! People must be able to predict outcomes so like cases need to be decided alike.

In order to predict outcomes, judges give reasons and describe the principles applied in making their decisions—these principles are collected into a set of predictable rules that are applied to determine outcomes in other cases. In effect, these principles become law known as precedents.

COMMON LAW: THE THEORY OF PRECEDENT

Certainty Versus Flexibility

stare decisis to stand by a previous decision

The Latin phrase **stare decisis**, meaning "to stand by a previous decision," defines the theory of precedent. It means decisions of higher courts must be followed by lower courts, most of the time.

There are limits to the stare decisis rule.

- First, although judges may be influenced by all prior decisions, they are only bound (required) to follow decisions of a higher level court. Decisions of lower courts have influential value only.

distinguish identify a factual difference that renders a precedent inapplicable to the case before the court

- Second, precedents bind only the exact same circumstances. No two sets of facts are identical in every respect—even when the same parties are involved, the time must be different. Judges can **distinguish** the current case from an earlier precedent by dwelling upon factual differences. In this way, they are able to adjust the law (rather slowly) to changing circumstances and values.

Still, the foundation of the common law legal system is the theory of precedent. We look to past court decisions to find relevant principles and apply them to new situations. Accordingly, a large part of the study of law involves the study of previously decided cases.

The theory of precedent does make it difficult for judges to respond quickly to change in society. A decision that seemed quite acceptable in 1985 may be entirely out of step with current social standards. Changing an existing precedent is possible but takes time.

Accommodating Change

overrule declare an existing precedent no longer binding or effective

In order to **overrule** an established precedent, the same matter must be addressed by a court higher than the one establishing the initial precedent. As will be discussed under the sections on systems of courts, courts are organized into a hierarchy involving three basic levels: courts of first instance (trial courts); appeal courts that hear appeals from the trial courts; and the Supreme Court, which is the highest level of appeal and hears only "important" cases from the appeal courts. Courts are reluctant to overrule precedents established at the same level. The danger in overruling decided cases too freely is that doing so would undermine the needed consistency and predictability in law. Obviously, Supreme Courts must be able to overrule themselves; otherwise, old precedents could never change without legislative intervention. The Canadian Supreme Court often does this.[1] It is rarer for other courts to overrule themselves.[2]

---

[1] See statement by Cartwright, J., in *R v Binus*, [1968] 1 CCC 227 at 229: "I do not doubt the power of the court to depart from a previous judgment of its own . . . ." It should be noted, however, that the court did not overrule itself in this case.

[2] In 2007, the Ontario Court of Appeal took the unusual step of overruling its own 2005 precedent on real-estate fraud, candidly describing the 2005 case as "incorrectly decided." See *Lawrence v Maple Trust Co et al* (2007), 84 OR (3d) 94, which overruled *Household Realty Corp Ltd v Liu* (2005), 261 DLR (4th) 679 (CA).

THE SOURCES OF LAW

The law in every legal system, civil or common law, is made up of law from both sources, court decisions and legislation. The difference, as noted, is the importance of each source. Legislation is the most important source of law in a civil law jurisdiction.

Judge-made law is the oldest form of law, and it is the premier source of law in a common law jurisdiction, but it is important to remember that even in a common law legal system, the government also makes law when it passes legislation, and in a civil law system judges still decide cases.

Legislation: Government Made Law

We begin with legislation. The words *legislation*, *statutes*, or *acts* are interchangeable. Legislation is passed by Parliament and by provincial legislatures depending upon the constitution's allocation of power.[3] Every province has passed statutes providing for the creation of municipal governments and for their supervision. These statutes give municipalities the power to make law and to raise revenue for the benefit of their citizens. Municipal bylaws and regulations are a form of statute law. There is a vast category of **subordinate legislation** usually known as administrative law, created by administrative agencies. Statutes create various administrative agencies of government and give them the power to make rules and regulations that carry out the specific purposes set out in the legislation. The Ontario Securities Commission is an example of such an agency. Chapter 3 focuses on the use of administrative law to regulate business.

subordinate legislation law created by administrative agencies whose authority is granted by statute in order to carry out the purposes of the legislation

Legislation Framework
As already discussed in Chapter 1, sometimes legislatures enact statutes to **codify** existing case law precedents in an area rather than to change the laws, as, for example, in the passing of the *Sale of Goods Act* and the *Partnership Act*. Before these Acts were passed, the related law was found in a huge number of individual cases. The Acts did away with the slow task of searching through many cases and put all the existing law in one place.

codify summarize in a statute the existing common law rules governing a particular area of activity

Legislation may be either passive or active. Passive statutes simply state the law. They prohibit an activity formerly permitted or else remove a prohibition. They provide a framework of rules so people know what behaviour is legal and may govern themselves accordingly. However, passive statutes do not create a regime to supervise or punish infringing behaviour. Passive legislation leaves it to an injured party or a law-enforcement official to complain about any activity that has violated a statute of this kind and to begin court proceedings.

"Active" Legislation: Administrative Law and Government
"Active" legislation not only states the law but also creates a mechanism to supervise compliance and punish violators. The statute may authorize the government to offer subsidies to encourage a particular economic activity and to create an agency to supervise and to regulate the related trade or activity. Parliament itself is not the right body to run any program requiring continual supervision. The primary responsibilities of its members are to represent their ridings and to set policy through legislation.

Programs authorized by Parliament are executed by designated government officials—the term "executive" describes the agencies of government that carry out Parliament's will. Every government department, agency, and tribunal is established by the legislature in an authorizing statute. For example, the Canadian Radio-television and Telecommunications Commission is established under the *Broadcasting Act*, which sets out the Commission's purposes and grants it regulatory powers to carry

---

[3] Cabinet, in its formal role of adviser to the monarch, can also "legislate" within certain limited areas by issuing orders-in-council.

them out.[4] As will be discussed in Chapter 19, the Office of the Superintendent of Financial Institutions is the federal agency created to supervise and regulate the banking industry.[5]

Subordinate Legislation In exercising its regulatory powers and acting in its executive capacity, an administrative agency creates new law, which we described earlier as regulations or "subordinate legislation." Some subordinate legislation sets down broad criteria, such as regulating the type of guarantee that a licence applicant must supply to carry on a particular activity, and the amount and type of investment required as a precondition. Other subordinate legislation may be detailed and technical (fees for applications).

Important regulations, such as those setting out broad standards, require the approval of the Cabinet in the form of an order-in-council. The agency itself drafts these regulations, and the minister responsible for the agency brings them before the Cabinet. Lesser regulations may be authorized by the minister, the head of the agency, or even a designated officer of the agency.

The constitutional validity of these regulations may be challenged in the same way as any other statute, and misinterpretation of a regulation by the agency responsible for its administration may be appealed or reviewed by the courts.

CASE 2.1   Court Overturns Administrative Tribunal Decision

The Alcohol and Gaming Commission of Ontario supervises the granting of liquor licences to businesses under the authority of the *Liquor Licence Act*. The Registrar applied to revoke Famous Flesh Gordon's liquor licence because its proprietor was a member of the Hells Angels, a criminal organization. The administrative tribunal hearing the application refused to revoke the licence because the proprietor had no criminal record of his own. The Registrar appealed to the courts and won. The tribunal had applied the wrong standard of evaluation and the revocation application was returned to the board for reconsideration.[6]

As noted in Chapter 1, the growing complexity of society and government has increased the need for specialized oversight and control in such areas as banking, environmental protection, energy, transportation, communications, education, and welfare, and the list includes a growing number of business and professional activities that are believed to affect the public interest. Administrative law is an important tool used to regulate business behaviour in these areas, as will be apparent in Chapter 3 when we look at regulation of competition, consumer protection, and the environment. Other administrative law topics such as banking, labour relations, and intellectual property will be discussed in later chapters.

Interpreting Statutes Courts are often asked to decide what the words in a statute mean or whether legislation applies to the facts of a case. These decisions form precedents or offer guidance in subsequent cases. In this way, judge-made law and legislation are connected. In cases involving a statute, a court will only apply the legislation when the facts of the case are covered by the words in the statute; courts respect the legislature's intention when passing the statute. Judicial determination of the meaning of words used in a statute is known as **statutory interpretation**, and it requires a judge to examine much more than just the dictionary meaning of the words.[7]

statutory interpretation
determining the meaning of words in a statute by considering the legislative intent, purpose, and object of the statute, as well as the definition and entire context of the language

---

[4] *Broadcasting Act*, SC 1991, c 11.

[5] *Office of the Superintendent of Financial Institutions Act*, RSC 1985, c 18; *Bank Act*, SC 1991, c 46; *Trust and Loan Companies Act*, SC 1991, c 45.

[6] *Ontario (Alcohol and Gaming Commission of Ontario) v 751809 Ontario Inc*, 2013 ONCA 157.

[7] Elmer Driedger, *Construction of Statutes*, 2nd ed (1983) at 87; Ruth Sullivan, *Sullivan on the Construction of Statutes*, 6th ed (2014) at 7–15.

Canadian judges take a modern "holistic" approach to statutory interpretation that involves consideration of the entire context of the statute; the ordinary, custom, and trade usage of the language; as well as the objects, intent, and purpose of the government when it passed the law. The whole statute must be examined, as one section will not be given a meaning inconsistent with the terms or objects of another part of the statute.

The Supreme Court of Canada has applied this modern approach to statutory interpretation in many cases.[8] As well, the federal *Interpretation Act* directs a court to take a "fair, liberal and large" interpretation of statutes.[9]

CASE 2.2 Application of the Modern Approach to Statutory Interpretation

A farmer hired a contractor to level out the sand hills on his farm; the contractor removed the sand, sold it, and levelled the land with top soil. The contractor was charged with operating a pit without a licence as required by the *Aggregate Resources Act*. The Court of Appeal was asked to determine the meaning of the word "pit" used in the legislation. The Court found that the contractor's activities fit within the grammatical and ordinary meaning of the word "pit" and that the presence of exemption procedures in the legislation for those pits not producing aggregate demonstrates an intention of the legislature to include all excavating activities such as improvement of farmland in the meaning of the word "pit." The contractor was convicted.[10]

Case Law: Judge-Made Law

Now we turn to the other source of law: the courtroom. Every trial produces a judgment that interprets and applies the law to a set of facts. It resolves the dispute for the parties, but it also creates law.

The Common Law[11]

Case law precedents, not statutes, form the bulk of Canadian private law. A flow of reported cases from an organized national **system of courts** is needed to build precedents. This collection of case law precedents is also referred to as common law. Lawyers arguing a case may say to a judge, "At common law, the rule is . . . ," meaning that the existing precedents, taken together, give us this rule. Each court has a recognized position within the system of courts that determines the "rank" or importance of their decision in influencing judges in subsequent cases.

The earliest decisions were made, of course, without the benefit of previous precedent, so courts looked to a variety of outside sources for direction. Canadian courts looked to England's existing precedents when they had none of their own. English courts formed their earliest common law precedents by borrowing from **canon law**, Roman law, **feudal law**, and **merchant law**.

As the number of precedents increased, the need to draw on outside sources was reduced. English judges applied their precedents rigidly. Eventually, the common law became very formal, with much of its cumbersome procedure rooted in ancient customs and superstitions.

Equity

The early rigidity of England's common law precedents led to the development of a completely separate system of courts: the **courts of chancery**. If the common law courts rejected a request, an unhappy party could ask for help from the courts of chancery. These early English courts created exceptions to the common law

system of courts the organization of courts into a hierarchy that designates the responsibilities of the court and determines the importance of the precedent; the standard system has three levels: trial, appeal, and final appeal

canon law law created by the Church, which had its own jurisdiction and courts in matters pertaining to itself, family law, and wills

feudal law a system of land ownership rooted in sovereign ownership: land was handed down to lords who gave possession of parcels of land to lesser "royals" in exchange for military service and loyalty

merchant law rules and trade practices developed by merchants in medieval trade guilds and administered by their own courts

courts of chancery a system of courts under the king's chancellor and vice-chancellors developed from the hearing of petitions to the king—courts of equity

---

[8] *Re Rizzo & Rizzo Shoes Ltd* [1998] 1 SCR 27 at para 21; *Alberta (Information and Privacy Commissioner) v University of Calgary*, 2016 SCC 53 at paras 63–66; *Tran v Canada Public Safety*, 2017 SCC 50 at para 23.

[9] *Interpretation Act*, RSC 1985, c I-21, s 12.

[10] *R v 311578 Ontario Corp*, 2012 ONCA 604.

[11] Confusingly, the term "common law" has three different meanings: (a) the legal system of a common law country as opposed to a civil law country; (b) judge-made law (including equity) as opposed to statute law; and (c) strict legal rules as opposed to equity (flexible principles of fairness).

equity rules developed by the courts of equity as exceptions to existing rules of common law

equitable remedies new remedies created by the courts of equity to address situations where money damages did not solve the problem

contempt of court a finding by a court that a person has willfully refused to obey a court order and therefore will be punished

rules when they felt the precedent was too harsh. They became known as courts of equity, and the rules that they developed also created precedents called the principles of equity or, simply, **equity**. Equity and the common law contribute equally to the current legal system developed by today's judges.

The courts of common law offered very few remedies; they would award money damages only to a party injured by a breach of contract. Yet sometimes money alone was not adequate compensation.

By contrast, the courts of equity were prepared, if they thought fit, to grant **equitable remedies** such as specific performance—for example, in a situation such as Illustration 2.2, to order the defendant to convey the land. If the defendant refused, he would be jailed for **contempt of court** until he gave in and carried out the order. The threat of a medieval jail was highly persuasive!

ILLUSTRATION 2.2 Money not an Adequate Remedy

B owned two separate lots of land and agreed to buy the middle lot between them from S in order to build a large building on the three pieces once they were joined.

S changed his mind and refused to convey the middle lot. If B sued for breach of contract in a common law court, he would be awarded only money damages, an inadequate remedy since his building project would now be impossible.

In summary, the approach of the chancery courts was different from that of the common law courts. "Equity was a gloss on common law; it was a set of rules which could be invoked to supplement the deficiencies of common law or to ease the clumsy working of common law actions and remedies."[12] Remedies in equity were discretionary. The relative innocence of the petitioner and the hardship he suffered determined whether the individual could hope for equity's special type of intervention. It was equity that pioneered key legal concepts of trust and loyalty, and it was equity that considered the relative positions of the parties when applying the law. As equity developed over many years, its principles became as important as those of the common law.

CHECKLIST
Three Meanings of Common Law

The phrase "common law" can be confusing. It refers to three interrelated topics:

1. The English-based legal system—common law system—as opposed to the French-based civil law system
2. The original body of precedents developed by common law courts as opposed to the body of precedents known as equity, developed by the courts of chancery
3. The entire collection of case law or judge-made law as opposed to statutes or legislation

---

Merger of Law and Equity In 1865, the British Parliament passed an act merging the courts of common law and equity into the single system we know today, where one set of courts applies principles and precedents from both common law and equity.[13] The Canadian provinces passed similar acts shortly afterward.

---

[12] R. M. Jackson, *The Machinery of Justice in England*, 8th ed, J. R. Spencer, ed (Cambridge: Cambridge University Press, 1989) at 7.

[13] *Supreme Court of Judicature Act, 1873*, 36 & 37 Vict, c 66 and the *Supreme Court of Judicature Act, 1875*, 38 & 39 Vict, c 77.

Amalgamating the courts of common law and equity did not result in abandoning the philosophy of equity. The precedents also merged into one set of rules. Every judge now applies both sets of precedents. Judges exercise their discretion to apply an equitable principle when it appears warranted in the circumstances of a case. Today, equity provides a link between law and ethics.

THE SYSTEM OF COURTS

A major part of business law continues to be created by judges, so we should be familiar with the system of courts and their rules of procedure. Figure 2.1 illustrates the simple framework of the English common law court system. It is a good starting place because England has a single government, and its system of courts is easier to grasp than the more complicated federal structure existing in Canada.

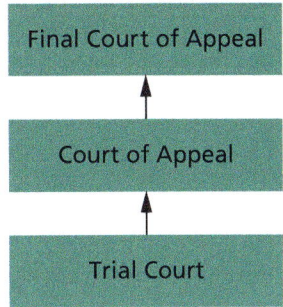

Figure 2.1 Basic Court System

The role of the three levels—courts of first instance, appeal courts, final court of appeal—is much the same in England as in Canada.

The Courts of First Instance—Trial Courts

Courts of first instance are also sometimes called courts of original jurisdiction because actions begin and trials take place in this court. This is the place where witnesses are called and an initial judgment is rendered.

The Court of Appeal

The Court of Appeal is the next level. Actions do not start in this court, but a party who is dissatisfied with the decision of a court of first instance may appeal to the Court of Appeal to reconsider the decision. The party who petitions for an appeal is called the **appellant**; the other party is the **respondent**. The appeal is not a new trial, and no witnesses are called. The court does not reconsider questions of fact because they were for the trial judge to decide, provided there was some evidence to establish the fact. The Court of Appeal proceeds on the basis of the written trial record, and lawyers for each side argue questions of law—with the appellant claiming that the trial judge erred in interpreting the law, and the respondent arguing to uphold the decision of the trial judge. The court may do one of four things:

1. Agree with the trial judge and dismiss the appeal;
2. Agree with the appellant and reverse the trial judgment entirely;
3. Change part of the trial judgment; or
4. Declare that the trial judge erred in failing to consider certain facts and send the case back for a **new trial** in the lower court.

appellant the party who petitions for an appeal

respondent the party who defends on an appeal

new trial a case sent back by the appeal court for retrial by the lower court

The Court of Appeal usually hears cases in a panel of three judges, but occasionally five judges may hear a very important case. The outcome is determined by a simple majority.

Final Court of Appeal—The Supreme Court

Parties dissatisfied with a decision of the Court of Appeal have one more chance—the ultimate court of appeal and the highest court in the land. Originally, the House of Lords (members of the peerage) had this responsibility. In 2009, an independent supreme court was formed in England with full-time salaried judges.

THE SYSTEM OF COURTS IN CANADA

The Canadian system of courts is a little more complicated than the basic English system. The Canadian Constitution divides legislative powers between the federal and provincial governments. It gives the provinces jurisdiction over the administration of justice—the organization and operation of police forces and the system of courts. It gives the federal government jurisdiction over trade and commerce, banking, bankruptcy, and criminal law—matters frequently litigated before the courts—as well as the exclusive right to appoint, and the obligation to pay, all Superior Court judges.[14] Therefore both levels of government must work together to operate a coordinated dual court system.

There are two Canadian court systems, a provincial system for each province and a federal system. Each system has three tiers: the courts of first instance or trial divisions, the intermediate provincial courts of appeal, and the final court of appeal for both systems, the Supreme Court of Canada. The names and jurisdictions of the courts differ somewhat from province to province, but in general they follow the same pattern as set out below. Figure 2.2 illustrates the structure of the Canadian Court System.

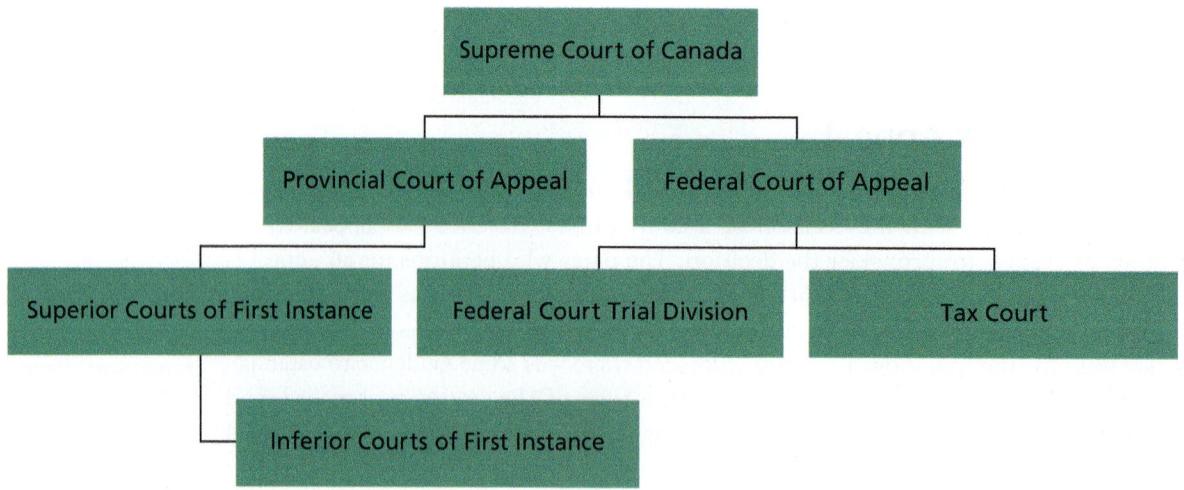

Figure 2.2 Canadian Court System

---

[14] The *Constitution Act, 1867*, ss 91, 92, 96, and 100. In all provinces, provincial judges are appointed and paid by the province to do specific legislatively created tasks.

The Provincial Court System

This system is the primary system of courts that deals with most matters of private and public law.

The Courts of First Instance The courts of first instance are trial courts where witnesses give evidence and initial judgments are made. The subject matter of the dispute determines which trial court hears the dispute. There are two branches of trial courts. The inferior trial courts are courts created by provincial legislation for a particular purpose such as minor criminal and family. The superior trial courts are the constitutionally created courts presided over by federally appointed judges and hear everything else. Individual provinces designate branches at each level to deal with specific topics. Most of the time, inferior trial court judgments are appealed to the superior trial court before they move to the intermediate appeal level.

Small Claims Court This court handles private disputes for smaller amounts of money. The maximum amounts have been increased in recent years but may vary considerably from one province to another.[15] Its procedure is quite simple and informal, so that the cost of taking action is small. The court is important to business because most consumer or client disputes and collections are handled in this court. Despite its small monetary limit, it is the busiest civil court.

Provincial Division This court decides very little, if any, private law. It hears criminal cases of almost every type except for the most serious offences such as murder, treason, sexual assault, and manslaughter. It may hold preliminary hearings in prosecution of these crimes to decide whether there is enough evidence to proceed to a Superior Court trial. No jury trials are held before Provincial Division judges. If an accused person elects (as one may) to have a jury trial, the case must be heard in Superior Court. Anyone charged with a criminal offence for which there can be a prison sentence of five years or more has the right to a trial by jury. In some cases where the prison sentence is less than five years, an accused person may also choose a jury.

A separate division of this court hears family questions of custody and support but not divorce. Some provinces set up a separate criminal division to act as a Youth Court where children and adolescents can be dealt with by special youth court judges rather than in the adult criminal courts.

Superior Trial Courts—Surrogate Court (or Probate Court) This court supervises the estates of deceased persons. It appoints an administrator to wind up the affairs of anyone who dies intestate (without leaving a will), settles disputes over the validity of wills and the division of assets, and approves the accounts of executors and administrators. Some provinces have merged this court into the Superior Court system.[16]

Superior Trial Courts—Superior Court This court has unlimited jurisdiction in civil (private) and criminal trials. It may be called the Court of Queen's Bench, Superior Court, or even Supreme Court depending upon the province. Federally appointed judges hear trials that deal with divorce and the most serious criminal matters, as well as all civil (private law) disputes above the jurisdiction of Small Claims Court. The court may also serve as a court of appeal for less serious criminal matters begun in Provincial Division. In Ontario, the Divisional Court is a branch of the Superior

---

[15] Alberta has the highest limit at $50 000; British Columbia, Nova Scotia, and Ontario limits are $25 000. In Ontario and Manitoba, Small Claims Court is a division of Superior Court, while other provinces maintain Small Claims Court as a civil division of the Provincial Court.

[16] Alberta, New Brunswick, Nova Scotia, and Saskatchewan.

Court of Justice, and it hears appeals from Small Claims Court and other administrative tribunals. Judges of the Superior Court of Justice also act as Divisional Court judges.

Intermediate Appellate Court—The Court of Appeal Each province has one intermediate appellate court, usually called the Court of Appeal. It performs the same function as the Court of Appeal in England. All matters arising in all the courts of first instance are appealed to the provincial court of appeal. This is the highest level of court in each province. The final level of appeal is to the Supreme Court of Canada, which hears appeals from all provinces and brings all provincial cases into the federal system.

The Federal Court System

Courts of First Instance There are two federal courts of first instance that handle disputes with the federal government or matters within its exclusive jurisdiction.

Tax Court of Canada The Tax Court hears appeals of taxpayers against assessments by the Canada Revenue Agency. The court hears only tax appeals and with relatively simple procedures. Either the taxpayer or the department may appeal its decisions to the Federal Court of Appeal.

The Federal Court of Canada The federal government maintains the Federal Court of Canada in two divisions: a Trial Division and an Appeal Division. The Federal Court has exclusive jurisdiction over such matters as disputes concerning ships and navigation and many sorts of lawsuits against the federal government itself. In the rather complicated areas of patents, copyright, and trademarks, the Federal Court has exclusive jurisdiction in some portions, but in others there is concurrent jurisdiction with provincial courts. A large area of concurrent jurisdiction remains, where a plaintiff may sue in either a provincial court or the Federal Court. For example, a person injured by the careless operation of a government motor vehicle may sue in a provincial court.

Intermediate Level Appeal—Federal Court of Appeal This court hears appeals from the Federal Tax Court and the Federal Court of Canada Trial Division. As noted, matters from the Federal Court of Appeal are appealed to the Supreme Court of Canada.

The Supreme Court of Canada

The Supreme Court of Canada is the final court of appeal in Canada for both the provincial and federal court systems. It consists of nine judges, and there is no higher court. In addition, it has special jurisdiction under the *Supreme Court Act*[17] to rule on the constitutionality of federal and provincial statutes when they are referred to the court by the federal Cabinet. In private actions, the appellant must obtain special leave from the Supreme Court to appeal.[18] Relatively few private matters are granted leave, so for many disputes, the provincial Court of Appeal is the last resort.

---

[17] RSC 1985, c S-26, s 53.

[18] *Ibid.*, s 40.

INTERNATIONAL ISSUE
The System of Courts in the United States

Both Canada and the United States have federal systems of government and common law legal systems, but there are major differences between their constitutions. In the United States, the individual states—at least theoretically—have more autonomy and have the residual power that in Canada rests with the federal government. Although under the Constitution the Canadian government has the power to create a full system of three-tier federal courts throughout Canada, Parliament has felt content to allow the provincial governments to organize one centralized set of provincial courts using their constitutional power over the administration of justice. The provincial courts decide cases of first instance (with the exception of the fields reserved exclusively to the federal and tax courts), with federally and provincially appointed judges deciding matters falling within their respective constitutional authorities.

On the other hand, the United States has two separate systems: a full system of federal courts—including a court of final appeal, the U.S. Supreme Court—that handles a large portion of litigation, although much less than the total handled by the state courts. Criminal law, for example, is a state matter, except in cases involving specific fields of federal jurisdiction, such as national defence, or in cases where an offence is committed in more than one state, such as moving stolen goods across state boundaries. The federal courts have jurisdiction in the following areas: bankruptcy; postal matters; federal banking laws; disputes concerning maritime contracts or wrongs; prosecution of crimes punishable under federal laws of the United States or committed at sea; actions requiring an interpretation of the U.S. Constitution, federal statutes, and treaties; and disputes between citizens of different states.

Most states also have an independent three-tier system of courts, with a final state appellate court. Unlike in Canada, there is no integration of the state and federal courts. Rarely, appeals are accepted by the U.S. Supreme Court when the appellant can convince the Supreme Court that a "substantial constitutional issue" is involved in a state matter.

Another fundamental difference between the two systems lies in their judicial selection processes. In Canada, all judges are appointed to a life term. Although the process varies somewhat for provincial and federal judges, most appointments begin with an application from a lawyer. The applicant is then screened by a selection committee; selected applicants are often interviewed by the committee. A list of acceptable candidates is then turned over to the Minister of Justice (or the provincial equivalent), who makes the final selection after consultation with Cabinet.

As noted in Chapter 1, the United States Supreme Court judges are appointed to a life term by the president, with a public confirmation process through the Senate. However, most state trial judges are elected for limited terms. In New York, the Democratic and Republican parties each select one candidate to represent their party in the state election so that only two names appear on the ballot. On January 16, 2008, the United States Supreme Court upheld this "partisan voting" process in *New York State Board of Elections v Lopez Torres*.[19] In other states, any candidate may run, but the electoral district may be so wide that minority voices are suppressed. In other states, the governor appoints the judge for the first term, and thereafter the judge must face the electorate to be renewed. This is known as retention election. Critics of retention elections worry that judges are tempted to make popular decisions in order to win re-election.

Questions to Consider

1. What are the arguments in favour of elected judges?
2. What are the disadvantages of judicial elections?
3. Discuss the pros and cons of life-term appointment.
4. In Chapter 1 we discussed the Ontario Court of Appeal decision that opened the door for same-sex marriage and the subsequent reference sent by Parliament to the Supreme Court of Canada. Why do you think the elected members of Parliament looked to the courts for direction on this issue?

Sources: Randolph N. Jonakait, *Checking Abuses of Power: The American Jury System* (New Haven, CT: Yale University Press, 2006) at Chapter 2; Gordon Van Kessell, "Adversary Excesses in the American Criminal Trial" (1992) 67 Notre Dame L Rev 427; Adam Liptak, "Rendering Justice, With One Eye on Re-election," *New York Times*, May 25, 2008, at 1, 13.

PROCEDURAL LAW: USING THE COURTS

The following is a general description of the procedures involved in a civil (private) lawsuit. Each province enacts regulations setting out the steps in a lawsuit, including forms, fees, and timelines. These regulations are known as the **rules of civil procedure**. Public law disputes have different procedures.

rules of civil procedure the provincial regulations that set out the steps in a private lawsuit, including forms, fees, and timelines

---

[19] 552 US 196 (2008).

Who May Sue?

Not everyone has the capacity to start an action. A living adult citizen of Canada has the broadest capacity—virtually unlimited access to the courts for any type of action. Generally speaking, non-Canadians may also sue as freely as citizens. A child (a person under the age of 18 or 19, depending on the province) is not permitted to bring an action alone but must be represented by an adult person. Similarly, an insane person cannot sue without a court-appointed representative. The estate of a dead person may sue on a deceased's behalf.

Generally speaking, corporations may sue and be sued, although foreign corporations may be subject to strict regulation and be required to obtain a provincial licence before bringing an action. For this purpose, a corporation is considered to be a legal "person" or "entity."

Greater difficulties arise when an action is brought by or against an **unincorporated collectivity**, a group of persons such as a social club, a church, a political party, or, perhaps most important, a trade union. In most cases, unincorporated groups are not recognized by the courts and may not sue or be sued. The position of trade unions varies. In some jurisdictions, it is possible to sue and be sued by a trade union, whereas in others it is not.

unincorporated collectivity a group of persons that in most cases is not recognized by the courts and that may not sue or be sued

Standing to Sue

Who has the right to advance a lawsuit? Generally speaking, only individuals whose rights are specifically affected have **standing** before the courts. The courts are concerned that especially litigious members of the public might clog the courts with matters in which they have no direct interest.

standing the right to bring a lawsuit

On the other hand, with growing awareness of damage to our environment through pollution and its impact on the safe supply of food and water, the risk of serious injury to large groups of persons has grown.

Some decisions of the Supreme Court of Canada have recognized the right of a taxpayer to sue when she believes public revenues are being improperly used, and the right of a movie viewer to bring an action when she believes his right to see a film has been taken away by a provincial censorship body.[20] Similarly, governments have invited the assistance of public interest plaintiffs in the enforcement of consumer protection standards.[21] The legislatures and the courts continue to work to achieve a balance between protecting the public interest and minimizing abuse of the judicial process.

Class Actions[22]

What if many people's interests are affected by the same conduct? Suppose the owner of a car wishes to sue the manufacturer to recover loss caused by a serious defect in the car, and the defect is known to exist in several thousand other cars of the same model. Who should sue? It would be unfortunate to clog the courts with hundreds, perhaps thousands, of repetitive claims in which all the essential facts and applicable laws had already been clearly established. Sometimes the amount in dispute is individually minor and not worth the cost of a lawsuit unless there is more than one

---

[20] *Nova Scotia Board of Censors v MacNeil* (1975), 55 DLR (3d) 632; *Minister of Justice of Canada v Borowski* (1981), 130 DLR (3d) 588; *Finlay v Minister of Finance*, [1986] 2 SCR 607; *Canadian Council of Churches v Canada*, [1992] 1 SCR 236.

[21] See e.g. *Business Practices and Consumer Protection Act*, SBC 2004, c 2, s 172. The important role of the public interest plaintiff is recognized by Justice Binnie in *Siedel v TELUS Communications*, 2011 SCC 15.

[22] W. K. Branch, *Class Actions in Canada* (Vancouver: Western Legal Publications, 1996); C. Jones, *Theory of Class Actions* (Toronto: Irwin Law, 2003). Also called class proceedings: *Class Proceedings Act, 1992*, SO 1992, c 6.

plaintiff and the multiple plaintiffs can pool their resources. Grouping parties with similar claims into one action is known as a **class action**, and the benefits include avoiding multiple actions and inconsistent results, allowing economic access to justice, and deterring wrongful behaviour of defendants.[23] Consumers often commence class actions against businesses over faulty products or services.

A court must approve the basis of a class action before the class action can proceed. There must be an identifiable class or group and common issues, and a class action must be the preferable procedure. If the court approves, then the class action is certified and the matter proceeds to trial as one action. The resulting judgment binds all class members; it makes the matter **res judicata**, and the case cannot be brought before the court again to contest legal liability. In our example of the defective car, if liability has already been established, other owners still have the right to have the court assess the amount of damage if the parties could not settle on an amount.[24]

Specific rules about bringing class actions vary by province.[25] Most class actions are brought by plaintiffs. Defendants complain that class actions encourage frivolous lawsuits that are so expensive to defend that unfounded claims are often paid to settle. The British Columbia and Ontario acts permit either a plaintiff or a defendant to apply to a court to have himself and others in his group declared to be a "class."

Procedure before Trial

An overall understanding of the steps in lawsuit is necessary for business administrators to work effectively with their legal advisers. Lawsuits progress through the courts in a form called an **action**, and most actions are begun by **issuing** and **serving** a **writ** or a statement of claim.[26] The statement of claim describes the reason for the action or the **cause of action**. A cause of action is an event or set of events that gives rise to legal liability. The statement of claim must describe both the facts and the legal principles that make up the cause of action.

> **plaintiff** the party that commences a private (civil) legal action against another party
>
> **class action** an action in which an individual represents a group of possible plaintiffs, and the judgment decides the matter for all members of the class
>
> **res judicata** a case that has already been decided by a court and cannot be brought before a court again
>
> **action** lawsuit
>
> **issuing** commencing the lawsuit by filing a copy of the statement of claim with the court office
>
> **serving** providing a copy of the issued claim to each defendant
>
> **writ** an ancient form required in order to take a grievance to court
>
> **cause of action** an event or set of events that gives rise to legal liability

---

ILLUSTRATION 2.3 Contents of a Claim

Tom buys an apple from a farmer, eats it, and becomes ill. Tom may commence an action for compensation for his suffering, lost time from work, and cost of medicine. The statement of claim must describe the facts of the event and the particulars of his loss. When, where, and from whom was the apple purchased? These would be the relevant facts as well as the particulars of the illness suffered. In addition, the claim must refer to the legal principles that apply to make the farmer responsible. In Tom's case, the claim would refer to the legal rules of contract law, product liability, and sale of goods that require a product to be fit for the purpose for which it was sold.

After a plaintiff has a statement of claim issued by the court, the document is served on the defendant. This is how the defendant learns by whom and for what he is being sued, so that he can prepare a defence; the plaintiff cannot proceed until the claim has been served. Obviously a defendant should immediately consult a lawyer after being served to act as **counsel**. It is a well-known saying that "he who acts on his own behalf has a fool for a client."

> **counsel** lawyer representing a plaintiff or defendant

---

[23] In *Western Canadian Shopping Centres v Dutton*, [2001] 2 SCR 534, the goals of class actions are discussed.

[24] The difficulties in maintaining a class action are illustrated in *Naken v General Motors of Canada Ltd* (1983), 144 DLR (3d) 385. For comment, see Fox (1984), 6 SCLR 335.

[25] *Class Proceedings Act*, RSBC 1996, c 50; CCSM c C30; SO 1992, c 6; SS 2001, c 12.01.

[26] Several provinces have simplified the process by abolishing the writ as a means of starting an action. The process now begins with the issue of a statement of claim.

Once a plaintiff has formally commenced an action and served the required documents on the defendant, why should they not go to trial immediately? It would waste time and money if a trial was held before the issues and evidence had been fully investigated. Time is needed to find witnesses, check documents, and research the law. Pre-trial procedure attempts to narrow the trial issues to those matters on which the parties disagree. The required pre-trial steps involve document preparation, tight time limits, and attendances, as follows:

- After receiving the **statement of claim**, a defendant who intends to contest the action files an **appearance** and replies with a **statement of defence**, admitting those facts not in dispute in the statement of claim and denying all others, and in addition setting out any other facts that the defendant intends to prove in court in support of his defence. Referring to Illustration 2.3, the farmer may admit to selling the apple but deny that it was the apple that made Tom sick. The statement of defence may also dispute the law.

- Next a plaintiff may deliver a reply disputing the added facts alleged by the defendant and adding any further facts believed necessary to cope with the defence.

- A defendant may have a claim of his own arising from the same facts. He will then **counterclaim** as well as defend. In turn the plaintiff will defend the counterclaim. Both claims will then be tried together. Collectively these documents are called the **pleadings**, and they tell the full story from both the plaintiff and defendant perspectives. Information left out of the pleadings will not be allowed into the trial.

- Depending upon the value of the claim, the next step is some form of **examination for discovery**, a process allowing either party to examine the other's evidence in order to narrow the issues further and to decide whether to proceed with a trial. Discovery allows a party to learn about the strength of the other party's case so that an informed decision about settlement can be made. Both parties must also produce their list of witnesses and relevant documents. Discovery of documents involves locating documents, preserving them, reviewing them for relevance, and producing them to the other side. Increasingly, documents are in electronic form, and production of these documents has become known as **ediscovery**. Once the forgoing steps are completed within the time limits, a party notifies court officials that the case is ready.

- Most provinces require a pre-trial or settlement conference with a judge or mediator after discovery is complete. During this confidential meeting, the issues in dispute are reviewed in an attempt to settle as many as possible or at least narrow the issues so that any eventual trial will be shorter.

The Trial

At trial the parties bring their evidence of all facts in dispute before the court. In private or civil actions, the **burden of proof** is on the plaintiff to prove her case. The standard of proof is the **balance of probabilities**—enough evidence to convince a judge that it is "more likely than not." This is done by bringing all the evidence of favourable facts before the court. The plaintiff asks the court to apply the law to the facts to come to a result favouring the plaintiff. The defendant, on the other hand, attempts to establish another version of the facts or at least to minimize the value of the evidence submitted by the plaintiff. The gap between the versions of the two parties is often astonishing. Sometimes the defendant will argue that even if the facts are as the plaintiff claims, the law does not support the request.

---

statement of claim document that starts a lawsuit containing a description of the facts and law that give rise to legal liability

appearance notice of an intention to defend an action

statement of defence a reply to a statement of claim, admitting facts not in dispute, denying other facts, and setting out facts in support of the defence

counterclaim a claim by the defendant arising from the same facts as the original action by the plaintiff to be tried along with that action

pleadings documents filed by each party to an action providing information it intends to prove in court

examination for discovery process allowing either party to examine the other in order to narrow the issues

ediscovery examination of electronic records and documents relevant to the dispute

burden of proof the responsibility to provide evidence

balance of probabilities more likely than not

Evidence is brought before the court through the sworn testimony of witnesses who produce relevant documents. Each side calls as witnesses those persons whose testimony is in their favour and cross-examines those witnesses called by the opposing party in an attempt to reduce their persuasiveness. Counsel may then re-examine its own witnesses to clarify any points dealt with in the cross-examination.

An opposing party may object to evidence introduced by another party for a number of reasons. It may not be relevant or it may be unreliable. One type of evidence that is not **admissible evidence** because it is considered unreliable is **hearsay**; that is, words attributed by the witness to a person not before the court. The reason for the hearsay rule is that the credibility of oral evidence cannot be properly assessed when it is secondhand, and therefore the original speaker should be subject to cross-examination and the scrutiny of the court. Witnesses must confine their evidence to the facts they know—they cannot give opinions about possible situations unless they are experts in the particular field. Although very technical, the rules of admissibility of evidence are intended to separate bad evidence from good.

After the court has heard all the evidence, each counsel makes a concluding presentation recommending the interpretation of the evidence and the law that is most favourable to their client.

> **admissible evidence** evidence that is acceptable to the court
>
> **hearsay** words attributed by a witness to a person who is not before the court

Judgment

After hearing all the evidence and the concluding legal arguments, the judge (or jury in some cases) must make a decision. In simple cases, the judge may give the decision at once or after a short recess, but in complicated and important cases, the judge will usually **reserve judgment** in order to have time to study the transcript of the facts and legal arguments and to compare the opinions in decided cases and textbooks. The judgment may be given orally in the court or in written form, and is reproduced in the law reports and in electronic databases. These judgments become the legal precedents that form the body of common law.

> **reserve judgment** postpone giving a decision after the hearing ends

Appeals

If either or both parties wish to appeal, they must make up their minds and serve notice within a time limit, usually 30 days or less.

As mentioned, most appeals take the form of a review by an appeal court of the written transcript of the trial forwarded to it from the trial courts. An appeal court also reviews proceedings of the trial court when a party contends that the trial judge erred in applying the law or in admitting or excluding certain evidence. If the appeal court agrees, it may order the case sent back to a new trial, directing the judge to correct the shortcomings of the first trial.

Costs

Who Pays for the Court System?

The courts provide a public service, a forum for peacefully settling disputes with the aid of government supervision and enforcement. The courts provide an essential alternative to parties taking matters into their own hands. Our governments pay the expenses of sustaining the court system, including the salaries of judges, registrars, clerks, and other employees, as well as the maintenance of court buildings. Litigants pay only a small portion of this overhead through charges made for specific services such as issuing a writ or registering a judgment against a losing defendant in order to enforce a claim. The term "**costs**" does not refer to the costs of running the court system; most of that is borne by the taxpayers. Instead it refers to legal fees and

> **costs** funds ordered by the court to be paid a party toward the expenses of the other party

disbursements that a party incurs in processing his claim or defence. The court will typically order the losing party to pay some portion of the costs of the winning party.

Solicitor–Client Fees
Initially each litigant pays the costs of hiring his or her own lawyers, although an important development in criminal and family disputes has been the system of **legal aid**, where the government pays for many legal services provided to low-income litigants. Legal aid is not particularly relevant to the business context.

A client pays a lawyer a **solicitor–client fee** as payment for time the lawyer spends working on the client's court action. As well, there are usually various expenses associated with a court case, such as court charges, travel costs when the case is heard or when evidence must be obtained at another location, and the usual array of out-of-pocket costs, all of which must be paid by the litigant. These direct costs of litigation are often substantial, especially if the original hearing is followed by an appeal, and, as we will discuss, they play an important part in an individual's decision to proceed with a lawsuit or settle.

legal aid a system where the government pays for many legal services provided to low-income litigants

solicitor–client fee payment for the time and expenses of a lawyer when representing the client

Party and Party Costs
Suppose a person is sued and defends himself successfully, with the court dismissing the action brought by the plaintiff. Should he be left with all the expense of defending an action that the court rejected? Or suppose a party demands payment for an injury wrongfully inflicted on her. The other party denies any liability; she then sues successfully. Should she have to bear the expense of her successful court action to recover a sum that the other party was legally obligated to pay?

Canada applies the "loser pays" rule. This means that a judge usually orders the losing party to pay at least part of the winning party's legal costs; this partial contribution is known as **party and party costs**.[27] Each province has a published scale of costs, varying with the level of court in which the case is heard, setting monetary amounts for the preparation of court documents by the lawyer and for time spent preparing the case and for each appearance or day in court. When a plaintiff wins a case, the court will award "x dollars damages, plus costs" against the defendant. If the defendant successfully defends the action, the court will dismiss the claim "with costs"—that is, party and party costs against the plaintiff. If the result of the action is a mixed one—for example, a plaintiff's claim succeeds in part and is rejected in part—the costs may be apportioned, or each party may be left to pay its own costs.

party and party costs a court order that shifts some of the winning party's costs to the losing side according to a published scale of fees

Total Costs of Litigation
A solicitor–client fee (the actual lawyer's bill) is almost always greater than an award of party and party costs. Therefore, even when a client wins a case with an award of costs in her favour, these costs will ordinarily cover only a portion of the fee charged by her lawyer; she will have to pay an amount over and above the costs recovered from the losing side. But she is considerably better off than the losing side with respect to the costs of the litigation; the loser must pay both party and party costs to the other side and a solicitor–client fee to his own lawyer, in addition, of course, to the amount of the judgment. In rare cases, when a judge believes the losing party behaved unreasonably, solicitor–client costs will be awarded. This means that the loser must pay the winner's entire solicitor–client fees.

Occasionally a client may believe that his lawyer has charged too high a fee for representing him in a court action, and the two are unable to reach a satisfactory settlement of the bill. If necessary, the client can have the matter referred to an officer of the court to assess the bill—that is, to set a fair fee for the service rendered in the action.

The Economics of Civil Litigation

Is it financially worth it to start an action? This is a key business law risk management question. First, there is always a risk of losing. A plaintiff who loses is not only denied the

---

[27] See G. D. Watson et al, *Civil Litigation*, 4th ed (Toronto: Emond Montgomery, 1991) at Chapter 4.

remedy sought but also must pay costs of the defendant. Even if the party seems certain of winning, it would generally be unwise to proceed with a claim that would occupy the time of the courts and incur heavy expenses in retaining a lawyer in order to collect a minor sum or to pursue a poor defendant or, conversely, to defend an insignificant claim.[28]

Second, apart from legal costs, businesses must examine the business costs of litigation. Often it may not be worth a business's time and effort to fight. For instance, a supplier of perishable goods such as potatoes might be offered payment of a reduced price by a buyer who claims that the potatoes had not arrived in as good condition as promised. The supply firm might decide that it is not worth the trouble to sue for the difference in price of, say, $200; nor would it wish to alienate the buyer, a good customer. It simply accepts the reduced price in full payment. On the other hand, the supply firm might think it necessary to fight the minor claim in order to discourage other similar claims.

A strategy should be developed for considering the impact of the litigation on all segments of the business. If the supply firm has had several similar complaints from customers and is concerned that the carrier has been careless in transporting the potatoes, it may decide to change carriers or to claim against the carrier. If the carrier should deny liability, the supplier would find it necessary to sue the carrier and "join" the buyer in the same suit in order to obtain a ruling. In other words, a party may have additional reasons besides the actual recovery of money for bringing an action for a relatively small sum.

Contingent Fees

Origins in the United States
In the United States, most courts do not follow the "loser pays" rule; a party, whether winner or loser, is required to pay only his own lawyer's fees. As a result, the **contingency fee** was developed to improve access to justice for poor litigants who might otherwise be denied the chance to pursue their claims.

Under a contingency fee arrangement, "the lawyer agrees to act on the basis that if the client is successful the lawyer will take as a fee a certain percentage of the judgment amount, and in the event that the client is unsuccessful the lawyer will make no charge for the services rendered."[29] From a prospective litigant's point of view—especially in a case where there may be a fairly poor chance of winning, but any award made will likely be for a large sum—a contingency fee arrangement might be the only practical way of bringing an action. A lawyer may take several cases and will be content to win one; the single contingency fee will cover his expenses in all the cases and leave him with substantial compensation for his work.

contingency fee a fee paid for a lawyer's services only if the client is successful; there is no charge if the client is unsuccessful

The Use of Contingency Fees in Canada
Canada was slow to adopt contingency fees as a result of concerns that such arrangements

- Encourage unnecessary and even frivolous litigation;
- Expose defendants to the costs of defending themselves against claims that have no merit;
- Encourage some clients to agree to unconscionably large percentage fees demanded by their lawyers;
- Drive up the cost of settlements and court awards and thus affect insurance premiums; and
- Cloud the judgment of the lawyer who becomes a stakeholder in the litigation.

---

[28] For discussion about the costs of litigation, see P. Puri, "Financing of Litigation by Third-Party Investors: A Share of Justice?" (1998), 36 Osgoode Hall LJ 515 (the Introduction).

[29] Warren K. Winkler, *Evaluation of Civil Case Management in Toronto Region*, 27 (Toronto, 2008), http://www.ontariocourts.ca/coa/en/ps/reports/rule78.pdf at 253.

> **ILLUSTRATION 2.4 Unnecessary Litigation**
>
> A is injured very seriously while skiing on an open slope. She complains that the accident was caused by an unmarked obstacle. Very likely, a court would find either that she accepted the risks voluntarily or that she was the author of her own misfortune through personal carelessness. Even so, if A is in a jurisdiction where a contingency fee agreement is available to her, she might well find it practical to bring an action on the small chance that the court would find the resort owner liable for the injury. She would probably not be able to afford the expense of litigation under the traditional solicitor–client way of charging fees.

Access to justice arguments prevailed, and most Canadian provinces now accept contingency fee arrangements, subject to supervision by the courts.[30] In 2004, Ontario was the last province to endorse contingency fees; the cap in Ontario states that the fee cannot exceed the amount of the plaintiff's recovery.[31] Although no statistics are available, it is generally agreed that contingency fees are most often used in class actions, and the combination has led critics to lament the explosion of American-style litigation. Criticism has focused on class actions involving individually minor claims where it appears that the lawyers make millions.[32]

> **CASE 2.3 Court Reduces Contingency Fee**
>
> National Money Mart, a payday loan company, was a defendant in a class action alleging that 210 000 Ontario borrowers were charged a criminally high rate of interest contrary to section 347 of the *Criminal Code*. The plaintiffs' lawyers were hired on a contingency fee basis with a written retainer that included a formula. Prior to trial, after multiple unsuccessful proceedings to have the action stayed and to block certification, National Money Mart settled the case. The settlement included a fee of $27.5 million for the class members' lawyers calculated according to the contingency fee agreement. Class action settlements require the approval of the court, and when the Ontario Superior Court reviewed the terms of settlement, Justice Perell valued the settlement at $30 million in cash and $58 million in debt forgiveness and reduced the plaintiffs' lawyers' fees to $14.5 million.[33] The fact that the class action led to new payday loan legislation in Ontario was relevant to the assessment of counsel fee, but the relatively low cash recovery of the individual class members was also relevant. On appeal to the Ontario Court of Appeal, the reduced $14.5 million contingency fee was found to be fair and reasonable in the circumstances.[34]

Settlement Out of Court

Advantages Illegal behaviour causes damage to a vast number of people, but only a small proportion of the victims sue. Even when a lawsuit is commenced, the disputes rarely go to trial. Most claims are settled before trial. **Settlement** is when one party agrees to pay a sum of money or do certain things in return for a waiver from the other party of all rights claimed in the lawsuit. Ontario's lawsuit settlement rate has been reported as high as 96 percent.[35]

settlement when one of the parties agrees to pay a sum of money or perform an act in return for a waiver by the other party of all rights claimed in the lawsuit

---

[30] *Justice Statute Law Amendment Act, 2002*, SO 2002, c 24; O Reg 195/2004; *Solicitors Act*, RSO 1990, c S-15, as amen. See also M. Trebilcock, "The Case for Contingent Fees: The Ontario Legal Profession Rethinks Its Position" (1985), 15 Can Bar LJ 360–8.

[31] "A Slice of the Settlement: Contingency Fees across Canada," *National* 13:9 (October 1986) 12.

[32] S. G. McKee, "The Canadian Challenge: Class Actions in Canada; A Potentially Momentous Change to Canadian Legislation," in J. Robson and O. Libbert, eds, *Law and Markets: Is Canada Inheriting America's Litigious Legacy* (Vancouver: Fraser Institute, 1997), https://www.fraserinstitute.org/sites/default/files/LawAndMarkets.pdf.

[33] *Smith v National Money Mart*, 2010 ONSC 1334 (CanLII).

[34] *Smith v National Money Mart*, [2011] OJ No 1321 (ONCA).

[35] Remarks of the Honourable Warren K. Winkler, "Civil Justice Reform—The Toronto Experience," University of Ottawa, Faculty of Law, September 12, 2007, available online at http://www.ontariocourts.ca/coa/en/ps/speeches/civiljusticereform.htm. See also Herbert N. Kritzer, "Disappearing Trials? A Comparative Perspective" (2004) 1(3) J Empirical L Stud 735 at 751, Figure 8.

Settlement provides quick compensation and avoids the expense of trial. Each party to a settlement also avoids the risk that the court will find against him. Since there are two sides to a story, there is some uncertainty in predicting which side will win. Of course, the stronger a person's claim appears to be, the more advantageous a settlement he will demand and usually obtain. Often a person starts legal proceedings to convince her adversary to seriously consider settlement. As a result, many actions are settled soon after they are started.

Why then are the courts and the relatively small body of decisions resulting from an enormous number of disputes so important? There are two main reasons. First, the decided cases create the law and supply the principles by which parties may assess the relative merits of their claims, predict the outcome of a possible court action, and strike a value for their claims. Second, the court is the last resort when all compromise fails. It settles the issue when the parties themselves cannot.

Growing Delay in the Court System
Despite the obvious advantages of settling disputes out of court, the number (not percentage) of cases going to trial has increased steadily over the years, indeed much faster than the growth in population. This might be because of the higher general level of education and the greater awareness of rights (especially since the *Charter of Rights and Freedoms* became part of our Constitution), the increased complexity of society, and the legal system generally. As well, the average length of a trial is increasing. Together the increase in number and length of trials has led to a backlog causing very long delays in actually getting most cases heard. In 2000, claims issued in Toronto languished in the system for just under two years before being resolved.[36] Since then, most provinces have designed simplified procedures and case management systems to move matters to trial more quickly.[37]

Delay often creates hardship. A plaintiff who has suffered serious injury might wait many years to be compensated; it might become much more difficult for witnesses to recall evidence. Indeed, sometimes one of the parties will die before the case is heard. As a result, rules have been adopted to encourage settlement.[38]

1. Parties must attend mandatory settlement conferences as part of pre-trial procedures. At this conference, judges offer opinions on possible trial outcomes and settlement offers.
2. The rules penalize parties who do not accept a reasonable offer of settlement. So, if a party rejects a reasonable offer to settle from the other party, and the court's subsequent judgment shows that the offer was a good one—that is, it orders substantially the same remedy as the offer made—the first party will be ordered to pay the costs incurred by the other party.
3. The use of alternative dispute resolution processes is encouraged by the courts. Some systems require mediation before trial.

Alternative Dispute Resolution

There have always been informal ways to resolve disputes rather than resorting to the courts, and over time, the rising costs and delays involved in using the court system encouraged a new emphasis on the alternatives. Today, many parties to disputes agree

---

[36] Warren K. Winkler, *Evaluation of Civil Case Management in Toronto Region*, 27 (Toronto, 2008), http://www.ontariocourts.ca/coa/en/ps/reports/rule78.pdf.

[37] Ontario has a simplified procedure for matters under $100 000. British Columbia has a pilot project testing a simplified procedure for Small Claims under $5000. Case management systems set timelines for completion of each step of the process, failing which the matter is dismissed. Toronto claims now average approximately one year in age before resolution.

[38] Rule 57(18), BC *Rules of the Supreme Court*; Rule 49, Ont *Rules of Civil Procedure*; Rule 10, NS *Rules of Court*.

arbitration a form of ADR where a dispute is referred to an arbitrator who adjudicates the matter, and the parties agree to be bound by the arbitrator's decision, although there may be a right to appeal to the courts

adjudicate hear parties and deliver a decision with reasons

mediation a form of ADR where a neutral third party who is acceptable to both sides acts as a mediator, assisting the parties to reach a settlement

not to go to court and instead to use the private procedures of alternative dispute resolution (ADR). The oldest form of ADR is **arbitration**—referring a dispute to an arbitrator who will **adjudicate** the matter; the arbitrator will hear the parties and their witnesses in private, less formally and more promptly than a court, and will deliver a decision with reasons. The decisions bind only the parties involved and are confidential. Arbitration was developed specifically with the business disputant in mind. The cost is borne entirely by the parties. The goal is party autonomy. Parties design their own process by selecting the rules, the forum, the arbitrator, and even the law that will be applied to the dispute. Often parties agree, through a term in their original contract, to refer any future dispute that may arise to arbitration. In the absence of a pre-dispute term, they may agree to arbitration after a dispute arises. Arbitration is also used in public sector disputes, in such areas as labour relations, workers' compensation, and international commerce (as discussed in Chapter 30). Normally, the parties agree in advance to be bound by the arbitrator's decision, but an appeal may go to the courts in some circumstances.[39] Recent decisions are limiting the availability of appeals to the courts.[40]

An increasingly important form of ADR is **mediation**. In mediation, a neutral third party acceptable to both sides acts as facilitator during settlement negotiations. The mediator has no power to make a binding decision but assists the parties in reaching a settlement. This is the ultimate form of party autonomy where parties not only design the process, like arbitration, but also design their own settlement. The mediator hears both parties, identifies and clarifies the issues, and explores middle ground that might be acceptable. Mediation can be evaluative—where the mediator offers an opinion on the substance of the dispute—or it may be facilitative—where the mediator guides the process only. It may focus on the legal rights of the parties, but it will often include a wider interest-based discussion. Mediation allows imaginative settlements not possible in courts and considers interests and factors beyond who would win in a courtroom.

The process usually begins with the mediator and both sides present, and after preliminary remarks by the mediator, each side presents its position; the mediator usually asks questions and tries to clarify those areas where the parties agree and disagree. Separate meetings may be held with each side to explore the prospects of agreement. All parties must adhere to basic rules of respect and confidentiality for an effective mediation.

While informal mediation has been used to settle disputes for many years, in the last two decades it has developed into a sophisticated procedure, and the success rate of reaching settlement is relatively high. There is a very large volume of literature on the subject.[41] As well, training courses are available across Canada at universities and through associations of mediators.

To be effective, a mediator must have the respect and confidence of both parties; key qualities are impartiality, sensitivity to each side's concerns, the ability to understand and analyze the disagreement, and the ability to present a creative approach to suggesting solutions.

Sometimes mediation can be abused. A party who does not really want to settle the dispute may agree to mediation in order to gain time by delay. When mediation fails, the parties ordinarily resort to arbitration or the courts.

---

[39] John C. Carson, "Dispute Resolution, Negotiation, Mediation and Arbitration in Ontario" (1993) 10(1) Bus & L 1.

[40] *Urban Communications Inc v BCNET Networking Society*, 2015 BCCA 297 (appeal dismissed 2016 SCC 45); *Sattva Capital Corp v Creston Moly Corp*, 2014 SCC 53.

[41] The 2001 Ministry of the Attorney General Evaluation of the Ontario Mandatory Mediation Program reported a 40 percent settlement rate, www.attorneygeneral.us.gov.on.ca/english/courts/manmed/exec _summary_recommend.pdf. The following four books are examples: G. Adams, *Mediating Justice: Legal Dispute Negotiations* (Toronto: CCH Canadian, 2003); R. M. Nelson, *Nelson on ADR* (Scarborough: Thomson Carswell, 2003); C. Picard et al, *The Art and Science of Mediation* (Toronto: Emond Montgomery, 2004); A. J. Pirie, *Alternative Dispute Resolution Skills, Science and the Law* (Toronto: Irwin Law, 2000).

CHECKLIST
Dispute Resolution Characteristics

Courts	Arbitration	Mediation
Public	Private	Private
Adjudication	Adjudication	Facilitated negotiation
Binding	Binding on parties	Non-binding
Precedent	No precedent	No precedent
Appealable	Limited appeals	No appeals
Enforcement	Court enforcement	Contractual enforcement

The advantages of ADR, both arbitration and mediation over courts, are as follows:

- Speed—cases are resolved by mediation or arbitration much more promptly than through the courts.
- Cost—speed in itself saves money; parties do have to pay the ADR fees themselves.
- Choice of adjudicator or mediator—unlike the courts, the parties can choose a person whom they believe to be especially suited to resolve the issue because of her experience and expertise in the area of the dispute.
- Confidentiality—the parties can agree to keep the dispute private to minimize harm to their business through disclosure of confidential information or encouraging others to bring similar complaints.
- Preservation of ongoing relations—since ADR is usually less adversarial than litigation, it is less likely to foster antagonism between the parties, and will allow them to continue to work together afterward.[42]

ADR has become important to legal risk management not only because of the foregoing advantages but also because of its wide availability and enforceability. The ADR movement—arbitration, in particular—grew out of commercial business disputes and was driven by the inability of domestic legal systems to handle international business disputes. Federal and provincial arbitration legislation was passed to promote arbitration and recognize and enforce arbitration awards through the courts.[43] Canadian courts follow a policy in favour of arbitration by upholding and enforcing arbitration agreements.[44] Organizations such as the International Chamber of Commerce facilitate arbitration among private sector international business partners. Domestically, private sector providers are widely available through organizations such as ADR Chambers and American Arbitration Forum, to name just a couple. Better Business Bureaus around the country offer ADR services to their members. By placing an ADR clause in a business agreement, businesses can take a proactive approach to legal risk management and ensure that if a dispute does arise it will not be resolved in the courts.

---

[42] For a general overview, see D. Paul Emond, *Commercial Dispute Resolution: Alternatives to Litigation* (Aurora, ON: Canada Law Book, 1989) or A. J. Pirie, *supra* note 41.

[43] *Arbitration Act*, RSBC 1996, c 55 (CAA); *Arbitration Act*, RSA 2000, c A-43; *Arbitration Act, 1992*, SS 1992, c A-24.1; *Arbitration Act*, CCSM c A120; *Arbitration Act*, RSY 2002, c 8; *Arbitration Act*, RSNWT 1988, c A-5; *Arbitration Act*, SNB 1992, c A-10.1; *Arbitration Act*, RSNS 1989, c 19; *Arbitration Act*, RSPEI 1988, c A-16; *Arbitration Act*, RSNL 1990, c A-14; *Quebec Code of Civil Procedure*, RSQ c C-25, art 940–51.2 (Arbitration legislation).

[44] *Ontario Hydro v Denison Mines Ltd*, [1992] OJ No 2948 at para 8; see *Deluce Holdings Inc v Air Canada*, [1992] OJ No 2382; *Buck Bros Ltd v Frontenac Builders*, [1994] OJ No 37; *Onex Corp v Ball Corp* (1994), 12 BLR (2d) 151; *Canadian National Railway Co v Lovat Tunnel Equipment Inc* (1999), 174 DLR (4th) 385 (ONCA); *Diamond & Diamond v Srebrolow*, [2003] OJ No 4004.

Mediation is also being embraced by the court systems. In Ontario, every civil (private) and estate action commenced in Toronto, Ottawa, and Windsor must undergo a three-hour mandatory mediation session before it may be set for trial. Saskatchewan also has a mandatory mediation program for civil actions filed in the Court of Queen's Bench. In Alberta, all Small Claims Court actions are screened and selected actions must enter mandatory mediation; civil actions in the Alberta Court of Queen's Bench may be moved to mediation by either party upon the filing of a notice. These provinces maintain rosters of approved mediators.[45]

Still, ADR has its limits and its critics. It is not right for every dispute. Situations that involve an imbalance of power between the parties can result in abuse. Parties might be forced unwillingly into ADR, or they might be bullied into undesirable settlements in mediation. Therefore, restrictions and protections have been put in place for certain types of conflicts. Family disputes cannot be arbitrated in Quebec, and Ontario has created a specially regulated and supervised form of family arbitration.[46] Consumers are another group that are being protected from mandatory ADR processes, with several provinces refusing to enforce pre-dispute arbitration clauses.[47]

Ethical Issue Access to Justice

One fundamental value in democratic nations is that all people should have access to justice. What does this mean? Is it enough that courts exist and are available for use? Are courts synonymous with justice? What about alternative dispute resolution processes? If courts and lawyers are too expensive, is access to justice denied?

Some of the provinces have taken steps to reduce the cost of litigation. For example, British Columbia and Ontario have simplified rules of procedure for claims of $100 000 or less. Simplified procedures expedite the path to trial with early disclosure requirements, limited pre-trial procedures, and reduction in the length of trials. Most Canadian provinces have Small Claims Court limits over $20 000 with Alberta's limit at $50,000. Most provinces incorporate mediation or settlement conferences into the pre-trial process in the hope that cases may settle before trial. Class actions allow small claims to be processed together.

What if disputants cannot access these simplified initiatives? Over the last decade, it has become common for big companies to insert mandatory arbitration clauses and waivers of class actions into consumer contracts so that consumers must arbitrate their disputes privately rather than go to court. Dell Computers, TELUS Communications, and Rogers Cable have all had such clauses upheld by the courts, effectively preventing consumers from processing lawsuits against them.[48] Is this effective legal risk management or a denial of consumer access to justice—or both? Balancing the interests of business and consumer is not easy.

Questions to Consider

1. Do class actions improve access to justice or promote frivolous lawsuits?

2. Is mandatory mediation or arbitration in conflict with the theory of alternative dispute resolution?

3. Should legal aid be available for private lawsuits?

Sources: "Does Justice Cost More Than It's Worth?," *Law Times*, December 11–17, 1995 at 1, 2; Beth Marlin, "Legal Update: Mandatory Mediation," *Canadian Lawyer*, November/December 1998; British Columbia Ministry of the Attorney General, "A General Overview of Rule 68, Which Allows for 'Expedited' Litigation," http://www.cfcj-fcjc.org/inventory-of-reforms/bc-supreme-court-rules-fast-track-litigation-part-15.

---

[45] Rules 24.1 and 75.1, Ontario *Rules of Civil Procedure*; Alberta Civil Practice Note No. 11; *The Queen's Bench Act, 1998*, SS 1998, c Q-1.01, s 42.

[46] Article 2639, *Civil Code of Quebec*, SQ 1991, c 64; *Family Statute Law Amendment Act, 2006*, SO 2006, c 1.; O Reg 134/07.

[47] Ontario and Quebec ban pre-dispute consumer arbitration clauses and class action waivers: *Consumer Protection Act, 2002*, SO 2002, c 30, ss 7, 8; *Consumer Protection Act*, RSQ c P-40.1, s 11.1. Alberta has legislation requiring government approval of consumer arbitration clauses: *Fair Trading Act*, RSA 2000, c F-2, s 16. See also Shelley McGill, "Consumer Arbitration Clause Enforcement: A Balanced Legislative Response" (2010) Am Bus LJ 361.

[48] *Dell Computers v Union des consommateurs*, 2007 SCC 34; *Kanitz v Rogers Cable Inc* (2002), 58 OR (3d) 299; *Seidel v TELUS Communications*, 2011 SCC 15. See also Shelley McGill, "Consumer Arbitration after Seidel v. TELUS" (2011), 51 Can Bus LJ 187.

Strategies to Manage the Legal Risks

This procedural laws described in this chapter highlight the need for strategies to reduce the legal risks associated with processing a dispute or court action.

Every business should have a protocol for managing disputes or complaints. Often, disputes wind up in court because they have been ignored. Similarly, once in the court system, timelines must be met or a party will lose its opportunity to be heard. Therefore, every business needs a system to manage complaints and monitor resolution or escalation. This system is important not only to the outcome of the specific dispute but also for business planning purposes. Data on the volume of disputes, their value, and resolution outcomes will help the business determine its legal resource needs and dispute resolution strategy.

The costs of legal services vary just as do the needs of the business. Written retainer agreements should define the scope of work and the basis upon which a fee will be charged. Relatively few types of claims are appropriate for contingency fee arrangements. The rest are billed on a fee-for-service basis. The hourly rate for time spent should be disclosed, as well as the number of hours expected. Similarly, disbursements for expert advice or assistance can be costly and should require pre-approval. Legal advice should not be only reactive—that is, after a dispute arises. Identified potential areas of risk should trigger proactive legal opinions.

Preferred methods of resolving disputes can be designated in advance in the contracts with suppliers, employees, and customers. The costs of defending a class action can be high, and therefore many businesses seek to avoid this risk by designating individual arbitration as the dispute resolution forum. This is done at the time of the original contract with the complainant and is most effective in business-to-business relationships. In business-to-consumer transactions, the effectiveness of this strategy will depend on the provincial legislation.

QUESTIONS FOR REVIEW

1. Distinguish the civil law system from the common law system.
2. Explain the theory of precedent and its values.
3. Describe the relationship between the courts of common law and equity.
4. What is the purpose of codifying law in a statute?
5. Why is subordinate legislation important?
6. How does the operation of an appeal court differ from that of a trial court?
7. Do you think motion pictures and television programs are responsible for a misconception about the way in which trials proceed?
8. Describe the basic difference between the systems of courts in the United States and in Canada.
9. What are the advantages of a settlement over a court trial?
10. Define *appellant, respondent, counterclaim, counsel, settlement, pleadings, party and party costs, res judicata*.
11. What is a "class action," and when do parties use them?
12. How does a judge decide a case when there is no precedent available in earlier decisions?
13. Explain why a legal rule in one province may differ from that in another province.

14. One of the major purposes of private law is to settle disputes between businesses. How can the settlement of a particular private dispute make a contribution to the business community as a whole?
15. "I was never ruined but twice; once when I won a lawsuit and once when I lost one." How can a successful litigant lose?
16. Explain the basis of a "contingency fee." How are contingency fees used in Canada?
17. What are the advantages that make ADR an attractive means of settling disputes?

CASES AND PROBLEMS

Continuing Scenario

The topics covered in this text have been chosen because they raise common legal issues that regularly confront businesses. Businesses face legal challenges every day. In order to highlight the ongoing interaction between law and business, we will follow one business throughout this text as it deals with an applicable legal issue in each of the following chapters. We begin with simple facts.

Ashley graduated from George Brown Culinary School as a pastry chef. She is opening a restaurant in Toronto. She will face legal issues as she starts the business, leases space, seeks professional accounting advice, sets up a website, creates her menu, finances expansion, hires employees, and deals with many other typical business issues. Follow Ashley as she grows her business in the Cases and Problems section at the end of each chapter.

Chapter 3
Government Regulation of Business

- **THE LEGAL FRAMEWORK FOR DOING BUSINESS IN CANADA**
- **CHALLENGING GOVERNMENT REGULATION OF BUSINESS**
- **COMPETITION**
- **CONSUMER PROTECTION**
- **ENVIRONMENTAL PROTECTION**
- **STRATEGIES TO MANAGE THE LEGAL RISKS**

Government controls business activity with legislation and regulations; regulations are the detailed rules imposed under the general power of the authorizing legislation. Regulations are used to manage business relationships with key stakeholders such as customers, competitors, and the public. In this chapter, we examine the Canadian regulatory framework within which business must operate, concentrating on three general areas of regulation that apply to most businesses: competition, consumer protection, and the environment. Other areas of regulation will be dealt with in later chapters of this text.

We examine such questions as:

- Who has the power to regulate?
- How are specific business sectors regulated?
- How can business use the law to eliminate oppressive regulation?
- How does competition law affect business arrangements?
- What are the consequences of consumer protection law for the consumer and for business?
- What are the main elements of environmental protection regulation?

THE LEGAL FRAMEWORK FOR DOING BUSINESS IN CANADA

regulation detailed legal rules enacted under the authority of an existing government statute typically by an administrative agency

Regulation is another word for *control*. Governments control business behaviour through regulation. A **regulation** is a detailed legal rule enacted under the authority of an existing government statute. In Chapter 2, we referred to this as subordinate legislation. For business to operate fairly and efficiently, an adequate legal and regulatory framework must be in place. However, excessive regulation can impose heavy costs and inhibit business activity; striking an appropriate balance is the challenge. Political parties are categorized as "left" or "right" based upon the level of government regulation they support. Parties "on the left" typically favour lots of government regulation, and parties "on the right" support minimal regulation. Therefore, the emphasis on government regulation will vary depending upon which party forms the government of the day.

During the 1980s and early 1990s, "deregulation" was a popular notion—freeing business from existing (excessive) government control. In many instances, direct government interference was merely replaced by a different sort of regulation, social regulation. **Direct regulation** occurs when the government controls such matters as prices, rates of return, and production levels. **Social regulation**, on the other hand, lays down standards that businesses must observe while carrying on their activities, in such areas as health, safety, and the environment. Chapter 2 describes how governments use their legislative powers to create legislation, subordinate legislation, and administrative agencies and tribunals.

direct regulation controls the characteristics of the product or service, such as pricing, profit margin, production level

social regulation sets standards about how the product or service is made or delivered, such as health, safety, and environmental standards

In this chapter, we examine how regulatory schemes may be challenged, a topic introduced in Chapter 1. We also look at some direct and social regulatory regimes designed to protect three key business stakeholders: consumers, competitors, and the public.

CHALLENGING GOVERNMENT REGULATION OF BUSINESS

Business does not always agree with the regulatory scheme imposed upon it by government. Chapter 1 identified three strategies that businesses may use to try to avoid complying with unwanted government regulation. They may ask a court to find that

- the regulation is invalid because the subject matter of the regulation is not within the constitutional jurisdiction of the relevant government,
- the regulation is invalid because it violates the *Charter of Rights and Freedoms*, and/or
- the administrative agency's application of the regulation is wrong, and the rule does not apply to the particular conduct.

Jurisdiction over "Business Activities" under the Constitution

In Chapter 1 we examined how the *Constitution Act, 1867* divides legislative power between the federal and provincial governments. The checklist below identifies key powers often used to regulate business. Under the provincial power to regulate municipalities, provinces have delegated local business regulation power to municipal councils. As a result, all three levels of government—federal, provincial, and municipal—regulate business activities.

> **CHECKLIST**
>
> ## The *Constitution Act, 1867*: Constitutional Power to Regulate Business Activities
>
> **Federal Powers, Section 91**
> - Regulation of trade and commerce
> - Specific industries such as banking, shipping and navigation, air transportation, and radio and television
> - Taxation
> - Intellectual property
> - Interest, legal tender, currency, bills of exchange and promissory notes
>
> **Provincial Powers, Section 92**
> - Property and civil rights
> - Municipalities (this section allows a province to delegate the power to regulate to a municipality)
> - Direct taxation within the province
> - All matters of a private nature within the province
> - Other specific industries such as road transportation, including trucking; and stock exchanges and securities trading

The definition of each power has taken years of case law to develop. The courts have defined the provincial power over "property and civil rights" very broadly, giving the provinces control over virtually all of private law, including contracts and most business transactions—matters that arguably could also fall in federal jurisdiction over "trade and commerce." Alternatively, the federal power over "trade and commerce" has been interpreted more narrowly to mean trade and commerce across borders[1] or where the national interest is involved in a way that is different from the provincial concern.[2] Therefore, it applies to matters of interprovincial and international commerce and usually not to matters conducted wholly within one province.[3] The production, storage, sale, and delivery of wheat is in federal hands on the basis that its major activity is international.

On the other hand, two sectors with a large interprovincial element remain almost exclusively within regulatory schemes of the provinces—road transportation, including trucking; and stock exchanges and securities transactions. In 2011, the Supreme Court of Canada rejected a proposed national *Securities Act* as overreaching the national concern aspect of the trade and commerce power. It held that regulating publicly traded companies was a provincial power and did not fit under the federal government's trade and commerce power.[4]

Inevitably there is overlap between the categories, and sometimes there are even conflicting rules, making it difficult for businesses and their lawyers to determine which regulations apply in a particular situation.

When a business wants to challenge a regulatory scheme, it begins by asking whether the legislature or agency that created the regulation had jurisdiction. As discussed in Chapter 1, questions about jurisdictional power are resolved using a two-step process that first determines the primary subject matter of the law and then identifies the power under which it fits.[5] Broad interpretations of any power will shelter many laws.

---

[1] *Citizen's Insurance Co. v Parsons* (1881), 7 App Cas 96; Federal power in general commercial matters is questioned when the issue falls within the boundaries of a province. See e.g. *MacDonald v Vapor Canada*, [1977] 2 SCR 134, and *Labatt Breweries v Attorney General of Canada*, [1980] 1 SCR 914.

[2] *Reference re Security Act*, [2011] SCC 66 at paras 46, 70.

[3] The U.S. Constitution's equivalent to our trade and commerce provision is "commerce among the several states." This phrase is given much wider interpretation and has expanded the powers of Congress, despite the interstate requirement of the words themselves: see *National Federation of Independent Business v Sebelius*, 567 US 519 [2012].

[4] *Reference re Securities Act*, *supra* note 2.

[5] See Chapter 1; *Reference Re Assisted Human Reproduction Act*, [2010] SCJ No 61 at para 19 (SCC).

pith and substance the true character of a law determined by examining its purpose and legal effect on those subject to it

During the first step, the court identifies the **pith and substance** of the law by looking at its true character or "main thrust"[6]: What does the law do, and why? The purpose of the law and its legal effect on those subject to it reveal the law's true character or subject matter.

CASE 3.1 Purpose of the Regulation

The City of Toronto passed a bylaw prohibiting the selling or consuming of shark fins. Shark fin vendors complained that the bylaw was beyond the power of the City, it unfairly discriminated against the Chinese community as shark fins are part of a traditional Chinese delicacy, and it hurt businesses that supply them. The bylaw was declared invalid because the *City of Toronto Act* gave the City the power only to regulate municipal issues. The purposes of the bylaw were to address the inhumane treatment of sharks occurring oceans away from the city and the global ecological threat—neither of these purposes fell within the municipality's power to regulate the social, environmental, or health needs of the city.[7]

In Case 3.1 the bylaw fails because the purpose of the bylaw did not fit within the regulatory power of the municipality.

The second step of the analysis (fitting the subject matter of the law into the appropriate constitutional power) is not as easy as it sounds. Some powers overlap, and some laws have **double aspects**, an aspect or purpose that falls within provincial power and another aspect that falls under federal power. Courts try to take a flexible view that accommodates overlapping jurisdiction, allowing concurrent application of multiple laws and encouraging intergovernmental cooperation.[8] Still, if valid federal and provincial laws affecting a business activity are incompatible with each other, the federal law overrides the provincial one.

double aspects laws that have an aspect that falls within provincial power and another aspect that falls under federal power

CASE 3.2 Double Aspects

The City of Hamilton passed a regulation dealing with the placement of equipment, including community mailboxes, on municipal roads so that local traffic flow, parking, and winter road conditions would be taken into consideration. A permit was required. Canada Post objected to the permit requirement, claiming location of mailboxes was outside the jurisdiction of the City because postal service is a federal power. The judge disagreed. The subject matter of the regulation involved the safety of people and property on municipal roads and fell within the provincial powers over local works and over property and civil rights. However, location of mailboxes also fell within federal power, and so the **federal paramountcy rule** determined the matter in favour of Canada Post. The bylaw was valid, but the permit requirement did not apply to Canada Post's mailboxes.[9]

federal paramountcy rule when valid federal and provincial laws conflict with each other, the federal law overrides the provincial one

Unlike Case 3.1, in Case 3.2 the bylaw was within the municipality's power, and yet it was still not enforced because it conflicted with a federal power.

In sum, the possible outcomes for a regulation that is challenged for lack of jurisdiction are as follows:

- The subject matter fits entirely within the power of the enacting body so the law is valid and enforceable.

- The subject matter does not fit within any power of the enacting body so the law is ultra vires or invalid.

---

[6] *Reference re Securities Act, supra* note 2 at para 66.

[7] *Eng v Toronto*, 2012 ONSC 6818; on deference to be shown to municipal bylaws see *Friends of Landsdowne Inc v Ottawa (City)*, 2012 ONCA 273.

[8] *Reference re Securities Act*, supra note 2 at para 57.

[9] *Canada Post v Hamilton*, 2016 ONCA 767

- The subject matter primarily fits within the power of the enacting body with only incidental (minor) effect on another body' power. The law will be valid and enforceable.[10]
- The subject matter primarily fits within the power of another body with only incidental (minor) connection to the enacting body's power. The law will be invalid and unenforceable.
- The subject matter has aspects that fall equally under two separate powers—one federal and one provincial. The laws from both jurisdictions will be valid unless they conflict, in which case the federal paramountcy rule will render the provincial law unenforceable.[11]

Business Regulations that Offend the *Charter*

Chapter 1 explains the process for a *Charter* challenge and highlights its relevance to business. Several examples of business regulations that violated the *Charter* are provided in Chapter 1. This section is only a summary of the key points made there.

- Even if a regulation is within the jurisdictional power of the government passing it, it may still be invalid if it infringes a right or freedom protected by the *Charter*.
- The business disputing the regulation must prove that it infringes one of the *Charter*'s rights or freedoms.
- An infringing regulation may still be valid if the enacting government proves that the infringement is justifiable.
- Advertising is covered by freedom of expression, but some restrictions on advertising have been found justifiable.[12]
- Unions are protected by freedom of association[13]

For the *Charter* to apply to a business situation, the business must show more than just an economic impact:

> [B]ecause there is an economic aspect to a *Charter* claim does not, for that reason alone, disqualify it . . . there have been numerous *Charter* cases in which there was an economic component or implication to a claim. On the other hand, where a claim is based solely on economic grounds, it [is] unlikely that a *Charter* claim could succeed.[14]

Corporations may invoke the *Charter*'s protection. In particular, a corporation should be allowed to rely on the *Charter* where it is charged with an offence or is the defendant in civil proceedings instigated by the government. No one should be convicted of an offence under an unconstitutional law or subject to any proceedings or sanction authorized by an unconstitutional law.[15]

---

[10] *Rogers Communication Inc. v Chateauguay (Ville)*, 2016 SCC 23 at para 37.

[11] *Ibid* at para 39.

[12] *Charter*, s 1(b), *Irwin Toy Ltd v Quebec* (1989), 58 DLR (4th) 577; *Rocket v Royal College of Dental Surgeons of Ontario* (1990), 71 DLR (4th) 68. In *UL Canada Inc v Attorney General of Quebec* (2003), 234 DLR (4th) 398, aff'd [2005] SCJ No 11, the Supreme Court of Canada agreed that a ban on the sale of yellow-coloured margarine did not violate the *Charter* freedom of expression. See *Griffin v College of Dental Surgeons of British Columbia* (1989), 64 DLR (4th) 652; *Urban Outdoor Trans Ad v City of Scarborough* (2001), 196 DLR (4th) 304; *Vann Media Ltd v Oakville (Town)*, 2008 ONCA 752; *R v Guignard* (2002), 209 DLR (4th) 549. See also *Carmichael v Provincial Dental Board of Nova Scotia* (1998), 169 NSR (2d) 294.

[13] *Charter*, ss 2(b) and (d). But see *Canadian Egg Marketing Agency v Richardson*, [1998] 3 SCR 157. Mobility rights do not extend to the right to conduct business anywhere in Canada without restriction.

[14] *Archibald v Canada* (2000), 188 DLR (4th) 538 at 545-6 (concerning restrictions on grain farmers under the *Canadian Wheat Board Act*, RSC 1985, c C-24).

[15] *Canadian Egg Marketing Agency v Richardson*, *supra* note 13. A national egg marketing scheme was not to be contrary to the *Charter*.

CASE 3.3 Advertising and Freedom of Expression

In 1988, the federal government introduced legislation prohibiting all advertising and promotion of tobacco products. The prohibition was challenged by a cigarette manufacturer.

The Supreme Court of Canada held that the legislation violated freedom of expression and was not justifiable. The objective of the legislation—to discourage the use of tobacco—was legitimate, but there was no direct scientific evidence showing a causal link between advertising bans and decreased tobacco consumption. The government had failed to show that a partial advertising ban would be less effective than a total ban. The impact on the complainant's rights was more than minimal, and the offending provisions of the legislation were declared to be of no force and effect.[16]

As a result of the court's ruling, the federal government adopted new legislation[17] restricting tobacco advertising, but in a way that was consistent with the ruling. The new law was challenged again but found not to infringe the Charter.[18]

An infringement will only be justified if the law's objective addresses a pressing and substantial concern, and the provisions are proportional to the objective (that is, that the impact of law on those subject to it is as small as possible given the objective).[19]

Regulation Improperly Applied in the Circumstances

Finally, a business may oppose the application of regulation on the basis that the regulation does not apply to its circumstances. This involves attacking the decision of whichever decision maker applied the regulation to the business situation. The decision maker could be a court or an administrative government commission, tribunal, or other official.

More and more often, regulatory schemes are shifting decision making away from the courts toward administrative tribunals with specialized adjudicators, not judges, ruling on matters covered by the authorizing legislation. The decisions of administrative adjudicators must be made fairly, reasonably, and in accordance with the power given to them by the legislation. This means that not only should the decision be right based upon the facts, it also must be one that the administrator is allowed to make and is arrived at after following fair procedures. The law about the actions and operation of administrative tribunals and decision makers is known as **administrative law**.

administrative law law about actions and operations of government administrators and administrative tribunals

"Active" legislative schemes are the foundation of administrative law and regulatory liability. The legislation outlines general principles and then delegates the power over the details to administrators named in the legislation itself. The administrators set specific standards, qualifying conditions, and procedures, and implement, enforce, and monitor compliance. As also noted in Chapter 2, the rules made by the administrators are called subordinate legislation.

Residential landlord and tenant law is regulated this way in most provinces. Disputes between landlords and tenants do not go to the courts but to specialized adjudicators that only deal with residential tenancies. The *Residential Tenancies Act* of British Columbia creates a director, who is then responsible for "the administration and management" of all matters under the Act, including forms, fees, and dispute resolution.[20] The Ontario Securities Commission is another example of an administrative agency that sets the rules for publicly trading stocks under the authority of the provincial *Securities Act* and then monitors compliance of traders, issuing companies, and licensees.

---

[16] *RJR-MacDonald Inc v Canada* (1995), 127 DLR (4th) 1.

[17] *Tobacco Act*, SC 1997, c 13.

[18] *JTI MacDonald Corp v Canada* (2002), 102 CRR (2d) 189. See also *Rothmans, Benson & Hedges Inc v Saskatchewan*, [2005] 1 SCR 188.

[19] *R v Oakes*, [1986] 1 SCR 103.

[20] SBC 2002, c 78, s 9.

If a business disagrees with the decision of an administrator, it may appeal the decision in the way described in the legislation, or it may attack the underlying authority or procedures followed to arrive at the decision through a process called judicial review. Judicial review involves the courts.

Judicial Review It remains the court's job to make sure that administrative decision makers exercise their power properly, even when the legislation that creates regulatory powers says the decisions are final with no appeal. The Federal Court has a general jurisdiction to review actions of federal boards and commissions,[21] and several of the provinces have enacted similar provisions with respect to provincial boards.[22] Even without such legislation, the courts have a general right to complete a **judicial review** of the legality of administrative acts and decisions.

judicial review a court's review of the legality of administrative acts and decisions

An administrative act or decision may be reviewed for several reasons:

- Misuse of authority—although the relevant legislation itself may be valid, the official or agency acted outside the scope of the authority conferred by the authorizing statute or refused to act when it did have authority.

- Procedural irregularity—the official or agency followed a process that did not match requirements of the statute; for example, public meetings required by the legislation were not held, or the prescribed notice was not given.

- Procedural unfairness—even when the legislation does not prescribe appropriate procedures, an official or agency is not entitled to act in a purely arbitrary manner.

Procedural fairness means that persons likely to be affected have a right to be heard and to have access to relevant documents. Adequate notice must be given of any public hearings, and the decision maker must act impartially, without any personal interest in the subject matter.

When courts review decisions, they are careful to show respect for the specialized expertise of the administrative tribunal. Therefore the standard of review applied to evaluate administrative decisions is usually "reasonableness."[23] As long as the decision is one of the possible acceptable outcomes available on the facts and law, it will be allowed to stand. It need not be the same decision the court would have reached. Only rarely in matters of general law (outside the tribunal's area of expertise) or of constitutional power or jurisdiction will the standard be "correctness," meaning it must be the same decision the court would have made.[24]

CASE 3.4 Judicial Review of Interpretation of Authorizing Statute

The British Columbia Director of Environmental Management gave Rio Alto Alcan permission to increase the amount of sulphur dioxide released into the air during the manufacturing of aluminum and approved an environmental impact monitoring plan. The union for the workers didn't like the monitoring plan and tried to appeal its approval. The Environmental Appeal Board refused the appeal, finding that approval of the monitoring plan was not a "decision" appealable under BC's *Environmental Management Act*. The union asked the court to review the Board's decision. The court used the "reasonableness" standard and found that the Board's interpretation of the word "decision" was not one of the possible outcomes available on the facts and the law. The Board's refusal to hear the appeal was set aside, and the appeal was set to be heard before the Environmental Appeal Board.[25]

---

[21] *Federal Court Act*, RSC 1985, c F-7, s 18.

[22] See e.g. *Judicial Review Procedure Act*, RSBC 1996, c 241; RSO 1990, c J.1.

[23] *Edmonton (City) v Edmonton East (Capilano) Shopping Centres Ltd*, 2016 SCC 47 at paras 22–24.

[24] *Dunsmuir v New Brunswick*, [2008] 1 SCR 190, 2008 SCC 9 at paras 58–61. Even when examining an administrative decision maker exercise of discretion with respect to the *Charter*, the standard of review is reasonableness: *Dore v Barreau du Quebec*, 2012 SCC 12 at para 58.

[25] *Unifor Local 2301 v Rio Tinto Alcan Inc*, 2017 BCCA 300.

> **CHECKLIST**
>
> ## Strategies to Prevent or Limit the Application of Government Regulation
>
> 1. Challenge the validity of the legislation on the basis of constitutional jurisdiction.
> 2. Challenge the validity of the legislation because it violates the *Charter of Rights and Freedoms*.
> 3. Appeal the decision of the administrative decision maker on one of the grounds set out in the legislation.
> 4. Seek judicial review of the administrative decision because it was outside the scope of the legislation or the process was flawed.

Next, we look at three regulatory regimes affecting most businesses: competition, consumer protection, and environmental protection.

COMPETITION

An essential characteristic of an efficient market economy is competition. If consumers and customers have a choice between the goods or services of competing firms, prices will be lower or quality better, or both. But an entirely unregulated market does not ensure competition. The most efficient firms will ultimately drive the less efficient out of business—at least in certain sectors of the market. They will then enjoy a monopoly, there will be no competition, and the benefits of a free market will be lost. The same might occur where two or more firms coordinate their actions and strategies in such a way as to divide up the market rather than compete for it. Therefore, governments intervene in order to preserve competition.

The *Competition Act*

To prevent unfair competition and abuse, the federal government used its trade and commerce power to pass the *Competition Act*,[26] creating a regulatory regime that controls three forms of anti-competitive behaviour:

- conspiracies,
- monopolies, and
- mergers.

Before examining the rules, two aspects of the Act are noted: exemptions and administrative enforcement.

Exemptions The Act does not apply to certain groups of people or certain businesses with their own regulatory oversight. In particular, the basic prohibition against conspiracies generally does not apply to the professions. Governing bodies of professions such as law, medicine, and public accountancy may establish agreements among their members dealing with such matters as qualifications, provided they are reasonably necessary for the protection of the public. Also exempt are agreements or arrangements among underwriters and others involved in the distribution of securities.

---

[26] RSC 1985, c. C-34. References to section numbers in this part of the chapter are to this Act, as amended. It underwent significant revisions in 2010.

Figure 3.1 Competition Bureau Enforcement Process

Enforcement The responsibility for administration of the Act is delegated to the Commissioner of Competition, as head of the Competition Bureau. Less serious regulatory offences known as civil matters or reviewable matters are managed by the Deputy Commissioner–Civil Matters and are ultimately referred to the Competition Tribunal (see Figure 3.1). This specialized tribunal has the power to grant or impose a variety of civil remedies and penalties. More serious cases involving **criminal offences** are investigated by the Deputy Commissioner–Criminal Matters and prosecuted through the courts by the attorney general. The Act creates a number of criminal offences, punishable by heavy fines and by imprisonment for up to five years. In one criminal case, fines totalling almost $90 million were imposed on a number of producers of vitamins participating in an international price-fixing ring.[27]

Normally, a person who is adversely affected by conduct that is prohibited by the Act lodges a complaint, and then it is the commissioner's responsibility to investigate and follow the appropriate procedure. However, section 36 also provides that an individual may bring a civil action for damages resulting from prohibited conduct or from contravention of an order of the tribunal.[28] This is rarely done because it is difficult and expensive to prove misconduct.

criminal offences most serious offences that require proof of mental intent with penalties imposed by the courts

Conspiracies

Competitors may not enter into agreements that hurt competition in their industry; these prohibited agreements are generally described as **conspiracies**. The *Competition Act* divides the agreements into three categories. The first group are agreements considered so harmful that they are completely banned without any proof that competition would actually be reduced. This type of conspiracy is a criminal offence handled by the courts. The second group involves less serious forms of conspiracies that are merely reviewable by the Competition Bureau. If the bureau determines that the agreement lessens competition, it will be subject to regulatory action by the tribunal. The

conspiracies agreements or arrangements between competitors to lessen competition

---

[27] *Commissioner of Competition v F Hoffmann-La-Roche Ltd* (1999) (guilty plea) see Competition Bureau—Penalties Imposed, https://www.justice.gov/sites/default/files/atr/legacy/2007/07/11/canada.pdf.

[28] The constitutionality of this provision was upheld by the Supreme Court of Canada in *City National Leasing Ltd v General Motors of Canada*, [1989] 1 SCR 641. See e.g. *Culhane v ATP Aero Training Products Inc* (2004), 238 DLR (4th) 112, where a claim of predatory pricing was not proven.

third category covers acceptable competitor agreements. The *Competition Act* has a registration process so parties may seek regulatory approval of their proposed agreement and thereby avoid liability.

Criminal Conspiracies: Section 45 of the *Competition Act*
Section 45 prohibits the most serious conspiracies. The negative impact on competition is assumed without proof. Section 45 makes it a criminal offence to conspire, agree, or arrange to:

- fix, maintain, increase, or control the price of a product or service (**price fixing**);
- allocate sales, territories, customers, or markets for the production or supply of the product or service (**market allocation**); or
- fix, maintain, control, prevent, lessen, or eliminate the production or supply of the product or service (**output restriction**).

price fixing fix, maintain, increase, or control the price of a product or service

market allocation divide sales, territories, customers, or markets for the production or supply of the product or service

output restriction fix, maintain, control, prevent, lessen, or eliminate the production or supply of the product or service

The Act designates these serious criminal conspiracies as indictable offences that are sent to court rather than the tribunal. Possible punishments include imprisonment for a term not exceeding 14 years or a fine not exceeding $25 million, or both.

"Conspires, Agrees or Arranges . . ." The essential requirement of section 45 is that two or more persons conspire together—that is, they enter into some sort of agreement. This is difficult to prove. Restrictive agreements are rarely in writing. There would be little point in drawing up a formal written agreement since it would not be enforceable and would be strong evidence of a criminal conspiracy. When investigating suspected offences, the Competition Bureau has wide powers to search premises and computer records, and to seize documents (s. 15 and 16). A court may "infer the existence of a conspiracy, agreement or arrangement from circumstantial evidence, with or without direct evidence of communication between or among the alleged parties to it" (s. 45(3)).[29]

CASE 3.5 Price Fixing Conspiracy

Members of the Canadian Steel Pipe Institute were concerned about the lack of price stability in their market, following a period of wide fluctuations and attempts by some firms to undercut their competitors. Public meetings were held and industry reports circulated, urging members to adopt an open pricing policy. The policy involved publication of price lists and notification of price changes.

The policy was a voluntary one, and each member was free to set its own price. Nevertheless, the evidence was that after the open price policy was instituted, bids submitted by members of the Institute were frequently identical.

The evidence to support the existence of an actual agreement comprised the following:

- the public statements made
- the publication of price lists
- the fact of identical pricing
- a communication from one firm to another to the effect that a third firm, which had been awarded a contract at a substantially lower price, was "not playing ball"

On that evidence the court inferred that an agreement existed among the members of the Institute.[30]

It is not necessarily a conspiracy if competitors' prices go up and down at the same time. Within an industry, prices will tend to be similar for similar products, a practice called **parallel pricing**; otherwise, businesses with higher prices would lose sales. One firm may tend to be the "price leader," so that if it raised or reduced its

parallel pricing the practice, among competing firms, of adopting similar pricing strategies

---

[29] Section 45(3) of the *Competition Act*, RSC 1985, c C-34.
[30] *R v Armco Canada Ltd* (1976), 70 DLR (3d) 287.

56 Part 1 The Law in Its Social and Business Context

prices, the others would quickly follow suit even though they had made no commitment to do so. Therefore, parallel pricing by itself is not evidence of conspiracy.

Other Criminal Conspiracies Apart from the activities listed above, the Act names three other agreements that are criminal conspiracy offences. In particular, it is an offence:

- to agree to withdraw or not submit a bid or to agree in advance on the details of bids to be submitted in response to a call for bids or tenders (**bid-rigging**) (s. 47);
- to conspire to unreasonably limit the opportunities for any person to participate in professional sport or to play for the team of her or his choice in a professional league (s. 48); and
- to implement in Canada a directive or instruction from a person outside Canada, giving effect to a conspiracy that would constitute an offence under the Act if done in Canada (s. 46).

bid-rigging agreeing not to submit a bid or agreeing in advance what bids will be submitted in response to a call for bids or tenders

Reviewable Conspiracies: Lessening of Competition

For this less serious group of conspiracies, the *Competition Act* does not define the types of agreements covered. Any agreement that lessens or has the potential to lessen competition may be reviewed by the Competition Bureau (s. 90.1). Thereafter, the Commissioner of Competition may seek enforcement proceedings before the Competition Tribunal. The available remedies are a cease-and-desist order or an order requiring some other form of corrective or modifying action. There are no fines or imprisonment imposed on the parties unless they fail to comply with the Tribunal's order, and no private cause of action for damages is allowed. Factors relevant to the determination that an agreement lessens competition include the impact of foreign competitors and the availability of substitute products. The Bureau created guidelines to support pro-competitive collaboration among competitors.[31]

Registered Agreements: Specialization Agreements

When competitors freely enter into an agreement under which each will discontinue producing a current product, the agreement is known as a specialization agreement. If the market efficiencies created by the agreement make up for any lessening of competition, the competitors may apply to the Competition Tribunal for approval of the agreement (s. 84–90). If the Tribunal approves the agreement, it will "register" it for a specific period of time. Registration exempts the agreement from both the criminal and regulatory conspiracy rules. This registry may be searched by the public.

Monopolizing

Conspiracy requires that two or more persons agree to restrict competition. A single person or firm that enjoys a monopoly or even a very powerful position in a particular market may also abuse its power in a manner that restricts competition. The Act identifies and restricts some improper distribution practices and labels some anti-competitive behaviour as an **abuse of dominant position**, which, though not a criminal offence, may be reviewed and prohibited by the Tribunal.

abuse of dominant position taking an unfair advantage of possessing a monopoly or dominant position in the marketplace

---

[31] Competitor Collaboration Guidelines http://www.competitionbureau.gc.ca/eic/site/cb-bc.nsf/eng/03177.html#ccg-2.4.1.

> ### ILLUSTRATION 3.1 Abuse of Dominant Position
>
> One of the most famous illustrations of improper distribution (tied selling) and abuse of market dominance is Microsoft's bundling of its Windows operating software with its internet browser and media player. Windows consumers could not get one product without the other. This had a devastating effect on other software suppliers. Microsoft's practice was challenged not only in the United States but also all around the world. In the European Union, Microsoft was ordered to separate the products, offer unbundled software, and share codes that would allow compatibility with other products. It was also fined $690 million plus costs. In February 2008, Microsoft was fined an additional $1.325 billion for failure to comply with the earlier rulings.[32]

Distribution Practices Generally, a supplier is entitled to choose its customers and is free to decide whether to supply a particular person or not, except where that refusal is part of a conspiracy or is related to a pricing offence. However, in circumstances where a vendor refuses to deal with a customer even though there is plenty of product and the customer is willing to pay the usual price, the tribunal may order a supplier to supply that customer (s. 75). This is done when the refusal negatively impacts the market.

Exclusive dealing, tied selling, and market restriction are also reviewable distribution practices. A supplier may make it a condition that the buyer deals only or primarily in the supplier's products (**exclusive dealing**); it may be a condition for the supply of one type of product that the buyer also deals in other products of the supplier (**tied selling**); or it may be a condition of supplying a customer that the customer markets the product only within a designated area (**market restriction**). Such practices are not forbidden, but section 77 provides that the tribunal may, on application by the commissioner, make an order prohibiting the practices or requiring them to be modified when they lessen competition.

exclusive dealing when a supplier of goods makes it a condition that the buyer should deal only or primarily in the supplier's products

tied selling when a supplier makes it a condition that, to obtain one type of product, the buyer must also deal in other products of the supplier

market restriction where a supplier makes it a condition that the buyer markets the product only within a designated area

predatory pricing where a seller temporarily reduces prices to an unreasonably low level with the aim of driving competitors out of business

discriminatory pricing where a seller makes a practice of discriminating between purchasers with respect to the price charged for goods or services

Abuse of Dominant Position Also reviewable by the tribunal is conduct amounting to an abuse of a dominant position. Examples of suspect behaviour include **predatory pricing**, which involves selling products at unreasonably low prices to drive others out of the market, and **discriminatory pricing**, which involves differentiating pricing between purchasers to give one group an advantage. In one example of predatory pricing, a valium manufacturer supplied the drug free to Canadian hospitals for a period of one year; this was viewed as an attempt to prevent other manufacturers of tranquillizers from entering the market.[33]

To prove abuse of dominant position, the commissioner must show that the accused business is in substantial control of a particular market sector and has engaged in an anti-competitive practice that has prevented, or is likely to prevent or substantially lessen, competition (s. 79). Section 78 sets out a non-exhaustive list of practices that are regarded as anti-competitive, such as buying up product to prevent a decrease in prices and requiring that a supplier refrain from selling to a competitor or sell only to certain customers.

The applicability of section 79 depends largely upon the identification of the relevant product and market. The firm usually argues for a broad definition so that more

---

[32] *United States v Microsoft*, 87 F Supp 2d 30 (DDC 2000) aff'd in part 253 F 3d 34 (DC Cir 2001) This action subsequently settled under terms approved at 2002 WL 31439450 (DDC Nov 1, 2002); Kevin O'Brien, "European Court Rejects Microsoft Antitrust Appeal," *New York Times*, September 17, 2007, http://www.nytimes.com/2007/09/17/technology/17cnd-soft.html; Bo-Mi Lim, "Microsoft Loses Antitrust Case Before S.-Korean Regulator," *Washington Post*, December 7, 2005, http://www.washingtonpost.com/wp-dyn/content/article/2005/12/07/AR2005120700137.html; Steve Lohr, "Europe's Latest Blow to Microsoft," *New York Times*, September 17, 2007, https://bits.blogs.nytimes.com/2007/09/17/europes-latest-blow-to-microsoft/?_r=0.

[33] *R v Hoffmann-LaRoche Ltd* (1980), 28 OR (2d) 151, aff'd [1981] OJ No 3075.

product substitutes are available, while the commissioner proposes a narrower definition so that fewer products or a smaller geographic area will be taken into account.[34]

> **CASE 3.6 Defining the Market**
>
> NutraSweet accounted for more than 95 percent of all Canadian sales of the sweetener aspartame—a product used mainly in the soft-drink industry. One other firm, Tosoh, accounted for the rest of the market.
>
> Tosoh complained to the Competition Bureau that NutraSweet had entered into exclusive purchasing contracts with its customers. If they wished to buy aspartame from NutraSweet, they had to agree to buy only from NutraSweet.
>
> This raised the question of defining the relevant market. Was it the market for aspartame or for sweeteners generally, and was the market Canada or the world?
>
> The tribunal considered the evidence of cross-elasticity of demand between the various types of sweeteners and concluded that there was, at most, only weak evidence of competition between aspartame and other sweeteners. Customers were unlikely to switch to other sweeteners on account of the conditions imposed by NutraSweet. Similarly, although aspartame was available in other countries, transportation costs were low, and there were no tariff barriers, the tribunal concluded that the relevant market was Canada. Prices in Canada differed significantly from prices in other countries, suggesting that Canada was a distinct geographic market and that customers were unlikely to switch to imported aspartame.
>
> NutraSweet was dominant in this narrowly defined market, and the tribunal found that it used its market power to keep other suppliers out of Canada, with the effect of lessening competition significantly.[35]

> **CHECKLIST**
>
> **Restricting Competition**
>
> Competition may be reduced by conspiracies between a number of producers or by monopolizing on the part of a single producer.
>
> Criminal conspiracies include
>
> - price fixing,
> - market allocation,
> - restriction of supply,
> - bid-rigging, and
> - sport professional restraint of play.
>
> Any agreement among competitors that lessens competition is subject to review by the commission and prohibition by the tribunal.
>
> Reviewable monopolizing distribution practices include
>
> - refusal to supply,
> - exclusive dealing,
> - tied selling, and
> - market restrictions.
>
> Any anti-competitive behaviour by a business in substantial control of a market that lessens competition is an abuse of power and is reviewable by the tribunal. Examples include
>
> - discriminatory pricing,
> - predatory pricing,
> - exclusive dealerships,
> - tied selling arrangements, and
> - marketing restrictions.

---

[34] See e.g. *Canada (Director of Investigation and Research, Competition Act) v Southam Inc*, [1997] 1 SCR 748 at paras 14–20. See also *Canada (Commissioner of Competition) v Canada Pipe Co*, 2006 FCA 233; *(Canada) Commissioner of Competition v Toronto Real Estate Board*, 2014 FCA 29 at para 14, leave to appeal denied.

[35] *Director of Investigation and Research v NutraSweet Co* (1990), 32 CPR (3d) 1; see also Competition Bureau Abuse of Dominance Guidelines http://www.competitionbureau.gc.ca/eic/site/cb-bc.nsf/eng/03497.html

Mergers

One way to combat monopolizing is to try to prevent monopolies from forming. To this end, section 92 of the *Competition Act* gives the tribunal power to prevent a merger from proceeding, in whole or in part, and to set conditions, where it concludes that the merger is likely to prevent or significantly lessen competition in Canada. The tribunal may act only after the commissioner has carried out a full investigation of a proposed or completed merger. The initial review may be followed up with a second request for information in complex mergers.

merger the amalgamation of two or more businesses into a single business entity

Merger is broadly defined (s. 91) to include the acquisition, by the purchase of shares or assets or by amalgamation, combination, or other means, of control over, or of a significant interest in, the business of a competitor (horizontal merger), supplier, customer (vertical merger), or other person (conglomerate or diversification merger). "Control" apparently means legal control—that is, ownership of more than 50 percent of the shares or voting rights of another corporation, but a "significant interest" may be something less than legal control.[36] Most likely to lessen competition are horizontal mergers between competing firms, since the number of competitors is effectively reduced when one such firm obtains control over another. But vertical mergers, where a business takes control of its suppliers or its distributors, may also reduce competition by increasing the market control of large firms. Diversification will only rarely have an anti-competitive effect.

To decide whether a merger is likely to have a significant effect on competition, the tribunal is required (by section 93) to consider a variety of factors, including whether

- the existence of foreign competition is likely to ensure that a reduction of competition within Canada will not have adverse consequences;
- the "target" firm is in poor economic health and would likely not have continued in business;
- acceptable substitutes exist for the products affected;
- there are barriers that might prevent new competitors from entering the market;
- effective competition will still exist after the merger; and
- the merger will eliminate a vigorous, effective, and innovative competitor.

Even if it is determined that a proposed merger will substantially and detrimentally lessen competition, it may still be justified on grounds of economic efficiency (s. 96). The creation of a larger firm, pooling the assets and skills of the parties, may produce gains—such as improved products, increased exports, or reduced reliance on imports—that offset some of the negative effects on competition.[37]

Although the tribunal has the power to "unscramble" a completed merger within one year after closing, this is unlikely for two reasons. First, there are pre-notification requirements for large mergers involving firms whose combined revenues exceed $400 million per year or whose assets exceed $88 million (2017). A party proposing a large acquisition must inform the bureau before proceeding.[38] Consequently, the mergers most likely to affect competition are reviewed before they take place. Second, where it is reasonably clear that a merger will not have anti-competitive consequences, the review process can be avoided by obtaining an advance ruling from the commissioner.

---

[36] The Act does not define significant interest—the Bureau considers the qualitative and quantitative impact of the acquisition. See Competition Bureau, Merger Enforcement Guidelines, October 6, 2011, available on the Competition Bureau website.

[37] See *Commissioner of Competition v Superior Propane Inc* (2002), 18 CPR (4th) 417, aff'd (2003) DLR (4th) 55 (FCA).

[38] Section 110. Pre-notification thresholds change annually, see Competition Bureau Canada, News Release (March 3, 2017) 2017 pre-merger notification transaction-size threshold, https://www.canada.ca/en/competition-bureau/news/2017/03/2017_pre-merger_notificationtransaction-sizethreshold.html. Under the *Investment Canada Act*, additional conditions apply in the case of acquisition of a Canadian firm by a foreign firm.

CASE 3.7 Attaching Conditions to Merger Approval

Bell (BCE Inc.) proposed a takeover of Astral Media Inc. for $3.38 billion. The Competition Bureau reviewed the proposed merger. To preserve consumer choice in television programming, Bell was required to sell several specialty television channels, including the Family Channel, Teletoon, the Cartoon Network, Disney XD, and others, in order to obtain Competition Bureau approval. The broadcasting regulator (Canadian Radio-television and Telecommunications Commission) was also free to impose other conditions on the deal.[39]

CONSUMER PROTECTION

Consumers are broadly defined as individuals who purchase goods and services from a business for their personal use and enjoyment. The definition does not include organizations or individuals using goods or services for a business activity or resale. Consumer protection statutes apply to both the sale of goods and the supply of services such as home repairs, carpet cleaning, and the preparation of income tax returns. They regulate the behaviour of manufacturers, distributors, importers, advertisers, and retailers.

consumers individuals who purchase goods and services from a business for their personal use and enjoyment

Why Is Consumer Protection Legislation Necessary?

Protective legislation is necessary because modern business methods have increased risks for consumers. Figure 3.2 shows some of the ways modern developments have affected consumers.

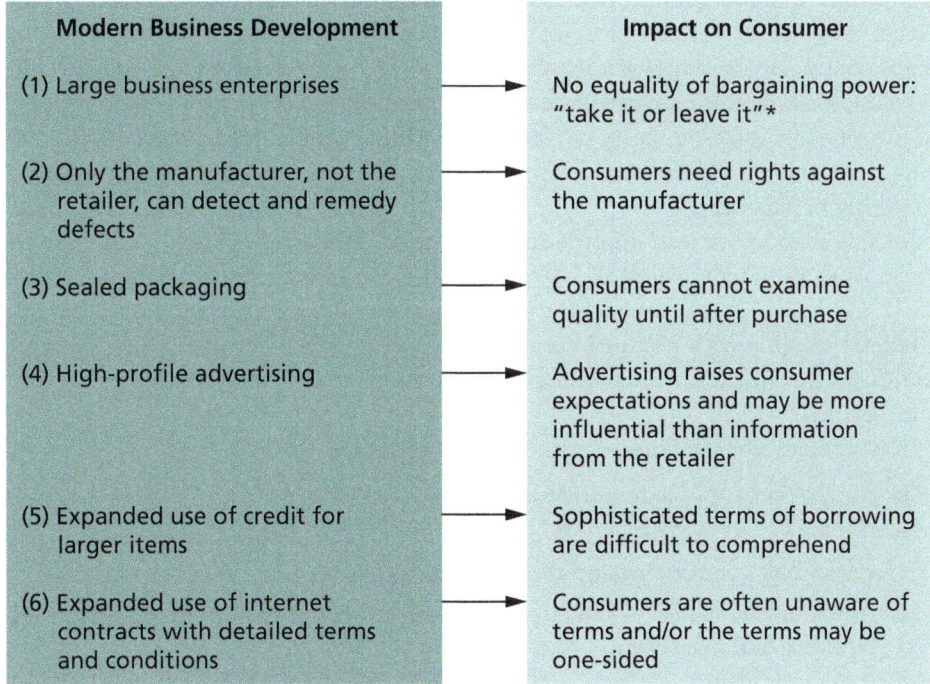

Figure 3.2 The Modern Business Environment

*George Mitchell (Chesterhall) Ltd v Finney Lock Seeds Ltd, [1983] 1 All E.R. 108 at 113: "The freedom was all on the side of the big concern.... The big concern said 'Take it or leave it.' The little man had no option but to take it."

---

[39] *The Commissioner of Competition v BCE Inc*, CT 2013-002 (Consent Agreement March 4, 2013).

Consumer protection is one of those topics that falls under concurrent jurisdiction of both federal and provincial governments; every Canadian province, as well as the federal government, has legislation. The result is a collection of individual statutes that often overlap.

CASE 3.8 Who Protects a Bank's Customers?

Credit card customers started a class action against several banks seeking reimbursement of undisclosed foreign currency charges. Prior disclosure was required under the Quebec *Consumer Protection Act*. The banks argued that the provincial legislation did not apply to them because the Constitution put banks under the exclusive jurisdiction of the federal government. The Supreme Court of Canada held that Quebec's consumer protection legislation enhanced rather than conflicted with the objectives of the *Bank Act*, and so it applied to federally regulated banks.[40]

The federal government is trying to organize its legislation under a comprehensive Consumer Protection Action Plan,[41] beginning with the adoption of the Canada *Consumer Product Safety Act* (CCPSA).[42] The CCPSA applies many of the existing consumer protection strategies to a wider range of products and adds some new initiatives. The two most important CCPSA initiatives are mandatory recall power for Health Canada and regulatory and criminal liability for corporate directors and officers.[43]

Principal Types of Consumer Legislation

Some consumer risks are contractual—arising from a one-sided agreement made with the business. Onerous terms, high cost of credit, and low negotiating power are contractual risks. Therefore, one type of consumer protection legislation regulates consumer contracts, including pressure sales tactics, onerous terms, disclosure, and cancellation rights; this type of legislation falls primarily under provincial jurisdiction, and it generally takes a "passive" form in which consumers enforce their own rights. This type of legislation is addressed in the chapters dealing with contracts, and specifically in Chapter 14.

In this chapter, we focus on the second type of consumer protection legislation. It is broader in scope, is typically "active" with an administrative agency to enforce it, and addresses business behaviour involving the public. This legislation is primarily federal, dealing with national concerns such as health, safety, and mass communication in the form of advertising and labelling; many federal statutes address multiple risks.

Key non-contractual consumer protection issues are

- regulation of misleading advertising;
- regulation of quality standards affecting labelling, safety, performance, and availability of servicing and repairs; and
- regulation of high risk industries that deal with the public through licensing, bonding, and inspection.

---

[40] *Bank of Montreal v Marcotte*, 2014 SCC 55 at paras 62–67; *see also Amex Bank v Adams*, 2014 SCC 56.

[41] Health Canada, Harper Government's *Canada Product Safety Act* Comes into Force, News Release, June 20, 2011.

[42] SC 2010, c 21.

[43] *Ibid.*, ss 42, 43.

Misleading Advertising There are both regulatory and criminal offences that punish sellers of goods and services for misleading representations. The *Food and Drugs Act* addresses advertising of food, cosmetics, and **devices**. The Act is administered by Health Canada and enforced by the Canadian Food Inspection Agency. It is a regulatory or even criminal offence to:

devices medical apparatus and test kits such as pregnancy tests

- label, package, treat, process, sell, or advertise any food or drug in a manner that is false, misleading, or deceptive or is likely to create an erroneous impression regarding its character, value, quantity, composition, merit, or safety (s. 5, 9)[44]
- label, package, sell, or advertise a product in a way that it is likely to be mistaken for a regulated cosmetic (s. 17)
- label, package, sell, or advertise a device in a false, misleading, or deceptive way (s. 19)

As already discussed, the federal *Competition Act* is the most comprehensive legislation regulating business conduct, and so, not surprisingly, it also deals with advertising and false claims. It contains a general prohibition of misleading representations made for the purpose of promoting the supply or use of a product or of any business interest.[45] Specifically, the Act makes it an offence to make false or misleading representations about the following:

- qualities of a product
- length of life
- warranties[46]
- guarantees
- performance claims
- test results[47]

CASE 3.9 Unproven Performance Claims

The Competition Bureau fined Rogers Communications Inc. $10 000 000 because it made two performance claims without proper testing when it launched its new Chatr cell phone campaign in television, internet, and radio ads across the country. Both performance claims related to dropped call rates, claiming Chatr's dropped call rate was lower than other providers and customers would have no worries about dropped calls. Rogers appealed. The court held that the proper test of a false or misleading advertisement under the *Competition Act* was whether or not the average wireless consumer who is credulous, is technically inexperienced, and does not take more than ordinary care when observing the entire advertisement is likely to form a false general impression. In order for the ads to be neither false nor misleading, the fewer dropped calls claim needed to be true in all Chatr markets. Rogers failed to conduct adequate and proper tests in the Calgary and Edmonton zones and in Toronto and Montreal. The complaints were upheld for those advertisements.[48]

The Act defines the word "product" as including goods and services. Liability extends to importers of goods, even though the misrepresentation may have been

---

[44] RSC 1985, c F-27, s 5(1). Labels and advertising are also controlled by the *Weights and Measures Act*, RSC 1985, c W-6. Other federal statutes regulate the sale of meat, livestock, fruit, vegetables, and honey.

[45] *Competition Act*, *supra* note 29, s 52.

[46] *Ibid.*, s 74.01.

[47] *Ibid.*, s 74.02.

[48] *Canada (Competition Bureau) v Chatr Wireless Inc*, 2013 ONSC 5315 (CanLII).

made outside Canada. This is clearly aimed at American manufacturers who target Canadian consumers. Misleading advertising during telemarketing is addressed separately.

dual offence an offence under the *Competition Act* that may be either a criminal or a regulatory offence, depending upon the seriousness of the conduct

Misleading advertising is a **dual offence**. Depending upon the seriousness of the non-compliance, it may constitute either a criminal or a regulatory offence. The criminal offence carries a maximum penalty of 14 years' imprisonment, a substantial fine, or both. The regulatory penalty is a maximum fine of $200 000 and/or one year's imprisonment (s. 52(5)).

Other reviewable "deceptive market practices" are exclusively regulatory offences.[49] These include **bait-and-switch advertising**, making performance claims that lack proper substantiation, and making misleading savings claims and misrepresenting the original price of a sale item. Such practices are subject to review by the Competition Tribunal, which may order the offender to refrain from such conduct for up to 10 years and may impose fines of up to $10,000,000 on corporations (s. 74.1).

bait-and-switch advertising advertising a product at a bargain price but not supplying it in reasonable quantities

CASE 3.10 Criminal Offence Involves Intention

Alan Benlolo and his brothers Elliot and Simon were the principals in two internet directory scams known as yellowbusinesspages.com and yellowbusinessdirectory.com. Between May and August, they sent out four different bulk "advertising" mailings to over 600 000 prospects. The mailings looked remarkably like a Bell Canada invoice, and some contained a version of the Yellow Pages "walking fingers" logo. Each "invoice" requested payment of $25.52. After several warnings from the Competition Bureau, the brothers were convicted of the criminal offence of making false and misleading representations contrary to section 52(1) of the *Competition Act*. Alan and Elliot were sentenced to three years in prison and fined $400 000.

The brothers appealed the sentences, claiming that the conduct should have been characterized as a deceptive market practice and dealt with as a regulatory offence, thereby eliminating any possible jail time. The Court of Appeal upheld the sentences, saying that criminal charges and significant jail time were appropriate because these individuals opened bank accounts for their "business," incorporated the operating corporations, designed the mailings, and arranged for their distribution. They were intentional architects of a fraud, not legitimate businesspeople who stepped over a line.[50]

As noted, the Canada *Consumer Product Safety Act* (CCPSA) focuses on harmful or dangerous products. It is an offence for a manufacturer or importer to advertise a product that is a danger to human health or safety or is the subject of a recall (s. 8). Retailers and advertisers may be convicted of an offence if they know the product is dangerous or recalled. Again, the CCPSA offences are dual offences that will be treated as criminal offences in serious circumstances.

Provinces also have legislation dealing with misleading advertising. In addition to prohibiting such advertising and imposing fines against sellers, consumers affected by misleading statements may start their own lawsuits. For instance, Ontario's *Consumer Protection Act* declares it to be an "unfair practice" to make "a false, misleading or deceptive consumer representation," which may include a wide variety of representations about the "sponsorship, approval, performance characteristics, accessories, uses, ingredients, benefits or quantities" that the goods or services do not have.[51] There is a long list of examples of deceptive representations. The Act also creates "an unconscionable

---

[49] *Competition Act, supra* note 29, ss 74.01-74.07.

[50] *R v Benlolo* (2006), 81 OR (3d) 440 (On CA). See also *Canada (Competition Bureau) v Yellow Pages Marketing BV*, 2013 ONCA 71.

[51] *Consumer Protection Act, 2002*, SO 2002, c C-30, s 14.

consumer representation" as a type of unfair practice that includes such conduct as simply asking a price that "grossly exceeds the price at which similar goods or services are readily available to like consumers."[52] A consumer subjected to an unfair practice may terminate the contract and "where rescission is not possible . . . the consumer is entitled to recover any payment exceeding the fair value of the goods or services received under the agreement or damages, or both" (s. 18(2)).[53] In addition, the court may award exemplary or punitive damages against the business. Similar protection exists in other provinces.[54]

Ethical Issue **Corporate Social Responsibility and Self-Regulation of Advertising**

It can be difficult to determine when an ad is misleading, and therefore only the most obvious abuses are acted upon by the government. In an effort to raise the level of professionalism in advertising and foster public confidence, Advertising Standards Canada (ASC), an industry body formed in the 1960s, developed the Canadian Code of Advertising Standards. The code goes far beyond inaccurate or misleading ads, and addresses advertisements that:

- target children,
- contain violence,
- play on fears, or
- offend public decency.

This voluntary code of conduct is widely adopted by advertisers, advertising agencies, and the media. A dispute resolution process is also available to resolve consumer and competitor complaints.

Questions to Consider

1. How does compliance with the Canadian Code of Advertising Standards promote corporate social responsibility?
2. What are the arguments in favour of and against endorsing the ASC code?
3. When is an ad too violent or offensive to public decency?

Regulation of Labelling, Product Safety, and Performance Standards

Public health and safety standards for consumer products are another topic of federal legislation. Some standards address the quality of the product itself; other standards ensure that the consumer is informed about the product's characteristics and risks. For example, the *Consumer Packaging and Labelling Act*[55] sets out comprehensive rules for packaging and labelling consumer products, including requirements for identifying products by their generic names and stating the quantity of the contents. The Act also standardizes package sizes to avoid confusion.

The *Textile Labelling Act*[56] requires clothing to have labels with the generic name of the fabric. The federal care labelling program encourages manufacturers to include recommended procedures for cleaning and preserving the fabric. The Ministry of Labour administers this Act, and offences are processed through the courts.[57]

The *Hazardous Products Act*[58] is one of many statutes that deal with harmful products. In 2010, control over products so dangerous that their manufacture is banned in Canada was transferred to the CCPSA. This Act deals with "controlled" products that must be manufactured and handled in conformity with regulations under the Act and

---

[52] *Ibid.*, s 15(2)(b).

[53] *Ibid.*, s18(2).

[54] See e.g. *Trade Practice Act*, RSBC 1996, c 457; *Fair Trading Act*, RSA 2000, c F-2.

[55] RSC 1985, c C-38.

[56] RSC 1985, c T-10.

[57] *Department of Industry Act*, SC 1995, c 1, s 9 establishes the framework for the many regulatory regimes assigned to this government agency.

[58] RSC 1985, c H-3.

includes such items as bleaches, hydrochloric acid, and various glues containing potent solvents. The Minister of Health[59] has broad discretion to regulate products deemed to be a threat to public health or safety, which includes warning symbols and container type, and to appoint investigators. In British Columbia, the Workers' Compensation Board administers the requirements of this Act.

Regulations under the *Motor Vehicle Safety Act*[60] set national safety standards for motor vehicles (whether manufactured in Canada or imported) and accessories such as seat belts and booster seats. Manufacturers must give notice of vehicle defects to Transport Canada and to all purchasers of the defective vehicles. Each of the above-described federal statutes creates regulatory and/or criminal offences for non-compliance.

The *Food and Drugs Act*[61] is a comprehensive statute regulating many aspects of foods and medical and cosmetic products, since virtually all of them, if improperly processed, manufactured, stored, or labelled, may adversely affect consumers' health or safety. Provisions deal with sanitary production, contamination prevention, the listing of ingredients contained in products, and the dating of products having shelf lives shorter than 90 days. The Act is administered jointly by the Canadian Food Inspection Agency and Health Canada. They have the power to search, seize, examine, and recall products, including imports.

ILLUSTRATION 3.2 The Importance of Inspections and Recalls

The 2008 tainted meat outbreak involving Maple Leaf Foods illustrates the importance of effective inspection and recall procedures. More than 30 people died from eating various products containing tainted meat, and a $100 million class action lawsuit was commenced.

The Canadian Food Inspection Agency came under heavy criticism when the publication of a 2005 report revealed that the government was aware of problems in its system, including irregular inspections, delays in warning the public, unclear recall protocols, and limited resources, years before the tainted meat deaths.[62]

The passage of the CCPSA in 2010 addressed some of the system's earlier failures.[63] It applies to manufacturing, importing, selling, and distributing a broad range of products that could endanger the health or safety of Canadians. The Act empowers Health Canada to inspect premises, products, and records and expands mandatory recall power beyond food products.

> 32. (1) If an inspector believes on reasonable grounds that a consumer product is a danger to human health or safety, they may order a person who manufactures, imports or sells the product for commercial purposes to recall it.[64]

If the business does not comply, Health Canada may carry out the recall itself and bill the business for the cost. The CCPSA also requires mandatory disclosure of defect incidents, increases penalties for non-compliance, and expands criminal liability to

---

[59] *Ibid.*, ss 2, 20, 21.

[60] SC 1993, c 16.

[61] RSC 1985, c F-27.

[62] Robert Cribb, "Food Alarms Rang in '05," TheStar.com, September 24, 2008, www.thestar.com/News/Canada/article/504671; Joanna Smith, "Two More Firms Jointly Launch Class Action Against Maple Leaf," TheSpec.com, August 27, 2008, www.thespec.com/news-story/2103464-two-more-firms-jointly-launch-class-action-against-maple-leaf.

[63] SC 2010, c 21.

[64] *Ibid.*, s 32(1).

include corporate directors and officers. The process is now much more transparent, and the latest recalls and safety alerts are published on the Health Canada website.[65]

Regulation of Specific Businesses by Licensing, Bonding, Inspection, or Other Regulation

Licensing of businesses is another common method of protecting consumers. We will discuss the licensing of professions in Chapter 5. Licensing is also used to regulate the providers of a variety of goods and services. A familiar example is the inspection and licensing of restaurants by municipal authorities to ensure sanitary conditions in the preparation of food.

Provincial consumer protection acts allow regulatory boards to suspend or revoke licences and to hear complaints. Most provinces require registration of door-to-door salespersons. Collection agencies—often accused of using high-pressure tactics and harassment to collect outstanding debts—are also subject to similar registration requirements.

After some highly publicized failures of travel agencies in which consumers who had paid for holiday packages lost their money, some provinces passed legislation to license travel firms in much the same way as door-to-door sellers and collection agencies. In addition, travel agents must be bonded in order to guarantee consumers against loss of prepaid travel; industry-wide Travel Assurance Funds accomplish the same purpose.

ILLUSTRATION 3.3   Licensing as Consumer Protection

The payday loan industry provides an interesting illustration of provincial and federal cooperation in consumer protection regulation. In 2004, the questionable lending practices of the payday loan industry caught the attention of the press. *The Toronto Star* reported that the combination of administrative charges, interest, and insurance fees typically collected on a two-week payday loan amounted to the equivalent of an annualized interest rate of 390–891 percent, even though it is a criminal offence to charge more than 60 percent per annum.

Since banking and interest are matters of federal jurisdiction, the federal government acted first by amending the *Criminal Code* to allow provinces to regulate this lending industry and set their own interest rate caps. Since then, British Columbia, Manitoba, Nova Scotia, Ontario, and Saskatchewan have passed legislation regulating the industry. Licensing, bonding, reporting, and disclosure requirements are common to most of the provincial schemes, but not all have capped the interest rates. Manitoba set an interest rate cap of 17 percent per annum. Ontario's legislation sets an actual cost-of-borrowing cap of $21 per $100 borrowed for loans of 62 days or less. This results in a higher rate of interest for shorter loans. Ontario also mandates disclosure and preserves the right to bring a class action.[66]

Sometimes consumers do not want to be protected.

ILLUSTRATION 3.4   Consumers Ignore Protections

Consider the taxi industry that has been the subject of municipal licensing, bonding and insurance regulations for over half a century. Operators required permits before offering rides to the public. Many operators spent large amounts of money to obtain one of the limited number of taxi permits. Then along came Uber, essentially operating a private ride service without complying with any of the existing regulations. Taxi drivers lobbied the municipalities to enforce the regulations but Uber drivers were so numerous and consumer support was so strong that ultimately municipalities were forced to rewrite their regulations to recognize the new manner of delivering private transportation to consumers.[67]

---

[65] http://www.healthycanadians.gc.ca/recall-alert-rappel-avis/index-eng.php

[66] *Criminal Code*, RSC 1985, c C-46, s 347.1; provincial payday lending regulations: BC Reg 57/2009, Alta Reg 1572009; NS Reg 248/2009; Man. Reg 99/2007, Man Reg 50/2010; *Payday Loans Act*, 2008, SO 2008, c 9; O Reg 98/09. Joanna Smith and Robert Benzie, "Payday Loan Crackdown," TheStar.com, April 1, 2008, www.thestar.com/News/Ontario/article/407813.

[67] See e.g. *Mississauga (City) v Uber Canada Inc*, 2016 ONCJ 461; *Edmonton (City) v Uber Canada Inc*, 2015 ABQB 214; Taxi drivers sued Uber in class actions: *Konjevic v Uber Technologies Inc*, 2016 ONSC 7804.

CHECKLIST

Federal Regulation of Consumer Protection

Topic	Legislation	Administrative Agency
Misleading Advertising	Food and Drugs Act	Health Canada Canadian Food Inspection Agency
	Competition Act	Commissioner of Competition Competition Bureau
Labelling, Product Safety, and Performance	Canada Consumer Product Safety Act	Health Canada
	Consumer Packaging and Labelling Act	Canadian Food Inspection Agency, Minister of Agriculture and Minister of Industry
	Food and Drugs Act	Health Canada Canadian Food Inspection Agency
	Textile Labelling Act	Minister of Industry
	Hazardous Products Act	Minister of Health
	Motor Vehicle Safety Act	Transport Canada

ENVIRONMENTAL PROTECTION

The environment is another area protected by government regulation. Most businesses need professional advice to navigate the complicated environmental regulatory schemes applicable to their industry. Non-compliance will trigger costly clean-up costs as well as fines and penalties.

The Legislative Framework

All three levels of government exercise regulatory jurisdiction over the environment. The protection of the environment is clearly within the competence of the provinces, but matters such as air and water pollution are national problems and require national solutions. Municipalities also pass bylaws to provide local environmental protection and to restrict activities deemed to be harmful.

CASE 3.11 Environmental Damage Across Borders

Corporations operating in Manitoba, Ontario, and Saskatchewan were found to have improperly discharged mercury into rivers that drained into Manitoba. The Manitoba government passed a regulatory scheme requiring the companies to compensate fishermen for loss suffered as a result of mercury contamination. The Supreme Court of Canada held that, although creating a civil cause of action for damages caused by pollution was within provincial jurisdiction, Manitoba did not have power to impose liability in respect of acts done outside the province.[68]

Federal Legislation The most important federal legislation is the *Canadian Environmental Protection Act* (CEPA) administered by Environment Canada.[69] Separate statutes address specific types of pollution or dangers to the environment.[70]

---

[68] *Interprovincial Corp Ltd v R*, [1976] SCR 477.

[69] SC 1999, c 33. The Act consolidated a number of earlier statutes, among them the *Clean Air Act*, the *Environmental Contaminants Act*, the *Ocean Dumping Control Act*, and parts of the *Canada Water Act*.

[70] Most notably is *Nuclear Energy Act*, RSC 1985, c A-16; *Fisheries Act*, RSC 1985, c F-14; *Pest Control Products Act*, SC 2002, c 28; *Transportation of Dangerous Goods Act*, SC 1992, c 34.

The *CEPA* applies to all elements of the environment—air, land, and water, all layers of the atmosphere, all organic and inorganic matter and living organisms, and any interacting natural systems of the foregoing components. The Act takes a coordinated intergovernmental approach to environmental policy and requires the minister of the environment to create a national advisory committee with representatives from every province, territory, and Aboriginal government (s. 6). The committee advises on environmental quality objectives and recommends guidelines and codes of practice to the minister (s. 54), taking a precautionary (preventive) strategy. There is a public registry of all regulations, policies, guidelines, proposed regulations, and court proceedings (s. 12–14). Separate parts of the *CEPA* deal with subjects such as toxic substances, hazardous wastes, nutrients, international air pollution, and ocean dumping, as well as reactive measures for emergencies and clean-up. Any substance listed in Schedule 1 is considered toxic and subject to special controls. Substances not yet classified must be assessed by Health Canada and Environment Canada before they can be imported or manufactured.

In the case of an abnormal environmental event, the person who owns or controls the substance or activity has a duty to report and take remedial action. Environment Canada will investigate, issue emergency orders and clean-up orders, and may lay charges if it finds non-compliance with environmental standards.

Part 10 of the *CEPA* deals with enforcement and designates enforcement officers as peace officers with the power to search, seize, and arrest (s. 217–224). Any contravention of the *CEPA* or its regulation is a criminal offence with minimum fine and maximum fines ($1 000 000) and three years of imprisonment, or both. Fines double for second offences. This is separate from the costs of the clean-up. The *CEPA* imposes a personal duty on officers and directors of corporations to comply with the Act, and they are personally subject to the same penalties (s. 280, 280.1).

CASE 3.12 Duty to Report

During blasting of rock to widen a highway, rock debris escaped and flew 90 meters, damaging homes and cars in the area. This was a dangerous and abnormal result, so the contractor reported the incident to the Ministry of Labour and the Ministry of Transport but failed to report the incident to the Ministry of Environment. The contractor was convicted of the offence of failing to report an incident. It appealed all the way to the Supreme Court of Canada without success. The event was out of the ordinary and not trivial, as it produced adverse effects; therefore, reporting was necessary.[71]

Provincial Legislation All provinces have a "general" environment protection law,[72] supplemented by various statutes referring to specific types of environmental protection. Examples are statutes relating to air pollution,[73] water conservation and pollution,[74] transportation of dangerous goods,[75] and waste management.[76]

---

[71] *Castonguay Blasting Ltd v Ontario (Environment)*, 2013 SCC 52.

[72] See e.g. *Environmental Management Act*, SBC 2003, c 53; *Environment Act*, SNS 1994–95, c 1; *Environmental Protection Act*, RSO 1990, c E-19.

[73] See e.g. *Environmental Management and Protection Act, 2010*, SS 2010, c E-10.22; *Environmental Protection and Enhancement Act*, RSA 2000, c E-12.

[74] See e.g. *Environmental Protection and Enhancement Act*, RSA 2000, c E-12; *Environment Act*, SNS 1994–95, c 1.

[75] See e.g. *Dangerous Goods Handling and Transportation Act*, CCSM c D-12; *Dangerous Goods Transportation Act*, RSO 1990, c D.1.

[76] See e.g. *Environmental Management Act*, SBC 2003, c 53.

Environmental Impact Assessment Review

It is much better to prevent injury to the environment than to try to remedy it after it has occurred so the CEPA takes a precautionary approach. Environmental impact assessment review processes are required at the federal level by the *Canadian Environmental Assessment Act* (CEAA)[77] and in all provinces. Regulations under the CEAA identify specific types of projects that may require an environmental assessment. For these projects, the developer must submit a summary of the project to the Canadian Environmental Assessment Agency, and the Agency has 45 days to decide if an assessment is required. Selected projects will be reviewed by a panel of independent experts. Public hearings are held in the communities likely to be affected. The review board submits its findings to the minister responsible or to the whole cabinet, which makes the final decision about the future of the project based upon whether or not it will have significant adverse environmental effect.

The federal process is concerned about environmental effects on matters within federal jurisdiction (such as fishing), on federal land or on environments outside the project's host province or outside Canada, or on Aboriginal land, culture, health, or traditions.[78] Governments have a constitutional duty to notify, consult, and accommodate Aboriginal groups on projects affecting their interests.[79] Conditions may be attached to any approval. The process must be completed within 365 days.

> **CASE 3.13 Environmental Impact on Aboriginal Tradition**
>
> The British Columbia Minister of Forests, Lands and Natural Resource Operations gave approval to Glacier Resorts to develop a ski resort in Jumbo Valley after a 20-year-long consultation, modification, and approval process involving the BC Environmental Assessment Office, among others. The Ktunaxa First Nation opposed the development because the land held religious significance as the home of the Grizzly Bear Spirit and development would oust the Spirit. On judicial review the Supreme Court of Canada found that the Minister's approval was reasonable.[80] Participation in various regulatory processes, including that of the Environmental Assessment Office, satisfied the constitutional duty to consult and accommodate Aboriginal groups. There is no constitutional guarantee of complete accommodation; approval was upheld.

The scope and the procedures of the review process vary from one jurisdiction to another. Where multiple jurisdictions are involved, the federal Minister of the Environment may substitute the provincial process for the federal one.

Enforcement and Liability

Although private enforcement of environmental standards is possible using the private lawsuits in nuisance or negligence, the enforcement of environmental laws is usually a public matter. Legislation provides public authorities with a variety of enforcement tools. Polluters may be ordered to stop harmful activities, to remedy existing situations, and to pay the costs of clean-up. Owners of contaminated property may be forbidden from dealing with that property, even if they did not cause the contamination. Environmental legislation normally creates a number of offences, punishable by

---

[77] SC 2012, c 19.

[78] *Ibid.*, s 5.

[79] *Constitution Act, 1982*, ss 35, 35.1; *Rio Tinto Alcan Inc v Carrier Sekani Tribal Council*, 2010 SCC 43 at para 31; The regulatory process may fulfill this duty: *Chippewas of the Thames First Nations v Enbridge Pipelines Inc*, 2017 SCC 41; Aboriginal Consultation and Accommodation Guidelines For Federal Officials http://www.aadnc-aandc.gc.ca/eng/1100100014664/1100100014675.

[80] *Ktunaxa Nation v British Columbia (Forests, Lands and Natural Resource Operations)*, 2017 SCC 54.

fines and, in serious cases, by imprisonment. Since most major polluters are corporations, which cannot be sent to prison, the statutes frequently impose personal liability on corporate directors and officers for pollution offences of their companies.

INTERNATIONAL ISSUE
Bribery of Foreign Officials

This chapter describes a number of regulations that require businesses to seek government approval. Would an ethical Canadian business ever consider bribing the Commissioner of Competition to obtain approval for a merger? Of course not; in Canada, bribery of Canadian public officials is unacceptable, and government corruption is prohibited through a number of *Criminal Code* offences, including bribery, fraud, influence peddling, and money laundering.

International attitudes concerning the bribery of government officials vary widely. In some cultures it is considered normal, if not acceptable, to bribe an official to get a favourable or at least more rapid response.

The Organisation for Economic Co-operation and Development's (OECD) Convention on Combating Bribery of Foreign Public Officials in International Business Transactions calls for member nations to adopt legislation that criminalizes bribery of foreign officials. Canada ratified the treaty and passed the *Corruption of Foreign Public Officials Act* (*CFPOA*). This Act makes it a crime to confer any benefit, directly or indirectly, to a public official "in order to obtain or retain an advantage in the course of business." It covers any global bribery where there is a real and substantial link between the offence and Canada. The maximum penalty under the Act is 14 years in prison. Progress on the fight against corruption must be reported to Parliament on an annual basis.

In 2002, Hector Ramirez Garcia, a U.S. immigration officer working at the Calgary airport, was sentenced to six months in jail and deported to the United States after accepting bribes from an Alberta company, Hydro Kleen Systems Inc., in violation of the *CFPOA*. The company was also convicted and received a $25 000 fine. In 2013, the director of a technology company was convicted of agreeing to offer a bribe to the Indian Minister of Civil Aviation in order to obtain an Air India contract.

The United States has similar legislation known as the *Foreign Corrupt Practices Act*. Other Canadian steps taken to reduce bribery include inserting anti–money-laundering provisions in the *Income Tax Act* and amending the *Criminal Code* to expand its applications to organizations.

Question to Consider

1. Should Canada attempt to regulate international business conduct by extending the reach of its criminal law beyond its borders? Is there a better way to stop bribery?

Sources: *Corruption of Foreign Public Officials Act*, SC 1998, c 34 as amended; *R v Karigar*, 2013 ONSC 5199; *R v Watts*, [2005] AJ No 568.

Strategies to Manage the Legal Risks

This chapter provides only a general overview of the main categories of government regulation of business. Industry-specific rules change regularly. Businesses need a system in place to routinely update the regulatory information as new guidelines are adopted and to maintain compliance on an ongoing basis. Some requirements are mandatory, in the form of regulations enforced through inspection and penalties. Naturally, these must be complied with, or even directors and officers risk punishment. Other standards are recommendations only, such as guidelines, codes of practice, and policies. Although these recommendations may not be mandatory, non-compliance may give rise to civil liability for those harmed—therefore, the best strategy is to conform to all recommended best practices.

Product safety is one of the major objectives of several pieces of legislation discussed in this chapter, and it is no longer a concern for just the product manufacturer. Every business involved in the manufacture, import, distribution, advertisement, or sale of a product may be liable for defects or misrepresentations. Those involved in the supply chain must inform themselves about the compliance of their distribution partners. Naturally, indemnity clauses (under which the offending party agrees to cover all costs of the defect) play a key role in managing the risk, but they may be of little help if the other businesses are foreign or insolvent. Insurance should be obtained not only for the damage caused to outside parties but also for the losses to the business itself when expensive recalls must be undertaken and funded.

Businesses need not accept all regulations imposed on them by government; sometimes the rule is beyond the power of the government, violates the *Charter*, or does not cover the subject conduct. Rather than waiting to complain until after their implementation, management should participate in the development of regulations. Many regulators, such as the securities commissions and the environmental protection agencies, release discussion papers seeking comments on proposed regulation. Businesses have the opportunity to respond individually or through industry-wide associations. Shaping the regulation before it is adopted is much easier and cheaper than attempting to invalidate it after enactment. This is just one of the uses of industry-wide associations. They may also be useful to supply current information about required standards of behaviour and in the development of best practices. However, caution must be exercised when developing industry-wide solutions through an association of competitors.

QUESTIONS FOR REVIEW

1. What strategies are available to business to avoid the application of government regulation?
2. How does the Constitution divide the power to regulate business among the various levels of government in Canada?
3. Which provisions of the *Charter* have particular application to business activity?
4. What changes to the business environment strengthened the need for consumer protection legislation?
5. What are the principal forms of misleading advertising that are prohibited by the *Competition Act*, and what are the consequences?
6. What is a conspiracy? How does the *Competition Act* categorize conspiracies?
7. How does a court determine if competition has been unduly lessened?
8. Give examples of the principal types of abuse of dominant position.
9. Why is it thought necessary for governments to control mergers?
10. Why are horizontal mergers more likely to affect competition than other types of mergers?
11. Why is the determination of the relevant market essential to the application of competition law?
12. What is the purpose of environmental impact assessment review?

CASES AND PROBLEMS

1. Continuing Scenario

    Before opening her restaurant, Ashley contacted O'Brien's Food Service Ltd. to be her frozen poultry supplier. Because she was new to the business, and her volume would be low, O'Brien's quoted her a price of $25 per case of frozen chicken breasts. Adam, O'Brien's salesman, told her in an email that the price was only $20 per case for restaurants that ordered more than three cases a week. Ashley could not be sure she would need this much chicken, so she proceeded on the initial quote. The following day, Adam stopped by the restaurant with the customer application form describing the price as "as quoted" and told Ashley that with every order of chicken she must also take two cases of frozen meatballs at a cost of $15 a case. Meatballs are not on Ashley's proposed menu—she does not want them. Adam tells her that it is both or nothing. Ashley says she needs time to think about it. Is there anything wrong with O'Brien's practice? What can Ashley do?

2. Dr. Carpenter relocated her dental practice to premises in a new shopping mall and placed an advertisement to that effect in the local newspapers. The notice conformed with the advertising standards of the dental profession in the province, but one of the newspapers decided to print a "human interest" story and did an interview with Dr. Carpenter. The story was printed without first having been shown to Dr. Carpenter, and a number of advertisements for dental supplies appeared on the same page. At the same time, Dr. Carpenter ordered a sign announcing the change of premises, which she intended to be displayed in the window of her old premises. Instead, by mistake, the sign was displayed in a public area of the shopping mall.

    The professional association considered that the sign and the advertisements that accompanied the newspaper article constituted breaches of the professional advertising code and gave notice to Dr. Carpenter of a disciplinary hearing, which could result in the cancellation or suspension of her licence to practise.

    On what grounds, if any, can the validity of the disciplinary hearing and the professional regulations be challenged?

3. Red Square Records Inc. is a Canadian corporation holding the sole rights to import and distribute in Canada discs and tapes produced by a Russian company, Krasnayadisk. For some years, Red Square has been importing two labels that have proven very popular, partly because of their low price. It has been selling the discs to dealers at $4.99 each, and they are retailed at prices ranging from $6.99 to $8.99.

    Recently, Krasnayadisk introduced a new label, on which it is releasing previously unavailable archival recordings that are of great interest to collectors. Red Square has started to import the discs and makes them available to retailers at $18.99 each.

    Steve's Records Inc., a Canadian firm that owns a large chain of record stores across Ontario, had been selling large quantities of the cheaper Krasnayadisk recordings, and its customers had shown a lot of interest in the new label. However, many were deterred by the high price. Steve's found another source for the new label—a dealer in the United States, who was prepared to supply Steve's at a price of $11.99 per disc. This enabled Steve's to sell the new label at a much lower price than any of its competitors.

    Some months ago, Steve's received a letter from Red Square saying if Steve's did not stop purchasing the new label from the United States, Red Square would no longer be willing to supply Steve's with the two cheaper labels. Steve's ignored the warning and continued to import the new label.

    A few weeks ago, Steve's ordered some discs from Red Square and was informed that Red Square would no longer supply Steve's. The cheaper labels are also available in the United States, but at the same price of $4.99, and with higher shipping costs.

    Is there any action that Steve's can take against Red Square's refusal to supply it?

4. Truenorth Press Inc. owned both of the daily newspapers in Bayville. The papers were relatively unsuccessful compared to Truenorth's other dailies throughout Canada and faced stiff competition for advertising revenue from a large number of small community newspapers that circulated in the same distribution area. Those community newspapers contained local news stories and advertisements from mainly local firms, appeared once or twice a week, and were distributed free of charge.

Truenorth embarked on a campaign to acquire the community papers and, within one year, obtained control of 20 publications, including the two papers with the largest circulation.

A group of citizens—readers, who feared that there would be fewer local stories, and small firms, who feared that their advertising rates would be increased once Truenorth gained control of the remaining papers—held a number of public meetings to express their concern.

Is there any legal action they could take?

Part 2 Torts

Chapter 4
The Law of Torts

- THE DEVELOPMENT OF TORT LAW
- THE BASIS FOR LIABILITY
- INTENTIONAL TORTS
- UNINTENTIONAL TORTS
- STRATEGIES TO MANAGE THE LEGAL RISKS

The word *tort* is originally French, meaning "wrong." A **tort** is improper behaviour by one person that causes injury to another, sometimes intentionally but more often unintentionally. The injury may be physical (to the person or property of the victim), emotional, or financial.

Tort law identifies situations where the person who causes an injury must compensate the victim.

tort a wrongful act causing harm to the person or property of another

In this chapter we examine such questions as:

- What is the basis for tort liability?
- What are intentional torts?
- What constitutes "negligence"?
- How does the law of negligence apply to particular situations, such as the liability of manufacturers and of the owners or occupiers of land?
- What remedies are available to tort victims?

THE DEVELOPMENT OF TORT LAW

The purpose of tort law is to compensate victims for harm caused by the activities of others. Usually punishment is left to criminal law, if the conduct in question also amounts to a crime.[1] For example, when a person punches an enemy in the nose, the victim may sue the attacker for the tort of battery, and the government may also charge the attacker with the criminal offence of assault causing bodily harm.

A tort identifies a situation that creates a right to claim compensation for harm. When dealing with harm caused by someone else, the underlying question for society is who should bear the loss—the victim, the person who caused the harm, the group that benefits most directly from the activity, such as all motor vehicle owners, or an even larger group such as taxpayers generally. Tort law is one way of apportioning loss, along with other approaches such as insurance and government compensation schemes.[2]

Initially, societies had simple rules for imposing responsibility for injurious conduct. Anyone who caused direct injury to another had to pay compensation. There was no investigation into the reasons for the injury or whether the conduct of the injurer was intentional or unintentional. This type of liability is called **strict liability**. Over time, societies recognized that compensation should only be given if the injurer was in the wrong or at fault. This required an investigation into the way the harm happened. At first, only direct injuries were recognized by the courts—running another person down or striking a blow. Gradually the courts recognized indirect or consequential injuries. For example, A carelessly drops a log in the road and does not bother to remove it. After dark, B trips over the log and is seriously injured. In early law, B would have been without a remedy. Eventually, the courts recognized that A's act was as much responsible for the injury to B as if A had struck B with the log.[3]

Today's tort law involves two principles: the fault of the defendant (that is, whether the behaviour was improper), and the causation of harm (that is, whether the plaintiff's injury was the result of the defendant's conduct).

strict liability liability that is imposed based upon causation regardless of fault

THE BASIS FOR LIABILITY

Fault

Fault, in the context of tort law, refers to blameworthy or culpable conduct—conduct that in the eyes of the law is unjustifiable because it intentionally or carelessly disregards the interests of others. One reason for basing liability upon fault is a belief in its deterrent effect. People will be more careful if they must pay for the consequences of their carelessness. Highly publicized damage awards should influence the behaviour and practices of other similar manufacturers or surgeons, for example. Even though many activities triggering tort liability—driving a car, operating a factory or store, practising medicine—are covered by insurance, a claim will still increase premiums and make insurance more difficult to obtain. Although carelessness is even more likely to be deterred by the likelihood of criminal penalties (for example, consider dangerous driving), not all tortious behaviour amounts to a crime.

fault unjustifiable injurious conduct that intentionally or carelessly disregards the interests of others

---

[1] Sometimes courts award "punitive damages," discussed later in this chapter under "Remedies."

[2] See generally C. Sappideen and P. Vines, eds, *Fleming's Law of Torts*, 10th ed (Prymont, N.S.W.: Lawbook Co, 2011). See also A. M. Linden and B. Feldthusen, *Canadian Tort Law*, 10th ed (Makham: LexisNexis, 2015).

[3] This example paraphrases a classic statement of the law from *Reynolds v Clarke* (1726), 93 ER 747.

Compensation based on fault also has disadvantages. Accident victims who cannot establish fault on the part of some other person go uncompensated. Alternatively, when fault is established, the victim may be overcompensated, especially where the plaintiff is sympathetic, or the defendant is a large corporation, or conduct is considered particularly bad.[4]

Strict Liability

Most but not all tort liability is based upon fault. Strict liability applies in only a few areas of tort law. For example, a person who stores potentially dangerous substances or materials on his land, which accidentally escape, is liable for any resulting damage even if he is blameless.[5]

ILLUSTRATION 4.1 Strict Liability for Escape of Toxic Chemical

A manufacturer stored acid in a large container on his property. The container was accidentally punctured by a visitor's truck, and the acid leaked out and damaged a neighbouring farmer's crops. The manufacturer is liable to compensate the farmer. The risk of that type of damage is a burden that the manufacturer must bear as the price for storing dangerous chemicals on his land. (The truck driver may also be liable for the damage if he is found to be at fault.)

Some activities are inherently dangerous regardless of the amount of care taken—for example, transporting high explosives. It seems logical that a person knowingly undertaking an inherently dangerous activity should be strictly liable for resulting damage, regardless of fault. Why? Because that person could charge for his services according to the degree of risk and could carry adequate insurance to compensate for possible harm done to others. In Canada strict liability is most often imposed through legislation. In the absence of legislation, Canadian courts typically consider fault to be the primary basis of liability. However, the expected level of care rises as the danger increases. As a result, in many cases involving hazardous activities, the defendant finds that the standard of care is so high that it is virtually impossible for him to show that he has satisfied it.[6] The effect is much the same as strict liability.

Public Policy

Whether liability should be based on fault, on strict liability, or on some other principles is an important question of **public policy**. Policy objectives change as our social standards change. These standards force the law to adapt in many ways, ranging from direct government legislative intervention to subtler influences on judge and jury in determining liability and the amounts of compensation awarded.

public policy economic, social, and political considerations or objectives that are believed to be beneficial to society as a whole

The most radical policy proposal would eliminate fault for all personal injuries and compensate victims through government-run compensation schemes. Most Canadian jurisdictions have adopted some form of this policy in automobile accident claims

---

[4] In the United States high jury awards of punitive damages are more common, which has driven "tort law reform" capping damages; see Michael I. Kraus, "'Pain And Suffering' And The Rule Of Law: Why Caps Are Needed" at https://www.forbes.com/sites/michaelkrauss/2014/04/17/pain-and-suffering-and-the-rule-of-law-why-caps-are-needed/#466ec18e799c.

[5] *Rylands v Fletcher* (1868), LR 3 HL 330. In Canada, the *Rylands v Fletcher* rule requires a non-natural use of the land and damage caused by accidental escape or unintended consequences. See *John Campbell Law Corporation v Owners, Strata Plan 1350*, 2001 BCSC 1342. See also *Smith v Inco Ltd*, 2011 ONCA 628, 107 OR (3d) 321, leave to SCC denied (refinery found not to be a non-natural use and no mishap so strict liability not applicable).

[6] *Smith v Inco Ltd*, ibid at para 93.

no-fault insurance a system of compulsory insurance that eliminates fault as a basis for compensation

workers' compensation a scheme in which employers contribute to a fund used to compensate workers injured in industrial accidents regardless of how the accident was caused

through a system of compulsory **no-fault insurance**. Another example of an alternative to the fault approach is found in the regulatory scheme governing **workers' compensation** in Canada. Under this scheme, workplace accidents are seen as the inevitable price of doing business. Employers must contribute to a fund that is used to compensate workers injured in workplace accidents, even when the employer is blameless and the injury is the result of the employee's own carelessness. Tribunals, rather than courts, decide on compensation.

Vicarious Liability

An employer is held liable when it is responsible for a tort committed by an employee. For example, an employer may instruct an employee to perform a dangerous task in an improper way or fail to properly train an employee. In such cases the employer is at fault, and it may be that there is no fault on the part of the employee.[7]

However, even employers without fault may be liable for harm caused by the acts of an employee when those acts arose in the course of employment. This is an example of strict liability—liability without fault. An employer may even be found liable when he has given strict instructions to take proper care or not to do the particular act that causes the damage, and he may be held liable for criminal—as well as intentional and unintentional—tortious acts of an employee, when the acts further the employer's aims.[8] This principle is called **vicarious liability** and results in an employer being liable to compensate persons for torts committed by an employee in the course of employment. (Figure 4.1.)

vicarious liability strict liability of an employer to compensate for torts committed by an employee during the course of his or her employment

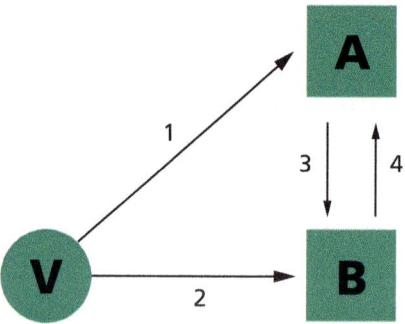

Figure 4.1 Vicarious Liability

The victim, V, is injured by A while A is acting in the course of his employment for B. V can sue A [1]. V can also sue the employer, B [2], who will normally have a greater ability to pay. (In practice, V is likely to sue both A and B.) If V does sue A, it is possible that A will have a right to be indemnified by B [3]. Or, if B has to compensate V, B may be able to sue A [4]. These rights [3 and 4] could arise under the contract of employment.

There are two public policy reasons for taking this approach. First, although an employee is personally liable for the torts he commits while acting for himself or his employer, employees often have limited assets available to pay compensation for the potential harm they can cause. Second, it seems only fair that the person who makes the profit from an activity should also be liable for any loss. These two policies off set by concern not to foist undue burdens on business enterprises.[9]

Even with no-fault schemes and strict liability, the most common approach to compensation of injury remains tort liability based upon the principles of fault and causation.

---

[7] See *Edgeworth Construction Ltd v ND Lee & Associates Ltd* (1993), 107 DLR (4th) 169.

[8] *British Columbia Ferry Corp v Invicta Security Service Corp* (1998), 167 DLR (4th) 193; *Bazley v Curry*, [1999] 2 SCR 534 at para 10.

[9] *Bazley v Curry*, ibid at para 26.

INTENTIONAL TORTS

Torts may be intentional or unintentional. Intentional torts are those where the activity or conduct is done deliberately, not by accident. Unintentional torts are those where the behaviour itself is accidental and not done deliberately. In both cases, the harm may be unexpected, and intention relates only to the behaviour, not the resulting damage. Consider, for example, the intentional tort of battery that arises from non-consensual physical contact. A person may intend to shake your hand, and therefore the contact is intended. However, the person does not intend to break your fingers while doing it—the harm remains unintended. Still, battery occurs.

Harm or damage must occur for any tort to be actionable. For example, one of the oldest intentional torts is **trespass**—entering upon another person's land without permission. Most of the time very little damage is done if someone merely steps upon another's land. There would be no point in suing unless the landowner could establish some loss—a damaged garden or fence, perhaps.

trespass unlawful entering, or remaining, on the land of another without permission

The list of torts continues to grow as courts impose liability for new behaviours causing harm. In this chapter, we focus on the most common torts and those most applicable to the business context.

Assault and Battery

One of the earliest torts was "trespass to the person." The present-day intentional torts dealing with trespass to the person are **assault** (the threat of violence) and **battery** (the actual physical contact). This behaviour may be a criminal offence, and the attacker may be fined or imprisoned. He may also be liable (in tort) to compensate his victim, though assault and battery cases are rarely fruitful against "attackers." Battery cases are common in the medical and sport contexts. The essence of a battery is the unlawful touching of a person without consent; a surgeon who operates on a patient without consent may commit a battery. As well, when a player exceeds the "accepted" level of contact in the specific sport, a battery has occurred. The defence most often presented to a battery is consent, either express or implied.

assault the threat of violence to a person

battery unlawful physical contact with a person

CASE 4.1 Consent in Sport

Steve Moore, a National Hockey League (NHL) player with the Colorado Avalanche, experienced a fractured spine and serious head injury after being hit from behind by Todd Bertuzzi of the Vancouver Canucks during the final game of the regular 2004 season. Moore sued Bertuzzi for damages arising from battery and sued the Vancouver Canucks for vicarious liability. The case was settled before going to trial, but the question that remains is what amount of physical contact exceeded the acceptable level impliedly consented to in the sport given that many believe fighting is part of hockey.[10] This is one of those rare cases that triggered three types of liability. In addition to the tort lawsuit, Bertuzzi pled guilty to criminal charges and was also disciplined (fined and suspended) by the NHL.

Nuisance

There are two nuisance torts. **Public nuisance** protects the public interest and access to public places. It applies to blocking public roads, interfering with the use of public amenities such as parks, and emitting dangerous substances in public places. Government agencies usually sue wrongdoers on behalf of the public as a whole.

public nuisance unreasonable interference with the lawful use of public amenities or the public interest

---

[10] See *R v Bertuzzi*, [2004] BCJ No 2692; *Moore v Bertuzzi*, 2012 ONSC 3497 (CanLII); Patrick Thornton, "Rewriting Hockey's Unwritten Rules: *Moore v Bertuzzi*" (2009), 61 Me L Rev 2005.

Occasionally, an individual who is able to show a special injury that is substantially greater than that suffered by other members of the public may bring an action for compensation.[11]

private nuisance substantial and unreasonable interference with an occupier's use and enjoyment of land

The tort of **private nuisance** protects an occupier's right to the reasonable use and enjoyment of its own land, without substantial interference from direct or indirect activity on neighbouring property. It covers things like noxious fumes, excessive noise, or contaminating liquids poured into rivers or seeping through the soil. The term "occupier" includes not only the owner of land but tenants as well.

Private nuisance can cause physical damage to the property or its occupiers, or interfere with the use of amenities on the property. It requires proof that the interference is substantial and also that it is unreasonable.[12] This is a two-step analysis. The interference must be found to be substantial before any assessment of reasonableness is undertaken.

Occupiers do not have the right to absolute freedom from trivial annoyances; the interference must be more than "slight" or "trifling." The degree of interference is assessed from the occupier's perspective. But in the reasonableness part of the analysis, courts must weigh competing interests and consider a number of factors, including the degree of interference with the occupier's use and enjoyment of the land, the character of the neighbourhood, and the utility or economic importance of the offending activity.[13] The level of interference that a community as a whole already tolerates and that individual members of it can be expected to tolerate also varies according to local conditions. The defence often advanced is that although interference might be substantial, it is not unreasonable. The reasonableness of interference from adjoining lands in an industrial area will be quite different from those in a holiday resort area. Increasingly, governments try to establish the reasonableness of interference through regulation of environmental protection or noise and zoning bylaws.

CASE 4.2 Two Step Analysis: Substantialness and Reasonableness

The defendant trucking company, KJS Transport, had an unpaved (sand and gravel) parking lot. The dust that was generated when trucks moved across the lot created a problem for the neighbouring lighting manufacturer, TMS Lighting. TMS sued KJS for private nuisance. The court found that the interference was substantial because it went on daily for five years—frequency, duration, and degree all pointed to substantialness. The unreasonableness was found in character of the neighbourhood, the sensitivity of the plaintiff's manufacturing business to airborne dust, and the fact that it was entirely resolved once the lot was paved.[14]

False Imprisonment and Malicious Prosecution

false imprisonment unlawfully restraining or confining another person

A tort that has significant importance to shoplifting in the retail business environment is the tort of **false imprisonment**. False imprisonment consists of intentionally restraining a person, without lawful justification, either by causing his confinement or by preventing him from leaving his location. The *Criminal Code* gives peace officers broader powers to arrest than private citizens.[15]

Actual physical restraint is not necessary, or even the threat that it will be applied. A reasonable fear that a store detective might shout, "Stop, thief!" would be enough restraint to amount to an imprisonment. There is a real risk of liability for civilians in confronting

---

[11] *Ryan v Victoria (City)*, [1999] 1 SCR 201 at para 52.

[12] *Antrim Centre Ltd v Ontario Transport*, 2013 SCC 13 at paras 19, 21–28, 53–54; See also *Smith v Inco Ltd*, *supra* note 5 (mere chemical alteration of the soil (increased nickel levels) did not amount to harm.)

[13] *Antrim Centre Ltd*, ibid.

[14] *TMS Lighting Ltd v KJS Transport Inc*, 2014 ONCA 1.

[15] *Criminal Code*, RSC 1985, c C-46, ss 25, 30-35, 494-95.

a suspected offender without strong evidence that a crime has actually been committed. For example, the store manager who detains a suspected shoplifter when no shoplifting had in fact occurred might not have a defence against an action for false imprisonment, even if he believed the suspect had stolen goods. **False arrest**, a tort often used in the same context, ordinarily includes a false imprisonment but has the additional feature of holding the victim with the intention of turning him over to the police for prosecution.

Someone who honestly makes a complaint to the police about a suspected crime is not liable for false imprisonment if the suspected criminal is arrested by the police as a result of the complaint, but it later turns out no crime was committed. For example, if a store detective reports a suspected shoplifter to a police officer, and the police officer arrests the alleged shoplifter, the store detective is not liable for false imprisonment and nor is the police officer who had reasonable and probable grounds to arrest. It is much safer to report suspicious activities to the police and let them decide whether an arrest is reasonably justified than to attempt a citizen's arrest. False complaints can attract liability for **malicious prosecution** if there is no honest belief that a crime was committed. The elements of malicious prosecution are (1) unsuccessful charges against the plaintiff (2) initiated by the defendant (3) without reasonable and probable grounds, and (4) with malice or other improper purpose.[16]

false arrest causing a person to be arrested without reasonable cause

malicious prosecution causing a person to be prosecuted for a crime without an honest belief that the crime was committed

Defamation

The two **defamation** torts are **libel** (written defamation) and **slander** (spoken defamation). In both, torts involve making a false or insulting statement that causes injury to the private, professional, or business reputation of another person. In defamation cases, the courts will not award damages unless the plaintiff can demonstrate that the defendant's remarks, taken as a whole, would discredit the plaintiff's reputation in the mind of an ordinary person. Over exaggerations, generalizations, or unbelievable remarks will be less likely to cause injury as the ordinary person would not be influenced by them.[17] Defamation torts require publication—that is, communication of the offending (written or oral) statement to someone other than the person defamed. This can be done electronically on websites or by some hyperlinking sites that repeat or endorse the linked content.[18]

One defence against defamation is that the alleged defamatory statements are true; the onus is on the defendant to prove the truth of the statements. In some circumstances there is immunity from defamation suits. Words spoken in parliamentary debate, in proceedings in law courts and inquests, and before royal commissions are subject to **absolute privilege**. The aim is to promote candid discussion; as a result, even intentional and malicious falsehoods uttered in Parliament are immune from action in the courts.

In other cases, a **qualified privilege** applies. For example, a person may be asked to disclose information or give an opinion about another person, as in a letter of reference from a former employer. The person supplying the letter would be reluctant to express an honest opinion if he might later have to prove everything he had stated in a court of law. Consequently, the law gives a qualified privilege to anyone giving such information. Provided he gives it in good faith, with an honest belief in its accuracy, he is not liable for defamation even if the statements turn out to be untrue.

Provincial libel and slander legislation[19] give journalists a **"fair comment"** defence when they have researched and offered a reasonable opinion, honestly believing it to be

defamation making an untrue statement that causes injury to the reputation of another person

libel written defamation

slander spoken defamation

absolute privilege complete immunity from liability for defamation

qualified privilege immunity from liability for defamation provided a statement was made in good faith

fair comment publication of a researched and reasonably held opinion that is honestly believed to be true

---

[16] *Miazga v Kevello Estate*, 2009 SCC 51.

[17] *Bon Malhab v Diffusion Métromédia CMR Inc*, 2011 SCC 9.

[18] *Crookes v Multimedia Foundation Inc*, 2011 SCC 47.

[19] *Libel and Slander Act*, RSO 1990 c L-12; *Libel and Slander Act*, RSBC 1996, c 263, *Alberta Defamation Act*, RSA 2000, c D-7.

responsible communication on matters of public interest a statement that is published in the public interest and is done responsibly

true.[20] Another reporting defence, **responsible communication on matters of public interest**, was created by the Supreme Court in 2009 (Case 4.3).[21] It is broader and applies when a matter is of substantial concern to segments of the public and when inclusion of a defamatory statement is important for the fact that it was made, not its truth. Both of these defences are blocked if the reporting is done with malice.[22]

CASE 4.3 Responsible Reporting

A newspaper published an article describing the opposition of local residents to a proposed private golf course development and included the suspicion of one resident that the developer was exercising political influence to obtain the necessary government approvals. The developer was invited to comment on the story before its publication but did not do so. The developer sued in defamation and won at trial. The Supreme Court of Canada ordered a new trial, stating that the defences of fair comment and responsible communication on matters of public interest were applicable and should have been considered at trial.

Even truthful reporting can trigger liability under relatively new intentional torts protecting privacy, such as "intrusion on seclusion" and "public disclosure of private facts."[23] These torts impose liability where there is intentional exposure of private affairs made without lawful justification that causes embarrassment. Invasion of privacy is discussed in Chapter 32.

Other Intentional Torts Related to Business

It is usually the government (not the courts) that sets standards for fair competition. In 2014, the Supreme Court confirmed that "Competition between businesses regularly involves each business taking steps to promote itself at the expense of the other. . . . Far from prohibiting such conduct, the common law seeks to encourage and protect it. The common law recognizes the economic advantages of competition."[24] Therefore, there are only a few "economic" torts targeting competitive business behaviour, and they are narrowly interpreted.

Torts related to carrying on business include unlawful interference with economic relations and inducing breach of contract. Usually if A convinces B to break his contract with C, C will sue B for the breach of contract. However, C may also sue A for the tort of **inducing breach of contract**.[25] As discussed in the next section, this tort is becoming increasingly popular in the employment context, where B may have limited resources as compared to A. C must prove that C and B had a contract and A knew it. A's intentional actions caused B to breach the contract, and this caused C damage.[26]

inducing breach of contract intentionally causing one party to breach her contract with another

unlawful interference with economic relations attempting by threats or other unlawful means to induce one person to discontinue business relations with another

The tort of **unlawful interference with economic relations** also involves three parties. Business A commits an unlawful act against B in order to hurt C's business. B would always have the right to sue A for the unlawful act; this tort also gives C the right to sue. A simple example is if A threatens B with violence if B continues to do

---

[20] *Simpson v Mair*, 2008 SCC 40.

[21] *Grant v Torstar Corp*, 2009 SCC 61 (the facts are discussed in Case 4.3).

[22] *Awan v Levant*, 2016 ONCA 970.

[23] *Jones v Tsige*, 2012 ONCA 32; *Doe 464533 v ND*, 2016 ONSC 54; *Intimate Image Protection Act*, CCSM c I87, s 11.

[24] *AI Enterprises v Bram*, 2014 SCC 12 at paras 29–31 (citing *OBG Ltd v Allan*, [2007] UKHL 21 at para 142).

[25] See e.g. *Ernst & Young v Stuart* (1997), 144 DLR (4th) 328; *Gainers Inc v Pocklington Holdings Inc* (2000), 194 DLR (4th) 109. The conduct may be reviewable under the *Competition Act*, RSC 1985, c C-34; see *Harbord Insurance Services Ltd v Insurance Corp of British Columbia* (1993), 9 BLR (2d) 81.

[26] *Johnson v BFI Canada Inc*, 2010 MBCA 101 at paras 52–54; *Alleslev–Krofchak v Vlacom Limited*, 2010 ONCA 557, leave to SCC denied.

business with C. The elements of this tort are both an intention to interfere with C's business and **unlawful means** used against a third party.²⁷ Originally, the law in this area was mainly concerned with the activities of labour unions, which now fall within the sphere of labour relations legislation. Now, unlawful acts done to influence customers, suppliers, and investors form the basis for many lawsuits.

unlawful means conduct triggering civil liability under common law

CASE 4.4 Unlawful Act of Bribery

The plaintiff corporation was one of the principal suppliers of car seat covers to Canadian Tire. A marketing company retained by one of its competitors bribed an employee of Canadian Tire to switch suppliers, with the result that the plaintiff lost future business. The Supreme Court of Canada held the marketing company liable for unlawful interference with the plaintiff's economic interests.²⁸

A second group of economic torts relates to false advertising in relation to another's products. A person commits the tort of **product defamation** when he intentionally makes false and disparaging statements about the products of another person—for example, a business competitor. A dishonest trader might also try to cash in on an established reputation by passing off his own goods as those of a competitor—for example, by using a similar label or form of packaging. Passing off is considered in Chapter 20. Breaches of copyright and of patent or trademark rights are also forms of tort; they too are dealt with in Chapter 20. Regulatory liability for unfair competition is considered in Chapter 3.

product defamation making false and damaging statements about the products of another person

Ethical Issue Employee Recruitment

Employers recruit skilled and experienced employees using advertisements and recruitment consultants (also known as headhunters). The usual result is an employee quitting her current job to join a new employer. In such cases, has the new employer committed the tort of inducing breach of contract? No—provided the employee gave the current employer proper notice, no tort has been committed. However, liability could attach if the new employer encourages the employee to ignore notice or other contractual obligations.

Recent focus has been on confidentiality obligations. It is common for employers to include confidentiality requirements in employment contracts. If an employee leaves to join a competitor, the former employer may be concerned that the employee will breach the confidentiality agreement. In addition to suing the employee, it is becoming common to sue the competitor for inducing breach of contract.²⁹

An alternative strategy for employers is to agree not to poach executives from each other, invoking a no-hire policy. One such alleged agreement between Google, Apple, and other Silicon Valley giants has triggered a U.S. class action from 64 000 employees, as well as a U.S. government investigation into anti-competitive behaviour.

Questions to Consider

1. How can an employer hire experienced employees without being accused of inducing breach of contract?

2. What are the competing ethical values involved in changing jobs?

Sources: Scott Deveau, "Rivals CP Rail and CN Rail Forge executive poaching accord," *Financial Post*, February 4, 2013; *In Re: High-Tech Employee Anti-Trust Litigation*, U.S. District Court, N. Cal. Case No.: - CV-2509-LHK (Oct. 24, 2013) leave to appeal denied, U.S. Court of Appeal, 9th Cir, Jan. 14, 2014.

---

[27] *AI Enterprises Ltd*, *supra* note 24 at paras 23, 28; *1175777 Ontario Ltd v Magna International Inc* (2001), 200 DLR (4th) 521.

[28] *671122 Ontario Ltd v Sagaz Industries Canada Inc*, 2001 SCC 59. The competitor was held not to be vicariously liable, since the marketing company was an independent contractor.

[29] In 2003, BellSouth and Cingular Wireless sued Sprint for luring vice-chairman Gary Forsee to Sprint. They obtained a temporary injunction blocking Mr. Forsee's move. Ultimately, Mr. Forsee was allowed to join Sprint subject to restrictions on the activities he could undertake; Bloomberg News, "Sprint Is Sued by BellSouth and Cingular" http://www.nytimes.com/2003/02/08/business/sprint-is-sued-by-bellsouth-and-cingular.html.

UNINTENTIONAL TORTS

Unintentional torts involve harm caused by accidental behaviour, not done deliberately or on purpose. The incident happens unexpectedly, by mistake or accident. It follows that the resulting harm is also unintentional.

Negligence

negligence carelessly causing injury to the person or property of another

The most common and popular tort is the unintentional tort of negligence. The concept of **negligence** is quite simple: Anyone who carelessly causes injury to another should compensate the victim for that injury. Negligence is a flexible tort that covers a wide variety of situations.

Elements of Negligence

Four elements must be proven by the plaintiff to succeed in a negligence cause of action.[30] The first element concerns the identity of the plaintiff—should the defendant have been aware of the risk of harm to this victim? The second element relates to the behaviour of the defendant—did the defendant's conduct fall below the appropriate standard of behaviour required in the circumstances? The third and fourth elements involve what harm was suffered and whether the defendant's conduct "caused" the plaintiff's "injury."

> **CHECKLIST**
> ### Elements of a Negligence Action
> To establish negligence, a plaintiff must prove four things (on the balance of probabilities):
> 1. The defendant owed the plaintiff a duty of care.
> 2. The defendant breached the required standard of care.
> 3. The plaintiff suffered injury or damage.
> 4. The defendant's conduct caused the plaintiff's damage.

duty of care a relationship so close that one could reasonably foresee causing harm to the other

1. Duty of Care Plaintiffs must establish that a **duty of care** is owed to them by the defendant. Duty focuses on the relationship between the parties and the likeliness of the plaintiff being hurt. For example, a duty of care is owed by a doctor to a patient or a motor vehicle driver to a pedestrian.

There is no finite list of situations when a duty of care exists. Whether a person owes a duty of care in particular circumstances is determined in two steps.

First, the closeness of the relationship between the plaintiff and defendant is examined to see if it was reasonably foreseeable that the defendant's conduct would cause harm to the plaintiff.[31] The parties must have a direct or connecting link to each other—this is known as proximity. As well, since the defendant cannot be expected to anticipate all the possible consequences of his actions, the duty will arise only where

---

[30] *Mustapha v Culligan*, 2008 SCC 27 at para 3; *Saadati v Moorehead*, 2017 SCC 28 at para 13; *Benavides v Insurance Corporation of British Columbia*, 2017 BCCA 15 at para 17.

[31] *Childs v Desormeaux*, 2006 SCC 18 at para 47; *Hill v Hamilton-Wentworth Regional Police*, 2007 SCC 47 at para 20; *Fullowka v Pinkerton's of Canada*, 2010 SCC 5 at para 18; *Livent v Deloitte & Touche*, 2017 SCC 63.

an ordinary person, sometimes called "the reasonable man," in the defendant's position would have foreseen the risk of harm to the plaintiff or to someone in the plaintiff's position. The key words are **proximity** (meaning "closeness") and **foreseeability** (meaning "predictability").

proximity   closeness

foreseeability   predictability

CASE 4.5   Proximity and Foreseeability of Harm

Two boys, ages 16 and 15, stole a car from Rankin's Garage & Sales; neither boy had a driver's licence. The car was unlocked with the keys in it. The driver had never driven before and earlier that night consumed alcohol that his mother supplied and smoked marijuana. The car crashed in a single vehicle accident. The 15-year-old passenger suffered catastrophic brain damage and sued Rankin's.

The Supreme Court of Canada held that Rankin's did not owe a duty of care to the injured passenger. Although theft was reasonably foreseeable, the risk of personal injury harm caused by unsafe driving was not reasonably foreseeable.

Harm is not reasonably foreseeable just because it is possible; there must be a factual connection to the unsafe driving. Illegality of the conduct does not automatically eliminate a duty of care.[32]

Courts have sometimes held that a duty of care is owed to persons other than the individual who is directly injured. For example, a negligent driver was held to be liable to a parent who suffered severe nervous shock when she saw her child, who was standing nearby, run down and killed.[33] In that case, the court considered the parent's injury to be foreseeable.

The second step considers policy concerns. If both proximity and foreseeability exist, then a duty of care is owed unless there are policy reasons that justify reducing or removing it.

The Supreme Court of Canada summarized the test for duty of care in one sentence: "Whether such a relationship exists depends on foreseeability, moderated by policy concerns."[34] Policy concerns consider the effect that recognizing a duty of care will have on other legal obligations, the legal system, and society generally.[35] Concerns include such things as the increase in lawsuits or the ability to insure against a huge new potential legal risk.

Sometimes a statute imposes duties. Breach of these statutory duties may trigger liability in negligence if people are injured as a result. Courts will hold public bodies liable for the negligent performance of their statutory duties. Municipalities have been held liable to homeowners for issuing building permits for defective designs or for not carrying out proper inspections of construction works.[36] A public body may be liable even where the statute imposes no duty but merely confers a discretionary power on it—for example, to maintain a highway—if it is negligent in the exercise of that power.[37] Government often relies on the second step, relating to policy concern, to argue that a duty should not be imposed on it. The courts will normally not impose liability for core policy positions adopted by a government body,[38] but once a policy decision has been made (for example, to guard against rocks falling onto a highway), the body will be liable if it is negligent in carrying out that policy.

---

[32] *Rankin (Rankin's Garage & Sales) v JJ*, 2018 SCC 19 at paras 2, 26, 40.

[33] *Hinz v Berry*, [1970] 1 All ER 1074. Contrast with *Schlink v Blackburn* (1993), 18 CCLT (2d) 173, where the plaintiff was home in bed when his wife was injured in a motor accident; his nervous shock occurred later when he was told of the accident.

[34] *Mustapha v Culligan of Canada Ltd*, *supra* note 30 at para 4, relying on *Anns v Merton London Borough Council*, [1978] AC 728 (HL).

[35] *Cooper v Hobart*, [2001] 3 SCR 537.

[36] *City of Kamloops v Nielsen*, [1984] 2 SCR 2; *Rothfield v Manolakos* (1989), 63 DLR (4th) 449.

[37] *Rausch v Pickering (City)*, 2013 ONCA 740; but see *House v Baird*, 2017 ONCA 885.

[38] *R v Imperial Tobacco Canada Ltd*, 2011 SCC 42 at paras 90–95.

CASE 4.6(i) Government Agency Owes a Duty of Care

G was injured when an electrical power line came loose and struck her car while she was driving under an overpass on a busy multi-lane controlled-access highway. The public utility company was stringing new wires across the overpass. The Ontario Court of Appeal held that the public utility owed a duty of care to G because "it was reasonably foreseeable that a careless act by the appellant in its work along the overpass above the highway could result in injury to users of the highway and there were no policy considerations to negative or limit the duty."[39]

standard of care the level of care that a person must take in the circumstances

2. Standard of Care

The **standard of care** focuses on the behaviour of the defendant. The defendant's conduct is compared to the level of care that a reasonable person would take in the same circumstances. If the defendant's conduct falls short of that required of the reasonable person in equivalent circumstances, he has breached the standard of care. At trial the plaintiff must establish the standard of care applicable to the circumstances and then produce evidence that the defendant's behaviour fell below that standard.

Every person must take reasonable care to avoid causing foreseeable injury to other persons and his or her property. It is often said that the required level of care is that of the ordinary reasonable person, or "the person on the Yonge Street subway."[40] However, the standard of care necessarily varies according to the type of activity and person involved. The standard expected of a brain surgeon when operating is that of a competent brain surgeon rather than that of the person in the subway.

The risk of harm and cost of eliminating it are considerations in setting the standard—a defendant need not take "all" care, only "reasonable" care.[41] It is not practical to take every possible precaution where the risk of serious damage or injury is small, but where there is danger of a major catastrophe, it would be unreasonable not to take every known precaution.

CASE 4.6(ii) Reasonable Care, Not All Care

In Case 4.6(i), the evidence showed that the electrical wires fell because vandals visited the unattended job site during a lunch break and released the security ropes. G claimed that the public utility company fell below the standard of care by failing to take reasonable steps to secure the wires and the site. The trial judge agreed, but the Court of Appeal held that the company's conduct did not fall below the standard of care. The method of security had been used for years without incident. Vandalism occurred in broad daylight on a frequently travelled road. The workers had never encountered vandalism in their combined 60 years of work experience. Given the unlikely prospect of vandalism during a short daylight absence from the site, the method of security used was sufficient to satisfy the standard of care.[42]

Failure to strictly comply with the Electrical Utilities Safety Association Manual did not amount to a breach of the standard of care in the circumstances.

Normally, when legislation describes the appropriate standard of care for particular activities, it will be considered the lowest acceptable standard of care. For example, the safety standards for the food industry are prescribed by statute, and those standards are frequently a good indication of where a court will set the negligence threshold. In rare cases such as Case 4.6(ii), a breach of a statutory standard does not of itself make the defendant civilly liable to a person injured as a result of the breach.[43]

---

[39] *Garratt et al v Orillia Power Distribution Corporation* (2008), 90 OR (3d) 161 at 171 (although a duty of care was owed, the defendant's behaviour did not fall below the standard of care).

[40] Linden and Feldthusen, *Canadian Tort Law*, *supra* note 2 at 126–7.

[41] *Ediger v Johnston*, 2013 SCC 18 at para 52; *House v Baird*, *supra* note 37 at paras 33, 37.

[42] *Garratt et al v Orillia Power Distribution Corporation*, *supra* note 39 at 174.

[43] *R v Saskatchewan Wheat Pool*, [1983] 1 SCR 205; *El Dali v Panjalingham*, 2013 ONCA 24, leave denied.

3. Damage to the Plaintiff
Damage involves some form of harm or injury to the plaintiff. Damage is always a requirement of tort liability, as compensation for loss is its goal. Harm can take the form of personal injury, including physical or mental injury, property damage to the land or goods of the plaintiff, and sometimes purely economic loss, including loss of value or profit, even worsening losses.[44] It must be real, not hypothetical.

Proof of mental injury does not require diagnosis of a specific psychiatric disorder. Just as with physical injury, assessment of damage is concerned with symptoms and effects rather than labels. To prove mental injury, a plaintiff must only show that the mental, psychological, or cognitive impact is serious and long lasting—it is more than "the ordinary annoyances, anxieties or fears" that come with living in society. Expert evidence from a psychiatrist is helpful but not mandatory.[45]

4. Causation of Damage
Causation focuses on the strength of the connection between the harm suffered and the behaviour of the defendant. The defendant's actions must have "caused" or contributed to the plaintiff's injury. If there is no real and substantial connection between the two, the negligence claim fails.

Causation is established using the "but for" test—the plaintiff must show that "but for" the negligent conduct of the defendant, the injury would not have occurred.[46] No matter how improper a person's conduct might be, he will not be held liable for damage that he did not cause. In a medical negligence case involving a baby born with brain damage, the Supreme Court of Canada found that the slow reaction times of a nurse and doctor fell below the standard of care, but this was not the cause of the damage; even if the need for cesarean birth had been identified earlier, the baby would still have been born with brain damage and so the nurse and doctor were not liable.[47] Evidence of causation considers the facts of the particular case. Statistical generalizations about cause and effect are not conclusive evidence of causation in particular cases.[48]

causation connection between the injury and the breach of the standard of care

When the "but for" test establishes that multiple defendants each caused or contributed to damage to the plaintiff, all will be held liable and damages apportioned between them.[49]

CASE 4.7 Multiple Defendants

A bar owner allowed a customer to drink too much and then threw the customer out to walk home along a country road, where he was hit by a careless motorist. Both the bar owner and the motorist were held to have contributed to the cause of accident and therefore the customer's injury.[50]

---

[44] *Livent v Deloitte*, 2016 ONCA 11.

[45] *Saadati v Moorehead, supra* note 30 at paras 35–38, 40.

[46] *Resurfice Corp v Hanke*, 2007 SCC 7 at paras 18–29; *Clements v Clements*, 2012 SCC 32 at para 8.

[47] *Cojocaru v British Columbia Women's Hospital and Health Centre*, 2013 SCC 30 at paras 110–15. See also *Ediger v Johnston, supra* note 41.

[48] *Benhaim v St Germain*, 2016 SCC 48 at paras 74–78.

[49] See e.g. *Negligence Act*, RSBC 1996, c 333; RSO 1990, c N-1. *Economy Foods & Hardware Ltd v Klassen* (2001), 196 DLR (4th) 413, a fire was caused by the negligence of one defendant but spread, causing additional damage, due to the failure of the second defendant to install an adequate system of sprinklers.

[50] *Menow v Honsberger and Jordan House Ltd*, [1974] SCR 239. See also *Murphy v Little Memphis Cabaret Inc* (1998), 167 DLR (4th) 190; *Renaissance Leisure Group Inc v Frazer* (2004), 242 DLR (4th) 229. By contrast, the Supreme Court of Canada held that a rest.. irant serving alcohol to a group was entitled to assume that a non-drinker would be driving; consequently, it was not responsible for the accident: *Mayfield Investments Ltd v Stewart* (1995), 121 DLR (4th) 222. So far, "social hosts" (for example, at a private party) have not been held liable in the same way as "commercial hosts": see *Childs v Desormeaux, supra* note 31.

Sometimes the involvement of multiple defendants hinders the identification of the precise cause of the damage. In exceptional circumstances, when the "but for" test cannot establish causation for reasons beyond the control of the victim, the court may use a "material contribution to risk" test. This test finds causation when the type of injury suffered is that for which the behaviour of the defendant created an unreasonable risk. Imagine that two hikers carelessly throw rocks into the river, hitting a swimmer; it is unclear which hiker's rock caused the injury. The material contribution (rather than the "but for" test) would allow liability to be assigned to both hikers.[51]

Remoteness of Damage   All damage resulting from the negligent act will not necessarily be compensated. Even when a person is considered to have factually caused the injury, he may not be considered to have legally caused the injury if it is too **remote**. The type of damage must be reasonably foreseeable. Unusual or extreme reactions will be considered too remote.

remote   unrelated or far removed from the conduct

"Reasonably foreseeable" has been defined as a real risk: "one which would occur to the mind of a reasonable man in the position of the defendant . . . which he would not brush aside as far-fetched."[52] A court undertakes an objective assessment of what a reasonable defendant would foresee as likely injury to the average defendant. The damage is considered from the perspective of the "normal" victim—a person of "ordinary fortitude." It is not based on the actual circumstances of the particular plaintiff.

CASE 4.8   Extreme Reactions

A consumer saw a dead fly in a bottle of water as he replaced a canister in his home. The observation was so upsetting that he developed serious mental disorders, including anxiety and phobias. The trial judge found that the mental injuries were caused by the incident and awarded damages of approximately $340 000. The judgment was overturned by the Court of Appeal, and leave to the Supreme Court of Canada was granted. The Supreme Court did not interfere with the trial judge's finding that the mental illness was caused by the incident but found that mental illness was not a reasonably foreseeable type of damage in the circumstances. The average person would not suffer a mental disorder as a result of seeing a fly in a water bottle. This was an extreme reaction by a plaintiff with particular vulnerabilities. The same reaction would not be expected in a person of ordinary fortitude. The plaintiff could not recover because the damage was too remote.[53]

The "reasonable foreseeability test" referred to in Case 4.8 should not be confused with the legal doctrine of "thin skull" or "egg shell" plaintiff, which requires a defendant to take the victim as he or she finds him:

> The law of negligence . . . draws the line for compensability of damage, not at perfection, but at reasonable foreseeability. Once a plaintiff establishes the foreseeability that a mental injury would occur in a person of ordinary fortitude . . . the defendant must take the plaintiff as it finds him for the purpose of [quantifying] damages.[54]

The thin skull doctrine allows the injured plaintiff to recover all of her damages even though they may be much greater than an ordinary plaintiff would have suffered. If the type of damage is considered reasonably foreseeable, the court will compensate the victim for her actual damage. When a teenager negligently started his father's snowmobile, which escaped from his control, crossed a schoolyard, and collided with a gas pipe just outside the school causing gas to escape into the school and explode, he was held liable for all the resulting damage. The damage was considered to be of a

---

[51] *Resurfice Corp, supra* note 46 at para 27; *Clements, supra* note 46 at paras 14–18.
[52] *Overseas Tankship (UK) Ltd v Miller Steamship Co Pty Ltd (The Wagon Mound No. 2)*, [1967] AC 617, 643; *Hughes v Lord Advocate*, [1963] AC 837.
[53] *Mustapha v Culligan, supra*, note 30 at paras 16–18.
[54] *Ibid* at para 16.

general type that might reasonably have been foreseen even if the actual extent of the damage was unusually high.[55]

Defences to Negligence: The Plaintiff's Own Conduct

A defendant may dispute all of the plaintiff's evidence on duty of care, breach of the standard of care, damage, and causation. In addition, defendants may allege that the plaintiff's own conduct or that of another defendant provides a partial or full defence to negligence. The courts at one time took a rather narrow and mechanical approach to this issue. If the defendant could establish that the plaintiff contributed in any way to her own loss, the plaintiff would fail, even if the defendant was mainly at fault. The harshness of the **contributory negligence** rule was changed by legislation pioneered in Canada.[56] The rule now allows judges and juries to apportion damages according to their opinion of the respective degree of responsibility of all of the parties.

contributory negligence a partial defence to a negligence action when the plaintiff's or another defendant's conduct also contributed to the injury

> **CASE 4.9 Apportioning Liability Among All Parties**
>
> The plaintiff, a passenger in a truck, was injured when the driver lost control on sharp curve in the road. The plaintiff knew the driver had been drinking before he accepted the ride. The judge held the plaintiff 15 percent to blame; the driver 50 percent, for driving too fast and while impaired; and the municipality 35 percent, for not placing a sign warning of the curve.[57]

Courts often find contributory negligence in a passenger's failure to wear a seat belt.[58]

Another partial defence arises after the injury has occurred. Every plaintiff must act quickly and reasonably to repair or heal her injury. Even when the victim is not to blame for the accident itself, her own post-injury conduct may contribute to the extent or seriousness of her original injuries—for example, when a plaintiff refuses to seek medical treatment and worsens her condition. In some cases, the courts have decided that part of the damages were due to the plaintiff's unreasonable conduct and were therefore not recoverable.[59] A plaintiff is expected to act reasonably to minimize, or **mitigate**, any damage suffered. This principle is discussed further, in the context of contract law, in Chapter 13.

mitigate duty to act reasonably and quickly to minimize the extent of damage suffered

Voluntary assumption of risk is a complete defence to a negligence action and is available to a defendant when the plaintiff was aware of the risk of harm prior to undertaking the activity and consented to it. Sometimes the defendant knows damage may occur and advises the plaintiff. We have all seen a "slippery when wet" sign after floors have been washed. If, after being fully advised of the risk or danger associated with the behaviour, the plaintiff continues the behaviour and is injured in the predicted way, the defendant will not be found liable since the plaintiff voluntarily assumed the risk. This is the legal risk management strategy underlying the use of medical consent forms advising patients of the risk of surgery prior to an operation. The challenge is that the exact risk must be described or the defence is not applicable.

voluntary assumption of risk a defence to a negligence action when the plaintiff was aware of the risk and continued with the activity anyway

---

[55] *Hoffer v School Division of Assiniboine South*, [1973] WWR 765 (SCC). The father and the gas company that installed the pipe were also held liable.

[56] Ontario passed the first statute in 1924; *Negligence Act*, RSO 1990, c N-1, s 3.

[57] *Housen v Nikolaisen* (2002), 211 DLR (4th) 577.

[58] A driver of a vehicle may be held negligent for failure to ensure that a child passenger is wearing a seat belt: *Galaske v O'Donnell* (1994), 112 DLR (4th) 109 (SCC); see also *Heller v Martens* (2002), 213 DLR (4th) 124.

[59] See *Janiak v Ippolito* (1985), 16 DLR (4th) 1 (SCC).

The Relevance of Insurance

Often the defendant has insurance that will cover the loss and defend it in the lawsuit. Sometimes the plaintiff has insurance that will cover the loss, too. In the case of property damage, for example, both plaintiff and defendant are normally insured. When a plaintiff recovers first from its own insurance company, the right to claim against the defendant passes to the insurance company. It "stands in the insured person's shoes"—that is, **subrogation**. The company gets the plaintiff's cause of action and may sue the defendant and collect (see Figure 4.2). Similarly, if V recovers her loss, or part of it, by suing T, then to that extent she cannot afterward recover from her own insurance company.

subrogation where one person becomes entitled to the rights and cause of action of another

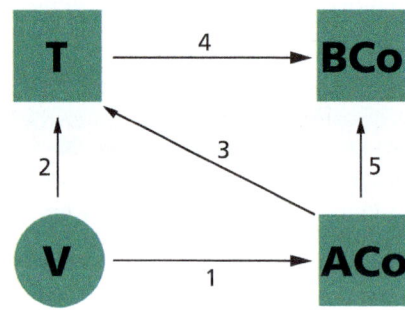

Figure 4.2   Insurance

Victim V is injured in an accident, caused by the negligence of tortfeasor T. V is insured by ACo, and T by BCo. V may claim under her policy with ACo [1], or may sue T [2]. If V claims under her policy, ACo may bring proceedings (in V's name) against T [3]. T could then claim under his policy with BCo [4]. Alternatively, ACo might settle with BCo [5].

In practice, it is normally simpler for V to recover under her insurance policy, leaving the company to decide whether or not to sue T. One reason is that under the policy, V may be entitled to recover the full extent of her loss, even though she might have been partly at fault. If she sued T, the damages might be reduced on account of her own contributory negligence. Another reason is that T might have insufficient funds to pay the claim. If T also has insurance, the two insurance companies may settle the question of payment between themselves, without resorting to expensive litigation. However, just as often, the two insurance companies litigate the action in the names of their insureds.

Product Liability

One of the most important business law torts involves the liability of manufacturers for injury or loss caused by defects in their products: **product liability**. This tort is a form of negligence customized to the manufacturing context. Consider who should bear the loss in each of the following four illustrations.

product liability   a negligence tort imposing liability on manufacturers for harm caused by defective products

---

ILLUSTRATION 4.2   Contaminated Product

X runs a small refreshment booth at a beach and buys his supplies from Y Bottling Co. Ltd. He sells a dark-green bottle of ginger ale to A, who gives it to her friend, B. B drinks half the contents and becomes violently ill. The balance is found to contain a decomposed snail. B is hospitalized and is unable to return to work for several weeks.

> ### ILLUSTRATION 4.3 Defective Parts
>
> P buys a Q Company sports car from Dealer R. On being driven away from the showroom, the car loses a defective front wheel and collides with a parked vehicle, injuring the occupant, S.

> ### ILLUSTRATION 4.4 Detecting the Defect
>
> A Ski Shop sells M thermal underwear manufactured by O Company. The underwear contains a too much of the heating chemical, which when it comes in contact with perspiration causes M to have a severe skin burn.[60]

> ### ILLUSTRATION 4.5 Improper Use of Product
>
> J buys a bottle of cough medicine, manufactured by the K Company, from her local drugstore. She drinks two beers, takes a dose of the medicine, and goes to bed. During the night she has a heart attack. The cough medicine is extremely dangerous if taken with alcohol, but there was no warning on the package.

A buyer of defective goods may always sue the vendor for breach of contract. However, the buyer may not always be the injured user, and the vendor may not be at fault. In Illustration 4.2, X sold the soft drink to A rather than to B, the injured party: There was no contract with B. Similarly, in Illustration 4.3, the injured person, S, has no contractual relationship with Dealer R. In these circumstances, contractual remedies are not available. The tort of product liability fills this gap. Product liability involves (with some modification) the familiar elements of negligence—duty of care, breach of the standard of care, damage and causation.

Duty of Care   Even though the manufacturer does not deal directly with the ultimate consumer or user of its product, that consumer is foreseeable and in fact the target of the manufacturer's business. Therefore, manufacturers owe consumers a duty of care. The famous British case of *Donoghue v Stevenson*,[61] first recognized this duty in a situation similar to Illustration 4.2. Illustration 4.3 is drawn in part from the United States case *MacPherson v Buick Motor Co*,[62] also recognizing a manufacturer's duty to the ultimate user.

In the decades since *Donoghue v Stevenson*, courts continue to recognize this duty to protect consumers and other members of the public. The complexity and sophistication of modern manufactured products makes it increasingly difficult for consumers and distributors to detect dangers in those products and places manufacturers in a position of growing responsibility for the safety of consumers. In Case 4.8, dealing with the fly in the water bottle, the Supreme Court of Canada declared that it is well established that a manufacturer of consumable goods owes a duty of care to the ultimate consumer.[63] Some provinces extend this duty to other businesses involved in distribution chain.[64]

Proving Breach of the Standard of Care   Establishing that manufacturers owe a duty of care to consumers and others who might be injured is only a first step to

---

[60] Based on facts from *Grant v Australian Knitting Mills*, [1936] AC 85.

[61] [1932] AC 562.

[62] 111 NE 1050 (1916).

[63] *Mustapha v Culligan*, *supra* note 30 at para 6.

[64] New Brunswick expanded this duty in the *Consumer Product Warranty and Liability Act*, SNB 1978, c C-18.1, s 27.

imposing liability. Not only must the product be defective, the injured party must also prove (on the balance of probabilities) that the manufacturer fell below the standard of care in its production, inspection, design, or distribution. This can be a challenge.

In product liability cases, the plaintiff may not have direct evidence on the specific defect or how the defect occurred. The product may be destroyed or the process confidential. The law takes these difficulties of proof into account. A plaintiff may initially meet his burden of proof using circumstantial evidence from which manufacturer's negligence can be inferred. Rather than identifying exactly how the manufacturer fell below the standard of care, the plaintiff need only prove that the uncharacteristic malfunction of the product is the most likely cause of his injury and that a substandard manufacturing process is the most likely reason for the malfunction. The existence of a recall notice will help with this inference. The judge or jury will use the **circumstantial evidence principle** to infer that the manufacturer breached the standard of care. Thereafter, it will be up to the defendant manufacturer to show that it was not at fault. It could establish a different reason for the defect such as improper assembly by the user or at least that it took all reasonable precautions to prevent defective goods from reaching the distribution system. The manufacturer will be found liable unless it produces evidence to satisfy the court that, on balance, it was not at fault and met the standard of care when producing the product.[65]

circumstantial evidence principle an initial case of negligence may be established by drawing reasonable inferences from the circumstances surrounding the product manufacture and failure

In Illustration 4.4, the manufacturing company was placed in a dilemma. If the inspection process permitted the defective underwear to pass through undetected, the system was inadequate, and the company was therefore negligent. If the inspection process was virtually foolproof, as the manufacturer claimed, then one of its employees must have been personally at fault, making the manufacturer vicariously liable. The court held that the plaintiff "need not lay his finger on the exact person in all the chain who was responsible or to specify what he did wrong. Negligence is found on a matter of inference from the existence of defects taken in connection with all the known circumstances."[66] Manufacturers who choose to reduce costs by omitting necessary safety features or by adopting quality control processes that are below prevailing industry standards will have difficulty rebutting the inference of negligence. In the long run, the savings in production cost may be outweighed by increased insurance premiums for product liability.

Inherently Dangerous Products

Illustration 4.5 is an example of the expansion of manufacturers' negligence to include properly produced but inherently dangerous products. Even though a product is not defective in any way, harm might be caused if the product is not used appropriately. Courts have ruled that manufacturers owe a duty to consumers to give proper warning of known dangers or dangers they ought to have known.[67] In some industries, government regulations dictate the type of warning that must be given, thereby establishing a standard of care that must be met. In other industries, the appropriateness of the warning will vary depending on the anticipated user group of the product. Consider children's toys as opposed to cleaning products—the appropriate placement, language, size, and symbols of the warning will be very different for these products.

---

[65] *Johansson v General Motors of Canada Ltd*, 2012 NSCA 120; *Benavides*, *supra* note 30 at para 17

[66] *Johansson*, *ibid* at para 81 (citing *Grant*, *supra* note 60 at 101).

[67] *Lambert v Lastoplex Chemical Co Ltd*, [1972] SCR 569 (inflammable lacquer); *Buchan v Ortho Pharmaceutical (Canada) Ltd* (1984), 28 CCLT 233 (Ont HCJ) (side effects of contraceptive pills); *Plas-Tex Canada Ltd v Dow Chemical of Canada Ltd*, 2004 ABCA 309 (defective resin). The duty to warn may be excluded by an express contractual provision; see *Bow Valley Husky (Bermuda) Ltd v Saint John Shipbuilding Ltd* (1997), 153 DLR (4th) 385 (SCC). For an interesting analysis of the duty to warn, see D.W. Boivin, "Factual Causation in the Law of Manufacturer—Failure to Warn" (1998–99) 30 Ottawa L Rev 47.

The **duty to warn** is a continuing one, owed to consumers of the product. If, after a product has been placed on the market, the manufacturer becomes aware of potential dangers in its use, it must issue appropriate warnings to the public.[68] Sometimes, however, the duty may be satisfied by issuing the warning to a "learned intermediary." In *Hollis v Dow Corning Corp*,[69] the Supreme Court of Canada considered that the warning of the dangers of silicone breast implants should have been given to the physicians who would perform the implant operation. Had this been done, a direct warning to the public might not have been necessary.[70] We are all familiar with the warnings associated with prescription drugs, now delivered not only to the dispensing pharmacist but also to the consumer through television advertisements.

A plaintiff whose claim is based on a breach of the duty to warn must show not only that the duty was owed and that the warning was deficient but also that, had a proper warning been given, she would not have used the product or would not have used it in the way she did—that is, the failure to warn influenced her behaviour, which caused the injury.[71] If a user continues in the behaviour after being warned of the risks, he has voluntarily assumed the risk, and the manufacturer will not be liable. A recall notice is a form of warning that, if ignored, may defeat a consumers claim for injury.

duty to warn manufacturer's responsibility to make users aware of the risks associated with the use or misuse of the product

INTERNATIONAL ISSUE
Tobacco Litigation

Tobacco is the most infamous inherently dangerous product of our time. Huge damage awards against U.S. tobacco manufacturers are well known. Individual smokers who have become ill as a result of smoking have received large sums in compensation. For example, a Florida court awarded US $145 billion in punitive damages in a duty-to-warn class action on behalf of 700 000 smokers and former smokers. Two years later, a Los Angeles court awarded US $28 billion in punitive damages to a single plaintiff (though this was reduced on appeal to a mere US $28 million). State governments have also launched proceedings to recover the extra healthcare costs that they have incurred in treating tobacco-related illnesses. A settlement was reached under which the major tobacco companies agreed to pay a group of states a total of US $246 billion over a 25-year period.

Tobacco litigation in Canada is a more recent development. Claims for compensation have been brought both by individuals[72] and in the form of class actions.[73]

Canadian governments have also joined in the action. The federal government brought an action to recover healthcare costs in New York State, presumably in the expectation of obtaining much larger damages than a Canadian court was likely to award. The action was dismissed on a technicality, having cost the government about $13 million in legal fees. Meanwhile, British Columbia passed a statute specifically entitling the government to recover healthcare costs.[74] The first

---

[68] *Nicholson v John Deere Ltd* (1989), 57 DLR (4th) 639.

[69] (1995), 129 DLR (4th) 609.

[70] The physician might then be liable if he operated without explaining the risk to the patient; this is discussed in Chapter 5.

[71] In *Hollis v Dow Corning Corp, supra* note 69, the Supreme Court of Canada preferred a subjective approach to causation in product liability cases; would the plaintiff have used the product if she had known of the risk? See also *Arndt v Smith* (1997), 148 DLR (4th) 48 (SCC), where warning would not have altered conduct.

[72] See *McIntyre Estate v Ontario* (2003), 218 DLR (4th) 193. That case is notable in that the Ontario Court of Appeal permitted the action to be brought on a contingency-fee basis.

[73] *Caputo v Imperial Tobacco Limited* (2004), 236 DLR (4th) 348. The action was dismissed for failure to establish an identifiable class.

[74] *Tobacco Damages and Health Care Costs Recovery Act*, SBC 1998, c 45.

statute was declared unconstitutional by the B.C. Supreme Court.[75] A replacement statute was promptly enacted[76] and declared constitutional by the Supreme Court of Canada.[77] In the federal government's latest health cost recovery litigation, the Supreme Court of Canada had to decide if the federal government itself could be held liable for failure to warn consumers about the dangers of "light" cigarettes and whether it could be considered a "manufacturer" for its role in developing and promoting light cigarettes. The answer was no.[78]

Questions to Consider

1. Should individual smokers be compensated for smoking-related illnesses? How can one prove the illness was caused by smoking? Are today's smokers responsible for their own misfortunes? Should they be held contributorily negligent?

2. What is the basis for the claims to recover healthcare costs? Should governments that have permitted the sale of cigarettes, knowing the health risks, and that have collected vast amounts of tax on their sale, be entitled to compensation for the costs of providing healthcare?

3. Is it appropriate for a government to enact a statute for the specific purpose of allowing it to bring a claim? Is that a form of retroactive legislation?

(For a historic view of issues relating to tobacco liability, see G. Edinger, "The Tobacco Damages and Health Care Costs Recovery Act" [2001] 35 *Canadian Business Law Journal* 95.)

Occupier's Liability

Another important business law tort evolving from negligence addresses the liability of occupants for injury or loss suffered by visitors to their premises. Again this tort involves the four elements of negligence: duty of care, breach of standard of care, and causation of damage to the plaintiff. However, in the context of "property" negligence, issues arise such as: Who owes a duty? To whom is a duty of care owed? What standard of care must an occupier meet?

occupier's liability a negligence tort imposing liability on occupants of land for harm suffered by visitors to the property

Who Is an Occupier?
Courts created the tort of **occupier's liability** to address negligence of land owners and occupants; subsequently, provincial occupier's liability legislation refined the rules. Occupiers physically or legally control premises. The statutory definitions of premises include land, structures, and ships. As well there can be more than one occupier. Occupiers of municipal sidewalks, for example, include the municipal owner and the adjacent commercial property owner who uses it to display goods or serve customers.[79]

To Whom Is the Duty Owed?
Three different categories or types of visitors exist to whom a duty could be owed—invitees, licensees, and trespasser. Before the legislation, the standard of care owed was different for each type of visitor. The highest duty was owed to an **invitee**—that is, a person permitted by the occupier to enter for business purposes (for example, a shopper). The duty owed by an occupier to an invitee is to take care to prevent injuries from hazards or dangers of which the occupier is aware and also those of which, as a reasonable person, he ought to be aware. By contrast, the duty owed to a **licensee**—any other visitor entering with the express or implied permission of the occupier—was simply to remove concealed dangers of which the occupier had actual knowledge.

invitee a person permitted by an occupier to enter premises for business purposes

licensee a visitor (other than an invitee) who enters premises with the consent of the occupier

---

[75] *JTI-Macdonald Corp v British Columbia* (2000), 184 DLR (4th) 335.

[76] *Tobacco Damages and Health Care Costs Recovery Act*, SBC 2000, c 30. The government of Newfoundland and Labrador has enacted a similar statute: *Tobacco Health Care Costs Recovery Act*, SNL 2001, c T-4.2.

[77] *British Columbia v Imperial Tobacco Canada Ltd*, 2005 SCC 49.

[78] *R v Imperial Tobacco Canada Ltd*, *supra* note 38.

[79] See e.g. *Occupiers' Liability Act*, RSO 1990, c O.2, s 1; *Occupiers' Liability Act*, CCSM c O8, s 1 (includes water); *MacKay v Starbucks Corporation*, 2017 ONCA 350 at paras 10–16. But see *Beheyt v Chrupalo* (2004), 244 DLR (4th) 688, holding an owner is not necessarily the "occupier" for the purposes of the legislation.

Legislation in most Canadian provinces[80] removed the distinction between invitees and licensee so all visitors lawfully on the premises must be kept reasonably safe. The occupier must take care to prevent harm from hazards or dangers that he is aware of or should have been aware of on his land. Not every risk of injury is a danger or hazard—some risks are ordinary demands of everyday life. They do not give rise to liability.

CASE 4.10 Danger or Ordinary Risk?

An escalator at a Sears store stopped working. Signs were placed at the bottom and top of the escalator saying that it was temporarily out of service and an elevator was available nearby. Initially, yellow tape blocked access to the escalator, but it was removed by the next day, when a shopper walked up the stopped escalator, tripped, and fell near the top, breaking her elbow. It was unclear whether the signs were visible, but the shopper did not see any. Sears argued that the stopped escalator was not a danger but an ordinary risk of everyday life for which a warning is superfluous or unnecessary. The shopper knew the escalator was stopped when she climbed it. The Court disagreed; the stopped escalator was not an ordinary risk arising out of the demands of everyday life but a danger for which Sears owed a duty of care. Sears was liable.[81]

A trespasser enters premises unlawfully without an invitation from or the permission of the occupier and is either unknown to the occupier or, if known, would be refused permission. A duty is still owed to a trespasser, but the standard of care that must be met is lower than that for expected visitors. It is minimal—the occupier must not set out deliberately to harm the trespasser or recklessly disregard the possibility that his acts might injure a trespasser. An occupier must not set traps for a trespasser, and warning signs are required.

Occupier's liability legislation has codified the reduced standard of care for trespassers stating that trespassers assume risks. Still, owners of large vacant properties, such as developers, conservation authorities, golf course owners, and municipalities, face big challenges in minimizing occupiers' liability risks, despite provincial legislation intended to reduce the standard of care for rural occupiers.

CASE 4.11 Lower Standard of Care

A kinesiology professor and former Olympic athlete went cross-country skiing in a park owned by the defendant conservation authority. The park was available to residents for recreational use even in the winter. When skiing down a berm onto the lake, she hit a concrete wall and fractured her ankle. The wall was not marked and was hidden by snow and ice. The defendant denied liability based on the provincial legislation's lower standard of care of reckless disregard for safety. The trial court held that the lake was not a trail within the provisions of the *Occupiers' Liability Act*, and the defendant should have warned users about the concrete wall it had installed. The Court of Appeal overturned the judgment, saying that the professor assumed the risk of skiing onto the lake. There was no reckless disregard.[82]

As in most negligence actions, if a visitor continues the activity after being properly warned about hazards or the risks, he will have voluntarily assumed the risk, and the occupier will not be held liable for any resulting damage.

---

[80] E.g. RSA 2000, c O-4, s 5; RSBC 1996, c 337, s 3; CCSM c O-8; SNS 1996, c 27; RSO 1990, c O.2, s 1(a). In Newfoundland and Labrador, much the same result has been achieved through the courts by "restating" the common law to the effect that an occupier now owes a duty to all lawful visitors to take reasonable care: see *Gallant v Roman Catholic Episcopal Corp for Labrador* (2001), 200 DLR (4th) 643.

[81] *Sears Canada Inc v Bartram*, 2004 BCSC 509. See for example *MacKay v Starbucks Corporation*, supra note 79; *House v Baird*, supra note 37.

[82] *Schneider v St Clair Region Conservation Authority* (2008), 89 OR (3d) 150 revs'd 2009 ONCA 640, leave denied. See also *Waldick v Malcolm*, [1991] 2 SCR 456, where court held risk not willingly assumed.

> ## CHECKLIST
> ### Negligence Torts
>
> Elements to prove basic negligence:
>
> 1. A duty of care is owed.
> 2. The applicable standard of care is breached.
> 3. The plaintiff suffers injury or damage.
> 4. The defendant's conduct caused the damage.
>
> Other types of negligence that have been refined to adapt to common situations:
>
> - product liability for defective products causing injury
> - duty to warn for inherently dangerous products
> - occupier's liability for injuries on land
>
> Defences applicable to negligence actions include
>
> - contributory negligence;
> - voluntary assumption of risk; and
> - failure to mitigate damage.

Remedies

damages a sum of money awarded as compensation for loss or injury

The purpose of the law of torts is to compensate an injured party; therefore, the usual remedy for a tort (intentional or unintentional) is an award of a sum of money, known as **damages**, to compensate for physical and economic losses. Physical losses are the costs of repairing damaged property or treating injured people; economic losses are losses in monetary value such as lost profits or wages. Courts were slow to award damages for only economic loss without some corresponding physical damage, but now this is common.[83] Sometimes courts award damages to cover preventive expenditures.

CASE 4.12 Potential Damage

A land developer hired the defendant construction company to build an apartment building, which was later sold to the plaintiffs. About 10 years later, a section of cladding fell from the ninth floor. Defects in the construction were found, and the plaintiffs had the entire cladding replaced. They successfully sued the defendants for the cost of the repairs.

Although no damage had been suffered, apart from the cladding on the ninth floor, the Supreme Court of Canada held that it was foreseeable that, without the repairs, there was a strong likelihood of physical harm to persons or to property. It was right that the defendants should be liable for the cost of replacing the rest of the cladding. In reaching that conclusion, the court recognized the strong underlying policy justification of providing an incentive to prevent accidents before they happen.[84]

punitive damages damages awarded with the intention of punishing a wrongdoer

The purpose of damages is to restore the plaintiff, so far as is possible, to the position she would have been in if the tort had not been committed. If the victim cannot be returned to her pre-injury position, amounts for loss of enjoyment of life will be awarded. The object of awarding damages is not to punish the wrongdoer, though **punitive damages** may be awarded in extreme cases to show the court's disapproval of intentional conduct, such as assault, libel or malicious prosecution.[85]

---

[83] *Hedley Byrne & Co Ltd v Heller & Partners*, [1964] AC 465.

[84] *Winnipeg Condominium Corp No 36 v Bird Construction Co*, [1995] 1 SCR 85.

[85] *Rollins v Niagara Regional Police Service*, 2016 ONSC 7735.

Setting the amount of an award involves special and general damages. **Special damages** refer to monetary or pecuniary items that have fixed costs and can be more or less accurately calculated—medical bills, the cost of repairing a car, or actual lost wages. **General damages** include less precise, more speculative items, such as future loss of earnings due to disability, and non-pecuniary losses, such as awards for the "pain and suffering" of losing a limb or one's sight. Obviously, it is impossible to put an exact money value on health, happiness, and loss of enjoyment, but courts attempt to do so. Damages for pain, suffering, and loss of enjoyment are awarded for the purpose of providing substitute pleasures to make the life of the injured person more bearable.[86] They have thousands of precedents to guide them.

special damages money to compensate for quantifiable injuries

general damages money to compensate for injuries that cannot be precisely expressed in monetary terms

In rare cases, remedies other than damages may be available. Where a defendant has wrongfully taken the plaintiff's property, the court may order its return or **restitution**. Courts may also grant an **injunction**—that is, order the defendant to refrain from committing further acts of a similar nature under threat of imprisonment for contempt of court. For example, an injunction may restrain the defendant from committing a nuisance or from trespassing on the plaintiff's land. Less frequently, courts grant a **mandatory injunction**, ordering the defendant to take some positive action, such as removing a fence blocking the plaintiff's right-of-way to her property.

restitution an order to restore property wrongfully taken

injunction a court order restraining a person from doing, or continuing to do, a particular act

mandatory injunction an order requiring a person to do a particular act

CASE 4.13 Injunction

Verdun, a former newspaper editor, opposed the merger of two insurance companies. After the merger was complete, Verdun continued to voice criticism about Astley, the former president of one of the insurance companies. Verdun's comments turned personal and were voiced orally at shareholders' meetings of major financial institutions across Ontario and written in letters of complaint. Even after Astley won damages in libel and slander lawsuits, Verdun continued to voice his opinion about Astley and published a book with libelous comments. The court ordered a permanent injunction against Verdun restraining further publication of remarks about Astley, because it was clear that the $650 000 damage award had not ended the defamation. The court also ordered a mandatory injunction, requiring Verdun to remove existing blog postings. When Verdun violated the injunction, he was convicted of contempt of court and sentenced to 90 days' house arrest.[87]

INTERNATIONAL ISSUE

Strict Liability or Negligence?

Jurisdictions around the world take differing approaches to assigning liability for defective and dangerous products. As we have seen, Canadian courts apply modified principles of negligence to determine liability. However, in many states in the United States, and also in the European Union, strict liability applies to manufacturers of consumer goods, eliminating the obligation for the plaintiff to prove that the manufacturer fell below the standard of care. The impact of strict liability is different in the European Union as opposed to the United States because the European Union does not allow contingency fees, applies the loser pays rule, and caps damages at 70 million euros per defect.

Questions to Consider

1. What impact do you think cost rules and damage caps have on product liability litigation?

2. What do you think will happen to the price of the goods if the manufacturer is strictly liable for all damage caused by a product?

Sources: Product Warranty Directive 1999/44/EC; Product Liability Directive 85/374/EEC; European General Product Safety Directive 2001/95/EC; Smith, "The EC Directive on Product Liability: A Comparative Study of its Implementation in the UK, France and West Germany" (1992) *Legal Issues in European Integration 101*; Roger Meiners et al, *The Legal Environment of Business* (Mason: Cengage Learning, 2009) at 169; *Greenman v Yuba Power Products*, 59 Cal 2d 57 (1963).

---

[86] *Milna v Bartsch*, [1985] BC No 2762; *Andrews v Grand & Toy Alberta Ltd*, [1978] 2 SCR 229; *Thornton v Prince George School District No 57*, [1978] 2 SCR 267; and *Arnold v Teno*, [1978] 2 SCR 287.

[87] *Astley v Verdun*, 2011 ONSC 3651; 2013 ONSC 2998; 2013 ONSC 6734.

Strategies to Manage the Legal Risks

The potential tort liability of a business affects every functional area of the business. The business may be vicariously liable for the negligent or even the intentionally wrongful acts of its employees. It may be liable for injuries caused by defects in the products it sells. It may be liable for injuries sustained by visitors to its premises or caused by harmful substances escaping from those premises.

On the other hand, the business might suffer the harm. Its property might be damaged by the negligent act of some other person, or a competitor might unlawfully interfere with its economic interests.

Legal risks of this nature cannot be entirely eliminated, but they can be reduced by following a risk management strategy, as discussed in Chapter 1, in particular by

- increasing business awareness of potential legal risks;
- assessing the size and likelihood of legal risks and obtaining professional legal advice before undertaking new ventures;[88]
- considering all risk management strategies, including avoiding, reducing, and transferring the risk;
- transferring the risk by insuring against damage to one's own property and against liability to others (insurance is considered in more detail in Chapter 16);
- alerting, advising, and warning potential users of identified risks so they may be considered to assume them; and
- implementing internal quality control practices within the organization consistent with prevailing industry standards.

QUESTIONS FOR REVIEW

1. What is the origin of the word "tort," and what does it mean?
2. What is the principal purpose of tort law?
3. What is meant by "strict liability"? Should liability ever be "strict"?
4. Who should bear the loss resulting from an automobile accident? What are the alternatives?
5. What is the main justification for the principle of vicarious liability?
6. What must a plaintiff prove in order to succeed in a negligence action?
7. How do the courts determine the appropriate standard of care to be expected of a defendant?
8. Is the "but for" test an appropriate way of determining causation?
9. What is meant by "economic loss"?
10. Should an injured party be able to recover damages despite the fact that her own conduct was negligent and contributed to the injury?
11. Is it relevant in a tort action that the injured party has taken out insurance against the loss sustained?
12. When is a manufacturer under a duty to warn?
13. What is the test in most Canadian provinces for establishing the liability of occupiers for injury to lawful visitors? Are trespassers treated differently?

---

[88] Failure to obtain legal advice may even amount to contributory negligence in some circumstances: see *M Tucci Construction Ltd v Lockwood*, [2000] OJ No 3192.

14. What is the difference between a public and a private nuisance?
15. What constitutes false imprisonment?
16. Distinguish between libel and slander. What is meant by "privilege" in the context of defamation?
17. Describe the difference between fair comment and responsible communication on matters of public interest.
18. What are the requirements for establishing that the tort of unlawful interference with economic interests has been committed?
19. What are "punitive damages"? Should they be awarded in tort actions?
20. What is an injunction?

CASES AND PROBLEMS

1. Continuing Scenario

    Ashley is preparing to open her restaurant and interviewing potential staff at her rented restaurant location. Ashley's landlord, ABC Ltd., has allowed her into the premises before the start of the lease so that she can complete some improvements. Gerald is a tiling contractor whom Ashley has hired to put down a porcelain tile floor, and he has unpacked his tools—including a tile saw—in the middle of the dining room area. When Ashley completes her interview with Shelley, an applicant for the position of hostess, Shelley turns to leave and trips over the tile saw, cutting her leg. Shelley does not want Ashley to know so she does not complain. She does not go to the hospital until three days later after she hears that she did not get the job. The cut is so deep that it requires stitches to close, and the doctor tells Shelley that she should have come to the hospital immediately. Now it will leave a permanent scar.

    What are Shelley's causes of action? Against whom? Explain your reasons. Would it have made a difference if Ashley's lease had already started? Why or why not?

2. Sullivan and his friend Williams were having a quiet drink together one evening in the Tennessee Tavern when they got into an argument with four men at the next table, who had obviously had a fair amount to drink and were looking for a fight. There was a brief scuffle when one of the four men attacked Sullivan. The scuffle was broken up by two members of the tavern staff.

    The tavern owner had the four men ejected by the back door of the tavern. He then told Sullivan and Williams to leave by the front door. They did so, only to be confronted by the four, who viciously attacked them, causing serious injury to Sullivan. Sullivan brought an action against the owner of the tavern, alleging that he was partly responsible for causing the injuries.

    Should Sullivan succeed?

3. Smiley, a buyer for Carrefour Fashions, entered the store of a rival firm, Boulevard Boutique, in order to find out what were the latest lines they were carrying. He was recognized by Maldini, the manager of Boulevard. Maldini called the store detective, Rocco, and ordered him to "keep an eye" on Smiley while he (Maldini) called the police.

    Maldini called the police, informing them that he had a "suspected shoplifter" on the premises. Smiley did not attempt to leave before the police arrived, assuming that Rocco would prevent him if he tried to do so.

    Smiley accompanied the police officers to the police station, where they accepted his explanation for why he was in the store and released him.

    What claim might Smiley have against Boulevard, Maldini, or Rocco? Does Boulevard have any cause of action against Smiley?

4. Prentice, an encyclopedia salesman, telephoned Hall and arranged to visit her at her apartment to show her his firm's latest volumes. When he entered the apartment building, owned by Newman, Prentice found the staircase lighting was out of order. He attempted to climb the stairs in the dark and fell on a loose step, breaking his leg. Hall knew of the faulty light and the loose step but had not thought to warn Prentice. No one had told Newman of either defect.

    What claim does Prentice have against either Hall or Newman?

5. Princess Properties Inc. is the owner of a large office building constructed in the 1930s. Renovations were carried out by Fundamental Construction Ltd. in 1975, during which fireproofing material, containing asbestos, was installed. Princess did not know that the material contained asbestos and had relied on Fundamental to select appropriate insulating material.

    In the course of further renovations in 1987, the existence of the asbestos material was discovered. Princess had it removed because it was considered a health hazard.

    Princess brought an action for the cost of removing the material and for lost rent against

    (a) Fundamental Construction Ltd;

    (b) the architects, who had specified the use of the material in 1975; and

    (c) the manufacturers of the material.

    On what basis might Princess have a valid claim against each of these defendants, and what are the principal issues that would have to be determined at trial?

6. Taylor had a student loan that was in arrears. Collection of the loan had been transferred from the original lender to Kneecap Collections Inc., a collection agency. When Kneecap demanded payment, Taylor questioned the amount that was being claimed, which was substantially larger than the amount of the original loan. Kneecap did not provide any explanation and made a further demand for immediate payment. Taylor replied that he would not pay unless he received a satisfactory explanation.

    Kneecap's goons then started a campaign of harassment. They made violent threats to Taylor and repeatedly telephoned his employer, making various false statements about Taylor. They told his employer that Taylor had defrauded them, that he had a court order against them, and that he was secretly working part-time for a competitor firm. As a result, even though Taylor denied all of these allegations, he was fired by his employer.

    What remedies might Taylor have against Kneecap?

7. Brown is a farmer who raises chickens on a large scale. The baby chicks require a continuous supply of oxygen to survive, and the necessary equipment for that purpose is connected to the electric power supplied to the farm. Brown installed an auxiliary battery-operated power generator in the barn to be available as an emergency backup. He also had a battery-operated power failure detector installed in his bedroom so that if the power in the farmhouse failed, a warning signal would alert him to the danger of loss of power to his operation.

    Chauncey is a driver for Gardiner Transport Ltd. While driving the company's tractor-trailer, Chauncey allowed the vehicle to wander onto the shoulder of the road where it struck overhead wires. As a result, electric power service in the area was interrupted for a period of five hours. The interruption extinguished the supply of oxygen to Brown's barn, and several thousand chickens died. Unfortunately, Brown had failed to replace the battery in the alarm detector in his bedroom, and so, on the one occasion he needed it, it did not work.

    Brown brought an action for damages of $30 000 against both Chauncey and Gardiner Transport Ltd. to compensate him for the loss of his chickens. At the trial, a witness estimated that about 50 percent of chicken breeders use power failure detectors.

    Discuss the merits of Brown's case. Explain with reasons what the court's decision would probably be.

Chapter 5
Professional Liability: The Legal Challenges

- **PROFESSIONAL LIABILITY: THE LEGAL CHALLENGES**
- **LIABILITY OF PROFESSIONALS**
- **TORT LIABILITY FOR INACCURATE STATEMENTS**
- **PROVING NEGLIGENT MISREPRESENTATION**
- **THE ROLE OF PROFESSIONAL ORGANIZATIONS**
- **MULTI-DISCIPLINARY PARTNERSHIPS**
- **STRATEGIES TO MANAGE THE LEGAL RISKS**

This chapter describes the different ways that legal liability is imposed on professionals: contract, fiduciary duty, tort, and statute. It emphasizes how tort law affects professionals—such as accountants, architects, doctors, engineers, and lawyers—but the principles apply to any expert giving advice.

In this chapter we examine such questions as:

- What are the special duties owed by professionals to their clients and others?
- How do the obligations differ when they derive from contract? A fiduciary relationship? Tort law?
- When are professionals in fiduciary relationships?
- How does a plaintiff prove negligent misrepresentation?
- How do professional organizations influence standards for professional conduct?
- What extra legal challenges are presented when different professionals practise together in one firm?

PROFESSIONAL LIABILITY: THE CHALLENGE

Professional services are one of the fastest-growing and most important sectors of the economy, but there is a significant risk of economic harm from negligent or fraudulent conduct by professionals.

The term "professional" describes people who have specialized knowledge and skills that are relied upon by clients and others. Usually professionals belong to professional organizations and are licensed by those bodies to offer services to the public. Professionals assist clients in making good and well-founded business decisions. The use of professional services reduces but does not eliminate business risk. When a client seeks and relies on professional advice that turns out to be wrong, a question arises: Should the professional be liable for the economic loss suffered by the client or someone else who acts on the incorrect advice?

Several causes of action are available to hold professionals responsible for incompetence or incorrect advice. A professional may be found liable for breach of contract if there is a contract with the victim. Liability may also be imposed by tort law or statute. Finally, sometimes the professional must honour "fiduciary" responsibilities separate from any tort or contractual obligations. The causes of action discussed in this chapter are not restricted only to professionals, but they are the major legal risk for professionals.

It can be challenging to determine when liability for professional incompetence should be imposed. Some favour wide liability of professionals to encourage careful behaviour and because they can cover any damages by increasing fees and purchasing insurance protection. However, if courts award damages to compensate everyone who relies on incorrect advice, the increased costs will likely discourage people from entering the profession and increase the price of advice beyond reach. A proper balance must be found.

In most professions, liability insurance is a mandatory part of the licensing requirements. Insurance premiums rise when there is uncertainty concerning liability or high damage awards. Professional fees, in turn, increase to cover insurance costs. As fees rise, clients expect more for their money and, if disappointed, are more likely to sue. This is the "vicious circle" that presents a challenge for the courts.[1]

LIABILITY OF PROFESSIONALS

Liability arises from three relationships, generating multiple causes of action:

- The contractual relationship generates a breach of contract cause of action.
- The fiduciary relationship generates a breach of fiduciary duty.
- The tort of negligent misrepresentation is available when a tort duty of care is owed.

In most cases, the professional stands in a contractual relationship with a client. A professional in a position of authority may be in a special relationship of loyalty, giving rise to a fiduciary duty. Sometimes a statute imposes liability. As well, professionals, like anyone else, owe a duty of care to persons who may foreseeably be injured by their negligence.

Contracts

An agreement to provide professional services to a client contains a promise, whether stated expressly or not, to perform those services competently. A breach of that

---

[1] See B.R. Cheffins, "Auditors' Liability in the House of Lords: A Signal Canadian Courts Should Follow" (1991) 18 CBLJ 118 at 125–7; quoted with approval by LaForest, J., *Hercules Managements Ltd v Ernst & Young* (1997), 146 DLR (4th) 577 at 593.

promise is a breach of the contract, and the client may then sue for damages. The next part of this text is devoted to the law of contracts, and subsequent chapters will discuss liability for breach of a contractual promise, including a promise to perform with due care. When no contract exists between the professional and the injured party, fiduciary liability and tort liability are the alternatives.

Fiduciary Duty

Sometimes a professional's duty extends beyond the terms of the contract. When a person is in a "special" vulnerable relationship with a professional, the law imposes a **fiduciary duty** on that professional.[2] This fiduciary duty can arise even when the professional provides services free of charge or no contract exists.

fiduciary duty a duty imposed on a person who stands in a special relation of trust and loyalty to another

The first step to imposing liability for breach of fiduciary duty is establishing that the relationship is a fiduciary one. In *Alberta v Elder Advocates of Alberta Society*,[3] the Supreme Court of Canada identified three characteristics of fiduciary relationships:

- The fiduciary (often a professional) undertakes to act in the best interests of the beneficiary (often the client).
- The beneficiary is vulnerable to or at the mercy of the fiduciary's control or discretion.
- A legal or practical interest of the beneficiary could be harmed by the fiduciary's exercise of discretion or control.

Some statutes designate specific positions as fiduciary—trustees and corporate directors are examples. Some professional relationships are obviously fiduciary, such as lawyer–client and doctor–patient.[4] But not every professional relationship is automatically a fiduciary one, and these must be evaluated using the above criteria. For example, the broker and client relationship depends on the particular facts of the case. Vulnerability is only one factor applicable to the assessment of the fiduciary nature of a financial advisor—others are client relationship, trust, reliance, discretion, and the standards expressed in a professional code of conduct.[5]

CASE 5.1 Fiduciary Relationship

The Hunts, a retired couple in their 70s, set up an investment account with Mr. Schram of TD Evergreen. Mr. Schram considered Mr. Hunt a person of average investment knowledge. The investment account was "non-discretionary"—that is, no trade was to be completed without Mr. Hunt's express authorization.

Schram sold 1349 of the Hunts' 1472 shares in BCE without authorization. By the time Mr. Hunt learned of the sale, the BCE stock price had risen, and the Hunts sued for the lost profit. The Hunts claimed breach of contract and breach of fiduciary duty. The Court of Appeal found that the unauthorized sale amounted to a breach of contract but denied the claim for breach of fiduciary duty because the relationship was not a fiduciary one. It lacked the necessary degree of discretion and control; Schram could not exercise unilateral power over the account. Although there were some health and age issues, vulnerabilities alone did not establish a fiduciary relationship.[6]

---

[2] *Nocton v Lord Ashburton*, [1914] AC 932 at 943–58; *Hedley, Byrne & Co Ltd v Heller & Partners Ltd*, [1964] AC 465 at 486.

[3] 2011 SCC 24 at para 36.

[4] *Lac Minerals Ltd v International Corona Resources Ltd*, [1989] 2 SCR 574 (describing these as per se fiduciary relationships).

[5] *Hodgkinson v Simms*, [1994] 3 SCR 377.

[6] *Hunt v TD Securities Inc* (2003), 229 DLR (4th) 609 (OCA).

If a fiduciary relationship exists, the law imposes additional obligations on the professional beyond those expressly stated in the contract or required under tort law. The professional must:

- act honestly, in good faith, and only in the best interests of the client;
- avoid all conflicts of interest; and
- account for all property held or administered on behalf of that beneficiary.[7]

The second step to imposing fiduciary liability involves determining if the professional's behaviour breaches the fiduciary's obligations. For example, a lawyer who entered into a business arrangement with a long-standing client, without disclosing his own precarious financial situation, was held to be in breach of his fiduciary duty to the client.[8] Liability for breach of fiduciary duty may arise without any negligence.

CASE 5.2 Breach of Obligations

Hodgkinson retained Simms, a tax accountant, to give him tax-wise investment advice. On Simms's advice, Hodgkinson invested in a number of multiple unit residential buildings (MURBs) as tax shelters and lost heavily when the value of the MURBs fell during a decline in the real estate market. The advice was perfectly sound at the time it was given, but Hodgkinson would not have followed it if he had known that Simms was also acting for the developers of the MURBs. The Supreme Court held that Simms was in a conflict of interest that breached his fiduciary duty to Hodgkinson and was liable for Hodgkinson's loss.[9]

conflict of interest a duty is owed to a client whose interests conflict with the interests of the professional, another client, or another person to whom a duty is owed

As Case 5.2 illustrates, a fiduciary should not place herself in a **conflict of interest** and must not profit, or attempt to profit, at the client's expense. A fiduciary obligation requires complete loyalty to the other party in the relationship. Consequently, a professional who acts on behalf of two or more clients who have competing interests (for example, the vendor and the purchaser of a piece of property) could find it impossible to fulfill her duty to them both.[10]

CASE 5.3 No Actual Conflict

A bookkeeper employed by a law firm voluntarily lent money to the financially struggling firm without being asked to do so. Separate and apart from the loan and as part of her employment contract, the bookkeeper received free legal services for the preparation of her will. When the firm was unable to repay the loan, the bookkeeper sued for breach of contract, negligence, and breach of fiduciary duty. The Supreme Court of Canada held that although solicitor–client relationships are inherently fiduciary, the loan transaction fell outside the scope of that relationship. Not all lawyers' duties toward clients are fiduciary. As well, there was no actual conflict of interest between the firm's duties to her in connection with the will and the loan. The breach of fiduciary duty claim failed.[11]

---

[7] *Manitoba Metis Federation Inc v Canada (Attorney General)*, 2013 SCC 14 at para 47.

[8] *Korz v St. Pierre* (1987), 61 OR (2d) 609; *Strother v 3464920 Canada Inc*, [2007] 2 SCR 177.

[9] *Hodgkinson v Simms*, supra note 5. See also *Martin v Goldfarb* (1998), 163 DLR (4th) 639 and *Strother*, supra note 8. See also *Eastern Power Ltd v Ontario Electric Financial Corporation*, 2010 ONCA 467.

[10] *Chapters Inc v Davies, Ward & Beck LLP*, [2000] OJ No 4973, aff'd [2001] OJ No 206 (the Ontario Court of Appeal prohibited a law firm, one of whose lawyers had represented two bookstores in an amalgamation five years earlier, from acting for a prospective purchaser of the amalgamated company because the confidential information acquired in the earlier transaction meant there would be a conflict between the firm's duty to its previous clients, which prohibited disclosure of the information, and its duty the new client).

[11] *Galambos v Perez*, 2009 SCC 48, [2009] 2 SCR 678.

> ### Ethical Issue Auditor Conflict of Interest
>
> Before their demise, Enron was the seventh largest public corporation in the United States, and Arthur Anderson LLP was one of the big five accounting firms, employing 85 000. The energy giant's collapse into bankruptcy cost investors billions of dollars, left the accounting firm a mere shell of its former self, and exposed massive fraud by management, consultants, and auditors.
>
> The Enron affair highlighted the many conflicts of interest that arise when a corporation's external auditors also act as its accountants, business advisers, or management consultants. In theory, a corporation's auditors are appointed by its shareholders; their task is to objectively review the financial management of the corporation's affairs and to report any irregularities to the shareholders. In reality, the auditors are usually selected by the management, and the shareholder appointment is a formality. They consequently owe their position to the very people they are meant to supervise, an obvious conflict of interest.
>
> A second conflict of interest arises when the auditors are themselves members of a firm that also has contracts to supply accounting and management services to the audited corporation. If auditors judge the directors too harshly, they jeopardize those contracts and risk an important source of income for their firm. This was Arthur Andersen's situation.
>
> To address these conflicts of interest and other governance problems, the United States passed the *Sarbanes–Oxley Act* of 2002 (SOX), which
>
> - prohibits a company from hiring the same accounting firm to provide both auditing and consulting services, and
> - places auditor selection under the control of independent directors who do not work at the company.
>
> The application of SOX is not limited to American companies—it applies to foreign companies trading on an American exchange. As we will discuss in Chapters 26 and 27, Canada immediately felt the impact of SOX and adopted many of the SOX provisions.
>
> **Questions to Consider**
>
> 1. Are there other possible solutions to minimize conflicts of interest?
> 2. Is it appropriate for American legislation to apply to Canadian corporations?
> 3. Accountants have always been under a duty to avoid conflicts of interest. Why was this existing duty not sufficient to prevent the auditor/consultant conflict?
>
> Sources: L. McCallum and P. Puri, *Canadian Companies' Guide to Sarbanes-Oxley Act* (Markham: LexisNexis Butterworth, 2004); *Chicago Tribune*, The fall of Andersen, Sept 1, 2002, http://www.chicagotribune.com/news/chi-0209010315sep01-story.html.

Tort Liability

When a professional deliberately or carelessly causes damage to a client, the client may sue in contract or in tort.[12] In a case where a solicitor was negligent in arranging a mortgage that was later found to be invalid, the Court held that the client was entitled to sue for breach of contract or tort.[13] A contractual relationship does not exclude a negligence duty of care—it coexists with and independently of the promises in the contract.[14]

> ### CASE 5.4 Contract and Tort
>
> A government investigation of a credit union revealed many irregularities, including various unauthorized and unsecured loans. The credit union brought a negligence action against its former auditors, claiming that they ought to have discovered the irregularities if the audits had been conducted properly.
>
> The auditors were negligent and were held liable for the credit union's losses. Auditors must perform the contract services in compliance with the standards of the profession. However, the credit union was contributorily negligent, in failing to properly supervise its loan manager, and was 30 percent to blame.[15]

---

[12] *Queen v Cognos Inc*, [1993] 1 SCR 87.

[13] *Central Trust Co v Rafuse* (1986), 31 DLR (4th) 481.

[14] *Oz Optics Ltd, v Timbercon, Inc*, [2010] OJ No 1963 at para 86, varied on appeal 2011 ONCA 714.

[15] *Capital Community Credit Union Ltd v BDO Dunwoody*, [2001] OJ No 4249.

The more difficult challenge is non-clients. Tort liability expands the range of possible plaintiffs beyond clients who have paid for the advice. "Other" people rely on a professional opinion given to a single client or to the public at large, as, for example, when:

- an auditor expresses an opinion on the fairness and accuracy of the client firm's financial statements, which is given to lenders, potential investors, shareholders, etc.
- engineers or architects recommend design specifications for structures that, if faulty, may present risks to occupiers and visitors
- bankers or credit analysts give assessments of creditworthiness for their customers that come to the attention of other lenders
- accountants provide a corporation with a valuation of the business or its shares, and the valuation is intended for the use by purchasers and lenders
- a doctor gives a professional opinion to another doctor concerning the second doctor's patient

third-party liability liability to some other person who stands outside a contractual relationship

These "others" are known as third parties, and any liability to them is referred to as **third-party liability**. Third-party liability is common for accountants, real estate agents, and insurance agents. A real estate agent contracts with the vendor of the property; an insurance agent usually contracts with the insurance company for which she arranges insurance.[16]

In the course of their work, however, these agents work closely with "other" persons—applicants for insurance and prospective purchasers of houses. Although the commissions are paid by the insurance companies and property vendors, the "other" persons with whom these agents deal frequently rely on their advice. (See Figure 5.1.)

This creates the very difficult question of where, precisely, to draw the line in deciding when a professional owes a duty of care to "other" persons, not clients, for negligent or inaccurate advice.

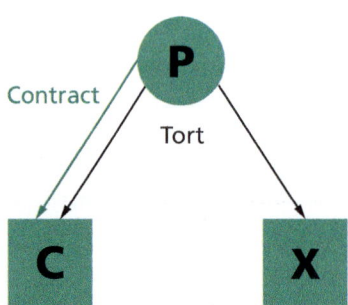

Figure 5.1 Contractual and Tort Liability

The professional P owes both a contractual duty and a duty in tort to client C. The only duty owed to a third party X is a duty in tort. (There may be occasions when a fiduciary duty is owed to C or to X.)

Statutory Liability

Provincial legislation sometimes creates a statutory cause of action for damages arising from misrepresentations. Real estate agents are subject to statutory duties.[17]

---

[16] By contrast, an insurance broker usually acts as agent for the insured: see the discussion in *Adams-Eden Furniture Ltd v Kansa General Insurance Co* (1996), 141 DLR (4th) 288, and see Chapter 16.

[17] *Sharbern Holdings Inc v Vancouver Airport Centre Ltd*, 2011 SCC 23, considering B.C. real estate legislation.

Securities legislation imposes liability on directors, officers, lawyers, actuaries, and other advisors of publicly traded companies for misrepresentations contained in financial documentation, as well as other documents, including press releases and prospectuses. This legislation widely defines the eligible plaintiffs as anyone completing a trade while the misrepresentation remains uncorrected without any obligation to prove they knew of or relied on the misstatement.[18] There is no concern over high damage awards because the statutory cause of action imposes a cap on damages.[19]

Choosing a Cause of Action

Sometimes a professional may be liable in tort but not in contract, or may be liable for breach of fiduciary duty without having been negligent. Other times, the professional may be liable in both contract and in tort, and also for breach of the fiduciary duty. A court will not award triple the damages; the plaintiff must choose. Does it matter whether the client sues for breach of contract, breach of fiduciary duty, or negligence?

The choice might be important. The facts or available evidence may fit into one cause of action better than another. The rules governing the time limits for bringing an action might make it advantageous to sue in one or the other.[20] As we saw in Case 5.3, a client's own contributory negligence may be raised as a defence in a tort action. Any term of the contract that excludes or limits liability will be raised as a defence in a contract action.[21] As Case 5.1 also demonstrates, the problem can be avoided by alleging breach of contract, negligence, and breach of fiduciary duty causes of action, in the alternative.[22]

The choice of cause of action might also affect the amount of damages awarded. The principles for determining the amount of damages are not exactly the same in contract as in tort.[23] In the case of breach of fiduciary duty, a defendant may be under a **duty to account** for any profit derived from the breach in addition to or as an alternative to damages. However, courts have said that higher damage awards should not be allowed merely because a claim is characterized as breach of fiduciary duty as opposed to breach of contract or tort.[24]

duty to account the duty of a person who commits a breach of trust to hand over any profits derived from the breach

---

[18] *Securities Act*, RSO 1990, c S-5, ss 130–8.14; RSBC 1996, c 418, ss 131–40; RSA 2000, c S-4, ss 203–11.095. For a discussion of the statutory liability, see *Kerr v Danier Leather Inc*, 2007 SCC 44; *LBP Holdings Ltd v Hycroft Mining Corporation*, 2017 ONSC 6342.

[19] See e.g. Ontario, *ibid.*, s 138.7. See e.g. certified class action brought by stockholders under the Ontario legislation: *Silver v IMAX Corporation et al*, 2009 CanLII 72334, [2012] ONSC 4881; 2013 ONSC 6571 (settled). Statutory and common law misrepresentation causes of action arising from estimates of earnings per share and non-compliance with GAAP standards in 2005 financial statements.

[20] Time limit for causes of action is normally calculated from the moment when the material facts are discovered or when a reasonable person would have discovered them, rather than when the breach occurs, as is the general rule in contract. *Ferrar v Lorenzetti, Wolfe*, 2012 ONCA 851.

[21] *Central Trust Co v Rafuse*, *supra* note 13; *London Drugs Ltd v Kuehne & Nagel International Ltd* (1992), 97 DLR (4th) 261. See also *McDonnell v Richter*, [2010] AJ No 794.

[22] Where the plaintiff sues in both contract and in tort, the defence of contributory negligence can be raised against both claims; see *Crown West Steel Fabricators v Capri Insurance Services Ltd* (2002), 214 DLR (4th) 577, appealed [2003] BCJ No 1076 (only as to costs): contrast *Caners v Eli Lilly Canada Inc* (1996), 134 DLR (4th) 730, where the action was brought only in contract.

[23] See Chapter 4, under the heading "Remedies," and Chapter 13, under the heading "The Measurement of Damages."

[24] Some uncertainty remains: see *Hodgkinson v Simms*, *supra* note 5 *Martin v Goldfarb*, *supra* note 9 at 652; Waddams, "Fiduciary Duties and Equitable Compensation" (1996), 27 Can Bus LJ 466; *Northwest Territories (Commissioner) v Portz*, 27 CCLT (2d) 241, [1996] 3 WWR 94.

TORT LIABILITY FOR INACCURATE STATEMENTS

Fraudulent Misrepresentation

A misrepresentation is an untrue statement. If it is made knowing it is untrue or without an honest belief in its truth, and with the intention to mislead some other person, the misrepresentation is fraudulent and amounts to the intentional tort of **deceit**. A victim who relies reasonably on the statement and suffers a loss may recover from the person who made it. The tort of deceit may also be committed when a person deliberately conceals or withholds information. The elements of deceit are:

deceit an intentional tort imposing liability when damage is caused by a false statement made with the intention of misleading another person

1. a false representation is made by the defendant;
2. the defendant has some level of knowledge of the falseness (actual or recklessness);
3. the false representation causes the plaintiff to act; and
4. the plaintiff's actions result in a loss.[25]

CASE 5.5 Deceit

A bank allowed a customer to invest in a company that owed a substantial debt to the bank. The bank's employees knew that the company was on the verge of insolvency but did not disclose this fact to the customer. The bank committed deceit and was held liable to compensate the customer.[26]

fraudulent misrepresentation
deceit

negligent misrepresentation
an unintentional tort imposing liability when an incorrect statement is made without due care for its accuracy, and injury is caused

Deceit, also known as **fraudulent misrepresentation**, requires at least some knowledge or willful disregard for the falseness of the information. The unintentional tort of **negligent misrepresentation** does not require knowledge of the falseness of the information, only carelessness in its creation.

Negligent Misrepresentation

Negligent misrepresentation is the unintentional tort of negligence modified to accommodate the very common situation where poor advice leads to financial loss. The usual negligence components of duty of care, breach of the standard of care, injury to the plaintiff, and causation of damage apply. However, these components are not an easy fit for the typical negligent misrepresentation scenario of inaccurate advice because information passes so quickly from one person to another, and it is the listener's actions after hearing the advice that give rise to the economic loss. Over time courts adjusted the standard negligence elements to fit the increasingly common scenarios where flawed advice from accountants, bankers, lawyers, and other experts is relied upon.

The first case to recognize negligent misrepresentation was the English case of *Hedley Byrne v Heller & Partners*,[27] which inspired the Canadian tort and still provides a good example of its application and the importance of putting disclaimers on opinions.

When considering whether a duty of care was owed, the court found that although Heller neither dealt with nor even knew the identity of Hedley Byrne, Heller did know

---

[25] *Bruno Appliance and Furniture, Inc v Hryniak*, 2014 SCC 8 at para 20.

[26] *Sugar v Peat Marwick Ltd* (1988), 55 DLR (4th) 230.

[27] *Hedley Byrne v Heller & Partners*, [1964] AC 465.

CASE 5.6 Origin of Negligent Misrepresentation

Easipower asked Hedley Byrne, an advertising agency, to handle its advertising account. Since Hedley Byrne would have to extend credit to Easipower in arranging the advertising, it asked its own bank to obtain credit information on Easipower, and in particular whether Easipower would be "good for" a line of credit. The bank manager made inquiries from Heller & Partners (Easipower's bankers) about Easipower's creditworthiness, without revealing Hedley Byrne's identity, saying only that a customer had inquired. Heller wrote back saying that Easipower would be good for the debt. At no time did Hedley Byrne communicate directly with Heller, but its own bank did inform it of the full contents of the letter, including the disclaimer of responsibility. Hedley Byrne then accepted Easipower as a client and allowed Easipower to run up a large debt. Shortly afterward, Easipower became insolvent and was unable to pay. Hedley Byrne sued Heller for the resulting loss, claiming it was caused by Heller's negligent misrepresentation of Easipower's creditworthiness.

that its information would be used by a customer of the other bank. It therefore owed that customer a duty of care. More investigation should have been taken before expressing an opinion about the financial state of Easipower, so the standard of care was breached. However, the court held that, because the **disclaimer** of responsibility was added, Hedley Byrne could not rely on the information.

disclaimer an express statement to the effect that the person making it takes no responsibility for its accuracy

This case extended liability to a wider group than those with direct contact to the advice giver and introduced the key concept of reliance in addition to causation.

PROVING NEGLIGENT MISREPRESENTATION

The Supreme Court of Canada set the five requirements for proving negligent misrepresentation when it imposed liability for negligent misrepresentations made by an employer during a pre-employment job interview in *Queen v Cognos Ltd*.[28]

CHECKLIST
Elements of Negligent Misrepresentation

The five requirements for proving negligent misrepresentation are

1. there must be a duty of care based on a "special relationship" between the representor and the representee;
2. the representation in question must be untrue, inaccurate, or misleading;
3. the representor must have acted negligently in making the misrepresentation—that is, he or she must have fallen below the standard of care required of a professional making such a representation;
4. the representee must have reasonably relied on the negligent misrepresentation; and
5. the reliance must have been detrimental to the representee, that is, damages resulted.[29]

The Duty of Care—Special Relationship

A duty of care is established in two steps. First, using the criteria of **proximity** and **foreseeability**, the court decides if the particular facts give rise to a duty. If so, the court next decides if there are public policy reasons to negate the duty.[30]

proximity closeness and directness of the relationship of the subject parties

foreseeability reasonableness of the of plaintiff's injury

---

[28] [1993] 1 SCR 87. Test applied in *R v Imperial Tobacco Ltd*, 2011 SCC 42.

[29] *Cognos, ibid* at para 33; see also *Sharbern, supra* note 17 at para 121; *LBP Holdings, surpa* note 18 at para 77.

[30] *Cooper v Hobart*, 2001 SCC 79; *Livent v Deloitte & Touche*, 2017 SCC 63.

Proximity Proximity describes the closeness of the relationship between the plaintiff and defendant, and it is examined before foreseeability Two factors are important:

- the nature of the defendant's undertaking to provide the representation or service, and
- the plaintiff's right or entitlement to rely on the representation in the circumstances.[31]

Foreseeability Foreseeability is about the injury. Was it a reasonably foreseeable consequence of the plaintiff's reliance on the negligent representation? There is some overlap with proximity here in that the purpose of the information is relevant. Still, foreseeability alone could yield almost limitless liability. For example, auditors of a public corporation know the financial statements will be read and relied upon by many groups of people—lenders, investors, proposed purchasers, etc. The Supreme Court of Canada first considered the large number of possible plaintiffs in *Hercules Management Ltd v Ernst & Young*.[32]

CASE 5.7 Duty of Care and Indeterminate Liability

Shareholders in two corporations brought an action against their accountants, alleging that audits of the corporations' financial statements had been negligent, leading to investment losses and losses in the value of their shareholdings. Their claim failed.

The Supreme Court of Canada held that (a) there was no contractual relationship between the auditors of a corporation and its shareholders; (b) the auditors owed shareholders no duty of care in respect of their personal investments.

As to the existence of a duty of care, the court applied the two-part test.[33] First, the court found that the shareholders were foreseeable, but this use of the audit was not within the purpose for which it was provided and would create a huge pool of plaintiffs. In the second branch of the test, the extent of liability was found to be too unpredictable.[34] When the number of plaintiffs or magnitude of their losses are undeterminable, public policy concerns will restrict the duty owed.

Residual Policy Considerations Policy considerations will negate a duty of care when

- the law already provides a remedy,
- a duty creates unlimited liability to an unlimited class or for an unlimited time, or
- other broad policy reasons exist.[35]

In *Hercules* (Case 5.7), there was a legitimate policy concern over indeterminate liability—it would be impossible to anticipate the number of plaintiffs, the value of the risk, or the length of time. This policy concern justified limiting the duty to only those plaintiffs who used the information for the purpose for which it was given. As a matter of law, the only purpose for which shareholders receive an auditor's report is to provide them with information in order to oversee the management and affairs of

---

[31] *Livent*, ibid at paras 24–30.

[32] *Hercules Managements Ltd v Ernst & Young* (1997), 146 DLR (4th) 577.

[33] *Ibid*; Originated in *Anns v Merton London Borough Council*, [1978] AC 728 at 751–2 (HL). Subsequently revised by *Cooper v Hobart*, 2001 SCC 79.

[34] See e.g. *Childs v Desormeaux*, 2006 SCC 18; *Mustapha v Culligan of Canada Ltd*, 2008 SCC 27; *Hill v Hamilton-Wentworth Regional Police Services Board*, 2007 SCC 41.

[35] *Livent*, supra note 30 at para 40; *The Los Angeles Salad Company Inc v Canadian Food Inspection Agency*, 2013 BCCA 34.

the corporation—not for the purpose of guiding their personal investment decisions.[36] The purpose of the representation was critical. Therefore, no duty of care was owed to the shareholder for damage to personal investments. Importantly, the Court stated that auditors owe a duty of care to the audited corporation itself. This finding established auditor client as a recognized category, important for when the Supreme Court considered auditor duty of care again in *Livent v Deloitte & Touche* (Case 5.8).[37]

> **CASE 5.8   Previously Recognized Relationship Categories**
>
> Livent's auditors, Deloitte & Touche, failed to disclose or uncover the fraud being perpetrated by Livent's management during successive annual audits in 1996 and 1997. There were many red flags that Deloitte failed to act upon, and this allowed its audit client, Livent, to go deeper and deeper into debt. When new management discovered the fraud, Livent was forced into receivership. Livent, by its receiver, sued Deloitte for negligent misrepresentation related to the statutory audits.
>
> The Supreme Court of Canada found Deloitte liable for negligent misrepresentation associated with the audits because the auditor–client relationship was recognized in *Hercules* as giving rise to a duty of care, and Livent's use of the audited statements was for the legal purpose of a statutory audit. When the facts of the case fall into a previously recognized category, proximity of the relationship is deemed established, and there is no need to reconsider residual policy considerations. The court need only determine if there is a reason to distinguish this case from the previous one and that the consequences or injury are reasonable.[38] Deloitte was liable for $40 million in losses.

In *Livent*, the Court emphasized that **indeterminate liability** means unclear or unknown not high or undetermined. The goal is not to insulate professionals from high liability. It is to protect them from unknown liability. High liability can be factored into the decision to provide the advice and at what price.

Duty of care for negligent misrepresentation is not restricted to financial information provided by professionals such as accountants and bankers.[39] Salespeople may be held liable for representations made about the products they sell.[40] Municipalities may be liable for losses suffered by purchasers of land who rely on incorrect information from zoning departments.[41] Engineering firms who negligently prepare construction drawings and specifications for land owners could be liable for the builder's losses.[42]

Courts remain cautious about extending the duty of care too far. For example, the British Columbia Court of Appeal held that a government department, which had negligently certified to a leasing corporation that a piece of contaminated land had been fully cleaned, was not liable to an investor who bought shares in the leasing corporation. The relationship between the Crown and the plaintiff was not close enough to establish a duty of care, and even if a duty of care was owed, it would be negated by the policy consideration of indeterminate liability.[43] In 2011, the federal government was held not to owe a duty of care to consumers for statements made about the

indeterminate liability inability to determine the size, time, or possible plaintiffs so that the magnitude of liability cannot be reasonably predicted

---

[36] *Livent*, *supra* note 30 at paras 59–61; consistent with an earlier case where an auditor negligently prepared accounts for a corporation, knowing they were to be shown to a potential purchaser of the corporation: *Haig v Bamford* (1976), 72 DLR (2d) 68.

[37] *Livent*, *supra* note 30.

[38] *Livent*, *supra* note 30 at paras 64–67.

[39] A law firm was held liable for a negligent statement regarding the secured status of a loan: *347671 BC Ltd v Heenan Blaikie*, [2002] BCJ No 347.

[40] *JB Printing Ltd v 829085 Ontario Ltd*, [2003] OJ No 1230, aff'd (2004) 192 OAC 313 (ONCA).

[41] *Bell v City of Sarnia* (1987), 37 DLR (4th) 438; *The Los Angeles Salad Company Inc*, *supra* note 35.

[42] *Edgeworth Constructions Ltd v ND Lea & Associates Ltd* (1993), 107 DLR (4th) 169. Company liable, individual engineers employed by the firm, who prepared the drawings, did not owe a duty to the contractor.

[43] *Border Enterprises Ltd v Beazer East Inc* (2002), 216 DLR (4th) 107.

reduced health risks of mild cigarettes; the relationship was close enough but policy concerns negated it.[44] In another case, there was no liability for safety certification of a defective smoke alarm system. The parties did not have the necessary close and direct relationship to justify imposing a duty of care. Even if a prima facie duty of care did exist, policy considerations would negate the duty, since to do so would effectively create an insurance scheme for dissatisfied purchasers.[45]

Accuracy of the Statement

It is easy to determine the accuracy of a factual statement. If a taxpayer incurs a late payment penalty because his accountant told him the wrong due date for payment of his taxes, the mistake is easily established with proof of the correct date. However, professionals often provide expert opinions, such as "the company is financially sound" or "the stock is a good investment." These opinions or "value judgments" are considered facts when expressed by an expert but are more difficult to prove wrong. The accuracy of the statement is assessed as of the time the information was given; the fact that the statement becomes untrue later does not necessarily establish that it was untrue at the time it was made. This rule does not apply to opinions about the future, such as the "good investment" opinion. This speaks to the future performance of the stock, and therefore future events will establish its truthfulness. Inaccuracy alone is not enough to establish liability. The crucial link in the third element: Why was the advice wrong? Professionals are not required to be perfect. To trigger liability, the inaccuracy must result from the failure of the professional to meet the required standard of care.

CASE 5.9 Inaccuracy Not Enough

Hodgins wished to add an indoor swimming pool to his house. Through his contractor, he sought the advice of the local hydro-electric commission on heating the addition. An employee of the commission gave an estimate of the electric heating cost, and in reliance on the estimate, Hodgins specified electric heating for the extension. The estimate proved to be much below the actual costs. Hodgins sued the hydro-electric commission for negligent misrepresentation. Although the estimate was clearly inaccurate, the employee was found not to have been negligent in its preparation.[46]

The court explicitly rejected a hindsight approach, saying that only information and practices available at the time should be considered to decide if reasonable skill, competence, and diligence were used when preparing the estimate. Experts testified that the heat loss calculations were made the same way other experts in the field would have done at the time. It is not sufficient that the plaintiff establish merely that the estimate was wrong; he must go further and establish that the incorrect estimate resulted from a lack of skill, competence, or diligence on the part of the preparer.[47]

The Standard of Care for Professionals

Professionals must take reasonable care before making a representation. The professional must "exercise such reasonable care as the circumstances require to ensure that the representations made are accurate and not misleading."[48] Professional behaviour should be compared to the reasonable behaviour of other professionals in that same profession when providing the same type of advice.

---

[44] *Imperial Tobacco, supra* note 25.

[45] *Hughes v Sunbeam Corp (Canada) Ltd* (2003), 219 DLR (4th) 467.

[46] *Hodgins v Hydro-Electric Commission of the Township of Nepean* (1975), 60 DLR (3d) 1.

[47] *Ibid* at 4.

[48] *Cognos, supra* note 28 at 121; *Sharbern, supra* note 17 at para 123.

The approach taken in the *Hodgins* case (Case 5.9) was to compare the quality of professional work done or advice given with the prevailing standards of the profession at the time. A professional must exercise the same degree of skill and possess the same level of knowledge as is generally expected of members of that profession.[49] The courts will normally consider multiple sources of evidence in determining what those standards are. Many professions publish a code of conduct for their members or guidelines to be followed in particular types of work. These can usually be taken as setting an appropriate standard. The accounting profession has a statement of generally accepted accounting principles (GAAP), and accountants who fail to comply with GAAP are considered to have fallen below the standard of care. Sometimes legislation sets the steps that must be followed to join or practise the profession—if the expert is not properly qualified but still gives advice, this will fall below the standard of care.

Frequently, the courts also hear the testimony of practitioners who state what they consider to be a proper standard. Sometimes, of course, professional opinion is divided—for example, about the best medical treatment in a particular circumstance. In such a case it will normally be sufficient that the defendant has followed a well-recognized practice, even though some other procedure might arguably have been better.[50]

Sometimes simply complying with normal professional standards is not an adequate defence.[51] Established standards alone should not be allowed to become a means for protecting members of a profession from liability.[52] As pointed out in the Hodgins case, sometimes a professional undertakes a task that is beyond the usual skills of her profession; she cannot then rely on the normal professional standard. The degree of skill and knowledge must be commensurate with the particular task undertaken.

Omissions The standard of reasonable care includes not omitting essential information. Providing partial or incomplete information in response to an inquiry can be negligent misrepresentation where the professional has a duty to the plaintiff to make the disclosure in question.[53]

CASE 5.10 Things Left Unsaid

Fine's Flowers Ltd. experienced a serious loss from frozen flowers and plants in its greenhouse. The freezing conditions were caused by failure of a water pump, which interrupted the supply of water to boilers that heated the greenhouse. Fine's had arranged extensive insurance with the same agent for many years. It relied on the agent to recommend appropriate coverage and paid the necessary premiums without question. The insurance company refused to cover the loss because Fine's policy did not cover the failure of water pumps.

Fine's sued the agent, claiming he owed a duty of care to notify the customer of the insufficient coverage. The agent defended on the grounds that such a duty of care was too broad and sweeping; it was not the standard to know everything about a client's business or to anticipate every conceivable form of loss. The court held that, on the facts of the case, the standard required the agent to warn the policy holder, and Fine's succeeded in recovering damages from the agent. The agent's behaviour was a negligent omission.[54]

---

[49] Inexperience is not relevant: a newly qualified professional is held to the same standard as an experienced one. However, within a profession, a higher standard may apply to a specialist than to a general practitioner.

[50] *Belknap v Meekes* (1989), 64 DLR (4th) 452; *Ter Neuzen v Korn* (1995), 127 DLR (4th) 577; *McLintock v Alidina*, [2010] OJ No 49.

[51] *Hodgins*, *supra* note 46.

[52] See e.g. *Roberge v Bolduc*, [1991] 1 SCR 374.

[53] *Manufacturer's Life Insurance Co v Pitblado & Hoskins*, 2009 MBCA 83 at para 106.

[54] *Fine's Flowers Ltd v General Accident Assurance Co et al* (1974), 49 DLR (3d) 641, aff'd (1977), 81 DLR (3d) 139 (could also be classified as a breach of a special fiduciary relationship between Fine's Flowers and the insurance agent). See also *Martin v Goldfarb*, *supra* note 9, *Fletcher v Manitoba Insurance Co*, [1990] 3 SCR 191, and *CIA Inspection Inc v Dan Lawrie Insurance Brokers*, [2010] OJ No 3313 at paras 7–14.

As noted in Chapter 4, a surgeon who operates on a patient without the patient's consent commits the tort of battery. In this context, "consent" means informed consent. Before operating, the surgeon should explain the procedure and the possible risks to the patient. The modern tendency has been to hold a doctor liable in battery only when it can be said that there has been no genuine informed consent at all. However, the courts have recognized a patient's right to full information about the risks inherent in a treatment, and the omission of relevant information is a breach of the duty to obtain informed consent, possibly also resulting in negligent misrepresentation.[55]

The court also considers a second question: Would a reasonable person in the position of the plaintiff have decided against the procedure upon a proper disclosure of the risks?[56] If the court is satisfied that the answer is yes, then it is also saying that the failure to inform was not only a breach of the standard of care but also caused the harm—and the patient will be awarded damages in compensation. But where the court is satisfied that the patient would still have consented even if the risk had been explained, the physician will not be liable.[57] This is a question of reliance or relevance of the information to the decision of the plaintiff.

Reliance and Detriment

The essence of causation, in the context of negligent misrepresentation and the professional–client relationship, is reliance. Did the client reasonably rely and act upon the advice of the professional? Would the client have acted in that way if he had not received that advice? The advice must be used by the plaintiff to make the decision that triggered the loss, and it must be reasonable for him to do so in the circumstances.

CASE 5.11 Opinion Not a Factor in Decision to Act

An investment company became interested in acquiring control of an apparently prosperous family business. The company commissioned a report on the proposed acquisition from a well-known firm of investment analysts. The report estimated the family business to be worth more than $4 million and considered it to be a sound investment. Without reading the report, the directors of the investment company decided they should move quickly—they had heard rumours that there was another prospective purchaser. They purchased all the shares in the family business for $3.5 million. Afterward, they learned that a major asset of their acquisition was almost worthless and that they had paid much more than the shares were worth.[58] Despite their negligence, the analysts were not found liable since the opinion was not relied upon and therefore did not cause the loss.

reliance acting in a certain way because one believed the information received

The plaintiff's **reliance** on the misrepresentation must be reasonable. Should the information be used in the way that it was? Were other more appropriate sources available for use? Again purpose will be relevant; the professional will argue reliance is only reasonable when done in furtherance of the purpose for which the advice was given.[59]

An interesting issue was raised in *Avco Financial Services Realty Ltd v Norman*.[60] At trial, the defendant finance company was held liable for a negligent misrepresentation

---

[55] Alternatively, it may be treated as a breach of fiduciary duty: see *Seney v Crooks* (1998), 166 DLR (4th) 337.

[56] *Hopp v Lepp* (1980), 112 DLR (3d) 67; *Reibl v Hughes* (1980), 114 DLR (3d) 1.

[57] *Kitchen v McMullen* (1989), 62 DLR (4th) 481.

[58] Case 5.11 is based in part on *Toromont Industrial Holdings v Thorne, Gunn, Helliwell & Christenson* (1977), 14 OR (2d) 87 (some damages were awarded, however, on other grounds). See also *Martin v Goldfarb*, *supra* note 9.

[59] *Livent*, *supra* note 30 at para 86 (rejecting the distinction between advice and information).

[60] (2003), 226 DLR (4th) 175.

for failing to point out to the plaintiff that he would need to renew a life insurance policy if he wished to renew his mortgage; the plaintiff was found contributorily negligent by not inquiring further into the terms of the mortgage. On appeal, it was argued that the two findings were mutually inconsistent. If the plaintiff's reliance on the misrepresentation was reasonable, then he could not have been negligent himself. Alternatively, if he was negligent, his reliance on the statement would not have been reasonable. Court of Appeal rejected both arguments. The two findings could coexist. It could be reasonable to rely on a statement but negligent to rely exclusively upon it.[61]

Finally, a loss must be caused by acting upon the information. As in all torts, there is no liability without a loss. With respect to negligent misrepresentation, **detrimental reliance** means worsening one's situation after acting upon the false information. The loss is often purely economic, that is, financial.

detrimental reliance the worsening of one's situation after acting upon false information

THE ROLE OF PROFESSIONAL ORGANIZATIONS

Responsibilities and Powers

Most major professions—medicine, nursing, dentistry, accounting, law, engineering, and architecture—are governed by professional organizations established under, and to some extent regulated by, provincial statutes. A typical professional organization has a governing council composed mainly of elected representatives of the profession, but it may also have external lay representatives appointed by the government to provide an impartial voice in decision making and to represent the public interest. Professional bodies have a number of special responsibilities:

- to set educational and entrance standards for candidates wishing to become members;
- to examine and accredit educational institutions that prepare candidates for membership;
- to set and adjust standards of ethical conduct and professional competence;
- to hear complaints about and administer discipline to members who fail to live up to the established standards; and
- to defend the profession against attacks that it considers unfair and to look after the general welfare of the profession.

The governing statute typically gives members of the organization the exclusive right to use a professional designation to identify themselves and often also gives members the exclusive right to practise their profession.[62] Anyone who identifies himself as a member or attempts to practise when not accredited as a member may be—and usually is—prosecuted for committing an offence under the provincial statute.

Two important consequences flow from these powers. First, the right to discipline gives the organizations great power over individual members—expulsion or suspension for an extended period might destroy a member's means of livelihood. Second, exclusivity gives these self-governing professions great power over the quality and cost of their services to the public, and there is consequently a strong public interest in the affairs of the organizations.

---

[61] See also M *Tucci Construction Ltd v Lockwood*, [2000] OJ No 3192, aff'd [2002] OJ No 440.

[62] For example, the exclusive right to practise applies to medicine and law but not to some areas of accounting.

CASE 5.12 Not the Purpose of the Association

Schilling entrusted $600 000 to an accountant, Hofman, to invest for him. Hofman absconded with the money. Hofman was a former member of the Association of Certified General Accountants of British Columbia and, having recently been disciplined for other offences, had been forced to resign from the Association and stripped of his accounting designation. Schilling sued the Association, alleging negligence in not preventing Hofman from continuing to practise—as a result of which Hofman had been able to defraud Schilling.

The British Columbia Court of Appeal held that the Association was not liable. There was no duty of care owed to the public requiring the Association to bring a criminal prosecution against a former member or to inform potential clients of his resignation.[63]

The Supreme Court of Canada faced a similar issue in *Cooper v Hobart*.[64] In that case, an investor entrusted funds to a mortgage broker, who dealt with those funds in an unauthorized manner. The investor brought a negligence action claiming damages against the Registrar (appointed by a statute regulating the mortgage-brokering profession). The plaintiff claimed that the broker's licence should have been suspended earlier. The court held that the Registrar owed no duty of care to individual investors. The regulatory scheme required the Registrar to balance a number of competing interests in order to protect the public as a whole. The decision to suspend a broker involved both policy and quasi-judicial elements that were inconsistent with a duty of care to investors. To impose a duty of care in such circumstances would be to create an insurance scheme for investors at the cost of the taxpaying public.[65]

Codes of Conduct

code of conduct a common standard of behaviour that may take the form of a values statement or a prescribed set of rules often used by a professional organization setting out the duties and appropriate standards of behaviour to be observed by its members

Professional bodies pass bylaws and require their members to observe a **code of conduct**. As noted, such codes can be important as evidence of what constitutes an appropriate standard of professional care and can help to determine the extent of the duty owed by members to their clients. Additionally, codes of conduct can impose ethical standards on their members over and above any legal requirements. Normally responsibilities to the public, the profession, other members of the profession, and clients are addressed, sometimes in multiple codes of conduct. Examples of typical codes of conduct can be found on organization websites; for example, the Canadian Association of Management Consultants addresses all these responsibilities in one code available on its website.[66]

CASE 5.13 Standards of Behaviour

The College of Pharmacists of B.C. adopted a bylaw that prohibited pharmacists from participating in loyalty rewards programs. They did so because incentifying the purchase of prescription drugs was not in the public interest. Several grocery stores with pharmacies challenged the bylaw in court and lost. Great deference will be shown to a professional association when setting the appropriate standard of behaviour for its members in furtherance of the public's interest. The rule must only be reasonable.[67]

---

[63] *Schilling v Certified General Accountants Assn of British Columbia* (1996), 135 DLR (4th) 669.

[64] (2001), 206 DLR (4th) 193. See also *Edwards v Law Society of Upper Canada* (2001), 206 DLR (4th) 211, holding a law society not liable for failure to issue a warning that an investigation was being conducted into the handling of a lawyer's trust account.

[65] The governing statute of the professional organization may provide for immunity in respect of acts done in good faith in the performance of a duty or exercise of a power under the statute; see, for example, *Regulated Health Professions Act, 1991*, SO 1991, c 18, s 38, considered in *Rogers v Faught* (2002), 212 DLR (4th) 366.

[66] http://www.cmc-canada.ca.

[67] *Sobeys West Inc v College of Pharmacists of British Columbia*, 2016 BCCA 41.

Discipline

One of the most important responsibilities of professional bodies is to maintain and improve standards. That may involve disciplining members of the profession. Most professions inevitably have a minority of members who act in an unprofessional, unethical, or illegal manner. The usual response of governing bodies is to punish serious cases of unethical conduct by expulsion or suspension. (There may also be provision for some form of compensation to the injured client by the governing body itself.) These actions are quite apart from any criminal prosecution of the wrongdoer or from private (civil) liability actions.

The more pervasive and difficult cases are those arising from alleged breaches of professional standards of skill and care. In what may be considered isolated cases of negligence, governing bodies ordinarily leave the matter to the regular courts, where an injured client may bring an action. However, in repeated cases of violations, or where the conduct of the professional is such that her competence to remain in practice is called into question, the governing body will take disciplinary action in the same manner as it would for unethical conduct.

A disciplinary hearing is usually conducted by a discipline committee consisting of experienced members of the profession. In addition, the governing council usually designates one or more other members or a separate committee to act as "prosecutor." Both the prosecutor and the accused member may be represented by lawyers. Ordinarily, the finding of a discipline committee takes the form of a recommendation to the governing council of the organization, which then acts on the recommendation to expel, suspend, reprimand, or acquit. Disciplinary proceedings must follow principles of natural justice and fairness[68] and may be reviewed by the regular courts.

CASE 5.14 Right to a Hearing

Manitoba's Law Society requires its member lawyers to complete 12 hours of continuing professional development (CPD) annually, failing which they are automatically suspended from the practice of law. One such suspended lawyer unsuccessfully challenged the law society's right to suspend without a hearing. The Supreme Court of Canada held that mandatory CPD was a reasonable requirement, and suspension was a reasonable penalty to obtain compliance. Lack of hearing or appeal was not unreasonable given the warnings that proceeded suspension and because lawyers can end the suspension by complying with the rules.[69]

Conflict of Duty toward Clients, the Profession, and the Courts

A member of a professional body faces a dilemma when required to testify in court proceedings affecting a client or patient. On the one hand, the member is expected to reply to questions under oath when examined and cross-examined in court; on the other hand, the member's testimony may appear to be a breach of confidence in the professional relationship with the client. A member or student member of a professional organization probably has a duty to ask the court for a ruling before divulging any information obtained in a confidential capacity.

---

[68] For a discussion of this duty see *Mondesir v Manitoba Assn of Optometrists* (1998), 163 DLR (4th) 703. Where the disciplinary body is established by statute, its procedures are also subject to the *Charter*: see *Costco Wholesale Canada Ltd v British Columbia* (1998), 157 DLR (4th) 725.

[69] *Green v Law Society of Manitoba*, 2017 SCC 20.

A professional who learns that a client may be engaged in or is contemplating possibly illegal activities may experience a further problem of interpreting her professional duties to the client. Obviously, the professional must not assist the client (except to advise on possible illegality) and, in dissociating herself from the client's activities, might have to terminate the relationship. A professional would not normally be obliged to reveal confidential knowledge to prosecuting authorities; such information is said to be covered by **privilege**. However, where keeping silent would create a serious threat to public safety, the public interest requires disclosure.[70]

privilege the right of a professional to refuse to divulge information obtained in confidence from a client

INTERNATIONAL ISSUE
Solicitor–Client Privilege

As discussed earlier, the United States' *Sarbanes–Oxley Act* of 2002 (SOX) was enacted in response to major corporate scandals, including that of Enron. It gave the Securities and Exchange Commission the power to regulate the conduct of attorneys. One measure known as "up the ladder" reporting[71] requires very specific conduct from lawyers acting for public corporations. If a lawyer becomes aware of improper activities within the corporation, he or she must report the activity up the chain of command, all the way to the board of directors.

The controversial part of the reporting requirement is known as "noisy withdrawal." If a corporation refuses to discontinue the improper activity, then the lawyer must withdraw her services and report the improper activity to the Securities and Exchange Commission.

The American Bar Association (ABA) raised strong objections to the "noisy withdrawal" proposal because it undermined the solicitor–client privilege and addressed the issue in its model codes of conduct. Rule 1.13 defines the degree of knowledge needed to trigger an obligation to report organizational illegality. Although lawyers may (but are not obligated to) report details of the violations to the SEC,[72] the SEC does require the fact of the withdrawal to be reported and requires identification of the "tainted SEC filing." This obligation applies notwithstanding any ABA rule to the contrary.

Questions to Consider

1. Why would the ABA object to "noisy withdrawal"?
2. Is there a public interest argument to counter the position of the ABA?
3. How does optional reporting affect the privilege?

Sources: U.S. Securities and Exchange Commission, "Final Rule: Implementation of Standards of Professional Conduct for Attorneys," 17 CFR Part 205, September 26, 2003, https://www.sec.gov/rules/final/33-8185.htm; American Bar Association, Model Rules of Professional Conduct. Rules 1.6; 1.13; *Sarbanes–Oxley Act*, 17 CFR §§ 205.3(d) (2010); SEC Release No. 33-8150; Theodore L. Banks and Frederick Banks, *Corporate Legal Compliance Handbook* (Wolters Kluwer, NY, 2013) at 3-58 to 3-63.

MULTI-DISCIPLINARY PARTNERSHIPS

Traditionally, professionals carry on their practices either alone or in partnership with fellow members of the same profession. Some professions forbid their members to incorporate. In some professions—for example, law—it has, in the past, been unlawful for a lawyer to practise in partnership with a non-lawyer. In this way, the law firm's entire activities are subject to law society oversight, and individual lawyers remain personally liable to clients and the public. However, these rules are changing.

Legislation has been adopted in a number of provinces to permit the creation of "professional corporations." We discuss these further in Chapter 25. Professionals choosing to incorporate as professional corporations remain personally liable for their torts and fiduciary duties. The other major development is the changing attitude toward "multi-disciplinary partnerships" (MDPs). The main focus of the current debate on

---

[70] *Smith v Jones* (1999), 169 DLR (4th) 385 (SCC) (a psychiatrist and an alleged serial rapist). See *Canada (Privacy Commissioner) v Blood Tribe Department of Health*, 2008 SCC 44 (prioritizing solicitor–client privilege over access rights).

[71] Title 17, Code of Federal Regulations, Part 205, s 205.3.

[72] *Ibid.*, s 205.3(6)(d)(2).

MDPs is on the combining of accountants and lawyers into a single firm. MDPs of this type are common in Europe, where the major international accounting firms have established their own legal departments. Advocates of MDPs claim that they benefit clients whose problems cannot readily be compartmentalized into legal and non-legal, and they provide a more efficient "one-stop shop" for business clients who require both accounting and legal services. There are also concerns, including the possibility that professional duties and codes of conduct could conflict,[73] and the increased sizes of firms and diversity of services may give rise to more conflicts of interest between clients.

Although the legal profession's licensing bodies historically opposed MDPs,[74] in 2010 British Columbia joined Ontario and Quebec in allowing lawyers to participate in MDPs provided the lawyers remain in control and non-lawyers abide by the law societies' rules.[75]

Strategies to Manage the Legal Risks

The rules governing most professions require members to carry public liability insurance to protect members (and their partners) from liability for unintentional wrongdoing. Anyone providing opinions to the public should have third-party liability coverage. Other preventive measures should also be taken. The risks of contractual liability are reduced when a written retainer (or contract) includes a detailed description of the scope of work and opinions to be provided to the client. Disclaimers should be used to exclude work not undertaken and limit liability for opinions expressed. A disclaimer's description of the purpose for which the information is being provided, as well as a restriction on who may use or rely on the opinions, will reduce the risk of tort and fiduciary liability.

Sometimes professionals give advice for free as part of volunteer work or marketing campaigns. Disclaimers limiting scope, use, and purpose of the work should also be applied to these services, as neither tort nor fiduciary liability depends upon being paid for the advice.

Of course, reducing the number of mistakes is the most effective preventive measure. Professionals should regularly participate in continuing education and professional development programs to ensure they are practising at the standard of their profession. Indeed, most professions set annual mandatory professional development requirements; without such mandatory requirements, the profession itself might be held liable for negligent omission—failing to monitor the competence of its members. With respect to fiduciary liability, screening for conflict of interest should be done before a new client is accepted in an effort to flag situations where the interests may conflict with existing clients. Software is available that can automatically search existing files for names, addresses, or other details that are already in the system.

Even liability arising from intentional behaviour such as fraud, deceit, or breach of fiduciary duty can be reduced if professionals practising in partnerships adopt control mechanisms requiring more than one professional to work on or be familiar with every file. The more people are involved in and familiar with a file, the more difficult it is to conceal fraudulent (or negligent) behaviour.

---

[73] See Noel Semple, "Canada: Legal Services Regulation in Canada: *Plus Ca Change?*" in A. Boon, ed, *International Perspectives on Regulating Lawyers and Legal Services* (Hart, 2017) at 105–107.

[74] In *Black v Law Society of Alberta*, [1989] 1 SCR 591, the Supreme Court of Canada struck down a rule that Alberta lawyers could not enter into partnership with lawyers from outside the province. The decision was based on the mobility rights provisions of the *Charter*, but arguably the right of association would have been equally applicable.

[75] Law societies in Alberta, Saskatchewan, and Manitoba are currently studying *Alternative Business Structures: Innovating Regulation: A Collaboration of Prairie Law Societies*, Discussion Paper, Nov. 2015, https://www.lawsociety.sk.ca/media/127107/INNOVATINGREGULATION.pdf.

QUESTIONS FOR REVIEW

1. What are the arguments in favour of imposing a wide liability on professionals?
2. What is the main effect of increased use of liability insurance?
3. What is the nature of the fiduciary duty owed by a professional? In what way can that duty be wider than a contractual duty?
4. Can a client choose to sue a professional adviser in either contract or tort? What factors will influence the decision?
5. Why were the courts initially reluctant to recognize liability for negligent misstatements to persons who are not clients?
6. How did the decision in *Hedley Byrne v Heller & Partners* address the issue in Question 5?
7. What is the test now applied in Canada to determine whether a professional owes a duty of care to a person for a negligent misstatement?
8. How does a fiduciary duty differ from the duty of care owed in negligent misrepresentation?
9. What must a plaintiff prove to establish negligent misrepresentation?
10. When will a professional be liable for an omission?
11. What are the objections to a "hindsight" approach in determining the appropriate standard of professional care?
12. What is the essence of causation in most professional–client relationships?
13. What are the main responsibilities imposed or assumed by professional bodies?
14. Should professional bodies be allowed to discipline their members, or should discipline be left to the courts?
15. What are the potential advantages and possible disadvantages of multi-disciplinary partnerships?

CASES AND PROBLEMS

1. Continuing Scenario

   One of the most important pieces of equipment for a restaurant business is the stove. Ashley wanted to make sure she installed the right one in her new restaurant, so she did lots of research on the internet to identify the possible selections. After visiting several manufacturers' websites, she narrowed her choice down to two commercial ranges: the FOX 950, a gas cooktop with an electric oven for $5000, because cooking with gas was flexible; and the more expensive Hiking 760 for $7000, an electric oven with an induction cooktop, because it gave off less heat and the kitchen would remain cooler. She visited the Restaurant Association website and saw that the Association ranked the Hiking induction cooktop first in its category. Later, when discussing the cost of kitchen appliances with Bill, her insurance agent, Bill told Ashley that she would get a reduced insurance rate for an induction range because the risk of fire was less. In the long run this could offset the higher price. Bill referred her to Smith's Appliance, where he knew she could see both floor models. Bill neglected to tell Ashley that Smith's Appliance was owned by his parents. The clerk at the appliance store said both ranges were excellent, and her choice depended on whether the flexibility of gas or the coolness of induction was most important to her; the clerk's personal preference was induction. Ashley called Bill from the store, and he confirmed that induction would mean a $500 savings on her property insurance premium. Bill knew this because a previous client had saved this much; he did not think it was necessary to call the insurance company for a quote.

   Ashley ordered the Hiking induction stove and paid the extra $2000. Unfortunately, once the stove was installed and working, the kitchen was not cool. The electric oven threw so much heat that it was necessary to reconfigure the air conditioning to cool down the kitchen at a cost of $4000. As well Ashley's insurance premium was not reduced because her water heater was fuelled with gas, and the insurance company felt the fire risk remained the same.

Does Ashley have a claim against Bill? the Restaurant Association? Smith's Appliance? Discuss the possible causes of action and Ashley's damages.

2. Mitchell was the owner of a landscaping business. He came to know "Simpson," an apparently successful businessman who engaged in various speculative investments. In reality, "Simpson" was a former lawyer whose real name was Anderson and who had been disbarred and convicted of a number of offences involving fraud.

Mitchell and Anderson became friendly, and Anderson persuaded Mitchell to join him in a number of investments, which, at first, seemed to be successful. In the course of their business dealings, Mitchell said that he thought it would be sensible for him to retain the services of a lawyer: Anderson recommended that he see a lawyer named Gordon.

Gordon quickly realized that Mitchell's business associate, "Simpson," was actually Anderson, whom he had known before Anderson's conviction. Gordon acted for Mitchell in a number of transactions, but despite his knowledge of Anderson's background, he said nothing about it to Mitchell.

A year or so later, Mitchell discovered that most of the investments undertaken with Anderson (both before and after becoming a client of Gordon) turned out to be complete failures. Apparently, Anderson had siphoned off most of the value of the properties they had bought.

Mitchell brought an action against Gordon, claiming that Gordon should have told him of Anderson's history and that, if he had done so, Mitchell would have terminated the relationship.

Identify Mitchell's cause of action and what Mitchell needs to prove. Should Mitchell succeed?

3. Hedgeways Construction Inc. is a company specializing in highway construction. In response to a public invitation from the Government of British Columbia to tender for an important road construction project, it submitted what turned out to be the winning bid.

The detailed description of the project in the tender invitation document contained a number of important inaccuracies. As a result, the cost of completing the project was substantially greater than Hedgeways had estimated, and it ended up suffering a loss on the project.

The tender invitation document issued by the province contained a statement to the effect that any representations made therein were "general information" only and were not guaranteed by the province. The actual specifications and engineering drawings in the document had been prepared by Brown and Green, two qualified engineers employed by the firm Black and Associates Ltd., who had contracted with the province to provide the specifications.

What claim, if any, does Hedgeways have against (a) the provincial government, (b) Black and Associates, and (c) Brown and Green?

4. Hopkins Steel Ltd. was a long-established corporation operating in Ontario. A few years ago it decided to change its bank and moved its account to the Canadian Business Bank. Before accepting the account, the bank made various inquiries and, in particular, examined the audited accounts of Hopkins over the preceding three years. The accounts showed a consistent record of profitability, growing steadily over the years. With this information the bank agreed to extend a line of credit to Hopkins and, over the following year or so, made advances to it totalling more than $2 million.

Shortly thereafter, Hopkins ran into serious trouble and eventually was forced into bankruptcy with debts in excess of $2 million.

The bank brought a claim against Cross, Jones, and Sparrow, the accounting firm that had audited the annual accounts of Hopkins during the years in question. The bank claimed that the accounts for the preceding years, which it had examined before granting the loans, were inaccurate and had been negligently prepared and that Hopkins was already in serious trouble before the bank accepted it as a client.

In each case, the audited accounts contained the following statement:

> We have examined the balance sheet of Hopkins Steel Limited as at [date] and the statements of earnings, retained earnings, and changes in financial position for the year then ended. Our examination was made in accordance with generally accepted auditing standards, and accordingly included such tests and other procedures as we considered necessary in the circumstances.

According to the evidence, during the years in which Cross, Jones, and Sparrow provided services to Hopkins, it also from time to time provided further information with respect to Hopkins to third parties, such as creditors and a bonding insurer for the company, and provided Hopkins with a number of copies of its financial statements and audit reports.

Does the bank have any claim against the accounting firm?

5. Prince, a chartered accountant employed as a controller and living in Calgary, was bored with his job. He applied to an Ottawa-based software company that was advertising for a chartered accountant to help in the development of new accounting software. At the job interview, Paulson, the manager of research and development, described the new venture and told Prince that the position would involve advising on accounting standards for many new products, addressing such things as cash-flow management, inventory controls, accounts receivables, and more. Prince was told that the company would commit significant funds to the project for the next 10 years. This position was the first of many accounting jobs. It was implicit that Prince (if hired) would become senior management, supervising the subsequent hires. Formal plans were still before the executive committee but would be in place before the start date of May 1. This was exactly the type of new challenge Prince was looking for, so when Paulson called to offer him the job of manager, financial standards, Prince accepted immediately. A few days later he received the employment contract by email, signed it, and returned it by courier. The job description said that Paulson would supply accounting expertise as required by the employer. Prince and his wife quit their jobs, sold their house in Calgary, bought a smaller, more expensive house in Ottawa, and moved across the country.

When the executive committee met in April to consider the development plan, they decided the plan was too aggressive and approved only the development of one aspect—cash-flow management. The project would be funded for only five months. Prince commenced work on May 1 and helped design the cash-flow software. When he asked Paulson about the next phase, he was told only that it was not firm yet. No other accountants were hired, and after five months, Prince was transferred to the accounting department to do typical controller work similar to his job in Calgary. He was unhappy with the transfer and quit.

Identify the possible causes of action, and assess their chances of success. Would it make a difference to your answer if the contract of employment included a term that the employer might transfer or reassign the employee to another position within the company at any time and a term that said that all agreements between the parties were included in the written document?

6. Hansen practised for a number of years as an investment counsellor, advising clients on how to invest their savings. He was as a Member of the Association of General Investment Counsellors, which entitled him to use the letters "M.A.G.I.C." after his name.

Over the years, the association (AGIC) received numerous complaints about Hansen. Many of his suggested investment schemes turned out to be disastrous, and there were strong suspicions that not only was he wholly incompetent, but he was also defrauding some of his clients.

Two years ago, after one particularly serious complaint, Hansen was called to attend a meeting of the disciplinary committee of AGIC. The committee informed him that, in view of the long history of complaints against him, it proposed to deprive him of his membership and to inform the Attorney General's department of the most recent complaint, about which there was at least a suspicion of fraud.

Hansen, who was a very persuasive talker, eventually convinced the committee not to report him and to allow him to resign from the association rather than being dismissed. He signed an undertaking that he would not practise again as an investment counsellor and would no longer describe himself as "M.A.G.I.C."

Despite the undertaking, Hansen very soon resumed his practice, in his old office, and continued to use his title. Soon afterward, he was consulted by Thaler, who said she had heard excellent reports about him from a friend. Hansen quickly talked Thaler into entrusting her life savings to him. It appears now that Hansen has disappeared to an island in the South Pacific, taking Thaler's money with him.

Thaler has commenced proceedings against AGIC, claiming that if the association had reported Hansen to the proper authorities and had taken steps to see that he abided by his undertaking to AGIC, Hansen would not have been in a position to defraud her.

What claim does Thaler have against AGIC?

Part 3 Contracts

Chapter 6
Formation of a Contract: Offer and Acceptance

- THE ROLE OF CONTRACT LAW
- THE NATURE OF A CONTRACT
- THE NATURE OF AN OFFER
- THE COMMUNICATION OF AN OFFER
- WRITTEN OFFERS
- THE LAPSE AND REVOCATION OF AN OFFER
- THE ELEMENTS OF ACCEPTANCE
- TRANSACTIONS BETWEEN PARTIES AT A DISTANCE FROM EACH OTHER
- UNILATERAL AND BILATERAL CONTRACTS
- FORMATION OF INTERNET CONTRACTS
- STRATEGIES TO MANAGE THE LEGAL RISKS

In this chapter we describe the essential requirements of a contract and, in particular, how a contract is formed.

In this chapter we examine such questions as:

- Why is a contract enforceable in law?
- How is a contract formed?
- How do we determine the terms of a contract?
- Why are standard form contracts used? What are their benefits and dangers?
- How does an offer come to an end?
- What is the difference between unilateral and bilateral contracts?

THE ROLE OF CONTRACT LAW

Contracts are voluntary legal relationships. They are not legal obligations forced upon everyone like tort or criminal liability. Parties choose to make a contract and only then become legally obligated to comply with its terms. Contract law empowers parties to create legal obligations that would otherwise not exist. Sometimes, though, inequality of bargaining power or expertise between parties results in unfair contracts. Contract law has rules to address these situations.

THE NATURE OF A CONTRACT

Contracts begin with a promise, but not all promises become contracts. Although there may be a moral obligation to keep all promises, there is not necessarily a legal obligation. Contract law sets the rules for how ordinary promises become legally binding promises. "The most popular description of a **contract** is also the most exact one, namely that it is a promise or set of promises which the law will enforce."[1] Which promises will the law enforce? There are four basic requirements to form a legally enforceable contract: offer, acceptance, consideration, and intention. This chapter addresses offer and acceptance; consideration and intention are discussed in Chapter 7.

contract a set of promises that the law will enforce

THE NATURE OF AN OFFER

A contract does not come into existence until an offer has been made by one party and accepted by the other party. An **offer** is a description of a promise or set of promises one party, the **offeror**, is willing to make, subject to the willingness of the other party, the **offeree**, to agree to the same promises. When the offeree accepts the offer by agreeing to the description of promises or requests, the offer is transformed into a contract. The promise is no longer tentative. Both the offeror and offeree are bound to carry out their promises.

offer a description of a promise one party is willing to make, subject to the agreement of the other party

offeror the person making the offer

offeree the person to whom the offer is made

A mere invitation to do business is not an offer capable of forming a contract. The display of a coat in a store window does not amount to an offer to sell; a catalogue does not guarantee that the goods pictured or described will be delivered to all who try to order them. These are simply merchandising or advertising devices to attract customers and to start negotiations for a contract of sale. A prospective customer, acting in response to the invitation, may make an offer, and the seller may in turn accept or refuse.

Advertisements to sell goods at a certain price are generally mere invitations to the public to visit the place of business. A business is not expected to sell the goods to everyone who reads its advertisement. Its supply is limited, and it cannot precisely predict the number of readers who will be seriously interested. If the advertisement were taken to be an offer, and too many people accepted it, the business would be liable for breach of contract to all those who accepted and to whom it could not supply the advertised goods.

However, this does not mean that advertisements can never be offers; the courts have sometimes held them to be offers when their wording supported this interpretation. An advertisement to sell a fixed number of items at a fixed price to those who accept first, an offer of a reward for information or for the return of a lost object, or a reward to any person using a preventive medicine who still catches an illness all may be valid offers. This group of advertisements forms a very small proportion of advertisements—the exception rather than the rule.

---

[1] P. H. Winfield, *Pollock's Principles of Contract*, 13th ed (London: Stevens & Sons, 1950) at 1.

CASE 6.1 Display not an Offer

When self-service supermarkets and drugstores appeared, the courts needed to decide whether the display of merchandise in itself amounted to an offer—and the act of the customer in taking the merchandise from the shelf amounted to an acceptance—or whether the display was merely an invitation to the customer to make an offer by taking the merchandise to the cashier. The question was important, because legislation made it unlawful to sell certain medicinal products unless the sale was supervised by a registered pharmacist.[2]

Placement of a registered pharmacist near the cashier was satisfactory. The judge said:

The mere fact that a customer picks up a bottle of medicine from the shelves in this case does not amount to an acceptance of an offer to sell. It is an offer by the customer to buy, and there is no sale effected until the buyer's offer to buy is accepted by the acceptance of the price.[3]

THE COMMUNICATION OF AN OFFER

The form of an offer is not important as long as it is heard and understood. The offeror could say, "I offer to sell you my car for $500," or "I will sell you my car for $500," or even "I'll take $500 for my car." All are equally good offers containing a tentative promise to sell the car if the buyer agrees to pay the stated price.

In most situations, an offeror communicates orally or in writing, but she can also express an offer by conduct without words. A taxi driver opening the door of her cab or a bidder raising his finger at an auction may also be offers.

An offeree cannot accept an offer until she is aware of it. Crossed offers provide an example of this rule.

ILLUSTRATION 6.1 Crossed Offers

A tells B she is interested in selling her car. The next day, A writes to B offering to sell her car for $1500; B has also written a letter crossing A's letter in the mail offering to buy the car for $1500. There is no contract: B was unaware of A's offer when he wrote and so his letter could not be an acceptance; similarly, A was unaware of B's offer—A's letter, too, could not be an acceptance. Unless either A or B sends a subsequent acceptance, no contract will be formed.

Similarly, we cannot be required to pay people who do work for us without our knowledge. We are entitled first to receive an offer to do the work, which we may then accept or reject. A person for whom work has been done without his request, and without his knowledge, may well benefit from it; but as he has not accepted any offer to do the work, he has no contractual obligation to pay for it.

Suppose, however, that goods or services are provided to a person without his request but in circumstances where he has an opportunity to reject them. The general contract law rule is that if he accepts the services or uses the goods, he is presumed to have accepted the offer and to have promised to pay the price. This rule triggered unconscionable selling practices that tempt consumers to bind themselves to pay for goods they did not request. Many provinces have passed legislation to reverse the rule, at least as it relates to consumers. For example, section 12 of British Columbia's *Business Practices and Consumer Protection Act*[4] states the following:

> (1) A consumer has no legal obligation in respect of unsolicited goods or services unless and until the consumer expressly acknowledges to the supplier in writing his or her intention to accept the goods or services.

---

[2] *Pharmaceutical Society of Great Britain v Boots Cash Chemists (Southern) Ltd*, [1952] 2 All ER 456.

[3] *Ibid* at 458.

[4] SBC 2004, c 2.

(2) Unless the consumer has given the acknowledgment referred to in subsection (1), the supplier does not have a cause of action for any loss, use, misuse, possession, damage, or misappropriation in respect of the goods or services or the value obtained by the use of the goods or services.

Section 13 of Ontario's *Consumer Protection Act*[5] contains a similar provision; however, consider section 68, which reads:

(1) Despite section 13, a consumer who . . . receives a credit card from a credit card issuer without applying for it shall be deemed to have entered into a credit agreement with the issuer with respect to the card on first using the card.

WRITTEN OFFERS

Standard Form Contracts: Their Risks and Benefits

Offers do not have to be in writing. However, businesses that sell to the general public often present the terms of their offers in pre-printed documents delivered to their customers, or they post notices containing terms on their business websites. Sometimes both methods are used together, with the delivered document referring to the terms posted in the notice. Common examples are tickets for theatres and airlines, hotel bookings, credit card agreements, online purchases, and insurance policies.

Almost without exception, a person receiving any one of these documents is neither asked nor expected to read, approve, or change the terms. If the customer took the time to read it and suggest changes, the agent of the offeror would probably become very annoyed. She would say, "Take it or leave it." As a practical matter, an offeree cannot change any terms of a **standard form contract**, also known as a *contract of adhesion*. There is no real element of bargaining. He must accept the offer as is or not at all. Often, as when travelling by airline, there may be no other practical means of transportation between two points; an offeree does not have the choice of refusing—he must accept if he is to make his trip. In this situation, an offeror business is strongly tempted to disregard the interests of its offerees, the general public, and give itself every advantage, and it rarely resists this temptation.

standard form contract an offer prepared in advance by the offeror, including terms favourable to the offeror that cannot be changed by the offeree but must be accepted as is or rejected in their entirety, also known as a contract of adhesion

Still, in fast-paced retail situations, the standard form contract is needed. Imagine waiting in line at the car rental office in an airport while each would-be passenger bargained separately for each term in his contract! Contract law recognizes the business need for standard form contracts while guarding against abuse from unequal bargaining power.

There are four methods of protection from this inequality in bargaining. First, if the business falls within an area regulated by a government board, the terms of its contracts are subject to board approval. When boards operate effectively, the public is usually well protected, and unreasonable terms are excluded—for example, the Canadian Radio-television and Telecommunications Commission. Second, specific types of agreements may be subject to legislation—for example, the *Wireless Service Agreement Act* expands cancellation rights in cell phone contracts.[6] Third, segments of the public, such as consumers, are offered special protection. Consumer protection legislation provides disclosure requirements and post-acceptance cancellation options. Finally, in the vast range of unregulated activity, the public receives only as much protection as the courts can find in the general law of contract.

---

[5] SO 2002, c 30, Sch A.

[6] SO 2013, c 8.

Notice of Terms

As a general rule, without legislative intervention, the courts will normally give effect to the terms of a commercial contract freely entered into, even a contract of adhesion.[7] An ordinary written commercial contract between business entities does not require notice of special terms; it is each party's responsibility to review the document.[8] Suppose, however, that an offeree is not a business person or does not know that the offer contains a certain term, or the terms are not all included in one document. She purchases a ticket to attend a baseball game. A clause on the back states that the management reserves the right to remove the ticket holder at any time without giving reasons. She does not know or suspect that the ticket contains such a term. If she satisfies the court that she did not know of it and that there was fraud or misrepresentation, then the court will ask what steps the business took to bring the term to the attention of its customers. If the court decides that the steps were insufficient, the ticket holder is not bound by the term; and if she has been wrongfully ejected from the baseball park, she will have the same remedy as if the term had not been on the ticket.

On the other hand, if the court finds that the business did what was reasonably necessary in the circumstances to bring the term to the notice of its customers, then the ticket holder is bound by the term whether she knew of it or not. Each "ticket case" is decided on its own facts, and there is no firm list of requirements for what is or is not sufficient notice.

CASE 6.2 Tickets

In *Parker v South Eastern Railway Co*,[9] Parker deposited his suitcase in the luggage room of a railway station, paid a fee, and received a ticket, on the face of which were the words "See back." On the reverse side of the ticket, it was stated that the railway was not liable for loss in excess of £10.

The bag was lost, and Parker sued the railway for his loss, £24. On appeal, the court decided that the issue was whether the railway had done what was reasonably necessary to notify customers of the term. The court ordered a new trial because the trial judge had not asked the jury to decide this question.

The fact that the front of the ticket in Case 6.2 contained the words "See back" is important. If a ticket—or other document given to the customer at the time of purchase—contains a short and clear reference to other terms appearing either on the reverse side or posted on a sign or website, it is likely that "reasonably sufficient notice" of those terms has been given.

A sign in a parking lot disclaiming liability for loss or damage to cars or contents may not in itself be reasonably sufficient notice to bind those who park their cars there. We have to ask whether the ticket or voucher received when a customer parks her car contains a clear reference to the sign and whether, in the circumstances, a customer ought to recognize the term stated on the sign as part of the contract she is making with the operator of the lot. A printed ticket or receipt containing the words "subject to the conditions as exhibited on the premises" may be enough to tie the sign to each contract. The sign must, of course, be displayed prominently, but this in itself might not be sufficient; the fact must be brought home to the customer at the time of making the contract. The operator of the parking lot, garage, or other place of storage cannot safely assume that he may exempt himself from liability merely by putting up

---

[7] *Seidel v TELUS Communications*, 2011 SCC 15 at paras 2, 36. But see *Douez v Facebook*, 2017 SCC 33.
[8] *Suhaag Jewellers Ltd v Alarm Factory Inc*, 2016 ONCA 33.
[9] (1877), 2 CPD 416.

a sign.[10] Ever wonder why you are asked to agree to the terms and conditions when you visit a website? The website's owners are proving they brought the terms to your attention.

> The best way of proving [that a customer has knowledge of the terms] is by a written document signed by the party to be bound. Another way is by handing him, before or at the time of the contract, a written notice specifying certain terms and making it clear to him that the contract is in those terms. A prominent public notice which is plain for him to see when he makes the contract would, no doubt, have the same effect.[11]

A court may find that there was adequate notice of usual, expected terms that the offeree chose not to read, but greater effort must be made to give notice of a surprising, shocking, or unusually unfair term. Again, if the offeree signs a document, a strong presumption arises that she has accepted all the terms it contains; avoiding the consequences becomes much more difficult.[12]

CASE 6.3 Limitation of Liability Not Unusual

A clause on the back of a car rental contract signed by the renter said that the renter was responsible for all theft if the renter was negligent, and the renter must keep doors, windows, and ignition locked when not in the car. The renter left the car unlocked and running outside an Edmonton bar between 1:00 and 3:00 in the morning. The Alberta Court of Appeal held that the clause was not unusual, unexpected, or onerous and therefore did not require special measures. Nor was the physical arrangement of the contract difficult to read, surprising, or tricky. Therefore, the clause applied, and the renter was held liable for the damages arising from the theft of the vehicle.[13]

The prospects of persuading a court to disregard onerous terms imposed in a written and signed document do improve somewhat[14] if there is misrepresentation or an unconscionable result, as we shall see in Chapter 9.

THE LAPSE AND REVOCATION OF AN OFFER

Lapse

When an offer has lapsed, the offeree can no longer accept it even if he is unaware that it has lapsed; it has become void and no longer exists. An offer may **lapse** in any of the following ways:

a. when the offeree fails to accept within a time specified in the offer
b. when the offeree fails to accept within a reasonable time, if the offer has not specified any time limit
c. when either of the parties dies or becomes insane prior to acceptance

Predicting what amounts to a "reasonable time" is often difficult. To say it depends upon the circumstances of each case may not seem helpful. The Supreme

lapse the termination of an offer when the offeree fails to accept it within a specified time, or if no time is specified, then within a reasonable time

---

[10] *Watkins v Rymill* (1883), 10 QBD 178. It is different if the customer leaves the keys in the car at the request of the parking lot operator, because a bailment for storage and safekeeping is implied. See Chapter 17, infra. See also *Brown v Toronto Auto Parks Ltd*, [1954] OWN 869; *Samuel Smith & Sons Ltd v Silverman* (1961), 29 DLR (2d) 98; *Hefferon v Imperial Parking Co Ltd* (1973), 46 DLR (3d) 642.

[11] *Olley v Marlborough Court Ltd*, [1949] 1 All ER 127 at 134.

[12] See *978011 Ontario Ltd v Cornell Engineering Co* (2001), 2001 CanLII 8522, 53 OR (3d) 783, 12 BLR (3d) 240 (ONCA), leave refused [2001] SCCA No 315.

[13] *Budget Rent-A-Car of Edmonton Ltd v University of Toronto*, 1995 ABCA 52, (1995), 165 AR 236.

[14] *Tilden Rent-A-Car Co v Clendenning* (1978), 18 OR (2d) 601; *DJ Provencher Ltd v Tyco Investments of Canada Ltd* (1997), 42 BLR (2d) 45.

Court of Canada discussed how the subject matter of the contract may provide a clue for deciding whether a reasonable length of time has elapsed in an offer to buy or sell:

> Farm lands, apart from evidence to the contrary . . . are not subject to frequent or sudden changes or fluctuations in price and, therefore, in the ordinary course of business a reasonable time for the acceptance of an offer would be longer than that with respect to such commodities as shares of stock upon an established trading market. It would also be longer than with respect to perishable goods such as food products. The fact that it was land would tend to lengthen what would be a reasonable time but other circumstances must also be considered.[15]

The "other circumstances" include the manner in which an offer is made and whether its wording indicates urgency. Often when a prospective purchaser makes an offer to buy property, she specifies that the offer must be accepted within 24 hours. The restriction is in her interest because it gives the vendor very little time to use this "firm offer" as a means of approaching other possible purchasers and bidding up the price.

Revocation

Notice of Revocation
An offeror may be able to revoke (that is, withdraw) an offer at any time before acceptance, even when it has promised to hold the offer open for a specified time. The offeror must provide notice of revocation to make it effective.

ILLUSTRATION 6.2 Receive Revocation Before Acceptance

A Inc. sends a letter by courier on January 15 to B offering to sell its warehouse to B for $800 000, stating that the offer is open only until January 19 and that it must have heard from B by then. B receives the letter on January 16 and immediately prepares a letter of acceptance. Before B sends his reply on the morning of January 17, A changes its mind and telephones B saying that it withdraws its offer.

The revocation is valid because it has reached B before he has accepted. Accordingly, B can no longer accept A's offer.

In Illustration 6.2, the offeror clearly revoked the offer before its acceptance. Its direct communication of the revocation left no doubt about the offeree's knowledge of it. The legal position of the parties is less certain if the offeree merely hears rumours that the offeror has revoked or hears that the offeror has made it impossible to carry out the offer because it has sold the property to someone else. The court will consider the offer revoked if it would be unreasonable for the offeree to suppose that the offeror still intended to stand by its offer.[16] Nevertheless, making an offer to sell a particular item to one party and then selling it to another without having directly withdrawn the offer to the first party is always poor business practice and maybe unethical. Quite apart from damage to goodwill, the offeror runs the risk of the first offeree accepting and of the offeror then being in breach when unable to fulfill both contracts.

Options

An offeree may obligate an offeror to keep its offer open (that is, not to revoke it) for a specified time in a couple of ways: (1) the offer itself may specify that it is irrevocable; or (2) a subsequent contract called an **option** may be made to keep the offer open. In an option, the offeree makes a contract with the offeror in the following general terms: The offeree agrees to pay a sum of money as consideration (discussed in

option a contract to keep an offer open for a specified time in return for a sum of money

---

[15] *Barrick v Clark*, [1950] 4 DLR 529 at 537.

[16] See *Dickinson v Dodds* (1876), 2 Ch D 463. See also *Hughes v Gyratron Developments Ltd*, [1988] BCJ No 1598.

Chapter 7); in return the offeror agrees (1) to keep the offer open for a specified time and (2) not to make contracts with other parties that would prevent the offeror from fulfilling its offer (that is, to give the offeree the exclusive right to accept the offer). Without consideration, an option is unenforceable.[17] Options can be a useful tool for business decision making.

ILLUSTRATION 6.3   Business Use of Options

PreciseComp pays $3000 to A for the right to buy her farm within three months for $350 000 and also buys similar option agreements from other farmers in the vicinity. In this way, PreciseComp can find out at a modest cost whether all the necessary property will be available for a new plant and what the total cost will be. It need not take up or **exercise an option**—that is, accept the original offer to sell any of the farms. The relatively small sums paid for the option agreements are simply the cost of a feasibility study for the projected plant. Alternatively, PreciseComp could require each of the farmers to honour the options and sell at the agreed price—provided PreciseComp accepts the offers contained in the options within the specified time.

In Illustration 6.3, the farmers are in the position of offerors who, for an agreed period of time, are not free to withdraw their offers without being in breach of the option. The parties are really contemplating two contracts: first, the option agreement itself, and second, the actual sale that will take place only if the option is exercised.

exercise an option accept the offer contained in an option

Rejection and Counter-offer by the Offeree

Business negotiations usually involve the exchange of offers and counter-offers, but until an offer by one side is accepted without alteration, modification, or condition by the other, there is no contract; the parties have no legal obligation to each other. When an offeree receives an offer and, though interested, chooses to change some of its terms, he has not accepted; rather, he has made a counter-offer of his own, amounting to rejection of the offer. Only when acceptance is without qualification is a contract formed.

The making of a counter-offer is a rejection of the earlier offer and brings it to an end. If the offeror in turn rejects the counter-offer, the original offer does not revive. Only if the offeror agrees to re-offer it may the offeree accept the original offer. However, when an offeree merely inquires whether the terms offered are the best he can expect, it does not amount to a rejection.

ILLUSTRATION 6.4   Counteroffer Is Rejection

A sent an email to B offering to sell her car for $2000. B replied by email, "I will give you $1900 for the car." Two days later B sent an email again to A saying, "I have been reconsidering. I will accept your offer to sell for $2000 after all."

In Illustration 6.4, there is no contract. B's counter-offer of $1900 brought the original offer to sell for $2000 to an end. Although B has phrased her final statement in the form of an acceptance, she is doing no more than making a fresh offer of her own that A may or may not wish to accept. Perhaps someone else has offered A $2100 for the car in the meantime. If, when A made the offer to sell for $2000, B had simply inquired whether this was the lowest A would go, the offer would have continued to stand. B would continue to be free to accept it within a reasonable period of time, provided A did not revoke her offer first.

---

[17] *Sail Labrador v Challenge One (The)*, [1999] 1 SCR 265 at para 42.

THE ELEMENTS OF ACCEPTANCE

Positive and Unconditional

Acceptance must be certain and unconditional, and must be a positive act, whether in words or in conduct. If acceptance is by conduct, the conduct must refer unequivocally to the offer made—for example, shaking hands at the conclusion of negotiations is generally regarded as an acceptance of the last offer.

On the other hand, an individual's conduct may happen to comply with the means of acceptance set out in an offer and yet not amount to an acceptance. Suppose A walks her dog around the park every evening. B leaves A a note saying that she will have accepted B's offer to buy her car for $2000 if she walks her dog in the park that evening. A need not abandon her normal conduct to avoid accepting the offer and having the contract forced upon her.

For the same reason, an offeror cannot insist on silence as a mode of acceptance and so require the offeree to act in order to reject the offer.

ILLUSTRATION 6.5 Unsolicited Goods

Sanger, a sales representative for Ion Electric Supply Inc., demonstrated a new high-speed Auto-analyzer for Glover, the owner of a car repair service. The price was $2500. Glover thought the device was useful but overpriced: "At $1500 I might consider buying it." Sanger said he could not reduce the price and removed the machine. Two weeks later, an Auto-analyzer arrived with a letter from Sanger stating: "When I reported how impressed you were with our analyzer to the manager, he said it would be worth selling one even at a loss just to break into the market in your city. Our price is reduced, only to you, to $1750. That is below cost. If we don't hear from you in 10 days we shall assume you have accepted this exceptional buy and will expect payment of our invoice."

There will be no contract even if the offeree, Glover, does not reply and simply allows the machine to sit idle; but he may well be bound if he takes the risk of using the machine, even to experiment with it.

---

negative option billing a practice of adding services and sending bills without request and relying upon the customer to cancel if they don't wish the service

Silence can be a sufficient mode of acceptance only if the parties have habitually used this method to communicate acceptance in previous transactions or have agreed between themselves in advance that silence is sufficient, as where books are regularly delivered under a contract for membership in a publisher's book club. Provincial consumer protection legislation regulates business practices involving unsolicited goods and **negative option billing**. If a consumer mistakenly pays for unrequested services, he may request a refund.[18]

Communication to the Offeror

Generally speaking, an offeree must communicate acceptance to the offeror. Some types of offers, however, can be accepted without communication because the offeror asks only that the offeree perform an act, implying that the act will amount to acceptance. The offeror may, in other words, do away with receiving notice of acceptance and be bound to the terms of the proposal as soon as the offeree has performed whatever was required of him in the offer.

---

[18] See e.g. *Business Practices and Consumer Protection Act*, SBC 2004, c 2, ss 12–14 and *Consumer Protection Act, 2002*, SO 2002, c 30, Sch A, s 13.

CASE 6.4 Rewards or Incentives

Carbolic Smoke Ball Company placed an advertisement in a newspaper promising to pay £100 to anyone who used one of its smoke balls three times daily for two weeks and still contracted influenza. Mrs. Carlill bought a smoke ball and used it following the instructions supplied and contracted influenza. She sued the Smoke Ball Company on its promise to pay £100. As a part of its defence, the company pleaded that Mrs. Carlill had never communicated her intention to accept its offer. The court found in favour of Mrs. Carlill.[19] It held that the offer had implied that notice was not necessary because the company had asked only that readers should buy and use the smoke balls. Performance of the conditions set out was a sufficient acceptance without separately notifying the company.

The *Carlill* case also established that an offer may be made to an indefinite number of people whose individual identities remain unknown to the offeror even after they have accepted. If the offer had been addressed to a particular group of persons, then only members of that group could have accepted.

The Moment of Formation

The moment a contract is formed by acceptance of an offer, each party is bound to its terms. Accordingly, we must be able to analyze business negotiations so we can identify:

- who made the offer,
- when it was communicated,
- when and by whom the offer was accepted, and
- when acceptance was communicated.

Buying an automobile from a car dealer provides a good example of the importance of knowing when and how an offer is accepted.

ILLUSTRATION 6.6 When the Contract is Formed

Car sales agents employed by a dealer normally have no authority to enter into contracts with customers. The management of the dealership retains the final word on both price and credit terms; the agent's task is to persuade any prospective buyer to submit an offer at a specified price. When the agent takes the customer's offer to the sales manager, the manager may agree by signing the offer (the positive act), and the agent will return to the customer to tell them (communication of acceptance). This is the moment of acceptance when the contract is formed. Alternatively, the manager may strike out the proposed price and insert a higher one with a request that the prospective buyer initial the change. In so doing, the manager rejects the customer's offer by making a counter-offer. No contract is formed unless and until the customer initials the counter-offer. Communication of acceptance is effective when the agent becomes aware of the initialing of the document and does not wait until the manager is told.

The common business practice of **inviting tenders** is a more complicated method of forming a contract. The purpose of inviting tenders may be to obtain firm offers from the tenderers for a fixed quantity of goods and services over a stated period, or it may be to explore the market of available suppliers and develop the best terms for proceeding with a project. When the object is to obtain firm offers, the most satisfactory tender should become the basis for a contract between the inviter of the tenders and the successful bidder. This is normal practice when a government or business calls for tenders for the construction of a large project. In fact, the Supreme Court of Canada has described the tender process as two contracts. It held that inviting tenders amounted to an offer to enter into a construction contract if selected according to the

inviting tenders seeking offers from suppliers

---

[19] *Carlill v Carbolic Smoke Ball Co*, [1892] 2 QB 484. See also *Grant v Prov of New Brunswick* (1973), 35 DLR (3d) 141, and *Dale v Manitoba* (1997), 147 DLR (4th) 605.

established criteria.[20] Submission of a bid is considered acceptance and forms a contract. Any refusal to fairly consider the bid would be breach of contract. The party inviting the tenders promises—in return for the tenderer taking the trouble to prepare and submit its tender—to fairly and equally consider all tenders and to accept the most attractive tender compliant with the specifications.

If the inviting party fails to fairly and consistently consider all tenders, it will be liable since it has breached the "tender contract."[21] If all goes well, the successful bidder enters into a second contract for the construction project. Bidders must carefully prepare their bids so they comply with the tender specifications, or they will not be considered.

In other circumstances, there is no intention to form a contract upon the receipt of tenders, and the call for tenders expressly denies any. The purpose of inviting tenders is to identify a supplier as the appropriate source of work to be done or goods to be supplied, if required for a future project. For example, a municipal corporation may invite tenders by private trucking firms for the removal of snow from city streets during the coming winter. The selection of the successful bidder need not be followed up by a contract to remove whatever snow may fall—no one knows how severe the winter might be. The successful bidder has made a **standing offer**, and the municipality may then make specific requisitions for snow removal as needed over the winter season.[22] The terms of the invitation to tender will describe which purpose is intended.

standing offer an offer that may be accepted as needed from time to time

---

Ethical Issue — When Is There a Duty to Negotiate in Good Faith?

Suppose a party enters into negotiations to purchase a business only for the purpose of gaining insight on how best to launch a successful competing business. What if a television network enters negotiations over the purchase of programming not with a view to completing a contract but in order to satisfy the regulator that no purchase is possible?[23] In these situations, a party may be accused of negotiating in "bad faith." Canadian law does not recognize a duty to bargain in good faith unless there is a special relationship between the negotiating parties.[24]

Tendering is one area of contract law where obligations of good-faith negotiations exist. Bidders must be treated fairly and equally, but the law falls short of imposing a negligence duty of care.[25] Another example where good faith is required is the negotiation of options to renew an existing contractual relationship, and sometimes the contract expressly requires it.[26]

Questions to Consider

1. Should the law recognize a duty to negotiate all contracts in good faith? Why or why not?
2. How could a business protect its competitive information during sale negotiations?

---

[20] *Ron Engineering & Construction Eastern Ltd v Ontario*, [1981] 1 SCR 111. The Supreme Court affirmed the two-stage contract approach in *Design Services Ltd v Canada*, 2008 SCC 22.

[21] See *Martel Building Ltd v Canada*, [2000] 2 SCR 860; *Blackpool and Fylde Aero Club Ltd v Blackpool Borough Council*, [1990] 1 WLR 1195. For further obligations that may be implied on inviting tenders, see *MJB Enterprises Ltd v Defence Construction (1951) Ltd et al*, [1999] 1 SCR 619.

[22] See *Powder Mountain Resorts Ltd v British Columbia*, [2001] 11 WWR 488 (BCCA); *Mellco Developments Ltd v Portage Le Prairie (City)* (2002), 222 DLR (4th) 67 (M CA).

[23] *Westcom TV Group Ltd v CanWest Global Broadcasting Inc*, [1997] 1 WWR 761 (BCSC).

[24] See *Martel*, supra note 21 at para 73; *978011 Ontario Ltd*, supra note 12 at para 32; *Molson Canada 2005 v Miller Brewing Company*, 2013 ONSC 2758 at para 89.

[25] *Ron Engineering*, supra note 20; *Martel*, supra note 21; recently followed in *IPC Investment Corporation v Sawaged*, 2011 ONCA 827; *Design Services Ltd*, supra note 20; *Envoy Relocation Services Inc v Canada*, 2013 ONSC 2034.

[26] *Empress Towers Ltd v Bank of Nova Scotia* (1990), 73 DLR (4th) 400 (BCCA). For a discussion of interpreting an express term to negotiate in good faith, see *Molson Canada 2005*, supra note 23.

> **CHECKLIST**
>
> ## Ways in Which an Offer Comes to an End
>
> Once an offer has been made, it can end in a number of different ways:
>
> - The offer may lapse when the offeree fails to accept within the time stated in the offer, or if no time limit is stated, within a reasonable time.
> - The offeror revokes the offer before the offeree has accepted.
> - The offeree rejects the offer or makes a counter-offer (which is, in effect, a rejection).
> - The offeree accepts before any of the three above has occurred (in which case the offer ends and is replaced by a contract between the parties).

TRANSACTIONS BETWEEN PARTIES AT A DISTANCE FROM EACH OTHER

Method of Acceptance

If the offer expressly states how acceptance must be communicated, then it must be completed in exactly that way. When the offer is silent and the parties are at a distance, an offeree may communicate acceptance in any reasonable way given the circumstances and expectations of the parties.[27] An offer made by mail may reasonably be taken as allowing acceptance by mail. Ordinarily, any faster mode may be used: a fax, email, or telephone call in response to a letter can be valid acceptance. It may be reasonable that an offer made orally in the presence of the offeree be accepted by letter. If the offeror merely allows for acceptance by some means other than post as, for example, by telephone or in person, the offeree may still accept by post. It depends upon the pattern of negotiations between the parties and the business realities of the circumstances.

The ordinary rule is that acceptance by mail is communicated when sent—that is, when a properly addressed and stamped letter of acceptance is dropped in the mail.[28] The reasoning behind the "postal rule" is that an offeror who chooses to use the post office to send an offer is assumed to be willing to have the same means used for acceptance and to take a chance that the post office will be efficient in delivering it.

For all other forms of acceptance, the offeror is not bound unless and until the acceptance reaches him—and it must reach him before the offer has lapsed. When his stated preference is for a mode speedier than mail, there is increased risk that his offer will have lapsed before the letter of acceptance arrives. In these circumstances, the acceptance is not valid when dropped in the mailbox (as it would be if acceptance by mail were reasonably contemplated) but only when received.[29] Even when an offeror invites acceptance by mail, he may change the postal rule by stating in the offer that it will be effective only when received. He may state that acceptance by letter is invalid—it must be made in person. The terms of the offer will always override the general rules.

When instantaneous means of communication such as telephone or text are used, the offeror must receive the acceptance before he is bound. One court considered the

---

[27] *Henthorn v Fraser*, [1892] 2 Ch 27 at 33. See *Charlebois v Baril*, [1928] SCR 88. See also *Loft v Physicians' Services Inc* (1966), 56 DLR (2d) 481, where a letter posted in a mailbox but never received was held to be adequate notice to the defendant.

[28] S.M. Waddams, *The Law of Contracts*, 4th ed (Toronto: Canada Law Book Company, 1999) at 76–7; also *Sibtac Corporation Ltd v Soo; Lienster Investments Ltd, Third Party* (1978), 18 OR (2d) 395 at 402. The same principle applies when correspondence is sent by courier service: *R v Weymouth Sea Products Ltd* (1983), 149 DLR (3d) 637.

[29] *Premium Properties Limited v Subway Franchise Restaurants of Canada, Ltd*, 2014 ONSC 3150 at para 17.

implications of the telephone line going dead so that the offeror did not hear the offeree's words of acceptance. The court concluded that the acceptance would be ineffective and that the offeror would have no contractual liability.[30] The common sense of this rule is that the offeree would know that the line went dead and that his acceptance might not have been heard. He must then verify that his acceptance was received.

Similarly, fax, email, and text acceptance is not effective until received.[31] Ecommerce legislation establishes that acceptance may be completed by electronic mail and that email is deemed to be received when it is capable of being retrieved by the recipient—that is, arrives in the mailbox.[32] The legal issues that can arise generally in ecommerce are discussed more fully in Chapter 31.

Methods of Revocation

Revocation by instantaneous means of communication is subject to the same rules as acceptance, discussed above—it must reach the offeree.

However, the rule concerning withdrawal of an offer by post differs from the usual rule concerning the time of acceptance. Revocation by post is effective only when notice is actually received by the offeree, not when the sender drops it in the mailbox. As a result, the offeree may accept, and a binding contract may be formed after revocation of the offer has been mailed but not yet received.

ILLUSTRATION 6.7 Revocation Compared to Acceptance

Chen, in a letter mailed January 15, offered to sell his business to Baker for $70 000. The letter was received by Baker on January 17. On January 19, Baker mailed her letter of acceptance, which did not reach Chen until January 21. On January 18, however, Chen had decided to withdraw his offer and mailed a letter to Baker revoking it. This letter did not reach Baker until January 20.

Chen's revocation arrived too late. There was a valid contract on January 19 when the acceptance was mailed. Chen was bound from the moment the letter was dropped into the mailbox.

What is meant by the requirement that a revocation be "actually received"? Is it "received" when delivered to the place of business or residence of the offeree, or must it reach her in person? The general rule is that, unless the offeror knows or ought to know that the revocation will not reach the offeree at her usual address, delivery at that address establishes the fact and time of revocation, and the offeree is deemed to have notice from that time. This rule applies to other means of communication; if an offeror can establish that his revocation by courier or fax arrived at the offeree's usual address, it will be effective.

Determining the Jurisdiction Where a Contract Is Made

Parties to a contract are often in different provinces or countries at the time they enter into the arrangement. If a dispute arises, knowing where the contract was formed can be important, since the law in the two places may be different. The place—the **jurisdiction**—where the contract was formed is an important factor in deciding which law applies. The general rule is that a contract is formed at the place where the acceptance becomes

jurisdiction the province, state, or country whose laws apply to a particular situation

---

[30] *Entores, Ltd v Miles Far East Corporation*, [1955] 2 QB 327 at 332.

[31] See *Eastern Power Ltd v Azienda Communale Energia & Ambiente* (1999), 178 DLR (4th) 409 (Ont CA); *Brinkibon Ltd v Stahag Stahl Und Stahlwarenhandelsgesellschaft mbH*, [1983] 2 AC 34 (HL).

[32] Most provinces have adopted legislation in conformity with the *Uniform Electronic Commerce Act* prepared by the Uniform Law Conference of Canada; see e.g. *Electronic Commerce Act, 2000*, SO 2000, c 17, s 22(3).

effective. That place is determined by the moment in time when the contract is formed. When an offeror invites an acceptance by mail, the contract is formed at the moment when—and so at the place where—the acceptance is dropped into the mailbox. When an instantaneous means of communication such as text, email, or telephone is used, the contract is not formed until the offeror receives the acceptance, and that is at the place where he receives it.

UNILATERAL AND BILATERAL CONTRACTS

Bilateral: Offer of a Promise for a Promise

Most offers require a promise or agreement about future performance from the offeree and the offeror; acceptance is a promise to perform in the future. For example, if A Motors offers to sell a truck to B Inc. for $32 500 and B Inc. replies accepting the offer, a contract is formed though neither party has as yet performed anything. In effect, A Motors has promised to sell the truck for $32 500, and B Inc. in return has promised to buy it for $32 500; the two parties have traded promises. If either party should refuse to perform its promise, then the other would have a right to sue: both parties are bound to perform. This type of contract is called a **bilateral contract** because it has two stages—first, promises are made to form the contract, and later, they are fulfilled.

bilateral contract a contract where offeror and offeree trade promises and both are bound to perform later

The most common business transaction, the credit sale, is an example of a bilateral contract: It is not until well after the contract is made that the goods are delivered by the seller and paid for by the buyer. Similarly, in a contract of employment, the employer promises to pay a wage or salary, and the employee promises to work for a future period.

In bilateral contracts, each party is both a **promisor** and a **promise**; each has a future obligation to perform as well as a right to performance by the other. In a court action, the party who sues as the promisee alleges that she has not received the performance to which she is entitled. The promisor may offer one or more defences as reasons why his conduct should be excused and why he should not be ordered to pay damages for **breach of contract**.

promisor a party who is under an obligation to perform a promise according to the terms of the contract

promise a party who has the right to performance according to the terms of the contract

breach of contract a cause of action where a party to the contract claims that the other party has not fulfilled its promises

Unilateral: Offer of a Promise for an Act

Less often, an offer is accepted by performance. As in the *Carlill* case (Case 6.4), an offer may invite acceptance simply by the offeree performing its conditions without first communicating acceptance. An offer of a reward is accepted by anyone to whom the offer is made if she performs the required conditions, such as providing information or returning a lost article. As in the *Carlill* case, the offer may be accepted by multiple offerees, unless otherwise stated.

When offers are of a type that can be accepted by performance without prior communication, the resulting contract is called a **unilateral contract**. Once the offeree has performed, she need not do anything more—except, of course, request payment. All obligation now rests with the offeror to perform his half of the bargain. Some offers require the offeree to perform a series of acts over a long period.

unilateral contract a contract in which the offer is accepted by performing an act or series of acts required by the terms of the offer

Usually, offers state whether acceptance can be made by performance and specify time limits and manner of performance in order to limit the number of unilateral contracts that can be formed. Bilateral contracts are more common, and courts treat offers as calling for bilateral rather than unilateral action when the language does not clearly state otherwise.[33] The advantage of treating an agreement as bilateral is that both parties know they are bound from the moment the offeree communicates acceptance.

---

[33] *Sail Labrador*, *supra* note 17 at para 41.

subsidiary promise an implied promise that the offeror will not revoke once the offeree begins performance in good faith and continues to perform

Where the courts do not find it possible to interpret an offer as bilateral, they may still try to help the offeree by implying a **subsidiary promise** that the offeror will not revoke once the offeree begins performance in good faith and continues to perform. The offeree's effort, time, and money spent toward performance will not be wasted.[34] The obvious difficulty is that the offeror may not know when the offeree has started performance. Of course, the subsidiary promise is merely implied, and it may be excluded by an express term to the contrary in the offer.

CASE 6.5 Difference Between Bilateral and Unilateral

The parties entered into a lease of a charter boat for a five-year term. At the same time, the owner and the lessee agreed that, provided the lease went well, the lessee had the option to buy the boat at the end of the lease. The Supreme Court of Canada was asked to decide whether the option to buy the boat at the end of the lease was one term of the bilateral lease contract or whether it was a unilateral contract on its own. This was important because the lessee's late rental payments were a minor breach of the lease and could impact the lessee's right to exercise the option to purchase. The Court stated:

> A bilateral contract is a contract in which both parties undertake obligations through an exchange of promises. Acceptance of a bilateral contract as a general rule, occurs when the offeree communicates its counter-promise to the offeror. In contrast a unilateral contract is one in which a party makes a promise in return for the performance or forbearance of an act. There is no counter-promise to perform or forbear. In this way, a unilateral contract is a contract in which only one party undertakes a promise. This promise takes the form of an offer which can only be accepted by performance of the required act or forbearance. Such performance provides the other party's consideration, allowing it to enforce the original promise.[35]

In this case the option was a term of the bilateral contract because it was connected to the lease in several ways: the rental payments were the consideration, it was contained in the same document and involved the same property, and it was dependent on the performance of the lease.

FORMATION OF INTERNET CONTRACTS

Internet contracts are common in the consumer context. Businesses selling online use standardized terms and conditions just as in the physical world. As will be discussed in more detail in Chapter 31, two key types of legislation govern the formation of online contracts: ecommerce and consumer protection. The ecommerce legislation has modernized contract formation rules to allow "clicking an icon" to satisfy the acceptance and communication requirements of contract formation.[36]

Consumer protection legislation deals with the problems surrounding long, detailed standard terms linked to an order webpage. Most provinces (most notably Alberta, British Columbia, and Ontario) regulate internet consumer agreements. However, these new statutory provisions may, in fact, alter the traditional rules of offer and acceptance in internet contracts.

Section 38 of the Ontario *Consumer Protection Act, 2002* states that before a consumer enters into an internet agreement, the supplier shall disclose specific information about, among other things, the total price of the good or service, the terms of payment, and warranties. Subsection 38(2) states: "The supplier shall provide the consumer with an express opportunity to accept or decline the agreement . . . ."[37] This suggests that the internet consumer is the offeree, and it seems to contradict the general rule discussed in this chapter: that a retailer advertising goods for sale is making only an invitation to consumers to make offers—and typically in retail sales the consumer is the offeror.

Since an internet consumer is considered the offeree, after seeing the terms required to be disclosed by the supplier, she will be bound by the terms of the internet

---

[34] See *Brackenbury v Hodgkin*, 102 A 106, 116 Me 399 (1917); *Errington v Errington*, [1952] 1 All ER 149.

[35] *Sail Labrador, supra* note 17 at para 33.

[36] See e.g. *Electronic Commerce Act, 2000, supra* note 32, s 19.

[37] Ontario *Consumer Protection Act, 2002*, SO 2002, c 30, Sch A, s 38(2).

contract at such time as she clicks an "I accept" icon on her computer screen. However, some etailers specifically design their websites with multiple acceptances before a "submit" icon is finally clicked. This would appear to satisfy the legislative "agreement to terms" requirement before the entire offer to purchase is submitted. The contract is not formed until the retailer communicates acceptance with a confirmation number.

INTERNATIONAL ISSUE
Jurisdiction and Internet Contracts

Online contracting has greatly increased the number of international contracts in which the offeror is in one jurisdiction while the offeree is in another. As we have already described, the laws may be different in each location, and jurisdiction is often determined by the place of acceptance. To reduce the likelihood that the rules relating to the formation of electronic contracts might be different in each jurisdiction, the United Nations has undertaken a number of initiatives:

- United Nations Convention on the Use of Electronic Communications in International Contracts (2005)
- United Nations Commission on International Trade Law (UNCITRAL) Model Law on Electronic Signatures (2001)
- UNCITRAL Model Law on Electronic Commerce (1996)

Still, international variation exists. For example, some Canadian consumer protection legislation extends protection to Canadian consumers even when they are involved in international contracts governed by a foreign jurisdiction.

Questions to Consider

1. Should Canadian provinces coordinate their legislation to avoid international inconsistency?
2. How can a business use its online contractual terms and conditions to ensure that foreign consumers are aware of the law that applies to the contract?

UNCERTAINTY IN THE WORDING OF AN OFFER

A vague offer may prove to be no offer at all, and the intended acceptance of it cannot then form a contract. If the parties enter into a loosely worded arrangement, a court may find the agreement too ambiguous and uncertain to be enforced. A court will not enforce an agreement to agree; there must be certainty about essential terms.[38]

Examples of lack of certainty in the terms of a contract are a promise to give a "fair" share in the profits of a business; a promise to "favourably consider" the renewal of the present contract "if satisfied with you";[39] and a promise made by the buyer of a race horse to pay an additional amount on the price "if the horse is lucky."[40]

Even when the wording of a contract seems uncertain, a clear enough meaning might be found in evidence of local customs or trade usage that gives a new precision to the terms. The courts have a policy of trying to making contracts effective wherever possible; they hold that (1) anything is certain that is capable of being calculated or ascertained, and (2) where a contract may be construed as either enforceable or unenforceable, they will favour the interpretation that will see the contract enforced. Problems about meaning and certainty will be examined in greater detail in Chapters 9 and 10.

A contract for the sale of goods is different from a contract for the sale of land or shares in a proposed corporation. Where the parties have agreed on the quantity, the *Sale of Goods Act* provides that the price in a contract of sale of goods "may be left to be fixed in manner thereby agreed, or may be determined by the course of dealing between the parties" and that "[W]here the price is not determined in accordance with the foregoing provisions the buyer must pay a reasonable price."[41]

---

[38] *Olivieri v Sherman* (2007), 86 OR (3d) 778 at paras 45–51 (certainty is to be determined based upon an objective reading of the offer not on the subjective intent of a party).

[39] *Montreal Gas Co v Vasey*, [1900] AC 595.

[40] *Cuthing v Lynn* (1831), 109 ER 1130.

[41] See e.g. RSBC 1996, c 410, s 12; RSO 1990, c S.1, s 9; RSNS 1989, c 408, s 11.

CASE 6.6 Contract to Make a Contract

In *Brixham Investments Ltd v Hansink*,[42] both parties signed a letter providing for incorporation of the company and for entering into a further agreement. The letter did not set out the share allocation of the parties in the proposed company. When one party decided not to proceed with the project, the other sued for breach.

The Court considered whether the document was binding despite the lack of an agreement about share allocation. It held that, although a court will imply certain terms that arise by necessary inference (for instance, if the letter referred to the parties as "equal partners"), where the document did not deal in any way with this crucial question of share allocation, the court will not construct an agreement between the parties. Accordingly, the document did not constitute a binding contract.

In other words, "The law does not recognize a contract to enter into a contract."[43]

Strategies to Manage the Legal Risks

Disputes often arise between offeror and offeree when too little attention has been paid to the requirements of offer and acceptance or the terms of the offer. Since all terms of the contract must be in the offer prior to acceptance of it, offerors should take some simple steps to ensure a contract is properly formed:

- Advertisements should clearly state that they are not offers capable of being accepted.
- Where possible, offers should be made in writing, especially for bilateral contracts where time will elapse between the exchange of promises and their performance.
- If many similar transactions are likely, standard form contracts should be prepared in advance for use in all subsequent transactions.
- Standard form contracts should be designed so that one-sided, onerous, or unusual terms are brought to the attention of the non-drafting party.
- Standard form contracts should exclude any advertisements, representations, or pre-contract discussions as terms of the contract.
- If statements made by salespersons or in advertisements are important, they should be included in the terms of the offer.
- A specific time for acceptance should be set, after which the offer will lapse.
- The offer should set the manner for acceptance (both the act and the mode of communication).
- Essential terms should be clear or have a manner set for determination.

Offerees should also take steps to limit their legal risks:

- Ensure that acceptance is made within the designated time period and by the designated manner.
- Review standard form contracts or online terms and conditions to identify one-sided or onerous terms prior to acceptance.
- Alter an offer only when the intent is to reject it and make a counter-offer; if the intention is only to clarify its meaning, the clarification should be discussed with the offeror prior to its lapse.

---

[42] (1971), 18 DLR (3d) 533.

[43] *Von Hatzfeldt-Wildenburg v Alexander*, [1912] 1 Ch 284 at 289.

QUESTIONS FOR REVIEW

1. Distinguish an offer from a promise.
2. What is a standard form contract? Describe the different ways in which it may be accepted.
3. Explain the importance of notice of terms in a standard form contract. To what extent does the law protect the interest of the public in standard form contracts?
4. Describe the ways in which an offer may come to an end.
5. What is the legal effect of a counter-offer?
6. "We cannot be obligated by people who do work for us without our knowledge." Why?
7. What elements are required for an acceptance to be effective?
8. What does it mean to "purchase an option"?
9. What does it mean to "invite tenders"? When is a contract normally created in the tendering process?
10. Can acceptance be effective from the moment a letter of acceptance is mailed even when the offer was not itself made through the mail?
11. Explain the different rules that apply to offer and acceptance when, rather than using the postal system, the parties communicate by telephone.
12. Should the same offer and acceptance rules apply to the sending of responses by fax or email? Why?
13. Explain the difference between unilateral and bilateral contracts.
14. Did the *Carlill* case concern a unilateral or a bilateral contract?
15. What is the effect of an agreement in which the parties state that certain terms will be discussed and agreed upon at a later date?
16. Give an example of circumstances in which the rule "An offer must be communicated before it can be accepted" would operate.
17. Is it true that an acceptance must be communicated before a contract can be formed?
18. May a person withdraw a bid he makes at an auction sale before the fall of the hammer?

CASES AND PROBLEMS

1. Continuing Scenario

    Very few customers came to the grand opening of Ashley's restaurant on Monday morning, so she placed an ad in the following Thursday's local newspaper saying "Grand Opening Saturday Morning—Join Ashley for coffee and let her satisfy your sweet tooth." Bill and Marlene saw the ad and went to the restaurant on Saturday. They sat down at a table and waved over a waitress who was holding a coffeepot. They did not even look at the menu on the table. The waitress came over to the table, and Bill pointed to his cup; she filled it up with coffee. She turned and looked at Marlene; Marlene nodded, and her cup was also filled. The waitress then asked if she could get them something, and Bill said, "Surprise us with something to 'satisfy our sweet tooth.'" The waitress returned with two cinnamon buns. Bill picked up the bun and took a bite. It was much too sweet; he did not like it, so Marlene did not even touch hers. They got up and left the restaurant without paying. The menu listed coffee at a price of $1.75 and cinnamon buns at $2.50. Do Bill and Marlene have a contract with the restaurant?

2. Friday evening after closing, Sackett's Appliances placed an ad in its window: "This weekend only, five Whirlwind dishwashers, reduced from $1199 to $599! Shop

early!" Martens saw the ad later that evening. She appeared the next morning at 9:00 a.m. when Sackett's opened its doors and stated to the clerk she would take one of the Whirlwind dishwashers. The clerk replied that the ad was a mistake; the price should have been $999. Martens demanded to speak with the manager and insisted on Sackett's honouring its offer to sell at $599. The manager said, "I'm sorry, madam, but that machine cost us more than $800. We cannot sell it at $599." Martens said Sackett's was in breach of contract and she would see her lawyer about it.

Is Martens right? Explain.

3. Garrett is the manager of Aristo Condos Inc. and is in charge of selling vacant units in the Aristo Towers. On October 4, Heilman examined several of the units with Garrett and said he thought the prices a bit high but would think about it. Several days later, on October 7, Garrett sent Heilman an email stating, "I will sell you any one of the units we examined together (numbers 14, 236, 238, or 307) for $275 000. I am sending you all the details by courier." Garrett then sent by courier to Heilman a formal offer containing all of the necessary terms, including the required down payment and acceptable mortgage financing.

Later that day after he had received the email message, but before he had received the letter, Heilman emailed Garrett, "I accept your offer with respect to unit 307."

Has a binding contract been formed by Garrett's email? In what circumstances might this question become the basis of a dispute between the parties?

4. Last year, Lambert bought a car on August 15 and insured it with the Reliable Insurance Company, for whom Drake was the local agent. On the following July 29, Drake telephoned Lambert about renewing her policy and learned she was on vacation at her summer cottage. Acting on behalf of Reliable Insurance, Drake wrote to Lambert at her cottage: "As you know, your car insurance policy with us expires on August 15. We will renew this policy on the same terms unless notified to the contrary by you. You may sign the application form and pay after you return to the city."

On her way back from her holidays on August 16, Lambert struck and injured a pedestrian with her car. The pedestrian claimed $100 000 damages from Lambert, and on referring the matter to the Reliable Insurance Company, Lambert was informed that her policy of insurance had expired without renewal on August 15.

Discuss Lambert's legal position.

5. A province and its largest university created a program by which the province would give funding to disadvantaged students. Students were told by the university that they would receive funding over four years, and on that basis, they enrolled in the program. The students dealt only with the university. In the third year of the program, the province restructured it so that students had to obtain their maximum Canada Student Loan before being eligible for funding.

The students sued for a declaration requiring the province to pay them at the original funding level for the full four years on the basis of a binding contract with the province. They claimed that they reasonably believed they had a contractual arrangement with the province not to alter the terms and conditions of the funding arrangement. The province defended by stating that there was no contract with the students because they had not communicated their acceptance to it but dealt only with the university; if anyone was bound, it was the university.

Discuss the merits of each party's argument. Who do you think should succeed?

6. Purcell was in failing health and advertised to sell his retail computing equipment business. Quentin was familiar with Purcell's business operations; he sent Purcell a detailed offer to buy for $450 000, paying $75 000 as a cash down payment, with the balance payable in instalments over two years. Purcell promptly sent an email

to Quentin stating: "The price and all the other terms seem fair, except that I need substantially more cash by way of down payment—say, $125 000. Tell me how high you are willing to go." Quentin replied by email, "There is no way I can increase the cash payment."

Purcell replied the next day, "Okay. I've thought about it, and given the state of my health, I have decided to accept your offer." By then, Quentin had heard that the business had suffered because of Purcell's declining health, and he refused to go through with the purchase. He asserted that since Purcell had refused his offer, there was no deal.

Is Quentin right? Has Purcell any basis for claiming there is a binding contract with Quentin?

7. Daly, a U.S. citizen, began negotiations with Stevens of Vancouver to investigate and stake mineral claims at the head of the Leduc River in British Columbia. Daly had discovered evidence of deposits there some 20 years earlier.

On January 13, Daly wrote, "A large mining company in Boise is showing an interest. To protect my interest it will be necessary for me to arrive at some definite arrangement soon." Stevens replied on January 17, "Perhaps we can make some arrangement this summer to finance you in staking claims for which I would give you an interest. I would suggest that I should pay for your time and expenses and carry you for a 10 percent interest in the claims." Daly replied on January 22, "Your proposition appeals to me as being a fair one."

Soon after, Daly was called to active duty in the United States Naval Reserve Engineering Corps and was sent to the Marshall Islands. Correspondence continued with some difficulty, but on February 28, Daly wrote, "As I informed you in a previous letter, your offer of a 10 percent interest for relocating and finding these properties is acceptable to me, provided there is a definite agreement to this effect in the near future."

On March 5, Stevens wrote, "I hereby agree that if you will take me in to the showings, and I think they warrant staking, I will stake the claims and give you a 10 percent interest. The claims would be recorded in my name and I will have full discretion in dealing with them—you are to get 10 percent of the vendor interest. I can arrange to get a pilot here."[44] Daly replied on April 12, "If you will inform me when you can obtain a pilot, I will immediately take steps for a temporary release in order to be on hand."

On June 6, Stevens wrote, "I was talking to a prospector who said he had been over your showings at the head of the Leduc River, and in his opinion it would be practically impossible to operate there, as the showings were behind ice fields that, along with the extreme snowfalls, make it very doubtful if an economic operation could be carried on. I now have so much work lined up that I doubt if I would have time to visit your showings and do not think I would be warranted in making the effort to get in there due to the unfavourable conditions. I must advise you, therefore, not to depend on making this trip, and suggest if you are still determined to go in, to make some other arrangements."

Daly did not reply. On his return from the Marshall Islands the following year, he did, however, follow up his interest in the property. He discovered that in July, Stevens had sent prospectors into the area and, as a result of their investigations, had staked claims in his own name and later sold them to a mining development company. Daly brought an action against Stevens claiming damages for breach of contract.

Should Daly succeed in his action? Explain.

---

[44] *Dawson v Helicopter Exploration*, [1955] SCR 868.

8. The City of Cameron was growing and needed to expand its water purification plant. It wanted to buy two hectares of land adjacent to the current purification plant from Margot Nurseries, a thriving fruit and vegetable business owning 40 hectares of prime land. As the two hectares were particularly important to Margot, she bargained for a substantial price to pay for the relocation of her business's sorting and packaging area.

The city bargained very hard and threatened to expropriate the land—as it had power to do under the provincial *Expropriation Act*—if a deal could not be reached. Finally, in exasperation, Margot handed the director of the purification plant a detailed written statement of the terms upon which she would sell, with the offer to be open for 10 days. She asked for a price of $200 000, with $50 000 paid on acceptance. She would permit the city to begin excavation on the nearest one-quarter hectare, but it must delay moving onto the remainder of the land for 60 days so that she could make the needed relocation. When Margot handed the director the offer, she stated that if the city began excavations on the one-quarter hectare, that would be acceptance of her offer.

Within a week, city workers began excavating about 20 metres into Margot's land, and two days later she was served with a notice of expropriation under the *Expropriation Act*, offering her a price of $80 000. Under the Act, if the parties do not reach a settlement, a court will hear evidence about the market value of the land and the costs caused by compulsory displacement to the owner; it then awards a sum in compensation and orders the owner to give up possession.

Margot, claiming that the city had accepted her offer before the expropriation proceedings were started, sued the city for damages for breach of the contract. Discuss the arguments of each side, and give your opinion on who should succeed. What general issue of public policy arises when a legislature grants powers of expropriation to municipalities?

Chapter 7
Formation of a Contract: Consideration and Intention

- THE MEANING OF CONSIDERATION
- GRATUITOUS PROMISES
- ADEQUACY OF CONSIDERATION
- MOTIVE CONTRASTED WITH CONSIDERATION: PAST CONSIDERATION
- RELATION BETWEEN EXISTING LEGAL DUTY AND CONSIDERATION
- GRATUITOUS REDUCTION OF A DEBT
- EQUITABLE ESTOPPEL
- THE EFFECT OF A REQUEST FOR GOODS OR SERVICES
- THE USE OF A SEAL
- INTENTION TO CREATE LEGAL RELATIONS
- STRATEGIES TO MANAGE THE LEGAL RISKS

Before an accepted offer becomes a legally binding agreement, two other essential requirements must be present: consideration and the intent to create a contract.

In this chapter we examine such questions as:

- What is the nature of consideration?
- How do we distinguish promises with consideration from gratuitous promises? from motive for making a promise? from an existing legal duty to perform?
- What is equitable estoppel?
- What other ways are there to make a promise binding?
- Why is it essential that parties intend their promises to be legally binding, and how is intention established?

THE MEANING OF CONSIDERATION

bargain each party pays a price for the promise of the other

consideration the price for which the promise of the other is bought

An accepted offer is not an enforceable contract unless it has consideration. The accepted offer must form a **bargain**—where each party pays a price or gives value for the promise obtained from the other party. In a unilateral contract, the price paid for the offeror's promise is the act done by the offeree. In a bilateral contract, the price paid for each party's promise is the promise of the other. This price is called consideration. In short, **consideration** is "the price for which the promise [or the act] of the other is bought."[1]

A promisor usually bargains for a benefit to himself, such as a promise to pay money, deliver goods, or provide services; but it need not be directly for his own benefit. So long as the promisor bargains for the other party to do something—or to promise to do something—that she otherwise would not do, the promisor will have received consideration.

ILLUSTRATION 7.1 Promise to Alter Conduct

Adams, a creditor of Brown, threatened to sue Brown for an overdue debt. Brown's friend Cox then promised to pay Brown's debt to Adams if Adams would refrain from suing Brown, and Adams agreed.

If Cox failed to pay Adams as agreed, and Adams sued him for breach of contract, she would succeed. To establish consideration she need only show that she changed her conduct—that is, that she refrained from suing Brown—in return for Cox's promise. The "price" she agrees to pay for Cox's promise need not confer a direct benefit on him.

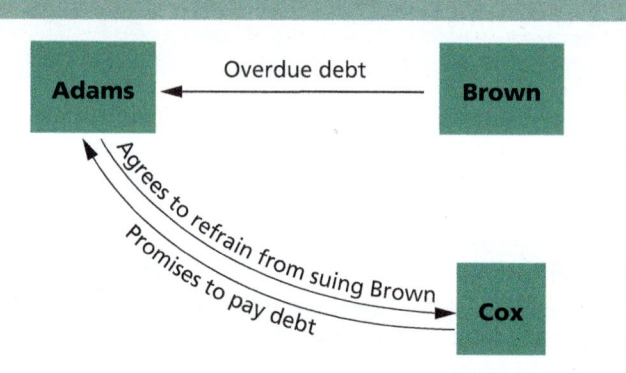

GRATUITOUS PROMISES

gratuitous promise a promise made without bargaining for or accepting anything in return

With some exceptions discussed later, consideration is necessary to make a contract legally binding. A person may, of course, make a promise to another without bargaining for anything in return. A promise made in the absence of consideration is a **gratuitous promise**, and even when accepted by the offeree, the promise is not a contract enforceable in law. A promise to make a gift and a promise to perform services without remuneration are common examples of gratuitous promises. Such arrangements are not legal contracts.

The law does not prevent performance of a gratuitous promise. It simply does nothing to help if the promisor does not perform; the promisee has no legal remedy—he cannot seek compensation for loss of the benefit he was promised. Ethically, most people perform their gratuitous promises.

What about charitable donations? Charities seldom find it in their interest to sue those who have made pledges but do not perform. They rely upon their prospective donors' sense of honour; they understand that people might become reluctant to give pledges if charities were likely to sue them for non-payment.

Occasionally donors have died before honouring large pledges, and charities have sued their estates.[2] A charity claiming payment will be asked what price it paid for the

---

[1] P.H. Winfield, *Pollock's Principles of Contract*, 13th ed (London: Stevens & Sons, 1950) at 133.
[2] See e.g. *Governors of Dalhousie College v Boutilier*, [1934] 3 DLR 593.

pledge. A court may find consideration if the charity began a specific project, such as constructing a building, in response to the donor's promise. The court must, however, be able to find an implied request from the promisor—if not an explicit one—that the charity undertake the project as the "price" of the pledge. When a pledge is for general funds, the charity can make it legally binding if it uses a seal on its pledge cards or offers something to the donor in return, such as membership rights. The use of a seal is discussed later in this chapter.

> **CASE 7.1 Consideration for Charitable Pledges**
>
> Dr. and Mrs. Marquis met, worked, and volunteered at the Brantford General Hospital; they became regular donors. After Dr. Marquis's death, Mrs. Marquis promised to give the hospital $1 000 000 over five years. The hospital foundation requested permission to name the coronary care unit after the couple. Mrs. Marquis signed the pledge and gave the first year's installment of $200 000. Unfortunately, she died the next year. In her will, she left one-fifth of her estate to the hospital. The estate refused to pay the outstanding $800 000 on the pledge, claiming the estate gift replaced it. The foundation argued that it was entitled to both. The pledge was an enforceable contract, and the consideration was the promise to name the coronary unit. The court disagreed. It was the foundation that suggested the naming; Mrs. Marquis never requested it. It was a voluntary act of gratitude. In addition, it was not a promise given by the foundation because the board had not yet approved the name.[3]

As long as a gratuitous promise remains unperformed, the promisee has no right to a remedy. If the promise is performed—a gift is made. If the donor later changes her mind, she cannot demand return on grounds of lack of consideration. Once she has voluntarily made the gift, it is no longer her property, and she does not own it, except in rare cases of undue influence, as discussed in Chapter 9.

ADEQUACY OF CONSIDERATION

Although the consideration given in return for a promise must have some value, the court does not make sure the parties have made a fair bargain. If a party agreed to a grossly inadequate consideration for his promise, then that was up to him. It is not the task of the courts to assess the adequacy of the consideration; relative value is too subjective a concept.

If there is some allegation of wrongdoing by one party, a court might look at adequacy of consideration because it might point to fraud, duress, or undue influence exerted on the promisor. There would need to be other evidence of fraud before the court would hold that the promise is voidable at the promisor's option. Courts have become increasingly concerned with protecting the interests of weak parties such as consumers from unconscionable conduct.[4]

When parties agree to settle a dispute out of court, consideration can be a challenge. Typically one party pays another to drop a lawsuit or to waive their right to start a lawsuit. However, if the other party's case was weak, and he would have lost in court, is his promise not to sue, therefore, worthless and not really consideration for the promise to pay something in settlement? The answer is no—lawsuits are expensive and unpleasant no matter who wins, and promising not to start or continue a lawsuit is sufficient consideration when the party honestly believed he had a case.[5]

---

[3] *Brantford General Hospital Foundation v Marquis Estate* (2003), 67 OR (3d) 432.
[4] See Chapter 9. Unconscionable consideration is now the subject of consumer protection legislation. See e.g. *Consumer Protection Act, 2002*, SO 2002, c 30, Sch A, s 15.
[5] *Haigh v Brooks* (1839), 113 ER 119; *Famous Foods Ltd v Liddle*, [1941] 3 DLR 525; *Fairgrief v Ellis*, [1935] 2 DLR 806.

If this were not the rule, no one could ever be sure that a settlement was binding; subsequent information might upset a settlement made in good faith.

MOTIVE CONTRASTED WITH CONSIDERATION: PAST CONSIDERATION

As noted, consideration is the price that makes the promisor's promise binding. However, the promisor's reason for making the promise, the motive, is irrelevant, whether it be gratitude, a sense of honour, duty, affection, or charity, or even part of an unworthy scheme. Motive cannot change a gratuitous promise into a binding contract, nor can it reduce a binding promise into a merely voluntary obligation.

CASE 7.2 Timing of Consideration

In *Eastwood v Kenyon*,[6] Eastwood, who was the guardian of Mrs. Kenyon while she was a child, personally borrowed money in order to finance her education and to maintain the estate of which she was sole heiress. On coming of age, she promised to reimburse him; after her marriage, her husband, Mr. Kenyon, promised Eastwood to pay back the sum, but he did not. Eastwood sued Mr. Kenyon, claiming that Kenyon had a moral duty to honour his promise, but his action failed. Eastwood had not given any consideration in return of Kenyon's promise to repay. Kenyon's promise happened well after the earlier loan was made, and his motive, a sense of gratitude, was not consideration.

If one person promises to reward another who has previously done an act gratuitously or given something of value, the promise is not binding. That promise is gratuitous—just like the benefit that the promisee had earlier conferred upon the promisor. Another approach is to say that the motive of the promisor was to return the kindness of the promisee, and, of course, motive and consideration are not the same thing. The benefit previously conferred upon the promisor is often called **past consideration**. Since there is no element of bargain—that is, of the benefit being performed in return for the promise—the expression is really contradictory, for "past consideration" is no consideration at all.

past consideration a gratuitous benefit previously conferred upon a promisor

Ethical Issue Promises

Ethically, it is wrong to break any promise seriously made, and a promisor has a moral duty to perform. If every promise were legally enforceable simply because the promisor had a moral duty to do as he said he would, we would not need the doctrine of consideration. In civil law legal systems, where **moral cause** may be sufficient to make a promise binding, courts must probe internally into a promisor's motive in order to establish moral obligation. Although the doctrine of consideration has been attacked as causing unfair decisions in some instances (and undoubtedly it sometimes does), it has the benefit of being an objective rather than a subjective test.

Questions to Consider

1. What difficulties arise when evaluating motives to establish moral obligations?
2. Is moral cause a more appropriate standard than consideration?

moral cause moral duty of promisor to perform his promise

RELATION BETWEEN EXISTING LEGAL DUTY AND CONSIDERATION

Where A has an existing contractual duty to B, a later promise by B to pay A something extra to perform that obligation is not binding. Performance by A is not good consideration for the later promise because A was already contractually bound to

---

[6] (1840), 113 ER 482.

perform. Indeed, A's failure to do so would have been a breach of contract. For example, a promise to members of a crew to increase their pay if they did not desert their ship was held to be unenforceable.[7] The existing contracts of employment between the crew and the employer bound the crew to perform their duties faithfully. On the other hand, a term of such contracts is that the ship be seaworthy. If it proves unseaworthy, the crew members are released from their obligation, and then, of course, there will be consideration for the promise to increase their pay if the crew stays with the ship.[8]

The situation sometimes arises where one party threatens to default on its obligation to perform and leave the other party to sue for breach. A common example occurs in construction projects.

ILLUSTRATION 7.2 Extra Payment for On Time Completions

A Inc. contracts to build an office building for land developer B. A Inc. runs into unexpected difficulties and informs B that it is thinking of abandoning the project. However, B has already leased out large parts of the building. If A Inc. abandons the job, B will lose valuable time finding another builder to complete the project and will be in breach of leases he has made.

To avoid these difficulties, B offers to pay A Inc. an extra $500 000 in order to complete construction on time. A Inc. accepts and completes on the agreed date. B may refuse to pay the additional sum on the grounds that he received no new consideration for his promise: A Inc. was already bound by its contract to complete on time.

Canadian courts take the view that this conduct is a form of economic blackmail by the party threatening to abandon the contract, and so they hold that there is no consideration for the promise to pay an extra sum.[9] However, a supplier intent on economic blackmail can still exact a legally enforceable promise from its customer to pay an increased price by delivering a paperclip (or any other item of negligible value) to her in return for the promise or by insisting that the customer make her promise under seal (as discussed later in this chapter).

Consideration already given will not support new promises when parties try to modify an existing contract, even though such changes are not always an unfair exploitation of the promisor. So far, the Canadian courts have been reluctant to recognize this reality,[10] although an English case has allowed a construction company to recover a promised extra sum for completion.[11] The court was satisfied that there was no economic duress; the construction company had not exerted undue pressure, and both parties benefited from performance. As well, if the second agreement resolves some uncertainty or dispute over the entitlements arising from the pre-existing contract, Canadian courts will find the subsequent contract has consideration.[12]

"Clarifying an unclear term in a long-term contract, in order to create certainty and to avoid future costly disputes, enures to the parties' mutual benefit, and is something of value that flows from and to each contracting party. It thus serves as a functional form of consideration."[13]

---

[7] *Stilk v Myrick* (1809), 70 ER 1168.
[8] *Turner v Owen* (1862), 6 ER 79.
[9] See *Gilbert Steel Ltd v University Construction Ltd* (1976), 67 DLR (3d) 606.
[10] See Stephen Waddams, "Canadian Contract Law, 1970–2010" (2011) 50 Can Bus LJ at 416–17.
[11] *Williams v Roffey Brothers & Nicholls (Contractors) Ltd*, [1990] 1 All ER 512. See *Greater Fredericton Airport Authority Inc v NAV Canada*, (2008), 290 DLR (4th) 405 at para 31 (holding that a threat to break the contract amounts to duress).
[12] *Richcraft Homes Ltd v Urbandale Corp*, 2016 ONCA 622.
[13] *Ibid* at para 47.

A related problem arises when a stranger—a "third party" to a contract—promises to pay a sum to the promisor for his promise to perform already existing obligations to the promisee.

> **ILLUSTRATION 7.3 Third Party**
>
> As in Illustration 7.2, A Inc. has made a contract to construct a building for B. C, who has a lease as principal tenant in the building, promises to pay A $100 000 if A completes the building on time. Is there consideration for C's promise?[14] Since A is already under a duty to B to construct the building on time, what further price does A give for C's promise?

A can enforce C's promise, and further, if A failed to perform, A would be liable to actions by both B and C.[15] A has given new consideration by promising C to complete on time and making himself liable to C if he fails to do so. The situation where the later promise is made by the promisee in the original contract differs from that where it is made by a third party to that contract.

Suppose A's duty to perform is a public duty required by law, as where A is a police officer. If B promises to pay A for services as a police officer, the court is confronted with two problems—the question of public policy and of consideration. If police officers are asked to do something that they are already bound to do or something that will interfere with their regular duties, the court worries that the promise to pay them tends to corrupt public servants; the court will likely find the promise unenforceable on grounds of public policy. On the other hand, if the court finds that the officers have been requested to do something beyond their duties and not in conflict with them, it will likely find consideration and hold the promise binding, as where a company agreed to pay for a special police guard during a strike and was held to be bound by its promise.[16]

GRATUITOUS REDUCTION OF A DEBT

The consideration requirement can lead to some other unsatisfactory results, especially in debt collection transactions.

> **CASE 7.3 Settling for Less**
>
> In the famous case of *Foakes v Beer*, a debtor owed a large sum of money to his creditor, and payment was overdue. The creditor agreed to accept a series of installments of the principal, and to forgo her right to interest, if the debtor paid promptly and regularly. The debtor paid the full principal as agreed, but the creditor then sued for the interest. She succeeded on the grounds that her promise to accept less than the total sum owing—that is, principal plus accrued interest—was a gratuitous promise and did not bind her.[17]

This rule is unrealistic. For a number of sensible reasons, a creditor, C, may find it beneficial to settle for a reduced amount rather than insist on full payment. First, the compromise may avoid placing a debtor in bankruptcy where, by the time all other creditors' claims have been recognized, C might end up with less money than if she

---

[14] *Shadwell v Shadwell* (1860), 142 ER 62.

[15] *Scotson v Pegg* (1861), 158 ER 121; *Pao On v Lau Yiu Long*, [1979] 3 WLR 435.

[16] *Glasbrook Brothers v Glamorgan County Council*, [1925] AC 270.

[17] *Foakes v Beer* (1884), 9 App Cas 605. *Process Automation Inc v Norsteam Intertec Inc & Arroyave*, 2010 ONSC 3987 (still the common law rule, para 88).

had accepted a reduced sum. Second, the proposed reduction may enable the debtor to persuade friends to lend him enough money to take advantage of it and make a fresh start. Third, the debtor may simply not have the assets to enable him to pay in full, so that a court judgment against him would not realize more than the reduced amount. Finally, C may urgently need at least part of the sum owed her for other commitments. She may be happier to take the lesser amount at once, instead of later collecting the full account with all the delays inherent in a legal action.

The rule in *Foakes v Beer* can be avoided in several ways. First, early payment before the due date is sufficient new consideration to make an agreed reduction in the debt binding on the creditor. So if the debtor pays $600 one day in advance in settlement of a $1000 debt due the next day, the agreement to accept $600 is binding. The court will not inquire into the adequacy of the consideration; if the creditor chooses to reduce the debt by $400 in order to receive payment one day in advance, she may bind herself to do so.

Second, the rule in *Foakes v Beer* applies only to reduced payments of money. It does not apply to the transfer of goods or to the provision of services. Since an individual may make a contract for a clearly inadequate consideration if he so desires—he may agree to pay $1000 for a trinket, a cheap watch, or a package of cigarettes—similarly, he may agree to cancel a $1000 debt on receiving any one of these objects. In effect, he is trading the debt for the object, and such an agreement is valid, provided he agrees to it voluntarily. The result of this reasoning creates a paradox: If a person agrees to accept $900 in full settlement of a $1000 debt, he may later sue for the balance successfully; if a person accepts $500 and a string of beads worth 10 cents in full settlement of a $1000 debt, he will fail if he sues for the balance.

Third, the rule in *Foakes v Beer* applies only to agreements between a creditor and debtor. A third party, who is not bound to pay anything to the creditor, may offer to pay the creditor a lesser sum if she will cancel the debt. A creditor who accepts such an offer is bound by her promise and will fail if she later sues the debtor.[18] The result is the same as if the third person had purchased the debt from the creditor.

The rule in *Foakes v Beer* has been restricted by statute in British Columbia, Alberta, Saskatchewan, Manitoba, and Ontario.[19] Under any of these acts, when a creditor accepts part performance (that is, a lesser sum of money) in settlement of a debt, and the debtor actually pays the reduced amount, the entire debt is extinguished. The payment must be acknowledged to be a full settlement of the debt. The creditor may still be able to go back on her promise to accept a lesser sum of money before the sum is actually paid.

Finally, the rule in *Foakes v Beer* is avoided if the creditor agrees in writing and under seal to reduce the debt. The concept of a "seal" is discussed later in the chapter.

EQUITABLE ESTOPPEL

Suppose a person makes a gratuitous promise to another, fully intending to keep it, but later finds it inconvenient to perform. Meanwhile, the promisee has quite reasonably relied on the promise and has incurred expenses he would otherwise not have made. What happens if the promisor subsequently defaults? According to the strict rules of contract law, the answer is—nothing at all. The gratuitous promise remains gratuitous, the promise cannot be enforced, and the promisee suffers the burden of his expenses.

---

[18] *Hirachand Punamchand v Temple*, [1911] 2 KB 330.

[19] *Law and Equity Act*, RSBC 1996, c 224, s 43; *Judicature Act*, RSA 2000, c J-1, s 13 (1); *Queen's Bench Act, 1998*, SS 1998, c Q-1.01, s 64; *Mercantile Law Amendment Act*, CCSM c M-129, s 6; and *Mercantile Law Amendment Act*, RSO 1990, c M.10, s 16. See *Process Automation Inc, supra* note 17.

The principle of equitable estoppel may provide some relief. As noted in Chapter 2, equitable principles were developed by old English courts to soften the harshness of strict rules. The above described situation may be resolved more fairly if the equitable concept of "estoppel" is applied.

Estoppel Based on Fact

estopped prevented

When one person asserts as true a certain statement of fact and another relies on that statement to his detriment, the maker of the statement will be **estopped** (prevented) from denying the truth of his original statement in a court of law, even if it turns out to have been untrue.

ILLUSTRATION 7.4 Relied on Statement

A purchased a retail shoe business from X in rented premises owned by B. After a few months, A mentions to her landlord, B, that the business does not have an adequate sales area and that she would like to turn a back room into a display and fitting salon. The room contains a number of pieces of old furniture that she believes belong to B and that she would like to get rid of. B says, "That furniture belonged to X, and you acquired it when you bought the business. You can do as you like with it." A replies, "I thought it was yours. That's what X told me." "No, it's yours," B answers.

The tenant next door to A is present and hears the conversation.

That evening, when B reports the incident to his wife, she becomes furious and reminds B that several antique pieces given to them by her grandmother are stored in the back room of the store. When B arrives at the shoe store the next morning, the furniture is gone. He then sues A for the value of the antique furniture.

B would fail because A can prove in her defence that B said that the furniture was A's, and the court would estop B from asserting the true state of the facts.

Estoppel applies to an assertion of existing fact; but does it also apply to a promise of future conduct? This question has presented a problem for the courts. The truth of existing facts is an objective matter that can easily be determined by evidence. Future promises are a different matter.

On the grounds of fairness, courts exercised their equitable jurisdiction to estop (prevent) the promisor from claiming he was not bound by his gratuitous promise. This reasoning extended the idea of factual estoppel to promises. The principle has been called **promissory estoppel or equitable estoppel** because the court is acting "equitably" to override a strict common law rule.

promissory estoppel or equitable estoppel the court's exercise of its equitable jurisdiction to estop a promisor from claiming that she was not bound by her gratuitous promise where reliance on that promise caused injury to the promisee

The doctrine of equitable estoppel originated well over a century ago in the leading case of *Hughes v Metropolitan Railway Co*,[20] and is currently limited to use by the promisor only as a defence against a claim where a legal relationship already exists between the parties.

CASE 7.4 Extending a Deadline

Metropolitan Railway, a tenant under a 99-year lease of a large block of buildings, was required to keep the building in good repair. The penalty for failure to do so would be termination of the lease. Hughes served notice that repairs were needed and gave the tenant six months to complete them. The tenant then suggested that Hughes might be interested in buying back the remaining years of the tenant's 99-year lease. The lease was a valuable one as rents to subtenants had risen greatly over the long years of the master lease. When Hughes expressed interest in the proposal, the two sides began serious negotiations. Hughes agreed that repairs could be delayed, since they would result in an increased sale price of the lease.

---

[20] (1877), 2 App Cas 439.

> After several months, negotiations broke down, and the tenant then proceeded with the repairs. They were not finished within six months of the original notice but were complete within six months of the end to negotiations. Hughes sued for forfeiture of the lease, and had he succeeded he would have obtained the remaining years free.
>
> The court held that the suspension of the repair notice during negotiations prevented Hughes from reverting to his strict legal rights in the lease. The notice became effective again only on negotiations being broken off, when the tenant could no longer rely on Hughes's implied promise to delay the repair deadline.

While a gratuitous promise may still be withdrawn, its withdrawal is not allowed to prejudice the promisee in respect of any past reliance on it. Notice of withdrawal (or an end to circumstances in which the promise is implied) may restore the promisor's rights to any future performance still owed by the promisee. In the *Hughes* case, the landlord was entitled, after the negotiations had broken down, to require repairs to be made within the six-month period provided in the lease.

Therefore, equitable estoppel applies in situations when

1. some form of legal relationship already exists between the parties;
2. one of the parties promises (perhaps by implication only) to release the other from some or all of the other's legal duties to him; and
3. the other party, in reliance on that promise, acts in a way that alters his position and would make it a real hardship if the promisor reneges on his promise.[21]

In these circumstances, if the promisor ignores his promise and sues to enforce his original rights, the promisee could use equitable estoppel to *defend* the action against him.

In *Conwest Exploration Co v Letain*,[22] the Supreme Court of Canada pushed the doctrine quite far, possibly suggesting that equitable estoppel might be used as a cause of action.[23] The facts were complicated, but the essential ones for our purposes can be summarized as follows in Case 7.5.

CASE 7.5 Option Expiry Date

> A held an option to purchase certain mining claims. Before the date of expiry of the option, B, the grantor of the option, impliedly agreed to its extension. (As in the *Hughes* case, it appeared to be in his own interest to do so.) As a result, A did not hurry to complete the required task under the option before the original expiry date, but he did try to exercise the option shortly afterward, before B had given any notice that he wished to return to his strict legal rights. In an action brought by A asking the court to permit him to exercise his option, the court did not allow B to revert to the original expiry date, and A's action succeeded.
>
> B implicitly promised to extend the original option period, while legal relations existed between the parties. On the one hand, it can be argued that this decision amounts to no more than an application of the *Hughes* case. On the other hand, the opposing view is that once the original option had expired, without an extension having been granted for additional consideration, no existing legal relationship between A and B remained; they were as strangers. Accordingly, to permit A to succeed is to permit him to use equitable estoppel as a cause of action. So far, the Canadian courts have not embraced this second view.

Injurious Reliance

In the United States, the principle of equitable estoppel has been expanded to allow the injured party to force the promisor to perform the promise.[24] Courts in some

---

[21] See e.g. *Central London Property Trust, Ltd v High Trees House, Ltd*, [1947] KB 130.
[22] (1964), 41 DLR (2d) 198. See also *Re Tudale Exploration Ltd and Bruce et al* (1978), 20 OR (2d) 593 at 597, 599.
[23] See e.g. *Crabb v Arun District Council*, [1976] Ch 179; *Paul v Lam*, 2011 BCSC 980.
[24] *Ricketts v Scothorn*, 77 NW 365 (1898).

injurious reliance loss or harm suffered by a promisee who, to his detriment, relied reasonably on a gratuitous promise

states assert that since the promisor by his conduct induced the injured party to rely on his promise, the promisor must honour his promise to prevent an injustice. This principle, known as **injurious reliance**, is a cause of action, not just a defence.[25]

The U.S. term "injurious reliance" and the English term "equitable estoppel" are essentially two sides of the same coin: Injurious reliance looks at the situation from the point of view of enforcement, whereas equitable estoppel views it from the position of the defence.

INTERNATIONAL ISSUE
Will Injurious Reliance Be Adopted by the Canadian Courts?

In the American doctrine of injurious reliance, a promisee might have a cause of action against a promisor who makes and then breaks a gratuitous promise on which the promisee has relied to his detriment. The Canadian courts have been prepared to recognize some gratuitous promises as binding but only to prevent a promisor from breaking a gratuitous promise and then suing the promisee. It is often said that Canadian courts accept the doctrine of promissory (equitable) estoppel as a "shield" (that is, a defence) but not a "sword" (that is, a cause of action). Recent decisions of Canadian appeals courts make one wonder if the Canadian common law will ever fully embrace the American notion of injurious reliance.

In *Maracle v Travellers Indemnity Co of Canada*,[26] the Supreme Court of Canada summarized the principles of promissory estoppel as follows:

> The principles of promissory estoppel are well settled. The party relying on the doctrine must establish that the other party has, by words or conduct, made a promise or assurance which was intended to affect their legal relationship and to be acted on. Furthermore, the representee must establish that, in reliance on the representation, he acted on it or in some way changed his position.[27]

In *Maracle*, although it did not expressly adopt the doctrine of injurious reliance, the Supreme Court of Canada did not seem to limit the doctrine to its traditional place as a defence. Professor Waddams has since written: "It may therefore be suggested that the Commonwealth law is moving, though rather slowly, in the direction of [the American position in the Restatement of Contracts] towards the protection of promisees by reason of and to the extent of subsequent reliance."[28]

However, evidence in court opinions of this trend to adopt injurious reliance or promissory estoppel as a cause of action remains limited.[29] In a 2003 decision[30] of the British Columbia Court of Appeal, Madam Justice Huddart wrote:

> While it may be, as Professor Waddams suggests, that the law is moving slowly toward a more generous approach to promissory estoppel than that said by Sopinka J. in *Maracle v. Travellers Indemnity Co.* to be well settled, I can see little evidence of that movement in Canadian authorities.

Some evidence of movement is apparent in the 2008 Ontario Superior Court decision of *Hepburn v Jannock Limited*,[31] where an employee's claim for a promised wage increase was allowed on a number of grounds, including promissory estoppel.

Questions to Consider

1. Why do you think the Canadian courts seem slow to widen the scope of the doctrine of promissory estoppel to allow for injurious reliance as a cause of action?
2. Do you think the next time the Supreme Court of Canada has the opportunity to address the subject of promissory estoppel, it should endorse the American principle of injurious reliance as a cause of action?

Source: Waddams, *The Law of Contracts*, 4th ed. (1999) at 141–2, 154–5.

---

[25] American Law Institute, Restatement of Contracts, Section 90 (Washington, 1932).

[26] (1991), 2 SCR 50.

[27] *Ibid* at 57.

[28] Waddams, *The Law of Contracts*, 4th ed (Toronto: Canada Law Book Company, 1999) at 141–2, 154–5.

[29] An Ontario Court of Appeal decision, *Doef's Iron Works Ltd v MCCI*, [2004] OJ No 4358, states in paragraph 2: "It is well established that promissory estoppel can be used only as a shield and not as a sword." See *Conwest Exploration Co v Letain*, [1964] SCR 20, 41 DLR (2d) 198; *Reclamation Systems Inc v The Honourable Bob Rae*, 1996 CanLII 7950, (1996), 27 OR (3d) 419 (ONSC).

[30] *NM v ATA*, 2003 BCCA 297.

[31] (2008), 63 CCEL (3d) 101 at paras 109–26.

THE EFFECT OF A REQUEST FOR GOODS OR SERVICES

When one person requests the services of another, and the other performs those services, the law implies a promise to pay. Such a promise is implied between strangers or even between friends, if the services are rendered in a customary business transaction. But a promise to pay is not usually implied when the services are performed between members of a family or close friends; although the services were requested, the circumstances may show that the parties expected them to be given gratuitously because of friendship, kindness, or family duty.

Even though neither party mentions price, the implied promise is for payment of what the services are reasonably worth—that is, for payment *quantum meruit*. Difficult though it may be when the services are not usual professional services with a recognized scale of fees, the court will still fix a fee that it considers to be reasonable.

After the requested services have been performed, the parties may agree on what they consider to be a reasonable price. If so, neither of them can later change his mind and ask the court to fix a reasonable price. In effect, by agreeing to a price, each party has given up his right to refer the matter to the court.

ILLUSTRATION 7.5 Reasonable Price

A asks computer programmer B for technical assistance. Afterward, A asks B what her fee is, and B suggests a certain sum. A refuses to pay it. In an action for payment for services performed, the court may give judgment in favour of B in the amount she requested or for some other amount that it finds reasonable.

If instead A agrees to the figure suggested by B but later changes his mind about paying, the court would not concern itself with what it considered reasonable: It would give judgment in favour of B for the amount earlier agreed upon by the parties.

The performance of requested services creates an existing obligation to pay a reasonable price for them, and by later agreeing upon a fixed price, the parties have done away with the need for an implied price. Subsequent payment of the fixed price satisfies all obligations owed by the party who requested the services.

We must be careful to distinguish this position from the situation arising when a promise is made for a past consideration.[32] If, for example, A promises to pay B $100 after B has given her and her family an excellent dinner, A is not bound, since she is under no existing legal obligation at the time she makes her promise. If, however, A agrees to pay B $100 after B has requested catering services, A would be bound; in fact, A was already bound to pay B a reasonable price, and she and B have simply agreed later upon what this price should be.

The principle of *quantum meruit* applies to goods supplied on request as well as to services rendered. Generally, a court has less difficulty ascertaining the reasonable worth of goods than of services.

THE USE OF A SEAL

In medieval times, when few people could read or write, a serious promise or covenant was often recorded by a cleric. He would read the covenant to the **covenantor**, who would then show his consent by impressing his coat of arms into a pool of hot sealing

covenantor one who makes a covenant

---

[32] *Lampleigh v Braithwait* (1615), 80 ER 255.

document under seal a covenant recorded in a document containing a wax seal, showing that the covenantor adopted the document as his act and deed

deed a document under seal, which today is usually a small, red, gummed wafer

wax poured at the foot of the document. Usually the coat of arms was worn on a signet ring. By impressing his seal in this way, the covenantor adopted the document as his act and deed. To this day a **document under seal** is still called a **deed** and requires *no consideration*. Methods of sealing a document evolved over time, including embossing the coat of arms directly on the paper. Today the usual method is to glue a small, red, gummed sticker to a document.

A seal must be affixed (or the word "seal" written) on the document at the time the party signs it. The word "seal" printed on the document in advance presents difficulties. It may simply indicate the place where the parties are to place a red paper wafer. In *Royal Bank of Canada v Kiska*,[33] the bank used a printed form of guarantee that included the word "seal" and also the words "Given under seal at . . ." and "Signed, sealed and delivered in the presence of . . . ." The bank manager did not affix a red paper wafer until sometime after the promisor had signed and without the promisor's instructions to do so. Laskin, J. (later Chief Justice of the Supreme Court of Canada) commented:

> The respective words are merely anticipatory of a formality which must be observed and are not a substitute for it. I am not tempted by any suggestion that it would be a modern and liberal view to hold that a person who signs a document that states it is under seal should be bound accordingly although there is no seal on it. I have no regret in declining to follow this path in a case where a bank thrusts a printed form under the nose of a young man for his signature. Formality serves a purpose here and some semblance of it should be preserved.[34]

Although some lower courts[35] have held that the words "given under seal" are sufficient without the need to affix a red paper wafer, the Supreme Court endorses the role of the seal in Canadian common law:

> To create a sealed instrument, the application of the seal must be a conscious and deliberate act. At common law, then, the relevant question is whether the party intended to create an instrument under seal.[36]

A promise made properly under the seal of the promisor does not require consideration to make it binding. Historically, signing under seal was considered an act done with great care. It is still considered so today. The seal says, in effect, "I fully intend to be bound by this promise." Its presence means that the court will not, as it otherwise would, insist upon consideration to hold the promisor bound.

Any offer may be made under seal and so becomes irrevocable. When a business firm or public body invites tenders and requires them to be submitted under the seal of the tenderer, the legal effect is much the same as when an option is given: The tenderer cannot withdraw without being liable in damages.[37]

Certain documents, such as a deed of land and a mortgage, traditionally required a seal even if there was consideration. Electronic registration of these documents has changed some of the seal requirements. These documents will be explained as they arise in later chapters.

Although a seal is an alternative to consideration, it does not do away with any of the other requirements needed to make a promise enforceable.

---

[33] (1967), 63 DLR (2d) 582.

[34] *Ibid* at 594, per Laskin, J. (later Chief Justice of the Supreme Court of Canada).

[35] *Canadian Imperial Bank of Commerce v Dene Mat Construction Ltd and others*, [1988] 4 WWR 344 (NWTSC); *Hongkong Bank of Canada v New Age Graphic Design Inc*, 1996 CanLII 1898 (BCSC); *Romaine v Romaine*, 2001 BCCA 509.

[36] *Friedmann Equity Developments Inc v Final Note Ltd*, [2000] 1 SCR 842 at para 36.

[37] See *Sanitary Refuse Collectors Inc v City of Ottawa*, [1972] 1 OR 296 at 308–9.

INTENTION TO CREATE LEGAL RELATIONS

Even when an apparently valid offer has been accepted and consideration is present, there is no contract formed unless both sides intended to create a legally enforceable agreement. There must be agreement or "meeting of the minds" on all the essential terms of the deal and a mutual intention to create a legally binding contract.[38] The parties' behaviour should show an intention to contract from the view of an objective reasonable bystander.[39] Since parties do not ordinarily think about the legal effects of their bargains, the law considers all the circumstances to conclude an agreement appears to be seriously made. A presumption in favour of an intention to contract also arises where parties have signed a commercial document.

It is not necessary to inquire into the parties' subjective state of mind when they made their agreement and to decide whether they truly had such an intention—an impractical and time-consuming task. Instead, the law determines intention corresponding with the reasonable objective meaning of his words and actions.[40] The presumed intention is especially strong in dealings between strangers and in commerce generally.

A defendant may dispute intention by using the external or objective test of the reasonable bystander. If to such a person the outward conduct of the parties lacked a serious intention to make an agreement, then no binding contract results. It is easier to rebut the presumption in arrangements between friends or members of a family, where it is often clear there was no intention to create legal relations. For example, claiming that a failure to show up for a dinner invitation would give the host a right to sue for breach of contract appears unreasonable to us, even though the host went to considerable trouble and expense. Many domestic arrangements between spouses are on the same footing.

In the commercial context, disputes over intention often arise when negotiations are concluded orally with a written contract to be produced after the fact. Is there an intention to contract at the conclusion of the oral negotiations or not until the written document is signed? Ultimately, each case will be determined on its own facts, objectively viewed.

CASE 7.6 Objective Evidence of Intention

Allen owned a business that his friend Wallace wanted to buy. They signed a letter of intent describing their general understanding of how the sale would proceed. The details were to be negotiated and reduced to writing in a binding share purchase agreement within 40 days. Each hired lawyers, and the terms of the share purchase agreement were negotiated between them, term by term. By the time the proposed agreement was in final form, the 40 days had long passed, and Allen had changed his mind. He refused to sign the purchase agreement or close the deal. Wallace sued alleging breach of contract and demanding Allen complete the sale. Allen took the position that no legally binding agreement existed as the parties never intended that the letter of intent would be a contract. The trial judge agreed; the importance of signing the final agreement was evident in the language of the letter of intent. However, the Court of Appeal viewed the evidence much differently. It found, first, that signing the letter of intent triggered a legal presumption that one who executes a commercial document intends to be bound by it. Second, notwithstanding the express requirement that a further agreement was to be signed, the Court of Appeal found intention to form a contract in the language of the letter of intent—words such as "it is agreed" and "upon acceptance." Finally, intent to be bound was also evident by their conduct. Allen announced his retirement after signing the letter of intent, and Wallace began working at the business. Damages for breach of contract were granted.[41]

---

[38] *Olivieri v Sherman* (2007), 284 DLR (4th) 516 (ONCA) at para 41 (applying general law of contract to settlement agreements).

[39] *Ron Ghitter Property Consultants Ltd v Beaver Lumber Co*, 2003 ABCA 221 (CanLII) at para 9.

[40] *Lindsey v Heron & Co* (1921), 64 DLR 92 at 98–9.

[41] *Wallace v Allen* (2007), 85 OR (3d) 88, appeal allowed (2009), 93 OR (3d) 723 (ONCA).

The requirement of an intention to contract has been important in interpreting the legal effect of advertisements. In *Carlill v Carbolic Smoke Ball Company*,[42] discussed in Chapter 6, the company pled that its promise to pay a £100 reward was no more than a "mere puff" and was not to be taken seriously. This defence lost any credibility because the advertisement itself stated, "£1,000 is deposited with the Alliance Bank, Regent Street, showing our sincerity in the matter." A 100 years later, Pepsi made the same legal argument about its "Pepsi Points" promotion.

CASE 7.7 Rewards

PepsiCo launched a rewards program where customers earned points for each Pepsi product purchased. Points could be redeemed for merchandise from the Pepsi catalogue, and extra points could be purchased for 10 cents a point. Unfortunately, a TV commercial promoting the points program showed a teenager arriving to school in an AV-8 Harrier Jump Jet with a caption "Harrier Jet 7,000,000 Pepsi Points." Leonard collected some points and sent Pepsi a cheque to purchase the remaining points to bring him to the necessary 7 000 000. PepsiCo successfully defended Leonard's breach of contract action to obtain the jet. The court held that, even if the commercial was an offer, intention was lacking. No reasonable person could believe that PepsiCo seriously intended to convey a jet worth approximately $23 000 000 for redemption of Pepsi points.[43]

The seriousness of the intention was assessed based upon the objective standard of what a reasonable person would believe. To make its intentions clear, Pepsi modified the commercial to add the words "just kidding" beneath the caption. Other possible legal effects of advertising will be discussed under the topics of misrepresentation in Chapter 9.

Strategies to Manage the Legal Risks

Parties must be clear about their intentions to contract. Businesses offering rewards programs now commonly require participants to register online or create an account by visiting the company's website. As part of the enrolment process, the customer must accept the company's standard terms and conditions, which will exclude advertisements and limit entitlements. This reduces the legal risk of customers believing the advertisement is intended as the offer. As well, an advertisement should give viewers notice that it is for informational purposes only and that any described offer is subject to terms and conditions set out on the business's website.

Standard form contracts may be used to clarify uncertainty regarding the existence of consideration. Most contracts include a phrase acknowledging the existence of consideration—for example: "in consideration of the mutual promises expressed herein and one dollar, receipt of which is hereby acknowledged." Out of an abundance of caution, the signature line will have the symbol of a seal beside it and be prefaced with the phrase "signed, sealed and delivered." In this process, some consideration is present (however modest). The parties have confirmed its existence, and the reference to a seal may make consideration unnecessary in any event.

---

[42] [1892] 2 QB 484.
[43] *Leonard v PepsiCo, Inc*, 88 F Supp 2d 116 (SDNY 1999), aff'd 210 F 3d 88 (2d Cir. 2000); Ann C. Morales, "Pepsi's Harrier Jet Commercial Was Not a Binding Offer to Contract" (2000) 28(2) Academy of Mark. Science J 318–20.

Businesses sometimes include in their contracts an express term that, in the event of its breach, a party's right to sue the other is restricted. Although such an understanding may be recognized by the courts,[44] it does not mean no contract is formed. Users should be aware of the limitations of such terms. These terms come in two variations: exemption clauses, discussed previously as a means of limiting liability, and choice-of-forum clauses redirecting the dispute away from the courts, as discussed in Chapter 2. Either term may be unenforceable if it applies only to the weaker party such as a consumer or franchisee.[45] Unconscionability will be discussed more generally in Chapter 9.

Finally, parties to existing legal contracts should take great care when modifying or amending their arrangements. New documentation signed under seal should be completed so that changes are binding upon both parties. Settlement of lawsuit or repayment of existing indebtedness should similarly be documented under seal.

QUESTIONS FOR REVIEW

1. Describe how a promise may become binding although the promisor receives no benefit herself.
2. How might the above situation apply to a promise of a charitable donation?
3. How "valuable" does consideration have to be to make a promise binding? When might a court review the value of consideration?
4. Describe the nature of consideration in an out-of-court settlement.
5. Why is gratitude not a sufficient consideration to bind a promisor?
6. In what ways might the common law rules about the need for consideration be unsatisfactory for business purposes in altering an existing contract? How can the defect be remedied?
7. Describe how one important defect in the consideration rules has been remedied by statute in five of the provinces.
8. Describe the differing points of view taken in "equitable estoppel" and "injurious reliance."
9. Explain the requirements necessary to successfully apply equitable estoppel.
10. What question remains unresolved in the application of the concept of injurious reliance by the Canadian courts?
11. How does *quantum meruit* differ from doing a friend a favour?
12. Explain the nature of a seal and its legal importance in Canada.
13. A firm of public accountants has for years been auditing the accounts of a charitable organization without charge. It now appears that the treasurer of the organization has absconded with a sizable amount of money and that an application of generally accepted auditing standards would have disclosed the defalcation in time to avoid the loss. Has the charitable organization any recourse against its auditors in these circumstances?
14. What factual situations give rise to a presumption that parties intended to create a legally binding contract?

---

[44] *Rose and Frank v Crompton*, [1925] AC 445; *Kanitz v Rogers* (2002), 58 OR (3d) 299 (SCJ).

[45] See e.g. *Consumer Protection Act, 2002*, *supra* note 4, ss 7–8 (banning pre-dispute arbitration clauses and class action waivers); *Sale of Goods Act*, RSO 1990, c S.1, s 53 (allowing rights to be varied if variation applies to both parties).

15. A supplier's invoice for goods has the following common term printed on it: "Terms—Net price 30 days; 2 percent discount if paid within 10 days." If the buyer pays the price less 2 percent within 10 days, can the supplier later sue successfully for the sum deducted?

CASES AND PROBLEMS

1. *Continuing Scenario*

   Ashley's restaurant business is off to a slow start. Her cash flow is low, and she cannot afford to pay all of her regular bills—she must pay her food suppliers, so she meets with her landlord and asks if she can pay only 50 percent of her rent for the next six months. She expects business will improve by then, and she will be able to repay the arrears with 150 percent rental payments beginning in the seventh month. The landlord orally agrees, and Ashley thanks him in a follow up email. Two months later, Ashley's landlord is approached by the manager of a prosperous chain of restaurants who is looking for space in this complex. He is willing to pay more than double Ashley's full rent. The landlord would like to evict Ashley's restaurant and rent the space to this chain, so he sends Ashley an immediate demand for payment of all the arrears of rent within two weeks or he will evict her for non-payment of rent. Evaluate Ashley's legal position. What is the status of the reduced rent conversation? Does it make a difference if Ashley paid only 25 percent of her rent during the first two months of the arrangement?

2. Burowski ran an office supplies business and donated one evening a week of her time helping run a bingo for charity. There, she met another donor, Adams, an investment broker. They worked well together for a few months. One evening, Burowski said to Adams that she was rather confused about her investment portfolio; she wondered where she might get advice. Adams suggested they have a coffee together after the bingo hall closed. They spent about an hour discussing Burowski's portfolio, and Adams made some suggestions about how she might improve her holdings. Burowski suddenly remembered she was late returning home to her babysitter and left quickly, thanking Adams as she got up from the table. A week later she received a bill from Adams for $150 for "professional advice."

   Discuss whether Adams has contractual grounds for making this claim.

3. The town of Broomville, along with local arts and athletic groups, decided to erect a new community centre for sports, music, and theatre. The total estimated cost was $18 000 000. In April, Jane Borkus, president and CEO of the largest local industry, Autotech, promised to match every dollar raised through other donors, up to $9 000 000. Both she and the delighted town mayor, Geoff Johns, made the announcement over the local television station and in a joint statement in the town's newspaper. Borkus said the deadline would be 12 months.

   The following January, the campaign was proceeding extremely well: Other donors had pledged $5 500 000, and Borkus presented a cheque for $4 000 000 as Autotech's "down payment and pledge of goodwill."

   Unfortunately, in March, Autotech lost its major contract to supply car parts to one of the big three auto manufacturers. Anticipating a large loss at year's end, Borkus withdrew the pledge and asked for the return of the down payment.

   What arguments may be made on behalf of the town both to keep the money paid and to require Autotech to honour its commitment? What do you think the decision would be?

4. (a) Matsui's bank manager recommended Roberts, a business consultant, to help Matsui appraise a suitable business investment. Matsui wished to buy control of a business and was prepared to pay $200 000 or so if Roberts could find a satisfactory business.

At Matsui's request, Roberts devoted most of his time from May to February of the following year investigating three businesses in which Matsui was interested. They did not discuss Roberts's rate of remuneration for performing these services. Finally, after consultation with Matsui, Roberts managed to obtain an option for him to purchase the shares of the A.C. Electrical Co. Ltd., one of the three companies identified by Matsui. When Matsui learned of Roberts's success in obtaining the option, he promised to pay Roberts $50 000 for his services. Roberts said that would be fine.

Matsui later decided not to exercise the option and refused to pay Roberts the $50 000. Roberts brought an action against him for this sum. In defence, Matsui asserted that it was expressly agreed that if, as a result of Roberts's services or efforts, Matsui actually made a purchase, he would pay a suitable commission to Roberts, but unless Matsui made such a purchase, Roberts would be entitled to nothing. Roberts denied that Matsui's undertaking had been qualified in this manner. Faced with this conflict of evidence, the trial judge stated that he accepted the evidence of the plaintiff in preference to that of the defendant.

What is the main issue? Should Roberts succeed? Why or why not?

(b) Suppose instead that the parties had discussed $50 000 as the appropriate fee before the services were rendered and then when Matsui learned of Roberts's success in obtaining the option, he was so elated as to promise him $10 000 more. What issue would arise if Roberts found it necessary to sue Matsui for the $60 000?

5. Harris N. Dealer was sole proprietor of a profitable computer data centre, which he sold as a going concern to Alice B. Wheeler for the price of $180 000. The price was paid—$30 000 in cash and the balance in the form of a contract under Wheeler's seal, which read in part as follows:

> For value received Alice B. Wheeler promises to pay Harris N. Dealer the sum of one hundred and fifty thousand dollars ($150 000) in 10 years from April 1, 2009, together with interest at 8 percent per annum from April 1, 2009, payable monthly on the first day of May 2009 and on the first day of each and every month thereafter until payment of the principal sum on April 1, 2019.
>
> After ten (10) days' default in any interest payment due under this agreement the whole amount payable shall become immediately due.
>
> March 29, 2009. Alice B. Wheeler [SEAL]

Dealer and Wheeler remained on friendly terms throughout the balance of 2009. Wheeler was somewhat dilatory in making her monthly payments of $1000 interest, so that by the end of the year she had made six of the eight monthly payments required by then on dates more than 10 days after they were due. Dealer had acquiesced in the arrangement without complaint, though the parties had never expressly agreed on any change in the due dates and Dealer seemed merely to have been indulgent with his debtor. Unfortunately, however, the parties had a serious personal disagreement early in 2010. On February 5, 2010, the January 1 interest payment then being 35 days overdue, Dealer wrote to Wheeler as follows:

> This letter will serve to inform you that, an interest payment due under the terms of the contract dated March 29, 2009, being in default for more than 10 days, the whole amount under the contract is now due.
>
> I hereby demand immediate payment of the principal amount of $150 000 and outstanding interest.
>
> H. N. Dealer

Wheeler immediately paid the outstanding interest but refused to pay the principal sum. Dealer brought an action against her for $150 000.

Develop fully the arguments for both the plaintiff and the defendant. State with reasons, including reference to a relevant case or cases, whether the action should succeed.

6. Waymart Ltd., a full service department store, introduced a customer rewards program to encourage loyalty among shoppers and increase sales of low volume products. The program allowed customers to accumulate "W dollars" with each purchase at the store; these dollars could be redeemed toward purchases of select items. The bottom of each customer receipt states its W dollar value, and customers simply bring the receipt to the store and "spend it like money."

Every Monday, the store manager designates slow-moving products eligible for purchase with W dollars. Eligible products vary weekly depending upon which items have not sold. The marketing department put together a TV advertisement showing a family enjoying a summer afternoon in their backyard. An eight-person hot tub sat beside new patio furniture while one person barbecued on an expensive grill. The family was eating hamburgers and drinking lemonade from pretty plastic glasses. The caption read "Fulfill your dreams with W dollars."

Susan was planning to buy a $5000 hot tub at another store when she saw the advertisement, so she began collecting Waymart receipts. She bought all her groceries, household, and family supplies at Waymart, as did her mother and sister. Together they collected $3000 worth of W dollars in just four weeks, but she never saw a hot tub in the store. She did see patio furniture and barbecues, but she never saw them marked as eligible W dollar products. She went to the customer service counter and asked about buying a hot tub using her points as part of the purchase price. The clerk told her that Waymart did not carry hot tubs and that the W dollar campaign applied to lower priced items such as groceries and dishware.

Can Susan sue for breach of contract? Give reasons for your opinion. What could Waymart have done differently to protect itself from this legal risk?

Chapter 8
Formation of a Contract: Capacity to Contract and Legality of Object

- **THE BURDEN OF PROVING ESSENTIAL ELEMENTS OF A CONTRACT**
- **LIMITED CAPACITY**
- **THE ROLE OF LEGALITY IN THE FORMATION OF A CONTRACT**
- **CONTRACTS AFFECTED BY STATUTE**
- **CONTRACTS ILLEGAL BY THE COMMON LAW AND PUBLIC POLICY**
- **STRATEGIES TO MANAGE THE LEGAL RISKS**

In this chapter, the discussion of the essential elements of a contract continues with two elements usually assumed to be present unless shown otherwise. The first is capacity to contract, and the second is the legality of the subject matter of the contract.

We examine such questions as:

- How does capacity of a minor depend on the nature of the contract?
- What are "necessaries"?
- What are the effects of other types of contracts?
- What are a minor's obligations upon attaining the age of majority?
- To what extent is the contractual capacity of the following classes of persons treated differently: Aboriginal peoples? corporations? labour unions? persons of diminished mental capacity?
- What is the difference between void and illegal contracts?
- What are gaming contracts?
- How are contracts affected in different ways by statute?
- What contracts are illegal by common law and public policy?

THE BURDEN OF PROVING ESSENTIAL ELEMENTS OF A CONTRACT

As discussed in Chapter 6 and Chapter 7, once a plaintiff proves that there was offer, acceptance, and consideration for the promise, the court will ordinarily presume an intention to create legal relations. At that point, the court will also presume that two additional elements are present: (1) The defendant has the capacity to make a contract, and (2) the contract is legal. However, if the defendant shows that she did not have the capacity to enter into the contract or that the contract was not legal, she will be released from her contractual obligations.

The Meaning of Capacity to Contract

When forming a contract, we usually assume the other party has the capacity to make a contract and is bound by it, but this is not always so. We would not expect a four-year-old child to be able to buy a $100 computer game; at that age, she would lack the competence—the **legal capacity**—to understand the meaning of a legally binding contract. Even if the requirements of Chapter 6 and Chapter 7 are met, as a matter of policy the law may excuse one party, such as the four-year-old child, from her obligations. Of course, in most cases, a lack of capacity is not so obvious; one party reasonably assumes the other has capacity to enter into a contract.

In addition to age, there are other reasons that contracting parties may lack capacity and, as a result, attempt to **repudiate** their contracts. This chapter discusses the rights and remedies available to both sides in such contracts.

legal capacity competence to bind oneself legally

repudiate reject or declare an intention not to be bound by

LIMITED CAPACITY

Minors (or Infants)

A **minor or infant** is a person who has not attained the **age of majority** according to the law of her province. Historically, the age was deemed to be 21, but it now varies according to the legislation in each province.[1] The general rule is that a contract made by a minor is not binding on her but binding on the other side, whether or not the other person is aware that he is dealing with a minor. When a minor owns assets or needs to contract, her legal **guardian** or parents are ordinarily empowered to look after her affairs.

The purpose of these rules is to protect minors, but still exceptions are needed so that a minor is not disadvantaged. For example, without an exception a minor in need of food or clothing—**necessaries**—might be unable to find a vendor willing to sell her these things on credit because the vendor could not force her to pay for them. Therefore, the first exception relates to contracts for necessaries.

minor or infant a person who has not attained the age of majority according to the law of his or her province

age of majority the age at which a person is recognized as an adult according to the law of his or her province

guardian a person appointed to manage the affairs of a minor in the place of his or her parents

necessaries essential goods and services

Necessaries and Beneficial Contracts of Service
A minor is bound by any contract for supply of necessaries, essential goods, and services. However, she is not bound to pay the contract price as such, but rather a reasonable price[2] on the same basis as *quantum meruit*, discussed in Chapter 7. In the absence of evidence that the minor has been charged a higher price than other customers, the court usually regards the contract price as evidence of what a reasonable price should be.

---

[1] It is usually 18 or 19 years. See e.g. *Age of Majority Act*, RSBC 1996, c 7 (19 years); RSNS 1989, c 4 (19 years); CCSM c. A-7 (18 years); *Age of Majority and Accountability Act*, RSO 1990, c A.7, s 1 (18 years).

[2] See *Sale of Goods Act*, RSO 1990, c S.1, s 3.1.

The courts have identified the following as necessaries: food, clothing, lodging, medical attention, legal advice,[3] and also transportation—but transportation includes only the means of getting the minor to and from work and does not include the purchase price of vehicles even if they are used by the minor in carrying on a business[4] or as a means of going to work.[5]

A minor is also bound by **beneficial contracts of service**: contracts of employment or apprenticeship when they are found to be for his benefit and not exploitative. Participating in a business venture is quite different: The courts are more hesitant to find such an arrangement to be for a minor's benefit, whether the minor is in business for himself[6] or in partnership with others.

beneficial contracts of service
contracts of employment or apprenticeship found to be for a minor's benefit

CASE 8.1 Terms not Beneficial

A 17-year-old hockey player signed a contract with an amateur hockey club that required him to play exclusively for the club for three years for minimal remuneration and to pay to the club 20 percent of his future earnings during his first three years as a professional hockey player. When the hockey player wanted out of the contract, the club sued him for breach of contract. The suit was dismissed because the court said the contract was not "on the whole" beneficial to the hockey player and was voidable at his option.[7]

All the terms of contract, taken together, will determine if it is beneficial to the minor; one harsh term will not be enough release the minor.

Contracts Without Liability for a Minor

A minor may always repudiate (back out of) a contract for non-necessaries even where the non-necessaries are clearly beneficial to him. The purchase of a truck for use in his business may well be very useful to a minor. Even so, the truck is not a necessary.[8] A fairly large number of things have been held to be necessaries. Each case must be decided on its own facts, and judges are reluctant to enlarge the class. When a minor is living at home and supported by his parents, his purchases are less likely to be considered as necessaries than when he is on his own. The court assumes that a minor living at home is provided for.

A minor may not be liable for necessaries he has ordered but not yet received. Accordingly, he can repudiate a contract of sale before the goods are delivered.[9] The point is underlined in the *Sale of Goods Act*, which defines necessaries for an infant in terms of goods sold and delivered.[10]

A minor who repudiates a contract for non-necessary goods will, if the goods are still in his possession, be required to return them to the seller in whatever condition they may be at the time; the effect of repudiating the contract is to revest the property in the vendor.[11] Similarly, when the minor is a seller rather than a buyer in a contract

---

[3] *Miller v Smith & Co*, [1925] 2 WWR 360 (Sask. CA) at 377; *Helps v Clayton* (1864), 144 ER 222.

[4] *Mercantile Union Guarantee Corp v Ball*, [1937] 2 KB 498.

[5] *First Charter Financial Corp v Musclow* (1974), 49 DLR (3d) 138 (BCSC).

[6] *Mercantile Union Guarantee Corp v Ball, supra* note 4.

[7] *Toronto Marlboro Major Junior "A" Hockey Club et al v Tonelli et al* (1979) 23 OR (2d) 193.

[8] *Supra* note 6.

[9] Furmston, *Cheshire, Fifoot and Furmston's Law of Contract*, 16th ed. at 543–9.

[10] See e.g. RSBC 1996, c 410, s 7; RSO 1990, c S.1, s 3 (1); RSNS 1989, c 408, s 5(1).

[11] *Louden Manufacturing Co v Milmine* (1908), 15 OLR 53 at 54; *McGaw v Fisk* (1908), 38 NBR 354; S.A. Williston, *A Treatise on the Law of Contracts*, 4th ed. by R.A. Lord, Vol. 5 (New York, NY: Lawyers Cooperative Publishing, 1993) at 113.

for the sale of goods, he cannot repudiate the contract to recover the goods delivered unless he returns the money paid.[12]

There is nothing to prevent a minor from purchasing non-necessaries if he can find a vendor who is prepared to sell to him. This is most likely when the minor purchases goods for cash.[13]

Ordinarily a seller cannot rely on a statement by a minor that his parents will pay for the purchase.[14] Provincial family law legislation may impose liability on parents for necessaries only.[15] Authority to bind the parents may also be implied from the fact that parents have paid the account for a previous purchase by their child without complaint. Apart from these possibilities, a vendor needs express authority from the parents before being able to bind them.

Contracts Indirectly Affecting a Minor
A minor who has benefited from a contract for non-necessaries will not be able to recover money already paid, though he will be able to repudiate his remaining liability.

CASE 8.2 Received the Benefit

T, a minor, agreed to become tenant of a house and to pay L, the landlord, a certain amount for the furniture in it. T paid part of the sum, gave a promissory note for the balance, then occupied the house and had the use of the furniture for several months. Later T brought an action to have the contract rescinded and to recover from L the money he had paid. The court held that T could avoid liability on the note, but that he was not entitled to a return of what he had paid.[16]

An adult can recover money lent to a minor only if the minor used the sum to purchase necessary goods.[17] If the borrowed money was used to pay for a vacation, the lender cannot recover the debt. Minors' contracts that are not binding under the common law may be altered by statute. For example, the *Canada Student Loans Act*[18] states that a guaranteed bank loan to a student "is recoverable by the lender from the borrower as though the borrower had been of full age at the time the loan was made."

A minor's freedom from liability is limited to contract; she remains liable for torts such as negligence, assault, defamation, or deceit.

Contractual Liability of Minors upon Attaining Majority
A minor's liability to pay for necessaries and beneficial contracts of service continues after she attains majority, and in addition, she may become liable for obligations that could not be enforced against her while she was a minor. A non-necessary contract is a **voidable contract**, of which there are two types.

voidable contract a contract that may be rendered non-binding at the option of one of the parties

In the first type, the minor acquires "an interest of a permanent, continuous nature." This class of contracts involves ongoing obligations paid in installments, such as cell phone services, car leases, and fitness club memberships. If she wants to be released from these obligations, she must repudiate or back out of such a contract

---

[12] Williston, *ibid.*, Vol 5, s 9:16 at 113–33. The right to repudiate may be lost when the infant comes of age.

[13] Problems may arise for the minor if the goods have been used or damaged. This problem is discussed under the heading of "Rescission" in Chapter 13.

[14] Hailsham, *Halsbury's Laws of England*, 4th ed rev, Vol. 5(2) 24 (London, UK: Butterworths, 1993) at 343–51.

[15] *Family Law Act*, RSO 1990, c F. 3, s 45(2); it is a criminal offence to fail to provide the necessaries of life to a minor. See *Criminal Code*, RSC 1985, c C-46, s 21.1(b).

[16] *Valenti v Canali* (1889), 24 QBD 166.

[17] Hailsham, *supra* note 13 at 175.

[18] RSC 1985, c S-23, s 19.

promptly upon reaching the age of majority, or she will be liable just as if she had entered into the contract after coming of age. In contracts of this type, the minor loses the right to repudiate by not doing so promptly after coming of age or by accepting the benefits of the contract after that time.

The second and more common type of voidable contract does not create an interest of a continuous nature and is not binding upon a minor unless she expressly **ratifies** or confirms the contract after attaining majority—that is, she acknowledges the contract and promises again to perform. Some provinces require ratification to be in writing and signed by the minor.[19] This type includes a minor's promise to pay for non-necessary goods or for services performed once at her request, such as buying a television or computer. A promise to pay for necessary goods not delivered by the time she becomes of age also requires ratification.

ratifies acknowledges and promises to perform

Some provinces, such as British Columbia, have passed legislation clarifying these rules.[20]

Other Persons of Diminished Contractual Capacity

The law protects persons of unsound mind or incapacitated through alcohol or drugs in the same way as a minor: They are bound to pay a reasonable price for necessaries; other contracts are voidable at their option but enforceable against the other contracting party.

In practice, a person who was drunk or insane at the time of making a contract often has a difficult problem of proof. A minor can more easily prove his age than can a person establish that he was so intoxicated or insane as not to know what he was doing.

There is an additional burden of evidence on the party seeking to avoid the contract. He must show not only that he was incapable of a rational decision at the time of the agreement but also that the other party was aware of his condition. Unfortunately for the person who was so insane or drunk that he did not know what he was doing, his own observations about the other contracting party are unlikely to be reliable, and the necessary evidence must then be adduced from all the surrounding circumstances.

As with voidable contracts generally, the party seeking to avoid must act promptly upon emerging from his state of incapacity. Unless repudiation comes within a reasonable time, the privilege is lost. It is also too late to repudiate if, after regaining sanity or sobriety, the party accepts the benefits of the contract.

With an aging population, we face a growing problem of diminished contractual capacity among older adults. In dealing with an aged person, it can be difficult to tell whether she is simply physically frail or also has diminished mental capacity that might leave a contract with her open to subsequent attack.

Bankrupt Debtors
During bankruptcy proceedings, a debtor is under certain contractual disabilities (except for necessaries) until after he receives a discharge from the court. We will discuss these disabilities more fully in Chapter 29.

Corporations

Since a corporation is a "legal fiction"—it is a legal creation[21]—it has no physical existence: It cannot think or act or sign its name as a natural person can. Nevertheless, the law gives corporations the capacity to make contracts or enter into any obligation that

---

[19] *Statute of Frauds*, RSO 1990, c S.19, s 7; RSNS 1989, c 442, s 9.

[20] *Infants Act*, RSBC 1996, c 223, s 19.

[21] These creations of the law are described variously as "a legal person," "a legal entity," an entity having "separate legal status," and "corporate persons." For further discussion, see Chapter 25.

a natural person possesses; business corporations' statutes give this capacity. Legislatures have not extended to all corporations the widest possible contractual capacity. Public corporations, such as municipalities and Crown corporations, are restricted to the limited power conferred by the statutes creating them. Obligations that they may claim to undertake but that are outside the ambit of the statute will, if challenged, be declared by the court to be ultra vires (beyond their powers) and, therefore, **void**. The promisee cannot enforce such obligations against the corporation. The legal consequences of ultra vires contracts are often complex and difficult.

void never formed in law

The law relating to principal and agent determines whether the person or persons claiming to act on behalf of a corporation have the power to bind it in contracts. (We will deal with this in Chapter 17.) The matter is especially important for a corporation because, not being a natural person, it must make all its contracts through agents. Corporation officers who have the necessary authority usually issue the corporation's signature for important contracts and formal documents, such as share certificates, bonds, debentures, deeds, and mortgages, by impressing the company seal using an embossing device.[22] For ordinary day-to-day business, the signature of an authorized officer alone is used.

Labour Unions, Associations, and Other Organizations

In our legal system, the fact that a group of individuals gets together and forms an organization—be it a social club, charity, religious community, or labour union—does not make that group into a legal entity (unless it incorporates). Only after the unincorporated group has applied to the appropriate government agency and been recognized as a separate legal person will it be capable of entering into contracts.[23] Despite their significant role in our economy, for the most part the legal status of labour unions remains limited, though the law varies significantly from province to province, and the rules for recognition (certification) of a union are set out in legislation and are quite complicated. (See Chapter 18 under "The Legal Status of Trade Unions.")

By contrast, the legal status of business corporations as employers is clearly settled. The differences between the two are evident in the processes for negotiation and enforceability of collective agreements between corporations and labour unions. The business's management has the capacity to make an offer in the course of negotiating a collective agreement. However, any acceptance of that offer by the union must be subsequently ratified by a majority of the union members before it is binding. As for enforcement, most provinces do have statutes[24] that provide for arbitration in the event of a dispute arising out of the collective agreement. If an employer does not implement the decision of the arbitrator, the union may apply to a labour relations board for permission to prosecute and for this purpose is given legal status. If a union rejects the arbitrator's decision and causes an illegal strike, damages have occasionally been awarded against the union; the enforceability of such decisions is a matter of debate. In those provinces where an employer may seek permission to prosecute a union for such a strike, the union's liability derives from a statutory provision and not from the union's contractual capacity.

representative action an action brought by one or more persons on behalf of a group having the same interest

Despite their indefinite status, labour unions may bring actions or defend against them when they so wish. By a legal technique known as a **representative action**, a union may expressly or impliedly authorize one or more persons to represent it in

---

[22] In most provinces it is no longer necessary for a corporation to have a seal, although it is still common practice to do so.

[23] For religious communities in Ontario, for example, see *Religious Organizations' Lands Act*, RSO 1990, c R-23.

[24] See e.g. *Labour Relations Code*, RSBC 1996, c 244, s 82(2); *Labour Relations Act*, SO 1995, c 1, Sch A, s 41; *Trade Union Act*, RSNS 1989, c 475, s 19(1).

court simply as a group of individuals having a common interest in a particular case. As a result, union officials may bring or defend a representative action on behalf of the union's members. Chapter 18 reviews the processes involved in a unionized workplace.

Aboriginal Peoples

Terminology can be confusing in this area. The definition of **Aboriginal peoples** in the Canadian Constitution includes Indian also referred to as **First Nation peoples**, Inuit, and Métis peoples of Canada.[25] The legal position and contractual capacity of Indians is addressed by the *Indian Act*.[26] It restricts contractual capacity with respect to assets and land "on a reserve" and involves issues of long-standing conflict (s. 89).[27] Under the *Indian Act*, land is designated or reserved for use and occupation by Indian bands. Reserve land is held by the Crown in trust for the benefit of the particular Indian band as a whole, including future generations (s. 18). It is not owned by individual Indian occupants, is not available as security for the claims of creditors, and any attempt to dispose of it to an outside party is void unless the transaction has been approved by the Minister of Indigenous Services.

Aboriginal peoples Canadian Indian, Inuit, and Métis peoples

First Nation Canadian Indigenous people who are not Métis or Inuit

Those living on reserves may manufacture and sell goods to outsiders. Land and property on a reserve are not subject to seizure for payment of debts (s. 89). About half of all Indians live on a reserve; those living off-reserve have unrestricted contractual capacity, and off-reserve property is not exempt from seizure.

The *Indian Act* recognizes over 600 **Indian bands** (groups of Indians for whose benefit land or money are held by the Crown) but does not definitively describe the bands' legal status or capacity as is done with corporations. Courts have struggled to define the nature of a band's legal status. Typically, bands are considered a special type of unincorporated association.[28] They have representative capacity similar to that of a labour union and may sue or be sued in their band's name. They also may enter into contracts in the band's name.[29]

Indian bands groups of Indian persons for whose benefit land or money are held by the Crown as described in the *Indian Act*

Aboriginal communities existed before Crown sovereignty and therefore do not derive their existence or authority from the *Indian Act* (whether identified as a band in the *Indian Act* or not). Many First Nation or other Indigenous groups have self-government arrangements, enacted in legislation or through modern treaties that address and clarify the Nation/group's legal status, typically assigning full capacity as a natural person and as a nation.[30] The inadequacies of the *Indian Act* were voiced by the British Columbia Assembly of First Nations:

> the lack of a simple and clear recognition of legal status and capacity has been a thorn in the side of our First Nation governments. This is why, for certainty, all sectoral and comprehensive governance arrangements directly address the legal status and capacity of the Nation and the governing body to act on behalf of the Nation.[31]

---

[25] *Constitution Act, 1982*, s 35(2).

[26] RSC 1985, c I-5. Section 4 excludes Inuit people from the application of the Act; Section 5 defines Status Indians.

[27] See e.g. Lionel J. Trupman, "The Gathering Storm of Inheritance Law in Canada: The *Indian Act*—Paternalism or Fiduciary Protection?" *Canadian Lawyer Magazine*, January 2017 at 30–32.

[28] *Orr v Alook*, 2013 ABQB 86.

[29] *Wilson v British Columbia*, 2007 BCSC 1324 at para 50.

[30] See e.g. *Westbank First Nation Self-Government Act*, SC 2004, c 17; *Tsawwassen First Nation Final Agreement Act*, SC 2008, c 32.

[31] Puglaas (Jody Wilson-Raybould) and Tim Raybould, BCAFN Governance Toolkit: A Guide To Nation Building (West Vancouver, BC: British Columbia Assembly of First Nations, 2011) at 45, http://bcafn.ca/wp-content/uploads/2016/06/Governance-Toolkit.pdf.

Indigenous people international global term referring to a variety of Aboriginal groups

In 2017, the federal government adopted the global term **Indigenous peoples** and renamed the relevant ministries Indigenous Services Canada and Crown-Indigenous Relations and Northern Affairs Canada. Moving forward, the government–Indigenous relationship (including legal capacity) will be managed according to the guiding principles modeled after the United Nations Declaration on the Rights of Indigenous Peoples.[32] Aboriginal title to land is a complicated issue discussed in Chapter 21.

CASE 8.3 Assets on the Reserve

A judgment creditor tried to collect its judgment by garnishing the bank account of the debtor, God's Lake Indian Band, an Indian band on a reserve in northern Manitoba. The bank account was with a financial institution in Winnipeg. The Supreme Court of Canada allowed the garnishment to proceed.

It held that the bank account was not actually situated on the reserve, nor was it "deemed to be" situated on the reserve within the meaning of the *Indian Act*. The creditor was entitled to collect.[33]

THE ROLE OF LEGALITY IN THE FORMATION OF A CONTRACT

illegal offends the public good or violates a statute

The object or purpose of a contract must be legal. A contract will be considered **illegal** if its purpose offends the public good (that is, it is contrary to public policy) or violates a statute. Courts presume that a transaction is legal unless a defendant produces evidence to show that it is not. It is relatively easy for judges to decide if a contract violates a statute. It is more difficult for judges to decide if a contract is contrary to public policy because there is no exhaustive list of public policies. Judges must decide for themselves whether the purpose of a particular contract offends the public good based on a general sense of what is good or bad for society as a whole.

unenforceable no court assistance or remedy is available to parties of the contract

The general rule is that an illegal contract is **unenforceable**. Courts will not assist parties trying to accomplish an illegal goal. In rare circumstances, a statute will specify that contracts that conflict with its provisions are void rather than unenforceable, and this leads to different results.

The Difference Between Void and Illegal Contracts

In circumstances where a statute states that a contract is void, no legally binding agreement is formed. In the eyes of the court, the contract does not exist, and the court will do its best to restore the parties to their pre-contract positions. The court may order the return of money paid or of property transferred. In addition, each party is released from the performance of any future obligations under the agreement. A court may find that only one term of a contract is void and that the remaining parts are valid. If

severed removed from the contract

it decides that the void term can be **severed** from the contract without doing injustice to the parties, it will enforce the remainder of the contract.

---

[32] See http://www.un.org/esa/socdev/unpfii/documents/DRIPS_en.pdf; Principles respecting the Government of Canada's relationship with Indigenous peoples, http://www.justice.gc.ca/eng/csj-sjc/principles-principes.html.

[33] *McDiarmid Lumber Ltd v God's Lake First Nation*, [2006] 2 SCR 846. The phrase "on a reserve" has been interpreted in the context of taxation in *Dube v Canada*, 2011 SCC 39. See also *Delgamuuk v BC* [1997] 3 SCR 1010 summarized in *Thomas v Rio Tinto Alcan*, 2013 BCSC 2303, leave refused.

Most of the time, illegal contracts are considered completely unenforceable, rather than void. The court will not get involved and will refuse to help any party who knowingly agreed to an illegal arrangement. Not only may a party not sue for money promised, but the court will not help recover any property already transferred. When both parties are aware of the illegal purpose, the plaintiff is without a remedy, and so the defendant may keep the ill-gotten gain. The end result is that, where both parties are equally in the wrong, the position of the defendant is the stronger. With illegal contracts, a court is less likely to sever the illegal part and enforce the rest.

It can be difficult to tell when a court will consider a contract unenforceable. Generally, the more reprehensible its purpose, the more likely the contract will be regarded as illegal and unenforceable, and a plaintiff will be denied any remedy. On rare occasions the statute will actually say whether an offending contract is void or unenforceable.

CONTRACTS AFFECTED BY STATUTE

Significance of the Wording of a Statute

Most statutes do not consider the consequences for a contract that conflicts with their purpose; they leave the matter for the courts to figure out on public policy grounds. However, on rare occasions a statute may prevent a particular type of contract from having any legal effect by stating that such agreements shall be void. Or it may go further and express disapproval by describing such agreements as "unlawful" or "illegal" or "unenforceable." A statute may even declare that performance of the agreement shall be a criminal offence, subject to prescribed penalties of a fine or imprisonment. Alternatively, legislation may be used to legalize behaviour that was previously considered to be against public policy. Examples of each type of statute are discussed below.

Examples of Contracts Void by Statute

Agreements Contrary to the Purpose of Legislation
Workers' compensation legislation provides an example of legislation that expressly declares some contracts void because they undermine its purpose. Any provision in an agreement between employer and employee depriving the employee of the benefits available under the legislation is void.[34] The legislation's purpose is to provide money to workers injured at work, and any contract that prevents that from happening undermines its purpose.

Another example is found in the *Bankruptcy and Insolvency Act*. Its purpose is to gather assets of a bankrupt person in order to pay his or her creditors and thereafter release the debtor from further obligation to pay. Obviously, disposing of the bankrupt person's assets before this happens conflicts with that purpose. Therefore, the statute contains a provision that if a person transfers property either by gift or for an obviously inadequate low price and becomes bankrupt within one year after, the transfer is void, and the property is available to the trustee in bankruptcy.[35] The trustee may recover the property and apply it to the claims of the bankrupt person's creditors. The same statute provides that a transfer of property by an insolvent person to one of several creditors with a view to giving that creditor a preference over the others is "void" if it occurs within three months preceding bankruptcy.[36]

---

[34] See e.g. *Workplace Safety and Insurance Act*, SO 1997, c 16, Sch A, s 16; *Workers' Compensation Act*, RSBC 1996, c 492, s 13; SNS 1994–95, c 10, s 87.

[35] *Bankruptcy and Insolvency Act*, RSC 1985, c B-3, s 95, see Chapter 29.

[36] *Ibid.*, s 95(1).

If legislation is silent about the fate of contracts affecting its purpose, a judge still has discretion to decide that a particular contract undermines the purpose of the legislation, and in such a case the contract will be unenforceable on public policy grounds.

Examples of Statutes Affecting Public Policy

Promises to Pay a Betting Debt
One example involving both public policy and statutes is betting. Historically, debts resulting from bets were not considered to be against public policy, nor was there legislation against betting; accordingly, bets were not void or unenforceable. Nevertheless, the English courts did not like enforcing wagers that were based simply on speculation about an unknown result, so the courts searched for reasons to refuse them. Sometimes they looked at the subject matter of the bet and found it to be against public policy, such as "bribing voters"—a wager with voters as to the outcome of an election in their constituency.[37]

In Canada, the *Criminal Code*[38] makes certain betting activities illegal. It is a criminal offence to keep a gaming house (s. 201) or to operate a pool (s. 202) or a lottery (s. 206) unless they fall under specified exceptions within the Code. Major exceptions include lotteries operated by a province or by an organization licensed by a province (s. 207).

All provinces have gaming control statutes and commissions that supervise the issuing of licences for lotteries, race courses, and casinos.[39] Some statutes make specific reference to the enforcement of gambling contracts:

> No person may use civil proceedings to recover money owing to the person resulting from participating in or betting on a lottery scheme within the meaning of section 207 of the *Criminal Code* (Canada) conducted in Ontario unless the lottery scheme is authorized under subsection 207(1) of the Code.[40]

The *Criminal Code* does address the ability to pass title to an asset through an unlicensed lottery:

> Every sale, loan, gift, barter or exchange of any property, by any lottery, ticket, card or other mode of chance depending on or to be determined by chance or lot, is void, and all property so sold, lent, given, bartered or exchanged is forfeited to Her Majesty. (s 206(5))[41]

Most of the Canadian cases on betting refuse to enforce the debts, although some decisions have allowed a creditor to succeed, usually when the money is lent to the debtor but the creditor is not a participant in the bet.

The parties to a **wager**—an agreement between two parties in which each has at the time some probability of winning or losing—must be distinguished from a **stakeholder** who manages a betting arrangement for a fee and redistributes winnings. Organizations that manage lotteries, racetracks, and casinos are stakeholders and therefore not a party to a wagering agreement. They do, however, remain legally accountable for performing their task as stakeholders.[42] A number of contracts commonly regarded as being of a legitimate business nature have a significant element of

wager an agreement between two persons in which each has some probability of winning or losing

stakeholder a person or organization that manages a betting arrangement for a fee and redistributes winnings

---

[37] *Allen v Hearn* (1875), 1 TR 56; *Gilbert v Sykes* (1812), 16 East 150 at 162.

[38] *Criminal Code*, RSC 1985, c C-46, ss 201–9.

[39] See e.g. *Gaming Control Act*, SBC 2002, c 14; *Gaming Control Act*, SNS 1994–95, c 4.

[40] *Gaming Control Act*, SO 1992, c 24, s 47.1.

[41] *Criminal Code*, supra note 38, s 206(5).

[42] *Ellesmere v Wallace*, [1929] 2 Ch 1; *Tote Investors Ltd v Smoker*, [1968] 1 QB 509.

speculation in them—insurance contracts, stock exchange transactions, and "futures" transactions in commodities. Insurance statutes, in particular, require that contracts of insurance not be regarded as wagering contracts if they are to be enforceable.

Insurance Contracts Contracts of insurance form an important class of commercial transactions. Typically, an individual does not hope to win the "bet" with the insurance company but rather hopes that, should the feared loss occur, he will receive a measure of compensation. The fear of loss is expressed in the idea of insurable interest. For a person to have an insurable interest, he must have a financial benefit from the continued existence of the property or life insured or suffer some financial detriment from its loss or destruction. Provincial insurance acts state that an insurance contract is invalid unless the party making the contract has an insurable interest in the property or life insured.

Insurance statutes define the circumstances where an insurable interest exists. With respect to life insurance, for policies on an individual's own life or on certain members of her family, it is not necessary to show a financial interest—a detriment is presumed to exist in the loss of that life. But for all other persons, a policy holder must show that he has a financial interest in the person whose life is insured, such as a debtor or a business partner. The acts waive the requirement of an insurable interest only when the person whose life is insured consents in writing to placing the insurance.[43] Insurance contracts are discussed more fully in Chapter 16.

Stock Exchange Transactions Stock exchange transactions are speculative business contracts. The contract itself is an actual sale of personal property. Good faith contracts for the purchase and sale of shares are therefore valid and enforceable. If, however, the subject of an agreement is a wager about what the price of a particular security will be at a specified future time, without a good faith intention of acquiring, selling, or taking delivery of the shares, such an agreement is an offence under the *Criminal Code*, and accordingly it is illegal.[44]

Commodities trading, or "futures" as these transactions are sometimes known, involves contracts for the future delivery of goods. Whenever goods are purchased or sold for future delivery at a price agreed upon in advance, one contracting party may gain at the expense of the other because of price changes between the time of the contract and the time of delivery. Again, the speculative element in these contracts is incidental to a larger purpose of selling goods, and the contract is not illegal on the ground that it amounts to a wager.

INTERNATIONAL ISSUE
Internet Gambling

Provinces control gambling within their borders by licensing specific types of gambling for particular purposes. Naturally, this power to control gambling and issue licences has jurisdictional limits. Internet gambling makes it easy for gamblers to access sites outside a province and beyond the control of provincial gaming authorities. Therefore, private sector online gambling sites located (wholly or partially) within a province are illegal unless operated by the Province itself.[45] However, at present, foreign online gambling sites whose entire operations are outside Canada are not illegal.

Calls to regulate or prohibit offshore gambling focus on the risks associated with addiction, underage access, criminal

---

[43] See e.g. *Insurance Act*, RSBC 2012, c 1, s 45(2)(b); RSO 1990, c I.8, s 178(2)(b); RSNS 1989, c 231, s 180(2)(b).

[44] *Criminal Code*, *supra* note 38, s 383.

[45] Sites that are operated or sponsored by the Province itself are legal. See *R v Starnet Communications International Inc* (August 17, 2001) Vancouver 125795-1 (BCSC); *Criminal Code*, *supra* note 38, ss 201–9.

behaviour, and, of course, lost government revenues. Prohibition may be difficult in any event. American attempts to prevent offshore gambling sites from accessing U.S. gamblers triggered an international trade dispute. The World Trade Organization held that the U.S. prohibition violated the General Agreement on Trade in Services (1995) and authorized sanctions of (a modest) US $21 000 000 against the United States.

Questions to Consider

1. Should internet gambling be illegal?

2. Should the *Criminal Code* be amended to apply to offshore gambling sites that offer services to Canadian gamblers?

Sources: C. I. Kyer and D. Hough, "Is Internet Gaming Legal in Canada: A Look at Starnet," (2002) 1(1) CJLT; T. L. Mackay, "Internet Gambling in Canada Waits in Legal Purgatory," National Policy Working Group Policy Discussion Document, July 2004, Canadian Centre on Substance Abuse, http://www.jogoremoto.pt/docs/extra/LPjNQz.pdf; B. S. Klapper, "WTO Clears $21 Million US in Sanctions Vs. U.S.," Associated Press, December 21, 2007, http://www.antiguawto.com/wto/AP_WTOClears21MSanctionsVSUS_21Dec07.pdf; *Her Majesty the Queen v Pamajewon*, [1996] 2 SCR. 821.

Examples of Agreements Illegal by Statute

Some statutes describe certain types of agreements as illegal. An example is the *Competition Act*, discussed in a separate section below. Other statutes impose penalties for certain kinds of conduct without expressly addressing contracts. While the most important of these statutes is the *Criminal Code*, other examples are the *Income Tax Act*, which imposes penalties for false returns and evasion,[46] and the *Customs Act*, which assigns penalties for smuggling.[47] Any contract that involves illegal conduct is itself illegal, not because the statute refers directly to contracts, but because the common law holds that when the object of a contract is illegal by statute, then the contract itself is illegal. A spectrum of remedies is available to suit the specific situation.

CASE 8.4 Severance of Illegal Term

A loan agreement between two parties calls for 4 percent interest per month plus other payments, such as a commitment fee and monitoring fees, which, when taken together, exceed 60 percent. Section 347 of the *Criminal Code* makes it an offence to enter into an agreement to receive more than 60 percent interest.

The Supreme Court held that, although the interest and fees provision violated the statute and was illegal, the illegal portion could be severed from the contract and the agreement could be allowed to proceed in its severed form. The creditor was allowed to recover a maximum of 60 percent interest.[48]

Provincial statutes and municipal bylaws require the licensing or registration of various classes of business and professional people, ranging from taxicabs and local building trades to moneylenders, trading partnerships, real estate agents, investment advisers and stockbrokers, optometrists, and public accountants.[49] When such a person sues to collect for services provided, the defendant may raise as a defence that the plaintiff has not been properly registered for his trade and is therefore not legally entitled to bill for such services. If the defendant is part of the targeted group that the law is intending to protect, then a court may choose not to enforce the contract.[50]

---

[46] RSC 1985, c 1, s 239 (5th Supp).

[47] RSC 1985, c C-1 (2nd Supp), ss 110–16, 153–61.

[48] *Transport North American Express Inc v New Solutions Financial Corp*, [2004] 1 SCR 249.

[49] See Ontario statutes: *Business Names Act*, RSO 1990, c B.17, ss 2(6), 7(3); *Real Estate and Business Brokers Act*, SO 2002, c 30, Sch C, s 3; *Securities Act*, RSO 1990, c S.5, s 25; *Drug and Pharmacies Regulation Act*, RSO 1990, c H.4, s 139; *Public Accounting Act, 2004*, SO 2004, c 8, s 3(1).

[50] *Reimer v Friesen*, 2012 MBQB 32.

CASE 8.5 Purpose of the Law

K, an electrician, sued for services rendered to A, who defended by saying K was not licensed as an electrical contractor as required by the local bylaw. The court stated that the object and purpose of the bylaw was to protect the public against mistakes and loss that might arise from work done by unqualified electricians and, accordingly, held that the contract was illegal. The court would not assist K in his attempt to collect the account.[51]

Another decision held that an unlicensed electrician in a similar position could recover for the materials supplied, though not the fee for the services provided.[52]

In contrast, when an action is brought against a person who has not been licensed, the defendant cannot use his own misconduct in not complying with a statute as a defence to an action by an innocent person. This result is an application of the general principle that a person (whether as plaintiff or defendant) is not permitted to use evidence of his own wrongdoing for his advantage before the courts.

The courts are more flexible and sympathetic toward entirely innocent breaches of statutory requirements.

CASE 8.6 Flexible Approach

S, an American citizen, was lawfully admitted to Canada and applied for permanent residence status. While waiting for her status to be granted, she accepted a position without first obtaining a work permit as required under immigration regulations; S was unaware of the requirement. She and her employer paid premiums under the *Employment Insurance Act*, but when S was laid off, she was denied benefits because her employment contract was void for illegality.[53]

The court rejected the "classic model of illegality" and stated that the consequences of declaring a contract illegal could often be too extreme. It was preferable to adopt a general principle rather than a rigid rule, and to refuse to give relief only where it would be contrary to public policy to do so. To allow this claim would not offend the policy of making benefits available to a person innocently unemployed. Nor would it encourage illegal immigrants to come to Canada to work illegally. S was not an illegal immigrant, and she acted in good faith. The Act only imposed sanctions against those who knowingly obtained work without a permit. The court gave S the right to collect employment benefits.

Examples of Agreements Made Legal by Statute

Attitudes about socially acceptable behaviour change over time, and therefore attitudes about what is in the public good also change. Legislation is sometimes passed to make previously illegal contracts legal. As discussed, statutes have been passed to legalize otherwise illegal betting; Section 204 of the *Criminal Code* makes betting on horse racing legal, as well as private bets between individuals not engaged in the "business" of betting.

Arbitration agreements are another example of previously unenforceable contracts being made legal by statute. Historically, courts considered any contract that blocked access to the courts to be against public policy and therefore unenforceable.[54] Canadian attitudes toward arbitration changed in the 1990s, and most provinces passed arbitration legislation embracing arbitration agreements and leaving only a few

arbitration agreements contracts that require all disputes to be resolved in arbitration, not the courts

---

[51] *Kocotis v D'Angelo* (1957), 13 DLR (2d) 69 (ONCA); but see *Sidmay Ltd et al v Wehttam Investments Ltd* (1967), 61 DLR (2d) 358, aff'd (1968), 69 DLR (2d) 336; *Chung v Idan*, [2006] OJ No 299 at paras 52–3 (QL) aff'd 2007 ONCA 544.

[52] *Monticchio v Torcema Construction Ltd* (1979), 26 OR (2d) 305.

[53] *Re Still and Minister of National Revenue* (1997), 154 DLR (4th) 229. But see *Koo v 5220459 Manitoba Inc*, (2010) 254 Man R (2d) 62.

[54] John D. McCamus, *The Law of Contracts* (Toronto, ON: Irwin, 2005) at 440.

possible reasons for a court to find an arbitration agreement unenforceable.[55] Now attitudes toward consumer arbitration are changing again, and some provinces have passed legislation declaring consumer arbitration agreements contained in standard form purchase contracts unenforceable.[56] The illegal arbitration clause may be severed from the purchase agreement, and any disputes may be resolved in the courts.

To avoid continuously changing legislation, most decisions about the legality of a contract are left to the courts to be decided on public policy grounds with the help of past cases.

CONTRACTS ILLEGAL BY THE COMMON LAW AND PUBLIC POLICY

The Common Law

common law precedents developed over time from the decisions of many cases

The **common law** has identified certain types of conduct that harm others and has granted remedies, usually in the form of damages, to persons harmed by that conduct. Generally, the conduct is considered a private wrong or tort, and so whenever a contract involves or requires the commission of a tort, the contract is illegal.

Among the torts that typically arise in an agreement are slander and libel, trespass, deceit (fraud), and, in particular, inducement to break an existing contract with someone else.

CASE 8.7 Inducing Breach of Contract

The Wanderers Hockey Club learned that Johnson had signed a contract to play for the following season with another club managed by Patrick. The Wanderers' manager persuaded Johnson to enter into a second contract with it for the same season by offering him a higher salary. Johnson tore up his contract with Patrick, but as things turned out, he failed to perform his new contract with the Wanderers, which then sued him for breach of contract.

The action failed on the grounds that no cause of action can arise out of a wrongdoing; it had been obvious to both parties that the second contract with the Wanderers could not be performed without breaking the earlier contract with Patrick.[57]

An agreement may not have as its primary purpose the commission of a wrongful act, but what if it contains an undertaking by one party to indemnify the other against damages arising from any tort committed in the course of performing the contract?

CASE 8.8 Commission of Any Tort

W. H. Smith & Son's contract to print the *Vanity Fair* newspaper for Clinton included a term that Clinton would indemnify it against libel claims. Thereafter, the paper published an article containing statements libelous to Parr's Bank. W. H. Smith settled the claim against it by paying Parr's Bank a sum of money and sued Clinton to recover the money. The action failed because the court refused to assist in the recovery of money to indemnify against wrongful behaviour—publishing libelous statements.[58]

---

[55] See e.g. *Arbitration Act*, RSA 1991, c A-43, ss 6–7; *Teal Cedar Products Ltd v British Columbia*, 2017 SCC 32.

[56] *Consumer Protection Act, 2002*, SO 2002, c 30, ss 7–8; Quebec and Alberta have also limited enforcement of consumer arbitration agreements.

[57] *Wanderers Hockey Club v Johnson* (1913), 14 DLR 42. See also *Fabbi et al v Jones* (1972), 28 DLR (3d) 224.

[58] *Smith v Clinton* (1908), 99 LT 840.

There are important exceptions to this rule for contracts of insurance. For example, an insurance policy that promises to indemnify a motorist for the damages he may have to pay to third parties as a result of his negligent driving is neither void nor illegal; automobile insurance for public liability and property damage is valid. Similar policies of insurance are designed to protect professional people against the consequences of their negligence in the course of practice, and such policies are also valid. However, the insurance protects the policyholder from negligence only—that is, from unintentional wrongdoing, and not from intentional behaviour, such as fraud.

In addition, a person or a business may exempt itself from liability for negligence by the terms of a contract. A railway or other carrier may state in its standard form contract for the shipment of goods (bill of lading) that it shall not be liable for damage to goods in excess of a stated amount, whether caused by the negligence of its employees or not. The temptation to include such exemption clauses is great, and as a result these contracts are often subject to government regulation.

Public Policy

Even though a contract does not contemplate the commission of a crime or of any of the recognized torts, it may still be regarded as illegal because it is contrary to public policy. If the court decides that a particular contract is prejudicial to the interests of Canada, its relations with foreign countries, its national defence, its public service, the values of society as a whole, or the administration of justice within the country, the court will declare the contract illegal although its performance is neither a tort nor a crime in itself.

CASE 8.9 Bribing a Witness

The plaintiff, Symington, promised the defendants (who were anxious to see a person named Ball convicted of illegal manufacture of alcohol) to give evidence that would assure Ball's conviction. The defendants promised to pay Symington $1000 for each month of imprisonment in Ball's sentence. Symington gave testimony, and Ball was sentenced to 12 months' imprisonment. Symington received only part payment and sued for the balance.[59]

Symington's suit failed on grounds of public policy that the agreement tended to pervert justice. In summarizing his reasons, Mr. Justice Martin said:

This is so direct and inevitable an incentive to perjury and other concomitant nefarious conduct that it cannot be in the public interest to countenance a transaction which is dangerous to such an exceptional degree to the administration of criminal justice.[60]

The arrangements by which a person accused of a crime may be released under bail are intended to be fair and humane.[61] However, they require that the party putting up the bail shall forfeit the bail money should the prisoner abscond. Accordingly, a promise either by the accused or by a third party to indemnify the party putting up bail is illegal.[62]

Public policy interests extend beyond the administration of justice, incorporating general values beneficial to a free society such as free speech and the right to profit from one's work.

---

[59] *Symington v Vancouver Breweries and Riefel*, [1931] 1 DLR 935.

[60] *Ibid* at 937.

[61] See M. L. Friedland, *Detention Before Trial* (Toronto: University of Toronto Press, 1965); *Criminal Code*, supra note 38, ss 763–71.

[62] *Herman v Jeuchner* (1885), 15 QBD 561; *Consolidated Exploration and Finance Co v Musgrave*, [1900] 1 Ch 37.

> ### Ethical Issue Confidentiality Clauses and Public Policy
>
> Employment and research contracts often contain clauses that require the employee or the funded researcher to maintain confidentiality about sensitive information. Such information might include the company's financial affairs, its marketing plans, the products it is developing, or the progress of research it is sponsoring. There are good reasons for these clauses. Businesses do not want their competitive position undermined by having private information end up in the hands of their rivals. They do not want the price of their stock or the reputation of their products to be affected by rumours and gossip. Courts award damages and sometimes grant injunctions for breach of confidentiality clauses.
>
> However, what if the clause prevents a person from disclosing information that shows that a company's products place consumers or patients at risk? In that case, ethical and public policy concerns arise.
>
> Dr. Nancy Olivieri, a professor of medicine at the University of Toronto and a leading researcher at the Hospital for Sick Children, received funding from Apotex, a drug manufacturer, to conduct clinical trials on a new drug.
>
> A few years into the trial, Dr. Olivieri became concerned that the drug was not effective and that dangerously high levels of iron were building up in the livers of some of the patients in the trial. When she reported her concern to the drug company and the hospital research ethics board, the company terminated the trial at the Toronto site. When she made her findings public, Apotex accused her of violating the confidentiality agreement she had signed and threatened to sue her. The company also asserted that her methods were suspect, and her findings were unsupported by other researchers. While Dr. Olivieri published her research findings in the highly respected *New England Journal of Medicine*, Apotex did not submit its data for publication.
>
> During the conflict, Dr. Olivieri received strong moral support from a number of her colleagues, many of whom thought the hospital had not properly supported and defended her. Eventually, Dr. Olivieri and the hospital reached a settlement of their differences.
>
> **Questions to Consider**
>
> 1. Should confidentiality agreements be enforced if doing so would prevent risks from being disclosed to the public? How can the proper balance be established between a company's interest in protecting sensitive information and the public's interest in knowing about risks to health and safety?
>
> 2. What legislation, if any, do we need to protect employees and researchers who disclose information about products or activities that pose a risk to consumers or patients?
>
> 3. Should medical and physical safety risks be the only exceptions? What about risks to our privacy? Consider the situation of Edward Snowdon, the former NSA and CIA contractor who breached his confidentiality obligations when he disclosed massive government surveillance practices.
>
> Sources: Susan Jeffrey, "Research Conflict," *The Medical Post*, January 21, 1997; Michael Valpy, "Science Friction," *Elm Street*, December 1998; University of Toronto Faculty Association Press Release, December 17, 1998; Joint Release, The Hospital for Sick Children and Dr. Nancy Olivieri, January 26, 1999; Marina Jimenez, "Olivieri, Foes Take Battle Over Drug to Ottawa," *National Post*, October 5, 1999.

Agreements in Restraint of Trade

The courts consider competition a necessary and important element of economic life, and agreements that diminish competition are undesirable and against public policy. Some **agreements in restraint** of trade—known as **non-competition agreements**, **non-solicitation agreements** and restrictive covenants—are unenforceable, whereas others may violate the *Competition Act* and trigger regulatory or criminal sanctions.

Even if a contract contains a **restrictive covenant** (a term in restraint of trade) that is found to be against public policy, the term might not invalidate the entire contract. The courts may refuse to enforce the offending term while treating the remainder of the contract as valid. The courts initially presume that any term in restraint of trade is against public policy, but the party seeking to enforce the covenant may **rebut** the presumption if it can demonstrate that it is a reasonable arrangement between the parties and does not adversely affect the public interest.

Rebutting the presumption is particularly likely for two of types of contracts in restraint of trade:

- agreements between the vendor and the purchaser of a business in which the vendor undertakes not to carry on a similar business in competition with the purchaser or solicit former customers or employees

agreements in restraint agreements that restrict competition, also known as non-competition agreements, non-solicitation agreements, or restrictive covenants when they are included in a larger contract

non-competition agreements agreements that restrict a person's right to carry on a business that competes with that of the other party or to work for a business that competes

non-solicitation agreements agreements that prevent a person from contacting the other party's customers, employees, or suppliers with a view to moving their business or employment

restrictive covenant a term in restraint of trade, that is, a promise not to carry on a competing business activity

rebut overcome

- agreements between employer and employee in which the employee undertakes that after leaving her present employment, she will not compete against the employer, either by setting up her own business or by taking a position with a competing business or by soliciting the employer's customers or other employees

The courts begin by presuming that any term in restraint of trade is against public policy and is void and unenforceable, but this presumption is not absolute. It may be overcome by the party seeking to enforce the covenant if that party can prove that the agreement is a reasonable arrangement between the parties and does not adversely affect the public interest.[63] The two types of contracts discussed next are the ones most frequently considered by the courts, however, they are not treated exactly the same. Parties negotiating a sale of a business receive greater freedom to contract than do those negotiating employment contracts; therefore the court must identify the type of contract it is in order to determine in which category the restrictive covenant falls.[64]

Agreements between Vendor and Purchaser of a Business

An important asset of a business is its goodwill—that is, the trade and commercial connections it has established through years of carrying on business under its name and in a particular location. The vendor of a business can persuade the purchaser to pay for the goodwill only if he can make a binding promise that he will do nothing in the future to diminish or destroy the value of what he is selling. To do so, he must be free to promise the purchaser that he will not enter into any business that is likely to compete with the business he is selling: There will then be no danger of his attracting old customers away and so diminishing its value. After the sale, it is important that the law enforce reasonable undertakings of this kind made by the vendor, or else the purchaser, fearing she will be deprived of a valuable part of the asset she has purchased, will refuse to pay the vendor's price.

Therefore, the law recognizes that both purchaser and vendor of a business may find a mutual advantage in a restrictive covenant and that such a restraint is not against the public interest. As well, the parties usually deal with each other on a more or less equal footing in striking a bargain with respect to both the price and the protection asked for by the purchaser. The vendor's covenant not to compete with the purchaser as a term of an agreement for the sale of a business may be enforced if it can be shown that the restrictions placed on the vendor are reasonable in view of the nature of the trade or practice sold.

Whether a particular restriction is so broad that it offends the public interest is for the court to decide. On the one hand, a clause forbidding the vendor ever to enter business again anywhere would, for most types of business, be more than is needed to protect the purchaser and would be considered to deprive the public of the benefits of the vendor's abilities; accordingly, it would be void. On the other hand, a term by which the vendor undertakes for a stated period of time (or perhaps even within his lifetime) not to set up the same business again within a specified area that reasonably describes the area of competition may well be reasonable in the opinion of a court and consequently valid. The size of the area and the period of time denied to the vendor vary with the nature of the business.

---

[63] *Shafron v KRG Insurance Brokers*, 2009 SCC 6 at para 27.

[64] *Payette v Guay Inc*, 2013 SCC 45 at paras 2–3.

> ### ILLUSTRATION 8.1 Selling a Practice
>
> A dentist in Saskatoon sells his practice to a young graduate, promising that he will not practise again anywhere in Canada. The retiring dentist has a change of heart, however, and two years later sets up a practice in the same city. The other dentist brings action to obtain a court injunction restraining him from doing so.

In these circumstances a restrictive clause that denies the seller a right to practise anywhere in Canada is more than is necessary to protect the interests of the purchaser. To argue that a covenant in restraint of trade is not against public policy, it is necessary to show at least that it is reasonable between parties. The scope of this covenant, in view of the nature of a dental practice, is unreasonable, and it is therefore void. The purchaser would fail to obtain the injunction, although if the covenant had been confined to the city of Saskatoon for, say, a period of three years, it would probably have been valid.[65]

With rare exceptions, the courts have refused to take on the task of narrowing to a "reasonable scope" the area or the time within which the seller is not to set up business.[66] The basic objection to reducing a covenant is that it rewrites the contract of the parties; it gives a purchaser who has demanded an unreasonable restriction the benefit of the court's opinion about the allowable maximum area not considered detrimental to the public interest. It would also discourage the vendor from taking the risk of opening a new business. If a restrictive clause is held to be too wide or it is written describing alternatives, it is highly unlikely that courts will narrow it to a reasonable scope. The clause will be unenforceable and a vendor who might otherwise have been bound by a reasonable restriction is free of the restraint. The lesson for the purchaser is that he should demand no more than a reasonable restriction, erring on the conservative side rather than demanding too much.

The next case illustrates how the nature of a business may be important in determining what is a reasonable restriction on its vendor.

> ### CASE 8.10 Separating Multiple Restrictions
>
> Nordenfelt had been a manufacturer of guns and ammunition. He transferred his patents and business to Maxim Nordenfelt Guns and Ammunition Co. Ltd. and covenanted that for 25 years he would not engage, except on behalf of this company, either directly or indirectly in the business of a manufacturer of guns or ammunition or in any other business competing or liable to compete in any way with the business of the company. Later, Nordenfelt entered into an agreement with other manufacturers of guns and ammunition, and the plaintiff company brought an action to enforce the covenant.
>
> The court divided the clause into two parts: first, the promise not to engage in the manufacture of guns or ammunition, and second, the promise not to engage in any other business competing or liable to compete with the plaintiff company. The court held that the second promise was an unreasonable restriction and declared it void. But it also held it could sever the second promise from the first and that the first promise was a reasonable restriction. Accordingly, it granted an injunction to restrain Nordenfelt from working for any other business that manufactured guns and ammunition.[67] Even though this is an 1894 case, it remains important today, quoted by the Supreme Court of Canada in 2013 and by the British Columbia Court of Appeal in 2017.[68]

---

[65] See e.g. *Lyons v Multari*, (2000), 50 OR (3d) 526 (CA).

[66] See *Goldsoll v Goldman*, [1915] 1 Ch 292; *Attwood v Lamont*, [1920] 3 KB 571; *Canadian American Financial Corp v King* (1989), 60 DLR (4th) 293; *Bonazza v Forensic Investigations Canada Inc*, [2009] OJ No 2626 at paras 13–15 (QL) (severance as applied to a clause drafted in the alternative).

[67] *Nordenfelt v Maxim Nordenfelt Guns and Ammunition Co Ltd*, [1894] AC 535.

[68] *Infra* note 69.

Although the courts will not save unreasonable restrictions by redrafting them or narrowing their effect, they will sever an unreasonable restriction from one that is reasonable provided they are two distinct ideas and can be severed without changing the meaning of the reasonable restraint.

Agreements between Employee and Employer Non-competition agreements in employment contracts are subject to stricter rules, making it more difficult to convince courts that covenants between employee and employer restricting the future economic freedom of the employee are reasonable and not in restraint of trade.[69] In an employment contract, there is no payment for goodwill, and bargaining power is unequal; an employer is able to impose terms on an employee that the latter must accept if he wants the position. Later he may find that the covenant, if valid, makes it virtually impossible for him to leave his employer in order to accept another position in the vicinity: He would have to sell his house and become established in another city. In protecting employees by striking down unreasonable restraints, the courts at the same time serve a second public interest—they protect the mobility of labour and so encourage more efficient allocation of human resources.

We must distinguish agreements that relate to activities undertaken after an employee leaves his present employment from those that address the employee's behaviour during employment. The law recognizes a full-time employee's primary duty of loyalty to the employer, and an absolute promise not to engage in any other business during the term of the employment is valid, whether that business competes with the employer or not. Similar agreements between partners that are operative during the life of the partnership are also binding.

An employer seeking to enforce a restrictive covenant usually asks the court for the equitable remedy of an injunction to restrain the defendant. A restrictive covenant may be enforced if it is unambiguous and

- the claimant has a proprietary interest worthy of protection;
- the interest cannot be adequately protected with less restrictive measures; and
- the non-competition clause in the agreement is reasonable by reference to
  - the activity prohibited,
  - the geographical area of the prohibition, and
  - the duration of the prohibition.[70]

The courts readily accept that trade secrets, secret processes, confidential information, and connections or relationships with customers and other employees are proprietary interests worthy of protection.[71] Still, the clause must be the most appropriate way to protect the interest and must be reasonable as to the activity restricted, the geographic area covered, and the duration of the restriction. Courts will consider whether a less onerous form of non-solicitation clause—a restriction on marketing to a previous employer's customers—would have sufficed in the circumstances. If so, a complete ban on competition will be unenforceable.[72] However, in employment contracts the court will not sever the offending part and substitute the lesser requirement, nor will it rewrite an ambiguous or unreasonable restrictive covenant in order to make it enforceable.[73]

---

[69] *Payette v Guay*, 2013 SCC 45 at paras 2-3; *IRIS The Visual Group Western Canada Inc v Park*, 2017 BCCA 301 at paras 19–23.

[70] *IRIS, ibid* at para 43.

[71] *Ibid* at paras 26–28.

[72] *JG Collins Insurance Agencies Ltd v Elsley*, [1978] 2 SCR 916 at 926; *Lyons v Multari* (2000), 50 OR (3d) 526 (CA).

[73] *Shafron, supra* note 63 at paras 36–42.

CASE 8.11 Higher Standard

Shafron sold his insurance agency to KRG Western and continued as an employee of the purchaser and subsequent owners under an employment contract with a restrictive covenant. The covenant prohibited Shafron from being employed in the business of insurance brokerage within the "Metropolitan City of Vancouver" for three years after leaving KRG. Within one year of leaving KRG, Shafron began working as an insurance salesman for another agency, and KRG sued. The geographic location was found to be unclear and ambiguous as there is no such place as the "Metropolitan City of Vancouver." Ambiguous clauses will naturally be unreasonable as the restriction is unclear. However, the Court of Appeal severed the word "metropolitan" and found the remaining phrase "City of Vancouver" unambiguous and reasonable so it was enforceable. The Supreme Court of Canada overturned the Court of Appeal. First, it found the agreement to be an employment agreement subject to higher standard of scrutiny than a sale of business contract. Second, although it agreed that the geographic restriction was ambiguous, it disagreed with severing the word "metropolitan" as this amounted to rewriting the clause for the parties. Severance should not be used for restrictive covenants in employment contracts.[74]

CHECKLIST
Enforcement of Agreements in Restraint of Trade

Agreements in restraint of trade are presumed against public policy and unenforceable subject to limited exceptions:

- They may be enforceable in two contexts: sale of business and employment.
- The party seeking enforcement must first prove the clause is clear and unambiguous—if not, it will be unreasonable and unenforceable.
- If the clause is unambiguous, it must also be proven to be reasonable as to restricted activity, geographic area, and time period.
- Employment agreements will be subject to greater scrutiny than business sales.
- The party seeking enforcement in the employment context must prove they have a proprietary interest worthy of protection and that the clause is the least restrictive way to protect it
- Severance is not available to cure an employment contract.

A third class of agreements in restraint of trade—agreements among manufacturers or merchants to restrict output or fix the selling price of a commodity or service—is examined in Chapter 3.

Strategies to Manage the Legal Risks

With respect to capacity issues and the risk that a contract may be rendered void, businesses must take steps before contracting to confirm the capacity of the other party. Government databases may be searched to determine the status of a business and its accurate name. Sole proprietors, partnerships, and corporations must register business names, and these records may be searched. Attention to this detail before the contract is formed will ensure that the named party is actually a legal entity and is bound by the obligation. Similarly, the age of an individual party may be confirmed through

---

[74] *Ibid.*

identification at the time of purchase. If the nature of the business involves contracting with minors, the contract should be structured to require immediate payment, so the burden will be on the minor party to nullify the agreement and not on the business to try to enforce it.

With respect to legality, business managers should familiarize themselves with industry-specific legislation that may render contracts void or unenforceable if not properly prepared in accordance with their provisions. Generally, applicable consumer protection statutes will also void non-complying contracts. Finally, non-solicitation, confidentiality, and non-competition agreements should only be employed in employment, partnership, and business sale contexts. Even in these circumstances, the terms must be reasonable in light of industry norms and the history between the parties. A severance clause should be included so that offending provisions may be removed without preventing enforcement of the balance of the contract.

QUESTIONS FOR REVIEW

1. Is a minor bound to pay the agreed contract price for necessaries? Explain.
2. What element is necessary for a contract of employment to bind a minor?
3. What obligation does a minor have when she repudiates a contract for non-necessary goods? Explain the policy reason for the rule.
4. Are minors' contracts for non-necessaries always voidable when the minors attain majority?
5. What two types of minors' contracts must be distinguished for the purpose of determining the liability of the minors after they become of age?
6. Give examples of persons of diminished contractual capacity. What special problems do such persons face when they want to deny responsibility under a contract?
7. Under what circumstances may a contract voidable at the option of one of the parties cease to be voidable?
8. What is the nature of the legal problem that adds to the uncertainty of an action against a trade union?
9. (a) When Jones was 17 years old, she took her stereo into the Mariposa Service Centre for an extensive repair job that cost $175. If she does not pay, can the Mariposa Service Centre sue her successfully?
   (b) After Jones becomes of age, she picks up the repaired stereo and does nothing to repudiate her liability to the Mariposa Service Centre. Can the Mariposa Service Centre recover the money now?
   (c) Upon becoming of age, Jones tells the manager of the Mariposa Service Centre in a telephone conversation that she will pay the $175. Can the Mariposa Service Centre recover now?
10. For what types of organization is a representative action important? Explain.
11. Why may it be important to a party to a dispute to show that a void contract is not also illegal?
12. How can we tell whether the intention of the legislature is to make a certain type of agreement illegal as well as void?
13. What are "wagering" contracts, and are they legal? What government legislation should be considered when answering this question?
14. What quality must an insurance contract possess to prevent it from being a wager and therefore void?
15. What kinds of business contract may have an element of wagering incidental to the main purpose of the transaction?

16. Explain how restrictive covenants play a role in the sale of an active business.
17. What exception is there to the rule that an agreement is illegal if it purports to indemnify a person against the consequences of his own wrongdoing?
18. What factors does a court consider when determining if a restrictive covenant in an employment contract is legal and enforceable?
19. Discuss the courts' attitude toward the subsequent use of trade secrets acquired by a former employee.

CASES AND PROBLEMS

1. Continuing Scenario

    The most important hiring decisions Ashley will make are for the chef and hostess positions. The hostess will be the face of the restaurant; regular customers will build a relationship with the hostess. The chef's food will keep customers coming back, and the chef's reputation will spread across the community. Ashley intends to share all her business skills with these two people. However, she worries that, once trained, they could open their own restaurants and divert her customers to their businesses. How can Ashley use the employment contract to protect herself from this business risk? What are the limits of the contractual protection? Does it make a difference if she makes the chef a partner in her business? Draft the necessary clause.

2. For most of a year, Harrison acted as agent for the purpose of obtaining options on property on an island in British Columbia on behalf of the Western Development Company, which planned to develop the island industrially. These plans became known to the property owners on the island, and some of them, believing their holdings to be indispensable to the plan, sought to obtain prices much higher than the market value established there for farm or residential purposes.

    Harrison obtained, for a consideration of $1, an option to purchase within one year the property of Mrs. Foy for $200 000. Harrison had negotiated the price with a Miss Foy and a widow, Mrs. Sheridan; he had offered $1000 a hectare, which was the maximum he had been authorized to offer, but the two women had insisted upon $2000 a hectare. He had then reluctantly agreed to take an option at the price demanded, explaining that his principals would not likely take up the option at such an exorbitant price. Miss Foy had next insisted that a further $10 000 be added to the price for the barn; Harrison had agreed to that, too.

    It was only when the option agreement was prepared for signing that Harrison learned that he had not been dealing with the registered owner of the property but with her daughters, both of whom resided there. They told him that Mrs. Foy was a very old lady and was bedridden. Harrison was taken to the bedroom, where he explained, carefully and accurately, the terms and effect of the option. Mrs. Foy appeared to understand what he was saying, nodding and smiling and from time to time saying, "Yes." At that point Harrison turned to Miss Foy, who was standing at the foot of the bed, and asked her, "Do you really think your mother understands the difference between an option and an agreement to sell her land?" Miss Foy replied, "Yes, I think she understands." Then Mrs. Sheridan asked Harrison if, before getting her mother to sign, he would wait until they could get the family lawyer to be present. Harrison, exasperated with slow pace of negotiations, replied that he was not prepared to put up with any further delay or discussion of terms. He asked Mrs. Foy to sign the option agreement. She did not sign her name but made a cross under the direction of one of her daughters, who explained to Harrison that her mother used to be able to sign her name but that her hand was now too unsteady.

    Harrison's principals did, in fact, elect to take up the option within the year to obtain property at the agreed price of $200 000; they had taken up the options on the adjoining properties and needed Mrs. Foy's property to complete the land they required. The two daughters said that the option agreement was "not worth the paper it was written on" because Mrs. Foy was insane at the time of her signing. The principals sued to have the option agreement enforced. It was brought out in evidence that Mrs. Foy was, indeed, insane, a fact of which Harrison denied any knowledge at the time; it was also shown that the fair market value of the property as a farm at the date of the option agreement was about $140 000.

Should a court enforce the agreement? Why or why not?

3. During the 2007–08 season, Harvey ("Ace") Tilson played hockey for the Medicine Hat Broncos of the Western Junior Hockey League, scoring 30 goals and assisting on another 35 goals. In recent years, many players in this league had been offered contracts to play professional hockey upon completion of their junior eligibility. They remained eligible to play in the league until the year in which they reached the age of 21.

In October 2006, Tilson signed a two-year contract with the Medicine Hat Broncos Hockey Club that was to terminate before the start of the hockey season in the early fall of 2008. However, at the beginning of training camp in September 2007, the manager of the Broncos presented Tilson and the other players with a new three-year contract. This contract contained a new set of standardized conditions of employment prescribed by the league and, by agreement among the clubs, was presented to all players in the league on a "take it or leave it" basis; the players understood that if they did not agree to waive their existing contracts and sign the new one, they would not be able to play in the league and their professional prospects would be severely harmed. The new contract included the following clauses:

1. This contract supersedes all previous contracts between the Club [Medicine Hat Broncos Hockey Club] and the Player [Harvey J. Tilson].

2. The Club employs the Player as an apprentice hockey player for the term of three years commencing 2008 and agrees, subject to the terms of this contract, to pay the Player a salary of $750.00 per week plus an allowance for room and board of $400.00 per week, with these payments to terminate at the last scheduled game of the Club each year.

3. The Player acknowledges that if his hockey skills and abilities develop to the degree that he is tendered and accepts a contract of employment with a professional hockey club, then the Club shall be entitled to compensation for its contribution to his development, and in consideration for such contribution by the Club, the Player agrees to pay the Club a sum equal to 20 percent (20%) of his gross earnings attributable to his employment with such professional hockey club during a period of three (3) years beginning on the date at which he first represents and plays for that professional hockey club.

4. The Player agrees that during the term of this contract he will loyally discharge his obligations to the Club and that he will not play for or be directly or indirectly employed by or interested in any other amateur or professional hockey club. The Player agrees that the Club shall have the right, in addition to any other legal remedies that the Club may enjoy, to prevent him by appropriate injunction proceedings from committing any breach of this undertaking.

5. The Player acknowledges that, if in breach of his obligations under section 4, the Player plays for any other hockey club, the Club will lose his services as a skilled hockey player and will suffer a loss of income from reduced paid attendance at hockey games and broadcasting rights and that a genuine estimate of the amount of this loss would be the salary that the Player can earn as a hockey player for any other amateur or professional club.

The manager of the Broncos advised the players to take their copies of the contract home and discuss the contract with their parents. He added that a signed copy had to be in his hands by the beginning of the following week. Tilson's parents actively encouraged him to sign the contract, and Tilson returned a signed copy to the manager on September 5, 1997.

Tilson played for the Broncos in the 2007–08 season until March 21, 2008. On that day he became 18 years of age, the age of majority in Alberta. On March 22, 2008, in a letter to the club written by his lawyer, Tilson repudiated the contract "without in any way acknowledging the validity thereof." On the same day, in the company of his lawyer, he signed a Pan-American Hockey Conference contract with the Calgary Whippets Hockey Club Ltd. for three seasons commencing September 1 of each of 2008, 2009, and 2010, providing for annual salaries of $170 000, $180 000, and $190 000, respectively.

At the time, the 2007–08 season was almost over, and the Broncos had qualified for the playoffs and were the favourite to win the Junior Cup. Tilson offered to stay with the team at his regular weekly salary and allowance during the 2008 playoffs if the Broncos Club would sign an agreement that Tilson's three-year hockey contract with it would expire when the playoffs ended. The Broncos refused and brought an action against Tilson, seeking an injunction to restrain him from breaking his contract or, in the alternative, damages for its loss for being deprived of his services for the next two years.

Explain the legal issues raised in this dispute, and offer with reasons an opinion about the probable outcome of the action.

4. Assume the facts of Problem 3, with the exception that the Broncos Club did sign the agreement proposed by Tilson in March 2008; that Tilson had played with the team during the 1998 playoffs; and that the Broncos Club had then brought its action against Tilson. What line of reasoning might the Broncos use to support the argument that the March 2008 agreement was not binding on it? Would it be a good argument? Cite any relevant case or cases.

5. Marbett noticed that the ceiling on the upper floor of her house had become damp from water seepage. She mentioned the problem to her neighbour, who remarked that Marbett's house was 25 years old and probably needed new roofing; he recommended that she contact Riley, who had recently repaired his roof. Marbett phoned Riley, and he came promptly to inspect the roof. He said he would replace it for $1800 within a few days. Marbett signed a contract to have the job done.

The day the work was being completed, Marbett was told by a friend that Riley did not have the required municipal licence for a roofing contractor. The friend said she believed Marbett did not have to pay Riley for the roofing work because the contract was illegal. Is the friend correct? Give reasons for your opinion.

6. Flanders & Co., a Montreal firm of wine importers, chartered the ship *Bacchus* from its owners, Swan Ltd., to transport a cargo of wine from Madeira to Montreal. The contract of charter party included a term to the effect that the charterer, Flanders & Co., should be liable for an additional $2500 for each additional day at the port of destination if the unloading of the ship were delayed for any reason.

Unknown to either party, the wine was a prohibited product under the federal *Food and Drugs Act* because of a preservative used in its production.

When the ship reached Montreal, customs officers refused permission to unload pending determination of the cargo's compliance with the federal act. The investigation and report from the government laboratory in Ottawa took 10 days; it was determined by customs officials that it would be illegal to import the wine, and the cargo was finally transferred at dockside to another ship for shipment to New York.

When Flanders & Co. refused to pay the additional $25 000 caused by the delay, Swan Ltd. sued for the amount. What defence might Flanders & Co. offer? Would Swan Ltd. succeed?

7. John Gifford and his friend Karl Holtz were enthusiastic followers of the commodities market, the market in which such products as wheat, cotton, tobacco, and coffee are bought and sold for future delivery. However, they did not have sufficient capital to engage in the market themselves, and so they played a game: They would

"buy and sell" futures in various commodities under three-month contracts for delivery and then "settle" their fictional gains and losses on the delivery date. Karl did very well in the game and over a two-year period "earned" over $100 000 at John's expense.

One day John finally said to Karl, "I think I have a real winner here: The price of coffee is going to rise sharply in the next three months. At what price do you want to sell to me?"

Karl disagreed with John's prediction and replied, "I'll sell you $20 000 worth of coffee at today's price. The price is going to drop, and you'll lose as usual."

"For once, not only am I right, but I'm prepared to back up my words. Are you?" asked John. "Let's make this a real transaction. If the price goes up, you pay me the difference. If it goes down, I pay you."

"Okay, it's your funeral. It's a deal," Karl replied, and they shook hands on it.

Three months later, the price of $20 000 worth of coffee had risen by 30 percent, making John richer by $6000. When John demanded payment, Karl said he didn't have that much in the bank but grudgingly gave John three cheques for $2000 each, one payable immediately and the other two postdated one month and two months, respectively.

John cashed the first cheque at Karl's bank at once. A month later, he used the second cheque to buy a used car from Grace Bukowsky. She has not yet presented it to Karl's bank for payment. John still has the third cheque.

Karl has heard from a friend studying law that the whole transaction might be "illegal." Give him your opinion with reasons.

Chapter 9
Contract Issues: Mistake and Misrepresentation

- **SETTING ASIDE A CONTRACT**
- **THE NARROW MEANING OF MISTAKE**
- **VOID AND VOIDABLE CONTRACTS**
- **MISTAKES ABOUT THE TERMS**
- **MISTAKES ABOUT THE SUBJECT MATTER**
- **MISTAKES ABOUT THE IDENTITY OF A PARTY TO A CONTRACT**
- **MISTAKES ABOUT THE NATURE OF A SIGNED DOCUMENT**
- **MISREPRESENTATION**
- **CONSEQUENCES OF MISREPRESENTATION IN CONTRACTS**
- **UNDUE INFLUENCE**
- **CONSUMER PROTECTION**
- **DURESS**
- **STRATEGIES TO MANAGE THE LEGAL RISKS**

What happens when a party realizes the contract is not the one that was intended? A party may believe a mistake has been made.

In this chapter we examine such questions as:

- What are common, mutual, and unilateral mistakes?
- What are the legal consequences of a mistake
  - about the meaning of the words?
  - about the existence or qualities of the subject matter?
  - about the identity of the parties?
- What is misrepresentation in contract, as opposed to tort?
- What are the legal consequences of a contractual misrepresentation?
- What remedy is available to the victim of undue influence or duress?
- Do consumers receive extra protection?

SETTING ASIDE A CONTRACT

Setting aside a contract is not an easy task. In the interests of commercial certainty, courts tend to hold parties to the bargains they make. However, in rare circumstances, courts recognize the need to set aside a contract. This chapter considers several equitable principles that allow a party to be released from a contract and returned to a pre-contract position. Relief may be available when there has been a mistake or a misrepresentation. As well, if one party has pressured the other into agreeing, the principles of undue influence and duress may apply. In addition, consumers are given statutory protection from some improper business behaviour. The availability of relief depends upon the factual circumstances of each case and the rules discussed below.

THE NARROW MEANING OF MISTAKE

Sometimes parties regret entering into a contract—perhaps it turns out to be different from what was expected, or they decide it was unwise. They made a "mistake" and wish to be released from it.

"Legal mistake" is not the same as "mistake" in its more general, everyday context. To say, "I made a mistake going for a walk without my umbrella" after getting wet in a storm means I later regret acting in a particular way. Just because things do not turn out as expected does not mean a legal mistake has been made. Errors in judgment do not legally justify avoiding one's legal obligations under a contract. To excuse performance too easily would undermine certainty in contractual arrangements. Parties would be reluctant to rely on their contracts. Therefore, only certain kinds of mistakes will make a contract **void** or **voidable** and thereby qualify for **equitable relief**. The rules of equity require that any party asking to have a contract set aside must also be prepared to return whatever benefit he or she received under the contract.[1] If a mistaken party cannot restore the subject matter of the contract to the other party—for instance, the goods have been consumed or have substantially deteriorated—the mistaken party loses the right to **rescind**.

To understand the law of mistake, we need to look at two issues—who is mistaken and what they are mistaken about. Generally, mistakes must be about facts, not the law itself. Typically, the mistakes relate to the terms of the contract, the subject matter of the contract, or the identity of the party. When both parties to the contract are mistaken about the same facts, it is a situation known as a common or mutual mistake. In a *common mistake*, both parties believe the same erroneous fact—the car is black, when it is really navy blue. In a *mutual mistake*, both parties are mistaken but believe something different from each other—one party believes the car is black, and the other believes it is charcoal grey, when the car is really navy blue. If only one party is mistaken, and the other knows the truth, it is a situation known as a *unilateral mistake*. In each of these types of mistake the court will decide whether to hold the parties to the bargain, however mistaken, correct the mistake for the parties, or rescind the contract completely.

void a contract that never existed and passed no rights

voidable the contract exists until set aside by a court; rights may pass to third parties before it is set aside

equitable relief a discretionary remedy first developed by the courts of equity to undo an injustice

rescind set aside; undo or revoke a contract and return the parties as nearly as possible to their original positions

VOID AND VOIDABLE CONTRACTS

If the court finds there has been a mistake—in the legal sense of the word—the contract may be declared either void or voidable, or, in special circumstances, the mistake may be corrected (rectified). As noted in Chapter 8, if a contract is void, it means that,

---

[1] Under "Equitable Remedies." See also Waddams, *The Law of Contracts*, 4th ed (Toronto: Canada Law Book Company, 1999) at 444–54.

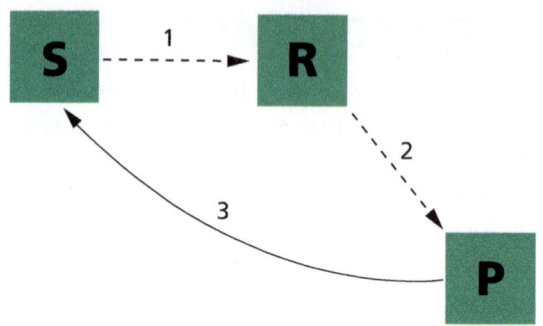

Figure 9.1 Void Contract

1. S "sells" goods to a rogue, R. R does not gain title.
2. R purports to resell the goods to P, the innocent purchaser. P does not gain title.
3. S may sue and recover the goods from P or any subsequent holder.

in law, it was never formed at all. In this sense, calling an agreement a void contract is a contradiction—if a contract is void, there is no contract. It means the contract is ineffective from the very beginning. No rights, title, or ownership pass to anyone under a void contract. Consider Figure 9.1.

If the court decides the contract between S and R is void, the second contract also fails. P can have no greater rights than R, so he will have to return the goods to S and sue R for his losses. Unfortunately, R is often penniless or has disappeared, and any judgment against him will be worthless.

Unlike void contracts, voidable contracts exist until they are **set aside** by the court. Prior to that time, rights, title, and interests pass as set out in the contract. Rescission is an equitable remedy that rescinds a contract. If the contract is rescinded after R has received the goods, R will have to return both title and possession to the seller. The difference between void and voidable contracts does not matter if the goods are still in the possession of the original parties when the contract is set aside. But if the goods have been conveyed to an innocent third party prior to the contract being set aside, then the consequences of void and voidable contracts are quite different. The courts of equity thought that taking the goods away from a subsequent purchaser was too harsh in some circumstances and so created a category of mistakes that only render a contract voidable, allowing a subsequent innocent purchaser to keep the goods, even when the first contract is rescinded. Consider Figure 9.2.

set aside rescind; undo or revoke a contract and return the parties as nearly as possible to their original positions

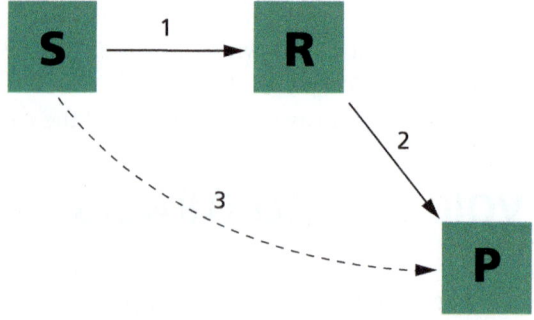

Figure 9.2 Voidable Contract

1. S "sells" goods to a rogue, R. R, despite his deceit, obtains title.
2. R purports to sell the goods to P, the innocent purchaser. P obtains title to the goods.
3. S cannot recover the goods from P.

In order to receive protection, a third-party purchaser must be innocent and have paid value for the goods. A seller's attempt to recover goods will not be blocked by someone who buys knowing about the fraud.

In summary, if a contract dispute concerns only the two original parties, whether the court declares it void or merely voidable might not matter. In either event, the court may order the return of property that has passed between the parties. But if the property has been transferred to an innocent purchaser, the original owner may recover it only if the original contract is declared void, not voidable. Whether any given contract is void or voidable will be determined by the type of mistake and the reasonableness of the behaviour or understanding of the parties. In the following discussion, we look at how courts use the classifications of void and voidable contracts and common, mutual, and unilateral mistakes to decide what should be done in specific situations.

MISTAKES ABOUT THE TERMS

Words Used Inadvertently

In Case 9.1, one party inadvertently uses the wrong words in stating the terms of a contract. The result is a one-sided or **unilateral mistake** by the careless party. It seems only fair that the consequences of such an error should fall on the one who caused the problem. However, when it is clear to an objective observer that the first party made a mistake in expressing the terms of the contract—the price might be absurdly low or quite unrelated to the range of prices quoted by both sides during negotiations—then the contract may be voidable for mistake.

unilateral mistake a situation in which only one of the parties believes there is a mistake in the contract

CASE 9.1   Typo

In *Webster v Cecil*,[2] the parties were negotiating about the sale to Webster of land owned by Cecil. Initially Cecil refused Webster's offer of £2000. Later Cecil made a counter-offer to Webster, mistakenly offering the land for £1250. Immediately after he mailed his letter, Cecil realized his error and sent a second letter stating that the price should have been £2250, but the second letter arrived after Webster mailed his acceptance. Webster sued to enforce the contract and failed. The court found that he could not possibly have believed that £1250 was the intended offer price and granted rescission of the contract.

How does a court exercise the discretion to grant relief? It considers the behaviour of each party and whether the other party (upon receiving the mistaken document) should have realized a mistake was made. Deciding whether a party could have relied reasonably on the words used in an offer is not always easy. Perhaps the offeree should have questioned the offeror to ask whether the offeror really meant them; on the other hand, the offeree could have believed that the offeror simply intended to make the offer so attractive that the offeree would find acceptance hard to resist. After all, a change might have occurred in the offeror's circumstances.

Errors in Recording an Agreement

Sometimes a contract contains an error, but a party does not wish to be released from the obligation. Instead, he wants to have the original deal enforced. If the final written version of the contract does not accurately reflect the original agreement, it need not be declared voidable for mistake. The mistake may be corrected—rectified. If both parties are under a shared or **common mistake**, rectification is a simple matter. The court will order rectification of the document if, at the time the document was signed,

common mistake a situation in which both parties believe the same misunderstanding or mistake about the contract

---

[2] (1861), 54 ER 812.

it did not reflect their shared common intention.[3] It is necessary to show that the parties were in complete definite and unambiguous agreement upon the terms of their contract but by an error wrote them down wrongly.[4] Rectification will only be allowed in cases where the agreement between the parties was not correctly recorded in the final form of their agreement; it is not used to alter the original agreement to avoid unexpected effects.[5]

Unfortunately, if one party stands to benefit from the error in recording, he may insist the final version represents the true bargain and resist any attempt to correct the document by denying a common mistake. In this case, the party claiming the arrangement was improperly recorded may ask the court for **rectification** of the contract based upon unilateral mistake only if the following conditions are met:

(a) The court is satisfied there was a complete oral agreement between the parties, free from ambiguity and not conditional on further adjustments.

(b) The parties did not engage in further negotiations to amend the contract.

(c) The mistake in the written document may have, but does not have to have, occurred as a result of fraud.

(d) When the written document was signed, the defendant knew or should have known of the mistake and the plaintiff did not.

(e) Any subsequent attempt to enforce the inaccurate written document would be equivalent to fraud.[6]

It is not easy to establish the conditions necessary for rectification based on unilateral mistake. If the terms were ambiguous in the original agreement or if the parties carried on subsequent negotiations, a court is very reluctant to alter the final document. Rectification will not correct an error in judgment, nor is it a substitute for due diligence.[7]

> **rectification** correction of a written document to reflect accurately the contract made by the parties

Misunderstandings About the Meanings of Words

In this type of mistake both parties to a contract agree to the words actually used—neither party put them forward accidentally, nor were any of the terms subsequently recorded incorrectly. However, the parties place different meanings on those words. In most instances, such disagreements can be treated as questions of interpretation (see Chapter 10). A court will decide which meaning is the more reasonable in light of the circumstances, including those things each party ought to have known about the subject matter of the contract and about the intentions of the other party. In some cases, the court will decide that the meaning an offeror gives to her own words was the more reasonable one. If so, the offeree will be bound by the terms as understood by the offeror. In other cases, the court will decide that the offeror was unwise to use the words as she did and that the offeree interpreted them more reasonably. In that event, the offeror will be bound by the contract as the offeree understands it.[8]

---

[3] *McLean v McLean*, 2013 ONCA 788 at para 44; *Shanahan v Turning Point Restaurant Ltd*, 2012 BCCA 411 at para 30.

[4] *Rose v Pim*, [1953] 2 All ER 739 at 747; *Brisebois v Chamberland et al* (1991), 77 DLR (4th) 583.

[5] *Canada (Attorney General) v Fairmont Hotels Inc*, 2016 SCC 56 at paras 3, 13.

[6] *Ibid* at paras 14–15, citing *Sylvan Lake Golf & Tennis Club Ltd v Performance Industries Ltd* (2002), 209 DLR (4th) 318 (SCC) at para 31. See also *Hepburn v Jannock Limited* (2008), 63 CCEL (3d) 101.

[7] *Fairmont Hotels, ibid*.

[8] See *Lindsey v Heron* (1921), 50 OLR 1.

In rare cases, both parties have equally reasonable (or unreasonable) interpretations of the words, and holding one party to the other's interpretation would be unjust—a **mutual mistake** exists. Such a contract is void for mistake as to the meaning of the terms. Case 9.2 describes the classic example from the case of *Raffles v Wichelhaus*.[9]

mutual mistake a situation in which both parties believe a mistake exists in the contract but their understandings of the mistake are different

CASE 9.2 Equally Reasonable Interpretations

The contract was for the sale of cotton that was to arrive in England from Bombay on board the ship *Peerless*. By a remarkable coincidence two ships called *Peerless* were sailing from Bombay, one in October, the other in December. Neither party was aware there were two ships. The seller believed he contracted to sell cotton on the later ship; the buyer believed he contracted to buy cotton on the earlier ship.

A delay of two months in the shipment of a commodity subject to market fluctuations is a major difference in terms. When the cotton arrived on the later ship, the buyer refused to accept it or pay for it. The seller sued for breach of contract, and the buyer pleaded mistake in defence. The defence succeeded because the court could not decide which ship *Peerless* was meant. A reasonable person would have been unable to decide the contract was for cotton on one ship rather than the other.

MISTAKES ABOUT THE SUBJECT MATTER

Mistake About the Existence of the Subject Matter of a Contract

The most fundamental mistake is one about the very existence of the subject matter. If, at the time the contract was made, the subject matter, such as goods in the hold of a ship at sea, had been destroyed (unknown to either party), a case of shared common mistake exists. A fair way to enforce the contract is hard to imagine. Is the buyer required to pay the price for goods that cannot be delivered? Is the seller liable for breach for non-delivery? No—this is a clear example of a void contract.

This rule, as it applies to the sale of goods, has been incorporated in the *Sale of Goods Act*, which provides that "where there is a contract for the sale of specific goods and the goods without the knowledge of the seller have perished at the time the contract is made, the contract is void."[10] Of course, if the seller was aware the goods had perished, his attempt to sell them would be fraudulent, and the buyer could recover damages by suing in tort for deceit.

Mistake About the Value of the Subject Matter

Finding a solution that is fair to both parties is much more difficult when the subject matter of a contract is still in existence, but its qualities (and therefore value) are radically different from those contemplated by the parties. One party may be paying far too much for what he will receive. The other party may receive a windfall. The willingness of a court to grant relief depends upon the reasonableness of the expectations of the parties.

In some types of transactions, the parties are expected to know that the subject matter may quickly rise or fall in value, and any change in value is one of the risks expected in the contract. Consider, for example, real estate speculators or commodities traders.

---

[9] (1864), 159 ER 375. See also *Angevaare v McKay* (1960), 25 DLR (2d) 521, and *Staiman Steel Ltd v Commercial & Home Builders Ltd* (1976), 71 DLR (3d) 17.

[10] *Sale of Goods Act*, RSBC 1996, c 410, s 10.

However, when the subject matter of the contract is understood, described, or represented to have particular characteristics that give it value, then mistakes about those characteristics and the corresponding value may trigger relief. The mistake as to value may be as to its quality or quantity. In *Hyrsky et al v Smith*,[11] the purchased parcel of land turned out to be only half the size that was expected. The court held that:

> If the mistake as to quantity is so substantial that in essence it changes the quality of the subject-matter, then a proper case for rescission may exist.[12]

The Manitoba Court of Appeal rescinded a contract for the purchase of a BMW because the car was not the described model and was built to American and not Canadian standards.[13] This was a substantial difference that went to value of the vehicle.

Under the principle of *caveat emptor*, a buyer is expected to inspect the goods and satisfy himself as to their character, quality, and value. However, when a misrepresentation has been made by the seller, or where discovery is impossible, or both parties believe the same mistaken characteristics (common mistake), rescission may be available. If the purchaser moves quickly, the contract is voidable. Delay will close the door.

CASE 9.3 Delay

A purchaser bought a painting of a cathedral from an art gallery. Both the buyer and the gallery believed the painting was painted by John Constable (1736–1837), a famous landscape painter. The purchaser took the painting home and hung it on his wall for five years before complaining that it was not painted by Constable. The court held that too much time had passed to give the purchaser any remedy for mistake or misrepresentation.[14]

MISTAKES ABOUT THE IDENTITY OF A PARTY TO A CONTRACT

Mistakes as to the identity of a party to the contract are unilateral mistakes often involving fraud, where an innocent party is deliberately tricked into believing the other party is someone he is not. If an existing identity is assumed (rather than a fabricated identity), the contract will be void, as was the outcome in the classic English case of *Cundy v Lindsay*.[15]

CASE 9.4 Existing Identity

Lindsay, an Irish manufacturer, was persuaded to send goods on credit to a thief, Alfred Blenkarn. Blenkarn signed an order for goods with an indistinct signature that appeared to be "Blenkiron & Co.," a reputable firm with offices on the same street but at a different number from that of Blenkarn. Lindsay did not check the street number but simply shipped the goods to Blenkarn, who then sold the goods to Cundy for cash and absconded. Cundy was unaware of the fraud. Lindsay learned the true facts when he attempted to collect payment from Blenkiron & Co.; he then sued Cundy for return of the goods, claiming that the sale to Blenkarn was void.

The court held that as Lindsay intended to sell to "Blenkiron & Co." and only to them, Blenkarn obtained the goods entirely without Lindsay's agreement. A mistake by the duped seller about the identity of the other party made the contract void. Since there was no contract between Lindsay and Blenkarn, ownership of the goods remained with Lindsay. Cundy was required to return them or pay damages.

---

[11] (1969), 5 DLR (3d) 385.

[12] *Ibid* at 392.

[13] *Ennis v Klassen*, [1990] 4 WWR 609 (also considered an innocent misrepresentation).

[14] *Leaf v International Galleries*, [1950] 1 All ER 693 (CA).

[15] (1878), 3 App Cas 459.

The decision in *Cundy v Lindsay* offends the general principle that between two innocent parties, both victims of a fraud, the loss should be borne by the more careless of the two. Lindsay had shipped goods on credit without a careful check of the street address of Blenkiron & Co.; as a result of Lindsay's carelessness, Blenkarn gained possession of the goods. But Cundy was blameless. Between the two, we might expect that Lindsay would bear the loss; yet the decision that the contract was void led to a hardship upon Cundy. It is not surprising that the courts attempted to limit the application of this case.

The year after Cundy, in *King's Norton Metal Co v Edridge*,[16] a thief once again obtained goods on credit, working more cleverly than had Blenkarn.

CASE 9.5 Fabricated Identity

Using a convincing but fake letterhead with the picture of a large factory and the name of a non-existent firm—Hallam & Co.—Wallis sent an order for goods to the plaintiffs, a firm of metal manufacturers. The plaintiffs sent Wallis the goods; he resold them and absconded. The plaintiffs, claiming that their contract with Hallam & Co. was void, sought to recover the goods from the innocent purchaser.

The action failed. The court held that they must have intended to contract with someone, and since there was no "Hallam & Co.," it could only be with the writer of the letter, even though he was a very different person from the party they had in mind. Accordingly, although the contract was declared voidable, title to the goods had passed to Wallis! The plaintiff could recover the goods from Wallis so long as he still had them, but meanwhile Wallis could pass title to an innocent purchaser.

The difference between *Cundy v Lindsay* and the *King's Norton* case is that in *King's Norton* there is only one party with whom the vendor might have contracted (Wallis, alias Hallam & Co.). In *King's Norton*, the assumed identity was fake or non-existent, but two separate entities existed in *Cundy v Lindsay* (Blenkarn and Blenkiron & Co.). Though an innocent purchaser may be excused for failing to see the significance of this distinction, the *King's Norton* case limits the application of *Cundy v Lindsay* to situations where the thief assumes an existing (real) identity.

In both cases, the parties dealt by mail at a distance. The same difficulty about identity can occur when the initial seller and the impersonator confront each other in person, but the law is clearer in this context—the contract will only be voidable.

CASE 9.6 In Person Purchases

In *Phillips v Brooks*,[17] the English Court of Appeal held that the plaintiff jeweller intended to sell pearls to the man who appeared in his shop, even though the man falsely identified himself as a reputable and wealthy member of the community and whom the jeweller knew by name but not in person.

The contract was voidable and not void. Consequently, an innocent purchaser from the impersonator was protected and able to keep the pearls, despite the jeweller's claim that he intended to deal only with the reputable named person and not the fake who had appeared in his shop.

Canadian courts continue to follow these English cases. In one case, the Supreme Court of Canada held that a car rental company had "consented" to the rental of a car to an impersonator who gave a false identity.[18] Subsequent purchasers are better protected when the first transaction takes place face to face than when the transaction takes place by post, phone, or internet.

---

[16] (1879), 14 TLR 98.

[17] [1918–19] All ER 246.

[18] *Terry v Vancouver Motors U-Drive Ltd and Walker*, [1942] SCR 391.

MISTAKES ABOUT THE NATURE OF A SIGNED DOCUMENT

Non Est Factum

non est factum "it is not my doing"

Non est factum ("it is not my doing") is an ancient principle created in medieval times when most people could not read or write and usually signed documents by making a mark or imprinting with a seal. In those days, illiterate people relied on the literate party to describe the nature of the document. If the literate party materially misrepresented the nature of the document, it would be declared void. The concept was later extended and misused to allow people to carelessly sign documents without reading them. This is no longer the case today.

In 1971, in *Saunders v Anglia Building Society*,[19] the House of Lords declared that a careless signer could not avoid liability by pleading *non est factum*. Despite the fact that the plaintiff was a 78-year-old widow who had just broken her glasses, the court found her careless in signing a deed she had been unable to read, and accordingly she was bound by the document. In 1982, the Supreme Court of Canada followed the *Saunders* case saying:

> This principle of law is based not only upon the principle of placing loss on the person guilty of carelessness, but also upon recognition of the need for certainty and security in commerce [of those persons who rely on signed documents] . . . the application of the principle . . . must depend on the circumstances of each case.[20]

The defence of *non est factum* is only available to someone who, as a result of misrepresentation, has signed a document mistaken as to its nature and character and who has not been careless in doing so.[21] In the age of internet contracting, buyers are expected to agree to terms everyone knows they did not read—no one should expect to escape liability under a contract simply because of failure to take the necessary time to familiarize oneself with its contents.

MISREPRESENTATION

Contract Versus Tort

In addition to cases of mistake, a court may also set aside a contract if a misrepresentation has occurred. As noted in Chapter 5, a misrepresentation is an untrue statement or omission that is believed and relied upon by another party. It may amount to a tort when it is made fraudulently or negligently. However, when a person makes an innocent misstatement, no tort is committed. If that person later discovers her error, she must inform the other party of the true situation as soon as she can. An innocent misrepresentation becomes fraudulent or negligent if the party responsible fails to correct it when in a position to do so.

material could reasonably be expected to influence or induce the decision of a party to enter into a contract

In contract law, any **material** misrepresentations—be they innocent, negligent, or fraudulent—give rise to the right to rescind a contract. If the maker of the misrepresentation also acted fraudulently or negligently, the court may grant damages against the wrongdoer. However, if she made the misrepresentation innocently and without negligence, no damages will be awarded; the injured party's remedy is restricted to the right to rescind the contract.

---

[19] [1971] AC 1004.

[20] *Marvco Colour Research Ltd v Harris* [1982] 2 SCR 744 at 789–97.

[21] *Bulut v Carter*, 2014 ONCA 424 at para 18.

A misrepresentation is not a term of the contract. It is a statement or impression usually made or formed during the pre-contract bargaining that is not included in the subsequent offer. A misrepresentation that is incorporated into the offer becomes a term of the contract and will give rise to a breach of contract action with much broader remedies.[22] It can be difficult to distinguish between circumstances where the representation became a term of the contract and those where it did not.[23] Most standard form contracts specifically declare that there are no representations other than those contained in the written terms of the contract.

Occasionally, courts have found statements about goods and services in advertisements and sales promotion material, read by a prospective buyer before contracting, to be terms of the contract.[24] More commonly, statements in advertisements are considered representations, not terms. A false assertion is a misrepresentation only if it is made as a statement of fact. Most statements of opinion do not amount to misrepresentations unless they are **expert opinions**—these are considered equivalent to statements of fact. Most advertisements include disclaimers.

expert opinions opinions given by a person who purports to have specialized knowledge of a subject

ILLUSTRATION 9.1 Opinion vs. Fact

If a car advertisement states that "this car is the best car we have ever made," the remark is just an expression of opinion. But if the ad says instead that "the car gets 100 kilometres per litre of gas in highway driving," a representation of fact has been made.

If the ad says "the Canadian Automobile Association declares this car to be the best car in its class," this is an expert opinion that will be treated as a statement of fact.

CONSEQUENCES OF MISREPRESENTATION IN CONTRACTS

When a party who relied upon a material misrepresentation learns the truth, the contract is voidable at the option of the victim. She must renounce the agreement promptly. If she allows an unreasonable length of time to pass without repudiating or she takes further benefits under the contract, she will lose her right to rescind. If she has sustained out-of-pocket expenses in performing the contract or has paid money to the other party before becoming aware of her right to rescind, she may be entitled to a money award known as an **indemnity or compensation** in addition to rescission.[25]

indemnity or compensation a money award given as a supplement to rescission for loss sustained in performing a contract

Ethical Issue Employment Résumé

In February 2006, David J. Edmondson resigned from his position as president and CEO of RadioShack Corp. after it was discovered that he had lied on his résumé. His résumé indicated that he earned a psychology degree from Pacific Coast Baptist College. After the college denied granting the degree, Mr. Edmondson acknowledged the error.

A résumé (and its corresponding covering letter) introduces an employment candidate to the employer. It describes the educational experience and work history of the candidate. An employer often decides whether to interview a candidate based on the information contained in the résumé. Most prospective employees design their résumés to

---

[22] See Chapter 13, sections on implications of breach and damages.

[23] The closer the misrepresentation was to the time the agreement was made, the easier it is for a court to conclude that it is a term. See *Dick Bentley Productions Ltd v Harold Smith Motors Ltd*, [1965] 2 All ER 65. See also *Esso Petroleum Co Ltd v Mardon*, [1976] 2 All ER 5 (CA).

[24] *Goldthorpe v Logan*, [1943] 2 DLR 519; *Murray v Sperry Rand Corp* (1979), 96 DLR (3d) 113.

[25] *Whittington v Seale-Hayne* (1900), 82 LT 49.

emphasize their strengths and minimize their weaknesses. However, the résumé must fairly and accurately present the background of the candidate, or it becomes a misrepresentation that may induce an employer into entering an employment contract.

Questions to Consider

1. Is it acceptable to omit past employment if it is not relevant to the employment sought? What if the candidate was fired from the previous employment?
2. What types of résumé "inaccuracies" should allow an employer to rescind the employment agreement?
3. Should Mr. Edmondson be entitled to his contractual severance package?

Sources: Associated Press, "RadioShack CEO David J. Edmondson Resigns," CBS News, February 21, 2006, http://archive.is/8dw7c; Associated Press, "RadioShack CEO's Résumé Raises Questions," MSNBC Business, February 14, 2006, www.msnbc.msn.com/id/11354888.

Misrepresentation by Silence or Omission

Not all misrepresentations are expressed in words; conduct or even silence may amount to a misrepresentation. Particular types of contracts and relationships give rise to disclosure obligations. If the requirements are not met, a misrepresentation exists by silence or omission. Special relationships of trust between the parties, such as fiduciary relationships, give rise to a duty to disclose all pertinent information; certain types of contracts, such as insurance contracts, give rise to the duty of **utmost good faith**. The nature of the relationship or type of contract will determine if such a duty exists in the circumstances.

utmost good faith a duty of disclosure owed when a special relationship of trust exists between the parties

The requirement of utmost good faith almost always exists in a continuing business relationship. Partnership depends on mutual trust, and, accordingly, partners owe a general duty of utmost good faith to each other in all their transactions. Similarly, directors and officers owe a duty of good faith toward their corporation. Consider the following examples of specific types of contracts and relationships that have obligations to disclose. Failure to properly disclose will render the resulting contract voidable.

Contracts of Insurance

Insurance contracts have a duty of utmost good faith that requires a party seeking insurance to disclose to the insurance company all pertinent information relating to the risk the insurance company is being asked to assume. If relevant information is withheld, the insurer may refuse to pay the insurance claim. Information relevant to life insurance contracts will include health details and the refusal of coverage by another company. Fire insurance disclosure requirements are governed by legislation in most provinces,[26] and failure to disclose a previous fire has been held to be a fraudulent omission under the *Insurance Act*.[27] Public liability insurance—for motor vehicles, for example—presents a special difficulty because denial of coverage is likely to deny innocent third parties compensation when the negligent insured withheld previous driving information. Therefore, the courts impose a duty on insurers to investigate applicants before agreeing to insure, especially when information appears false to a reasonable insurer.[28] As well, automobile insurance legislation makes coverage of third-party losses mandatory up to the statutory minimum.[29]

---

[26] See e.g. *Insurance Act*, RSBC 2012, c 1, ss 17, 29(1); RSO 1990, c I.8, s 148; RSNS 1989, c 231, Sch to Part VII, s 1.

[27] *Sherman v American Institute Co*, [1937] 4 DLR 723.

[28] *Armstrong v Northwest Life Insurance Co of Canada* (1990), 72 DLR (4th) 410 at 414; *State Farm Mutual Automobile Insurance Co v General Accident Assurance Co of Canada*, [1995] NBJ No 405 (C.A.); *Coronation Insurance Co v Taku Air Transport* (1991), 85 DLR (4th) 609; *Campanaro v Kim* (1998), 112 OAC 171.

[29] *Schoff v Royal Insurance Company of Canada*, [2004] 10 WWR 32 (Alta CA); *Insurance Act*, RSA 2000, c I-3, s 57(1); RSO 1990, c I.8, s 251(1). The statutory minimum coverage is $200 000 in Alberta and Ontario.

Contracts Involving the Sale of Corporate Securities
Promoters or directors naturally know more about a corporation's affairs and prospects than does the investing public from whom subscriptions are being solicited. Therefore public corporations are legislatively required to give the investing public information about any new issue of shares or bonds in a statement called a prospectus or sometimes in other documents such as circulars, letters, or notices published in newspapers.[30] Inaccurate, missing, or misleading information will attract not only the remedy of rescission but also the statutory right to claim damages from any person involved in the preparation and release of the document.

Contracts Involving the Sale of Goods
As will be discussed in Chapter 14, the *Sale of Goods Act* restricts the doctrine of **caveat emptor** for the sale of goods. It offers buyers the right to rescind contracts for the sale of goods if the vendor fails to disclose a problem with the ownership of the goods. Similarly, misrepresentations or omissions about the quality or characteristics of the goods give a similar right to rescind under the *Sale of Goods Act*. These remedies are not offered to contracts involving services or land. Land contracts have particularly narrow remedies for representation. First, no obligation exists to disclose defects in title, and second, complaints about any misrepresentation must be raised before title is transferred or any right to rescind is lost.[31]

caveat emptor let the buyer beware

Contracts with Consumers
In *Tilden Rent-A-Car Co v Clemdenning*, the Ontario Court of Appeal suggested that there was a special onus on suppliers dealing with consumers to point out terms in standard form contracts that differed from what a consumer might reasonably expect.[32] Current consumer protection legislation goes much further by imposing a statutory obligation on specific industries to disclose such things as cost of credit, total interest and principal repayment schedules, and business contact information.[33] Failure to meet the disclosure requirements gives the consumer the right to cancel or rescind the contract. Even after compliance, some statutes still offer consumers a **cooling-off period** during which a consumer may cancel or rescind without any reason whatsoever. Today's fast-paced online marketplace is dominated by standard form contracts prepared by businesses that few, if any, consumers have an opportunity to read before accepting. The legislation gives consumers time to read the document by way of a cooling-off period.

cooling-off period a time during which a consumer may cancel (rescind) a contract without any reason; length of the time period is set in provincial legislation

UNDUE INFLUENCE

Undue influence is the domination of one party over the mind of another to such a degree as to deprive the weaker party of the ability to make an independent decision. A contract formed as a result of undue influence is voidable at the option of the victim. The victim may avoid the contract only if he acts promptly after he is freed from the domination. If he acquiesces or delays, the court will refuse to assist him.

Undue influence is often an issue in disputes involving contracts, gifts, or bequests under a will. Generally speaking, the principles governing undue influence in all these

undue influence the domination of one party over the mind of another to such a degree as to deprive the weaker party of the will to make an independent decision

---

[30] See e.g. *Securities Act*, RSO 1990, c S.5, s 1(1) at paras 25, 38, 56, 122, 130, 130.1, 138.3.

[31] Except for serious defects that would be impossible for the purchasers to discover. See e.g. *Sevidal v Chopra* (1987), 64 OR (2d) 169, where the court held that the vendor had a duty to disclose that radioactive soil had been found on the property after the contract was made but before completion date.

[32] (1978), 18 OR (2d) 601 at 609 (citing Waddams, "Contracts Exemption Clauses Unconscionability Consumer Protection" [Comments; 1971]), 49 Can. Bar Rev. 578 at 590–1.

[33] See e.g. *Consumer Protection Act, 2002*, SO 2002, c 30, Sch A; *Business Practices and Consumer Protection Act*, SBC 2004, c 2, ss 19(1), 21.

circumstances are the same. Usually undue influence arises when the parties stand in a special relationship to each other. One party has a special skill, position, or knowledge, causing the other to place confidence and trust in him. Typical examples of this relationship are doctor and patient, lawyer and client, religious leader and believer, and parent and child.

Burden of Proof

A party alleging undue influence must satisfy the court that, in the circumstances, domination was, in fact, exerted by the other party expressly for the purpose of securing some advantage.[34]

It is easier to prove undue influence if a special relationship existed: The law presumes undue influence was exerted in contracts favouring the party in the dominant position, as, for example, in relationships of doctor–patient or lawyer–client. In the absence of a special relationship, it is more difficult for a party to demonstrate undue influence, but he might still be able to show, for instance, that he was in a desperate financial state at the time of the contract. Once the alleged victim shows that circumstances existed that were likely to lead to undue influence, the burden shifts to the dominant party to prove that undue influence was not exerted by him.[35]

Arrangements Involving Spouses

A spouse may set aside a transaction if he or she can prove actual undue influence. As well, some marital relationships will raise a presumption of undue influence. This is true when one spouse traditionally relies upon the other for major decisions. If a spouse is experienced in business and has persuaded the other, who has had little or no business experience, to pledge her separate assets as security or act as **guarantor** for his business transactions, a presumption arises, and the dominant spouse must establish that no undue influence was applied. Otherwise, the weaker spouse may rescind the contract with the lender. Two cases illustrate how undue influence may be viewed in spousal relationships.

guarantor one who agrees to pay the debts of another person if that person defaults

CASE 9.7   Notice of Special Relationship

In order to obtain an increased credit limit for his company, the shareholder agreed to give the bank a mortgage on the family home. The home was jointly owned by the shareholder and his spouse. The spouse was brought to the bank and signed the mortgage documents without explanation or independent legal advice. Eventually the company failed, and the bank claimed the house. The spouse successfully blocked the bank's attempt to seize the house because the bank was on notice of the special relationship and failed to inquire into undue influence.[36]

CASE 9.8   No History of Dominance

Both spouses co-signed a guarantee of the husband's business loan to fund a "tax driven real-estate investment" without independent legal advice. There was no evidence of actual undue influence, and the history of the relationship was not one where the wife placed trust and confidence in the husband to make all major decisions. The wife was a real-estate agent who responded to the bank's request for income disclosure directly. The loan went into default. The marriage failed, and the husband went bankrupt. The bank sued the wife, the court found no evidence of actual undue influence, and the relationship did not give rise to a presumption. Therefore, the bank won, and the guarantee was enforceable.[37]

---

[34] *Kavanagh v Lajoie*, 2014 ONCA 187 at para 19.

[35] *Geffen v Goodman Estate*, [1991] 2 SCR 353.

[36] *Barclays Bank plc v O'Brien*, [1993] 4 All ER 417. See also *Gold v Rosenberg*, [1997] 3 SCR 767 (affirming reasoning).

[37] *Bank of Montreal v Duguid* (2000), 185 DLR (4th) 458.

Importance of Independent Legal Advice

The presence or absence of independent legal advice was important to the outcome of the foregoing cases. This is because independent legal advice received by the weaker party prior to signing the contract rebuts any presumption of undue influence. The legal advice must come from a lawyer not associated with the transaction or the other parties. Lenders aware of a special relationship between co-debtors are obligated to inquire into the possibility of undue influence. The standard risk management strategy is to require each party to obtain a certificate of independent legal advice from the lawyer of his or her choice, certifying that the transaction has been explained and the party is entering the agreement voluntarily, without any pressure or influence.

CONSUMER PROTECTION

Contracts between parties of unequal bargaining power that are unfairly advantageous to the powerful parties may be considered **unconscionable contracts** and voidable at common law. The plaintiff seeking to void the contract must prove that the defendant abused its bargaining power and preyed upon the plaintiff, or that the bargain was improvident.[38]

unconscionable contracts contracts where there is unequal bargaining power between the parties, and the powerful party gets an extremely advantageous deal

Most provinces have also adopted legislation specifically defining unconscionable contracts and deceptive business practices that will also render a contract voidable at the option of the consumer. In British Columbia, for example, rescission is available for unconscionable practices, including putting undue pressure on a consumer, and deceptive practices, including claiming goods or services have sponsorship, grade, style, or quality they do not possess. False advertising was discussed in Chapter 3, but note that such false claims amount to representations from which consumers will be given relief.

Loan transactions are among the most heavily scrutinized consumer contracts, with tight regulations about disclosure of cost of borrowing, maximum interest rates, terms of credit, and more.[39] The *Criminal Code* even makes charging an interest rate in excess of 60 percent an offence.[40] Consumers also have expanded remedies; courts may sever the offending interest terms entirely or lower the rate below the criminal rates.[41] Consumers receive these added protections because of their less powerful position in the purchase relationship, their relative inexperience with the type of transaction, their lack of participation in the creation of the contract, and the short time within which they must make their decisions. Unfortunately, few consumers are aware of their cancellation rights and allow them to expire without ever taking the time to examine the terms of their contracts.

INTERNATIONAL ISSUE
Regulating Payday Loans

As discussed, unconscionable loans with excessive interest provisions have been the subject of provincial legislation for a long time. However, the North American explosion of "payday" loans has revealed vagueness in existing legislation and prompted action.

Payday loans are short-term (daily or weekly) advances of small amounts of money (usually under $1000). Lenders charge not only interest but also application fees and service charges. When calculated on an annualized basis, the total

---

[38] *Bank of Montreal v Javed*, 2016 ONCA 49 at para 7.

[39] *Unconscionable Transactions Act*, RSA 2000, c U-2; RSNB 2011, c 233; *Unconscionable Transactions Relief Act*, CCSM c U20; RSPEI 1988, c U-2.

[40] RSC 1985, c C-46, s 347. See *Garland v Consumer's Gas Co*, [1998] 3 SCR 112.

[41] *Mira Design v Seascape Holdings*, [1982] 1 WWR 744 (BCSC). See Waldron (1994) 73 Can Bar Rev 1.

charges often exceed 300 percent of the principal borrowed, well above the criminal rate of interest.

In the United States, payday loans are governed by state legislation. Common restrictions include

- capping the charges on a fixed basis rather than a percentage basis (for example, Iowa describes the maximum interest charge as $15 per $100 over the term of the loan),
- capping the principal amount that can be borrowed (for example, Illinois describes the maximum amount that can be borrowed as $1000 or 25 percent of a borrower's monthly gross income), and
- capping the number of renewals.

In Canada, most provinces have passed legislation that regulates the payday loan industry.[42] Common restrictions include

- licence requirements for lenders,
- cost-of-borrowing (all charges) disclosure requirements,
- cooling-off periods during which a consumer can cancel the agreement, and
- capping cost of borrowing.

Lenders argue that any cap must exceed the criminal rate of interest because the default rate on payday loans is extremely high.

Questions to Consider

1. Should Canadian limits adopt the American approach of capping the cost of borrowing on a fixed rather than percentage basis?
2. What is the rationale behind the American limit on the number of renewals?
3. How should the cap relate to the criminal rate of interest?
4. Why not ban payday loans completely?
5. How will jurisdictional variation in the regulation of payday loans affect the development of the industry?

Sources: National Conference of State Legislatures, http://www.ncsl.org/research/financial-services-and-commerce/payday-lending-state-statutes.aspx; Canadian Consumer Finance Association, https://canadiancfa.com.

DURESS

duress actual or threatened violence or imprisonment as a means of coercing a party to enter into a contract

Duress consists of actual or threatened violence or imprisonment as a means of coercing a party to accept a contract. The effect of duress is similar to that of undue influence. The contract is voidable at the option of the victim. The threat of violence need not be directed against the party being coerced—it may be a threat to harm the victim's spouse, parent, or child.

Historically, duress was a concept recognized by the common law courts and was narrowly interpreted by them. Today, duress is not strictly confined by the courts to the circumstances just described. Sometimes, the concepts of duress and undue influence appear to overlap. The concept of economic duress is one example; it focuses on **coercion** as an illegitimate or inappropriate application of pressure.[43]

coercion improperly forced payment under protest

CASE 9.9 Job Threat

Stott was a securities salesman employed at Merit Investments Corp. A term of his contract required him to cover all bad debts of his clients. In the case of one client, Stott's boss ordered him to close out the account. Stott took the position that he should not have to cover the loss because he was ordered to close the account. Stott was called into the boss's office and asked to sign a written promise to pay the debt. When Stott argued that he was not responsible, the boss replied, "You are probably right, but if you don't sign, it won't go well with you at the firm, and it would be very difficult for you to find employment in the industry."[44] Stott signed the promise to pay. The Ontario Court of Appeal found that there was coercion and that Merit had applied illegitimate pressure. The conduct would justify rescinding the agreement based on economic duress if Stott had acted immediately to repudiate it. Unfortunately, Stott complied with the agreement and did not complain until two years later when he left Merit's employment.

---

[42] Manitoba was the first: Man. Reg. 99/2007; see also *Payday Loans Act, 2008*, SO 2008, c 9.

[43] Coercion involves four factors: (a) protest, (b) available alternative, (c) lack of independent advice, and (d) post-contract steps to avoid it. See *Pao On v Lau Yiu Long*, [1980] AC 614 (P.C.).

[44] *Stott v Merit Investment Corp* (1988), 63 OR (2d) 545 at para 12.

Strategies to Manage the Legal Risks

A business can reduce the risks associated with mistake and misrepresentation by making sure all the information produced and relied upon by it and others is accurate. Carefully researched claims and thorough investigation before agreeing to sell or purchase will result in fewer errors. Credit checks will confirm the identity of parties, title searches will determine ownership of the product, and careful examination of proposed contracts will ensure that terms are as expected. Written rather than oral contracts are preferred. If dealing without a written document, retain emails or pre-agreement documentation until the contract is fully performed. These may be useful to clarify meaning if a dispute arises.

Standard form contracts prepared in advance will ensure that common provisions are appropriately worded and key words are defined. In addition to exemption clauses, most standard form contracts include an **entirety clause**, a clause that specifically excludes any outside terms, conditions, or representations and confines the agreement between the parties to the single written document. This clause prevents a party from arguing that they relied on a representation when the contract they signed says they did not. Express warranties relating to replacement and repair of the product will help to clarify expectations for the product and reduce surprises.

entirety clause a term in a contract stating that the whole agreement is contained in the written documents, and there are no other terms, conditions, representations, or warranties

Each party in special relationships or power imbalances should seek independent legal advice during negotiations. Consumers should receive full copies of contracts at the time of purchase, and businesses should ensure the appropriate cooling-off period has expired before relying upon the agreement. Any consumer contracts should comply with the requirements of the applicable consumer protection legislation, recognizing that contracts involving certain identified activities are heavily regulated. Sales staff should be trained and supervised so that no unapproved representations or inducements are made during the pre-sale process. Naturally, pressure tactics or threats are unacceptable.

QUESTIONS FOR REVIEW

1. What are common, mutual, and unilateral mistakes?
2. When will a party be granted a remedy for mistakenly using a term in a contract?
3. When parties use a term but intend it to have quite different meanings, how does the court resolve the difference?
4. What conditions must be satisfied before a court will order rectification? Under what circumstances is a court unlikely to grant such a remedy?
5. Describe the difference between void and voidable contracts. What are the consequences of each for innocent third parties?
6. Jameson appears at Klemper's Jewellery and asks to buy an expensive watch on credit. She identifies herself as Johnson, a wealthy local financier. Klemper agrees and hands over possession of the watch to Jameson. Jameson immediately pawns it at Larry's. Klemper sees the watch in Larry's window the next day. Explain whether he may reclaim it as his own without paying Larry. Are there any further facts that might influence your opinion?
7. What are the consequences of an innocent misrepresentation in contract rather than tort? What if the representation later becomes a term of the contract?

8. H's business is in financial difficulties, and he offers the bank a mortgage on the family home, which is in his wife's name. What precautions should the bank take when having the wife sign the contract? Why?

9. Why are consumers a protected class of purchasers? Describe two forms of protection available to them.

CASES AND PROBLEMS

1. Continuing Scenario

    Ashley saw the perfect French "bistro-" style chair for her restaurant when she attended a furniture expo and contacted Ben, the sales representative for the chair's Canadian distributor, Just Like Home Inc. Ben tells Ashley the price of the chosen chair, product #7733, is $150 if 15 or fewer are ordered, and the price drops to $125 for orders of 16 to 50. Ashley orders 40 chairs and signs Just Like Home's standard form contract, which states that there are no representations or warranties, and it is the entire agreement between the parties. Unfortunately, when the chairs arrive, they are the wrong ones. Ashley checks the contract and sees that the product number has been incorrectly recorded as #3377. These chairs are not the same quality and have a price of $100 for orders of 16 to 50. Ashley wants the other chairs; Ben has left the company, and her new contact, Jill, insists the contract has been performed. The current price of the #7733 chairs is $145 for orders of 16 to 50, and Ashley will need to pay the higher price if she wants them plus the 25 percent restocking fee for returning the other chairs. What can Ashley do?

2. Paul, a third-year university student, was in the habit of selling his used textbooks at the conclusion of each term. He usually recouped about 50 percent of their original cost. Unfortunately, when he posted his accounting textbook for sale online, he quickly discovered that a new edition of the book had been published, and there was little interest in his edition. He contacted the publisher using a fictitious name and requested a sample copy of the new edition. He told the publisher he was an accounting instructor considering adopting the book for a new course being introduced at the university. As a result, the publisher agreed to supply a copy of the new edition, provided that Paul paid the shipping cost and agreed to review the book for the publisher. Paul agreed. When Paul received the sample book, he promptly posted it for sale online. Joan, a second-year student at another university, was happy to purchase the new edition for 75 percent of the bookstore price. When Joan accessed the textbook website using the code provided with the book, the publisher became aware that the book was in the hands of a student and not an instructor. The publisher never would have agreed to release the book to a student without payment of the full list price. The publisher blocked Joan's access to the textbook website and demanded she return the book. If the matter goes to court, will Joan have to return the book? Why or why not? What recourse will Joan have against Paul?

3. Smart was Hull's lawyer for many years and not only handled legal matters for Hull but gave him important advice on business matters as well. At one stage, Hull owed Smart about $8500 for professional services. Smart suggested to Hull that the account could be conveniently settled in full if Hull would transfer his new 10-metre sailboat to Smart. Hull hesitated at first, but realizing how indispensable his relationship with Smart had been and how important it was that Smart should continue to respect the confidential nature of his private business affairs, he transferred the sailboat to Smart.

    A few months later Hull's daughter, who greatly enjoyed sailing, returned from graduate studies in Europe and persuaded her father to sue for recovery of the sailboat. On what grounds could Hull seek the return of the sailboat? Explain how the onus of proof will operate in the resulting legal action and indicate the probable outcome.

4. On arriving at Vancouver airport, Mr. Clemson, a frequent traveller, rented a car from Tilford Car Rentals Ltd., as he had done many times before. The clerk asked him whether he wanted additional collision insurance coverage, and as usual Mr. Clemson said, "Yes." The clerk added a fee of $10 a day for this coverage. She then handed the contract to Clemson, and he signed it in her presence. She was aware he did not read the terms of the contract before signing it.

   Clemson's signature appeared immediately below a printed statement that read, "I, the undersigned, have read and received a copy of above and reverse side of this contract." On the back of the contract, in small type and so faint on Mr. Clemson's copy as to be hardly legible, there was a series of conditions, one of which read:

   > Notwithstanding the payment of an additional fee for limitation of liability for collision damage to the rented vehicle, customer shall be fully liable for all collision damage if vehicle is used, operated or driven off highways serviced by federal, provincial or municipal governments and for all damages to vehicle by striking overhead objects.

   The clerk placed Clemson's copy of the contract in an envelope and gave him the envelope and car keys. He got in the car, placed the contract in the glove compartment, and drove to a nearby shopping plaza to buy a gift. While driving in the plaza parking lot, he collided with another car, causing damage of $2500 to his rented car. The car rental agency claimed he was personally liable for repairs under the terms of their contract. Clemson refused to pay for the car repairs, and Tilford Car Rentals Ltd. sued him for breach of contract.

   Outline the nature of the arguments available to Tilford Car Rentals Ltd. and of the defences available to Clemson. Express an opinion, with reasons, about whether the action is likely to succeed.

5. H. Golightly is a professional football player who has played for the Toronto Mercenaries ("Mercs") for the past three football seasons. The Toronto Mercs are a member of the Eastern Conference of the Trans-Canada Football League. Golightly lives in the southern United States during the off-season.

   Golightly had an exceptionally good season last year and was in a strong bargaining position for negotiating his salary for this season when he met with Rusty Trawler, the general manager of the Mercs, last January. The parties discussed salary possibilities for the next two seasons in a tentative way but adjourned their meeting, expecting to come to final terms in early April.

   In February, at the Trans-Canada Football League's annual meeting in Vancouver, it was decided to increase the number of regular games scheduled to be played in the Eastern Conference to 16, up from the usual 14 over many previous seasons, commencing with the current season. By contrast, the Western Conference already had a schedule of 16 games for several seasons; this decision brought the Eastern Conference in line with the Western Conference. It received wide publicity in the news media of the various cities with teams in the Eastern Conference.

   On April 3, Golightly telephoned Trawler from Biloxi, Mississippi, and they agreed to meet on April 6 in the offices of O.J. Berman, Q.C., Golightly's solicitor in Toronto. The meeting between Golightly, Trawler, and Berman lasted about three hours. Eventually it was agreed that Golightly should be paid $150 000 for the current season and $225 000 for the following year, plus further amounts for playoffs and bonuses. Two separate contracts were signed to cover the two seasons. At the time, neither Golightly nor his lawyer, Berman, had any knowledge that the number of league games in the Eastern Football Conference had been increased to 16 from 14. In fact, the parties did not refer in any way to the number of games in their meeting in Berman's office. Trawler made no mention of the increased schedule. The contracts simply stated:

> The Player agrees that during the term of this contract he will play football and will engage in activities related to football only for the Club and will play for the Club in all its Conference's scheduled and playoff games.

The contract also contained a clause to the effect that the player could be traded to a team in the Western Conference.

It was not until later, when Golightly reported for training, that he learned about the increase in the schedule. He then claimed that he would not have agreed to the salaries of $150 000 and $225 000, respectively, had he known about this change; he would have bargained for more. On Berman's advice, he brought an action to have these contracts set aside with a view to their renegotiation.

Express an opinion, with reasons, about whether this action should succeed.

6. Robelus Communications Inc. launched a new advertising campaign proclaiming that it was "Canada's Fastest" wireless network. It placed the statement in TV commercials, internet ads, and store signage. Mary was shopping in the mall and saw the sign. She decided to switch her plan to Robelus. After the change, Mary did not notice any difference to her service. She began to investigate and found out that the claim was based on industry comparisons from 2007. Most competitors had put new networks in place since 2007, and there was no available data to determine whose network was fastest. Mary had had to sign up for a three-year plan when she contracted with Robelus, and the standard form contract she signed included the following term:

> This is the entire agreement between the parties. There are no representations, conditions, warranties, conditions or terms save and except for those contained in this written agreement.

Can Mary get out of her three-year commitment? Do you need to know additional facts to form an opinion?

Chapter 10
Writing and Interpretation

- THE DISTINCTION BETWEEN SUBSTANCE AND FORM
- THE *STATUTE OF FRAUDS*
- CONSUMER PROTECTION LEGISLATION
- THE INTERPRETATION OF EXPRESS TERMS
- THE PAROL EVIDENCE RULE
- IMPLIED TERMS AS A METHOD OF INTERPRETATION
- STRATEGIES TO MANAGE THE LEGAL RISKS

Creating a written record of a contract makes good business sense, and failing to do so can have serious legal consequences. Every common law province has legislation requiring that some contracts be in writing to be enforceable. Even when a contract is put in writing, parties may disagree about its meaning. In this chapter, we identify which contracts must be in writing and discuss the rules for determining the meaning of the words used in a contract.

In particular, we examine such questions as:

- What legislation requires that certain contracts be in writing?
- What types of contracts are affected by the *Statute of Frauds*?
- How much writing is necessary to comply with the *Statute*?
- What is the effect of the *Statute of Frauds* on contracts that do not comply with the writing requirement?
- What are the writing requirements of the *Sale of Goods Act*?
- What writing requirements exist under general consumer protection legislation?
- What approaches are used to interpret the express terms in a contract?
- What is the parol evidence rule, and how do courts apply it?
- When are terms implied into a contract?

THE DISTINCTION BETWEEN SUBSTANCE AND FORM

The Benefits of a Written Record

In previous chapters, we used the term *formation of a contract* in a legal sense, not in a physical sense. The contract is formed when there is an accepted offer, consideration, and intention. Once created, the contract may exist in the parties' recollection of the spoken words, or it may be recorded in a written document or stored electronically, in the cloud, or on a computer. So the substance—the terms of the contract—may have a variety of physical forms or even no form at all, other than in the minds of the parties. In this chapter, we consider the rules that apply to the physical form of the contact. Contracts may be in one the following three forms:

1. contracts whose terms are entirely oral (spoken)
2. contracts whose terms are part oral and part written
3. contracts whose terms are entirely in writing, whether all in one document or spread through several documents, such as a series of letters

It is good business practice to keep some record of even the simplest transaction at the time it is made. For complicated contracts, it is best to have a complete written record signed by the parties. We forget things over time, especially when burdened with many details, and common sense tells us that relying on written records is better than on mere memory. The large majority of contractual disputes are not about the existence of contracts but about the differing recollections of the terms of the contract and the meaning of the words used. Very often, the reason a party sues over a contract is that he disagrees with its interpretation by the other party. In such cases, the court is asked to determine the meaning or interpret the contract, also known as **construing** the contract.

construing interpreting

When the court is asked to construe a contract, it tries to find the most reasonable meaning that can be attributed to the words in the circumstances. Over the years, courts have developed some strategies to assist them. To ensure there is some written evidence to aid a judge in establishing the meaning of contracts, provincial legislation imposes specific writing requirements for some types of contracts.

Legislation Dealing with Writing

Not all contracts require writing; very often oral contracts are legally enforceable. However, over time, legislators identified some high-risk contracts and required that they be in writing. Originally, *writing* meant *recorded on paper*; as will be discussed more fully in Chapter 31, writing requirements may now be satisfied through either paper or electronic means such as PDF documents and emails.[1]

Typically, the subject matter of the contract will dictate the applicable writing requirements, if any. For example, a mortgage will need to meet specific requirements in order to be registered against the land it charges. These may be set out in either the land registration or mortgage legislation. Rather than focusing on the huge number of statutes that impose precise details on specific transactions, this chapter focuses on the general writing requirements imposed by three common types of legislation affecting a wider range of contracts:

---

[1] *Leoppky v Meston*, 2008 ABQB 45; see also the *Personal Information Protection and Electronic Documents Act* and the *Interpretation Act*, including province-specific legislation such as the *Electronic Transaction Act* (Alberta) and *Electronic Commerce Act* (Ontario).

1. The *Statute of Frauds*—the first piece of legislation to impose writing requirements
2. The *Sale of Goods Act*—focusing on the most common type of business transaction, a purchase of goods
3. Consumer protection legislation—dealing with the most vulnerable type of party

Provincial variations exist in the application of these three classes of legislation, but every province imposes writing requirements through some combination of the three statutes.

THE *STATUTE OF FRAUDS*

The oldest piece of legislation dealing with writing is the *Statute of Frauds* passed in 1677 by the English Parliament.[2] It was subsequently adopted (with some changes) by most common law jurisdictions around the world, including some in Canada and the United States. British Columbia substantially revised it,[3] and Manitoba eventually repealed it entirely.[4] In the remaining common law provinces, the *Statute* remains in force in one form or another.

The *Statute of Frauds* makes certain types of contracts unenforceable unless they are in writing. An otherwise valid oral contract that falls within the *Statute* is unenforceable; neither party may sue on the contract. This allows a party to avoid performing a contract solely because it is oral—the contract might be perfectly valid in every other respect. It has often been said that by defeating the reasonable expectations of parties, the *Statute of Frauds* promotes more frauds than it prevents. For this reason, the courts have tried to limit the application of the *Statute* wherever possible. As a result, the scope of the *Statute* has been restricted by exceptions.

The Types of Contracts Covered by the *Statute of Frauds*

Originally, the *Statute of Frauds* covered six types of contracts:

i. A promise by an **executor or administrator** to pay estate debts out of his own money,
ii. A promise to answer for the debt, default, or miscarriage of another (guarantee),
iii. An agreement made in consideration of marriage,
iv. A contract dealing with interests in land,
v. An agreement not performed within one year of its making, and
vi. Ratification of debts incurred while a minor.

executor or administrator legal representative of the estate of a dead person

In New Brunswick and Nova Scotia, the *Statute* still covers five of these six categories (excepting minors).[5] In other provinces, rules about minors and marriage contracts have been moved to family law statutes, and contracts lasting longer than a year are covered under consumer protection legislation.[6] Guarantees, land, and executor's promises are the categories addressed in most of the remaining provinces' *Statute of Frauds*. We focus on guarantees and interests in land as the categories most relevant to business.

---

[2] *Statute of Frauds: An Act for the prevention of frauds and perjuries*, 29 Charles II, c 3 (1677, U.K.).

[3] The *Law Reform Amendment Act*, SBC 1985, c 10, s 8 repealed the *Statute of Frauds* and established new writing requirements now found in the *Law and Equity Act*, RSBC 1996, c 253 (dealing with land and guarantees). Alberta and Saskatchewan have adopted the original English *Statute*, while Ontario, Prince Edward Island, New Brunswick, and Nova Scotia have enacted their own similar statutes.

[4] RSM 1987, c F-158.

[5] Prince Edward Island retains the infant ratification category as well as guarantees RSPEI 1988, c S-6, ss 1, 2.

[6] See e.g. *Family Law Act*, SBC 2011, c 25, s 259; *Family Law Act*, RSO 1990, c F.3, s 52; *Matrimonial Property Act*, RSNS 1989, c 275, s 23.

Guarantees

A guarantee is a promise "to answer for the debt, default, or miscarriage of another"; it is a conditional promise to pay only if the debtor defaults: "If he does not pay you, I will." Only after the debtor has defaulted may the creditor claim payment from the guarantor.

In contrast, a person who makes a promise to indemnify a creditor makes herself primarily liable to pay the debt through her **indemnity**. When the debt falls due, the creditor may sue either the original debtor or the person who gave the promise to indemnify, or both. "Give him the goods, and I will see to it that you are paid" would usually be a promise to indemnify.[7] A promise by a purchaser of a business to its employees to pay back wages owed by the former owner would be a promise to indemnify.

This distinction is important because the courts have applied the writing requirements of the *Statute of Frauds* only to simple guarantees. Therefore, a guarantee must be made in writing to be enforceable, but a promise to indemnify is outside the *Statute* and is enforceable without being in writing. Even the class of guarantees that fall within the *Statute* has been narrowed; the courts have excluded those guarantees incidental to a larger contract where the element of guarantee is only one of many promises made in the contract.

indemnity a promise by a third party to be primarily liable to pay the debt

---

CASE 10.1 Type of Contract

Sutton & Co. were stockbrokers and members of the London Stock Exchange with access to its facilities. Grey was not a member, but he had contacts with prospective investors. The parties made an oral agreement by which Grey would receive half the commission from transactions for his clients completed through Sutton and was to pay half of any bad debts that might develop out of the transactions.

When a loss resulted from one of the transactions, and Grey refused to pay his half, Sutton & Co. sued him. Grey pleaded that his promise to pay half the loss was a guarantee and was not enforceable against him because it was not in writing. The court ruled that the whole arrangement between Sutton and Grey was much broader than merely guaranteeing the payment of a debt owing by a particular client and that the *Statute of Frauds* should not apply. Therefore, the agreement was enforceable, and Sutton & Co. obtained judgment against Grey.[8]

British Columbia has done away with the judge-made distinction between indemnity and guarantee by requiring that both types of promise be in writing.[9]

In contrast to the restricted meaning given to the words *debt* and *default*, the courts have given the word *miscarriage* a fairly wide meaning. They have interpreted a promise to "answer for the **miscarriage** of another" to mean "to pay damages for loss caused by the tort of another person," for example, by that person's negligence. The promise "I will pay you for the injury B caused you if B doesn't settle with you" must be in writing. On the other hand, the promise "I will pay you for the injury B caused you if you will give up absolutely any rights you have against B" is a promise of indemnity and need not be in writing to be enforceable.[10]

miscarriage an injury caused by the tort of another person

Land

Requiring that contracts concerning interests in land be in writing is necessary to protect the public record of land ownerships. The special qualities of land, in particular its virtual indestructibility and permanence, make the ability to ascertain the various outstanding interests and claims against land important. It is essential to have

---

[7] See Cheshire, Fifoot, and Furmston's *Law of Contract*, 13th ed at 212. It is the intention of the parties and not their language that determines whether the promise is a guarantee or an indemnity; *Western Surety Co v Brakop* (1994) 47 ACWS (3d) 589.

[8] *Sutton & Co v Grey*, [1894] 1 QB 285; *Bassie v Melnychuk* (1993), 14 Alta LR (3d) 31.

[9] *Law Reform (Enforcement of Contracts) Act, 1954*, 2 & 3 Eliz 2, c 34, s 1 (UK), and *Law and Equity Act*, RSBC 1996, c 253, s 59(6).

[10] *Kirkham v Marter* (1819), 106 ER 490; *Read v Nash* (1751), 95 ER 632.

verified written records of transactions affecting interests in land, and these records must be available over many years for inspection by interested persons and the public. Therefore, we have systems of public records where interested parties may search and discover who owns or claims to own the interests in land.[11]

Still, some contracts concerning land are considered too remotely connected with land to be protected by the *Statute*. The courts have held that agreements to repair or build a house, or to obtain room and board, are outside the *Statute*, whereas agreements to permit taking water from a well or to lease any land, house, or other building, or even a portion of a building, are within the *Statute*. Landlord and tenant statutes make oral residential leases enforceable, as we will discuss in Chapter 22.

Part Performance To prevent fraud, the courts developed an exception that allows some oral land contracts to be enforced despite the *Statute of Frauds*. It is called the doctrine of **part performance**. If the plaintiff can show that performance of the contract has begun and he has relied on its existence, the court would accept that performance as evidence of the contract without writing.[12]

part performance performance undertaken in reliance on an oral contract relating to an interest in land and accepted by the courts as evidence of the contract without writing

Not every act of performance under a contract qualifies as a substitute for a written document. The following conditions must be satisfied before the court will enforce the oral contract:

(a) The contract must be one concerning land.
(b) The acts of performance must suggest quite clearly the existence of a contract dealing with the land in question; they must not be ambiguous or just as possibly explained as part of a quite different transaction. The must fulfill the "very purpose" of the contract.[13]
(c) Activities of either the plaintiff or the defendant may be considered acts of performance, but the plaintiff must have relied on the existence of the contract and suffered a loss if the contract is not enforced. This is detrimental reliance.[14]

The act(s) of part performance do not need to disclose all the terms of the contract, just support the existence of the contract, and then the court will enforce it according to the terms orally agreed (and proven).

CASE 10.2 Acts of Part Performance

The Province of Nova Scotia built a new highway through the middle of Ross Hill's farm. When it expropriated the land, it promised Mr. Hill that he would be permitted to "move people, cattle and equipment" back and forth across the highway. The Province built ramps and gates to allow for Hill's use. Twenty-seven years later, the Province tried to deny that an equitable interest in land had been created for Hill. The Supreme Court of Canada held that "the actions of the province [spoke] louder than any written document." Building and maintaining the gates and ramps were clear and unequivocal acts of part performance, and Hill relied upon them to his detriment. Higher compensation for the expropriated land would have been sought if access had not been promised. Therefore, the oral contract was exempt from the *Statute of Frauds*, and the court upheld Hill's interest in the land.[15]

---

[11] British Columbia retains the requirement of writing for contracts concerning interests in land. *Law and Equity Act*, RSBC 1996, c 253, s 59(3). *Law of Property Act*, 1925, 15 & 16 Geo 5, c 20, s 40 (UK).

[12] *Hill v Nova Scotia (Attorney General)*, [1997] 1 SCR 69 at paras 11–16; *Erie Sand and Gravel Ltd v Seres' Farms Ltd* (2009), 97 OR (3d) 241 at 252–65.

[13] *Erie Sand and Gravel Ltd, ibid* at 261–65.

[14] *B & R Development Corp (cob Abbey Lane Homes) v Trail South Developments Inc*, [2012] AJ No 1171 at para 35 (ABCA); *Erie Sand and Gravel Ltd, supra* note 12 at 257–61.

[15] *Hill v Nova Scotia (Attorney General), supra* note 12.

Typically, mere payment of a deposit, submission of an offer, or waiver of some of the conditions in the contract will not amount to part performance, as is demonstrated in Case 10.3.[16]

Requirements for a Written Memorandum

The actual writing requirements of the *Statute of Frauds* are quite vague. It requires only a "note or memorandum" of the contract "signed by the party to be charged" or by the party's authorized agent; it does not require complete detail of every term or both parties' signatures.

Electronic forms of documents satisfy the statutory requirement of being in "writing." Canadian courts have assumed that faxes or emails are sufficient to satisfy the writing requirement of the *Statute of Frauds*.[17] Other legislation is being amended to specifically address writing in the ecommerce environment. Electronic signatures and PDFs are sufficient. Chapter 31 specifically addresses these changes under "Formal Requirements."

All Essential Terms Must Be Included
The memorandum must contain all the *essential* terms of the contract, including the identity of the parties. If the contract is for the sale of land, for example, the memorandum must name the parties, describe the subject matter (the land), and set out the consideration to be given for it.

> **CASE 10.3   Key Terms**
>
> Wayne and Janet Gretzky made a written offer to purchase a cottage property, including a main house, guesthouse, and two-story boathouse for $1 860 000. All the terms and conditions were acceptable to the vendor except the date for vacant possession of the boathouse. The offer was rejected, and a counter-offer was made. At this point, oral discussions took place between the various agents and their clients, and a mutually agreeable date was established. However, the new date was not placed in the agreement, and no written memorandum of the boathouse possession term was made. Subsequently, the vendors refused to complete the deal, and the Gretzkys sued. The court found that vacant possession of the boathouse was obviously an important issue between the parties, and therefore it was an essential term not in writing. The contract failed to satisfy the *Statute of Frauds* and was unenforceable. The Gretzkys did not get the cottage.[18]

An exception exists for contracts of guarantee—the consideration for that type of promise need not appear in writing.[19]

The memorandum need not be wholly within a single document; several written notes may be taken together to satisfy the requirements of the *Statute*. Using more than one document to satisfy the writing requirement can be difficult if there are no cross-references within the documents. In one case, the court heard evidence that a signed letter beginning with "Dear Sir" was contained in a particular envelope that bore the name and address of the plaintiff and in this way linked the two pieces of paper as a sufficient memorandum.[20] The court justified its decision on the grounds that, even

---

[16] *Hunter v Baluke* (1998), 42 OR (3d) 553 at paras 64–75; *Erie Sand and Gravel Ltd*, *supra* note 12 at 265.

[17] See *Rolling v William Investments* (1989), 63 DLR (4th) 760. The Ontario Court of Appeal decided that faxing acceptance of an option was satisfactory acceptance, even though when the parties made the agreement in 1974, they "could not have anticipated delivery of a facsimile of the [accepted] offer by means of a telephone transmission." The court concluded that "Where technological advances have been made which facilitate communications and expedite transmission of documents we see no reason why they should not be utilized. Indeed, they should be encouraged and approved . . . . [The defendant] suffered no prejudice by reason of the procedure followed." See also *Leoppky v Meston*, 2008 ABQB 45 at paras 38–41.

[18] *Hunter v Baluke*, *supra* note 16.

[19] See e.g. RSO 1990, c S.19, s 6; RSNS 1989, c 442, s 8.

[20] *Pearce v Gardner*, [1897] 1 QB 688; *Harvie and Hawryluk v Gibbons* (1980), 12 Alta LR (2d) 72.

without oral evidence, it could reasonably assume that the letter was delivered in an envelope: It admitted oral evidence merely to identify the envelope.

Signed by the Defendant The *Statute* requires that the note or memorandum be signed by the party to be charged—that is, sued (the defendant)—and only that person, not the plaintiff. The plaintiff's own signature is irrelevant; if the defendant has not signed, the plaintiff's signature on the document does not help, and he cannot enforce the contract against the other party.

The courts have been lenient in prescribing what amounts to a sufficient signature; it need not be in the handwriting of the defendant. A printed name will suffice as long as it is intended to validate the whole of the document. For example, a letterhead on an invoice is designed to verify the sale of the goods described below without a signature and is sufficient. Ecommerce legislation now expands the notion of signature to include electronic signatures, as will be discussed in Chapter 31.

CASE 10.4 Emails

An unmarried couple entered into an agreement dividing the proceeds of sale of their home and its contents. One party refused to honour the deal as it violated the *Statute of Frauds* and asked the court to divide the proceeds of sale of the home. The court enforced the settlement agreement, finding that, although the *Statute of Frauds* applied to the agreement as it related to the sale of land, the emails exchanged by the parties satisfied the written "note or memorandum" requirement. The signing requirement was met by the typed first name on the bottom of the email—even though the email was sent from someone else's email account.[21]

Consequences for Contracts Within Its Scope

What do we mean when we say that the *Statute of Frauds* makes an oral contract unenforceable? This means the parties cannot use the courts to obtain a remedy. The courts recognize that an **unenforceable contract** still exists even though neither party is able to obtain a court remedy. Is this the same as saying it is void? The answer is a definite no. Although no action may be brought on the contract itself, the contract may still affect the legal relations between the parties in several ways.

unenforceable contract
a contract that still exists for other purposes but neither party may obtain a remedy under it through court action

1. Recovery of Money Paid under a Contract First, both parties to an unenforceable contract may, of course, choose to perform, but if they do not, recovery of any down payment made will depend upon which party repudiates the contract.

ILLUSTRATION 10.1 Down Payment

P orally agrees to buy V's house for $50 000 and gives a down payment of $5000, with the balance to be paid in 30 days.

Suppose that P then sees a more suitable property and refuses to pay the balance. The *Statute of Frauds* applies, and V cannot force P to buy V's house. On the other hand, P cannot by court action require V to return the payment. Although the contract is unenforceable, it still exists and may be used as a defence; V may retain the payment knowing that he will not be ordered by a court to return it.[22]

Suppose instead it is V who refuses either to complete the sale or to return the payment. P can sue successfully for the return of the payment. The court in these circumstances will not permit V to repudiate the contract and yet keep the payment received under its terms. Without an enforceable contract, no court will let him keep the deposit.

---

[21] *Leoppky v Meston*, 2008 ABQB 45 at para 45.

[22] See e.g. *Semchyshen v Semchyshen*, [2013] SJ No 342.

In this illustration, we can see the court will not permit the party who breaches an unenforceable contract to gain a further advantage. If the contract were found instead to be void, the problem of breach would not arise. A void contract cannot be "breached"; the remedy is rescission, as discussed in Chapter 9.

2. Recovery for Goods and Services Second, a party who has accepted goods and services under a contract that is unenforceable because of the *Statute* is not permitted to retain the benefit received without paying something for it. He would have to return the goods or pay a reasonable price for them, as was explained in Chapter 6 under the principle of *quantum meruit*.

3. Effect of a Subsequent Written Memorandum Third, a written document may come into existence after the contract has been formed, and it will still satisfy the *Statute*. As long as the document comes into existence before the action is brought on the contract, it provides the necessary evidence.

> **ILLUSTRATION 10.2   Writing Produced Later**
>
> P agrees orally to buy V's home. P then refuses to complete the contract, and V sends her a letter outlining the contract and demanding she carry out her obligations. P replies by letter saying that she has decided not to go through with the contract referred to in V's letter and that she is not bound since the contract is not in writing. Even though the statements in P's letter were intended to deny liability, the two letters taken together would amount to a sufficient memorandum to satisfy the *Statute* and make the contract enforceable.

4. Defendant Must Expressly Plead the *Statute* Fourth, a defendant who is sued upon an oral contract must expressly plead the *Statute* as a defence to the action. If he fails to mention it, the court will decide the case without reference to the *Statute*. The plaintiff will then succeed if he establishes that the contract, though oral, was validly formed.

5. Varying a Prior Written Contract Fifth, an oral contract may effectively vary or end a prior written contract even though the oral contract could not itself be enforced. An oral contract within the *Statute* is effective as long as a party does not have to bring an action to have it enforced.

> **ILLUSTRATION 10.3   Ending a Written Contract**
>
> P agrees to buy Roselawn from V under a written contract containing a promise by V to give vacant possession on a certain day. V then has unexpected difficulty in removing his tenants and tells P he will not be able to give vacant possession. P finds another property equally suitable to her and available with vacant possession. Rather than get into a dispute, the parties make a mutual oral agreement to call off the first contract. P releases V from his promise to transfer Roselawn with vacant possession in return for a release by V of P's promise to pay the purchase price. Afterward, V succeeds in removing his tenants and sues P to enforce the original written contract. P may successfully plead that the subsequent oral contract validly terminated the written contract.
>
> However, the oral contract cannot be sued upon directly. Suppose that, in addition to terminating the prior contract, V had orally agreed to give P an option on another property. Although the oral contract effectively dissolved the prior written contract, P could not sue upon the new promise to give an option because otherwise the court would be enforcing an oral promise for an interest in land.[23]

---

[23] See *Morris v Baron*, [1918] AC 1 for a similar result.

INTERNATIONAL ISSUE
Should the *Statute of Frauds* Be Repealed?

The *Statute of Frauds* was passed over three centuries ago, and the argument has been made that the historical reasons for creating it no longer exist. In Canada, more detailed consumer protection writing requirements reduce the *Statute's* impact. As previously noted, the *Statute* has been repealed in Manitoba and amended in Ontario and British Columbia. Perhaps it is time to replace or amend it throughout Canada. When the Province of Ontario amended its *Sale of Goods Act* to remove the writing requirements (see footnote 25), it did so for the express purpose of facilitating electronic commerce.

On the other hand, consider this statement from Mr. Justice Côté of the Alberta Court of Appeal:

> Over 20 years ago, it was fashionable to attack the *Statute of Frauds*, and indeed a number of jurisdictions have repealed large chunks of it. But Alberta has not touched s. 4. In my view, the trend of modern legislation is actually to call for more writing in contracts and commercial transactions. The idea that one can validly sell a valuable piece of land entirely by oral discussions runs contrary to the expectations of most lay people; one can almost say that absence of writing casts into doubt intention to create binding legal relations. So I feel no compulsion to undermine the *Statute*.[24]

Interestingly, provincial electronic commerce legislation like the Ontario *Electronic Commerce Act* addresses the issues of writing and signatures in electronic documents—not by avoiding the effect of legislation such as the *Statute of Frauds* but by seeking practical equivalents to those requirements in forming a contract.

Internationally, the trend may be different. Civil law jurisdictions, such as France, never had the *Statute of Frauds*. Even common law countries are moving away from writing requirements. England has repealed most of the *Statute of Frauds*. Article 11 of the United Nations Convention on Contracts for the International Sale of Goods reads:

> A contract for sale need not be concluded in or evidenced by writing and is not subject to any other requirements as to form. It may be proved by any means including witnesses.[25]

Questions to Consider

1. How are business relationships and commercial activity affected by complex legal rules about the enforceability of oral contracts?
2. Are there sound policy reasons for requiring some contracts to be in writing?
3. Are amendments adequate to address the problems arising from the *Statute of Frauds*, or would it be better to repeal the *Statute* and replace it with legislation that meets contemporary needs?
4. Can the *Statute of Frauds* coexist with ecommerce legislation?

Sources: *Austie v Aksnowicz*, [1999] 10 WWR 713, 70 Alta LR (3d) 154 (CA) at para 55; Law Reform Commission of British Columbia, Report on the *Statute of Frauds* (1997), available online at https://www.bcli.org/project/statute-frauds-1977; Manitoba Law Reform Commission, Report on the *Statute of Frauds* (1980); University of Alberta Institute of Law Research and Reform, Background Paper No. 12: *Statute of Frauds* (1979); Report No. 44 (1985); SO 2000, c 17.

Writing Requirements of the *Sale of Goods Act* Provinces other than British Columbia and Ontario[26] impose writing requirements in their *Sale of Goods Acts*. Although the specifics vary by province, the basic requirements are similar to those found in the *Statute of Frauds*—contracts for the sale of goods must be evidenced by some note or memorandum signed by the party to be charged, or they are unenforceable.

What Constitutes a Sale of Goods for the Purposes of the Writing Requirement?

Goods A sale of tangible moveable personal property is a sale of goods for the purposes of the writing provisions under this legislation. It does not apply to money or services. The challenge is that often contracts involve both the goods and services,

---

[24] *Royal Bank of Canada v Reddy*, 2007 ABQB 613.

[25] (1980), https://www.uncitral.org/pdf/english/texts/sales/cisg/V1056997-CISG-e-book.pdf.

[26] *Law Reform (Enforcement of Contracts) Act, 1954*, 2 & 3 Eliz 2, c 34, s 1 (UK); *Statute Law Amendment Act, 1958*, SBC 1958, c 52, s 17; *Statute Law Amendment (Government Management and Services) Act, 1994*, SO 1994, c 27, s 54.

such as a contract to provide materials and build a garage. If it is considered a contract for the sale of goods, it is subject to the writing requirements; if it is one for work and materials, it is not. The problem of defining a sale of goods is discussed in detail in Chapter 14. Typically, it will depend on the *essence* of the contract—the proportion of labour or service to goods or materials supplied under the contract.

Threshold Amounts   All provinces set a (very low) threshold value of goods supplied under the contract to trigger the writing requirement. Amounts vary from $30 to $50.[27] The contract may state a fixed price or set a formula for calculation, or the price may be determined by the past dealings between the parties.[28]

Evidence That Satisfies the Act

Unlike the *Statute of Frauds*, the *Sale of Goods Act* states expressly that a party to a contract for the sale of goods who cannot produce the required written memorandum may still enforce the contract if he can show one of the following kinds of conduct:[29]

(a) "acceptance" and actual receipt of the goods (or part) by the buyer, or
(b) part payment tendered by the buyer and accepted by the seller, or
(c) something "by way of earnest" given by the buyer to the seller.

acceptance any conduct by the buyer in relation to the goods that amounts to recognition of an existing contract of sale

Acceptance   In the *Sale of Goods Act*, the word **acceptance** has a special meaning. It means any conduct by the buyer in relation to the goods that amounts to recognition of an existing contract of sale. The buyer will have "accepted" the goods when she does anything that amounts to admitting she has a contract with respect to them.

part payment something tendered by the buyer and accepted by the seller after formation of the contract, to be deducted from the price

Part Payment   A **part payment** is a credit toward payment of the purchase price. Therefore, it must be made after the contract is formed and applied to reduce the debt created by the contract. It is not the same as the part performance exception for sales of land discussed under the *Statute of Frauds*, as a mere payment of money is usually capable of having alternative explanations.

earnest a token sum or article given to seal a bargain—now a rare practice

Earnest   Earnest differs from part payment in that it is not deducted from the price to be paid. Rather it is a token sum (or article) given to seal the bargain. Although giving something by way of earnest was common at one time, it is now rarely, if ever, done, and the reference to this practice is not of practical importance.

When Both Acts Apply

Both the *Sale of Goods Act* and the *Statute of Frauds* might apply to the same contract. They both apply, for example, where there is an oral agreement to sell goods that are to be delivered and paid for by installments over a period exceeding one year. The evidence may satisfy the requirements of the *Sale of Goods Act* if the buyer accepts some of the goods or makes part payment, but it does not comply with the *Statute of Frauds* because it is an oral contract that neither party can wholly perform within one year. Accordingly, it is unenforceable because of the *Statute of Frauds* but not because of the *Sale of Goods Act*.

The requirement of a written memorandum in the *Sale of Goods Act* is open to the same criticism as the comparable provision in the *Statute of Frauds*. Its limited

---

[27] The amount is $40 in Nova Scotia; $50 in Newfoundland and Labrador, Saskatchewan, and Alberta; and $30 in Prince Edward Island. These amounts are, of course, insignificant compared to their value over 100 years ago when the *Sale of Goods Act* was adopted.

[28] See e.g. *Sale of Goods Act*, RSBC 1996, c 410, s 12; RSO 1990, c S.1, s 9; RSNS 1989, c 408, s 11.

[29] *Sale of Goods Act*, RSNS 1989, c 408, s 7.

protection is hard to justify in today's marketplace; its arguably more important function is to imply terms into contracts for the sale of goods. A thorough discussion of the *Sale of Goods Act* is in Chapter 14.

CONSUMER PROTECTION LEGISLATION

A consumer is an individual who purchases goods or services for personal non-commercial use. Consumers have no power to negotiate terms of their contracts, so provincial legislation imposes some protective measures. Generally this legislation regulates the form (writing) and contents (terms) of consumer contracts, although with differing names and methods of protection.[30] The consumer protection statutes cover both goods and services and extend further than either the *Sale of Goods Act* or the *Statute of Frauds*, by dictating not only the evidence of writing but also the terms that must be included in that written document. High-risk industries and contracts formed using particular sales tactics are subject to even greater controls, including consumer cancellation options.

Consumer contracts that reach the threshold value must be in writing and include the following information:

- Detailed description of goods or services
- Itemized purchase price
- Detailed disclosure of cost of borrowing: this includes annualized interest rates and separate disclosure of other administration fees associated with the extension of credit
- Name, address, and contact information of the vendor
- Notice of statutory cancellation rights
- Complete copy provided to the consumer

Cancellation options are attached to contracts that are formed or performed in the following ways:

- Future performance contracts—this type of contract is one where the goods are supplied or payment is made at a future time.
- Direct sales contracts—this type of contract is formed when the seller contacts a consumer outside his place of business; for example, via door-to-door sales.
- Distance or remote contracts—this type of contract is formed when the parties are separated by distance; for example, by telephone marketing or promotional mailings.
- Internet contracts—the use of online sales is now regulated by most consumer protection legislation.

Some industries are required to include special terms in their consumer contracts. Designated industries considered high risk include the following:

- Time sharing—one Alberta provision requires that time-share agreements be signed by both business and consumer, and the text of the notice provisions cannot be smaller than 12-point font.[31]

---

[30] See e.g. *Business Practices and Consumer Protection Act*, SBC 2004, c 2; *Consumer Protection Act, 2002*, SO 2002, c C.30, Sch A; *Consumer Protection Act*, RSNS 1989, c 92.

[31] A Reg 105/10, s 2.

- Fitness or personal development—Saskatchewan's legislation requires these contracts to be in writing and include start and end dates, as well as a formula for reducing the amount owing if the club is not available on a specified date.[32]
- Lending (credit)—naturally, all provinces require very specific detailed descriptions of the interest calculations and the composition of the payment amounts.
- Credit card—among Manitoba's written requirements for credit card agreements are a written description of the method for determining the minimum required payments.[33]
- Leasing—many consumers do not understand how their car lease payments are calculated and the importance of the residual value of the vehicle at the end of the lease term. For this reason, Ontario's legislation requires lessors to provide a disclosure statement before the written lease is signed.[34]
- Motor vehicle repair—one Ontario provision prohibits a repairer from charging for work unless an estimate meeting the prescribed requirements has been given or waived. The estimate must be written and must show the make, model, and odometer reading of the vehicle, as well as a detailed description of proposed work.[35]
- Funeral services—the British Columbia legislation requires funeral services contracts to disclose in writing the address where the body will be stored pending disposition and the name of the bank where any prepaid funds will be held.[36]

Consumers are not bound by these contracts unless the business has complied with the requirements of the legislation. Provinces have set up agencies to hear consumer complaints as well as to investigate or even negotiate on the consumer's behalf. We discuss consumer protection legislation in more detail in Chapters 3 and 14.

Ethical Issue Do Writing Requirements Protect the Consumer or the Business?

Many of the consumer protection writing requirements involve disclosing onerous terms to the consumer as part of the written contract. As long as the consumer has received the written disclosure, she will be bound by the terms. In the fast-paced world of online contracting, few consumers have time to read the disclosed terms and have no power to bargain for a change in terms if they are dissatisfied. Onerous terms are presented on a take-it-or-leave-it basis. Furthermore, even when a cancellation right is available, finding a business that does not require agreement to similar one-sided terms might be impossible for the consumer. In this light, written disclosure requirements may not actually protect the consumer.

Questions to Consider

1. Do writing requirements protect the consumer or the business? Or both?
2. Rather than being given the right to cancel an agreement, should consumers be allowed to modify the terms and conditions before agreeing to them? Would consumers take the time to do this?
3. The European Union has a directive that identifies unfair terms and declares them unenforceable against a consumer. Is this a more fair approach?
4. In *Seidel v TELUS*, the Supreme Court of Canada said that unless the legislature intervenes, the courts will enforce contracts of adhesion that are freely entered into.[37] Should the courts ever help a consumer subject to a written contract filled with unfair terms? Consider Case 10.7, which shows how implied terms in the consumer contract can protect a consumer.

---

[32] *Consumer Protection Act*, SS 1996, c C-30.1, s 76.

[33] *Consumer Protection Act*, CCSM c C200, s 35.2.

[34] *Consumer Protection Act, 2002*, *supra* note 30, s 89.

[35] O Reg 17/05, s 51.

[36] *Business Practices and Consumer Protection Act*, *supra* note 30, ss 34–36.

[37] 2011 SCC 15 at para 2.

THE INTERPRETATION OF EXPRESS TERMS

Even when parties put their contracts in writing, disagreements about their meaning regularly occur. Words are at best an imprecise means of communicating thoughts. Simple words are capable of more than one meaning—ambiguous without the parties realizing it. Therefore, disagreements about express terms are a common business risk, and courts are regularly asked to decide what a contract means.

The Goal of the Courts: To Give Validity to Contracts

Courts must make difficult interpretation decisions. Declaring an agreement void because its wording is ambiguous might seem to be the easiest thing to do, but if the courts took this attitude, they would not be performing their role of encouraging reliance on seriously made agreements. Instead, they try to keep an agreement alive rather than brushing it aside as not binding. When it is possible to find one interpretation more likely in the circumstances than another, courts give ambiguous words that meaning and make the contract enforceable. The overriding goal is to ascertain the objective intent of the parties—that is, to determine intention of the parties and their reasonable understanding of the words used. Considerations of good faith may be involved.[38]

ILLUSTRATION 10.4 Unclear Meaning

Smith offers to build a set of cabinets for Doe for $1000, and Doe accepts. The next day, Smith appears and asks where the lumber is. Doe says, "You are supposed to supply it." Smith replies, "My price was for the work only, not for the materials."

One party might claim that the offer omitted an essential term (who should supply the lumber), and such a vague offer could not form a contract. However, if each side accepts that the agreement "to build a set of cabinets for $1000" is valid, Smith will claim that Doe should supply the lumber, and Doe will claim the opposite.

Legal Principles of Interpretation

What precisely did Smith promise when he agreed "to build a set of cabinets for $1000"? Determining the meaning of this phrase involves questions of law and fact; the legal principles of interpretation are applied to the particular factual circumstances surrounding the contract.[39] The legal approach to interpretation combines the **strict grammatical or plain-meaning of the words** used with the **surrounding contextual circumstances** in which the contract was formed.

The plain-meaning analysis considers the ordinary, grammatical, or dictionary meaning of the words. However, few words have a single "plain" or "ordinary" meaning. Browsing through a dictionary will show that many words have two or more definitions. In addition, the meanings of words change from time to time and place to place—or the combination or context of the words in a contract may make it obvious they have been used in a special sense.[40] Therefore, the plaining meaning of words is not usually considered in isolation.

The contextual circumstances surrounding the formation of the contract are vital to understanding the meaning of the words used. This requires examination of the

strict grammatical or plain-meaning of the words the ordinary, grammatical, or dictionary meaning

surrounding contextual circumstances the factual matrix in which the contract is formed including the purpose of the contract and the intent of the parties

---

[38] *Sattva Capital Corp v Creston Moly Corp*, 2014 SCC 53 at paras 47, 49; *Bhasin v Hrynew*, 2014 SCC 71 at para 45.

[39] *Sattva Capital Corp*, ibid at paras 47–48.

[40] *Investors Compensation Scheme Ltd v West Bromwich Building Society*, [1998] 1 All ER 98 at 115.

contract as a whole, the purposes of the particular parties in drafting their agreement, and their relationship. What did they intend? It stresses the circumstances surrounding the contract, the negotiations leading up to it, the knowledge of the parties, the nature of the industry, and any other relevant facts. Together, the plain meaning of the words used in light of the factual circumstances surrounding the parties provide the most reasonable and common sense approach to contract interpretation.

General Approach to Interpretation

The court begins with the dictionary definitions of the words used and the grammatical arrangement of their placement, then examines their meaning in the context of this contract, these parties, and the surrounding circumstances.

In Illustration 10.4, Smith promised "to build" the cabinets. Does "to build" include "to supply materials"? Literally, "to build" means only "to construct," but in many circumstances it may include "to supply materials." As an example, when a contractor undertakes to build a house, the price usually includes the price of materials. In the illustration, the words themselves are not conclusive either way. Since the words are ambiguous, the court will look outside the contract to the surrounding circumstances as a means of clearing up this uncertainty. It will hear evidence of any past transactions between the parties to learn whether materials have been included in previous building contracts between them. It will hear evidence of the negotiations leading up to the contract; perhaps Smith had quoted different prices varying with the kind of wood to be used; perhaps Doe made it clear earlier that she wanted a price including materials. Any of these facts, if established in court, would support the claim that "to build" in this contract meant "to supply materials" as well as labour.

Special Usage of Words

Words used in a contract may have a special meaning in the particular business, trade, or geographic location. For example, a dozen typically means 12, but a baker's dozen means 13. In Illustration 10.4, Smith might produce expert witnesses who testify that, in the carpentry trade, usage of the word "build" means labour only. Or he might show that, in that part of the country, the word always has that meaning.

Evidence of special usage is not necessarily conclusive. A court may decide the word was used in a general rather than a special way, perhaps because the user of the word was aware that the other party was not familiar with trade usage. In general, the courts construe words most strictly against the party who has suggested them because that party could have been more clear.[41]

Conflicting Testimony and Credibility

Parties to a contract may give conflicting evidence about the circumstances or conversations surrounding its formation. In order to decide which testimony to accept, the court will seek corroboration of one of their versions, if possible, from a non-party, from documentation, or from the actions of the parties in relation to the contract. When the only evidence in a case is the testimony of the disputing parties, the case becomes a "credibility contest." The judge has to assess the credibility of the witnesses and decide whose version seems more reasonable. Credibility includes both truthfulness and reliability. One person may not have seen or heard clearly, may not remember

---

[41] See *Manulife Bank of Canada v Conlin*, [1996] 3 SCR 415.

well, or may have observed only part of an event. Even though a witness is honest, his testimony might not be reliable and therefore not be credible. Judges must give reasons for why they find one witness more credible than another.

Special Contracts or Clauses

Some types of contracts and clauses require a different approach. **Standard form contract** are contracts prepared in advance by one party and presented to the other on a take-it-or-leave-it basis. In these contracts factual circumstances are less important because no prior negotiating takes place. Interpreting these contracts consistently is more important because they have precedential value beyond the parties before the courts.[42] There is a power imbalance between the parties resulting in an unlevel playing field. When interpreting an ambiguous term in a standard form contract, the court will prefer the interpretation advanced by the non-drafting party. Of course, it must be a reasonable interpretation. This rule is known as ***contra proferentem***.[43] It is also applies to the interpretation of ambiguous exemption clauses and consumer contracts, as will be discussed in Chapters 13 and 14 respectively.

contra proferentem a rule of contract interpretation that prefers the interpretation of a clause that is least favourable to the party that drafted the clause

Insurance Contracts Insurance contracts are an example of a type of standard form contract with special interpretation rules. Interpretation of ambiguous insurance contracts must avoid unrealistic results and seek consistent interpretations by:

1. following the contra proferentem rule,
2. construing coverage provisions broadly, and
3. interpreting exclusion clauses narrowly.[44]

Chapter 16 deals specifically with insurance contracts. Of course, as with all contracts, where the meaning of a contract is clear and unambiguous, the court will not resort to special principles of interpretation.

THE PAROL EVIDENCE RULE

The Meaning of Parol Evidence

Before a deal is made, the parties often spend time bargaining and negotiating, making offers and counter-offers, with both sides making concessions until finally they reach a suitable compromise. The bargaining may be carried on orally or in writing. In important contracts, the parties usually put their final agreement into a formal document signed by both sides. During the negotiation process, emails, phone messages, draft documents, faxes, and letters may be created and exchanged. These documents and recordings are collectively known as parol evidence. The word *parol* means extrinsic to or outside of the written agreement.[45] If a dispute subsequently arises over the meaning of the words used in the formal signed document, this parol evidence contains valuable information about the parties' understanding of the meaning of the words used in the final contract.

---

[42] *Ledcor Construction Ltd v Northbridge Indemnity Insurance Co*, 2016 SCC 37 at paras 31–32.

[43] The rule does not apply if the term is clear and unambiguous: *Hillis Oil & Sales Ltd v Wynnis Canada Ltd*, [1986] 1 SCR 57.

[44] *Ledcor Construction Ltd*, *supra* note 42 (citing *Progressive Homes Ltd v Lombard General Insurance Co of Canada*, 2010 SCC 33 at paras 24–27).

[45] See John D. McCamus, *The Law of Contracts* (Toronto: Irwin Law, 2005) at 193–207.

> ### CASE 10.5 Use of Parol Evidence for Interpretation
>
> When the seller asked the buyer, "What will you give me for 75 shares of Eastern Cafeterias of Canada?," the buyer said he would think about it and then make an offer. Later in the day the buyer replied, "I will give you $10.50 a share for your Eastern Cafeterias shares." The seller replied, "I accept your offer." The seller delivered the shares for Eastern Cafeterias of Canada Ltd. and received a cheque in full payment. The buyer then realized that Eastern Cafeterias Ltd. and Eastern Cafeterias of Canada Ltd. were two different companies and that he had the former company in mind when he made his offer to buy the shares. He stopped payment on his cheque.
>
> In defending the seller's lawsuit, the buyer claimed that his offer to buy "Eastern Cafeterias" was ambiguous, as he could have meant either company. He argued that since he and the seller were talking about two different companies, there was never any agreement, and no contract was formed. The court examined the pre-contractual unambiguous statement of the seller that referenced Eastern Cafeterias "of Canada" and interpreted the final agreement as referring to those shares. The defendant's use of the ambiguous term in the offer was in response to the plaintiff's earlier inquiry, and so the contractual language must be interpreted in the same way.[46]

Case 10.5 is an example of a court using parol evidence to establish the meaning of an ambiguous contractual term.[47]

The Meaning of the Parol Evidence Rule

parol evidence rule a rule preventing a party to a written contract from later using parol evidence to add to, subtract from, or modify the final written contract

The **parol evidence rule** puts a limit on what uses can be made of parol evidence. As we saw in Case 10.5, parol evidence can be used to help interpret ambiguous words used in a contract. It can also be used to address formation of the contract such as its legality, the capacity of the parties, mistakes, duress, undue influence, or fraud. However, it cannot be used to add a new term to a final written contract.

According to the parol evidence rule, once a final written contract has been formed, a party cannot later use parol evidence to add, subtract, contradict, or modify a term in that written contract.[48] The rule applies both to an oral agreement that has been reduced to writing and to a written agreement that has been set out in a more formal document. A party may still try to argue mistake or rectification, as discussed in Chapter 9, but otherwise the contract is final.

Exceptions to the Parol Evidence Rule

The Document Does Not Contain the Whole Contract
Once the parties have put their agreement into a document in its final form, the parol evidence rule precludes either party from adding terms not in that final agreement. However, sometimes the court may find that the written document was not intended to be the whole complete contract. Earlier in this chapter, we learned that the terms of a contract may be partly in writing and partly oral; if a party can show that the writing was not intended to contain the whole contract but was merely a part of it, then she may introduce evidence of additional oral terms using parol evidence.[49]

---

[46] *Scammell v Ouston*, [1941] 1 All ER 14 at 25.

[47] See also *Campeau v Desjardins Financial Security Life Assurance Co*, [2005] MJ No 448 (Man CA).

[48] *Sattva Capital Corp*, supra note 38 at para 59.

[49] See *King v Operating Engineers Training Institute of Manitoba Inc*, 2011 MBCA 80; *Gallen v Allstate Grain Co* (1984), 9 DLR (4th) 496, reviewing exceptions to the rule. But see *Norman Estate v Norman*, [1990] BCJ No 199 (BCSC).

> **ILLUSTRATION 10.5** Documents Created for Performance
>
> A, the owner of a fleet of dump trucks, agrees orally with B, a paving contractor, to move 3000 cubic metres of gravel within three months from Calgary to Carstairs for $18 000, and to provide any related documents that B may require for financing the project. To finance her paving operations, B applies for a bank loan, and the bank requests evidence that the paving work can be started immediately. B therefore asks A to sign a statement saying he will deliver 1000 cubic metres of gravel from Calgary to Carstairs within the next month for $6000. Soon after A starts to make the deliveries, he discovers he has quoted too low a price per cubic metre.
>
> He claims that his whole agreement with B has been reduced to writing and that he need move only the 1000 cubic metres of gravel referred to in the writing.
>
> The parol evidence rule does not apply. The written document for the bank was not intended to be a complete statement of the contract. Rather, it was drawn up as part of A's performance of his obligation under it. Accordingly, B may sue A for damages if A refuses to perform the balance of the contract, and for this purpose B may offer evidence of the terms of the original oral agreement.

Subsequent Oral Agreement The parol evidence rule does not exclude evidence of a separate oral agreement the parties may reach after they have entered into the written agreement. The subsequent oral agreement may change the terms of the written agreement,[50] or it may even discharge or rescind the prior contract altogether.[51] When such a claim is made, the court will hear evidence of a subsequent oral contract, but the contract must satisfy all the usual formation requirements: offer, acceptance, consideration, and intention.

Collateral Agreement A **collateral agreement** is an entirely separate undertaking agreed on by the parties at the same time (or prior to) the written agreement but not included in their written contract, probably because the written contract seemed unrelated or separate from it. The argument is that a collateral agreement may be enforced as a separate contract quite independent of the written document. Again, courts will only accept such a claim when all elements of formation are separately met for the collateral agreement (especially separate consideration) and when it does not contradict the terms of the written agreement.[52]

collateral agreement a separate agreement between the parties made at the same time as, but not included in, the written document

> **CASE 10.6** Contradictions in Terms
>
> A lawyer signed a written personal guarantee of the indebtedness of a company. The guarantee stated that it was continuous, meaning the lawyer would be responsible not only for the existing debts of the company but also for any future indebtedness the company would create after the signing of the guarantee. It also stated there were no representations, and liability would only end upon agreement in writing. When the company went bankrupt, and the bank called upon the lawyer to pay, the lawyer argued that there was a collateral agreement made at the time of signing that the lawyer would only be responsible for existing debts of the company, and he would be released from any indebtedness when guarantees from other directors were signed. The bank did obtain guarantees from other directors but argued that this in no way released the lawyer. The Supreme Court of Canada refused to allow evidence of an oral collateral agreement. The guarantee was a complete final agreement, and therefore its terms could not be modified by extrinsic parol evidence. The alleged collateral agreement discharging the lawyer directly contradicted the terms of the guarantee, and therefore they could not consistently stand together. No exception to the parol evidence rule applied, and the lawyer had to pay the debts.[53]

---

[50] See *Johnson Investments v Pagritide*, [1923] 2 DLR 985.

[51] *Morris v Baron*, [1918] AC 1.

[52] *Hawrish v Bank of Montreal*, [1969] SCR 515 at 524.

[53] Ibid. See also *River Wind Ventures Ltd v British Columbia*, 2011 BCCA 79; but see *Corey Developments Inc v Eastbridge Developments (Waterloo) Ltd* (1997), 34 OR (3d) 73, aff'd (1999) 44 OR (3d) 95 for an example where the court refused to follow the parol evidence rule.

condition precedent any set of circumstances or events that the parties stipulate must be satisfied or must happen before their contract takes effect

Condition Precedent A **condition precedent** is any set of circumstances or events the parties agree must be satisfied or must happen before their contract takes effect. It may be an event beyond the control of either party, such as a requirement that a licensing board approve the transfer of a business, or a student graduating before a contract of employment takes effect. Courts will admit evidence of an oral condition precedent even when the written contract expressly states that the parties' rights and duties are governed exclusively by the written terms. The courts are prepared to recognize and enforce a condition precedent agreed to orally even when the subject matter of the contract falls within the scope of the *Statute of Frauds* or the *Sale of Goods Act*. Once a court accepts a contention that the parties did indeed intend to suspend the operation of their contract subject to a condition precedent, then the whole of the contract is suspended, including any term attempting to exclude the admission of such evidence.

ILLUSTRATION 10.6 Financing Condition Precedent

B offers to sell a car to A for $14 000. A agrees orally to buy it, provided he can persuade his bank to lend him $10 000. The parties agree orally that the contract will operate only if the bank makes the loan and that otherwise the contract will be void. They then make a written contract in which A agrees to pay B $14 000 in 10 days, and B agrees to deliver the car to A at that time. The writing does not mention that the contract is subject to A obtaining the bank loan. The bank refuses to lend the money to A, who then informs B that the sale is off. B sues A for breach of contract and contends that their oral understanding about the bank loan is excluded by the parol evidence rule.

The parol evidence rule does not apply, and B will fail in his action. In his defence, A must show that there was an oral understanding suspending the contract of sale unless and until he could obtain the necessary bank loan. It is risky to rely on this exception because of the difficulty in proving the oral conversation. It is always better to put any conditions precedent in the written document.

CHECKLIST

Exceptions to the Parol Evidence Rule

A court will admit parol evidence about a missing term when

- the written agreement does not contain the whole agreement;
- the missing term is part of a subsequent oral agreement;
- the missing term is part of a collateral agreement for which there is separate consideration; or
- the missing term is a condition precedent to the written agreement.

IMPLIED TERMS AS A METHOD OF INTERPRETATION

It is difficult for parties to expressly address every possible scenario in a contract. Therefore, the express terms of a contract may not deal with the situation now facing the contractual parties. In such circumstances, a court may imply a term into the contract. An **implied term** is a term not expressly included by the parties in their agreement but which, in the opinion of the court, they would, as reasonable people, have included had they thought of the possibility of the subsequent difficulty arising. A term will be implied if it is obviously necessary to accomplish the purpose of the contract.

implied term a term not expressly included by the parties in their agreement but which, as reasonable people, they would have included had they thought about it

Terms Established by Custom or Statute

Implied terms usually result from long-established customs in a particular trade or type of transaction. They were accepted by business people because they made good sense or because they created certainty in transactions without the need to spell out every detail. In time, the courts fell into line with this business practice: When a party failed to perform in compliance with an implied term, the courts would recognize its existence and enforce the contract as though it had been an express term.

> **ILLUSTRATION 10.7   Fit for the Purpose**
>
> A asks B, a tire dealer, to supply truck tires for his five-tonne dump truck. B then shows A a set of tires and quotes a price. A purchases the tires. The sale slip merely sets out the name and the price of the tires. Later A discovers these tires are not safe on trucks of more than three tonnes' capacity and claims B is in breach of the contract.
>
> On these facts, there was no express promise by B that the tires would be safe for a five-tonne truck or any other type of truck. Nevertheless, the court would hold that, under the circumstances, there was an implied term that the tires should be suitable for a five-tonne truck. It would say that, in showing A the tires after he had made his intended use of them clear, B, as a regular seller of such tires, implied they would be suitable for A's truck.

This approach applies to all kinds of contracts, but in some fields—especially the sale of goods, insurance, partnership, and landlord and tenant relations—a large and complex body of customary terms has developed. In many jurisdictions, these customary terms have been codified in a statute that sets out in one place all the implied terms previously established by the courts for a particular field of law. For instance, court decisions in cases similar to Illustration 10.7 led to a specific provision in the *Sale of Goods Act*.

> **ILLUSTRATION 10.8   Legislation Implying Terms**
>
> Alberta's *Sale of Goods Act*[54] implies the following terms into contracts for the purchases of tangible property:
>
> - The seller is the owner of the goods with the authority to sell them.
> - The goods match the description given to the buyer by the seller.
> - The goods match the sample of the goods viewed by the buyer.
> - The goods are not subject to any liens.
>
> The implied terms of the *Sale of Goods Act* are also implied into consumer contracts for sale or lease of goods and services. Most statutory terms implied into consumer contracts cannot be waived.

> **CASE 10.7   Waiver Ineffective**
>
> Szilvasy bought a new home and took over the lease of the rented hot water heater. It sprang a leak and caused $16 000 of damage to the basement. Szilvasy sued for breach of contract. She alleged that the water heater was not fit for the intended purpose. Reliance Home Comfort defended the action, saying the lease contract did not include an express term on fitness for purpose, and it did include a clause exempting Reliance from liability for water damage. The court held that section 9 of the *Consumer Protection Act* implied a term of fitness for purpose into the contract, and this implied warranty could not be waived or varied by the express exemption clause. The water heater was not fit for the purpose because it leaked. Judgment was for the consumer.[55]

---

[54] *Sale of Goods Act*, RSA 2000, c S-2.

[55] *Szilvasy v Reliance Home Comfort*, 2012 ONCA 821, considering *Consumer Protection Act, 2002*, *supra* note 30, s 9.

Reasonable Expectation of the Parties

Sometimes the courts will imply terms reasonably necessary to make a contract effective; if not, the fair and reasonable expectations of a party would be defeated. Courts may consider it necessary to encourage good faith in contracting.[56]

However, the court will not go further than is necessary and will not make a new contract for the parties. Nor will it imply a term that is contrary to the expressed intent of the agreement. A term will be implied on grounds of business efficacy. Parties should therefore consider carefully what unstated assumptions are needed for performing their contract; they need to bring as many of the important possibilities as they can think of into the terms of the written contract.

As a general rule, when parties deal expressly with a matter in their contract, a court will not insert an implied term that deals with the same matter in a different way. If the parties have been diligent in canvassing the foreseeable possibilities for future dispute, a court may conclude that they intended to deal in a comprehensive way with all future events so that no further terms should be implied.[57]

However, even in lengthy and complex contracts, the parties might not have dealt with what later turns out to be a crucial matter. Courts will sometimes come to the conclusion that a term may be implied so that the purpose of the contract will be fulfilled.

CASE 10.8 Implied Term and Intention

Nickel Developments Limited (Nickel), the owner of a new shopping centre in Thompson, Manitoba, signed a long-term lease with Canada Safeway Limited containing several renewal options. Safeway was to be the "anchor" tenant, and its supermarket would use more than half of the centre. The rest of the space contained 12 other non-competing retail units.

After 30 years of operation, Safeway closed its supermarket but continued to occupy the space. For some time, Safeway had been operating another supermarket in a competing shopping centre in Thompson. It decided it could not continue operating the two in a town that had gone through a lengthy recession; it would be better to close down the premises leased from Nickel. Rather than allow its lease to expire, leaving open the prospect of unwanted competition, Safeway chose to exercise its option to renew the lease for a final term of five years and go on paying the rent in order to keep the space vacant. It already knew one of its supermarket competitors was interested in taking over the space and was communicating with Nickel.

Nickel served notice on Safeway, demanding possession of the leased space, claiming that Safeway had failed to comply with the implied term to use the leased premises "only as a supermarket" and for no other purpose. It stated that "vacancy by design" was not the kind of use intended. Safeway defended by stating there was no term in the lease expressly requiring it to keep operating its supermarket or prohibiting it from leaving the space vacant during the lease.

The Court of Appeal agreed with Nickel and held that there was an implied term in the lease that the space would be continuously used as a supermarket. It stated:

> A lessee which effectively shuts down half of a shopping centre and fundamentally alters the original concept cannot, absent very unequivocal language, unilaterally alter the arrangement between the landlord and the tenant which had been followed through the entire term of the lease . . . there must be "continuous use" as a supermarket, and that promise does not include the right to intentionally maintain and renew long-term "non-use."[58]

In this case we can see that the court could view the conduct of Safeway to be contrary to the intention of both parties in signing the contract and maybe not in good faith.

---

[56] *Bhasin v Hrynew, supra* note 38 at para 44.

[57] See *Cooke v CKOY Ltd* (1963), 39 DLR (2d) 209; *Shaw Cablesystems (Manitoba) Ltd v Canadian Legion Memorial Housing Foundation (Manitoba)* (1997), 143 DLR (4th) 193.

[58] *Nickel Developments Ltd v Canada Safeway Ltd* (2001), 199 DLR (4th) 629.

Strategies to Manage the Legal Risks

Written documents are the best way to prove the existence of a contract, and it should be standard business practice to create written contracts. The first step toward managing the legal risks associated with oral and written contracts is to determine what legislative writing requirements are applicable to the particular business. This requires familiarity with the legislation applicable to the subject matter of the business transaction, such as land development or funeral services, and also with legislation governing the sales and marketing strategy employed to form the contract, such as internet or direct sales.

The best way to ensure that terms advantageous to the business are enforceable against a consumer is through the use of a detailed standard form contract that meets the requirements of consumer protection legislation. Careful, consistent choice of language with clear, unambiguous meaning will avoid interpretation problems later. The consumer protection approach adopted by most provinces is to require disclosure first and allow a revocation period after the written document is signed. In this way, disclosure requirements actually help businesses bind consumers to onerous terms.

An oral agreement can be fortified with follow-up emails that confirm the terms after the fact. This subsequent behaviour can remedy defects caught by the *Statute of Frauds* and may be helpful to a court when determining the meaning of what was expressly agreed upon.

There are a number of strategies for reducing interpretation disputes:

- Incorporate a definition section into a contract, explaining the meaning of key words, and then be consistent with the use of those words throughout the contract.
- Begin the contract with a statement of the purpose of the agreement; this will help the court when interpreting and implying terms.
- Save pre-contract memos, emails, and the like (parol evidence) for assistance in the interpretation of the terms of the written contract.
- Include an "entirety" clause in the contract that states that the contract contains the whole agreement, and no separate oral or implied terms exist. This will invoke the parol evidence rule and limit a court's power to imply terms. The clause should specifically reference subsequent oral agreements if those are to be excluded as well.[59]
- Include a "severability" clause that allows a court to cut out an ambiguous term for which the meaning is not clear without destroying the entire contract.
- Prepare standard form contracts ahead of time for use in simple deals—these can include all of the aforesaid terms.
- Refer customers to standard terms and conditions on websites that provide detailed information.
- Request clarification of language included in an offer if it is vague prior to acceptance.
- Naturally, legal assistance in the drafting of a contract will avoid some pitfalls.

---

[59] *Turner v Visscher Holdings Inc* (1996), 23 BCLR (3d) 303 (CA).

QUESTIONS FOR REVIEW

1. Distinguish among the different outcomes for contracts that are unenforceable, voidable, and void.
2. What are the consequences of failure to comply with consumer protection legislation as opposed to the *Statute of Frauds* or *Sale of Goods Act*?
3. Explain the difference between a guarantee and an indemnity. Is there any policy basis for treating the two differently?
4. What is the difference between part performance and part payment?
5. State which of the following contracts are affected by a statutory requirement that would permit the promisor to plead that the contract cannot be enforced against her because evidence of the terms is not available in the required form:
    a. A and B, having entered into a written agreement as purchaser and vendor, respectively, of a piece of land, later agree by telephone to call off the sale.
    b. C enters into an oral contract with D, a contractor, to build a house for C.
    c. E is the proprietor of a business that requires a bank loan. E's father, F, tells the bank manager that if the bank approves the loan and E does not repay it, he (F) will.
    d. G, just before she graduates from university, accepts a job at a manufacturing firm. In the exchange of letters between G and her employer, nothing is said about the duration of G's employment or the need to actually graduate.
6. Give an example of when a party to an unenforceable contract may nevertheless recover money he has paid to the other party.
7. Why doesn't a dictionary definition of a word clarify its meaning in a contract? Give an example.
8. Explain and give an example of special usage of a word.
9. What are the primary goals of a court in interpreting a contract?
10. Name four ways in which a party may persuade a court that the parol evidence rule does not apply to the term or terms it asserts were part of the contract.
11. What is an implied term? Give an example from question 5.
12. When a contract is subject to a condition precedent, does the contract nevertheless still exist? May either party simply withdraw from the contract before the condition precedent has been met? Again, consider question 5.

CASES AND PROBLEMS

1. Continuing Scenario

    Before opening her restaurant, Ashley contacted O'Brien's Food Service Ltd. to be her frozen poultry supplier. Because she was new to the business and her volume would be low, O'Brien's quoted her a price of $25 per case of frozen chicken breasts. Adam, O'Brien's salesman, told her in an email that the price was only $20 per case for restaurants that ordered more than three cases a week. Ashley could not be sure she would need this much chicken, so she proceeded on the initial quote. The next day, Adam stopped by the restaurant with the customer application form describing the price as "as quoted" and told Ashley that because she had no history in the business, he needed a guarantor for her account. Jim, Ashley's father, was at the restaurant that day painting the dining room. Jim overheard Adam's request and volunteered to be the guarantor. He gave Adam his personal information to insert into the application form. Ashley signed the form, which stated that "upon acceptance by O'Brien's the application and corresponding terms and conditions would form the entire agreement between the parties."

At the end of Ashley's first year of business, she reviewed her chicken volume and discovered she was ordering at least four cases or more each week. However, she was still being charged $25 per case. When she contacted Adam about this, he said there was no agreement to reduce her price. Ashley was angry and responded that she would not be paying this week's $320 bill, and that would even up the amount. Adam threatened to sue her father if Ashley refused to pay. What rules of writing and interpretation are raised in this question? How will the court decide what price is a term of the contract? Will Jim be liable for this week's bill?

2. On January 15, Tonino and Logan signed a lease in which Logan agreed to rent her commercial office space to Tonino at $2000 per month for three years, commencing February 1. Tonino took possession as agreed. In March of the same year, Tonino and Logan agreed orally that Tonino would pay an additional $250 per month in rent upon the completion of some alterations and repairs to the premises within three months. Logan completed the alterations and repairs in April, but Tonino refused to pay anything but the $2000 a month specified in the lease. In August, Logan sued Tonino for the additional rent.

   What points must the court settle in reaching its decision, and what should the decision be?

3. M, N, O, and P each owned 25 percent of the shares in Resort Hotel Inc. As a result of a bad season, the hotel had a cash-flow problem. M arranged to borrow $25 000 from a friend, Q, and to lend it to the hotel on condition that if the hotel did not repay the funds, his three co-owners, N, O, and P, would each pay $5000 to M. The three agreed to the arrangement. Subsequently, the hotel defaulted, and M repaid the $25 000 to Q. He requested payment from N, O, and P but they refused to pay.

   M sued the three for $5000 each; they defended claiming that their promises were "guarantees," and since they were not in writing they were unenforceable. M claimed that their obligations were part of a larger transaction to protect their shared interests in Resort Hotel and, therefore, were not mere guarantees. Whose argument should succeed? Give reasons.

4. The manager of Jiffy Discount Stores ordered a carload of refrigerators from Colonel Electric Company by telephone. When the refrigerators arrived at the warehouse, the transport employees and Jiffy's employees began unloading them. When about half of them were unloaded, the manager arrived and asked to examine one. An employee uncrated one refrigerator, and after looking it over, the manager stated it was not the right model and ordered the transport employees to take them back. The refrigerators were returned to Colonel Electric Company, and the company sued Jiffy Discount Stores for breach of contract. It was proven that the manager was mistaken, and the refrigerators did conform to the telephone order. What legislation applies here? Explain what the result should be.

5. Carter left a position where he was earning $48 000 a year to accept a position as general manager of Buildwell Limited at the same annual salary. All negotiations leading up to his appointment were carried on orally between Carter and Webster, the president of Buildwell Limited. Both parties assured each other in various conversations that the employment would last "for life"; they agreed that each year Carter would receive a bonus, and that if he was not satisfied with it, he could terminate his employment, but that the company could not terminate his employment unless he "did something wrong."

   Over the succeeding few years, Carter's salary was increased from $4000 to $5000 per month, and he received, in addition, annual bonuses of up to $4000. A letter to Carter announcing his last bonus was signed by both the president and vice-president of the company and included the words, "And we want you to know that with all the experiences we are going through in connection with the business, your efforts are appreciated."

Shortly afterward, Webster died, and immediately the company dismissed Carter without explanation, paying him one month's salary. Carter then attempted to go into business for himself but without success. He sued Buildwell Limited for wrongful dismissal, claiming breach of his employment contract. Can Buildwell Limited successfully plead the *Statute of Frauds*?

6. In February, Baldwin Co. Ltd., a woollens manufacturer, contracted to sell 500 pieces of blue serge to Martin Bros. tailors, at a price of $40 000, as stated in a written memorandum signed by both parties. After 220 pieces of the cloth had been delivered, a dispute arose between the parties: Martin Bros. complained of delay in delivery, and Baldwin Co. Ltd. complained of failure to pay for the goods delivered. Baldwin Co. Ltd. sued Martin Bros. for the price of the goods delivered, and Martin Bros. counterclaimed for damages for non-delivery.

   In August, before the case came to trial, the parties orally agreed to a settlement and to substitute for the original contract a new one in which Martin Bros. would have an additional three months to pay for the goods and have an option of buying the remaining 280 pieces at the prices in the earlier contract. The following November, Martin Bros. paid the amount due on the original 220 pieces of cloth and placed an order for the remaining 280 pieces under the option agreed to in the substituted contract. Baldwin Co. Ltd. refused to deliver these pieces, the agreed price being no longer profitable to them. Martin Bros. then sued Baldwin Co. Ltd. for damages for breach of contract (failure to deliver). Should this action succeed?

7. John Brown, a retired widower, said to Mrs. Adele Barber that if he could find a suitable house and if she would move into it as a housekeeper, help operate it as a rooming house, and take care of him, he would give her the house on his death. Mrs. Barber agreed. Mr. Brown purchased a house that he operated as a rooming house until his death five years later. During this period Mrs. Barber served as housekeeper; she prepared the necessary food and made other household purchases, always turning over to Mr. Brown the balance of the board money received from the tenants. She received no remuneration for her services other than her own board and an occasional allowance for clothing.

   Mr. Brown made no provision in his will for Mrs. Barber, and following his death Mrs. Barber brought an action against the executors of his estate for specific performance of his promise. In evidence, Mrs. Barber offered the testimony of her two daughters, her son, and her son-in-law, who were present at the time of the original conversation between her and Mr. Brown. The executor contested the action. What legal considerations are relevant to a decision in this case? State whether Mrs. Barber's action would succeed.

8. Provinco Grain Inc. was in the business of selling seeds and buying and reselling the crops grown from the seeds sold. Its sales manager approached Quinlan, a farmer in the Lower Fraser Valley in British Columbia, to grow an early crop of buckwheat for the Japanese market. Quinlan, an experienced farmer, was interested because it would be a valuable market. However, he had never grown the crop before and said he was worried about weeds; he understood they could be a serious problem. The sales manager replied that he need not worry—the buckwheat would smother any weeds. Quinlan bought seeds and signed a printed document stating that Provinco Grain Inc. gave no warranty as to "the productiveness or any other matter pertaining to the seed . . . and will not in any way be responsible for the crop."

   Quinlan planted the seeds, but weeds destroyed the crop, and he suffered a substantial loss. He sued Provinco for damages on the basis that the sales manager's statement was a collateral warranty and a deliberate, material misrepresentation. With regard to the misrepresentation, the court found that the sales manager believed it to be true: he came from Saskatchewan where buckwheat did indeed suppress the weeds. Provinco further defended by claiming that the signed contract exempted it from all liability pertaining to the seeds and subsequent crop. Accordingly, any statement on this subject by the sales manager would be excluded by the parol evidence rule.

In reply, Quinlan's lawyer claimed that the sales manager's warranty was about the risk of weeds, and it did not contradict the terms of the signed contract pertaining to the seed itself. It was on the basis of that warranty that Quinlan signed the contract.

Give your view of each party's position and what the likely result would be.

9. Chénier sold the surface and minerals in her land in Alberta for $104 000 to Werner under an agreement for sale (an installment sale that reserved Chénier's ownership in the property until a specified amount of the price was paid). Werner defaulted payment, giving Chénier the right to recover possession by court action. Chénier started proceedings, but they were not yet complete when it became apparent that the land was very valuable. Werner entered into a petroleum and natural gas lease with Imperial Oil Ltd. and received a cash bonus of $110 000, which he intended to use to settle his debt to Chénier. At about the same time, Chénier, anticipating the recovery of her property by court order, entered into a similar lease of the same property with California Standard Oil Co. At the time Chénier gave her lease to California Standard Oil Co., she told the company's agent that her ability to lease the property depended upon winning her court action against Werner and that she could give the lease only if the company's agent gave her a signed statement acknowledging she (Chénier) did not have any right to lease the mineral rights until the court action against Werner went through. The agent gave her a statement to that effect, and Chénier and California Standard Oil Co. entered into a lease of the mineral rights that made no reference to the statement signed by the company's agent and also contained a paragraph stating the lease contained the whole of the agreement.

Werner tendered the balance of the purchase price to Chénier, but she refused it and proceeded with the court action. The court dismissed Chénier's petition for recovery of the property. She was, therefore, unable to lease the property to California Standard Oil Co., and that company sued her for breach of contract. Should the action succeed?

Chapter 11
Privity of Contract and the Assignment of Contractual Rights

- **PRIVITY OF CONTRACT**
- **EXCEPTIONS TO THE PRIVITY OF CONTRACT RULES**
- **ASSIGNMENT OF RIGHTS**
- **EQUITABLE ASSIGNMENTS**
- **STATUTORY ASSIGNMENTS**
- **NOTICE TO THE PROMISOR**
- **THE ASSIGNEE'S TITLE**
- **ASSIGNMENTS BY OPERATION OF LAW**
- **NEGOTIABLE INSTRUMENTS**
- **STRATEGIES TO MANAGE THE LEGAL RISKS**

A contract creates rights and duties between the parties who enter into the agreement; the rights may have an economic value that one party wishes to transfer to an outsider—a person who was not a party to the contract. Or a party may wish to arrange for her duties under the contract to be performed by another person.

In this chapter we examine such questions as:

- Who can enforce the obligations described in a contract?
- What are the legal consequences of an outsider performing a party's obligations under a contract?
- How are trusts used to create rights for an outsider to a contract?
- In what other circumstances or special types of contracts do outsiders have the right to enforce a contract?
- How may contractual rights be transferred to an outsider, and what are the consequences?
- What are negotiable instruments, and why are they important in business?

PRIVITY OF CONTRACT

Scope of Contractual Rights and Duties

When parties make a contract, they create a small body of law for themselves. Its power to affect behaviour should be confined to the parties who agreed to it. A person outside the contract, who did not agree to its terms, should not have rights or duties under it.

This reasoning seems sound and represents the general rule of contract law. However, sometimes situations arise where justice or business convenience require that a contract affect the rights of people outside it. In the law of contract, a person who is not a party to a contract is called a **third party** to the contract. In this chapter, we explore the effect contracts have on third parties.

third party a person who is not one of the parties to a contract but is affected by it

The general rule is that a contract does not give any benefits to or impose any obligations on third parties. To win a contract lawsuit, the plaintiff must prove **privity of contract** with the defendant—that is, he must show they are both parties to the same contract.

privity of contract the relationship that exists between parties to a contract

---

ILLUSTRATION 11.1 Privity of Contract

A, a carpenter, owes $4000 to B. A offers to renovate C's kitchen if C promises to pay off A's debt to B. C accepts the offer, and A completes the renovation. A and B have a contract; A and C have a contract; but B and C have no contract with each other. As a third party to the contract for renovation, B cannot enforce C's promise to pay the debt; there is no privity of contract between them.[1] Consequently, if C fails to pay B, B cannot sue C but may still sue A for the debt. A may then sue C for his failure to carry out his promise to pay B and will recover damages of $4000 plus any costs he suffered as a result of B suing him. This result is a simple application of the privity of contract rule and is illustrated in Figure 11.1.

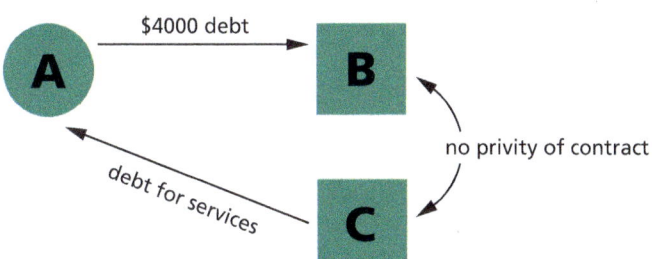

Figure 11.1 Privity and Consideration

Another reason for preventing a third person from suing on a contract is that the third party has not given consideration for the promise. Not only must consideration for a promise be given by a party to the contract, but also it must be given by the party seeking to enforce the promise. As we saw in Chapter 6, signing the contract under seal could solve B's problem.

The privity of contract rule can have harsh consequences when it prevents a third person from enforcing a contract when the whole object was to benefit him. Therefore, a number of exceptions have developed over time. In fact, tort law developed as an exception to the privity of contract rule.

---

[1] *Price v Easton* (1883), 110 ER 518.

Comparison with Rights and Duties in Tort

Liability of Sellers of Goods
We saw in Chapter 10 that a consumer who purchases goods from a retailer receives the benefit of an implied term that the goods are reasonably suited for the purpose for which they are sold. If a person buys a can of salmon that turns out to be poisonous and that seriously harms her, she may successfully sue the retailer for breach of the implied term that the fish was suitable to eat. But members of her family could not sue for breach of contract because the contract of sale was with the buyer, and only she can sue successfully for breach of contract. Other members of the family have no privity of contract with the seller and no rights under the contract. However, they may be able to sue in tort, and statutes may impose liability. New Brunswick has legislation that gives the user of a consumer product a right to sue the seller.[2] As well, Canada's *Consumer Product Safety Act* imposes some duties on sellers that could trigger tort liability.[3]

Liability of Manufacturers
As we saw in Chapter 4, although members of the family have few rights against the retailer, the manufacturer may be liable for negligence. The tort duty of care extends well beyond the parties to the contract to include those persons that a reasonable person could foresee as likely being harmed. The buyer, too, may sue in tort since she has no contract with the manufacturer.[4] In perhaps the most famous case of the 20th century, *Donoghue v Stevenson*,[5] the British House of Lords decided that manufacturers are liable in tort to the consumer for damages caused by their defective products. As noted, New Brunswick's *Consumer Product Warranty and Liability Act* and Canada's *Consumer Product Safety Act* extend product liability throughout the distribution chain.

Builders, engineers, architects, and designers owe a similar tort duty of care to subsequent owners and occupants of the buildings they build.[6] Their tort liability extends beyond the parties to the original building contract. These examples show that tort liability fills a void left by the privity of contract rule.

Tort Liability and Vicarious Performance

Sometimes a business takes on more work than it can complete, or a job requires more specialized skills than it has. In these circumstances, the business may hire a "subcontractor" to complete the excess or specialized work on its behalf. This is **vicarious performance**—finding a third party to perform someone else's contractual obligations. However, the original promisor cannot escape contractual liability for performance of its own contractual obligations by sending a substitute.

Vicarious performance is acceptable provided the contract does not specify personal performance.[7] As in Illustration 11.2, whether a party is expected to perform personally or whether she may employ someone to perform vicariously might not always be clear.

vicarious performance a third party performs contractual obligations on behalf of the promisor who remains responsible for proper performance

---

[2] *Consumer Product Warranty and Liability Act*, SNB 1978, c C-18.1.

[3] *Consumer Product Safety Act*, SC 2010, c 21, ss 6, 7.

[4] Liability for "breach of implied collateral warranty" is sometimes imposed when a representation amounts to a warranty: see *Shanklin Pier Ltd v Detel Products, Ltd*, [1951] 2 KB 854; See also *Cummings v Ford Motor Co of Canada*, [1984] OJ No 43; *Murray v Sperry Rand Corp et al* (1979), 23 OR (2d) 456; for contrary, see *Olsen v Behr Process Corporation*, [2003] BCJ No 627.

[5] [1932] AC 562. The Supreme Court of Canada reiterated its acceptance of the manufacturer duty of care: *Mustapha v Culligan of Canada Ltd*, 2008 SCC 27 at para 6; and cited *Donoghue* most recently in *Rankin (Rankin's Garage & Sales) v JJ*, 2018 SCC 14.

[6] *Winnipeg Condominium Corporation No 36 v Bird Construction Co Ltd*, [1995] 1 SCR 85 at 121.

[7] All contracts with corporations must be carried out by their agents or employees.

> **ILLUSTRATION 11.2 Personal Performance**
>
> A Co. contracts with a public accountant, B, to have its accounts audited. B sends C, a senior accountant, to carry out the audit program. May A Co. object? This is a type of work that can be carried out competently by a qualified accountant and ordinarily would not require B's personal performance unless A Co. had expressly bargained for it. Consequently, the vicarious performance by C is permissible, and A Co. is not entitled to reject the tender of such performance.

Although the third party to the contract who takes over performance does not face contractual liability, he may face tort liability. If an employee commits a tort such as negligence while vicariously performing a contract for his employer, the injured party may sue both the employer for vicarious liability and the employee personally in tort. Since the employer ordinarily has "deeper pockets" than its employee, the injured party almost always sues the employer but may sue the employee as well, in case the court should find that the employer is not liable because the damage did not occur in the course of employment. Therefore, an employer remains liable for defects in vicarious performance not only in contract but also in tort.

> **ILLUSTRATION 11.3 Vicarious Liability**
>
> Suppose that in Illustration 11.2, C does such an inadequate job that he fails to detect a material error in the accounts, and as a result A Co. suffers a loss. A Co. must look to B for damages for breach of contract. However, if C's poor work amounted to negligence, C would be personally liable to A Co. in tort, and B would also be vicariously liable in tort for C's negligence.

As will be discussed later in this chapter,[8] a properly worded exemption clause contained in the contract could protect a third party from tort liability for vicarious performance.[9] Employers often protect themselves from tort and contractual liability by placing an **exemption clause** in a contract. Such a clause restricts the application of the privity of contract rule as it prevents a party with privity from enforcing the terms of the contract and may extend protection beyond the parties to a contract.

exemption clause a clause in a contract that exempts or limits the liability of a party or third parties

> **ILLUSTRATION 11.4 Exemption Clauses**
>
> Some exemption clauses exclude all liability, whereas others limit a party's liability to a fixed amount. An example of an exemption clause excluding liability is as follows:
>
> > The purchaser agrees that the company, its officers, employees, and agents shall not be liable for any claim, demand, cause of action, damage, harm, loss, or injury whatsoever, whether in contract or tort, arising from any activities carried out in furtherance of the performance of this contract.
>
> An example of a clause limiting liability to a fixed amount is as follows:
>
> > The liability of the airline, its agents, and employees for any claim, whether in tort or contract, arising from the loss, delay, or damage of baggage is limited to $50 per bag.

---

[8] See "The Principled Exception" in this chapter and discussion in Chapter 13.

[9] *London Drugs v Kuehne & Nagel International* (1992), 97 DLR (4th) 261. See also *Kirby v Amalgamated Income Limited Partnership*, [2009] BCJ No 1555; *MANB & W Diesel v Kingsway Transports Ltd* (1997), 33 OR (3d) 355.

EXCEPTIONS TO THE PRIVITY OF CONTRACT RULE

Trusts

What Is a Trust? Suppose a mother wishes to provide financial security for her son in case she dies while he is a child. In her will, she sets aside money to be invested and directs that the income be used to care for her son. The fund will require someone to look after it—that is, to invest it and to pay money out for the child's care. The fund is called a **trust**; the person—or perhaps a trust company—who looks after the fund is called a **trustee**. The child is the **beneficiary**. A trust has been defined as "any arrangement whereby property is transferred with the intention that it be administered by a trustee for another's benefit."[10] In this definition and in the example, the trust is created by the transfer of property to the trustee in the will for the benefit of the child.

What if, after the mother dies, the trustee refuses to pay any income for the benefit of the child? We know the trust fund was set up by the mother for the child's benefit and not for that of the trustee. What rights has the child as beneficiary of the trust? Although under common law rules the trustee becomes the legal owner of the trust, the rules of equity recognize that the son has an interest. He is the fund's true owner—the **beneficial owner**—and equity has procedures that may compel a trustee to carry out its duties under the **trust agreement** even though the beneficiary is a third party. A trust may be created not only in a will (on death) but also in any agreement that conveys property to a trustee on the understanding that it will be used for the benefit of a third-party beneficiary.

The trust concept has important applications in business. For example, income trusts are a form of business association where the business transfers its assets to a trustee for the benefit of the unit holders. Unit holders must be able to compel the trustee to comply with the terms of the trust.

A trust is created by operation of law when the creditors of a business convince the court that their debtor is no longer capable of paying its debts as they fall due. The court will order that the property of the bankrupt debtor be transferred to a trustee in bankruptcy who will sell the assets and distribute the proceeds to the creditors.

How Trusts Affect Third Parties: Constructive Trusts How is the concept of a trust related to contracts and the rights of third parties? The beneficiary of a trust is a third party to the trust agreement (contract). The beneficiary is neither the person who created the trust nor the person who is appointed to administer it; yet the rules of equity allow the beneficiary to enforce the terms of the trust.

Sometimes the contract containing the promise is not expressly described as a trust, and the promise may be only one part of a larger deal. In some circumstances, equity recognizes that a person holding property is really a trustee, and others are entitled to a share of the property. A trust of this kind is called a **resulting trust** or a **constructive trust**.[11] When a court accepts this argument, the restrictions of the privity of contract rule do not apply.

trust an arrangement that transfers property to a person who administers it for the benefit of another person

trustee a person or company who administers a trust

beneficiary a person who is entitled to the benefits of a trust or the person entitled to receive insurance monies

beneficial owner a person who, although not the legal owner, may compel the trustee to provide benefits to him

trust agreement the document that conveys property to a trustee to be used for the benefit of a third-party beneficiary

resulting trust a trust relationship recognized when the conduct of the parties demonstrates the intention to hold property for the benefit of the other

constructive trust a trust relationship imposed by the court to prevent a party from being unjustly enriched by keeping property that should benefit another

CASE 11.1 Resulting Trust

A, B, and C entered into a partnership agreement, a term of which stated that if one of the partners should die, his widow would receive a share of the future profits of the firm. When A died, the surviving partners refused to pay a share of the profits to A's widow.

The court held that although the widow was not a party to the partnership agreement, that agreement had created a trust in her favour.[12] Her husband, as promisee of the term in the partnership agreement, had become a trustee of her interest. On his death, his executor became the trustee in his place, and the executor was successful in obtaining the share for the widow.

---

[10] *Black's Law Dictionary*, 10th ed (St. Paul, MN: West Publishing, 2014).

[11] *Kerr v Baranow* 2011 SCC 10 at para 2.

[12] *Re Flavell* (1883), 25 Ch D 89. For an interesting later case, see *Beswick v Beswick*, [1968] AC 58.

Unfortunately, parties to a contract are not likely to be aware of the subtleties of a resulting or constructive trust. As a result these principles are not a reliable means for avoiding the privity of contract rule.

Insurance

Typically, in a contract (or policy) of life insurance, a person pays a premium in exchange for a promise from the insurance company to pay a sum of money on his death to a specified person—a spouse, say—who is not a party to the insurance contract. Each province has a statute that gives a beneficiary the right to force the insurance company to pay out the contract.[13] Similarly, in a contract of automobile insurance, the company may promise to indemnify not only the owner but also anyone driving with his consent. If a person driving with consent injures a pedestrian and is required to pay damages, she may in turn sue the insurance company to recover her loss, even though she was not a party to the insurance contract.[14] Chapter 16 deals with the law of insurance.

The Undisclosed Principal

A further exception to the rule requiring privity of contract occurs when one of the contracting parties, unknown to the other, proves to be an agent of someone else: The person for whom the agent was acting, known as an **undisclosed principal**, may sue or be sued on the contract. The subject is discussed more fully in Chapter 17.

undisclosed principal a contracting party who, unknown to the other party, is represented by an agent

Contracts Concerning Land

The rules of privity of contract do not apply in land law. People who acquire an interest in land are subject to the rights and obligations created in earlier contracts that are recorded on the public registry system. This is true even though the new owner is not a party to the previous contracts. For example, if the owner of land leases it to a tenant who promises to pay rent and keep the property in good repair, and the owner then sells it, the tenant must perform the promises for the new owner. The value of the land on the market would be substantially lowered if the tenant could ignore promises made to the former owner. Similarly, the new owner must respect the tenant's rights to remain on the property until the lease expires. Otherwise, tenants would always be in jeopardy of being evicted when land is sold. Land law will be discussed in Chapters 21, 22, and 23.

Express Language in the Contract

Enurement Clause An **enurement clause** in a contract extends rights under the contract—typically it says the contract will "bind" or "enure to the benefit" of successors, assigns, or heirs. Such a clause could be used to justify "relaxing" the privity of contract rule so that the identified third parties listed in the clause may enforce the rights under the contract.[15] As this type of clause is very common, such an interpretation significantly alters the privity rule.

enurement clause a clause in a contract that extends the rights and benefits to those inheriting from a party, succeeding the party, or taking an assignment from a party

---

[13] See e.g. *Insurance Act*, RSO 1990 c I.8, s 195; RSBC 1996, c 206, s 53; RSNS 1989, c 231, s 197.
[14] See e.g. *Insurance Act*, RSO 1990, c I.8, s 239; *Insurance (Vehicle) Act*, RSBC 2012, c 1, ss 29, 127.
[15] *Brown v Belleville (City)*, 2013 ONCA 148.

CASE 11.2 Intention to Benefit Third Parties

In 1953, a municipal storm drain was built on the property of a farmer, and the municipality agreed to maintain and repair the drain as needed. The agreement was registered on the title to the farmer's land, but after six years the maintenance stopped. The farmer died, and the property was resold many times until the Browns became owners in 2003. The municipality had merged with the City of Belleville. The Browns could not get the City of Belleville to fix the storm drain, so they sued in 2011. Belleville claimed (among other things) the Browns lacked privity of contract and could not enforce the agreement as they were not parties to it; in fact, neither was the City of Belleville. The Ontario Court of Appeal disagreed with the City of Belleville. There was a clause in the agreement stating that the agreement was binding on and for the benefit of the parties "and their respective heirs, administrators, successors, and assigns." The Browns were the "successor" owners of the property who, according to the term of the contract, were intended to benefit from the agreement. This clause justified "relaxing" the privity of contract rule. The City of Belleville was also a successor of the local municipality.[16]

The Principled Exception—Exemption Clauses Typical exemption clauses limit the liability of a party to the contract for damages arising in both breach of contract and tort. When the parties to the contract intend, an exemption clause may also extend that protection to third parties, including agents, employees, subcontractors, consultants, directors, officers, and others involved in the performance of the contract. In this way an exemption clause protects the business from liability for its own breach of contract or negligence, plus any vicarious liability for the torts of employees or other third parties. The Supreme Court of Canada identified two criteria that will determine if a third party may rely on contractual provisions to protect it from liability.[17] Two questions are asked:

1. Did the parties to the contract intend to extend the protection to the third party claiming it?
2. Are the activities of the third party within the scope of the contract generally and the exemption clause in particular?[18]

If the intention of the parties is to extend protection to the particular third party, and the type of work is part of the contract performance and within the scope of the clause, the exemption clause will protect the third party from liability. Application of this exception will vary depending upon the facts of each case.

CASE 11.3 Employee Protection

London Drugs contracted with Kuehne & Nagel to store a new piece of equipment worth $7500. The standard form storage contract contained an exemption clause limiting liability to $40 per item damaged. Two employees of Kuehne & Nagel dropped the piece of equipment. London Drugs sued Kuehne & Nagel and both employees. The Supreme Court held that the employees were also protected by the contract's exemption clause. The language of the standard form contract was intended to apply to employees, and the employees were acting in the course of employment.[19]

principled exception allows third parties to rely upon a contractual exemption clause when the parties to the contract intended to include them and their activities come within the scope of the contract and the exemption clause

This exception to the privity rule is sometimes called the **principled exception**, and it was developed because courts felt that the privity of contract rule should not stand in the way of commercial reality and justice.[20]

---

[16] *Ibid* at paras 80–111.

[17] *Fraser River Pile & Dredge Ltd v Can-Dive Services Ltd* (1999), 176 DLR (4th) 257.

[18] *Ibid* at para 32.

[19] *London Drugs, supra* note 9.

[20] *Ibid* at paras 212, 258, 262

INTERNATIONAL ISSUE

Has Privity of Contract Lost Its Relevance?

Exceptions to the privity of contract principle allow some non-parties to enforce the obligations of a contract. In most of Canada, these exceptions are limited to specific types of contracts or specific clauses with identified non-party beneficiaries. As noted, insurance contracts and trust agreements are such exceptions. In Case 11.3,[21] the Supreme Court of Canada extended the protection of contractual exemption clauses to non-parties identified by the exemption clause, and the Ontario Court of Appeal allowed successors to sue to enforce a contract in *Brown v City of Belleville*.[22]

Some jurisdictions have made sweeping changes to the privity of contract rule. New Brunswick's privity of contract rules were first changed with the passage of the *Consumer Product Warranty and Liability Act* in 1978.[23] Then, in 1994, the privity rule was completely abolished in favour of the identified beneficiary concept: Section 4(1) of the *Law Reform Act* reads:

> A person who is not a party to a contract but who is identified by or under the contract as being intended to receive some performance or forbearance under it may, unless the contract provides otherwise, enforce that performance or forbearance by a claim for damages or otherwise.[24]

An intended beneficiary's right to sue has been recognized since 1859 in the United States. In *Lawrence v Fox*,[25] Fox promised Halley he would pay Halley's debt. When Fox failed to make the payment, the New York Court of Appeal allowed the unpaid creditor (Lawrence) to sue Fox directly.

In 1999, England passed the *Contracts (Rights of Third Parties) Act, 1999*,[26] which allows non-parties to enforce any contractual obligation if the contract benefits them or specifically authorizes them to do so. Similar legislation exists in Australia and New Zealand.

Questions to Consider

1. Should all provinces abandon the privity of contract rule in favour of a third-party beneficiary rule?
2. Should the law make a distinction between an intended beneficiary and an incidental beneficiary?
3. Should the law make a distinction between defendants and plaintiffs?

Sources: R.L. Miller and G.A. Jentz, *Business Law Today*, standard ed, 7th ed (Florence, KY: South-Western College/West, 2006) at 325–44; J. Edelman, "Taking Promises Seriously" (2007) 45(3) *Canadian Business Law Journal* 399–413; M.H. Ogilivie, "Re-defining Privity of Contract: *Brown v Belleville (City)*," (2015) 52(3) Alta L Rev 731.

ASSIGNMENT OF RIGHTS

Sometimes one party is not willing to wait for the other party to perform the contract and wants to receive his benefit immediately. The party may need money now. In such cases, the impatient party may transfer the unperformed right or benefit of the contract to a third party who is willing to wait for performance. This is known as an *assignment* and is an important exception to the privity of contract rule.

The Nature of an Assignment

Businesses often make use of assignments to secure financing from a lender by assigning the right to collect their accounts receivable to the lender in exchange for credit now. Only rights or benefits may be assigned, not contractual obligations or liabilities. Assignments usually involve two contracts: The first contract creates the unperformed right, which is subsequently assigned to a third party in the second contract.

---

[21] *Ibid.*

[22] *Brown*, *supra* note 15.

[23] *Supra* note 2. This Act entitled non-parties to sue for breach of the statutory warranties implied into a contract of sale. The exception is not limited to consumers but includes any organization involved in the chain of distribution, such as retailers, wholesalers, and importers.

[24] *Law Reform Act*, RSNB 2011, c 184, s 4(1).

[25] 20 NY 268 (1859).

[26] 1999, c 31 (Eng.).

> **ILLUSTRATION 11.5 Promise to Pay**
>
> A Ltd., a building contractor, has just completed a building for B. Under the terms of their building contract, B still owes A Ltd. $10 000, to be paid one month after the completion of the building. In a second contract, A Ltd. purchases $12 000 worth of materials from X Corp. In exchange for the materials, A Ltd. agrees to pay $2000 in cash and assigns to X Corp. the rights to the $10 000 still owing to A Ltd. under the building contract. As a result, X Corp. collects the $10 000 directly from B when the debt falls due.

assignor a party that assigns its rights under a contract to a third party

assignee a third party to whom rights under a contract have been assigned

assignment the transfer by a party of its unperformed rights under a contract to a third party

In Illustration 11.5, the contractor A Ltd. is the **assignor** of its right to payment of $10 000 from B, the promisor in the building contract. A Ltd. assigns the right to payment to X Corp., a third party to the building contract but the **assignee** in the materials contract. The materials contract is an **assignment**. Provided B receives notice of the assignment, then B must perform for the assignee X Corp. instead of for the original party, A Ltd. X Corp. now stands in the place of A Ltd.

Contractual rights are valuable and are considered a type of personal property. The $10 000 still owing under the building contract in Illustration 11.5 is an example of this form of intangible personal property. Its value is obvious. Intangible property differs from tangible property, such as jewellery or furniture, which may be possessed physically. Tangible property has a concrete existence, whereas a right to demand performance of a contract has no concrete existence—it is valuable only because it is enforceable in the courts. The rights to intangible property—to things that have value only because they may be enforced by action in the courts—are called **choses in action**. The unpaid $10 000 in Illustration 11.5 is a chose in action. The rights to tangible property that may be possessed physically are known as **choses in possession**. There are many types of choses in action, including patents, copyrights, stocks, bonds, funds deposited in a bank account, rights to collect the proceeds of an insurance policy, rights of action against persons who have caused injury, and rights under contracts generally.

choses in action rights to intangible property such as patents, stocks, and contracts that may be enforced in the courts

choses in possession rights to tangible property that may be possessed physically

> **CHECKLIST**
>
> ## Third Parties Who May Play a Role in a Contract
>
> There are many ways in which a third party to the original contract may acquire rights under it or become subject to duties to perform:
>
> - through vicarious performance, such as an employee carrying out the obligations of one of the parties to the contract
> - when an exemption clause applies to a third party
> - through a trust where a trustee confers benefits on a third party
> - through an insurance contract under which the insurer promises to pay a third party in the event that a particular risk occurs
> - when an agent makes a contract on behalf of an undisclosed principal
> - when a party acquires an interest in land and becomes subject to rights and duties owed to a third person previously registered against the land
> - when contractual rights are assigned to a third party

The Importance of Assignments

Choses in action are used to accumulate wealth such as savings in bank accounts and the ownership of shares and bonds. These assets are put to work as capital of corporations. In other words, this device links personal saving to business investment. In some less-developed countries, where citizens have little confidence in their legal system, it has been a major problem to persuade individuals who own tangible property to abandon their preference for investment in gold, jewels, and real estate and to accept a portfolio of mortgages, shares, and bonds as an alternative form of property. As a result, active capital markets in these countries have been slow to develop.

This chapter addresses the assignment of contractual rights generally; a discussion of the specific features of such choses in action as mortgages, shares, bonds, and negotiable instruments is reserved for later chapters.

The Role of Equity

An assignment of rights (choses in action) and a sale of goods (choses in possession) are similar. Each involves the transfer of an asset to another party. In an assignment, the subject matter of the transfer is an intangible asset—an unperformed contractual right; in a sale, the subject matter of the transfer is the ownership in goods. The first rules about how to complete an assignment of contractual rights were developed by the courts of equity and were called "equitable" assignments.

EQUITABLE ASSIGNMENTS

Equitable assignments require only that a clear intention to **assign** all or part of a contractual benefit be shown either orally or in writing. The assignee receives the benefit of the contract from the promisor. If legal action is necessary to collect from the promisor, the assignee must make the assignor a party as well. All three parties—the assignee, the assignor, and the promisor—must be part of the legal action. This is because if an assignor assigns part of her rights only, she remains vitally interested in the result of any action by the assignee against the promisor. If the court should decide that the promisor is not bound to perform any part of his obligations, its decision would adversely affect the assignor as well as the assignee.

assign transfer to another person outside the contract

ILLUSTRATION 11.6 Part of the Benefit

A owes B $10 000 under a contract. At the same time, B owes $6000 to X Finance Co. B assigns $6000 of her account receivable from A to satisfy X. Subsequently, A refuses to pay X; X sues A for the $6000.

If the court were to decide that A was not bound to pay anything on the debt because, say, the contract between A and B was within the *Statute of Frauds* and there was an insufficient memorandum of it, B would also be affected for she could not claim her remaining $4000 of the debt either.

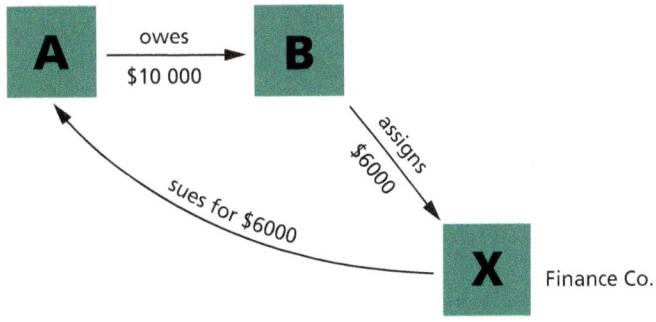

Assignment of Part of a Debt

In an assignment of part of a debt, as in Illustration 11.6, both the assignee and the assignor are equally anxious that the court find the debtor (that is, the promisor) liable. The assignor B must have her own chance to argue and to introduce evidence. For example, she might well have in her possession a memorandum sufficient to comply with the *Statute of Frauds*, and her evidence might be decisive in holding the debtor liable.

Similarly, in an action brought by B against A, the court would require that X Finance Co. also be made a party.

For the purposes of Illustration 11.7, assume the assignor assigns only part of its rights; the promisor is willing to perform his obligation, but he does not know what part he should perform for the benefit of the assignee and what part for the benefit of the assignor.

ILLUSTRATION 11.7 Competing Claims

A owes $100 000 to B Inc., due in 12 months. B Inc. needs short-term financing and borrows $80 000 from X Bank, repayable in 12 months. Under their loan agreement, B Inc. gives X Bank a conditional assignment of its account receivable from A as security for repayment of the loan under the following terms: As long as B Inc. pays the interest on its loan every three months, the bank will not be entitled to notify A of the assignment; but if B Inc. fails to pay the interest or fails to pay the $80 000 on the due date, the bank may advise A to pay it that sum plus unpaid interest, in reduction of his debt to B Inc. In other words, the assignment is conditional upon the default of the borrower, B Inc.

If, at the end of the year, the bank notifies A that B Inc. has assigned his account and demands that A pay the bank, A cannot afford to do so until he has verified the default and the amount owing. He must check with B Inc. Suppose B Inc. claims it has paid the bank $60 000 of the debt. A is in a quandary: He is aware of the competing claims and fears that if he pays one party and guesses wrong, the other may sue him successfully and collect the amount in dispute a second time. In such a case, A should hand over the sum claimed by the bank to the court as custodian and let B Inc. and the bank settle their dispute before a judge.

An equitable assignment also occurs when the subject of the assignment is an aggregate of book debts (accounts receivables) whose balances fluctuate over time.

ILLUSTRATION 11.8 Fluctuating Value

Fribble Corp. owes $160 000 to Tower Bank under a demand loan. Fribble is required to make regular monthly payments on the loan and to provide the bank with semi-annual financial statements. Fribble reported substantial losses six months ago and was slow in making two subsequent interest payments. The bank threatened to call the loan unless it received additional security. Fribble then gave the bank a conditional assignment of its accounts receivable, including several large accounts, some of them running to tens of thousands of dollars.

Fribble receives frequent payments on these accounts from its customers and also ships its products to them from time to time so that the account balances fluctuate substantially. Fribble promised to make its monthly interest payments without fail; otherwise, the bank would call the loan and notify Fribble's customers of the assignment.

In these circumstances the assignment is conditional not only because it depends on a future event (default by Fribble) but also because the value of the accounts receivable varies according to the state of accounts between Fribble and each of its customers at any given moment.

In Illustrations 11.6, 11.7, and 11.8, all the parties have a vital interest in the assignment and must necessarily be bound by the same court decision. The requirement of equity that the assignor and the debtor(s) be made parties to the assignee's action is fair in cases where the assignor retains an interest in the contract.

STATUTORY ASSIGNMENTS

Reform

In many business transactions, an assignor does not want to retain any rights under the contract; he assigns them entirely to the assignee, and there is no need for him to remain involved in subsequent court actions. Such a requirement only increases the expense of the action by bringing in a party who has no real interest.

Legislation removed this requirement. An assignee may sue the promisor without joining the assignor in the lawsuit provided that:

(a) the assignment was absolute (unconditional and complete),
(b) it was in writing, and
(c) the promisor received notice of it in writing.

Most of the provinces in Canada have passed statutes setting out these requirements.[27] An assignment that complies with these requirements is known as a **statutory assignment**. Any other assignment is called an **equitable assignment**. Note that the statute did not change the effect of assignment—allowing an assignee to enforce the contract; it merely provided a streamlined procedure for hearing actions that meet the requirements laid down by statute.

statutory assignment an assignment that complies with statutory provisions enabling the assignee to sue the other party without joining the assignor to the action

equitable assignment an assignment other than a statutory assignment

The Requirements of the Statute

It is not always convenient in business to meet the requirements of the statute, and many assignments remain equitable rather than statutory. For instance, with regard to requirement (a), an assignment is not complete if a balance remains to be paid to the assignor after the assignee is paid—the assignor still has an interest in the contract. Nor is an assignment unconditional when the amount assigned varies according to the state of accounts between the assignor and his debtor; this situation exists when the balance of the account assigned fluctuates because the assignor continues to sell goods or services on credit to the debtor (the customer) or the debtor reduces the balance assigned by making payments on account to the assignor. The balance assigned is not fixed and may need to be verified from the assignor's records. In neither of these situations is the assignment absolute.

The need for (b)—writing in support of the statutory assignment—is reasonable. If the assignment were oral, the assignee would have to call the assignor as a witness to prove the assignment was actually made. Even then oral recollections can be unreliable and imprecise. In most cases, a written assignment signed by the assignor at the time of the assignment is the most reliable evidence. Only if there is a rare allegation of serious fraud, such as forgery, will further evidence be required to prove the assignment. Similarly, (c)—the requirement that the promisor receive the notice of assignment in writing—simplifies proving that the promisor knew of the assignment. It is good business practice and common sense to send written notice by registered letter when important rights are in question in any transaction.

NOTICE TO THE PROMISOR

The Effect of Notice on the Promisor

To be effective, all assignments require that notice be given to the promisor, but that does not mean the promisor's consent is required. A promisor ignores a notice of an

---

[27] See e.g. *Conveyancing and Law of Property Act*, RSO 1990, c C.34, s 53; *Law and Equity Act*, RSBC 1996, c 253, s 36; *Judicature Act*, RSA 2000, c J-2, s 20; RSNS 1989, c 240, s 43(5). The statutory provisions are somewhat different in certain provinces. See e.g. *Choses in Action Act*, RSS 1978, c C-11, s 2 and the *Law of Property Act*, CCSM c L90, ss 31(1), (5).

assignment at his own risk. Confronted with a demand for payment from one who claims to be an assignee, the promisor should, of course, require proof of the assignment to protect himself against a possible fraud, but once he has had an opportunity to satisfy himself that there has been an assignment, he must make further payments to the assignee. If he continues to make payments to his original creditor, he can be sued by the assignee and required to pay the amount a second time.

> **CASE 11.4 Impact of Notice**
>
> Brian Wholesalers Ltd. buys a large quantity of goods on credit from Akron Manufacturing Inc. and defaults payment. Brian offers to pay Akron by assigning certain of its accounts receivable owed by retail merchants with excellent credit ratings. Akron agrees to this settlement and takes an absolute assignment of the debts, the largest of which is owed by Woolridge's Department Store. Akron sends Woolridge's a notice, signed by an officer of Brian, stating that the account has been assigned to Akron, and encloses a request that Woolridge's pay Akron. Woolridge's inadvertently ignores the notice and pays Brian, which shortly afterward becomes bankrupt. Akron sues Woolridge's for payment of the debt again. Woolridge's paid Brian at its peril after receiving valid notice of the assignment, and Woolridge must pay Akron again.[28]

The Effect of Notice from Multiple Assignees

The ability to assign contractual rights is an important exception to the doctrine of privity of contract. Someone other than the original party to a contract is permitted to claim the benefit of rights under the contract. Indeed, more than one person may claim to be the assignee of the same right. An unscrupulous creditor might sell the right to collect the same debt to two different persons by assigning it to each of them. The debtor is then faced with two demands for payment. Which of the two innocent assignees is entitled to payment? And which is left only with an action for fraud against the assignor?

The law is clear. The assignee who first gave notice to the debtor is the one entitled to payment. This rule, like the rule that the debtor must receive notice of assignment before it affects him, offers the only fair treatment to the debtor. Otherwise, a debtor would be in a very insecure position, never being sure when he makes payment whether someone else to whom he should have paid the money may turn up later. An assignee who receives his assignment first might be slow in notifying the debtor, and the second assignee might notify the debtor first.

The second assignee is still entitled to payment by the debtor—unless he knows of the prior assignment at the time of the assignment to him. If he knows of that prior assignment, he is a party to the fraud. He cannot take payment ahead of the first assignee without becoming liable to him. In order to determine who is entitled to the debtor's performance, the court must ascertain the validity and extent of every right claimed by contending assignees.

Mercifully, the debtor need perform his obligation only once—provided he acts prudently when it is unclear whose claim should prevail. As is suggested in Illustration 11.7, it may be necessary to pay the money into court and leave the court to decide the validity and extent of the claims by contending assignees.

THE ASSIGNEE'S TITLE

An Assignee "Takes Subject to the Equities"

subject to the equities The assignee takes title subject to any rights the promisor has against the assignor

A fundamental rule is that an assignee can never acquire a better right to sue the promisor than the assignor had. In legal terms, the assignee's claim is "**subject to the equities**": Her claim is subject to any rights the promisor had against the assignor before the promisor received notice of the assignment. Any valid defence the promisor had against the assignor, with whom he originally contracted, will also protect him from liability to the assignee.

---

[28] See *Brandt's Sons & Co v Dunlop Rubber Co Ltd*, [1905] AC 454.

If a person takes an assignment of rights under a contract originally induced by the fraudulent misrepresentation of the assignor, the assignee will have no better chance to enforce her claim than if she had been the perpetrator of the fraud herself. In other words, if a debtor is the victim of fraudulent misrepresentation, the contract remains voidable at his option despite any assignment of the contractual rights. (The debtor cannot, however, sue the assignee for damages for the tort of deceit. He must sue the assignor, the person actually guilty of the fraud.) In addition to fraudulent misrepresentation, a promisor may use as any defence against an assignee mistake, undue influence, duress, and the fact that he received no consideration for his promise.

The position of an assignee is in marked contrast to the position of a person who obtains title to goods under a similarly flawed contract. For instance, we have seen in Chapter 8 that in spite of his fraud, a person may obtain title to goods so that, in turn, he may pass on valid title to a subsequent innocent purchaser, who may retain the goods against the claim of the person fraudulently persuaded to part with them.[29] But a person who obtains contractual rights by fraud does not, by assigning these rights, give an innocent assignee the right to enforce them against the defrauded promisor. Therefore, an innocent assignee is in a much more vulnerable position than is an innocent purchaser of goods.

The Right to Set Off

An important defence of a promisor is his right to **set off** any debt owed to him by the assignor at the time the assignment is made.

set off the right of a promisor to deduct an existing debt owed to him by the promisee

ILLUSTRATION 11.9 Outstanding Amounts Owing

A is employed by B at a salary of $550 per week, payable at noon Saturdays when the business closes. On Thursday, A borrows $200 from B. On Saturday, A fails to appear at work on time. When he telephones an hour late, they argue, and B informs A that he is fired and tells him not to bother coming back. On Monday, A sues B for $550 in the small claims court. B may reduce the amount owning to A by both the $200 loan owed by A and the $50 A would have earned had he come to work on Saturday morning. After the set off the court judgment against B will only be for $300.

Suppose that, instead of suing B, A had assigned his claim for salary to his neighbour X for $500. X would take the claim, subject to the equities between A and B. Even though X did not know of B's loan to A and of A's failure to work on Saturday, B would be able to set off these amounts if X sued him: X would recover $300 from B, the same amount as A could recover.[30]

Until an assignee gives the promisor notice of the assignment, acts of either the assignor or the promisor or their agents may prejudice the assignee's rights. So it is important for an assignee to give notice as soon as possible. If he delays, his rights may deteriorate.

ILLUSTRATION 11.10 Timing of Notice

Williams owes Mehta $900. Mehta assigns the debt to Young on May 1. Young neglects to notify Williams, and on May 11, Williams, unaware of the assignment, pays Mehta $300 on account. Because of her failure to notify Williams, Young, the assignee, may now recover from Williams only $600 and must look to Mehta for the $300 already paid.

---

[29] This result follows because fraud makes the contract voidable, not void. See Chapter 8 and *King's Norton Metal Co v Edridge* (1879), 14 TLR 98; *Lewis v Averay*, [1971] 3 All ER 907.

[30] Provincial legislation may provide that an assignment of wages, or any portion, to secure payment of a debt is invalid. See e.g. *Wages Act*, RSO 1990, c W.1, s 7(7); *Assignment of Wages Act*, RSS 1978, c A-30, s 3; *Labour Standards Code, 1972*, RSNS 1989, c 246, s 89.

When a creditor—a building contractor, say—assigns rights to partial payment before it has completed performance, the assignee may be subject to an additional risk. Even when the assignee has given notice to the debtor (the party entitled to completion of the project), the debtor may be able to use defences based upon developments after the time of notice. The assignor's (builder's) subsequent failure to complete performance may cause the debtor damages, which he can set off against the assignee's claim. In other words, an assignee's rights under a contract that is still incomplete are imperfect and subject to proper completion of the contract.[31]

A general assignment of accounts receivable is an important business device for securing credit. The common law provinces each have statutes making such assignments void against the assignor's creditors unless the assignment is registered in a public office where its terms are available for inspection. The purpose of these statutes is to protect prospective creditors. They may inspect the registry to discover whether some assignee has a prior claim against the assets of a person who has applied to them for credit. The reasons for providing public notice are considered in Chapters 23 and 28.

Ethical Issue   Credit Cards

Credit cards have become one of the most common forms of payment for goods and services. There are several ways of setting up a credit card arrangement and organizing the legal relationships among the parties. Three-party credit card transactions (except when the card is issued by the merchant itself, such as a department store) are assignments of contractual rights. A business accepts a credit card and assigns to the credit card company its own right to payment for goods or services purchased on credit. The credit card issuer pays the business for goods purchased with the credit card. The customer, by entering into a contract with the credit card company, consents to the assignment and agrees to pay the credit card issuer, rather than paying the business directly.

The credit card industry is well financed by charging businesses a small percentage of credit card sales (2–10 percent, depending on volume), by charging cardholders an annual fee, and by collecting interest on unpaid balances. Retailers are subject to agreements that prevent them from surcharging credit card transactions to cover this fee. When considering the anti-competitive nature of the prohibition, one scholar wrote:

> This means that businesses that accept credit cards are forced to charge all customers the same higher prices in order to cover the costs of accepting credit card transactions. As a result, non-credit consumers (food stamps, cash, checks, debit) end up subsidizing credit card consumers and, indirectly subsidizing the entire credit card industry.[32]

Australian legislation allows businesses to charge credit card customers a higher price than customers paying cash. In an attempt to assist both merchants and consumers, the Canadian government (Financial Consumer Agency of Canada) produced a code of conduct for the credit and debit card industry.

Questions to Consider

1. Should cash customers be charged the same price as credit card customers when credit card customers cost the retailer more?
2. Why should credit card companies get to collect fees from both the customer and the retailer?
3. Who should bear the loss in the case of online credit card fraud: the consumer, the retailer, or the credit card issuer?

Sources: A.G. Guest and Eva Lomnicka, *An Introduction to the Law of Credit and Security* (London: Sweet & Maxwell, 1978) at para 366; E. Warren, "Antitrust Issues in Credit Card Merchant Restraint Rules," *Discussion Paper for The Tobin Project Risk Policy Working Group*, May 6, 2007; Financial Consumer Agency of Canada, https://www.canada.ca/en/financial-consumer-agency/services/merchants/rights-merchant.html.

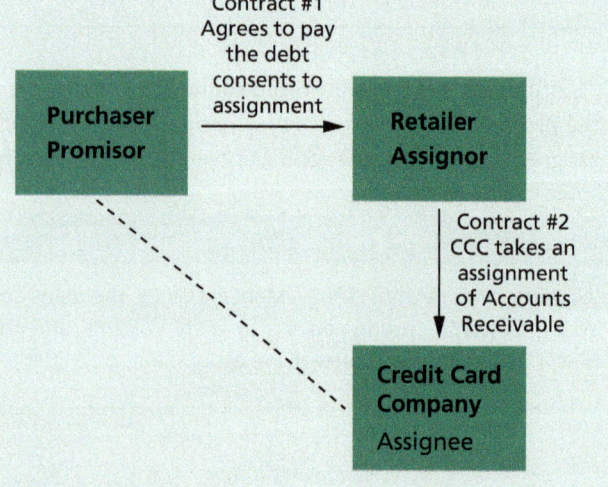

---

[31] *Young v Kitchen* (1878), 3 Ex D 127.

[32] E. Warren, "Antitrust Issues in Credit Card Merchant Restraint Rules," *Discussion Paper for The Tobin Project Risk Policy Working Group*, May 6, 2007 at para 2.

ASSIGNMENTS BY OPERATION OF LAW

Death

When a person dies, the law automatically assigns his rights and obligations under outstanding contracts to a personal representative. If the deceased person leaves a will naming a representative, the representative is called an **executor**. If the deceased failed to name an executor in the will (or the executor refuses to assume the position) or leaves no will (that is, dies **intestate**), the court will appoint a personal representative called an administrator. A representative does not have to perform a contract requiring personal services; the skill of the deceased cannot be demanded of the representative.

The task of an executor or **administrator** is to pay all just claims against the deceased's estate, to complete performance of any outstanding contractual obligations of the deceased not requiring personal skill, to pursue all claims the deceased had against others, and then to distribute the assets according to the will—or, in the case of an intestate person, to distribute them to the heirs according to statutory provisions.[33]

> **executor** the personal representative of a deceased person named in his or her will
>
> **intestate** when a person dies without leaving a will
>
> **administrator** the personal representative of a person who dies intestate

Bankruptcy

A person carrying on business who becomes insolvent may realize his position is hopeless and may voluntarily apply for bankruptcy proceedings to avoid further loss to his creditors and injury to his name. Or it may be creditors who begin bankruptcy proceedings against a reluctant debtor by petitioning the court for an order known as a **receiving order**. If the creditors satisfy the court that their debtor is insolvent, the court will declare him bankrupt and appoint a licensed trustee to take charge of his property. Then the duty of the trustee is to liquidate the assets and settle the creditors' claims.

> **receiving order** a court order to commence bankruptcy proceedings

Bankruptcy is covered in Chapter 29. The relationship between a bankrupt person and the trustee in bankruptcy is one of assignment. In the proceedings, the court assigns to the trustee the bankrupt person's assets, which include contractual rights and liabilities.[34]

Assignments resulting from death and from bankruptcy proceedings started by creditors differ from other assignments in that they are involuntary; they take place "by operation of law." An individual's affairs are seldom completely in good order when either of these events occurs, and an assignment creates an artificial extension of the assignor's legal existence until his affairs can be wound up.

NEGOTIABLE INSTRUMENTS

Their Nature and Uses

Chapter 19 examines the law affecting negotiable instruments in more detail. However, since negotiable instruments are a special type of assignment, it is important to review their differences here. A **negotiable instrument**—including a bank draft, promissory note, or cheque—is a written document containing a promise, express or implied,[35] to pay a specific sum of money to a named person or to the "bearer" (the person in possession of the document).

> **negotiable instrument** a written contract containing a promise, express or implied, to pay a specific sum of money to a designated person or to "bearer"

---

[33] The assets of an intestate person will be distributed to the heirs as set out in provincial statutes. See e.g. *Estates Administration Act*, RSO 1990, c E.22; *Intestate Succession Act*, RSNS 1989, c 236, s 153; *Estate Administration Act*, RSBC 1996, c 122, Part 7.

[34] A licensed trustee may, however, with the permission of inspectors appointed by the creditors, disclaim any lease of property of the bankrupt debtor: *Bankruptcy and Insolvency Act*, RSC 1985, c B-3 (as amended), s 30(1)(k).

[35] According to the wording of a cheque, the drawer does not directly promise to pay its amount, but she does promise by implication that sufficient funds will be available in her bank account for the bank (the drawee) to take and pay the cheque when it is presented.

Usually, a negotiable instrument is created to satisfy a payment obligation in a prior contract. A buyer delivers a negotiable instrument in payment for goods or services received. But delivery of the instrument does not complete the promisor's obligation. If he does not honour the instrument when it falls due and is presented to be paid, the promisee has the choice of suing under the original contract or suing for failure to honour the instrument. The negotiable instrument creates its own obligation to pay separate from the contract that triggered it. Often a promisee chooses to sue on the negotiable instrument because it is easier.

The unique aspects of the law of negotiable instruments arise when a promisee assigns an instrument to a third party.

Negotiability Compared with Assignability

negotiation the process of assigning a negotiable instrument

endorse sign one's name on a negotiable instrument

holder a party who acquires a negotiable instrument from the transferor

The process of assigning a negotiable instrument is known as **negotiation**. A promisee or payee of an instrument may negotiate it in one of two ways. If the instrument is payable to bearer, he need only deliver it to a third party; if the instrument is payable in his name, he must **endorse** his name upon it and then deliver it. Negotiation is really a special type of assignment in which the new **holder** of the instrument acquires from the transferor (named payee) the rights and benefits of the instrument.

In a sense, negotiation is a privileged type of assignment that, for reasons of business convenience, is freed from the restrictions that apply to an ordinary assignment of contractual rights. It differs from an assignment of rights generally in the following important respects.

Notice to the Promisor
As noted, notice takes two forms for regular assignments: First, written notice is necessary before an assignee may take advantage of a statutory assignment; and second, notice protects an assignee against the risk of the promisor being unaware of the assignment and paying the assignor or other assignees. However, notice is not necessary for the transfer of a negotiable instrument—indeed, it is irrelevant—because the promisor is liable to pay only one person, the holder of the instrument at the time of payment. Even if the promisor receives notice of the assignment, neither she nor her bank will pay the assignee unless and until the assignee presents the instrument. The promisor pays her debt only once—to the holder of the instrument at the time of the demand and in exchange for the instrument. In effect she pays for the return of her negotiable instrument. The legal right to be paid is embedded in the document itself so that the right moves in unison with the physical document and will be paid as directed by the instructions on the document when it is presented by the holder.[36]

ILLUSTRATION 11.11 Notice Not Relevant

Steele receives his monthly paycheque of $3500 from Union Foundry Co. Ltd. He negotiates it to Comfy Furniture Mart for $2700 worth of furniture and $800 cash. Steele then falsely tells his employer that he has inadvertently destroyed the cheque by throwing it into the garbage, and he persuades Union to pay him a second time. When Comfy presents the original cheque for payment, Union must honour it even though Comfy gave no notice of the assignment.

If instead Steele had assigned to Comfy a claim against Union for arrears of wages (a contractual right not represented by any negotiable instrument) and if Comfy did not immediately notify Union of the assignment, Union could defeat the claim of Comfy, as assignee, by establishing that it had already paid Steele before receiving notice.

---

[36] *Bills of Exchange Act*, RSC 1985, c B-4, ss 16, 84, 86, 126; *Canada Trustco Mortgage Co v Canada*, 2011 SCC 36 at paras 21, 25, 27, 40, 51.

Defences of the Promisor A person who writes a cheque in payment for goods may be able to deny payment of the cheque when he discovers the vendor has tricked him. If sued by that original vendor, his defence will prevail. However, defences available against the vendor originally named as payee on the cheque will not work against a subsequent holder of the cheque. An assignee for value of a negotiable instrument may succeed in an action against the promisor where the assignor himself would not have succeeded. Even when a promisor is induced to sign a negotiable instrument because of fraud or undue influence, he may be sued successfully by a subsequent innocent holder who has given consideration for the instrument. This rule does not apply to consumers—consumer negotiable instruments remain subject to the equities.[37]

A defrauder may transfer enforceable rights under a negotiable instrument in much the same way that she can pass valid title to goods to an innocent purchaser. Similarly, a person who has given a negotiable instrument in payment for an illegal consideration loses the defence of illegality against an innocent holder of the instrument for value. This is a key difference from an ordinary assignment of rights discussed earlier in this chapter. The regular assignee never acquires a better right than the assignor had; the debtor retains her defences against all assignees.

ILLUSTRATION 11.12 Holder in Due Course

Bacchus contracted with Hermes for the illegal transportation of liquor into Saskatchewan and gave Hermes his cheque for $2000 for services rendered. The police discovered and confiscated the liquor, and Bacchus then asked his bank to stop payment on the cheque to Hermes.

In the meantime, Hermes had endorsed the cheque to pay a debt to an innocent trade creditor, Argus, who knew nothing of the illegal contract for which the cheque had been issued. Argus learned that payment of the cheque had been stopped when he attempted to cash it at the bank. Argus sued Bacchus on the dishonoured instrument.

Bacchus might have used the defence of illegality successfully in an action brought against him by the party with whom he contracted—Hermes. But he must pay the holder of the cheque, Argus, if (as appears probable) Argus can prove he took the instrument unaware of its illegal origin and gave value for it.

By contrast, if Hermes's claim for $2000 against Bacchus had remained simply in the form of an account receivable, no one to whom Hermes might have assigned the account receivable would have obtained a better right to collect it than Hermes himself had.

An exception to this principle exists for consumers. Consumer negotiable instruments (except for cheques) remain subject to any defence or set off that the consumer has against the original seller.[38]

Form of Action A holder of a negotiable instrument can sue in her own name; it is not necessary for her to join in the action of any of the other parties who have signed the instrument along the way.

Commercial Importance of Negotiability

For hundreds of years, businesses have benefited from the advantages of negotiable instruments as a special class of readily assignable promises, free from the formalities and many of the risks of an ordinary assignment of contractual rights. The law reduces

---

[37] See the *Bills of Exchange Act*, RSC 1985, c B-4, s 191, restricting the rights of finance companies to assert the status of a holder in due course. See also the *Business Practices and Consumer Protection Act*, SBC 2004, c 2, s 15.

[38] *Bills of Exchange Act, ibid*, ss 190–1.

the possibility of abuse through fraud, undue influence, duress, and illegality by requiring a holder of a negotiable instrument to show that he was unaware of the origin of a tainted instrument and that he or some previous holder of the instrument must have given value for it.[39]

Modern banking practice is based upon the relatively secure position of an innocent holder for value of a negotiable instrument. Banks are able to cash cheques or accept them for deposit without exhaustive inquiry into the background of the transactions out of which they arose, since, as innocent holders for value, they are immune from the earlier flawed nature of the transaction. Without such a rule, banking would be much slower and less reliable for business and the public generally.

Despite these advantages, negotiable instruments are losing their place in low value transactions and being replaced by debit and credit card transactions. Their heavy dependence on the paper and physical world means they are now usually restricted to high-value transactions.

Currency

Money is a special type of negotiable instrument authorized by statute and designed to circulate with maximum ease.[40] Therefore, rules of transferability, notice, and negotiation are even more relaxed for this type of negotiable instrument to make it easy for currency to change hands quickly.

CHECKLIST
Principles of Assignment

Equitable Assignments

- partial or conditional in nature; promisor must receive notice of assignment before obligated to pay
- assignor must participate in any lawsuit
- subject to the equities

Statutory Assignments

- provincial statutory requirements: complete (not partial), unconditional, and written
- promisor to receive notice of transfer before being obligated to pay
- assignor need not participate in any lawsuit
- subject to the equities

Negotiable Instruments

- federal statutory requirements: *Bills of Exchange Act* applicable to promissory notes, cheques, bills of exchange
- promisor need not receive notice before obligated to pay
- previous holders need not participate in any lawsuit
- not subject to the equities (except for consumers)
- currency special rules

---

[39] The requirements are somewhat more technical than described here: the holder must be a holder in due course. See Chapter 19.

[40] *Currency Act*, RSC 1985, c C-52; *Bank of Canada Act*, RSC 1985, c. s 25 (notes that are a first charge on the assets of the Bank of Canada).

Strategies to Manage the Legal Risks

Every person responsible for performance of a contract should be named as a party to it. Persons wishing to enforce the terms of a contract should sign it under seal so any lack of consideration is not a barrier to enforcement. If it is important that only the original parties complete the transaction, then the contract should include a clause that specifies personal performance and another clause that prohibits assignment of any rights under the contract. Alternatively, assignment could be allowed with prior written consent of the other party. Exemption clauses should name all possible participants in the performance of the contract so they too benefit from its protection.

Credit arrangements should be designed to allow maximum flexibility with minimum liability. This means that, when giving a promise to pay, a debtor should preserve all possible defences for use against any subsequent assignee. This means resisting the use of negotiable instruments in favour of the standard type of contract where the promise to pay is incorporated into the original purchase agreement. As well, the contract should state that subsequent assignees are bound by the terms of the contract. By contrast, when receiving another party's promise to pay, maximum flexibility will be achieved when a separate negotiable instrument is obtained. This will be easier and more valuable to transfer.

Assignments, other than partial or conditional assignments, should be completed in writing, and immediate notice should be sent to the promisor. This reduces the likelihood of new defences arising or loss of priority to competing claims from other assignees.

QUESTIONS FOR REVIEW

1. Define the following terms: *third party, assignor, constructive trust, beneficiary, chose in action*.
2. Give an example of vicarious performance by a party other than an employee.
3. How has the privity of contract rule been modified with respect to insurance?
4. Describe the significance of exemption clauses in contracts performed by third parties.
5. P contracted with Q to move equipment from one of Q's buildings to another site. R, an employee of P, damaged some of the equipment. What facts must Q establish in order to hold P liable for R's conduct?
6. Describe the exception made for consumer negotiable instruments.
7. A debtor owed his creditor $2000. The creditor assigned her right to collect this debt to another person, X. The assignee, X, delayed in sending notice to the debtor that he was now the party entitled to payment. Before receiving any notice of assignment, the debtor paid his original creditor $750 on account. How have X's rights been affected?
8. Anderson, a skilled mechanic, agreed to do some car repair work for Bartlett. Anderson was busy when the car was delivered for repair and gave his friend Gauche the work to do, without consulting Bartlett. Gauche sent Bartlett a bill for the repair work. Bartlett refused to pay. Is he justified?
9. Give two examples of involuntary assignments.
10. What are the requirements for a statutory assignment? Describe the business advantages associated with such assignments.
11. Explain the two types of assignment by operation of law.
12. Is notice required to assign a negotiable instrument? Explain.

CASES AND PROBLEMS

1. Continuing Scenario:

   Ashley asks her accountant for advice about which form or forms of payment she should allow her restaurant customers to use and how she should protect herself from the risks involved:

   a. Ashley has arranged to supply several hotels close by with muffins and pastries she bakes for her own customers. The hotels have asked to be billed at the end of each month and be given 30 days to pay. This will mean large outstanding debts for 60 days. How should she respond, and why?

   b. In addition to payment by cash and debit cards, the restaurant customers surveyed asked for credit cards and cheques. Describe how the law treats these types of transactions.

2. King, a building contractor, completed the construction of a house for Harris. At completion, Harris owed King a balance of $15 000. King then borrowed $10 000 from the Brandon Bank. In consideration for this loan, King assigned to the bank as much of his account receivable from Harris as should be necessary to repay the sum borrowed plus interest and any further sums for which he might become indebted to the bank. Is the bank, as assignee, entitled to sue Harris without the assistance of King's testimony?

   Suppose instead that King had borrowed $20 000 from the Brandon Bank and in partial settlement assigned the whole of the $15 000 due to him from Harris. Are these changed facts in themselves sufficient to entitle the bank to sue Harris without joining King in the action?

3. The University of Ashcroft Business School offers one-week executive courses. For its October program on marketing strategies, Ashcroft's dean managed to make a deal with Professor Bertoff, a famous specialist in the field, to give the opening lecture and remain at the business school for two full days. Less than a week before the program was to begin, Bertoff sent an email to the dean that his country's government had requested him to chair a crucial international meeting on trade policy; he would send his associate, Professor Colbert, a more junior but quite well-known person in the marketing field, to deliver the lecture prepared by Bertoff himself and to remain on campus for the two days.

   The dean is quite upset, but he has no alternative but to allow Colbert to fill in. He wishes to know whether he has a good case against Bertoff. Give your opinion with reasons.

4. Garbutt was dismissed by her employer, Carter Computers Inc., for allegedly dishonest conduct. She hired Harkin to be her lawyer and represent her in grievance arbitration for wrongful dismissal. Harkin was successful; the arbitrator found that Garbutt had been wrongfully dismissed and that she was entitled to be compensated for her losses.

   During negotiations to settle the amount of compensation, Garbutt gave Harkin a signed direction to Carter Computers to pay 30 percent of the settlement proceeds to Harkin. He delivered a photocopy of the direction to Carter Computers' in-house lawyer, but she told him that Carter Computers would honour only an original signed copy.

   The next day the parties reached a settlement of $20 000. Before the in-house lawyer received the original copy of the direction, she instructed the payroll department to issue a cheque to Garbutt for the full amount of the settlement proceeds. Harkin sued the defendant for failure to pay him the $6000.

   Summarize the arguments of each side, and give your opinion of whether Harkin should succeed.

5. Keirson sold his taxi business to Martens, covenanting neither directly nor indirectly to carry on or be engaged in another taxi business within five kilometres of the place of business for five years from the date of sale. The agreement contained the

usual clause extending the benefit of the contract to the "assigns" (assignees) of the parties. Two years later, Martens resold the taxi business to Nelman, and shortly afterward, Keirson entered into another taxi business within the five-kilometre area. Nelman brought an action against Keirson for an injunction to restrain him from operating a competing business within the five-kilometre area. Should Nelman succeed?

6. B. Flatt and F. Major made a $250 wager about the outcome of the 2014 Olympic hockey final game. Flatt lost, and he gave Major a cheque for $250 drawn on his TD Canada Trust bank account. Major immediately took the cheque to Money Mart, presented it for payment, signed the back, and received the money (less Money Mart's cheque cashing fee). When Money Mart presented the cheque for payment to TD, it was discovered that Flatt had instructed his bank to stop payment on it. What are Money Mart's rights? Against whom?

7. Glashov purchased on credit from Brown a building for business purposes. In their agreement, Glashov covenanted that he would insure the property and assign the insurance to Brown, the vendor, as security for the amount that remained owing on the purchase price.

    Glashov insured the property with the Standard Insurance Company but neglected to inform the company that the proceeds in the event of a claim should be paid to Brown. The building was later destroyed in a fire.

    Immediately after the fire, three of Glashov's trade creditors sought payment of their claims and agreed to accept from him an assignment to them of the proceeds of the fire insurance. The trade creditors gave notice to Standard Insurance Company at once, before the amount of the loss had been established and before that company had admitted any liability under the policy. Brown, after learning what had happened, informed the insurance company that she wished to claim the insurance money due and supported her claim by showing to the company the terms of the agreement for sale. The insurance company paid the money into court for settlement of the dispute.

    What is the nature of the trade creditors' argument that they should have the insurance money instead of Brown? What possible defence or defences might Brown offer against this claim? To whom would a court order the payment of the insurance money?

8. Norton responded to a campaign for funds by the National Association for the Preservation of Wildlife (NAPW) by signing the following statement, which she gave to a canvasser for NAPW:

> $1250.00 Charlottetown, Nov. 2, 2015
>
> To assist in the purchase of conservation area sites and in consideration of the subscriptions of others, I promise to pay to the Treasurer of the National Association for the Preservation of Wildlife the sum of twelve hundred and fifty dollars, payable $500 on February 1, 2016, and $750 on August 1, 2016.
>
> Joan I. Norton

This and other similar agreements permitted the Association to acquire property for use as conservation areas.

In order to obtain cash immediately from some of the pledges made to it, including Norton's, NAPW sold (assigned) them to Simpson for an undisclosed cash sum. Simpson's secretary telephoned Norton to advise her of the assignment of her promise, and Norton confirmed she had made the pledge. Norton failed, however, to pay either of the installments to Simpson. Simpson brought an action against Norton for payment of the $1250.

Express, with reasons, an opinion about the probable outcome of this action.

Chapter 12
The Discharge of Contracts

- **THE WAYS IN WHICH A CONTRACT MAY BE DISCHARGED**
- **DISCHARGE BY PERFORMANCE**
- **DISCHARGE BY AGREEMENT**
- **DISCHARGE BY FRUSTRATION**
- **DISCHARGE BY OPERATION OF LAW**
- **STRATEGIES TO MANAGE THE LEGAL RISKS**

When a contract comes to an end—is discharged—neither party has any further obligations under it. This chapter examines the different ways of discharging a contract without breaching the contract, which is examined in Chapter 13. We also discuss the consequences of an event that makes performance impossible or pointless—a frustrating event—and its effects.

In this chapter we examine such questions as:

- What is "tender of performance," and what are its requirements and consequences?
- What are the various ways in which a contract may be discharged by agreement?
- How might a contract provide for its own termination?
- What are the shortcomings of common law rules in their ability to deal with frustration?
- How have statutory reforms dealt with these problems?
- What special problems arise from frustration as it applies to the sale of goods?
- What is meant by "discharge by operation of law"?

THE WAYS IN WHICH A CONTRACT MAY BE DISCHARGED

To **discharge a contract** means to cancel or end the obligations of a contract; to make an agreement or contract inoperative.[1] This chapter looks at four ways to discharge a contract: by performance, agreement, frustration, and operation of law. Breach of contract is reserved for separate treatment in Chapter 13.

discharge a contract cancel or end the obligations of a contract; make an agreement or contract inoperative

DISCHARGE BY PERFORMANCE

The Nature of Discharge by Performance

Parties who enter into a contract expect it to be discharged—ended—by performance. Their contract ends after they have both performed all their respective obligations satisfactorily. For a contract to be fully discharged by performance, both parties—not merely one of them—must fulfill all their promises. A bilateral contract, formed by the offer of a promise for a promise, goes through three stages: first, when neither party has performed its promise; second, when one but not the other party has performed; and third, when both have performed. Only at the final stage is the contract discharged by performance.[2]

Performance may take several forms, depending on the terms of the contract. It may mean supplying the services, delivering the goods, paying the purchase price, or any combination of these.

Tender of Performance

One party may attempt to perform, but the other party might refuse to accept the performance. An attempt to perform is called a **tender of performance**, whether accepted or rejected by the other party. If a seller properly tenders delivery of goods, and the buyer refuses to accept them, the seller is under no obligation to attempt delivery again and may immediately sue for breach of contract.

tender of performance an attempt by one party to perform according to the terms of the contract

A debtor who makes an unsuccessful but reasonable attempt to pay will be free from further liability for interest on the amount owing and generally will not have to pay court costs if he is later sued for the debt.

Refusing payment does not extinguish an existing debt. There is a legal principle that the debtor must seek out her creditor. She is not excused from tendering payment because her creditor is slow or hesitant about asking for it. The onus is on the debtor to find and pay her creditor.

DISCHARGE BY AGREEMENT

Waiver

Parties may discharge their contract by agreeing between themselves not to perform it. A **waiver** is an agreement not to proceed with the performance of an existing contract. If neither party has fully performed when they agree to call off the bargain, there is automatically consideration for the waiver of each party. Each still has rights and obligations outstanding, and a promise by one party to waive its rights is sufficient consideration for it being released from its obligations to the other.

waiver an agreement not to proceed with the performance of an existing contract

---

[1] *Black's Law Dictionary*, 6th ed. at 463.

[2] In a unilateral contract, formed by the offer of a promise for an act, the first stage is eliminated because the second takes place in the very formation of the contract through one party's performance; the last stage remains necessary for discharge by performance.

On the other hand, if one party has already fully performed its part but the other has not, the first party receives no consideration for giving a waiver of the other party's duty to perform. To be binding, its promise to release the other party should be under seal.

ILLUSTRATION 12.1 Consideration

Azim agrees to install a sound system in the Kent Theatre for $5500. Kent's right, under the contract, is to receive the benefits of the work, and Kent's obligation is to pay for the work. Azim's right is to receive the price, and his obligation is to do the work required. If they should mutually agree to call off their contract before Azim completes the work, there is consideration for the waiver. Azim promises to abandon a claim for payment; in return, Kent Theatre promises to abandon a claim for services. Each party's promise is the price paid for the promise of the other.

But suppose that Kent has paid Azim the $5500 and that to date Azim has only partly installed the system. At this stage, any undertaking by Kent that will "require neither completion of the work nor a return of any money" is without consideration and, therefore, not binding unless under seal.[3]

Neither party can impose a waiver on the other. A party who fails to perform without securing a waiver by the other commits a breach of the contract. As discussed in Chapter 13, the consequences of breach are quite different from discharge by agreement.

Substituted Agreement

Accord and Satisfaction

Sometimes performance becomes too difficult. One party may offer the other a monetary payment or some other substitute for performance if she discharges (releases) him from the original obligation. For example, a seller may find that he cannot obtain certain imported goods to fill an order and may offer other goods of equal quality, perhaps at a lower price, if the buyer releases him from his original promise. A promisee may be preparing to sue the promisor before a settlement is agreed on.

The distinction between a material alteration of the terms and **accord and satisfaction** is in the purpose of the arrangement. In a material alteration, the parties are primarily concerned with creating a new arrangement; the discharge of the old contract is incidental. In accord and satisfaction, the parties are seeking a way to end their existing arrangement; the new arrangement is only for that very purpose.

Accord and satisfaction is used to settle lawsuits. Processing a lawsuit is expensive, and success is not guaranteed, so settlement is encouraged. After trial, the loser must pay not only his own legal fees but the costs of the winning party too—this rule is designed to encourage settlement offers before trial. A winning party may forfeit their right to have their costs paid if they have refused a reasonable settlement offer. This rule is designed to encourage reasonable valuation of claims.[4] The consideration in such a settlement is the consent of each party to discontinue the lawsuit although usually the document is signed under seal.

accord and satisfaction a compromise between contracting parties to substitute a new contractual obligation and release a party from the existing one

Novation

Novation is another method of discharge. It occurs when the parties to a contract agree to terminate it and substitute a new contract. There are two types of novation:

- a material change in terms
- a change in parties

novation the parties to a contract agree to terminate it and substitute a new contract

---

[3] This statement remains subject to the discussion in Chapter 7, concerning the "Gratuitous Reduction of a Debt" and "Injurious Reliance."

[4] See e.g. Ontario, *Rules of the Small Claims Court*, O Reg 258/98, r 14.01.

If parties agree to a material alteration of the terms, one that goes to the root of the contract, they have, in effect, agreed to discharge their original contract and replace it with a new one. One material change would be to change the subject matter of the contract. For instance, car dealer B may inform A that he cannot deliver the car A has ordered without a lengthy delay. They agree to cancel the contract and substitute a new one. For a favourable price offered by B, A buys a car that B has in stock. It is not always easy to decide whether an agreed alteration leaves the original contract intact or amounts to novation.

CASE 12.1 Material Change in Terms

P, a building contractor, agreed to pay a penalty if he did not complete the construction work by a certain date. Before completion, P and the owner, Q, agreed that P should do some additional work on the same project. The changes made it impossible for P to complete the building by the original date. Q insisted that the penalty clause allowed him to deduct the penalty from the amount he still owed to P. The court held that the new agreement had discharged the old and that the penalty clause disappeared with it.[5]

When one of the parties to the contract "wants out," and the remaining parties agree that another party replaces the first party, they have discharged the original contract and replaced it with a new one. A common example occurs when a party purchases an existing business and assumes its outstanding liabilities as a part of the purchase price for the assets acquired. If the creditors accept the new owner as their debtor, either by an express agreement with it or by applying to the new owner for payment of claims against the former owner, the liability of the former owner may discharged and replaced by the liability of the purchaser.[6]

There must be evidence, either by words or conduct, of intention and agreement to abandon the original contract on the part of both the creditors and the new owner.[7] The burden of proof is upon the party claiming that there was novation to show that the other party has assumed all liabilities under a pre-existing contract and has acted on that contract.[8]

In good business practice, neither the vendor nor the purchaser of a business relies on implied novation with creditors. The two parties to the sale agree on what debts the new owner should assume and then call in the creditors to obtain their express consent to the substitution of a new debtor. In addition, to protect or herself, the purchaser of a business makes a careful examination of public records, requires the vendor to provide a declaration setting out the names of all its creditors and the amounts owing to them, and publicizes the sale. The statutory reasons for these procedures are considered more fully in Chapters 28 and 29, which discuss creditors' rights.

A Contract Provides for Its Own Dissolution

When negotiating a contract, one party may be worried about a possible future event affecting its ability or willingness to perform. If the other party is agreeable, the parties may include a term in the contract stating what should happen if this event occurs. Sometimes, a similar term maybe implied by trade usage or by the surrounding

---

[5] *Thornhill v Neats* (1860), 141 ER 1392. See also *Amirault v MNR* (1990), 90 DTC 1330. See *Jedfro Investments (USA) Ltd v Jacyk*, 2007 SCC 55: the parties must arrive at a new agreement, not merely enter into negotiations.

[6] *Re Star Flooring Co Ltd*, [1924] 3 DLR 269 at 272.

[7] *Toronto Star v Aiken*, [1955] OWN 613.

[8] See *Pacific Wash-A-Matic Ltd v RO Booth Holdings Ltd* (1979), 105 DLR (3d) 323.

circumstances of the agreement. Such a term is known as a condition precedent, a condition subsequent, or an option to terminate, depending upon what it says.

Condition Precedent

condition precedent a future act or event that must happen before the obligation to perform the promises arises

A **condition precedent** is a clause in the contract identifying a future act or event, other than a lapse of time, that must happen before the obligation to perform the promises arises.[9] Both parties' contractual obligations are dependent on an uncertain future event that is not under the control of either party.[10] If the condition is not met or waived, the parties need not perform. A condition precedent may be an oral understanding, or it may be a term in a written contract.

One could argue that the contract does not come into existence until after the condition precedent is fulfilled. However, a contract subject to a condition precedent does have some legal force even before the condition is met. The parties are not discharged from their promises unless and until the condition precedent becomes impossible to fulfill. The arrangement is, therefore, much more than an outstanding offer that can be revoked prior to acceptance. For example, in Illustration 12.2, if immediately after B received A Co. Ltd.'s acceptance, he accepted an offer for a higher-paying position with a different firm, he would be in breach of contract. The only reasons that will justify his refusal to take the job are a lack of housing or the promotion for his wife. Unless the contract says otherwise, both parties are obligated to wait and see if the condition precedent is met before their obligations to perform can be ignored.

ILLUSTRATION 12.2 Future Events

A Co. Ltd., located in Moncton, writes to B in Winnipeg offering him a good employment position. B replies by letter that he will take the position provided A Co. Ltd. finds satisfactory housing in Moncton for his family before the start of the school year. A Co. Ltd. accepts B's counter-offer by mail. The employer's obligation of finding the housing is a condition precedent.

Alternatively, B might reply that he will take the position if his wife, who works for a different firm, is not offered a promotion for which she has already applied. The failure to receive the promotion is a condition precedent.

Condition Subsequent

condition subsequent a future event that brings a promisor's liability to an end if it happens

A **condition subsequent** is a future event that, if it happens, brings a promisor's liability to an end. Liability is established when the contract is formed, but one of the parties has reserved for itself an "out" in certain circumstances.

A buyer of a ticket for a baseball game has the benefit of a term in his contract that if the game is rained out before a stated inning, he will be given a ticket for another game.

ILLUSTRATION 12.3 Condition Subsequent

Norton is a fourth year BBA student who requires one more credit to graduate. He plans to take the last credit over the Spring term while working full time. He interviews for employment with an accounting firm and describes is situation. Normally the firm requires new employees to first complete their BBA, but it offered Norton employment beginning June 1 on the condition that he will be terminated if he fails the last credit being taken in the Spring term. This is a condition subsequent because Norton works and is paid up until the point where he fails the course.

---

[9] *Newfoundland and Labrador (Human Rights Commission) v Newfoundland Liquor Corp*, 2004 NLCA 5 at para 66 (citing *Black's Law Dictionary*).

[10] *PS International Canada Corp (Seaboard Specialty Grains and Foods) v Palimar Farms Inc*, 2017 SKCA 78 at para 27.

In contracts for the shipment of goods, an **act of God** (the raging of the natural elements) may be a condition subsequent if it results in the destruction of the shipment. When a railway, trucking line, airline, or marine shipping company accepts goods for shipment, it undertakes to be liable for any damage if the goods arrive at their destination in a poorer condition than they were received in by the carrier. But there is also a term discharging the carrier from this liability if the goods are destroyed by an act of God. If the goods are only partly destroyed, the contract is not discharged completely; instead, the carrier is absolved from liability to the extent that the damage was caused to the goods by an act of God, and the carrier must deliver them as they are. Such a term is implied by trade custom, but most carriers take the added precaution of expressly stating the term in their bills of lading. Therefore, when shipping goods at the owner's risk, it is wise to insure against such loss.

act of God the raging of the natural elements

Option to Terminate A contract may include a term that gives one party, or perhaps both, the choice to bring the contract to an end before its performance has been completed, usually by giving notice. Exercising the choice results in discharge by agreement because this way to discharge the contract was agreed upon when drawing up the contract. For example, a contract of employment often contains an option to terminate, entitling the employer to dismiss an employee by giving the required notice, as explained in Chapter 18. Many residential leases have an option clause entitling the tenant to leave before the end of the term by giving notice to the landlord. In a contract for the purchase of a business, a buyer may insist on a term allowing it to discharge the agreement if the auditor of the financial statements of the business is unable to give an unqualified opinion on their fairness. In these circumstances, an auditor's qualified opinion (or unwillingness to express any opinion) would give the purchaser an option to terminate the contract.

The distinction between an option to terminate and the previously discussed conditions is that the discharge does not happen automatically. The party decides whether to trigger the discharge of the contract.

INTERNATIONAL ISSUE

Hamilton Hockey

The story of Jim Balsillie's dream to buy an NHL hockey team and move it to Canada is a tale of conditions precedent, conditions subsequent, and options to terminate.

A 2006 bid to buy the Pittsburgh Penguins failed because Balsillie was unwilling to promise that the team would remain in Pittsburgh. The agreement of purchase and sale contained a condition that the purchase be approved by the NHL Board of Governors before it became binding. The NHL Board would only approve the purchase if Balsillie agreed to a variety of new terms, including keeping the Pittsburgh location. As a result, Balsillie gave notice that he would not proceed with the purchase.

In 2007, negotiations with Nashville Predators again focused on league approval and on whether Balsillie would immediately move the Predators to Canada. Two contracts figured prominently in the ability to make such a move:

1. The existing lease of the Nashville arena: The lease included a term that allowed the Predators the option to end the lease early if average fan attendance at the games fell below 14 000. The City of Nashville took the position that the tenant could not take advantage of the option because it was in default under the lease.

2. A new lease (and management agreement) with the City of Hamilton for the use of Copps Coliseum. This lease agreement was entered into during the Predator negotiations. The deal contained a condition that it would automatically expire if Balsillie did not buy a team by December 30, 2007.

The publicity surrounding the Hamilton lease, and the acceptance of deposits on season tickets, drew the ire of the NHL Commissioner. In the end, the Board of Governors never considered the approval issue. The Predators completed a deal with a group of Nashville investors for much less than the Balsillie offer.

Questions to Consider

1. What kind of term was attached to the league approval of the Penguins sale: a condition precedent, a condition subsequent, or an option to terminate?

2. What kind of term was included in the City of Hamilton agreement: a condition precedent, a condition subsequent, or an option to terminate?
3. What kind of term was included in the Nashville arena lease: a condition precedent, a condition subsequent, or an option to terminate?

Sources: S. Brunt, "Balsillie Still in the Game," *Globe and Mail*, May 8, 2008; D. Schoalts, "Predators Inch Closer to Hamilton," *Globe and Mail*, June 13, 2007, http://www.theglobeandmail.com/sports/hockey/predators-inch-closer-to-hamilton/article1326638; Schoalts, "Tickets? Who Needs Tickets?" *Globe and Mail*, June 14, 2007, http://www.theglobeandmail.com/sports/tickets-who-needs-tickets/article1086841; P. Waldie and S. Stewart, "RIM Boss Buys NHL's Penguins," *Globe and Mail*, October 5, 2006, http://www.theglobeandmail.com/sports/rim-boss-buys-nhls-penguins/article1106862

DISCHARGE BY FRUSTRATION

It is not possible to anticipate all future events and address them with conditions in a contract. It would take too much time and money to negotiate long lists of unlikely events that would excuse performance. Therefore, courts excuse or discharge parties for failure to perform their contracts, when the contract is silent, if unforeseeable circumstances beyond the control of the parties make performance impossible, pointless, or radically different from that intended by the parties.[11]

Historically, courts viewed contractual promises as absolute, regardless of the reason for which they could not be performed.[12] Examples are covenants in commercial leases that require tenants to keep the property in good repair and to pay rent. As a result tenants found themselves liable for damages caused by fire, storms, and disasters, and liable for rent for the duration of the lease when the property was no longer useable.[13] Eventually, courts applied the doctrine of frustration to leases when the whole point of the lease has disappeared or become impractical.[14]

Several provinces have enacted legislation to expressly apply the doctrine of frustration to residential leases.[15] Most commercial leases will have a clause about frustration in the lease that addresses disasters rendering premises unusable. Frustration is also applied to real estate purchase agreements and to employment contracts when an employee is unable to work because of a disabling illness that is likely to continue for an extended period of time.[16]

doctrine of frustration the law excuses a party from performance when unforeseeable circumstances beyond the control of the parties make performance impossible, pointless, or radically different from that contemplated by the parties

Doctrine of Frustration

If the courts were to excuse a failure to perform for any flimsy excuse, there would be tremendous uncertainty in business affairs. Therefore, courts carefully consider when the **doctrine of frustration** should be applied. Sometimes the parties may include in their contract a term to deal with the particular risk that has occurred; if so, the courts

---

[11] John Swan, *Canadian Contract Law* (Toronto: LexisNexis, 2006) at 600–01; *Naylor Group v Ellis-Don Construction*, 2001 SCC 58 at paras 53–55 citing *Peter Kiewit Sons' Co v Eakins Construction Ltd*, [1960] SCR 361.

[12] *Budgett & Co v Binnington & Co*, [1891] 1 QB 35; *Hills v Sughrue* (1846), 153 ER 844.

[13] *Paradine v Jane* (1647), 82 ER 897; *Redmond v Dainton*, [1920] 2 KB 256; *Foster v Caldwell*, [1948] 4 DLR 70.

[14] *Cricklewood Property & Investment Trust, Ltd v Leighton's Investment Trust, Ltd*, [1945] AC 221; *Capital Quality Homes Ltd v Colwyn Construction Ltd* (1975), 9 OR (2d) 617; *Victoria Wood Development Corp Inc v Ondrey* (1977), 14 OR (2d) 723, affd (1978), 92 DLR (3d) 229 (ONCA); *First Real Properties Ltd v Biogen Idec Canada Inc*, 2013 ONSC 6281.

[15] See e.g. *Residential Tenancies Act*, SO 2006, c 17, s 19; *Residential Tenancies Act*, 2006, SS 2006, c R-22.0001, s 11.

[16] As to real estate purchases: *Maison Development & Construction Ltd v Jefferson*, 2015 BCSC 1329 (subject to the presence of a risk clause); as to employment: *Wightman Estate v 2774046 Canada Inc*, 2006 BCCA 424 at para 21.

will not accept the event as frustrating the parties' contract and will honour the limited protection provided in the contract.[17]

The doctrine of frustration has been summarized as follows:

> Frustration occurs whenever the law recognizes that without default of either party a contractual obligation has become incapable of being performed because the circumstances in which performance is called for would render it a radically different thing from that which was undertaken by contract. . . . It is not hardship or inconvenience or material loss itself which calls the principle of frustration into play. There must be as well such a change in the significance of the obligation that the thing undertaken would, if performed, be a different thing from that contracted for.[18]

More recently, frustration was described this way:

> When an unforeseen event or circumstance occurs after a contract is signed, both parties may be discharged from performance if the parties are not at fault and performance is impossible or there would be a radical change in the obligations the parties agreed to.[19]

The simplest cases are those where performance becomes literally and physically impossible, and this is how the doctrine of frustration first developed.

CASE 12.2 Physical Destruction

The producer of a concert booked a music hall, but it was destroyed by fire before the scheduled date of the concert. No one was found to blame for the fire. The producer sued the owner of the hall for damages for breach of contract to compensate for losses sustained in having to cancel the concert. The court held that the contract was discharged by frustration and refused to award damages. Had the court found instead that the owner of the music hall had broken the contract, it would have ordered him to pay damages.[20]

CASE 12.3 Illness

Robinson booked Davison, a pianist, to give a concert on an agreed date. Robinson incurred expenses in preparing for the concert: advertising, selling tickets, and hiring staff for the evening. At about 9:00 a.m. on the morning of the concert date, he received word from Davison that a sudden illness would prevent her from performing. Robinson had further expenses in cancelling the concert. When he sued Davison for damages for his loss, the court held that the contract had been discharged by frustration, and the action failed.[21]

Today, most personal performance contracts include express options to terminate for illness and require insurance to cover cancellation costs. Similar options to terminate are inserted in ticket sale contracts. Therefore, if the performer cancels her contract, the promoter may correspondingly cancel the audience contracts. As noted when the contract has a term anticipating the foreseeable circumstance, the doctrine of frustration does not apply.

Over time, the doctrine of frustration evolved to cover situations when actual performance remained physically possible but would have a very different meaning from the expectations of the parties when they made their agreement.

---

[17] *Teleflex Inc v IMP Group Ltd* (1996), 149 NSR (2d) 355; *Maison Development & Construction Ltd, supra* note 16 at paras 49–51; but see *Wightman Estate, supra* note 16 at paras 3–4.

[18] *Davis Contractors Ltd v Fareham*, [1956] AC 696 at 729.

[19] *Vista Sudbury Hotel Inc v The Oshawa Group Limited*, 2018 ONSC 1164 at para 28 citing *Focal Properties Ltd v George Wimpey (Canada) Ltd* (1975), 14 OR (2d) 295 (ONCA), aff'd [1978] 1 SCR 2; *Naylor Group Inc, supra* note 11 at paras 55–56.

[20] *Taylor v Caldwell* (1863), 122 ER 309. See also *Laurwen Investments Inc v 814693 NWT Ltd* (1990), 48 BLR 100.

[21] *Robinson v Davison* (1871), LR 6 Ex 269.

CASE 12.4 Radically Different

In July 1914 in England, the contractors Dick, Kerr & Co. agreed to construct certain reservoirs for a local water board within six years at a specified price; they started work immediately. In February 1916, during the First World War, the Minister of Munitions, acting under wartime statutes, ordered the contractors to cease work. Most of their plant and materials were then sold under the minister's directions.

After the war ended, the water board insisted that the contractors resume their work under the original terms, but the contractors refused to comply. Prices and conditions of supply had changed drastically from what they had been in 1916. The court held that the contract had been discharged by frustration, and the water board failed in its action.[22] In a more recent case, a two day delay in performance caused by flight cancellations related to the 9/11 terrorist attacks did not amount to a frustrating event—it did not render performance impossible, just temporarily delayed.[23]

The war was an unforeseeable and unanticipated event. Usually, the fact that contractual obligations prove to be more onerous than anticipated will not, by itself, discharge a contract by frustration. A business is not excused from performance just because the most convenient or inexpensive method of performance is not available. To excuse a promisor in these circumstances would mean almost any contract could be discharged, and no one would be held to their bargains. Frustration is available only in extreme circumstances that could not have been anticipated by the parties.[24] Price increases and labour shortages are to be expected.

CASE 12.5 Not Just More Expensive

In a written contract formed on June 15, 2016, Jeong agreed to purchase Wilkie's North Vancouver home for $2 668 000 on Oct 17, 2016. On August 2, 2016, the Province of British Columbia imposed a new foreign buyer tax on all real estate transactions. This meant the tax Jeong owed on the October closing rose from $58 040 to $458 240.

Jeong refused to complete the purchase, claiming that the contract was radically changed and therefore frustrated by the imposition of the new tax. She did not have the money to pay the higher tax. The court held that this was not frustration; hardship or increased expense were not frustrating events. Jeong forfeited the $180 000 deposit.[25]

Where the contract involves the sale of goods that are destroyed, it will only amount to a frustrating event if the specific goods or source of goods is a term of the contract; if not, the supplier must find and the buyer must accept replacement goods from a different source.

CASE 12.6 Specific Goods

A trucker in Parkhill contracted with a Toronto corn merchant to deliver a quantity of corn to shipping points in the Parkhill area specified by the corn merchant. It seemed that the trucker was to purchase the corn from certain Parkhill farmers. Unfortunately, the trucker was unable to obtain the required quantity of corn because of a local drought. The corn merchant sued for damages for failure to deliver according to the contract. The Court of Appeal agreed with the defendant trucker that if the source of the goods formed a term of the contract, the failure of the crop would have amounted to a frustrating event, excusing the trucker from performance. The majority of the court found that the contract had not expressly stated that the corn should be from a particular source, and it was unwilling to find an implied term to that effect. It held that the trucker should have obtained the corn from other suppliers and that it was liable for breach of contract.[26]

---

[22] *Metropolitan Water Board v Dick, Kerr & Co*, [1918] AC 119.

[23] *Allen v Taku Safari Inc*, 2003 BCSC 516 at paras 15–17.

[24] *Twentsche Overseas Trading Co v Uganda Sugar Factory Ltd* (1945), 114 LJPC 25 at 28. See also *Graham v Wagman* (1976), 14 OR (2d) 349 at 352: "I have never heard that impecuniosity is an excuse for non-performance of a promise" varied on appeal (1978), 21 OR (2d) 1.

[25] *Wilkie v Jeong*, 2017 BCSC 2131.

[26] *Parrish & Heimbecker Ltd v Gooding Lumber Ltd*, [1968] 1 OR 716 at 719–20; See also *PS International Canada Corp*, *supra* note 10.

Last, for a contract to be discharged by frustration, its performance must become impossible or purposeless after the agreement was made, for reasons beyond the control of the parties. This is not the same situation as one in which performance was impossible or purposeless at the very time the agreement was made. If the subject matter has ceased to exist at the time of the agreement, the agreement is void for mistake—as discussed in Chapter 9—not discharged by frustration.

Self-Induced Frustration

A party that deliberately makes performance impossible cannot rely on the doctrine of frustration to discharge his obligations. **Self-induced frustration** is really a breach of the contract. In most cases, the distinction between frustration and self-induced frustration is easy to see.

self-induced frustration a party willfully disables itself from performing a contract in order to claim that the contract has been frustrated

ILLUSTRATION 12.4 Self-Induced

(a) A Inc. contracts to transport top soil for B. On realizing that it has made a bad bargain, A Inc. sells its only dump truck and claims that it cannot fulfill the contract because of frustration. Obviously A Inc. has broken the contract.

(b) A Inc. contracts to transport top soil for B in an isolated northern community. Shortly after the contract is made, its truck (the only available one in the area) is destroyed by a tornado. The contract is discharged by frustration, and A Inc. is freed from its obligation to perform.

(c) A Inc. contracts to transport top soil for B. Its dump truck breaks down because of an employee's negligence, and there will be a long delay in its repair as the parties are in a small northern community. Because the situation is attributable to A Inc.'s negligence, the contract is not discharged, and A Inc. will be liable for breach of contract.

Not every fault or irresponsibility, however, will bar a party from claiming that the contract has been frustrated. It will depend upon how careless the owner was. Consider if the dump truck is stolen: The application of frustration may depend upon whether the truck was locked or the keys left in it.[27]

Ethical Issue Self Induced Frustration

Supposing a business has many contracts requiring the same performance but only limited ability to perform. Which contracts should be performed, and which customers should go unsatisfied? It is up to the business to choose which contract will not be performed. This is considered by the courts as a form of self-induced frustration.

A classic case involves applications for fishing licences from the Ministry of Fisheries.[28] The business had four boats that were each rented out for the season. The ministry granted the company only three licences, which could be allocated to any of the four boats. When sued by the fourth customer, the court rejected the business's defence of frustration because the business decided to breach the contract with the fourth customer.

When governments use their legislative power to release themselves from contractual performance, it is a form of self-induced frustration. In one example, the Newfoundland government restructured the public utilities board and eliminated the commissioner's position. When the commissioner sued for breach of contract, the Province claimed that the restructuring was a frustrating event. The Supreme Court of Canada disagreed. It was self-induced frustration, and the displaced commissioner had a right to compensation for breach of contract.[29]

---

[27] *Joseph Constantine Steamship Line Ltd v Imperial Smelting Corp Ltd*, [1942] AC 154 at 179. See also *Kendall v Ivanhoe Insurance Managers Ltd*, [1985] OJ No 1725; *Atcor Ltd v Continental Energy Marketing Ltd*, [1996] 6 WWR 274.

[28] *Maritime National Fish Ltd v Ocean Trawlers Ltd*, [1935] 3 DLR 12.

[29] *Wells v Newfoundland*, [1999] 3 SCR 199 at paras 51–55.

Questions to Consider

1. Is this a fair result for the fishing business? Would the doctrine of frustration apply if the business had not received any licences?
2. What factors should the business consider when deciding which contract(s) to perform?
3. What condition should the business place in the rental agreement to protect itself from this potential breach of contract liability?
4. Should governments be treated differently from private sector businesses?

CHECKLIST

Requirements of Frustration

1. Intervening Event
   - After formation of contract
   - Beyond control of parties
   - Not self-induced
   - Unforeseeable
   - Not addressed in contract
2. Impossible Performance
   - Physically Impossible
   - Radically different
   - Permanent, not temporary
   - Affects nature, meaning or purpose
   - More than inconvenience, hardship, or expense

The Effect of Frustration

Release of Further Performance Frustration discharges the contract at the moment of the frustrating event. If neither party has performed at all, frustration is a complete discharge of both parties from all obligations under the contract. But if one or both parties have partially performed before the frustrating event, one party could receive a windfall from the completed performance of the other party. This happened in the old case of *Cutter v Powell*.[30] A ship worker was to be paid on completion of a trip from Jamaica to Liverpool. He died en route when the voyage was nearly three-quarters complete. An action by his widow to recover a proportionate part of his wages failed; the obligation to pay never arose because he did not complete the journey.

The frustrating event was considered to discharge future obligations under it from the time of the frustrating event, but any obligations previously due still had to be paid.

CASE 12.7 Payments Already Due

In 1902, the plaintiff rented a London hotel room to view the coronation procession of Edward VII. It was the first coronation in over 60 years (since that of Queen Victoria); the demand and price for locations with a view were very high—for this room, £141, payable at once. The plaintiff was able to pay only £100 at the time and owed the remaining £41. The contract was frustrated when the king became ill and the procession was cancelled. The plaintiff failed to recover his £100, and the court held that since the remaining £41 was due and owing before the frustrating event occurred, he was still liable for that sum, too![31] The "solution" in this decision was to let the loss fall where it lies at the time of the frustrating event.

---

[30] (1795), 101 ER 573.
[31] *Chandler v Webster*, [1904] 1 KB 493.

Over time the **let the loss fall where it lies** approach was modified or "softened." In *Fibrosa v Fairbairn*,[32] the court decided a party could recover any payment made before the frustrating event as long as absolutely no benefit had been received from the other party before the frustrating event.

This left the problem of a seller's expenses already incurred. The case law would not apportion the loss between the parties by allowing a seller to retain some portion of an advance payment. It was a matter either of retaining the whole of the deposit or of returning it entirely.

let the loss fall where it lies the court will enforce the contract up to the moment of discharge—obligations due before the frustrating event remain; obligations arising after the frustrating event are discharged

Statutory Reform

To address the unfairness of the seller's situation, provincial legislation has been passed in all parts of Canada.[33]

Now when a frustrating event occurs after money is already due under the contract (whether paid or not), the *Frustrated Contracts Act* provides for the allocation or apportionment of losses between parties:

> [t]he court, if it considers it just to do so having regard to all the circumstances, may allow the party to retain or to recover, as the case may be, the whole or any part of the sums paid or payable.[34]

The recovery or retention is capped at the amount of the payment made or due. Any excess over the performing party's allowed loss will be returned to the payor. In addition, the acts authorize a court to award the performer a just proportion of any valuable benefit received by the other party, regardless of whether a deposit has been paid.

One possible gap remains. When a party has expended time and money in performance of a contract, but the other party, which was eventually to have received the benefit of the work, has (a) made no deposit and (b) not yet received any benefit—except in British Columbia, Yukon, and Saskatchewan—the first party is still without remedy and must bear the whole loss.[35] The *British Columbia Act* states: "a 'benefit' means something done in the fulfillment of contractual obligations, whether or not the person for whose benefit it was done received the benefit."[36] Therefore, in these three jurisdictions, expenditures made by the first party can be taken into account, and to the extent that the other party has received no benefit from them, the loss is divided equally.[37] This solution seems fair to both parties.

The Sale of Goods

If the contract is for the sale of goods, the *Sale of Goods Act* could also apply to a frustration situation. The Act states:

> Where there is an agreement to sell specific goods and subsequently the goods without any fault on the part of the seller or buyer perish before the risk has passed to the buyer, the agreement is thereby avoided.[38]

---

[32] *Fibrosa Spolka Akcyjna v Fairbairn Lawson Combe Barbour, Ltd*, [1943] AC 32. See also *KBK No 138 Ventures Ltd v Canada Safeway Ltd*, (2000) 185 DLR (4th) 650 (BCCA); *Palachik v Kiss*, [1983] 1 SCR 623 at 631.

[33] *Frustrated Contracts Act*, RSPEI 1988, c F-16; RSNB 2011, c 164; RSO 1990, c F-34; CCSM c F-190; RSA 2000, c F-27; RSNL 1990, c F-26; RSNWT 1988, c F-12; SS 1994, c F-22.2; RSY 2002, c 96. *Frustrated Contract Act*, RSBC 1996, c 166.

[34] *Frustrated Contracts Act*, RSO 1990, c F.34, s 3(2); See also *Frustrated Contract Act*, RSBC 1996, c 166, s 5(2).

[35] See *Appleby v Myers* (1867), L.R. 2 C.P. 651, discussed in Chapter 15 under "Quantum Meruit."

[36] *Frustrated Contract Act*, RSBC 1996, c 166, s 5(4).

[37] *Ibid*, s 5(3).

[38] 40 RSBC 1996, c 410, s 11; RSO 1990, c S.1, s 8; RSNS 1989, c 408, s 10.

Three conditions must be present for this section to apply:

- First, the goods must be specific—that is, "they must be identified and agreed upon at the time the sale is made."
- Second, the risk must still be with the seller—that is, the seller must still be responsible for the safety of the goods.
- Third, the cause of the frustration must be the perishing or destruction of the goods.

ILLUSTRATION 12.5 Specific Goods

A sends a fax to B offering to sell the load of flour sitting at the railroad station for $10 000, "risk to pass to you on delivery of the shipping documents in seven days' time." B accepts by return fax. Three days later a train on adjacent tracks is derailed and knocks over the freight car containing the flour. The contents are spilled out and ruined by rain, frustrating the contract.

Both parties are immediately discharged from liability under the contract. A cannot sue for the price, nor can B sue for failure to deliver. B can recover any deposit it has made. A's only remedy is against those responsible for the accident.

In Illustration 12.5, all three elements mentioned in the *Sale of Goods Act* are present, and the Act applies; consequently the *Frustrated Contracts Act* does not.[39] But if any one of these elements is missing, the *Sale of Goods Act* does not apply,[40] and the *Frustrated Contracts Act* applies in those provinces having the Act with an applicable rule; in the remaining provinces, the parties are left with the common law position up to and including the *Fibrosa* case.

CHECKLIST

The Effect of Frustration

- Step 1: Determine if any part of performance, benefit, or expenditure was provided before the frustrating event. If not, then all obligations are discharged, and no further inquiry is necessary. If the answer is yes, proceed to Step 2.
- Step 2: Identify the subject matter of the contract. If the contract deals with specific goods, and they have perished, then the rules of the *Sale of Goods Act* decide the effect of frustration.
- Step 3: If the *Sale of Goods Act* does not apply, determine if the applicable province's *Frustrated Contracts Act* has a rule that determines the effect of frustration in this situation.
- Step 4: The common law rules as set out in the *Fibrosa* case will decide all remaining cases.

Let's look at some examples of the parties in each of these circumstances.

In provinces where the *Frustrated Contracts Act* applies, the application of the Act is more easily understood if we begin with some examples.

---

[39] Except in British Columbia, where s 1(b) of the *Frustrated Contracts Act* states expressly that the Act applies even in these circumstances.

[40] See e.g. RSO 1990, c S.1, s 2(2)(c).

> **ILLUSTRATION 12.6** **Application of the *Sale of Goods Act***
>
> (a) A sends a fax to B offering to sell "one thousand sacks of number one flour from our warehouse stock for $5000, risk to pass to you on delivery of the shipping documents in seven days' time." B accepts by return fax. Three days later, the warehouse and contents are destroyed by fire without any negligence on A's part. The goods are not specific because they have not been segregated from the larger stock and earmarked for the buyer.
>
> (b) A sends a fax to B offering to sell "the carload of number one flour sitting at our rail siding for $10 000, risk to pass to you on delivery of the shipping documents in seven days' time." B accepts by return fax. Three days later, the government requisitions all of A's flour, including the carload sold to B, in order to help feed the victims of a flood disaster. Here the contract is frustrated by an event other than the perishing of the goods.

In neither of the examples in Illustration 12.6 does the *Sale of Goods Act* apply. Under the *Frustrated Contracts Act*, if B made a deposit and sued for its return, the court would consider whether A had incurred any expenses toward the completion of the contract and would take them into account in determining how much of the deposit B would recover. If B made no deposit, A could only recover the value of any benefit already conferred upon B.[41] So, if A delivered one sack of flour to B as a sample, it could recover the price of that sack but no more.

The *Frustrated Contracts Act* also states that the courts shall give effect to any special provisions made by the parties in anticipation of a frustrating event.

> **ILLUSTRATION 12.7** **Term in the Contract**
>
> A sends a fax to B offering to sell "the carload of number one flour sitting at our rail siding for $10 000, risk to pass to you upon acceptance of this offer. Delivery was in seven days' time." B accepts by return fax. Three days later the flour is destroyed in a derailment accident. The risk has already passed to the buyer when the frustrating event takes place.

In the above example, the parties have agreed expressly that the risk should pass to the buyer, which seems to indicate that the buyer would be liable for any loss caused by a frustrating event after the risk has passed. The buyer must then pay the price to the seller. Although both the Act and the express terms of the contract indicate this result, there are no reported cases directly on point. Ordinarily, buyers arrange to insure valuable goods not in their possession when the risk passes to them.

DISCHARGE BY OPERATION OF LAW

A contract may be discharged or its legal importance ended by a law of general application that advances the public good.

Bankruptcy Debtors who are unable to pay all their debts may obtain a release from those debts by making an assignment into bankruptcy. The federal *Bankruptcy and Insolvency Act* operates to discharge a bankrupt debtor from contractual liabilities after the processes of bankruptcy have been completed. The debtor is discharged, however, only if he qualifies for a certificate stating that the bankruptcy was caused by misfortune and without any misconduct on his part.[42] He is discharged only from the debts

---

[41] Except, as already noted, in British Columbia, where the court could give recovery for part or all of the expenses incurred, whether or not a benefit was conferred.

[42] RSC 1985, c B-3, s 175.

disclosed to the trustee. The trustee distributes the any assets of the debtor among the relevant creditors. No further collection efforts may be taken against the debtor. Chapter 29 deals with the law of bankruptcy.

Expiration of Limitation Period Every cause of action has an expiration date—a time limit within which a lawsuit must be started or the cause of action expires. A debt or other contractual obligation that has been neglected by a creditor for a long time becomes **statute barred**—that is, the creditor loses the right to bring a court action on it. Each province has a *Limitations Act* setting out the time at which a creditor loses its remedy. The *Limitations Act* "bars" (rather than completely discharges) a right of action if the promisee fails to pursue it within the time specified. The statute gives effect to the legal principle that the public interest requires a definite end to the opportunity to sue. The effect of the statute is really to banish the right of action from the courts rather than to extinguish it. The distinction is important because a claim may be rehabilitated and made enforceable by certain conduct of the promisor, as will be discussed in Chapter 29. The time period begins to run at the point when the cause of action arises or is discoverable by a reasonably diligent plaintiff.[43]

statute barred an action that may no longer be brought before a court because the party wishing to sue has delayed beyond the limitation period in the statute

Strategies to Manage the Legal Risks

Thoughtfully written contracts can give parties maximum control over how and when their contracts are discharged. Businesses should identify the circumstances in which they would not want to perform and include them as conditions subsequent to the agreement. If things need to happen before the business is interested in the deal, these should be added as conditions precedent. If there is still uncertainty about whether the business should proceed with the deal, an option to terminate upon written notice should be created. Of course the most flexibility is obtained when the conditions or options depend upon the businesses' satisfaction rather than outside experts.

Where one party will have to expend considerable time, effort, or funds in preparation for performance, the contract should call for deposits or partial payments to be made. The contract should also address return or forfeiture of the deposit if performance is not completed as expected.

Frustration is only available for unanticipated or unforeseeable events, and the rules are arbitrary, so it is much better if the contract deals with all possible obstacles. Before contracting, time should be spent imagining the variables that might occur, and customized frustration clauses should be included in the contract. For example, standard real estate agreements include a term setting out what will happen if the house burns down after the sale is agreed to but before the deal is completed. Businesses should maintain insurance policies until a deal closes.

Finally, if a dispute develops, any resulting settlement agreement, release, or waiver should be put in writing and under seal to avoid arguments surrounding lack of consideration.

---

[43] Limitation legislation (*such as Limitations Act*, 2002, S.O. 2002, c. 24, Sched. B.) usually defines when the cause of action arises or is discoverable. See *Canada (Attorney General) v Lamerman*, 2008 SCC 14.

QUESTIONS FOR REVIEW

1. What are the consequences for a creditor who refuses a tender of performance by the debtor?
2. Describe the nature of the consideration given by the parties to a waiver.
3. When a party admits liability for breach, what is his best course of action? Explain.
4. In what respect does the arrangement known as accord and satisfaction involve a discharge of a contract?
5. Describe the role of novation in the purchase of a going business.
6. Does a contract exist at all before a condition precedent has been satisfied? Explain.
7. Why may an "option to terminate" clause be described as a condition subsequent?
8. The principles of mistake and discharge by frustration may both relate to contracts in which the subject matter is non-existent. How do these principles and their remedies differ?
9. What else, apart from physical destruction of the subject matter of a contract, can result in frustration of the contract?
10. Is substantial hardship in performing sufficient to excuse a promisor from performing? Explain.
11. James had contracted to give a talk and demonstration on resolving human relations conflicts in small organizations for a management consulting firm. After dinner with his hosts the evening before his talk, he accepted a dare to slide down a lengthy banister on the main staircase of the hotel. James fell off partway down and suffered a concussion and a badly sprained ankle. He was unable to give his talk and has been sued for breach of contract. Give a brief opinion of the likely result.
12. In what important respect has the British Columbia *Frustrated Contract Act* provided a fairer solution when a contract is frustrated?
13. What three conditions are required for the *Sale of Goods Act* to apply to a frustrated contract? Does the Act apply to a case where the goods have been impounded by the government?
14. Suppose P contracts to buy 10 tonnes of corn grown in the county of Haldimand from S. Because of a local drought there is insufficient corn, but S can quite easily obtain corn of the same quality from the adjacent county of Frontenac. Has the contract been frustrated? Give reasons.
15. In what respect may bankruptcy bring about the discharge of contracts?

CASES AND PROBLEMS

1. Continuing Scenario

   In addition to serving customers in the restaurant, Ashley's restaurant does catering for weddings and corporate events. Jill books Ashley's restaurant to do part of the catering for her wedding—the hors d'oeuvres for the pre-dinner cocktail party and the wedding cake for the dessert (both the display cake and the individual pieces for guests to eat). Jill gives Ashley a $500 deposit on the quoted contract price of $3000. A month before the wedding, Jill calls to cancel because the groom has backed out. She requests return of her deposit, and the contract is silent about cancellation and deposit return. Ashley has not purchased any of the food yet; however, she did turn down another catering job for the same day. Can Ashley retain the deposit? Has the contract been frustrated? Would your answer change if Jill had called off the wedding rather than the groom? Is there a difference between supplying the wedding cake and the hors d'oeuvres?

2. Urban Construction Co. contracted with Mandel to build a small two-storey office building for $240 000. The contract contained a clause stating that the agreed price would be reduced by $500 for every business day the building was not completed after April 1. The price was to be paid on completion of the building.

During construction, Mandel asked Urban Construction Co. to alter certain specifications so a complete air-conditioning system might be installed at a later time with a minimum of inconvenience and so there would be an additional washroom on the second floor.

The building was completed April 17. Urban Construction Co. refused Mandel's tender of a cheque for $243 500 (comprising $240 000 less $6500 for 13 business days, plus $10 000, the agreed price for the extra work). Urban Construction Co. sued for $250 000, the full price without deduction.

Examine the validity of the arguments Mandel might use in defending the action.

3. Twilight Properties agreed to purchase land on the Vancouver waterfront from the Harbour Commission, conditional upon no changes being made to the zoning bylaw that permitted high-density development for building condominium units. Twilight then began negotiations with the city for a site plan for 650 units. Its chief executive officer, Moon, was very optimistic and immediately offered 500 units for sale. (He had a fallback plan to build only that number if the zoning and site plans were restricted by municipal authority.) Moon obtained agreements to purchase 110 units from individual purchasers, who paid deposits to Twilight of $20 000 per unit. Each contract contained a clause stating

> if the development does not proceed in accordance with Twilight Properties' plans, Twilight retains the right to terminate the contract without liability on or before June 30, 2015.

This date corresponded with the closing date in the agreement with the Harbour Commission. Units were to be available, and the deals closed one year later.

On June 30, 2015, Twilight completed the purchase of the lands, but the date passed without any approval of the site plan by the city. At the end of July, the Planning and Development Department of the city approved the site plan and sent it on to the city council. However, in October the city council refused to approve the plan and stated that it intended to reduce the number of units permitted on the property. The council instructed its secretary to write to Twilight and ask whether it would be willing to provide a guarantee to the original condominium purchasers that it would perform its commitments to sell the units should the development be approved. Twilight replied that the city's request was inappropriate and an interference with its private contract rights. At its November meeting, the city passed a more restrictive rezoning bylaw that would permit only 400 units to be built.

Immediately afterward, Twilight returned the deposits of the purchasers and stated that their agreements were terminated; it was not possible to proceed with the project as planned. The unit purchasers sued for breach of contract. Twilight defended by claiming that their contracts were frustrated by the actions of the city. Summarize the arguments for each side, and give your opinion about who should succeed.

4. The Dryden Construction Co. contracted with the Ontario Hydro Electric Power Commission to build an access road seven miles long from its Manitou Falls generating station to provincial Highway No. 105. The contract contained the following clause:

> The contractor agrees that he is fully informed regarding all of the conditions affecting work to be done and labour and materials to be furnished for the completion of the contract and that his information was secured by personal investigation and research and not from the Commission or its estimates and that he will make no claim against the Commission.

In fact, the area over which the road was to be built was under heavy snow at the time, and the temperature was very low. The description of the property proved to be inaccurate, there being much more muskeg than indicated. After these facts became known, the contractor claimed to be excused from the contract, alleging that it had been frustrated and that what was required amounted to an entirely different contract.

Is there a binding contract to build the road?

5. Gilman Steel Ltd. is a large fabricator of reinforcing steel. It makes its product from steel bars purchased from steel mills in accordance with engineers' specifications for particular projects. Universal Construction Corp. is an apartment construction company.

In September 2014, Gilman and Universal signed a contract for the supply of fabricated steel at a price of $253 per tonne for use in three apartment buildings to be built consecutively by Universal at different sites.

At the first building site, deliveries were made and paid for as agreed, and construction of that building was completed. Then in July 2015, steel mill companies announced increases in the price of unfabricated steel, to take effect in two stages. The price to Gilman would increase on August 1, 2015, by $8.50 per tonne and a second increase of a then-unspecified amount would become effective as of March 1, 2016.

In the changed circumstances, Gilman suggested a new contract for the second and third apartment buildings. Universal agreed to reconsider because it found that it would not require as much fabricated steel for the remaining two buildings as it had initially contracted for. The parties signed a new contract for the supply of fabricated steel at a price of $257 per tonne, a price that only partially passed on the increase to Gilman. Universal had thus agreed to pay a higher unit price for a smaller quantity of steel. The parties did not include in the contract a clause providing for an escalation of price because Universal expected to complete the remaining buildings before the next round of price increases in March 2016.

Construction of the second apartment building began in August 2015, and Gilman made numerous deliveries of steel. Universal accepted all steel delivered and regularly paid the amount billed on each invoice at $257 per tonne. The second building was completed in January 2016, and construction of the third was started.

On March 1, while the third apartment building was still far from completion, the steel mills announced the anticipated second price increase. Officers of Gilman, hoping to agree on another new contract, met with a senior officer of Universal. They asked Universal to consider a new contract since construction had not progressed as expected. Universal agreed to accommodate Gilman on the understanding that Universal would be given favourable consideration in the supply of steel for the construction of additional apartment buildings.

Gilman then prepared an agreement dated March 1, 2016, and mailed it to Universal. It was a duplicate of the preceding contract in July except that the price of the steel was increased. Universal did not sign or return the document, but it did accept deliveries of steel invoiced at the new rates without protest. Universal adopted a new method of payment, however, after March 1, 2016. It no longer paid by cheques based on the invoice amounts but in round figures that tended at first to overpayment; however, by the end of the construction, this procedure led to a net balance of some $25 000 owing by Universal.

As construction of the third apartment building neared completion, the comptroller of Gilman asked for payment in full of the account. Universal informed him that it expected some new mortgage money to become available enabling it to pay the account in full soon. At about the same time, officers of Universal met with Gilman's officers to discuss a contract for the supply of steel for a new apartment complex. Universal reminded Gilman that it had twice agreed to new contracts and asked whether Gilman could offer a good price. Gilman made an offer, and Universal said it would consider it. The meeting was conducted and concluded in an atmosphere of goodwill without complaint about the March price increase. Shortly afterward, Universal decided that the new offer was not attractive enough to accept and indicated for the first time that it would not pay the portion of the past due account that represented the increase in the March 2016 agreement.

Gilman Steel Ltd. sued Universal Construction Corp. for the balance owing according to its invoices.

a. Outline the nature of the defence or defences available to Universal.

b. Explain the nature of the argument or arguments that could be advanced for the plaintiff.

c. Indicate with reasons what the court's decision would likely be. (If you perceive any difference between what the law is and what it ought to be in a case of this kind, set out your reasoning separately from your prediction of what the decision is likely to be.)

6. Parker's Automatic Laundry Services Inc. installed coin-operated washing machines and dryers in an apartment building owned by Mountbatten Estates Ltd. under a five-year contract. The contract gave Parker's the exclusive right to install and maintain any laundry machines in the building. No one other than the employees of the laundry service company would be permitted to repair, remove, or replace any of the machines. A clause in the contract read:

> In the event the Proprietor [Mountbatten] sells or assigns its interest in the said premises, such Successor shall be fully bound by the terms of this agreement and before the Proprietor sells or assigns it shall obtain the consent in writing of the grantee or assignee to the terms of this agreement.

In return, Mountbatten was to receive 20 percent of the gross receipts collected from the use of the laundry equipment.

Six months later, Mountbatten sold the apartment building to Baldoon Holdings Ltd. for $2 500 000. The lawyer acting for Baldoon drew up the agreement of sale, one clause of which read:

> The Vendor [Mountbatten] warrants to the Purchaser [Baldoon] that the 10 washing machines and 10 clothes dryers located in the apartment building have been placed there by Parker's Automatic Laundry Service Inc. pursuant to an agreement with a five-year term, a copy of which is attached hereto.

Following its purchase of the apartment building, Baldoon continued for a time to operate the building much as before and retained the same manager. Parker's made the first quarterly payment to Baldoon three months after the purchase. At that time, Baldoon approached Parker's with a view to purchasing the 10 washing machines and 10 dryers and operating them itself, as owner of the building. Parker's refused, and Baldoon then instructed Parker's to remove its machines within two weeks. When Parker's failed to do so, Baldoon moved the machines to a locked storage area in the basement of the apartment building and replaced them with new washing machines and clothes dryers of its own.

Parker's Automatic Laundry Services Inc. brought an action against Baldoon Holdings Ltd. for breach of contract. Indicate with reasons what the result of this action will likely be, leaving aside the question of what the amount of damages should be, if awarded.

7. Diehl owned some land on which she planned to have a house built that would be suitable for her retirement the following year. She made a contract with Summers, a building contractor, to build a house for $80 000, the price to be paid in full on completion. The contract contained an unqualified promise by the contractor to complete the house at that price. When the house was about three-quarters

finished, Diehl stored some expensive furniture in a completed part and took out a $20 000 fire insurance policy on the furniture.

Two weeks later, before the house was completed, lightning caused a serious fire that did considerable damage to both the building and the furniture. Summers learned that Diehl would receive about $16 000 in insurance money. When Diehl asked him to go ahead and complete the house, Summers said, "I believe I'm no longer bound to go on, and if you do not pay me the insurance money, I will ask a court to declare that the contract has been frustrated. I'm willing to compromise if you pay me the insurance money." Diehl protested that she had lost considerably from the destruction of her furniture but finally said, "All right, go ahead and do the work."

When the house was completed, Diehl paid Summers $80 000 but refused to pay anything more. Summers sued her for $16 000 on the grounds that he had been led to believe he would receive this additional sum and would not otherwise have completed the contract.

At the trial, evidence was submitted that in contracts of this kind, builders frequently require an undertaking by the owner to insure the building during its construction against loss by fire and have the insurance company include a clause agreeing that, in the event of a claim, it would pay the insurance money first to the builder "insofar as his interest may appear." A copy of the written contract between Summers and Diehl was produced and showed that the contract did not include a term of this kind. The parties testified that neither of them had insured the building itself, as distinct from the contents. It was acknowledged that the contractor, Summers, would have had an insurable interest and could have insured the house himself to the value of the contract.

Develop the arguments for the plaintiff and the defendant, and offer an opinion about whether the action should succeed.

8. M Inc. chartered a vessel from Q Corp. under a five-year agreement that gave M an option to purchase the vessel at the end of the five-year term, subject to "full performance of all its obligations under the agreement, including delivery of prompt payments in accordance with the schedule in the agreement." The agreement required seven monthly installments each year on specified dates, "in cash, by way of Bank Transfer and/or certified cheques." The parties subsequently agreed informally that M would deliver seven postdated, uncertified cheques to Q at the beginning of each operating season, and they would be deposited on the specified dates.

There were no problems with the cheques for the first four years, but the cheque for the first payment in the fifth year was returned by reason of insufficient funds. The bank's refusal to honour M's cheque was due to an error by a bank employee. Q immediately wrote to M stating that the option to purchase was void and of no further effect because of M's failure to make the payment as required. Q also gave M instructions on how to remedy its late payment. M promptly made the payment with interest in accordance with Q's instructions. All remaining payments were made on time.

As prescribed in the terms of their agreement, M gave notice to exercise the option to purchase the vessel. Q insisted that the failure to make the first payment in the fifth year on time was a precondition to exercising the option and that, accordingly, the option was void. M Inc. sued Q Corp. to enforce the option agreement. Give your opinion of which side should succeed.

Chapter 13
Breach of Contract and Remedies

- **IMPLICATIONS OF BREACH**
- **HOW BREACH MAY OCCUR**
- **EXPRESS REPUDIATION**
- **ONE PARTY RENDERS PERFORMANCE IMPOSSIBLE**
- **FAILURE OF PERFORMANCE**
- **EXEMPTION CLAUSES**
- **TYPES OF REMEDIES**
- **DAMAGES**
- **THE MEASUREMENT OF DAMAGES**
- **TYPES OF DAMAGES**
- **CHALLENGES IN MEASURING DAMAGES**
- **EQUITABLE REMEDIES**
- **METHODS OF ENFORCING JUDGMENTS**
- **STRATEGIES TO MANAGE THE LEGAL RISKS**

Not all breaches are of the same importance, nor do they trigger all the same consequences or remedy. When one party commits a breach, the non-breaching party may have choices to make, and those choices depend on how the breach occurs, how serious it is, and what the losses are. The usual remedy—damages—may not always be sufficient; sometimes an equitable remedy will be more appropriate in the circumstances.

In this chapter we examine such questions as:

- What options are available to a non-breaching party when the other party
  - expressly repudiates the contract,
  - simply fails to perform at the agreed time, or
  - makes it impossible for itself to perform?

- How serious must the breach be to trigger various options?
- How do exemption clauses affect a non-breaching party's rights?
- What types of remedies are available to a non-breaching party?
- How are damages measured?
- When does a non-breaching party qualify for an equitable remedy?
- How is a judgment enforced?

IMPLICATIONS OF BREACH

A breach of any term in a contract entitles the non-breaching party to claim damages. However, serious breaches may also discharge a contract and release the non-breaching party from further performance of his or her contractual obligations. To discharge a contract, the breach must undermine the whole contract or a substantial part of the contract; only then is the option to discharge the contract available. The purpose of the contract must be defeated so that performance by the non-breaching party is rendered pointless.

Breach does not discharge a contract automatically (as does frustration or completed performance, for example). Even when a breach is sufficient to discharge the contract, the non-breaching party must choose to treat the contract as discharged and communicate its choice to the breaching party. Often the parties disagree over the importance of the breach and whether the non-breaching party is entitled to discharge.

Even when the non-breaching party would ordinarily have the right to treat its obligations as discharged, it loses that option in two situations. The first occurs when the innocent party decides to proceed with the contract and accept benefits under it, despite the breach. In the second, the innocent party may have received the benefit of the contract and not learned of the breach until this party's performance was already complete. Even in these circumstances, a breach of contract action claiming damages remains available.

ILLUSTRATION 13.1 Essential Term

(a) A agrees to sell 10 000 bags of potatoes to B with nutritional content printed on each bag in 28-point font (twice the size required by government regulation (14 point font)). By mistake, the information is printed in 20-point font. B may feel annoyed and believe that its merchandise display will not be as effective. B may sue A and collect damages for its loss, but it cannot reject the potatoes without itself committing a breach that might make it also liable for damages.

(b) A agrees to sell 10 000 bags of potatoes to B and to deliver them to B's warehouse on Wednesday in time for B to distribute them to its supermarket chain for a weekend special. A makes no delivery until late Friday afternoon. This is a breach of an essential term of the contract—delivery on Wednesday. B may reject the potatoes and discharge the contract, freeing itself from any obligation to pay for them. In addition, it may sue A for damages caused by failure to deliver on time. In the alternative, B may decide it still wants the potatoes, and it may accept them. In this event, the contract is not discharged: B is liable to pay the price for the potatoes, subject to a deduction for damages caused by the failure to deliver them on time. If B should accept the potatoes and then refuse to pay for them, A could sue B for the price, and B could counterclaim for its damages.

If the breach is of a significant or essential term, the party committing the breach is still bound, but the injured party may elect to discharge the contract or to affirm the contract so that it continues to bind both parties.

minor breach a breach of a non-essential term of a contract or of an essential term in a minor respect

major breach a breach of the whole contract or of an essential term so that the purpose of the contract is defeated

A major term may be broken in only a minor respect. Suppose in Illustration 13.1 that A delivers on time but is short by five bags. The quantity to be delivered is a major term, but delivering 9995 bags of 10 000 promised would be only a **minor breach** of that term and would not entitle B to reject the shipment. If, however, A delivers only 5000 bags, a **major breach** would have occurred, and B could elect to reject them. Conversely, a minor term may be breached in a major way: What if the mistaken font size was smaller than government regulations required? If this rendered the product unsellable or exposed the vendor to government penalties, the wholesaler may be justified in rejecting the potatoes. It is not always easy to decide whether a term of a contract is essential or of lesser importance, or whether the breach is a serious one. In all disputes concerning a breach, the first task is to determine the importance of the term breached.

conditions essential terms of a contract

Terminology concerning essential and non-essential terms can be confusing. For a variety of reasons stemming from 19th-century developments in contract law, essential terms became known as **conditions** and non-essential terms as warranties. These names are unfortunate because "condition" may easily become confused with "condition precedent" (discussed in Chapter 12), and "warranty" may be confused with its special meaning in a sale of goods (where it means a guarantee of quality of the goods or of their ownership—usually an essential term). Despite the confusion, use of the terms "condition" and "warranty" to distinguish essential from non-essential terms is common.

ILLUSTRATION 13.2 Online Pharmacies

The prices that drug manufacturers may charge for Canadian prescription drugs are controlled by the government regulatory board. This means Canadian prescription drugs are cheaper (often significantly) than their U.S. counterparts. Online pharmacies offer Canadian pricing to American consumers. Several American states no longer block access to cheaper drugs through Canadian online pharmacies.

Not surprisingly, drug manufacturers are unhappy with the potential for reduced American profits. The contracts under which the drugs are sold to the Canadian pharmacies include terms that prohibit the export of the drugs. Beginning in 2004, several drug manufacturers, including Merck and Pfizer Inc., took the position that the online pharmacies were in substantial breach of their sale agreements. The manufacturers elected to discharge the contracts and stopped supplying further drugs to the Canadian pharmacies.[1]

HOW BREACH MAY OCCUR

A party to a contract may break it

- by expressly repudiating (rejecting) its obligations,
- by acting in a way that makes it impossible to perform its promises, or
- by either failing to perform at all or tendering an actual performance that falls short of its promise.

EXPRESS REPUDIATION

express repudiation one of the contracting parties communicates to the other that it does not intend to perform as promised

Express repudiation happens when one of the contracting parties communicates to the other that it does not intend to perform as it promised. Repudiation can be by words or by conduct that shows an intention not to be bound by the contract.[2]

---

[1] "Canadian Internet Pharmacies: Buying Drugs from Canada—Small but Growing," *Senior Magazine Online*, www.seniormag.com/canadianpharmacy/articles/growing-use.htm (accessed June 15, 2018); "Canadameds Upset With Power Struggle of Drug Companies to Stop Mail Order Pharmacy Industry in Canada," *Medical News Today*, January 18, 2005, www.medicalnewstoday.com/articles/18997.php; "Merck Cuts Off Net Pharmacies," *Canadian Press*, January 21, 2005.

[2] *Potter v New Brunswick Legal Aid Services Commission*, 2015 SCC 10 at para 149.

If the repudiation is of the whole contract or of a substantial part of it, the promisee is entitled to treat the contract as being immediately at an end, to find another party to perform, and to sue for whatever damages it sustains. Before substituting a new party to proceed with performance, the promisee must inform the repudiating party that it is treating the contract as immediately terminated and is reserving its rights to sue for damages for breach. When express repudiation occurs before the time agreed for performance, it is known as **anticipatory breach** or anticipatory repudiation, and the non-breaching party has a choice to accept the breach or insist on performance.[3]

anticipatory breach an express repudiation that occurs before the time agreed for performance

A promisee that chooses to reject the anticipatory breach and insist on performance as stated in the contract takes a risk. Although failure to perform on the specified day would still be breach of contract (and trigger a claim for damages) intervening events may provide the promisor with an excuse for not performing—for example, a frustrating event could occur.

ILLUSTRATION 13.3 Anticipatory Breach

A Co. contracts with B Ltd. for the delivery to A Co. in six months of well-drilling equipment at an agreed price. A week later, B Ltd. discovers it has agreed to a price that is much too low and informs A Co. it will not deliver the equipment as promised. B Ltd. has committed an anticipatory breach of its contract with A Co., and A Co. need not wait until the delivery date to sue B Ltd.

As a promisee, A Co. is entitled not only to performance of the contract in six months' time but also to a continuous expectation of performance in the period between formation of the contract and its performance. During that period, A Co. may have entered into a drilling contract relying on delivery of the equipment. The concept is a basic one: a contract exists and has legal effect from the time of its formation, and not just from the time of its performance. Breach may occur before performance is due.

CASE 13.1 Contractual Obligations at an End

Atkinson's employment contract contained a clause that he would not work in competition with his employer in the same town for two years after the termination of his employment. The employer dismissed him without cause in breach of the contract. Atkinson recovered damages for wrongful dismissal and then began to work for a competitor within the district. His former employer sought an injunction to restrain him from competing but failed. The court held that the company had, by its dismissal, repudiated the entire employment contract, and this entitled Atkinson to consider his own contractual obligations at an end.[4]

Major breach amounting to repudiation may also occur at the time set for performance, and it too will free the aggrieved party from further obligations.

---

[3] *Brown v Belleville (City)*, 2013 ONCA 148 at para 5; J. Cassels and E. Adjin-Tettey, *Remedies: The Law of Damages*, 3rd ed (Toronto: Irwin Law, 2014) at 442–46. Same principles apply for repudiation and anticipatory breach: *Remedy Drug Store Co Inc v Farnham*, 2015 ONCA 576 para 44.

[4] *General Billposting Co v Atkinson*, [1909] AC 118, applied by the Supreme Court of Canada in *Potter*, *supra* note 2 at paras 35, 154.

> ### ILLUSTRATION 13.4 Mitigate the Loss
>
> X Inc., a distributor of specialty coffee equipment, agreed to supply B Ltd., a chain of retail kitchen stores, with a large quantity of new espresso machines, along with sample coffee "pods" so that customers could sample the coffees to promote the new product. Several days before delivery, the manager of X Inc. discovers the coffee makers are in stock but the demonstration coffee pods have not arrived and appear to have been lost during shipment. Knowing that B Ltd. plans to feature the new product, X Inc.'s manager should to notify B Ltd. so B Ltd. might be able to arrange for an alternative supply of pods and reduce its loss.

In these examples, repudiation takes the form of words or conduct affecting performance of the whole contract. As noted, if one party repudiates only a minor term of the contract, the other party is not entitled to treat the contract as discharged. When a business is unable to perform exactly as promised, a wise manager, as soon as she is aware of the situation, will notify the other party so it may take immediate steps to reduce any loss the breach may cause.

ONE PARTY RENDERS PERFORMANCE IMPOSSIBLE

An intentional or negligent act by the promisor that destroys its ability to fulfill its contractual promises amounts to breach of contract—this does not include an act that is an involuntary response to forces beyond its control. A deliberate or negligent act that makes performance impossible amounts to repudiation. The promisor may not have said so in words but has implied as much by her conduct. As with express repudiation, conduct that makes performance impossible or shows an intention not to be bound by the contract may take place either before or during performance.

> ### ILLUSTRATION 13.5 Performance No Longer Possible
>
> A agrees to sell her Ferrari sports car to B for $30 000, to be delivered in three weeks. A few days later, X, unaware of the agreement between A and B, offers A $35 000 for the car. A accepts and delivers the car to X that day. A is in breach of the contract with B the moment she makes the sale to X, and B may sue her as soon as he learns of it. A is not permitted to argue that she can still deliver the car on time by buying it back from X; B is entitled to a continuous expectation of A's performance until the day agreed for delivery arrives.

> ### Ethical Issue Good Faith Performance
>
> Civil law jurisdictions, including Quebec, have long recognized a general duty of good-faith performance. The *Civil Code of Quebec* states:
>
> > The parties shall conduct themselves in good faith both at the time the obligation is created and at the time it is performed or extinguished. (art. 1375)[5]
>
> The United States also recognizes a generalized duty of good faith. The United States *Restatement of Contracts*[6] describes it this way:
>
> > Every contract imposes upon each party a duty of good faith and fair dealing in its performance and its enforcement. (s. 205)[7]

---

[5] Article 1375 CCQ.

[6] In the United States, common rules of contracts and torts are collected into one statute. The *Restatement of Contracts* is such a statute, as is the *Restatement of Torts*.

[7] *Duty of Good Faith and Fair Dealing*, s 205.

Although difficult to define, good faith includes concepts of fairness, honesty, and consideration for the interests of the other party.

Canadian common law jurisdictions take a narrower approach[8] to good faith duty to perform. In 2014 the Supreme Court of Canada considered the issue in *Bhasin v Hrynew*.[9] The Court refused to recognize a general duty of good faith performance in all situations and instead declared "good faith performance" an organizational principle, not a free-standing rule. It is a standard that underpins and is manifested in more specific legal doctrines and may be given different weight in different situations (para 64). Good faith performance does not engage duties of loyalty to the other contracting party or a duty to put the interests of the other contracting party first but simply suggests parties perform contractual duties honestly and reasonably and not capriciously or arbitrarily.

Examples of this narrow topic specific approach to good faith are employment, insurance, and franchise contracts that carry some good faith obligations.[10] The newest manifestation of this common law organizational principle is the duty of honesty in contractual performance. This means parties must not lie or otherwise knowingly mislead each other about matters linked to performance.[11]

Questions to Consider

1. Should common law Canada recognize a general duty of good faith in contractual performance and enforcement? How does an organizational principle of good faith differ from a duty of good faith performance of the all contracts?

2. How does a duty of good faith differ from a duty of honesty?

FAILURE OF PERFORMANCE

Degree of Failure

Failure of performance usually becomes apparent only at the time set for performance. The degree of failure may vary. It may be a total failure to perform, it may be a grossly inadequate performance, or it may be a minor variation. There may be satisfactory performance of all but one of the terms of the contract or of only part of a main term. The extent of a failure affects the type of remedy available to the injured party.

Inadequate performance by the first party will again trigger the decision of whether the second party is excused or must still perform, as just discussed. The question is complicated in contracts requiring the delivery of goods by installments when the first quantity delivered fails to meet the amount called for in the contract, but future installments could make up the deficiency. Partial delivery may be merely inconvenient, or it may be completely unsatisfactory.

ILLUSTRATION 13.6   When is the Other Party Released from its Performance Obligations?

(a) The seller contracts to deliver 6000 tonnes of coal in 12 monthly installments of about 500 tonnes each. One of the terms is that the buyer is to provide the trucks to take the coal away. In the first month, the buyer sends sufficient trucks to take away only 400 tonnes. The buyer's default would not likely be sufficient to discharge the seller from its obligation to stand ready to provide the remaining 5600 tonnes over the following 11 months.[12]

(b) The seller agrees to deliver 150 tonnes of iron per month but delivers only 21 in the first month. Its default is very likely sufficient to discharge the buyer, which may then turn to another source of supply and sue for damages resulting from the breach.[13]

---

[8] *Transamerica Life Canada Inc v ING Canada Inc* (2003), 68 OR (3d) 457 (CA) at para 53.
[9] [2014] 3 SCR 494, 2014 SCC 71.
[10] *Wallace v United Grain Growers Ltd* (1997), 152 DLR (4th) 1 (SCC). See also *Honda Canada Inc v Keays*, 2008 SCC 39. *Bhasin*, *supra* note 9 at paras 54–56.
[11] *Bhasin*, *supra* note 9 at para 73.
[12] See *Simpson v Crippin* (1872), LR 8 QB 14.
[13] *Hoare v Rennie* (1859), 157 ER 1083.

Often, an innocent party is left with a dilemma. If she is really concerned about the seriousness of continuing defective performance, it is wise for her to seek legal advice before claiming to be discharged of her own obligations; otherwise, she risks being held liable for wrongful repudiation should a court find that the seller's default was only a minor breach.[14]

In a contract where one party is to perform by installments, the other may consider itself freed from liability only if it can offer convincing affirmative answers to both of these questions:

(a) Is there good reason to think future performance will be equally defective?

(b) Is either the expected deficiency or the actual deficiency to date important relative to the whole performance promised?

Doctrine of Substantial Performance

substantial performance
performance that does not comply in some minor way with the requirements of the contract

The doctrine of **substantial performance** states that a promisor is entitled to enforce a contract when it has substantially performed, even though its performance does not comply in some minor way with the requirements of the contract. The promisor's claim is, however, subject to a reduction for damages caused by its defective performance. The effect of the doctrine is that a promisee cannot use a trivial failure of performance to avoid its own obligations.[15] There can often be substantial disagreement over whether a failure in performance is serious or trivial.[16]

Duty of Honesty in Performance

The duty of honesty imposes a minimum standard of honesty onto all parties during performance of their contracts. One must not lie or mislead the other party about performance. The duty does not require loyalty or subordination of one's own interests to that of the other party, just a minimum level of honesty. The parties may not exclude the duty but may modify it with express terms in the contract.[17]

Overperformance

What happens when a party "overperforms" an existing obligation by paying more money than is owed? What about when it performs in a mistaken belief that an obligation existed, as when an insurance company pays a claim and then discovers the loss arose from a risk not covered by the policy? What happens when someone simply pays the wrong person? What are the consequences for the other party to the original contract who is still waiting for performance? What are the consequences for the "lucky" recipient of mistaken or overperformance?

When the "lucky" recipient knows the payment does not belong to him, the answer is straightforward: he cannot "snap up" a benefit that belongs to another person—a court will order him to restore it. The question becomes more difficult when the recipient honestly but mistakenly believes he is entitled to the benefit. **Quasi-contract** (named because the obligations may not arise as a direct result of contractual relations between the parties) uses the concepts of **unjust enrichment** and

quasi-contract an obligation that may arise not as a result of contractual relations but because one party has received an unfair benefit at the expense of the other

unjust enrichment an unfair benefit

---

[14] See e.g. *Agrifoods International Corp v Beatrice Foods Inc*, [1997] BCJ No 393.

[15] *Dakin & Co Ltd v Lee*, [1916] 1 KB 566.

[16] See *Miller v Advanced Farming Systems Ltd*, [1969] SCR 845; *Sail Labrador Ltd v Challenge One*, [1999] 1 SCR 265.

[17] *Bhasin, supra* note 9 at paras 72–78.

restitution to force the recipient of a windfall to repay it.[18] If, in all the circumstances, a court finds it would be an unjust enrichment to allow the recipient to keep the benefit, it will order restitution by finding a duty implied by law to pay for it.

With respect to the mistaken party's obligations under the original contract, performance to the wrong person is no performance at all, and the mistaken party remains obligated to perform to the correct party. Otherwise the original contracting party has experienced a total failure of performance. The above described rules of breach (major or minor) apply. To avoid breaching the original contract, the mistaken party will have to perform again.

restitution a requirement that an "enriched" defendant must restore or return the benefit to the donor *in specie* or by money

EXEMPTION CLAUSES

Purpose

Business parties use exemption clauses to protect themselves from liability for breach of contract for a number of reasons. First, exemption clauses allocate the risk so parties know who should insure against what. Next, they allow suppliers to charge lower prices, since the supplier need not increase its price to cover the costs and damages arising from customer lawsuits. Even if sued, the exemption clause will usually offer a complete defence, and the business can recover its legal costs from the unsuccessful litigant. Finally, if the supplier is in the position of using a standard form contract (especially if the contract is detailed with many other terms), it will, in most circumstances, have a distinct advantage over its customer and can design the clause in its favour.

Exemption clauses work reasonably well when the bargaining power and knowledge of the law are relatively equal between the parties. For example, one party may willingly assume a risk in return for a lower price; that party may already have adequate insurance coverage. Or the activity may be extremely hazardous: a charter airline may be unwilling to fly a client into northern mountain regions in winter except at the client's own risk. Generally speaking, however, the party preparing the standard form contract designs the exemption clause clearly to its own advantage, and the courts take a three-step analytical approach to deciding if a party should escape the effect of an exemption clause.[19]

Analytical Approach

Courts take a three-step approach to deciding whether or not to enforce an exemption clause. First, the court decides whether the clause covers the circumstances in question. If it does, the court moves to the second step and determines whether the clause was unconscionable at the time of contracting. If the clause is unconscionable, it will not be enforced. However, if it is not unconscionable, the court must decide a third and final question—whether there is a strong public policy reason against enforcement.[20]

Step One: Interpretation of Exemption Clauses

The first question is, "Does the clause apply to the facts?" The court must assess the intention of the parties by interpreting the words used in the clause to decide whether the clause applies to the given circumstances. Exemption clauses are typically written using very broad, flexible language. A supplier of machinery might exempt itself from "all liability for defects in the product supplied, for any negligence of its employees, and for any guarantees implied by custom or trade usage—except for guarantees expressly set out in the

---

[18] *Barafield Realty Ltd v Just Energy (BC) Limited Partnership*, 2017 BCCA 307 at paras 58–9.
[19] *Tercon Contractors Ltd v British Columbia (Transportation and Highways)*, 2010 SCC 4 at paras 21–23.
[20] *Ibid*; see also *Roy v 1216393 Ontario Inc*, 2011 BCCA 500 at para 22.

contract, such as replacing any defective parts for three months." Courts have taken the view that words must be interpreted in a manner that is consistent with other terms in the contract, its commercial purpose or context, and any relevant statutory scheme.[21] If there is ambiguity, it must be interpreted against the **drawing party** because that party had every chance to make the ambiguity more clear.[22] Even so, the courts respect the theory of freedom of contract, and in the absence of special rules (such as exist for common carriers) or special statutory protection (as in consumer protection legislation), they will not make a new contract for the parties. If an exemption clause applies to the breach that has occurred, the injured party—subject to the discussion that follows—has no remedy.

drawing party the contracting party that prepared the agreement or the particular clause

CASE 13.2 Situation Not Covered by the Clause

Purolator undertook to deliver a tender document from Cathcart's office to the office of Ontario Hydro. The bill of lading contained a clause stating that Purolator would not be liable for "any special, consequential or other damages for any reason including delay in delivery." The tender document was never delivered to Ontario Hydro.

In an action by Cathcart to recover lost profits, Purolator admitted that had the bid been received, it would have been accepted and that the loss of profit by Cathcart was $37 000. But Purolator claimed the clause exempted it from any liability. However, Cathcart succeeded in its action. The court construed the clause strictly against the drafter of the term, Purolator, even though the parties were of equal bargaining power. The clause, on its "true construction," covered only damages arising from delay, not from a complete failure to deliver.[23]

Step Two: Unconscionable Clauses If the clause covers the circumstances, it may still be unenforceable. Sometimes when there is a significant imbalance in the bargaining power of the parties, the stronger party takes an unfair advantage of the weaker one by extracting unfair or **unconscionable terms**. An unfair outcome alone is not sufficient to make a clause unconscionable; similarly inequality of bargaining power alone is not sufficient. An unconscionable term has both inequality in the process of creating the clause and an unfair outcome.[24]

unconscionable terms terms agreed to by parties of unequal bargaining power that give an unfair advantage to the powerful party over the weaker party

Usually, commercial contracts are negotiated by sophisticated business parties that lack imbalance in bargaining. However, consumer contracts are one-sided in favour of the retailer and are offered on "a take it or leave it" basis, with little time to review their contents. Some web retailers simply include a link on their ordering page to the "terms and conditions" of the purchase contract (including the exemption clause); others require the purchaser to scroll through all such terms and indicate acceptance before completing an order. In a leading case, *Microsoft v Rudder*,[25] where the consumer plaintiffs complained about the terms of Microsoft's standard form online licence, the Court likened scrolling through terms of an online contract to flipping through the pages of a multi-page paper contract. The judge in *Rudder* concluded that if a consumer clicked "I agree" at the end of a series of standard form terms, she would be bound by those terms, including, presumably, any exemption clause. Still, courts continue to examine exemption clauses very carefully and to refuse to protect a defendant when it would appear the clause is unconscionable.[26]

---

[21] *Tercon, supra* note 19 at paras 64, 65, 72.

[22] *Tercon, supra* note 19 at paras 62, 79; *Hunter Engineering v Syncrude*, [1989] 1 SCR 426; *Hillis Oil and Sales Ltd v Wynn's Canada, Ltd*, [1986] 1 SCR 57 at 68–9.

[23] *Cathcart Inspection Services Ltd v Purolator Courier Ltd* (1982), 34 OR (2d) 187.

[24] *Roy, supra* note 20 at paras 29–30.

[25] (1999), 2 CPR (4th) 474.

[26] *Monta Arbre Inc v Inter-Traffic (1983) Ltd* (1989), 71 OR (2d) 182. See also *Hunter Engineering v Syncrude, supra* note 22.

Step Three: Public Policy and Public Interest Finally, even if the wording of the clause applies to the situation, and the clause was not unconscionable at the time the contract was formed, a court may still refuse to enforce an exemption clause if the injured party can "point to some paramount consideration of public policy sufficient to override the public interest in freedom of contract."[27] Is there greater harm to the public interest if the offending conduct is protected? Conduct approaching criminal or fraudulent behaviour is well recognized as being against public policy, and therefore it would not be in the public interest to allow an exemption clause to insulate the offending party from liability for such conduct. In Case 13.3, the distinction between unconscionability and violation of public policy is blurred, but the end result is the same. The court may refuse to enforce the exemption clause that would protect the offender.

CASE 13.3 Public Policy Grounds

Dow Chemical sold plastic resin to its customer for use in the fabrication of natural gas pipelines. At the time of the sale, Dow knew the product was defective. Instead of disclosing the known defect to the buyer, Dow chose to try to protect itself by including exemption clauses in its sales contracts. After some years, the pipelines began to deteriorate, causing considerable property damage and human health risks from leaks and explosions. The Alberta Court of Appeal refused to apply the exemption clause, concluding that "a party to a contract will not be permitted to engage in unconscionable conduct secure in the knowledge that no liability can be imposed upon it because of an exclusionary clause."[28] When the Supreme Court of Canada reviewed the case, it agreed with the result but applied public policy grounds, saying "Dow was so contemptuous of its contractual obligation and reckless as to the consequences of the breach as to forfeit the assistance of the court. The public policy that favours freedom of contract was outweighed by the public policy that seeks to curb its abuse."[29]

TYPES OF REMEDIES

In addition to the right to treat the contract as discharged as a result of breach, an injured party may have several other remedies available, depending on the type of breach and the subject matter of the contract. They are as follows:

(a) damages

(b) equitable remedies—specific performance, injunction, and rescission

(c) *quantum meruit*

DAMAGES

The Purpose of an Award of Damages

Damages are awarded to place the injured party in the position he would have been in if the contract had been properly completed. The award is intended to compensate an injured party for the loss caused by failure to perform, not to punish the party liable for the breach. In this respect, the purpose of an award of damages in contract is similar to that in tort law—that is, compensation and not punishment. Still, knowing the injured party can force it to pay compensation usually deters a party from committing any breach it can avoid. There are exceptions.

---

[27] *Tercon, supra* note 19 at para 82.
[28] *Plas-Tex Canada Ltd v Dow Chemical of Canada Ltd*, 2004 ABCA 309 at para 53.
[29] *Tercon, supra* note 19 at para 119.

ILLUSTRATION 13.7 Decision to Breach

X Inc. contracts to supply 100 000 widgets at $2.00 each to Y Corp. It expects to earn a profit of $20 000 on the contract. Shortly afterward, X Inc. receives an offer to supply a different item to Z Ltd. at a profit of $60 000—but if it accepts the offer from Z Ltd., it will be unable to produce the 100 000 widgets for Y Corp.

X Inc. learns that a competing manufacturer can supply widgets of equal quality to Y Corp. at $2.25—that is, for $25 000 more than its own price. In these circumstances, X Inc. would gain financially if it were to forgo its profit of $20 000 on the contract with Y Corp. and pay that company $25 000 in damages for breach while earning $60 000 on the new contract—a net gain of $15 000. The duty of honesty in performance would require X Inc. to inform Y Corp. of its decision immediately.

As discussed later in this chapter, less often damages are awarded to compensate for non-economic injury (such as mental distress) and to punish bad faith or malicious behaviour.[30] Additional intangible costs incurred by a breaching party include harming continuing good relations with the affected customer as well as one's general reputation for honouring commitments.

Prerequisites for an Award of Damages

1. Loss Must Flow from the Breach   To qualify for recovery, damage must "flow naturally from the breach." This principle has been interpreted to mean that a loss resulting from breach must be within the foreseeable limits of what the parties would have expected as a likely consequence of a failure to perform, had they thought about it when they drew up their contract. Damages are not generally awarded to compensate an injured party for some unusual or unexpected consequence of breach.

CASE 13.4 Unexpected Consequence

A carrier failed to deliver a vital piece of machinery promptly to a sawmill as instructed by an employee of the mill. As a result, the sawmill had to suspend operations until the part arrived. The sawmill company sued the carrier for the losses suffered through the shutdown, but the court refused to award damages because the employee had not told the carrier about the vital nature of the machinery when the carrier agreed to transport it, and the carrier had no reason to foresee the loss.

If the carrier had been told of the importance of the item, it would likely have been liable for the loss—unless it exempted itself from liability and suggested the sawmill insure the shipment against risk of delay or loss. Or it would have placed the item in a higher category of freight to ensure greater care in delivery and charged a higher rate for its services.[31]

Sometimes a party does enter into a contract with knowledge of special liability if it fails to perform.

CASE 13.5 In Reasonable Contemplation of the Parties

An engineering company contracted to make a machine and deliver it by a given date. It then made a subcontract with the defendant firm to manufacture an essential part, clearly stating the date that the entire machine had to be completed for its customer. The defendant subcontractor did not manufacture the part on time, and because of the delay, the buyer refused to accept the machine. The engineering company sued the subcontractor for damages, including the loss of profit on the main contract and the expenses incurred uselessly in making the machine. It succeeded; the court agreed that the subcontractor should have foreseen the risk when the contract was made.[32]

---

[30] Cassels and Adjin-Tettey, *supra* note 3 at 11–12.

[31] *BC Saw Mill Co v Nettleship* (1868), LR 3 CP 499. See also *Hadley v Baxendale* (1854), 156 ER 145; *Koufos v C Czarnikow, The Heron II*, [1969] 1 AC 350; *Cornwall Gravel Co Ltd v Purolator Courier Ltd* (1978), 18 OR (2d) 551. Cassels and Adjin-Tettey, *supra* note 3 at 464.

[32] *Hydraulic Engineering Co v McHaffie Goslett* (1878), 4 QBD 670. See also *Telecommander Corp v United Parcel Service Canada Ltd*, [1996] OJ No 4664.

The critical determination is made based upon the actual and supposed knowledge of the parties at the time the contract was formed, not at the time the breach occurs.

2. Damages Must Be Mitigated A party that has suffered a loss as a result of breach of contract is expected to do what it can to minimize its losses. Recoverable damages will not include what it might reasonably have avoided. In this respect, **mitigation** in contract is similar to that in tort. A business that has contracted to sell perishable goods and had them rejected by the breaching party cannot let the goods spoil. Instead, it should resell them at the best obtainable price as quickly as it can if it wishes to recoup any resulting loss in an action for damages. Similarly, when a business has agreed to buy goods and the seller fails to deliver, the buyer should move to replace the goods from another supplier as soon as possible. The same rule applies when a contract of employment is broken by the employer. An employee, in suing for damages for wrongful dismissal, should be able to show she made every reasonable effort to find suitable alternative employment as a means of mitigating the loss.

In summary, an injured party can only recover for the losses resulting from the breach that could not be reasonably avoided. Any costs associated with mitigating or reducing the loss are recoverable as damages. It naturally follows that if a party acts in a manner that aggravates or increases the loss, it will be denied recovery for the additional damages.[33]

mitigation action by the injured party to reduce the extent of loss caused by the other party's breach

THE MEASUREMENT OF DAMAGES

Damages for breach of contract may arise from a number of different types of loss. Depending upon the facts of the case, any one type or combination of types of damages may be experienced by the non-breaching party and be eligible for compensation. Usually it is the court that assesses the amount of damage and assigns a value to a particular type of loss; however, sometimes parties set the value of possible damages in the terms of the contract.

Liquidated Damages

When forming a contract, parties may agree on the amount of damages to be awarded for any type of damage if a breach should occur. The actual value of any eventual loss may turn out to be greater or less than the agreed amount, but the injured party's recovery will be limited to the pre-set amount, provided it was a genuine attempt by the parties to estimate a loss. The contractual terms will conclusively govern the amount of damages awarded. Such provisions for **liquidated damages** can provide some economic certainty—each party will know the extent of liability or recovery at the start of the contractual relationship and may plan accordingly.

liquidated damages an amount agreed on to be paid in damages by a party to a contract if it should commit a breach

ILLUSTRATION 13.8 Pre-Estimate of Damage

P Inc. agrees to construct an office building for Q Properties Inc., with a completion date of May 31. Both parties agree that any delay will cause a loss in revenue to Q from prospective tenants. A term of the contract states that, for any delay in completion, Q may deduct $600 per day from its final payment of $100 000 to P, payable one month after Q obtains possession of the building. Such a term is binding upon both parties whether Q Properties Inc. suffers a larger or smaller loss because of delay.

---

[33] Cassels and Adjin-Tettey, *supra* note 3 at 428–30.

We must distinguish between a genuine attempt to anticipate or "liquidate" the consequences of a breach of contract and a **penalty clause**. If a term in the contract specifies an exorbitant or unconscionable amount, out of all relation to the probable consequences of breach, a court may find that it is intended merely to frighten a party into performance. Accordingly, the court will hold that it is a penalty clause and will disregard it and award damages based on an assessment of the actual loss suffered.

penalty clause a term specifying an exorbitant amount for breach of contract, intended to frighten a party into performance

A sum paid as a deposit on the formation of a contract, to be forfeited on failure to perform, is a common type of liquidated damages provision, but it is treated somewhat differently. Partly because the money has already been paid as a guarantee of performance and partly because of a long history of deposits being forfeited, courts are reluctant to overturn such provisions even when they seem harsh. If, however, the sum is described as a part payment or a down payment, the courts are more willing to examine whether its forfeiture would be a penalty.

At the other extreme, a term limiting liquidated damages to a very small sum may be tantamount to an exemption clause. For instance, if a term states that $1 shall be payable as full compensation for breach, the court will undertake the three-step analysis discussed under "Exemption Clauses."

Nominal Damages

Occasionally, a court may award nominal damages to acknowledge a breach of contract where there is no real loss experienced by the non-breaching party. A court award of $1 will at least acknowledge the validity of the plaintiff's claim where a question of principle is at stake. In general, when the amount in dispute is nominal, the likelihood that a "successful" plaintiff will still have to pay or share court costs discourages such litigation.

TYPES OF DAMAGES

Expectation Damages

expectation damages an amount awarded for breach of contract, based on expected benefits or profits

Expectation damages are the usual remedy for breach of contract—the value of the expected benefit of performance. The basic calculation is as follows:

Expectation damages = (Expected position of the plaintiff if the contract had been performed) − (The actual position the plaintiff is in after the breach of contract)

An award of expectation damages for breach of contract contrasts sharply with the measurement of tort damages where recovery is limited to actual harm or loss suffered.[34] Expectation damages in contract look to the future and value expected future profits of the aborted transaction. For example, breach of a contract to sell a limited edition baseball may include an award for the expected rise in value of the baseball—that is, the lost investment value. This would not be the case for a contract to supply baseballs for use in a Little League game. In this second case, only the mitigation cost of buying replacement baseballs from another source would be recoverable.

opportunity cost the lost chance of making a similar contract with a different promisor

An award for expectation damages may also be based upon lost **opportunity cost**—this is because a party will have given up an opportunity to make a similar contract with someone else in order to contract with the breaching party. Illustration 13.9 demonstrates the approach courts take in the calculation of expectation damages.

---

[34] *Ibid* at 18.

> **ILLUSTRATION 13.9 Calculation of Expectation Damages**
>
> Suppose, first, that a buyer is in breach by refusing to accept delivery of the goods purchased. In an action for damages,[35] the first consideration is whether the seller's supply of goods exceeds the demand for them—that is, whether the seller can supply goods to all prospective customers.
>
> If so, the buyer's breach results in the seller losing the profit on one sale, regardless of the resale of those same goods to a second buyer: the seller would have made the second sale even if the first buyer had accepted the goods, and would have made two sales instead of one. Accordingly, the seller may recover damages from the first buyer amounting to the lost profits on their contract of sale.

However, if the seller has limited supply, and it could not have filled a second order if the first buyer had accepted the goods, the seller's damages will be measured, first, by its additional expenses in taking reasonable steps to find a second buyer, and second, by any loss in revenue as a result of having to accept a lower sale price to dispose of the goods. The seller may suffer no damages at all if it resells for the full contract price (or more) without additional selling expenses.[36]

Suppose, instead, a seller breaks its contract by failing to deliver on time. If the buyer can obtain the goods elsewhere, the damages will be reasonable expenses incurred in seeking an alternative supply and any additional price the buyer has had to pay above the original contract price. Of course, if the buyer obtains an alternative supply for the same or a lower price than that in the original contract, there will be no damages without added expenses in seeking the new supply.

Consequential Damages

Consequential damages are, in a sense, secondary losses, one stage removed from the immediate effects of breach. Nevertheless, they may be both serious and reasonably foreseeable at the time of contracting, so that a defendant will be liable to compensate for them. Suppose a seller fails to deliver goods that the buyer was to use as components to build another product for resale. Damages arising from the buyer's breach of the subsequent sale contracts are consequential damages. The seller will be liable for the lost profits on any resale transactions, and damage claims may also include claims against the buyer by its own customers as a result of its unavoidable default on contracts with them.

consequential damages
secondary losses incurred by the non-breaching party that were foreseeable at the time of contracting

> **CASE 13.6 Consequences of Breach**
>
> Lakelse Dairy Products purchased a new bulk-milk tank truck from General Dairy Machinery (GDM) to transport milk to its production facility. GDM specialized in building such vehicles and warranted that it was fit for the purpose. However, the truck had serious flaws—there were cracks in the tank where milk remained in sufficient quantities that when the milk deteriorated and went bad, new shipments of milk were affected. Lakelse hired experts to find the source of the problem.
>
> It took several months to uncover the defect in the truck. Meanwhile, a substantial amount of milk had to be discarded, and some had to be taken back from customers. When the source of the problem was discovered, Lakelse had to lease another tank truck. It sued GDM successfully, not only for the direct loss in value of the defective tank truck and the cost of leasing another truck but also for the lost profits that would have been made on the discarded milk if it had been sold by Lakelse at market value.[37]

---

[35] The *Sale of Goods Act* may allow the vendor to sue for the price instead of damages.
[36] In one sense, the first buyer's breach enabled the seller to make the second sale. See *Apeco of Canada Ltd v Windmill Place* (1978), 82 DLR (3d) 1; Cassels and Adjin-Tettey, *supra* note 3 at 28.
[37] *Lakelse Dairy Products Ltd v General Dairy Machinery & Supply Ltd* (1970), 10 DLR (3d) 277.

Consequential damages may arise in any contract, not only in the sale of goods. For instance, failure to repair the heating system of a concert hall as promised in time for a performance in midwinter could lead to the cancellation of the program, making the heating contractor liable for the losses due to cancellation as well as for damage to the building by frozen pipes, since both are foreseeable harms.

General Damages

The term *general damages* describes an estimated amount for intangible injury that a court may award, over and above specifically proven losses for harm. Damage cannot be calculated in precise monetary terms, but the court believes such an award is necessary to compensate the aggrieved party fairly. For example, if a surgeon undertook to improve the appearance of a professional entertainer by performing plastic surgery on her nose, but the result was disfigurement, a court would have to decide what general damages, over and above specific out-of-pocket medical and hospital expenses, would compensate the plaintiff for the effects of this failure on her state of mind and professional morale. A U.S. court has, in fact, awarded general damages for breach of contract in such circumstances.[38]

Reliance Damages

> **reliance damages** costs of expenditures and wasted effort reasonably made in preparation for performance

As an alternative to expectation damages, which place the injured party into the position it would have been in if the contract had been properly performed, an injured party may claim **reliance damages**, which compensate the injured party for wasted time, effort, and expenses preparing for performance—in essence putting the injured party back in their pre-contract position. Sometimes reliance damages yield a larger amount than expectation damages, usually when mitigation efforts have been very successful.

Suppose a management consultant contracts to spend three months advising a manufacturing company on the reorganization of its operations. During the two months prior to commencement of the contract, the consultant spends time assembling and preparing customized material. Just prior to the start date, the client cancels the contract. Even if the management consultant replaces the lost fee with another consulting opportunity, she has still lost the time, effort, and expenditures involved in the preparation. Now it is merely wasted effort—not needed for the substituted job—that she could have used more productively for other contracts. In these circumstances, the consultant may recover as reliance damages the costs of all expenditures and wasted effort that were reasonably made in preparation for her performance of the first contract.[39]

Punitive Damages

Punishment is not the purpose of contract damages; however, in rare circumstances courts have awarded punitive damages for malicious or bad faith behaviour of the breaching party.[40] In *Whiten v Pilot Insurance Company*, the Supreme Court of Canada confirmed the trial judge's award of $1 000 000 in punitive damages in a case concerning the defendant's refusal to pay a claim under a property insurance policy (or

---

[38] *Sullivan v O'Connor*, 296 NE 2d 183 (1973). Damages of $13 500 were awarded. See Cassels and Adjin-Tettey, *supra* note 3 at 251.

[39] *PreMD Inc v Ogilvy Renault LLP*, 2013 ONCA 412 at paras 65–70.

[40] Cassels and Adjin-Tettey, *supra* note 3 at 346–53. See e.g. *Ribeiro v CIBC* (1992), 13 OR (3d) 278; *Wallace v United Grain Growers Ltd* (1997), 152 DLR (4th) 1 (SCC).

contract). In its decision, the Court held that, while punitive damages in contract law are exceptional, they are appropriate if there has been "high-handed, malicious, arbitrary, or highly reprehensible misconduct that departs to a marked degree from ordinary standards of decent behaviour."[41]

This kind of "values-based" assessment of behaviour may lead to inconsistent and unpredictable results. In *Fidler v Sun Life Assurance Co of Canada*,[42] the British Columbia Court of Appeal's award of punitive damages arising from the five-year denial of long-term disability benefits was set aside by the Supreme Court because the conduct was not malicious or oppressive. Although rare, punitive damages are possible in extreme circumstances. Courts will exercise this discretion cautiously.

CHALLENGES IN MEASURING DAMAGES

Mental Anguish

In tort law, courts recognize pain, suffering, nervous shock, and humiliation as harms for which they should grant recovery as part of general damages. In an increasing number of contract cases, mental anguish or distress resulting from breach is recognized as a form of non-economic harm entitled to compensation. The Supreme Court of Canada stated that the purpose of recognizing mental distress in an award of damages is "to substitute other amenities for those that have been lost, not to compensate for the loss of something with a money value . . . [and] to provide more general physical arrangements above and beyond those directly relating to the injuries, in order to make life more endurable."[43]

Courts initially awarded this type of damage for contracts that promised some form of pleasure such as vacations or luxury items. Now, damages for mental distress may be awarded in any breach of contract action if this type of damage was reasonably foreseeable by the parties at the time the contract was created.[44] In one case, mental anguish damages were awarded against an airline for breach of contract in transporting the plaintiffs' dogs[45] as compensation for the mental suffering endured when they learned that their dogs suffocated while being carried in the baggage compartment of an airplane. The law is still evolving in this area, and it is not clear whether the plaintiff must suffer some psychological illness or whether mere mental suffering or distress is sufficient.[46] Wrongful dismissal and lost holiday cases often consider this type of general damage.

1. Wrongful Dismissal Mental anguish often occurs when an employee is fired, especially after long years of service. Apart from direct financial loss, for which he is entitled to compensation, the dismissed employee may feel humiliated and suffer a serious loss of confidence. When the Supreme Court of Canada considered this type of damage, it confirmed that although "normal distress and hurt feelings resulting from dismissal are not compensable . . . [mental anguish damages may be awarded] when the employer engages in conduct during the course of dismissal that is unfair or in bad faith such as [behaviour that is] untruthful, misleading or unduly

---

[41] *Whiten v Pilot Insurance Co*, 2002 SCC 18.
[42] [2006] 2 SCR 3.
[43] *Lindal v Lindal* (1981), 129 DLR (3d) 263 at 272–3.
[44] *Fidler, supra* note 42 at para 42. But see *Healey v Lakeridge Health Corporation*, [2010] OJ No 417 (distinguishing *Fidler*).
[45] *Newell v CP Air* (1976), 74 DLR (3d) 574.
[46] See *Kotai v Queen of the North*, [2009] BCJ No 2022, where the court held that the plaintiff must suffer from a psychological illness, not just distress.

insensitive."[47] Examples of behaviours that meet this test are lying about the reason for dismissal or defaming the reputation of the employee.[48] The plaintiff must prove the psychological harm for which mental anguish damages are claimed; it will not be presumed by the court.

CASE 13.7 Damages for Breach of Employment Contracts

K worked for his employer for 11 years on the assembly line and then as a data entry clerk. After being diagnosed with chronic fatigue syndrome, he was frequently absent, which resulted in his firing. At trial, K was awarded damages for lack of notice and mental anguish, and punitive damages related to allegations of discrimination and failure to accommodate his illness. The Supreme Court of Canada overturned the punitive damage awards, saying the discretion to grant punitive damages should be exercised cautiously for only harsh, vindictive, extreme, or malicious conduct, which was not present in the subject case.[49]

We discuss employment in Chapter 18.

2. Lost Holidays Many contracts, such as those for holiday travel and accommodation, are intended to confer an experiential rather than economic benefit. Unless courts take into account disappointment caused by the loss of an anticipated holiday, a vacationer would be without remedy apart from the return of any money paid. A return of that money would hardly be ample compensation to a vacationer who discovers at the airport that there is neither a flight nor any possibility of arranging an alternative holiday at the last minute. Therefore damages for ruined holidays often include damages for mental distress, inconvenience, upset, disappointment, and frustration caused by the loss of the holiday.[50]

Cost of Performance Versus Economic Loss

The following U.S. case provides a striking example of the difficulty in deciding on the appropriate standards for measuring damages in circumstances that fall outside traditional categories of economic loss.

CASE 13.8 Potential Windfall

Owners of a farm containing coal deposits leased it to a mining company for five years. The operation was strip mining, in which coal is scooped from open pits on the surface, scarring the land. The owners insisted on including a term in the lease requiring the company to restore the surface at the expiration of the lease by moving earth in order to level the pits. At the end of the lease, the company vacated without restoring the land, and the owners sued for damages.

Breach was admitted by the company. However, the court was faced with the following dilemma: the cost of restoring the land as promised would be $29 000, but the market value of the farm would increase by only $300 as a result of the restoration. The owners claimed damages of $29 000, measured by the "cost of performance," and the company countered that it was liable only for damages of $300—the "depreciated [market] value"—caused by the breach. The court found that an award of $29 000 to the plaintiffs would have given them a windfall of $28 700; it awarded damages of only $300.[51]

---

[47] *Honda Canada Inc v Keays*, 2008 SCC 39 at paras 56–7, referring to *Wallace v United Grain Growers Ltd* (1997), 152 DLR (4th) 1 (SCC) at para 98, and *Vorvis v Insurance Corporation of BC*, [1989] 1 SCR 1085.

[48] *Honda, ibid* at para 59.

[49] *Honda, supra* note 47 at paras 62–78.

[50] *Jarvis v Swan Tours Ltd*, [1973] QB 233; *Elder v Koppe* (1974), 53 DLR (3d) 705; *Keks v Esquire Pleasure Tours Ltd*, [1974] 3 WWR 406; *Wolf v Advance Fur Dressers Ltd*, 2005 BCSC 1097.

[51] *Peevyhouse v Garland Coal & Mining Company*, 382 P 2d 109 (Okla 1963). See also *James v Hutton & J Cool & Sons Ltd*, [1950] 1 KB 9; *D Karrasch Construction Ltd v Telosky*, 2010 BCSC 423.

The choice of economic value over cost of performance recognizes the basic purpose of damages—there must be a loss. If the non-breaching party is no worse off as a result of the failure to perform, it does not matter how much performance would have cost the breaching party.

EQUITABLE REMEDIES

Reasons for the Intervention of Equity

Historically courts gave only money damages for breach of contract. But sometimes money damages alone are inadequate. For example, suppose a purchaser buys a "classic car" because it belonged to his great grandfather. If the vendor refuses to complete the deal, no amount of money will fulfill the purpose of the contract. The most sensible remedy would be to order the vendor to transfer the car to the purchaser on payment of the purchase price. The inadequacy of the common law damages led to the development of special equitable remedies, such as specific performance. Failure to comply with an equitable remedy places a defendant in "contempt of court" and can lead to a fine or imprisonment.

Prerequisites for an Equitable Remedy

Equitable remedies are discretionary—that is, the court decides whether, in view of all the circumstances, good reasons exist to go beyond the ordinary common law remedy of damages. First, the court must be satisfied that damages will not adequately compensate the loss; thereafter, an equitable remedy is granted to a plaintiff that complies with the established principles of equity. The following are among the more important requirements:

(a) A plaintiff must come to court with "clean hands"—that is, he must not himself have acted unethically; if he has, his claim will be limited to money damages.

(b) A plaintiff must not delay in bringing an action. The faster the request is made, the more likely a court will grant an equitable remedy.

(c) As we noted in Chapter 9 on "Mistake," a court will refuse to intervene on equitable principles when to do so would negatively affect an innocent purchaser.

(d) The plaintiff must have paid meaningful consideration for the defendant's promise; promises given under seal or in exchange for a nominal sum do not qualify.

(e) Finally, a plaintiff must ordinarily be a party against whom the remedy would be awarded were he the defendant instead. For example, because a court will not grant an equitable remedy against an infant defendant when a contract is voidable at his option, neither will it grant that remedy in his favour as a plaintiff. This factor is hard to justify on grounds of fairness and is not always followed.

Specific Performance

Specific performance is an order requiring a defendant to do a specified act, most often to complete a transaction. In a real estate sale agreement, specific performance is commonly ordered, provided the purchaser can prove the piece of land is unique, and no other will suffice.[52] This is difficult to do if the land is purchased for investment or

specific performance an order requiring a defendant to do a contracted-for act, usually to complete a transaction

---

[52] *Semelhago v Paramadevan*, [1996] 2 SCR 415; *Carttera Management Inc v Palm Holdings Canada Inc*, 2011 ONSC 2573 (holding the subject property was not unique).

development purposes only.[53] Still if uniqueness is proven, a vendor will be ordered to deliver all documents necessary to transfer of ownership, on payment of the purchase price.

In situations where the court might be obligated to supervise a defendant, specific performance will not be granted. As a result, performance that depends on the personal skill or judgment of a defendant does not lend itself to an order for specific performance. An artist who repudiates a contract to give a concert will not be ordered to perform; to do so would be to invite a disgruntled performance. The plaintiff will be awarded of money damages.

Courts rarely grant specific performance of a contract for the sale of goods—damages are considered adequate compensation, unless the contract is for the sale of a one-of-a-kind item. Antiques, heirlooms, rare coins, and works of art are possible examples. Shares in a corporation may also be considered property for which specific performance is an appropriate remedy, especially when a plaintiff's primary purpose is to obtain a controlling or substantial interest in the business.

Injunction

An injunction is a court order restraining a party from acting in a particular manner; in relation to contract, it prohibits a party from committing a breach. For the remedy to be available, the courts require the contract to contain a **negative covenant**: a promise not to do something. However, the covenant need not be stated expressly as a prohibition but may simply be a logical consequence of an express promise. Accordingly, an express promise by a tenant to use leased premises for office space would likely be construed to contain an implied promise not to use them for a nightclub; the landlord could obtain an injunction prohibiting their use for a nightclub. The negative tone of an injunction also avoids the supervision problem discussed above. Any evidence of the prohibited activity is a violation of the injunction, and the court does not need continuous supervision.

negative covenant a promise not to do something

In some circumstances, a court will grant an **interlocutory injunction**—a temporary injunction—to restrain immediate harm from being done, pending formal resolution of the dispute at trial. Courts are reluctant, however, to grant even a temporary injunction of this kind in personal service contracts, and a party must establish that irreparable harm will be done without an injunction. A typical example involves a breach of contract action claiming specific performance of a real estate transaction. The plaintiff may ask the court to prohibit the sale of the land by the vendor to anyone else until after the trial. Obviously, the purchaser could not get a specific performance remedy if the vendor had already sold the land to a third party.

interlocutory injunction a temporary injunction preventing immediate harm from being done before the full trial of the matter

In rare cases, an interlocutory injunction may be granted against a non-party to the lawsuit or the contract but only when that non-party is so involved in the wrongful acts of others that they facilitate the harm.[54]

Rescission

rescission setting aside or rescinding a contract in order to restore the parties as nearly as possible to their pre-contract positions

As discussed in Chapter 9, **rescission** involves returning a party as nearly as possible to the position that existed before the contract was made at all. In other words, the contract is set aside or rescinded. This is not usually the focus of a remedy for breach—those strive to place the parties, as nearly as possible, into the position that would have existed if the contract had been properly formed. However, if a breach is

---

[53] *Strategic Acquisition Corp v Starke Capital Corp*, 2017 ABCA 250 at paras 34–5.

[54] *Google v Equustek Solutions*, 2017 SCC 34.

serious enough to discharge the plaintiff from her own obligations, she may elect rescission, provided it is feasible to return the parties substantially to their pre-contract positions. An aggrieved party must choose between the two remedies—she cannot have both. Naturally, if it is not possible to return the parties to their pre-contract positions, the court will not order it. People elect rescission whenever they decide to return defective goods to the store for a refund rather than suing for cost of repair or replacement.

Quantum Meruit

As discussed in Chapter 7, a *quantum meruit* claim arises when valuable benefit is conferred at the request of a promisee. *Quantum meruit* may also be claimed when a serious breach occurs, and the non-breaching party has partially performed his obligations. The non-breaching party may elect to treat the contract as discharged or to rescind but still deserves payment for the value previously conveyed. Such circumstances are common in construction contracts when breach occurs after commencement of the work but prior to completion. The partially performing party may ask the court to assess the fair market value of the work already done and thereby receive compensation on a *quantum meruit* basis. The assessment is based upon the benefit conferred, not the cost of doing the work.

quantum meruit the fair amount a person deserves to be paid for benefit conferred

---

CHECKLIST

Breach of Contract Remedies

Common law damages
- expectation damages
- consequential damages
- general damages
- reliance damages
- punitive damages

Equitable remedies
- specific performance
- injunction
- rescission
- *quantum meruit*

METHODS OF ENFORCING JUDGMENTS

When a plaintiff obtains judgment for a sum of money, he becomes a **judgment creditor**, and the defendant a **judgment debtor**. If the judgment debtor is financially sound, the stigma of the court judgment is usually sufficient to motivate voluntary payment. If, however, the debtor resists payment or is in financial difficulty, the judgment creditor may then move to enforce payment. There are legal procedures by which a judgment creditor may seize as much of the debtor's property as is necessary to satisfy the judgment. If the assets are insufficient, she may seize more assets in the future when they

judgment creditor a party who has obtained a court judgment for a sum of money

judgment debtor a party who has been ordered by the court to pay a sum of money

become available. Judgments remain enforceable for a long time after judgment, often 20 years before they require renewal.

The most usual collection procedure is to register the judgment with the office of the sheriff of the county or district in which the debtor resides and to request the sheriff to **levy execution** against the assets of the debtor to satisfy the judgment. An **execution order** gives the sheriff authority to seize and sell various goods and arrange for a sale of the debtor's lands after an appropriate grace period.[55] Additional procedures exist to seize money in a bank account, the contents of a safety deposit box, or income from a trust fund. A creditor may also obtain a **garnishee order** against a debtor's wages. The order requires the employer to retain a portion of the debtor's wages each payday and forward the sum to the creditor to be applied against the judgment. If the judgment creditor does not know where the debtor works, banks, or owns land, it may summon the judgment debtor to appear for a judgment debtor examination. The debtor must attend and disclose, under oath, the details of his finances. Failure to appear at an examination or knowingly providing false information is considered **contempt of court** and may be punished by imprisonment.

A judgment debtor is not considered a criminal. Honest inability to pay is not punished; only willful failure to comply or fraudulent concealing of assets will trigger punishment such as imprisonment.

levy execution to seize and sell a debtor's chattels or arrange for a sale of his lands

execution order an order that gives the sheriff authority to levy execution

garnishee order an order requiring the debtor's employer to retain a portion of the debtor's wages each payday and surrender the sum to the creditor

contempt of court a finding by a court that a person has willfully refused to obey a court order and therefore will be punished

INTERNATIONAL ISSUE

Enforcement of Foreign Judgments

Sometimes the assets of a judgment debtor are located in a foreign jurisdiction. A judgment creditor must seek the foreign court's recognition of its judgment before it may seize the asset. In Canada, common law provinces recognize each other's judgments (and those of the United Kingdom) through a simple registration process. An enforcing court will recognize the judgment provided the granting court had a real and substantial connection to the matter and followed its own jurisdictional rules. It does not matter if the defendant participated or agreed to the jurisdiction of the granting court.[56] Within Canada, there is confidence that the judicial systems offer procedural fairness, and there is no need for examination of the correctness of the decision.

The Supreme Court extended the application of this narrow procedural fairness and jurisdiction test to foreign judgments from other countries such as the United States. In *Beals v Saldanha*,[57] the Court recognized a judgment from Florida that granted damages of $210 000 plus $50 000 of punitive damages. This was somewhat controversial because circumstances of the case stemmed from an $8000 real estate transaction, and there was no evidence to support punitive damages. The dissent felt that the excessive damages and the lack of notice associated with this outcome was a barrier to the recognition of the judgment. However, the majority disagreed, and the judgment was recognized.

Questions to Consider

1. Should foreign judgments containing excessive damage awards be recognized by Canadian courts if the same damages would not be recoverable here?
2. Is it relevant to consider whether the foreign court easily recognizes Canadian judgments?

Sources: H.S. Fairley, "Open Season: Recognition and Enforcement of Foreign Judgments in Canada After *Beals v. Saldanha*" (2005), 11(2) ILSA *Journal of International and Comparative Law* 305–18; J.S. Ziegel, "Enforcement of Foreign Judgments in Canada, Unlevel Playing Fields and *Beals v. Saldanha*: A Consumer Perspective" (2003) 38 *Canadian Business Law Journal* 294–308.

---

[55] See e.g. *Execution Act*, RSO 1990, c E.24, s 2; *Court Order Enforcement Act*, RSBC 1996, c 78, s 71.
[56] *Morguard Investments v De Savoye*, [1990] 3 SCR 1077; *Club Resorts Ltd v Van Breda*, 2012 SCC 17.
[57] [2003] 3 SCR 416.

Strategies to Manage the Legal Risks

There are a number of proactive steps a business can take that will reduce the costs and losses associated with breach of contract, should one occur. The first step is to determine the risks that are likely to make performance difficult for the business or the customer and quantify the value of those risks. The business should adopt some or all of the following strategies to manage the risks:

- A party may obtain insurance against the risk and raise its price accordingly.
- It may "self-insure"—that is, charge a higher fee and build up a reserve fund to pay any claim that arises later from harm to a customer.
- For reoccurring transactions, the business should develop a standard form contract that specifically addresses the risks from the business's perspective.
- It may include an exemption clause in the contract to exclude any liability for the risk and transferring the risk of harm to its customer.
- Parties may include liquidated damage clauses to quantify the risk ahead of time and provide incentive for parties to perform.
- Contracts may require the payment of a deposit, installments, or the posting of a performance bond, to be released only after full performance. In this way, an injured party will have some funds available to them in the event of a breach, avoiding collection problems.
- Parties should identify essential terms of the contract, breach of which would trigger their discharge from the contract. This will avoid arguments about the seriousness of the risk.
- Businesses should keep detailed records of expenses incurred in preparation for or reliance upon a contract. Expenses associated with mitigation should also be documented.

Whenever a business is unable to perform exactly as promised, a wise manager will notify the other party as soon as she is aware of the inability to perform. In this way, the non-breaching party may take immediate steps to mitigate any loss the breach may cause, minimizing unnecessary reliance and consequential damages.

QUESTIONS FOR REVIEW

1. Why does a major breach not automatically discharge a contract? Give an example.
2. Describe two ways in which anticipatory breach may occur.
3. In what types of contracts does it become particularly difficult to ascertain whether a breach is sufficient to allow the injured party to be freed from its part of the bargain? Explain.
4. Describe why the doctrine of substantial performance is of practical importance.
5. What is the reasoning behind the requirement that an injured party mitigate its losses?
6. When a buyer refuses to accept delivery of goods, explain the significance of supply and demand when determining the value of damages suffered.
7. Explain the attitude of the courts toward exemption clauses.
8. Give an example of strict interpretation of an exemption clause.

9. In what circumstances might a court grant an interlocutory injunction?
10. When a judgment debtor refuses to pay the judgment, what recourse does the judgment creditor have?
11. Describe the nature and purpose of liquidated damage clauses and how they are distinguished from penalty clauses.
12. Define expectation damages, consequential damages, and specific performance. Give an example of each.

CASES AND PROBLEMS

1. *Continuing Scenario*

   In the coat room at Ashley's restaurant, a posted sign says "Not responsible for loss or damage." Joan arrives for lunch, hangs her coat in the coat room, and is seated in the dining area. After lunch, Joan begins feeling ill and goes to the hospital, where it is determined that Joan got food poisoning from the chili she ordered and ate at Ashley's restaurant. When Joan contacts Ashley for compensation, she is told that Ashley is "not responsible for loss or damage" because the sign is an exemption clause. Will the alleged exemption clause protect Ashley from liability? How will the court approach the analysis?

2. Stellar Construction Inc. agreed to build a new Olympic swimming pool for the Thomson Aquatic Centre for $450 000. The completion date was May 1. Thomson visited the pool on April 23 and was very disappointed with the quality of the tiles and caulking on the edges of the pool. She complained at once to Urqhart, Stellar's onsite manager.

   Urqhart said the tiles and caulking complied with the specifications, but if Thomson wanted them replaced, there would be a delay of two weeks for completing the project. Thomson insisted that the quality was inadequate but that she needed to have the pool ready by May 3 when she had scheduled the grand opening celebration of the renovated centre. Urqhart replied that she would have to choose between a delayed opening and accepting the tiles as is. Thomson then said, "Leave it. We'll settle it later."

   Stellar continued its work and completed the project on May 2, in time for the grand opening. The final payment of $100 000 to Stellar was due May 15, but Thomson refused to pay it. She claimed that she had an independent appraisal of the tile work, that it would cost at least $50 000 to have the work done, and that the pool would have to be closed for two weeks, causing substantial losses in revenue to the aquatic centre.

   Stellar sued Thomson for the $100 000, denying that Thomson's complaint was valid. It was established that the tiles failed to meet the specifications in the contract between the parties and that replacing them would indeed cost $50 000 plus the cost of business disruption. However, the diminished appearance of the pool caused by the tiles reduced the value of the pool by no more than $15 000.

   Give your opinion about whether it was Thomson's choice to replace or leave the tiles. In either case, would Stellar's failure to perform amount to a minor or major breach?

3. In December, Carvel Estates Ltd., a real estate developer, contracted to buy 24 large suburban lots from Dalquith Enterprises Inc., with the transaction to close May 15. Carvel had hired an architect and intended to build expensive "upmarket" homes. The plans for each house were at an advanced stage by late March, when, without any prior notice, Dalquith sent Carvel a cheque refunding Carvel's down payment. Dalquith informed Carvel it could not go through with the deal because Dalquith's parent corporation had applied for a zoning change and wished to construct luxury condominiums on the site. Dalquith also stated it had discussed the situation with the owner of land adjacent to the site Carvel had

purchased, and the owner was willing to discuss selling an equivalent number of lots to Carvel.

Carvel's manager was very upset because the firm would have been ready to begin work immediately after the May 15 closing date. Carvel refused to consider the alternative lots offered by Dalquith. Carvel commenced an action, requesting transfer of the property and damages for any additional costs as a result of delay in the project. Name the remedy Carvel is requesting, and explain whether it is likely that Carvel will succeed. If not, what other remedies might be available to Carvel?

4. Complicated Machinery Co. Ltd. manufactures and assembles heavy equipment for industry. It accepted an order from Northern Paper Co. for a large machine that would automate certain processes; one of the terms of the order was that the machine was to be completed by October 31. The contract further stated that if the machine was not completed by October 31, Complicated Machinery Co. Ltd. would pay Northern Paper Co. $1000 for each week of delay. The manager of Northern Paper Co. had written in a letter accompanying the offer: "Until the machine is in full operation it is hard to say what our savings will be. A thousand dollars a week is a rough guess."

Complicated Machinery Co. Ltd. failed to deliver until December 26, eight weeks late. It billed the paper company for the full price less $8000 (eight weeks at $1000). The paper company discovered that the machine actually saved $2400 weekly in production costs. It therefore tendered as payment the full price less $19 200 (eight weeks at $2400). Which party is correct, and why?

5. Brown, a painting contractor, made an oral contract with Hilton to paint the interior of Hilton's house for $1600, to be paid on completion of the work. Brown ran into difficulty when he painted the walls of the living room because the paint was pulled into the wall by the porous plaster. He had the same problem when he applied a second coat. He then realized what was causing the trouble and applied what is known as a "sealer," so that the next coat would adhere properly. Leaving the living room until the sealer was dry, he began painting the dining room.

At that point, Hilton inspected the work and complained to Brown that the colour of the paint was not the colour she had selected. Brown became very annoyed and emphatically announced he would quit the job. Hilton urged him not to abandon the work without first seeing her husband, but in a huff he removed his materials and equipment. When he abandoned the work, Brown still had to finish painting the living room and had not begun to paint several other rooms in the house. It also appeared that the woodwork had been painted without having been sanded and would have to be stripped and repainted. Brown brought an action against Hilton for $890, claiming $230 for materials and $660 for 33 hours' work. Should he succeed?

Part 4 Special Types of Contracts

Chapter 14
Sale of Goods and Consumer Contracts

- **THE *SALE OF GOODS ACT***
- **TERMS IN A CONTRACT OF SALE**
- **TITLE TO GOODS**
- **REMEDIES OF THE SELLER**
- **THE SELLER'S LIABILITY**
- **REMEDIES OF THE BUYER**
- **CONSUMER CONTRACTS**
- **BUSINESS SALES TACTICS TARGETING CONSUMERS**
- **TERMS IN CONSUMER CONTRACTS**
- **CONSUMER REMEDIES**
- **STRATEGIES TO MANAGE THE LEGAL RISKS**

Contracts for the sale of goods are the most common type of contract and are identified by the subject matter of the contract—goods. Over time, they generated a vast amount of case law, which was eventually collected into one statute—the *Sale of Goods Act*.

Consumer contracts are contracts between—consumers and business. A variety of statutes attempt to level the imbalance of power between consumers and business.

In this chapter we examine such questions as:

- What does the *Sale of Goods Act* do?
- What are the terms that it implies into a contract of sale?
- How is the ownership of goods transferred?
- To what extent is the seller liable for defective or unsatisfactory goods?
- What are the remedies available to buyers and sellers?
- What is a consumer contract?
- What pressure sales tactics are regulated?
- What additional terms are implied into a consumer contract?
- What additional remedies are available to a consumer?

THE *SALE OF GOODS ACT*

History of the *Sale of Goods Act*

When the term *contract* is used, the type of contract that usually comes to mind is a contract for the sale of goods. Goods have been sold for centuries, and the number of cases that developed was so immense that the British Parliament simplified the rules by putting them all in a comprehensive statute called the *Sale of Goods Act*. All the common law provinces in Canada subsequently passed similar acts.[1]

The *Sale of Goods Act* did not change the law. Its organized the existing law, with clarification where necessary to resolve conflicts between competing principles. The cases decided before the Act recognized several implied terms that were added to every contract for the sale of goods, unless they were inconsistent with the purposes of the contract or were expressly excluded by the parties. Those terms were **codified**, or collected in the Act—they are now implied into every contract covered by the *Sale of Goods Act*. We discuss these implied terms in the next section of this chapter.

codified existing common law rules collected and put in statute form

---

CHECKLIST
Application of the *Sale of Goods Act*

The *Sale of Goods Act* applies to

- sales (and agreements to sell)
- goods (not services, unless other legislation extends the protection)
- all parties to the sale contract, including businesses, consumers, individuals, and corporations

The *Sale of Goods Act* does not apply to

- exchanges of goods (barter)
- bailments or leases (see Chapter 15)
- consignments (see below)
- non-contractual transfers of property or goods
- sales of land or intangible property
- supply of services (see consumer protection exception)

Contracts of Sale

In the *Sale of Goods Act*, a contract of sale "is a contract whereby the seller transfers or agrees to transfer the property in the goods to the buyer for a money consideration, called the price." Money must form a part of the transaction. A straight barter of goods where no money changes hands does not come within the statute.

---

[1] The various provincial *Sale of Goods Acts* are fairly similar, but the numbering of sections differs from one province to another. In this chapter, we quote from the *Ontario Act* and give the corresponding section numbers in Alberta, British Columbia, Newfoundland and Labrador, and Manitoba as well as other provinces where applicable.

agreement to sell a contract of sale in which the transfer of ownership in the goods is deferred to some future time

The Act distinguishes between a sale and an **agreement to sell**. In a sale, the seller transfers ownership or title in goods to the buyer at the moment the contract is made. In an agreement to sell, the transfer is deferred until a future time; that time is either a specified date or an indefinite date that depends on the fulfillment of a particular requirement. The Act applies to both sales and agreements to sell. An agreement to sell may be formed even when the goods are non-existent. A contract to sell goods to be manufactured in three months' time or to sell a crop at a stated price per bushel once it has grown are examples of agreements to sell. An agreement to sell is a binding contract, as are other contracts containing promises of future conduct.

consignment the transfer of only possession of goods from one business to another for the purpose of offering for sale

A contract of sale is different from a **consignment**. The difference is confusing, since the word *consignment* is used in two different senses. In common usage, a consignment is simply a shipment of goods from one person or business to another in performance of a contract of sale. Here, the consignor is a seller and the consignee a buyer. But in a more technical sense, a consignor may send goods to an agent (consignee) who will offer them for sale at their new location on behalf of the consignor. In this instance, ownership in the goods does not pass between the consignor and consignee: If the consignee sells the goods, the title passes directly from the consignor to the purchaser. Expensive items displayed in a jeweller's shop, for example, may not be part of the jeweller's own stock-in-trade but simply may be held on consignment from a manufacturer or wholesaler. The distinction between sale and consignment may be important, since it will determine if the *Sale of Goods Act* applies.

CASE 14.1 Consignment

Win Sun Produce, a family business engaged in importing fruit and vegetables, agreed with Pacific Produce, a large wholesale fruit and vegetable business, to supply Pacific with a container shipment of 950 boxes of pomelos imported from Thailand. The pomelos were delivered to Pacific, together with a "purchase order" invoicing the pomelos at $47 per box. A "load sheet," signed by the person at Pacific, referred to the "consignment" as having been received. Pacific had not previously stocked pomelos and found that they did not sell well. Pacific asked Win Sun to take back 140 boxes, which Win Sun did, crediting Pacific with the sum of $6580.

Pacific was still unable to sell all the remaining pomelos, and eventually many of them rotted. Win Sun claimed the balance of the price. Pacific contested this, claiming the pomelos had been supplied on consignment and still belonged to Win Sun.

The British Columbia Court of Appeal ruled that the contract was one of sale. The word *consignment* in the load sheet had been used in the sense of "shipment." If the contract had been one of consignment, there would have been no need for Pacific to ask Win Sun to take some back or for Pacific to have been credited with part of the price.[2]

Goods

goods personal property, excluding both money and choses in action

For the *Sale of Goods Act* to apply, the subject matter of the contract must be **goods**, which the Act (section 1(1)) defines as meaning "all chattels personal, other than things in action and money."[3] Property is divided into two main classes: real property and personal property. Real property is confined to interests in land. All other property is called personal property. Personal property is also divided into two categories: intangible property, known as choses ("things") in action; and tangible property, known as

---

[2] *Win Sun Produce Co v Albert Fisher Canada Ltd* (1998), 111 BCAC 295, varying cost order [1999] BCJ No 294, leave denied [1998] SCCA No 522 (QL).

[3] *Sale of Goods Act*, RSO 1990, c S.1, s 1(1).

goods or chattels. In Chapter 11, we discussed choses in action in relation to the assignment of contractual rights. In contrast to choses in action, which have a value because they represent binding obligations, goods derive their value intrinsically from the utility or satisfaction they provide.

There is also a distinction between contracts for the sale of goods and contracts for services. The distinction is not always an easy one to make. For example, in contracting to have a house constructed, a boat built, or a central heating system installed, the buyer agrees to pay for a finished product as well as for the labour that produced it. A court may have to decide whether it was the work or the materials that constituted the essence of the contract. If the final value is mainly the result of the skill and labour that have gone into its preparation, the contract will be one for work and materials and not for "goods" as defined by the Act.[4] In practice, the distinction is not always important, since some of the legal principles that apply to contracts for work and materials are much the same as provisions in the *Sale of Goods Act*. For example, the Supreme Court held that a contract for work and materials is also subject, as a matter of common law, to an implied condition of fitness, analogous to the condition of fitness implied in contracts for the sale of goods.[5] This is not true in every case.

CASE 14.2 Services or Goods

The plaintiff was infected with HIV as a result of artificial insemination performed by her physician in 1985. The physician screened the donors and took the usual precautions according to the standard practice in Canada at that time (when no test was available to detect the virus in blood or semen). The trial jury found the physician negligent and awarded damages of $883 800, but the finding of negligence was overturned on appeal.

The plaintiff also based her claim on another ground. The physician had supplied "goods," namely, the semen. The semen was not fit for the purpose for which it was supplied, the plaintiff claimed, and therefore there was a breach of the "seller's" duty under the *Sale of Goods Act*.

The Supreme Court of Canada ruled

1. that the contract was one for the supply of services, not of goods,
2. that the courts should be wary of implying terms in contracts for the supply of services, especially when the contract involved the supply of products that carry inherent risks.

The physician had not been negligent and should not face a stricter liability for goods that are incidental to the service supplied than that imposed by the normal duty of care.[6]

Ownership and Possession

The words *ownership* (legal title) and *possession* (physical control) involve difficult legal problems. We understand the distinction in everyday activity, as when we lend possession of an object to someone yet retain ownership of it. We correctly assume that if that person refused to return the object, we would have a remedy in the courts to protect our ownership or title.

---

[4] The examples mentioned—a house, a boat, and a central heating system—have all been held to be contracts for "work and materials"; see *Hodgkinson v Hitch House Ltd* (1985), 60 OR (2d) 793, aff'd [1987] 60 OR (2d) 797. By contrast, a restaurant meal has been held to be "goods." *Gee v White Spot Ltd* (1986), 32 DLR (4th) 238.
[5] *AG of Canada v Laminated Structures & Holdings Ltd* (1961), 28 DLR (2d) 92, 100–1, aff'd *Laminated Structures & Holdings Ltd v Easter Woodworkers Ltd*, [1962] SCR 160. Also see *Spanos v Dufferin Tile & Marble Inc*, 2007 CarswellOnt 8625.
[6] *Ter Neuzen v Korn*, [1995] 3 SCR 674. See also *Pittman Estate v Bain* (1994), 19 CCLT (2d) 1, a case involving HIV-tainted blood.

The separation of ownership and possession occurs frequently in contracts for the sale of goods: When the contract is a sale that passes title to the buyer immediately, possession often remains with the seller or with a carrier for some time afterward. By contrast, under installment sales contracts, a vendor often keeps title to goods until the last payment is made while possession passes to the buyer immediately.

TERMS IN A CONTRACT OF SALE

The *Caveat Emptor* Principle

caveat emptor let the buyer beware

The legal saying **caveat emptor** is one of the few Latin phrases most people know. *Caveat emptor* means "let the buyer beware"—that is, the risk is with the buyer. He must investigate the purchase or suffer the consequences. However, it is not a rigid rule but a flexible general principle limited by customary business practice and the *Sale of Goods Act*.

The *caveat emptor* principle applies where the goods in existence are specific items that may be inspected by the buyer and when the seller has made no misrepresentations about them. In these circumstances, it is a sensible rule. The buyer has the opportunity to exercise her judgment by examining the goods, and if she distrusts her own judgment or has doubts, she may bargain for an express term stating the goods have the particular quality she requires.

Caveat emptor encourages buyers to determine if the goods are what they want before they contract to buy. However, in certain circumstances, the principle could invite abuse by fraudulent sellers. For example, a buyer sometimes relies upon the knowledge or expert judgment of the seller, or a buyer may place special confidence or trust in the seller. Consequently, various implied terms that protect buyers are found in the *Sale of Goods Act*.

Statutory Protection for the Buyer: Implied Terms

condition a major or essential term of the contract, the breach of which may relieve the injured party from further performance

warranty a lesser or non-essential term that, when breached, does not relieve the injured party from performance

retail sales sales of consumer goods by retail businesses, in the ordinary course of their business, to private individuals

Conditions and Warranties The *Sale of Goods Act* uses the word **condition** to mean a major or essential term of a contract, the breach of which relieves the injured party from further duty to perform the contract. The Act uses **warranty** to mean a lesser or non-essential term, the breach of which does not relieve the injured party from the bargain—she must perform her side, but she may sue for damages. In this chapter, we use the two words with the meanings given them by the Act. Some terms implied by the Act are conditions, and others are warranties.

In the majority of provinces, the terms are only implied if there is no express provision to the contrary in the contract. In some provinces, however, the most important implied terms cannot be excluded in the case of **retail sales**—that is, sales of consumer goods by retail businesses to private individuals in the ordinary course of business. In New Brunswick, the warranties are set out in a separate statute—the *Consumer Product Warranty and Liability Act*.[7] Saskatchewan originally followed the same approach but has since incorporated the warranties into its *Consumer Protection Act*.[8] British Columbia, by contrast, simply provides in its *Sale of Goods Act* that the implied warranties and conditions cannot be excluded in the case of retail sales or leases.[9]

---

[7] SNB 1978, c C-18.1, ss 7, 24.

[8] SS 1996, c C-30.1, s 48, replacing the *Consumer Products Warranties Act*. In Manitoba, the statutory warranties are also contained in the *Consumer Protection Act*, CCSM c C200, s 58.

[9] RSBC 1996, c 410, s 20.

Seller's Title *Caveat emptor* applies to the qualities of goods, not their ownership. Inspection by the buyer normally does nothing to indicate who owns the goods. In offering to sell goods, the seller impliedly represents that he has the right to do so. The (Ontario) *Sale of Goods Act* implies title conditions and warranties (unless a different intention is shown):

(a) An implied condition that the seller has a right to sell the goods; in the case of an agreement to sell the seller will have a right to sell the goods at the time when the property is to pass;

(b) An implied warranty that the buyer will enjoy quiet (undisturbed) possession of the goods; and

(c) An implied warranty that the goods will be free from any lien, charge or encumbrance unknown to the buyer before or at the time when the contract is made.[10]

An example of the **implied term as to title** is provided in Illustration 14.1.

implied term as to title it is implied that the seller has a right to sell the goods

---

ILLUSTRATION 14.1 Right to Sell

Alberti purchases a second-hand refrigerator from Blake. It later turns out that Cowan, Blake's roommate, was the owner of the refrigerator. Cowan retakes possession of the refrigerator from Alberti.

In the contract of sale between Alberti and Blake, there is an implied promise by Blake that he had a right to sell the refrigerator, that Alberti should have quiet possession of it (that is, not have physical possession of it interrupted), and that it would be free from any encumbrance in favour of a third person (that is, no third person would have a right to the property). None of these requirements was satisfied. Alberti is therefore entitled to sue Blake for breach of contract based upon an implied condition of title to the refrigerator and receive a damage award.

Description Where the actual goods are not available for prior inspection, the buyer often makes his decision to buy based on a description of the goods contained in a catalogue, included on a website, or written on a sealed package. The resulting contract is a contract for the sale of goods by description. The Act sets out the circumstances in which there is an **implied term as to description**—that is, that the goods will match the description given by the seller.[11]

implied term as to description it is implied that goods sold by description will conform to the description

This means the goods will meet the specifications in the description and have the characteristics described. The word *description* applies to a generic characteristic of the goods (for example, that blouses offered for sale are cotton blouses instead of polyester blouses) and not to words of praise about the blouses (for example, "It is classic and elegant.").

ILLUSTRATION 14.2 Characteristics of the Goods

ProMotors sold Bridges an electric motor for use in his workshop. The motor was described in the ProMotors catalogue as "heavy-duty, double bearing." After only three months' use, the motor burned out. It turned out that the motor supplied had only a single bearing, although that was not apparent until the motor was taken apart following the burnout.

Bridges may sue ProMotors based on the breach of an implied term to the effect that the goods will correspond with the description. While the expression "heavy-duty" may be a matter of opinion, "double bearing" is clearly a factual description within the meaning of the Act.

---

[10] *Sale of Goods Act*, ON, s 13. The corresponding provisions in the Alberta, British Columbia, and Newfoundland and Labrador acts are RSA 2000, c S-2, s 14; RSBC 1996, c 410, s 16; RSNL 1990, c S-6, s 14.

[11] *Sale of Goods Act*, ON, s 14; see also AB, s 15; BC, s 17; NFLD, s 15.

Providing a sample good for inspection does not remove the implied term about description; the goods must still match any description given. In fact, it may expand the description as the characteristics of the sample can be considered to form part of the description.

> ### CASE 14.3 Symbol as Description
>
> A hotel chain ordered tableware, after having inspected samples. The tableware was delivered over a period of three years. The purchasers had no complaint regarding the earlier deliveries but discovered that the sets delivered later did not have the same manufacturer's embossed stamp on the back. They rejected the goods and sued for damages. The court held that the stamp, which had been on the sample, formed part of the description of the goods, and the vendor was in breach of the implied warranty.[12]

Sale by Sample Sometimes sample goods are displayed for prior inspection by the buyer without any corresponding description. In such cases, the Act inserts into the contract an **implied term that goods correspond with sample**. The Act provides the following:

In the case of a contract for sale by sample, there is an implied condition

(a) that the bulk will correspond with the sample in quality;

(b) that the buyer will have a reasonable opportunity of comparing the bulk with the sample; and

(c) that the goods will be free from any defect rendering them unmerchantable that would not be apparent on reasonable examination of the sample.[13]

implied term that goods correspond with sample the actual goods supplied will correspond to that sample in type and quality

> ### ILLUSTRATION 14.3 Ordinary Examination
>
> The plant supervisor at High Grade Printing Company examined a sample of choice quality paper supplied by Universal Paper Co. Ltd. and approved its purchase. When the paper was used in one of the books printed by High Grade, it turned yellow, and the entire run had to be done again. High Grade sued Universal Paper for breach of contract. In defence, Universal Paper pleaded that the paper supplied was exactly the same as the sample on which the purchase was based and that a chemical test of the sample would have revealed the defect.
>
> The printing company should succeed in its action if it can show the defect would not have been apparent on an ordinary examination and that an ordinary examination would not include a chemical test.

Suitability and Quality The general rule is that the buyer must satisfy himself as to the suitability, fitness for purpose, and quality of the goods. There are two exceptions:

1. Where the buyer, expressly or by implication, makes known to the seller the particular purpose for which the goods are required so as to show that the buyer relies on the seller's skill or judgment, and the goods are of a description that it is in the course of the seller's business to supply (whether he is the manufacturer or not), there is an implied condition that the goods will be reasonably fit for such purpose, but in the case of a contract for the sale of a specified article under its patent or other trade name, there is no implied condition as to its fitness for any particular purpose.

---

[12] *Coast Hotels Ltd v Royal Doulton Canada Ltd*, [2000] BCJ 2115, 2000 BCSC 1545.

[13] *Sale of Goods Act*, ON s. 16; see also AB, s. 17; BC, s. 19; NFLD, s. 17.

2. Where the goods are bought by description from a seller who deals in goods of that description (whether he is the manufacturer or not), there is an implied condition that the goods shall be of merchantable quality, but if the buyer has examined the goods, there is no implied condition as regards defects that such examination ought to have revealed.[14]

The first exception, **implied term of fitness**, offers protection to a buyer who has a particular purpose in mind for the goods and relies on the seller's expertise in selling this type of goods. The buyer should declare this purpose specifically if it is not one of the general uses for such goods but the court can find purpose and reliance were inferred by actions.

> **implied term of fitness** it is implied that the goods are of a type that is suitable for the purpose for which they are bought

ILLUSTRATION 14.4 Undeclared Purpose

Slack buys 30 metres of clothesline wire from a hardware store and uses it as a cable for a homemade elevator in his barn. The wire breaks with him in the elevator, causing him injury. He sues the hardware dealer for breach of contract damages.

Slack will not succeed because (1) he did not expressly state the particular purpose for which he intended to use the wire and so did not rely on the seller's skill and judgment, and (2) the use to which he put the wire was not a normal use for clothesline wire so could not be inferred.

A purpose need not be stated in so many words if it is obvious. When buying cakes in a bakery, one need not state, "I propose to eat these." The essential requirement is that the buyer relied upon the seller's skill and judgment.[15]

CASE 14.4 Familiarity with Purchaser's Work

Lavalin ordered 57 000 kilograms of welding electrodes from Carbonic for use in a project involving the fabrication of a cross-country gas transmission line. The electrodes turned out to be incapable of producing a satisfactory weld in a vertical position. Lavalin had made known to Carbonic the fact that the electrodes were to be used in a gas transmission line, apparently assuming that Carbonic's engineers would know the electrodes would have to be capable of functioning in a vertical position. In fact, Carbonic had no experience in pipeline work.

The court held that Carbonic had implied it was familiar with pipeline work and that Lavalin had relied on Carbonic's skill and judgment. Lavalin was entitled to damages for the costs incurred with respect to the acquisition and handling of the useless electrodes.[16]

The implied condition of fitness does not apply when an article is sold or requested under its trade name:

> The mere fact that an article sold is described in the contract by its trade name does not necessarily make the sale a sale under a trade name. Whether it is so or not depends upon the circumstances.... In my opinion the test of an article having been sold under its trade name within the meaning of the proviso is: did the buyer specify it under its trade name in such a way as to indicate that he is satisfied, rightly or wrongly, that it will answer his purpose, and that he is not relying on the skill or judgment of the seller, however great that skill or judgment may be?[17]

---

[14] *Sale of Goods Act*, ON s. 15; see also AB, s. 16; BC, s. 18; NFLD, s. 16. See *Borgo Upholstery Ltd v Canada*, [2004] NSJ No 7 (NSCA).

[15] *Chaproniere v Mason* (1905), 21 TLR 633; *McCready Products Ltd v Sherwin Williams Co of Canada Ltd* (1985), 61 AR 234. The seller's failure to provide adequate instructions as to use of the product and to warn of possible dangers may constitute a breach of the warranty: see *Caners v Eli Lilly Canada Inc* (1996), 134 DLR (4th) 730.

[16] *SNC-Lavalin International Inc v Liquid Carbonic Inc* (1996), 28 BLR (2d) 1.

[17] *Baldry v Marshall*, [1925] 1 KB 260 at 266–7.

CASE 14.5 Reliance on Expertise

Nikka Trader, a Vancouver-based exporter of Canadian goods, hired Gizella Pastry to create a mouse cake for export to Japan, after confirming Gizella's extensive experience with the Japanese market in a meeting with Gizella's export sales manager. Over the next several years, Gizella created several custom products for Nikka, specifically designed to pass easily through Japanese customs. In 2007, Gizella advised that the price of the Kona Pie cookies, one of the custom Japan products, would need to increase unless margarine was substituted for butter in the recipe. Nikka agreed to the substitution. After the substitution, the Kona Pie cookies were detained and quarantined at Japanese customs because the margarine contained a banned substance. Nikka sued Gizella for damages arising from breach of the implied term of fitness for purpose—the cookies were not fit for export to Japan. The Court held that when Nikka was asked to agree to the butter substitution, Gizella knew the cookies would still be exported to Japan, Gizella was an expert on exporting products to Japan, and Nikka relied on Gizella's expertise. This was all that was necessary to prove breach of the implied warranty as to fitness for purpose under British Columbia's *Sale of Goods Act*. Fitness for sale in Canada did not satisfy the implied warranty of fitness for sale in Japan. The use of the trade name Kona Pie on the order form did not preclude the implied warranty when the other factors of knowledge, expertise, and reliance were present. Nikka was entitled to its damages.[18]

The second exception deals with quality of goods rather than their particular purpose. To establish a breach of condition under this exception, the buyer need not show she relied on the seller's skill and judgment but only that the buyer could not have discovered the defect.[19]

implied term of merchantable quality it is implied that the goods are in reasonable condition and free from defects that would make them unsuitable for use

To satisfy the **implied term of merchantable quality**, goods should be in such a condition that a reasonable buyer, fully acquainted with the facts and condition of the product, would buy them without a price reduction and without special guarantees.[20] The word *reasonable* is important; especially in the case of the sale of used goods, there is no warranty that the goods are entirely free from defect.

The implied condition relates to the quality of the goods at the time of the contract, yet it may be some time later that the defect is discovered. It does not apply if the defect did not exist at the time of the sale but developed later, perhaps due to misuse by the buyer. A buyer must prove that an article that ceases to function properly was defective at the time of sale. A new car that develops transmission problems within a few months is likely to have been defective all along; one that runs well for several years before developing a fault may well have been in satisfactory condition at the time of sale.

CASE 14.6 Time of Sale

McCann bought an electric blanket from Sears. More than 10 years later it caught fire, causing damage to McCann's bedroom. McCann brought an action for breach of contract on the grounds that there was an implied condition that the electric blanket was reasonably free from defect. The court held that, in view of the time that had elapsed (during which the blanket had functioned without any problems), the buyer had failed to satisfy the burden of proving that the defect existed when the blanket was bought.[21]

In practice, it is often difficult to tell which exception is the more relevant to a buyer's complaint, as the two tend to overlap.[22]

---

[18] *Nikka Traders, Inc v Gizella Pastry Ltd*, 2012 BCSC 1412.

[19] *Wren v Holt*, [1903] 1 KB 610.

[20] *Australian Knitting Mills Ltd v Grant* (1933), 50 CLR 387 at 418; also *Bristol Tramways v Fiat Motors*, [1910] 2 KB 831 at 841.

[21] *McCann v Sears Canada Ltd* (1998), 43 BLR (2d) 217, aff'd (1999) 122 OCC 91.

[22] The two warranties are not identical. In *Wharton v Tom Harris Chevrolet Oldsmobile Cadillac Ltd*, [2002] BCJ No 233, a defective stereo system in a luxury car was in breach of the fitness warranty, although it did not render the car unmerchantable.

CHECKLIST

Implied Terms in a Contract for the Sale of Goods

Subject to certain exceptions and qualifications, the *Sale of Goods Act* implies the following contractual terms into contracts for the sale of goods:

- an implied condition that the seller has (or will have) a right to sell the goods
- an implied warranty that the buyer will have and enjoy quiet possession of the goods
- an implied warranty that the goods will be free from any undisclosed charge or encumbrance
- an implied condition that the goods will correspond with the description under which they are sold
- an implied condition that the goods will be reasonably fit for the purpose for which they are required if that purpose was made known to the seller
- an implied condition that the goods will be of merchantable quality
- in the case of a sale by sample, an implied condition that the bulk will correspond with the sample

Exemption Clauses

The *Sale of Goods Act* states:

> Where any right, duty or liability would arise under a contract of sale by implication of law, it may be negatived or varied by express agreement or by the course of dealing between the parties, or by usage, if the usage is such as to bind both parties to the contract.[23]

Therefore, a seller may include in a standard form contract of sale an express term exempting it from the liability normally imposed by the implied terms under the Act.

The courts interpret such terms very narrowly, so clear and direct language must be used to contract out of the statutory protections.

CASE 14.7 Clear Language

Syncrude ordered 32 gearboxes from Hunter, a manufacturer, to drive its conveyor belts in the Alberta tar sands project. Syncrude provided specifications of what the gearboxes were required to do, and Hunter designed them to meet those specifications.

The contract contained an express term guaranteeing the gearboxes for two years. When the period had expired, the gearboxes developed faults that were found to be due to faulty design. Syncrude could not succeed in an action on the express term because the two-year period had elapsed, but the Supreme Court of Canada held that the implied term of fitness under the Act could still be relied on. The existence of an time limited express warranty was not interpreted as displacing the statutory warranties.[24]

If the words used in an exemption clause do not precisely describe the type of liability disclaimed, the courts will normally find that the implied liability is still part of the contract. If a seller includes an express term that "all warranties implied by

---

[23] *Sale of Goods Act*, ON s 53.; see also AB, s 54; BC, s 69; NFLD, s 56.

[24] *Hunter Engineering Co v Syncrude Canada Ltd* (1989), 57 DLR (4th) 321 (SCC). See also *Fording Coal Ltd v Harnischfeger Corp of Canada* (1991), 6 BLR (2d) 157.

statute are hereby excluded," the seller will avoid liability under all those implied terms that are warranties but not under those that are conditions.[25] If the seller expressly promised that the goods would be of a certain quality or type, an exemption clause that refers only to implied terms will not free him from obligations under this express term.

> ### CASE 14.8 Express Terms
>
> Allan agreed to purchase a car from Lambeth Motors Ltd. In the contract the car was described as "a new, 190-horsepower, six-cylinder sedan." There was also a clause, inserted by the seller, that "all conditions, warranties, and liabilities implied by statute, common law, or otherwise are hereby excluded." After taking delivery, Allan discovered the car was not new and had only four cylinders, and he sued for damages.
>
> The exempting clause referred only to implied terms. The undertaking that the car was new and had six cylinders was an express term in the contract of sale. The seller had therefore failed to exempt itself from liability.[26]

The courts have also held that a seller cannot completely exempt himself from all performance under the contract. They will not give effect to an exemption clause that gives a seller immunity from action if he delivers goods that are totally different from those contracted for by the buyer or if he delivers goods to which he does not have good title.[27] In effect, the courts have held that a contract for the sale of goods would be deprived of all meaning if a seller's obligation were merely to deliver the goods "if he felt like it." Chapter 13 also discusses the court's approach to enforcing exemption clauses.

> ### Ethical Issue Exemption Clauses
>
> Exemption clauses are an important tool used by businesses to limit their exposure to liability. As the foregoing discussion indicates, the *Sale of Goods Act* recognizes and preserves the legality of an exemption clause. This position prioritizes the freedom to contract over the protective policy reflected in the implied terms. This priority is not absolute. The Supreme Court recognizes that an exemption clause may be unenforceable for public policy reasons such as a seller's criminal or fraudulent behavior.[28] This is the exception rather than the rule when dealing with commercial contracts.
>
> However, it may not be possible to contract out of the implied terms in the consumer context. In a complete reversal of the *Sale of Goods Act*, the Ontario *Consumer Protection Act* voids any "term or acknowledgement, whether part of the consumer agreement or not, that purports to negate or vary any implied condition or warranty under the *Sale of Goods Act*" (section 9(3)).[29] This places the retailer in a precarious situation. Few retailers manufacture their own goods; the chain of distribution usually involves a manufacturer and a wholesaler. The retailer is bound by the implied terms of the *Sale of Goods Act* when dealing with consumers but may be unable to rely on them when pursuing the manufacturer or wholesaler of the goods.
>
> **Questions to Consider**
>
> 1. Does this represent a fair result in today's marketplace?
> 2. Which legislation should be changed?

---

[25] *Gregorio v Intrans-Corp* (1994), 115 DLR (4th) 200 (ONCA); *Tercon Contractors Ltd v British Columbia (Transportation and Highways)*, 2010 SCC 4 at paras 21–23 (describing a three-step approach to exemption clause interpretation).

[26] *Andrews Bros Ltd v Singer & Co Ltd*, [1934] 1 KB 17.

[27] *Pinnock Brothers v Lewis and Peat Ltd*, [1923] 1 KB 690; *Karsales (Harrow) Ltd v Wallis*, [1956] 2 All ER 866; *Canadian-Dominion Leasing Corp Ltd v Suburban Superdrug Ltd* (1966), 56 DLR (2d) 43.

[28] *Tercon*, *supra* note 25.

[29] Ontario *Consumer Protection Act, 2002*, SO 2002, c 30, Sch A, s 9(3).

Payment

Many contracts of sale set out the time of payment expressly—in others it may be implied from the terms of the contract and the particular circumstances. When the contract itself gives no guidance, the courts assume that delivery and payment are to happen together; the transaction is presumed to be a cash sale. But this presumption may be rebutted by the circumstances in which the contract is made. For example, when payment from a customer is accepted by credit card, the buyer is normally entitled to delivery of the goods immediately, before payment by the credit card company.

The courts interpret the time set for payment as a warranty unless the parties have expressed themselves otherwise. Therefore, a seller is not entitled to rescind the contract of sale and have the goods back simply because payment is not made on time. He must be content with a breach of contract action for the price of the goods. A seller may insist on a term entitling him to retake possession in the event of non-payment. This provision is characteristic of the installment sale, to be considered separately in Chapter 28.

Delivery

Delivery terms should specify the date and time, the location, and the quantity to be delivered. A term specifying the quantity of goods to be delivered is a condition. If the term is broken—that is, if the seller delivers a substantially different quantity—the buyer is free to reject the goods. Her right to do so exists whether a greater or lesser quantity than promised is delivered. The buyer may, of course, choose to take all or part of what is delivered. If she does so, she must pay for what she takes at the contract rate.

The time specified for delivery is also usually a condition, so that if the goods are not delivered on time, the buyer may rescind the contract. She is free to look elsewhere for the goods she needs as soon as she learns they will not be available on time. If the parties agree that the goods are to be delivered as soon as they are available, without specifying a time, then delivery must occur within a reasonable time, taking into account all the circumstances.

The place of delivery is normally either the seller's place of business or wherever the goods happen to be located at the time of the contract. The parties may, however, express a different intention—for example, that the goods should be delivered to the buyer's home—or their intention may be implied from trade custom.

An offer for sale sometimes states, along with the asking price, the terms of delivery. It may, for example, quote wheat at so much per bushel FOB Winnipeg, or steel at so much per tonne CIF Hamilton. *FOB* means that the seller will place the goods at that location "free on board" the type of transportation specified. When a *CIF* (cost, insurance, freight) price is quoted, the seller undertakes to arrange insurance and to ship the goods to the buyer. (These and other standard terms are widely used in international trade and are discussed further in Chapter 30.) Another common type of contract is the *COD* (cash on delivery) contract in which the seller undertakes to deliver the goods at the buyer's place of business or residence.

Risk of Loss before Delivery

The contract should also describe who is required to insure the goods throughout the delivery process. If the goods are damaged or lost during delivery, ideally the contract will indicate who—the buyer or seller—must compensate for the loss. If the contract does not expressly state when the risk of loss (responsibility for damage to or destruction of the goods) moves from the seller to the buyer, the courts typically imply a term that reflects the ownership of the goods. Whoever owns the goods at the time of loss is the one who is at risk. The risk of loss follows the title to the goods unless the parties have agreed otherwise: The party that has title ordinarily suffers the loss.[30] For this reason, we must identify the moment in time when ownership passes from seller to buyer—when does title pass?

TITLE TO GOODS

Who May Pass Title?

Ordinarily goods are sold by a person who is not their owner and who does not sell them under the authority or with the consent of the owner. The buyer acquires no better title to the goods than the seller had, unless the owner of the goods is by conduct precluded from denying the seller's authority to sell.[31]

Only the owner, or a person authorized by the owner, can pass a good title to goods. The *Sale of Goods Act* allows two main exceptions: certain sales made by an agent (considered below) and sales made under any special common law or statutory power of sale or under a court order.

The Effect of Agency When a business ships goods to its agent for the agent to sell, the effect of the consignment is to give the agent (the consignee) the appearance of ownership in the eyes of the public. Statutes in the various provinces give the agent the same authority to deal with the goods as their owner has.[32] The agent may, therefore, validly pass title to anyone who purchases the goods in good faith, even though the sale may not be authorized or is on terms forbidden by the owner (the consignor).

Seller or Buyer in Possession A seller could mistakenly sell the same goods twice, or a buyer could resell goods before she actually owns them. The Act protects an innocent purchaser who "buys" the goods in the normal course of business without notice of any defect in the seller's title.[33]

CASE 14.9 Innocent Purchaser

Western Environmental acquired the assets of a Canadian oil refinery that was being closed down. It proceeded to sell off various assets of the refinery, including a quantity of pipe, which it sold to the plaintiff, Epscan, for $260 000. It was agreed that Epscan would cut and remove the pipe over the following three months. Before it could do so, Western sold the same pipe to another Canadian corporation, Bartin, and was paid $162 000. Epscan learned that Bartin was removing the pipe and sued Bartin for conversion. Meanwhile, Western and its employees had disappeared.

At trial, Epscan was awarded damages for the conversion. On appeal, the Alberta Court of Appeal held that Bartin was protected under the *Sale of Goods Act*.[34] The vendor, Western, remained in possession, there were no suspicious circumstances, and Bartin had no knowledge of Epscan's interest.[35]

---

[30] For an example of this rule, see *AMS Equipment Inc v Case*, [1999] BCJ No 124.

[31] *Sale of Goods Act*, ON, s 22; AB, s 23; BC, s 26; NFLD, s 2.

[32] See e.g. *Factors Act*, RSO 1990, c F.1, s 2; RSA 2000, c F-1, s 2; *Sale of Goods Act*, BC, s 59.

[33] *Sale of Goods Act*, ON, s 25; AB, s 26; BC, s 30; NFLD, s 27. An exception may apply where the situation is governed by the *Personal Property Security Act* (discussed in Chapter 29).

[34] AB, s 27(1), now s 26(1).

[35] *Bartin Pipe & Piling Supply Ltd v Epscan Industries Ltd* (2004), 236 DLR (4th) 75.

A buyer who does not take immediate possession of goods when title passes runs the risk that a fraudulent seller may resell them to an innocent third party who will obtain a good title. A similar risk exists where a seller allows the buyer to take possession of goods before title has passed.[36]

When Does Title Pass?

As already noted, the risk—of loss or damage—generally passes with the title (ownership) to goods. It is therefore essential to know when title passes; usually the contract expressly says. If not, the *Sale of Goods Act* has five rules that determine when title passes.[37]

The *Sale of Goods Act* Rules for Passing of Title
Unless otherwise agreed, the *Sale of Goods Act* provides that title to goods passes from the seller to the buyer as follows.

- Rule 1: where there is an unconditional contract for the sale of **specific goods** in a deliverable state, when the contract is made
- Rule 2: where there is a contract for the sale of specific goods and the seller is bound to do something to the goods to put them into a deliverable state, when the buyer has received notice that it has been done
- Rule 3: where there is a contract for the sale of specific goods in a deliverable state but the seller is bound to do something to ascertain their price, when the buyer has received notice that it has been done
- Rule 4: where goods are delivered to the buyer on approval or on "sale or return," when the buyer signifies his approval, or does some other act adopting the transaction, or when the buyer retains the goods beyond a reasonable time
- Rule 5: where there is a contract for the sale of **unascertained goods** or **future goods** by description, when goods of that description and in a deliverable state are **appropriated** to the contract by one party with the assent of the other

specific goods goods in existence, identified and agreed upon as the subject matter of the sale

unascertained goods goods that have not been set aside and agreed upon as the subject of a sale

future goods goods that have not yet been produced

appropriated designated as the subject matter of the contract

Bills of Lading

Historically a paper **bill of lading** was the essential document of all commercial sales transactions, and it travelled with the goods and was signed by each new custodian. The purpose was to transfer title and to record changes in possession. Today a broadly similar result is now achieved through an electronic exchange of data and documents.

bill of lading a document signed by a carrier acknowledging that specified goods have been received by it for shipment

REMEDIES OF THE SELLER

Lien

One way to ensure payment for goods is to withhold delivery until payment is made. While the goods remain in an unpaid seller's possession, the seller has a **lien** on the goods regardless of whether title has passed to the buyer. The seller has a claim or charge on them for their agreed price and can refuse to release them until full payment is made. Once the seller delivers the goods to the buyer, however, he normally loses this special lien. The right of lien is based upon possession and is gone if possession passes in good faith to the buyer.[38]

lien a right of a person in possession of property to retain that property until payment

---

[36] Usually fraud is involved, but that is not necessarily so; see *Sun Toyota Ltd v Granville Toyota Ltd*, [2002] BCJ No 847 (QL).

[37] ON, s 19: see also AB, s 20; BC, s 23; NFLD, s 20.

[38] An exception to this rule applies when an unpaid seller repossesses goods under the provisions of the *Bankruptcy and Insolvency Act*; this exception is discussed below under the heading "Repossession."

The lien remedy arises in the following situations:

(a) where the contract does not state that the buyer is to have credit, so that payment may be required upon delivery

(b) where the goods have been sold on credit, the term of credit has expired without payment being made, and the seller still has possession of the goods

(c) where the buyer becomes insolvent before delivery[39]

In (c), a seller who refuses to deliver is excused only if the buyer is insolvent. A seller should be sure of the facts before exercising the right of lien; otherwise, he takes the risk that the buyer may subsequently sue for breach of the promise to deliver. It is not enough simply to hear that the buyer's financial position is questionable.

A seller may waive his right of lien—and rely on the buyer's credit—in two ways. He may waive the right by implication, as in the usual credit sale, simply by agreeing to deliver before payment is due. Second, he may voluntarily deliver the goods before he needs to do so.

Repossession

Once possession passes in good faith to a buyer, the seller loses the right to repossess the goods even if the buyer fails to pay for them. Bankruptcy law creates an important exception to the rule.[40] Where a seller has delivered goods to a buyer and the buyer, before having paid in full for the goods, becomes bankrupt or insolvent within 30 days, the seller may make a written demand for the return of the goods. The demand must be presented to the trustee in bankruptcy or receiver appointed to manage the debtor's affairs within 15 days after the buyer goes bankrupt. The right to repossess applies only to goods that were delivered in relation to the buyer's business, not to consumer goods. The goods must still be in the possession of the buyer, must be identifiable, and must be in the same condition as they were when sold. If the price has been partly paid, the seller has a choice between repossessing a portion of the goods in proportion to the amount still owing and repossessing all of the goods and refunding the amount already paid. The right of repossession ranks above any other claim to the goods, except those of a subsequent purchaser who has bought the goods for value and in good faith, without notice of the unpaid seller's claim.

Resale

After exercising a right of lien under the *Sale of Goods Act*, an unpaid seller may give notice to the buyer and resell the goods to a third party. The new purchaser obtains good title to them. The right of resale is especially helpful when the goods are perishable but is not confined to such emergencies.

This right also arises whenever a buyer commits a breach by refusing to accept goods. Resale is the way a seller mitigates his loss. If the seller makes a reasonable effort to get a good price on resale but obtains a lower price, he may sue the original buyer for the deficiency.

Damages for Non-Acceptance

A critical factor in determining the seller's damages when a buyer refuses the goods is whether the seller is in a position to supply more goods than prospective customers might order. If so, the seller's damages are measured by the profits lost due to the

---

[39] Section 39 (BC). "Insolvent" is not a defined term under the *Sale of Goods Act*.

[40] *Bankruptcy and Insolvency Act*, RSC 1985, c B-3, s 81.1.

buyer's breach; if not, damages are generally measured by any deficiency in the resale price of the rejected goods compared with the original contract price.

> **ILLUSTRATION 14.5 Calculating Damages**
>
> Read examined a used accordion for sale in Crescendo Music Stores Ltd. She agreed in writing to buy it for $600 provided the bellows were repaired and gold monogram initials were affixed to it. Before the repairs were made, Read informed Crescendo that she had decided to take up the saxophone instead and refused to accept the accordion. Crescendo sued Read.
>
> The appropriate action would be for damages for non-acceptance because the title had not passed to Read at the time of her repudiation. If the music store had more used accordions in stock than it had customers wanting to buy them, it would have sustained damages equal to the profit it would have made had Read purchased the instrument as she promised.
>
> If the store had no other used accordions and was able to resell the accordion, but for less than $600, it would have sustained damages equal to the difference between the two prices. If the repairs and changes had been made but Read had not been notified before she repudiated the contract, title would still not pass to her, and the seller may claim additional damages for its expenses. Crescendo should be able to recover the cost of affixing the gold monogram but not that of repairing the bellows.

Action for the Price

When title has passed to the buyer, a seller is entitled to the full price regardless of whether the buyer has taken delivery. If the buyer rejects goods after title has passed to her, she is rejecting what she already owns.

> **ILLUSTRATION 14.6 Full Price or Lost Profit**
>
> Anderson bought a sound system on display at Burton's Appliance Store for installation at her dental office. The system was tagged "sold" with Anderson's name on it, and Anderson signed a form identifying the purchase and stating its price. On her way back to the office, Anderson saw another model in the window of Modern Electronics Ltd. and decided that she would prefer it. She refused to take delivery of the sound system from Burton, and Burton sued her for the full price of the machine.
>
> The action would succeed. At the time Anderson attempted to repudiate the contract of sale, title had already passed to her. If Burton sues for the price, however, he must be willing and able to deliver the sound system.

The conclusion in Illustration 14.6 is based on a strict application of the *Sale of Goods Act*. When the seller still has the goods, courts may want to see mitigation efforts. If the buyer is a consumer, special cancellation options are available, as discussed later in this chapter. Most retail businesses make it a practice to include return options in their consumer sales contracts.

Retention of Deposit

In a contract of sale may include a term that, in the event of breach, the party in default shall pay the other a specified sum of money by way of liquidated damages. As discussed in Chapter 13, the court will enforce such a term if the amount specified is a genuine estimate by the parties of the probable loss. Depending upon the circumstances, an amount paid by a buyer as a deposit may be treated as liquidated damages in the event of her default. In many contracts of sale, the reason the seller demands a deposit is to protect himself at least to that extent in the event of the buyer's non-acceptance. The intention is clear that the deposit will be forfeited upon breach by the buyer.[41]

---

[41] See *Stockloser v Johnson*, [1954] 1 QB 476. If the contract provides for a non-refundable deposit but the deposit has not been paid, for example, when the purchaser has stopped payment on the cheque, the vendor is entitled to recover the agreed sum: *Vanvic Enterprises Ltd v Mark*, [1985] 3 WWR 644.

deposit a sum of money paid by the buyer to the seller, to be forfeited if the buyer does not perform her part of the contract

down payment a sum of money paid by the buyer as an initial part of the purchase price

Legally speaking, there is a difference between a **deposit**, which is intended primarily to provide a sanction to induce performance of the contract by the buyer, and a **down payment**, which constitutes a part payment of the purchase price and is unrelated to the seller's loss in the event of breach by the buyer. If the title to the goods has already passed to the buyer at the time the buyer repudiates, the seller is entitled not only to retain the down payment but also to sue for the balance of the price. If title has not yet passed, the seller is entitled to retain out of the down payment any damages for non-acceptance he can prove and is accountable to the buyer for any remaining surplus.[42] If the seller has no damages, he must return the down payment in full.

THE SELLER'S LIABILITY

Breach of a Term

Generally, breach of a warranty gives rise to only an action for damages, but a breach of a condition entitles the injured party to discharge the contract as well as to sue for damages for any loss suffered. The *Sale of Goods Act*, however, creates exceptions where a buyer will not be entitled to terminate the contract and return the goods, even though the seller has breached a condition.[43]

First, the buyer must keep the goods and be content with damages when the broken contract of sale does not contemplate delivery by installments (is not severable), and the buyer has indicated an intention to keep the goods or treated them in a way inconsistent with the seller's ownership of them.

A second situation might arise where the right to repudiate would be lost when the contract is for specific goods, and the title has passed to the buyer even though the goods are still in the seller's possession. However, when the seller has committed a breach of condition by offering unsatisfactory goods to fill the contract, such a result would seem surprising. So courts tend to ignore this part of the section.

In Case 14.10, we see the consequences for the buyer when the seller breaches a condition but the buyer has accepted the goods.

CASE 14.10   Consequences of Accepting Goods

Leaf purchased a painting of Salisbury Cathedral that the seller, International Galleries, represented to him as the work of the famous artist Constable. When Leaf attempted to resell the picture five years later, it was discovered that it had not been painted by Constable but by a much less-famous artist. Its value was consequently only a small fraction of what both the seller and buyer had thought.

Leaf tried to return the picture to International Galleries and recover the purchase price. The court held that the *Sale of Goods Act* applied, so that Leaf did not have the right to treat the contract as being at an end. Since he did not sue for damages, as he might have done, his action failed.[44]

Wrongful Withholding or Disposition by the Seller

When the title to goods has already passed to the buyer, a seller who refuses to deliver them according to the terms of the contract commits a tort; the buyer may sue the seller for damages for **wrongful detention**. Sometimes the buyer may obtain a court order for the delivery of the goods. If, in addition to a failure to deliver, the seller

wrongful detention the refusal by the seller to deliver goods whose title has passed to the buyer

---

[42] *Stevenson v Colonial Homes Ltd* (1961), 27 DLR (2d) 698.

[43] ON, s 12(3); see also AB, s 13(4); BC, s 15(4); NFLD, s 13(4).

[44] *Leaf v International Galleries*, [1950] 2 KB 86.

transfers the goods to a third party, he will have disposed of goods that do not belong to him; the buyer may sue for damages for the tort of conversion—that is, for converting the buyer's goods to his own use or purposes.

REMEDIES OF THE BUYER

A buyer has a range of possible remedies in contract, in tort, and under consumer protection legislation, which were discussed in earlier chapters.

In tort and in contract, a buyer's usual remedy will be to claim damages for breach of contract. In Chapter 13, under the heading "Expectation Damages," we discussed the measure of damages available to a buyer when the seller fails to deliver. If delivery is merely delayed and the buyer still accepts the goods, the measure of damages is the value the goods would have had for the buyer if they had been delivered on time, less their actual value when delivered.

As an alternative to damages, a buyer may be able to claim the equitable remedy of specific performance or of rescission; both of these remedies were discussed in Chapter 13. The *Sale of Goods Act* gives the court discretion to order specific performance of a contract for the sale of goods—that is, to order the seller to deliver the goods to the buyer. Generally, the court does not grant this remedy when a seller refuses to deliver, because money damages are nearly always an adequate remedy. Where the goods have a unique value for the buyer, however, the court may exercise its discretion in her favour and order specific performance.

INTERNATIONAL ISSUE

International Sale of Goods

In 1980, the United Nations Commission on International Trade Law (UNCITRAL) developed a set of uniform rules for international sale of goods. The Convention on Contracts for the International Sale of Goods (CISG) establishes substantive rules relating to the formation of a contract, buyers' and sellers' obligations, and remedies. Its goals are to overcome the problems associated with conflicting principles of law between buyer and seller jurisdictions and provide certainty and consistency in the resolution of international trade disputes. It applies to sales of commercial goods between businesses in different countries (providing the countries subscribe to the convention). It does not apply to sales for personal or household use (consumer transactions).

In 1992, the convention became law in Canada,[45] and federal and provincial legislation has been adopted to implement its terms.[46] This means that when a dispute arises in a contract covered by the convention, a Canadian court should apply the rules of the convention rather than the domestic laws relating to sale of goods. Parties may specifically opt out of the application of CISG by inserting a term in their contract (article 6). The United States and China have implemented the convention, but the United Kingdom has not.

Questions to Consider

1. If the goal of the convention is to create uniformity and certainty, why is "opting out" allowed?
2. What would be a business's rationale for contractually opting out of CISG?

Sources: CSIG Canada, www.osgoode.yorku.ca/cisg; "International Sale of Goods (CISG) and Related Transactions," UNCITRAL, www.uncitral.org/uncitral/en/uncitral_texts/sale_goods.html; R. Sharma, "The United Nations Convention on Contracts for the International Sale of Goods: The Canadian Experience" (2005) 36 *Victoria University of Wellington Law Review* 847–58, available online at www.victoria.ac.nz/law/research/publications/vuwlr/prev-issues/vol-36-4/cisg-sharma.pdf

---

[45] *International Sale of Goods Contracts Convention Act*, SC 1991, c 13.

[46] *International Conventions Implementation Act*, RSA 2000, c I-6; *International Sale of Goods Act*, RSBC 1996, c 236; *International Sale of Goods Act*, RSNL 1990, c I-16; *International Sale of Goods Act*, RSO 1990, c I.10.

CONSUMER CONTRACTS

We discussed regulation of consumer contracts and consumer protection in Chapters 3 and 10. In this chapter, we focus on how the contractual relationship between the parties—the business and the individual consumer—is controlled by legislation. As noted in Chapter 6, the unequal bargaining positions in consumer transactions leave the consumer at the mercy of business, ultimately resulting in one-sided contracts presented to the consumer on a take-it-or-leave-it basis. A standard form contract is prepared in advance by the business party with the goals of reducing potential liability for the business and eliminating consumer rights. The legislation described below does not ban these one-sided contracts entirely; instead it controls the use of pressure sales tactics, inserts terms into the contract, requires notice and disclosure of onerous terms, and gives the consumer a chance to back out once they have time to consider these terms.

A **consumer** is an individual (not an organization) purchasing a product or service for personal, family, household, non-business purposes. In Chapter 6, *standard form contract* was defined as an offer prepared in advance by the offeror, including terms favourable to the offeror that cannot be changed by the offeree but must be accepted as is or rejected. Businesses typically use standard form contracts in their dealings with consumers. These agreements, also known as contracts of adhesion, typically favour the business party, and so consumer protection legislation tries to level the playing field.[47]

consumer an individual (not an organization) purchasing a product or service for personal, family, household, non-business purposes

Consumer Protection

In addition to the *Sale of Goods Act*, most provinces have developed separate legislation addressing the specific needs of the consumer. Consumer protection legislation applies to the sale of goods as well as to the supply of services, and extends the warranties described in the *Sale of Goods Acts* to goods that are leased, traded, or otherwise supplied.[48] Unlike the *Sale of Goods Act*, consumer protection legislation does not apply to business-to-business commercial transactions. As discussed in Chapter 10, it targets the practices of particularly "high risk" business sectors such as time shares, travel, and fitness industries. Sometimes custom legislation exists to address particular products such as energy or tickets.[49]

BUSINESS SALES TACTICS TARGETING CONSUMERS

Problematic business sales tactics often result in unwanted consumer contracts; consumer protection legislation regulates these tactics by ensuring the necessary detailed information is supplied to the customer, by adding cancellation options to the contract or by blocking the contract's enforcement.

Pressure Selling

As a response to high-pressure door-to-door selling methods, most provinces enacted legislation making the **direct sales contract** non-binding on consumers.[50] Consumers

direct sales contract a contract formed at a place other than the business's place of business

---

[47] See e.g. *Business Practices and Consumer Protection Act*, SBC 2004 [BPCPA], c 2; *Fair Trading Act*, RSA 2000, c F-2; *Consumer Protection Act, 2002*, SO 2002, c 30, Sch A; *Consumer Protection Act*, CCSM, c C200, s 58.

[48] *Consumer Protection Act*, ON s 9 (ON). See also *Consumer Product Warranty and Liability Act*, SNB 1978, c C-18.1.

[49] See e.g. *Energy Consumer Protection Act, 2010*, SO 2010, c. 8; *Ticket Sales Act, 2017*, SO 2017, c 33, Sch 3.

[50] See e.g. BPCPA, ss 17, 20, 21.

are given a cooling-off period after contracting, during which they may terminate the contract by giving written notice to the seller. Upon doing so, the consumer has no further obligation under the contract and may recover any money already paid. This marks an important change from the common law rule that the rights and liabilities of the parties are established at the time the contract is formed.

The statutory cooling-off periods vary in length from two to ten days. In some provinces, it is based on the time when the contract is entered into; in others, from the date on which a copy of the contract is received by the buyer. The legislation applies to both goods and services, but in some provinces it does not apply to sales under $50. Cooling-off periods are also used to address the inequities of other distance contracts such as those entered into using the internet or by telephone, or anytime the contracting parties are separated by distance.

In some provinces, door-to-door sales of electricity, gas, or energy products such as furnaces and water heaters are prohibited, and contracts arranged this way are void.[51]

Unsolicited Goods

Pressure selling can also take the form of sending goods not ordered by the consumer, hoping the recipient will pay for them. Consumer protection statutes expressly state that use of unrequested goods by the recipient does not amount to an acceptance of the seller's offer. A recipient of unsolicited goods may use them without becoming liable for their price.[52] The purpose of the provision is to discourage sellers from sending unsolicited goods to consumers, and it seems to have been quite effective. Some provinces have taken a similar approach to unsolicited credit cards.[53]

Telemarketing

The federal *Competition Act*[54] defines **telemarketing** as "the practice of using interactive telephone communications for the purpose of promoting, directly or indirectly, the supply or use of a product or for the purpose of promoting, directly or indirectly, any business interest."[55] It can be a pressure sales tactic because it targets people in their homes who are not considering any purchases. Sometimes callers mislead purchasers about their intentions and leave out important information. Therefore, the cooling-off period and disclosure requirements apply to these contracts.

telemarketing the use of telephone communications for promoting the supply of a product or for promoting a business interest

In addition, under the *Competition Act*, deceptive telemarketing is a criminal offence, punishable by a maximum of 14 years in prison and a fine within the discretion of the court; or a fine of up to $200 000 may be imposed on summary conviction. The provisions also extend criminal responsibility to directors and officers of a corporation when its employees are found guilty of deceptive telemarketing. In 1999, a Quebec court imposed a record $1 million fine for deceptive telemarketing and imposed the first-ever jail sentences. The firm's president and several of the firm's sales agents were sentenced to six months in jail.[56]

---

[51] See e.g. *Energy Consumer Protection Act, 2010, supra* note 49, s 9.1; *Consumer Protection Act*, RSA 2000, c 26.3.

[52] See BPCPA, ss 12, 13, 14; *Consumer Protection Act*, ON, s 13.

[53] See BPCPA, s 96; *Consumer Protection Act*, NS, s 23; ON, s 13 (although use of the card triggers an agreement, s 68).

[54] RSC 1985, c C-34.

[55] Internet communications, automated pre-recorded messages, and consumer-instigated calls to a customer relations line are not covered.

[56] American Family Publishers et al, Competition Bureau Annual Report 98/99.

Callers must disclose the name of the company they represent, the purpose of the call, the kind and value of the product or service being promoted, the terms or restrictions relating to delivery of the product to customers, and other specified information. Additionally, the provisions prohibit telemarketers from conducting contests where the participant can receive prizes only after she makes some kind of prior payment or from offering gifts or prizes for buying a product unless the value of the gift is disclosed. It is also illegal for telemarketers to offer a product for sale at a price grossly in excess of its fair market value, where delivery of the product is conditional on prior payment by the customer.

In 2008, a National Do Not Call List was established by the Canadian Radio-television and Telecommunications Commission.[57] Once a consumer registers his number, telemarketers must not call to solicit unless the telemarketer is a registered charity, is a political party, or has an existing business relationship with the consumer. Registration is effective for a period of three years. Corporations face a possible $15 000 fine for each violation. Canadian anti-spam legislation, discussed in Chapters 31 and 32, regulates bulk emailing and online solicitations.

TERMS IN CONSUMER CONTRACTS

Legislated Terms

Provincial statutes provide protection for consumers by implying terms into the contract or requiring businesses to expressly state certain terms in the contract. First, the implied terms under the *Sale of Goods Act* with respect to seller's right to sell, merchantability, and fitness, etc., are made added to contracts—goods and services—with consumers; sellers cannot escape liability by requiring buyers to sign exemption clauses.[58]

> **CASE 14.11 No Waiver of Implied Warranty**
>
> Szilvasy bought a new home and took over the lease of the rented hot water heater. It sprang a leak and caused $16 000 of water damage to the basement of the home. Szilvasy sued for breach of contract. She alleged that the water heater was not fit for the intended purpose. Reliance Home Comfort defended the action, saying the lease contract did not include an express term on fitness for purpose, and it did include a clause exempting Reliance from liability for water damage. The Ontario Court of Appeal held that section 9 of the *Consumer Protection Act* implied a *Sale of Goods Act* term of fitness for purpose into this leasing contract, and this implied warranty could not be waived or varied by the express exemption clause. The water heater was not fit for the purpose because it leaked. The consumer contract was breached by the business.[59]

This approach, of imposing contractual liability on sellers by inserting compulsory terms in consumer contracts, has been taken further in the Saskatchewan and New Brunswick statutes, which imply additional warranties and extend protection to third persons who were not parties to the contract, such as members of the buyer's family.[60]

Second, consumer protection legislation requires businesses to give consumers subject to pressure sales tactics or involved in high-risk industries specific detailed

---

[57] *Telecommunications Act*, SC 1993, c 38, s 41; *Telecom Decision* CRTC 2008-6.

[58] See e.g. *Consumer Protection Act*, NS, s 26(3); ON, s 9(2)(3), BPCPA, s 3.

[59] *Szilvasy v Reliance Home Comfort*, 2012 ONCA 821, considering the combined impact of Ontario's *Consumer Protection Act* and *Sale of Goods Act*.

[60] *Consumer Protection Act*, SS 1996, c C-30.1; *Consumer Product Warranty and Liability Act*, SNB 1978, c C-18.1.

information about their transaction. This includes obvious information about the names, addresses, and phone numbers, as well as notice of how to cancel their contracts. The cooling-off period and cancellation rights created for high pressure sales tactics must be expressly described in the contract, along with instructions about how to exercise the option to cancel. Failure to include the statutory information results in the contract being void or unenforceable.[61]

Finally, all terms in the consumer contract (whether implied or express) that are capable of more than one reasonable interpretation must be given the interpretation most favourable to the consumer.[62] This is an application of the *contra proferentem* rule because business will have drafted the contract.

Exemption Clauses

As repeatedly stressed, exemption clauses (also known as exculpatory clauses or limitation of liability terms) are regularly used by business to restrict their liability—arising from breach of contract, tort, or statute. As noted, some provinces contain their scope in the consumer context.[63] Most importantly, they are not capable of excluding liability for breach of either the implied *Sale of Goods Act* warranties or any of the obligations imposed on business under the consumer protection legislation. Business cannot "contract out" of the duties imposed upon it by the statutes discussed in this part.

Repossession

A standard form consumer contract involving goods typically contains a term giving the lender or seller a repossession remedy should the consumer default. For example, the contract may authorize the seller to take back the goods from the consumer if installment payments are not kept up or to sue for the entire balance due under the contract if the consumer defaults in a single installment payment. Consumer protection statutes in some provinces state that the seller's remedy of repossession is lost once the buyer has paid a specified proportion (for example, two-thirds) of the purchase price, and other statutes limit the circumstances in which a seller or creditor can enforce an acceleration clause, which is a provision in the contract that stipulates that the entire unpaid balance of the price is immediately payable should the buyer default.[64] A further example occurs in the law of landlord and tenant, where some provinces have abolished a landlord's self-help remedy of seizing a residential tenant's goods for arrears of rent.[65]

Arbitration and Class Actions

Some businesses try to prevent consumers from using the courts to enforce their rights, particularly class actions and small claims court. This is done by placing a term in the contract that designates individual arbitration as the only process that may be used to resolve any disputes with the business arising from the contract. Consumers waive their right to participate in class actions. This discourages most consumer claims

---

[61] Alta Reg 191/99.

[62] *Consumer Protection Act*, ON, s 11; BPCPA, s 18(2); *Seidel v TELUS Communications*, 2011 SCC 15 at para 2.

[63] In British Columbia, New Brunswick, Ontario, and Saskatchewan, the warranties cannot be contracted out of in the case of retail sales.

[64] See e.g. *Personal Property Security Act*, RSO 1990, c P.10, s 66(2), stating that a consumer may redeem seized property without paying full purchase price by merely paying arrears in installments.

[65] See e.g. *Residential Tenancy Act*, SBC 2002, c 78, s 26(3)(a).

because such claims are usually worth so little money that it does not make sense to pursue them individually. It only makes monetary sense to collect all consumers with the same complaints into one class action. This works in every province except Ontario, Alberta, and Quebec—the consumer protection legislation in these provinces makes arbitration clauses in consumer contracts void and unenforceable.[66] Consumers in other provinces will have the arbitration term in their contracts enforced.

Severance

Businesses that operate in multiple provinces often use the same standard form contract across the entire country. They manage the differences between provincial consumer protection laws by including whatever terms they want plus a term that states that any term deemed to be illegal, void, or unenforceable may be severed or cut out of the contract, leaving the balance of the contract to be enforced. This is known as a severance clause, and it prevents the entire contract from being struck down when one of its clauses is illegal.

Financing Arrangements and Disclosure of the True Cost of Credit

Consumer protection statutes require that detailed description of all financial arrangements between business and consumer be included in the written contract, a copy of which must be given to the consumer. These disclosure requirements apply to all contracts where a buyer of goods or services or a borrower of money repays the debt by installments. They require sellers and lenders to give their customers a detailed statement of the terms of credit in dollars and cents and in percentage terms as an effective annual rate of interest, as well as any charges for insurance and registration fees. Payments must be broken down separately and aggregated to show a total cost of borrowing. A customer is not bound by the contract if the seller fails to comply with the requirements.[67]

The *Criminal Code* sets a maximum "legal" interest rate, and the federal *Interest Act* requires that interest rates in written contracts be expressed in annual percentages.[68] Non-compliance makes interest agreements void and unenforceable.

Many vendors who sell goods to consumers on the installment plan assign their consumer credit contracts to finance companies. Typically, a vendor assigns the contract to a finance company and receives immediate payment of a sum that is less than the full amount to be paid by the buyer. The buyer then receives notice of assignment and makes the installment payments to the finance company. The general rule about assignment of contractual rights, as discussed in Chapter 11, is that an assignee "takes subject to the equities" and acquires no more enforceable claim than the assignor had. There is little doubt that a vendor can more readily find an assignee to buy its installment receivables if the assignee acquires rights against the buyer that are not subject to any complaints the buyer (consumer) may have about the goods.

Therefore, vendors and finance companies looked for a way around the general rule about assignments by using a negotiable instrument: A buyer was required to sign a promissory note for the balance of the purchase price plus finance charges, and this note, along with the conditional sale contract, was endorsed by the vendor to the finance company. As a result, the finance company became a holder in due course of

---

[66] *Consumer Protection Act*, ON, ss 7,8; , AB, s 16; , CQLRc P-40.1, s 11; *Seidel, supra* note 62 at para 2.

[67] See e.g. *BPCPA*, Part V; *Consumer Protection Act*, ON, Part VII.

[68] RSC 1985, c I-15, s 4.

the note, theoretically immuned to any "personal defences" the buyer might have against the vendor. Until the matter was corrected by legislation, a consumer might be liable to a finance company with no opportunity to refuse to pay for the goods if they proved defective or if the dealer refused to perform its warranties. An amendment to the *Bills of Exchange Act* made finance companies subject to consumers' defences against sellers.[69]

Another way around the rule was to use the contract of sale itself to waive the consumer's rights by a rather special kind of exempting clause: The consumer was asked to sign a standard form contract of sale containing a clause (sometimes referred to as a "cut-out clause") agreeing that any assignee of the contract (for example, a finance company), when seeking to enforce the debt, would not be subject to the defences that the debtor (consumer) might have against the assignor (dealer). As noted in Chapters 11 and 28, most consumer protection acts now state that an assignee of a consumer credit contract shall have no greater rights than the assignor and is subject to the same obligations.[70]

The purpose of these statutes is to make the costs of obtaining credit clearer to the prospective debtor, who is then able to compare offers of credit and to shop around for the lowest effective rate of interest.

Some provincial consumer legislation imposes higher standards of financial disclosure on particular industries. Under the Ontario *Consumer Protection Act*, time share, personal development, leasing, and motor vehicle repair contracts are required to contain special terms, including detailed financial disclosure and cost-of-borrowing calculations. Several provinces regulate the payday lending industry, imposing relatively high caps on lending rates, under an exception to the general *Criminal Code* limit.[71]

CONSUMER REMEDIES

Consumers may sue for damages arising from breach of implied terms or prohibited practices under consumer protection legislation. They may do this individually or collectively in a class action. Many provinces call for **exemplary damages** to be awarded to the consumer when the seller's behaviour has been willful or deliberate.[72] And if the consumer loses the lawsuit against the seller, some provinces prohibit a judge from ordering the consumer to pay the costs of the seller, which is common in other types of lawsuits.[73]

exemplary damages money over and above losses to punish bad behaviour

CASE 14.12 Consumer Damages

The consumer's truck was destroyed in a fire caused by a defective daytime running light module. Neither the manufacturer nor dealer gave any assistance to the consumer despite knowing of the defective module for years before this incident. No recalls were issued. The consumer sued for breach of the *Sale of Goods Act* warranties pursuant to the Saskatchewan *Consumer Protection Act*. The Supreme Court of Canada held that this was an appropriate case for exemplary damages under the Saskatchewan *Consumer Protection Act* as the manufacture and dealer acted wilfully in choosing to ignore the consumer's request for compensation.[74]

---

[69] RSC 1985, c B-4, s 191.

[70] See e.g. BPCPA, 7, ss 15–16; *Consumer Protection Act*, NS, s 25; ON, s 83.

[71] See e.g. *Payday Loans Act, 2008*, SO 2008, c 9; O Reg 98/09; BC Reg 57/2009; Alta Reg 157/2009.

[72] *Consumer Protection Act*, SK, s 65; ON, s 100(3).

[73] *Consumer Protection Act*, SK, s 66 (unless the action was frivolous or vexatious).

[74] *Prebushewski v Dodge City Auto (1984) Ltd*, 2005 SCC 28.

> **CHECKLIST**
>
> ## Relevant Legislation
>
> Business sales tactics targeting consumers
>
> - Provincial consumer protection statutes
> - *Competition Act*
>
> Terms added to a consumer contract
>
> - Provincial consumer protection statutes
> - *Sale of Goods Act(s)*
> - *Interest Act*
> - *Bills of Exchange Act*

Strategies to Manage the Legal Risks

The *Sale of Goods Act* is a statute designed to address the legal risks associated with the sale of goods. However, for sellers, it adds risk to a contract silent on such things as quality and ownership. The key to managing these risks lies in the ability to contractually vary, limit, or exclude some of the implied protections. This is most important for business-to-business transactions, as most provincial consumer protection legislation prohibits any variation or limitation in consumer transactions. Where possible, vendors should design standard form contracts to:

- limit, vary, or exclude the implied protections of the *Sale of Goods Act*
- use clear and unambiguous language when excluding liability
- cover all forms of protection by referring to all warranties, conditions, or terms, whether implied by statute or common law
- specify their own return policy and warranty for repair or replacement of goods
- state when title passes and which party has the obligation to insure the goods in the interim and during transit
- confirm the purchaser's inspection and acceptance of the goods while excluding reliance on any representations, skill, or expertise of the vendor
- adopt language for installment payments (deposit or down payment) that reflects the desired result

Businesses must respect the legislative limitations imposed on the use of consumer standard form contracts. Therefore, in the consumer context, standard form contracts should include all required detail and notices together with a severance clause to save the contract if offending clauses are struck down. Sales strategies should be cross-referenced against required disclosure and cooling-off provisions. Telemarketers must be trained to comply with restrictions on their practices. Finally, businesses should be aware of industry-specific requirements and consider variation across the provinces in which they do business.

QUESTIONS FOR REVIEW

1. What was the principal purpose of the original *Sale of Goods Act*?
2. Distinguish between ownership and possession.
3. How are "goods" defined in the *Sale of Goods Act*? What types of personal property are not within the definition?
4. Is a contract for the installation of a central heating system a contract for the sale of goods?
5. What is the distinction between a sale and an agreement to sell?
6. What is meant by a "consignment"?
7. When does the *caveat emptor* principle apply to the sale of goods?
8. Distinguish between the implied term as to fitness and the implied term of merchantable quality.
9. What is the significance of an article being sold under its trade name?
10. What terms are implied in the case of a sale by sample?
11. What does it mean to say that the courts interpret the time set for payment as a warranty unless the parties have expressed otherwise?
12. What determines who bears the risk of loss when goods that are the subject matter of a contract of sale are destroyed?
13. When does title pass in the case of specific goods that are in a deliverable state?
14. In what circumstances can a person who is not the owner of goods pass a good title to them?
15. What is the distinction between unascertained goods and future goods?
16. What is a "bill of lading"?
17. When does an unpaid seller have a lien on the goods sold? When is there a right of repossession?
18. Who is a consumer?
19. What is the purpose of a cooling-off period?
20. How does the *Competition Act* attempt to prevent fraudulent telemarketing?

CASES AND PROBLEMS

1. Continuing Scenario

    Ashley wants to put fresh flowers on the tables in her restaurant. She wants the flowers to last longer than seven days without losing petals or wilting, and she wants them to match her decor—white, blue, and yellow. Finally, they must have a very mild scent so as not to interfere with the pleasant food smells. She goes online and locates a flower shop within a few blocks of her restaurant. She goes to the shop and speaks to Gladys, who suggests the Generosia blue hydrangea—it is the only blue flower they carry, although they have many yellow ones. Gladys shows her a sample she has in the cooler—the flower is a round ball approximately the size of a baseball. Ashley loves it. Gladys describes the blue hydrangea as long lasting, low fragrance, and blue. In particular, the ones grown by Generosia are very intense blue and large. Ashley places an order for 50 Generosia blue hydrangeas to be delivered every Friday morning so they will be fresh for the weekend diners.

    The first week, the order arrives on time. The flowers are big and blue, but by Tuesday they are drooping and beginning to look wilted. The next week, the flowers are not quite as big, and they also wilt by Tuesday. Ashley calls Gladys and is told to call Generosia, the grower. When Ashley speaks to the customer service agent from Generosia, she is told that hydrangeas are not long lasting flowers—they need lots of water and will wilt within five days. He also says the Generosia blue are especially likely to droop because of the weight of the extra big flower.

Ashley wants Gladys's flower shop to refund all her money plus some compensation for the inconvenience of having to replace the flowers. What are her rights? Would your answer be different if these flowers were ordered for Ashley's home?

2. On a Friday afternoon, Harris went into a store owned by Kabul Karpets Inc. and saw a large Uzbek carpet, which she immediately decided would be perfect on the wall of her sitting room. She promptly bought the carpet for $2000, paying by credit card.

    Because of the large size of the carpet—and the smallness of her car—she asked the store to deliver it and was told they would do so on the following Monday. The sales assistant attached a "sold" notice to the carpet with a small piece of adhesive tape, leaving the carpet prominently displayed on the wall of the store.

    The following Monday morning, Lewis saw the carpet through the store window and at once realized it was just what he was looking for to hang on his study wall. He entered the store, paid $2000 by credit card, and had the carpet loaded into his large van. The shop assistant who served Lewis was not the same one who had been on duty on the Friday, and the "sold" notice had somehow become detached from the carpet and presumably had been swept up by the cleaners. On the Tuesday, Harris phoned the store to inquire why her carpet had not been delivered.

    Who owns the carpet? Is there a remedy if the carpet is not perfect for the study wall?

3. Dorothy receives a phone call during the dinner hour from a company selling magazine subscriptions; at first, she tries to get off the phone and tells the caller she is not interested. However, she recalls that her son's birthday is coming up so she asks the caller if they have *Golf Magazine*; they do. The caller tells her that she will get a better price if she orders two magazine subscriptions rather than just one; he tells her it is no problem to have the magazines sent to different addresses. Therefore, she orders *Golf Magazine* to be delivered to her son's home and *Better Homes & Gardens* for herself. The caller tells her she is getting 24 months at 50 percent off of the in-store price. She agrees to pay by monthly installments and gives her credit card information. The first month, *Golf Magazine* is delivered to her home and not her son's; when she looks at the back of the magazine in search of a phone number to call, she sees the in-store price and realizes it is the same as the price she is paying.

    Discuss Dorothy's remedies. Does it make a difference if she never received a full copy of the magazine subscription contract?

4. Gabrieli bought a truck from a dealer, Transit Inc. Gabrieli signed a "purchase order" on May 12, at which time Transit ordered the truck from the manufacturer. It was agreed that the sale was subject to Gabrieli's being able to arrange suitable financing.

    Three weeks later, Gabrieli informed Transit that she had been able to obtain a loan from her bank and was in a position to give Transit a bank draft for the full price. Transit confirmed that the arrangement was satisfactory. On August 2, the truck was delivered to Transit from the manufacturer. Transit called Gabrieli, telling her, "Your truck is here and ready for you to collect." Gabrieli went straight to the Transit premises, handed over the bank draft, and received the keys, papers, and truck. At that time, Transit's sales manager also handed her a number of other documents, including one the manager described as "your warranty," which he asked Gabrieli to sign. Gabrieli did so. The document gave a limited one-year warranty for defects but excluded implied warranties and excluded liability for consequential damages.

    The truck proved to be defective and soon developed a number of faults. Gabrieli took the truck back to Transit on numerous occasions for various repairs, but these were mostly unsuccessful. Finally, after more than two years of unsatisfactory operation, Gabrieli returned the truck to Transit and demanded her money back.

    Transit denied liability, pointing to the one-year warranty that excluded the statutory implied warranties.

    Is Gabrieli entitled to any remedy? Why or why not?

5. Benner's Sawmill Inc. entered into a contract with Chen to purchase a quantity of timber growing on land leased by Chen. A price of $150 per cubic metre was agreed, and the quantity set at approximately 600 cubic metres. Chen was to cut and trim the timber ready for collection by Benner's, who paid an initial deposit of $15 000. Benner's asked its insurance company about insuring the timber and was told the timber could not be insured until it had been felled, trimmed, and "timber-marked" (that is, marked with a provincially registered mark applied by swinging a timber hammer and striking the wood surface at both ends).

   Some weeks later, Chen phoned Benner's and informed them that the timber had been cut, trimmed, and stacked. The total price was $94 000 (the quantity being a little more than 600 cubic metres). When asked if the timber had been timber-marked, Chen replied that it had not. He was going away on a short vacation but would see to it as soon as he returned. In accordance with the contract, Benner's sent Chen a cheque for the full price, less the deposit already paid.

   Before Chen returned from vacation, his sheds were destroyed by fire. When Benner's demanded the timber or their money back, Chen replied, "Sorry, but it was your timber that burned."

   Advise Benner's.

6. The Granite County School Board placed an order with Borough Furniture Ltd, a furniture manufacturer, for 2500 folding chairs. Before placing the order, an officer of the board examined a number of chairs produced by Borough (as well as chairs of other manufacturers). Eventually, they settled on one particular model but required a number of modifications to be made. Borough produced a prototype of the chair, which was examined by the officer, who expressed satisfaction.

   Borough delivered a first batch of 500 chairs and continued with the manufacture of the remaining 2000. A few days after the first delivery, it was found that the chairs tipped rather easily and were unsuitable for use in classrooms. The board refused to take delivery of any more chairs and demanded that Borough take back the 500 they had delivered. Borough claimed they had made the chairs according to the board's specifications and demanded payment for the full 2500.

   Which party has the better claim?

7. In December, Winnipeg Seafoods Ltd. orally agreed to purchase from Lakehead Fish Wholesale Co. 1000 five-kilogram boxes of frozen Lake Superior herring at $1.40 per kilogram. The fish were being stored in the cold storage warehouse of a third party, the Bailey Co. of Thunder Bay. The Bailey Co. operated as a storage company that processed and stored fresh fish. At the time, it held some 1500 boxes of this type of fish in storage.

   Because Winnipeg Seafoods was short of storage space, it did not want the fish shipped to it but preferred to have it remain in the warehouse at Thunder Bay. Lakehead Fish then arranged with Bailey to transfer the storage account to the name of Winnipeg Seafoods in respect of the 1000 boxes, and Lakehead Fish sent an invoice for $7000 to Winnipeg Seafoods. The invoice indicated that the merchandise was in storage at Bailey's in Thunder Bay. Immediately afterward, Bailey sent its invoice to Winnipeg Seafoods for one month's storage charges, payable in advance. Winnipeg Seafoods did not pay either of these accounts. The price of frozen herring started to fall in the middle of January. The fish were held in storage until the end of January and then processed to prevent spoilage. On February 2, Winnipeg Seafoods returned the invoice of Lakehead Fish with an accompanying letter to the effect that it had decided to "cancel the order." Lakehead Fish then sued Winnipeg Seafoods Ltd. for the price of the fish, $7000, or in the alternative, for damages for non-acceptance.

   Should it succeed?

8. Ebrahim bought a used car from Cival Autos Inc. for $8000. The car was described by Cival as follows: "one careful owner only, low mileage, excellent condition." In fact, Cival's manager was aware that the car had had three previous owners, the

most recent of whom had been convicted of dangerous driving following a collision in which the car had sustained serious damage. He also knew that the odometer had been altered and that the car was generally in very poor condition.

Very soon after Ebrahim took delivery, the car started to develop problems. At first he took the car back to Cival, where he was told that the problems were minor and that they had "fixed" them. After three such visits to Cival, Ebrahim took the car to an independent garage, and the true facts about the car became known.

Apart from the normal remedies in contract and tort, is there any other legal action that Ebrahim can take against Cival?

Chapter 15
Bailment and Leasing

- **BAILMENT**
- **RIGHTS AND DUTIES OF A BAILEE**
- **SPECIAL TYPES OF BAILMENT**
- **LEASING**
- **TYPES OF CHATTEL LEASE**
- **REASONS FOR CHATTEL LEASING**
- **COMMON TERMS IN CHATTEL LEASES**
- **RIGHTS OF THE PARTIES**
- **STRATEGIES TO MANAGE THE LEGAL RISKS**

Ownership and possession of goods do not always go together. Bailment and leasing are two common types of contract in which ownership and possession are separated. Leasing of personal property is a form of bailment, although from a business point of view, leasing has a very different function from other forms of bailment. A lease of personal property—a chattel lease—is frequently regarded as a form of financing or an alternative to sale. By contrast, most other types of bailment involve parting with possession of an item only temporarily—for storage, repair, or transportation. Legally, however, they share the same essential features.

In this chapter we examine such questions as:

- What is the legal nature of bailment?
- What are the principal types of bailment contract?
- What are the rights and duties of the parties to a contract of bailment?
- What are the principal types of chattel lease?
- Why are leasing contracts used, and why have they become so important?
- What are the terms that are commonly found in leasing contracts?
- What are the respective rights of the lessor and the lessee?

BAILMENT

Definition

bailment possession of personal property without ownership

bailor owner or transferor of the goods

bailee party accepting possession of goods from a bailor

Bailment is the transfer of possession of personal property without a transfer of ownership; the receiving party agrees to return the property at a later time. The transferor of the property, usually its owner, is called the **bailor**, and the person who receives custody of it, the **bailee**. During a bailment, the bailee must take care of the bailor's goods.

Nature of Bailment

The nature of bailment can be illustrated by comparing it to other common transactions or relationships—in particular, sale, trust, debt, and licence:

- Sale: A sale transfers ownership, with or without a change in possession. By contrast, a bailment does not alter ownership but requires a change in possession.
- Trust: The creation of a trust gives legal ownership to the trustee, and the beneficiary acquires an equitable interest in the subject of the trust. Possession is not relevant; the property could be in the possession of the trustee, the beneficiary, or the creator of the trust.
- Debt: A deposit of money in a bank or trust company creates a creditor–debtor rather than a bailor–bailee relationship. It is not bailment because only property of equal value is returned, not the exact asset given. By contrast, a deposit of specific items of personal property for safekeeping with a bank or trust company does create a bailment.[1]
- Licence: A bailment requires a transfer of possession and a voluntary acceptance of the common law duty of safekeeping. A licence amounts to no more than a grant of permission to make use of the licensor's land on the understanding that possession of any chattel is not transferred, and responsibility for guarding the chattel is not accepted.[2] For example, the owner of a parking lot normally does not accept responsibility for storage of the vehicle and grants only a licence to use the spot.[3] Alternatively, when a vehicle is left at a garage for servicing, the garage owner does assume responsibility for its safekeeping.[4]

Most bailments are contractual and involve payment, but a bailment can also occur without a contract between a bailor and bailee. The essential elements of bailment are delivery of possession without the intention to transfer title and with the intention that the property will be returned to the bailor. These elements may exist without a contract, as when the owner of a car lends it gratuitously to a friend. A bailment may also be involuntary; if a customer leaves a coat behind in a restaurant, the restaurateur becomes a bailee of the coat and cannot refuse to return it at the customer's request.

Bailments may benefit the bailor or the bailee, or both parties. By their nature, contractual bailments are intended to benefit both parties. One party obtains the service desired, and the other receives payment. A non-contractual or **gratuitous bailment**

gratuitous bailment a bailment where one party provides no consideration, or where there is no intention to create a contractual relationship

---

[1] *Royal Bank of Canada v Reynolds* (1976), 66 DLR (3d) 88; *Cuvelier v Bank of Montreal* (2002), 212 NSR (2d) 17.

[2] *Heffron v Imperial Parking Co et al* (1974), 3 OR (2d) 722 at 727.

[3] *Bata v City Parking Canada Ltd* (1973), 2 OR (2d) 446. *Heffron v Imperial Parking Co et al*, *supra* note 2.

[4] *Hertz Canada Ltd v Suburban Motors Ltd*, [2000] BCJ No 830.

may be for the benefit of either party. In the examples given above, the bailment of the coat benefits the bailor, whereas the loan of a car benefits the bailee.

Sub-Bailment

In a sub-bailment, after receiving the property from the bailor, the bailee transfers possession to someone else, a **sub-bailee**.

sub-bailee a person who receives a bailment of property from a bailee

CASE 15.1 Creation of Sub-Bailment

After Mason's mother died, he contracted with Thompson Funeral Home to have her body cremated and her ashes stored in an urn. The urn was to be held until after Mason's father died, when Mason would then make a decision about what was to be done. When Mason's father died four years later, Thompson cremated the remains and placed them in another urn. Thompson sought Mason's instructions about what to do with the two urns, but Mason was still not sure where he wanted to bury them. Mason instructed Thompson to send the urns to Westside Cemetery for burial in common ground. Common ground involves one storage vault without marker, which allows easy retrieval, so Mason would be able to move them later. Thompson sent the urns to Westside as instructed. When Mason contacted Westside 10 years later, the urns could not be found. Mason sued Thompson and Westside in bailment. The court held that the urns and ashes were Mason's property. A bailment contract was formed with Thompson, and Mason had authorized a sub-bailment to Westside. Both the bailee and sub-bailee owed Mason a duty to take care of the urns as instructed. The urns were lost by Westside, and only Westside was held liable.[5]

To avoid liability when creating a bailment relationship between the bailor and the sub-bailee, the bailee must obtain permission or consent from the bailor for the sub-bailment, and the sub-bailee must be aware of the bailor's interest. For usual or expected sub-bailments, permission may be implied. Obvious examples of sub-bailment include postal or courier services used to transport the bailed goods.

CASE 15.2 Delivery as Sub-Bailment

Punch took her diamond ring, worth $11 000, to Savoy's Jewellers in Sault Ste. Marie for repair. Savoy was unable to make the repair, so they sent it to Walker Jewellers in Toronto. Savoy sent the ring by registered mail and stated the value for insurance purposes as $100. Apparently, this was normal trade practice.

After Walker repaired the ring, it returned the ring to Savoy's using a delivery service operated by Canadian National (CN). Again, the value was declared as $100. The contract between Walker and CN limited CN's liability for loss or damage to the declared value of $100. The ring was never delivered to Savoy.

Punch sued Savoy's, Walker, and CN. The court found that Savoy was a bailee, and both Walker and CN were sub-bailees. All three owed a duty of care directly to Punch, and the burden on each of them was to show it was not responsible for the loss or for inadequately insuring the ring.[6]

In *Punch v Savoy's Jewellers Ltd* (Case 15.2), the court held that the clause in the contract between CN and Walker, which limited CN's liability, could not be relied on by CN against either Savoy or Punch, since they were not parties to the contract and lacked privity. All three parties were found liable. Is this fair?[7] Suppose, for example, that Punch agreed that Savoy's liability should be limited to $100 when it sent the ring by registered mail; why should CN and Walker not be entitled to rely on a similar limitation in their contracts? This question was considered in *The Pioneer Container* (Case 15.3 below).

---

[5] *Mason v Westside Cemeteries Ltd*, 1996 CanLII 9113, 135 DLR (4th) 361 (O SC).

[6] *Punch v Savoy's Jewellers Ltd* (1986), 26 DLR (4th) 546.

[7] Contrast *London Drugs Ltd v Kuehne and Nagel International Ltd* (1992), 97 DLR (4th) 261.

> **CASE 15.3** Terms in the Sub-Bailment Contract
>
> The plaintiffs hired Hanjin Container Lines to ship goods from the United States to Hong Kong. The contract with Hanjin contained a term that "the carrier shall be entitled to sub-contract *on any terms* the whole or any part of the handling of the goods" (italics added). Hanjin contracted with Pioneer Container to ship the goods on the last leg of their journey, from Taiwan to Hong Kong. The goods were lost in a collision off the coast of Taiwan. The bill of lading contract between Hanjin and Pioneer contained a term that the contract should be governed by Chinese law, and any dispute should be determined in Taiwan.
>
> The plaintiffs sued the defendants in Hong Kong. The defendants objected that, under the terms of the bill of lading, they could be sued only in Taiwan. The court ruled that, although there was no contract between the plaintiffs and the defendants, the plaintiffs had authorized the sub-bailment and effectively consented to the terms of the sub-bailment.[8]

RIGHTS AND DUTIES OF A BAILEE

Liability under Contract and Tort

Sometimes bailed goods are lost, damaged, or destroyed while in the possession of a bailee. Who is liable for the loss suffered? When the bailment is the result of a contract, its terms, either express or implied by trade custom, establish the duties, level of care, and liabilities of the bailee for the goods in its possession. All bailees are, however, under a duty to take care of property bailed to them. The duty of care required by the law of torts applies to circumstances not covered expressly or impliedly by the bailment contract and applies also to gratuitous bailments involving no contract at all. The required standard of care varies according to the type of bailment.

Sometimes, a contract of bailment includes a term that the bailee is not liable for damage to the goods while in her custody, even when the damage is caused by negligence in the course of performing the contract. The courts construe this type of exemption clause very strictly against the bailee. If the goods are damaged for any reason not related to the actual performance contemplated by the contract, the bailee is not protected by the exemption clause.[9]

> **CASE 15.4** Narrow Interpretation of Exemption Clause
>
> An army officer took his uniform to the dry cleaners to be cleaned. The cleaners gave him a receipt in which they disclaimed all liability for damage arising in the course of "necessary handling." The uniform was never returned, and when the officer sued for its value, the cleaners relied upon the exemption clause. It was established that the loss arose when the cleaning firm sent the uniform to someone else for cleaning. The court found that the wording of the contract required personal performance by the bailee. The damage had not taken place during "necessary handling." The exemption clause did not apply, and the cleaners were held liable for the loss.[10]

Although the law of bailment is derived from principles of both tort and contract law, bailment is a distinct relationship governed by its own rules. When goods are damaged or lost while in the possession of a bailee, it is often difficult for the bailor to ascertain exactly how the harm occurred. Since a bailee is better able to establish the facts, the law of bailment places the burden of showing that she was not negligent on the bailee. She must offer some reasonable alternative explanation for the loss and show she met the standard of care. This burden of proof makes it easier for a bailor to sue under the rules of bailment than under the ordinary rules of tort.

---

[8] *The Pioneer Container*, [1994] 2 AC 324.

[9] *Solway v Davis Moving & Storage Inc* (2002), 62 OR (3d) 522, leave dismissed [2003] SCCA No 57.

[10] *Davies v Collins*, [1945] 1 All ER 247.

The Standard of Care

The required level or standard of care varies according to the type of bailment. The standard is lowest when the bailment is both gratuitous and for the benefit of the bailor, as when A permits B to leave her car in A's garage without charge. After all, the bailee is doing the bailor a favour; but even a gratuitous bailee is liable for gross negligence.

The standard of care is highest on a bailee when the bailment is gratuitous and for the benefit of the bailee, as when one borrows a friend's car for personal use. The bailor receives no valuable consideration, so it is fair that, in such circumstances, the bailee should compensate the bailor when damage to the goods results from even slight carelessness on the bailee's part. In **bailments for value**, the standard of care falls between that of gratuitous bailments for the benefit of the bailee and those for the benefit of the bailor. (A bailee who allows a friend to leave her car in the bailee's garage is not under as high a duty of care as would a warehousing firm being paid to store the car.) Generally, a bailee for value is expected to take the same care of goods as a prudent and diligent person should take of goods belonging to those with whom she transacts business—a standard of care that is at least as high and probably higher than she might choose to apply to her own goods.

bailments for value contractual bailment

CASE 15.5 Reasonable Precautions to Prevent Theft

A car rental firm left one of its cars at a garage for routine servicing. The car was locked and left overnight in an unsecured parking lot adjacent to the garage. During the night, a thief broke into the locked office where the car keys were kept (with tags on them in order to identify the car), stole the key to the rental car, and drove it away.

The rental firm claimed damages for the loss of the car. The court held that there had been no breach of its duty of care on the part of the garage. It had taken reasonable precautions to prevent loss. The loss was a result of the efforts of a "truly determined thief."[11]

CASE 15.6 Not Enough Done to Prevent Theft

Duckworth owned a classic sports car that was damaged in an accident. He took the car to Superior Autobody to have repairs done and left a deposit of $500. The shop did not have an alarm system and did not have padlocks on the latches of the overhead doors. Keys were left in the ignition to allow easy removal. Thieves broke in and stole the car, which was never recovered. The court held that the repairers were bailees for value and were liable for the loss since they had failed to take appropriate care of the car while it was in their charge.[12]

The standard also varies according to the type of goods bailed and the extent of the promise to look after the goods. In interpreting both express and implied promises of the bailee, the courts consider all the circumstances. If the property is very valuable and easily damaged, the standard of care required will be higher. You must take greater care with expensive jewellery than with a bicycle stored in your shed. In the words of one judge, "The substantial question must always be, whether that care has been exhibited which the special circumstances reasonably demand."[13]

---

[11] *Hertz Canada Ltd v Suburban Motors Ltd*, supra note 4.

[12] *Duckworth v Armstrong* (1996), 29 CCLT (2d) 239.

[13] *Fitzgerald v Grand Trunk Railway* (1880), 4 OAR 601 at 624. See *Solway v Davis Moving & Storage Inc*, supra note 9.

Some special classes of bailee are subject to higher standards of care because they deal with the public generally. These include common carriers and hoteliers or innkeepers, discussed later in this chapter.

Rights and Remedies

Damages and *Quantum Meruit*

In a contractual bailment, the bailee has the usual contractual remedies for breach by the bailor. Because of the character of bailment, the main concern of a bailee is collecting compensation for services rendered.

When a bailee has performed her part of a contract, as when a warehouse returns goods that have been stored with it, the usual remedy is an action for the contract price. Occasionally a bailee may not be able to complete performance, as when a carrier has contracted to transport goods in several installments but the bailor delivers only part of the goods for shipment. The carrier may then sue *quantum meruit* for the value of the services it has performed and for damages compensating it for its loss of profits.

Lien

An important additional remedy available to a bailee is a lien on the bailed goods in its possession. This gives the bailee a right to retain possession of the goods until the bailor pays what is due for the services. The bailor cannot normally repossess the goods until he has paid the sum due. Generally, a right of lien arises only when the services have been performed and payment is already due.

ILLUSTRATION 15.1   When Lien Right Arises

Pliable Plastics Ltd. has very little storage space for its manufactured products. It enters into an arrangement with Stately Storage Limited whereby Pliable Plastics delivers its products for storage on a daily charge basis and, when the products are sold, picks them up again for delivery to the buyer. Storage charges are billed and become payable every three months.

Stately Storage has no lien upon the goods stored with it until the end of the three-month period and until it has billed Pliable Plastics. If, after two-and-one-half months have passed, Pliable Plastics sells a portion of the stored goods, Stately Storage must surrender the goods on demand to Pliable Plastics or to a buyer who presents proper documents. When three months have expired and Stately Storage bills Pliable Plastics, Stately Storage has a lien for all the accrued storage charges upon the goods remaining in the warehouse at that time.

As noted in Chapter 14, the lien of an unpaid seller is a possessory remedy; an unpaid bailee loses her lien on the bailed goods as soon as the bailor obtains possession of them without deceit or fraud.

A right of lien under common law rules is available to any bailees who perform services such as repairs or improvements to goods bailed with them, to innkeepers, to common carriers (who are under a duty to accept goods from anyone so long as they have space for them), and also to professional people like lawyers and bankers (who have a common law right of lien over documents in their possession when they have performed services related to the documents). Various statutes give liens in other types of bailment, and even though they may have a common law or statutory right of lien, many businesses acting as bailees make the lien right a term in their contracts with customers.

The Right of Sale

The right of lien is valuable to a bailee because the bailor usually needs to recover his goods, and to do so he must first pay off overdue charges. If, however, the bailor is unable to pay off the charges—say, he becomes insolvent—the bailee is left with goods she cannot use because she has no title to them, and yet she has the burden of storing them. The bailment contract may contain a right of sale, and various statutes give bailees who have a lien upon goods stored with them an additional right to sell the goods.

The exact provisions of the statutes vary in detail, but generally they require (1) that a certain time elapse after payment falls due; (2) that advance notice be given to the bailor of the bailee's intention to sell; (3) that the sale be advertised; and (4) that it be held by public auction. Until the time of sale, the owner of the goods (or other person entitled to possession) is usually entitled to recover them on payment in full of the bailee's charges.[14] The proceeds of the sale are used, first, to reimburse the bailee for her costs of holding the sale and, second, to pay the overdue charges for her services. Any surplus belongs to the bailor.

SPECIAL TYPES OF BAILMENT

There are various types of bailment, and both the common law and the statutory rules vary to some extent according to the type of bailment.

Storage and Safekeeping

A warehousing firm that accepts goods for storage and a bank that rents a safety deposit box are bailees for storage or safekeeping and are under a duty to take care of the goods stored with them.

The terms of a contract may reduce liability; for example, if the bailor specifically directs where the goods are to be placed, the liability of the warehouse keeper will be restricted to complying with those instructions.

A warehouse firm is not customarily obliged to insure goods stored with it against loss by fire unless it has expressly contracted to do so.[15] Ordinarily, a bailee must return to the bailor the exact goods stored. When, however, the goods stored are **fungible goods** (that is, replaceable with identical goods also in storage), the bailee's liability is discharged when she returns to the bailor goods of the exact description in the warehouse receipt. For example, when a quantity of grain of a specific grade is stored in a grain elevator in bins containing other grain of the same grade, the elevator company is bound to deliver not the exact grain that was bailed with it but an equivalent quantity of the same grade.

At common law, a warehousing firm did not obtain a right of lien on goods stored with it unless it had specifically bargained for the lien. Now all common law provinces have legislation giving a warehouse a right of lien on goods stored with it for the amount of its charges.

The statutes contain words such as "every warehouser has a lien on goods deposited with the warehouser for storage whether deposited by the owner of the goods, or by the owner's authority or by any person entrusted with the possession of the goods

fungible goods goods that may be replaced with different but identical goods

---

[14] See e.g. *Warehouse Lien Act*, RSBC 1996, c 480, s 7; *Repair and Storage Liens Act*, RSO 1990, c R-25, s 22.

[15] See *Neff v St Catharines Marina Ltd* (1998), 155 DLR (4th) 647. The warehouse firms must exercise due care to prevent fire: *Hogarth v Archibald Moving & Storage Ltd* (1991), 57 BCLR (2d) 319.

by the owner or by the owner's authority."[16] The statutes further provide that "a warehouser may sell by public auction, in the manner provided in this section, any goods on which the warehouser has a lien for charges which have become due."[17] The statutes set out the details of the notice that must be given and the way in which the sale is to be advertised and held. The aim is to give adequate protection to the bailor or owner while giving the bailee a reasonably prompt method of obtaining payment.

Repairs and Work on a Chattel

Bailment is often a normal consequence of contracts made for the maintenance of, or repairs to, various articles, as when a truck is delivered to a garage for repair, or when an electronics firm receives business machines for servicing. A repairer who works on these articles on her own premises is a bailee for value. In accepting the work, the repairer undertakes to do it in a competent manner, employing the skill she professes to have and to have the work done by the promised time. The bailee is also under a duty to take care of the article while it is in her possession, just as a warehousing company.[18] Failure to do so is a breach of contract on the bailee's part, and a breach may entitle the bailor to deny payment for work already done or to sue for damages. The bailor is also entitled to the return of the chattel.

As noted earlier, the common law gives a repairer a lien on the goods for the value of the work done. The common law right does not extend to the right to sell the goods, but some of the provinces give an additional statutory right to the repairer to sell the goods once the repair charges are three months overdue.[19]

Transportation

The law identifies three types of carriers.

1. A gratuitous carrier is anyone who agrees to move goods from one place to another without reward.
2. A private carrier is a business that undertakes on occasion to carry goods for reward but reserves the right to select its customers and restrict the type of goods it is willing to carry.
3. A **common carrier** is a business that holds itself out to the public as a transporter of goods (or passengers) for reward.

common carrier a business that holds itself out to the public as a transporter of goods for reward

The public nature of a common carrier is that it does not discriminate among those who request its services, nor does it reserve the right to refuse an offer of goods for shipment when it has the means of shipping them. A common carrier may restrict its services to a certain area and to certain goods that are suitable for carriage by its equipment. Most railway and steamship companies are common carriers, as are some trucking companies and even gas and oil pipeline companies. Airlines may repudiate the status of a common carrier by reserving the right to refuse goods. The *Canada Transportation Act* regulates air and rail carriers.[20] A proprietor of an amusement ride

---

[16] BC *Warehouse Lien Act, supra* note 14, s 2; *Warehousemen's Lien Act*, RSNS 1989, c 499, s 3. In Ontario, warehousing is covered in the *Repair and Storage Liens Act supra* note 14; section 4(1) gives a similar lien to a "storer" of goods.

[17] BC *Warehouse Lien Act, supra* note 14, s 4; NS *Warehousemen's Lien Act, supra* note 16, s 5. In Ontario, a storer has a similar right: *Repair and Storage Liens Act, supra* note 14, s 4(7).

[18] *Letourneau v Otto Mobiles Edmonton (1984) Ltd*, [2002] AJ No 825.

[19] See e.g. *Repairers' Lien Act*, RSBC 1996, c 404, s 2; ON *Repair and Storage Liens Act, supra* note 14, s 3(3) (60 days overdue).

[20] SC 1996, c 10.

is not a common carrier because the ride's purpose is not to transport but rather to thrill.[21] Alternatively, the operator of an escalator may be a common carrier when it moves passengers between destinations.[22]

A carrier's liability for damage to goods in the course of transit depends upon the type of carrier. All carriers are bailees and always have some responsibility for the goods under their control. Even a gratuitous bailee must exercise at least the diligence and care to be expected of a reasonable person in handling her own property.

The duty of care required of a private carrier is greater. It owes a degree of care commensurate with the skill reasonably expected of a competent firm in its line of business. The liability of a common carrier is still greater, although it may take advantage of certain recognized defences.

A common carrier undertakes to indemnify the shipper (the bailor) against loss whether the loss occurs through the carrier's fault or not. The carrier is, therefore, an insurer as well as a bailee.[23] This rule makes sense: Its practical effect is to relieve the shipper of the burden of producing evidence that it was the common carrier's lack of care that caused the loss or damage. In most circumstances, it would be impossible for the carrier to gather this evidence. The shipper need only prove (1) that the carrier received the goods in good condition, and (2) that the carrier delivered them in bad condition or failed to deliver them at all. The burden is then on the carrier to establish that the cause of the loss was within one of the recognized defences available to common carriers. These defences are

- an act of God;
- inherent vice in the goods; and
- default by the shipper.

It is not enough for a common carrier to show that it was not negligent—it has only those three defences. An "act of God," refers to a natural catastrophe; fire is not an act of God unless caused by lightning. Even when the cause of the loss is a natural catastrophe, the carrier may still be liable if it has negligently contributed to the loss, for example, by failing to install a sprinkler system. A common carrier may also avoid liability if it can show that the goods had an **inherent vice** at the time of shipment; for example, the goods may have been in a combustible condition or may have had latent defects that made them more susceptible to breakage than is typical of goods of their category.

inherent vice a latent defect or dangerous condition of goods

A common carrier can offer a third defence: that the shipper has been guilty of a breach of duty or is in some way at fault. A contract for the transportation of goods includes an implied promise on the part of the shipper that the goods are safe to carry. The shipper's breach of this duty releases the carrier from its part of the bargain, and if the goods cause damage to the carrier's equipment, for instance by exploding, the carrier may successfully sue for damages.

Unless otherwise agreed,[24] a common carrier is liable for the full value of goods lost or destroyed. However, the carrier may, and frequently does, limit the amount of its liability when the shipper does not declare the value of the goods. Where the shipper declares less than the full value of the goods to the carrier, in order to pay a lower freight charge than it would have paid had it declared their true value, the carrier is not released from its duty, but its liability is limited to the declared value.

---

[21] *Mallais v DA Campbell Amusements Ltd* (2007), 84 OR (3d) 687 (ONCA).

[22] *Kauffman v Toronto Transit Commission*, [1960] SCR 251.

[23] *Canadian National Railway Co v Harris*, [1946] SCR 352 at 369–370.

[24] *Canada Transportation Act*, supra note 20, s 137; *Mitsubishi Heavy Industries Ltd v Canadian National Railway Co*, 2012 BCSC 1415 at para 23.

INTERNATIONAL ISSUE
International Transport of Goods

The global marketplace has created an explosion in international transportation of goods. Often, multiple carriers move the goods across borders and over roads, rail, and water. Sometimes a "multimodal transport operator" coordinates the movement of the goods from one carrier to the next. Goods may be in sealed containers, unavailable for inspection by any of the carriers.

If the goods arrive damaged, it is very difficult to determine when (or in which carrier's possession) the damage occurred and what jurisdiction's rules or laws should be applied in the circumstances.

The global community has been trying to unify the liability rules for international carriage but has had little success. The 1980 United Nations Convention on International Multimodal Transport of Goods failed to attract support and never came into force. The United Nations Conference on Trade and Development (UNCTAD) produced rules in 1992, but their effectiveness depends on the private sector incorporating the terms into their agreements. Although a review of the 1992 rules was commenced over 10 years ago, adoption of new multimodal rules has not occurred despite the prevailing view that existing liability framework does not take into account modern changes in transport patterns, technology, and markets. New rules for transportation by sea were adopted by the UN in 2008.

Question to Consider

1. How should liability be assigned when the point of damage cannot be established and multiple carriers are involved?

Sources: Based on United Nations Commission on International Trade Law (UNCITRAL) website, www.uncitral.org; UNCTAD website, www.unctad.org; M. Faghfouri, "The International Regulation of Liability for Multimodal Transport—In Search of Uniformity" (2006) 5(1) *WMU Journal of Maritime Affairs* 95–114; Report by the UNCTAD secretariat for United Nations Conference on Trade and Development Jan. 2003, "Multimodal Transport: The Feasibility of an International Legal Instrument" (available at www.unctad.org); The United Nations Convention on International Carriage of Goods Wholly or Partly by Sea, also known as the "Rotterdam Rules," December 2008. Nnenna Ifeanyi-Ajufo, "International Multimodal Transport Business and the Regulation of Electronic Commerce" (2015) 35 *Journal of Law, Policy and Globalization* www.iiste.org; ISSN 2224-3259 https://iiste.org/Journals/index.php/JLPG/article/view/20913.

Innkeepers

innkeeper a person or firm that maintains an establishment offering lodging to any member of the public

Under common law, the word **innkeeper** refers to a person or establishment offering lodging to any member of the public. An inn, or a hotel, differs from a boardinghouse, whose owner may pick and choose whom he is willing to accommodate, and also from a restaurant, which offers only food to guests. Most provincial statutes, however, have broadened the definition considerably.

All businesses offering accommodation to the public are under a duty to take reasonable care of the belongings of their guests and patrons. Like warehousing firms, they are liable for damage or loss caused by their negligence or the negligence of their employees. Under the common law, however, innkeepers are also liable for the loss or theft of their guests' goods. There is, however, an important difference between goods bailed to a common carrier and goods left in the room of a hotel guest: The bailor of goods to a common carrier gives them over completely to the care of the carrier, whereas the hotel guest shares the responsibility with the hotel, since he or she has control over the goods when occupying the room. Accordingly, a hotel may avoid liability if it can show that the disappearance was due to the carelessness of the guest. A hotel is liable for damage to the goods of its guests—as distinct from its liability for their disappearance through loss or theft—only if the damage was caused by the negligence of the hotel's employees.

The strict liability of an innkeeper at common law has been modified by legislation in most provinces. Usually, the innkeeper is liable only where the goods have been stolen, lost, or damaged through the willful act, default, or neglect of the innkeeper or an employee, or where the goods have been deposited expressly for safe custody with the innkeeper.[25] The innkeepers acts of the various provinces usually also give the right to sell the goods of guests by public auction if their bills remain unpaid for a specified period.[26]

Pledge or Pawn

Although the two terms "pledge" and "pawn" have the same legal significance, a "pawn" refers only to transactions with a pawnbroker. A **pledge or pawn** is a bailment of personal property as security for repayment of a loan. The borrower is the pledgor and the creditor the pledgee. The subject matter of a pledge may be goods left with a **pawnbroker**, for example, or share certificates left with a bank.

A pledgee is a bailee for value and must exercise such care as is reasonable in the ordinary and proper course of its business. A pledgee obtains a lien on the personal property pledged with it, and the pledgor cannot recover possession of the goods until it repays the debt for which they are security. In addition, by pledging the goods, the pledgor gives authority to the pledgee to sell the pledged goods upon default and to reimburse itself out of the proceeds of the sale for any costs incurred as a result of the default and for the amount of the unpaid loan. The surplus, if any, belongs to the borrower.[27] Rights in pledged property are governed by the personal property security system, discussed in Chapter 28.[28]

pledge or pawn a bailment of personal property as security for repayment of a loan where possession passes to the bailee

pawnbroker a business that loans money on the security of pawned goods

CHECKLIST
Types of Bailment

- gratuitous bailment for the benefit of bailee
- bailment for value (contractual bailment)
- gratuitous bailment for the benefit of the bailor
- sub-bailment

Special types of bailment

- storage and safekeeping
- repairing
- transportation
- innkeeping
- pledge or pawn

LEASING

Leasing of personal property is a major growth industry and has become a multibillion-dollar business in Canada and the United States. At the consumer level, automobile leasing is a common alternative to purchasing on credit. In business, it is common to lease capital equipment, such as heavy machinery and aircraft. Leasing is a bailment for value usually governed by the terms of a detailed standard form contract.

---

[25] See e.g. *Hotel Keepers Act*, RSBC 1996, c 206, s 3; *Tourist Accommodation Act*, SNS 1994–95, c 9, s 11; *Tourism Industry Act*, RSPEI 1988, c T-3.3, s 9. In some provinces, strict liability is retained but only up to a fixed amount: *Innkeepers Act*, RSNL 1990, c I-7, s 3 ($200); *Innkeepers Act*, RSO 1990, c I-7, s 4 ($40).

[26] RSBC 1996, c 206, s 2; RSO 1990, c I-7, s 2; SNS 1994–95, c 9, s 10; RSPEI 1988, c T-3.3, s 8.

[27] In some provinces ownership passes to a pawnbroker after a specified period; see e.g. *Pawnbrokers Act*, RSO 1990, c P. 6, ss 20–2.

[28] See e.g. *iTrade Finance Inc v Bank of Montreal*, 2011 SCC 26 (Pledges, tracing and PPSA).

lease (1) an agreement where the owner of property allows another person to have possession and use of the property for a specific period in return for the payment of rent and (2) the agreement between landlord and tenant creating the leasehold interest

lessor the owner of the leased property; when applied to land, known as a landlord being a grantor

lessee the person who takes possession of the leased property; when applied to land the lessee is a tenant, the person to whom an interest in a leasehold estate is granted

hire-purchase an agreement to lease an item of property with an option for the lessee to purchase it at the end of the stipulated term

The essence of a **lease** is that the owner of an item of property, referred to as the **lessor**, rents the property to the **lessee**—that is, allows the lessee to have possession and use of the property for a specific period, in return for the payment of rent. Leasing traditionally has been associated with real estate—leasing, or renting, a house, an apartment, or office space for a business has always been an alternative to purchase. We consider leases of land in Chapter 22.

Although renting personal property, or chattels, has always been recognized by the law, such contracts were comparatively rare until recently because goods and chattels are transportable, and a lessee might simply disappear with the leased property and stop paying rent for it. Modern systems of registration of property rights have reduced this risk.

The other factor that led to the great increase in the leasing of personal property was the realization that a lease could be used as a security device. This was first recognized in England more than 100 years ago, in the leading House of Lords decision of *Helby v Matthews*,[29] which recognized a hiring agreement with an option to purchase at the end of the hiring term as an effective method of selling goods on credit. In a typical **hire-purchase** agreement, the lessee/purchaser agrees to lease an item of property for a specified number of years, paying a monthly rental, with an option to purchase it at the end of the term—provided the rent has been paid in full—for a nominal amount, such as $1 or for whatever balance remains owing on the negotiated purchase price.

This type of transaction is well known in Canada, principally as a means of marketing automobiles. In reality, it is a method of purchasing on credit and, as such, is an alternative to the conditional sale and to the chattel mortgage. However, not all chattel leases are intended as security devices.

TYPES OF CHATTEL LEASE

chattel moveable personal property or goods; not land

Two main types of **chattel** lease exist: operating leases, or "true" leases, where the intention is that possession will revert to the owner at the end of the term; and purchase leases, where it is anticipated that the lessee will eventually become the owner. Purchase leases can be further subdivided into security leases, where the credit is provided by the lessor/vendor, and finance leases, where a third party finances the transaction on credit.

Operating Leases

operating lease a lease under which there is no intention to transfer ownership

In an **operating lease**, since there is no intention to transfer ownership, the term tends to be relatively short—substantially less than the expected working life of the property leased. Examples include a car rental for a weekend or a month and the renting of specialized machinery for the duration of a construction contract or of farm machinery for the harvest season.

Purchase Leases

Long-term leases in which payments add up to the value of the property are more likely to be purchase leases. When determining the true nature of a lease, courts consider the position of the parties, their intention, and the true effect of the transaction.[30]

---

[29] [1895] AC 471. See also *Langille v Keneric Tractor Sales Ltd*, [1985] NS J No 118.

[30] *Re Speedrack Ltd* (1980), 1 PPSAC 109; *Adelaide Capital Corp v Integrated Transportation Finance Inc* (1994), 111 DLR (4th) 493.

In practice, however, this test has been difficult to apply and has led to contradictory results. The accounting profession has developed a more objective approach to determine whether to classify a lease as an operating lease or a purchase lease. A lease is treated as a **purchase lease**, or "capital lease,"[31] if one of three conditions exists:

- Title passes automatically to the lessee at the end of the lease or on the exercise of a "bargain purchase option."
- There is a non-cancellable term for at least 75 percent of the economic life of the asset.
- The present value of the minimum lease payments exceeds 90 percent of the market value of the asset at the time the lease commences.[32]

purchase lease a lease whereby ownership is intended to change hands at the end of the lease term

The distinction between an operating lease and a purchase lease is important for accounting purposes. If a lease is a purchase, or "capital," lease, the asset and the accompanying liability must be recorded in the balance sheet of the lessee/purchaser. From a taxation perspective, the distinction determines whether the lease payments are rental payments—and thus deductible by the lessee in determining the profits of the business—or are installments of the purchase price and not deductible (apart from any interest element). It also determines which party is regarded as the true owner and entitled to claim capital cost allowances in respect of depreciation of the asset. From a legal perspective, all lessors' interests should be registered under Personal Property Security legislation to ensure priority over other creditors of the lessee.[33]

Security and Finance Leases

In the typical purchase lease arrangement, it is the lessor who effectively provides the credit. The lessee pays what is, in reality, the purchase price by installments—in the form of "rent." Until the price is paid in full, the lessor has a security interest by virtue of his continued ownership of the leased property—hence the expression **security lease**. As discussed in Chapter 28, the lessor should perfect his security interest in the leased property by complying with the provincial personal property security legislation in order to maintain priority in the leased property over other creditors of the lessee.

security lease a purchase lease in which the lessor provides the credit

An alternative that is becoming increasingly common is for a third person, such as a financial institution, to provide the credit financing. In this type of transaction, commonly known as a **finance lease**, the supplier of the goods sells them to the financer, who in turn leases them to the lessee. The financer is technically the owner of the goods, even though it probably has never had possession of them and will ultimately pass title to the lessee. Again, financiers should register notice of their security interest pursuant to Personal Property Security legislation discussed in Chapter 28 in order to maintain priority in the leased property.

finance lease an arrangement where a third person provides credit financing, becomes the owner of the property, and leases it to the lessee

The major auto manufacturing companies commonly establish their own leasing companies to provide consumer financing in this manner. Figure 15.1 gives a comparison of purchase and finance leases.

---

[31] Also known as "lease-to-own."
[32] CICA Handbook, section 3065. See also Canada Revenue Agency Interpretation Bulletin IT-233R.
[33] *Mitsui & Co (Canada) Ltd v Royal Bank of Canada* (1995), 123 DLR (4th) 449; *Adelaide Capital Corp v Integrated Transportation Finance Inc, supra* note 30. See Chapter 28.

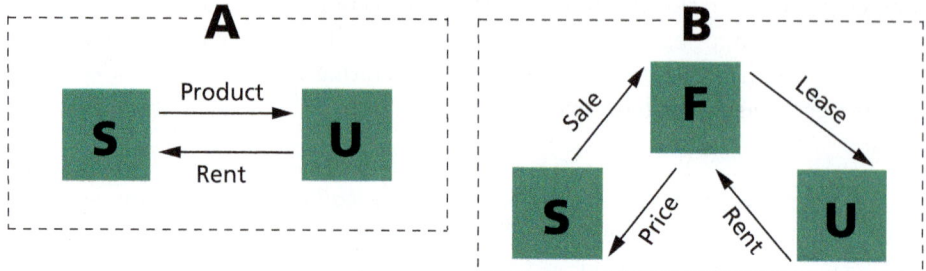

Figure 15.1 Comparing Purchase Lease and Finance Lease
In (A), a conventional purchase lease, the supplier, S, leases the property to the user, U, who pays rent in return. In (B), a finance lease, the supplier, S, sells the property to the financer, F, who in turn leases it to the user, U. U pays rent to F.

Sale-and-Leaseback

sale-and-leaseback a transaction in which the owner of property sells it and immediately leases it back from the new owner

A business with cash-flow problems may enter into a **sale-and-leaseback** transaction to raise working capital. The business sells assets for cash and leases them back in return for future rental payments. The leaseback may take the form of an operating lease or a purchase lease. In the latter case, the effect is similar to raising cash by mortgaging the asset.

REASONS FOR CHATTEL LEASING

A business may be reluctant to purchase an item that may be used only for a limited period, even though it may be possible to resell that item when it is no longer needed. An operating lease will normally be a more convenient, and frequently less expensive, alternative to purchase.

The advantages of purchase leases and finance leases are less obvious. The lessor's perception may be that continued ownership of the asset, until payment has been made in full, provides more security in the case of default or insolvency of the lessee than would a conditional sale or chattel mortgage, though that view is questionable under personal property security legislation, which treats all forms of security interests the same.[34] The lessee may find it preferable to lease assets as a form of off-balance-sheet financing—that is, since the asset is not owned by the business, it does not appear on the balance sheet, but neither does the future rental obligation appear as a liability. The net result is to record a lower debt-to-assets ratio than would be the case if the asset had been purchased with borrowed funds. Whether that is in fact the case depends upon the proper classification of the lease for accounting purposes.

Initially, the main business reason for preferring leasing lay in the way the transaction was treated for tax purposes. Some of these tax advantages have been countered by legislation, but the rapid growth of leasing, and especially of international leasing, owes much to ingenious tax planning.

Consumers often prefer leasing for expensive depreciating items such as cars because down payments are low and payments are easier to incorporate into their financial capabilities.

COMMON TERMS IN CHATTEL LEASES

The following terms are commonly found in chattel leases.

---

[34] See *Re Giffen*, [1998] 1 SCR 91. See Chapter 28; finance leases may be purchase money security interests that have special priority.

Duration

The lease normally sets out the time period during which it is intended to continue in force. In purchase lease arrangements, this is usually a fixed number of years. Operating leases may not contain a fixed term but rather provide for termination by one party or the other on giving notice. If the term of the lease is shorter than the period for which the lessee is likely to want to use the asset, it is common to include an option for renewal or balance to purchase the asset.

Rent

Most leases provide for equal monthly or quarterly payments of rent, usually payable in advance. In a lease-to-own contract, the rent is calculated with reference to the normal selling price of the asset, with an additional "interest" element to take account of the period over which it is payable. Operating lease rentals take more account of the probable depreciation of the asset over the period of the lease and of the cost to the lessor of the asset, with an appropriate profit margin.

Consumer protection legislation imposes credit disclosure requirements on consumer leases and gives consumers cooling-off periods for cancellation.[35]

Insurance and Other Costs Payable by the Lessee

In short-term operating leases, the lessor normally insures the leased asset and bears the costs of maintenance and repairs. In longer leases, and especially in purchase leases, the lessee is usually required to covenant to keep the asset insured, to maintain it properly, and to pay the costs of maintenance and repairs. Sometimes the lessee is required to provide a "residual guarantee"—that is, a guarantee that the lessor will receive a minimum resale value at the end of the lease or, if not, the lessee will be responsible for the difference. This ensures that the lessee takes good care of the asset.

Purchase Option

A purchase lease always contains an option for the lessee to purchase the asset at the end of the term, usually for a relatively small amount. In practice, a distinction is made between fair-market-value (FMV) leases and lease-to-buy (LTB) leases. In FMV leases, the purchase option corresponds to an estimate of the value of the asset at the end of the lease term; in LTB leases, the price is nominal (for example, $1). This difference is reflected in the rental payments—an FMV lease will have lower monthly payments than an LTB lease. Operating leases sometimes also include a purchase option, at a price to be agreed upon, with the price reducing over the lease term to offset depreciation.

Consent to Assignment (Sub-Bailment)

Purchase leases will prohibit the assignment of the lease without the prior written consent of the lessor. This is really a sub-bailment and likely to arise in purchase leases involving motor vehicles. Lessees cannot simply find someone to take over the payments of the purchase lease and give them the vehicle. As discussed in Chapter 11, the right to assign may be contractually limited. Sub-bailment also requires express or implied permission of the bailor.

---

[35] See e.g. *Consumer Protection Act, 2002*, SO 2002, c 30, Sch A, ss 86–90.

> ### CASE 15.7 Consent to Transfer
>
> Delta Hotels rented several street and roof signs from Wallace Sign Company for display on one of its hotel properties. Twenty years later Delta transferred the hotel and the sign leases to the subsequent owners of the hotel property, Coastal Motels, without Wallace's permission. When Coastal stopped paying rent on the signs, Wallace sued Delta for arrears of rent. The court held that Wallace never consented to the sub-bailment by Delta to Coastal Motels. Therefore, Delta was liable to Wallace for the condition of the signs and the arrears of rent.[36]

Early Termination—Minimum Payment

For new or nearly new leased assets, the depreciation in its value will often be greater than the amount of rent payable in the early part of the lease term. Consequently, it is usual for the lessor to insist on a minimum rental payment, to act as a deterrent against default or early termination. In some provinces, consumers receive protection from such clauses, as consumer protection legislation caps the maximum amount of compensation a lessor can receive for early termination.[37]

> ### CHECKLIST
> ### Standard Terms in a Lease Contract
>
> A lease contract will normally include terms that address the following:
>
> - the duration of the lease
> - the rent payable
> - the party responsible for maintenance and insurance
> - the expected residual value of the goods at the end of the term
> - whether there is an option to renew
> - whether there is an option for purchase and, if so, the terms of the option
> - what is to happen if the lease is terminated before the end of its prescribed term
> - the requirement that any transfer (sub-bailment) of the bailed goods must have the lessor's prior written consent
> - consumer protection requirements

Implied Terms

quiet possession *a warranty that there will be no interference with the lessee's possession or use of the asset*

The law implies a warranty of **quiet possession**—that is, there will be no interference with the lessee's possession or use of the asset so long as the rent is paid and other terms are complied with.[38] Implied warranties, such as the warranty of fitness, are equally applicable to purchase lease contracts as they are to sales.[39] Lessors impliedly warrant that the leased equipment is reasonably fit for the purpose for which it was leased.[40] Some doubt exists as to whether this warranty is limited to defects of which the lessor ought to have been aware. A number of provinces have resolved these doubts by extending to consumer leases the implied warranties that apply in the case of sale of goods. For example, in British Columbia the warranties implied under the *Sale of Goods Act* apply

---

[36] *Wallace Sign Crafters West Ltd v Delta Hotels Ltd*, 1994 CanLII 1510.

[37] See Ontario *Consumer Protection Act, 2002, supra* note 35, s 90; O Reg 17/05, s 76 (formula for calculating maximum); see also Alberta, British Columbia, and Saskatchewan.

[38] See e.g. *Sale of Goods Act*, RSBC 1996, c 410, s 16.

[39] *Ibid.*, s 18; see *Astley Industrial Trust Ltd v Grimley*, [1963] 1 WLR 584.

[40] *Griffith SS Co v Western Plywood Co*, [1953] 3 DLR 29.

equally to retail leases,[41] and in Manitoba and Saskatchewan, the implied warranties under the *Consumer Protection Act* are expressly made applicable to consumer leases.[42]

As with all bailments for value, the contractual terms set the standard of care. If silent, the standard of care required of a lessee who rents equipment is to take such care as is prudent and usual in the industry for those who own the equipment.

CASE 15.8   Condition of the Equipment

Roxburgh rented a portable steam engine from Reynolds to power a wood-cutting saw. The engine exploded immediately after it was put into use, killing one worker and injuring another. Reynolds sued Roxburgh for the value of the destroyed engine and boiler. He alleged that Roxburgh had not tested the steam gauge and safety valve before running the machine. The court applied the rule that "the hirer of a chattel is required to use . . . the degree of diligence which prudent men use . . . in keeping their own goods of the same kind."

However, the court held that this standard of care did not require the lessee to test the safety gauge and valve. Accordingly, the defendant was not in breach of his duty as a lessee and was not liable to pay for the destroyed steam engine.[43]

The question of who was liable for the injuries to the workers—the lessor or the lessee—was not raised in the case.

RIGHTS OF THE PARTIES

The Lessor

The principal remedies available to the lessor are the right to sue for rent that is due and unpaid, and the right to retake possession of the leased property at the end of the lease or upon earlier default by the lessee. When a lessee contracts to hire a chattel for a given period, she remains liable for the whole rental, even if she finds that she has overestimated the time needed to use the equipment. A lessor may agree to take equipment back ahead of time and to reduce the rental charges; when he does so, he is consenting to a discharge of the original lease contract and to replacing it with a substituted agreement.

The lessor is entitled both to retake possession of the chattel and to sue for damages for loss of bargain in respect of the rent that would have been payable if there had been no default or for any minimum rent stipulated in the contract.[44] Additionally, if the lessee is in breach of her duty to take proper care of the leased property, the lessor will have an action for damages for the loss. Damages should be calculated in accordance with the general principles applied to a breach of contract action. Again consumers who default late in the lease are protected from repossession.

The Lessee

As noted, the lessor impliedly warrants that the lessee shall have quiet possession and, probably, that the goods are fit for the purpose for which they are hired. Consequently, the lessee is entitled to sue for damages if she is wrongfully dispossessed during the term of the lease or if she suffers loss because of some defect in the goods.

The law is less clear in the case of finance leases where the supplier sells an article to the financer, who in turn leases it to the actual user, the lessee. The lessee's contract is with the financer, although most of her dealings will have been with the supplier, with whom she has no contract. Where the supplier has made express representations to the

---

[41] RSBC 1996, c 410, s 20.
[42] CCSM c 200, s 58; SS 1996, c 30.1, s 48.
[43] *Reynolds v Roxburgh* (1886), 10 OR 649 at 655.
[44] *Keneric Tractor Sales Ltd v Langille* (1987), 43 DLR (4th) 171.

lessee to induce her to enter into the contract, a collateral contract may be implied between supplier and lessee—that is, in return for the supplier's warranty that the goods conform to a particular quality or have a particular characteristic, the lessee agrees to enter into the contract with the financer, a contract that is of benefit to the supplier.[45]

The lessee would have the usual contractual remedies against the financer, although in practice finance leases routinely exclude all implied warranties on the part of the lessor.

Ethical Issue Consumer Leases

A common complaint about leasing contracts is that the consumer lessee rarely knows the terms of the contract—how much is she really paying, and what happens if she wishes to terminate the lease?

During the term of the lease, circumstances may change. The lessee may lose her job and be unable to keep up the payments or may move and find that the leased article is no longer suited to her needs. It is then that she discovers that she cannot just stop payments and return the article. In the majority of cases, the lease terms are quite fair—it is simply that the terms were never properly explained to the lessee. But in some cases, the terms that apply on early termination can be quite harsh.

Some provincial consumer protection legislation (including that of Ontario, British Columbia, Alberta, and Manitoba) specifically addresses the harshness of consumer leasing contracts through the following requirements and limitations:

- a written disclosure statement showing the itemized costs of the lease, including the financed amount, interest rates and calculations, and implicit financing charges
- caps on termination penalties equal to three months of average payments (British Columbia and Alberta cap this amount if the goods have been returned)
- disclosure and restrictions on form and content of advertising (not in the B.C. statute)

Questions to Consider

1. Does a disclosure requirement provide sufficient protection? Should there be a set of statutory implied terms to protect consumers, as in some provincial *Sale of Goods Acts*?
2. Does capping the termination penalties unfairly penalize lessors?
3. Why is leasing less popular with the auto industry since the 2008 economic crisis?

Strategies to Manage the Legal Risks

Bailments and leases benefit from written contracts that describe and limit the expectations and obligations of both parties. The type of bailment will determine the terms of the contract and how effective any exemption clause will be. Businesses must be familiar with industry-specific and province-specific legislation that will influence the form and contents of any contract. For example, Ontario carriers cannot be bound by any requirement to deliver to a particular address or by a particular time unless the requirement is in writing and signed by both shipper and carrier.

Best practices should be developed with the onus of proof in mind. Bailors should document the pre-transfer condition of the goods. Signed acknowledgments of the condition of the goods at the commencement and conclusion of the bailment protect both bailor and bailee. Pictures should be taken. Record keeping during the bailment is fundamental for a bailee who must prove it met the standard of care. Bailees must keep pace with the best practices of their competitors and ensure that measures to protect goods in their care meet or exceed these standards. Bailees should obtain consent to any sub-bailment or include a standard authorization in the contract. To preserve the availability of the bailee's lien rights, goods should not be released to the bailor until full payment is received. Finally, insurance coverage for the bailed goods remains a vital component of any bailment risk management strategy.

---

[45] See *Hallmark Pool Corp v Storey* (1983), 144 DLR (3d) 56; *Shanklin Pier Ltd v Detel Products Ltd*, [1951] 2 KB 854.

QUESTIONS FOR REVIEW

1. What is the principal difference between an operating lease and a purchase lease?
2. Distinguish between a security lease and a finance lease.
3. What warranties will normally be implied in a chattel lease?
4. What are the main perceived advantages of leasing capital assets as opposed to borrowing in order to purchase them?
5. Why would a business enter into a sale-and-leaseback transaction?
6. If a lessee defaults in paying the rent, is the lessor entitled to retake possession of the leased property as well as to sue for the rent owing?
7. Give an example of (a) a non-contractual bailment and (b) an involuntary bailment.
8. Distinguish between a bailment and a licence. In what circumstances is the distinction especially important?
9. What factors determine the standard of care to be expected of a bailee?
10. What is a "sub-bailment"?
11. In what circumstances may a bailee claim a lien on bailed goods?
12. What does it mean that goods are "fungible"? How does that affect a bailee's liability?
13. Who normally bears the loss if goods left in a warehouse are stolen or destroyed?
14. Distinguish between a common carrier and a private carrier.
15. What does it mean to say that a common carrier "is an insurer as well as a bailee"?
16. What are the principal defences available to a common carrier when goods in its possession are damaged or lost?
17. Is a hotel keeper liable if a guest's property is stolen from his room?
18. What is meant by a "pledge"?

CASES AND PROBLEMS

1. Continuing Scenario

   At Ashley's restaurant, there is an open coat room with hooks on the wall. There is a posted sign that says "For the use and convenience of our customers only—not responsible for loss or damage." Joan and Gloria arrive for lunch, and Joan hangs her coat in the coat room; Gloria wears her coat to the table. Partway through lunch Gloria removes her coat and places it on the chair beside her. The waiter asks Gloria if she would like him to take her coat. She says yes, and he takes it to the coat room. After lunch, Joan and Gloria go to the coat room and discover that both coats are missing. Gloria's coat had her car keys in the pocket, and unfortunately Gloria's car was parked in one of the free parking spaces reserved for Ashley's customers. It is gone too. Is Ashley liable for the lost coats? How will the court approach the analysis for Joan's missing coat? Will Gloria's coat be treated differently? How about Gloria's car? Explain your reasons.

2. Intrepid Exploration Inc. is a comparatively small corporation engaged in exploring and drilling for oil in shallow coastal waters, usually as a subcontractor for major companies. Intrepid's owners recently entered into a contract with Globres Inc., one of those major companies, to provide specialized drilling services in a project off the New Brunswick coast. Intrepid anticipated making a substantial profit on the contract.

   Intrepid found that, to perform the contract, it would need a high-pressure drilling unit of a particular type that it did not own. Normally such units are custom-made, cost about $500 000, and take about six months to construct. Fortunately, Intrepid was able to locate such a unit, which was owned by Banditoil, a rather larger corporation in the same line of business as Intrepid. The unit was not in use at the time and was unlikely to be needed by Banditoil for at least 18 months.

Intrepid negotiated a contract with Banditoil to lease the drilling unit for 12 months, with an option to renew for six months, at a monthly rental of $15 000. Before Intrepid took delivery of the drilling unit, Globres informed Intrepid that it was unwilling to have Intrepid do the work contracted for and that it was awarding the contract to another corporation, Cutprice Inc. Globres claimed to be entitled to do so under a clause in the contract, a claim that Intrepid contested. Intrepid immediately informed Banditoil that it no longer needed the drilling unit. Banditoil acknowledged receiving the information and replied that it was considering what action, if any, to take.

Intrepid received a demand from Banditoil for payment in full of the sum of $180 000 under the lease contract. Intrepid also learned that Cutprice has agreed to rent the same drilling unit.

What is the extent of Intrepid's liability toward Banditoil?

3. Firth contracted with Dave the Mover Inc. to have her furniture and household effects moved from her house, stored for a week (until she moved into her new home), and then delivered to the new home. Firth told Dave's manager that she was particularly concerned about security, since the effects included some rare and valuable antiques and artifacts. She was told there was nothing to worry about. The articles would remain in the trailer until delivery at her new home, and the trailer would be locked at all times and parked in their yard, which was securely fenced, locked at night, and kept under regular supervision.

The trailer was kept in the yard as promised for several days, but one night, after a heavy snowfall, it was moved and parked, unattended, on a public street while the yard was being plowed. While it was parked on the street, the trailer was stolen.

Firth claimed damages for the full value of the goods lost. Dave's admitted liability but pointed out that the bill of lading limited damages to $0.60 per pound weight of the goods, which came to just over $7000, a small fraction of their true value.

Firth admitted she was aware of the limitation when she entered into the contract but claimed she only agreed to it because of the assurance that the trailer would be properly supervised at all times.

Should Dave's be allowed to rely on the limitation clause?

4. Nerdley is a skilled interior designer who decided to go freelance after years of being employed by a large construction company. Although accustomed to using a computer in her work, she understands very little about their characteristics and specifications, having always relied in the past on other specialist employees of the company for advice and assistance.

Nerdley realized she would need to acquire her own computer equipment. She was told by a friend that Millennium Electronics had "the best prices in town" and a competent sales staff. She visited their local store, briefly explained to Boffin, a salesperson, what she perceived her needs to be, and eventually decided to acquire two computers, a printer, and various other items of equipment. Boffin assured her they were "state of the art" and should be able to do everything she needed them to do.

The total price came to around $11 000. Nerdley then asked about credit and was told Millennium recommended a leasing agreement with a finance company it normally used in such cases. Under the agreement, Millennium sold the equipment to the finance company for $10 500, and Nerdley entered into a lease agreement with the finance company under which she agreed to make 36 monthly payments of $400, with an option at the end of the three-year period to buy the equipment for a further $400. The lease was on a standard printed form and included the following clause:

> The lessee acknowledges that the equipment hereby leased was personally selected by the lessee for business purposes and purchased by the lessor at the lessee's request from a supplier designated by the lessee. The lessee takes full responsibility for such selection and waives all defences predicated on the failure of the said equipment to perform the function for which it was designed or selected and further acknowledges that such failure shall not be deemed to be in breach of this lease.

Nerdley soon discovered the computer did not have sufficient memory to operate some of the sophisticated design programs she used, and the printer did not have sufficiently high definition to reproduce her designs adequately.

When she attempted to take the equipment back to Millennium, she was told the problems had nothing to do with them and that she should take it up with the finance company. Advise her.

5. 4D Enterprises Ltd. hired Jung to design and develop a website for its business. According to the agreement, Jung was to install the servers and all necessary software and to test the system fully. To enable him to do so, 4D delivered to him the two computers that would be used.

During the following three weeks, 4D phoned Jung several times to ask how the work was going. Each time, Jung assured them that it was "coming along fine" and would be ready soon. 4D started to become anxious, as they had expected the work to be done within two or three days. They made some enquiries and heard a few rather negative reports about Jung's work. As a result, they decided to find someone else to do the work and asked Jung to return their computers. Jung refused, claiming he had done a substantial amount of work on the project, and demanded payment in full of the agreed amount.

Is Jung entitled to keep the computers until he has been paid?

Chapter 16
Insurance and Guarantee

- **INSURANCE AND THE MANAGEMENT OF LEGAL RISK**
- **INSURANCE TERMINOLOGY**
- **REGULATION OF INSURANCE BUSINESS**
- **TYPES OF INSURANCE**
- **SPECIAL ASPECTS OF INSURANCE CONTRACTS**
- **GUARANTEE**
- **STRATEGIES TO MANAGE THE LEGAL RISKS**

The two types of contracts dealt with in this chapter redistribute risk. They often form part of a business's legal risk management strategy. Insurance enables a business to shift the risk of loss—from damage to its own property or liability for damage to someone else's person or property—to an insurance company. In return, the business pays for that protection. A contract of guarantee allows a lender or creditor to reduce the risk of non-payment by obtaining a promise from a third person to pay the debt if the debtor defaults.

In this chapter we examine such questions as:

- What is the nature of the contract of insurance?
- What role does insurance play in risk management?
- What types of insurance protect against liability or loss in the operation of a business?
- What are the special characteristics of insurance contracts?
- What is the legal nature of a guarantee?
- How may a guarantee be discharged?
- What are the rights and liabilities of a guarantor?

INSURANCE AND THE MANAGEMENT OF LEGAL RISK

Insurance is a method of purchasing protection against a possible loss. The insured agrees with an insurance company that, in return for the payment of a premium or regular premiums, the company will compensate the insured if a specified loss occurs. The insurance company calculates the amount of payment required based on experience with the type of risk in question. A business faces two main types of "legal" risk:

- the risk that its own property or assets might be destroyed or damaged as a result of an accident or due to the fault of some other person
- the risk that it may be held liable for some loss or injury caused to another person and/or their property

In the first type of risk, no one may be responsible, as in the case of storm damage, for example. Or, if the loss was caused by another person, tracing that person might be impossible, or he might have insufficient funds to pay compensation. Even when recovery is possible, legal proceedings are likely to be time-consuming and expensive. With this type of risk, it is possible to estimate the extent of the possible loss—you cannot lose more than the total value of all your assets.

The second type of risk, known as third-party or public liability, is more open-ended. A business may be able to make an estimate of its potential liability. If you sell 100 000 cars of a particular model, it may be possible to calculate, based on experience, that a given number of defects will pass the inspection system, and of those, a certain percentage will cause serious injury. However, other calculations will be impossible—a shopper may trip on an uneven floor tile and suffer a crippling injury, resulting in a damage award of hundreds of thousands of dollars. (By contrast, an insurance company can make the calculation, based on the experience of thousands of similar businesses.)

A business could set aside a reserve or contingency fund to meet future claims. The more realistic alternative is to purchase insurance coverage.

INSURANCE TERMINOLOGY

An **insurance policy** is a document that describes the terms of an insurance contract. The insurance company providing the protection is called the insurer; the party contracting for the insurance protection is the insured.[1] The **premium** is the price paid by the insured for the insurance coverage specified in the policy. The premium may be paid in a single sum, but more often it is paid yearly or at some other shorter interval throughout the term of the insurance.

The four key issues for an insurance contract are

- the nature of the risk covered (cause of the loss)
- the amount for which it is insured (extent of **coverage**)
- the duration of the protection (**term** of the policy)
- the amount of the premium

The terms of a policy may require the insurer to pay the insurance money, in the event of a claim, to the insured, to the insured's estate, or to some other person

insurance policy the document describing the terms of a contract of insurance

premium the price paid by the insured to purchase insurance coverage

coverage maximum amount payable for an insured risk

term the duration of the policy

---

[1] In life insurance, we distinguish between the insured and the life insured when the subject of the insurance is the life of someone other than the party contracting for insurance.

beneficiary a person who is entitled to the benefits of a trust or the person entitled to receive insurance monies

rider additional provisions attached to a standard policy of insurance

endorsement written evidence of a change in the terms of a policy

insurance agent an agent or employee of an insurance company

insurance broker an independent business that arranges insurance coverage for its clients

designated as **beneficiary**. When an insured requires additional coverage—that is, wider protection than is available under the insurer's standard form policy—additional clauses are added to the contract by attaching a **rider**. When the parties agree to a change in the terms of an existing insurance contract, they may do so without rewriting the entire policy but rather by attaching a separate **endorsement** to the policy.

An **insurance age** is an employee or agent of the insurance company whose function is to arrange contracts with persons seeking insurance protection for themselves. By contrast, an **insurance broker** conducts an independent business and generally acts for the insured rather than for the insurer.[2] A broker is a specialist in insurance problems who advises on the coverage required and arranges insurance with the companies best suited to provide it. However, the distinction between an agent and a broker is not always a clear one. In practice, an insurance agent often gives advice to the insured about the appropriate coverage, and it is possible in some cases for an agent, or a broker, to be considered to be acting as agent for both the insurer and the insured and to owe a duty to both.[3]nt

CASE 16.1 Duty to Advise

Miller was injured in a motor vehicle accident caused by the negligence of a person who was underinsured. Miller purchased an insurance policy from an agent of the Guardian company. He requested full coverage, but the agent did not suggest that the policy should contain an "underinsured motorist endorsement," which was available at a modest premium. As a result, Miller was not fully covered for the accident that occurred.

The court held that the agent had a duty to advise the insured on suitable coverage, and since the agent was acting as the agent of the insurance company, the company was also liable.[4]

insurance adjuster a person who appraises property losses

personal insurance insurance against death, injury, or ill health of an individual

property insurance insurance against damage to property

term insurance personal insurance that provides coverage for a limited period only

An **insurance adjuster** is an expert in the appraisal of property losses and provides these services to insurance companies for a fee. When a claim has been made, the adjuster gives an opinion to the insurer about whether the loss is covered by the insurance contract and, if so, what the amount of the loss is.

Insurance can be subdivided into **personal insurance** and **property insurance**. Personal insurance, as the name implies, covers risk to life and health, and includes life insurance, medical insurance, accident and disability insurance, and workers' compensation. All other types of insurance are property insurance. Life insurance is unique in that the risk insured against is certain to materialize eventually, though in the case of **term insurance**, it may not occur during the period covered by the policy.

REGULATION OF INSURANCE BUSINESS

Each province has one or more statutes regulating the insurance business within its borders. The main purpose of these statutes is to protect the public by requiring responsible behaviour on the part of insurance companies and others in the

---

[2] See *Adams Eden Furniture Ltd v Kansa General Insurance Co* (1996), 141 DLR (4th) 288, leave denied [1997] SCCA No 42.

[3] See the discussion of an agent's duty in Chapter 17.

[4] *Miller v Guardian Insurance Co of Canada* (1997), 149 DLR (4th) 375, leave denied [1997] SCCA No 480; *Fine Flowers Ltd v General Accident Assurance Co* (1974), 49 DLR (3d) 641, aff'd (1977), 81 DLR (3d) 139. Contrast *Planidin v Insurance Corporation of British Columbia* (2004), 245 DLR (4th) 511, where it was held that the insurer owes no duty to provide advice on the extent of the coverage of a policy. Motor vehicle insurance coverage is subject to legislative minimums, the details of which are beyond the scope of this chapter.

business. Among other matters, the statutes authorize the appointment of a superintendent of insurance to oversee the operations and financial responsibility of licensed insurers within the province, describe the terms that must be included in insurance policies, and define the extent to which an insurer may limit its liability. In addition to these provincial statutes, the federal *Insurance Companies Act*[5] provides for compulsory registration of federal and foreign insurance companies wishing to carry on insurance business in Canada and for voluntary registration of provincial insurance companies. Its aim is to ensure financial stability in the insurance industry by providing a system of inspection and by requiring statements and returns from these companies.

TYPES OF INSURANCE

Insurance against Loss or Damage

You can insure against loss or damage to your own property or assets, and you can insure against liability to others for their losses. Until recently, it was usual to insure against different risks in separate insurance policies. Some types of insurance—for example, fire insurance and marine insurance—go back several centuries. Typically, a business will insure against

- damage to buildings and contents (inventory, fixtures, and equipment) due to fire or storm,
- loss due to theft, and
- loss of or damage to vehicles used in the business.

In addition, it might take out insurance against

- loss of profit due to interruption of business activities,
- bad debt losses (credit insurance),
- losses caused by theft or fraud of employees (fidelity insurance), and
- loss due to injury to or death of important personnel (key-person insurance).

The precise extent of the coverage will vary from policy to policy and from one insurance company to another. Determining precisely what types of losses are covered is of crucial importance; insurance policies are filled with exclusions and limits. For example, does fire insurance also cover relocation expenses or loss of profit while the business is unable to operate? Does it include damage to a client's property that happens to be on the premises at the time of the fire? One case held that insurance against accidental damage to the insured's photocopying machines did not cover damage due to faulty manufacture because this was not an accident.[6]

In most instances, the insurer is liable either for the cost of repairing damaged property or for the value of the destroyed property. Value takes into account the condition of the property immediately before destruction. You may purchase insurance for full replacement value, but this higher protection is more expensive.

An insurance contract frequently contains a **deductible clause**, under which the insured is required to pay the first $500 (or some higher amount) in respect of

deductible clause a clause requiring the insured to bear the loss up to a stated amount

---

[5] SC 1991, c 47.
[6] *Celestica Inc v ACE INA Insurance* (2003), 229 DLR (4th) 392. This case was distinguished on the facts in *Chanore Property Inc v ING Insurance Co of Canada* (2010), 94 CLR (3d) 223.

each claim. A deductible feature gives the insured a greater incentive to take care of the insured property and, by eliminating small claims, makes the insurance cheaper.

Insurance against Liability

As noted in Chapters 4 and 5, businesses may be sued and held liable to others in various ways, including liability for their own acts, or the acts of their employees, that cause damage to their customers, distributors, suppliers, and the general public. The type of insurance that covers this risk, known as **public liability insurance**, obligates the insurer to defend the insured against lawsuits and plus pay the amount of any judgment, up to the policy limit. As long as the claim alleges facts and damage that might be covered by the policy, the insurer must defend the lawsuit.[7] When a court is interpreting a policy to determine if the insurer must defend the insured in a lawsuit brought by a third party, policy terms describing coverage are given a broad meaning, and exclusionary clauses are interpreted narrowly.[8]

public liability insurance insurance to cover damage to others caused by the business, also known as third-party liability

Businesses will normally insure against

- liability for negligent acts and omissions,
- liability for defective products,
- liability for the dangerous state of their premises, and
- liability for breach of their professional duty of care.

Public liability insurance is compulsory for most professions, and provincial legislation requires that owners of motor vehicles carry third-party liability insurance.

Comprehensive Insurance

Rather than issue multiple policies, each providing protection against specific risks, comprehensive general insurance policies are available to cover most types of damage to the insured's property as well as liability to others. Such insurance tends to be expensive; however, the great advantage lies in the completeness of the coverage—unexpected risks do not fall into the cracks between two or more separate policies.

CASE 16.2 Does the Policy Cover the Loss?

Goderich insured grain stored in its elevator under an "all risks" insurance policy that covered "all risk of direct physical loss or damage . . . except as excluded." The policy excluded "loss or damage caused directly or indirectly by . . . dryness of atmosphere, changes of temperature, heating, shrinkage, evaporation." Some of the stored grain was devalued due to a condition known as "heated grain." The cause of the heated grain could not be established, but there was no evidence of external causes. Goderich's claim under the insurance policy was denied by the insurance company. The court held that the loss was covered by an "all risk" policy, and the insurance company had not shown that the cause was within the exclusion.[9]

---

[7] *Monenco Ltd v Commonwealth Insurance Co*, [2001] 2 SCR 699.

[8] *Progressive Homes Ltd v Lombard General Insurance Co of Canada*, 2010 SCC 33 at para 19.

[9] *Goderich Elevators Ltd v Royal Insurance Co* (1999), 169 DLR (4th) 763. The court applied one of the "general principles of interpretation of insurance policies," that "coverage provisions should be construed broadly and exclusion provisions narrowly."

INTERNATIONAL ISSUE
Medical Malpractice Insurance

Many professions require their members to insure against public liability for malpractice (negligence) or breach of their duty of care. Even if not mandatory, it is advisable to do so. Unfortunately, the cost of malpractice insurance has escalated rapidly—and that cost is passed on to the client.

In the United States, it is not uncommon for doctors to pay $100 000 a year or more in premiums. Premiums are assessed based on the physician's specialty and location. In Florida, rates increased by 60 percent between 2000 and 2004, and an obstetrician's premium in Dade County (Florida) was $201 376 in 2003.[10] By contrast, an obstetrician's premium in Minnesota was only $17 431. This difference in rates could have an impact on physician's decision about where to practice, affecting the availability of care and specialist expertise in certain states. Some states have introduced tort reform, including damage award caps and limits on plaintiffs' lawyer fees.

Things are not quite as bad in Canada—an Ontario obstetrician's premium was $78 120 in 2005 and was not any higher in 2016.[11] In 2004, the Canadian Health Research Foundation reported that the number of medical malpractice lawsuits was steadily declining. Such lawsuits peaked in 1996 but had declined by 23 percent by 2004. As in the United States, however, the size of the average settlement is increasing.[12] Other professions face similar challenges. Accountants, in particular, have been hit with huge damage awards that increase their insurance costs and have argued that liability should be denied if it will make insurance more difficult or expensive to obtain.[13]

Questions to Consider

1. Which of the following do you consider to be most responsible for the differences between the Canadian and American malpractice insurance premiums? Explain your choice.
   (a) high legal fees
   (b) excessive damages awards
   (c) lack of competition in the insurance industry
2. Can you suggest other ways of tackling the problem of skyrocketing malpractice insurance premiums?

SPECIAL ASPECTS OF INSURANCE CONTRACTS

Legality of Objects—Wrongful Act of the Insured

A general principle of insurance law is that the courts will not enforce a contract of insurance when the claim arises out of a criminal or deliberate wrongful act by the insured.[14] Two reasons are commonly given for this rule: (1) It would be contrary to public policy to allow the insured to profit from his own crime, and (2) it would be contrary to the purpose of insurance to allow the insured to recover compensation for a loss that he had deliberately caused himself. Therefore, a beneficiary under a life insurance policy who murders the insured is not entitled to claim,[15] and an arsonist is not entitled to recover under a policy of fire insurance.[16] However, the

---

[10] U.S. General Accounting Office, "Medical Malpractice, Excerpts from Medical Malpractice and Access to Health Care (GAO-03-836)," https://www.gao.gov/products/GAO-03-836.

[11] Canadian Medical Protection Association, 2005 Fee Schedule, www.cmpaacpm.ca; as to 2016, see Robert Cribb "The High Cost of OB/GYN Mistakes in Ontario", TheStar.com, Nov 28, 2015, https://www.thestar.com/news/canada/2015/11/28/the-high-cost-of-obgyn-mistakes-in-ontario.html.

[12] "Myth: Medical Malpractice Lawsuits Plague Canada", MythBusters, Canadian Health Service Research Foundation, March 2006, www.chsrf.ca; Cribb, *supra* note 11.

[13] *Livent v Deloitte & Touche*, 2017 SCC 63.

[14] *Beresford v Royal Insurance Co*, [1938] AC 586.

[15] *Demeter v Dominion Life Assurance Co* (1982), 132 DLR (3d) 248, where the husband who was convicted of the murder of his wife was the owner and beneficiary under personal policies issued on the life of his wife. See also *Brisette Estate v Westbury Life Insurance Co*, [1992] 3 SCR. 87; *Lachman Estate v Norwich Union Life Insurance Co* (1998), 40 OR (3d) 393.

[16] See *Scott v Wawanesa Mutual Insurance Co* (1989), 59 DLR (4th) 660.

courts have limited the scope of the public policy exception; it will not prevent recover if the loss occurred as an unintended consequence of the insured's deliberate wrongful act or if recovery is by heirs or beneficiaries not involved in the wrongful act.[17]

> **CASE 16.3 Unintended Consequences**
>
> A dentist died as a result of substance abuse, the dangers of which were obvious and were presumably known by him. The insurance company refused to pay under a policy of insurance that he had taken out on his life, claiming that his death resulted from his own intentional act. The court held that, although the act of administering the substance was deliberate, the deceased had no intention of committing suicide. His estate and heirs were entitled to claim under the policy.[18]

Insurance companies tend not to rely upon the common law principle and frequently insert an express provision that coverage does not extend to damage or injury resulting from an intentional or criminal act of the insured.[19]

Insurable Interest

An insurance contract is distinguished from a wager by the fact that the insured has an insurable interest; the contract shifts a genuine risk of loss from the insured to the insurer. An **insurable interest** is the genuine loss that would be suffered by the insured from damage to or destruction of the thing insured, or from the death of or injury to the person insured. Insurable interest is not confined to ownership of property. A person who owns all the shares in a corporation does have an insurable interest in the corporation's property; the Supreme Court of Canada held that an insurable interest exists where an insured benefits from the property's existence and is prejudiced by the property's destruction.[20] Obviously, damage to the property of the corporation would necessarily reduce the value of his shares. Similarly, a tenant might have an insurable interest in leased premises he uses for his business, since he may suffer financial and other loss if the premises are destroyed or damaged.[21] Although the insured need not be the owner of the insured property, he must have some form of interest in that property.[22]

When the contract is for life insurance, the person buying the insurance must either obtain the written consent of the person whose life is to be insured or have an insurable interest at the time the contract is formed, though not necessarily at the time of death of the person whose life is insured. When the contract is for property insurance, the insured must have an insurable interest at the time the contract was formed; otherwise the contract is void. And, since the purpose of insurance is to indemnify for

insurable interest genuine risk of loss that may be suffered from damage to the thing insured

---

[17] *Oldfield v Transamerica Life Insurance Co of Canada* (1998), 43 OR (3d) 114, aff'd (2002), 210 DLR (4th) 1; See also *Desjardins Financial Security Life Assurance Company v Emond*, 2017 SCC 19 (deceased life insured driving illegally; beneficiaries of life insurance not excluded).

[18] *Bertalan Estate v American Home Assurance Co* (2001), 196 DLR (4th) 445; *American International Assurance Life Company Ltd v Martin* (2003), 223 DLR (4th) 1.

[19] See e.g. *British Columbia Insurance Corp v Kraiger* (2002), 219 DLR (4th) 49 (arson); *Hodgkinson v Economic Mutual Insurance Co* (2003), 235 DLR (4th) 1 (defamation). Where coverage is for accidental damage, it is not sufficient that the event is unexpected: see *Co-operators Life Insurance Co v Gibbens*, [2009] 3 SCR 605.

[20] *Kosmopoulos v Constitution Insurance Co* (1987), 34 DLR (4th) 208. It is unclear whether a holder of only a small proportion would be found to have an interest.

[21] *Evergreen Manufacturing Corp v Dominion of Canada General Insurance Co* (1999), 170 DLR (4th) 240.

[22] See *Assaad v Economic Mutual Insurance Group* (2002), 214 DLR (4th) 655.

loss suffered, the insured must still have an interest at the time the claim arises; otherwise there will be no loss to be recovered by the insured.

> **CASE 16.4** Insurable Interest in Property at Time of Loss
>
> The owner of mortgaged premises insured them against damage by fire. Subsequently, the owner failed to keep up the mortgage payments, and the mortgagee foreclosed. While the mortgagor was still in possession, the premises were destroyed by fire. On a claim by the mortgagor under the insurance policy, the Court held that the foreclosure had extinguished all rights and interest of the mortgagor in the property and had vested the title in the mortgagee. Therefore, the mortgagor no longer had an insurable interest in the premises.[23] For this reason, mortgagees require their names be added to insurance policies.

Formation of the Contract

A proposal drafted by an insurance agent is usually a mere invitation to treat, not an offer. The offer to purchase insurance coverage is made by the party seeking the insurance protection—the prospective insured—by signing an application form. What constitutes acceptance by the insurer? We need to know so we can tell when the insurance is in force. These questions are usually answered by provincial legislation or the offer itself.

With life insurance, the applicant's offer is not accepted until the insurance company delivers the policy. It is a condition precedent to delivery of the policy that the first premium be paid.[24]

Property insurance is managed differently than for life insurance. An agent dealing in property insurance may have agency contracts with a number of insurance companies. Each contract gives the agent authority to sign and deliver policies and renewal certificates and generally to bind the company concerned; a business seeking property insurance can obtain the desired protection immediately, before paying the premium or receiving a policy. The agent need only prepare a memorandum or binder for the agency's records as evidence of the time and nature of the request for insurance. When immediate protection is required, an insured should be satisfied that the agent has an agency contract with the proposed insurer.

Renewal

Property insurance is written for a specified period of time (usually a number of years). Frequently, the intention is that the insurance should be renewed at the end of the period, and it is not uncommon for the insured to fail to renew it on time. What is the situation in the meantime? A common practice is for an insurance company, or its agent, to prepare a renewal policy or memorandum and send it to the insured shortly before the current policy expires. This acts as a reminder that the insurance protection is about to cease if not renewed. But unless there is evidence of an agreement between the company and the insured that they intend the delivery of a renewal policy or memorandum to create a new contract of insurance, or such an agreement can be inferred from their past dealings with one another, the act of delivering the renewal policy amounts to no more than making an offer to the insured. No contract is formed until the insured communicates acceptance, and because the offer is open, at most, for a reasonable time, the insured cannot wait indefinitely.

---

[23] *Walton v General Accident Assurance Co of Canada* (2000), 194 DLR (4th) 315.

[24] See e.g. *Insurance Act*, RSBC 2012, c 1, s 48.

CASE 16.5 Offer to Renew

The insured's auto insurance policy expired on February 5, 1989. About a month before, the insurance company sent him an offer to renew if the premium was paid before February 5 and a "pink slip" certifying that the insurance was in effect until August 5, 1989. The insured did not pay the renewal premium and was injured in an accident on February 20.

The Supreme Court of Canada held that the pink slip did not amount to a renewal of the contract. It was sent to the insured for convenience only and did not bind the company.[25]

Absent legislation to the contrary (such as exists for mandatory motor vehicle coverage in some provinces), a policy that expires for non-payment of renewal does not need any formal termination process.

CASE 16.6 Reasonable Time to Accept

A premium payment for a live insurance policy was due on July 26. The grace period expired, and the company sent a "late payment" notice offering to receive late payment under certain conditions. Four months later, the company sent a letter to the insured saying that the policy was "technically out of force" and that immediate payment of the premium was required. In February of the following year, the company sent a further letter, stating that the insurance had lapsed. The letters did not come to the insured's attention until April. Finally, in July, he sent a cheque. By then, his life had become uninsurable, and he died a month later.

The Supreme Court of Canada held that the July payment was too late. The company had offered to renew the policy, but that offer was open only for a reasonable time.[26]

Interpreting Terms of the Contract

If the terms of an insurance policy are clear and unambiguous, then they will be given their stated meaning. However, if there is ambiguity in the language, the insured has an advantage. An insurance policy is an example of a standard form contract—it is prepared unilaterally in advance by the insurer so ***contra proferentum*** rules are applied against the insurer. Terms describing coverage are interpreted broadly or inclusively to give the widest reasonable application; terms that exclude coverage are interpreted narrowly.[27] Any remaining ambiguous words are given the meaning most favourable to the insured. Courts take the view that clauses exempting an insurer from liability in specific circumstances must be stated in clear and unambiguous terms if they are to be binding.[28]

contra proferentum preference for the interpretation of a term that favours the non-drafting party

CASE 16.7 Intended Meaning

A group of tenants brought a class action against the owner of an apartment complex, claiming they became ill after breathing carbon monoxide leaking from the apartment furnace. The apartment owner had a commercial liability insurance policy, but the policy contained an exclusion clause for "pollution liability." The insurance company claimed that the clause exempted it from liability.

The court held that, although carbon monoxide could be considered a pollutant, the clause was intended to exclude coverage for damages from environmental pollution. The clause should be strictly and narrowly interpreted against the insurer. It was not intended to apply to circumstances such as a leak from a faulty furnace.[29]

---

[25] *Patterson v Gallant* (1994), 120 DLR (4th) 1 at para 35.

[26] *Saskatchewan River Bungalows Ltd v Maritime Life Assurance Co* (1994), 115 DLR (4th) 478.

[27] *Progressive Homes Ltd*, *supra* note 8 at paras 21–24.

[28] *Somersall v Friedman* (2002), 215 DLR (4th) 577 (SCC) at paras 46–48. See e.g. *British Columbia Ferry Corp v Commonwealth Insurance Co* (1985), 40 DLR (4th) 766.

[29] *Zurich Insurance Co v 686234 Ontario Ltd* (2002), 222 DLR (4th) 655, leave denied [2003] SCCA No. 33.

Good Faith, Fairness, and Disclosure

Insurance contracts are contracts of the **utmost good faith**. This means parties to the contract must act fairly and with integrity in their dealings with each other. A misrepresentation renders a contract voidable; in Chapter 9, we noted that an insurer may avoid paying a claim if it can show that the insured did not exercise the utmost good faith when applying for insurance.[30] In particular, full disclosure must be made of all material facts and circumstances that are known, or should have been known, to the insured.

utmost good faith to act with fairness and integrity

CASE 16.8 Full Disclosure

A corporation took out an insurance policy against losses caused by dishonest employees. The corporation's accountant stole over $20 million over a 10-year period. The fraud could have been easily detected from the corporation's financial statements. The Court held that the insured corporation had constructive knowledge of the fraud and had a duty to disclose it. Therefore, it was not entitled to recover under the policy.[31]

The disclosure requirement is applied even when the loss is unrelated to the facts the insured should have disclosed.[32] However, exceptions have also occurred. For example, an incorrect statement by the insured that a night watchman would be present on the premises every night was held not to be material when the actual loss occurred in the afternoon.[33] As well, the insured need not disclose information of a general nature that should be well known to the insurer: An asbestos manufacturer was not required to inform its insurer that there were health risks related to working with asbestos, so long as the likelihood of exposure to asbestos was disclosed.[34]

In *Coronation Insurance Company v Taku Air Transport Ltd*,[35] the Supreme Court of Canada went so far as holding that the utmost good faith principle should not apply at all in the highly regulated field of aviation insurance. The requirement that air carriers have insurance for their passengers was primarily intended for the benefit of the public, whose protection should not depend entirely on the good faith of the carrier. Consequently, the failure of a carrier to fully disclose its past safety record did not invalidate the policy. The insurance company had a duty at least to check its own files and the public records.[36]

An insurer may insert terms in an insurance contract to extend the obligation of the insured even beyond that imposed by the requirement of utmost good faith. The application form signed by the party seeking insurance may contain a provision that the applicant warrants the accuracy—not merely the truthfulness—of any declarations made. If in these circumstances an applicant for life insurance replies in the negative to the question "Have you any disease?" and proves later to have had a disease of which she was unaware, the insurer may avoid its liability. The courts

---

[30] *Haraba v Wawanesa Mutual Insurance Company*, 2017 ABQB 190 at paras 4, 25 (one co-insured makes a misrepresentation that might affect the ability of innocent co-insureds to collect under the policy).

[31] *JJ Barnicke Ltd v Commercial Union Assurance Co of Canada* (2000), 5 BLR (3d) 199.

[32] See *Lachman Estate v Norwich Union Life Insurance Co* (1998), 40 OR (3d) 393.

[33] Case *Existological Laboratories Ltd v Century Insurance Co* (1982), 133 DLR (3d) 727, aff'd [1983] SCJ No 61.

[34] *Canadian Indemnity Co v Canadian Johns Mansville Co*, [1990] 2 SCR 549.

[35] [1991] 3 SCR 622. See also *MacNeil (Litigation Guardian of) v Bryan*, (2009) CCLI (4th) 96.

[36] The crash victims still did not recover compensation. The aircraft was carrying more passengers than provided for in the policy, and the policy was consequently void.

dislike this type of provision and insist on strict proof by the insurer that the question was answered inaccurately.

Insurance contracts other than for life insurance contain a statutory term that the insured shall notify the insurer promptly of any change that is material to the risk and within the control or knowledge of the insured. Such a term then gives the insurer some options. It may either cancel the insurance and return the unexpired portion of the premium, or inform the insured that the insurance will continue only on payment of an increased premium. Prompt notice by the insured in these circumstances is a condition precedent. An insurer is absolved from liability under the policy if it does not receive such notice. Insurance contracts normally also contain a term requiring the insured to notify the insurer promptly of any loss that occurs. Failure to give notice promptly may also free the insurer from liability to pay the claim.

Ethical Issue   Insurer Bad Faith

Insurance companies must also act with utmost good faith toward their insureds. The manner in which an insurance company must behave in cases of disagreement over coverage was addressed the 2002 Supreme Court of Canada in *Whiten v Pilot Insurance*.[37] It held that Pilot acted in bad faith during the management of the claim, and this entitled the insured to $1 000 000 in punitive damages. Pilot alleged arson with little or no evidence to support such an allegation. Pilot rejected independent advice that the claim should be paid and even influenced an independent investigator to change his opinion. In the circumstances, the Court held that Pilot breached its duty of good faith. This duty requires prompt and fair treatment of the insured.

In 2006, the Supreme Court awarded punitive damages again when an insurer unreasonably denied disability benefits in *Fidler v Sun Life Assurance Co*. Mental anguish damages that stemmed from the long delay in receiving benefits were also allowed.[38] Since *Whiten*, insurers are required to balance their right to investigate with the responsibility not to unduly delay the processing of claims, not to pursue unfounded defences, and to treat the insured fairly.

Question to Consider

1. What claim investigation strategies should an insurance company employ to avoid allegations of bad faith?

The duty of good faith is owed by both insured and insurer, and applies to the making of the contract as well as its performance.[39] An insurer must deal with claims fairly both in the manner in which it investigates and values a claim and in the way it defends any lawsuit. It must not take advantage of its position of power over a vulnerable insured.

CASE 16.9   Costs

Wilson was injured in two motor vehicle accidents one year apart. He underwent surgery and rehabilitation for the next decade; the cost of each was covered by his insurance. When a new claims adjuster took over the case, benefits were terminated despite reports recommending continued treatment from those involved with Wilson's care. Only the consultant hired by the insurer suggested that treatment was unnecessary, and he did so without meeting Wilson or any of those treating Wilson. The Saskatchewan Court of Queen's Bench held that the insurer was "looking for an excuse to terminate benefits" and that it had breached its duty of good faith. The Court also held that the insurer manipulated the rules relating to witnesses and settlement offers in order to disadvantage Wilson. Damages and solicitor client costs were awarded.[40]

---

[37] [2002] 1 SCR 595.

[38] *Fidler v Sun Life Assurance Co*, [2006] 2 SCR 3.

[39] *Zurich Insurance Co v Ison TH Auto Sales Inc*, [2011] OJ No 1487 at para 29 (citing *Whiten*, *supra* note 37).

[40] *Wilson v Saskatchewan Government Insurance*, [2011] 2 WWR 154, punitive damages varied on appeal 2012 SKCA 106.

Subrogation

If a storeowner has obtained fire insurance for her premises and suffers a loss because of a fire negligently caused by her neighbour, she can recover from her own insurance company without having to sue the neighbour. However, she cannot recover twice. She cannot subsequently sue the neighbour for the same damages. As a result, as long as she is fully insured, she will have no incentive to sue her neighbour. If that ended the matter, many people would escape liability for their careless acts. Therefore, under general principles of insurance law, when an insurer has *fully* compensated an insured for all losses, it is entitled to "step into the shoes of the insured" and sue the person liable for the loss.[41] But the **right of subrogation** cannot place the insurer in a better position than the insured.

right of subrogation the right to assume the insured's "legal" rights against the wrongdoer after the paying compensation for all the insured's damages

CASE 16.10 Same Position as the Insured

A fire damaged leased premises, apparently due to the negligence of the tenant. The landlord was fully indemnified by its insurer, who brought an action for damages against the tenant by way of subrogation. In the lease, the landlord had covenanted to insure against damage by fire, and the tenant had agreed to pay a proportionate share of the landlord's cost of insuring. The tenant covenanted to repair the premises, except for insured fire damage.

The court held that the terms of the lease indicated that the tenant had bargained for the right to be free of liability for fire arising from its negligence. Regardless of the terms of the policy between the insurer and the landlord, the insurer could have no better claim against the tenant than the lease gave to the landlord.[42]

Recovery

In many types of insurance, property is insured for a stipulated amount (usually the estimated value of the property), and the insurer's liability is limited to that amount. However, it is a basic principle of insurance law that the insured may not recover more than the amount of the actual loss. For example, if a business insures its warehouse against damage by fire for $300 000, but the warehouse is actually worth only $275 000, that lower amount is the maximum that may be recovered. A person or business might think of saving premium costs by insuring property for less than its total value, since fires and accidents rarely result in total loss. Insurance companies often insert a clause in the contract stating that an insured that does not purchase coverage of at least a stated percentage of the value of the property (usually 80 percent) will become a "co-insurer" proportional to the lower coverage, along with the insurance company, for any loss that results. The insured would not recover the total loss, even though the loss itself was less than the face value of fire insurance policy.

Sometimes the same loss is covered by two or more separate insurance policies (especially where different risks are insured separately rather than under a single comprehensive policy). That does not permit the insured to recover twice for the same loss, and where the policies are issued by different insurance companies, they will have to determine which one must bear the loss or how it must be shared.[43]

The fact that the insured received insurance proceeds does not mean the defendant or tortfeasor is not liable—the insurance proceeds are not deducted from the damages

---

[41] *Zurich Insurance, supra* note 39 at paras 32–41.

[42] *Amexon Realty Inc v Comcheq Services Ltd* (1998), 155 DLR (4th) 661; *Orion Interiors Inc v State Farm Fire and Casualty Co*, 2016 ONCA 164.

[43] *Family Insurance Corp v Lombard Canada Ltd* (2002), 212 DLR (4th) 193; *Unger v Unger* (2003), 234 DLR (4th) 119.

payable by the defendant. This is known as the private insurance exception and is justified on the basis that the plaintiff has paid premiums in consideration of the insurance coverage.[44]

Assignment

A life insurance policy of the type that accumulates a cash surrender value is an item of property—a chose in action—which the insured may assign for value, for example, by giving a conditional assignment of the policy to a bank as security for a loan. If the insured defaults on the loan, the bank is entitled to the cash surrender value up to the amount due on the loan. The insurer's consent to an assignment of life insurance is not necessary, although the insurer is entitled to notice. The risk of the insurer is not affected by an assignment of the benefits of a life insurance contract.

In contrast, property insurance is not assignable without the consent of the insurer. The reason for this rule is that an assignment substitutes a new person as the insured, and the personal qualities of the insured may be relevant to the risk assumed by the insurer. When a person sells a house or an automobile, there is usually unexpired insurance on the property; the purchaser must therefore renegotiate the insurance with the insurer, possibly at different premium rates. On the other hand, after a risk materializes and an insurance claim is established, an insured may assign the claim (say, to creditors) without the consent of the insurer.

GUARANTEE

The Nature of a Guarantee

guarantee a promise to perform the obligation of another person if that person defaults

A **guarantee** usually arises in one of three common business situations:

- A prospective creditor may refuse to advance money, goods, or services solely on the prospective debtor's promise to pay for them.
- A creditor may state that it intends to start an action against its debtor for an overdue debt unless the debtor can offer additional security to support a further delay in repayment.
- A prospective assignee of rights under a contract may be unwilling to do so if he only receives the promise of payment in the original contract.

In each of these circumstances, the creditor or assignee may be reassured if he also receives a third party's promise to perform the obligation of the debtor if the debtor defaults. The debtor is then called the principal debtor, and his obligation is known as the principal or primary debt. The person who promises to answer for the default of the principal debtor is called the guarantor or surety, and her promise is a guarantee or contract of suretyship.

There are three important characteristics of a guarantee. First, the guarantor makes the promise to the creditor, not to the principal debtor. A promise made to a debtor to assist in the event of default is not a guarantee, and since the promise is not made to the creditor, the creditor cannot recover on it. Second, a guarantee is a secondary obligation arising only on default of the primary debt. For this reason it is a contingent liability, in contrast to the absolute liability of the principal debtor. A creditor has no rights against the guarantor until default by the principal debtor.

---

[44] *Krawchuk v Scherbak*, 2011 ONCA 352 at paras 98–101 (citing *Cunningham v Wheeler*, [1994] 1 SCR 359).

> **ILLUSTRATION 16.1 Common Guarantee Situations**
>
> (a) Crown Autos Ltd. agrees to sell a sports car to Tomins, provided that her uncle, Gilmour, guarantees payment. Gilmour agrees to assist his niece, and both join in signing an installment purchase agreement whereby Tomins promises (as principal debtor) to make all payments promptly, and Gilmour promises (as guarantor) to pay off the debt if Tomins defaults.
>
> (b) Arthur purchases a truck from Bigtown Trucks Ltd. under an installment agreement. After Arthur making half of his payments, he defaults. Bigtown threatens to retake possession of the truck. Arthur asks Bigtown to give him an extra six months to pay if he can obtain a satisfactory guarantor. Bigtown agrees, and Arthur's friend Campbell signs a contract of guarantee, promising to pay the balance in six months if Arthur fails to do so.
>
> (c) Perez buys a freezer from Quincy and gives a promissory note payable in 60 days for the full purchase price. Quincy is in need of cash and takes the note to her banker, who agrees to give her cash for it, less a 5 percent charge. Quincy endorses the note in favour of the bank—that is, she signs it when assigning it to the bank and thereby guarantees payment if Perez defaults.

Third, a guarantor's duty to pay arises immediately on default by the principal debtor. The creditor need not first sue the debtor. Strictly speaking, the creditor need not even notify the guarantor of the default before starting an action to enforce the guarantee. As a practical matter, however, the creditor always makes a demand on the guarantor before suing. Of course, the guarantee contract may stipulate that the creditor must first sue the debtor. It is more common that the guarantee specifically releases the creditor from any obligation to proceed against the debtor first. There is no obligation on the creditor to monitor the performance of the principal debtor, it is the guarantor who should do this.[45] Figure 16.1 illustrates the relationships involved in a guarantee.

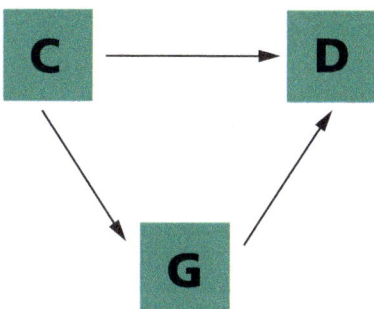

Figure 16.1 Liability on a Guarantee

The creditor, C, may sue either the principal debtor, D, or the guarantor, G, once D has defaulted. Normally, G will be entitled to sue D to recover what she has paid on D's account.

> **ILLUSTRATION 16.2 Guarantee Not Indemnity**
>
> William tries to rent a launch from Boat Rentals Ltd. but is refused because of his youth. William's father, a reputable businessman, informs the manager of Boat Rentals that if the company rents the launch to his son, he will be responsible for any damage caused by his negligent acts if his son does not reimburse the company for such damage. Boat Rentals accepts his offer.

---

[45] *Bank of Montreal v Javed*, 2016 ONCA 49 at para 24.

In Illustration 16.2, the guarantee is rather like a contract of insurance in which the father is the counterpart of an insurer, and the boat rental firm is the counterpart of the insured. If William's father had undertaken absolutely (without reference to a failure by his son to make good the loss himself) to assume any costs of his son's possible negligence, his promise would have been an indemnity and even more like a contract of insurance.

The distinction between guarantee and indemnity is important in that the liability of a guarantor depends on the default and liability of the principal debtor, whereas the liability under a promise of indemnity stands alone. If a person guarantees the debt of a consumer debtor, and the obligation is not binding under consumer legislation (for example, for failure to deliver a written statement of the terms of credit), the guarantor is not bound to pay either. On the other hand, a promise of indemnity is independent of any obligation of the person who benefits from that promise.

Continuing Guarantee

A continuing guarantee covers a series of transactions between a creditor and its principal debtor. A guarantor may, for example, agree to guarantee X Co.'s account with supplier Y up to an amount of $5000. In a series of purchases by X Co. and payments by it, X Co.'s indebtedness to Y will fluctuate considerably. At any given date during the currency of the guarantee, the guarantor is contingently liable for the debt, to a maximum of $5000. A continuing guarantee is often given for a specific length of time, and debts contracted afterward are not the liability of the guarantor. In any event, the death of a guarantor ends liability with respect to further transactions, although the guarantor's estate remains contingently liable for the debt existing at death.

A guarantor may limit liability under a continuing guarantee until a specified date. If the principal debtor has not defaulted or been sued by that date, then the guarantor's liability terminates. The variety of terms of a guarantee is virtually limitless, and they depend only upon the ability of the parties to reach agreement.

Consideration

To be a legally enforceable promise, the guarantee must be given either under seal or for consideration. Usually a guarantor makes the promise in writing and under seal. If not, what is the consideration for a guarantee?

Consideration is clearest when the guarantor receives an economic benefit—when she obtains a higher price as an assignor of an account receivable because she is willing to guarantee payment by the debtor. More frequently, the guarantor does not receive any economic benefit for her promise; but as noted, consideration need not confer an economic benefit on the promisor. The essential element of consideration is simply that the promisee pays a price for the promise of the other party. The creditor gives sufficient consideration for the promise of the guarantor by performing some act or forbearing to do some act at the request of the guarantor. The guarantor's request need not even be express; it may be implied from the circumstances.

ILLUSTRATION 16.3   More Time Before Suing

Creely threatens to sue Dobbs for his missed payments. Dobbs asks for 60 days to raise the money; Creely refuses to give the extra time unless Dobbs obtains a guarantee from his cousin Guara. Guara signs a guarantee, so Creely allows Dobbs a further 60 days. When Dobbs defaults payment again, Creely sues Guara.

Creely gave consideration because Guara impliedly requested Creely to give Dobbs extra time to pay.

Discharge of Guarantee

The liability of a guarantor may be discharged by bad behaviour of the creditor but only for the most serious misconduct.[46] The Supreme Court of Canada set down the following principles:[47]

1. The guarantor will be discharged if the creditor breaches the terms of the contract of guarantee. For example, where a creditor commenced proceedings against the principal debtor without giving notice to the guarantor and making it a party to the proceedings, as required by the contract of guarantee, the guarantor was discharged.[48]

2. The guarantor will be discharged if the principal contract between the creditor and the debtor is varied without the guarantor's consent and in a manner that is not obviously to the benefit of the guarantor. The rationale for this rule is that the guarantor has undertaken to underwrite a particular risk and is entitled not to have that risk materially altered to his detriment. For example, where an individual guaranteed a mortgage to a bank for a three-year term, and prior to the end of the term, the mortgagor and the bank renewed the mortgage for a further term at a higher rate of interest, the guarantor was held not liable when the mortgagor subsequently defaulted. The guarantor had not been given notice of the renewal and did not sign as guarantor on the renewal form; he was relieved from liability on his original guarantee.[49]

3. If the creditor acts in breach of its contract with the principal debtor, and that breach materially affects the risk assumed by the guarantor, the guarantor will be discharged. When a bank, having agreed to give a family company more time to pay off its debt, in return for a personal guarantee from its principal shareholders, made a demand for immediate payment and put the company into receivership, the guarantors were held to be discharged.[50] But in another case, where a bank appointed a receiver without first demanding repayment from the debtor, the guarantor was held not to be discharged since, on the evidence, there was nothing the debtor could have done even if it had been given proper notice.[51]

4. Finally, when the creditor does something that impairs the value of any security given by the principal debtor, but without materially affecting the guarantor's risk under the original contract of guarantee, the guarantor is entitled to be partially discharged from her obligation, but only to the extent that the value of the security is reduced.[52]

Less serious misconduct entitles the guarantor to damages from the creditor.

Rights of the Guarantor on Default

Defences   A guarantor may defend a creditor's action on any grounds that would be open to the principal debtor. If a debtor has a good defence because of the

---

[46] *Ibid* at paras 19–20.

[47] *Pax Management Ltd v Canadian Imperial Bank of Commerce*, [1992] 2 SCR 998.

[48] *Bank of British Columbia v Turbo Resources Ltd* (1983), 23 BLR 152.

[49] *Manulife Bank of Canada v Conlin* (1996), 139 DLR (4th) 426 (SCC). See also *Royal Bank of Canada v Bruce Industrial Sales Ltd* (1998), 40 OR (3d) 307.

[50] *Bank of Montreal v Wilder* (1986), 32 DLR (4th) 9 (SCC).

[51] *Royal Bank of Canada v Nobes* (1982), 49 NSR (2d) 634.

[52] *Rose v Aftenberger* (1969), 9 DLR (3d) 42. See also *Bank of Montreal v Korico Enterprises Limited* (2000), 50 OR (3d) 520.

misrepresentation of the creditor in selling the goods, the guarantor will as well. A guarantor may reduce the outstanding amount by any claim the debtor has against the creditor, as when the debtor has performed services for the creditor that also remain unpaid.

If the principal contract is void—as, for example, in the case of a prohibited loan to a company—then any guarantee will also be a nullity.[53] Although not absolute, the general rule is that a contract made with an infant is not void but merely unenforceable against the infant and would not necessarily prevent the enforcement of a guarantee.

Subrogation   Subrogation, as described earlier, also applies to a guarantee. A guarantor who pays off the creditor becomes subrogated to the rights of the creditor against the debtor and the debtor's assets. She may sue the debtor for the amount she has paid the creditor and for any expenses she has incurred because of the debtor's default. She is also entitled to an assignment of any security the creditor holds.

A guarantor may choose to pay off the creditor and become subrogated to its rights as soon as the debt falls due. She need not wait for the creditor to make a demand or to sue. The guarantor may wish to act even when the creditor is content to wait. The guarantor may have ascertained that the debtor is failing and may wish to take action before the debtor becomes insolvent.

Requirement of Writing

Chapter 10 discussed that a contract of guarantee must be in writing and signed by the guarantor to be enforceable against him. This requirement has been retained even in those jurisdictions where the *Statute of Frauds* has largely been repealed.[54] Most guarantees, such as those given to a bank, are in writing, regardless of whether writing is required by law.

Strategies to Manage the Legal Risks

Insurance and guarantee contracts are valuable risk management tools that virtually every business uses. Their effectiveness depends upon their form and content, as well as compliance with the legislation that governs their use. Scope of coverage is the most important term of an insurance contract. Typical insurance contracts contain many exclusions, and coverage may be denied if full disclosure has not been made at the time of contracting. Therefore, careful attention must be paid to exclusions and riders attached to policy, and a comprehensive insurance policy is less likely to create gaps in coverage. Renewal dates should be monitored, and any material change in circumstances (that is, risk) should be reported to the insurer immediately.

Businesses using guarantees to reduce the chances of bad debts among their accounts receivable should prepare written documents under seal. A guarantor's right to subrogation means any dealings with the primary debtor or security should be completed with the full knowledge and agreement of the guarantor.

---

[53] *Communities Economic Development Fund v Maxwell*, [1991] 3 SCR 388; *Jer-Mar Foods Ltd v Arrand Refrigeration Inc*, [2010] OJ No 1119. In *William E Thompson Associates Inc v Carpenter* (1989), 61 DLR (4th) 1, the interest rate exceeded the maximum permitted under the *Criminal Code*, but the guarantee of the principal sum only was held to be severable and enforceable.

[54] Only Manitoba does not require a guarantee to be in writing: *Act to Repeal the Statute of Frauds*, CCSM c F158. In Alberta, the requirement is more stringent. A guarantee by an individual must also be acknowledged before a notary public: *Guarantees Acknowledgement Act*, RSA 2000, c G-11.

QUESTIONS FOR REVIEW

1. What are the two principal types of "legal risk" that a business may insure against?
2. Distinguish between an insurance agent and an insurance broker.
3. What are the principal types of insurance that a business is likely to need?
4. What are the advantages and disadvantages of "comprehensive" insurance?
5. What is meant by an "insurable interest"?
6. Does a shareholder have an insurable interest in the property of his corporation?
7. What is the legal position where an insured fails to renew an insurance policy by the due date?
8. Is it necessary for an insured to notify the insurer of changes of circumstance that occur after the policy enters into force?
9. Can an insurance policy be assigned to a third person?
10. What is "subrogation"?
11. In what business circumstances are guarantees commonly required and given?
12. To whom does a guarantor give her promise?
13. What normally constitutes the consideration for a guarantee?
14. How may a guarantee be discharged?
15. Does a contract of guarantee have to be in writing?

CASES AND PROBLEMS

1. Continuing Scenario

    Ashley's parents, Jim and Shelley, want to assist her in building the business, so in 2009 they signed limited guarantees for the principal sum of $128 000, with interest, at bank prime rate plus 1.5 percent in favour of the Monarch Bank. The guarantees were given to secure a line of credit for Ashley and were provided for (1) a $100 000 term loan with interest at bank prime plus 2.25 percent and (2) a revolving demand loan for general operating purposes. The revolving loan was not to exceed the principal sum of $125 000, and the lending was subject to an accounts receivable margin requirement. Interest under the revolving loan was at prime plus 1.5 percent per annum. The revolving loan contained a provision under which the bank agreed to apply specified credit balances to repay the loan.

    In 2012, Ashley's business seemed to be doing fine so she told her parents she no longer needed their help. Jim and Shelley gave the bank notice in writing that they were ending their liability in accordance with the guarantee. (Their understanding was that this fixed their maximum liability at the amount then outstanding under the loan.) At the time of the notice, their liability under the revolving loan was $95 000.

    After receiving the notice, the bank converted the revolving loan into a fixed loan without the knowledge or consent of Jim and Shelley. In 2013, Ashley renegotiated the loan arrangements to comprise (1) a $100 000 term loan with interest at prime plus 2.5 percent and (2) a fixed operating loan with interest at prime plus 2 percent and with more flexible margin requirements. If Ashley defaults on the loan, will the bank be able to sue Jim and Shelley to enforce the guarantees?

2. Whitehorse Furniture Ltd. took out a fire insurance policy on its premises with Kansafe Insurance Co., with the coverage being arranged through an insurance broker, J&H Ltd. Whitehorse did not inform J&H that it had made a previous substantial claim against another insurance company (for a fire in which arson was suspected) and that there had also been two previous fires at its premises that had caused little or no damage. Consequently, Kansafe was also unaware of those facts.

Another fire occurred at the Whitehorse premises. When Kansafe learned of the previous fires, it initially denied liability because of the non-disclosure. Whitehorse claimed that it had not thought the earlier fires were relevant. Since J&H had not asked any questions about previous fires or claims, Whitehorse had not mentioned them. Kansafe eventually agreed to settle the Whitehorse claim and made a payment of $550 000, without admitting liability.

Subsequently, Kansafe brought an action against J&H, alleging that it had been negligent in not making proper inquiries of Whitehorse and in failing to disclose important information when it applied for the insurance coverage on behalf of Whitehorse.

Should Kansafe succeed against J&H?

3. Perennial Manufacturing Inc. carried on a foundry business in premises leased from Sharbo Investments Ltd. Perennial arranged a contract of fire insurance with the Commonwealth Insurance Co. The insurance covered equipment, business interruption, and the value of the building. At the time when the insurance was arranged, Vandervelde was the controlling shareholder of both Perennial and Sharbo. He later sold his shares in Perennial and no longer had an interest in that corporation.

The building burned down. Perennial claimed on the insurance policy, and Commonwealth paid out $700 000 for the loss of stock and equipment, business interruption, and extra expenses. It refused to make any payments for the loss of the building on the ground that the building was not owned by Perennial. (It was not insured by Sharbo.)

Is that a valid defence to the claim?

4. Two years before her death, Desai placed a term life insurance policy for $400 000 on her own life. Her friend Trumble was named beneficiary.

In her application for insurance, Desai described her occupation as "business administrator," Trumble was described as her "business associate," and she stated that her net financial worth was $100 000. None of those statements was entirely accurate. Although she had studied business administration, she was then working as an office cleaner. She did not have a business relationship with Trumble, and her net worth was considerably less than $100 000.

Desai was subsequently murdered by Trumble. Desai's sister claimed on the policy as executrix. The insurance company refused to pay.

What defences are available to the insurance company?

5. Blackgold Investments Limited required additional financing. Its directors decided to assist the company by raising the sum of $500 000 on their own credit. The corporation then applied for a loan with Merchant Bank, on the terms that a guarantee would be signed jointly by all the directors. The guarantee was on a standard form provided by the bank and included the clause:

> This guarantee shall be binding upon every person signing the same, notwithstanding the non-execution thereof by any other proposed guarantor.

Four directors signed the guarantee in the office of the bank manager in Calgary. Then it was sent to Edmonton, where four other directors signed it together. They noted the absence Fowler's signature, the corporation's president (also a director), and agreed among themselves that they were signing only on the condition that the guarantee would not be delivered to the bank until Fowler signed as well.

When the guarantee was returned to Calgary, it was given to the bank manager with instructions that it was not to be treated as having been delivered to the bank as an operative instrument until Fowler had signed. In the end, Fowler refused to sign because he did not want to reduce his own line of credit at the bank. Nevertheless, the bank manager advanced the corporation $500 000, and the corporation gave the bank its promissory note for that amount.

Blackgold subsequently defaulted on the note, and the bank claimed the sum owing from those directors who had signed the guarantee. They refused to pay on the grounds that the guarantee would not operate unless and until all directors had signed. The bank sued them to enforce the guarantee.

Explain whether this action should succeed.

6. Maria owned a policy that insured the life of her husband, Paul, and named her as the beneficiary. Paul also owned two policies, each of which insured his life and named Maria the beneficiary. The couple subsequently separated.

    About a year after the separation, Paul died while on a trip to Bolivia. An autopsy revealed a number of condoms filled with cocaine in his digestive tract. One of the bags had burst, causing his death. The circumstances indicated the death was accidental. It was agreed that the husband's ingestion of the cocaine amounted to possession of a narcotic and was a crime under the laws of Bolivia and of Canada.

    When Maria wrote to the insurance company, claiming payment under the policies, the company refused to pay on the ground that the claims resulted from a criminal act of the life insured.

    Should Maria be entitled to recover?

Chapter 17
Agency and Franchising

- **DEFINING AGENCY**
- **CREATION OF AN AGENCY RELATIONSHIP**
- **DUTIES OWED BY AN AGENT TO THE PRINCIPAL**
- **DUTIES OWED BY THE PRINCIPAL TO THE AGENT**
- **THE AUTHORITY OF THE AGENT**
- **RIGHTS AND LIABILITY OF PRINCIPAL AND AGENT**
- **TERMINATING AN AGENCY RELATIONSHIP**
- **FRANCHISING**
- **STRATEGIES TO MANAGE THE LEGAL RISKS**

Two types of contract that allow a business to expand its operations are agency and franchising. The contract of agency has ancient origins, whereas franchising, by contrast, is a relatively recent phenomenon.

In this chapter we examine the following issues:

- What is agency?
- How is an agency relationship created?
- What are the duties of the agent and the principal?
- What is the extent of the liability of the principal and of the agent to third parties?
- How is an agency relationship terminated?
- What is the legal nature of franchising?
- What are the usual contents of a franchising agreement?
- What are the rights and duties of the parties to a franchising agreement?

DEFINING AGENCY

Agency is a relationship in which one person, known as an **agent**, is authorized by another person for whom she acts, known as a **principal**, to form contracts with third parties on the principal's behalf. The relationship between agent and principal is usually a contractual one, with the agent being paid by the principal. Employment is the obvious example. A person may also act gratuitously as an agent, in which case she is bound by all the duties imposed by agency law.

A distinction is sometimes made between a **dependent agent** and an independent agent. A dependent agent is one who acts exclusively, or mostly, for a single principal. Insurance agents, for example, are sometimes dependent agents, representing only one insurance company.[1] Agency may be created by the terms of an employment contract in which an employer (as principal) delegates to an employee (as agent) the authority to make contracts. However, the functions of agency and employment may be entirely separate; an agent need not be an employee, just as not all employees are agents. Sometimes it is difficult to determine whether an agent is an employee; usually, a self-employed agent is compensated solely by commissions and does not receive any salary, but that is not always conclusive. The distinction is important in employment law and is discussed further in Chapter 18; it is also important for income tax purposes.

An **independent agent** is not an employee and usually acts on behalf of several principals or clients. Lawyers frequently act as agents for their clients in the settlement of lawsuits. Stockbrokers are agents for clients who place orders with them to buy or sell shares. Auctioneers have authority to sell goods for their principals. A person may be a **commission agent**—that is, one who sells on behalf of a principal to third parties and receives compensation through commissions on those sales.

The Supreme Court of Canada recognizes that "Society today simply could not function without the services of agents."[2] A corporation, as an entirely artificial "person," can enter into contractual relations only when its officers and employees act as agents on its behalf. Agency plays an important role in partnerships. Each partner is an agent of the other partners, with very wide authority to act on behalf of the firm. Sometimes the term "agent" is used in a general sense to mean "representative." The so-called real estate agent does not have authority to sell the property of a client—instead, her role is to introduce prospective purchasers, and the client contracts directly with the purchaser. Without the power to contract, a representative is not an agent in the legal sense.

agent a person acting for another person in contractual relations with third parties

principal the person on whose behalf the agent acts

dependent agent an agent who acts exclusively, or mostly, for a single principal

independent agent an agent who carries on an independent business and acts for a number of principals

commission agent one who sells on behalf of a principal to third parties and receives compensation through commissions

CREATION OF AN AGENCY RELATIONSHIP

Any person who has the capacity to contract may appoint an agent to contract on his behalf. An agent's power to contract on behalf of her principal is limited to the capacity the principal possesses. If a minor appoints an agent, the contracts made for him by the agent are as voidable as if he had made them personally. However, a minor may act as an agent and bind her principal in contracts with third parties, even where she would not bind herself.

Agency involves two relationships: first, the relationship between principal and agent, usually expressed in the form of an **agency agreement**, and second, the relationship between the principal and third parties with whom the agent makes contracts on the principal's behalf (see Figure 17.1).

agency agreement the agreement between principal and agent whereby the agent undertakes to act on behalf of the principal

---

[1] See Chapter 16 on insurance.
[2] *R v Kelly*, [1992] SCJ No 53, (1992), 92 DLR (4th) 643 at para 26.

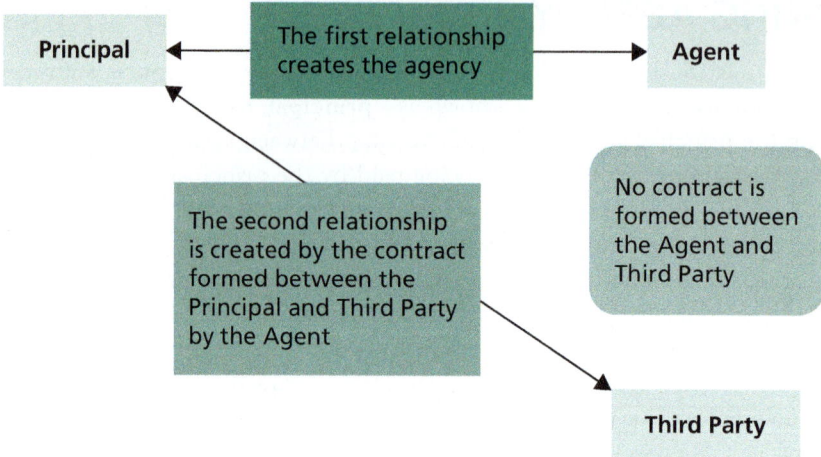

Figure 17.1 Agency Relationships

By Agreement

The easiest way to create an agency relationship is by agreement. An agency agreement may be express or implied, oral, written, or in writing under seal. If an agency agreement is to extend beyond one year, it must be in writing to be enforceable in those provinces where the relevant section of the *Statute of Frauds* continues to apply.[3]

The agreement should clearly define the limits of the agent's authority; how far she can go in making a contract with a third party without obtaining further instructions from the principal. An agency agreement may give an agent a wide general authority to make contracts, or her authority may be narrowly restricted to making a specific contract.

An agent should always have authorization in writing if she wishes to issue promissory notes or draw cheques in the name of her principal, and she should sign them in a way that makes it clear that she is acting in a representative capacity; otherwise she may be personally liable for the promise.[4]

power of attorney a type of agency agreement authorizing the agent to sign documents on behalf of the principal

A **power of attorney** is a special type of express agency agreement.[5] Normally, a power of attorney is issued under seal, since an agent who does not receive authority under seal cannot be authorized to sign documents under seal on behalf of the principal.

Other Ways to Create an Agency Relationship

An agency relationship may be implied through the conduct of the principal and the agent. If the principal has allowed the agent to act like his agent in dealings with third parties, agency will be implied. This is an application of the estoppel principle—when someone allows another to believe something, he cannot later deny it. In these circumstances, agency is created by estoppel.

Agency may also be created retroactively. If an unauthorized agent negotiates a contract with a third party on another's behalf, that person may subsequently approve the agent's behaviour and adopt or ratify the contract as his own. In this case, agency

---

[3] See e.g. *Statute of Frauds*, RSO 1990, c S.19.

[4] See *Bills of Exchange Act*, RSC 1985, c B-4, s 51(1).

[5] See *Power of Attorney Act*, RSBC 1996, c 370; *Powers of Attorney Act, 2002*, SS 2002, c P-20.3; *The Power of Attorney and Mental Health Amendment Act*, CCSM c P97; *Substitute Decisions Act, 1992*, SO 1992, c. 30.

is created by ratification. These concepts (ratification and estoppel) are considered later in this chapter under "The Authority of the Agent." Often, a principal admits that an agency relationship exists but still disputes his liability to a third party because the agent exceeded the power or authority he was given. Again, the behaviour of the principal may be used to imply authority in the agent.

DUTIES OWED BY AN AGENT TO THE PRINCIPAL

Duty to Comply with the Agency Agreement

The duties of an agent are determined by the terms—express and implied—of the agreement with the principal. A number of rights and duties, typically implied by custom as terms of the agency agreement, may be expressly excluded from an agreement. The breach of any term, whether express or implied, gives the innocent party the usual remedies against the other for breach of contract. For example, if an agent exceeds his express authority, and the principal suffers damage, the principal may claim any loss that results from the agent's breach of duty.

Duty of Care

An agent owes a duty of care to her principal, even when she acts for free. The level of skill expected of the agent depends upon the task and the agent's apparent competence for the purpose.

The courts generally regard notice to an agent as being the equivalent of notice to her principal. An agent therefore has a duty to be diligent in keeping her principal informed about all important developments affecting their relationship.

Personal Performance

An agent's usual responsibilities include personal performance and the exercise of her judgment, skill, and discretion on the principal's behalf. Because of the high degree of confidence and trust necessary in an agency relationship, an agent cannot delegate her duties to another without the principal's prior agreement.

However, there are exceptions where the nature of the agency relationship or trade usage give the agent implied authority to delegate some or all of her duties. For example, when a bank acts as agent for its customers, it may require the services of other banks to represent it in countries where it has no branches. When a corporation is appointed as an agent, it can only perform through sub-agents, namely, its directors or employees.

When an agent has implied authority to perform through a sub-agent, there is generally privity of contract between only the principal and the agent. The principal has no claim for breach of contract against the sub-agent. The agent must in turn recover from the sub-agent.

Good Faith

An agent owes a fiduciary duty to the principal.[6] This duty of good faith requires that an agent be loyal, act in the best interests of the principal, and keep the principal fully informed. If she is authorized to buy property at a certain price and learns that it can

---

[6] *R v Kelly*, supra note 2 at para 33. See Gerald Fridman, *Canadian Agency Law* (Markham: LexisNexis, 2009) at 106–21 (noting exceptions); *Knoch Estate v Jon Picken Ltd*, [1991] OJ No 1394 (ONCA). The duty may be varied by contract: *Kelly v Cooper*, [1993] AC 205.

be obtained more cheaply, she is bound to inform the principal. If she buys at the lower price, she must pass on the savings to the principal, rather than make a secret profit for herself.[7]

Money that comes into an agent's possession in respect of contracts made for the principal belongs to the principal, although the agent may be entitled to withhold her commission. She should keep separate records so she can account to the principal for money received. An agent who fails to keep proper accounts may be liable to her principal for any shortfalls.[8]

In most circumstances, an agent will not be acting in good faith when she serves two principals in the same transaction without their knowledge and consent. This is allowed only if they are both aware of the arrangement and have consented to it. However, the practice is still discouraged. The two principals will normally have conflicting interests, as each will want to get the best possible bargain. By considering both their interests, the agent places herself in a conflict of interest.

An agent who agrees to be paid a commission for acting on behalf of a vendor breaches his duty if he also accepts a commission from the purchaser. He may have to return both commissions.[9] An agent who arranges a sale for his principal to a purchasing corporation in which the agent is a director or shareholder also breaches his duty. He is not entitled to commission and may be liable for the principal's losses because he has conflicting interests.[10]

An agent also has a conflict of interest if she enters into a contract on her own behalf with the principal, without his knowledge and approval—for example, buying property from or selling property to the principal.

Under the *Criminal Code*, it is a criminal offence for an agent to corruptly demand or accept any remuneration from a third party in the conduct of her principal's business affairs.[11] The third party that offers such a bribe or kickback is also criminally liable.

DUTIES OWED BY THE PRINCIPAL TO THE AGENT

A principal does not owe a fiduciary duty to the agent. Where the agency is created by contract, the principal's duties will be set out in the contract. For other agencies, the law imposes only two duties on a principal:

- the duty to compensate the agent for his or her effort (by commission or otherwise)
- the duty to pay the agent's expenses and compensate for losses

In the absence of an express compensation term, an agent is entitled to a reasonable fee—another example of *quantum meruit*. A term is implied into the contract prohibiting the principal from acting in a way that interferes with the agent's ability to earn commission.[12]

A listing agreement between a prospective seller and a real estate agent frequently states that the agent is entitled to commission when she introduces to the seller a prospective purchaser who is "ready, willing, and able to purchase." A completed sale is not required, so the purchaser's refusal to perform will not deprive the

---

[7] *McCullough v Tenaglia* (1999), 40 BLR (2d) 222, aff'd [1999] OJ No 4401.

[8] See *Killoran v RMO Site Management Inc* (1997), 33 BLR (2d) 240.

[9] *Andrews v Ramsay* [1903] 2 KB 635.

[10] *Salomons v Pender* (1865), 195 ER 682.

[11] RSC 1985, c C-46, s 426 (1). See also *R v Kelly, supra* note 2.

[12] *Pure Energy Marketing Ltd v Ramarro Resources Inc*, [2003] AJ No 1105.

agent of commission.[13] Some listing agreements require commission to be paid if the vendor accepts an offer during the term of the listing. Again, completion of the sale is not necessary. A prospective seller should insist that the listing agreement contain a term that the agent is not entitled to commission unless and until a sale is completed.

Some provinces have statutes rendering a contract to pay commission to a real estate agent unenforceable unless it is in writing and signed by the prospective seller of the property. In these provinces, when an agreement for an agent's services is entirely oral, the agent does not acquire an enforceable right, even though she may have introduced a willing and able purchaser to the client.[14]

Even if an agency agreement is silent, there is an implied term that the principal will reimburse the agent for all reasonable expenses incurred when acting within the scope of her authority. The principal is under no obligation to reimburse an agent for unauthorized acts unless he ratifies them.

Ethical Issue Insurance Broker Compensation

Independent insurance brokers offer insurance products from a number of different insurance companies. They are often considered agents of the insured and owe the insured a duty of good faith. However, they are paid by the insurance companies. A potential conflict of interest arises for two reasons:

- Not all insurance companies pay the same percentage of commission.
- Some companies pay an additional amount of "contingent commission" based on the overall business placed with the company.

It is possible that an unethical insurance broker may recommend a particular product in order to maximize his own commission, rather than considering the best interests of the consumer. The Code of Conduct governing Ontario insurance brokers requires a broker to disclose any real or potential conflict of interest associated with the transaction and not to charge or accept a commission that is not fully disclosed to the consumer. The Insurance Council of British Columbia requires licencees to disclose that a commission is paid and by whom but not the exact amount.

Questions to Consider

1. Is disclosure a satisfactory solution for this conflict of interest?
2. What other measures would you recommend?

Sources: *Registered Insurance Brokers Act*, RSO 1990, c R.19, *General Regulations*, RRO Reg 991, s 14 (7.1), (8); Insurance Council of British Columbia Licencee Responsibilities, s 8, https://www.insurancecouncilofbc.com/licensee-resources/licensee-responsibilities.

THE AUTHORITY OF THE AGENT

The purpose of agency is to allow one person (the agent) to form contracts on behalf of a second person (the principal) with a third person (the third party). Whether a contract comes into existence depends upon the authority the agent possesses. An agent's authority may be either actual or apparent.

Actual Authority

Actual authority may also be either express or implied. Express authority is the authority given orally or in writing by the principal. It may be set out in the agency agreement or might be given subsequently in separate instructions.

actual authority the authority given expressly or impliedly to the agent by the principal

---

[13] *Columbia Caterers & Sherlock Co v Famous Restaurants Ltd* (1956), 4 DLR (2d) 601.

[14] See e.g. *Real Estate Act*, RSA 2000, c R-5, s 22; *Real Estate Trading Act*, SNS 1996, c 28, s 26. But see *Real Estate and Business Brokers Act, 2002*, SO 2002, c 30, Sch C, ss 33(3), 36 and O Reg 567/05, s 1, suggesting that representation agreements may be oral and may not even specify the commission charged.

Implied terms may supplement the express authority in the contract. When a principal expressly authorizes an agent to make a purchase of, say, Italian wine from Tuscany, the agent would also have implied authority to make a contract for shipment of the goods to Canada.

Authority may be implied by commercial usage or by conduct. For example, if a person is appointed as an insurance agent, it is implied that she possesses the usual authority of such an agent, except to the extent that the usual authority is expressly restricted. Similarly, a person appointed as company secretary will have all the usual authority of a company secretary, in the absence of express limitations.[15] Actual authority may also be inferred from the conduct of the parties. If an agent purchases goods for the principal without having express authority to do so, but the principal pays for the goods without complaining, that act may amount to an implied authority to act in the same way in the future.

Apparent Authority

In most cases, a third party will not have any knowledge of the contents of the agency agreement or of any special restrictions upon an agent's authority. The third party can only rely upon the **apparent authority** of the agent—that is, the authority that the third party is entitled to assume the agent possesses. Consequently, agency law provides that a contract is valid and enforceable, even when the agent had no actual authority to enter into it—if she had the apparent authority to do so. However, as we have already noted, by acting beyond the limits of her authority, the agent has breached her duty to the principal and is liable to compensate him for any loss suffered as a result.

apparent authority the authority that a third party is entitled to assume the agent possesses

Like actual authority, apparent authority can arise in two ways: by commercial usage and by conduct (holding out).

Usual Authority
An agent has the apparent authority to act in the manner that is usual for that type of agent in that type of business, unless the third party knows, or ought to know, of any restriction upon that authority. As far as the third party is concerned, apparent authority is frequently the same as actual, implied authority; but if there is a restriction on the agent's usual authority, of which the third party is unaware, the agent will possess apparent authority but not actual authority.

CASE 17.1 Usual Not Actual Authority

Garrod and Parkin entered into a partnership to run a car repair business. Parkin was to be the active partner; Garrod provided most of the financing. Garrod insisted that the agreement contain express provision that the business was not for the buying or selling of cars. Parkin later sold a car belonging to a customer who had left it with the firm for repairs, without the knowledge of the owner, and disappeared with the proceeds. The car was later recovered by the owner, and the purchaser, who had innocently bought the car from Parkin, brought an action against Garrod (for breach of the implied condition in the contract of sale that the seller has title). The court ruled that, in selling the car, Parkin was acting as agent for Garrod since, in partnership law, each partner is an agent for the other partners. Parkin had no actual authority to sell the car because of the express provision in the partnership agreement, but he did have apparent authority. Selling used cars is a common part of the car repair business.[16]

If the third party is aware of a restriction on the agent's authority, or ought to be aware because there are suspicious circumstances, then the third party cannot claim that there is an apparent authority.[17] If the proposed contract is not within an area

---

[15] *Panorama Developments (Guildford) Ltd v Fidelis Furnishing Fabrics Ltd*, [1971] 2 QB 711.

[16] *Mercantile Credit Co Ltd v Garrod*, [1962] 3 All ER 1103. See also *Financial Management Inc v Associated Financial Planners Ltd* (2006), 56 Alta LR (4th) 207 (ABCA).

[17] *32262 BC Ltd v 411676 Alberta Ltd* (1995), 29 Alta LR (3d) 415.

ordinarily entrusted to such agents, or if its consequences are of unusual importance for the principal and the third party, the third party should first check with the principal about the agent's authority. For example, an agent who is authorized to sell goods is not necessarily authorized to accept the purchase money, particularly where payment to the agent is not customary trade practice or where the principal has sent an invoice to the third party requesting payment. If the third party pays the money to the agent, and the agent absconds, the third party may have to pay the money again to the principal.[18]

Holding Out Even when an act or contract falls outside the usual authority of a particular agent, the agent may still possess apparent authority because she has been represented by the principal as having that authority. The principal may be estopped (prevented) from denying liability on a contract with a third party because of conduct known as **holding out**: when a principal acts in a way that suggests agency. The behaviour may be by words or conduct, and includes such things as honouring similar contracts made for it by that person in the past. If the behaviour may be reasonably interpreted by the third party as consistent with the agent having authority, the principal cannot deny the authority of the agent.[19]

holding out representing by words or conduct that a person is one's agent or has a particular authority

---

ILLUSTRATION 17.1 Pattern of Behaviour

Able contracted with Prado, a fashion accessories retailer, to act as Prado's purchasing agent in western Canada. The agency contract expressly stated that contracts in excess of $25 000 require Prado's prior approval. All previous contracts for purchase of costume jewellery from X varied between $10 000 and $20 000. Recently, Able placed an order with X for $40 000 worth of jewellery, without first consulting Prado. X did not question the order and two weeks later received payment from Prado, as usual. Prado reprimanded Able, reminded her of the $25 000 limit, and told her not to exceed that limit again without approval. Despite the warning, Able placed another order with X for $30 000. Can Prado refuse to pay? No.

Able clearly did not have actual authority to enter into either contract. In the first ($40 000) contract, Prado might have argued successfully that, because of the unusually large amount, Able did not have apparent authority either. But in the case of the second ($30 000) contract, Able almost certainly has apparent authority. By paying X on the first occasion, without mentioning the limit to X, Prado held out A as having authority, at least up to $40 000.

Holding out may also apply when an agency agreement ends. If an agent continues to enter into contracts for the principal after the agency ends, and third parties receive no notice of the termination, the principal is bound by the contracts. This is of practical importance when a partner retires from a partnership, since partners customarily act as agents for the partnership in contracts with outside parties such as suppliers.

Ratification

Sometimes a person pretends to be an agent, knowing she lacks authority but hoping the proposed principal will later adopt the contract. Subsequent adoption by the principal is called **ratification**. The need for ratification arises either because the person purporting to act as agent is not one or because she has limited authority and has exceeded it.

ratification subsequent adoption by the proposed principal of a contract made by an agent acting without authority

---

[18] *Butwick v Grant*, [1924] 2 KB 483.

[19] *Doiron v Devon Capital Corp* (2003), 232 DLR (4th) 732 (ABCA). But see *McRae Management Ltd v Breezy Properties Ltd* (2008), 74 RPR (4th) 50.

> **CHECKLIST**
> ## An Agent's Authority
>
> An agent's authority may be
> - actual, or
> - apparent.
>
> Actual authority may be
> - express, or
> - implied from (1) commercial usage or (2) conduct.
>
> Even when an agent does not have actual authority, she may have apparent authority, derived from
> - commercial usage (usual authority), or
> - holding out.

When a principal ratifies, the effect is to establish the contract with the third party retroactively, as if the agent possessed actual authority at the time she made the contract. The principal, agent, and third party are then in the same position regarding the contract as if the agency relationship had existed from the beginning.

A named principal need not state his ratification expressly. It may be implied from the fact of his assuming the benefits of the contract, or perhaps even from failing to notify the third party of the absence of authority when it is discovered.[20] Ratification cannot be partial. A principal cannot accept the benefits without also reimbursing the agent for her costs. He cannot ratify only those aspects of the transaction that prove to be to his advantage but refuse to ratify the balance of the contract. A principal must also ratify within a reasonable time to be able to claim the benefit of a contract.[21]

Not all contracts made by an agent without authority may be ratified by the principal; a principal may not ratify a contract made for him if, at the time the contract was made, he would have been unable to enter into the contract himself.

ILLUSTRATION 17.2   Time to Ratify

A places fire insurance on P's building, without P's authority. After buildings burn down, P tries to ratify the insurance contract. The ratification is not effective because at the time P attempts to ratify, the buildings are already destroyed, and it is too late for P to insure them.[22]

ILLUSTRATION 17.3   Third-Party Rights

A, without authority from P, accepts T's offer to sell a large quantity of canned goods to P. Before the delivery date, T learns that A had no authority, so T makes another contract to sell the same goods to X. Ratification by P will now be ineffective because someone else has rights to the goods.

---

[20] *Community Savings Credit Union v United Assn. of Journeymen and Apprentices of the Plumbing and Pipefitting Industry*, [2002] BCJ No 654.

[21] *Metropolitan Asylums Board Managers v Kingham & Sons* (1890), 6 TLR 217.

[22] See *Portavon Cinema Co Ltd v Price and Century Insurance Co Ltd*, [1939] 4 All ER 601 at 607.

A principal cannot ratify when the rights of an outsider are affected and must ratify within a reasonable time.

Finally, a principal cannot ratify if, at the time the agent made the contract, the agent failed to name the intended principal or at least mention the existence of a principal whose identity could then be ascertained. An undisclosed principal cannot ratify a contract made without his authority.

When an agent purports to accept an offer "subject to the ratification of my principal," the later ratification will not be retroactive. This exception is simply an application of the rules of offer and acceptance. A conditional acceptance by an agent is not acceptance at all. The offeror may revoke the offer at any time before acceptance. In these circumstances, the eventual "ratification" of the principal is really only an acceptance of the original offer.

CHECKLIST
Ratification

An agent's contract with a third party may be ratified
- expressly or impliedly;
- within a reasonable time;
- by a named principal;
- if the rights of an outsider are not affected; and
- if, at the time of creation and ratification, the principal was capable of making the contract.

RIGHTS AND LIABILITY OF PRINCIPAL AND AGENT

When an agent makes a contract with a third party on behalf of her principal, who is liable on the contract—the agent or the principal? The answer should be "the principal," but it depends upon a number of factors. Was the agent acting within the scope of her authority in making the contract? Was the identity or existence of the principal disclosed to the other party? There are three possible outcomes:

- The principal alone is liable on the contract.
- The agent alone is liable.
- Either the principal or the agent may be held liable.

The Principal Alone Is Liable on the Contract

An agent is not liable for contracts made for her principal when the agency relationship is functioning properly. After creating the contract, the principal is liable for performance and is the one able to enforce it against the third party. Further, an agent has no liability to the third party even when she acts outside her real authority, so long as she acts within her apparent authority. She may be liable to the principal for breach of the agency agreement.

To protect against liability, an agent should indicate that she acts as agent and should identify the principal. The following are examples of signatures that accomplish this purpose:

"The Smith Corporation Limited, per W.A. Jones"
"W.A. Jones, for The Smith Corporation Limited"

Sometimes, an agent may persuade a third party to enter into a contract with her principal, without disclosing the exact identity of the principal. She may describe herself as agent for a party who does not want to reveal his name. For example, an agent may negotiate in this way in order to obtain options for the purchase of individual pieces of land intended for assembly into a large block. The reasoning is that if the prospective purchaser is a large developer, the disclosure of his identity and purpose might induce some owners to hold out for much higher prices. In this situation, although the principal was not named in the contract, it was made on his behalf and with his authority, and he alone is liable on, and entitled to enforce, the contract. The third party has no rights against the agent.[23]

The Agent Alone Is Liable on the Contract

When an agent contracts on terms that she is the real contracting party, though she is in reality acting or intending to act for an undisclosed principal, the agent alone has rights and liabilities relative to the third party. The principal can neither sue nor be sued on the contract. In the next section we look at what happens if the existence of a principal is discovered by the third party after contracting with the agent personally.[24]

Either the Principal or the Agent May Be Held Liable on the Contract

Sometimes a person who is an agent does not mention her status and deals with a third party without making it apparent that she is acting as an agent. In that case, the third party is entitled to sue the agent on the contract. That is fair, since the third party may have been influenced by the personal credit and character of the agent. What are the third party's rights if and when it discovers the existence and identity of the principal? If the contract was one that the agent had authority to make, the third party has the option of holding either principal or agent liable for performance of the contract, but not both. If the third party sues and obtains judgment against the agent before it learns of the real principal, it has no rights against the principal.[25] If, however, the fact of agency becomes known before judgment, the action may be discontinued, and fresh proceedings taken against the principal.

Rights of the Undisclosed Principal

An undisclosed principal can enforce a contract made with a third party on his behalf and with his authority.[26] To succeed, an undisclosed principal must show that the contract was made with his authority. If the agent had no real authority, the undisclosed principal cannot ratify the contract and enforce it. If he were allowed to do so, he would be in a position to choose whether to be bound by the contract. Nor can the third party hold the principal liable in such a case. See Figure 17.2 to compare contractual liability in various agency situations.

---

[23] See *QNS Paper Co v Chartwell Shipping Ltd* (1989), 62 DLR (4th) 36; *Lang Transport Ltd v Plus Factor International Trucking Ltd* (1997), 143 DLR (4th) 672.

[24] *Jade West Holdings Ltd v Canada Zau Fu Trade Ltd*, 2002 BCSC 420.

[25] *Kendall v Hamilton* (1879), 4 App Cas 504.

[26] A major exception to this rule are contracts that are essentially personal in nature: *Collins v Associated Greyhound Racecourses*, [1930] 1 Ch 1.

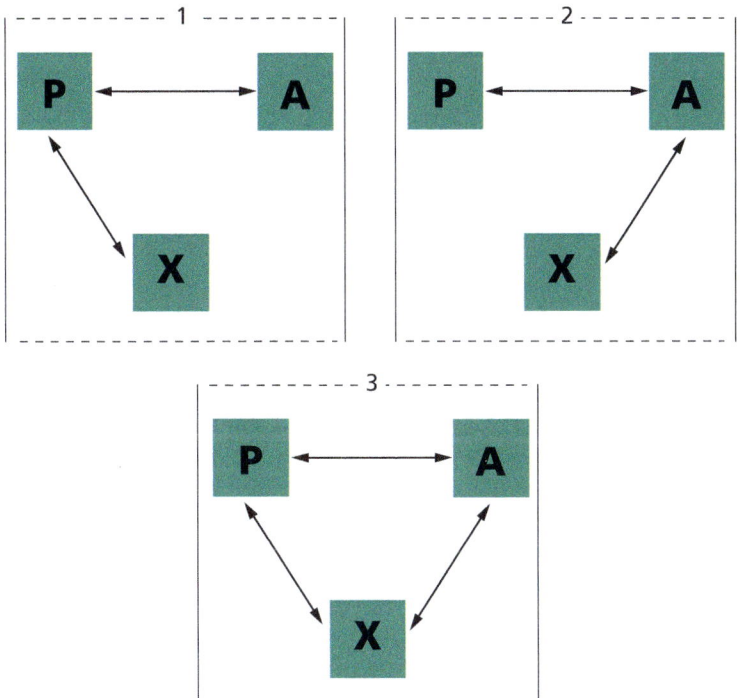

Figure 17.2   Liability on Agency Contract

(1), An agency contract exists between the principal (P) and the agent (A). A, acting within her authority, actual or apparent, negotiates a contract with a third person (X). That contract is legally formed between P and X. (2), A describes herself as principal and does not disclose the existence of P. The result is that the contract is between A and X. (3), A says nothing about her status as agent. X is entitled to assume that A was acting on her own account and can sue A. But if A was in fact acting on behalf of P, X can choose to sue P instead.

CASE 17.2   Neither Authority nor Knowledge

A Co. was a management company controlled by the owner of a shopping mall. It entered into a contract to rent an electronic sign from T for use in the shopping mall. Later, P Co. bought the mall; A Co. continued to manage the mall as its agent. T was unaware of the change of ownership. No mention of P Co.'s ownership was made when T and A Co. renewed the sign rental contract. P Co. refused to honour the contract and was sued by T. The British Columbia Court of Appeal held that P Co., the undisclosed principal, was not liable on the contract. The agent had no authority, and the plaintiff had no knowledge of the principal's existence. The plaintiff's right of recovery was limited to A Co.[27]

Liability for Torts

When an agent commits fraudulent misrepresentation during negotiations, even though the principal did not authorize the misrepresentation or had forbidden it, the third party may rescind the contract, just as if the principal had made the misrepresentation himself. If the agent was acting within her apparent authority, the third party may sue the principal as well as the agent for the tort of deceit.[28] An agent may be similarly liable to the third party for negligent misrepresentation.[29]

---

[27] *Sign-O-Lite Plastics Ltd v Metropolitan Life Insurance Co* (1990), 49 BCLR (2d) 183.

[28] *Lloyd v Grace, Smith & Co Ltd*, [1912] AC 716. If the principal was innocent of the fraud, he may in turn sue the agent for damages to compensate for the loss.

[29] See *Avery v Salie* (1972), 25 DLR (3d) 495; *Krawchuk v Scherbak* 2011 ONCA 352.

Generally, a principal is vicariously liable for torts committed by his agent while acting within the scope of her actual or apparent authority, whether the agent is an employee or an independent contractor.[30] As discussed in Chapter 4, the actual tortfeasor (the agent) remains liable for her torts, even though the principal is liable as well.

CASE 17.3 Vicarious Liability

D was contracted to sell annuities for an insurance company. He persuaded W to buy an annuity, and W paid the purchase money by cheque, made out to D. D did not purchase the annuity and instead ran off with the money. W sued the insurance company for return of the purchase money.

The court held the insurance company liable because (1) D received the money as its agent, acting within the scope of his authority to sell annuities; (2) D committed the tort of deceit, and the company was vicariously liable since D was acting within the scope of his agency contract; and (3) the company was directly liable for its own negligence in hiring D and putting him in a position of trust, because D had a known history of improper dealings.[31]

Breach of Warranty of Authority

No contract is formed when a person holds herself out to be an agent but has no authority, actual or apparent, and the named principal does not ratify. The situation may arise because the alleged agent has acted fraudulently; she may give the name of a reputable party as principal in order to obtain goods on credit. The seller may sue in tort for deceit against the fraudulent agent, though the action may not be worth pursuing. An action in tort will also lie where an agent makes a negligent misrepresentation that she has authority she does not possess.[32]

Breach of warranty of authority occurs when an agent creates the impression of agency when none exists.[33] An agent may innocently act without authority when she mistakenly believes she has the necessary authority, or, unknown to her, her principal has become bankrupt or insane or has died. No contract between a third party and the principal can be formed after the principal has lost contractual capacity or has ceased to exist. And no contract is formed between the agent and the third party either, because there was no intention that the agent should be a party to the contract. However, the third party may bring an action against the agent for breach of **warranty of authority**.

warranty of authority a person falsely represents that she has authority to contract on behalf of the principal

An agent may be liable if she acts expecting ratification by the principal that never occurs or if she contracts on behalf of a non-existent principal. These are examples of breach of warranty of authority. The damages will be the amount necessary to put the other party in the position in which he would have been had the warranty been true.[34]

CASE 17.4 Calculation of Damages

The plaintiff owned shares in a corporation of which he was the treasurer. He was dismissed from that position, and in the course of negotiations, the defendant, a solicitor, purportedly acting on behalf of the majority shareholders, made an offer to buy out the plaintiff's shares. The solicitor did not have authority to make the offer, and the majority shareholders refused to go through with the purchase. In the meantime, the shares were de-listed and became worthless.

The solicitor was held to be in breach of warranty of authority, and the plaintiff was entitled to damages representing his loss of bargain—namely, the difference between the price offered and their new value, which was zero.[35]

---

[30] *Thiessen v Mutual Life Assurance Co of Canada* (2002), 219 DLR (4th) 98. See also *Straus Estate v Decaire*, [2011] OJ No 737 at paras 48–56, aff'd 2012 ONCA 918.

[31] *Wilson v Clarica Life Insurance Co*, [2002] BCJ No 292.

[32] *Attis v Ontario*, 2011 ONCA 675 at para 18.

[33] *Alvin's Auto Service Ltd v Clew Holdings Ltd*, [1997] SJ No 387.

[34] *Attis*, supra note 32 at paras 19–20; *Delta Construction Co Ltd v Lidstone* (1979), 96 DLR (3d) 457.

[35] *Salter v Cormie* (1993), 108 DLR (4th) 372 (ABCA).

TERMINATING AN AGENCY RELATIONSHIP

An agent's authority may be terminated on any of the following situations:

- at the end of a time specified in the agency agreement
- at the completion of the particular project for which the agency was formed
- on notice by either the principal or the agent that he wishes to end the agency
- on the death or insanity of either the principal or the agent
- on the bankruptcy of the principal
- on an event that makes performance of the agency agreement impossible

Where no specific term is fixed for an agency relationship, it is implied that either party may end the relationship by giving reasonable notice to the other. If, however, the agreement is for a specified time, early withdrawal by either principal or agent without the consent of the other constitutes a breach of contract.

When an agency ends for reasons other than bankruptcy, death, or insanity of the principal, the principal should bring the termination to the attention of third parties likely to be affected.

FRANCHISING

Agency and franchising appear similar. Both are methods that permit a business to expand rapidly. In both, the proprietor of the original business—the principal or the franchisor—invokes the assistance of other persons or business entities to reach out to a wider public. Independent agents market the principal's products, just as franchisees market the franchisor's products. In law, however, there are important differences between the two relationships. Franchisees are not in an agency relationship with the franchisor.

The Nature of Franchising

Canada has the second largest franchise industry in the world, behind the United States.[36] Franchises account for close to 50 percent of all retail sales in Canada. Franchising is much more than just fast food; it spans business sectors from hotels and office supplies to real estate agencies, and car repairs.

Despite its economic importance, "franchising law" was slow to develop in Canada. In some provinces without legislation, the franchising law is still found in the general principles of contract and tort law and more specific areas of law, such as consumer protection and intellectual property law. Legislation governing franchising has been adopted in Alberta, Manitoba, Ontario, Prince Edward Island, New Brunswick, and British Columbia and is discussed later in this chapter.

In a franchising relationship, one party, the franchisor, grants a licence to the other party, the franchisee, to sell its product and use its name, trademark, and business model in return for payment of a franchise fee. However, a franchise normally amounts to considerably more than the mere granting of a licence. It involves a substantial degree of control by the franchisor over the operation of the franchisee's business. The franchisee, nevertheless, operates as an independent business and is not simply an

---

[36] For statistics on franchising, see http://www.franchise101.net/canadian-franchise-statistics.

employee or agent of the franchisor. It does not sell or contract "on behalf" of the franchisor. As described by one judge:

> [F]ranchising promises to provide the independent merchant with the means to become an efficient and effective competitor of large integrated firms. Through various forms of franchising, the manufacturer is assured qualified and effective outlets for his products, and the franchisee enjoys backing in the form of know-how and financial assistance.[37]

When it operates well, franchising provides benefits to both the franchisor and the franchisee. However, "to say that franchising is a risky business is, if anything, an understatement."[38]

In theory, franchises offer the investor an opportunity to reduce the risk of failure by adopting a proven business concept, and it is true that franchises tend to fail less frequently than independent businesses that are started from scratch. But franchising is not a guarantee of success, and potential investors need to do their homework carefully.

Contents of a Typical Franchising Agreement

A franchise is created when the franchisor and franchisee enter into a contract, referred to as the **franchise agreement**. Since the franchisor normally makes a substantial number of such agreements—Subway has more than 20 000 franchises worldwide, including more than 2000 in Canada alone—whereas the franchisee normally enters into only one such agreement, the agreement is usually the franchisor's standard form contract, often accompanied by a disclosure statement and an operating manual for the franchisee. Typically, the agreement will deal with the following subjects.

franchise agreement an agreement under which a franchisor grants to the franchisee a right to market the franchisor's products

Consideration Provided by the Franchisor
The essential feature of the agreement is the grant to the franchisee of a right, or licence, to sell goods or services supplied by or made to specifications provided by the franchisor. The agreement further allows the franchisee to use trademarks, trade names, logos, secret processes, and so on that belong to the franchisor.

Although the above features are also found in simple licensing agreements, a franchise agreement goes further. It normally provides for training the franchisee in the operation of the business and for ongoing supervision, assistance, and management services. The franchisor frequently assists in the design of the business premises—usually to a standard design—and in establishing accounting, inventory control, and purchasing systems. It is also common for the franchisor to provide financial assistance to the franchisor through loans or guarantees.

Franchising lets independent entrepreneurs take advantage of well-known and widely recognized trade names and reputations. The franchisor usually undertakes to provide advertising and promotion on a national or regional scale. The franchisee's rights are limited to a geographic area.

Consideration Provided by the Franchisee
The franchisee is required to provide an initial contribution of capital. The size of the contribution varies widely, according to whether premises and equipment are purchased (and perhaps custom built) or leased from the franchisor or from some other person. Additionally, the franchisee agrees to pay for the services and assistance provided by the franchisor. Normally, there is an initial franchise fee, and there are ongoing payments, which may take the form of a percentage of the revenues of the franchise, rentals for premises or equipment, payments for management services, or contributions to the cost of advertising campaigns.

---

[37] *United States v Arnold, Schwinn & Co*, 388 U.S. 365 (1967) at 386.

[38] *Country Style Food Services Inc v Hotoyan*, [2001] OJ No 2889.

Franchisors also earn revenue from exclusive supply arrangements. Sometimes, the franchisee acts as a retailer for products manufactured or supplied by the franchisor; the franchisee normally agrees to sell only the franchisor's products. In other franchises, the franchisor primarily sells an idea or a process; the actual goods sold to the public may be manufactured locally according to a set formula, and usually the franchisee purchases the components only from suppliers approved by the franchisor.

Conduct of the Business
A franchise agreement commonly provides for a substantial degree of supervision by the franchisor. The franchisee must agree to give the franchisor right of access to carry out inspections as well as to provide proper accounts and regular information. Usually, the franchisee is required to promise that the business will be carried on only in accordance with the franchisor's regular operating instructions and that no other competing business will be carried on by the franchisee. Since it is the franchisor's reputation that is the basis of the arrangement, the franchisee also promises to protect the goodwill, trademarks, and trade secrets of the franchisor. A franchise agreement may also include expensive obligations to renovate or redecorate premises in accordance with the franchisor's specifications. Participation in the franchisor's online program will require the franchisor to coordinate websites, share data, and maintain security.

CASE 17.5 Breach of Contract

Robin's Foods was a franchisor of doughnut stores. A numbered Ontario corporation owned one of the franchises. The numbered corporation, in addition to operating the franchise, supplied wholesale doughnuts to other shops for resale. The packaging did not identify the doughnuts as Robin's doughnuts, and the doughnut mix used was not the same mix required by Robin's. The sale of the wholesale doughnuts was done secretly on a cash basis and not recorded in the accounts provided to Robin's.

The court ruled that the secret activity constituted a breach of the franchising agreement, entitling Robin's to treat the agreement as terminated.[39]

Termination of the Franchise
Serious breaches of the franchising agreement amount to repudiation of the agreement, allowing the other party to treat it as terminated. Additionally, the agreement normally contains detailed provisions regarding the duration and termination of the relationship. Franchising usually involves a substantial investment by both parties and an expectation that the relationship will continue for a number of years. Consequently, the agreement typically provides for a long fixed term, followed with an option to renew, and requires a substantial period of notice to terminate, with penalties for premature termination.

To protect the franchisor against assignment of the franchise to an unsuitable operator, the franchise agreement normally stipulates that any assignment of the franchisee's interest may only be made with the consent of the franchisor.[40]

Restrictive Covenants
Franchises are usually territorial in nature. A franchisee is assigned a particular area—a county, city, or part of a city—in which to operate, and the franchisor often undertakes not to grant any other franchise within the same territory. In return, the franchisee agrees not to carry on business outside that territory.

An obvious risk taken by franchisors is that their franchisees, having operated a franchise successfully, will gain valuable experience and information, and establish relationships with customers and suppliers that they will take to an independent business of their own. To guard against this danger, the franchisee is normally required to execute a non-competition agreement stating that it will not, for a given number of years after termination of the agreement, carry on a similar or competing business

---

[39] *1017933 Ontario Ltd v Robin's Foods Inc*, [1998] OJ No 1110.
[40] See *Kentucky Fried Chicken Canada v Scott's Food Services Inc* (1998), 41 BLR (2d) 42.

within a stipulated radius from the franchise location. As noted in Chapter 8, such covenants may be unenforceable if they are an unreasonable restraint on trade.

Intellectual Property Rights   Intellectual property involves things such as trademarks, copyright, patents, and industrial designs, as discussed in Chapter 20. Protection of these rights is at the heart of a franchisor's business and the value of the franchise. Agreements will describe these intangible assets and reserve ownership to the franchisor, restrict use by the franchisee to activities within the franchise business, and prohibit copying, variation, or misuse of these assets. The computer operating system will be among these assets. Franchisees will not be allowed to install unapproved software into the system for fear it will be incompatible with or corrupt the system. The agreement will specify requirements for software, hardware, and security. These costs are most often at the expense of the franchisee, at times designated by the franchisor.

CASE 17.6   Non-Competition Agreement

Hohnjec had been the holder of a franchise granted by Yesac Foods to operate a restaurant in Barrie, Ontario. Subsequently, after termination of the franchise, Hohnjec opened a restaurant in Toronto. The new restaurant was not similar in concept to the Yesac franchise.

Yesac sought to enforce a provision in the franchise agreement, which purported to prevent the franchisee from engaging "in any other business . . . related to the food, beverage or restaurant business." The court held that the clause, which had no time or geographical limitations, was invalid and unenforceable.[41]

Dispute Resolution   Franchising agreements are intended to run for a number of years and contain a substantial number of provisions, each of which could become the subject of dispute. To avoid the expense and the possible ill will involved in litigation, it is not uncommon for franchise agreements to contain a provision adopting alternative dispute resolution methods. Such a provision may, for example, oblige the parties to submit to mediation before the contract may be terminated for alleged breach by one of the parties.[42] Franchisees often resort to class actions to resolve common disputes.

ILLUSTRATION 17.4   Class Actions

The Great White North Franchisee Association is a group representing over half of the North American Tim Hortons franchisees. They took the unusual move of launching two separate multimillion-dollar class actions against Tim Hortons owner Restaurants Brand International Inc. (RBI), within one year. The first class action, commenced in June 2017, claimed $500 million in damages from RBI and that four of its top executives mismanaged the Tim Hortons advertising fund. In October 2017, a second class action for $850 million claimed that RBI was trying to intimidate franchisees so they would not join the Association and attempting to strip franchises from the franchisees who founded the group.[43] Central to the second class action is any legislative right to associate. Neither action is certified at the time of this writing, and an earlier 2012 Ontario action alleging Tim Hortons mismanagement was denied certification.[44] Still, it is easy to wonder how much damage is done to the value of the franchise by such large scale public feuding between franchisee and franchisor.

---

[41] *Yesac Creative Foods Inc v Hohnjec* (1985), 6 CPR (3d) 398. See also *Kardish Food Franchising Corp v 874073 Ontario Inc*, [1995] OJ No 2849; *Cash Converters Pty Ltd v Armstrong*, [1997] OJ No 2659; *Nutrilawn International Inc v Stewart*, [1999] OJ No 643.

[42] See e.g. *Toronto Truck Centre Ltd v Volvo Trucks Canada Inc* (1998), 163 DLR (4th) 740; *Ellis v Subway Franchise Systems of Canada Ltd*, [2000] OJ No 3849 (where the contract provided for arbitration in the state of Connecticut).

[43] Hollie Shaw, "Tim Hortons franchisees sue corporate parent for $850M alleging bullying and intimidation," Oct 6, 2017, http://business.financialpost.com/news/retail-marketing/tim-hortons-franchisees-sue-corporate-parent-for-850m-alleging-bullying-and-intimidation.

[44] *Fairview Donut Inc v The TDL Grp Corp*, 2012 ONCA 867.

> **CHECKLIST**
>
> ## Contents of a Typical Franchise Agreement
>
> Franchise agreements usually cover the following:
> - activity and geographic limits of the franchise
> - services to be provided by franchisor (training, management services, advertising, etc.)
> - licensing of trademarks, know-how, etc.
> - provision of financial assistance
> - capital to be provided by franchisee
> - franchise fee
> - ongoing payments by franchisee (percentage of receipts, payments for services, etc.)
> - arrangements for supply of materials and inventory
> - provisions governing conduct of business (supervision, accounting, renovations, etc.)
> - duration of relationship
> - termination of relationship (notice, restrictions on assignment, penalties, etc.)
> - restrictive covenants—confidentiality, and non-competition and non-solicitation agreements
> - covenants relating to intellectual property and system operation
> - procedures for resolving disputes

Legal Relationships Created by Franchising

The relationship between franchisor and franchisee is a contractual one between independent entrepreneurs. The Supreme Court of Canada has held that the relationship between the parties is not fiduciary.[45] Nevertheless, the ongoing nature of the relationship imposes a duty of good faith on both parties—requiring prompt, honest, fair, and reasonable dealings with each other[46] and actions to protect and enhance the value of the brand.[47]

In particular:

> Part of the obligations in this special relationship with the franchisee includes a positive obligation to disclose accurate financial information to a prospective franchisee at the time of entering into a franchise agreement. Misrepresentations may result from silence or omissions.[48]

> **CASE 17.7** Franchisor Misrepresentation
>
> Neish entered into a franchise agreement with Melenchuk. He received financial statements that purported to be historical records for the franchise. In fact, the records did not relate to the particular outlet but rather were reconstructed records of other outlets. The records significantly misrepresented the profit and loss situation of the outlet. Neish's bank provided financing based on the financial records provided.
>
> Subsequently, Neish had to borrow more money to keep the business alive. When he could not borrow any further, he abandoned the business. He brought an action seeking compensation for his losses.
>
> The court found that there was no evidence that Melenchuk knew the records were actually misleading so as to constitute fraud. However, he had been negligent in putting the records together and was liable for negligent misrepresentation and breach of contract. Neish was entitled to damages for his lost investment.[49]

---

[45] *Jirna Ltd v Mister Donut of Canada Ltd* (1973), 40 DLR (3d) 303.

[46] *Shelanu Inc v Print Three Franchising Corp* (2003), 226 DLR (4th) 577; *Healy v Canadian Tire Corp*, 2012 ONSC 77 (two-way street).

[47] *Allied Domecq Retailing International Canada Ltd v Bertico Inc*, 2015 QCCA 624 at paras 30–32.

[48] *Machias v Mr Submarine Ltd*, [2002] OJ No 1261.

[49] *Neish v Melenchuk* (1993), 120 NSR (2d) 239. See also *Nutrilawn International Inc v Stewart*, *supra* note 41.

With respect to customers, franchising is entirely different from agency. The franchisee contracts with members of the public on its own behalf, not as agent for the franchisor. There is no contract between the customer and the franchisor, though the franchisor might be considered, in some cases, as having held out the franchisee as having authority to act on its behalf and consequently be estopped from denying an agency relationship. When defective goods have been manufactured or supplied by the franchisor, it may, of course, be liable in tort.

Various Franchise Models

We tend to think of franchising in one way—someone contracts directly with the franchisor to operate one or more single units within a designated territory. However, other models exist involving intermediaries. Area representatives may be designated to recruit franchisees within a territory; these recruiters would execute distinct representation agreements. Alternatively, master franchisees may be authorized to actually award unit franchises to new sub-franchisees within their territory. Tim Hortons and Burger King follow this model of master and sub-franchisees, which require master franchisees to enforce standards of the franchise operation.[50]

Franchise Legislation

At least six provinces—Alberta, Manitoba, Ontario, Prince Edward Island, New Brunswick, and British Columbia—have legislation regulating franchises operated within their province.[51] The purpose of the legislation, as described by the courts, is "to protect the franchisee," and this has resulted in broad and generous interpretation in favour of the franchisee.[52] The most important features of these laws, which are broadly similar, are as follows.

Mandatory Franchisor Disclosure
Franchisors are required to give every prospective franchisee a copy of the franchisor's disclosure document at least 14 days before the signing of a franchise agreement or the payment of any consideration.[53] The disclosure document must comply with the requirements of regulations. It must give specified information about the business, the franchisor, the franchisor's associates, and the franchise system, including financial statements and reports (s 4 [AB]; s 5 [MB, ON, PEI, NB, BC]) plus any other material facts that may "significantly" affect the price of the franchise.[54] Disclosure must be updated to inform of material changes between the time of first disclosure and agreement execution. Information must be site specific to the territory under consideration.[55]

---

[50] Restaurant Brands International Inc., 2016 Annual Report to the United States Securities and Exchange Commission Form 10-K , p. 15, http://www.rbi.com/Cache/1500096187.PDF?O=PDF&T=&Y=&D=&FID=1500096187&iid=4591210.

[51] *Franchises Act*, RSA 2000, c F-23; *The Franchise Act*, CCSM c F156; *Arthur Wishart Act (Franchise Disclosure)*, SO 2000, c 3; *Franchises Act*, RSPEI 1998, c F-14.1; *Franchises Act*, SNB 2007, c F-23.5; *Franchises Act*, SBC 2015 c 35. Quebec has some provisions in its *Civil Code*.

[52] *6792341 Canada Inc v Dollar IT Limited*, 2009 ONCA 385 at para 72; *Addison Chevrolet Buick v General Motors of Canada*, 2016 ONCA 324; *405341 Ontario Ltd v Midas Canada Inc*, 2010 ONCA 478.

[53] Ontario legislative exceptions for confidentiality agreements are pending. *Cutting Unnecessary Red Tape Act, 2017*, SO 2017, c 20, Sch 9.

[54] *Arthur Wishart Act*, supra note 51, s 1(1); It is not possible to contract out of the legislative disclosure requirement; *MAA Diners Inc v 3 for 1 Pizza & Wings (Canada) Inc*, [2003] OJ No 430, aff'd [2004] OJ No 297 (QL).

[55] *Mendoza v Active Tire & Auto Centre Inc*, 2017 ONCA 471 (considering s 6(2) of *Arthur Wishart Act*, supra note 51), but see *MDG Kingston Inc et al v MDG Computers Canada Inc et al* (2008), 92 OR (3d) 4 (ONCA) (considering the effect of inadequate disclosure on the franchise agreements arbitration clause).

Failure to provide the required disclosure gives the franchisee the right to rescind the agreement within two years; unsigned disclosure is not disclosure.[56] Misrepresentations in the document entitle the franchisee to compensation from the franchisor and impose personal liability on the officers or directors who have signed the disclosure document. Courts look for strict technical compliance with disclosure requirements.[57] The disclosure requirements generally do not apply in the case of a sale between franchisees.

CASE 17.8 Prior Disclosure

The franchisor made general non-site-specific disclosure to a prospective franchisee, which qualified renovation cost estimates subject to variables specific to the eventual site. The franchise agreement was signed before the site was chosen. The agreement allowed for the franchisee's active participation in the site selection and gave the franchisee the right to opt out of the agreement with a full refund if it did not like the selected site. The site was picked and renovated. After operating in the location for a few months, the franchisee wanted out. The trial court allowed rescission of the franchise agreement, saying the non-site-specific disclosure was so deficient that it amounted to no disclosure at all. The Court of Appeal overruled the lower court, saying the franchisor had provided the franchisee with sufficient information to make an informed decision.[58] In reaction to this decision, the Ontario legislation is being amended to remove site designation and confidentiality agreements from the prior disclosure requirement.[59]

Fair Dealing All acts say that a franchise agreement imposes a duty of fair dealing in its performance and enforcement on each party (s 7 [AB.]; s 3 [MB, ON, PEI, NB, BC]). This probably does no more than codify the common law duty of good faith.[60]

Right to Associate In the past, some franchisors have tried by various means to prevent their franchisees from getting together to "compare notes" and, perhaps, to take class action against what are perceived to be unfair practices. The Acts (s 8 [AB]; s 4 [MB, ON, PEI, NB, BC]) expressly recognize a "right of association" among franchisees; a franchisor may not prohibit or restrict its franchisees from forming an organization and may not penalize them in any way for doing so.

No Waiver Most provincial legislation blocks any attempt to restrict application of the legislation by voiding any contractual term that ousts the law of the province or waives the rights given under the statutes (s 16 [AB], s 13 [BC] s 11 [MB, NB, PEI, ON]). There is some uncertainty about whether this non-waiver will void mandatory arbitration clauses and class action waivers. A clause requiring disputes to be resolved by individual arbitration may be viewed as a waiver of the right to associate;[61] however, the express legislative intent to preserve the right to court access in the face of contractual choice of arbitration is lacking.[62]

---

[56] Peter Dillon, "Canada: It's Like Watching a Car Crash in Slow Motion" (2017) 37(2) Franchise LJ,265 at 282–84.

[57] *Ibid.*

[58] *Raibex Canada Ltd v ASWR Franchising Corp*, 2018 ONCA 62.

[59] *Cutting Unnecessary Red Tape Act, 2017*, supra note 53.

[60] See *Machias v Mr Submarine Ltd*, supra note 48.

[61] *405341 Ontario Ltd v Midas Canada Inc*, supra note 52.

[62] *1146845 Ontario Inc v Pillar to Post Inc*, 2014 ONSC 7400; See *MDG Kingston Inc et al v MDG Computers Canada Inc et al*, supra note 55 (arbitration clauses must meet the ADR disclosure requirement—or are subject to a right to rescind).

INTERNATIONAL ISSUE
Foreign Franchisors

The location of a franchisee's business or territory determines the application of provincial legislation. If the franchise territory is in the province, then the provincial legislative rights and requirements apply no matter where the franchisor is located.

A franchisor or the franchisor's associate (an entity that controls the franchisor) may be a foreign corporation or may be taken over by a foreign corporation during the term of the franchise agreement. Such was the case for Tim Hortons franchisees. In 2014 the iconic Canadian brand merged with Burger King under Restaurant Brands International Inc., a Canadian multinational firm, controlled by 3G Capital, a Brazilian investment company. This major merger in the Canadian fast-food industry required Competition Bureau approval to protect competition in the industry and approval by Investment Canada to assess the impact of foreign control over a Canadian business. The merger easily obtained Competition Bureau approval, but Investment Canada attached the following conditions to the merger, some specifically addressing the risk to franchisees:

- to work with Tim Hortons franchisees to maintain 100 percent of existing employment levels at Tim Hortons franchises across Canada;
- to expand Tim Hortons by opening new restaurants, both in the United States and globally, at a significantly greater pace than currently planned;
- to establish the headquarters of the new company (formed by Tim Hortons and Burger King) in Oakville, Ontario, to maintain significant employment levels at that facility and to list the company on the TSX;
- to manage Tim Hortons as a distinct brand, without co-branding of any locations in Canada or in the United States;
- to maintain the Canadian franchisee rent and royalty structure at current levels for a five-year period;
- to maintain 100 percent of Tim Hortons's current charitable work and involvement in communities across Canada; and
- to have Canadians comprise at least 50 percent of the membership of the Tim Hortons brand Board of Directors.[63]

Franchisee dissatisfaction is running high following the merger. In addition to launching the two class actions discussed in Illustration 17.4, franchisees pressured Investment Canada to investigate non-compliance with the above described conditions specifically related to store renovation plans and response to minimum wage hikes.[64]

Questions to Consider

1. Is Investment Canada the right body to protect domestic franchisees from abuse by foreign franchisors?
2. Should franchise legislation be amended to improve protection for franchisees when control of the franchisor changes? If so, what measures would you propose?

Strategies to Manage the Legal Risks

It is best for both principal and agent to have a written, signed copy of an agency agreement in order to minimize future misunderstandings about the terms of the arrangement. Neither should rely on principles of implied or apparent authority. Where the actual authority of an agent varies from that expected or usual in the industry, a principal should publicize the restrictions to those dealing with his agent. This will reduce the likelihood of liability for unwanted contracts based upon apparent authority.

Agents should protect themselves from unwanted liability by ensuring that their agency contract includes indemnification by the principal and that any exclusion clause in the third party's contract expressly refers to agents. Care should be taken when signing documents to ensure that the agent's representative status is disclosed to third

---

[63] Competition Bureau Canada, Press Release, Oct 28, 2014, http://www.competitionbureau.gc.ca/eic/site/cb-bc.nsf/eng/03828.html; Industry Minister Statement, Dec 4, 2014, https://www.canada.ca/en/news/archive/2014/12/statement-industry-minister-james-moore-proposed-acquisition-tim-hortons-burger-king.html?_ga=2.163841535.196302086.1523730195-36307786.1523730195.

[64] Adam Burns & Ian Bickis, "Ottawa probing Tim Hortons franchisee dispute with RBI," The Canadian Press, April 14, 2018, http://nationalpost.com/pmn/news-pmn/canada-news-pmn/ottawa-probing-tim-hortons-franchisee-claims-rbi-failing-to-honour-commitments.

parties, even where the name of the principal is not. Finally, as an agent is a fiduciary, conflicts of interest must be avoided. Agents should not act for both parties, even if both consent. If conflicts arise with the agent's own interests or those with whom he is connected, immediate disclosure to all persons affected is necessary.

Franchising agreements are typically standard form contracts prepared by the franchisor and presented to the franchisee on a take-it-or-leave-it basis. Therefore, franchisees must examine the terms carefully before agreeing. Often there are onerous fees for advertising. Regular capital expenditures will be required to keep physical and electronic systems in conformity with the franchisor standards. Disclosure requirements in those provinces with legislation may give an uninformed franchisor an option to rescind. This will not be the case in other provinces.

Franchisors must treat the protection of their intellectual property as a priority. This property is at the heart of the value of each franchise. Chapter 20 describes the steps necessary to establish ownership in copyrights, trademarks, and patents. Agreements must preserve ownership and restrict use to only that authorized. Proprietary interests in software systems for the operation of the franchise are no less important than the logos. Agreements should ensure that electronic data generated by the franchisee is shared with the franchisor. Such data provide valuable strategic planning information.

QUESTIONS FOR REVIEW

1. Distinguish between dependent agents and independent agents.
2. Is a "real estate agent" a true agent?
3. What is a power of attorney?
4. What is the effect when a principal ratifies a contract made on its behalf by an agent who lacked the authority to enter into the contract?
5. What are the limits of ratification by a principal?
6. How does an agent acquire actual authority?
7. How does an agent acquire apparent authority?
8. What is meant by "holding out"?
9. Is an agent entitled to delegate her duties to some other person?
10. Why should an agent not act for both parties to a transaction? What are the probable legal consequences of doing so?
11. In what circumstances may an agent be held liable on a contract that he has negotiated?
12. Can an undisclosed principal enforce a contract made on her behalf?
13. What is meant by "breach of warranty of authority"?
14. Distinguish between a franchise and a licence.
15. What restrictions are usually placed on a franchisee carrying on other business activities?
16. What is the relationship between a franchisor and the eventual customer of the franchisee?
17. Is the relationship between franchisor and franchisee a fiduciary relationship?
18. What are the principal additional protections given to franchisees by the Alberta, Ontario, PEI, and New Brunswick legislation?

CASES AND PROBLEMS

1. Continuing Scenario

   Gail and Kevin are frequent guests at Ashley's restaurant. Karen is their favourite server because she allows them to substitute different menu items without charge and sometimes even arranges custom take-out menus. Therefore, when they became engaged, they went to talk to Karen about catering the wedding. They knew Ashley's restaurant did catering because it was advertised on the menus. Karen agreed to sit down with them and plan the menu even though this was not her job—Ashley negotiated all the catering contracts herself. Karen had packed and served many catered menus, and she knew what the restaurant could do. She let Gail and Kevin look at a catering menu the restaurant was putting together for another client that weekend. They loved everything on it, and Karen told them the same price as the existing order. Gail and Kevin agreed to the price, so Karen took a $200 deposit and wrote the date in the restaurant's calendar. When Ashley returned, Karen told her about the order. Ashley was not happy with Karen's behaviour and told her not to do it again. Two days later Ashley looked at the calendar and realized the restaurant had too many orders to fill for that weekend and told Karen they could not cater Gail and Kevin's wedding. Has a contract been formed? With whom? Explain your answer.

2. Halloran entered into a contract with Scallop Petroleum Ltd. to manage one of Scallop's gas stations. The contract set out detailed arrangements for the operation of the station. It provided that all inventory should be the property of Scallop until sold and that all proceeds of sale belonged to Scallop, out of which Halloran was to receive a fixed percentage as commission. Halloran was required to maintain two bank accounts, to pay all sales receipts into one of those accounts, and to provide Scallop with regular records of all transactions.

   Initially things worked well. Then Halloran became less diligent in furnishing accounts, and Scallop began to notice various other irregularities. Halloran's records were inadequate, and an investigation revealed a shortfall in the sales account of about $80 000, which appeared to have accrued over more than a year. Scallop suspected Halloran of theft, and the police were called in. Their investigation was inconclusive; it seemed probable that the money had been stolen by a former employee of Halloran, who could not be traced.

   Halloran was cleared of all involvement in the theft. However, it became clear that he had not been operating the station in accordance with the instructions set out in the contract. For example, he had been keeping cash and credit card receipts in a freezer and in a locked tin box, instead of paying them into the bank as required.

   Scallop gave Halloran notice that it was terminating their relationship; it refused to pay Halloran commission on the previous month's sales, and brought an action against him for the balance of the $80 000.

   Is Scallop entitled to succeed?

3. Da Silva entered into a franchising agreement with Snacks Unlimited Ltd. to operate a fast-food outlet in Regina. Under the contract, the store was to make and sell hot dogs and hamburgers, the ingredients were to be of a specified quality, and the products were to be made to uniform standards. The premises were to be equipped and maintained according to a prescribed format and would have the decor and distinctive sign of "Snacks." Large sales were anticipated since Snacks was already a well-known operation and had carried on extensive advertising.

   The franchising agreement signed by Da Silva required him to do five things:
   - pay a franchise fee of $40 000
   - pay a royalty of 2 percent on gross sales
   - pay an annual fee of $10 000 for advertising services provided by Snacks

- buy his store equipment from Snacks
- buy his ingredients from sources indicated by Snacks

The agreement set out detailed provisions about how the business was to be conducted and concluded with the words, "The relationship between the parties is only that of independent contractors. No partnership, joint venture, or relationship of principal and agent is intended."

Da Silva operated the business successfully for two years and showed a reasonable profit. Last year, he discovered that the firms from whom he was required to purchase his supplies were paying substantial rebates to Snacks. On the question of whether he had paid prices higher than the prevailing market prices for comparable supplies, it was difficult to generalize. For some materials, this was true; for others, he paid much the same price, and in some instances even a somewhat lower price. In any event, Snacks had instructed all the suppliers to have no dealings or negotiations with its franchisees that might indicate the true nature of the arrangements made with them for rebates.

Da Silva sued Snacks for an accounting of these undisclosed profits and rebates and an order requiring them to be paid over to him.

Discuss the merits of his case, and indicate with reasons whether his action should succeed.

4. On a number of occasions over the past two years, Longhaul Transport Ltd. had carried goods belonging to Factorplus Products Inc. The shipments were arranged by a broker, Transshipments Inc. Longhaul invoiced Transshipments, which in turn invoiced Factorplus. The normal procedure was for Transshipments to pay Longhaul out of funds received by it from Factorplus. Longhaul was aware that the goods belonged to Factorplus and was under the mistaken impression that Transshipments was simply a division or subsidiary of Factorplus, rather than an independent broker.

Following one major shipment, Longhaul invoiced Transshipments but was not paid; Transshipments had received no payment from Factorplus in respect of the shipment and refused to pay the shipping charges.

Advise Longhaul whether it should sue (a) Transshipments, (b) Factorplus, or (c) both.

5. Strauss, an experienced business administrator, became unemployed six years ago when his firm "downsized." He decided to set up his own business. He was interested in the lawn care business and thought that a franchised operation provided the best chance for quick success.

After examining a number of lawn care franchises, Strauss concluded that a firm called Sodmaster Inc. was the franchisor best suited to his requirements. Strauss contacted Sodmaster and had several discussions with the area manager for Eastern Ontario. Strauss was provided with a vast amount of information about Sodmaster's operations, including various projections of costs and profits based on the operation of other Sodmaster franchises. Strauss also visited other franchisees and talked with them about their experiences.

According to the financial projections in the booklet given to him by Sodmaster, a franchise with a gross annual revenue of $200 000 would normally make a small loss (after allowing for a modest management fee); one with revenue of $400 000 would show a reasonable profit, and one with revenue of $800 000 or more would show an excellent profit. Potential franchisees were warned that it was unusual to break even in the first year of operation. The projections were essentially accurate, based on the actual experience of Sodmaster franchises, though the booklet failed to say that only one of the franchises actually grossed more than $800 000 per year.

Strauss also made his own projections of his probable revenues and decided to go ahead and purchase a franchise for Frontenac County, Ontario. He agreed to pay a franchise fee of $40 000 ($25 000 payable immediately and the balance after two years) and to pay royalties of 6 percent on gross revenues. He also entered into the usual restrictive covenants not to carry on a competing business within 30 km of the franchise area for a period of five years after termination of the franchise. In order to get started, Strauss borrowed money on the security of his home and, in all, invested about $100 000 of his own money.

The business did not work out nearly as well as Strauss had expected. In his first year, he had sales of only $60 000 (when he had anticipated twice that figure), and he made a loss of $75 000. The second year's sales reached $100 000 (with a loss of $12 000); by the third year, sales had risen to $180 000, still with a small loss; in the fourth and fifth years, Strauss's sales levelled out at a little more than $200 000, and he was still making a loss.

Because of his financial problems, Strauss never paid the remaining $15 000 owing on the franchise fee, and he also fell behind early on in the payment of the royalties. Eventually Sodmaster informed Strauss that they would not be prepared to renew the franchise at the end of its five-year term. Strauss then abandoned the franchise and set up his own lawn care business in the same area.

Sodmaster brought an action against Strauss, claiming payment of the balance of the franchise fee, the unpaid royalties, and an injunction to restrain the breach of the restrictive covenant. Strauss counterclaimed for damages, alleging he had been misled into entering into the franchise agreement in the first place. Who should succeed? Would your answer change if only 18 months had passed?

Chapter 18
The Contract of Employment

- DEVELOPMENT OF EMPLOYMENT LAW
- RELATIONSHIP OF EMPLOYER AND EMPLOYEE
- EMPLOYMENT RELATIONSHIP AT COMMON LAW
- THE EMPLOYER'S LIABILITY TO THIRD PERSONS
- NOTICE OF TERMINATION OF INDIVIDUAL EMPLOYMENT CONTRACTS
- DISMISSAL WITHOUT NOTICE
- WRONGFUL DISMISSAL
- EMPLOYEE WELFARE LEGISLATION
- COLLECTIVE BARGAINING
- LABOUR DISPUTES
- THE LEGAL STATUS OF TRADE UNIONS
- STRATEGIES TO MANAGE THE LEGAL RISKS

Employers contract with employees either individually or collectively in unionized workplaces. Modern legislation provides protection for workers, as do trade unions, with the collective bargaining process and the system of regulation in place to facilitate resolving disputes.

In this chapter we examine such questions as:

- What is the difference between an employer's liability in contract and in tort?
- What are the grounds for dismissal "with cause"?
- What is "wrongful dismissal," and what are its consequences?
- What are the effects of human rights requirements, and pay and employment equity statutes?
- What are the consequences of regulation on general working conditions?

- How is mandatory retirement affected by the *Canadian Charter of Rights and Freedoms*?
- How are employment conditions affected by workers' compensation and occupational health regulations?
- What are the implications of a collective agreement for the individual employee?
- What is the legal status of trade unions?

DEVELOPMENT OF EMPLOYMENT LAW

The principles of modern employment law come from the common law rules defining the **relationship of master and servant**. This law developed long ago when the employer (master) always had separate contracts with each employee (servant); welfare legislation and trade unions were unknown. Today, the individual contract of employment remains the most common form of employment relationship, but the economic and social changes of the past century have changed the employment relationship in two respects:

relationship of master and servant the contractual relationship between an employer and an employee

- First, legislation sets minimum standards for safe and fair working conditions that override any contractual terms; this branch of the law as is known as employee welfare legislation.
- Second, employees may organize into trade unions and collectively negotiate one agreement; a separate body of law known as labour law or the law of collective bargaining governs the relationship between employers, trade unions, and the employee members.

This chapter deals with individual employment relationships, employee welfare legislation, and collective bargaining.

We cannot cite all the relevant statutes in the space available, and employment law changes frequently. Therefore, the chapter gives only a general overview of the law. More detail can be found in the resources cited in the footnotes.[1]

RELATIONSHIP OF EMPLOYER AND EMPLOYEE

Compared with Agency

The relationship of employer and employee is established by a contract that gives one party, the employer, authority to direct and control the work of the other party, the employee. The services that are contracted for may or may not include making contracts with third parties as agent for the employer.

The same person is often both an employee and an agent. For example, a purchasing agent for a company has the responsibility to order goods on the company's credit and has authority to do so within the limits of her agency. She is also a company employee and subject to the direction of management. Other employees may have limited duties as agents of their employer: The driver of a delivery truck is an employee who may only act as an agent when taking the truck into a garage for servicing and binding the employer to pay the charges. In many types of employment,

---

[1] See J.R. Sproat, *Wrongful Dismissal Handbook*, 7th ed. (Toronto: Thomson Canada, 2015); W. Rayner, *Canadian Collective Bargaining Law*, 3rd ed. (Toronto: Carswell, 2017).

an employee—a lathe operator, for instance—has no reason to enter into contracts on behalf of the employer and no authority, express or implied, to do so.

An agent may have no recourse against a principal that terminates the agreement without notice. By contrast, an employee, as we shall see, often has a right of action for damages for wrongful dismissal in comparable circumstances.

Both principals and employers may be liable in tort for the acts of their agents and employees, respectively. For various reasons—some historical and some related to the different functions of agents and employees—the liability of an employer may be wider than that of a principal; the basis for vicarious liability is not the same for principals and employers. Accordingly, when a third party is injured, it may be important to establish whether the wrongdoer was acting as an employee, an agent of a firm, or an independent contractor.

Compared with Contractors

Contractors may be dependent or independent. An **independent contractor** agrees to do a specified task within a specific time, such as building a house. Contractors are not employees because the contractor is free from the supervision and control of the person engaging him. His job is to complete a specified result within a specific time, but he may do so in his own way. Whether an individual is an employee or independent contractor will depend upon the level of control over the task, the ability to work for others (exclusivity), and the financial importance of this client to the contractor (economic dependence). The checklist below lists factors used to assess the level of independence and exclusivity in a relationship.

independent contractor contractors that is not exclusive, permanent, and economically dependent on one client

CHECKLIST
Characteristics of Independent Contractors

- hired to complete a task or deliver a result for a fee
- owns the tools necessary to do the work
- controls hours and time of work
- controls how the work is done
- may work for others
- no tax, pension, benefit, or government deductions withheld from payment
- invoices for work done and charges GST/HST
- pays own expenses
- assumes the risk of profit or loss[2]

Independent contractors do not receive any of the legal protection employees enjoy. An independent contractor's rights are confined to those described in their contract. When an independent contractor takes on a job, any liabilities incurred by him in carrying out the task are almost entirely his own, subject to the terms of the contract.[3] Vicarious liability is not applied to someone who hires an independent contractor. Employee tax and pension holdbacks are also not applicable.

---

[2] 671122 Ontario Ltd v Sagaz Industries Canada Inc, 2001 SCC 59 at paras 34–48; For discussion of control and dependence, see *McCormick v Fasken, Martineau, DuMoulin, LLP*, 2014 SCC 39.

[3] See *Vic Priestly Landscaping Contracting Ltd v Elder* (1978), 19 OR (2d) 591 at 601–5. An exception to this rule is the construction lien and holdback obligations of an owner of land who hires contractors to improve the land; see Chapter 28.

> ### ILLUSTRATION 18.1 Independence
>
> Imperial Builders contracted with Parkinson Corp. to build a building. During the construction work, Miss Chance, walking on the sidewalk far below, is injured by a falling brick. The accident is the result of inadequate protection for pedestrians provided by Imperial. Imperial—not Parkinson Corp.—would likely be solely liable for Chance's injury unless Parkinson was negligent in hiring an incompetent contractor or some known hazardous activity.[4]

dependent contractor contractors with a level of exclusivity and permanence that makes them economically dependent on one client

Dependent contractors operate midway between employees and independent contractors. Although they have their own businesses and control over the completion of their tasks, dependent contractors work primarily with one client over a long period of time and therefore are economically dependent on that client.[5] Common law grants them one of the legal protections of employees. Dependent contractors must be given reasonable notice of termination of the relationship.[6]

EMPLOYMENT RELATIONSHIP AT COMMON LAW

At common law, the relationship of employer and employee carried with it responsibilities about

- the employer's liability to third persons,
- the notice required to terminate the relationship,
- the limited reasons an employer could terminate the relationship without notice, and
- assessment of damages for wrongful dismissal.

These rules remain applicable to individual employment contracts.

THE EMPLOYER'S LIABILITY TO THIRD PERSONS

Liability in Contract

Often, parties to a contract do not intend to perform personally—corporations cannot do so—and they expect employees or an independent contractor will perform. The promisor remains liable for satisfactory performance, as when a construction firm undertakes to build a building according to specifications and hires a subcontractor to put up the structural steel, but the subcontractor does defective work. The construction firm is liable for breach of contract no matter who did the improper work.

Liability in Tort

Employers are liable to third parties for damages arising from any tort an employee may commit in the course of employment. They may be primarily liable if they have been negligent in the selection, training, or supervision of the employee, or they may be vicariously liable (without fault) simply because of the employment relationship.

---

[4] *Savage v Wilby*, [1954] SCR 376; *Chappell's Ltd v Municipality of County of Cape Breton*, [1963] SCR 340; *Sickel v Gordy*, 2008 SKCA 100 at paras 48–49.

[5] *TCF Ventures Corp v The Cambie Malone's Corporation*, 2017 BCCA 129 at paras 19–24; *McKee v Reid's Heritage Homes Ltd*, 2009 ONCA 916; *Keenan v Canac Kitchens*, 2016 ONCA 79.

[6] *Ibid.*

The employer need not have authorized the wrongful act; all the injured party need establish is that the employee caused the damage while working.[7]

> **ILLUSTRATION 18.2   Vicarious Liability**
>
> Adair is a sales representative employed by Magnum Computers. While doing a sales demonstration at a client's office, he negligently breaks the client's existing projector. He has committed a tort in the course of his employment; the owner of the damaged projector may sue both Magnum Computers and Adair. This is a typical example of vicarious liability.

However, if the employee is not engaged in the employer's work at the time of the tort, as when she takes time off to attend to some personal matter, the employer is not liable; only the employee is liable. Neither is the employer liable if the employee delegates the work to someone else without the employer's consent.

> **ILLUSTRATION 18.3   Unauthorized Activities**
>
> Adair injures a neighbour's projector as a result of negligently using the company equipment to host an in-home theatre event for the neighbourhood, without permission or knowledge of his employer. As noted in a Nova Scotia judgment in a similar case, Adair has "departed from the course of his employment and . . . embarked upon an independent enterprise—'a frolic of his own'—for purposes wholly unconnected with his master's business."[8] He alone is liable; Magnum Computers is not. It is important that Adair was not representing himself as an employee at the time of the act.

> **ILLUSTRATION 18.4   Intentional Wrongful Acts While Working**
>
> While delivering a computer, Adair becomes embroiled in an argument with a customer about the quality of the product. He pushes the customer, who falls and injures himself. Is Magnum Computers vicariously liable to the customer for the assault?

Illustration 18.4 is a challenging example. When an employee commits an unauthorized intentional wrong, an employer may be liable if the act is sufficiently related to conduct carried out in the authorized course of employment, and there is significant connection between the employment's creation of the risk and the wrongful behaviour.[9]

Adair's conversation about his employer's product during delivery is an authorized part of Adair's employment, so his employer is most likely liable for the assault even though it is not behaviour condoned by the employer. When the behaviour is less clearly related to business operation, connection is assessed using five factors: opportunity, employer's goals, friction in the employer's business, power of the employee, and vulnerability of the victim.[10]

---

[7] Allen M Linden and Bruce Feldthusen, *Canadian Tort Law*, 10th ed. (Toronto: LexisNexis, 2015) at 591.

[8] *Hall v Halifax Transfer Co Ltd* (1959), 18 DLR (2d) 115 at 120.

[9] *Bazley v Curry*, [1999] 2 SCR 534 (for purposes of victim compensation and deterrence).

[10] *Ibid*; *Douglas v Kinger*, 2008 ONCA 452 at paras 21–24.

CASE 18.1 Five Factors

An intoxicated passenger was sexually assaulted by a taxi driver. She sued the employing taxi company in negligence and vicarious liability. The negligence claim failed because the driver had no criminal record or prior history that the company should have discovered during the hiring process. The vicarious liability claim failed because the connection to employment was not strong enough. The attack was only coincidentally connected to the taxi company's business—it afforded opportunity. However, the attack did not relate to the business goals and did not arise from business friction with the passenger, and the employee's status did not confer power over the passenger, although she was in a vulnerable state of intoxication. The policy goal of deterrence would not be advanced by imposing liability.[11]

NOTICE OF TERMINATION OF INDIVIDUAL EMPLOYMENT CONTRACTS

Express Term in the Contract

fixed term a contract of employment with defined start and end dates

When an employer hires an employee for a **fixed term**, no notice of termination is necessary on the part of either party. The relationship naturally comes to an end on the date when the fixed time period expires. Neither one has a right to expect anything more from the other at the end of the specified time. If the employer terminates the contract before the expressed end date, the employee is entitled to be paid out to the end of the term.[12]

Alternatively, employment contracts of fixed or indefinite length may contain an option to terminate. Such a clause will describe the process to be followed for either party to bring the contract to an end. It will usually specify a required amount of advance notice. In most provinces and at the federal level as well, the minimum length of notice and benefits is required by statute, and any attempt by an employer to impose a term shorter than the minimum is void.[13] Adding an early termination term to the employment contract after the start of employment will require new consideration.[14]

Implied Term of Reasonable Notice

notice advance warning that the employment relationship will end

When employment contracts do not say how or when they will come to an end, the common law implies a term requiring reasonable **notice** of termination. Notice of termination involves telling an employee in advance that the employment relationship will end.

Often, employers and employees do not discuss when the employment relationship is to end, nor do they expressly agree on the length of notice required to terminate employment. They may intend the hiring to be by the month, or the year or some other length of time, renewable for successive periods, and possibly lasting for many years. Or, as more often happens, they may simply regard the employment as a general or **indefinite hiring**.

indefinite hiring a contract of employment for an undetermined length of time, with no expectation of termination or described end date

When no evidence about the intention of the parties is given to the court, it may infer a yearly or a monthly hiring from the pay periods. Usually a hiring is indefinite, even though the employee is paid by the week.

---

[11] *Ivic v Lakovic*, 2017 ONCA 446.

[12] *Howard v Benson Group Inc*, 2016 ONCA 256.

[13] See e.g. *Labour Standards Act*, RSS 1978, c L-1, s 44.2; *Labour Standards Code*, RSNS 1989, c 246, s 72; *Employment Standards Act, 2000*, SO 2000, c 41, s 54 as applied in *Machtinger v HOJ Industries Ltd* (1992), 91 DLR (4th) 491 (SCC) and *Rizzo & Rizzo Shoes Ltd, (Re)*, [1998] 1 SCR 26; *Wood v Fred Deeley Imports Ltd*, 2017 ONCA 158.

[14] *Holland v Hostopia.com Inc*, 2015 ONCA 762.

Length of Reasonable Notice

Reasonable notice must be given—but exactly how much notice is *reasonable?* The answer is: It depends. Each case is unique, and length of notice varies depending on the circumstances. For indefinite hiring, length of reasonable notice depends upon a variety of factors and the circumstances of the employment; it usually varies between one and six months, and occasionally it is as long as two years or more in special circumstances.[15] Key considerations (known as the "*Bardal* factors") are the length and character of employment, the age of the employee, and the availability of similar employment, given the education, training, and experience of the employee.[16] Senior executive compensation settlements are often higher.[17] Since the legislative provisions referred to above are minimum requirements only, reasonable notice periods and contractual notice terms are usually substantially longer.

If an employer wants to dismiss an employee immediately, it may satisfy its obligation to give reasonable notice if it pays the employee for a period equal to the time required for reasonable notice. This is known as **payment in lieu of notice**. Employers commonly terminate this way to avoid friction with the now-terminated employee. If, for example, a court finds that reasonable notice in the circumstances is three months, and the employee had been given only one week's salary in lieu of notice, it will order payment of the balance of three months' salary.

reasonable notice the acceptable length of advance notice of termination considering the length and character of employment, the age of the employee, and the availability of similar employment, given the education, training, and experience of the employee

payment in lieu of notice payment of the amount of compensation the employee would have earned during the reasonable notice period

CHECKLIST

Factors Relevant to Length of Reasonable Notice: *Bardal* Factors

- length of employment
- character of employment
- age of employee
- education or training of employee
- experience of employee
- availability of similar employment in the industry (market conditions)

This is not an exhaustive list of relevant factors, and the importance of individual factors will vary with the circumstances of the particular case.

An employee who decides to leave voluntarily must give the employer the same amount of notice as he himself would be entitled to receive for dismissal. If he does not do so, the employer may, if it considers it worthwhile, sue the employee for damages equal to the loss caused by this breach of contract.[18] Few employers ask for more than two weeks' notice for the same reasons they would rather pay an employee in lieu of giving notice.

---

[15] See *Bardal v The Globe and Mail Ltd* (1960), 24 DLR (2d) 140; *Stevens v Globe and Mail et al* (1992), 86 DLR (4th) 204; *Keenan v Canac Kitchens Ltd*, 2016 ONCA 79 at para 30 (special circumstances).

[16] *Bardal, supra* note 15. The balancing and weight given to each factor is not uniformly applied. See *Love v Acuity Investment Management Inc*, 2011 ONCA 130 at paras 13–24; *Bramble v Medis Health & Pharmaceutical Services Inc* (1999), 175 DLR (4th) 385 (NBCA), *Cronk v Canadian General Insurance Co* (1995), 128 DLR (4th) 147 (ONCA.). See also *Honda v Keays*, [2008] 2 SCR 362 at 379–80 Specialized short-term employment may be entitled to longer notice: *Pakozdi v B & B Heavy Civil Construction Ltd*, 2018 BCCA 23 at para 29.

[17] Eric Dash, "Executive Pay: Has the Exit Sign Ever Looked So Good?" *New York Times*, April 8, 2007, https://www.nytimes.com/2007/04/08/business/yourmoney/08axe.html.

[18] *RBC Dominion Securities Inc v Merrill Lynch Canada Inc*, 2008 SCC 54.

An employee is justified in leaving without giving the usual notice if she can show she was "forced to quit." For example, she is not required to work under dangerous conditions that the employer refuses to correct. An employee also has grounds for leaving immediately if she is ordered to perform an illegal act. The employer has broken the contract, freeing the employee from her obligations, for it is an implied term that the employer will maintain a safe place to work. If an employer substantially changes an employee's job, for example, by a **demotion** or a geographic transfer, the employee is not obliged to accept the change. Under such circumstances, the unilateral change amounts to **constructive dismissal**, and the employee is entitled to receive reasonable notice.[19]

demotion transferring an employee to a job with less responsibility and/or income potential

constructive dismissal a substantial change to an employee's job that amounts to termination of the existing employment

DISMISSAL WITHOUT NOTICE

An employer need not give notice of termination when it can show that the employee was dismissed for good reason or "just cause." **Dismissal for cause** is allowed when an employee's conduct amounts to a breach of the employment contract. The employer is entitled to consider itself discharged from any further obligations and to terminate the contract at once. As we know, in contract law, generally not every petty breach would have this result. Just cause exists if the behaviour

dismissal for cause dismissal without notice or further obligation by the employer when the employee's conduct amounts to breach of contract

- violates an essential term of the employment contract,
- breaches the faith inherent in the relationship, or
- fundamentally or directly conflicts with the employee's obligations to the employer.[20]

Less serious violations require **progressive discipline** such as warnings or counselling before dismissal.

The collective bargaining process has developed the idea further. In some jurisdictions, employees are given additional protection by statute.[21]

progressive discipline imposing increasingly serious consequences for each event of improper employee behaviour beginning with a warning and ending with dismissal

Misconduct

Misconduct may be dishonest or criminal behaviour associated with employment, such as embezzlement or fraud, or related to conduct outside of employment. Either way, it is behaviour that undermines the core of the employment relationship. An employee guilty of grossly immoral conduct that might bring the employer's business into public disrepute, disturb the morale of other employees, or cause the employer direct financial loss may be dismissed at once. Conviction for a crime is grounds for immediate dismissal, especially when it involves immoral conduct such as stealing or fraud.[22]

A business is entitled to place confidence in its employees, and depending on the nature of the employment, evidence of a lack of integrity is often grounds for dismissal. An employee's deception need not cause financial loss to his employer. It is enough that the employer can no longer trust him.[23]

---

[19] *Farber v Royal Trust Co*, [1997] 1 SCR 845; but see *Brown v Pronghorn Controls Ltd*, 2011 ABCA 328.
[20] *McKinley v BC Tel*, [2001] 2 SCR 161 at para 48.
[21] See e.g. *Employment Standards Act, 2000*, SO 2000, c 41.
[22] *Pliniussen v University of Western Ontario* (1983), 2 CCEL 1.
[23] *Werle v Saskenergy Inc* (1992), 103 Sask R 241.

> **CASE 18.2 Dishonesty**
>
> Fernandes, a private school teacher, was dismissed without notice because he created false marks and inaccurately inflated grades and then lied to the school vice-principal to it cover up. He sued for wrongful dismissal and lost. The Court of Appeal found that "one of a teacher's most important professional obligations is to fairly and properly evaluate and assess student progress . . . Fernandes' misconduct could not be reconciled with his obligations as a teacher. It was fundamentally and directly inconsistent with Mr. Fernandes' obligations to the School and to his students."[24] The behaviour was sufficiently serious that it justified immediate dismissal without notice.

Employers may set their own standards of conduct or misconduct. Codes of conduct addressing activities such as harassment, discrimination, privacy, and use of technology are used to set standards of appropriate behaviour for employees. Provided the employee is made aware of the code, she may be dismissed for code violations.

Disobedience

Willful disobedience of a reasonable and lawful order from an employer is grounds for immediate dismissal without notice. An accurate **job description** and identified chain of command help an employer avoid employee confusion about expected behaviour and disobedience. The concept of disobedience is broad enough to include situations where the employee does not directly disobey but acts in a manner inconsistent with the usual loyalty expected of that kind of employee. Again the nature of the conduct in light of surrounding circumstances will determine if dismissal is warranted or a less drastic consequence.[25]

job description a description of the responsibilities of a position, including objectives, qualifications, and supervisor

Incompetence

The degree of skill an employer may demand depends partly on the representations made by the employee when seeking the position and partly on the degree of skill ordinarily to be expected of an employee of that category and rate of pay. Again, accurate job descriptions and recruitment activities reduce the likeliness of hiring an incompetent applicant. If an employee accepts a position on the understanding that she is capable of doing a particular kind of work, and it becomes apparent that she cannot, in fact, do this work satisfactorily, the employer may then dismiss her without notice. On the other hand, incompetence as a cause for dismissal becomes more difficult to justify the longer an employee remains employed.[26] An employer must make an effort to remedy incompetence with training and education. Only after these efforts fail can the employer dismiss without notice.

Illness

Permanent disability or constantly recurring illness entitles an employer to consider the contract at an end, regardless of any terms in the contract requiring notice. An employer cannot, however, recover damages from an employee for breach of contract in these circumstances; the contract is discharged by frustration and not by breach. Human rights legislation imposes a duty on employers to accommodate an employee's disability. A disabled person's employment may only be terminated after all reasonable efforts to accommodate the disability have been exhausted. Many employers offer disability benefits to employees as part of the compensation package.

---

[24] *Fernandes v Peel Educational & Tutorial Services Limited (Mississauga Private School)*, 2016 ONCA 468 at paras 7, 112.

[25] *Ibid* at para 105.

[26] See *Duncan v Cockshutt Farm Equipment Ltd* (1956), 19 WWR 554; *Bardal*, *supra* note 15.

Discovery of Cause

Sometimes an employer has a general dissatisfaction with or mistrust of an employee and dismisses him apparently without cause. If the employer should later discover there was in fact cause for dismissing the employee without notice, it could use these grounds to defend a subsequent action by the employee for wrongful dismissal.[27] The courts admit such evidence even if it becomes known after the action has started.

An employer must undertake a thorough, objective, unbiased, and fair investigation into allegations of cause. Courts will award aggravated or punitive damages against an employer who terminates on the basis of false accusation or alleges cause in a lawsuit without evidence to prove it.[28]

Progressive Discipline

Only the most serious events of cause entitle an employer to immediately terminate an employee after the first incident. The conduct must be considered in context and be so serious as to amount to a total breakdown in the employment relationship.[29]

The employer bears the burden of proof. Most circumstances require an employer to show that the employee was previously warned that the offending conduct is unacceptable and further occurrences will result in termination.[30] Even a series of events may not justify dismissal if the employer has failed to warn the employee in the past. Ignoring the initial events may be seen as condoning or accepting the behaviour, and the employer may forfeit the right to complain later.[31] The British Columbia Supreme Court stated that

> the employer must provide the employee with a clear warning which specifically informs the employee that his or her job is in jeopardy. The employer cannot employ oblique language when warning the employee that his or her employment may be terminated. It is not sufficient for the employer to merely criticize the employee's performance or simply urge improvement.[32]

Courts expect a structured approach to dismissal for cause showing progressive discipline, noting all infractions and warnings on an employment record, and exhausting all less severe consequences before resorting to dismissal. An employer must be able to establish that training or education was attempted when relying on incompetence. If the employer allows unacceptable behaviour to continue without comment or correction, it may be taken as accepting or condoning the behaviour and release the right to consider it cause.

An employee's interest in a job is more than just contractual; work provides a sense of identity, self-worth, and emotional well-being.[33] In particular, the growing remedy of reinstatement, discussed in the next section, suggests a kind of ownership. With this in mind, before an employee is dismissed—and deprived of an "interest" in his job—he is entitled to a fair hearing. The employer should confront him with the allegation and provide an opportunity to explain his acts and minimize their significance.[34] An employer must show good faith and fair dealing in their approach to dismissal.[35]

---

[27] See e.g. *Lake Ontario Portland Cement v Groner* (1961), 28 DLR (2d) 589; *Bannister v General Motors of Canada Limited* (1998), 40 OR (3d) 577.

[28] *Honda Canada v Keays*, supra note 16; *Lau v Royal Bank of Canada*, 2017 BCCA 253.

[29] *McKinley*, supra note 20.

[30] *Rajakaruna v Peel (Regional Municipality)* (1981), 10 ACWS (2d) 522; *Elgert v Home Hardware Stores Ltd*, 2010 ABQB 65 at para 40.

[31] *Varsity Plymouth Chrysler (1994) Ltd v Pomerleau* (2002), 23 CCEL (3d) 148.

[32] *Bomford v Wayden Transportation Systems Inc*, [2010] BCJ No 2080 at para 5.

[33] *Reference Re Public Service Employee Relations Act (Alta.)*, [1987] 1 SCR 313 at 368.

[34] See *Reilly v Steelcase Canada Ltd* (1979), 26 OR (2d) 725; *Pulsifer v GTE Sylvania Canada Ltd* (1983), 56 NSR (2d) 424; *Pilato v Hamilton Place Convention Centre* (1984), 45 OR (2d) 652.

[35] *Lau* supra note 28.

Adverse Economic Conditions

Adverse economic conditions do not excuse an employer from its implied obligation to give employees reasonable notice of termination. An employer might overcome this implied obligation by getting his employee to agree expressly that in adverse economic conditions he may be dismissed without notice. However, when a right to notice is required by statute, even an express agreement to give it up is ineffective; the statute prevails, and the employer must still give notice or wages in lieu of notice.

Some statutes permit an employer to temporarily lay off employees without notice for periods as long as three months under certain economic conditions prescribed by regulation.[36]

WRONGFUL DISMISSAL

If the employer does not follow the rules for cause or reasonable notice, the employee has a cause of action against her employer for breach of the employment contract, known as wrongful dismissal. An employee must show she was an employee who was fired without reasonable notice. An employer often defends by claiming either that the employee was dismissed for cause and not entitled to notice or that reasonable notice was given. If the employer's defence fails, the employee is entitled to damages and/or reinstatement.

Damages

The purpose of an award of damages is to place an injured party in the position it would have been in if the contract had been completed; for an employment contract, proper completion means terminating the employment with the appropriate reasonable notice. To calculate the damages, the length of reasonable notice is multiplied by the employee's rate of pay and the value of fringe benefits. Any bonus the employee would have been eligible for during the notice period is added to damages.[37] As noted earlier, the length of the notice period is set using the following factors:

> the character of the employment, the length of service of the servant, the age of the servant and the availability of similar employment, having regard to the experience, training and qualifications of the servant.[38]

Additional Damages In addition to damages for the lack of notice, employers may be liable for other aggravated or "moral" damages[39] when they act in bad faith, use hardball tactics, or humiliate an employee causing harm. Employers are under an obligation to behave fairly, honestly, candidly, and reasonably when dismissing an employee. When the bad faith or malicious behaviour of the employer adds to the harm caused—as where the employer falsely makes it appear that the employee was dismissed for serious misconduct or where the employee is terminated in a public or humiliating

---

[36] *Canada Labour Code*, RSC 1985, c L-2; *Canada Labour Standards Regulations*, CRC, c 986, s 30; *Employment Standards Act, 2000*, SO 2000, c 41, s 56.

[37] *Paquette v TeraGo Networks Inc*, 2016 ONCA 618.

[38] *Bardal, supra* note 15 at 145, per McRuer, CJHC; *Machtinger v HOJ Industries Ltd*, [1992] 1 SCR 986.

[39] *Capital Pontiac Buick Cadillac GMC Ltd v Coppolla*, 2013 SKCA 80 at para 26 (upholding an award of $20 000 of moral damages).

way—damages may be assessed against the employer for mental anguish, pain and suffering, or, in extreme circumstances, punitive damages.[40] Some provinces allow damages for human rights violations to be assessed as part of a wrongful dismissal action.

> ### CASE 18.3 Moral Damages
>
> Doyle was sexually harassed by a co-worker for nine years before she complained to her employer. The employer made only a cursory investigation of the complaint and then fired Doyle. Doyle's supervisor was told to "dig up dirt" on Doyle's performance. Doyle was told her job was not in jeopardy and she would be given a chance to improve when, in fact, her termination was already planned. Doyle's medical condition (depression) was disclosed to her supervisor in breach of her privacy; and during her termination meeting, Doyle's keys were taken from her purse, and her car was brought to the exit. She was pressured to sign a release. This was evidence of untruthful, misleading, and unduly insensitive employer conduct. Collectively this conduct was appropriate for moral damages. It is not just conduct at the moment of termination that may be considered but also conduct that is a component of the manner of dismissal. Doyle was entitled to $60 000 in moral damages in addition to 10 months' reasonable notice and human rights damages for sexual harassment.[41]

Mitigation

A party injured by breach of contract is expected to act reasonably in order to mitigate her loss. Mitigation in the wrongful dismissal context means finding another job. Accordingly, the employer may be able to defeat or reduce the employee's claim for damages by proving she has not made a serious attempt to obtain reasonably comparable work elsewhere. If the employer shows the employee had an opportunity to work elsewhere but declined it, the court will reduce the award of damages by the amount the employee might have earned during the required term of notice. However, a dismissed employee is not required to take any work simply to mitigate her loss; if the only work available is substantially below what she might reasonably expect based on her qualifications and experience, she may refuse it without negative impact on any subsequent award of damages. Nor need she move to a distant location, requiring her to relocate. If she does accept a lower-paying job, she will be entitled to the difference in remuneration during the term of notice.

In rare circumstances, the employee may be expected to mitigate by accepting alternative employment with the dismissing employer.[42] This is most common in constructive dismissal situations. Employees are not expected to work in hostile or humiliating environments, and in most situations, this precludes returning.[43] Expenses for looking for another job are recoverable as a cost of mitigation.

Reinstatement

In addition to damages, employees may seek other remedies such as reinstatement—a form of specific performance in which the court orders the employer to give the

---

[40] See *Honda Canada Inc v Keays, supra* note 16 (damages can include mental anguish, punitive, or moral damages); *Strudwick v Applied Consumer & Clinical Evaluations Inc*, 2016 ONCA 520 (awarding 24 months' notice plus $35,000 mental distress, $70,000 aggravated, $55,000 punitive, and $40,000 human rights damages). See also *Fidler v Sun Life Assurance Co of Canada*, [2006] 2 SCR 3, and *Wallace v United Grain Growers Ltd.* [1997] 3 SCR 701.

[41] *Doyle v Zochem Inc*, 2017 ONCA 130.

[42] *Evans v Teamsters Local Union No 31*, 2008 SCC 20. The test is whether a reasonable person would accept the offer to return to work: *Turner v Indirect Enterprises Inc*, [2009] OJ No 6345 at paras 9–10, aff'd [2011] OJ No 621.

[43] See e.g. *Renard v Facet Decision Systems Inc*, [2010] BCJ No 2694, but see *Chevalier v Active Tire & Auto Centre Inc*, 2013 ONCA 548 (employee was expected to accept offer of re-employment).

employee his job back. We noted in Chapter 13 the reluctance of courts to order specific performance of contracts of service. However, the impersonal nature of most large business enterprises has diminished the strength of this argument. Indeed, reinstatement has become the norm as the remedy for wrongful dismissal under collective agreements. Reinstatement also occurs at universities; professors who have been wrongfully dismissed are ordinarily entitled to reinstatement.

Non-union employees in industries within the federal jurisdiction have a statutory right to reinstatement. The *Canada Labour Code* (s. 240) provides that adjudicators may order reinstatement of a non-unionized employee if he has completed 12 consecutive months of employment with the employer.[44] The *Quebec Labour Standards Act* and the *Nova Scotia Act* create a similar right for employees in those provinces.[45] Human rights legislation also offers reinstatement as a remedy in discrimination complaints.[46]

CHECKLIST

Remedies Available in a Wrongful Dismissal Action

A. Damages:
- payment in lieu of notice
- damages for mental anguish or pain and suffering
- special damages associated with the cost of mitigation
- moral, aggravated, and/or punitive damages for employer bad faith
- reduction for failure to mitigate their damages

B. Reinstatement

Ethical Issue   Protection of Employee Privacy

Employee misuse of workplace technology is a common and so are surveillance and monitoring of employee technology use. To justify surveillance, employers argue that telephones, internet service, and computers are company property. Therefore, the employer has the right to ensure they are used only for work rather than for personal purposes and that employees are not jeopardizing the security of confidential and private information. Employers also cite their duty to maintain a secure and safe workplace—including the protection of employees against sexual harassment—as justification for monitoring employees.

The American Management Association, in conjunction with the ePolicy Institute, has been surveying the use of employee monitoring for decades. In 1993, only 33 percent of employers reported using some form of monitoring. However, by 2001 usage had risen to 79 percent.[47] Common forms of technological monitoring include the following:

- data shadowing
- video surveillance
- GPS tracking

One of the most controversial forms of monitoring involves biometrics. Biometrics use digital scans of personal features such as fingerprints and retinas to control access to computers, work premises, and so on.

The federal *Personal Information Protection and Electronic Documents Act* (PIPEDA) provides that "organizations" must obtain consent of "individuals" to the collection, use, and disclosure of personal information, except where it would be

---

[44] *Canada Labour Code*, RSC 1985, c L-2, s 240.

[45] *An Act Respecting Labour Standards Act*, RSQ 1991, c N-1.1, ss 124–8; *Labour Standards Code*, RSNS 1989, c 246, ss 71(1) and 26(2)(a).

[46] See e.g. *Human Rights Code*, RSO 1990, c H.19, s 45.2; *Hamilton-Wentworth District School Board v Fair*, 2016 ONCA 421.

[47] American Management Association, Electronic Monitoring & Surveillance Survey, Executive Summary 2001, 2005, 2007, http://www.plattgroupllc.com/jun08/2007ElectronicMonitoringSurveillanceSurvey.pdf

"inappropriate" to do so. Section 4 extends the application of PIPEDA to personal information collected in some employment relationships (except an employee's name, title, business address, or telephone number). Surveillance of employees is not expressly forbidden by PIPEDA, but employers must use the least invasive form of surveillance and should give the employee advance notice.

The Office of the Privacy Commissioner of Canada hears complaints about the appropriateness of workplace surveillance under PIPEDA. In one case, the employer's stated purposes for using web cameras included security of the workplace, especially from theft, and monitoring of employee productivity. The surveillance was found inappropriate because there were less intrusive ways for the employer to achieve these goals, noting that

> Continuous, indiscriminate surveillance of employees... was based on a lack of trust and treats all employees with suspicion when the underlying problems may rest with a few individuals or with a management plan that may not be entirely sound.[48]

In other words, the position of the assistant commissioner was that the "cost to human dignity," in the form of the right to privacy, must be a factor in the assessment of the appropriateness of surveillance.

Questions to Consider

1. Is it appropriate to "reduce privacy to a contractual right," as one commentator has put it? If a prospective employee is asked in a job application if she would consent to the electronic monitoring of her work by the employer, and she declines to give her consent, is the employer entitled to reject her application?

2. Is privacy of personal information a "fundamental human right"?

Sources: Privacy Commission of Canada, Commissioner's Findings, August 14, 2002, http://www.privcom.gc.ca; Anik Morrow, "Privacy and Data Protection," Paper for Ontario Bar Association Institute, January 24, 2002; B. McIsaac, R. Shields, and K. Klien, *Privacy Law in Canada*, student ed. (Toronto: Thomson Canada, 2007); *Eastmond v Canadian Pacific Railway*, [2004] FCJ No 1043; M.A. Geist, "Computer and E-mail Workplace Surveillance in Canada: The Shift From Reasonable Expectation of Privacy to Reasonable Surveillance," (2003) 82(2) Canadian Bar Review 152; Shelley McGill and Mark Baetz, "Technology Use Codes of Conduct: Is It a Choice Between Shaping the Organizational Culture and Effective Legal Enforcement?," (2012) 15(2) *Employee Rights and Employment Policy Journal* 101.

EMPLOYEE WELFARE LEGISLATION

Background

Unfair and dangerous working conditions in the 19th century led to employee welfare legislation. Both federal and provincial governments used legislation to force employers to improve working conditions for employees.

The first reform statutes dealt with the minimum age of workers, maximum hours of work, safety devices for machinery, the maintenance of safe work premises, and liability on employers when an employee was injured at work. Current statutes attempt to level the playing field among employees with equal pay and anti-discrimination measures. The disparity in bargaining power between employer and employees is reduced for unionized workers. However, many categories of work remain non-unionized, and contracts are negotiated individually. Employee welfare legislation sets a minimum standard of fair working conditions for all employees.

Federal and Provincial Jurisdiction

In Canada, the activities of a small but important group of businesses are under federal jurisdiction, and, for them, the rights and duties of employers and employees are governed by federal legislation. These industries include banking, shipping, air transport, interprovincial transportation and telephone systems, radio, and the operations of federal Crown corporations.[49] The remainder of businesses—the bulk of industrial and commercial enterprise—are subject to provincial rather than federal employee welfare legislation.

---

[48] PIPEDA Case Summary #2004-279, ARCHIVED http://www.privcom.gc.ca Surveillance of employees at work (issued July 26, 2004) (Section 3; subsection 5(3)).

[49] *Constitution Act, 1867*, s 91.

Employee Rights

Human Rights The *Canadian Charter of Rights and Freedoms* is the constitutional authority for human rights protection. According to section 15 of the *Charter*:

> Every individual . . . has the right to the equal protection and equal benefit of the law without discrimination and, in particular without discrimination based on race, national or ethnic origin, colour, religion, sex, age or mental or physical disability.[50]

The *Charter* applies to government behaviour, not to the private sector; similar human rights legislation passed by each province and the federal Parliament governs employment behaviour in the private sector.[51] Generally speaking, the acts require equal treatment in employment and prohibit

> all discriminatory practice . . . to refuse to employ or continue to employ an individual, or . . . to differentiate adversely . . . on a prohibited ground,[52] that is, on the basis of race, national or ethnic origin, colour, religion, age, sex, sexual orientation, gender identity, gender expression, genetic characteristics, marital status, family status, disability and conviction for which a pardon has been granted.[53]

Employees may file complaints against current, prospective, and former employers that will be adjudicated by an administrative tribunal set up under the legislation, or they may add damages for human rights violations to a common law claim for wrongful dismissal filed in the courts.[54] Employers must not only comply with the human rights legislation themselves but also ensure that co-workers in the workplace do the same. Employers are responsible for "hostile workplaces" and must take steps to free the workplace from harassment.

Disability Human rights statutes require employers to accommodate disabled employees or prospective employees unless the employer can demonstrate that such accommodation will result in undue hardship for them, considering the cost, outside sources of funding, if any, and health and safety requirements.

CASE 18.4 Disability Not Factor in Termination

The employer coal mine implemented a drug dependence policy for the safety of the workplace. Employees were to disclose addiction and receive treatment; employees who did not comply would be terminated if an accident occurred. S did not tell his employer of his cocaine habit, and when his loader was involved in an accident, he was terminated for cause. He filed a human rights complaint. The Supreme Court upheld the Alberta Tribunal's decision that the employee was terminated for breach of the policy (misconduct), not for an addiction disability. Therefore the employer did not have to reasonably accommodate the employee's disability.[55]

Employees must participate in accommodation process by releasing medical information. Other factors relevant to undue hardship are problems of morale of other employees or interchangeability of workforce and facilities. The financial cost will be

---

[50] *Part I of the Constitution Act, 1982, being Sch B to the Canada Act 1982 (UK), 1982, c 11.* Section 28 emphasizes that *Charter* rights "are guaranteed equally to male and female persons."

[51] See e.g. *The Human Rights Code*, RSBC 1996, c 210; RSO 1990, c H-19; SS 1979, c S-24.1; CCSM c H-175; *Alberta Human Rights, Citizenship and Multiculturalism Act*, RSA 2000, c H-14.

[52] *Canadian Human Rights Act*, RSC 1985, c H-6, ss 7(a) and (b).

[53] *Ibid*, s 3(1), amended to include "sexual orientation" by SC 1996, c 1 and gender identity and expression by SC 2017, c 13. Human rights legislation applies to employees, not partners in a partnership: *McCormick v Fasken Martineau DuMoulin, LLP, supra* note 3.

[54] See e.g. *Ontario Human Rights Code, supra* note 51, ss 27–31.7 (Ontario Human Rights Commission), s 46.1 (Civil Remedy); *Strudwick, supra* note 40.

[55] *Stewart v Elk Valley Corp*, 2017 SCC 30.

viewed in proportion to the size of the employer's operation, as will the ease with which the workforce and facilities can be adapted to the circumstances.[56]

> **CASE 18.5   Undue Hardship**
>
> After 14 years of employment with the Hamilton Wentworth School Board, Fair developed generalized anxiety disorder, depression, and post-traumatic stress disorder because of her high stress job as supervisor (regulated substances, asbestos) and its potential for personal liability. She took a leave of absence and sought treatment. When Fair's psychiatrist determined that she was ready to return to work with accommodations that reduced stress and excluded work involving personal liability, the School Board could not find a suitable position. Fair filed a human rights complaint. The Court of Appeal upheld a tribunal order reinstating Fair. In a large employer like the School Board, there were multiple alternative positions that could have accommodated Fair, including two supervisory positions that became vacant during the accommodation process. The employer had not proven undue hardship, and the Court did not believe that the employer would have to create a surplus position or displace an incumbent employee to accommodate Fair.[57]

Sexual Harassment   Human rights legislation prohibits harassment in the workplace on any protected ground, not just sex. Sexual harassment includes unwelcome vexatious comments or conduct about gender, sexual orientation, gender expression, or gender identity, and specifically lists solicitation, advances, and threats or reprisals for rejection. Knowledge is relevant; to be harassment the offender must know or should reasonably know the behaviour is unwelcome. Sometimes freedom of expression issues overlap harassment complaints, and in one such case sexist postings on a blog associated with the union, not the employer's workplace, were not considered sexual harassment and were outside the scope of human rights legislation.[58]

Hostile Workplace   Sometimes the discriminatory treatment does not come from the employer but from co-workers. It is the employer's duty to intervene to reduce the hostility between employees and discipline the offending co-worker if necessary.[59] Sensitivity training is one common employer strategy.

Constructive Discrimination   A non-discriminatory rule, qualification, or factor may still be a discriminatory practice if the result or impact is to exclude or disproportionally impact members of a protected group. This is true unless said rule, qualification, or factor is reasonable and done in good faith. Dress codes or uniform policies often have discriminatory impact for particular religious groups. Courts are likely to treat a school uniform policy differently from hospital operating room dress codes.

Pay Equity   Pay equity legislation is directed toward eliminating gender discrimination in remuneration. There are two ways of assessing the wage gap between men and women. The more traditional is through the principle of "equal pay for equal work." The law prohibits different levels of pay for substantially the same kind of work performed in the same establishment, requiring substantially the same skill, effort, and responsibility and performed under similar working conditions.[60]

The second approach requires a focus not on the similarity of the jobs but on their **comparative value** to the employer—the concept of "equal pay for work of equal value" or "comparable worth."[61] The legislation requires employers to pay employees

comparative value   equal pay for work of equal value

---

[56] *Hamilton-Wentworth District School Board v Fair*, supra note 46 at paras 52–59.

[57] *Ibid*.

[58] *Taylor-Baptiste v Ontario Public Service Employees Union*, 2015 ONCA 495.

[59] *British Columbia Human Rights Tribunal v Schrenk*, 2017 SCC 62.

[60] *Ontario Human Rights Code*, supra note 46, s 5.

[61] This standard applies to both public and private sectors in areas of federal jurisdiction and in Quebec and Ontario. See Canadian Pay Equity Compliance Guide (North York, ON: CCH Canadian Ltd., 1990). Manitoba, New Brunswick, PEI, and Nova Scotia have pay equity legislation applicable to public sector only.

performing jobs traditionally done by women the same as those performing jobs done by men if the jobs are of equal or comparable value. The main task is to give a meaning to the word "value." It is not the same as current market value of work but rather involves evaluating based upon criteria such as effort, training necessary, skills required, and contribution of the work. This model depends on the existence of a male-dominated comparable.[62]

Once a job evaluation results in a finding that one group of employees is paid too little in comparison with another, the employer must increase the wages of the lower-paid group. This may substantially raise the labour costs of an employer, making it likely that the employer will contest the job evaluation.

Usually, someone must file a complaint in order to trigger enforcement of the legislation. However, for **systemic discrimination**, the complaint system is less effective than a regulatory model that not only prohibits wage discrimination but also places positive obligations on employers to scrutinize their pay practices and ensure that these practices comply with the legislation.

systemic discrimination discrimination that is pervasive throughout an employer's workforce

At present, the regulatory model applies to the public sectors in Manitoba, New Brunswick, Newfoundland and Labrador, Nova Scotia, and Prince Edward Island; and in Ontario to both the public sector and to private sector employers who employ 10 or more persons. Throughout the rest of Canada, the complaints system alone remains in force.[63]

Employment Equity

Employment equity requires employers to treat individual applicants for jobs equally, regardless of personal characteristics. It strives to make the workforce reflect the various underrepresented classes of disadvantaged persons in the general population.

The federal *Employment Equity Act*[64] applies to all employers with 100 or more employees, "in connection with federal work, undertaking or business as defined in section 2 of the *Canada Labour Code*." Employers are required to conduct a "workforce analysis"—that is, to obtain relevant information about the personal characteristics of their current employees, in order to determine underrepresentation of designated groups—women, visible minorities, Aboriginals, and persons with disabilities—in the workforce generally. In addition to information from their current employees, employers must seek the same information from job applicants before determining whether certain applicants should be given preference. Employers are required to review their formal and informal hiring policies in order to remove all systemic discrimination against the designated groups and to set goals and timetables for achieving representation based on the working-age population within each employer's community. Finally, they must prepare a plan to carry out their goals, including monitoring systems to assess their progress. Critics claim this is a quota system.

Ontario had legislation similar to the federal Act,[65] which applied to all public sector employment and to private sector employers with more than 50 employees. It became a major issue in the 1995 provincial election; the Progressive Conservative Party vowed to repeal the legislation and did so after it was elected to power.[66] No other province has passed similar legislation.

---

[62] *Centrale des syndicats du Québec v Quebec (Attorney General)*, 2018 SCC 18.
[63] *The Pay Equity Act*, RSO 1990, c P-7, s 3.
[64] Federal *Employment Equity Act*, SC 1995, c 44.
[65] *Employment Equity Act*, SO 1993, c 35.
[66] *Job Quotas Repeal Act*, SO 1995, c 4.

Mandatory Retirement and the *Charter of Rights and Freedoms*

Mandatory retirement schemes expect workers to leave their jobs, usually at age 65, and enjoy retirement, thereby making room for younger workers seeking employment. However, as people live longer and save less, courts and governments have been forced to re-evaluate the legality of mandatory retirement.

Section 15 of the *Charter of Rights and Freedoms*, which guarantees "equal protection and benefit of the law without discrimination . . . based on . . . age," was first used by public sector employees wishing to remain in their jobs to challenge mandatory retirement provisions. Next, the *Charter* was used to challenge provincial human rights legislation that exempt mandatory retirement from age discrimination provisions. Challengers claimed that mandatory retirement based solely on age, without regard to the health or competence of an employee, is arbitrary and discriminatory and therefore offends the *Charter*.[67] By 2005, all Canadian jurisdictions had abolished mandatory retirement and extended protection against age discrimination to workers over 65.[68]

Defenders of mandatory retirement schemes claim that, because the schemes are socially desirable, under section 1 of the *Charter* they are valid because they are a "reasonable limit prescribed by law" and "can be demonstrably justified in a free and democratic society." The British Columbia and New Brunswick human rights statutes prohibit discrimination based on age but not if it is part of a *"bona fide"* retirement plan.[69] This is because many pension plans and collective agreements depend upon a fixed retirement age to value contributions and benefits. In the past, the Supreme Court of Canada allowed such schemes in a group of four decisions dealing with complaints made by employees of hospitals, community colleges, and universities.[70] However, more recent cases suggest that societal attitudes have changed, and bona fide retirement plan exceptions may violate the *Charter*.[71] In all provinces, mandatory retirement schemes may be upheld when they are a genuine occupational requirement.[72]

Regulation of Working Conditions

Each province has multiple statutes prohibiting child labour, regulating the hours of work of young persons, and providing for the health and safety of employees while at work. Sometimes provincial inspection agencies are created to see that these requirements are complied with. Other statutes rely on a complaints-based model.

All provinces and the federal government set statutory minimum wage rates and grant discretionary power to certain government agencies to fix a minimum wage that

---

[67] *McIntire v University of Manitoba* (1981), 119 DLR (3d) 352, followed by *Newport v Government of Manitoba* (1982), 131 DLR (3d) 564. Both cases held that section 6(1) of the *Human Rights Code*, SM 1974, c 65, made mandatory retirement provisions void.

[68] See e.g. Abolition of Compulsory Retirement Act, SQ 1982 c 12.

[69] See e.g. *Air Canada Pilots Assn v Kelly*, *infra* note. 71. See B.C. *Human Rights Code*, RSBC 1996, c 210, s 13(3); see also NB *Human Rights Act*, RSNB 2011, c 171, s 4(6). A similar section in the *Canada Human Rights Code* was repealed in 2012.

[70] *McKinney v University of Guelph*, [1990] 3 SCR 229; *Harrison v University of British Columbia*, [1990] 3 SCR 451; *Stoffman v Vancouver General Hospital*, [1990] 3 SCR 483; *Douglas/Kwantlen Faculty Association v Douglas College*, [1990] 3 SCR 570.

[71] *Air Canada Pilots Assn v Kelly*, [2011] FCJ No 152 at paras 98–156, reversed 2012 FCA 209, leave denied; *Greater Vancouver Regional District Employees' Union v Greater Vancouver Regional District*, 2001 BCCA 435; *Assn of Justices of the Peace of Ontario v Ontario (Attorney General)* (2008), 92 OR (3d) 16; *New Brunswick (Human Rights Commission) v Potash Corporation of Saskatchewan Inc*, 2008 SCC 45.

[72] *Air Canada Pilots Assn.*, *supra* note 71 at paras 98–156, 353–85. *British Columbia (Public Service Employee Relations Commission) v British Columbia Government and Service Employees' Union*, 1999 3 SCR 3.

varies with the industry. The legislation sets limited working hours of, with some exceptions, eight hours a day and a maximum of 40 or 48 hours a week. These statutes also require overtime rates if the number of hours worked exceeds the specified maximum.[73]

All provinces provide for annual vacations with pay and protect employment during paternity leaves. The most frequent requirement is for employers to grant their employees one week's paid vacation after one year of work. Some provinces also require public holidays with pay and minimum notice of termination.

Employment Insurance

The *Employment Insurance Act*[74] manages a federal employment insurance fund to which both employers and employees contribute through mandatory payroll deductions according to a published schedule of rates. Coverage is not extended to persons who are receiving retirement pensions, self-employed, employed by a spouse, or employed by provincial governments, foreign governments, and international organizations.[75] The employer must account for all employee contributions and, along with its own contributions, regularly send them to the government. Benefits are payable out of the fund to workers who have contributed in the past and become unemployed. These benefits are not available in some circumstances, one of which is loss of work caused by a labour dispute in which the employee is on strike. Other employees, not on strike but "locked out" because a plant or business is shut down by a strike, remain eligible for benefits.

Most important, if an employee voluntarily leaves employment without just cause—or is justifiably dismissed for misconduct—she will not be eligible for benefits.

Workers' Compensation

Each province has a statutory no-fault compensation scheme[76] for employees injured at work so that employees do not have to pursue negligence actions against their employers.

The statutes require employers to contribute to a fund that is used to pay employee claims. Workers' Compensation Boards hear employees' claims and set the amount of compensation and the terms of return to work. To succeed, an employee need only show that the injury was caused by an accident in the course of employment. The principles of contributory negligence, negligence of a fellow employee, and assumed risk do not apply. An employee's claim will fail only if it is shown that the accident was caused substantially by his willful misconduct. Even then, the employee or the dependents will recover if the accident has caused death or serious disablement. This system avoids the costs and hazards of litigation. As well, since an employee claims recovery from a compensation board and not from his employer, he need not fear prejudicing his future with the employer.

Variations in Provincial Reforms
Coverage varies somewhat among the provinces. Generally included are workers in the following industries: construction, mining, manufacturing, lumbering, fishing, transportation, communications, and public

---

[73] See e.g. *Employment Standards Act, 2000*, SO 2000, c 41.

[74] *Employment Insurance Act*, SC 1996, c 23.

[75] *Ibid.*, s 5(2).

[76] See e.g. *Workers' Compensation Act*, RSBC 1996, c 492; SNS 1994–5, c 10; *Workplace Safety and Insurance Act, 1997*, SO 1997, c 16, Sch A.

utilities. Industries are classified according to the degree of hazard. Exemptions may include casual employees and employees of small businesses employing fewer than a stated number of workers. For employees excluded from the usual workers' compensation benefits, several provinces have added a second part to their legislation, defining the employer's liability for injuries caused by defective plant or equipment or by the negligence of other employees, and granting employees a right to damages in spite of contributory negligence on their part. In other jurisdictions, the common law rules still apply to casual employees and to those in small businesses.

Occupational Health Provincial occupational health and safety legislation takes a proactive approach to preventing injury in the workplace.[77] It requires a business to establish an in-house committee to identify, investigate, and correct dangers in the workplace. Government inspections are randomly carried out, and companies may be fined for failing to remedy a dangerous situation. Injuries in the workplace automatically trigger an investigation. Employees have the right to refuse to perform unsafe work without breaching their employment contract.[78] In Ontario, harassment in the workplace is considered an occupational health and safety issue.[79]

INTERNATIONAL ISSUE

Global Employment Standards

On April 24, 2013, more than 1100 workers were killed when a garment factory building collapsed in Bangladesh. This was another tragic reminder of the wide variation in wages and employment conditions that exist around the world. Two prominent initiatives aimed at harmonizing and improving employment standards in developing nations are

- the United Nations (UN) Global Compact, and
- the Organisation for Economic Co-operation and Development (OECD) Guidelines for Multinational Enterprises.

Both initiatives take a corporate social responsibility approach. The UN Global Compact is a set of 10 principles addressing human rights, labour, the environment, and corruption. A business voluntarily undertakes to participate in the compact and, in so doing, agrees to adopt policies and operations furthering the compact's objectives and to publicize the results of their progress. The four principles dealing with labour are

- freedom of association and the right to collective bargaining,
- elimination of all forms of forced and compulsory labour,
- effective abolition of child labour, and
- elimination of discrimination in respect of employment and occupation.

Many of Canada's largest companies participate in the Global Compact, including Rio Tinto Alcan, Bombardier, Enbridge, Hydro-Québec, and Petro-Canada.

The OECD guidelines are also voluntary standards, but they are the recommendations of the participating governments to the multinationals within their respective jurisdictions. Canada is a participating country. The guidelines include eight standards addressing employment and industrial relations that are more detailed than those in the Global Compact.

Questions to Consider

1. Do you think voluntary compliance with these international codes of conduct is more likely to be achieved through the business network approach of the Global Compact or the government-backed approach of the OECD? Why?

2. Discuss the pros and cons of the broad general principles of the Global Compact as distinct from the more detailed set of standards of the OECD.

Sources: "The Ten Principles," The United Nations Global Compact, https://www.unglobalcompact.org/what-is-gc/mission/principles; Organisation for Economic Co-operation and Development, The OECD Guidelines for Multinational Enterprises (Paris: OECD Publications, 2000), https://www.oecd.org/corporate/mne/1922428.pdf.

---

[77] Some provinces, such as British Columbia, cover this issue in the workers' compensation legislation, whereas others have separate legislation: *Occupational Health and Safety Act*, RSO 1990, c O.1.

[78] See e.g. *Occupational Health and Safety Act*, RSO 1990, c O.1, s 43(3); see also *Dionne v Commission scolaire des Patriotes*, 2014 SCC 33 at para 20.

[79] *Ibid*., ss 32.0.1–32.0.7; it is also a human rights issue.

COLLECTIVE BARGAINING

The Process

The process of negotiating terms of employment with a group of employees rather than individually is known as **collective bargaining**, and the right to do so is protected by the constitutional freedom of association.[80] For industries within federal jurisdiction, the *Canada Labour Code* regulates how collective bargaining is done.[81] Provincial legislation regulates collective bargaining for all other industries.[82] These Acts state that all employees are free to belong to trade unions and that membership in a trade union does not provide the employer with grounds for dismissing an employee. The Acts also require employers to recognize the representative union as the bargaining agent for employees for reaching an agreement on the general terms of their employment.

If an employer is unwilling to recognize a trade union voluntarily, as often happens, the union must apply to be certified before it can proceed to bargain for the employees. **Certification** is an acknowledgment by an administrative tribunal (called in some provinces a **labour relations board**) that a particular union has won sufficient membership to justify its role as exclusive bargaining agent for the employees. This arrangement has the practical advantage of confining the negotiations to a single representative of the employees, and it avoids the confusion of rival unions claiming the right to act as bargaining agents for a group of employees. We must distinguish between a bargaining agent and a bargaining unit: A **bargaining agent** is a union that has the exclusive right to bargain with the employer on behalf of the bargaining unit. The **bargaining unit** includes a specific group of employees eligible to join the union, whether they join or not.

collective bargaining establishing conditions of employment through negotiation between an employer and the collective bargaining agent for its employees

certification an acknowledgment by an administrative tribunal that a particular union commands sufficient membership to justify its role as exclusive bargaining agent for the employees

labour relations board an administrative tribunal regulating labour relations

bargaining agent a union that has the exclusive right to bargain with the employer on behalf of the bargaining unit

bargaining unit a specified group of employees eligible to join the union

Content of a Collective Agreement

When an employer and union reach an agreement, the members vote to approve or ratify the agreement, and the terms are placed in a contract called a collective agreement. The terms usually include a definition of the employees covered, an acknowledgment by the employer that the contracting union is their recognized bargaining agent, an outline of the steps that both parties must take in settling **grievances**, seniority provisions in the promotion and laying off of employees, wage rates, hours, vacation periods and other fringe benefits, the duration of the collective agreement, and the means by which it may be amended or renewed. Often there is a clause acknowledging that maintaining discipline and efficiency of employees is the exclusive task of the management of the company, subject to the right of an employee to lodge a grievance.

grievances disputes arising under the collective agreement

The agreement almost invariably forbids strikes or lockouts as long as the agreement continues to operate; indeed, most provinces require that such a term be included. The employees covered do not generally include those employed in a confidential capacity, those who have managerial responsibilities such as the authority to hire or discharge others, or those employed as guards or security police in the protection of business property. Some provinces have also excluded certain professional groups such as engineers, although the recent tendency has been to include professions.

The terms of a collective agreement set the procedure for dismissing employees, replacing the common law rules for reasonable notice of dismissal, grounds for

---

[80] *British Columbia Teachers' Federation v British Columbia*, 2016 SCC 49 (declaring unconstitutional provincial legislation that removed some issues from collective bargaining).

[81] RSC 1985, c L-2.

[82] See e.g. *Labour Relations Code*, RSBC 1996, c 244; *Labour Relations Act, 1995*, SO 1995, c 1, Sch A; *Trade Union Act*, RSNS 1989, c 475.

dismissal, progressive discipline, and reinstatement. Only if the collective agreement prescribes working conditions above the level required by existing legislation does it replaces employee welfare legislation in protecting the interests of workers. Human rights legislation continues to apply.

First Collective Agreement Frequently the most difficult collective agreement to reach is the first one after certification: The union is new, and its local members are inexperienced (even if they have advice from other union officials); management is unaccustomed to working with a union; and sometimes hostility and bitterness between employer and employees lingers from the certification process. In response to the problem, most provinces and the federal government have legislation providing for "first contract arbitration."[83] If the parties cannot reach agreement on a contract within the time stated in the Act, then the applicable provincial or federal labour board may impose a first contract on them after hearing the parties in an arbitration.

LABOUR DISPUTES

Types of Disputes

There are four major types of disputes affecting trade unions: jurisdictional disputes, recognition disputes, interest disputes, and rights disputes.

jurisdictional dispute two or more unions compete for the right to represent a particular group of employees

recognition dispute an employer refuses to recognize the union as the employees' bargaining agent

interest dispute an employer and the union disagree about the particular terms to be included in the collective agreement

rights dispute an employer and the union differ in their interpretation or application of terms in an existing collective agreement

1. A **jurisdictional dispute** is a disagreement between unions competing for the right to represent a group of employees. For instance, the type of work the employees do might seem to bring them within the terms of reference of two different trade unions. A single operation of drilling a hole through both metal and wood might raise a question of whether the worker should belong to the metalworkers' or the woodworkers' union.
2. A **recognition dispute** arises between an employer and a union when the employer insists on negotiating employment contracts directly with its employees and resists a union demand that it be recognized as the employees' bargaining agent.
3. An **interest dispute** arises when an employer and a union cannot reach agreement about the terms to be included in a collective agreement.
4. A **rights dispute**, commonly known as a grievance, is a difference of opinion between employer and union on the interpretation or application of terms in a collective agreement already in existence.

Legislative Regulation of Dispute Resolution

Labour statutes provide machinery that either eliminates or minimizes the need to resort to strike action in each of the four main types of dispute mentioned above. Certification procedure, briefly considered in the preceding section, has done much to resolve jurisdictional disputes and is the only legal means of settling recognition disputes.

Provincial statutes require both employer and employees to follow a series of procedures designed to aid in the settlement of interest disputes:

- First, they require a genuine attempt over a specified period to bargain to reach agreement.[84]

---

[83] RSBC 1996, c 244, s 55; RSQ 1991, c C-27, s 93.1; RSM 1987, c L-10, s 75; SO 1995, c 1, Sch A, s 43.

[84] In Canada, an employer need not bargain with a union that has not been certified and with which it has not previously made a collective agreement. In the United States, an employer must bargain with a union representing the majority of its employees, whether it is certified or not.

- Second, if the parties fail to agree, they must submit to **conciliation procedure**—that is, continue to bargain with the help of a conciliation officer or board.
- Third, if the parties still fail to agree, the conciliator will file a "no board report"; the employer cannot declare a lockout, nor can the union begin strike action, until a further specified **cooling-off period** has elapsed after the no board report.

For a rights dispute, the law imposes **arbitration procedure**; the parties are bound by the interpretation placed on the collective agreement by an arbitrator. In conciliation procedure, the parties are not bound to accept the solution proposed by the conciliation officer, but in arbitration procedure, the decision of the arbitrator is binding.

Only in interest disputes is there the possibility of lawful strike action, and then only after the prescribed conciliation procedure and cooling-off period. A strike is illegal if the preliminary procedures set down by statute have not been followed or, even when they have been followed, if the strike is not conducted according to carefully defined rules. The conduct of a strike by the union must be free of compulsion, intimidation, and threat. Furthermore, a strike may become unlawful if it is undertaken with an intent to injure another party and not with the intent of improving the employment interests of the strikers.

Although strikers are entitled to picket at or near the place of the employer's business, they must do so peaceably and only for the purpose of obtaining or communicating information. Statements made on placards or in literature distributed at the scene of the picketing must be correct and factual. Mr. Chief Justice McRuer of the Ontario Supreme Court outlined the scope of these rights as follows:

> It is one thing to exercise all the lawful rights to strike and the lawful rights to picket; that is a freedom that should be preserved and its preservation has advanced the interests of the labouring man and the community as a whole to an untold degree over the last half-century. But it is another thing to recognize a conspiracy to injure so that benefits to any particular person or class may be realized. Further, if what any person or group of persons does amounts to a common law nuisance to another what is being done may be restrained by injunction.[85]

This is a complicated area of law, and we attempt only a basic overview in this section. Authorities listed in the bibliography at the end of this text offer a complete description.

conciliation procedure bargaining with the help of a conciliation officer or board

cooling-off period a time during which the employer cannot declare a lockout nor can the union begin a strike

arbitration procedure the procedure in a rights dispute that binds the parties to accept the interpretation of the collective agreement by an arbitrator

Implications of the Collective Agreement for the Individual Employee

The parties to a collective agreement are the employer and the representative union; generally, each party is a large organization or institution, and the individual employee does not actively participate in negotiating the terms of employment. The union may also be a large organization with smaller segments known as locals representing specific workplaces. The union bargaining team is elected by the members of the local. Since nearly all the bargaining is done by the union, comparatively little ground is left for an employee to negotiate with the employer at the time of making an individual contract of employment.

The province of Quebec has a unique piece of legislation that takes this process a step further. The terms of a collective agreement may apply even to workers who are not members of the bargaining unit for which the union was entitled to negotiate.[86] Under the legislation, when a union has bargained for a certain rate of pay with one

---

[85] *General Dry Batteries of Canada Ltd v Brigenshaw*, [1951] OR 522 at 528.
[86] *Collective Agreement Decrees Act*, RSQ 1991, c D-2.

or more large employers within the industry, the parties may apply to the Minister of Labour for a decree extending the provisions of the collective agreement to all other employers and employees within the industry or trade in the province or within a region of the province. To succeed, the application must show that the collective agreements already written have acquired a dominance and importance for establishing conditions of labour within the industry or region. The effect is to establish a minimum wage law within the area covered by the decree, and to extend the terms of the collective agreement to workers within the industry not represented when the contract was made.

Unions have the dominant role in bargaining on behalf of individual workers; often workers do not have the freedom to choose whether to belong to the union and do not like the terms that the union negotiates on their behalf. In *Bonsor v Musicians' Union*, the plaintiff, who had been wrongfully expelled from the union and found it impossible to earn a living as a musician without being a member, said "I will be a member by force because I am forced to be a member."[87]

After hearing the plaintiff, the judge commented that a collective agreement is less like a contract and more like "a legislative code laid down by some members of the union to be imposed on all members of the union. They are more like by-laws than a contract."[88]

THE LEGAL STATUS OF TRADE UNIONS

trade union an organization of employees formed for purposes that include the regulation of relations between employees and employers

Under labour relations legislation, a **trade union** is defined as an organization of employees formed for purposes that include the regulation of relations between employees and employers.[89] They are empowered to bargain and appear before labour relations boards in order to bind them to the board's rulings; a representative action provides a possible means by which unions may sue or be sued in the courts. Still confusion exists about their precise legal status and relationship with their members because they lack the separate legal identity afforded to corporations.

In a famous British case from 1901, trade unions were declared to be a "quasi-corporate" body that could be sued.[90] Decades later the Supreme Court of Canada stated that

> The Legislature, by giving the right to act as agent for others and to contract on their behalf, has given them [trade unions] two of the essential qualities of a corporation in respect of liability for tort since a corporation can only act by its agents.[91]

The Court concluded that since a trade union could own property and employ agents, it must be suable for torts committed by them. This led some provinces to expressly make unions suable entities,[92] whereas others such as Ontario enacted statutory provisions that restrict the possibility of an action against a trade union for torts.[93]

In the process of deciding Case 18.6, the Supreme Court of Canada recognized contractual liability:

---

[87] [1954] Ch 479, overturned on appeal [1956] AC 105).

[88] *Bonsor v Musicians' Union*, [1954] Ch 479 at 485.

[89] See e.g. *Labour Relations Act, 1995*, SO 1995, c 1, Sch A, s 1.

[90] *Taff Vale Railway Co v Amalgamated Society of Railway Servants*, [1901] AC 426.

[91] *International Brotherhood of Teamsters v Thérien*, (1960), 22 DLR (2d) 1 at 11; See e.g. *UNA v Alberta (Attorney-General)* (1990), 89 DLR (4th) 609.

[92] For legislation expressly making unions suable entities, see *Labour Relations Code*, RSBC 1996, c 144, s 154; *Industrial Relations Act*, RSNB 1973, c I-4, s 114(2); *Trade Union Act*, RSS 1978, c T-17, s 29, as amended by SS 1983, c 81, s 9.

[93] *Rights of Labour Act*, RSO 1990, c R.33, s 3.

CASE 18.6 Contractual Liability

Trade union members wanted to sue former members of their union for breach of the union's constitution—they framed the action as a breach of contract action between members. The Supreme Court held that there was no contract between members. Instead, each member had a contract with the union itself, so if there was a breach, it was the union's cause of action.[94]

> It follows that unions must have sufficient legal personality to enter into contracts of membership, and that this is an aspect of union affairs for which legislatures have impliedly conferred legal status on unions . . . the time has come to recognize formally that when a member joins a union, a relationship in the nature of a contract arises between the member and the trade union as a legal entity.[95]

Strategies to Manage the Legal Risks

When dealing with individual employment relationships:

- Establish job related criteria for job applicants—this will avoid consideration of the personal characteristics of prospective employees in violation of human rights legislation.
- Initially hire employees on short fixed-term contracts that naturally come to an end.
- Replace implied terms for reasonable notice of termination in employment of indefinite length with express contractual terms designating the amount of notice that will serve to terminate the agreement.
- Create detailed job descriptions and codes of conduct describing employee responsibilities, and share them with prospective employees as part of the employment contract.
- Create, publish, and follow a protocol for progressive employee discipline.
- Document infractions and responses.
- Follow consistent warning and discipline processes that allow employees to respond to allegations.
- Offer incompetent employees training or education opportunities.
- Dismiss employees privately, at the end of the day, and in the most sensitive, fair, and respectful manner possible.

When dealing with independent contractors:

- Respect the characteristics of an independent contractorship to avoid confusing the relationship for one of employment.
- Require independent contractors to carry their own liability insurance, and obtain a promise to indemnify the business if it is held liable for substandard work or negligence of the independent contractor.
- Ensure that exemption clauses in contracts with customers extend protection to independent contractors completing work under it.

When dealing with a unionized workforce, specialized legal advice should be obtained to guide management through the processes, especially when interest- or jurisdictional-based disputes arise. For rights-based disputes, the grievance process of arbitration should be followed. Parties should commence negotiations well in advance of the expiration of the existing collective agreement so that a new contract may be in place before the former's end.

---

[94] *Berry v Pulley*, 2002 SCC 40.

[95] *Ibid* at paras 46–49.

QUESTIONS FOR REVIEW

1. Briefly describe two employees, each of whom has varying degrees of responsibility as agent.
2. How does an independent contractor differ from an employee? From a dependent contractor?
3. Give an example of circumstances where an employee commits a tort, but his employer is not liable. What element is necessary to make the employer liable?
4. After earning his B. Comm. degree, Bruce was hired as a junior accountant by Cargo Wholesale Inc. He received favourable assessment letters and salary increases after year one and year two. At the end of his third year, he received his final paycheque with a letter stating that he was dismissed for incompetence. What points might Bruce argue to show that he was wrongfully dismissed?
5. Norman is hired as a waiter in a restaurant at a summer resort without any discussion about the length of his employment contract. He receives a weekly paycheque. He is let go without notice at the end of the summer. Explain whether he has been wrongfully dismissed.
6. On what grounds is a business justified in dismissing its employees without notice?
7. What are the main factors to be taken into account when assessing damages for wrongful dismissal?
8. When is reinstatement an unlikely remedy for wrongful dismissal?
9. Why is it not effective to define pay equity solely in terms of the market value of comparable jobs?
10. Describe factors relevant to an employer's obligation to accommodate a disabled employee.
11. Describe briefly the benefits of and problems with compulsory retirement.
12. Under workers' compensation legislation, who pays compensation to an injured employee? How are the funds raised?
13. Describe some of the main elements in a collective agreement.
14. In certain provinces and in federal jurisdiction, what happens when the parties do not succeed in making a deal for their first collective agreement?
15. What is the difference between a jurisdictional dispute and an interest dispute?
16. Collective agreements have been described by some commentators as being more like legislation for individual workers. Explain.
17. Quality Meat Packers Ltd. has major factories and warehouses from coast to coast. How does this fact complicate the company's collective bargaining with its employees?

CASES AND PROBLEMS

1. *Continuing Scenario*

    Benson was hired as a waiter at Ashley's restaurant; he had 15 years of table service experience even though he was just 30 years old. Six months after he began work, Ashley learned that Benson had behaved inappropriately at the restaurant, insulting several customers after he had too much to drink. Ashley called Benson on the telephone and told him he would be fired if he ever drank alcohol at work again. Two months later, there was another incident at work when Benson was rude to customers. Benson was not working at the time and had only stopped by the restaurant to pick up his jacket. Ashley was furious: She dismissed Benson and gave him two weeks' payment in lieu of notice.

    Benson sued for damages for wrongful dismissal, claiming 12 months' salary.

Ashley did not claim that she dismissed Benson for drinking while on duty; in fact, Ashley was not aware of such conduct. She argued that two weeks' notice was all that Benson should receive. However, at the trial, evidence of other employees and patrons of the restaurant established that Benson had been drinking at work on many occasions after Ashley's warning.

Should Benson's action succeed? Why? Would your answer be different if Ashley had simply demoted Benson to kitchen dishwasher (where he wouldn't see customers) with a reduction in pay?

2. Taxi drivers owned their own taxis and worked for Welcome Taxis Ltd. The taxi company called them "independent contractors" and distinguished them from employees in that they were not covered by the *Employment Insurance Act*. Although the company neither owned nor leased the vehicles, the drivers were required to comply with the company's directions about the dispatch services and how the vehicles were operated. They were also obligated to use the company's bookkeeping and fuel provision services—and the company could suspend or discharge the drivers for any breach of its rules.

   The Ministry of National Revenue decided to assess Welcome and require it to pay premiums for each of its drivers as an employee. Welcome appealed to the court, and the trial judge concluded that such a degree of control was exercised by the taxi company over the drivers that all the drivers were in insurable employment, pursuant to section 6(e) of the Act. The taxi company brought an application for judicial review to the Federal Court of Appeal. The following arguments were made:

   - *By Welcome Taxis Ltd.*—The drivers were owners or operators of their own businesses within the meaning of section 6(e) of the Regulations. The trial judge erred in considering only the factor of control to the exclusion of other relevant factors. Another consideration was who owned the tools of the trade. Not only did the drivers own the vehicles, but also they were in a position to gain a profit or suffer a loss from the operation of the business. The degree of financial risk taken by the drivers was considerably more than that taken by the company. The drivers were in a position to delegate their driving duties, which indicated independent status. Given the chance of profit, the relative degree of financial risk, and the ability of the drivers to "operate their own business," they were not employees of the company.
   - *By the Ministry of National Revenue*—Under a traditional employee/independent contractor analysis, the drivers appeared to be in business for their own account, as independent contractors. However, the breadth of section 6(e) was broad enough to extend the conventional meaning of "employment." The company exercised a great deal of control over the drivers. Although it did not own or lease the vehicles, it retained the right to cancel the lease agreement or exercise its option to purchase the vehicle if the drivers should fail to observe its rules. The trial judge had not erred in applying a liberal interpretation of section 6(e) and finding that the drivers were included in insurable employment.

   Which argument do you think should succeed in the Court of Appeal? Give reasons for your opinion.

3. C. W. Jonas was a conductor employed by the East-West Railway Company. While the passenger train on which he was working was standing in a railway station, it was struck by another train. Because of the negligent operation of the train, Jonas was severely injured. He sued the East-West Railway Company for damages for negligence.

   In defence, the railway company produced its copy of an employment contract signed by Jonas. The contract included the following clause:

   > The employee, C. W. Jonas, agrees that in consideration of employment and wages by the Great East-West Railway Company, he will assume all risks of accident or casualty incident to such employment and service whether caused by the negligence

of the Company or of its employees or otherwise, and will forever release, acquit, and discharge the said Company from all liability. The employee waives all rights to worker's compensation that might otherwise arise under this contract.

Without rendering a decision, discuss the public policy considerations inherent in a dispute of this kind.

4. Devellano operated a retail food supermarket that bought 60 percent of its merchandise from Prairie Wholesale Grocers Limited. Because of a wage dispute, the employees of Prairie Wholesale Grocers, who were members of the Office and Shop Clerks Union, went on strike. An official of that union then telephoned Devellano to enlist her support and apply economic pressure on Prairie Wholesale Grocers by reducing purchases from it. When Devellano refused, members of the union picketed her supermarket. They stopped cars on their way into the parking lot of the supermarket and distributed leaflets, intimating, inaccurately, that Devellano's store was controlled by Prairie Wholesale Grocers. The placards used while picketing contained the words "Devellano's Supermarket" and "Strike" in large letters, although none of Devellano's own employees were on strike. As a result, Devellano lost customers and sued the union for damages and an injunction to restrain the picketing of her premises.

Discuss the defences available to the union, and state whether they would succeed.

5. Lucy Anang was hired as a chemist by the Plastic Toy Co. Her employment contract stated that, following termination of her employment with the company, she would not work for any competitor in the province for five years or at any time in the future disclose to anyone any information about secret processes used by Plastic Toy Co. Anang had worked in the laboratory of the company for a period of about three years when she was given two months' notice of dismissal.

After her dismissal, Anang tried to earn a living as a consulting chemist. The plant supervisor at Plastic Toy then learned that she was disclosing certain information about manufacturing processes to one of the company's chief competitors. Specifically, it appeared that she had disclosed secret processes related to the production of equipment used in the colouring of toys, processes of value to the company.

Plastic Toy Co. sued Anang for damages and for an injunction restraining her from disclosing further information. One of Anang's defences was that no injunction could be granted to deprive her of the right to practise her profession as a chemist. What is the likelihood that the action will succeed?

Suppose instead that Anang had left Plastic Toy Co. because she had received an offer of a higher salary from a competitor of Plastic Toy. The management of Plastic Toy had no evidence that she disclosed any of its secret processes to her new employer but was concerned that she might do so. Is it likely that Plastic Toy could obtain an injunction restraining Anang from working for its competitor? What conflicting policy issues must the court resolve?

6. In May 1986, the directors of Universal Printing Co., publishers of a newspaper with a large circulation, approached Bell to persuade him to become their assistant advertising manager. They suggested that, if he accepted, he would probably succeed the present advertising manager upon that manager's retirement. At the time, Bell held a responsible position with an advertising agency and was 42. During the discussions, Bell emphasized that his present position was a very satisfactory one, that it was important at his age that his employment be permanent, and that he would not consider a change that did not offer the prospect of a position lasting for the balance of his working life.

After careful consideration, Bell accepted the position offered at a salary of $65 000 a year. He was promoted to advertising manager in 1994, and in the period from May 1986 to July 2002, his salary was increased regularly until it reached an annual sum of $160 000. In addition, every year he received a discretionary

Christmas bonus approved by the directors and a special distribution pursuant to a profit-sharing plan confined to selected employees and made under the sole direction of the principal shareholder of Universal Printing Co. Ltd. Bell's receipts under the profit-sharing plan were $23 600 in 1999, $20 400 in 2000, and $17 000 in 2001.

In August 2002, the president of Universal Printing Co. Ltd., T. G. Dodds, called Bell into his office and, after some opening pleasantries about Bell's prowess in golf, told Bell he thought another advertising manager he had in mind could produce better results for the company. Dodds told Bell that if he could see his way clear to resigning forthwith, he might have three months' salary in lieu of notice. Bell replied that he could not afford at this stage in his career to admit to the incompetence implied in a resignation and refused. Later in the afternoon, his secretary brought him the following letter:

August 8, 2002

Dear Mr. Bell:

This is to confirm the notice given to you today of the termination of your employment with Universal Printing Co. Ltd. as of this date. Enclosed is a cheque for your salary to date. Your pension plan has been commuted to a paid-up basis that will pay you $3500 a month commencing at age 65.

T. G. Dodds

Bell at once made efforts to secure other employment and by December 8, 2002, found a position with an advertising agency at a salary of $42 000 a year. If he had remained a further year with Universal Printing Co. Ltd., the paid-up value of his pension would have increased to $6500 per month.

Bell brought an action against Universal Printing Co. Ltd. for damages for wrongful dismissal. What amount of damages, if any, should he recover? Are there any additional facts you would like to know?

7. In September, Knowles, the owner of a professional hockey club, began negotiations with Meyer, a professional hockey player, for Meyer's services for the following two years. The two agreed orally to a salary of $3000 a week for Meyer during the training and playing seasons. At the time, Meyer asked whether players would be covered by workers' compensation insurance if injured. Knowles replied that the club's lawyer had advised that players were not covered, but that in any event he was having written contracts drawn up by the lawyer in which a clause would provide that every player would be insured against injury and that if a player were disabled, he would be looked after.

Written contracts were then prepared and presented to all the players (including Meyer) for signing. The contracts in their written form stated the agreed salary for each individual player and outlined the usual conditions regarding the player's obligations to the club, but there was no reference to insurance protection against injury or to the employer's obligation in the event of a player being disabled.

Meyer played for the team for six weeks and then received a serious injury to his eye during a hockey game. He was immediately taken to the hospital. At the end of the game, Knowles announced to Meyer's teammates in the dressing room that he would pay Meyer's salary to the end of the season.

Knowles paid Meyer's salary to the date of his injury and refused to pay any additional sum. Meyer brought an action for damages claiming $45 000 representing his salary for the remaining 15 weeks of the playing season; $500 for the cost of an artificial eye; and $100 000 general damages as compensation for the loss of his eye.

Discuss the issues raised by these facts, and explain whether Meyer's action is likely to succeed.

Chapter 19
Banking and Negotiable Instruments

- WHAT IS A BANK?
- REGULATION OF BANKS
- REGULATION OF NON-BANK FINANCIAL INSTITUTIONS
- WHAT IS A NEGOTIABLE INSTRUMENT?
- NATURE AND USES OF NEGOTIABLE INSTRUMENTS
- PREREQUISITES FOR PAYMENT
- NEGOTIABILITY
- METHODS OF NEGOTIATION
- PURPOSES OF ENDORSEMENT
- LIABILITY OF PARTIES
- PROVING LIABILITY
- HOLDER IN DUE COURSE
- DEFENCES
- CONSUMER BILLS AND NOTES
- MODERN ALTERNATIVES TO CASH
- STRATEGIES TO MANAGE THE LEGAL RISKS

Banks are central to many business activities, including depositing, transferring, and borrowing money. For centuries, negotiable instruments were the main method of paying debts and moving funds. Recently, the traditional payment system has been transformed by the electronic transfer of funds. This chapter discusses the legal environment of the banking industry and the specific rules applicable to the instruments that move money.

In this chapter we examine such questions as:

- What is a bank?
- How are banks regulated?
- What are negotiable instruments?
- What is meant by negotiability?
- What are the methods, purposes, and consequences of endorsement?
- What is the liability of various parties to a negotiable instrument?
- What defences are available to the parties?
- Are consumer bills and notes treated differently?
- What new rules apply to the electronic transfer of funds?

WHAT IS A BANK?

A bank is one type of financial institution. It provides financial services, investment counselling, and money management services and operates payment, credit, and charge card plans. Banks may not carry on insurance, auto leasing, or securities businesses. Some banks get around this restriction by conducting such businesses through corporate groups, discussed in Chapter 25.

Banks can be sorted into three categories: **domestic banks** (Canadian), **subsidiaries** of **foreign banks**, and bank branches of foreign banks. The rules controlling a bank's operations vary depending upon the bank's category. Despite its name, the Bank of Canada is not a typical bank. It is the government's bank, and it acts as the bank for banks. It is responsible for monetary policy, payment clearing systems, and currency and oversees the economic and financial welfare of Canada.[1]

domestic bank a bank incorporated in Canada in compliance with the *Bank Act*; publicly owned and traded on a Canadian stock exchange

subsidiary an entity controlled by another entity

foreign bank a bank incorporated in a country other than Canada according to that country's banking laws

REGULATION OF BANKS

The Canadian Constitution gives the federal government the exclusive power to regulate banks, so the rules are the same for banks in every province. The *Bank Act* is the key statute, and the Office of the Superintendent of Financial Institutions (OSFI) is the overseeing regulatory body that supervises the banks.[2] The Superintendent must approve the operations of any bank (foreign or domestic) before it may accept deposits, lend money, or make investments (s. 51), and it may punish (fine or shut down) a bank that does not follow the rules.

The *Bank Act* describes the requirements for incorporation and the share structure of a bank. A domestic bank must be incorporated in Canada, publicly owned, and traded on a Canadian stock exchange. The *Bank Act* outlines corporate governance processes, regulates recordkeeping and auditing responsibilities, and sets the **capital adequacy** and **liquidity** requirements (s. 485). Banks must hold a certain percentage of capital (assets) in liquid (easily cashable) forms. Regulations promote efficiency, stability, and public confidence in the banking industry and therefore the national economy.

During the 2008 financial crisis, no Canadian bank failed or needed "bailing out." Six of Canada's largest domestic banks are designated as **systemically important banks**.[3]

capital adequacy sufficient assets as compared to liabilities

liquidity how quickly and easily an asset is convertible into cash

systemically important banks large domestic banks that OSFI identifies as having a major impact on the Canadian financial system

---

[1] *Bank of Canada Act*, RSC 1985, c B-2, Preamble, ss 18, 25; *Currency Act*, RSC 1985, c C-52.

[2] *Bank Act*, SC 1991, c 46 as amended. (The *Bank Act* is reviewed (and updated) every five years); *Office of the Superintendent of Financial Institutions Act*, RSC 1985, c 18.

[3] Royal Bank of Canada, Toronto Dominion Bank, Bank of Montreal, Bank of Nova Scotia, Canadian Imperial Bank of Commerce, and National Bank of Canada.

They are subject to extra regulation regarding share structure and liabilities because their success or failure could have major impact on Canada's financial system as a whole (ss. 485.01, 484.1(3)). Canadian banking requirements about capital and liquidity align with global rules established after the 2008 financial crisis.[4]

The rules applicable to bank accounts, such as interest paid or fees charged, must be set out in an account agreement with the customer (s. 440). Banks must have established procedures for dealing with complaints (s. 455). The Financial Consumer Agency of Canada imposes additional consumer protection measures on banks,[5] and a bank must also comply with the requirements of the *Canada Deposit Insurance Corporation Act* (ss. 413, 437) in order to accept deposits.[6]

REGULATION OF NON-BANK FINANCIAL INSTITUTIONS

Non-bank financial institutions are trust and loan companies, cooperatives and credit unions, and insurance companies. They are controlled by both federal and provincial regulation. The OSFI also supervises these financial institutions according to provincial and federal regulatory legislation (see Table 19.1).

These financial institutions may also accept deposits and make loans. It is hard to distinguish non-bank financial institutions from banks. The key differences are outlined in Table 19.2.

Although all financial institutions must protect the privacy of customer information,[7] an exception is made when **money laundering** is suspected. All financial institutions must comply with the *Proceeds of Crime (Money Laundering) and Terrorist Financing Act* and report suspicious or large cross-border transfers of funds to **FINTRAC**.[8]

money laundering transfer of proceeds of crime to conceal their origin

FINTRAC Financial Transactions and Report Analysis Centre of Canada

Table 19.1 Legislation for Non-Bank Financial Institutions

Non-Bank Financial Institution	Applicable Federal Legislation	Example of Applicable Provincial Legislation
Trust and loan companies	*Trust and Loan Companies Act*	*Financial Institutions Act* (BC)
Cooperative credit associations	*Cooperative Credit Association Act*	*Credit Union Incorporation Act* (BC)
Insurance companies	*Insurance Companies Act*	*Financial Institutions Act* (BC)
Federal credit unions	*Bank Act*	

Table 19.2 How They Differ from Banks

Non-Bank Financial Institution	Difference from Banks
Trust and loan companies	Are fiduciaries and trustees for money, trust, and estates
Cooperative credit associations	Are owned by their members, not the public
Insurance companies	Sell insurance against risk
Federal credit unions	Are owned by their members, not the public

---

[4] Basell III Accord.

[5] *Financial Consumer Agency of Canada Act*, SC 2001, c 9.

[6] RSC 1985, c C-3.

[7] *Personal Information and Protection of Documents Act*, SC 2000, c 5.

[8] SC 2000, c 17; http://www.fintrac.gc.ca/intro-eng.asp.

INTERNATIONAL ISSUE
Combatting Money Laundering and Terrorism

Global financial institutions play a huge role in combatting money laundering and fighting terrorism. It is their responsibility to screen all financial transactions to identify suspicious activity, block it, and file a suspicious activity report with their regulator. Global regulators share information and identify trends, regions, and violators through membership in an association of 100 financial intelligence units. In Canada, FINTRAC performs this function; in the United States it is the Financial Crimes Enforcement Network (FinCEN).

Failure to properly screen and report results in significant fines for financial institutions. In 2016 FINTRAC fined Manulife Bank of Canada $1.2 million for money-laundering tracking violations.

A transaction could be suspicious because

- it involves a suspicious party,
- it involves a suspicious bank (or intermediary),
- it involves a suspicious industry, or
- it involves a suspicious or sanctioned geographic area.

For example, FinCEN identified the Los Angeles garment district as a geographic target area after reports revealed a money-laundering ring and netted a seizure of $90 000 000 (US) in cash. Miami's electronics industry was similarly identified. Banks must also enforce sanctions. Sanctions are financial restrictions used by governments or government organizations such as the UN to punish or persuade a particular group or country to change its behaviours. Sanctions may be imposed on a country or geographic area, a designated person or entity, or an economic sector such as oil or diamonds. Again, transactions must be screened to ensure they do not involve a sanctioned country, entity, or sector. Canadian banks enforce sanctions imposed by all organizations and treaties Canada participates in. Any breach of sanctions is a criminal offence that involves a significant fine against the bank and could lead to imprisonment for bank employees and executives.

A good example of the international aspect of sanction enforcement is Deutsche Bank. This German bank was fined $258 million (US) for doing business with Iran and Syria in violation of US sanctions. Six bank employees were fired.

Questions to Consider

1. Why do you think global regulators have put financial institutions in charge of detecting money-laundering crime and enforcing sanctions?
2. Do you think it is appropriate to punish a bank or imprison employees for failure to comply with detection obligations?

Sources: Financial Crimes Enforcement Network, https://fincen.gov/what-we-do; Egmont Group, http://www.egmontgroup.org/en/membership/list; Marco Chown Oved et al., "Manulife Admits It Was the Bank Fined $1.2 Million by Canada's Money-laundering Watchdog," TheStar.com, Feb 27, 2017, https://www.thestar.com/news/world/2017/02/27/manulife-admits-it-was-bank-fined-12-million-by-canadas-money-laundering-watchdog.html; FinCen Press Release Oct. 2. 2014, https://www.fincen.gov/news/news-releases/fincen-issues-geographic-targeting-order-covering-los-angeles-fashion-district; Jonathan Marino, "Deutsche Bank Fired Staff and Is Paying a $258M Fine for Violating Sanctions 27,000 Times," Business Insider, Nov 4, 2015, http://www.businessinsider.com/deutsche-bank-fined-for-violating-sanctions-2015-11.

WHAT IS A NEGOTIABLE INSTRUMENT?

A negotiable instrument is a document ordering the payment of money that may be transferred from one person to another. It is an alternative to carrying cash; examples are cheques and bank drafts. Negotiable instruments fall under federal jurisdiction, so the legal rules about creating and transferring them are standard across the country. The *Bills of Exchange Act*[9] sets out the legal rules. The last section of Chapter 11 introduced the special rules about negotiable instruments; re-reading that section will be helpful before proceeding with this chapter.

A **bill of exchange** is the original negotiable instrument; it is a document made by a purchaser or banker in one location instructing a colleague elsewhere to make a payment to a certain person or to the bearer of the document. Bills of exchange helped early exporters and importers do business across borders. A buyer in England who bought goods from a vendor located in Germany could arrange for payment for the

bill of exchange a written order by one party to another party to pay a specified sum of money to a named party or to the bearer of the document

---

[9] *Bills of Exchange Act*, RSC 1985, c B-4. When a footnote mentions a section only, the reference is to this Act.

goods by a banker in Germany, making it unnecessary to transport cash. For a small fee, the English buyer could arrange for an English firm dealing in bills of exchange to draw a bill on its agent in Germany, instructing him to pay the German vendor on a certain date. The vendor would accept the bill of exchange as payment for his product. At regular intervals, all the firms dealing in bills of exchange would get together and tally the "bills" they had honoured and pay each other any difference owing. This form of setting off credits eventually grew into more sophisticated government-regulated "clearing houses."

Today's payment system is overseen by the Bank of Canada. The clearing and settlement of payments is supervised by the Canadian Payments Association under authority of the *Canadian Payments Act*[10] and the rules set out in the *Payment Clearing and Settlements Act*.[11] Its members are the Bank of Canada, domestic banks, authorized foreign banks, loan and trust companies, and credit unions.

NATURE AND USES OF NEGOTIABLE INSTRUMENTS

Personal Property

Chapter 11 discussed—**choses in action**—and noted that negotiable instruments are a unique kind of chose in action. This chapter considers the unique characteristics of negotiable instruments that make them especially useful in business.

choses in action rights to intangible property such as unperformed contracts

Every negotiable instrument contains an express or implied promise made by one or more parties to pay the amount stated in the instrument. Unless there is other information, the promisee is presumed to have given good consideration for the promise. A negotiable instrument is normally a self-contained contract with the details of its terms written on it. Often a negotiable instrument is given to a vendor as payment for goods or services.

Types of Instruments

The most common types of negotiable instruments are bills of exchange (known as drafts), promissory notes, and cheques.

Share certificates could be negotiable instruments. The *Canada Business Corporations Act* states expressly that a share certificate whose transfer is not restricted by words printed on its face is a negotiable instrument.[12] However, it is very common for the articles of incorporation or unanimous shareholder agreement to restrict the transfer of shares, so most shares are not negotiable instruments.

Bills of Exchange (Drafts)

drawer the party who draws up the bill of exchange

drawee the party who is required to make payment on the bill of exchange

payee the party named to receive payment on the bill of exchange

A bill of exchange (see Figure 19.1) is a written order by one party, the **drawer**, addressed to another party, the **drawee**, to pay a specified sum of money to a named party, the **payee**, or to the bearer, at a fixed or determinable future time or on demand. A bill of exchange originates with a drawer (creditor) and directs a drawee (existing debtor) to acknowledge indebtedness and to agree to pay according to the terms stated in the document. A drawer sometimes designates itself as a payee. Most of the time it involves a third party; the drawer directs that the money be paid to some other person

---

[10] RSC 1985, c C-21, ss 3, 4, 5.

[11] SC 1996, c C-21, ss 3, 4, 5.

[12] *Canada Business Corporations Act*, RSC 1985, c C-44, ss 48(3), 49.

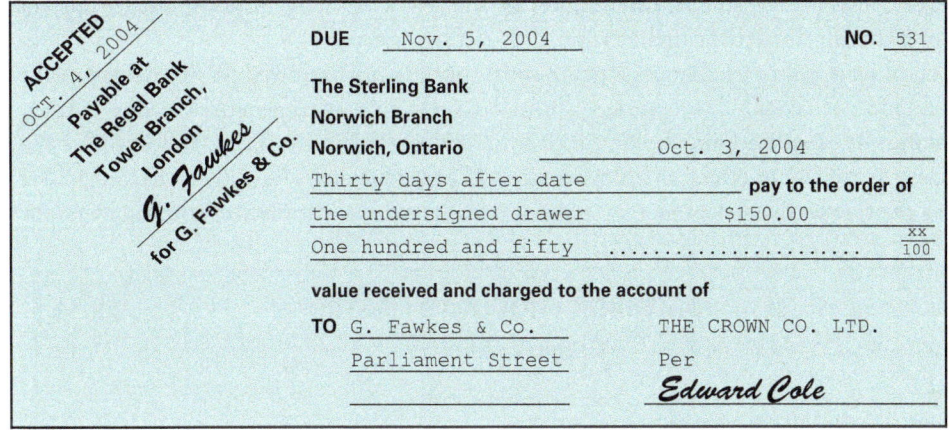

Figure 19.1   A Bill of Exchange (Accepted Time Draft)

or business to whom the drawer owes money. The drawer expects the debtor (drawee) to consent by signing the instrument together with the word "accepted" and the date; the drawee then becomes an **acceptor** who is obligated to pay the sum.

A bill of exchange may pass among a number of holders as an item of valuable personal property even before it has been accepted. It has value for a holder because the drawer, by drawing and delivering it, has made an implied promise guaranteeing its payment.[13] Its subsequent acceptance adds the express promise of the acceptor to pay the amount.

An acceptor may indicate that the bill is to be paid out of its bank account. The drawer (or a subsequent holder) may then leave the instrument with its own bank for collection and have it deposited in its account. That bank will present the bill to the acceptor's bank for payment out of the acceptor's account. After the amount is deducted from the acceptor's account, the cancelled bill of exchange is returned to the acceptor as evidence of payment, just as cancelled cheques are returned.

Bills of exchange vary depending upon the time of payment:

- **Demand draft**, payable immediately upon presentation without any days of grace before payment.
- **Sight draft**, which the drawee is ordered to pay "at sight." In Canada, three days of grace for making payment are allowed after presentation for acceptance.
- **Time draft**, payable a stipulated number of days, months, or other period "after date" (after the date stated on the instrument) or "after sight" (after presentation for acceptance). Three days of grace should be added in fixing the maturity of a time draft. A bill payable at a given time after sight is a time draft, not a sight draft. Presentation for acceptance is necessary whenever a bill is payable at sight or after sight, so that the time at which payment is due may be figured out.[14]

acceptor   the drawee who consents to the bill of exchange by signing it together with the word "accepted" and the date

demand draft   a bill of exchange payable immediately upon presentation without any days of grace

sight draft   a bill of exchange payable "at sight"—three days of grace are allowed after presentation

time draft   a bill of exchange payable within a stipulated period after the date stated on the instrument or after presentation

Promissory Notes

A **promissory note** is a written promise by one party, the **maker**, to pay a specified sum of money to another party, the payee, at a fixed or determinable future time or on demand. The maker is usually a debtor of the payee, and it prepares the instrument

promissory note   a written promise to pay a specified sum of money to another party at a fixed or determinable future time or on demand

maker   the party who signs and delivers a promissory note

---

[13] *Supra* note 9, s 129.

[14] *Ibid.*, ss 74, 76.

itself, though it may do so at the request of the payee. Usually, it is a two-party instrument between the debtor (maker) and the creditor (payee).

Unlike a bill of exchange, a promissory note is not required to be presented for acceptance. It contains an express promise to pay that is triggered by a due date or demand. To a subsequent holder, a promissory note that has been endorsed by the payee has the same effect as an accepted bill of exchange. The *Bills of Exchange Act* rules relating to the acceptance of bills of exchange do not apply to promissory notes.

```
                    SUPERIOR PRODUCTS LIMITED            No. 80013
                       Calgary, Alberta             April 26, 2004
  To
  THE STERLING BANK
     Lethbridge, Alberta

  Pay to the
  order of      C.B. BOWEN & CO. LTD.              $   400.00
  FOUR HUNDRED                                         DOLLARS
  ............................... XX/100

                                            SUPERIOR PRODUCTS LIMITED
                                       Per:   J. B. Riches
  Branch  0752
  Account 987654                         Per:   J.B. Walker
```

Figure 19.2   A Cheque

Cheques

cheque a bill of exchange drawn against a bank and payable on demand

A **cheque** (see Figure 19.2) is treated as a bill of exchange drawn against a bank and payable on demand.[15] From the point of view of the holder, a cheque contains the implied promise of its drawer that the drawer has funds on deposit at the bank sufficient to pay the cheque's amount, or that the amount is within the terms of a line of credit granted by the bank. For this reason, it is sometimes convenient to think of the drawer of a cheque as a "promisor." The bank on which the cheque is drawn is called the drawee bank. If the holder of the cheque takes it to his own bank for deposit in an account, once an equal amount is credited to the account, the holder's bank becomes the **holder in due course** of the cheque and will present it to the drawee bank through the payment settlement system mentioned above.

holder in due course a party who is not the original payee that acquires the cheque from that payee or a subsequent holder and is unaware of any defects

certification an undertaking by the bank to pay the amount of the cheque to its holder when later presented for payment

Certification   The *Bills of Exchange Act* does not mention the banking practice of certifying cheques.[16] **Certification** amounts to an undertaking by the drawee bank to pay the amount of the cheque to its holder when later presented for payment, and to ensure this result, the bank immediately deducts the amount of the cheque from the drawer's account. Certification takes the form of the bank's stamped acknowledgment, with date, on the face of the cheque. When a cheque is certified, the drawer is discharged from its promise; the drawee bank becomes liable to pay the certified amount to the payee.[17]

---

[15] *Ibid.*, s 164(2).

[16] See JD Falconbridge, *The Law of Negotiable Instruments in Canada* (Toronto: Ryerson, 1955) at 43.

[17] See B Crawford and JD Falconbridge, *Banking and Bills of Exchange*, 8th ed (Toronto: Canada Law Book, 1986) at 1791.

Occasionally, a supplier will refuse to release goods until paid by certified cheque. The buyer prepares a cheque payable to the supplier, has the drawee bank certify it, and then delivers it to the supplier. Or a payee may receive the cheque uncertified and, before releasing the goods, will have the bank certify it. Such a cheque is safer to hold than cash—a thief would have to forge an endorsement before being able to cash it. In addition, certification at the request of the holder prevents any attempt by the drawer to stop payment on the cheque. The bank must honour it.

Certification of a cheque is comparable to the acceptance of other types of bills of exchange.[18] Once certified, the bank assumes a liability to the holder for the amount of the cheque.

Postdated Cheques

The drawer may **postdate** a cheque by giving it a date later than the time when it is delivered to the payee. The bank must not pay the instrument before its date. Although a cheque is by definition payable "on demand," a holder's right to demand payment is not effective until the date on the cheque.

Postdating is convenient for a drawer who does not wish to pay in advance. It is common for a drawer to give a series of postdated cheques to meet future installment payments on a lease, for example.

postdate date a cheque later than the time when it is delivered to the payee

Stop Payment

After delivering a cheque, the drawer may learn that the payee is in serious breach of the contract between them. Before the cheque has been charged against its account, the drawer may countermand or **stop payment** by instructing its bank not to pay the cheque. The bank may require the drawer to agree that it will not be held responsible if, through its inadvertence, the cheque is paid out of the drawer's account in spite of the countermand.

Even a cheque certified at the request of its drawer and not yet delivered to the payee may be countermanded and the amount returned to the drawer's account at the bank. Since the bank has a liability on the certified cheque, it will reject the countermand unless the cheque is surrendered by the drawer for cancellation or the drawer agrees to indemnify the bank should the bank be sued for refusing to honour the cheque.

stop payment an instruction from the drawer of a cheque to the bank not to pay the cheque

Electronic Cheques

Just as paper cheques replaced sight drafts, time drafts, and promissory notes as the preferred manner of payment, electronic transfers of funds through electronic cheques, payment cards, and ecash are replacing paper cheques. This development is due in part to the speed and efficiency of electronic transfers. Many of the physical steps involved in processing a paper cheque can be completed much more quickly electronically using a digital image.

Electronic processing is known as **cheque truncation**.[19] The *Bills of Exchange Act* allows an "official image" of a cheque to be created by a bank and used for all purposes as though it were the original.[20] The Canadian Payments Association, created under the *Canadian Payments Act*,[21] regulates the size, form, and information contained on a paper cheque. The original paper cheque may be destroyed and the official digital image saved electronically.

A cheque, whether transferred electronically or physically—even one certified by a bank—is not legal tender. Strictly speaking, a creditor is entitled to payment in Bank

cheque truncation the physical movement of cheques is replaced by the electronic transfer of digital information

---

[18] The difference between certification and acceptance is confined to the circumstance where the drawee bank fails.

[19] Benjamin Geva, "Recent International Developments in the Law of Negotiable Instruments and Payment and Settlement Systems" (2007) 42 *Texas Int'l LJ* 685 at 688.

[20] *Supra* note 9, s 163.2.

[21] RSC 1985, c C-21, ss 3, 38, 39; see Canadian Payments Association Manual, available at http://www.cpa.ca (under Acts and Rules).

of Canada notes and in coins up to the designated amounts for each denomination. He cannot be forced to accept payment by cheque physically or electronically. However, to insist upon payment in cash would be inconvenient to both parties, and if a creditor refused a reasonable tender of payment by cheque and sued for payment in cash, court costs would likely be awarded against the creditor.

Finally, blank cheques are sometimes used as a source of information to initiate a separate electronic transfer of funds. A blank "void" cheque may be requested to facilitate regular automatic debits such as direct deposit of employee pay. Such a payment is sometimes referred to as an electronic cheque. This is not technically correct, as the act of voiding a paper cheque makes it legally incapable of being acted upon.

> **CHECKLIST**
>
> ## Classes of Negotiable Instruments
>
> The following negotiable instruments are governed by the federal *Bills of Exchange Act*:
>
> - bills of exchange (or drafts)
>   - demand drafts
>   - sight drafts
>   - time drafts
> - promissory notes
> - cheques
>   - postdated
>   - certified
>   - electronic

PREREQUISITES FOR PAYMENT

Until an instrument is delivered, a drawer, acceptor, or maker has no obligation to pay. After signing, he may still reconsider and tear it up before delivering it. A drawee has no liability in respect of a bill of exchange until after acceptance and delivery.

Delivery may be "actual"—the instrument being given directly by the promisor to the payee; or it may be "constructive"—simply by notice to the payee that the instrument is complete and ready for delivery.[22] Once an instrument has been delivered, the term "negotiation" is used to describe any subsequent transfer of it by the payee to a new holder, as well as any later transfers to other holders. The term "presentment" refers to the time when the instrument is finally submitted for payment to the named promisor or drawee bank. This final payment discharges the instrument or "cancels" the cheque.

NEGOTIABILITY

Meaning of Negotiability

negotiability the transfer of payment rights in a negotiable instrument

Negotiability is the transfer of rights in a negotiable instrument to new holders. It can happen over and over again. As noted in Chapter 11, their transfer is easier than ordinary assignments of contracts in three ways:

- A negotiable instrument may be transferred (or assigned) from one holder to another *without notice to the promisor*; the promisor only pays the holder who presents the instrument for payment.

---

[22] *Supra* note 9, s 38.

- A transferee of an negotiable instrument may sometimes acquire a *better right to sue* on the instrument than its predecessor had because fewer defences are available. Negotiable instruments are not **subject to the equities**.

- A holder may *sue in its own name* any other party liable on the instrument without joining any of the remaining parties.

subject to the equities subject to any rights or defences the promisor had against the original assignor

The three legal features described above make it more attractive to transfer negotiable instruments from one person to another than regular assignments of contracts.

To get the benefits of a negotiable instrument, the following requirements must be met:

(a) The promise or order must be in writing.

(b) The promise must be for payment of money only.

(c) The money promised must be an exact sum. It may be repayable in installments or with interest and still be a "sum certain."[23] But a promise to pay "the balance owing for services rendered" is not a sum certain.

(d) The promise or order must be unconditional so that the holder need not look outside the instrument to learn the implications of some qualifying phrase, such as "if the goods are delivered in good condition" or "subject to an allowance for poor material." A contract subject to a condition, though it may be valid between the immediate parties, lacks the certainty needed for a negotiable instrument: An attempt to transfer rights under it is a mere assignment.

(e) The negotiable instrument must be payable at a fixed or determinable future time or on demand.

(f) Negotiation (transfer) must be of the whole instrument, not for part of the amount.

(g) The negotiable instrument must be signed by the drawer (or authorized signing officers of a drawer business)[24] if it is a draft or cheque, or by the maker if a promissory note.

CHECKLIST

Formal Requirements of Negotiable Instruments

Negotiable instruments must:

- be in writing and signed by creator or drawer,
- be an unconditional obligation to pay a fixed amount of money,
- indicate a specific time when payment is due, and
- be a transfer of the whole obligation.

---

[23] *Supra* note 9, s 27. Problems arise where the instrument provides for payment of a fixed sum plus a variable or "floating" rate of interest, for example, "prime rate plus 2 percent." The Supreme Court of Canada has held that the sum must be capable of being ascertained by numerical calculation from the information contained in the instrument itself: *MacLeod Savings & Credit Union Ltd v Perrett*, [1981] 1 SCR 78. This does not mean the underlying debt fails just the status as negotiable instrument: See *Practicar Systems Inc v 696373 Alberta Ltd*, 2007 ABQB 143, 74 Alta LR (4th) 59 at para 112.

[24] The signer is personally liable unless he states that he signs in a representative capacity: section 51. The usual practice for a corporation is for its name to be printed on the instrument and for the officer to sign "per X" or "X, director."

Consequences When a Document Is Not Negotiable

Although a document may not amount to a negotiable instrument, it may still be enforceable between the original parties and be capable of assignment as an ordinary contractual right. In these circumstances, the *Bills of Exchange Act* does not apply, and the parties' rights are subject to the general rules governing contractual assignments, as discussed in Chapter 11.

METHODS OF NEGOTIATION

The methods of transferring the rights in a negotiable instrument to a new payee (holder) vary depending on whether it names a specific payee or not. If no payee is identified on the document, as when the space is blank or the words "payable to bearer," are used, it may be negotiated by simply giving the note to another person. This process is known as **delivery**, and it is all that is required to transfer an instrument that is in **bearer form**.[25] This is the same way a $10 bill is negotiated—it is just handed over to the next holder.

A negotiable instrument that names the person to be paid is known as an **order instrument**. In this case the named payee must sign over the instrument before delivering to a new holder. This signature is known as **endorsement**; essentially it is the payee's signature (traditionally on the reverse side of the instrument) transferring its right to the new holder, saying something like "pay to the order of James Bond." If the current named payee endorses it without naming a new payee (holder), it becomes bearer form for the next transfer. A party who takes delivery of an order instrument without the endorsement on it gets few legal rights[26] and has no right to demand payment from the original drawer or drawee.

Naming a payee is the safest approach because any attempt to negotiate it dishonestly amounts to the criminal offence of forgery.[27] The *Bills of Exchange Act* makes forgery one of the exceptions to the rule that a holder may acquire a better right than the transferor had. By contrast, because a bearer instrument may be negotiated by delivery only, a thief may successfully negotiate it without resorting to forgery. As a result, even if a bearer instrument was lost or stolen at some previous time, its holder can require the party liable to pay—but only if she can show that she acquired the instrument without knowledge of the loss or theft.[28]

Businesses rarely prepare negotiable instruments in bearer form, although, as we have noted, order instruments may be converted into bearer form by their holders. An employee, for example, may endorse her paycheque before taking it to the bank. If her endorsement is simply her signature, she has converted the cheque into a bearer instrument, and it becomes subject to the risks discussed above.

At one time, bank notes were promissory notes in bearer form; we still refer to paper money as "dollar bills." Now bank notes or dollar bills are designated as legal tender under the *Bank of Canada Act* and are readily negotiable by delivery only.[29]

delivery physically handing over a negotiable instrument to the next holder

bearer form a negotiable instrument that does not name a specific payee

order instrument an instrument that names the person to be paid

endorsement the named payee's signature on a negotiable instrument transferring the right to payment to the new holder

---

[25] It is also in bearer form when it is payable to an abstraction (for example, "Pay to Petty Cash") or to a fictitious or non-existent person: s 20(5). See *Westboro Flooring & Decor Inc v Bank of Nova Scotia* (2004), 241 DLR (4th) 257 (Ont CA); *Rouge Valley Health System v TD Canada Trust*, [2010] OJ No 5302 (Ont SC).

[26] He can sue the transferor who failed to properly endorse it. See Crawford and Falconbridge, *supra* note 17 at 1503.

[27] *Criminal Code*, RSC 1985, c C-46, s 374.

[28] N Elliott, J Odgers, and JM Phillips, eds, *Byles on Bills of Exchange*, 27th ed (London: Sweet & Maxwell, 2001) at 231, 445.

[29] *Bank of Canada Act*, *supra* note 1, s 25; *Currency Act*, *supra* note 1.

PURPOSES OF ENDORSEMENT

The primary purpose of endorsement is to transfer the right to collect payment to someone new. As described in the previous section, this may be done by an **endorsement in blank**, where the payee on an order instrument signs his name (and nothing else), thereby making it payable to bearer, or by a **special endorsement**, where the payee signs and specifies the next person to whom payment is to be made. For example:

Pay to Jane Bond
(signed) James Bond

endorsement in blank payee signs name only

special endorsement payee names next person to be payee

However, there are also other purposes or reasons for endorsing a negotiable instrument in a particular way.

A payee (the endorser) may want to end the negotiability of the instrument, making it impossible to transfer it to any subsequent holders. A **restrictive endorsement** will accomplish this by adding the words "for deposit only," with the endorser's signature. When endorsed "for deposit only," an instrument can only be deposited to the credit of the current payee's bank account. It is no longer possible to transfer it to someone new.

restrictive endorsement limits transferability

CASE 19.1 Endorsing a Cheque for Deposit

M was a lawyer who owed tax to the federal government. His law firm issued three cheques payable to M from its trust account. M endorsed each cheque "to be deposited" to the joint bank account M held with a third party at Canada Trustco Mortgage Co. The cheques were then delivered to Canada Trustco, the joint account was credited, and the cheques were sent for clearing. Minister of National Revenue sued Canada Trustco because at the time the cheques were deposited, the bank was subject to a "requirement to pay" notice. Any payments owed to M were to be redirected to the government. Canada Trustco denied owing any payments to M. The Supreme Court of Canada agreed. Just because M was the original payee on the face of the cheque did not mean that payment was to be made to M. A drawee is answerable to the drawer (law firm), and to whom the drawee must make payment is determined by the endorsements on the back of the cheque. When the cheques were presented, the instructions were to credit the joint bank account. At no time was Canada Trustco instructed to pay M alone.[30]

A holder may want to limit her own liability, making it impossible for subsequent holders to sue her if payment is not made. A qualified endorsement allows the holder to transfer rights in a way that blocks future liability as an endorser—for example, "Jane Bond, **without recourse**." Anyone giving value for the instrument is on notice that no remedy is available against Jane Bond should the party primarily liable default. In the absence of a qualified endorsement, an endorser is liable to subsequent endorsees.

without recourse no ability to claim against the endorser

The drawer of the negotiable instrument may have weak credit, and therefore the instrument requires additional security to make it attractive to new holders. An **anomalous endorsement** adds a new signature to the instrument from someone who has never been a payee; she signs the instrument solely to add her liability, as endorser or "guarantor," to that of the debtor who is primarily liable. It is not added for the purpose of negotiating the instrument; the additional endorser has never owned the instrument.[31]

anomalous endorsement an endorsement that is added as a guarantee to make it easier for the drawer to obtain credit on the bill

A bill endorsed in this manner is called an **accommodation bill**. The additional endorser usually signs to accommodate the drawer—that is, to make it easier for the

accommodation bill bill of exchange that contains an anomalous endorsement

---

[30] *Canada Trustco Mortgage Co v Canada*, 2011 SCC 36, [2011] 2 SCR 635 at para 51.

[31] *Supra* note 9, s 130. The endorser is liable to the payee even though the payee has not himself endorsed. *Robinson v Mann* (1901), 331 SCR 484. Also see *Byles on Bills of Exchange*, *supra* note 28 at 203.

drawer to obtain credit on the bill. An anomalous endorser contributes to negotiability because of her good credit standing.

An imposter may forge an endorsement. To protect itself from accepting a forged endorsement, a bank may require an **identification endorsement** from a third party identifying the person seeking to cash a cheque. For instance, it may require an endorsement in the following form:

> Jane Bond is hereby identified
> (signed) *Eve Moneypenny*

identification endorsement a third party confirms the identity of the endorser

Moneypenny is not liable for payment, as are other endorsers, if the party primarily liable defaults. Her liability is limited to the loss that would follow from having identified someone as Jane Bond who later proved not to be that person.

When a debt is paid by installments, it is up to the debtor to obtain a **partial payment endorsement** on the instrument by its holder each time an amount is paid. Otherwise she remains liable for the full original amount if it is subsequently negotiated to a holder who is unaware of the partial payments. An example of this type of endorsement is as follows:

partial payment endorsement the date and amount of a part payment to be deducted from outstanding balance of the instrument

> May 12, 2015
> Received in part payment, $175.00
> (signed) *James Bond*

CHECKLIST
Types of Endorsements

Types of Endorsement	Purpose	Words Required
Blank	Convert to bearer form	None
Special	Identify next holder	Name of next payee
Restrictive	End negotiability	"For deposit only"
Qualified	Limit liability	"Without recourse (liability)"
Anomalous	Add security	"As guarantor"
Identification	Confirm identity	"is identified"
Partial Payment	Reduce outstanding balance	Date and amount of payment

LIABILITY OF PARTIES

Many parties are involved in the creation, transfer, and payment of a negotiable instrument:

- Maker
- Drawer
- Promisor
- Acceptor
- Drawee
- Endorser
- Holder in due course

434 Part 4 Special Types of Contracts

The liability each party faces if the instrument is not paid or is dishonoured can vary. Liability begins with the responsibility for payment. **Dishonour** is the failure by the party who is primarily liable to pay the debt when it is due.

dishonor the failure by the party primarily liable to pay the instrument according to its terms

A Drawer or Maker

The maker of a promissory note is the primary promisor or debtor, and the maker promises to pay it when it comes due. The maker dishonours the note if he refuses to pay, and the maker will be held liable by a court for non-payment.[32]

The drawer of a draft undertakes that when the draft is presented, it will be accepted and paid by the drawee according to its terms, and if it is dishonoured by the drawee, the drawer will be liable to compensate the holder or any endorser who is compelled to pay it.[33] The drawer of a cheque undertakes that the cheque will be paid from his account on demand. If there are insufficient funds in his account, he is liable to the holder or to any endorser from whom the holder may recover. Because the parties to a cheque do not ordinarily expect a formal acceptance of it by the drawee bank, the drawer of the cheque becomes, for practical purposes, "the party primarily liable" (unless the cheque has been certified).

A bank follows instructions from its customer in disposing of the funds on deposit with it. Its authority to pay a cheque ends when its customer stops payment or when it receives notice of the customer's death.[34] Although a holder cannot then hold the bank liable, his rights against the drawer continue. By stopping payment, a drawer dishonours the instrument and may be sued by the holder. The death of the drawer makes the amount of the cheque a charge against the drawer's estate, and it becomes one of the debts the personal representative (executor or administrator) must settle.

A Drawee or Acceptor

By accepting a bill, a drawee undertakes to pay it according to the terms of his acceptance.[35] If the instrument is a draft, dishonour may take the form of either the drawee's refusal to accept or, if he accepts, his later refusal to pay.[36]

Banks as drawees of a cheque are only liable to the extent there are funds available in the drawer's account. Certification of a cheque puts the bank in the same position as an acceptor. Of course, the liability to pay only requires payment to the named payee or a proper holder in due course.

An Endorser

An endorser is liable to the current holder for the amount of the instrument should the party primarily liable dishonour it, but there are limits to this liability. If an endorser does not receive prompt notice of the dishonour from the holder, the endorser will not be liable.

If an order instrument is negotiated several times, a particular endorser's liability extends to any subsequent endorser as well as the current holder. He has no liability to prior endorsers—indeed, they are liable to him. The holder has a choice of endorsers to require payment from when the instrument is dishonoured, provided each of

---

[32] *Supra* note 9, s 185.
[33] *Ibid.*, s 129.
[34] *Ibid.*, s 167.
[35] *Ibid.*, s 127; *Canada Trustco Mortgage Co v Canada*, *supra* note 30 at para 51.
[36] *Supra* note 9, s 132(a).

them has received the necessary notice of dishonour.[37] In turn, an endorser who is held liable has recourse against any prior endorser but not against any subsequent one.[38] Assuming he cannot recover from the party primarily liable, the ultimate loser will be the first endorser (or the drawer if the instrument is a draft).

When an endorsement is forged, the drawer and any endorser prior to the forgery are not liable. The only holder who can recover from an endorser in these circumstances is one who has satisfied the conditions for qualifying as a "holder in due course," as explained later. When such a holder suffers a loss arising from a forged endorsement or the forged signature of the drawer, unless the forger can be caught and made to pay, the loss will ultimately be borne by the person who acquires the instrument immediately following the forgery.[39]

ILLUSTRATION 19.1 Negotiability in Action

A knew that C maintained an account at the B Bank. She drew a cheque on the B Bank payable to herself, forging C's signature as drawer. She then endorsed the cheque with her own signature and cashed it at a hotel operated by D.

D endorsed the cheque and deposited it in the hotel account at the X Bank. The X Bank presented the cheque for payment to the B Bank through the bank clearing system. The B Bank recognized the forgery and refused to pay the cheque out of C's account. The cheque was then returned to the X Bank.

The X Bank is entitled to recover the amount it had previously credited to D's account in respect of the cheque. The X Bank is the holder (in fact, a holder in due course), and D, as the endorser immediately after the forgery, is liable.[40] In this illustration, there is no other endorser between D and A, the perpetrator of the fraud. The loss must fall upon D unless A can be apprehended and the funds recovered from her.

For instruments in bearer form, no endorsement is required, so someone who transfers by delivery is not liable on the instrument as an endorser if the party primarily liable simply proves financially incapable of paying it.[41] However, he may be liable to the one person to whom he has negotiated the instrument, his immediate transferee, but only for such loss as that transferee would sustain if the instrument were not genuine—that is, if the instrument was not what the transferor represented it to be, or he was aware that it was valueless, or if he had no right to transfer it.[42]

PROVING LIABILITY

A court will impose liability for payment only if:

- the instrument was presented for payment,
- it was dishonoured,
- prompt notice of the dishonour was given to the defendant (if he is not the one who dishonoured it), and
- the lawsuit is commenced within the limitation period.

Presented for Payment

presents produces the instrument to the drawee bank, promisor, or maker for payment

Unless a holder **presents** the instrument for payment, endorsers will not have any liability to him. An instrument payable on demand must be presented for payment

---

[37] Alternatively, the holder may sue all the endorsers as codefendants in a single action and leave them to work out their individual liability among themselves.

[38] Ibid., s 100. Each endorser has, after receiving notice of dishonour, the same period for giving notice to earlier endorsers that the holder had after dishonour.

[39] Ibid., s 132(b).

[40] Ibid., ss 49(1) and (2).

[41] Ibid., s 136(2).

[42] Ibid., s 137.

within a reasonable time after its endorsement, and an instrument that is not payable on demand must be presented on the day it falls due.[43]

Notice of Dishonour

Neither an endorser nor a drawer will be liable in the absence of prompt, express notice of dishonour from the holder—it is not enough for the holder to show that the endorser or drawer heard about the dishonour from some other source.[44] Notice must be given not later than the business day next following the dishonour.[45]

Normally no special form of notice is required as long as the essential message is conveyed. However, a special form of notice of dishonour is required if the instrument is drawn, payable, or accepted outside Canada.[46]

Limitation Periods

The provincial legislation[47] sets the time period within which a lawsuit must be commenced. This limitation period begins to run from the maturity of the instrument, the time of the most recent payment made in respect of it, or any written acknowledgment from which a promise to pay may be implied—whichever is the latest date.

HOLDER IN DUE COURSE

The last and in some ways most important party to discuss is the holder in due course. This party deserves extra discussion because by definition she is an innocent third party who is not one of the original parties and therefore is not affected by unknown deficiencies in the instrument's creation or its previous transfers. The greater rights and protection available to holders in due course make them useful tools of commerce.

Requirements to Become a Holder in Due Course

The holder in due course must satisfy four conditions:[48]

(a) The holder must have taken the instrument complete and regular on its face.
(b) She must have acquired it before it was overdue and without notice of any prior dishonour.[49]
(c) She, or someone through whom she claims, must have given consideration ("value") for the instrument.[50]
(d) She must have taken the instrument in good faith and without notice of any defect in the title of the person who negotiated it.

When a cheque is delivered to a bank for deposit to an account, and the bank credits the account for the amount, the bank gets the protection of a holder in due course (s. 165(3)). Otherwise, banking would become impossibly slow, and banks

---

[43] *Ibid.*, s 85.

[44] *Ibid.*, s 98. See also Crawford and Falconbridge, *supra* note 17 at 1576.

[45] *Supra* note 9, s 96. Under some circumstances, a delay in giving notice may be excused (s. 104).

[46] *Ibid.*, s 111. The prescribed forms are set out in the Schedule at the end of the Act.

[47] The relevant period varies between two and six years; see the discussion of limitation periods in Chapter 29.

[48] *Supra* note 9, s 55.

[49] A subsequent holder will succeed to the rights of a holder in due course whether or not he himself satisfies all the essential conditions, unless he was a party to fraud or illegality affecting the instrument: section 56.

[50] *Supra* note 9, s 55 requires that she shall have taken the instrument "for value," but section 53 states that where value has been given at any time for a bill, the holder is deemed to be a holder for value.

would be reluctant to purchase negotiable instruments and hold them as assets. They would first have to make exhaustive inquiries to be sure that valuable consideration was given for an instrument and that it was free of fraud, illegality, duress, or undue influence. Banks would not risk acquiring instruments that might be subject to such defences when the time came to collect from the party primarily liable.[51]

CHECKLIST
Key Terms Relating to Negotiable Instruments

Parties	Actions
■ Maker	■ Delivery
■ Drawer	■ Acceptance
■ Promisor	■ Endorsement
■ Drawee	■ Negotiation
■ Endorser	■ Presentment
■ Holder in due course	■ Dishonour

DEFENCES

Quite a few defences could block liability, but their availability depends on the relationship between the parties and what was known at the time of the transaction.

ILLUSTRATION 19.2   Types of Parties

A draws a cheque in favour of B. B endorses it to the order of C. C endorses it to the order of D. D is the present holder of the cheque.

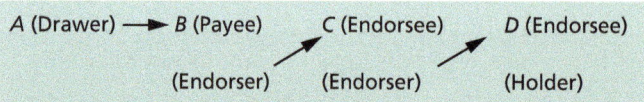

A and B, B and C, and C and D are immediate parties of each other. The remote party relationships are between A and C, A and D, and B and D. Whether the present holder, D, is a holder in due course will depend on whether he satisfies the four essential conditions described in the previous section.

Personal Defences

Personal defences are only available when the parties have dealt directly with each other. When a holder is trying to collect from the party immediately before him who conveyed the instrument to him, whether it is the maker or drawer or an endorser, that direct relationship between the parties means personal defences applicable to other contractual situations are also available to the defendant in an action based on a negotiable instrument. These defences are referred to as *mere personal defences* and include lack of consideration and a right to set off.

---

[51] As an additional protection, a bank will require the endorsement of the person from whom it acquires the instrument; but recourse against endorsers is at best a second resort, which banks naturally wish to avoid.

By contrast, personal defences are not available to a remote party who has had no direct dealing with the person suing her. **Remote parties** may only use title or real defences depending on what the plaintiff knew when she received the instrument. Defendants who are **immediate parties** may use any defence available to a remote party plus personal defences.

remote parties parties to an instrument who have not had direct dealings with one another

immediate parties the holder of an instrument and the party alleged to be liable on it who have had direct dealings with each other

Defect of Title Defences

If a holder takes the instrument knowing it is defective, or when there is an **irregularity on the face** of the instrument that should have alerted him to a problem, he is not a "protected" holder in due course, and therefore a defence based on a title defect will be defeat his claim. Title defect defences are available to any party sued by such a holder.[52] Title defects are as follows:

irregularity on the face something appears unusual on the document itself

(a) incapacity to contract as a result of drunkenness or insanity[53]
(b) discharge of the instrument by payment, or renunciation of a holder's rights in it
(c) absence of delivery when the instrument was complete at the time
(d) fraud, duress, undue influence, illegality
(e) want of authority in an agent to complete the instrument on behalf of the party primarily liable

Real Defences

The following defences are available to defeat a claim brought by any holder, even a holder in due course:

(a) incapacity to contract because of infancy
(b) cancellation of the instrument
(c) absence of delivery where the instrument is incomplete when taken
(d) fraud as to the nature of the instrument when the promisor is blind or illiterate
(e) a forged signature on the instrument
(f) want of authority, in someone who has represented himself as an agent, to sign on behalf of the party liable
(g) alteration of the instrument

Only real defences can be used to block the claim of a holder in due course. Therefore, a holder in due course has the best chance of success in collecting payment because the fewest number of defences are available against his claim.

CHECKLIST
Available Defences

Defences available against the plaintiff (suing for payment):

Status of the Plaintiff	Personal Defences	Title Defect Defences	Real Defences
Immediate party	✓	✓	✓
Holder (other than due course)		✓	✓
Holder in due course			✓

[52] For a full discussion, see Crawford and Falconbridge, *supra* note 17.
[53] *Supra* note 9, ss 55 and 57(2).

CONSUMER BILLS AND NOTES

The general rules about negotiable instruments can be unfair to consumers. When installment payments stretch over a long period of time, the seller might assign the contract to a finance company and receive immediate payment. The consumer would receive notice of assignment and make the installment payments to the finance company. The general rule about assignment of contractual rights, as we saw in Chapter 11, is that an assignee acquires no better claim than the assignor had. Therefore, if the buyer had some claim against the seller, for breach of warranty or because the contract was induced by some misrepresentation, that claim can normally be asserted against the assignee. Some merchants and finance companies used negotiable instrument to block these consumer defences. The buyer was required to sign a promissory note for the balance of the purchase price plus finance charges, and this note, along with the conditional sale contract, was endorsed by the merchant to the finance company. The finance company became a holder in due course of the note, immune to any personal or title defect defences the buyer might have against the original merchant.

This loophole was closed by the *Bills of Exchange Act*,[54] which removed the protection otherwise accorded to a holder in due course in consumer credit arrangements. The Act requires that every consumer bill or consumer note be prominently and legibly marked on its face with the words "consumer purchase" before or at the time the instrument is signed by the purchaser or by anyone signing to accommodate the purchaser (that is, a guarantor).[55] It also provided that the right of the holder of a consumer bill or consumer note to have the whole or any part thereof paid by the purchaser or a guarantor is subject to any defence or right of set-off that the purchaser would have had in an action by the seller on the bill or note.[56]

Therefore, a consumer buying on credit may use all the personal defences (formerly available only against the seller) to defend against a finance company that sues him as holder of his promissory note.

MODERN ALTERNATIVES TO CASH

Bank drafts and cheques were the original substitutes for cash. In the 1950s and 1960s, credit cards surpassed both cash and cheques as the preferred method of payment. Credit cards assured retailers that funds were available and reduced the risk of bad debts experienced with payment by cheque. Early in the new millennium, direct debit cards displaced credit cards in an increasing proportion of transactions; the current decade is trending toward virtual wallets and even digital currency. These modern alternatives are reducing the reliance on paper negotiable instruments and cash. Between 2008 and 2015, the number of cash and cheque transactions fell by 30 and 35 percent, respectively, while the number of online e-wallet and electronic person-to-person transactions rose by more than 1000 percent.[57]

Digital transfers of funds happen quickly and therefore reduce the risk that intervening events will disrupt payment; however, the speed and volume of these transactions puts great pressure, responsibility, and trust on the payment system providers who process the transfers.

---

[54] See also the discussion of this issue in Chapter 3, under the heading "Consumer Protection."

[55] *Supra* note 9, s 190(1). If not so marked, the instrument is void in the hands of either the seller or the finance company (s. 190(2)).

[56] *Ibid.*, s 191.

[57] Department of Finance Canada, "A New Retail Payments Oversight Framework," https://www.fin.gc.ca/activity/consult/rprof-cspd-eng.asp (citing Canadian Payment Methods and Trends: 2016, Payments Canada Discussion Paper No 7, November 2016).

Regulation of the Electronic Transfer of Funds

No comprehensive regulatory scheme covers all digital transfers of funds—big gaps exist. Since 2011 the federal government has released several task force reports on the future of payment systems, each of which proposed legislation to regulate digital payment services and providers and recommended a public oversight body for the digital payment industry.[58] The federal government retains the power to recognize new payment systems under the *Canadian Payments Act*, and all reports have pointed to an expansion of the federal regime.[59]

Regulations already cover the major national payment and clearing systems that deal with large value payments or high volume. The Large Value Transfer System (LVTS) is a wire transfer system that provides real-time validation or rejection of payments based on certain risk control tests. It is designated as systemically important to the Canadian economy, so the Bank of Canada oversees this system pursuant to the *Payment Clearing and Settlement Act*, and Payments Canada administers the daily operations.[60]

The Automated Clearing Settlement System processes a high volume of transactions (99 percent of daily Canadian transactions). It is designated as a prominent payment system and therefore is also subject to Bank of Canada oversight and controls.[61] **Payment card** (credit, debit, and gift) providers are regulated under the *Payment Card Networks Act* and supervised by the Financial Consumer Agency of Canada.[62] Notice that the forgoing regulations (like banking regulations) focus on supervising specific providers, and those providers process the transactions.

The **retail electronic payments** genre is defined by low-value everyday transactions conducted through a variety of different payment methods that could be processed through different low-volume private sector payment systems. It is the least regulated category partly because of the exploding number of system providers flooding the market. It is estimated that Canadian startups in this business will grow from 100 in 2016 to more than 1000 by 2021.[63] The federal government's 2017 task force report suggests that regulation would be most effective if it was triggered by the type of payment rather than the system operator. The same rules would apply to any system provider involved with everyday payment methods such as credit cards, online payments, pay deposits, debit transactions, preauthorized payments, and person-to-person money transfers.

Some proposed regulations are as follows:

- to maintain a trust account at a financial institution covered by *Canada Deposit Insurance Act*
- to provide a user disclosure agreement
- to meet privacy and security standards
- to offer dispute resolution processes

payment cards   credit or debit or gift cards

retail electronic payments   low-value everyday transactions conducted through a variety of different payment methods, such as debit, credit cards and etransfers

---

[58] "The Task Force for the Payments System Review, Moving Canada into the Digital Age," December 2011, http://paymentsystemreview.ca/wp-content/themes/psr-esp-hub/reports/rf_eng/files/assets/downloads/publication.pdf; Department of Finance Canada, 2015 Consultation Paper "Balancing Oversight and Innovation in the Ways We Pay" https://www.fin.gc.ca/activty/consult/onps-ssnp-eng.asp; Department of Finance Canada, "A New Retail Payments Oversight Framework" *supra* note 57.

[59] *Canadian Payments Act*, RSC 1985, c C-21, s 37.

[60] Lana Embree and Paul Miller, "Improving the Foundation of Canada's Payment System," 2015 *Bank of Canada Review* 26–34, available online at http://www.bankofcanada.ca/wp-content/uploads/2015/05/boc-review-spring15-embree.pdf.

[61] *Ibid*.

[62] SC 2010, c 12, s 1834.

[63] *Supra* note 57 (citing the Business Development Bank).

The proposed regulations would apply only to transactions based in legally regulated currency. Virtual currency remains outside the financial institution system and so far is unregulated as a form of fund transfer, save and except for anti-money laundering. The *Proceeds of Crime (Money Laundering) and Terrorist Financing Act* recently added "dealers in virtual currencies" as businesses subject to tracking and reporting obligations.[64]

Ethical Issue The Digital Future of Money

A 2002 report of the Organisation for Economic Co-operation and Development entitled "The Future of Money" concluded that the disappearance of physical money is inevitable; it is just a question of time. It suggested that a coordinated transition to digital payments would be good for the world economy for a number of reasons, including the following:

- the elimination of the high costs associated with the transfer and protection of physical forms of money, including cash, cheques, bills of exchange
- the decrease in underground, illegal, and even terrorist activities as a result of the ability to track the movement of money

If all transactions were digital, there would be a comprehensive record of all our financial activities. It would track where we went, what we earned, and how we spent it. It would reveal personal information about our preferences, religious and charitable affiliations, and medical conditions. As will be discussed in greater detail in Chapters 31 and 32, the potential for abuse and misuse of this record has privacy advocates and ethicists very concerned. Should the government be allowed to use this record to assess income tax? Should the police be allowed to view this record to investigate suspected criminal activity? Should a business be able to use this record in order to target a market? What security measures would be necessary to protect the record of digital movement of funds from abuse? Who should be allowed to offer payment services? A 2013 report of the Financial Consumer Agency of Canada highlighted the many risks of digital payment for consumers, including profiling, malware, and fraud, and recommended that all payment service providers be subject to the same regulation and security requirements.

Would your privacy be better protected if you avoided legal currency and opted for digital currency? Digital or cryptocurrencies such as Bitcoin are emerging. They lack a centralized monetary authority and so far remain out of reach of regulators.

Questions to Consider

1. Contrast the advantages and disadvantages of electronic money transfers as compared with physical methods.
2. Should individuals have a right to keep their financial activities private?
3. How will a move to digital transactions affect developing or emerging economies?
4. Do you think digital currency increases rather than decreases the risk of illegal activities?

Sources: Organisation for Economic Co-operation and Development, "The Future of Money" (Paris: OECD Publications Service, 2002), http://www.oecd.org/dataoecd/40/31/35391062.pdf; "The Economist Explains: How Does Bitcoin Work?" April 11, 2013, http://www.economist.com/blogs/economist-explains/2013/04/economist-explains-how-does-bitcoin-work; Steve Trites et al., "Mobile Payments and Consumer Protection in Canada, Research Division, Financial Consumer Agency of Canada," December 2013, http://www.fcac-acfc.gc.ca/Eng/resources/researchSurveys/Documents/FCAC_Mobile_Payments_Consumer_Protection_accessible_EN.pdf.

Despite the speed and efficiency of electronic payment methods, it does not appear that the world is ready to eliminate negotiable instruments. After severe public backlash, the United Kingdom abandoned its plan to end the use of cheques by 2018. Rather than abolishing cheques entirely, the Canadian government is leading by example and phasing out its own use of cheques by 2016.[65] Although the law governing negotiable instruments developed in the paper world, it is slowly being adapted to function in the electronic world as well.

---

[64] Amendment to s 5(h) not yet proclaimed in force; dealers in virtual currency to be defined in the regulations.

[65] Public and Government Service Canada, News Release, April 11, 2012. It costs 82 cents to produce a cheque and only 13 cents to complete a direct deposit.

Strategies to Manage the Legal Risks

Many retail businesses have already acted to minimize the risks associated with negotiable instruments. They do not accept cheques or bills of exchange as payment for goods. The wide availability of credit cards has reduced the need to accept these forms of payment, although there are costs for such services. Retailers offering financing involve a separate finance company to lend directly to the customer, rather than accepting a promissory note and transferring it to a factoring company. This provides immediate cash flow and reduces the defences that may be available to the customer against the lender. As noted above, this is less effective when the finance company is connected to the vendor or if the customer is a consumer.

For businesses that extend credit, cash cheques, and provide payment services, including banks and payday loan companies, forgery and false identity are major legal risks. Strict policies involving proof of identity, inspection of the physical cheque for any sign of irregularity, and implementation of high fees for dishonouring help to minimize the risks.

The modern digital climate has expanded the legal risks faced by banks and non-bank financial institutions in areas such as:

- Money laundering
- Cybercrime
- Terrorism financing
- Insider fraud
- Credit card fraud
- Mortgage fraud
- Hacking of private information
- Phishing

The heavy regulation placed on banks is done partly to protect them from these enormous legal risks, so willing compliance with regulatory requirements will reduce risk. Banks can build a culture of compliance by helping staff understand the purpose of regulatory compliance and committing resources to it.

QUESTIONS FOR REVIEW

1. Discuss the differences between banks and other financial institutions.
2. Describe the changing way in which banks are processing cheques.
3. What types of negotiable instruments are governed by the *Bills of Exchange Act*?
4. Describe differences between demand drafts, sight drafts, and time drafts in commercial practice.
5. Describe the three qualities of negotiable instruments that distinguish them from ordinary assignments. How do these qualities make them commercially useful?
6. Donna draws a cheque payable to Edgar for "a maximum of $1000 for carpentry work." Edgar completes the work while Donna is out of town and takes the cheque to his bank to cash it. The bank refuses on the grounds that it is not a valid cheque. Is the bank correct? Explain.
7. Describe the difference between a "bearer" instrument and an "order" instrument.
8. Explain the significance of a party transferring a negotiable instrument endorsed "without recourse." When is this type of endorsement used?

9. J delivers a cheque for $500 in payment for a secondhand computer purchased from K. K inadvertently leaves the cheque on a restaurant table. Q picks it up from the table, forges K's name, and cashes the cheque at the L Bank. K reports the loss of the cheque to J, who immediately informs her bank to stop payment. What rights does the L Bank have?

10. W delivers a cheque for $1000 in payment of a debt owed to X. X endorses the cheque to Y's Secondhand Shop to purchase a television set. Y endorses the cheque to her landlord, Z, in part payment of her monthly rent. When Z takes the cheque to his bank, the teller recognizes W's signature and has heard that he is in financial difficulty. She contacts W's bank and learns there are not sufficient funds in W's account. What should Z do to protect his claim?

11. Describe the requirements for a party to be considered a holder in due course.

12. You are the maker of a note in which you undertake to pay $500 to a moneylender on demand. Subsequently you pay an installment of $200 to the moneylender on this liability. What steps should you take to ensure you will not have to pay a further $500 at some later time?

13. Gower has drawn a time draft on Cohen payable three months after sight to Jenkins. The draft is complete and regular, with the possible exception of a clause that Cohen, the drawee, is "to pay the amount of this draft out of money due me on December 31 for professional services rendered." If Cohen refuses to accept the draft, does he owe its amount in future to Gower or to Jenkins?

14. The endorsements appearing on the back of each of three negotiable instruments are reproduced below. An asterisk following a name indicates an actual signature. Identify each of the endorsements by type, and explain its effect for the parties concerned:

    (a) Pay to John Factor, Without Recourse
    The Synthetic Textile Co. Ltd.
    per Terry Lean,*/Manager.
    John Factor*

    (b) Pay to James Hawkins,
    S. Trelawney*
    For deposit only,
    James Hawkins*

    (c) Pay to Archibald Grosvenor only
    Archibald Grosvenor*
    Archibald Grosvenor is hereby identified,
    Ralph Rackstraw*

15. Wilma purchased a used minivan, including a three-month warranty on parts and labour, from Xenon Used Cars Inc. for $10 000. She paid $1500 down and signed a promissory note for $8500, payable in monthly installments of $285 for three years. If any payment is missed by Wilma, the entire sum will fall due at once because of her default. Xenon immediately transferred the note to Yarrow Finance Corp. and received payment of $7750. Wilma received notice of the transfer with a request to make her monthly payments directly to Yarrow Finance. The van broke down repeatedly within the first month, and Wilma was unable to obtain proper repairs from Xenon. She refused to make the payments to Yarrow Finance, and it sued her for the full sum due. Describe the nature of Wilma's defence against Yarrow Finance and whether she will succeed.

CASES AND PROBLEMS

1. Continuing Scenario

    Ashley arranged a credit line at her bank; only Ashley or her father, Jim, were authorized to sign the credit line cheques. The cheques were kept in her office at the restaurant. Miranda was Ashley's assistant manager responsible for making the daily bank deposit and had regular access to Ashley's office. Over time, she became familiar with Ashley's signature and started preparing credit line cheques payable to herself. She would take them to the bank with the regular bank deposit and endorse the cheques for deposit to her account. On the one occasion when a bank teller questioned her, she said the cheque was for overtime she had worked. Only after Miranda quit did Ashley discover that over $2000 had been taken in the last two years. Ashley is now arguing with her bank over whether she should have to pay the outstanding $2000 withdrawn on the credit line. Identify the roles of the bank, Ashley, and Miranda. What negotiable instrument legal principles and defences are involved in this dispute?

2. On April 28, the University of Penticton made a note payable to the Baroque Construction Co. Ltd., three months after date. The amount of the note was expressed simply as "the balance due to you for construction of our Arts Building." On May 2 following, the Baroque Construction Co. Ltd. sold the note to a private financier, R. Jay, for $47 500, having shown him accounts and vouchers indicating a balance of $50 000 due from the university. On July 31, R. Jay presented the note to the treasurer of the university for payment and was advised by him that the construction contract with the Baroque Construction Co. Ltd. contained a guarantee clause and that serious defects had developed in the foundation of the Arts Building. The treasurer stated that the university was not prepared to pay the note for this reason. R. Jay countered with the argument that the defective work was not the slightest concern of his and that the proper officer of the university had signed the note. He then sued the University of Penticton on its note. Should he succeed? Give reasons.

3. On the afternoon of October 27, Connor supplied office furniture valued at $48 000 to Osmond. When the furniture was delivered, Connor received a certified cheque for $48 000 from Osmond. The cheque, drawn on Osmond's account at the Kelsey Bank, had been certified earlier that afternoon by the bank at Osmond's request. That morning, Osmond had deposited a cheque from a customer for $76 000; the cheque had not yet been cleared, but the bank took the risk that it would be honoured by the Portage Bank, where Osmond's customer had his account.

   On October 28, after having been informed by Portage that it would not honour the $76 000 cheque, the Kelsey Bank called Connor to say that certification had been revoked and that she should not attempt to negotiate the cheque. The next day, Connor presented the certified cheque for payment. The Kelsey Bank refused payment, and Connor sued the bank.

   Is the Kelsey Bank legally bound to honour the cheque? Explain.

4. Elston owned all the issued common shares of Ham Ltd. He lent Ham Ltd. $160 000 of his personal funds and obtained in return a promissory note from the company payable to his order.

   For personal reasons, Elston subsequently had to borrow money on his own account from the Atlas Bank. To secure this loan he delivered the Ham Ltd. promissory note to the bank, but without endorsing it. The bank gave no notice to Ham Ltd. that it was the transferee.

   Two months later, Elston sold his shares in Ham Ltd. to new owners who had no knowledge of the existence of the note. At the same time, Elston gave Ham Ltd. a general release of all claims he had against it in terms wide enough to include the company's obligation to him on the $160 000 note.

   Elston defaulted on his personal loan from the Atlas Bank, and it then demanded payment of the note from Ham Ltd. Ham Ltd. refused to pay, and the bank brought an action against it for $160 000.

   Should this action should succeed? Why or why not?

5. Allison opened a chequing account with the Picton Bank and signed an "Operation of Account" agreement; she agreed to notify the bank of any discrepancies and errors in her bank balance within 30 days of receiving her monthly statement and to notify the bank of any forgeries or frauds within her organization as soon as she became aware of them. Soon after, she hired Ralph, a new bookkeeper. Just two weeks later Ralph forged four cheques, worth $24 000, on Allison's chequing account. Ralph was very shrewd; he had done this while Allison's general manager, who was in charge of dealings with the bank, was on vacation. Each of the four cheques was made out to a fictitious payee named Quigley, and each was marked "for deposit only." Ralph had set up an account for Quigley in another bank, deposited the cheques, and within a few days withdrew all the money.

    The general manager discovered Ralph's fraud on the day he returned; he immediately told Allison about it, and she phoned the bank at once—but it was too late. Ralph had absconded. The Picton Bank refused to return the funds to Allison's account, claiming that she had been negligent. In reply, Allison claimed she had complied with the Operation of Account agreement.

    Outline the legal argument Allison would use and any defence of Picton Bank. Give your opinion on whether she should succeed.

6. As accountant at a branch of the Crown Bank, Cole misappropriated rent of $3000 due to the bank. When the bank inspector discovered these facts, the bank notified the Flin Flon Fidelity and Guarantee Co., which had previously bonded Cole for the bank, and claimed the $3000. The bonding company told Cole that it preferred not to prosecute if it could avoid it, and a possible way out would be for Cole to get his friends to come to his assistance. Cole then prevailed on his friend Smith to sign a promissory note payable 12 months after date in favour of the bonding company. When Smith dishonoured his note at maturity, the bonding company sued him. Should it succeed? Would the result be different if the bonding company had discounted Smith's note at its bank and Smith had refused to pay the bank at the note's maturity?

7. VanWyck drew a cheque payable to Lockhart but decided not to send it until he had examined the goods purchased from Lockhart to see whether they were satisfactory. VanWyck's clerk, Anderson, inadvertently gave the cheque to Lockhart without first getting permission from VanWyck. (Anderson normally had nothing to do with the preparation or delivery of VanWyck's negotiable instruments.) Lockhart endorsed the cheque for value to Snider, who took it without notice of the circumstances. When Snider attempted to cash the cheque, she discovered that VanWyck had requested his bank to stop payment on it. Snider sued both VanWyck and Lockhart for the amount.

    State with reasons the rights of the respective parties and the probable result of the action.

8. Originals Inc. held an auction of antique furniture and received a winning bid of $18 000 from Parker. Parker gave his cheque, drawn on the Regal Bank, to Originals Inc. and asked that the furniture be delivered to his warehouse the next day. Originals's clerk deposited the cheque at its bank the afternoon of the auction.

    When the furniture arrived the following morning, Parker examined the items on the delivery truck and realized most of them did not meet the description provided by the auctioneer. He rejected them, and the deliverer returned them to Originals Inc. Parker immediately telephoned his bank to stop payment on the cheque and then telephoned Originals to inform it of what he had done. Originals protested but accepted the furniture and said it would sue Parker.

    Regal Bank's employee erroneously overlooked Parker's stop payment order and paid the cheque to Originals. When the error came to light, the Regal Bank credited the amount of the cheque to Parker and brought an action against Originals Inc. to recover the amount of the payment. Originals claimed it was entitled to hold on to the funds because of breach of contract.

    Summarize the arguments of both sides. Who should succeed?

Part 5 Property

Chapter 20
Intellectual Property

- **THE NATURE OF INTELLECTUAL PROPERTY**
- **TRADEMARKS**
- **COPYRIGHT**
- **PATENTS**
- **INDUSTRIAL DESIGNS**
- **CONFIDENTIAL INFORMATION, TRADE SECRETS, AND KNOW-HOW**
- **TECHNOLOGICAL CHANGE AND INTELLECTUAL PROPERTY LAW**
- **STRATEGIES TO MANAGE THE LEGAL RISKS**

In this chapter, we review the various forms of intellectual property—trademarks, copyright, patents, and industrial designs.

In this chapter we examine such questions as:

- What is "intellectual property"?
- How is intellectual property acquired?
- What types of intellectual property are protected by law?
- What constitutes an infringement of intellectual property?
- What are the remedies for infringement?
- How does intellectual property law adapt to new technologies?
- How should the rights of inventors and innovators be balanced against the general public interest?

THE NATURE OF INTELLECTUAL PROPERTY

Forms of Intellectual Property

Intellectual property is intangible property that is the product of mental activity. The four most recognized forms of intellectual property are trademarks, copyright, patents, and industrial designs. Each type of intellectual property deals with ideas or inventions; originality is an essential feature. Each particular type of property is protected by its own rules and statutes, which are administered through the Canadian Intellectual Property Office (CIPO), an agency of the federal ministry of Innovation, Science and Economic Development.

Some intellectual property rights are protected solely by statute, and others are also protected by common law rules. For some interests, registration is essential, whereas other rights arise upon creation. Some types of intellectual property may fall within two different categories; others may fall into gaps between the categories so that no protection is provided. In addition, since intellectual property is essentially concerned with knowledge, information, and, above all, innovation, it is linked to technological progress. Rules are constantly being revised to address the new challenges. This chapter is designed to present a general overview of intellectual property rights and protections and some guidance on how to avoid infringing the rights of others. Specific rules may have changed since this edition's publication date; in fact, pending legislation (2018) will significantly change trademark law. Legislative jurisdiction over intellectual property is assigned to the federal government, and the legislation discussed below applies across the country.[1]

Not all ideas, information, or knowledge qualify as intellectual property; confidential information, trade secrets, and what is commonly referred to as "know-how," though sometimes protected by law, are not regarded as forms of property.

CHECKLIST

Forms of Intellectual Property

Canadian law recognizes the following basic forms of intellectual property:

- trademarks
- copyright
- patents
- industrial designs

Should Intellectual Property Be Protected?

Tort law protects intellectual property with causes of action such as passing off and product defamation. The increasing value of intellectual property motivated the government to create additional legislative protection. The scope of legislative protection remains a point of debate.

Advocates for protection claim that creators such as writers, inventors, and designers deserve compensation for their efforts and that without protection, creativity is discouraged. Opponents of protection claim that ideas and inventions—especially those concerning matters such as health, medicine, food production, and education—should belong to the whole world. They point to the heavy social costs of protection—higher prices due to

---

[1] *Constitution Act*, 1867, s 91(22–23). The Federal Court of Canada hears disputes over intellectual property.

the payment of royalties and licence fees, and inefficiency resulting from restrictions on the use of new techniques and from the abuse of monopoly power. Overprotection, as much as lack of protection, may hinder economic and social progress.

The problem, especially for a country such as Canada, which is both an exporter and importer of cultural and technological innovation, is to set the right balance. The United States emphasizes greater protection of "ownership rights," for example, by lengthening the period of copyright protection and criminalizing infringement (mostly for the benefit of large corporations).[2] Canadian courts and legislators show more concern for "user rights."[3]

TRADEMARKS

Nature of Trademarks

Section 2 of the federal *Trade-marks Act*[4] defines a **trademark** as follows:

(a) a mark that is used by a person for the purpose of distinguishing or so as to distinguish wares or services manufactured, sold, leased, hired, or performed by him from those manufactured, sold, leased, hired, or performed by others

(b) a certification mark

(c) a distinguishing guise

(d) a proposed trademark

trademark an identifiable feature or combination of features that is used by a person for the purpose of distinguishing his goods or services from those of others

Although the Act does not define the word "mark," any visual characteristic of goods or their presentation that serves to distinguish them from goods and services that do not have the same trade connection can be considered a "mark." CIPO is accepts applications for non-traditional marks such as sounds and three-dimensional marks.[5] Reforms anticipated in 2019 will change the Canadian conception of mark; see the Reform Checklist below.

A **certification mark** is a special type of trademark used to identify goods or services that conform to a particular standard, character, or quality; a typical example being the "TRUSTe" mark for internet security.[6] The owner of the certification mark may register it and license its use to other persons whose goods or services meet the defined standards. A **distinguishing guise** usually involves the shaping of goods or their containers, or a mode of wrapping or packaging that is distinctive—a Coca-Cola bottle, for example.[7]

certification mark a special type of trademark used to identify goods or services that conform to a particular standard

distinguishing guise the configuration of goods or their containers, or a distinctive mode of wrapping or packaging

---

[2] *The Sonny Bono Copyright Extension Act of 1998*, extending U.S. copyright protection by 20 years, to 70 years after the creator's death, is commonly known as the "Mickey Mouse Act" because of the benefit it conferred on the Walt Disney Company.

[3] See *Theberge v Galerie d'Art du Petit Champlain*, [2002] 2 SCR 336; *CCH Canadian Ltd v Law Society of Upper Canada*, [2004] 1 SCR 339; *Bell Canada v SOCAN* [2012] 2 SCR 326; *Alberta (Minister of Education) v Canadian Copyright Licensing Agency*, [2012] 2 SCR 345.

[4] *Trade-marks Act*, RSC 1985, c T-13. (Unless otherwise stated, statutory references in this part of the chapter are to this Act.) A new act ("*Trademarks Act*") is expected pursuant to the *Combatting Counterfeit Products Act*, SC 2014, c 32 (pending legislation).

[5] CIPO Practice Notice: Trade-mark consisting of a sound (Publication Modified: 2015-06-01); CIPO Practice Notice: Three-dimensional Marks (Publication Modified: 2015-06-01). New act will replace mark with "sign" that will incorporate distinguishing guise and add smells, holographs, and others.

[6] U.S. Trademark No. 3695190 registered October 2009 to True Ultimate Standards Everywhere Inc. Description of the mark: "The colors green, white, and black are claimed as features of the mark. The mark consists of a stylized 'e' in black with a white half circle arc above the 'e' and green background above the arc. The word 'TRUSTe:' appears in black letters above the green."

[7] A distinguishing guise must be more than purely functional: see *Kirkbi AG v Ritvik Holdings Inc* (2003), 228 DLR (4th) 297, aff'd [2005] 3 SCR 302 (Lego Block case). The new act will not protect utilitarian features of a trademark.

Business Names

Businesses operate using a variety of business names, domain names, brands, and trade names. Each of these names involves trademark. The name of an established business is a valuable asset that forms part of the goodwill of the business. A trademark may be and frequently is part of a business name, but the entire name may not be a trademark. For example, the word "Ford" is a trademark of the Ford Motor Company, but the full name is not a trademark. Common or **generic** words such as "company," "limited," or "commercial" are not trademarkable. Similarly, only portions of a domain name are eligible for trademark protection. Although a domain name is technically only an address, that portion of the name that is uniquely linked to goods or services may be registered as a trademark.[8] Businesses often register separate trade names to market different product lines or represent different divisions of a business (sometimes referred to as brands). For example, Cara Operations Limited owns the trademark "Harvey's" for its fast-food restaurant brand, as well as the advertising slogan "Harvey's Makes Your Hamburger a Beautiful Thing."[9] A business should investigate trademark protection and availability for its name, domain name, and any trade names before investing in them. Free online trademark searches are available through the CIPO website.[10]

> **generic** word or feature that is commonly used and not distinguishing

The names of all corporations, and those of some unincorporated businesses, must be registered with the government under which the business operates. Registration of a business name does not give a business the right to carry on business under that name if to do so would infringe the trademark of some other business. The government specifically excludes any suggestion that granting incorporation or registering a particular name guarantees the use of that name, and it specifically warns applicants of this limitation.[11] Therefore, a separate trademark search and registration should be completed. Since section 40(2) of the *Trade-marks Act* allows a proposed trademark to be registered, a business can gain trademark protection before it spends too much promoting its names. The federal government will investigate potential confusion between corporate names and require a business to change its name if necessary.

Protection of Trademarks

Common Law: The Tort of Passing off

The common law protects a trademark owner through the tort of passing off. A person commits the tort of passing off when she misrepresents goods, services, or a business in such a way as to deceive the public into believing those things are the goods, services, or business of some other person, thereby causing damage to the latter. A passing off action will protect the trademark owner from the sale of counterfeit goods, which is actually theft of goodwill.

> **goodwill** positive association that attracts customers toward the owner's wares or services rather than those of its competitor

The legal definition of **goodwill** is "the positive association that attracts customers towards the owner's wares or services rather than those of its competitor."[12] The name of the business and any mark associated with it form part of a business's intangible reputation and goodwill.

---

[8] For a historic perspective of this topic, see LK Jones, "Trademark.com: Trademark Law in Cyberspace" (1999) 37 Alta. L. Rev. 991. This issue is discussed further in Chapter 31.

[9] Canadian Trademark Registration Number TMA147423 (registered in 1966), TMA315056 (registered in 1986).

[10] See http://www.ic.gc.ca/app/opic-cipo/trdmrks/srch/tmSrch.do?lang=eng.

[11] When applying for federal incorporation with a specific name, the applicant is required by the federal government to perform a NUANS (Newly Upgraded Automated Name Search). Names likely to cause confusion are rejected. The federal government limits its investigation to the contents of this search, and applicants are warned to complete a trademark registration and monitor ongoing applications. See the Innovation, Science and Economic Development Canada website: http://www.ic.gc.ca.

[12] *Veuve Clicquot Ponsardin v Boutique Cliquot Ltee*, 2006 SCC 23 at para 50.

CASE 20.1 Distinctive

Ray Plastics Ltd. manufactured a successful tool—a combined snow brush, ice scraper, and squeegee—called "Snow Trooper." It supplied the tool to a number of large retailers, including Canadian Tire. Canadian Tire suggested to another of its suppliers, Dustbane Products Ltd., that it consider producing a similar type of tool. Dustbane did so, producing a tool that was virtually identical and at a lower price; it took over all of Canadian Tire's snow-brush business.

The court found that the design of the "Snow Trooper" was very distinctive, that it had been intentionally copied, and that this constituted the tort of "passing off." It awarded an injunction and damages to Ray Plastics.[13]

Elements of the tort of passing off are as follows:

- The plaintiff's goods, services, or business must enjoy a reputation that is of some value worth protecting, that is, goodwill.
- The defendant must have misrepresented its goods, services, or business as those of the plaintiff.
- There must be either actual confusion or a likelihood of confusion in the public's mind between the goods, services, or business of the plaintiff and those produced or licensed by the defendant.[14]
- The plaintiff must suffer or be likely to suffer damage in consequence of the Passing off.[15]

CASE 20.2 Goodwill and Point of Confusion

Vancouver Community College adopted its name in 1974, and Vancouver Career College was founded in 1995. Both use the acronym "VCC." Vancouver Career College's website is "VCCollege.ca," and it bid on keywords "VCC" and "Vancouver Community College" so that online searches of those key words would produce "VCCollege.ca" in search results. Vancouver Community College sought an injunction and damages, claiming passing off.[16]

As to goodwill, the British Columbia Court of Appeal did not require that "VCC" be universally known, just that a small percentage of the market associate the trademark with the community college. As to confusion, it was not necessary for the searcher to click on "VCCollege.ca" to establish confusion. Confusion is established at first impression of the domain name in the search results. Passing off was proven, and an injunction was granted.

Passing off need not be intentional, and confusion is assessed as the first impression of the average consumer in a hurry. Some argue that plaintiffs should not need to prove damage or actual confusion if the passing off is deliberate.[17] This view has limited success in the courts, and the argument is more effective under the statutory causes of action discussed next.

---

[13] *Ray Plastics Ltd v Dustbane Products Ltd* (1994), 57 CPR (3d) 474. See also *Eli Lilly and Co v Novopharm Ltd* (2000), 195 DLR (4th) 547, leave denied [2001] SCCA No 100, in which the shape and colouring of a drug capsule were held to be distinctive packaging. However, the combination of shape and colour must be unique or sufficiently unusual to clearly distinguish the product from other products: *Novopharm Ltd v AstraZeneca AB* (2003), 233 DLR (4th) 150, supp'l reasons [2006] FCJ No 854.

[14] This may simply be a mistaken belief that the defendant has a licence to produce associated goods—see *Paramount Pictures Corp v Howley*, [1992] OJ No 1921.

[15] See *Ciba-Geigy Canada Ltd v Apotex Inc*, [1992] 3 SCR 120. See also *Kirkbi*, supra note 7; *Paramount Pictures*, ibid.

[16] *Vancouver Community College v Vancouver Career College (Burnaby) Inc*, 2017 BCCA 41 at paras 44, 66, 70, 73; See also *Diageo Canada Inc v Heaven Hill Distilleries Inc et al*, 2017 FC 571.

[17] See *National Hockey League v Pepsi-Cola Canada Ltd* (1995), 122 DLR (4th) 412 (an advertising campaign that incorrectly associates a product with another's product may actually benefit that other product but might still amount to passing off).

CASE 20.3 Proof of Confusion

The defendant named its new hotel in Edmonton the "Fantasyland Hotel." An injunction was sought by Walt Disney Productions, which had used the name "Fantasyland" in connection with its amusement parks. The Alberta Court of Appeal refused the injunction. According to the court:

> Passing off cases fall into two broad categories. In the first are those where competitors are engaged in a common field of activity and the plaintiff has alleged that the defendant has named, packaged or described its product or business in a manner likely to lead the public to believe the defendant's product or business is that of the plaintiff. The second, and nowadays perhaps more common type of passing off, is where it is alleged that a defendant has promoted his product or business in such a way as to create the false impression that his product or business is in some way approved, authorized or endorsed by the plaintiff or that there is some business connection between the defendant and the plaintiff. By these means a defendant may hope to cash in on the goodwill of the plaintiff. The appellant argued the second type saying that using the name "Fantasyland" for its hotel created the false impression that the hotel was connected to Disney. Disney lost because the belief that the respondent is benefiting from the use of the name "Fantasyland" is not enough to found the tort of passing off without proof of confusion.[18]

Section 7 of the *Trade-marks Act*

The *Trade-marks Act* provides additional statutory causes of action that are closely related to the common law action of passing off. Section 7 prohibits the following:

- making a false or misleading statement tending to discredit the business, wares, or services of a competitor
- directing public attention to one's wares, services, or business in such a way as to cause or be likely to cause confusion in Canada between those wares, services, or business and the wares, services, or business of another
- passing off other wares or services as and for those ordered or requested
- making, in association with wares or services, any description that is false in a material respect and likely to mislead the public as to their character, quality, geographic origin, or mode of production

Section 7 gives wider protection in some cases, since it applies to the whole of Canada and is broader in scope than the passing off action.

Registered Trademarks

Unregistered trademarks are protected by both the passing off tort and section 7 of the *Trade-marks Act*. Additional advantages are available if a business registers its trademarks under the *Trade-marks Act*.

When a registered mark is used, there is no need to indicate that it is registered in order to obtain the benefits of registration, but it has become common practice, on labels and in advertisements, to use the symbol ® or ™, frequently accompanied by words such as "is the registered trademark of XYZ Inc."

---

[18] *Walt Disney Productions v Fantasyland Hotel Inc* (1998), 85 CPR (3d) 36, aff'd (2000), 4 CPR (4th) 370; [1994] AJ No 484, aff'd [1996] AJ No 415. Disney won an earlier case over the use of the name "Fantasyland" for a theme park in West Edmonton Mall: Use within the same genre or business activity is relevant. See *Walt Disney Productions v Triple Five Corp*, [1992] AJ No 571, aff'd [1994] AJ No 196. The use of the trademark "Playboy" in connection with magazines and hotels was held not to be confusing with the same name for hairstylists: *Playboy Enterprises Inc v Germain* (1978), 39 CPR (2d) 32, aff'd. (1979), 43 CPR (2d) 271. See also *Toyota Jidosha Kabushiki Kaisha v Lexus Foods Inc* (2000), 194 DLR (4th) 491.

Rights Obtained by Registration   Section 19 of the Act gives the owner of a valid registered trademark the exclusive right to its use throughout Canada in respect of the goods and services for which it was registered. No unauthorized person may then sell, distribute, or advertise any goods or services in association with a confusingly similar trademark or trade name (s. 20), or otherwise use the mark in a manner that is likely to have the effect of depreciating the value of the goodwill attached to it (s. 22). Registration provides a complete defence to a Passing off action. If another person claims he had already been using the mark, or a deceptively similar mark, before the registration, his only recourse is to attack the validity of the registration.[19] If, after a trademark has been registered, it is discovered that some other person had been using a similar trademark before the registered owner first used it, the first user may bring proceedings to have the registration "expunged"—that is, removed (s. 17).[20]

Registration gives the owner other advantages; normally it applies to the whole of Canada so that the right of exclusive use is not restricted to the area in which the owner actually does business and has established a reputation. A trademark that has been registered in Canada may also be registered in other countries that adhere to the International Convention for the Protection of Industrial Property.[21] Although a separate foreign application is currently required, the Canadian registration creates a presumption in favour of validity, distinctiveness, and ownership, and pending legislation will allow a single application to access 92 countries.[22]

Duration   A trademark registration is valid for a period of 15 years and may be renewed indefinitely. Reforms anticipated in 2019 will reduce the period to 10 years. The Registrar may from time to time request evidence that the trademark is still being used, and if it has been abandoned or is not renewed at the end of the 15-year period, it may be expunged from the register (ss. 44, 45, 46).

Requirements for Registration

The Mark   In order for a trademark to be registered, it must satisfy a number of conditions (s. 12). In particular, the mark must *not* be

(a) a word that is primarily merely the name or surname of an individual who is living or died within the preceding 30 years; a person may continue to use her own name despite the existence of a registered trademark (s. 19);

(b) clearly descriptive or deceptively misdescriptive of the character or quality of the wares or services, or of their place of origin;

(c) the name of any of the wares or services in connection with which it is used;

(d) likely to be confused with another registered trademark;

(e–f) a mark that is prohibited by sections 9, 10, or 10.1 of the *Trade-marks Act*; or

(g–i) a protected geographic indication, Olympic, or Paralympic mark.

Prohibitions (a), (b), and (c) ensure that the names of people and places, and descriptive words that are in common usage, are not taken out of circulation through registration by giving a monopoly to the registered owner. The intention of prohibition (d) is to carry out the main purpose of the Act. Trademarks are designed to be

---

[19] *Molson Canada v Oland Brewery Ltd* (2002), 214 DLR (4th) 473; *Philip Morris Products SA v Marlboro Canada Ltd*, [2012] FCJ No 878.

[20] *Masterpiece Inc v Alavida Lifestyles Inc*, 2011 SCC 27.

[21] This treaty arose out of the Paris Convention of 1883, and it remains in force today (obviously in an amended form). Participating states guarantee the protection of intellectual property rights to each other's regimes. World Intellectual Property Organization, administers treaties and facilitates international cooperation in intellectual property regulation. See http://www.wipo.int.

[22] Madrid Protocol implemented by *Combatting Counterfeit Products Act*, SC 2014, c 32.

distinctive, and such distinctiveness would be lost if two or more persons were allowed to register "confusingly similar" marks. Although each case of confusion must be determined on its own facts with regard to all the surrounding circumstances, section 6 provides a list of relevant considerations, including the nature of the wares, the degree of resemblance, and the nature of the trade. Finally, the legislation prohibits registration of marks that suggest an association with geographic locations, royalty, the government, or certain international organizations or professional groups, or that are scandalous or obscene. The government controls which agricultural, food, or liquor products can be associated with a particular geographic location—it maintains a list of **protected geographical indications** (s. 11.1) and designates exceptions for such things as parmesan cheese and Black Forest ham (s. 11.18(4.1)).

protected geographical indications word or feature that connects a wine, spirit, or food product to a geographic location

It must be distinctive, original, and not confusingly similar to some other registered mark. The applicant must identify the class of goods to which the mark will relate. The normal practice is to search the Trade-marks databank on the CIPO website for other marks that are visually or phonetically similar to the mark being proposed for registration;[23] U.S. searches might also be advisable. In

---

ILLUSTRATION 20.1 Eligibility Examples

(a) A mark consisting of the name of a historical figure, such as "William Shakespeare" or "John A. Macdonald," would probably be acceptable; even though it is very likely that there are living persons with those names—they are not "primarily merely" surnames. Similarly, fictitious names, such as "Captain Kirk" or "Darth Vader," are registrable because the public would not identify the names with living individuals. In one instance, an invented name, "Marco Pecci," was held to be registrable in the absence of evidence that such an individual actually existed.[24]

(b) Words, especially adjectives, that are merely descriptive (or misdescriptive) of the quality of the goods are not acceptable. "Instant" or "Super" would be rejected, though "Kold One" has been accepted when applied to beer.[25] The word "Golden" was held to be descriptive of a beer and therefore not registrable.[26]

(c) The use of a place name as descriptive of the quality or origin of goods is normally not permitted and may be assessed as a geographic indication. The mark "Toscano," applied to wine, was disallowed since that is the Italian name for wine from a famous region.[27] However, a producer was permitted to register the mark "Oberhaus" in relation to wine, despite the fact that there is a village called Oberhausen in Germany where wine is produced. It was considered unlikely that the Canadian wine-buying public would know of the place.[28]

(d) An applicant was allowed to register the trademark "Barbie's" for restaurant, take-out, catering, and banquet services despite the objections of Mattel Inc., owners of the famous "BARBIE" mark in association with dolls and doll accessories. The Supreme Court of Canada held that the doll and restaurant business appealed to different consumers, and confusion was unlikely. The average consumer is not so easily confused.[29]

---

[23] The federal government's online search system searches all federally (and some provincially) registered companies and trademarks. The CIPO's Canadian Trade-marks Database website also has database search capabilities: http://www.cipo.ic.gc.ca/eic/site/cipointernet-internetopic.nsf/eng/h_wr03082.html.

[24] *Gerhard Horn Investments Ltd v Registrar of Trade Marks*, [1983] 2 FC 878. See also *Jurak Holdings Ltd v Matol Biotech Laboratories Ltd*, [2006] TMOB No 36 at paras 23–7, aff'd [2008] FCJ No 1367.

[25] *Registrar of Trade Marks v Provenzano* (1978), 40 CPR (2d) 288.

[26] *John Labatt Ltd v Molson Cos* (1987), 19 CPR (3d) 88 (FCA), leave denied [1988] SCCA No 109.

[27] *Jordan & Ste Michelle Cellars Ltd v Gillespies & Co* (1985), 6 CPR (3d) 377. In that case, the words were also deceptively misdescriptive, since the wine was Canadian.

[28] *Stabilisierungsfonds fur Wein v TG Bright & Co Ltd* (1985), 4 CPR (3d) 526. Sections 11.11 to 11.19 of the *Trade-marks Act* contain names and geographical descriptions of origin approved by the government that may be used in connection with wines and spirits. See *Sociedad Agricola Santa Teresa Ltda v VinaLeyda Limitada*, [2007] FCJ No 1681.

[29] *Mattel, Inc v 3894207 Canada Inc*, [2006] 1 SCR 772. See discussion of confusion: *Veuve Clicquot Ponsardin v Boutiques Cliquot Ltee*, *supra* note 12 and *Masterpiece Inc v Alvida Lifestyles Inc*, [2011] SCJ No 27.

practice, the application to register is normally prepared and filed by a specialist trademark agent, who will give advice on the likelihood of an application being accepted. Reforms anticipated in 2018 will change the concept of mark.

Ownership and Use Registration creates a presumption of ownership. It does not make a person the owner of a trademark; that person must already be the owner at the time of registration. Even in the case of an approved application based upon proposed use, the mark will be registered only after the applicant has filed a declaration that it has started to use the mark in Canada. Reforms anticipated in 2019 will change the concept of mark.

The application to register may be based upon any one of the following grounds (s. 16):

- The mark has been previously used or made known in Canada.[30]
- The mark has been registered and used abroad, in a country that is a party to the international convention.
- The use of the mark is proposed in Canada.

Generally, the advertising of a trademark is not sufficient to constitute "use"; the goods to which the mark relates must have been sold or the services performed. Advertising alone may be sufficient to amount to "making known" the mark in Canada.

Opposition Proceedings

If the Registrar refuses registration, the owner may appeal that decision to the courts. If there is no objection by the Registrar, or an objection has been overcome, the Trade-marks Office issues a notice that the application has been approved for advertisement in the *Trade-marks Journal*, and, subsequently, the application must be advertised. Any person may file a notice of opposition within two months of the advertisement. Registration may be opposed on any of the following grounds:

- The application did not comply with the various formal requirements for filing.
- The mark is not registrable.
- The applicant is not the person entitled to registration.
- The mark is not "distinctive" (ss. 37, 38).

The opponent must give reasons for the objection, but the applicant still bears the onus of satisfying the Registrar that the trademark should be registered. Opposition proceedings are determined in the first place by hearing officers, with appeal to the Federal Court.

An objection that the mark is not registrable may be based on any of the elements set out in section 12 of the Act. One common reason is that the objector claims pre-existing rights to an identical or confusingly similar mark, whether or not it is registered. Determining what is "confusing" depends on all the surrounding circumstances, including the nature of the business concerned and the class of goods or services involved.[31]

---

[30] *Trade-marks Act, supra* note 4, s 16. Pending legislation will abolish prior use.

[31] Section 6(5) contains a non-exhaustive list; whether confusion is likely is determined on a balance of probabilities: *Masterpiece Inc v Alavida Lifestyles Inc, supra* note 20; *Veuve Clicquot Ponsardin v Boutiques Cliquot Ltee, supra* note 12.

CASE 20.4 Unlikely to Confuse

A small Ontario corporation, Pink Panther Beauty Corp., applied to register the name "Pink Panther" as a trademark for hair care and beauty supplies that it proposed to market. The application was opposed by United Artists, the well-known movie studio that owns the Pink Panther movies, the Pink Panther cartoon character, and the accompanying music. United Artists has its own "Pink Panther" registrations for movie-related services. It argued that the application by the Ontario corporation should not be granted because of the risk of confusion with its existing marks. Further, it claimed that the applicants were simply trying to cash in on the famous name.

The court allowed the Ontario corporation's application to register the mark. There was no likelihood of confusion, and the average consumer is not so devoid of intelligence as to confuse the applicant's beauty products with the complainant's movies.[32]

Actions for Infringement

Unauthorized Use

One major advantage of registration is that, unlike passing off, a registered trademark may be infringed by *any* unauthorized use of that mark or a confusingly similar mark by some other person. It is not necessary for the defendant to have attempted to pass off its products as those of the owner of the mark.

Any use of another's name or mark, even without any intent to deceive, infringes another's mark.[33] Comparative advertising, where one firm attempts to demonstrate that its product is superior to a rival's, may constitute a "use" of the rival's mark if the advertisement refers to the name or mark of the rival product.[34] An infringement may be accidental or deliberate; it is not necessary to show intent to damage the goodwill of the owner of the mark,[35] though such an intention may persuade a court to award punitive damages.

grey marketing acquiring authentic goods through legal channels, then importing or exporting them for sale in another country without the trademark owner's permission

CASE 20.5 Authentic Goods

In *Coca-Cola Ltd v Pardhan*[36] the well-known soft drink company brought an action alleging infringement of its trademark on the ground that the defendant bought quantities of the beverage in Canada and then exported it for resale without the consent of the manufacturer. Coca-Cola argued that the defendant's export amounted to infringement because exporting is deemed to be use under the *Trade-marks Act*.[37] The Federal Court of Appeal rejected the argument and found that improperly distributing authentic goods did not amount to infringement.[38] The court held that "goods which originate in the stream of commerce with the owner of a trademark are not counterfeit."[39] This practice is known as "**grey marketing**," where a company acquires authentic goods through legal channels and then imports or exports them for sale in another country without the permission of the international trademark owner.

---

[32] *Pink Panther Beauty Corp v United Artists Corp* (1998), 80 CPR (3d) 247 (FCA). The Supreme Court of Canada has held that this case should not be interpreted to suggest that some resemblance of linkage to the wares in question is necessary for confusion to exist. The wares or services in question do not have to be of the same general class; this is but one factor to consider: *Mattel, supra* note 29 at paras 57–71.

[33] *Walt Disney Productions v Triple Five Corp, supra* note 18. In *Pro-C Ltd v Computer City Inc* (2001), 205 DLR (4th) 568, the Ontario Court of Appeal held that a trademark was not "used" simply because it appeared on a passive website.

[34] *Eye Masters Ltd v Ross King Holdings Ltd* (1992), 44 CPR (3d) 459. Contrast *Future Shop Ltd v A & B Sound Ltd* (1994), 55 CPR (3d) 182.

[35] Even a "spoof" upon a trademark may be actionable: see *Source Perrier SA v Fira-Less Marketing Co Ltd* (1983), 70 CPR (2d) 61; *United Airlines Inc v Cooperstock*, 2017 FC 616.

[36] (1999), 85 CPR (3d) 489.

[37] *Supra* note 4, s 4(3).

[38] The purpose of section 4(3) is not to equate exporting with "use" but rather to enable Canadian producers who do not make local sales but simply ship their goods abroad to establish "use" in Canada for the purposes of obtaining Canadian trademark registration. See also *Molson Cos v Moosehead Breweries Ltd et al* (1990), 32 CPR (3d) 363. But see *Mars Canada Inc v Bemco Cash & Carry Inc*, 2018 ONCA 239.

[39] Citing *Smith & Nephew Inc v Glen Oak Inc et al* (1996), 68 CPR (3d) 153.

Jurisdiction and Remedies Both the civil provincial courts and the Federal Court of Canada have jurisdiction to hear an action for infringement. The appropriate provincial court may deal with both passing off and *Trade-marks Act* claims, but the resulting judgment will be enforceable in the specific province only. On the other hand, if an action is brought in the Federal Court, the judgment is enforceable anywhere in Canada. However, the Federal Court has jurisdiction to deal only with statutory actions brought under the *Trade-marks Act*. Normally, that should not cause any difficulty since, as we have seen, section 7 of the Act seems to provide greater protection to even unregistered trademark owners than does the common law tort of passing off.

The remedies that either court may grant are almost the same. If there is injury to the goodwill of the owner, then damages may be awarded; if the defendant has profited from the infringement, an account of profits may be ordered. The defendant may be restrained from further infringement by an injunction and may be required to deliver up or dispose of infringing materials. The court may also order the defendant to allow the plaintiff to search for and seize offending wares and relevant books and records,[40] and, in a statutory action, may impose a ban upon further imports of offending products.[41] Anticipated 2019 reforms would introduce new criminal offences.

Assignment, Licensing, and Franchising

An owner may transfer a trademark (a) whether or not it is registered, (b) either as part of or separately from the goodwill of the business, and (c) in respect of either all or some of the goods and services with which it is associated (s. 48). An owner may also license the use of a registered trademark under specific conditions set out in the licence (s. 50).

A transfer of the business operates to assign the trademark. If the mark is registered, the fact of the assignment may be entered on the register, but an assignment may be valid even if unregistered. If a mark is unregistered, the new owner may register it. A more difficult situation occurs when an owner keeps the business but assigns the trademark, perhaps because the business is discontinuing production of the associated goods. Confusion arises because, in the eyes of the public, the trademark may remain distinctive of the goods of the previous owner rather than those of the new owner, who consequently will not immediately have an established right to it.[42]

When licensing a trademark, the owner may want to continue to use the mark and also to allow use by one or more other businesses, usually in return for payment of a fee or royalty. This may be done by giving notice to the public that the use is under licence. In that case, use by the licensee is deemed to be use by the registered owner itself so as to preserve the distinctiveness of the mark (s. 50). A licensed user cannot transfer the right to use a mark, and a breach of any of the terms of the licence will normally constitute an infringement of the trademark.

Although a franchise agreement, as discussed in Chapter 17, usually involves much more than the licensing of a trademark, the franchiser will, in most cases, require that the franchisee market goods or services under the franchiser's trademark. Franchisers normally insist on strict conditions in the franchise agreement, relating to such matters as quality control, purchasing of supplies and equipment, advertising, and the use of

---

[40] Known as Anton Piller relief: see *Anton Piller KG v Manufacturing Processing Ltd*, [1976] Ch 55; *Coca-Cola Ltd v Pardhan*, [2003] FCJ No 22.

[41] The power to ban imports may be restricted by trade agreements.

[42] See *Wilkinson Sword (Canada) Ltd v Juda*, [1968] 2 Ex CR 137.

trademarks, trade names, designs, and the like. Breach of the agreement by a franchisee normally terminates its right to use the trademark so that continued use would amount to infringement.

CHECKLIST
Reform 2019

Change	Current *Trade-marks Act*	Pending *Trademarks Act*[43]
Definition	Mark	Sign, including three-dimensional shape, scent, taste, texture
Distinguishing guise	Separately defined	Included in sign
Length of term	15 years	10 years
Prerequisite for registration	Use	No prior use required
Class of associated goods	Canadian classifications	International classification categories
International registrations	Multiple applications	Single applications
Offences	None	New criminal offences

COPYRIGHT

Statutory Origin

Copyright law balances public access to creations of art and intellect with fair compensation for creators.[44] Unlike trademarks, copyright is entirely the creation of statute. There is no common law action for infringement of copyright. Copyright law first developed to protect the written word after the invention of the printing press; over time its scope grew to cover drawings, paintings, movies, and musical scores. Current rules address radio and television broadcasting, computer software, digital copying, and the internet.

Canadian copyright law is governed by the *Copyright Act*,[45] originally adopted in 1924 and substantially amended in 1988, 1993, 1997, and 2012.

International Treaties

International treaties try to standardize copyright protection across international borders. The Berne Convention is an agreement among more than 150 countries, including Canada. An author who is a citizen of a Convention country has copyright protection in Canada, and Canadian authors enjoy protection in other Convention countries. Canada also signed the Universal Copyright Convention, which gives a citizen of a contracting state the same copyright protection in another contracting state as it gives its own citizens. Therefore, a Canadian can obtain protection in the United States simply by following the American practice of marking the work with the symbol "©" or the word "copyright," followed by the name of the copyright

---

[43] *Combatting Counterfeit Products Act*, *supra* note 22.

[44] *Theberge v Galerie d'Art du Petit Champlain Inc*, *supra* note 3 at para 30.

[45] RSC 1985, c C-42. Unless otherwise stated, references in this part of the chapter are to this Act, as amended.

owner and the year of first publication. In 1997, Canada signed two treaties developed by the **World Intellectual Property Organization** that are especially concerned with the impact of new technologies and the internet on creators' rights: the WIPO Copyright Treaty (1996) and the WIPO Performances and Phonograms Treaty (1996). These treaties came into force in 2002 and require participating countries to adopt domestic legislation creating copyright enforcement remedies with significant infringement deterrence effect. In 2014, the Canadian Parliament finally ratified both treaties.[46] A proposed trade agreement between Canada, the United States and Mexico (USMC trade agreement not yet ratified) would require Canada to extend the length of its copyright protection within two years of its ratification.

World Intellectual Property Organization a specialized agency of the United Nations dedicated to harmonizing intellectual property laws and regimes worldwide

Reform—2012

As will be discussed in Chapter 31, computer technology and the internet have created unparalleled access to copyrighted material. They have also enabled instantaneous copying, distribution, and alteration of copyright material, aggravating tension between owners and users. Even ordinary good faith computer use involves copying that could technically violate traditional copyright law.

Since the signing of the 1996 WIPO treaties, the Canadian government has talked of copyright reform to address such activities as material. The 1996 WIPO treaties prioritized owners' rights. They called for criminalization of activities such as downloading, uploading, sharing, updating, burning, copying, and electronic storage, strong enforcement procedures and remedies, and support for security technology in the form of **digital rights management technology (DRMT)** and technological protection measures (TPM). Users argue that DRMT violates privacy rights and does not distinguish between acceptable and unacceptable copying. The pivotal year for Canadian copyright reform came in 2012,[47] when the Supreme Court decided five copyright cases,[48] and Parliament passed the *Copyright Modernization Act*. Together, these initiatives clarified the law with respect to fair dealing, technical copying, and the role of DRMT.

digital rights management technology (DRMT) a system collecting data about the licensing, payment, use, and authenticity of a work

As a result, Canada became the international standard for balancing both creator and user rights.[49]

Nature of Copyright

Rights of Owner What is commonly referred to as "copyright" is really a collection of distinct rights conferred by statute. The basic rights of the owner of copyright are as follows:

---

[46] *Copyright Modernization Act*, SC 2012, c 20 began the process of bringing Canadian copyright law into conformity with international treaties. Canada is not the only signatory country that has been slow to implement the corresponding domestic legislation. France, Germany, the European community, and the United Kingdom have also failed to implement the treaty provisions. The United States adopted the 1996 treaty provisions in the *Digital Millennium Copyright Act* (DMCA). Treaty compliance improved with the passage of *Combating Counterfeit Products Act*, increasing the penalties for importing, exporting, or possessing goods that infringe trademark or copyright.

[47] For a review of Canadian copyright reform issues, see Michael Geist, ed, *In the Public Interest: The Future of Canadian Copyright Law* (Toronto: Irwin Law Inc., 2005). See also Nathan Irving, "Copyright Law for the Digital World: An Evaluation of Reform Proposals" (2010) *Asper Rev. of Int'l Bus Trade L* 141–62; Michael Geist, *The Copyright Pentalogy—How the Supreme Court of Canada Shook the Foundations of Canadian Copyright Law* (University of Ottawa Press, 2013).

[48] *Rogers Communications Inc v Society of Composers, Authors and Music Publishers of Canada*, 2012 SCC 35; *Society of Composers, Authors and Music Publishers of Canada v Bell Canada*, 2012 SCC 36; *Entertainment Software Association v Society of Composers, Authors and Music Publishers of Canada*, 2012 SCC 34; *Alberta (Education) v Canadian Copyright Licensing Agency (Access Copyright)*, 2012 SCC 37; *Re: Sound v Motion Picture Theatre Associations of Canada*, 2012 SCC 38.

[49] Michael Geist, *The Copyright Pentalogy*, *supra* note 47 at iv.

INTERNATIONAL ISSUE
Canada–U.S. Tension

Arguably, the Canada–U.S. border is the easiest border to cross in the world, and in the internet age, information flows invisibly across the boundary. This is cause for concern for copyright owners and users as each country has different rules for the protection and use of copyrighted material. The U.S. copyright regime is dominated by the *Digital Millennium Copyright Act*, which puts the rights of creators first. Unauthorized downloading of copyrighted material is illegal, including peer-to-peer software and music transfers.[50] The use of DRMT is supported, and internet service providers (ISPs) are required to block access to infringing material and turn over the names of their subscribers who download and share material illegally. In addition, the *Sonny Bono Copyright Extension Act* provides copyright owners 70 years of posthumous protection, compared to Canada's 50 years. Proposed trade agreement between Canada, the United States and Mexico would require Canada to change to 70 years.

The current Canadian copyright regime supports user rights, sometimes in contrast to the U.S. approach. The private-use exceptions for uploading, downloading, and copying have been expanded, especially in the education category.[51] In an apparent recognition of everyday activities, time shifting (i.e., PVR recording) and **format shifting** (moving works between digital formats) are permitted.[52] Canadian privacy laws forbid the arbitrary release of subscribers' names by ISPs,[53] which has protected Canadians from the types of infringement lawsuits music producers have launched in the United States, and Canadian law does not require ISPs to block access to infringing material as American law does. Still, some 2012 reforms move Canada closer to the American position on DRMT. The *Copyright Modernization Act* makes it illegal to use or sell technology to circumvent digital locks or TPMs.[54] As a result, in 2013 the Office of the United States Trade Representative moved Canada off its intellectual property "Priority Watch List," where it was placed in 2009, returning Canada to the less serious "Watch List" of countries needing to improve their intellectual property policies.[55] Although still on the 2017 Watch List, Canada recently expanded the powers of Canadian customs officers to stop the flow of counterfeit goods, another area of U.S. discontent.

Questions to Consider

1. Should Canada synchronize its copyright regime with the United States in order to reduce tension between the countries?
2. Did Canada lose the ability to independently determine its own copyright direction when it signed the 1996 WIPO treaties?

---

format shifting transferring purchased material, such as music, from one of the owner's devices to another

royalty payments fees paid for permission to use another person's copyrighted material

- the right to produce or reproduce the work in question, or any substantial part of it, in any material form
- the right to perform or deliver the work in public
- the right to publish an unpublished work

The Act is "technologically neutral"—reproduction in any form (print, telecommunication, internet) is covered, and **royalty payments** should not differ according to the medium used to deliver the work to the end user.[56]

---

[50] See e.g. *Robertson v Thomson Corp*, [2006] 2 SCR 363.

[51] *Supra* note 45, s 80 specifically exempts private-use copying of music from infringement provisions; s 29 fair dealing includes exceptions for research, private study, education, parody, and satire; s 29.21 exempts user-generated non-commercial content; ss 29.22 deals with private use; s 29.4 deals with instruction.

[52] *Ibid.*, ss 29.22 and 29.23.

[53] In BMG *Canada Inc v John Doe* (2004), 239 DLR (4th) 726, partially aff'd (2005) 252 DLR (4th) 332 (FCA) (denying a request from a music producer that five major ISPs disclose the identity of customers who traded music downloaded from the internet).

[54] *Supra* note 45, s 41.1; see opposition by Jennifer Stoddart, Privacy Commissioner of Canada, to the Industry Minister, dated January 18, 2008.

[55] Office of the United States Trade Representative, 2007, 2008, 2009, 2010, 2011, 2012, 2013, 2017 Special 301 Reports, https://ustr.gov/issue-areas/intellectual-property/Special-301.

[56] *Supra* note 45, s 3; *Robertson*, *supra* note 50 at para 49; *Entertainment Software Association v SOCAN*, 2012 SCC 34 at para 9.

CASE 20.6 Technologically Neutral

The Society of Composers, Authors and Music Publishers of Canada (SOCAN), a collective association that charges royalties for performance and communication of copyrighted musical works, wanted payment for music included in downloaded video games. The Supreme Court denied the request, saying downloading was no different from buying a physical copy in a store, and additional payments applying to only downloaded copies would violate the principle of technological neutrality. The *Copyright Act* does not impose additional layers of protections and fees based solely on the method of delivery of the work.[57]

The Act lists examples of specific rights protected:

- the right to translate the work
- the right to convert the work from one form into another (for example, to convert a novel into a play, or vice versa)
- the right to make a recording or film of the work
- the right to communicate the work to the public by telecommunication
- the right to exhibit the work in public
- the right to authorize any of the above (s. 3)

The nature of copyright is best understood as the power of the owner of the copyright to prevent others from doing any of those things that only the owner has the right to do.

Copyright arises automatically, without any registration, application, or publication. The private act of creating a work gives rise to copyright protection without the need to publish the work to a wider audience. The author or creator of the work is the original owner and may assign the copyright. Copyright may be owned by the author of a book or by the firm that publishes it, by the composer of a piece of music or by the recording company, or it may be transferred to some person not connected in any way with the creation or production process, such as an heir or creditor of the author. However, there are other rights known as **moral rights**, which are personal to the author or creator and cannot be assigned to others.

moral rights the non-transferable rights of an author or creator to prevent a work from being distorted or misused

Moral Rights These include

- the right to integrity of the work;
- the right to prevent distortion or mutilation of the work;
- the right to prevent it from being used in association with some product, service, cause, or institution; and
- where the work is copied, published, or performed, the right to be associated with the work as author or to remain anonymous (s. 14.1).

The author of a play is entitled to have the authorship properly attributed to her when it is performed or, if she wishes to remain anonymous or use an alias, the right not to have her true identity revealed. The integrity of the work is infringed if the creator's honour or reputation is damaged (s. 28.2). An artist who paints a picture is entitled not to have it defaced.

---

[57] *Entertainment Software Association v SOCAN*, ibid.

CASE 20.7 Moral Right to Prevent Distortion

A sculptor who created a flock of flying geese, to be displayed in a shopping centre, is entitled not to have them decorated with red ribbons at Christmastime.[58] This is the case whether or not he still owns the copyright.

Limits to Copyright

There is no copyright in a mere idea or thought. Copyright attaches to the expression of an idea in a material form. As was stated in one leading case:

> An author has no copyright in ideas but only in his expression of them. The law of copyright does not give him any monopoly in the use of the ideas with which he deals . . . , even if they are original. His copyright is confined to the literary work in which he has expressed them.[59]

A playwright could "borrow" the plot from another person's novel, provided the play is expressed entirely in her own words. Such conduct might be considered to be unprofessional and to amount to plagiarism, but it would not by itself constitute an infringement of copyright.

Works in Which Copyright Exists

Copyright exists in every *original* literary, dramatic, musical, and artistic work (s. 5). "Originality" means the work must have originated from its creator; there is no requirement that it must be particularly imaginative, novel, or skillful. Nevertheless, for a work to be "original," it must be work independently created by its author and must display at least a minimal degree of skill and judgment. The fact that it may have involved substantial effort does not by itself mean the work has originality.

Literary Works The *Copyright Act* gives a non-exhaustive definition of "literary work." The expression "includes tables, computer programs and compilations of literary works" (s. 2). Still there must be some conversion into a lasting or retrievable form, such as writing, film, digital form, or sound recording. There is no copyright in spoken words as such.

CASE 20.8 Originality

Tele-Direct Publications Inc. sued American Business Information Inc., claiming copyright on its "Yellow Pages" directories because of the extra work done to arrange phone number information and add other data, such as fax numbers. The Federal Court of Appeal ruled that compilations of this nature, which simply rearrange existing data, are not typically copyrightable.

However, the Yellow Pages, taken as a whole and given the visual aspects of the pages and manner of their arrangement, are protected by copyright. The information they contain is not. The court concluded that Tele-Direct had exercised only a minimal degree of skill, judgment, or labour in its overall arrangement, which was insufficient to support a claim of originality so as to be entitled to copyright protection.[60] This analysis conforms with the 1996 WIPO Copyright Treaty, which includes databases if the data selection or arrangement amounts to an "intellectual creation."

---

[58] *Snow v Eaton Centre Ltd* (1982), 70 CPR (2d) 105. In *Theberge v Galerie d'Art du Petit Champlain Inc*, supra note 3, the Supreme Court of Canada ruled that moral rights are infringed only if the work is modified in a manner that is prejudicial to the honour or integrity of its creator.

[59] *Moreau v St Vincent*, [1950] Ex CR 198 at 202.

[60] *Tele-Direct (Publications) Inc v American Business Information, Inc*, [1998] 2 FC 22. See also *Edutile Inc v Automobile Protection Association* (2000), 188 DLR (4th) 132.

CASE 20.9 Spoken Words

A book was published about the late classical pianist Glenn Gould. The book was largely based on private interviews between Gould and the author, Jock Carroll. Gould's estate sued, claiming, among other things, that copyright in the interviews belonged to Gould. The court held that Carroll was the sole author and owner of the copyright in the notes and recordings of his interviews of Gould, and that neither Gould (nor his estate) had copyright in Gould's spoken words.[61]

In addition to books and magazine and newspaper articles, the term "literary works" has been held to include income tax tables, street directories, examination papers, insurance forms, parts catalogues, and the like. From this list, it is apparent that literary merit is not an essential element of a "literary work."

Computer Software Computer programs are protected by copyright as literary works (they can be part of a patent if it has a physical existence or manifests a discernable change). Section 2 defines "computer program" to mean instruction or statements expressed, fixed, embodied, or stored in any manner, for use directly or indirectly in a computer in order to bring about a specific result. However, not every part of a software program is necessarily protected by copyright; some parts of the program may be purely functional or minor modifications, and to copy those parts would not constitute an infringement.[62] The statutory provisions also contain certain exemptions, permitting the making of single copies for a specific purpose, such as a backup copy or reproducing the program in another form in order to render it compatible with a particular computer.

Dramatic Works A "dramatic work" is defined to include "any piece for recitation, choreographic work, or mime, the scenic arrangement or acting form of which is fixed in writing or otherwise," as well as "any cinematographic work, and any compilation of dramatic works" (Copyright in choreography s. 2. Government of Canada.). The category is sufficiently wide to include not only the older forms of drama, such as plays, operas, and ballets, but also most new forms of entertainment. The key words in the definition are "fixed in writing or otherwise." The text of a play and score of a musical comedy are protected since they are fixed in written form. But so are films, video recordings of dramatic works, and sound recordings of an interview.

Although an event such as a street riot or a plane crash, or perhaps even a football game, occurs independently of a person making a video of it, and is not itself a "dramatic work," videoing such an event can constitute the dramatic work of the videographer. Copyright subsists in video, and to copy the video would constitute an infringement of copyright.

Communication Signals and Telecommunications A "live" broadcast of an event is a communication signal—radio waves transmitted through space (without wires or cables) for reception by the public—and a broadcaster has copyright in the communication signals it broadcasts. These signals are protected by copyright despite the fact that they are not **fixed**.[63] A "live" broadcast is considered to be "fixed" even if it becomes fixed simultaneously with its transmission. In addition, communicating a work to the public by any form of telecommunication is an infringement of

fixed stored in a permanent or lasting form

---

[61] *Gould Estate v Stoddard Publishing* (1998), 161 DLR (4th) 321. Contrast *Hager v ECW Press Ltd*, [1999] 2 FC 287.

[62] *Delrina Corp v Triolet Systems Inc*, [2002] OJ No 3729; *Harmony Consulting Ltd v GA Foss Transport Ltd*, [2011] FCJ No 451.

[63] *Supra* note 45, s 21.

copyright unless the retransmission complies with the *Broadcasting Act*.[64] The definition of a telecommunication is much wider than a communication signal as it includes radio as well as wire, cable, visual, optical, or electromagnetic systems. This broad definition is why the internet is regulated by the broadcasting regulator: the Canadian Radio-television and Telecommunications Commission (CRTC).

Musical Works A "musical work" refers to a musical composition with or without words. A performance of a musical work is not within the definition but is separately protected. Separate protection is also given to sound recordings. The recording is itself regarded as a work in which copyright subsists, whether or not the work being performed also has its own copyright (s. 18). A recording of a live performance by a jazz musician, in which a new work is improvised, is protected by copyright even though the music itself was never written down. A recording of a performance of a symphony by Beethoven is similarly protected, even though any copyright in the symphony itself would long ago have expired.

Artistic Works An "artistic work" is defined by section 2 to include "paintings, drawings, maps, charts, plans, photographs, engravings, sculptures, works of artistic craftsmanship, architectural works, and compilations of artistic works."[65] Architectural work means "any building or structure, or model of a building or structure." For architectural works, copyright is restricted to the artistic character and design and does not extend to the processes or methods of construction. A trademark of distinctive design may also qualify as an artistic work and may be protected by copyright. In addition, plans and drawings of machinery or other devices may be protected by copyright as artistic works and at the same time may depict or describe an invention that is protected by patent. It is also frequently difficult to determine whether a particular piece of work is an artistic work, protected by copyright, or an industrial design, which may receive a different form of protection.

Performers' Performances A performance of an artistic, dramatic, or musical work qualifies for copyright protection separate and apart from the copyright given to the work itself. Unlike other works, performers receive copyright even if the performance is not converted to a fixed format. One of the rights section 15 gives a performer is the right to transform the performance into a material form. A live broadcast of a performance will be protected as telecommunication.

The Protection of Copyright

Registration Copyright comes into existence automatically on the creation of a work. Registration of copyright is not necessary, but the Act gives the option of registration (s. 54), and it does confer certain advantages on the registered owner. In particular, the certificate of registration creates a presumption that copyright subsists in the work and that the person registered is the owner of the copyright. Still, the advantages to be gained from registration are relatively small, and the practice is not widely used except by performing rights societies.

Duration of Copyright In Canada, a work is usually protected by copyright during the life of its author and for a further period of 50 years after the author's death (s. 6). Proposed trade agreement between Canada, the United States and Mexico might force Canada to extend the length of its copyright protection to 70 years after death.

---

[64] *Ibid.*, s 31. Regulation of broadcasting sometimes conflicts with copyright law. For a discussion of the interaction of the two, see *Reference re Broadcasting Act (Can)*, 2012 SCC 68.

[65] *Supra* note 45, s 2.

The deceased author's estate or an assignee of the copyright—for example, a publisher—may use the protection. The Act prescribes different terms for the following:

- Photographs are protected for 50 years from the making of the original negative or plate.
- Cinematographic works are protected for 50 years after first publication.
- Posthumous works—works not published before the death of the author—are protected for 50 years from the date of first publication.
- Jointly authored works are protected for 50 years after the death of the last surviving author.
- Crown copyright persists for 50 years from the date of first publication.

Ownership of Copyright Copyright belongs initially to the author or creator of a work. Copyright in a work may be jointly owned by two or more authors, such as the joint authors of a book. It is also possible for separate copyrights to exist in different parts of the same complete work; for example, the writer of the lyrics of a song may hold copyright in the words (as a literary work), and the composer may hold copyright in the music.

There are a number of exceptions to the general rule. Works that have been prepared or published by or under the direction of the government belong to the Crown, subject to contrary agreement. Most important is the rule that where the author of a work was employed by some other person and the work was made in the course of employment, copyright belongs to the employer—again, unless otherwise agreed.[66] This does not change the length of protection, which remains tied to the human author.

Section 14 provides that, when an author has assigned a work, copyright in it reverts automatically to the author's estate 25 years after the death of the author. However, the rule applies only in cases of sole authorship where the original copyright belonged to the author, and nothing to the contrary is said in the will.

Assignment and Licensing An owner of copyright may assign it, for payment of a royalty or by way of gift, or it may pass to heirs upon the death of the owner. An owner may also assign part of a copyright in a work or divide it territorially. For example, one person might own the copyright of a book in Canada and another in the United States. Authors often assign the copyright in a book to their publishing company in return for the payment of a royalty—for example, 10 percent of total sales revenue. The parties may attach a variety of conditions to an assignment, dealing with such matters as publication in other countries, translations, and reproduction in other forms.

Alternatively, an author may retain the copyright in a work but give the publisher a licence to print or reproduce and sell it, again normally in return for a royalty. An author may grant a licence for the single performance of a play or musical work, on a specified date at a particular theatre, or for the reproduction of an extract from a work in some other work—for example a collection of essays or a set of teaching materials.

A special arrangement is available for management of rights in literary, musical, and dramatic works, recordings, and performances. An author may assign her rights in the work to a **collective rights society** (ss. 2, 19, 81). In turn, the society grants licences for a fee, pays part of the fee to the author, and retains the remainder to cover the society's costs. The Copyright Board has authority to approve and to regulate the fee (tariffs) charged by the collectives. A collective society can only impose a fee for what

collective rights society a society to which authors of musical and dramatic works assign performing and communication rights and that grants licences and collects fees

---

[66] *Ibid.*, s 13(3). In *Hanis v Teevan* (1998), 162 DLR (4th) 414, copyright in computer software developed by an employee was held to belong to the employer university. A special rule (art 13) applies to employees of newspapers: but see *Robertson v Thomson Corp*, *supra* note 50 (dealing with freelance authors).

would otherwise amount to an infringement of copyright. Collectively managed tariffs have been imposed on many internet business activities, as discussed more fully in Chapter 31. SOCAN has attempted to impose fees on a number of activities that the Supreme Court decided do not infringe copyright.

CASE 20.10 Internet Service Providers

SOCAN applied to the Copyright Board for approval of a special tariff on Canadian ISPs applicable to internet transmissions of copyrighted music (known as Tariff 22). SOCAN's application was opposed by the Canadian Association of Internet Providers, which argued that ISPs did not commit any breach of copyright by transmitting or caching copyrighted music often from international sources.

The Supreme Court of Canada ruled that the ISPs committed no breach of copyright. They were merely intermediaries who provided the means of telecommunication. They were not communicators and could not be required to pay the tariff.[67]

Infringement of Copyright

What Constitutes Infringement? Copyright consists of a number of exclusive rights vested in the owner. An infringement occurs when another person, without the consent of the owner, does an act that only the owner has the right to do. An unauthorized public performance, communication, publication, or reproduction of a copyrighted work constitutes an infringement, as does the translation of a work, or recording, broadcasting, or exhibiting it in public. A person who purports to authorize some other person to do any of those acts, without the copyright owner's consent, also infringes copyright.

CASE 20.11 Downloading or Streaming?

SOCAN alleged that online music service providers that allow consumers to download or stream music are "communicating a musical work to the public by telecommunication" and thereby infringe copyright. SOCAN requested separate tariffs for downloading or streaming. The music service providers argued that each transaction was a private communication by the individual user and therefore should not be considered communication to the public. The Supreme Court distinguished between downloading and streaming; downloading is not communication by telecommunication but rather reproduction already covered by the existing royalty. Streaming, on the other hand, was held to be a communication "to the public" regardless of whether the members of the public receive their communications at the same place or time or at their own request.[68]

It is not necessary for the entire work to be copied to constitute an infringement of copyright; the unauthorized copying of a substantial part is sufficient. What amounts to a "substantial" part is a question of fact and degree and should be determined on a holistic not piecemeal basis.[69] A quotation of a few lines from a written work, especially if attributed to its author, does not constitute an infringement, but the quotation of several pages might. The offending copy need not be identical to the original work, and one cannot avoid liability simply by arranging the copied work in a different format or by making minor changes.

---

[67] *Canadian Association of Internet Providers v SOCAN*, (2004), 240 DLR (4th) 193.

[68] *Rogers Communications Inc v SOCAN*, 2012 SCC 35.

[69] *Cinar Corporation v Robinson*, 2013 SCC 73 at paras 26–29, 36.

> ### CASE 20.12 Original and Substantial
>
> Hager was the author of a book about famous Canadians of Aboriginal heritage, which included a nine-page chapter about country music star Shania Twain. The chapter was based on Hager's interviews with Twain and included many quotations from those interviews. Subsequently, Holmes was commissioned by ECW Press to write a book about Twain. The ECW book was found to contain substantial portions of Hager's work, including most of the direct quotations from the interviews with Twain. Hager sued ECW for breach of copyright. ECW argued that the quoted words of Twain were not protected by copyright because they were not the original work of Hager. It also claimed that the copying was not substantial (it amounted to about one-third of the Hager chapter) and that it constituted fair dealing for research purposes.
>
> These defences were rejected, and Hager was awarded damages, plus an accounting equal to 10 percent of ECW's profits from the sale of its book. The court held that Hager's work was protected by copyright because it was a product of her skill, judgment, and labour. Twain's quoted words were in response to Hager's questions and had been selected by Hager for inclusion in her book. The copying was substantial and could not be said to have been done for research purposes.[70]

The person who actually makes the copy is not the only one who may be liable for infringement of copyright. A theatre owner who permits the theatre to be used by a group of actors or musicians for a performance that infringes the author's copyright is infringing as well as the performers. Also, a bookseller who imports and sells a "pirated" edition of a copyrighted book infringes all with the illegal publisher. It is an infringement of copyright to authorize a person to do something the owner of the copyright has the sole right to do. A person who buys a book and lends it to a friend for the known purpose of photocopying it infringes the copyright in the book as much as the friend does. However, the manufacturing and selling of equipment that can be used for creating copies does not constitute authorizing an infringement.[71]

Notice of Infringement ISPs are currently considered more like manufacturers than theatre owners, not liable for infringement because they are only intermediaries for communication (s. 2.4(1)(b)). However, there is liability on ISPs that have notice of infringement and do nothing to stop it. The *Copyright Act* creates a "notice to notice" scheme requiring an ISP to give notice to a subscriber when it is aware of or receives notice of an alleged infringement. Canada rejected the more drastic U.S. "notice and takedown" scheme, which would obligate an ISP to withdraw service from an alleged infringer.[72] The notice to notice scheme also applies to other digital network provider. A weakness in the scheme is that the recipient of the notice is not obligated to do anything in response to the notice.

Fair Dealing and Other Permitted Uses Certain acts that would otherwise amount to infringement of copyright are expressly permitted by the *Copyright Act*. The most important exemption allows the fair use of copyright works for research, private study, education, parody, or satire (s. 29), for criticism and review (s. 29.1), or for news reporting (s. 29.2).

Copying a musical work or performance of a musical work for the private use of the copier is also not infringement (s. 80). Instead, tariff is collected from online music provider and manufactures of blank CDs; the money collected is distributed to musical work copyright owners (s. 82). Re:Sound is a collective society that collects a tariff

---

[70] *Hager v ECW Press Ltd*, *supra* note 61.

[71] *CBS Songs Ltd v Amstrad Consumer Electronics*, [1988] 2 All ER 484. The Act imposes a levy on the sale of blank cassette tapes and compact discs (ss. 82, 83).

[72] *Supra* note 45, ss 41.2, 41.26, 41.27(3). See Irving, *supra* note 47.

> **CASE 20.13 Fair Dealing in Research**
>
> A provincial law society provided various services to its members. These included providing photocopying machines in the library so that members could make copies of law reports and other documents and, for an additional fee, have library staff make copies of documents on request and fax or courier those copies to members. A publisher of law reports claimed that these practices constituted infringements of its copyright in the reports.
>
> The Supreme Court of Canada agreed that the publishers owned the copyright in the reports. Although the actual judgments of the courts are in the public domain, the reports contained headnotes and annotations that met the requirement of originality.
>
> However, the Court held that there was no infringement of that copyright by the law society. In particular, (1) the mere provision of photocopiers, which might be used to infringe copyright, did not constitute authorization to infringe; (2) the fax transmission of a single copy of a work to a single individual does not constitute "communication to the public" under the Act; and (3) under the fair dealing provisions of the Act, a person is permitted to use and copy copyrighted works for purposes of research. Research is not limited to non-commercial use, and lawyers carrying on their profession conduct research within the meaning of the Act.[73]

for musical works played by radio stations, pay audio services, satellite radio companies, gyms, nightclubs, restaurants, retail establishments, and hotels. A user may use copyrighted work to generate his own content for non-commercial purposes (s. 29.21, the so-called "YouTube exception"). Subject to a number of conditions, educational institutions are permitted to copy and reproduce works for purposes of instruction (s. 29.4).[74] Decisions vary depending upon the specific institution's copying policy.

> **CASE 20.14 Conflicting Decisions on Fair Dealing in Education**
>
> Access Copyright is a collective society representing authors and publishers of literary and artistic works. Access Copyright sought to renew its tariff agreement with school boards covering photocopying of sections of textbooks for distribution to students. The Supreme Court determined that photocopies made by teachers for distribution to students were part of class instruction and qualified as fair dealing. Photocopying part of textbooks qualified as research or private study, and the extent of the copying was fair given the purpose of education and instruction, the small amount copied, the limited alternatives, and the low effect on textbook sales.[75]
>
> In a subsequent, possibly conflicting decision, the Federal Court refused to apply the fair dealing exception when York University opted out of Access Copyright's tariff increase. The Court found York's copying policies were not fair and had virtually no safeguards to ensure compliance.[76]

Courts apply a two-step process to the determination of fair dealing. First the court determines if the activity is done for one of the allowable purposes described above (that is, research, private study). Second, the court decides if the activity is "fair" in light of its purpose, character, amount, or alternatives and the nature of the work and effect the activity has on the work.[77]

Remedies for Infringement
The usual civil remedies are available in cases of infringement of copyright, including the following:

- damages for profit or income lost by the owner, or for conversion of the owner's property

---

[73] *CCH v Law Society of Upper Canada*, supra note 3. Section 30.2(1) of the Act provides that a library or person acting under its authority does not infringe copyright to do anything on behalf of a patron that the patron could personally have done under the fair dealing exception. The library must not be established or operated for profit.

[74] It does not permit the reproduction of an entire work or a substantial portion thereof: *Alberta (Education) v Canadian Copyright Licensing Agency (Access Copyright)*, 2012 SCC 37.

[75] *Ibid*.

[76] *Canadian Copyright Licensing Agency v York University*, 2017 FC 669.

[77] *Alberta (Education)*, supra note 74 at para 12.

CASE 20.15 Consumer Research

SOCAN collects a royalty tariff from online music service providers that sell digital music. It wanted to apply a tariff to the 30- to 90-second free preview of the music that could be streamed by prospective purchasers. The Supreme Court held that previews were not copyright infringement because they fell under the fair dealing exception for research—consumers were doing research before their purchases. It was fair because there were no alternatives to hearing the music, the amount of dealing was modest, and its effect on the work was to increase sales. No new royalties or tariff were allowed.[78]

- accounting for profits made by the defendant as a result of the infringement (normally an alternative to damages)[79]
- injunction to restrain the defendant from further infringement and to require the surrender of any offending copies

Some criminal offences trigger fines up to $1 million and/or imprisonment for up to five years to deter bootlegging and pirating copyrighted materials (s. 42). **Statutory damages** for non-commercial infringement are capped at $5000 (s. 38.1). However, in the commercial context, the Supreme Court has given punitive damages.[80]

statutory damages damages a plaintiff may request instead of proving actual loss

PATENTS

Like copyright, the law of patents is entirely based on statute. At common law, an inventor had no inherent right to profit from his creation, and no law was broken by making use of another's invention. However, a patent differs fundamentally from copyright. Whereas copyright comes into existence automatically upon creation of the work, a patent exists only after a grant from the appropriate government body.

History The first federal *Patent Act* was adopted in 1869, largely based upon the existing American legislation rather than British or European models.[81] Canada's current *Patent Act*[82] was substantially amended in 1987, in part to bring Canada's law into partial conformity with international practice under the Patent Cooperation Treaty. The 1987 amendments changed a number of the specifically American features of our law. These amendments came into effect on October 1, 1989; patents granted or applied for prior to that date remain subject to the earlier law. Further substantial amendments, notably in respect of pharmaceutical products, were introduced in 1992 and 1993. The result is that there are distinct differences between Canadian patent law and U.S., British, and European rules.

International Treaties

Over 142 countries adhere to the Patent Cooperation Treaty administered by the World Intellectual Property Organization. It provides for the filing of a single international patent application, which then gives patent protection in all the signatory countries.[83] More than 160 countries belong to the Paris Union and comply with the

---

[78] *Society of Composers, Authors and Music Publishers of Canada v Bell Canada*, 2012 SCC 36. Intellectual property rights in relation to the internet are also discussed in Chapter 31.

[79] *Cinar v Robinson Corporation*, 2013 SCC 73 (discussing proof of profit and entitlement to non-pecuniary and punitive damages).

[80] *Ibid*.

[81] British and European patent laws are based in on the European Patent Convention (Convention on the Grant of European Patents, 1973, now in its 16th edition), which defines inventions (art. 52) based upon exclusions rather than an inclusive definition.

[82] RSC 1985, c P-4. References in this part of the chapter are to that Act.

[83] See Canadian Intellectual Property Office, Patent Cooperation Treaty Kit, https://www.ic.gc.ca/eic/site/cipointernet-internetopic.nsf/eng/wr02599.html.

Paris Convention for the Protection of Industrial Property, which gives an applicant one year from the date of filing in Canada to file in a member country. Canada belongs to both treaties. In 2014, Canada passed legislation to modify it pharmaceuticals patent process as part of its obligations under the Canada–European Union Comprehensive Economic and Trade Agreement (CETA).[84]

The Nature of Patents

An inventor or the legal representative of an inventor may obtain a patent that gives the applicant a monopoly over the invention for a period of 20 years (s. 44).[85] This secures the "exclusive right, privilege and liberty of making, constructing and using the invention and selling it to others to be used" (s. 42).

In exchange for this monopoly, the inventor must make the invention public, by filing an adequate description of the invention, so that others will be able to duplicate the invention freely when the statutory 20-year period expires.[86]

CASE 20.16 Full Disclosure

Pfizer opposed a request by Teva Canada to sell a generic version of Viagra, a drug already patented by Pfizer. Teva claimed that Pfizer's patent was invalid because the application did not meet the *Patent Act*'s disclosure requirements. It failed to specify which of the many compounds was effective for treating erectile dysfunction. The Supreme Court of Canada agreed with Teva—the application did not make proper disclosure. Since the patent system is a bargain—the inventor gets exclusive rights in exchange for disclosure of the invention—the logical consequence of insufficient disclosure is patent invalidity. Pfizer's Viagra patent was declared invalid.[87]

An inventor has a choice: (1) keep the invention entirely secret and continue to exploit it indefinitely but run the risk that some other person will sooner or later stumble upon the same invention or unravel the secret; or (2) reveal it and enjoy exclusive rights for a limited period only. Given the speed at which technological advances are now being made, and the generous period of protection, applying for a patent would seem advisable for inventions that have lasting appeal. However, obtaining a patent is a complex and fairly expensive business, and if an invention is likely to have only a short productive life, secrecy may be the better option. The alternatives of registering the invention as an industrial design or relying upon copyright protection of the plans or specifications and requiring confidentiality agreements should also be considered. But although copyright provides protection for a much longer period, that protection is more limited, since it extends only to the method of expression and not to the idea itself.

Patentable Inventions

Only "inventions" qualify for patent protection. The *Patent Act* defines an invention as "any new and useful art, process, machine, manufacture or composition of matter, or any new and useful improvement in any art, process, machine, manufacture or

---

[84] 2014 SC, c 39.

[85] The 20-year period runs from the date of filing the application.

[86] Some aspects of the patented invention may continue to be protected after the expiry of the patent, for example, under trademark law. It may be legal to use the invention but not to copy a distinctive shape or format. See *Eli Lilly and Co v Novopharm Ltd*, supra note 13; *Thomas & Betts Ltd v Panduit Corp* (2000), 185 DLR (4th) 150. Contrast *Kirkbi AG v Ritvik Holdings Inc*, supra note 7.

[87] *Teva Canada Ltd v Pfizer Canada Inc*, 2012 SCC 60.

composition of matter" (s. 2).[88] Three elements in the definition must be present for an invention to be patentable. It must be

- an art, process, machine, manufacture, or composition of matter, or an improvement to such;
- new; and
- useful.

Inherent in the notion of an invention is the requirement that it is something that possesses the quality of ingenuity and is not simply an obvious step that any person with ordinary skill in the field might have taken. It must be more than just an obvious next step given the state of prior knowledge in the field (known as prior art).[89]

Art, Process, Machine, Manufacture, or Composition of Matter

For an invention to be patentable, it must fall within one of these categories. The word "art" refers to the manual or productive arts, as distinct from the fine arts. A "process" means a method of manufacture or operation designed to produce a particular result—for example, a new process for the chemical cleaning of fabrics. "Machine" and "manufacture" are given their usual meanings, and a "composition of matter" refers to such things as chemical formulae that produce new compounds and substances.

A patent will not be issued solely for a scientific principle or abstract theorem, such as a mathematical formula (s. 27(8)). For these purposes, a computer program is equated to an abstract theorem and is not by itself patentable.[90] Computer-implemented inventions may be patented as a business method, a machine, or a product, provided they have a physical existence or manifest a discernible effect or change but not as computer programs, data structures, or computer-generated signals.

CASE 20.17 Patentable Subject Matter

Researchers at Harvard College developed a method of genetically altering mice to make them more likely to develop cancer following exposure to chemicals. This made the mice valuable for experimentation purposes. Harvard patented the invention in the United States (and in a number of European countries) and applied for a patent for the "Harvard mouse" (or "oncomouse," to give it its technical name) in Canada in 2002.

Registration was refused by the Patent Appeal Board and by the Federal Court. The process lacked the element of reproducibility required of a patent.

The Supreme Court of Canada (by a 5–4 majority) held that the oncomouse could not be patented.[91] Although some "lower" forms of life have been held to be patentable,[92] the majority considered that patenting higher life forms would involve a radical departure from the traditional patent regime and must only be done under the clear and unequivocal direction of Parliament. No clear direction existed. Harvard reduced the patent claims eliminating some of what the invention claims it can do, and a patent was awarded (it expires in 2020).[93]

Business Methods

Whether a business method is a patentable invention depends on its novel, useful, and ingenious contribution. Both in Canada and in the United States, business methods are processes eligible to be patented if they meet the regular

---

[88] *Supra* note 82, s 2.

[89] *Apotex Inc v Sanofi-Synthelabo Canada Inc*, 2008 SCC 61 (four-part test to obviousness).

[90] *Schlumberger Canada Ltd v Commissioner of Patents*, [1982] 1 FC 845.

[91] *Harvard College v Canada (Commissioner of Patents)* (2002), 219 DLR (4th) 577.

[92] Genetically modified yeast has been patented; see *Re Application of Abitibi Co* (1982), 62 CPR (2d) 81. However, in *Pioneer Hi-Bred Ltd v Canada (Commissioner of Patents)* (1987), 14 CPR (3d) 491 (FCA), aff'd (1989), 25 CPR (3d) 257 (SCC), it was held that a soybean variety developed by traditional plant cross-breeding was not patentable subject matter. The rights of plant breeders may now be protected under the *Plant Breeders' Rights Act*, SC 1990, c 20; see below, under the heading "Technological Change and Intellectual Property Law."

[93] CA1341442 (C)—2003-10-07.

requirements of the legislation. This is not so in countries covered by the European Patent Convention, which contains an express exclusion of "methods of doing business."[94]

CASE 20.18 Online Purchasing

Amazon.com applied for a patent of a "single click" online purchasing method whereby cookies stored in customer and server computer systems would recognize each other and exchange purchasing information without the purchaser having to check out or enter purchasing data. The patent was rejected, but Amazon.com won its appeal before the Federal Court. The Court held that the patent examiner wrongly applied the European definition of patentable inventions. Canadian law is different—business methods are patentable as an "art" or a "process" if they are new and useful with practical applications that manifest an effect of change. They should be assessed like any other invention.[95] It was sent back for assessment by the Patent Commissioner, who issued a patent in December 2011.

Novelty An essential element of an invention is that it be "new." A patent will not be granted for a machine or process that is already known or in use, even if it has not been patented by some other person.[96]

Until 1989, Canada had a "first-to-invent" system; that is, if two or more persons applied for a patent for the same invention, only the first inventor was considered the true inventor and entitled to the patent. The present law adopts the more common "first-to-file" system; in cases of conflicting applications, the application with the earlier filing date prevails (s. 28.4).

An invention for which a patent is claimed must be one that has not been disclosed to the public anywhere in the world before the filing date. The exception to this rule occurs when the inventor himself makes the disclosure, but even then he must file the application within one year of making the disclosure.

Utility For an invention to qualify as "useful," it must possess industrial value—for example, by making a process easier, cheaper, or faster. Promise of future use is not sufficient. Still the utility requirement is minimal; only a small "scintilla" of practical purpose is needed.[97] Also implied is that it be usable—that is, it should be reproducible and operable, so that a skilled worker, by following the specifications published in the patent, should be able to reproduce the invention and obtain the desired result.

Inventiveness An invention requires an element of ingenuity, considering the claim made and the state of the art. As we have noted, it must be more than an obvious step. As has been said:

> The question to be answered is whether at the date of invention . . . an unimaginative skilled technician, in light of his general knowledge and the literature and information on the subject available to him on that date, would have been led directly and without difficulty to [the] invention.[98]

How big is the difference or gap between from the prior state of the art and the inventive concept of the claim? The patent examiner must decide if it took inventiveness to bridge that gap or whether it was the obvious next step.

---

[94] *Amazon.com, Inc v Canada (Attorney General)*, [2010] FCJ No 1209, reversed [2012] 2 FCR 459 (FCA); *Bilski v Kappos*, 561 US (2010).

[95] *Ibid*. The Federal Court of Appeal agreed that business methods are patentable and reversed the lower court's holding that the Amazon method was patentable—this was for the Commissioner to assess. Australia also recognizes the patentability of business methods: *Grant v Commissioner of Patents*, [2006] FCAFC 120.

[96] The discovery of a new use for a known compound is patentable: see *Apotex Inc v Wellcome Foundation Ltd* (2002), 219 DLR (4th) 660.

[97] *Astra Zeneca v Apotex*, 2017 SCC 36.

[98] *Beecham Canada Ltd v Proctor & Gamble Co* (1982), 61 CPR (2d) 1 at 27; *Sanofi-Synthelabo*, supra note 90.

Obtaining a Patent

Only the inventor or the legal representatives of the inventor may apply for the grant of a patent. If an inventor has assigned the rights to an invention to another person or to a corporation, the assignee may apply. An employer usually owns inventions made by its employees and is the rightful applicant for a patent.[99]

Applications for patents are made to the Commissioner of Patents and are processed by the Patent Office, a branch of the CIPO. Individual inventors may pursue their own applications, but any other applicants must use the services of a registered **patent agent**. In practice, making an application is a highly complex and specialized matter, and is almost invariably handled by a patent agent.

The agent first makes a search of the online register of patents, and frequently also a search at the U.S. Patent Office, to ensure that no patent has already been granted in respect of the invention. Thereafter, the application, in a form prescribed by the Patent Rules, is prepared. The application has two key elements: (a) the **specification**, providing a full description and disclosure of the invention, its use, operation, or manufacture, and (b) the **claim**, setting out the features claimed to be new/inventive and in respect of which the applicant claims an exclusive right. Applicants want the claim to be broad to obtain the maximum benefit from the invention, but it must not be excessively wide so as to include matters that are obvious or already known, and thus render the claim invalid.

When an application has been filed, a further application must be made for the claim to be examined. The application is then public, and anyone can raise questions or protest it. The Patent Office appoints an examiner to consider the application. The examiner makes searches of patents, and frequently of technical publications, to ensure that the claimed invention is indeed novel and otherwise complies with the requirements of the *Patent Act*. The examiner scrutinizes the specification and claim to ensure that complete disclosure has been made and that the invention is described in a way that would enable other persons to utilize it once the period of protection has elapsed. The applicant may make amendments to the application in order to satisfy objections raised by the examiner. When the process is complete, the examiner determines whether or not a patent should be granted. An appeal from a rejection of the application may be made to the Patent Appeal Board and thereafter to the federal court.

When the application is successful, the Patent Office issues a "Notice of Allowance," and on payment of a fee (which is additional to the application fee), it issues the patent. Annual fees must be paid in order to maintain the patent. The fees, however, are relatively modest and vary according to the nature of the applicant entity; for example, an applicant that qualifies as a "small entity."[100]

patent agent a registered agent who pursues applications for patents on behalf of individual inventors

specification the description of the invention, its use, operation, or manufacture

claim a statement of the features claimed to be new and in respect of which the applicant claims an exclusive right

Enforcing Patent Rights

A patent owner receives the exclusive right of constructing, using, and selling the invention. An owner may assign patent rights to others or grant a licence for their limited or exclusive use. An assignment must be in writing and registered with the Patent Office. It is the same for an exclusive licence. Any unauthorized act that interferes with the patent owner's rights is patent infringement, and the patent owner may sue. Defendants in an infringement action may defend by alleging that the patent is invalid (s. 59).

Remedies The remedies available for patent infringement are damages, injunction, and accounting for profit (ss. 55 to 57). Damages can be based on the reasonable royalty fee that should have been paid for the period of infringement or on an accounting

---

[99] *Techform v Wolda* (2001), 206 DLR (4th) 171.
[100] A "small entity" means an individual inventor or a business concern that employs 50 or fewer persons, or is a university, and meets a number of other conditions.

of the actual profits made by the infringer and can cover the application processing time (before the patent was granted). The court may award costs "on an escalated scale" against a defendant who makes unfounded claims of invalidity.[101] As of 2018, the largest Canadian damage award for patent infringement was for $644 million, plus millions of dollars in costs, and it included an amount for increased market share obtained by the infringer arising from the association with the patented product; this was described by the court as "springboard profits."[102]

Patents and the Public Interest

The 20-year monopoly created by a patent confers a considerable advantage over business competitors and sometimes, if the patentee chooses not to use the invention, deprives the public of the benefit of the invention. There are many stories—most of them probably fabrications—of large corporations buying up inventions (such as everlasting light bulbs or electric cars) that threaten their business in order to suppress the invention. The patent regime attempts to protect the public in a number of ways.

Challenging a Patent

One of the most important functions of the patent examiner is to perform a purpose-based evaluation of an invention before granting a patent. Third parties, such as business competitors or rival researchers, may protest during a patent application or try to invalidate a patent after it is granted by bringing an **action for impeachment** in the Federal Court. The Attorney General of Canada may also bring such an action.

action for impeachment an action challenging the validity of a patent

As well, any person may apply to the Commissioner of Patents for re-examination of any claim of a patent. Upon receiving such a request, the commissioner establishes a re-examination board to examine the request.

CASE 20.19 Conflicting Dispute Resolution Processes

Research In Motion (now known as BlackBerry) found itself embroiled in a patent dispute in the United States that highlights the complications associated with multiple dispute resolution venues. NTP Inc. claimed that RIM's BlackBerry infringed NTP's patent rights, and NTP started an infringement action in the U.S. federal court in Virginia. In addition to defending the court action, RIM challenged the validity of the NTP patents through the patent re-examination process of the U.S. Patent and Trademark Office. RIM found itself in the confusing position of losing the court action[103] while achieving preliminary success in the patent challenges. RIM eventually settled both actions with a payment of over US $600 million for a licence of the NTP patents.

Abuse of Patent Rights

Another form of protection allows the Attorney General or any interested person to apply to the Commissioner of Patents when it is alleged that patent rights are being abused. An abuse occurs, for example,

- if demand for the patented article in Canada is not being met to a reasonable extent and on reasonable terms;
- if the patentee is hindering the creation of new industries or damaging the public interest by refusing to grant licences;
- if any trade, industry, or person engaged therein is unfairly prejudiced by the conditions attached to a patent; or
- if the existence of a patent has been used so as to unfairly prejudice in Canada the manufacture, use, or sale of any materials.

So far courts have not recognized a common law cause of action for abuse of patent rights. In 2017 a consumer class action on behalf of Viagra users who believed they

---

[101] *Mediatube Corp v Bell Canada*, 2017 FC 6.

[102] *Dow Chemical Company v Nova Chemicals Corporation*, 2017 FC 350.

[103] *NTP, Inc v Research In Motion Ltd*, (2005) 418 F 3d 1282 (US App); (2006) 546 US 1157.

were overcharged for the drug pursuant to an invalid patent was dismissed for failing to disclose a cause of action.[104]

Compulsory Licensing A patentee cannot simply hold a patent for the purpose of blocking trade. If it does not use the invention itself in a reasonable manner, it must sell it or grant a licence on reasonable terms. If this does not happen, another person who wishes to make use of the invention may apply for the grant of a **compulsory licence**, which may be ordered on terms that allow the applicant to work the patent while giving the patentee a fair return.

compulsory licence a licence granted to a person to work a patent without the consent of the owner of the patent

Pharmaceutical products are high demand products and enjoy a thriving generic drug industry in Canada, to the economic benefit of the Canadian consumer. The compulsory licensing scheme for patented medicines has special regulations that establish a framework for allowing generic drug companies to obtain the right to produce patented drugs on payment of a royalty to the patent owner. The regulations are extremely complex and have produced one of the most hotly contested areas of litigation.[105] In part due to the problems highlighted by this litigation, the regulations are frequently are central in trade negotiations with foreign partners. Generic pharmaceuticals were at the center of NAFTA negotiations and the recently negotiated trade agreement with the European Union. CETA amendments to the patented medicine regulations include adding discovery and witnesses to drug patent challenges, shifting the burden of proving invalidity to the generic, and expanding the patent owner's rights of appeal if the generic drug maker succeeds.[106]

Competition Law The *Competition Act*[107] provides a further form of protection of the public interest. It prohibits the exploitation of a patent in such a way as to unduly restrain trade or prevent or lessen competition, and authorizes the Federal Court to grant appropriate relief.

> ### Ethical Issue Drugs for AIDS
>
> Almost 5 million people are infected with AIDS in Africa; fewer than 100 000 are receiving treatment. The key reason is cost. The patented drugs necessary to treat AIDS cost between $8000 and $15 000 per person, per year. Generic drugs could reduce that cost to a few hundred dollars.
>
> The World Health Organization has urged that countries be allowed to produce generic drugs to counter the AIDS epidemic, and the World Trade Organization has now agreed to allow its members to do so in times of health crises.
>
> Canada's Access to Medicines Regime (CAMR), enacted in May 2004, is an example of compulsory licensing. It amends the *Patent Act* (s. 21.1) and the *Food and Drugs Act* to approve the production of generic drugs in Canada for export to countries that could not otherwise afford drugs to fight AIDS, malaria, tuberculosis, and other diseases. In September 2007, the first authorization was granted to a generic drug company to produce a patented HIV/AIDS drug for export to Rwanda. Critics complain that the system is too complicated, and few drugs have actually been sent.[108]
>
> **Questions to Consider**
>
> 1. Should Canadians also be entitled to benefit from cheaper drugs?
> 2. Should there be any restrictions on the production of generic drugs for fighting potentially fatal illnesses and diseases?

---

[104] *Low v Pfizer Canada Inc*, 2015 BCCA 506.

[105] See e.g. *Eli Lilly and Co v Novopharm Ltd* (1998), 161 DLR (4th) 1; *Merck Frosst Canada Inc v Canada* (1998), 161 DLR (4th) 47; *Sanofi-Aventis Canada Inc v Hospira Healthcare Corp*, [2009] FCJ No 1380.

[106] *Canada–European Union Comprehensive Economic and Trade Agreement Implementation Act*, SC 2017, c 6.

[107] RSC 1985, c C-34. See more in Chapter 30. The assignment of a patent could unduly lessen competition: see *Apotex Inc v Eli Lilly and Co* (2005), 260 DLR (4th) 202 (FCA).

[108] George Tsai, "Canada's Access to Medicines Regime: Lessons for Compulsory Licensing Schemes Under the WTO Doha Declaration" (2009) 49(2) Virginia J. of Int'l L. 1064; Bill C-393, 3rd Sess., 40th Parl., 2011 passed second reading but died when Parliament dissolved in May 2011; Bill C-398, 1st, Sess., 41st Parl., 2012, defeated at second reading on Nov. 28, 2012 (by seven votes); Paul Webster, "TRIPS drug amendment a start," CMAJ February 21, 2017 189 (7) E289; DOI: https://doi.org/10.1503/cmaj.109539.

INDUSTRIAL DESIGNS

Industrial designs comprise the fourth type of intellectual property registrable under the *Industrial Design Act*.[109] Originally enacted in 1868, the Act has been amended on a number of occasions. Extensive amendments enacted in 2014 to bring the Act into conformity with the international system would significantly change what is registrable, but these have not been proclaimed in force at the writing of this chapter.[110]

Meaning of "Industrial Design"

The Act (s. 2) defines "industrial design", Government of Canada as:

> features of shape, configuration, pattern or ornament and any combination of those features that, in a finished article, appeal to and are judged solely by the eye.

Features that are solely utilitarian or functional are not protected, nor is any method or principle of manufacture or construction. The Act applies to designs placed on an article, such as a decorative design on a dinner service, a crest or emblem on a sports shirt, or a design on a roll of wallpaper as well as the shape of the article itself, insofar as the design is ornamental and not dictated by the function of the article. The shape of a stacking chair or a knife handle may be registered. In order to secure registration, some degree of originality is required.

Protection by Registration

The Act permits the proprietor of an industrial design to register it and obtain exclusive rights to its use in Canada for a term of 10 years (s. 10). At common law, there is no property in an industrial design, except insofar as it may qualify for protection as a trademark. Protection is consequently dependent upon registration. A proprietor may apply to register a design with the Commissioner of Patents. Application must be made within one year of the first publication of the design (s. 6(3)). "Publication" in this sense means making the design available to the public—for example, by selling an article to which the design has been applied.

The only person entitled to apply for registration is the "proprietor," who is usually the designer, but if a client or customer commissioned and paid for the design, that person is considered to be the proprietor. If the design was produced by an employee in the normal course of employment, the employer will normally be the proprietor.

Registration gives the proprietor the exclusive right to apply the design to any article for the purpose of sale. However, in order to protect the design, each article to which the design is applied must be marked with the name of the proprietor, the word "Registered" or its abbreviation, "Rd," and the year of registration. A proprietor may assign or grant a licence for the use of a registered design, but the assignment or licence must be recorded on the register in order to preserve the exclusive right.

Remedies During the existence of the exclusive right, a registrant may bring an action for infringement against anyone who applies the design, or any imitation of it, to any article for the purpose of sale without their written consent. The action must be commenced within three years of discovering the infringement. The remedies include damages, injunction, and account for profits; however, to obtain anything other than an injunction, the registrant must prove that the infringer was aware or should have been aware of the registration. A number of summary offences, punishable by fine, also exist for deliberate infringement of industrial design rights.

---

[109] RSC 1985, c I-9. (Unless otherwise stated, references in this part are to this Act, as amended.)
[110] SC 2014, c 39; SC 2015, c 36.

Reform The pending amendments would change the criteria for registration to include novelty and public morality. The length the term of protection would change to 15 years from the application date if that was longer than 10 years after registration, and there would be an application process to access international registrations.

Overlap

It can be difficult to decide whether a design qualifies for patent protection or should be registered as an industrial design. Industrial designs are essentially ornamental, expressly excluding utilitarian function, whereas a patentable invention must be useful.

The same design or logo applied to an article as an industrial design may also be considered a trademark. Similarly, the ornamental shape of a container or wrapper may be registered as an industrial design as well as protected under trademark law as a "distinguishing guise." Protection as a trademark is clearly superior, since property rights in a trademark are not dependent upon registration and are not limited to a maximum period of 10 years. The two forms of protection are not mutually exclusive. A proprietor may register an industrial design and still claim protection for the design as a trademark.

The situation with respect to copyright is more complex. The *Copyright Act* does not protect designs that are used or intended to be used as models or patterns to be multiplied by an industrial process. If a design is applied to a useful article, and the article is reproduced in a quantity of more than 50, another person does not infringe copyright in the design simply by reproducing the article (s. 64). Therefore protection for the design can only be secured by registering it under the *Industrial Design Act*.[111]

CONFIDENTIAL INFORMATION, TRADE SECRETS, AND KNOW-HOW

Mere ideas or knowledge, however valuable, are not regarded as intellectual property in the strict sense of the term. The Supreme Court of Canada has ruled that confidential information is not property that can be the subject of theft under the *Criminal Code*.[112]

Confidential information still has commercial value. A secret manufacturing process—if it can be kept secret—may be more valuable not patented than patented. And a uniquely efficient way of operating a business, though not capable of being patented at all, may be worth millions in extra profits to its owner. Similarly, a list of customers or clients may constitute an important part of the goodwill of a business. Information can also be valuable to people other than its owner. Although not property in the strict sense, information can still be sold to others as, for example, where data are made available to subscribers to a computerized data retrieval service.

The holder of confidential information, trade secrets, or know-how is not entirely without legal protection, though such protection normally arises out of a contractual or fiduciary relationship. A seller may supply machinery or equipment to a buyer and at the same time license the buyer to use the seller's know-how or some secret process. It is usual to stipulate in the contract that the licensee will not divulge the secret to anyone else.[113] Similarly, as discussed in Chapter 18, some employment contracts

---

[111] *Copyright Act*, s 64(4). See *Bayliner Marine Corp v Doral Boats Ltd* (1986), 10 CPR (3d) 289.

[112] *R v Stewart*, [1988] 1 SCR 963; *R v Benson*, [2009] OJ No 239.

[113] In *Cadbury Schweppes Inc v FBI Foods Ltd* (1999), 167 DLR (4th) 577, the Supreme Court of Canada held that a manufacturer under licence who produced a competing product after the termination of the licence, using confidential information, was liable in damages for the loss suffered by the licensor.

include a restrictive covenant restraining the employee, if she leaves the employment, from making use of the employer's confidential information or divulging it to someone else. The employer may claim breach of contract and seek an injunction to prevent the employee from joining a competitor. As well, the employer may sue the competitor for the tort of inducing breach of contract. In other circumstances, a claim for breach of confidence arises if

- confidential information is communicated to someone in confidence, and
- the information is subsequently misused by the person to whom it was communicated.[114]

As will be discussed in Chapter 26, officers, company directors, and partners stand in a fiduciary relationship to their employers, corporations, or co-partners. To misuse or divulge confidential information acquired in the course of such a relationship may constitute a breach of fiduciary duty, which can be restrained by injunction or punished by an award of damages or an accounting for profits made as a result of the breach.[115] Distributing client information may breach privacy laws.

CASE 20.20 New Employer

A former employee of Apotex took up a new position with a competing firm, Novopharm. He brought with him confidential information about a process for making the drug Lovastatin. Apotex brought an action for an injunction restraining Novopharm from carrying out further research on the drug and for damages against the employee and against Novopharm.

The court held both the employee and the new employer liable. Novopharm knew, or ought to have known, that the information was confidential and had been obtained from Apotex. It was consequently liable for the breach of trust of its new employee.[116]

TECHNOLOGICAL CHANGE AND INTELLECTUAL PROPERTY LAW

The Harvard mouse case illustrates the legitimacy and possible limitations of genetic engineering, especially of human life forms. A related issue concerns the genetic modification of foods: Are genetically modified foods a great benefit to humankind that should be protected by patent law, or are they a potential cause of uncontrollable catastrophe? This debate was given a new focus in the recent case of the Saskatchewan farmer accused of infringing a patent for genetically modified canola.[117]

Two statutes were enacted to protect the rights of plant breeders and the designers of integrated circuits. The *Plant Breeders' Rights Act*[118] provides exclusive rights, similar to patent rights in respect of new varieties of plants, including genetically modified plants. To qualify, a plant variety must be clearly distinguishable from all other commonly known varieties of the species, be both stable and homogeneous, and be of a variety not yet sold in Canada. Application is made to a Commissioner of Plant

---

[114] See *Free Trade Medical Network Inc v RBC Travel Insurance Co* (2006), 215 OAC 230; *Lysko v Braley* (2006), 79 OR (3d) 721; *Sabre Inc v International Air Transport Assn*, [2011] OJ No 95, aff'd 2011 ONCA 747.

[115] See *LAC Minerals Ltd v International Corona Resources Ltd* (1989), 61 DLR (4th) 14. Misuse of confidential information by corporate directors or officers is discussed further in Chapter 26.

[116] *Apotex Fermentation Inc v Novopharm Ltd* (1998), 162 DLR (4th) 111.

[117] *Schmeiser v Monsanto Canada Inc* (2004), 239 DLR (4th) 271. The farmer had claimed that the genetically modified seed had blown onto his land. The Supreme Court of Canada upheld the grant of a patent for the seed but held that the farmer had obtained no benefit from its use and was not liable to compensate the patent owner.

[118] SC 1990, c 20.

Breeders' Rights, who may require or conduct such tests as are necessary to establish the novelty of the variety. A grant is for a term of 18 years, subject to payment of an annual fee, and confers the exclusive right to sell, produce, and use the variety.

The *Integrated Circuit Topography Act*[119] also provides exclusive rights similar to patent rights in the "topography" or design of integrated circuits (semiconductor chips) and in the circuits that incorporate such designs themselves. Registration is required, and protection is for a period of 10 years.

New technologies will continue to drive legislative reform.

Strategies to Manage the Legal Risks

Every business needs an all-encompassing IP strategy. Determining whether a concept, activity, or system is protected as a trademark, copyright, patent, or industrial design can be difficult. Sometimes a concept is entitled to protection in multiple categories. A copyrighted drawing may also be a trademark for a product (Mickey Mouse, for example). All available forms of protection should be sought.

A trademark is relatively easy to register and may be renewed indefinitely, so registration should be completed before a business invests heavily in naming a company or promoting a brand. Searches of trademark databases should be undertaken, as well as of corporate and business name registries. When licensing others, use should be confined to specific duration, activities, products, and geographic locations. To preserve the exclusivity of the mark, the business should defend or oppose all applications that might be even slightly similar.

Copyright protection arises automatically and does not require notice of copyright; still, notice of ownership through the universal symbol "©" is recommended. This may have a deterrent effect on would-be thieves. Computer technology producers should consider the use of DRMT to discourage the casual copier and also recognize that, although computer programs may be the subject of copyright, business methods or inventions involving computer programs are patentable.

Managing protection decisions is more difficult when dealing with patents. A business cannot delay funding for projects involving inventions—that is, patent or industrial design—until after protection is in place, as such projects require prior research and development. Patent applications are complicated and can take a long time. Products with a short window of marketability may not be worth the process. As well, the monopoly lasts only 20 years, so if the formula is complicated, longer protection may be available if the product is just kept secret.

Everyone involved in the business's IP or with the development of a new concept should be subject to a confidentiality agreement and an agreement establishing ownership of the property in the business. Employees must honour the confidentiality obligations owed to past employers. A breach of confidence cause of action is not confined to contractual relationships but may arise from fiduciary relations or any communication of confidential information. Businesses may be liable for any infringing behaviour carried on by their employees. An IP code of conduct should be developed to protect the integrity of the business's IP and to limit liability for the infringing behaviour of others. The code should set standards for use and misuse, and control use of technology by prohibiting downloading, uploading, sharing, and format shifting, except in accordance with defined rules.

Finally, IP risks must be assessed when international business strategies are formed. Although some international coordination has been undertaken, this is largely

---

[119] SC 1990, c 37.

in the areas of application, processing, and recognition. Other laws may still vary. In many countries, IP rights are routinely violated with little consequence. Ukraine and China are identified by the Office of the United States Trade Representative as presenting the greatest IP risk.[120] The specific grounds for this designation include the unfair, non-transparent system for collecting and distributing royalties to rights holders; the widespread (and admitted) use of illegal software; and failure to combat the widespread online infringement of copyright. China is a major source of counterfeit goods, violating trademarks, patents, copyrights, and industrial rights in the process. Most troubling is China's limited legal structure, enforcement, and political desire to stop this abuse. A business entering the Ukrainian or Chinese markets can take little comfort in Canadian IP protection. A good source of information on the IP habits of countries around the world is the Office of the United States Trade Representative. As noted, Canada is also on the USTR Watch List.

QUESTIONS FOR REVIEW

1. What types of intellectual property are protected by law?
2. What are the principal costs and benefits of protecting intellectual property?
3. What is a "trademark"?
4. What are the essential elements of the tort of passing off?
5. Are there any advantages to be gained in registering a trademark?
6. What is a "certification mark"?
7. On what grounds may the registration of a trademark be opposed?
8. What are the principal rights possessed by an owner of copyright?
9. In relation to copyright, what are "moral rights"?
10. Does copyright exist in computer software?
11. For how long does copyright usually last?
12. In what ways may a person become an owner of copyright?
13. What constitutes "fair dealing" in relation to copyright?
14. What qualities must an invention have in order to be patented?
15. Why might an inventor choose not to register a patent?
16. What is meant by an "industrial design"?
17. In what circumstances should a business owner require a confidentiality agreement?

CASES AND PROBLEMS

1. Continuing Scenario

   Ashley hired Jordan, a co-op culinary student from her alma mater, George Brown College, to work as a sous chef in her restaurant for the summer. Although Jordan's passion was food, he also had superior computer skills and, after examining the restaurant's website, volunteered to make some improvements. He made two visual and style changes—(1) he standardized the website colours to match the decor of the restaurant (white, blue, and yellow), and (2) he stylized the initials in the name into a visual symbol and repeated the use of this symbol throughout the website wherever the name formerly appeared. Ashley liked this symbol so much that she changed the front of the menu to include it, she had it etched into the glass on

---

[120] Office of the United States Trade Representative, 2017 Special 301 Report, *supra* note 55.

the restaurant windows, and she planned to put it on the sign outside when the current one was replaced. On the technical side, Jordan designed an online reservation system where customers could not only view and book available time slots but also designate the table they wanted from a colour-coded map of the restaurant. The map shaded tables that were already booked and colour-coded tables based on three levels of noise (secluded, active, high activity). Again, Ashley was thrilled; no other restaurant that she knew of had such a user-friendly process.

Jordan was a wonderful employee, but Ashley did not promise to hire him upon his graduation. Jordan was disappointed, but he easily obtained a job at Kate's Kitchen, another restaurant in Toronto. Soon after starting at Kate's, Jordan redesigned that restaurant's website using the same colour scheme as Ashley's, the same stylized font for the symbol (although the letters in the name were different), and—most upsetting to Ashley—the same reservation booking process complete with colour-coded table map.

Can Ashley do anything about this? Are there intellectual property rights in any of the website components, and if so, who owns them? What preventative steps should Ashley have taken?

2. In 1955, a successful novel entitled *Lolita*, authored by Vladimir Nabokov, was published. The novel recounts the story of a middle-aged man, Humbert Humbert, who becomes infatuated with his 12-year-old stepdaughter, Lolita, eventually descending to rape, murder, and madness.

In 1995, the Italian author Pia Pera wrote a book entitled *Lo's Diary*, which was subsequently translated into English. The book purports to tell the story of the affair as experienced by Lolita herself. The principal events of the earlier parts of the story are the same as described in the Nabokov book, though described from the very different perspective of the young girl. (Ms. Pera's book goes on to describe events that occurred after the two parted.)

The late Mr. Nabokov's son and executor threatened action for infringement of copyright. Should the action succeed? Why or why not?

3. A small Canadian corporation, Lexus Foods Inc., applied to register the name Lexus as a trademark for its range of canned fruit products.

The application was opposed by the Japanese manufacturer of the well-known Lexus model of automobiles. It argued that the application by the Canadian corporation should not be granted because of the risk of confusion with its existing marks. Further, it claimed that the applicants were simply trying to cash in on its famous name.

Is the objection a valid one? Why or why not?

4. Shamrock Homes Inc. is a major construction company that specializes in the construction of large residential developments. Brendan, its chief engineer, has worked out an entirely new method of planning a development, requiring the construction of a factory in which prefabricated components for houses are manufactured and assembled to speed up the construction of houses. The factory is specially designed to be converted into a shopping mall when all the houses are completed. Shamrock estimates that the new method reduces construction costs by as much as 15 percent.

Shamrock wishes to patent this new method, fearing that competitors will easily be able to copy it otherwise. Give your opinion as to whether the method is patentable.

5. Dolphin Marine Ltd. is a well-established firm with an excellent reputation for building racing sailboats. It has recently produced a new 12-metre model, the DM35X, with a fibreglass hull of novel design, which has been highly successful in a number of important races.

Kopikat Inc. is a small firm that has been building sailboats for a number of years with little success, either sporting or financial. Kenny, the controlling shareholder and president of Kopikat, buys one of the new Dolphin models, constructs a mould of the hull, and commences to produce a racer with a hull identical to the DM35X and with other features that are very similar. Kopikat is planning to market it at a price $8000 lower than the DM35X.

Has Kopikat infringed any right of Dolphin? Why or why not?

6. Richards, a freelance writer, wrote a long article on the devastating effects of a tsunami in Asia and submitted it to the *Global Post*, a leading newspaper that had published other articles by her. The newspaper agreed to publish her article in its December 2015 print edition.

In early 2016, the *Global Post* published a number of extracts from what it described as "the best GP articles of 2015" on its website. Included was Richards's tsunami article. Richards complains that (1) she had never agreed to the publication on the internet, and (2) in editing the article for the website, the newspaper had omitted important details so that the edited version did not properly represent the original work.

Does Richards have an action against the newspaper? Why or why not?

Chapter 21
Interests in Land and Their Transfer

- THE NATURE OF INTERESTS IN LAND
- ESTATES IN TIME
- INTERESTS LESS THAN ESTATES
- GOVERNMENT REGULATION OF LAND
- TRANSFERRING INTERESTS IN LAND
- REGISTRATION OF INTERESTS IN LAND
- STRATEGIES TO MANAGE THE LEGAL RISKS

Since land is the most long-lasting business asset and the "ultimate platform of human activity," the ownership of land is a primary concern both in private life and in carrying on business.

In this chapter we examine such questions as:

- What is land or real property?
- How is land owned?
- What is Aboriginal title?
- What are the various levels of ownership in land?
- How is ownership shared?
- What are the legal characteristics of "estates" and "interests less than estates"?
- How is condominium ownership structured?
- How are interests in land transferred and protected?

THE NATURE OF INTERESTS IN LAND

The Definition of Land

When we think of land, we usually think of its surface. In law, **land** includes not only the surface but also all that is under the surface, including the natural resources such as minerals or oil, and much of what is above and attached to the surface, including the buildings or trees. A landowner's entitlement to the air above the surface is restricted. Various statutes, international treaties concerning air travel, and municipal bylaws limiting the use of land reduce ownership of the air.[1] Aircraft may fly over land at a safe altitude, and buildings must not exceed a certain height.

The legal concept of land includes all things permanently attached to it—trees, buildings, and fences—known as **fixtures**. When A transfers her house and lot to B, the document describes the land only, according to its location and dimensions, but everything attached to the land goes with it. Lawyers do not draw a distinction between land and buildings as do businesses and accountants. For business purposes, the depreciation of buildings is reported, not of land; in law, the two are considered one when determining or transferring ownership.

Real Property or Real Estate

The Meaning of "Property"
Land is often referred to as real property or real estate, two terms that need some explanation. The term **property** means "everything which is the subject of ownership . . . everything that has exchangeable value or which goes to make up wealth."[2] By this definition, "property" refers to the thing itself, whether it is a piece of land or a piece of cheese or share certificates or the tangible things documents represent.[3] The person or entity that holds the ownership to the property is said to have **title** to the property: "ownership of a thing," or "title to a thing."

The Meaning of "Real"
The word "real" originated from an ancient remedy. Certain interests in land gave the owner the right to repossess it—this was referred to as a **real action**—rather than a personal action, an action for money damages without a right to recover the interest. Eventually the term "real" property came to refer to interests in land generally.

The Meaning of "Estate"
Land is permanent, except on the rare occasions when a piece of it slides into the sea. Its value may drop but it exists forever. Each owner of land is a temporary owner because eventually the land will pass to another owner. As a result, the law defines ownership of land based on the length of time that the owner is entitled to exclusive possession of the land and calls such ownership **estates in time**. Any interest in land that gives someone exclusive possession for some period of time is known as an estate.

Crown Grant

In 1763, the British government assumed the sole authority to acquire land from Indigenous nations through **treaties**. British subjects could acquire title to land from

---

land comprises the surface, all that is under the surface, including the minerals and oil, and most everything above and attached to the surface, including buildings and trees

fixtures all things permanently attached to land are deemed part of the land

property (1) everything that is the subject of ownership or (2) the legal interest in a thing

title holding ownership of a thing

real action an action to repossess an interest in land that had been interfered with

estates in time the right to exclusive possession of the land for a period of time

treaties sacred agreements between the Crown and Indigenous peoples with a solemn, special, public nature that rank above personal contracts but below international treaties

---

[1] See e.g. *Aeronautics Act*, RSC 1985, c A-2, s 5.4. The *Hydro and Electric Energy Act*, RSA 2000, c H-16, permits trespass by power lines without compensation.
[2] *Black's Law Dictionary*, 6th ed (St. Paul: West Publishing, 1990) at 1216.
[3] The lesser-known meaning of "property" is not the thing itself but the legal interest in the thing; *ibid*.

the Crown, not directly from Indigenous people.[4] The first transfer of title from the government to a private owner is known as the **Crown grant**. It conveys an estate in time to the new owner. Sometimes Crown grants impose restrictions on use or exclude some rights such as mineral rights or timber rights, and then ownership of these rights remain with the government.[5] The new owner could transfer his estate to a subsequent owner, but he could not create a greater interest than was received in the Crown grant.[6]

Crown grant the first transfer of an estate in time from the government to a new owner

During an owner's exclusive possession of the land, he may reduce the estate for those that come later. For instance, if the owner of land grants the city the right to put water mains across the land, that right prevents a subsequent owner from removing the pipes to build a building. Each subsequent holder of an estate in time owns the land minus any rights previously granted away. Rights dealing with the use of the land and not exclusive possession to it are referred to as **interests less than estates**. Land use is regulated by all levels of government, as discussed below.

interests less than estates interests in land that do not give the right to exclusive possession

A challenge to the Crown grant could undermine the title to all those receiving grants after or through it.[7]

Treaties and the *Indian Act* specifically "reserved" some land for exclusive use and occupation by identified Indian bands. This was the government's early version of shared ownership with First Nations and placed the government in a fiduciary role.[8] Over the years since enactment of the *Indian Act*, a more comprehensive view of Aboriginal title has slowly evolved with roots before 1763 and is not confined to reserve lands.

Aboriginal Title and Rights

Aboriginal land claims are the most common challenges to Crown authority or grants. First Nations, Indians, Métis, and Inuit peoples are collectively referred to as Aboriginal or Indigenous peoples or nations.[9] Aboriginal title and rights are not derived from the Canadian legal system or from colonial law; they are *sui generis*—a unique collective right stemming from Indigenous peoples' prior occupation and connection with the land.[10] The Canadian Constitution recognizes existing rights and treaties of Aboriginals and imposes a duty on provincial and federal governments to notify, consult, and accommodate Aboriginal interests when dealing with lands in which Aboriginal title or rights are claimed.[11]

sui generis a unique collective right stemming from Indigenous peoples' prior occupation and connection with the land

Aboriginal land claims take multiple forms and have multiple forums for resolution. **Specific land claims** allege that the Crown violated a treaty or improperly dealt with reserve land; this type of claim may be advanced through the courts or through the Specific Land Claims Tribunal.[12] The Aboriginal nation pursuing the claim elects

specific land claims claims involving treaty or reserve lands

---

[4] *Royal Proclamation, 1763*, RSC 1985, App II, No 1; Marcia Nickerson, "Characteristics of a Nation-to-Nation Relationship," Discussion Paper, February 2017 at 13. *Royal Proclamation* reserved "Hunting Grounds" for First Nations.

[5] *Wardle v Manitoba Farm Loan Association*, [1956] SCR 3.

[6] *Herbison v Canada (Attorney General)*, 2013 BCSC 2020 at para 26.

[7] But see *Chippewas of Sarnia Band v Canada* (2000) 51 OR (3d) 641.

[8] *Indian Act*, RSC 1985, c I-5 (consolidated in 1876); *Infra* note 22. There were over 500 treaties made between 1763 and 1930; Canada claimed "territorial sovereignty" over land not covered by treaties.

[9] Defining Indigenous peoples or nations is more complicated than this description portrays. Other relevant terms include First Peoples, First Nations, and Assembly of First Nations. There are 633 *Indian Act* bands spread across 2700 reserves; approximately 50 percent of First Nation peoples do not live on reserves.

[10] *Calder v Attorney General of British Columbia*, [1973] SCR 313; *Roberts v Canada* (1989), 57 DLR 4th 197; *R v Badger*, [1996] 1 SCR 771 at para 76.

[11] See *Constitution Act, 1982*, Schedule B to the *Canada Act 1982* (UK), 1982, c 11 ss 25, 35, 91(24) (existing rights as at April 17, 1982; federal government has jurisdiction over Indigenous peoples); see *Tsilhqot'in Nation v British Columbia*, 2014 SCC 44.

[12] *Specific Claims Tribunal Act*, SC 2008, c 22.

between the courts or the Tribunal. Treaty rights depend on context and the interpretation of the particular wording; ambiguity is resolved in favour of the Aboriginal party.[13] Use of Aboriginal oral histories to interpret treaty terms has been inconsistent.

Comprehensive land claims deal with lands that are not subject to a treaty but in which an Aboriginal interest, right, or title is claimed.[14] Courts are the forum for comprehensive claims.

comprehensive land claims claims involving land not covered by treaty nor part of a reserve

Aboriginal Title

Title is the strongest type of Aboriginal interest in land and is similar but not identical to the fee simple form of title discussed below. It gives the Aboriginal nation collective territorial control in the form of exclusive use and occupation, including proactive management of the land for modern uses and economic purposes.[15] This includes the right to benefit from the development of the land and its resources. Still, there are important limitations. The ownership is communal or collective for the benefit of present and future Indigenous generations, and the land cannot be put to uses that would destroy its traditional value. Title is inalienable (unsellable) except to the Crown, and it is subject to possible infringement by the Crown when justified for the public interest. Aboriginal title may exist in occupied land where the Aboriginal nation can establish that its use was sufficiently regular, continuous, and exclusive.[16] It does not depend on previous recognition by treaty or reserve.

CASE 21.1 Territorial Approach to Aboriginal Title

The Tisilhqot'in Nation, a semi-nomadic people made up of six Indian bands, occupied land in the interior of British Columbia; the land was not covered by a treaty or a reserve and included the Nemiah Valley. The Province wanted to allow timber harvesting in the Nemiah Valley. When negotiations with Tisilhqot'in Nation failed to produce an agreement, British Columbia issued the timber licences anyway. The Tisilhqot'in Nation responded with a blockade and a court action seeking invalidation of the timber licences and a declaration that the Nation had title to the lands. The legal battle lasted decades.

In 2014, the Supreme Court of Canada unanimously held that the Tisilhqot'in Nation's occupation established Aboriginal title in the land. Aboriginal title is not confined to specific settlements but extends to lands that were regularly used for hunting, fishing, or other resource-based activities and over which the group had effective control at the time of assertion of European sovereignty. The Court defined Aboriginal title as the exclusive right to decide how the land is used and the right to benefit from those uses, subject to the restriction that the uses must be consistent with the group nature of the interest and enjoyment of the land by future generations.[17] This was the first case to recognize Aboriginal title in non-reserve lands, to include the right to financially benefit, and to define occupation based on territorial, not site-specific, usage.

Aboriginal Rights

A right is a lesser form of interest recognizing a non-exclusive Aboriginal practice, custom, or tradition. A right entitles the Aboriginal nation to continue the use or tradition on a non-exclusive basis; it does not depend on the existence of Aboriginal title over the affected land.[18] Rights are recognized when the practice, custom, or tradition was integral to the culture of the Aboriginal community prior to contact with European societies; it requires an inquiry into the community's precontact way of life.[19] A right may coexist with the Crown's other uses or activities that are in the public interest.

---

[13] *R v Marshall*, [1999] 3 SCR 456 at para 51 (to avoid any appearance of sharp dealing by the Crown).

[14] Indigenous and Northern Affairs Canada—Land Claims, https://www.aadnc-aandc.gc.ca/eng/1100100030285/1100100030289.

[15] *Tsilhqot'in Nation v British Columbia*, supra note 11 at para 73.

[16] Ibid.; *Delgamuukw et al v The Queen* (1997) 153 DLR (4th) 193.

[17] *Tsilhqot'in*, ibid at paras 50, 73.

[18] *R v Côté*, [1996] 3 SCR 139 at para 38; *Delgamuukw et al v The Queen*, supra note 16 (Aboriginal title and rights rest with nations, not bands).

[19] *R v Van der Peet*, [1996] 2 SCR 507 at paras 46–60; *R v Sappier/R v Gray*, 2006 SCC 54.

> ### CASE 21.2 Rights Independent of Aboriginal Title
>
> An accused was convicted of fishing without a licence on a Quebec lake, contrary to Quebec's regulation.[20] The Supreme Court of Canada set aside the conviction because the accused was exercising his Aboriginal right to fish. Rights do not depend on the existence of Aboriginal title; they can exist when occupation is not sufficient to establish Aboriginal title. In this case there was an established Aboriginal right to fish on the lake that was unduly infringed by the requirement of obtaining a licence. The licence requirement interfered with the preferred means of exercising the fishing right.

Infringement of Aboriginal Title or Rights Governments may infringe on Aboriginal title or rights, even treaty rights, but only in "justifiable" circumstances. Aboriginal land disputes involve conflicting Aboriginal and public interests. Court actions result when agreement cannot be reached between the government and the objecting Aboriginal party.

A court will determine whether there is infringement on the Aboriginal right by the proposed activity or legislation. The onus of proving a *prima facie* infringement lies on the Aboriginal individual or group. Relevant factors include reasonableness, hardship, and preferred means of exercising a right.[21] If the court finds there is a right and it is infringed, the second step is to determine if the infringement is "justified." Justification requires the Crown to prove it had a valid legislative objective, and the plan is consistent with the Crown's fiduciary relationship with Aboriginal people.[22] The fiduciary responsibility requires that the Aboriginal interest be given priority.[23] Examples of Aboriginal rights that are given priority over non-Aboriginal rights are hunting, fishing, and harvesting for food. Commercial-scale harvesting requires existence of trade before European contact.[24]

Duty to Consult and Accommodate When proposed new uses or changes in use, such as cutting down trees or mining, could negatively impact Aboriginal interests, the government must consult with affected groups and make a genuine good faith effort to accommodate their interests. The purpose of the consultation duty is to promote the reconciliation of the pre-existing Aboriginal nations with the Crown. The consultation process will be scrutinized to ensure it advances the reconciliation objective.[25]

The duty to consult, sometimes described as honourable negotiation, exists even if the Aboriginal right or title has not been proven and is disputed; since it takes so long to prove such rights, it would be dishonourable of the Crown to restrict consultation to only proven rights.[26]

The extent of the duty to consult and accommodate varies on a case-by-case basis depending on the strength or weakness of the land claims; still, it does not give an Aboriginal objector veto power, nor does it require the Crown to reach an agreed solution.[27] Many lawsuits are the result of failed consultation processes, giving the Courts the ultimate power to decide if rights or title exist, if appropriate consultation was undertaken and if accommodation is necessary or possible. Sometimes the

---

[20] *R v Adams*, [1996] 3 SCR 101.

[21] *R v Côté*, *supra* note 18 at para 38.

[22] *R v Sparrow*, [1990] 1 SCR 1075; *Manitoba Metis Federation Inc v Canada (Attorney General)*, 2013 SCC 14 (honourable conduct and fiduciary duty); *Guerin v The Queen*, [1984] 2 SCR 335.

[23] *Delgamuukw et al v The Queen*, *supra* note 16; *R v Gladstone*, [1997] 2 SCR 723.

[24] *Marshall*, *supra* note 13.

[25] *Haida Nation v British Columbia*, 2004 SCC 3; *R v Van der Peet*, *supra* note 19 at paras 30–31. See also *Final Report of the Truth and Reconciliation Commission of Canada* (2015) http://www.trc.ca/websites/trcinstitution/index.php?p=890.

[26] *Haida, ibid*. See also *Manitoba Metis Federation Inc v Canada (Attorney General)*, *supra* note 22; *Badger*, *supra* note 10 at para 76 (the honour of the Crown is at stake when dealing with Aboriginal peoples).

[27] *Haida, ibid*.

business proposing the infringement (the proponent) undertakes negotiations directly with the Aboriginal group. This alone does not fulfill the Crown's duty.

> ### CASE 21.3 Administrative Tribunals
>
> Enbridge wanted to change the flow of an existing heavy crude pipeline in order to increase its capacity. The National Energy Board (NEB) held formal public hearing that gave an impacted Aboriginal group (Chippewas of the Thames) the opportunity to participate. The NEB ultimately approved the application with conditions that purported to address the Chippewas' concerns. The Supreme Court of Canada reviewed the NEB's process and found it was the proper administrative body with statutory power to consult, and it was clear to the Chippewas that the Crown was relying on the administrative tribunal to fulfill its duty. Reasons for the NEB decision included an explanation of how the Indigenous concerns were considered and addressed. The Crown's duty to consult was met.[28]
>
> However, in another case involving Petroleum Geo-Services's application to conduct seismic testing for oil and gas in Baffin Bay and Davis Strait, the Supreme Court found that the Crown's duty to consult was not met. The Inuit Clyde River group objected because the migration of marine mammals could be affected. The NEB approved the application without holding formal hearings, relying on written materials summarizing meetings between Petroleum Geo and the Inuit group. This did not discharge the Crown's duty to consult.[29]

Remedies Aboriginal land claim disputes are often settled by payment of compensation. Breach of treaty terms can result in an order for damages, usually for a maximum of 10 years before the commencement of the lawsuit.[30] Courts can also issue declarations about existence and priority of the right, title, or interest and declare government actions or legislation unconstitutional.

INTERNATIONAL ISSUE

Treatment of Indigenous Peoples' Land Claims

In 2007 the United Nations adopted the Declaration on the Rights of Indigenous peoples (UNDRIP). Among other things, it declares that "States shall provide effective mechanisms and redress for . . . any action which has the aim or effect of dispossessing [Indigenous peoples] of their lands, territories or resources" (article 8). Canada was one of only four countries that voted against UNDRIP's adoption (along with Australia, New Zealand, and the United States. Eleven others abstained. By 2010 Canada gave weak support to UNDRIP, saying "it was an aspirational document that was not legally binding and did not change Canadian law." Finally, in 2017, Canada endorsed UNDRIP and recognized the following principles, among others, to guide its dealings with Indigenous peoples:

- Meaningful engagement with Indigenous peoples aims to secure their free, prior, and informed consent when Canada proposes to take actions that impact them and their rights, including their lands, territories, and resources.
- Respecting and implementing rights is essential, and any infringement of section 35 rights must by law meet a high threshold of justification, which includes Indigenous perspectives and satisfies the Crown's fiduciary obligations.

Questions

1. What impact do you think international standards have on Canada's relationship with Indigenous peoples?
2. Contrast the principles described above with the legal standards for justification and duty to consult described in the forgoing section.

Sources: Department of Justice, "Principles Respecting the Government of Canada's Relationship with Indigenous Peoples," http://www.justice.gc.ca/eng/csj-sjc/principles-principes.html; United Nations Declaration on the Rights of Indigenous Peoples, https://www.un.org/development/desa/indigenouspeoples/declaration-on-the-rights-of-indigenous-peoples.html; CBC News, "Canada Endorses Indigenous Rights Declaration," Nov. 12, 2010, http://www.cbc.ca/news/canada/canada-endorses-indigenous-rights-declaration-1.964779.

---

[28] *Chippewas of the Thames First Nation v Enbridge Pipelines Inc*, 2017 SCC 41. See also *Ktunaxa Nation v British Columbia (Forests, Lands and Natural Resource Operations)*, 2017 SCC 54 (no breach of duty was found).

[29] *Clyde River (Hamlet) v Petroleum Geo-Services Inc*, 2017 SCC 40.

[30] *Canada v Lameman*, 2008 SCC 14 (limitation periods apply).

ESTATES IN TIME

Freehold Estates

The first category of estates in time is freehold estates. A **freehold estate** is indeterminate in time; it cannot be predicted how long the interest of the owner will last.

freehold estate an interest in land that is indeterminate in time

Fee Simple Estate This estate is the longest interest a person can own in land and is as close to complete ownership as the law allows. Everyday reference to land ownership means **fee simple**. The holder of the fee simple holds it for all time present and future. The holder of the fee simple may designate the next owner by selling it, transferring it, or leaving the property to someone in a will. Even if there is no will, the relatives of a deceased fee simple owner are entitled to inherit it. He may grant the whole of the fee simple away; he may grant away a lesser interest, keeping the rest for himself; or he may sever off smaller portions of the whole parcel and convey them to different persons.

fee simple the interest in land closest to complete ownership

---

ILLUSTRATION 21.1 Lesser Estates

(a) A, the holder of the fee simple in a farm, may grant it to his brother B for the rest of B's life. At B's death, it returns to A, or to A's heirs if A dies before B. A retains the fee simple subject to a life estate to B.

(b) A may grant the farm to a brother for life with the rest of the fee simple going to a niece, C, at the brother's death.

Illustration 21.1 provides examples of some ways a fee simple owner may carve out lesser estates. If the owner dies without relatives or a will, then the land is transferred to the government.

Life Estate A **life estate** is the right to exclusively use, possess, and deal with the land for one lifetime—usually for the life of the person who holds the estate, but not necessarily. The length of the life estate may be measured by the life of different person. A may convey his cottage to B for the rest of A's own life—if A dies within a few months, the life estate ends. B retains no interest in the cottage. This is rare. The more usual life estate is for the life of the person to whom the interest is given and often arises under the terms of a will. For example, the owner of a fee simple may, by the terms of her will, give a life estate in the family home to her spouse, who becomes the **life tenant**. She then directs that the rest of the fee simple pass to the children after the death of the spouse.

life estate an estate in land that lasts for the life of one person

life tenant a holder of a life estate

The balance of the fee simple, after a life estate has been carved out, is called either a reversion or a remainder. It is called a **reversion** when the grantor of the life estate reserves the balance of the fee simple for herself and her heirs (that is, it reverts to the grantor or her heirs after the life estate ends). It is called a **remainder** when it goes to some third person. The balance of the estate in example (a) in Illustration 21.1 is a reversion and in example (b) is a remainder. Unfortunately, life estates create many problems.

reversion the balance of a fee simple reserved to the grantor and her heirs at the end of a life estate

remainder the balance of a fee simple that goes to a third person at the end of a life estate

- First, it is difficult to sell land subject to a life estate. Very few people will buy only the remaining years of a life tenant's interest, an uncertain period of time. Only if both the life tenant and the **remainderman** join in the sale and together grant the whole of the fee simple will it likely be possible to sell the land.

remainderman a person who holds the reversion or remainder in a fee simple

- Second, a life tenant is limited in the changes she can make on the land without the consent of the remainderman. She cannot tear down buildings or cut down trees without the permission of the remainderman; she must leave the land to the remainderman substantially as she received it. On the other hand, she is under no duty to make repairs either, depending on the wording of the life estate.[31]

- Third, and again depending upon the wording of the grant, she cannot force the remainderman to contribute anything to the cost of substantial repairs and maintenance needed on the land, though they will ultimately be of benefit to the remainderman in preserving its value.

Life estates are not typically used in business. However, they are used for personal tax planning purposes and family situations. For example, parents may wish to transfer the fee simple in the family cottage to the children but retain a life estate to enjoy until their deaths. Capital gain is the children's, and tax will not be triggered on the death of the parents.

A spouse may wish to create a life estate in the family home for her second spouse and leave the fee simple to the children of her first marriage. This will allow the current spouse to continue to live in the home for life without disinheriting the children of the first marriage.

Leasehold Estates

leasehold an interest in land for a definite period of time

The other major category of estates is leasehold estates. A **leasehold** estate is an exclusive interest in land for a definite period of time—a week, a year, a hundred years, or any other specific period. This is the big difference between a freehold and a leasehold estate. A freehold estate is either for an infinite time (the fee simple) or an indefinite time (the life estate), but the leasehold is for a definite time. In a leasehold estate, the person to whom the interest is granted is called the lessee or tenant, and the grantor of the interest is called the lessor or landlord.

Historically, leaseholds have always been considered lesser estates than freeholds, even though leases for 100 years would almost invariably last longer than a freehold life estate. However, a leasehold interest must be created from a freehold estate and cannot last longer than the freehold from which it is created.

ILLUSTRATION 21.2 Limits of Life Estate

In her will, T gives A a life estate in the cottage with the remainder after A's death to X in fee simple. A leases the cottage to B Inc. for 100 years. Several months later, A dies. X, the remainderman, can take possession of the cottage and evict B Inc. X is not bound by the lease because A could not create a leasehold interest in the cottage to last longer than his own life estate.

The result in Illustration 21.2 is an application of the rule that a person cannot grant to another a greater interest than he himself holds.[32]

Leasehold interests share an important characteristic with freehold interests—a lease gives a lessee the right to exclusive possession of the land described in the lease. A lessee has the right to keep all persons off the leased land, including the lessor himself, unless the lessor has reserved the right to enter the property for inspection and repairs. The law concerning leasehold interests combines the strict concepts of real property, the flexible concepts of contract, and the changing policies of government

---

[31] *Estate of Lynn Louise Hawkins*, 2006 BCSC 1374.

[32] In Ontario, a life tenant may lease his estate for a term not exceeding 21 years, and the lease will be valid against the remainderman. If the life tenant dies, the lessee remains in possession and pays the rent to the remainderman for the balance of the lease: *Settled Estates Act*, RSO 1990, c S.7, s 32.

regulation. The legislative rules vary depending upon whether the purpose of the lease is residential or commercial.[33] Both types are discussed in Chapter 22, "Landlord and Tenant."

Sharing Title: Co-Ownership

Tenancy in Common   Two or more persons may share ownership of the same estate in land at the same time. They are concurrent holders of the estate. In the absence of any special agreement between them or of special terms set out in the initial grant, co-owners are deemed to be tenants in common. **Tenants in common** hold equal shares in the estate; each is entitled to the same rights over the property and an equal share of the income. Each interest is an undivided interest. One tenant cannot fence off a portion of the property for her exclusive use—each is entitled to the use of the whole property. However, tenants in common may agree to hold unequal shares, transfer the share of one to another, or divide and fence the property into exclusive lots. In addition, a tenant in common may transfer her interest to any third party without the consent of the others. When a tenant in common dies, her interest goes to her heirs, who continue to hold the interest with the other tenants in common. Business partners usually hold title to real property as tenants in common.

tenants in common   concurrent holders of equal undivided shares in an estate

Joint Tenancy   Another form of co-ownership is joint tenancy. Two or more persons become **joint tenants** only when expressly stated at the time the estate is granted to them or afterward by an express agreement among them. Joint tenancy is different from a tenancy in common because of the **right of survivorship**. Under the right of survivorship, the interest of a deceased joint tenant passes on his death to the surviving tenant instead of to the heirs of the deceased. If A, B, and C own a building in joint tenancy, upon C's death his interest will pass to A and B, who will continue to own the building in joint tenancy between them. C's interest does not go to his heirs.

joint tenants   concurrent holders, each of whom has a right of survivorship

right of survivorship   the right of a surviving tenant to the interest of a deceased joint tenant

Husband and wife often take title to their family home in joint tenancy. On the death of either spouse, the survivor automatically receives full title to the property. Joint tenancy is an advantage to the survivor because the house does not form part of the deceased partner's estate and become entangled in problems of **probate** (administration and settling of the deceased person's estate). Legal fees and probate costs are reduced.

probate   the process of administering and settling the estate of a deceased person

Severance   A joint tenant may end the right of survivorship at any time before his death without the consent of the other joint tenants. By a procedure called **severance**, he may turn his joint tenancy into a tenancy in common. If there are two or more other tenants remaining, they continue as joint tenants with each other, but are tenants in common with the one who has severed his joint tenancy. The most common method of severance is by a joint tenant granting his interest to a third party. The grant automatically turns the interest transferred into a tenancy in common with the remaining interests. A joint tenancy is also severed by giving a mortgage on one's share. However, a joint tenant cannot sever his share by disposing of it in his will. A will "speaks" only at death, and by that moment the deceased's share has already passed to the surviving joint tenant.

severance   a procedure that turns a joint tenancy into a tenancy in common

INTERESTS LESS THAN ESTATES

Easements

In addition to estates in time, there are other interests that permit use or benefit but do not give a right to exclusive possession.

---

[33] See e.g. *Commercial Tenancies Act*, RSO 1990, c L-7; *Residential Tenancies Act*, SO 2006, c 17.

easement a right enjoyed by one landowner over the land of another for a special purpose but not for occupation of the land

right-of-way an easement that gives the holder a right to pass back and forth over the land of another in order to get to and from her own land

An **easement** is a right enjoyed by one landowner over the land of another, for a special purpose rather than for the general use and occupation of land. The most common type of easement is a **right-of-way**. The holder of a right-of-way may crossover the land of another in order to get to and from her own land. She does not have the right to remain on the other's land or bring things on the land and leave them there or to obstruct others from using the land, but she can sue anyone who interferes with her right to pass. Other examples of easements are the right to hang eaves of a building over another's land and to drain water or waste materials from one piece of land over a watercourse on another's land. Adjoining landowners frequently have mutual easements over each other's land, such as a shared driveway or a narrow strip between houses to provide access for maintenance and repairs.[34] Once granted, an easement attaches to the land and binds subsequent owners—they cannot interfere with the exercise of the easement. Similarly, purchasers of the land benefiting from the easement acquire the former owner's easement rights.

dominant tenement the piece of land that benefits from an easement

servient tenement the land subject to the easement

Essential requirements of an easement, at common law, are that there must be a **dominant tenement** (a piece of land that benefits from the easement) and a **servient tenement** (the land subject to the easement) owned by a different person. The dominant tenement must be close to the servient tenement; how close is a subjective determination based on the facts of each situation. The owners of the dominant and servient tenements must each reasonably accommodate their joint use of the easement land.[35] If the right to enjoy another's land benefits a person, not another piece of land, then the right is only a personal right, known as a **licence**.[36]

licence a right to use another's land for the benefit of a person

Statutory Easements The term "easement" is sometimes used to describe certain statutory rights, such as the right granted to a telephone company to run wires and cables either underground or overhead on poles. The telephone company has the right to leave wires where they have been installed and to inspect and repair them when necessary. But often the telephone company owns no land in the area. The nearest land that could be considered a dominant tenement may be many kilometres away. Therefore, strictly speaking, the right is not an easement—it is a right created by statute.[37]

prescription the creation of an easement over adjoining land through exercising a right continuously and openly

Easements by Prescription In some parts of Canada, using another person's land may give an adjoining landowner an easement over his neighbour's land without a written grant. The method is called **prescription**, and an easement is created if a person

- continuously exercises a right for a period of at least 20 years,
- openly,
- without fraud, deceit, force, or threats against the owner of the land, and
- without consent or permission of the owner or payment to the owner.

An easement by prescription is recognized in some parts of Atlantic Canada and in parts of Manitoba and Ontario where land ownership is recorded in a registry

---

[34] See e.g. *Rose v Krieser* (2002), 212 DLR (4th) 123; *Fallowfield v Bourgault* (2003), 235 DLR (4th) 263. Alternatively, it could be a licence—a personal contractual right to use another's land—*394 Lakeshore Oakville Holdings Inc v Misek*, [2010] OJ No 4659 at paras 61, 69–70, aff'd *Mechanical Services Inc v Flesch*, 2011 ONCA 764.

[35] *Birch v Brenner*, 2017 BCCA 22 at para 33.

[36] *Mechanical Services Inc v Flesch*, *supra* note 34 at para 203.

[37] "Conservation Easements" created by the *Alberta Land Stewardship Act*, the *Conservation Land Act* in Ontario, and the *Conservation Easements Act* in Saskatchewan are more like building-scheme or restrictive covenants.

system. Easements by prescription are not recognized in the three western provinces or in parts of Manitoba, Ontario, and Atlantic Canada covered by land titles registration discussed below.[38]

Covenants

An owner of land may wish to restrict or control the use of land after she sells it; especially if she retains abutting property. She may wish to see the property kept in good repair or to prevent the operation of a noisy business that would interfere with neighbours' privacy. She may, of course, require the purchaser to do any or all of these things as part of the consideration for the contract of sale of the land. However, this would not bind any subsequent buyer. The solution is to create an interest in land that is binding upon all subsequent owners.

It is not possible to bind subsequent owners to positive duties (such as the obligation to plant trees). For public policy reasons "[n]o personal or affirmative covenant, requiring the expenditure of money or the doing of some act, can, apart from statute, be made to **run with the land**" even if there is an express agreement to the contrary.[39]

run with the land bind subsequent land owners

Restrictive Covenants

Covenants that require the owner to refrain from doing something will bind subsequent owners if registered on title. These negative covenants are known as "covenants running with the land," or **restrictive covenants**. They are subject to a rule similar to that concerning easements—there must be a piece of land subject to the covenant and another piece that receives the benefit of the covenant. A registered covenant recognized by the courts as running with the land is enforceable by any subsequent holder of the land benefiting from it against any subsequent holder of the land subject to it.

restrictive covenant a covenant requiring the holder of the land to refrain from certain conduct or certain use of the land

The party seeking to enforce it (the covenantee) must own land to be benefited by the covenant, the land must be identified in the document creating the covenant, and the document must be properly registered.[40] Covenants found to be highly unreasonable, against public policy, or not properly registered against the land will not be enforced by the courts against subsequent owners.

Remedies for Breach of a Covenant

If a landowner ignores a restrictive covenant and, for example, builds a fence or clothesline, the court may grant a mandatory injunction requiring the wrongdoer to tear down the prohibited fence or clothesline. If it is too late to repair the damage, as when the wrongdoer has cut down a row of 100-year-old oak trees, the court may award damages in lieu of an injunction.

Building-Scheme Covenants

A restrictive covenant that regulates land use over an entire neighbourhood or shopping centre is referred to as a **building-scheme covenant**; these are widely used by residential housing developers to control the uses and look of the subdivision. Covenants are included in the deed to each builder or homeowner. Typical residential covenants prohibit commercial use, limit building on the land to one-family dwellings, require minimum frontage or square footage per house, specify maximum fence heights, and ban outdoor clotheslines.

building-scheme covenant a restrictive covenant that regulates land use over an entire neighbourhood or shopping centre

---

[38] See e.g. Ontario *Land Titles Act*, RSO 1990, c L.5, s 51(1) (preserves prescriptive easements created before transfer to land titles). See also *Millstone Consulting Services Inc v Cleary*, [2008] OJ No 3106, aff'd [2009] OJ No 4510 (ONCA).

[39] *Amberwood Investments Ltd v Durham Condominium Corp No 123* (2002), 211 DLR (4th) 1; *Heritage Capital Corp v Equitable Trust Co*, 2016 SCC 19 at para 25; *Black v Owen*, 2017 ONCA 397.

[40] *Re Sekretov and City of Toronto* (1973), 33 DLR (3d) 257; *Canada Safeway v Thompson (City)*, [1997] 7 WWR 565. For statutory authority to modify or discharge a restrictive covenant, see e.g. *Conveyancing and Law of Property Act*, RSO 1990, c C-34, s 61(1); *Land Titles Act*, RSO 1990 c L.5 s 119.

If a once-reasonable covenant has become unduly restrictive or obsolete, an affected landowner may apply to the court to have the covenant terminated.[41] The court will require that the owner of the land for whose benefit the covenant was made be served with notice and given an opportunity to defend the covenant.

Covenants are gradually being replaced by municipal regulations in the form of zoning and building bylaws and development agreements (between developer and municipality), especially in newly developed areas. Nevertheless, covenants still play an important role in older parts of our cities and towns; sometimes they unduly restrict the development of an area.

Other Interests

Oil, Gas, and Mineral Leases
The right to extract minerals, oil, and gas (collectively described as mineral rights) from within or under the surface of land occupied by others is obtained through government approval and two separate "leases." One lease grants the right to the mineral, and the other grants permission to cross over the surface of the land during the extraction process.[42] Both leases are registered on the land's title. The owner of the minerals allows removal by the lessee (usually a private oil and gas company) using a lease that embodies both an interest in land and contractual rights to the mineral in exchange for payment of royalties.[43] Mineral rights may be owned by

- the Crown (if they are reserved in the Crown grant or if the land is Crown land, either provincial or federal),
- a First Nation (if the nation has Aboriginal title to the lands)[44], or
- the owner of the fee simple (if there was no reservation in the Crown grant).

Royalties for minerals on reserve lands are paid to the Crown for the benefit of the identified Indian band, and requests for extraction trigger the duty to consult.[45]

The owner of the surface land under which the mineral is located (regardless of whether the same owner owns the sub-surface minerals) grants access using a separate **surface rights lease**, like an easement,[46] which requires its own consideration. Alternatively, the extracting company may obtain a "right of entry" to surface lands or necessary adjacent lands from the applicable government's regulatory agency, such as the Alberta Surface Rights Board. Compensation will be paid to the affected landowners. Provincial or federal regulatory approval is required for the entire extraction project. It is a complicated process involving licencing, development oversight, environmental impact assessment, and restoration obligations.

Pipelines move oil and gas from the extraction sites to the market and involve multiple surface rights leases. In addition to surface rights legislation, pipeline construction, maintenance, and operator licencing are governed by specific regulatory requirements from provincial and federal governments.[47] The National Energy Board may approve pipeline projects, vary operating licences, and authorize work that crosses

surface rights lease grant from owner of land to allow access to minerals

---

[41] See e.g. *Property Law Act*, RSBC 1996, c 377, s 35; *Paterson v Burgess*, 2017 BCCA 298.

[42] *Surface Rights Act*, RSA 2000, c S-24, s12; *Surface Rights Acquisition and Compensation Act*, RSS 1978, c S-65, s 6; *Surface Rights Act*, CCSM c 5235; *Petroleum and Natural Gas Act*, RSBC 1996, c 361, s 9.

[43] An ancient interest in land known as a *profit à prendre* that permitted the lessee to remove material extracted from the ground. See *Bank of Montreal v Dynex Petroleum*, [2002] 1 SCR 146.

[44] *Tsilhqot'in*, supra note 11.

[45] *Indian Oil and Gas Act*, RSC 1985, c 1-7.

[46] For a discussion of the historic relationship between mineral and surface rights, see *Forty Ninth Ventures Ltd v British Columbia*, 2005 BCCA 213.

[47] See e.g. *Canada Oil and Gas Operations Act*, RSC 1985, c O-7, s 5.

provincial boundaries for reasons of public convenience and necessity.[48] Pipelines through or under navigable waters are also under the jurisdiction of the National Energy Board. Sometimes pipelines cross international boundaries with the United States (Alaska), and in such cases a special federal regulatory board called the Northern Pipeline Agency, along with an advisory council with provincial membership, supervises the project in accordance with international agreements.[49]

Licences A licence given to another person by an owner to use his land is personal and not an interest in land at all. If B gives his friend, A, permission to hold a garage sale on his front lawn, A becomes a "licensee" on B's land during the garage sale; she is not a trespasser. However, she has no "right" to remain on B's land, and if he should revoke permission, something he may do at any time, A would have only a reasonable minimum time to remove her goods and herself from B's lawn.

Contractual licences between enterprises create contractual rights binding between the original parties. They do not need to benefit any nearby land.

In summary, Figure 21.1 illustrates the various types of interests in real property we have discussed.

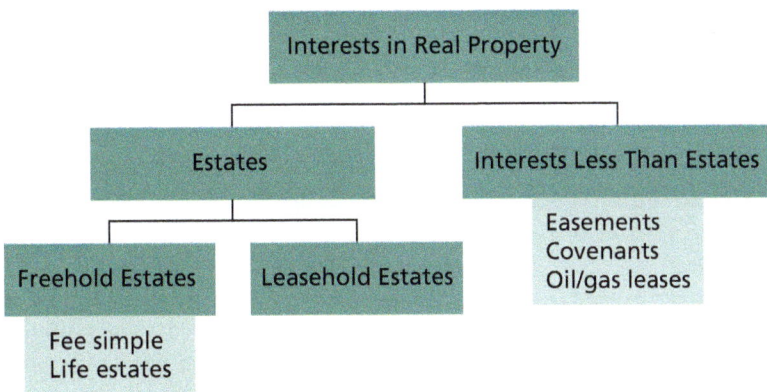

Figure 21.1 Interests in Real Property

ILLUSTRATION 21.3 Breach of Licence

The City of Brockville charges the Jazz Theatre Company a fee to use its municipal auditorium and grants it a licence to perform a play for one week. Revocation of permission to use the auditorium for that week would be a breach of contract. An injunction—or any other remedy such as damages—would be a contractual right enforceable only against the city. If the city sold the auditorium before the week scheduled for the performances, Jazz Theatre would have no rights against the purchaser.

GOVERNMENT REGULATION OF LAND

Use and Development

Landowners are not free to do whatever they want with their land. All three levels of government (federal, provincial, and municipal) regulate land use or development. Originally, fire and health hazards were the focus of regulation; now, municipal zoning bylaws prescribe the use and type of buildings that may be built. Building regulations prescribe minimum standards of quality for materials and the

---

[48] *National Energy Board Act*, RSC 1985, c N-7, s 52.

[49] *Northern Pipeline Act*, RSC, 1985, c N-26.

size of all parts of structures erected within an area. Planning bylaws set out requirements for roadways and for water and sewage services, and often prescribe the amounts of land a land developer must give to the municipality for use as school and park areas.

Provincial legislation regulates land development. Land development historically involved reconfiguring large blocks of land into new smaller parcels. The most common example is farm property that is converted into a residential subdivision of separate building lots. Two key components are involved: changing the allowed use—for example, from agricultural to residential; and changing the size of the parcel—for example, subdividing a farm into city-sized lots. Provincial planning legislation limits the right of an owner to subdivide his property into smaller parcels without prior permission of the municipality. This allows a municipality to control the density of an urban centre.

Increasingly, land development is focusing on repurposing previously developed sites, such as taking existing commercially developed sites and adapting them to residential use (converting a factory into lofts, for example). Municipal approval is also required for change of use. When regulating use, government power has limits. Surrounding properties and communities may object to municipally approved plans. The governmental body will need to show that it has met its constitutional duty to consult when Aboriginal interests are involved.[50]

CASE 21.4 Zoning Limits

The City of Kitchener's core neighbourhood had a variety of housing types ranging from heritage houses, high-rise condominiums, and apartment buildings to group homes, duplexes, older adults' residences, and public housing. Residents regularly complained about unmaintained properties and criminal activity such as drug dealing and prostitution. The City believed the "over-concentration" of "low income households" was an "unhealthy social environment" and passed a bylaw that required landlords to live in their buildings and banned all new facilities for the "targeted (low-income) population." A tenants' advocacy group challenged the bylaw, and the Ontario Municipal Board found that the bylaw failed to consider the needs of persons with disabilities as required by the provincial *Planning Act* and the *Charter of Rights and Freedoms*. It appeared to be "people zoning" rather than "use zoning." The City was given 15 months to redraft the bylaw. Instead, the bylaw was withdrawn completely.[51]

Another area of concern for redevelopment projects is protection of historical architectural sites, a concern reflected in provincial heritage legislation. This legislation allows municipalities to designate sites for preservation and monitor any proposed changes to them.

Growing public concern about environmental issues has led to provincial and federal environmental assessment and protection legislation, discussed in Chapter 3. Proposed development requires an environmental impact assessment before development can proceed.

Federal legislation regulates land use in areas of federal jurisdiction such as airports, national parks, natural resources, military sites, and Aboriginal lands. These matters often have interprovincial or international dimensions and involve considerations beyond those of the local community. Some land development projects involve all three levels of government regulation, as the following conflict illustrates.

---

[50] *Ktunaxa Nation v British Columbia (Forests, Lands and Natural Resource Operations)*, supra note 28.

[51] [2010] OMBD No PL050611; Terry Pender, "City Kills Cedar Hill Bylaw," *Waterloo Region Record*, June 22, 2011, B1.

CASE 21.5 All Levels of Government

The municipal government for Haldimand County gave all necessary approvals for a residential subdivision, known as Douglas Creek Estates, in Caledonia, Ontario. In July 1995, the developer registered a plan of subdivision and began selling lots. Also in 1995, Six Nations (a First Nation of 13 Indian bands) sued the federal and provincial governments, claiming interest in and title to Douglas Creek Estates (among other things), and warned the developer of the "dangers" associated with development. In February of 2006, Six Nations protesters took possession of the site. Occupation, protests, road blockages, and sometimes violent disruptions occurred. In March 2006, the protesters ignored a court-ordered injunction to leave the site. Negotiations between Six Nations, the Ontario government, and the federal government proceeded on an irregular basis.

In June 2006, the Ontario government agreed to pay $15 million to purchase the land from the developer plus additional compensation for lost profit. As the new fee simple title holder of the land, the Ontario government withdrew objections to the Six Nations occupation, despite the disapproval of surrounding neighbours.[52] The province, the police, and the municipality faced a class action lawsuit filed by residents, businesses, and contractors displaced by the occupation. The class action was settled in July 2011 with the creation of a $20 million compensation fund. Court approval of the distribution of the class action fund occurred in 2017.

Rights in the Matrimonial Home

For many centuries, a widow's principal security on the death of her husband was a common law right to **dower**—that is, a right to a life interest in one-third of the real property held by her husband in fee simple during their married life.

Dower was abolished in most provinces[53] and replaced by family law legislation that still recognizes the special interest that a spouse has in the family home, whether alive or dead. The legislation varies greatly from province to province.[54] Generally, statutory rights go much further than the ancient right to dower and include the right to refuse consent to any change in the title to the family home or to its sale. (A sale without consent is void.)[55]

Matrimonial property legislation complicates the use of the matrimonial home as collateral security for business loans or lines of credit.

dower a widow's right to a life interest in one-third of the real property held by her husband in fee simple before his death

Condominiums

The condominium is a provincial legislative solution to a shortage of housing and recreational areas in large urban centres. The legislation recognizes fee simple ownership of a **condominium unit** within a multiple-unit development, such as a high-rise apartment or town house block, without any interest in the surface land.[56] Condominiums may be residential housing or commercial and industrial developments.

condominium unit a unit in a multiple-unit development that is owned in fee simple without surface land

---

[52] *Henco Industries Limited v Haudenosaunee Six Nations Confederacy Council*, (2006) OR (3d) 721; *CBC News In Depth*, "Caledonia Land Claim," CBC News, November 1, 2006, http://www.cbc.ca/news2/background/caledonia-landclaim. See http://www.caledoniaclassaction.com; Province of Ontario, http://www.ontario.ca/government/six-nations-grand-river.

[53] Manitoba and Saskatchewan retain *Homesteads Acts*: CCSM c H80; SS 1989–90, c H-5.1, giving a surviving spouse a life interest in the entire family home. Alberta retains a *Dower Act*, RSA 2000, c D-15), which grants a life interest in the matrimonial home to a surviving spouse; see *Re Estate of Johnson, Rick*, 2017 ABQB 309.

[54] "Spouse" is restricted to married couples in some provinces; it includes cohabiting partners in British Columbia, Manitoba, and Saskatchewan. A restriction to married couples does not violate the *Charter*: *Nova Scotia (Attorney General v Walsh)*, 2002 SCC 83; *Kerr v Baranow*, 2011 SCC 10.

[55] See e.g. *Homesteads Act*, CCSM s H80, s 4; *Matrimonial Property Act*, RSNS 1989, c 275, s 8; *Family Law Act*, RSO 1990, c F.3, s 21.

[56] See e.g. *Strata Property Act*, SBC 1998, c 43; *Condominium Act*, SO 1998, c 19; RSNS 1989, c 85.

The Nature of Ownership in a Condominium A unit owner holds a fee simple estate in that unit and also obtains an undivided part ownership, shared with other unit owners, of the areas known as **common elements**. These include structures and areas external to the unit such as entrances, hallways, stairs, and elevators, and communal facilities such as laundries, recreation rooms, garages, and swimming pools. Each unit can be bought and sold, mortgaged, and passed to successors on death. It is separately assessed and taxed. Transfers do not affect the ownership of other units. A purchaser acquires a unit subject to several important conditions. In a multiple-unit building he must insure his unit; allow entry to make necessary repairs to services; and contribute to the cost of operation, upkeep, and the restoration of the common property. In addition, he becomes a voting member of the **condominium corporation** responsible for management of the property as a whole, and he is subject to the rules and regulations governing the development.

common elements structures and areas external to a condominium unit, including communal facilities

condominium corporation a corporation—whose members are the condominium owners—that is responsible for managing the property as a whole

Responsibility for Maintaining Units A unit owner is responsible for maintaining her unit. The boundaries of a unit are precisely defined in the organizing documents registered on the land title by the land developer. The definition of the unit identifies what is owned by the unit owner and what is owned by the condominium corporation. Things behind the drywall such as electrical and plumbing may still be the unit owner's responsibility to repair.

Maintenance and Management of a Condominium After the last condominium unit is sold, the developer turns over the management of the condominium corporation to the owners of the condominium units. Collectively they are responsible for managing the complex and maintaining the condominium common elements in a good state of repair. Typically, the unit owners authorize the corporation to hire a property management company to oversee the operation. Each unit owner pays a proportionate monthly amount toward the costs of maintenance and management known as **common area expense**; unpaid expenses may be registered as a lien against the owner's unit. Most legislation requires a condominium to undertake periodic property reviews, schedule routine maintenance, and maintain a **reserve fund** to cover the cost of major projects and emergencies. Prospective buyers receive a status certificate before buying that describes outstanding repair issues and the adequacy of the reserve fund, among other things.

common area expense unit owner's proportionate share of the costs of operating the corporation and maintaining the common elements

reserve fund money set aside for future major projects and emergencies

Financing and Insurance A unit owner must maintain fire and liability insurance on her unit to comply with mortgage requirements and the condominium rules. If something happens to the unit or the complex, the mortgage holders and insurers must consider the interests of the development as a whole, not just the specific unit owner. The most common method of dealing with the problem is through an "insurance trust." A trustee insures the entire building for the benefit of both the condominium corporation and every individual unit owner; each pays part of the premium proportionate to its interest.

Cooperative Housing

Cooperative housing is different from condominium ownership. In a cooperative housing development, a member buys a share in the cooperative corporation, which entitles the shareholder to occupy one of the units in the development. A risk of this type of home ownership is that the whole cooperative venture may flounder because of bad management and insolvency. All members are affected equally by the failure and may lose their equity investment, even though they may personally have been honouring their obligations and paying the required contributions for taxes and upkeep. Financing a share in cooperative housing presents difficulties of its own.

A member buys an equity share and has rights, similar to a leasehold interest, to occupy a unit. The method of borrowing money on the value of a share in a cooperative, combined with the right to occupy a unit, is more complicated than a mortgage on a fee simple interest.

CHECKLIST

Government Regulation of Land

Municipal	Provincial	Federal
■ Zoning bylaws ■ Property standards bylaws ■ Building permit regulations	■ Planning legislation ■ Environmental protection and assessment legislation ■ Heritage statutes ■ Family law statutes ■ Residential tenancies legislation ■ Commercial tenancies legislation ■ Condominium legislation	■ Environmental protection and assessment legislation ■ Land regulation as part of specific areas of federal jurisdiction such as • national parks • natural resources • Aboriginal peoples • airports • military

TRANSFERRING INTERESTS IN LAND

By a Sale or Gift

A living person may enter into a contract of sale or gift their interest to another person. Historically, a grant of land (known as a **deed of conveyance**) describing the grantor, the grantee, and the interest being transferred was originally signed and sealed by the grantor before a witness and registered on the title to the property. Electronic registration in combination with the Land Titles system's less formal **transfer** document has dispensed with signatures, witnesses, and seals.

When the owner grants only part of his land, the balance remains his. As noted earlier in this chapter under "Government Regulation of Land," some grants of only part of the land require prior approval of the municipality under planning control legislation.

deed of conveyance a document under seal that transfers an interest in land from the owner to another party

transfer under the land titles system, the equivalent of a grant; not required to be made under seal

On Death of the Owner
Interests in land are also transferred on the death of the owner, either by will or according to the rules of **intestate succession**. If a will identifies the person to whom the deceased wants to receive his interest, the executor of the estate will prepare the transfer to that beneficiary.[57] If the deceased dies intestate (without leaving a will), the interest passes according to statutory rules of inheritance to the holder's heir or heirs—that is, the interest passes usually to the closest relatives. If, for example, a widow with two adult children holds a fee simple ownership in a condominium unit and dies without a will, the children will become the co-owners of the fee simple. As noted earlier, if title is held in joint tenancy, the land will pass automatically to the surviving joint tenant.

intestate succession government rules that determine who gets the property of someone who dies without a will

By Compulsory Sale
A landowner may be forced to transfer her interest against her will. A creditor may hold a mortgage or obtain judgment against her in court and force the sale of the land to satisfy the debt (see mortgage remedies in Chapter 23).

---

[57] Subject to any rights of a surviving spouse, discussed above.

expropriation a private owner is forced by stature to transfer its land to a government body that needs it

A second type of compulsory transfer of land is **expropriation**. When a government body such as the federal government or a local school board requires land for its activities, it may proceed under statute to force the transfer of land to itself. It must pay compensation for taking the land, and if the parties cannot agree upon a price, the statute provides for arbitration or judicial proceedings to determine the fair market price to be paid.

Ethical Issue Expropriation

Expropriation can seem harsh as it prioritizes the public good over the individual property rights. The right to own property is not a constitutional right, but still the public expects the government to behave honourably and in good faith when exercising discretion to expropriate land and in setting "fair market" compensation. Defining what is in the public interest is challenging because it is rarely singular in nature and includes public safety, urban planning, infrastructure expansion, historical and environmental preservation, and even economic development. Fair market value is set objectively, and the loss of a sense of "home" may not be compensable. In 2012, Alberta established a property rights advocate to help private property owners voice their concerns during expropriation applications and ensure access to an independent tribunal for compensation assessment.

One of the most appalling examples of government expropriation of land for what some felt was in the "public good" at the time is the Canadian government's seizure of Japanese Canadian land and property during the Second World War. Thousands of Japanese Canadian residents were designated enemy aliens, forced to give up their land, and moved to "camps." The government sold their land to new owners. After the war ended, they were moved east or had the option to return to Japan. It took until 1988 for an apology to be issued and compensation to be paid.

Questions

1. What is the difference between public interest and majority public opinion?

Sources: *Expropriation Act*, RSA 2000 c E-13; *Property Rights Advocate Act*, SA 2012, c P-26.5; Maryka Omatsu, *Bittersweet Passage: Redress and the Japanese Canadian Experience*, (Toronto, 1992); *War Measures Act, 1914*, 5 George V, c 2, s 6 (repealed).

Adverse Possession

extinguish the title end the title of the owner and the owner's right to regain possession

adverse possession the exclusive possession of land by someone who openly uses it like an owner and ignores the claims of other persons, including the owner

limitation period the time period within which a right of action must be pursued or it is lost forever

Just as we saw with easements of prescription, at common law the continuous exclusive use of land could create an interest in it. An unauthorized occupant of land could **extinguish the title** of an owner and gain the title for himself. This is known as **adverse possession**, and it requires the following conditions:

- open, notorious, exclusive possession of the land (not necessarily by the same person)[58]
- possession without the consent of the owner[59]
- possession for the legislated **limitation period** for real property claims (for example, 10 years; longer against the Crown)[60]

Most Canadian jurisdictions using the land titles system of registration abolished transfer of title by adverse possession.[61]

---

[58] See e.g. *Shennan v Szewczyk* 2010 ONCA 679 at para 18; *Nelson (City of) v Mowatt*, 2017 SCC 8 at paras 17–18, 20.

[59] *Nadherny v 880474 Ontario Inc*, [2010] OJ No 2263.

[60] See e.g. *Real Property Limitations Act*, RSO 1990, c L.15, s 4 (10 years); *Limitations of Actions Act*, RSNS 1989, c 258, s 10 (20 years).

[61] See e.g. *Limitation Act*, RSBC 1996, c 266, s 12; *Real Property Act*, CCSM c R-30, s 61(2); *Land Titles Act*, RSO 1990, c L-5, s 51. In Alberta, a claim based on adverse possession may be registered: *Land Titles Act*, RSA 2000, c L-4, s 39. In Nova Scotia, adverse possession claims are allowed provided they do not affect more than 20 percent of the area of the parcel: *Land Registration Act*, SNS 2001, c 6, s 75.

REGISTRATION OF INTERESTS IN LAND

First in Time

Provincially regulated public registration systems record all interests in land.[62] Owners must register their interests, or the interests are not valid. The priority of each interest is determined based on the order of registration, with earlier registrations taking priority over subsequent registrations. Therefore, a purchaser should not rely on a properly executed grant of title unless it is registered in the public system. The date on the grant does not establish ownership; the date and time of registration does.

Two different registration systems operate in Canada: the registry system and the land titles system. Both systems adopt the "first in time" concept, also known as the **priority of registration** rule. This rule forces a purchaser to register her grant immediately.

priority of registration priority of interests in real property is determined based on the order of registration in the public system

Registry System

The registry system is the older of the two systems and is being replaced by the land titles system. This is because it is a labour-intensive system that places the responsibility for establishing good title on the users of the system or their real estate lawyers. Each transaction involving land requires an examination of the registered interests in order to establish the proper chain of ownership, identify any defects or other interests, and take corrective action. Each document must be examined to confirm that it meets the requirements to effectively deal with the interest. In the registry system, one cannot simply rely on the printed record or the fact of registration to confirm title; an evaluation of all documents registered in the title search period must be undertaken. Ownership may only be relied upon if a **chain of title** can be established throughout the search period. The specific length of the search period is usually set out in the legislation. Some registry systems limit the required search period to the proceeding 40 years, which can mean hundreds of registrations.[63] Failure to detect a defect in the chain of title will lead to liability in negligence for the real estate lawyer.

chain of title the series of grants over the title search period that can be traced to the current owner (vendor)

Land Titles System

The disadvantages of the registry system led to creation of the **land titles system**. It began in the western provinces and spread across Canada.[64] In the land titles system, each document is examined and must receive approval from the land titles examiners before it is allowed to be recorded against the title. As a result, the record of registration may be relied upon as a **certificate of title**. Section 23(2) of the British Columbia *Land Title Act* specifically states that the certificate of title is conclusive evidence in any court that the person named in the certificate is the holder in fee simple of the property.[65] The government guarantees the accuracy of the title as shown on the record. There are variations from jurisdiction to jurisdiction in the methods of recording and in the type of guarantee given by the government. The great advantage of the system is that a purchaser need not search through 40 or more

land titles system a system of land registration where the land titles office records outstanding interests in the land and certifies them as being correct

certificate of title summary of registered interests in a property, showing the owner and any mortgages, easements, or other interests held by others, which may be relied upon by the public

---

[62] Subject to very few exceptions such as adverse possession.

[63] *Registry Act*, RSO 1990, c R-20, s 112(1); *Limitations of Actions Act*, RSNS 1989, c 258, s 23.

[64] British Columbia, Alberta, and Saskatchewan; conversion is underway in Ontario, New Brunswick, Nova Scotia, and Manitoba.

[65] In British Columbia, the *Land Title Act*, RSBC 1996, c 250, s 23(2).

years of records to discover the state of the title. The land titles office produces a complete statement, valid to the moment the statement is issued. If errors occur, land titles systems have assurance funds available to compensate injured parties. A land titles system does not completely eliminate the need to search title—exceptions to the certificate must be separately searched—but it drastically reduces the work involved.

The land titles system does away with adverse possession and prescriptive easements, ensuring that only registered documents can affect the state of the title.[66] The older registry system makes no attempt to do this: Its purpose is simply to provide an inventory of title documents and let the searcher assess them. "Off title" searches must still be completed for such things as zoning compliance, utility arrears, and environmental regulation.

Electronic Registration Now all jurisdictions use electronic systems with three key components:

- electronic record keeping—a computerized databank of registered interests in land
- electronic search capabilities—the ability to electronically search existing registrations using assigned "property identifier numbers" (called PINs or PIDs)
- electronic registration of documents—paperless registration of interests completed online[67]

The electronic system is far more accessible than its paper predecessor. Still, the electronic system faces new problems such as viruses and crashes. One of the most serious threats is fraud. The elimination of signatures, witnesses, and paper, together with the wide access to the electronic system, has led to increased **title fraud**—the fraudulent transfer or mortgaging of land by a non-owner. This has led some provinces to restrict access to electronic registration, requiring evidence of good character and accountability before access is allowed.

title fraud fraudulent transfer or mortgaging of land by a non-owner

Claims That Are Not Registered on Title

Some unregistered claims or interests could still affect a landowner's title in both the registry and land titles systems. Therefore, potential purchasers often undertake "off title" searches or investigations.

Adverse Possession In jurisdictions where the registry system is still in use, adverse possession could displace a registered fee simple holder. Adverse possession is also still possible in some land titles systems: for example, adverse possession claims of less than 20 percent of the parcel of land are allowed in the Nova Scotia land titles system.[68]

A **survey** of the real property is one way to uncover small encroachments. It is a detailed drawing or map of the real property showing all the boundaries of the land and the location of all buildings, fixtures, encroachments, or overhangs. A survey can be used to

- confirm that the buildings are actually on the land being purchased,
- confirm that the location of all buildings complies with the municipal zoning bylaws,

survey detailed drawing or map of the real property showing all the boundaries of the land and the location of all fixtures, encroachments, or overhangs

---

[66] See e.g. the British Columbia *Land Title Act*, *ibid*, s 24, or the Ontario *Land Titles Act*, RSO 1990, c L.5, s 51.

[67] See British Columbia *Land Title Act*, *supra* note 65; Ontario *Land Registration Reform Act*, RSO 1990, c L.4 (applies to both registry and land titles systems); *Land Registration Act*, SNS 2001, c 6.

[68] Nova Scotia *Land Registration Act*, *ibid*, s 75; see also *Nelson*, *supra* note 58.

- identify any possible claims for adverse possession, and
- locate fences, driveways, etc., in relation to the boundaries of the property.

Arrears of Taxes Tax arrears attach to the real property as if they had been registered. If any of these claims appear after a purchaser has paid the vendor, the purchaser must pay them in order to protect her interest in the land. A prospective purchaser should request a tax certificate from the municipality showing any taxes outstanding and evidence from the provincial government of any arrears of corporation taxes.

Creditors' Claims A claim against land may arise when the vendor is a judgment debtor at the time of the sale—that is, he has been sued successfully by a creditor who has filed its judgment with the sheriff for the county or district. If a claim of this kind is outstanding (unpaid) at the time the land is sold, the judgment creditor may still require the sheriff to levy execution against the land—that is, seize and hold a sale of the land in order to recover the amount due under the judgment. The purchaser will then have to pay the debt to save the land. Accordingly, a purchaser should also make a search for executions in the sheriff's office to ensure that there are none before completing the sale. These records may also be searched electronically.

Tenant in Possession Another hazard to a purchaser may be created by a tenant in possession of the land. In most jurisdictions, short-term leases—usually for three years or less—need not be registered or even be in writing and are valid against purchasers who buy the interest of the landlord. A purchaser must inspect the property to see whether there are any tenants, and if there are, she should obtain an acknowledgment from them of the type of tenancy they claim to hold.

Title Insurance

The transfer of an interest in land is a complex transaction requiring careful examination of the registry or land titles records, the municipal and provincial bylaws and regulations, the local sheriff's office records, and the land itself. These complicated search requirements, as well as the risk of title fraud in electronic registration, have increased the popularity of **title insurance**. Title insurance allows a potential purchaser or lender to buy insurance covering defects in the title to the real property. Though many variations exist, basic title insurance usually covers

- title (fee simple estate) in the subject land,
- a defect, charge, lien, or other interest (discoverable in the public record),
- lack of access to the property, and
- costs of defending the title to the property.

title insurance a policy of insurance that compensates the policy holder for defects in a title

Additional coverage is available for such things as off-title risks, known defects in title, and survey-related issues. Title insurance takes away the need to prove negligence against a real estate lawyer for a subsequently discovered defect in title. However, it does not eliminate the need for a lawyer during a real estate deal. In some provinces, lawyers are specifically required to explain and offer title insurance to prospective purchasers.[69]

---

[69] Law Society of Upper Canada, Rules of Professional Conduct, Rules 2.02(10), 5.01.

Strategies to Manage the Legal Risks

The value of land is affected by the marketability of its title. Therefore, agreements to purchase land should allow a sufficient amount of time prior to completion to obtain a survey, investigate the state of the title, and confirm that the intended use of the land is legal. Potential purchasers should take advantage of four key sources of information (even before offering to buy the property) to reduce the risks of receiving defective title or paying too much for the property:

- Title registry—both registry and land titles systems offer publicly searchable databases that will reveal the number of mortgages currently on the property and the price paid by the current owner.
- Municipal zoning files—municipalities maintain zoning information on the subject property and can confirm allowed uses, issuance of building permits, and completion of inspections.
- Survey—this drawing is the only way to confirm the exact physical location of buildings and fences on the property, and since most of us value the building more than the land, it is important to confirm that the building is actually on the lot.
- Title insurance—the existence of an insurance policy that will pay out if title defects are later discovered is a valuable safety net, particularly for land in older neighbourhoods with complicated title histories. Lenders often require it, in any event.

When sharing land ownership for business purposes, tenancy in common is the usual arrangement. Most often, joint tenancy is reserved for personal relationships where the intention is to gift the property to the co-owner on death. Most businesses would incorporate a company to own the land and then divide the shares in the company to reflect the percentage ownership. Finally, if considering a condominium, review the creating documentation carefully to determine the parameters of the unit and the formula for calculation of the common expenses. These expenses vary depending on the condominium and may have a significant impact on the cost of maintaining the unit.

QUESTIONS FOR REVIEW

1. Define the terms "title," "real," "land," "property," and "estate."
2. What factors have encouraged the growth of public regulation of land use?
3. Describe the two main classifications of interests in land. Distinguish between freehold and leasehold estates.
4. How does the existence of a life estate make selling land difficult?
5. Describe the nature of the interest a spouse has in the family home. How did this interest evolve?
6. What is the difference between Aboriginal title and Aboriginal rights?
7. What are the principal differences between joint tenancy and tenancy in common?
8. Describe the two elements of ownership in a condominium and how they affect responsibility for maintenance.
9. What is the special nature of insurance for a high-rise condominium building?
10. In cooperative housing, who owns the property?
11. What are the reasons for limitation periods generally? How do they apply to land?

12. Distinguish between the circumstances under which an easement may be obtained by prescription and a title may be extinguished by adverse possession.
13. Describe the three typical characteristics of oil, gas, and mineral leases.
14. Distinguish between a restrictive covenant in a grant, a building-scheme covenant, and a zoning bylaw.
15. For decades, each winter Timson has openly entered the fields of an uninhabited farm adjoining his home and cross-country skied several times a week. He knows the Abel family who used to farm there, but they have moved to a town 25 kilometres away. The Abels have just sold the farm to Belsen, and he has erected a sign at the gate, "No Trespassing." Does Timson have a right to continue his cross-country skiing?
16. What is expropriation, and how does it take place?
17. What is the main difference between the registry system of registration and the land titles system?
18. How is electronic registration connected to the expansion of the land titles system?
19. What must a prospective purchaser of land do to ensure that the vendor has the right to transfer the property clear of any claims? Does the purchase of title insurance change this answer?
20. What is the purpose of a survey?

CASES AND PROBLEMS

1. Continuing Scenario

   Ashley's Restaurant has been in leased premises since it opened, and there are things she wants to change the next time she renegotiates her leasehold interest with the landlord. Her issues are as follows:

   (i) The lease prohibits any lit or neon sign that shows in the dark. Ashley would like this term removed. The landlord says he cannot change this as it was a covenant included in his grant from the developer in order to fit in with the very residential surroundings of the neighbourhood.
   (ii) Ashley would like an outdoor patio area for the summer months on the sidewalk in front of the restaurant. The landlord will not agree to this because he thinks the City won't like it.
   (iii) In the current lease, Ashley pays the landlord for tax bills associated with her unit. She would rather pay these directly to the City. The landlord does not want to let her do this.

   What are the legal reasons why the landlord is resisting each of Ashley's requests? The landlord is considering selling the complex; should Ashley be worried about a new owner evicting her business?

2. Rumford College was established in the centre of the city in the late 19th century when the city was still small. It was granted 20 acres at the time—about nine hectares—and occupied two hectares with its buildings and lawns, expanding to about four hectares over the years. As the city grew, the remaining five hectares became extremely valuable, and Rumford ultimately agreed to sell certain portions for commercial development. It sold one hectare to each of three developers, including a restrictive covenant with each grant limiting the height of any buildings to 20 metres so as to protect the view of Rumford's college towers. Two of the three developers erected buildings complying with the restriction. The third, Townhouse Inc., kept the land vacant.

   Savvy Developers Inc. wished to erect a 25-storey luxury apartment building in the area to a height about five times more than the 20-metre limit. In addition to paying market value to Rumford for one-half hectare of land, it offered to donate

$500 000 to the college's endowment fund if it would forgo the restrictive covenant to allow the construction of the apartment building. Rumford agreed and sold the land. When Townhouse learned about the deal with Savvy, it resold its hectare to Upper Developments Ltd., deliberately omitting the restrictive covenant from the grant.

Upper Developments then sought a declaration from the court that the restrictive covenant no longer applied because of the concession made to Savvy. How do you think this dispute should be resolved by the court?

3. Peter Green owned and operated Green's General Hardware as well as the lands and buildings where he carried on business. His younger brother, John, worked for him as manager, as did his daughter, Susan. Peter died, leaving a will in which he gave the business and real property to John for life, with the remainder to Susan at John's death. John and Susan could not agree on how to run the business. John wanted to push sales and expansion as quickly as possible; Susan feared that such action would make the business unstable—she preferred to build more slowly, consolidating the gains of the business. The dispute became heated, and John fired Susan. Within a few years the business was in serious financial difficulty. John had allowed several buildings, including a warehouse, to fall into disrepair. Susan sought by court action to force John to keep the buildings in good repair. Should she succeed? Why?

John died and left a will giving his whole estate, including the business and buildings, to his wife. Who is entitled to the business, and why?

4. Ferrand owned a summer cottage near Fredericton, New Brunswick. He sold it and delivered a grant to Simpson in exchange for $35 000 cash on June 10. On June 11, Simpson received a telephone call to return home to Newfoundland, where her mother was seriously ill. She left without registering her grant to the cottage. When Ferrand learned that Simpson had left the area, he called an acquaintance, Entwistle, and asked him whether he was interested in buying the cottage at a bargain price of $26 000. Entwistle had offered Ferrand that amount several months before, and Ferrand had refused. Entwistle eagerly accepted the offer on June 20 and paid Ferrand. On the same day, Entwistle received a grant to the cottage and registered it without knowledge of its prior sale to Simpson. Ferrand then absconded with the money from both sales.

Several weeks later, Simpson returned to find Entwistle occupying the cottage. When Entwistle refused to move, Simpson brought an action to have Entwistle put out and herself declared the owner.

The *Registry Act*, RSNB 1973, c R-6, contains the following provision:

> 19. All instruments may be registered in the registry office for the county where the lands lie, and if not so registered, shall . . . be deemed fraudulent and void against subsequent purchasers for valuable consideration whose conveyances are previously registered.

Will Simpson succeed in her action? Would the result be different if Entwistle had heard that Simpson had purchased the cottage before he paid Ferrand the $26 000? Give reasons.

5. Three owners of three abutting lakefront apartments buildings agreed to share use of their beach frontage, allowing all tenants to walk along the collective 200 meters of beach. They also agreed to share expenses of maintaining the fences and decks on one another's property. The agreement stated that they would bind future owners and was registered on title. When a new owner of one of the buildings refused to pay its share of expenses, the other owners sued. Will they succeed? Why or why not?

6. For over 30 years Montgomery owned two farms—Green Gables, on which he lived, and Wildwood. The two were separated by a farm owned by Cavendish.

Montgomery continually used a road across the Cavendish farm to go to and from Green Gables and Wildwood. The access to the road was through a gate on the boundary of the Cavendish property. During most of these years, Montgomery gave Cavendish a large turkey for New Year's, presumably as a gesture of goodwill and appreciation for the use of the road.

Three years ago, Montgomery sold Wildwood to Radoja. Radoja made relatively little use of the road over the Cavendish property (going across twice yearly to visit Montgomery with mortgage payments) until last year, when she also bought Green Gables. The old road then became valuable to Radoja as the most convenient access between her two properties. In the meantime, however, the Cavendish family had extended their lawn across the roadway, and Radoja's suddenly increased use of the road led to a dispute about her rights.

Cavendish sought a court injunction to restrain Radoja's use of the alleged right-of-way. Indicate, with reasons, whether the court will grant the injunction.

Chapter 22
Landlord and Tenant

- **THE NATURE OF THE RELATIONSHIP**
- **CLASSES OF TENANCIES**
- **COVENANTS**
- **REMEDIES OF THE LANDLORD**
- **REMEDIES OF THE TENANT**
- **TERMINATION AND RENEWAL OF A TENANCY**
- **ORAL LEASES**
- **SALE OF THE LANDLORD'S INTEREST**
- **LEASEBACKS**
- **RESIDENTIAL TENANCIES**
- **STRATEGIES TO MANAGE THE LEGAL RISKS**

There are many reasons why someone leases real property, whether in the form of vacant land, buildings and surrounding land, or just space within a building. The premises may be used for residential, recreational, and social or business purposes.

In this chapter we examine such questions as:

- What is the nature of the landlord-and-tenant relationship?
- What classes of tenancies may be created?
- What are the typical covenants put into leases?
- How are tenancies terminated and renewed?
- What are "fixtures," and why are they important?
- What are the consequences of a landlord transferring his interest?
- What are "leasebacks," and how are they used?
- Why are residential tenancies treated in a special way?

THE NATURE OF THE RELATIONSHIP

Definition of a Tenancy

A leasehold interest is created when a landlord (lessor) grants, to a tenant (lessee), exclusive possession of land for a term. A **term** is the definite period of time for which the interest lasts. The landlord divides her interest in the land between herself and the tenant by giving an interest to the tenant for a limited time and retaining the reversion. At the end of the term, the tenant must give up the land. The right to possession reverts to the landlord. The word lease is a short form for the creation of a leasehold interest and also refers to the agreement or contract between landlord and tenant creating the leasehold.

term an interest in land for a definite period of time

A leasehold interest is an estate in land.[1] When parties create a leasehold, certain rights and duties are given to both the landlord and the tenant. The requirements of land law are strict, and if they are not met, no estate in the land is created—the usual rights and duties between landlord and tenant do not arise. The consequences of failing to create a leasehold interest may be serious for either party but especially for a would-be tenant:

- He may be evicted by the owner at once.
- He has no right himself to evict strangers.
- In the case of residential tenants, he might not be covered by protective legislation.

The essential requirements for the creation of a leasehold are, first, that the tenant must obtain the right to exclusive possession, and second, that the tenancy must be for a definite or ascertainable period of time. Depending upon the length of the term of the lease (and the jurisdiction), the lease may have to be in writing.

The rules applicable to leasehold interests are found in the common law on real property interests, statutes passed by government, and the specific contractual covenants in the lease. Rules vary depending upon the proposed use of the property. All provinces designate **residential tenancies** as a separate class of tenancy and offer tenants special protection in residential landlord and tenant legislation.[2] They do so in order to recognize the special importance of basic shelter. The special statutory provisions applicable to residential tenancies are discussed in the final section of this chapter. Most of this chapter applies to **commercial tenancies** only, and separate legislation is applicable to this type of leasehold interest.[3] The rules applicable to residential and commercial tenancies are quite different from each other.

residential tenancies a lease of premises used as living accommodation

commercial tenancies a lease of premises used for a business or non-residential purpose

Exclusive Possession

Exclusive possession is the difference between estates in land and lesser interests in land. It gives control over the land rather than a right merely to use the land in common with others. A person who has a right to use land in common with others may be merely a licensee. A licensee enters upon land with the consent of the owner, as, for example, when he is allowed to go fishing in a farmer's stream. He is on the land lawfully, not as a trespasser, but he has no interest in the land. He does not have the right to exclude others from the land or to object to the activities of others.

---

[1] Estates in time were considered in Chapter 21.

[2] See e.g. *Residential Tenancy Act*, SBC 2002, c 78; *Residential Tenancies Act, 2006*, SO 2006, c 17.

[3] See e.g. *Commercial Tenancies Act*, RSO 1990, c L.7; *Commercial Tenancy Act*, RSBC 1996, c 57.

A tenant's right to exclusive possession gives him far greater power than a licensee. He may keep anyone off the land, and his landlord has limited rights to evict him from the land until the term ends. A tenant may prevent even the landlord from entering the land unless the lease gives the landlord a right to enter for a specific purpose, such as to view the state of repair of the property and to make repairs. The right to exclusive possession of land gives a tenant the ability to acquire other lesser rights—a tenant may acquire an easement over adjoining land for the duration of his tenancy in the same manner as the holder of a fee simple.

A person is considered to have exclusive possession if, under the terms of the lease, others are excluded or given only limited rights to use or have access over the land. Generally, it is not wise for a business to enter into a lease that grants a right of use to a third person or to the landlord, except (as already noted) for the limited purpose of inspecting the premises and making repairs.

Definite or Ascertainable Period A leasehold interest must begin on a fixed date, and it must end on a fixed or ascertainable date. The final date need not be stated if the period itself is definite. A lease that begins in March of a certain year to run for a week, a month, a year, five years, or 500 years is a valid leasehold interest because the date of expiry can always be worked out accurately. Long leases—for 99 years, or even for 999 years—are common in England but are rare in Canada, although terms of 25 to 50 years are not uncommon in the case of large commercial developments (see the discussion of leasebacks later in this chapter).

If the parties attempt to create a term for an uncertain period, the term is void, and no leasehold interest is created. Leases "for as long as the tenant holds a Tim Hortons franchise" or "until the tenant becomes insolvent" are void. However, parties who wish to have such a lease can accomplish their purpose through conditions subsequent or options to terminate. The requirement of certainty is satisfied if a lease ends at the latest upon a certain date but may be brought to an end at an earlier date upon the happening of a particular event. A lease from A to B for 10 years that may be terminated earlier "should B lose its Tim Hortons franchise" is a valid lease condition.[4]

Leasing Compared to Condominium Ownership

Non-residential condominiums are increasingly used instead of rental units for professional, office, retail, commercial, and even industrial purposes. Like leasing, condominiums reduce individual responsibility for exterior maintenance and improvements and spread the costs across multiple owners. Unlike leasing, they offer stability and security without the need to worry about fixed terms, renewals, or change in landlord. Other advantages to buying a commercial condominium unit include capital investment and tax advantages of ownership.

Among the disadvantages of owning a non-residential condominium are high initial capital investment and the carrying costs; maintenance costs are charged back to unit owners through common expenses and special assessments without the owner being able to control the timing. If the business grows and requires more space, adjacent units might not be available. Resale potential might not be good. In a mixed-use development, the developer may not have structured voting rights and cost allocations equitably. Poor management of the development might result in a loss in investment value.

---

[4] Bankruptcy law voids a termination clause triggered by bankruptcy because the lease is an asset; see *Bankruptcy and Insolvency Act*, RSC 1985, c B-3, ss 84.2(2),(5) and the discussion in Chapter 29. A trustee may assume the tenancy is preserved by provincial law; see e.g. *Landlord's Rights on Bankruptcy Act*, RSA 2000, c L-5, ss 1, 5.

CLASSES OF TENANCIES

Term Certain

A **term certain** is a tenancy that expires on a specific day; the term ends without any further act by either the landlord or the tenant. A lease of a restaurant at a summer resort "from May 24 to September 15" of a particular year and a long-term lease of a cold storage plant "from March 1, 2015, to February 28, 2025" are examples of typical commercial leases for a term certain. The tenant is expected to vacate before the end of the last day of the tenancy unless she has made new arrangements with the landlord. If she stays on without making any arrangements, she becomes an **overholding tenant**, liable for the payment of rent, but she may be evicted by the landlord. If, however, the landlord accepts further rent without protesting, a new tenancy may be created, as explained below.

term certain a tenancy that expires on a specific day

overholding tenant a tenant who remains on the premises without a new agreement with the landlord after the term of the lease expires

Periodic Tenancy

A **periodic tenancy** is a leasehold interest that renews itself automatically on the last day of the term for a further term of the same duration, unless either the landlord or the tenant serves notice to bring the tenancy to an end. A periodic tenancy may be created by a formal agreement, but in Canada it arises more often in an informal way when a tenant moves into possession and pays an agreed rent to the landlord at regular intervals as agreed between them, either in writing or orally. If, for example, a business pays rent on the first day of each month, the tenancy renews itself for another month without further agreement between the parties. A periodic tenancy also comes into existence when a tenant remains in possession after the tenancy with a term certain has expired and pays further rent to the landlord. The most common periodic tenancies are weekly, monthly, and yearly. The monthly tenancy is often called a **month-to-month tenancy**.

periodic tenancy a leasehold interest that renews itself automatically on the last day of the term for a further term of the same duration

month-to-month tenancy a periodic tenancy that renews itself monthly

The difference between a term certain and a periodic tenancy is this: A term certain ends automatically unless the parties make an arrangement to continue it; a periodic tenancy renews automatically unless either of the parties serves notice to end it. The requirements of notice are set out below, under "Termination and Renewal of a Tenancy."

Tenancy at Will

A tenancy at will is not a true leasehold interest because it does not last for a definite period, nor does the tenant have any right to exclude the landlord and remain on the premises. The tenant is there merely at the landlord's will, and the landlord may demand possession at any time without notice. The tenant does, however, have a reasonable time to gather up possessions and leave.

On the other hand, a tenant at will is under no obligation to remain in possession and pay rent—he may vacate possession at any time without notice. Such a tenancy may exist when the owner of real property allows a prospective purchaser to occupy the premises pending the conveyance of the title to the purchaser or when a landlord permits a tenant to remain on a day-to-day basis pending the wrecking of the building to make way for new construction. A tenancy at will may be gratuitous, or the landlord may exact a payment without turning the arrangement into a leasehold.

Tenancy at Sufferance

A tenancy at sufferance is not a true tenancy either. The typical example is that of an overholding tenant who entered into possession rightfully under a lease but now stays

trespasser one who enters without consent or lawful right on the lands of another or who, having entered lawfully, refuses to leave when ordered to do so by the owner

in possession wrongfully after the term has expired. Since he came into possession lawfully, he is not treated as a trespasser unless the landlord orders him to leave and he refuses. (Ordinarily, a **trespasser** is one who enters without consent or lawful right on the lands of another or who, having entered lawfully, refuses to leave when ordered to do so by the owner.) There is a key difference between a tenant at sufferance and a tenant at will. Although a tenant at will has no estate in the land and can be put out by the landlord, he is nonetheless there lawfully, by agreement. A tenant at sufferance also initially entered the premises lawfully but has no agreement with the landlord; his occupation of the land is merely tolerated by the landlord until the landlord acts to put the occupier out.[5]

COVENANTS

To Pay Rent

covenant a term, clause, or promise contained in a contract or lease

The **covenant** to pay rent is the consideration given for receiving the leasehold interest. Often leases describe the total rent to be paid during the whole term of the lease and then describe when payments are to be made. For example, the tenant may promise to pay the sum of $120 000 to lease a suite of offices for five years, to be paid in 60 monthly installments of $2000 due on the first day of each month.

The promise to pay rent is unconditional and must be performed despite any landlord misconduct. Only landlord actions that amount to eviction of the tenant discharge the tenant's obligation to pay rent.[6] If the leased premises are destroyed, in the absence of a specific term in the lease dealing with the problem, the tenant is still liable for the rent. She has purchased a leasehold interest consisting of a certain geographically defined area and must pay for it whether or not the building and amenities continue to exist for the full term. Sometimes, the doctrine of frustration applies to commercial leaseholds.[7] One example involves leasehold interests above the ground floor in a multi-story building. If a 10-story building burns down, the landlord cannot insist that a tenant on the ninth floor continue to be liable for rent.[8]

When a tenant leases only a portion of the landlord's building, the landlord usually retains control over heating, repairs, and maintenance. In these circumstances, it is common to state in the lease that liability to pay rent shall be suspended if the leased premises are substantially destroyed by fire or other cause, and not by the tenant's own negligence.

A tenant's covenant to pay rent is independent of any express promise by the landlord to make repairs to the property, and the tenant is not excused from paying rent on the grounds that the landlord has not performed her part of the bargain.

During the term, the landlord cannot increase the rent unless express provision has been made, as in the case where the parties agree that the landlord may increase the rent by an amount equal to any increase in property taxes. If the landlord wishes to increase the rent, she cannot do so until the term expires. She may, of course, bargain for an increase in any subsequent lease.

---

[5] *Gari Holdings Ltd v Lanham Credit Union* (2005), DLR (4th) 74 at para 37 (SKCA).

[6] *Cross v Piggott*, [1922] 2 WWR 662; *Northern Cartage Ltd v Motorway (1980) Ltd*, [1999] MJ No 323 at para 64.

[7] *National Carriers v Panalpina (Northern) Ltd*, [1981] AC 675. See also *Canadian Western Bank v 702348 Alberta Ltd*, [2009] AJ No 481 at para 55 (citing *Great Lakes Bick and Stone Ltd v Vanderlinder*, [1993] OJ No 2763 at para 18), aff'd [2010] AJ No 784 (ABCA); *Commercial Tenancy Act*, RSBC 1996, c 57, s 30.

[8] C Bentley, J McNair, and M Butkus, eds, *Williams and Rhodes: Canadian Law of Landlord and Tenant*, 6th ed (Toronto: Carswell, 1988) at 6–41.

Assignment and Subletting

Freedom to Assign A tenant may wish to assign the balance of the term of a tenancy before it expires. For example, the tenant's business may have become so successful that he requires larger premises, or he may have received an offer to sell the business as a going concern provided he assigns the balance of the lease to the purchaser so that the business may continue at the same location. A tenant, as owner of a leasehold interest, has (subject to the terms of the lease) the right to assign it. A tenant does not, however, terminate his personal liability to the landlord by assigning; the landlord may still hold him accountable for performance of those obligations if, after the assignment, the assignee does not perform them or goes bankrupt.[9] For this reason, a tenant should make it a term of the assignment of the tenancy that the assignee shall carry out all the tenant's covenants in the lease and indemnify him against any loss caused by the assignee's default.

The Landlord's Consent to Assignment

When leasing premises, a landlord is often concerned with the reputation of the tenant as well as with her ability to pay the rent. Having, for instance, the head office of a large corporation as a tenant in a new building might attract other tenants. A landlord may also be concerned about the type of business to be carried on for any of several reasons. Here are a few examples:

- the risk of unprofitable competition with the business of other tenants or with that of the landlord herself—a problem often arising in large business blocks and shopping centres
- noise, fumes, or traffic interfering with other tenants
- the wear and tear that certain businesses may inflict upon the premises

For these reasons, a landlord almost invariably requires a tenant to agree that she will not assign the lease without first obtaining consent (permission) from the landlord.

Still, if a landlord were free to withhold consent for any reason, the tenant might be placed in a difficult position. A landlord could arbitrarily refuse to give consent to an assignment that would in no way be harmful to her. Accordingly, tenants often require that the words "but such consent shall not be unreasonably withheld" be added to the covenant. In most provinces, these words are implied by statute as part of the covenant unless they are expressly excluded, and a tenant may apply to the court for an assessment of the reasonableness of any refusal.[10]

Subletting

A sublease is different from an assignment. An assignment is a transfer of the whole of the remainder of the tenant's term to the assignee; so long as the assignee performs all its covenants, the tenant retains no further right or interest in the lease. A sublease is a transfer of only part of the tenant's term to the subtenant. If the term given to the subtenant expires just one day before the expiration of the main lease (leaving the tenant with a reversion of one day), the tenancy of the subtenant is created not by an assignment but by a sublease. The tenant becomes the landlord of the subtenant.

---

[9] *Crystalline Investments Ltd v Domgroup Ltd*, [2004] SCJ No 3.

[10] See e.g. *Commercial Tenancies Act*, RSO 1990, c L-7, s 23.

The sublease may differ materially from the main lease in the rent payable, in any of the covenants given by either party, and in the extent of the premises sublet (the subtenant may hold only a portion of the premises leased to the tenant). In both sublease and assignment, the tenant remains liable to the landlord to perform all the covenants under the main lease. The discussion concerning the requirement of consent of the landlord for assignment applies equally to subleases.[11]

Restrictions on Use of Premises

A landlord is usually concerned with the proposed use of the premises. This is controlled by requiring a covenant in the lease that restricts the use of the premises to particular activities. Such covenants are also enforceable against the tenant's assignees and subtenants.

A tenant may, in turn, insist that the landlord give a covenant not to rent adjoining premises to a competing business; this is known as an **exclusive use clause**. If, however, the landlord should commit a breach by renting adjoining premises to an innocent third party unaware of the covenant, the tenant would have no rights against the other tenant. His remedy would be limited to an action for damages against the landlord.

exclusive use clause a landlord's promise not to rent adjoining premises to any other entity in the same or competing business as the tenant

Even in the absence of an express covenant, there is an implied covenant by the tenant to treat the premises in a "tenant-like manner"—that is, use them only for those purposes for which they are reasonably intended. A tenant could not turn a cold storage plant into a glue factory, or a restaurant into a hotel. In other words, a tenant may be prevented from carrying on activities for which the premises were not intended or zoned or that would cause excessive wear and tear.

Fitness for Occupancy

At common law, there is generally no covenant of fitness implied by a lessor in granting a commercial lease. The lessee takes the premises as she finds them and at her own risk. Unless a tenant obtained an express covenant in the lease concerning the fitness of the premises for a particular use, or unless the landlord made a misrepresentation, the tenant is responsible for her own investigation of the premises.[12] However, courts have suggested that the course of dealing between the parties may create an implied covenant that the premises will be fit for the lessee's purposes, if they are disclosed to the lessor, much as the implied condition of fitness arises in a sale of goods.[13]

A commercial landlord is not usually liable to a tenant or the tenant's customers, family, or guests for injuries caused by the unsafe condition of the rented premises, unless the landlord actually created the danger. However, where the landlord covenants to maintain and repair the premises, and fails to carry out that responsibility, occupiers' liability legislation generally equates her duty to visitors to the duty of an occupier.[14] In all other circumstances, the tenant, as the party in exclusive possession of the property, bears the responsibility that arises from injuries caused to persons in the leased premises.

---

[11] See *Zurich Canadian Holdings v Questar Exploration Inc* (1999), 171 DLR (4th) 457 (ABCA).

[12] Covenant relating to fitness for habitation is incorporated into residential tenancy legislation.

[13] *Telex (Austral/Asia) Proprietary Ltd v Thomas Cook & Sons (Austral/Asia) Proprietary Ltd*, [1970] 2 NSWR 257 (NSCA).

[14] *Occupiers' Liability Act*, RSBC 1996, c 337, s 6; CCSM c O.8, s 6; SNS 1996, c 27, s 9; RSO 1990, c O-2, s 8. See the discussion of occupiers' liability in Chapter 4.

Repairs

As a general rule, a landlord is not liable to make repairs to the property unless she expressly covenants to do so. Of course, a landlord has an economic incentive to maintain her property in good condition.

A landlord may, however, be liable to repair structural defects that develop, particularly if failure to repair would amount to an indirect eviction of the tenant and consequently a breach of the covenant for quiet enjoyment, as we shall see. For example, if a landlord fails to repair a leak in the roof of an office building and it results in the soaking and eventual crumbling of the ceiling and walls in an office suite, the tenant has an action against the landlord even where no covenant to repair has been given. In addition, when rented premises are in a large building, the landlord is responsible to the tenants for the maintenance of corridors, stairways, and elevators.

The general rule is that a tenant is not liable to make repairs to the premises unless he has expressly covenanted to do so. The rule is subject to two exceptions. First, as we have already noted, the tenant must not make such use of the premises that will cause excessive wear. Second, he is liable for committing **waste**. Waste may be voluntary—as when a tenant pulls down part of a building or otherwise damages it, or makes alterations that reduce its value. Alternatively, it may be permissive—that is, negligent—as when a tenant fails to repair a leak in the roof even though he is aware that more serious harm will result if he does not correct the problem.

waste damage to the premises that reduces its value

Usual Covenants in the Lease of a Building

When a tenant leases an entire building or property, the landlord frequently obtains a covenant from him to keep the property in good repair, reasonable wear and tear excepted. Accordingly, the tenant agrees to make such repairs as are necessary to keep the property in the same condition as when the lease began, except for normal depreciation. The tenant is not liable for damage caused by faulty construction or for deterioration in the property due to the normal forces of nature. Unless the lease exempts the tenant, however, the tenant's covenant to repair includes liability to make good any loss by fire or storm. Often a tenant exempts himself from liability in this respect by qualifying the covenant to repair with the words "loss by fire, lightning, and tempest excepted."

When a tenant leases only part of a building, the landlord usually undertakes to provide various services such as heat, water, and elevator service, and also to keep the premises in good repair. There is an important difference between a covenant to repair given by the tenant and one given by the landlord. A tenant is in possession of his premises and should be aware of their falling into disrepair—it is not up to the landlord to remind the tenant or give notice.

In contrast, the landlord, not being in possession of the tenant's premises, is not presumed to be aware of any disrepair in them, and her duty to repair does not arise until the tenant gives her notice. A landlord who undertakes to repair the premises often reserves the right to go on the premises at reasonable hours and inspect and view the state of repair. Reserving this right, however, does not place any duty upon her to make inspections or to repair until she has received notice from the tenant.

Quiet Enjoyment

The whole purpose of a lease is to give the tenant possession and the right to "enjoy" the premises during the term of the lease. Accordingly, the landlord gives a **covenant of quiet enjoyment** either impliedly, simply by granting the lease, or expressly, in a specific covenant for that purpose. The covenant refers to disturbance and has two aspects. First, it is an assurance that the landlord has good title to the property at the

covenant of quiet enjoyment a landlord's promise that nothing will interfere or disturb the tenant's possession and use of the premises

time she gives the lease; second, it is a covenant that, subsequent to the making of the lease, the landlord will not herself interfere or permit anyone obtaining an interest in land from her to interfere with the tenant's enjoyment of the premises.

ILLUSTRATION 22.1 Breach of Covenant

(a) Greer owns a piece of land, including some warehouses. A mining company survey shows valuable ore deposits. She grants the company a long-term mining lease, and the company begins extensive mining excavations. Subsequently, she leases the warehouses to Atkins Inc., which intends to use them to store heavy machinery. Atkins discovers that the mining operations involve regular movement of mining equipment on and off the property, making it difficult for Adler to access the warehouses. Since Greer authorized the mining company's activities before granting Atkins Inc. its lease, Greer has allowed the mining company to interfere with Atkins's use of the property. Therefore, Greer breached her covenant to Atkins Inc. for quiet enjoyment.

(b) Mendoza leases a suite of offices to McAdam and McCollum, an accounting firm. Subsequently, he leases the area on the floor directly above to a machine shop. The machine shop operations create noise and heavy vibrations, making it impossible for the accountants to work. Mendoza is in breach of his covenant.

Breach of the covenant of quiet enjoyment no longer requires physical interference with the enjoyment of the premises. Substantial noise, smell, or vibration that seriously interferes with the comfort or convenience of a lessee will be recognized as a breach of the covenant of quiet enjoyment. The interference must be substantial and permanent, and a court may reduce the rent of the tenant during the period of interference.[15]

Insurance

In the absence of a covenant in the lease, neither landlord nor tenant is under a duty to insure the premises for the benefit of the other. In most cases, of course, the landlord insures the premises to protect her own investment. If the leased property consists of an entire building or a group of buildings under the complete control of one tenant, especially if the lease is for a long term, the lease may impose on the tenant full responsibility for the premises, including obtaining insurance.

The complexity of liability and insurance problems increases when there is a large number of business tenants, each with its own employees, as in a large office building or a shopping mall. Who is liable for the loss if an employee should negligently cause a fire that substantially destroys a mall? Providing insurance protection and allocating risk through the use of exemption clauses requires great expertise.[16]

The question of insurance is closely tied to the problem of what should happen to the tenancy in case of severe damage to the premises by fire, flood, or storm. Failure to make proper provision can lead to great hardship, particularly for the tenant. A tenant may not get much benefit from a lease stating that, if the premises are substantially destroyed, the liability to pay rent is suspended until the building is repaired; such a clause may place the tenant at the mercy of the landlord. While the landlord decides what to do, the tenant, although not paying rent, is temporarily out of business. If he leases premises elsewhere, he may find that when the building is repaired, he is liable to pay rent for both locations.

---

[15] *Stearman v Powers*, 2014 BCCA 206 (defining quiet enjoyment). See *Caldwell v Valiant Property Management* (1997), 145 DLR (4th) 559. A tenant's right to quiet enjoyment extends to non-interference with the guests whom she might invite to visit her: *Cunningham v Whitby Christian Non-Profit Housing Corp* (1997), 33 OR (3d) 171.

[16] See *Greenwood Shopping Plaza Ltd v Beattie*, [1980] 2 SCR 228, where employees were held personally liable and could not take advantage of an exemption clause as third parties, but see more recent cases where the rule of privity was relaxed to give employees protection under their employer's exemption clause: *London Drugs v Kuehne & Nagel International Ltd* (1992), 97 DLR (4th) 261. See also *Laing Property Corp v All Seasons Display Inc* (1998), 53 BCLR (3d) 142, aff'd (2000) 6 BLR (3d) 206 (BCCA).

A lease should state that the repairs must be made within a certain time and that, if they are not made within that time, the tenant then has the option of terminating the lease rather than waiting until the premises are restored. Another possibility is to give the tenant the right to make the repairs himself and to deduct the costs from future rent.

Provision of Services and Payment of Taxes

When a tenancy is for a portion of a building only, and the landlord retains control over the building as a whole, it is usual for the landlord to covenant to provide heat, water, electricity, and occasionally even telephone service. When the tenancy is for the whole of the building, it is usual for the tenant to provide all these things himself.

Generally, property taxes are paid by the landlord when the tenant leases only a portion of the building. If the lease is of the whole of the building, the taxes may be paid by either party. As long as the agreement is clear, who pays is not important. If the landlord pays, the rent will be that much higher; if the tenant pays, then the rent is that much lower. In the absence of an agreement on the matter, it is the landlord's duty to pay the taxes. Often, the cost of these items is passed on to the tenant in the form of **additional rent**. Some leases include a term that each tenant must pay his proportionate share of maintenance expenses, utilities, and taxes. Tenants should carefully review the formula used to determine proportionate share, as it is often based upon the area of the leased premises as a percentage of the total area of the building. The definition of "total area of the building" could include all hallways and common areas, or it could be restricted to rentable areas. The most expensive scenario is if the area of the building only includes actually rented areas, resulting in the tenants, not the landlord, assuming the cost of unrented space.

additional rent a tenant's proportionate share of maintenance costs, utilities, and taxes

CHECKLIST
Covenants in a Lease

This is not a complete list of covenants; covenants vary depending upon the circumstances of the lease. In every lease, however, covenants that should be checked carefully by both parties are those concerning the following:

- term
- payment of rent
- restrictions on assigning or subletting the premises
- restrictions on the use of the premises
- fitness for occupancy
- responsibility for repairs
- quiet enjoyment of the premises
- responsibility for insurance
- responsibility for provision of services such as access (for example, elevators), heating, and electricity
- responsibility for payment of property taxes
- calculation of additional rent
- covenant for exclusive use
- options to terminate and renew
- ownership of leasehold improvements

REMEDIES OF THE LANDLORD

A landlord may seek a remedy when a tenant's breaches a covenant in the lease provided the landlord has not waived the breach. Accepting payment of rent after the landlord is aware of a breach and without specifically preserving the right to act on the breach may waive it. Waiver depends upon the type of breach.

> **CASE 22.1 Ongoing or Single Breach**
>
> Contrary to the terms of the lease, the tenant operated an illegal marijuana dispensary out of the premises. The landlord accepted a rent payment even after it was aware of the dispensary. It was clear to the court that the landlord did not intend to waive the breach even though there was no express reservation. The court held that waiver did not apply to situations involving repeated conduct. Acceptance of rent on one or even many occasions does not waive subsequent repeated breaches of the lease. Every day the dispensary operated was a new breach.[17]

Damages and Recovery of Rent

A landlord may sue for damages caused by a tenant's breach of any covenant. However, the right to recover rent requires further discussion and often presents a dilemma. If a tenant abandons the premises and pays no further rent, the old rules concerning interests in land placed the landlord in a predicament. On the one hand, by leaving the premises vacant and insisting on her rights under the lease, she could claim the entire rent due under it. In land law, apart from any statutory provisions to the contrary, there is no duty to mitigate damages as there is in contract law. Still, the tenant might never be able to pay, so doing nothing could be expensive. The landlord could terminate the lease and relet the property to a new tenant, but she lost all right to future rent and could only collect arrears at termination from the former tenant. If the landlord tried to sublet the premises "on behalf of the defaulting tenant" in order to reduce her loss but keep the right to collect rent for the entire term, she risked being seen as accepting the **surrender** by the tenant, thereby terminating the lease and freeing the tenant from future obligations to pay rent.

surrender abandonment of the premises by the tenant during the term of the lease

Courts now recognize that a lease creates both an interest in land and a contract, and so the principles of contract law are applied to resolve the landlord's dilemma. If a landlord wishes to terminate the lease and to continue to hold the tenant liable for future losses of rent, she may do so by informing the tenant at the time of termination that she will hold him responsible for all future losses arising from his breach. A landlord may mitigate her losses without losing her rights against the defaulting tenant.[18] The Supreme Court of Canada acknowledges that a landlord has no duty to mitigate if she chooses not to assume control of the premises.[19] However, if the landlord does terminate the lease and gives notice to seek future damages, she must mitigate her damage.[20] The law is complicated in this area, and a commercial landlord should obtain a legal opinion before acting to terminate the tenancy.[21]

---

[17] *1028840 BC Ltd v The Heritage Dispensary Clinic Society*, 2018 BCSC 82.

[18] *Highway Properties Ltd v Kelly, Douglas & Co Ltd* (1971), 17 DLR (3d) 710; *Manufacturers Life Insurance Co v Executive Centre at Manulife Place Inc*, [2011] AJ No 320; *Langley Crossing Shopping Centre v North-West Produce Ltd*, 2000 BCCA 107 at para 44; *Learmonth v Letroy Holdings Ltd*, 2011 BCSC 143 at paras 40–50, aff'd 2012 BCCA 262.

[19] *Highway Properties Ltd.*, ibid.

[20] *BG Preeco 3 Ltd v Universal Exploration*, [1987] 6 WWR 127 (as long as the claim is for rent due and not damages, there is not duty to mitigate). See also *AGC Flat Glass North America Ltd v CCP Atlantic Specialty Products Inc*, [2010] NSJ No 140.

[21] See e.g. *Smith v Busler*, [1988] BCJ No 2739; *Globe Convestra Ltd v Vucetic* (1990), 15 RPR (2d) 220. See also *Transco Mills Ltd v Percan Enterprises Ltd* (1993), 83 BCLR (2d) 254; *Jade Agencies Ltd v Meadow's Management Ltd*, [1999] BCJ No 214.

With respect *only* to residential tenancies, the duty to mitigate is clearer. Several provinces have amended their landlord and tenant laws as follows:

> A landlord or tenant who claims compensation for damage or loss that results from the other's non-compliance with this Act, the regulations or their tenancy agreement must do whatever is reasonable to minimize the damage or loss.[22]

Eviction

This remedy is sometimes called the landlord's **right of re-entry**. The right of re-entry for failure to pay rent is a term implied by statute, if not expressly included in the lease. The period for which rent must be in arrears before a landlord is entitled to re-enter and evict the tenant varies considerably from province to province and is longer in the case of residential tenancies. Before evicting a tenant in default, the landlord must follow the procedure laid down in the legislation of the province.

Leases often provide that the landlord may re-enter and evict the tenant for breach of any of the other covenants in the lease. Since eviction amounts to a **forfeiture**—that is, forfeiting (losing) the remainder of the term to the landlord, the court is very reluctant to permit eviction for breach of any covenant other than one relating to payment of rent, use of the property, or assignment of the lease. A court may grant a tenant relief against forfeitures either under the general principles of equity or under various statutory reliefs found in provincial legislation.[23] Generally speaking, so long as the tenant corrects the breach and proves it will not reoccur, the court will restrain the landlord from evicting him and will declare the lease to be valid under its original terms.

right of re-entry a landlord's remedy of evicting the tenant for failure to pay rent or breach of another major covenant

forfeiture to lose or give back to the landlord the balance of the term of a lease

Distress

Distress is the landlord's right to distrain for rent—that is, to seize assets of the tenant found on the premises and sell them to recover arrears of rent. Usually, the landlord authorizes a bailiff to distrain on the property of the tenant. The right to distrain does not arise until the day after the rent is due and a demand for payment has been made. A landlord cannot prevent the tenant from removing goods from the premises even as late as the day the rent is due. She may, however, object if the tenant is clearly removing all the goods in order to avoid the landlord's power of distress. If the tenant removes the goods in spite of the landlord's objection, or later removes them fraudulently to prevent the landlord from asserting her rights after the right has arisen, the landlord may follow the goods and have them seized in another location, provided they have not been sold in the meantime to an innocent purchaser.[24] The time limit within which a landlord may seize goods in this fashion varies from province to province.

A landlord is not permitted to exercise the right of eviction and simultaneously or subsequently exercise a right of distress. The right to distrain is limited to situations where the relationship of landlord and tenant remains in existence.[25]

Certain personal property is exempt from seizure—necessary household furniture, a limited supply of food and fuel, and mechanic's tools. A commercial lease may contain a term by which the tenant "contracts out" of its right to exemptions should the landlord

distress the right of the landlord to seize assets of the tenant found on the premises and sell them to realize arrears of rent

---

[22] *Residential Tenancy Act*, SBC 2002, c 78, s 7(2); CCSM c R119, s 55(2); SO 2006, c 17, s 16.

[23] See e.g. *Commercial Tenancies Act*, RSO 1990, c L-7, s 20; *Courts of Justice Act*, RSO 1990, c C.43, s 98; *Law and Equity Act*, RSBC 1996, c 253, s 24.

[24] See *Albo v Concorde Group Corp* (2004), 235 DLR (4th) 465, where the purchaser was a party to the fraud.

[25] *2105582 Ontario Ltd (Performance Plus Golf Academy) v 375445 Ontario Limited (Hydeaway Golf Club)*, 2017 ONCA 980 at paras 43–45; *Mundell v 796586 Ontario Ltd* (1996), 3 RPR (3d) 277. *Delane Industry Co Ltd v PCI Properties Corp*, 2014 BCCA 285.

distrain for rent.[26] If the landlord mistakenly seizes the goods of third parties such as customers or consignors, they must be released on proof of ownership. The landlord may also seize equipment or appliances purchased on the installment plan and not fully paid for, but before selling them she must first pay the balance owing to the seller.

CASE 22.2 Goods Owned by Creditor

A bakery bought an oven, dough mixer, and other bakery equipment on an installment payment plan and placed them in the leased premises in which it carried on business. The credit agreement stated that the equipment remained the property of the manufacturer until the purchase price was paid in full. The bakery ran into financial difficulties and stopped paying the installments and its rent. The landlord attempted to distrain the bakery equipment, and the manufacturer wanted to repossess the equipment. The Court held that the landlord could distrain the equipment only after it paid the balance owing to the manufacturer.[27]

Injunction

If a tenant uses the premises in a manner that would be in breach of a covenant restricting use, the landlord may obtain an injunction ordering the tenant to cease the prohibited use. An injunction may be obtained against certain types of use, even when they are not expressly prohibited under the terms of the lease, if they are inconsistent with the bylaws or general design and ordinary use of the property. For example, a landlord could obtain an injunction to prevent a house ordinarily used as residential property from being turned into a medical clinic.[28]

Normally, if a landlord is entitled to obtain an injunction, she also has the right to re-enter the property and evict the tenant. She will make her choice based on the circumstances and, in particular, on whether the lease is an otherwise desirable one from her point of view.

Bankruptcy of the Tenant

Under the *Bankruptcy and Insolvency Act*, a landlord has priority over the proven claims of general unsecured creditors in the event of the tenant's bankruptcy for the amount of three months of rent arrears.[29] For any additional arrears, she ranks among the general creditors. Any term that automatically terminates a lease upon the bankruptcy of the tenant is void.[30] This preserves the asset for use by the trustee in bankruptcy. The purpose of the three months' preference is to encourage landlords to be a little more patient with a defaulting commercial tenant. Inability to pay rent may be only temporary, but eviction will close down the business, probably causing greater hardship to both the tenant and other creditors of the tenant. Provincial landlord and tenant acts recognize the right of a trustee in bankruptcy to repudiate an outstanding lease without further liability[31] or, with proper notice, to continue to use the premises for

---

[26] Distress for residential tenancies has been abolished in some provinces.

[27] *Emcan Bakey Equipment & Supply Ltd v DMI Property Management Inc*, [2010] OJ No 2315.

[28] *McCuaig v Lalonde* (1911), 23 OLR 312.

[29] RSC 1985, c B-3, s 136(1)(f), as amended by SC 1992, c 27 (and an additional amount of three months of accelerated rent after bankruptcy). In the absence of bankruptcy proceedings, a landlord's priority under provincial legislation is usually greater than three months.

[30] *Ibid.*, s 84.2.

[31] Repudiation does not terminate the lease. It terminates the liability of the lessee but not of any guarantor: *KKBL No 297 Ventures Ltd v IKON Office Solutions Inc* (2004), 243 DLR (4th) 602. Where a lease has been assigned, repudiation by the assignee's trustee does not terminate the liability of the original lessee: *Crystalline Investments Ltd v Domgroup Ltd* (2004), 234 DLR (4th) 513.

so long as may serve the purpose of liquidating the tenant's assets and to pay rent at the rate specified in the lease.[32] Recognizing that in some circumstances the unexpired term of the lease may have value, a trustee may also assign the lease to a new tenant in circumstances that are acceptable to the court.[33] A landlord's right to distrain also ends when a tenant goes bankrupt.

REMEDIES OF THE TENANT

Damages

A tenant may recover damages from the landlord arising from breach by the landlord of any of her covenants. The wrongful eviction by the landlord is a breach of the covenant for quiet enjoyment. Similarly, if a landlord distrains upon more goods than were reasonably necessary to satisfy a claim for arrears of rent, the tenant may recover damages. If the landlord or her bailiff, in attempting to distrain upon the goods of the tenant, enters the premises illegally—that is, by use of force—she will be liable for damages for trespass. A tenant is entitled to prevent an exercise of the power of distress by keeping the premises continually locked, but in these circumstances the threat of distress can be an ongoing harassment to the tenant.

If a landlord has expressly covenanted to keep the premises in good repair or to rebuild them if they are destroyed, her failure to do so will be a breach not only of the covenant to repair but also of the covenant for quiet enjoyment.

Injunction

A tenant may also obtain an injunction to restrain a landlord from a continuing breach of the covenant of quiet enjoyment. A court will grant an injunction against a landlord for interfering with quiet enjoyment caused by a continuing nuisance such as vibrations, noise, or fumes escaping from the landlord's premises. The court will not grant an injunction, however, where it would be futile to do so—for example, where vibration caused by the landlord has so damaged the structure that it has been condemned as unsafe for occupation, destroying its usefulness to the tenant. The tenant's remedy is to vacate the premises and seek damages. An important covenant often given by a landlord to a retail tenant is a promise not to lease premises in the same building or shopping centre to a competing business. When a breach occurs, an injunction restraining the second tenant from carrying on the competing business will be granted only if the second tenant was aware of the covenant.

Termination of the Lease

When a landlord's breach of the covenant of quiet enjoyment has made the premises unfit for the tenant's normal use and occupation, the tenant, in addition to any other remedy, may terminate the lease and vacate the premises. Upon vacating, the tenant ends any further liability to the landlord. The landlord's breach must make the entire premises unfit for the tenant's use—amounting to a total eviction—before the tenant has this option.

If the landlord's interference is only with part of the premises, or is only a nuisance or inconvenience rather than amounting to a total eviction, the tenant remains bound to pay the rent and cannot terminate the lease. His remedies are then an action for damages for the injury suffered and an injunction to restrain further breach.

---

[32] See e.g. *Commercial Tenancy Act*, RSBC 1996, c 57, s 29; *Commercial Tenancies Act*, RSO 1990, c L.7, ss 38(2) and 39(1); *Landlord and Tenant Act*, CCSM c L-70, ss 46(2) and 47(1).

[33] See e.g. *Landlord's Rights on Bankruptcy Act*, RSA 2000, c L-5, s 8.

TERMINATION AND RENEWAL OF A TENANCY

Surrender

A term certain expires automatically without notice. Although not required by law, a landlord often delivers a reminder to the tenant that the lease is about to expire and that he must vacate on the date of expiry. Upon vacating the premises, the tenant surrenders them to the landlord.

A surrender may also take place during the term of a tenancy by express agreement between landlord and tenant, as when a tenant no longer desires to keep the premises and pays the landlord a sum of money to release him from obligations for the balance of the term. A landlord may also bargain for the tenant's surrender of the remainder of the term when she needs vacant possession in order to sell the property or wishes to make substantial alterations or to demolish the building.

Suppose a tenant abandons the premises without making an agreement to surrender to the landlord. As discussed above, a landlord may be presumed to have treated an abandonment as a surrender of the premises when she relets to another tenant or takes possession of the premises herself to make use of them for her own purposes. Often it may be difficult to decide from the circumstances whether the landlord has accepted an abandonment and so released the tenant from further obligation to pay rent. Since abandonment is usually committed by an insolvent tenant, the landlord's rights against the tenant may have little practical value.

Forfeiture

In our discussion of a landlord's remedies, we noted that breach of certain covenants by a tenant (such as failure to pay rent) entitles the landlord to evict the tenant and impose a forfeiture of the lease. Once the forfeiture takes place, the relationship of landlord and tenant is terminated. The tenant has no further obligations under the lease, although he may be liable because of his breach before forfeiture for damages suffered by the landlord. Similarly, if a landlord has attempted to impose forfeiture by improperly evicting her tenant—entitling the tenant to consider his obligations under the lease at an end—the relationship of landlord and tenant is terminated, but the tenant may still recover damages for the landlord's breach of covenants.

Termination by Notice to Quit

Periodic Tenancies

notice to quit notice of an intention to bring the tenancy to an end

A periodic tenancy renews itself automatically unless either the landlord or the tenant serves **notice to quit** on the other party—that is, serves notice of an intention to bring the tenancy to an end. Notice to quit served by a tenant is sometimes called notice of intention to vacate. In weekly, monthly, or quarterly tenancies, the length of notice required to bring the tenancy to an end is one clear period of tenancy. In other words, one party must give the other notice on or before the last day of one tenancy period for the tenancy to come to an end on the last day of the next period.

The common law rule that six clear months' notice is necessary to terminate a yearly tenancy at the end of the first year or any succeeding year of the tenancy applies to commercial leases in all provinces except New Brunswick, Nova Scotia, Quebec, and Prince Edward Island. In these provinces, only three clear months' notice is required. Common law and statutory notice periods are of little importance because virtually all commercial leases specify their own notice of termination requirements for fixed term leases.

> **ILLUSTRATION 22.2 Calculating Length of Notice**
>
> West Side Corp. rents a small warehouse from Bernstein on a monthly basis, commencing March 1, at a rent of $1250 per month. The following September, West Side buys a warehouse building with possession available on November 1. West Side must serve Bernstein with notice to quit on or before September 30 if it wishes to terminate the tenancy on October 31. October is then a clear month. If, however, it does not serve notice until after September 30—say, on October 3—October is no longer a clear month, and West Side Corp. is not able to terminate the tenancy until November 30. In these circumstances, November will be the clear month.

> **ILLUSTRATION 22.3 Yearly Renewal**
>
> Bok leases the Greenbrier summer hotel in Alberta from O'Brien at a yearly rental of $30 000, commencing April 1, 2012. The yearly tenancy will renew itself automatically each April 1 unless either party gives six clear months' notice before April 1—that is, on or before September 30 of the preceding year. If Bok wishes to vacate the property by March 31, 2019, he must serve notice on or before September 30, 2018. If he serves notice on October 1, 2018, it is too late; the tenancy will automatically renew itself on April 1, 2019, and continue to March 31, 2020. Therefore, the maximum time that may elapse between giving notice and terminating the tenancy may be 18 months less a day, that is, from October 1, 2018, to March 31, 2020.

Tenant Remaining in Possession after the Expiration of a Fixed Term If a tenant remains in possession after the expiration of a fixed term, he becomes a tenant at sufferance and may be evicted by the landlord at any time on demand. What happens, however, if the landlord accepts further rent from the tenant? A periodic tenancy then arises on all the terms of the original lease except those that are inconsistent with a periodic tenancy. An example of an inconsistent term would be a covenant by the landlord to redecorate the premises every three years during a 12-year term. This covenant would not become part of a subsequent periodic tenancy.

Generally speaking, if a periodic tenancy arises after the expiry of a fixed term expressed in years (for example, a lease for five years at an annual rental of $8400 payable in installments of $700 per month), then the periodic tenancy created will be a yearly tenancy. If instead the term certain is stated as a term of months (say, a lease for eight months at a monthly rent of $700), then the periodic tenancy created will be a monthly one; similarly, if the term certain is expressed in terms of weeks or quarter-years, a succeeding periodic tenancy will be weekly or quarterly, respectively.

Parties May Set Their Own Terms for Notice

The requirements for a valid notice to quit discussed above are those that apply in the absence of express agreement; the parties to a lease usually agree to vary them to suit their own needs. Landlord and tenant may agree that some period less than six months is sufficient notice for either party to terminate a yearly tenancy. Remaining in possession after giving notice to quit can attract contractual penalties in addition to damages and eviction. For example, in British Columbia, a tenant who remains in possession after the date mentioned in his notice is liable for double the rent.[34]

Renewal

A lease for a fixed term, particularly a lease of premises for a retail store, often provides for a renewal at the option of the tenant. Asking for such an option makes good business

---

[34] *Commercial Tenancy Act*, RSBC 1996, c 57, s 16.

sense. One option permits the tenant to terminate the tenancy at the end of the original lease if the business is unsuccessful or so successful that larger premises are needed, yet he has the security of exercising the option if the business proves successful.

Landlords usually require some increase in rent for the renewal term and sufficient notice to obtain a new tenant if the option is not exercised. Rent increases may be tied to the consumer price index or some other measure of the rate of inflation. At least three months' notice from the tenant that he intends to exercise the option is typical.

Fixtures

As noted in Chapter 21, land includes everything fixed to it. Trees, fences, and buildings form part of the land, but they are distinguished from the land itself in that they are called fixtures. Technically, a grain elevator, a stand of timber, and a large office building are all fixtures, although in the everyday language of business they are not usually called fixtures. An object that is affixed to a fixture (such as a furnace installed in a building) is also a fixture. It is in this more restricted sense that the word is often used.

General Rules for Ownership of Fixtures

Whether an object is a fixture or not may determine who owns it. Generally, an object permanently affixed to a building becomes a part of the building and of the real property itself. In a sale of land, the vendor cannot remove fixtures that were attached at the time of the contract of sale; they conveyed to the purchaser. Similarly, since fixtures belong to the landlord, a tenant cannot remove them.

In a sale of land, the purchaser and vendor usually agree between them what fixtures remain with the land. If the vendor wishes to take certain fixtures away, he expressly reserves that right in the agreement of sale, and the sale price may be adjusted accordingly. In tenancy, however, a problem may arise after the lease begins. The tenant may attach objects to the premises for his own benefit without any agreement with the landlord. A creditor may see the secured chattels transformed into fixtures when the tenant installs them into leased premises. Questions arise whether he may take them away when he vacates the premises or whether the landlord or creditor is entitled to them.

The result would be very harsh if a tenant temporarily attached valuable objects to the building, unaware of the consequences of so doing, and later discovered he could not remove them under any circumstances. In such a case the landlord would reap an unjust benefit. Understandably, the law has developed more flexible rules in these circumstances than in a sale of land. To apply the rules, we must decide, first, whether the object has become a fixture, and second, if it has become a fixture, whether it belongs to those classes of fixtures that may be removed by a tenant. The safest course of action is to negotiate the fate of tenant leasehold improvements as part of the lease.

Fixture or Not?

There is no finite definition to decide if something is a fixture also known a leasehold improvement.[35] Each situation is decided on its own facts based on the answer to a number of questions:

- Has the object been fastened to the building with the intention that it become a fixture?
- What use is to be made of it?

---

[35] *2105582 Ontario Ltd (Performance Plus Golf Academy) v 375445 Ontario Limited (Hydeaway Golf Club)*, 2017 ONCA 980 at para 40 (fixtures are the same as leasehold improvements).

- How securely and permanently is it attached?
- How much damage, if any, will be caused to the building by its removal?

A picture hanging on a hook in the wall is not a fixture. A partition nailed and bolted to the walls of the building is a fixture. But what would we conclude about the following—a table that has been bolted to the floor to prevent delicate machinery on it from being jarred; machinery bolted to the floor to prevent vibration; a display stand tacked to a wall so that it will not topple over; or a neon sign held in place by guy wires bolted to the roof of the building?

Ordinarily, objects not bolted or anchored in any way but merely resting on their own weight are presumed not to be fixtures. Objects attached in any way create a presumption that they are fixtures, although this presumption may be rebutted by asking what a reasonable person would intend when attaching the object (for instance, the display stand mentioned above). When objects are held not to be fixtures, they may be removed by the tenant at any time. If the tenant should inadvertently forget to remove them from the premises when the lease expires, they still remain the property of the tenant and may be claimed afterward.

The uncertainty can be avoided if the parties expressly agree in the lease that a particular object is to remain the property of the tenant; the agreement is conclusive.

Tenant's Fixtures

Even when it is decided that an object has become a fixture, the tenant may still have the right to remove it if he can show that either (a) it was attached for the convenience of the tenant or for the better enjoyment of the object, as when it is purely ornamental, or (b) it was a **trade fixture**—that is, an article brought onto the premises for the purpose of carrying on some trade or business, including manufacturing. These fixtures are collectively called **tenant's fixtures**. A tenant may remove them before the end of his tenancy, provided that in doing so he does not cause permanent damage to the structure of the building, and he repairs what damage is done. If, however, a tenant leaves without removing his fixtures, and the term expires, they are presumed to become part of the premises and the property of the landlord. Tenant's fixtures include only those fixtures brought onto the premises by the tenant himself. Fixtures installed by the landlord or left by preceding tenants are the landlord's property from the time of installation or from the beginning of the tenancy and may not be removed.

trade fixture an object attached to the premises for the purpose of carrying on a trade or business

tenant's fixtures trade fixtures or any other fixtures attached for the convenience of the tenant or for the better enjoyment of the object

ORAL LEASES

In most jurisdictions, when a tenant is in possession under a short-term lease of three years or less, the lease need not be in writing in order to satisfy the *Statute of Frauds*, although, of course, a written lease is advisable in any event.[36] Leases of longer than three years are usually unenforceable if they are not in writing. If, for example, a tenant enters into an oral lease for five years, and the landlord later changes her mind and refuses to let the tenant into possession, the tenant is without remedy. If, however, the tenant is already in possession and has paid rent, the doctrine of part performance, as discussed in Chapter 10 under the *Statute of Frauds*, will apply. Under the rules of equity, the court will order the landlord to give the tenant his lease in the terms originally agreed between them. A landlord too may obtain specific performance and hold the tenant bound to a long-term lease if, after taking possession, the tenant wishes to avoid the lease and vacate the premises.

---

[36] See e.g. *Statute of Frauds*, RSO 1990, c S.19, s 3, and RSNS 1989, c 442, s 3; *Carter v Irving Oil Co*, [1952] 4 DLR 128 at 131; Bentley, McNair, and Butkus, *Williams and Rhodes: Canadian Law of Landlord and Tenant*, supra note 8 at 2:1–2.

SALE OF THE LANDLORD'S INTEREST

Relationship Between a Tenant and a Purchaser of the Landlord's Interest

In a lease, a landlord grants away a right to possession of her land for a term and reserves to herself the right to possession at the end of the term—that is, the reversion. She also receives the benefit of the tenant's covenants, including the promise to pay rent. When a landlord sells land subject to a lease, she parts with both the reversion and the benefits of the covenants given by the tenant. A purchaser acquires the whole interest in the land subject to the outstanding lease and is bound to both the rights and duties of the former landlord. We may ask, "How can a purchaser receive both the rights and duties of the landlord when the tenant was not a party to the sale and there is no privity of contract between purchaser and tenant?" The answer is that the lease is more than just a contract. It also creates an interest or estate in the land, resulting in **privity of estate**. Neither landlord nor tenant can destroy the privity of estate by claiming that the original contract of lease does not bind them. Their respective interests in the land create the relationship between them. Notice of leases longer than three years should be registered with the applicable land titles registry to give prospective purchasers notice of the tenant's interest.

privity of estate the relationship between tenant and landlord created by their respective interests in the land that passes to a transferee of the interest

Privity of Contract with the Former Landlord

The creation of privity of estate with a new landlord does not bring to an end privity of contract with the former landlord. Although a landlord may sell her reversion, she still remains personally liable on her covenants to her tenant, in particular, the covenant for quiet enjoyment. If the new landlord should interfere with the covenant for quiet enjoyment in an irreparable manner, the tenant, if he chooses, may sue the original landlord in contract. He might well have to do so if the new landlord has subsequently become insolvent or has little in the way of assets. The doctrine of privity of estate is a concept of real property and does not apply to personal property.

Relationship Between a Tenant and the Landlord's Mortgagee

The leasehold estate acquired by a tenant, like other interests in real property, is valid against parties that subsequently acquire an interest in the land provided land registration requirements are met (that is, notice of lease in the land titles system). If, after leasing her land, the landlord borrows against it under a mortgage, the mortgagee's (that is, the lender's) interest will be subject to the rights of the tenant. If the mortgagor (the landlord–borrower) defaults, the mortgagee may claim the reversion but is not entitled to evict the tenant. So long as the tenant observes the terms of the lease, the mortgagee is bound by it and cannot obtain possession, except as provided under the lease.

On the other hand, when the landlord mortgages her land before leasing it, the tenant is, in theory at least, at the mercy of the mortgagee if the landlord defaults, unless the mortgagee concurred in the lease at the time it was given. However, it is almost always in the best interest of the mortgagee to collect the rent rather than put the tenant out and try to obtain a new tenant. The risk to a tenant is greater if the lease is a long-term one and if, at the time of default, the value of the premises for leasing purposes has increased substantially beyond the current rent. For this reason, it is wise for a tenant to obtain the agreement of the mortgagee before entering into a long-term lease.

The Need to Register a Long-Term Lease

To preserve priority of his leasehold interest over subsequently acquired interests, a tenant should always register notice of a long-term lease in the land registry or land title system. Otherwise, the interest may be destroyed if the landlord fraudulently sells to a bona fide purchaser without notice of the tenancy. The requirements for registration vary by province. In some provinces, leases as short as three years must be registered, whereas in others, only leases over seven years need be. Leases under three years need not be registered in any province.[37] The safest course of action is to register notice of all leases on the title to the land.

LEASEBACKS

An established company with a good record of earnings is often able to arrange financing of the acquisition of a new building by a long-term leasing device known as a **leaseback**. First, the business obtains a short-term loan, usually from a bank, to finance construction of the building. As soon as the building is completed, the business sells it to the finance company and pays off its bank loan. The finance company then leases the building back to the business. The lease is usually for a period of 20 or 25 years, with the lessee business receiving an option to renew for additional periods. The lessee business acts very much as the owner of the property rather than as a tenant, paying for all repairs, maintenance, insurance, and property taxes during the currency of the lease.

leaseback a financial arrangement enabling a business to buy a building and sell it to a financial institution that, in turn, gives a long-term lease of the property back to the business

The leaseback device has several advantages for the lessee business. First, the business has a relatively easy means of financing its expansion once a willing financial institution is found to undertake the project. Second, in terms of financing, a leaseback may be more advantageous than buying the property and mortgaging it because a mortgagee will not generally provide the full value of the project (as the leaseback does), leaving the company to raise the balance. Third, there may be tax advantages for the lessee business.

From the point of view of a lessor financial institution, rented property represents an investment of funds that not only provides regular rental revenue that includes the amortization of the cost of the property but also gives the lessor ownership of the entire property at the expiration of the lease. Any improvements in the building added by the tenant and any inflation in land values accrue to the benefit of the landlord. In addition, if the lessee business gets into financial difficulty, the legal formalities in evicting it are simpler and quicker than those required for a mortgagee to foreclose on a mortgage.

The leaseback, as compared with other leases, is a relatively long, detailed, and complex document, often carefully setting out the rights a tenant has in making alterations and adding fixtures to the building, as well as in the types of trade it may carry on. Sometimes the lessor may impose restrictions on the future borrowing of the lessee business, as a means of ensuring that it will not enter into obligations so great as to impair its ability to pay the rent.

Sometimes a leaseback includes an option for the lessee business to purchase the premises at the end of the term. The price at which the option may be exercised by the lessee may be determined in a variety of ways. It may be simply a specified sum of money, or it may be calculated by a formula taking into account, for example, whether the option is exercised at the end of the original term or the end of a renewal.

---

[37] See e.g. *Land Titles Act*, SNB 1981, c L-1.1, s 27(1); RSBC 1996, c 250, s 20(3).

RESIDENTIAL TENANCIES

Changing Needs of Residential Tenants

The demand for rental accommodation has spawned large developments of high-rise apartment buildings in most urban Canadian cities. The typical city tenant now lives in a large apartment complex and may not have even met his landlord. He has come to regard himself as a consumer of housing and to think of his relation with his landlord as based on a contract for services rather than an acquisition of an estate in land. Provincial legislation addresses the unique needs of the residential tenant with specific legislation applicable only to residential tenancies.

Ethical Issue   Discrimination

Provincial human rights legislation protects tenants and prospective tenants against discrimination based on such things as race, colour, gender, ancestry, sexual orientation, lawful source of income, and age. However, exceptions exist; for example, British Columbia allows older adults' buildings, reserved for persons over the age of 55. Ontario allows same-gender buildings, occupied by either all men or all women. Landlords are also allowed to select tenants based on income information and credit checks.

Questions to Consider

1. Do you think these protections and exceptions are enough to prevent discrimination against students?
2. Are the poor protected? Consider the role of publicly subsidized housing.

Source: *Human Rights Code*, RSBC 1996, c 210, s 10; RSO 1990, c H-19, ss 4, 21.

Legislative Protection for Tenants

Residential tenancy legislation varies considerably from province to province, but certain basic features are commonly found in most of the laws:

- Restrictions are imposed on the landlord's right to demand security deposits.
- Landlords are required to maintain the premises in a reasonable state of repair.
- Tenants are relieved from paying rent in the event of certain breaches of covenant by the landlord or if the lease contract is frustrated.
- The landlord's remedy of distress is abolished.
- The landlord has a duty to mitigate any loss caused by the tenant's breach.
- The landlord may not arbitrarily or unreasonably withhold consent to an assignment or subletting.
- It is more difficult to evict a tenant, even for non-payment of rent.
- Restrictions are imposed on the amount of rents and rent increases.
- Special tribunals and procedures have been established to deal with disputes.

As a general rule, the landlord in a residential tenancy is prohibited from requiring any security deposit in excess of one month's rent, and even that sum may only be applied to the payment of rent for the last rent period under the tenancy agreement. The landlord must also pay interest on the amount of the deposit at a specified rate.[38] Ontario requires all residential tenancies to use the same legislated standard form.[39]

---

[38] *Residential Tenancies Act, 2006*, SO 2006, c 17, ss 105, 106. The rules about security deposits vary considerably from province to province. See e.g. *Residential Tenancy Act*, SBC 2002, c 78, ss 17–22; *Residential Tenancies Act*, CCSM c R.119, ss 29–36.1.

[39] Ontario Residential Lease Template, http://www.mah.gov.on.ca/Page18704.aspx.

The legislation makes the landlord liable for maintaining residential premises in a good state of repair fit for habitation and further states that the tenant's knowledge of the lack of repair before the lease is irrelevant.[40]

In commercial tenancies, the failure of a landlord to perform her own covenants, even if they were major terms, does not release the tenant from the obligation to pay rent unless the landlord's breach amounted to an eviction of the tenant. The legislation makes some promises or covenants in a residential lease interdependent, so that breach by one party of a condition frees the other from his or her obligations.[41] Before withholding rent, a tenant should review the rules; some provinces require the rent to be deposited with the tribunal pending resolution of a dispute.

The doctrine of frustration is expressly declared to apply to residential tenancies,[42] so that a tenant is no longer liable to pay rent for the balance of the term when the premises became uninhabitable through no fault of his own or to restore the property if it was destroyed during the tenancy.

The landlord's remedy of distress has been abolished.[43] The requirements when a tenant wishes to move from the premises are eased—a landlord may not arbitrarily or unreasonably withhold consent to an assignment or subletting.[44]

Nor can a residential tenant be evicted as easily. Termination by notice to quit requires notice even for a term certain tenancy that would otherwise end without any act by either landlord or tenant.[45] In the absence of notice to quit, a tenancy is deemed to continue as a periodic tenancy. In addition, the notice period is longer in some provinces. In Ontario, for example, all tenancies other than weekly tenancies require at least 60 clear days' notice prior to the termination date, and weekly (or daily) tenancies require 28 days, on the part of both landlord and tenant.[46] Landlords are precluded from terminating tenancies and evicting tenants except for a serious breach of the lease by a tenant; or because at the end of the current lease the landlord wishes to repossess the premises for occupation by herself or her immediate family; or because the premises are going to be torn down or substantially altered in order to be used for different purposes such as conversion to commercial premises.[47]

Finally, the legislation imposes restrictions in many cases on the amount of rent that may be charged and on increasing existing rents.[48]

INTERNATIONAL ISSUE

Rent Control

Affordable housing is a necessity in a healthy community, and ensuring its supply involves balancing the interests of tenants and landlords. When housing prices or unemployment rates rise, the demand for rental units increases. In a purely supply-and-demand scenario, low vacancy rates would lead to escalating rents. Tenants might be required to move out at the end of their term unless they were willing to pay large (unaffordable) rent increases. As a result, it is common for provinces to fix the amount of rent that can be charged or limit the amount of any rent increase. The distinction between these two controls is made clear by reviewing the history of rent controls in Ontario. Prior to 1998, the

---

[40] Ibid.; SBC 2002, c 78, s 32; CSSM c R.119, s 59; SO 2006, c 17, s 20.

[41] SBC 2002, c 78, ss 45, 47; SO 2006, c 17, ss 12(4).

[42] SBC 2002, c 78, s 92; CSSM, c R.119, s 105; SO 2006, c 17, s 19.

[43] SBC 2002, c 78, s 26; CSSM c R.119, s 192; SO 2006, c 17, s 40.

[44] SBC 2002, c 78, s 34; CSSM c R.119, s 43; SO 2006, c 17, s 95.

[45] See e.g. SBC 2002, c 78, s 57; SO 2006, c 17, s 47.

[46] SO 2006, c 17, ss 44(1), (2) and (3).

[47] SO 2006, c 17, ss 48, 49, 50.

[48] SBC 2002, c 78, s 41; CSSM c R.119, ss 117, 118; SO 2006, c 17, ss 110–36.

Ontario rent control system established a baseline legal rent for each existing or new rental unit.[49] Thereafter, only annual rent increases were allowed at the prescribed percentage (tied to the consumer price index). This cap on rent increases applied regardless of any change in tenant. Since 1998, the system provides protection from unreasonable rent increases only to existing or continuing tenants (subject to some exceptions). When a new tenant rents the unit, the landlord may set a new rent based upon market conditions, without regard to past rental rates or increases.[50] In 2017, Ontario removed a previous rent control exemption applicable to buildings built after 1991.

In the United States, rent control is implemented at the municipal level in accordance with governing state legislation. As of 2003, only 125 cities had some form of rent control, including New York, San Francisco, Washington DC, and Los Angeles. Several states have banned rent control entirely, including Florida and Illinois. In 1995, California restricted rent control protection to existing and continuing tenants. In 2008, California voters defeated a proposition that would have abolished rent control entirely.

The worldwide trend is mixed: Both China and Japan have eliminated rent control, whereas countries in the Middle East seem to be embracing it. Dubai and Qatar implemented new rent control programs in 2005 and 2007, respectively.

Questions to Consider

1. What are the arguments for and against rent control?
2. Why is Ontario's current stabilization system hailed by some as a fair compromise?

Sources: Prince Christian Cruz, "The Pros and Cons of Rent Control," Global Property Guide, January 19, 2009, www.globalpropertyguide.com/investment-analysis/The-pros-and-cons-of-rent-control (accessed April 17, 2018); Peter Dreier, "Californians Defend Rent Control," Rooflines, June 5, 2008 www.rooflines.org/941/californians_defend_rent_control (accessed April 17, 2018).

Strategies to Manage the Legal Risks

In commercial tenancies, the interests of landlords and tenants and their respective creditors often conflict. Priority is usually determined by the wording of the covenants in the lease, the contents of the credit agreement, and the timing of notice and registration under land titles and personal property systems. Therefore, careful attention needs to be paid to all of these steps.

From the tenant's perspective, ownership of goods, trade fixtures, and leasehold improvements should be spelled out in the lease. Options to renew or terminate should also be established, as well as the right to assign any unexpired term. This gives the tenant the maximum amount of flexibility for the expansion, stability, or relocation of their business. However, tenants should remember when assigning a lease that they remain liable to the landlord if the assignee defaults or goes bankrupt. Since a tenant does not have a common law right to withhold rent for breaches by the landlord, the lease should designate specific incidents that suspend the obligation to pay rent, including destruction or damage to the premises.

When considering multi-unit locations, the tenant should focus on two key concerns. First, the additional rent charged for the share of maintenance and operation of the entire development is often more complicated than traditional rent. Careful attention to the formula for its calculation can save money. The second issue relates to the presence of competing businesses; an exclusivity clause restricting the landlord from renting to competitors is fundamentally important to the success of the location. The exclusion should be as broad as possible to give the tenant the greatest flexibility in his business model. Finally, with respect to all leases, multi- or single unit, notice of lease should be registered within the provincial land titles system so that all prospective purchasers and mortgagees have prior notice of the tenant's leasehold interest.

---

[49] *Rent Control Act 1992*, SO 1992, c 11, replaced by the *Tenant Protection Act*, SO 1997, c 24. Landlords could apply for permission to increase rents above guidelines in prescribed circumstances.

[50] *Residential Tenancies Act, 2006*, SO 2006, c 17, ss 110–36 (maximum 2.5 percent increase).

From the landlord's perspective, the two greatest concerns are payment of rent and care of the premises. If the tenant should go bankrupt, the rights of the landlord to deal with the unexpired term or to distrain goods are supplanted to those of the trustee. Any clause purporting to end the lease due solely to the bankruptcy of the tenant is void. However, other triggers for options to terminate, such as the tenant ceasing to carry on business at the premises, are enforceable and may give the landlord the opportunity to end the lease prior to the trustee assuming control. When faced with an absconding tenant, the landlord should proceed cautiously, depending upon the desire to terminate the tenancy or not. Legal advice should be sought. Obligations to mitigate vary. With respect to care of the premises, precise notice obligations should be imposed on the tenant to advise of deterioration at its earliest indication.

Creditors of both landlords and tenants must be aware that the right to seize and sell the financed asset, whether it is the landlord's land or the tenant's goods, may be displaced by rights under the lease. Goods of the tenant may become attached to the landlord's land as fixtures. A landlord's right to distrain may take precedence over the creditor. Reserving title to the goods in the creditor's name until the full purchase price is paid will help to give the creditor priority. Registration of the credit agreement under the provincial personal property system (discussed in Chapter 28) is vitally important.

Mortgagees of the landlord may also be subordinate to the interests of a commercial tenancy shorter than three years, even if it is not registered on title. Taking an assignment of rents for the mortgaged premises in all cases of mortgaging commercial property will ensure that rents can be applied to delinquent mortgage payments of the landlord. Notice of assignment of rents should be registered on the land title so new tenants have notice.

QUESTIONS FOR REVIEW

1. Define *tenancy at will, term certain, overholding tenant, subletting, eviction, forfeiture, surrender,* and *quiet enjoyment.*
2. What are the risks for a tenant if he limits his right to exclusive possession of the premises? Explain.
3. Should a leasehold interest be shown as an asset (with an equal and offsetting liability) on the balance sheet of a business? If so, at what amount?
4. Describe the difficulty caused by the strict covenant to pay rent as it relates to frustration in contract law.
5. What are the concerns of a landlord with respect to a tenant's right to assign the remainder of a leasehold interest?
6. Lewis owns a five-bedroom house next to his own home in Niagara-on-the-Lake and rents it to Tessa for three years. Tessa then applies for a licence to operate a bed-and-breakfast on the premises. Lewis objects to such use of the house. Would he have any legal recourse against Tessa?
7. Describe the usual responsibilities of a landlord for repairs when a tenant leases only part of a building. How does this situation differ from a lease of an entire building?
8. Turner rented a store from Lauren on the ground floor of a multi-story building as an art gallery to sell paintings and small statues. Turner's hours of business were normal retail business hours. A few months later, Lauren leased the adjoining store to Rockbar Inc. It played very loud music from noon until Turner's closing time. The music, especially the thumping sounds, could be heard clearly in Turner's store and interfered with normal conversation. Does Turner have any remedies?

9. How would you suggest that responsibility for insuring the premises be allocated in a large shopping mall? Describe the most difficult aspects of the problem.
10. What is the dilemma for the landlord when a tenant abandons the premises during the term of the lease?
11. Describe the landlord's duty to mitigate after a tenant abandons the premises.
12. In what way may a tenant be in a difficult position when the premises burn down, even if the lease states that the rent is suspended until the premises are rebuilt?
13. What property is exempt from a landlord's right to distrain?
14. Under the common law, how long a period of notice must be given to terminate a yearly tenancy? What is the meaning of "clear" as it relates to notice?
15. Oscar leased Blackacre from Brenda for five years at a monthly rent of $1200. Neither of them seemed to notice when the lease had expired. For several months, Oscar continued to pay his rent on the first day of each month. Brenda now needs to take possession of Blackacre for a large construction project. How much notice must she give to Oscar?
16. Explain the importance of renewal clauses in business leases.
17. How is the relationship of a tenant affected by his landlord's sale of her interest to a purchaser? What is the nature of the new relationship?
18. Stroll leases a warehouse for a term certain of five years. During the second year of the lease, the landlord, Vernon, mortgages the land. At the end of the fifth year of the lease, Stroll and Vernon enter into another lease for a further five years. Explain the difference, if any, in Stroll's position in the first term and in the second term insofar as the mortgage is concerned.
19. (a) What are three characteristics that make leaseback arrangements attractive to lessee businesses?
    (b) What are the characteristics that make them attractive to lessor financial institutions?
20. Describe briefly the reasons for treating residential tenancies differently from commercial tenancies.

CASES AND PROBLEMS

1. Continuing Scenario

    Ashley is approached by a land developer about opening a third location in the new strip mall being constructed in a subdivision on the edge of Ottawa. The developer is offering her a great deal on reduced rent for two years and customized premises because he is having trouble attracting tenants as the surrounding area is still under construction with few residents in occupancy. Ashley has the draft lease documents to review—what additional terms should be inserted into the lease to address the following concerns?

    - The area may not have the population base to sustain enough business for the restaurant to be profitable; a restaurant should have a significant following once it has been open for six months.
    - If she is able to attract a clientele, she does not want to face large rent increases or be forced to move at the end of one term just as she is building a reputation.
    - The developer may be so desperate for tenants that he will rent to anyone—undesirable tenants would be veterinary clinics, walk-in medical clinics, and hair salons as well as other competing restaurants.
    - The developer is offering to customize the space with all the improvements Ashley usually does for herself—upholstered benches, walk-in refrigerator, and custom signage. These are items she would want to re-use in another location if this spot does not work out.

2. Ms. Bone, the owner of a downtown block of stores, rented one of them to Mr. Bull, who opened a retail china shop on the premises. Bull's tenancy was from year to year. He had a number of display cases built with glass doors to keep their fragile contents out of the reach of curious customers. The cases were secured to the wall by three-centimetre nails. Bull also purchased and installed heavy-duty air-conditioning equipment, which was connected to the water supply and anchored to the floor.

    Several years later, Bull was adjudged bankrupt on a petition of his creditors. At the time, he owed Bone $3600 for three months' rent. The trustee in bankruptcy remained in possession of the store pending liquidation of the business assets. The trustee claimed the display cases and air conditioner for the benefit of Bull's general creditors, but Bone claimed them as lessor of the store.

    Discuss the respective rights of Bone and of the trustee in bankruptcy.

3. Kruger leased a warehouse to Pool Corp. for a fixed term of eight months at a rent of $3000 per month, commencing January 1 and expiring August 31. Pool did not move out on August 31 and tendered its cheque for $3000 to pay the rent for September. It was accepted by Kruger. On October 1, Pool's manager appeared at Kruger's office with another cheque for $3000. Kruger said he had inspected the warehouse and was disappointed by the rough treatment the building was receiving from Pool's employees. When the manager replied that he could hardly expect otherwise in a busy operation, Kruger stated it was not worth his while to rent it under those conditions unless he received at least $4000 per month. The manager refused to pay that much and tendered the company's cheque for $3000. Kruger refused the cheque and ordered Pool to "clear out of the warehouse at once." The manager left and mailed the cheque to Kruger, who simply held it and did not cash it.

    On November 1, Kruger called Pool by telephone and asked if the company would pay $4000. The manager replied, "No." Kruger said that he was at the end of his patience and had given Pool a full month to reconsider. He sent a bailiff to evict Pool that very day, cashed its cheque for the previous month, and sent it a demand for "the $1000 still owing."

    Pool was forced to move its stock to a more expensive warehouse at once and suffered some damage to its goods when they were moved into the street by the bailiff. It sued Kruger for losses of $8000 caused by the eviction. Should it succeed? Give reasons for your opinion.

4. Rogers, a dance teacher, was looking for space to operate a dance studio. She visited premises on the second floor of Hart's building four times with other people who concluded that the premises were suitable for the purposes intended. Rogers signed a lease, and with Hart's approval, she installed a special dance floor, cabinets, dance bars, and mirrors and did painting and electrical work, including installation of light fixtures. She then began her classes.

    Hart immediately noticed that the building began to vibrate. Within 24 hours he had a special beam installed, but the vibrating continued. Hart hired a structural engineer at once to examine the building. The engineer concluded that the vibration was caused by harmonic pressure created by the coordinated movement of the dancers. He stated that the vibration could not be avoided by structural changes, and it could ultimately cause the building or parts of it to collapse. Hart worried about the safety of the patrons of the restaurant situated under the dance studio, as well as of Rogers herself and her students. Three days after classes had begun, he told Rogers that the classes had to stop.

    Rogers immediately began to look for new premises and took the position that, by preventing her from continuing dance classes, Hart terminated the lease without notice. She sued Hart for damages for the cost of all the improvements she had made, the cost of moving, and general damages for loss of business.

She argued that, because the defect in the premises was latent and did not become apparent until after she had begun the dance lessons, it was unreasonable to ask her to ensure the soundness and safety of the premises. It was Hart's problem as landlord to deal with.

Give your opinion of Rogers's claims and whether they should succeed.

5. Allgate Realties Ltd. constructed a new building suitable for a restaurant in a suburb of Calgary. Streeter, the manager, invited Kratinsky to examine it. Kratinsky already owned and operated a restaurant in the city and was hesitant. Streeter assured him that the suburb was growing rapidly, with new businesses about to open as well as new housing developments being built. He offered Kratinsky a five-year lease, including a sale to him of the building at the end of the lease. Kratinsky finally accepted; he opened the restaurant three months later.

Almost no new construction took place in the area; the restaurant was isolated, and business was very poor. Within six months, Kratinsky closed the restaurant and refused to pay further rent, claiming that Allgate had made serious misrepresentations and was in breach of the contract. Allgate responded that there were no covenants in the lease referring to future development in the area and that Kratinsky remained bound by the lease and sale of the property.

Whose argument do you think will prevail?

6. Ivan Drugs Inc., a drugstore chain, leased premises from Hay Investments Ltd. in its shopping mall. The lease was for 10 years, at a "base" rent of $46 200 per year in monthly installments of $3850, plus Ivan's share of the taxes, insurance, and common expenses of the mall. Ivan also agreed to pay an additional 6 percent of gross annual sales as rent, to the extent that its gross sales exceeded $770 000 for the year ($46 200 represents 6 percent of $770 000). The lease also contained a usual covenant allowing Ivan to assign the lease with consent of Hay.

In the first three years, Ivan's sales exceeded $1 500 000, and it duly paid the additional sums to Hay. However, during the third year a much larger shopping mall was opened across the street from Hay's mall. Ivan, fearing its sales at the current location would suffer, leased larger premises at the new mall and moved from its old premises, leaving them vacant. Ivan continued to pay the "base" rent and its share of the taxes, insurance, and common expenses but paid no additional rent based on its sales in the new mall.

Partly as a result of receiving diminished rent, Hay was unable to obtain extensions of its mortgages or new financing for the mall and was in financial difficulty. Hay served notice on Ivan to enforce the original agreement according to its terms and to pay rent based on sales that could be attributed to Ivan's business if it had remained in Hay's mall. Hay Investments Ltd. asserted that Ivan Drugs Inc. had impliedly promised to carry on business for the full term of the lease.

Give your opinion of the validity of Hay's claim and what you think the result should be.

7. Frost Investments Limited owned three adjoining buildings downtown that it rented to various tenants as office space. All three buildings were heated centrally from a single heating plant in Building No. 1. The Generous Loan Company occupied offices in Building No. 3 under a lease in which the lessor, Frost, covenanted to maintain the heat continuously above 15 degrees Celsius from October 1 to May 24, except for weekends. In January, a serious fire occurred in Building No. 2, breaking the heating connections between Buildings No. 1 and No. 3. The damage was so serious that Frost decided to demolish Building No. 2 and rebuild.

In the meantime, Generous Loan Company suffered a significant drop in business because of very low temperatures in its offices. It eventually vacated the premises and leased other quarters at a higher rent. It then sued Frost, claiming damages of $1750 for the additional amount of rent it had to pay the new landlord for what otherwise would have been the balance of the term of its lease with Frost and

$6000 for its estimated loss of profits. Frost counterclaimed for rent for the balance of the term of the lease, seven months at $2150 per month. What do you think the decision should be?

8. Tagom rented a service station from Oil Can Limited for a term of 12 months, commencing July 1, at a rent of $975 per month payable on the first day of each month. The lease contained the following clause:

> If the lessee shall hold over after the term . . . the resulting tenancy shall be a tenancy from month to month and not a tenancy from year to year, subject to all the terms, conditions, and agreements herein contained insofar as same may be applicable to a tenancy from month to month.

On May 28 of the following year, Oil Can sent Tagom a notice stating that he must give vacant possession on the expiry of the lease. On June 30, Oil Can representatives visited Tagom and asked him what he intended to do. He replied that he would not leave the premises "peacefully." Tagom remained in possession on July 1 and sent a cheque by registered mail to Oil Can as rent for that month. Although the area superintendent had given instructions to the accounting department not to accept any rent from Tagom, a junior clerk deposited it in the company bank account. Soon afterward, a senior officer discovered the error, informed Tagom that the act of the clerk in accepting the cheque had been inadvertent and against instructions, and delivered a refund cheque from the company to Tagom for $975. Tagom returned the cheque.

Was a new tenancy created, or could Oil Can obtain a court order for immediate possession?

Chapter 23
Mortgages of Land and Real Estate Transactions

- **THE ESSENCE OF MORTGAGE LAW**
- **RIGHTS OF THE MORTGAGEE AND MORTGAGOR**
- **THE MORTGAGEE'S REMEDIES UPON DEFAULT**
- **SALE BY A MORTGAGOR OF HIS INTEREST**
- **SECOND MORTGAGES**
- **MORTGAGEE'S RIGHTS COMPARED WITH RIGHTS OF OTHER CREDITORS**
- **TRANSFERRING A MORTGAGEE'S INTEREST IN LAND**
- **PROVINCIAL VARIATIONS**
- **REVERSE MORTGAGES**
- **MORTGAGE FRAUD**
- **A TYPICAL REAL ESTATE TRANSACTION**
- **STRATEGIES TO MANAGE THE LEGAL RISKS**

Mortgages play a central role in financing land purchases. In this chapter we discuss the nature of mortgages, the rights and obligations of both lenders and borrowers, and the steps in a typical real estate transaction.

In this chapter we examine such questions as:

- What is a mortgage, and what are the important mortgage terms?
- What are the rights of the mortgagor and mortgagee?
- What remedies are available to the mortgagee?
- What is a "second mortgage," and how is it used?
- In what ways are a mortgagee's rights different from those of other creditors?

- What is an "offer to purchase"?
- What are the usual steps in a real estate transaction?
- What is the process of "closing" the transaction?

THE ESSENCE OF MORTGAGE LAW

The Mortgage as a Contract

A **mortgage** document creates two things: an interest in land and a loan contract containing a number of important terms.[1] The most important terms are the **mortgagor**'s (borrower's) personal promise to pay off the debt and the **mortgagee**'s (lender's) promise to discharge its interest in the land upon repayment. The most important promises of the mortgagor are:

(a) to pay the principal debt and accrued interest, either at the **maturity date** or in installments as agreed by the parties,[2]

(b) to keep the property adequately insured in the name of the mortgagee,

(c) to pay taxes on the land and buildings, and

(d) to keep the premises in a reasonable state of repair.

Interest charged on the principal sum is expressed as an annual percentage rate, and the mortgage specifies the **calculation period**—stages when interest is added to the principal. Periodic payments are usually required, and they are commonly a blend of interest and principal. The amount of each payment is determined by the **amortization period**—the maximum length of time it should take to repay the entire debt (interest and principal). Spreading the debt over a longer amortization period reduces the size of each periodic payment but increases the total amount of the debt. The interest rate is set for a specific time period—typically much shorter than the amortization period—that is known as the **term** of the mortgage. At the expiration of the term, the mortgage must be paid off, renewed at a new agreed-upon interest rate, or refinanced with a new mortgagee. Together, these provisions establish the financial arrangement for the mortgage loan. They are first described in the **mortgage commitment** letter, in which the parties initially agree to borrow and lend.

Mortgages almost always contain an **acceleration clause**, which states that upon default of any installment, the whole of the principal sum of the mortgage and accrued interest immediately comes due. Default accelerates the maturity date, and the mortgagee may pursue all its remedies.

The most important promises of the mortgagee are:

(a) to execute the necessary discharge of the mortgage upon repayment in full, and

(b) to leave the mortgagor in possession and not interfere with his use and enjoyment of the mortgaged premises so long as the mortgagor observes all his covenants.

The mortgagor signs the mortgage, and the mortgagee merely accepts the document without signing it. Since the mortgagee's promises are set out as provisos or standard charge terms—some are simply implied by the common law and statutory principles of mortgage law—its acceptance of the document binds it to the mortgage terms.

mortgage a loan contract that gives the lender an interest in the borrower's land as security for a debt

mortgagor a borrower who gives his lender an interest in his land as security for repayment of a debt

mortgagee a lender who accepts an interest in land as security for a loan

maturity date the end of the term when debt must be repaid

calculation period stages at which accrued interest is added to principal

amortization period length of time it should take to repay an entire debt with the specified payment schedule

term the time period during which an interest rate is fixed and principal lent

mortgage commitment document in which parties to a mortgage initially agree to borrow and lend

acceleration clause upon default in a payment the entire principal sum accrued interest comes due immediately

---

[1] *Leatherman v 0969708 BC Ltd*, 2018 BCCA 33 (different limitation periods may run for mortgage and debt).

[2] Except in Alberta and Saskatchewan, where a mortgagor cannot be sued personally for the mortgage debt. See provincial variations, *infra* note 8.

Although some mortgages are private transactions between two individuals, most real estate mortgage lending to individual borrowers is done by financial institutions—insurance companies, trust companies, and banks.

The Mortgage as an Interest in Land

The concept of the mortgage as an interest in land developed through case law and is now summarized in provincial legislation. Originally, a mortgage was an actual conveyance of the **legal title** to a fee simple interest in land by the mortgagor to the mortgagee as security for a debt. The transfer of title had two conditions: first, that the mortgagor could remain in possession of land as long as payments were up to date, and second, that the mortgagor was entitled to have the legal title returned to him upon full payment of the debt. However, if the appointed day passed without the debt being repaid, the conditions then expired, and the mortgagee owned the interest absolutely.

legal title an interest in land recognized by the common law

The Mortgagor's Right to Redeem

It seemed unfair to allow a mortgagee to keep title to land in situations where only a small amount of the debt remained unpaid. The courts of equity created a remedy for these cases of hardship. If the mortgagor pled hardship and tendered payment of the debt in full, the court would acknowledge his interest in the land and permit him to **redeem** it. It would order the mortgagee to reconvey the land to the mortgagor. This right to redeem obtained by the mortgagor from a court of equity is known as the **equity of redemption**, and it is often called simply "the equity." This is the source of the modern business term "equity," meaning the interest of the proprietors of a business in its total assets after allowing for mortgagees' claims.

redeem have the land reconveyed to the mortgagor

equity of redemption the right of the mortgagor to redeem mortgaged land on payment of the debt in full

The Mortgagee's Right to Foreclose

The courts of equity also recognized that limits needed to be placed on a mortgagor's equity of redemption. A mortgagor should not be entitled to redeem his property years later, after the mortgagee had significantly improved the land. The courts agreed that after a reasonable period of time had passed, the right to redeem the property should expire and the mortgagee could then safely treat the land as his own. The foreclosure period became generally accepted as six months from the date of the hearing in the case. Provincial mortgage legislation now establishes minimum time periods within which a defaulting mortgagor may redeem, after which his interest is foreclosed.

Why Mortgagees Rarely Take Possession
Although a mortgagee can take possession upon default of the mortgagor, in practice, a mortgagee rarely does so until after it has obtained **foreclosure**. There are exceptions, such as when it believes that the mortgagor has no intention of trying to redeem, when the property is vacant, or when the premises become dilapidated. There are three main reasons for not going into possession:

foreclosure an order by a court ending the mortgagor's right to redeem within a fixed time

- First, a mortgagee generally wants its money rather than the mortgagor's property, and it would prefer to encourage the mortgagor to pay off the debt.
- Second, its possession would be uncertain, since the mortgagor might at any moment tender payment, redeem his interest, and demand possession.
- Third, it must account for any benefit it receives from occupation of the land and deduct it from the amount owing if the mortgagor tenders payment, losing any material advantage gained from taking possession.

Land Titles System

The land titles system, created through provincial legislation, has changed the legal nature of a mortgagee's interest in land. Under the land titles system (which is being used in most areas across Canada, as discussed in Chapter 21), a mortgage is called a **charge**, a mortgagor is a **chargor**, and a mortgagee is a **chargee**.[3] Charges are no longer, strictly speaking, conveyances of the legal title. Rather, they are liens or encumbrances recorded on the title to the land, for which the ordinary remedy is to force a sale of the land and then apply the proceeds toward repayment of the debt.[4] Despite this significant legal distinction, basic mortgage procedure and remedies remain mostly unchanged. Chargors execute a charge document containing the terms of the loan and a personal promise to pay, remain in possession of the land, and, upon payment in full, are entitled to a discharge of the charge. If there is default, the chargee is given the right to dispossess the chargor, foreclose his interest, and sell the property. The chargor still has a "redemption period" during which he may tender full payment of the debt and stop the foreclosure or sale of the property.[5] The mortgagee's remedies are discussed more fully below.

charge a lien or encumbrance on land

chargor mortgagor

chargee mortgagee

Registration

A mortgage or charge must be registered in the appropriate registry or land titles system, as discussed in Chapter 21. Its paper document is converted to electronic form that identifies the parties and the land involved. The priority of the mortgage interest is determined by the order of registration.[6] Consequently, if a mortgagee fails to register its mortgage, a subsequent purchaser will be unaware of the mortgage and will acquire title free from it. Similarly, a subsequent mortgagee has priority over an earlier mortgage if it registered first. Failure to register may result in the complete loss of the land as security, although the mortgagor's personal covenant to pay would still survive. Registration of the mortgage is public notice of its existence.

RIGHTS OF THE MORTGAGEE AND MORTGAGOR

The Mortgagee

Although the courts of common law and equity are merged, and most registry systems have been converted to land titles, the interests of the mortgagee and mortgagor are still interpreted according to the remedies and principles developed before the merger.[7] If the mortgagor defaults on any of the terms of the mortgage, the mortgagee has the following remedies:

(a) It may sue the mortgagor on his personal covenant to repay, just as any creditor may sue any debtor who is in default, and obtain a personal judgment against him in most provinces.

(b) It may dispossess the mortgagor and occupy the land itself (or put in a tenant). As noted above, this is not an attractive remedy until after foreclosure.

---

[3] Mortgages throughout Ontario, including those regions under the registry system, have been converted to charges and no longer represent legal title to the land: *Land Registration Reform Act*, RSO 1990, c L-4, ss 1, 6.

[4] *Land Titles Act*, RSA 2000, c L-4, ss 1(e), 1(o), 103.

[5] *Land Registration Reform Act*, *supra* note 3, s 6(3).

[6] See e.g. Alberta *Land Titles Act*, *supra* note 4, s 14.

[7] The old terminology concerning legal and equitable title, rights, and remedies remains in common use.

(c) It may sell the land under its contractual or statutory power of sale and apply the proceeds to pay the debt, as explained below.

(d) It may proceed with a court action for foreclosure and eventually destroy the mortgagor's right to redeem and, usually, the mortgagee's right to sue on the personal covenant as well.[8]

A mortgagee frequently chooses a combination of these remedies.[9]

The Mortgagor

The rights of a mortgagor after default are as follows:

(a) He may repay the mortgage loan together with interest and all expenses incurred by the mortgagee at any time, up to and including the date of the order of foreclosure, and obtain a release of his land.

(b) He may obtain an accounting for any benefits obtained from the land by the mortgagee and deduct them from the amount owing on redemption.

(c) If sued on his covenant to repay after foreclosure, he may require the mortgagee to prove that it is ready and able to reconvey the land upon repayment.

(d) If sued on his covenant to repay after sale of the property under power of sale, he may attack the sale price or sale expenses as unreasonable and have the amount outstanding reduced.

(e) He may also obtain relief against the consequences of an acceleration clause. If he pays all prior accrued payments, performs all other terms of which he may have been in default, and pays all costs incurred by the mortgagee, a court will permit him to continue to make regular payments under the original terms of the mortgage.[10]

(f) He may ask a court to stop the foreclosure proceedings and hold a sale instead (as discussed below).

THE MORTGAGEE'S REMEDIES UPON DEFAULT

There are advantages and disadvantages to each of the various remedies listed above. In this section, we examine the basic procedures, benefits, and drawbacks of the primary remedies.

Foreclosure

The process of obtaining foreclosure consists of three stages:

- Upon default, the mortgagee goes to court and asks for an order setting a time limit within which the mortgagor can redeem.

---

[8] See e.g. British Columbia, Alberta, Manitoba, and Saskatchewan, where a final order of foreclosure extinguishes the right to sue on the personal covenant of the mortgagor: *Property Law Act*, RSBC 1996, c 377, s 32; *Law of Property Act*, RSA 2000, c L-7, s 40; *Mortgage Act*, CCSM c M200, s 16; *Limitation of Civil Rights Act*, RSS 1978, c L-16, ss 2(1)–(2), 6. In Ontario, a mortgagee may only sue on the covenant after foreclosure if it is in a position to reconvey the property to the debtor: *Price v Letros*, [1973] OJ No 2260 at paras 7–9 (ONCA); *L-Jalco Holdings Inc v Marino*, [2011] OJ No 419 at paras 67–73, aff'd 2011 ONCA 639.

[9] There are rules about how or in what order the remedies may be enforced. For example, a judge may stop a foreclosure and turn it into a sale: *Law and Equity Act*, RSBC 1996, c 253, s 15; *Real Property Act*, RSPEI 1988, c R-3, s 72.

[10] *Mortgages Act*, RSO 1990, c M.40, ss 22(1), 23(1); Alberta *Law of Property Act*, *supra* note 8, s 38.

- Once the redemption period has expired, the court issues a final order of foreclosure that ends any further claim of the mortgagor and the claims of any other subsequent registered interests.
- Upon registration of the final order of foreclosure, the mortgagee is recognized as the owner of the property.

As the owner of the property, the mortgagee is deemed to accept the land in full satisfaction of the debt; it no longer has any right to demand payment.[11] Most mortgagees do not want to be landowners. Therefore, foreclosure is an attractive remedy only when the value of the property is high and the amount of the debt is low. However, in these circumstances, the mortgagor is likely to redeem.

In some provinces (discussed below), if a mortgagee starts a foreclosure action and the mortgagor believes the land is worth more than his mortgage debt, the mortgagor or any other subsequent secured creditor may ask the court to hold a sale instead.[12]

Sale by the Court

A mortgagee may request that the land be sold under the supervision of the court (or in some of the western provinces, under the supervision of the registrar of titles), with the sale to be either by tender or by auction.[13] Some jurisdictions permit the mortgagee or its agent to bid; others prohibit such bidding. The sale must be advertised for a specified period and carried out according to provincial statutes and regulations. In some jurisdictions, the court or registrar sets a reserve price below which no tenders will be accepted. The reserve price is not disclosed. When the tenders are opened, the highest one is accepted if it is over the reserve price. If no bid is above the reserve price, then the land remains unsold and the mortgagee may resort to its other remedies.

When a sale produces a successful bid, the mortgagee is entitled to recover the principal sum owing, accrued interest, and expenses of the court action and the sale. If the sale produces a smaller sum, the mortgagee may obtain judgment against the mortgagor for the deficiency. If the sale is for a larger sum, the surplus is returned to the mortgagor or her other secured creditors of the land.

Sale by the Mortgagee

Most mortgages—and, in some jurisdictions, the statutes governing mortgages—give the mortgagee a contractual and statutory **power of sale** that may be exercised privately without court action or supervision, although advance notice to the mortgagor is generally required. A mortgagee may exercise its power of sale at any time after default, subject to any statutory period of grace. By completing the proper transfer document and outlining the power of sale process, the mortgagee may validly transfer the title to the land to any third party. The sale must, however, be a genuine sale and not a fraud upon the mortgagor. A mortgagee may not sell to itself either directly or through an agent. Whenever a mortgagee exercises a power of sale, it is under a duty to take reasonable steps to obtain a fair price for the land. If the mortgagor can show that the mortgagee sold for an unreasonably low price, the court will reduce the deficiency accordingly or give the mortgagor judgment for any surplus she should have received.

power of sale a right upon default to sell mortgaged land

---

[11] Some provinces allow an action on the personal covenant if the mortgagee still has the property: *supra* note 8. Proceeding on separate security such as a chattel mortgage or security agreement may still be possible: *Aros Investments Ltd v Picchi*, 2003 BCSC 78.

[12] BC *Law and Equity Act*, *supra* note 9, s 15; PEI *Real Property Act*, *supra* note 9, s 72.

[13] Alberta *Law of Property Act*, *supra* note 8, s 40.

The same rules concerning the proceeds of a sale apply here as in a sale by the court. If there is a deficiency, the mortgagee may still sue the mortgagor for the sum; if there is a surplus, it must be returned to the mortgagor or to the remaining secured creditors.

INTERNATIONAL ISSUE

Mortgage Crisis

Over the past two decades, the United States experienced a major crisis in its mortgage industry. Homeowners defaulted on residential mortgages in record numbers, and the resulting explosion in power-of-sale and foreclosure proceedings created a glut in the real estate market and a decline in housing prices. The National Consumer Law Center reports that between 1980 and 2005, American foreclosures increased almost 300 percent, while home ownership increased by only 5 percent. The *Los Angeles Times* reported a record 47 171 foreclosures in California during the first quarter of 2008, more than four times as many as in the first quarter of 2007. By May 2011, one in every 103 housing units in Nevada was in foreclosure.

Some factors contributing to the high number of defaults were

- loans given to borrowers with poor credit,
- misleading lending terms that included low interest-only payments to start (teaser rates) with large balloon payments of principal required at the end of the term, and
- mortgages with no down payments, or fully financed housing purchases.

As a result, homeowners found themselves with mortgages they could not afford to maintain after the initial low-interest term. They could not refinance due to falling real estate values, and they could not sell because too many other homes were already for sale at low prices.

Suggested legislative initiatives to ease the crisis and prevent future instability in the mortgage market include the following:

- regulating lending criteria
- restricting predatory lending practices
- extending low "teaser" rates
- altering foreclosure and power-of-sale procedures to provide greater protection for mortgagors

Possible changes to foreclosure and power-of-sale procedures include the following:

- longer redemption periods
- restrictions on possession rights
- expanded defences available to mortgagors

In 2011, the foreclosure rates were still paralyzing economic recovery, and attorneys general in several states were investigating the foreclosure practices of lenders after documentation discrepancies and inaccurate calculation of indebtedness were reported.

Canadian banking and tax regulations may have protected Canada's housing market from the American crisis of 2008. In 2018, concern over house price inflation, primarily in Toronto and Vancouver, led Canada's federal banking regulator to raise lending requirements to make it more difficult for new purchasers to qualify for high ratio mortgages from federally regulated banks and financial institutions.[14]

Questions to Consider

1. What measures do you think best protect both mortgagors and mortgagees?
2. In this market, which remedy best protects a mortgagee?
3. Is it possible that the U.S. income tax rule that allows homeowners to deduct mortgage interest from taxable income contributed to the foreclosure crisis? Why?

Sources: Peter Y Hong, "Foreclosures in State Hit Record," *Los Angeles Times*, April 23, 2008, http://articles.latimes.com/2008/apr/23/business/fi-foreclose23; FEDERAL RESERVE SYSTEM, 12 CFR Part 226, Regulation Z; Docket No. R-1305, Truth in Lending; August 18, 2007 https://www.federalreserve.gov/boarddocs/meetings/2008/20080714/draftfedreg.pdf; Ruth Simon and Nick Timiraos, "California and Illinois Expand Foreclosure Probe," *Wall Street Journal*, May 26, 2011, available at http://online.wsj.com/article/SB10001424052702304066504576345422453284118.html; Pam Bennett, "The Aftermath of the Great Recession: Financially Fragile Families and How Professionals Can Help," The Forum for Family and Consumer Issues NC State University, http://ncsu.edu/ffci/publications/2012/v17-n1-2012-spring/bennett.php.

---

[14] Office of the Superintendent of Financial Institutions, Residential Mortgage Underwriting Practices and Procedures, Effective January 1, 2018, http://www.osfi-bsif.gc.ca/Eng/fi-if/rg-ro/gdn-ort/gl-ld/Pages/b20_dft.aspx.

SALE BY A MORTGAGOR OF HIS INTEREST

Financial Arrangements

A mortgagor struggling to keep up with mortgage payments may need or want to sell his property before the maturity date. A mortgagor may transfer the property to a new purchaser, but the existing mortgage must be dealt with as part of the financial arrangements between the two.

ILLUSTRATION 23.1   Sale with Outstanding Mortgage

BCD Trust Co. has a $100 000 mortgage on Adam's farm. If Adam sells the farm to Rona for $160 000, how is the price to be paid by Rona?

There are three possibilities:

- First, Rona may pay Adam the full $160 000 and obtain an undertaking from Adam that he will pay off the mortgage to BCD Trust Co. This is high risk.
- Second, Rona may pay $60 000 to Adam for Adam's equity of redemption and a further $100 000 to BCD Trust Co. in full payment of the mortgage.
- Third, Rona may pay Adam $60 000 and accept the farm subject to the mortgage; that is, Rona will herself assume responsibility for paying off the mortgage. The third possibility is really a variation of the second: Instead of paying the mortgage off at once, Rona simply pays it off as it falls due. This is known as an **assumption of the mortgage**.

The first possibility in Illustration 23.1 rarely occurs because Rona takes the risk that Adam's other creditors might obtain the purchase money through court action, or Adam might abscond so that the funds never reach BCD Trust Co., leaving Rona to pay BCD in order to redeem the mortgage. She might end up paying $260 000 for the farm instead of $160 000. The second option can be very expensive for two reasons. First, by the terms of the mortgage, the mortgagor may not have the right to pay off the mortgage before the due date without a substantial penalty; this is a **closed mortgage**. Also, purchasers rarely have the full purchase price in cash. Land transactions are almost invariably financed by a mortgage. If interest rates have risen, the purchaser will wind up replacing a low interest mortgage with a new higher interest mortgage. Therefore, the third option is most attractive for Rona; however, Adam may not agree.

If the purchaser lacks the cash to pay fully for the vendor's equity and needs more financing than the vendor's existing mortgage provides, she will arrange a new mortgage for a larger sum of money and then use the proceeds of the new mortgage to pay off the existing mortgage, with the balance going toward the cash portion of the purchase price.

assumption of the mortgage   a subsequent purchaser takes over the responsibility of paying off the vendor's existing mortgage

closed mortgage   a mortgage that does not permit early repayment of the debt without a substantial penalty

Effect of Default by the Purchaser
If the purchaser, Rona, defaults on payment of the assumed mortgage:

- Adam's sale of the farm to Rona does not affect BCD's rights as mortgagee; BCD retains all its rights against the land. BCD may obtain possession and sell the land. It may also recover from Adam, the original mortgagor, on his personal covenant—his contractual obligation—to repay the debt. This continuing liability discourages many vendors from agreeing to an assumption by the purchaser. Some provinces limit the right to sue an original mortgagor on a personal covenant in a residential mortgage if the mortgagee has approved the new purchaser.[15] Once the new purchaser renews the mortgage for a subsequent term, his own personal covenant (given upon renewal) replaces that of the original mortgagor.

---

[15] BC *Property Law Act, supra* note 8, ss 23, 24; *Real Property Act*, CCSM c R.30, s 77.2; RSPEI 1988, c R-3, s 79.

If BCD sues Adam, what rights does Adam have upon paying off the mortgage?

- Adam may successfully sue Rona for the full sum of money he was required to pay to BCD. When Rona assumed the mortgage and agreed to pay it off, the law implies that the promise to pay off the mortgage includes a promise to indemnify Adam—that is, to protect Adam from any liability under it. As well, by paying off the mortgage, Adam has, in effect, purchased the mortgagee's rights. He becomes subrogated to the mortgagee's rights and is, in effect, the mortgagee to whom Rona is now a mortgagor. At this point, Adam may use all the remedies against Rona that BCD Trust Co. might itself had against the land and the mortgagor.

Instead of suing Adam, may the mortgagee BCD sue the purchaser Rona directly?

- At common law, BCD could not sue Rona because the mortgage (alone) does not create privity of contract (or estate) between BCD and Rona. However, most lenders will not allow their mortgage to be assumed unless the purchaser signs a contract with them, agreeing to make all the remaining payments. This contract is known as an **assumption agreement** and gives BCD privity of contract (and a breach of contract cause of action) with Rona. In addition, some provincial mortgage legislation gives the mortgagee a statutory right to sue the purchaser, Rona, directly, while Rona holds the land.[16] If she sells it to yet another purchaser, Bill, then Bill becomes liable to pay the mortgage, and Rona is released from her statutory obligation to the mortgagee. As a last resort, BCD may obtain an assignment of Adam's right to indemnity discussed in the preceding paragraph. As a practical matter, Adam will often agree to assign his right in order to avoid having the mortgagee sue him on his covenant in the mortgage.

assumption agreement a contract between the mortgagee and the new purchaser in which the new purchaser agrees to comply with all the requirements in the original mortgage

SECOND MORTGAGES

Uses of a Second Mortgage

A prospective purchaser often finds she does not have sufficient money to buy land that is already subject to a mortgage. An existing landowner may wish to use some of its existing equity in land to renovate the property. Second mortgages (that is, mortgages registered after one prior mortgage) are commonly used for both reasons. Less common are third and fourth mortgages. The subsequent mortgages rank behind prior registered mortgages, and their interests may be wiped out by the remedies of the first mortgagee.

Rights of a Second Mortgagee

A second mortgagee has rights similar to those of a first mortgagee except that he ranks behind the first mortgagee in priority of payment out of the proceeds of the land. If the mortgagor defaults on payment of both mortgages, the first mortgagee may start an action for foreclosure. The second mortgagee may decide to stand by and do nothing. If the first mortgagee completes the foreclosure, the interests of both mortgagor and the second mortgagee are destroyed. The second mortgagee loses his security in the land and is left with only a right of action for debt against the mortgagor, who may be insolvent.

If the first mortgagee proceeds with a sale under power of sale, or sale by the court, the proceeds will be paid, first, to satisfy the first mortgage debt and

---

[16] Ontario *Mortgages Act*, *supra* note 10, ss 20(2), (3).

expenses of the sale, and second, to satisfy the second mortgage debt. The second mortgagee will be paid only to the extent that there is any surplus after paying off the first mortgagee. Of course, the sale may bring in more money than the total amount owed on both mortgages, and in that case the excess will go to the mortgagor.

If the first mortgagee begins a foreclosure action, the second mortgagee has the same opportunity to redeem as the mortgagor—that is, to pay off the first mortgage himself and receive an assignment of it. Thereafter he may commence his own foreclosure action, or he may proceed with either of the two remedies of sale, taking the risk that a sale may not bring in enough to pay off the two sums he has invested.

Risks for a Second Mortgagee When the Mortgagor Defaults

A second mortgage always provides that default on the first mortgage is also immediate default on the second mortgage—that is, a breach of the mortgagor's obligation to protect the second mortgagee's interest in the land—and the second mortgagee may immediately act upon the usual remedies. In the absence of such protection, a second mortgagee might find himself in the following position:

(a) Payment of the second mortgage is not yet due, so there is no default on it.

(b) The first mortgage, having an earlier due date, is in default, and the first mortgagee promptly pursues one of its remedies against the land—foreclosure, sale by court, or exercise of the power of sale.

(c) The result of either of these remedies would be to destroy the second mortgagee's interest in the land.

In a sale either by the court or by the first mortgagee, to the extent that the sale brought in more than the debt due on the first mortgage, the second mortgagee would receive compensation, but he might well recover only a part of the debt. To avoid these risks, a second mortgagee may himself act promptly to pursue his remedies.

Sometimes a mortgagor defaults on only the second mortgage, or, if he has defaulted on the first as well, the first mortgagee might be quite satisfied with the adequacy of its security and be willing to "sit tight" and see what the subsequent mortgagees and creditors intend to do. The first mortgagee need not worry since it has priority in the land, and no one can affect its position. If the second mortgagee forecloses, he becomes the owner of the property, subject to the prior interest of the first mortgagee. He must now make the payments and assume the responsibilities of the original mortgagor. A second mortgagee rarely proceeds by sale, but in such circumstances, the purchaser would obtain title clear of the mortgagor's interest and the second mortgage but, of course, still subject to the first mortgage. In either case the new owner must make satisfactory arrangements with the first mortgagee.

Subsequent Mortgages after a Second Mortgage

Each successive mortgage ranks in priority according to its registration. Each subsequent mortgage gives all the usual remedies to the mortgagee, subject to the prior rights of any earlier mortgagee. Each subsequent mortgagee takes a greater risk as creditor for several reasons:

- First, the land is subject to a larger financial debt, and any drop in price will injure the security of the last mortgagee most.

- Second, a succession of mortgages on one piece of land usually indicates financial instability and poor management on the part of the borrower.
- Third, failure by a subsequent mortgagee to act promptly in case of default may result in the destruction of its secured interest in the land, if a prior mortgagee exercises its power of sale or right to redeem first.
- Fourth, the cost of redeeming multiple prior mortgages will be high—in order to prevent foreclosure of its interest.

Therefore, interest rates are higher on subsequent mortgages and lenders frequently demand additional security, such as mortgages on other lands or personal property or guarantors, before approving mortgage applications.

MORTGAGEE'S RIGHTS COMPARED WITH RIGHTS OF OTHER CREDITORS

general creditor a creditor that has no security other than the debtor's promise to pay

secured creditor a creditor that has collateral security in the form of a recognized claim against specified assets of the debtor

A creditor with only the debtor's promise to pay is a **general creditor**, and its claim ranks as a general claim. A creditor that has security—that is, a recognized interest in specified assets of the debtor, is a **secured creditor**. If the debtor becomes insolvent, the general creditors must wait until the claims of the secured creditors have been satisfied out of the specified assets. When the sale of a specified asset brings in more than the amount owing to the secured creditor, the surplus becomes available to the general creditors. A mortgagee is a secured creditor in the land. After a sale of the mortgaged land by the mortgagee, the sale proceeds first go to satisfy the mortgage debt and sale expenses. Any surplus is returned to the mortgagor; if the mortgagor is insolvent, the surplus goes to his general creditors. However, if there is a deficiency—that is, the specified security realizes less than the amount owed to the secured creditor—the secured creditor then ranks with the general creditors for the deficiency.

ILLUSTRATION 23.2 Distribution of Proceeds of Sale

(a) Harper operates a retail business with some land worth about $320 000. He mortgages the land for $250 000 to Commerce Trust Co. Unfortunately, he becomes insolvent and is declared bankrupt. A trustee is appointed and sells the land (for $270 000) and Harper's other assets (for $38 000). The proceeds of sale will be distributed as follows:

Assets		Liabilities	
Bank balance from:		Commerce Trust Co.	$247 000
sale of land	$270 000		
sale of other assets	38 000	General creditors	85 000
TOTAL	$308 000	TOTAL	$332 000

The assets would be distributed as follows:

Commerce Trust Co.	$247 000
General Creditors	61 000
	$308 000

The mortgagee receives 100 cents on each dollar of debt owed to it from the sale of the land. The land sale produces a surplus of $23 000, which is added to the $38 000 realized from all other assets and is paid out rateably to the general creditors. Here, they receive 61 000 ÷ 85 000 of each dollar of indebtedness—about 72 cents on each dollar.

(b) If the sale of the land only brings in $200 000, the distribution of proceeds is as follows:

Assets		Liabilities	
Bank balance from:		Commerce Trust Co.	$247 000
sale of land	$200 000		
sale of other assets	38 000	General creditors	85 000
TOTAL	$238 000	TOTAL	$332 000

Note: We obtain the figure of $132 000 by adding the deficiency of $47 000 on the mortgage debt to the total unsecured debt of $85 000. In these circumstances the mortgagee receives a total of over $213 000 from a debt of $247 000—about 86 cents on each dollar of debt. On the other hand, the general creditors suffer much more severely: They receive about 24 500 ÷ 85 000 of each dollar of indebtedness—about 29 cents on each dollar. The general creditors' position is worsened because the mortgagee becomes a general creditor for the deficiency in the sale of the land, dividing the assets among a larger group of claims.

The assets would now be distributed as follows:

Creditors	Secured	General	Total
Commerce Trust Co.	$200 000		
plus $\frac{47\ 000}{132\ 000} \times 38\ 000$		$13 530	$213 530
General Creditors			
$\frac{85\ 000}{132\ 000} \times 38\ 000$		24 470	24 470
	$200 000	$38 000	$238 000

TRANSFERRING A MORTGAGEE'S INTEREST IN LAND

Assignment

A mortgagee may not want to wait for the mortgage due date in order to collect. The mortgagee may sell its mortgage at the best price it can get. The sale of a mortgage is a transaction involving both contractual and real property aspects. The mortgagee assigns its rights to the covenants made by the mortgagor and grants or transfers its interest in the land to the purchaser (assignee) of the mortgage. Sometimes, in order to obtain a higher price, an assignor–mortgagee guarantees payment—that is, if the mortgagor defaults in payment, the assignor, on the assignee's demand, will pay off the mortgage and take back an assignment of it. In most sales, however, a mortgagee sells the mortgage outright, and the purchaser takes the risk of default together with all the usual remedies of a mortgagee.

A purchaser of a mortgage, as an assignee of contractual rights, is bound by the usual rules of assignment in contract. As noted in Chapter 11, the debtor—in this case, the mortgagor—is not bound by the assignment until receiving notice of it, and the assignee takes the mortgage subject to the equities and the state of the mortgage account between mortgagor and mortgagee. Assignments are registered on the title to the land, and this constitutes notice.

Discharge of Mortgages

Effects of a Discharge
When a mortgagor or a subsequent purchaser pays off the whole of the mortgage debt at maturity of the loan, she is entitled to a discharge

from the mortgagee. A discharge operates both as an acknowledgment that the debt has been paid in full and as a cancellation of the interest or encumbrance on the land. To clear his title to the property, the mortgagor promptly registers the discharge in the land titles office.[17] In areas where the registry system still exists, a discharge from the mortgagee operates to reconvey the legal title of the land to the mortgagor.

Arrangements for Prepayment of Mortgage Debt

A mortgage sometimes contains a contractual provision permitting the mortgagor to repay the mortgage early and to obtain a discharge before the end of the term. Sometimes conditions are attached to prepayment. Often a mortgagee requires notice, usually three months, before prepayment. This will provide time for the mortgagee to find a new investment. A mortgagee usually requires payment of a bonus—for example, three months' interest in lieu of notice—or it may require both notice and a bonus. Flexible mortgage-prepayment clauses often contain various other prepayment possibilities. A mortgagor may be permitted to prepay part of the debt rather than all of it, in order to make good use of extra earnings and to reduce the interest payable on the mortgage loan. A mortgage that permits repayment "at any time without notice or bonus" is called an **open mortgage** and may charge a higher interest rate.

open mortgage a mortgage permitting repayment of the debt at any time without notice or bonus

discharge statement mortgagee's calculation payment necessary to obtain a discharge of the mortgage

Early discharge of a mortgage requires the mortgagee to calculate the exact amount due by deducting all payments and adding in all bonuses or penalties, late or discharge fees, and accrued interest to the date of payment. The calculation is shared in a **discharge statement**.

CASE 23.1 Privacy and Discharge Statement

Royal Bank of Canada (RBC) obtained a $26 000 judgment against Mr. and Mrs. Trang and started sale proceedings against the Trangs' home. The home was subject to a first mortgage held by Scotiabank. RBC would rank behind Scotiabank for proceeds of sale, so RBC requested a mortgage statement to determine the amount of the Trangs' equity in the property. Scotiabank refused to produce the discharge statement, claiming it violated the debtor's privacy. The Supreme Court of Canada order Scotiabank to produce a discharge statement for RBC, saying, "A mortgage discharge statement is not something that is merely a private matter between the mortgagee and mortgagor, but rather is something on which the rights of others depends, and accordingly is something they have a right to know."[18]

---

partial discharge a discharge of a definite portion of the mortgaged lands

Partial Discharges

A mortgage may also permit the mortgagor to prepay a specified portion of the mortgage debt and to obtain a **partial discharge**—that is, a discharge of a defined portion of the mortgaged lands. Partial discharges are common when the mortgagor is a land developer. The developer may own a large piece of undeveloped land and wish to sell off a part free from any encumbrance; or he may wish to build a large building on a particular part of the land and may require financing in the form of a large, new mortgage—which he cannot obtain except as a first mortgage. Partial discharges play an important role in the financing of land development.

---

[17] A fraudulent mortgagee may deprive a mortgagor of the land when the mortgagor has neglected to obtain a discharge and register it: *Dicker v Angerstein* (1876), 3 Ch D 395.

[18] *Royal Bank of Canada v Trang*, 2016 SCC 50 at para 45.

PROVINCIAL VARIATIONS

The variations in mortgage law and remedies among the provinces and territories in Canada are considerable. Although the basic provisions are similar, the specifics differ according to the economy of the province and the character of business within it. Some examples are discussed below.

The Mortgagee's Rights

In British Columbia, in that portion of Manitoba under the registry system, and in Ontario, New Brunswick, Prince Edward Island, and Newfoundland and Labrador, a mortgagee may foreclose the equity of redemption in the manner already discussed. In Alberta, Saskatchewan, and Manitoba, the usual remedy is sale by the court.[19] If the sale does not produce any satisfactory bids, then the mortgagee may proceed to foreclose, but foreclosure is a rare remedy in those provinces. In all provinces, a mortgagee may request the court or registrar to hold a sale of mortgaged land and, except in Nova Scotia, may sell under a power of sale if it is provided for either by statute or under the terms of the mortgage.[20] In Nova Scotia, although the court issues an order of "foreclosure and sale," foreclosure is not really permitted. The court must hold a sale. Saskatchewan requires mortgagees to seek prior leave of the court before undertaking any action (foreclosure, sale, possession or personal) against a mortgagor.[21]

Non-recourse Mortgages Most provinces eliminate a mortgagee's right to sue the mortgagor for any deficiency after foreclosure is completed. Mortgage deficiency judgments remain available when power of sale or judicial sale are undertaken. This is not true in Alberta and Saskatchewan. In those two provinces, a mortgagee has no right to sue on the covenant to repay; remedies are restricted to realizing on the land only.[22] If the value of the property does not cover the debt, the mortgagee has no recourse against the mortgagor.

The Mortgagor's Rights

Except for New Brunswick, provinces permitting a mortgagee to start an action for foreclosure also allow the mortgagor to request the court to hold a sale, provided she deposits a sum of money as security for the costs of the sale if it produces no acceptable bids. Therefore, a mortgagor may prevent the mortgagee from acquiring the mortgagor's interest in the land. This right of the mortgagor can be an important protection when the land is worth substantially more than the mortgage debt. She should be able to sell the equity of redemption at its market value and pay off the debt. In all jurisdictions, a mortgagor has the right to redeem the land by paying off the entire debt before foreclosure or sale.

REVERSE MORTGAGES

A recent development in Canadian law has been the recognition of the European concept of the **reverse mortgage**. It can be a benefit, especially to older citizens who are retired and are "house rich and cash poor." Typically, a homeowner purchased a house

reverse mortgage a form of mortgage under which no repayment is due until the mortgagor sells or dies

---

[19] See e.g. Manitoba *Real Property Act*, *supra* note 15, s 138; Ontario *Mortgages Act*, *supra* note 16, s 40(2).
[20] See e.g. Manitoba, *ibid*, s 135.
[21] *Land Contracts (Actions) Act*, RSS 1978, c L-3.
[22] Alberta *Law of Property Act*, *supra* note 8, s 40; Saskatchewan *Limitation of Civil Rights Act*, *supra* note 8, s 2. Applies only to purchase money mortgages not insured under Canada Mortgage and Housing program. See also *National Trust Co v Mead*, [1990] 2 SCR 410.

many years earlier and has paid off the mortgage debt on the property; she owns it without debt. Suppose her retirement income is very small, and her house has increased substantially in market value.

Using the reverse mortgage concept, she may give a mortgage on her house and receive a lump sum or a periodic payment based on the market value of the property, prevailing interest rates, and actuarial calculations of her life expectancy. She remains in possession of the house while the principal and interest on the reverse mortgage accrue; no repayment is due until she sells the house or dies. When one of these two events occurs, and if the market value of the house is greater than the accrued debt, the lender pays the excess to the owner or her estate. If the value of the house is less than the accrued debt, then the lender absorbs the deficiency.[23]

The aging population and increased life expectancy has made the reverse mortgage more common.[24] There are wide variations in the design of reverse mortgages. Provinces regulate the reverse mortgage contract with mandatory disclosure and cooling-off periods.[25]

MORTGAGE FRAUD

A rise in "mortgage fraud"[26] is associated with the "hot" real estate market in many Canadian cities, automation of the land registration systems, and the increase in technology-related identity theft.

This mortgage fraud—which takes as its primary victim mortgage lenders but also creates costs for homeowners and society generally—can take two forms.

The first involves identity theft; one fraudster assumes the identity of a registered land title holder, while a second "conspirator" assumes the identity of a purchaser. An agreement of purchase and sale is drawn up and used to obtain mortgage financing, which is never repaid. When the mortgage goes into default, the true owner of the property is surprised to learn of power-of-sale proceeding by an unknown lender.

The second type involves the artificial inflation of the value of a property, through multiple "flips" of properties (a property is purchased and then immediately resold at an inflated price, so as to increase the purported value of the property and increase the amount of mortgage financing) or through misrepresentations of the purchase price using falsified purchase agreements or phony appraisers.

While the mortgagees are defrauded of the mortgage amount, homeowners are also affected. In the case of identity fraud, not only will the real homeowner have to convince the mortgagee that he is not the debtor, but also he will likely have to spend additional money to restore his credit rating and pay land registry and legal fees to correct his title on the register. Additionally, the costs of mortgage fraud borne by the mortgage lenders will inevitably be passed on to mortgagors in the form of higher lending costs. The initial response by the courts was not favourable to the homeowner;[27] the lender was entitled to enforce its remedies. Eventually, in 2007, courts

---

[23] See e.g. Manitoba *Mortgage Act*, *supra* note 8, s 31(2).

[24] See the Canadian Centre for Elder Law Studies, Consultation Paper on Reverse Mortgages (B.C. Law Institute, February 2005).

[25] Manitoba was the first to adopt legislation directed specifically at reverse mortgages. See Part III of the Manitoba *Mortgage Act*, *supra* note 8.

[26] See Canada Mortgage and Housing Corporation, Mortgage Fraud, https://www.cmhc-schl.gc.ca/en/co/buho/plmayomo/plmayomo_004.cfm.

[27] *Household Realty Corp v Liu*, (2005), 261 DLR (4th) 679 (ONCA).

overruled past precedents. In *Lawrence v Maple Trust Co*, the fraudulent mortgage was ruled invalid, and the innocent homeowner's title was cleared.[28] The Ontario land titles legislation was amended to invalidate fraudulent documents.[29] The losing party, either the duped lender or the innocent homeowner, is entitled to make a claim against the Land Titles Assurance Fund. Other legislation strengthens the proof of identity requirements for the registrar of land titles and imposes a duty on the real estate industry to protect against mortgage fraud.[30]

Fraudulent registration of any document in a real property transaction is a criminal offence with a maximum penalty of five years in prison.

Ethical Issue   Money Laundering and Solicitor–Client Privilege

As part of a federal anti-terrorism initiative, the federal government enacted the *Proceeds of Crime (Money Laundering) and Terrorist Financing Act*. Under the federal legislation, professionals and financial institutions are required to report suspicious transactions or large cash payments of $10 000 or more. An independent government agency (FINTRAC) investigates and analyzes reports and tracks cross-border movements of currency.

Lawyers were among the professionals covered by the Act, and real estate lawyers were particularly affected since their work involves receiving large sums of money from their clients.

The Federation of Law Societies of Canada launched a successful court challenge of the law. It argued that requiring lawyers to report on their clients was a violation of solicitor–client privilege and a breach of the constitutional right to independent counsel. The courts agreed with the Federation's position and restricted the application of the new law. As a result, the Minister of Finance introduced amendments to the Act exempting lawyers from its reporting requirements.

In recognition of the fact that preventing money laundering is a worthy goal, the Federation developed model rules for lawyers' codes of professional conduct. The model "know your client" rule requires lawyers to confirm their clients' identities with independent documents and collect information such as addresses and occupations. The model "no cash" rule prohibits lawyers from accepting cash payments of $7500 or more (per client).

Accounting firms, real estate brokers, agents, and developers are not exempt from the reporting obligations and remain subject to search provisions of the legislation.

Questions to Consider

1. Do you think law societies are in a better position to deal with money laundering than FINTRAC?
2. This is another example of a conflict between two worthy goals. What are the arguments that justify the priority of solicitor–client privilege?

Sources: *Proceeds of Crime (Money Laundering) and Terrorist Financing Act*, SC 2000, c 17; Department of Finance Canada, "Reviewing Canada's Anti-Money Laundering and Anti-Terrorist Financing Regime," https://www.fin.gc.ca/activty/consult/amlatfr-rpcfat-eng.asp#ftn8; *Law Society of British Columbia v Attorney General of Canada* (2002), 207 DLR (4th) 736 (BCCA); *Canada (Attorney General) v Federation of Law Societies of Canada*, 2015 SCC 7; Federation of Law Societies of Canada, "Model Rules to Fight Money Laundering and Terrorist Financing" https://flsc.ca/national-initiatives/model-rules-to-fight-money-laundering-and-terrorist-financing.

A TYPICAL REAL ESTATE TRANSACTION

The Circumstances

Vincent owns the land and office building at 99 Main Street, legally described as Lot 27, Plan 7654, in the City of Oshawa (Property Identification Number (PIN) R234). In

---

[28] [2007] 84 OR (3d) 94 (ONCA); but see *Reviczky v Meleknia* (2008), 88 OR (3d) 699, where the court felt the victim had an opportunity to avoid the fraud.

[29] The Ontario *Land Titles Act*, RSO 1990, c L.5, s 78(4.1), invalidates fraudulent documents registered after October 19, 2006. However, the amendment does not invalidate the chain of documents stemming from the document—only the initial fraud.

[30] See e.g. A Reg 174/08; Alberta *Land Titles Act*, *supra* note 4, s 43.1; *Real Estate Amendment Act, 2006*, SA 2006, c 29, s 2.

addition to Vincent's office, the building holds three other offices. One is rented to a dentist, the second to an auto insurance company, and the third to a chartered accountant. Vincent wishes to retire and decides to sell the building. Ideally, Vincent contacts his lawyer, Vale, before competing any of the next steps.

Vendor Lists the Property for Sale

Vincent hires a real estate agent to help him find a buyer for the property. After Vale's review, Vincent signs a standard form **listing agreement** that appoints the agent and

listing agreement contract between the vendor and his real estate agent creating the obligation to pay commission

- designates a list price (selling price) and term (length of the agent's appointment);
- gives the agent the exclusive right to advertise the property on MLS (Multiple Listing Service) and via the internet and television during the term of the listing;
- consents to the use and distribution of property, listing, and sale information;
- allows the agent to show the property to prospective buyers, either individually or collectively at "open houses";
- requires Vincent to pay the agent a commission (usually a percentage of the sale price) if the agent "procures an offer" at the list price or Vincent accepts an offer at any price;[31] and
- directs Vincent's lawyer to pay the commission directly to the agent out of the sale proceeds.

> **CASE 23.2 Use of Listing Data**
>
> The Toronto Real Estate Board's standard form listing agreement includes consent to distribute property information to other real estate agents via the online MLS. It describes retaining, compiling, and publishing information "during the term of the listing and thereafter." The Toronto Real Estate Board's attempt to prohibit its members from sharing historic or "sold" data obtained from MLS with prospective clients via their virtual office websites was struck down by the Federal Court of Appeal. There was no privacy violation; the listing agreement clause was broad and unrestricted. It allowed "any other use in connection with the listing, marketing and selling of real estate."[32]

The Offer to Purchase

Hi-Style Centres Ltd. operates a chain of clothing stores and wants another location. Hi-Style's lawyer, Harmon, is retained to review each offer and counter-offer before signature. Hi-Style's first offer to purchase the building for $600 000 is rejected, and Vincent counter-offers $675 000. This is rejected, and Hi-Style makes a counter-offer. These are the essential terms:[33]

(a) purchase price of $645 000, is payable as follows:
  (i) $25 000 as a deposit by certified cheque attached to the offer;
  (ii) assumption of the first mortgage of about $375 000 held by the Grimm Mortgage Company;

---

[31] If the vendor accepts an offer after the expiration of the term of the listing from a purchaser introduced to the property by the agent.

[32] *TREB v Commission*, 2017 FCA 236 at para 164.

[33] An offer to purchase may also include other terms, the importance of which vary according to the circumstances and, in particular, the nature of the property.

(iii) give back to Vincent a second mortgage of $125 000 (interest and other terms set out in detail);

(iv) pay the balance on closing date (completion date).

(b) sale closing date is 90 days after the date of the offer.

(c) Hi-Style may search the title and submit **requisitions** (questions concerning claims against Vincent's title) within 60 days of acceptance of the offer. Vincent promises to deliver a copy of any survey of the lot, which he has in his possession, for examination by Hi-Style. If serious claims against Vincent's title are raised, and Vincent cannot answer them satisfactorily, the contract will be terminated, and the deposit returned to Hi-Style. If requisitions are answered satisfactorily or no requisitions are submitted within 60 days, it is presumed that Hi-Style accepts Vincent's title as satisfactory.

(d) Vincent is to remain in possession, and the building is to remain at his risk until closing. He promises to keep the building insured to its full insurable value and provide vacant possession in substantially the same condition as it was at the time of making the contract.[34]

(e) Vincent is to pay all taxes and insurance until closing and deduct from the amount due at closing all outstanding current expenses, such as accrued water and electric bills, and unpaid taxes. Hi-Style will arrange its own insurance to commence on the day of closing.

(f) Vincent warrants that
  (i) the three suites of offices are leased to tenants as stated at rents of $1250 monthly per suite under leases expiring two years after date of closing for Suite No. 1; two years and four months after closing for Suite No. 2; and Suite No. 3 as a monthly tenancy only.
  (ii) He will deliver the original of the two leases and assignments of the leases on closing, an acknowledgment from the third tenant that she is only a monthly tenant, and signed notices to the tenants that Hi-Style is the new landlord to whom they are to pay their rent.

(g) The offer is conditional on:
  (i) Hi-Style obtaining a satisfactory property inspection report. The condition may be waived by Hi-Style.
  (ii) Grimm Mortgage Company approving Hi-Style's assumption of the first mortgage within 10 days of acceptance, failing which the offer is null and void.

(h) The offer is open for two days, and acceptance must be communicated to the office of the lawyer for Hi-Style in Oshawa before 5:00 p.m. on the second day;

(i) There are no other oral or written representations or warranties save and except for those contained in this written offer.

requisitions questions concerning claims against a seller's title to property

Accepting the Offer and Waiver of Conditions

Vincent accepts Hi-Style's counter-offer and signs four copies. The agent sends two signed copies back to Hi-Style (one for Hi-Style's lawyer, Harmon) prior to 5:00 p.m., retaining the other copies for Vincent and his lawyer, Vale.

---

[34] Standard form purchase agreements usually include a frustration clause. For example, if the building is destroyed or seriously damaged, Hi-Style may elect to take over the premises and to receive the proceeds of all insurance, or it may elect to terminate the contract, with Vincent to suffer the loss, if any.

The agent and Hi-Style, with Harmon's assistance (if necessary), immediately request Grimm's approval of Hi-Style's assumption of the first mortgage; credit checks and financial disclosure will be necessary. When the approval is obtained, Hi-Style signs a waiver of condition, copies of which are received by Vincent and both lawyers before expiration of the 10-day time period.

The condition on satisfactory property inspection report may be in the form of an option to terminate, condition precedent, or condition subsequent (as defined in Chapter 12). It gives Hi-Style the right to have a professional of its choice visit the property and report on its physical soundness. If Hi-Style is not happy with the condition of the property as revealed in the report, it may terminate the contract.

The property inspection report is important for a number of reasons. First, the general rule of *caveat emptor* applies to land purchases—it is up to the buyer to satisfy himself about the condition of the property. There are some exceptions; for example, under fraudulent misrepresentation (that is, where the vendor conceals defects of which he is aware), the vendor remains liable. Sometimes a vendor supplies a written **property condition disclosure statement** that describes his knowledge of the property (the age of roof, etc.). Inaccuracies in this document can be misrepresentations. Another exception exists for a **latent defect** not discoverable by a purchaser when doing ordinary inspection. If a vendor is aware of such a defect, he must disclose it. However, a **patent defect**, one apparent by ordinary inspection, need not be disclosed by the vendor.

caveat emptor let the buyer beware

property condition disclosure statement written statement of vendor's current actual knowledge of the property's condition

latent defect defect not readily apparent to an ordinary purchaser during an ordinary inspection

patent defect a defect discoverable by a purchaser during an ordinary inspection

---

CASE 23.3 Vendor Property Condition Disclosure Statement

The vendor supplied the purchaser with a Property Condition Disclosure Statement that said the roof of the building was six years old. The purchaser waived the profession home inspection condition and closed the transaction without one. After closing, the purchaser discovered that parts of the roof were much older and sued to have the purchase set aside based on fraudulent misrepresentation. The British Columbia Court of Appeal held that *caveat emptor* applied. The age of the roof was not a latent defect that had to be disclosed. The vendor honestly believed the roof was six years old, and the vendor's current actual knowledge of the state of the property met the disclosure statement obligation.[35]

Preparations for Completing the Transaction

Verifying Title and Possession
As the purchaser's lawyer, Harmon takes the following steps:

1. First, she discusses the purpose and availability of title insurance with the purchaser. The insurance policy compensates for any title defects, zoning noncompliance, or tax arrears that are discovered after closing. Title insurance is usually a mandatory requirement if new mortgage financing is being arranged. In our scenario, Hi-Style may choose title insurance (as most purchasers do), and, if so, obtaining a survey and completing title and off-title searches will be unnecessary. The lawyer can proceed to preparation of the documentation. However, if Hi-Style decides against title insurance, Harmon will complete the following steps.

---

[35] *Nixon v MacIver*, 2016 BCCA 8.

2. Harmon orders an electronic search of the title to the lot (referencing the PIN) and also compares the survey received from Vincent with the plan of the whole area as filed in the registry office, to make sure there are no discrepancies in the boundaries of the lot and to learn whether there are any outstanding claims registered. In the registry system, it will be necessary to hire a title searcher to review actual documents (a step not necessary in land titles).
3. Harmon conducts "off title searches" by sending letters to various agencies with the necessary fee. For example, she writes to the city tax department asking for a certificate showing the state of real property taxes, both arrears and current, and to Oshawa's zoning and building department requesting confirmation that the property complies with current zoning and there are no outstanding work orders and deficiency notices under municipal bylaws. Most of these searches (and fees) are unnecessary if title insurance is purchased.
4. Harmon writes to the Grimm Mortgage Company asking for a mortgage statement showing what the exact amount outstanding on the mortgage will be, including accrued interest, on the date of closing and for the assumption agreement for Hi-Style to sign.
5. She asks her client to arrange insurance for April 15 and to examine the premises carefully to confirm that the building is occupied by the tenants and by Vincent, as stated in the contract, and that no other persons appear to be exercising an adverse claim over any part of the premises. Harmon may advise Hi-Style to hire a surveyor to make a new survey and compare it with the old, although not if title insurance is being purchased.
6. Harmon completes an electronic search of execution claims (judgments) that may be filed against the vendor.
7. After collecting all the aforesaid information, Harmon writes a requisition letter to Vale identifying all discrepancies she has found in the title and off-title searches and requesting that Vale correct any problems. Harmon must make sure that Vale receives this letter by the requisition date. In the letter Harmon asks for copies of all leases. She asks Vale to obtain tenant acknowledgments—standard form questionnaires describing the terms of the tenancy, the state of premises, and the status of rent and security deposits. Harmon also confirms who will be preparing the electronic documents.

Preparing the Documents for Closing Vincent's lawyer, Vale, prepares a transfer and second mortgage (charge), the documents both lawyers will authorize for electronic registration. Harmon examines them and approves their contents. Most real estate lawyers have a software package that generates all necessary documents in registrable form. Still, both lawyers check the details against identification supplied by their clients to confirm accuracy. A few days before closing, each lawyer meets with his or her respective client and reviews the draft documents and **statement of adjustments** (discussed below). The electronic registration system no longer requires the vendor to sign the transfer. However, both vendor and purchaser are asked to sign an authorization and direction allowing their lawyers to electronically register the documents in the form presented. Other tangible documents are signed and delivered on closing. Vale has prepared a charge document for the second mortgage, and Hi-Style will sign this and acknowledge receipt of standard charge terms. Both clients sign undertakings to readjust the accounts after closing if there is a mistake on the statement of adjustments (as discussed below).

statement of adjustments
a document setting out all the items—both credits and debits—that must be adjusted between the parties to arrive at the correct amount to be paid on closing

Re: Lot 27, Plan 7654, in the City of Oshawa
Hi-Style Centres Ltd. purchase from Vincent

STATEMENT OF ADJUSTMENTS
as at April 15

	Vendor	Purchaser
1. SALE PRICE		$645 000.00
2. Deposit paid by purchaser	$ 25 000.00	
3. (a) Principal amount first mortgage to Grimm Mortgage Co. to be assumed by purchaser	373 580.60	
(b) Plus interest, April 1 to 15 at 10.5%	1 612.03	
4. Second mortgage back to vendor	125 000.00	
5. Total taxes for current year, $8695.00, vendor paid first two installments totalling $4000. Vendor share is 105 days ($23.82/day = $2501.30) overpayment charged to purchaser.		1 498.70
6. Rent received in advance (deposits):		
(a) Suite #1: 1.5 months	1 875.00	
(b) Suite #2: 1.5 months	1 875.00	
(c) Suite #3: 0.5 months	450.00	
7. BALANCE DUE ON CLOSING	117 106.07	
	$646 498.70	$646 498.70

Preparing for Closing Harmon finds that Vincent's title to the land is in good order, and she is satisfied with Vale's response to her requisition letter. She receives a mortgage statement (consistent with Vincent's representation) and an assumption agreement from Grimm. A few weeks before the date of closing, Vale prepares a document called a statement of adjustments (see above) reconciling the financial items, both credits and debits, that must be adjusted between the parties to arrive at the correct amount to be paid by Hi-Style to Vincent on the date of closing. The closing date is to be April 15.

The Closing

Exchanging Documents Since all registrations can be completed online, the lawyers agree to close the deal without a face-to-face meeting. Each lawyer sends a package of documents to the other's office to be held in escrow (an agreement that the documents and keys will not be released, used, or registered without the prior authorization of the other). Vale's package includes

(a) the undertaking to readjust,

(b) the original copies of the leases to Suites No. 1 and No. 2,

(c) the properly executed assignments of each lease,

(d) the acknowledgment of the tenant in Suite No. 3 that she is a monthly tenant at a rent of $900 payable in advance,

(e) the notice signed by Vincent to each tenant of Suites No. 1, No. 2, and No. 3 informing tenants of the change of ownership and requesting them to pay all future rent to Hi-Style, and

(f) keys to the building.

On the morning of April 15, Harmon updates all her searches and electronically transfers $117 106.07 to Vale's trust account. Both lawyers access the electronic registration system and authorize the registration of the transfer and the charge (second mortgage). The assumption agreement has been provided to Grimm, and the corresponding first mortgage is already on title. The new second mortgage will rank behind it.

Delivering Possession   Vale agrees not to release the funds he has received until registration is complete. On rare occasions, the vendor's lawyer may agree not to release the funds until the purchaser confirms possession. To avoid conflict, the vendor should arrange to be completely out of the premises by the time the deal is closed and to leave remaining keys for the purchaser. Vincent has vacated the premises the day before, and the Hi-Style manager picks up the keys, goes to the building, and finds the store vacant. The transaction is complete.

After the Closing   Each lawyer still has things to do. Vale will write to the city tax office to inform them of the change of ownership. Vale will pay the commission owed to the real estate agent from the proceeds of sale in accordance with the direction in the listing agreement.

Harmon will communicate with Vale to see that all these things have been completed. She will write to each of the tenants to inform them of the change of ownership, enclosing Vincent's notice and giving them the address at which Hi-Style would like the rent to be paid.

Finally, the lawyers will return all the documents to their respective clients and make a full written report of all details, and the transaction will be complete.

The Distinctiveness of Each Transaction   The terms of each sale of land should be tailored to meet the specific requirements of the parties in the circumstances. Our fictional illustration does not deal with every detail that might arise in the circumstances; rather, it is intended to illustrate the steps in a real estate transaction.

Strategies to Manage the Legal Risks

The typical real estate transaction is far less complicated if the land is registered in the land titles system or if title insurance is purchased. Expecting real estate purchasers and mortgagees to restrict their endeavours to only land titles property is illogical; however, buying title insurance for every real estate transaction, whether in registry or land titles systems, is sound strategy. This does not eliminate the need for legal representation in real estate transactions, as lawyers generally control access to the electronic registration system, and immediate registration is the key to protecting priority of any interest in land. Lawyers should be involved early in the transaction, ideally prior to submitting the offer to purchase. Conditions and warranties are more likely to be effective if they are drafted by a lawyer and included in the offer to purchase.

Mortgages remain the most common way to finance the purchase of land, and the amortization and calculation periods, term, prepayment options, and fixed or floating interest rates will have a dramatic impact on the financial feasibility of the financing and its long-term cost. Mortgagees are required to disclose the full cost of borrowing as part of consumer protection measures, and these should be reviewed carefully before accepting a commitment. If the arrangement proves to be too expensive, the property may be sold with an existing mortgage on it—however, the mortgagee will require full payment (plus penalty if inside the term) or will allow the new purchaser to assume the payments. In the latter case, the financial soundness of the new purchaser is just as important to the vendor as to the mortgagee since the vendor remains liable for the payments.

If a mortgagor goes into default, and the mortgagee commences foreclosure, the value of the property relative to the outstanding mortgage indebtedness will dictate whether the mortgagor should request a sale instead of foreclosure. Generally, where the value of the property greatly exceeds the indebtedness, a sale is more advantageous to the debtor. This will give the debtor his equity in the property. Mortgagees should proceed with sale rather than foreclosure when the debt is close to or exceeds the value of the property. This will preserve the right to proceed on the personal covenant.

QUESTIONS FOR REVIEW

1. Describe the contractual aspects of a mortgage.
2. How does a mortgagee's interest in land under the land titles system differ from the type of interest a mortgagee receives under a registry system?
3. Describe the two harshest of the common law rules for mortgagors. How did equity remedy this?
4. Why does a mortgagee rarely take possession immediately on default by the mortgagor?
5. Define *foreclosure, acceleration clause, redemption, charge*, and *power of sale*.
6. In a sale of mortgaged land by the court, what are the consequences for the mortgagor if there is a deficiency? If there is a surplus?
7. When a purchaser acquires land from the mortgagor and defaults, who may the mortgagee sue? Why? Are there any exceptions to this rule?
8. What are the main options open to a second mortgagee when the mortgagor defaults?
9. In addition to timely repayment of the loan, what other duties does a mortgagor assume?
10. M, a mortgagee, wishes to sell you a $20 000 mortgage on Blackacre. M states that Q, the mortgagor, is already in default, but M needs money quickly to proceed with another transaction. M offers to assign the mortgage to you for $16 000. Name the two most important things you would need to verify before accepting the offer.
11. Distinguish between a general creditor and a secured creditor.
12. Greenacre, a five-hectare field in a new subdivision, is available for sale. You would like to divide it into 20 lots, develop eight of them yourself, and eventually sell off the remaining 12 lots. Describe an important term you would want in the mortgage you need to finance the purchase.
13. Why would a mortgagor who has defaulted request the court to hold a sale of his property rather than allow the mortgagee to foreclose?
14. What is the appeal of a reverse mortgage on their home to a retired older adult couple?
15. In our "typical real estate transaction," explain why Vincent might not agree to take back a second mortgage.
16. How does title insurance change the tasks that the purchaser's lawyer must complete? Discuss the consequences of title insurance.

CASES AND PROBLEMS

1. Continuing Scenario

    Ashley needs an increase in the credit line for the restaurant business. The existing outstanding balance of the business's unsecured credit line is $23 450, and she wants it raised to $50 000. The bank will not agree to the increased limit without getting security in the form of a mortgage on land. Since all the restaurant's locations are leased, the only available property is Ashley's home, where she lives with her husband and co-owner, Michael. It has a market value of $450 000 and a first mortgage in favour of another bank with $300 000 outstanding. Michael is willing to give the mortgage but wants the payments as low as possible (in case he and Ashley need to cover them) and does not care if that increases the amount of the debt. Ashley thinks current interest rates are going to fall, so she wants the opportunity to lower her rate at the earliest possible time. Explain how Ashley and Michael should negotiate term, interest rate, calculation period, and amortization period in order to address both of their concerns. What conditions should the bank demand in order to address the first mortgage and Michael's interest in the home?

2. Four years ago, Azoic Wholesalers Ltd. purchased a warehouse building for $550 000. To finance the purchase, the company paid $75 000 in cash and gave a 7.5 percent first mortgage to the Reliable Insurance Company for $315 000 and an 11 percent second mortgage of $160 000 to the vendor. The vendor subsequently sold the second mortgage to Sharpe Realties Ltd. for $145 000. All documents were duly registered. For the next few years, Azoic Wholesalers Ltd. managed to pay interest on both mortgages and somewhat reduce the principal.

    Azoic Wholesalers Ltd.
    STATEMENT OF CONDITION AT DATE OF DISTRIBUTION

Assets		Liabilities	
Bank balance from:		Reliable Insurance Co.	
sale of building	$425 000	(first mortgage)	$296 000
sale of all other assets	78 000	Sharpe Realties Ltd. (second mortgage)	151 000
Total available cash	503 000		
Deficiency of assets	83 000	General creditors	139 000
	$586 000		$586 000

    Azoic Wholesalers Ltd. subsequently became insolvent and was declared bankrupt. A trustee in bankruptcy was appointed, and all the assets of the company sold. The statement above shows its financial condition after all assets were liquidated.

    Calculate how the available cash will be distributed to the various creditors.

3. Fedorkow purchased a 100-hectare farm on the St. John River in New Brunswick for $90 000. He paid $12 000 cash and gave back a mortgage of $78 000 to the vendor, Bowes. The mortgage was payable over a 15-year period, with interest at 8.5 percent in installments of about $630 per month. Within a year, Bowes fell ill and decided to retire to a warm climate. She sold the mortgage to Manor Mortgage Co. with only a slight discount on the amount then outstanding because she personally guaranteed payment by Fedorkow.

    A year later Fedorkow received an offer to purchase his frontage on the St. John River, an area of about five hectares, for $32 000. He visited the offices of Manor Mortgage Co. and asked if it would be interested in giving a discharge of the mortgage over the five hectares. Manor Mortgage Co. agreed to do so provided Fedorkow gave a $1000 bonus and a further $12 000 in reduction of the mortgage debt. The parties carried out the arrangement, and the five hectares were discharged from the mortgage, leaving the mortgage on the remainder of the farm. Subsequently, Fedorkow defaulted on the mortgage, having also let the farm fall into disrepair. Manor Mortgage Co. sued Bowes as guarantor of the mortgage debt for the balance of $31 560 then outstanding.

Should Manor Mortgage Co. succeed? Explain.

4. Expecting to make a quick profit, Pender purchased two hectares of land in a suburban community outside Fredericton for $85 000. He paid $20 000 in cash and obtained a loan for $65 000 by mortgaging the property to Quincy for two years with interest at 11 percent. Under the terms of the mortgage, Pender was to make quarterly payments of $5000 plus interest, with the balance of the principal sum and interest due at the end of two years. Pender's attempts to sell the land failed because the suburb did not develop as he had hoped. He paid the first quarterly installment but missed the second.

Quincy took possession shortly after the default in payment and applied for foreclosure. The market for land in the area continued to weaken, and shortly after he obtained a final order of foreclosure, Quincy advertised the property for sale "under the mortgagee's power of sale." He accepted the highest offer of $50 000 and sued Pender for the deficiency of $10 000 plus accrued interest and the costs of obtaining foreclosure and conducting the sale, for a total of $15 600.

Pender defended by claiming that Quincy had given up all rights against him when he foreclosed Pender's equity of redemption, unless he could return the land. Quincy argued that he retained the choice to exercise his power of sale with a claim for any deficiency.

Which argument do you believe is more sound? Explain.

5. Keller owned and operated the Serene Bed & Breakfast near Sarnia for many years. It was a small business, and her health was not good. She decided to sell but found the market very limited. Jepson agreed to purchase Serene Bed & Breakfast from her for $195 000 if she agreed to take back a second mortgage. On March 31, Jepson paid Keller $30 000 on closing, assumed the first mortgage of $150 000 held by Huron Co-op Inc., and gave Keller a second mortgage for the balance of $15 000.

The spring and summer tourist seasons were very poor, and Jepson lost money during the first six months. He defaulted on payments to both mortgagees and informed them that he could not carry on. Huron replied that it intended to commence foreclosure proceedings immediately. Both Jepson and Keller then met several times with the manager of Huron at his office to try to work out the most convenient arrangement and keep expenses to a minimum, avoiding court costs. They agreed to avoid court proceedings by Jepson's conveying the property to Huron—and Keller would also transfer her interest as second mortgagee to Huron in return for the nominal sum of $100.

Several months later Keller learned that Jepson owned a substantial interest in a large retail hardware store; Jepson earned a good salary there as manager. She requested that he pay the unpaid debt on the second mortgage, but he refused on the basis that Keller could no longer reconvey the interest she held, having already transferred it to Huron. Keller believed she was entitled to repayment and sued Jepson.

Give your opinion of the defence raised by Jepson and whether Keller should succeed.

6. Lawlor purchased a small house from Cloutier at a price of $80 000. She paid $15 000 in cash and gave Cloutier a first mortgage for the balance. A year later, when Lawlor had reduced the principal amount of the mortgage to $52 000, she suffered financial reverses that made it impossible for her to continue to repay mortgage principal as required. Cloutier brought an action against Lawlor and on

May 15 obtained an order for foreclosure, with the deadline for payment by Lawlor specified as November 15.

On July 10, the insurance of $50 000 on the house expired, and Lawlor renewed it while she was seeking to refinance with a new mortgagee. A few weeks later, the house was seriously damaged by fire; the insurance adjuster appraised the loss at $35 000.

Both Cloutier and Lawlor immediately claimed the insurance money. The insurance company refused to pay Cloutier on the grounds that the insurance policy contained no mortgage clause that would have assigned to him rights in any claim "in so far as his interest may appear." The insurance company also refused to pay any part of the loss to Lawlor on the grounds that she had no insurable interest in the property.

Discuss the validity of the claims of Cloutier and Lawlor. Assume that there is no evidence to show that the fire was other than accidental in its origin.

7. Three years ago, the Lister Co. Ltd. borrowed $200 000 from the Hi-Rise Bank. Lister Co. was in the textile business and gave a real estate mortgage on one of its buildings as collateral security for the bank loan: The mortgage provided security in the land, building, and fixtures in the building.

The company was later adjudged bankrupt on a petition of its creditors. A question arose about whether a certain piece of expensive machinery in the mortgaged building was in fact a fixture against which the bank would retain priority in liquidation. The trustee in bankruptcy, representing the general creditors, claimed it was not a fixture, so that the proceeds from its sale would be applied to all creditors' claims and not solely to that of the bank as mortgagee.

An officer of the bank and the trustee in bankruptcy went personally to inspect the machine but were unable to agree whether it could be described as being "permanently" affixed. The bank then started legal action to have its claim as mortgagee of the machine confirmed. At this point, the trustee offered as a compromise to recognize the bank's priority to the extent of $20 000, a sum much less than the probable resale value of the machine. The bank accepted the offer and withdrew its action.

A few days later the bank learned that at the time it took the mortgage on the building, the machine in question had been affixed to a cement floor in the plant in a permanent way, but that the building had since been renovated and the machine had been reattached much less securely to the new floor. Neither the bank nor the trustee had this information when they contracted to substitute $20 000 in cash for the mortgage claim. The trustee refused to waive the agreement, however, and the Hi-Rise Bank brought an action asking the court for rescission of that contract and an order acknowledging its claim as a secured creditor with respect to the machine.

Discuss the nature of the argument on which the bank would base its claim, and indicate whether its action should succeed.

Give an opinion on the probable outcome of this litigation with reasons.

8. Victor Contractors Ltd. financed the construction of a high-rise apartment tower in Hamilton by receiving "draws" on first mortgage financing as work progressed. Rail Canada Pension Fund held the first mortgage for $10 700 000. The mortgage contained the following clause:

> The Mortgagor [Victor Contractors Ltd.] covenants and agrees with the Mortgagee [Rail Canada Pension Fund] that, except with the prior consent of the Mortgagee (which consent shall not be unreasonably withheld), it will not enter into any agreement for the sale, transfer or other disposition of the mortgaged premises.

On May 31, Victor Contractors agreed to sell the apartment building to Steel City Developers Corp. for $16 000 000. Steel City Developers paid a deposit of $75 000 and agreed to assume the existing first mortgage. The closing date was December 1, with the balance due on closing. The contract included the following clause:

> This Agreement is conditional upon the Vendor [Victor Contractors Ltd.] being able to obtain within 30 days following this date the consent of the first mortgagee [Rail Canada Pension Fund] to this sale and to the assumption of the first mortgage obligations by the Purchaser [Steel City Developers Corp.].

When Victor Contractors requested consent from Rail Canada Pension Fund, its manager stated that he would have to be satisfied with the financial capability of Steel City Developers and wished to see its audited financial statements. The secretary–treasurer of Steel City Developers refused to produce the statements on the grounds that her company had a firm policy of never disclosing its financial affairs to anyone except its bank because this policy gave it an advantage over its competitors.

With matters at an impasse, the solicitors for Steel City Developers finally wrote on June 28, informing Victor Contractors that since, as vendor, it had been unable to obtain the consent of the first mortgagee as required, "This Agreement is now null and void." In reply, Victor Contractors wrote, "It is clear that your letter of June 28 written on behalf of your client constituted a wrongful renunciation of the contract of sale and purchase."

Victor Contractors then sued Steel City Developers for specific performance or, alternatively, for damages for breach of contract. Steel City Developers counter-claimed for the return of the deposit of $75 000.

Outline what you consider to be the main issue that the court will have to resolve in this case, and offer with reasons an opinion about the probable outcome. Why would Rail Canada Pension Fund have insisted upon a right to satisfy itself of the financial capability of any purchaser of the apartment building?

Part 6 Business Organizations: Their Forms, Operation, and Management

Chapter 24
Sole Proprietorships and Partnerships

- CHOOSING THE APPROPRIATE FORM OF BUSINESS ORGANIZATION
- SOLE PROPRIETORSHIPS
- PARTNERSHIPS
- THE NATURE OF PARTNERSHIP
- THE CREATION OF A PARTNERSHIP
- THE LIABILITY OF A PARTNER
- THE RELATIONSHIP BETWEEN PARTNERS
- TERMINATION OF PARTNERSHIP
- LIMITED PARTNERSHIPS
- LIMITED LIABILITY PARTNERSHIPS
- JOINT VENTURES
- INCOME TRUSTS
- STRATEGIES TO MANAGE THE LEGAL RISKS

This chapter examines unincorporated business entities—sole proprietorships, partnerships, joint ventures, and income trusts, with the main emphasis on partnerships.

In this chapter we examine such questions as:

- Why are partnerships formed?
- What is the legal nature of a partnership?
- Why is it important to establish whether a partnership exists between persons carrying on a business?
- How are partnerships created?
- What are the usual contents of a partnership agreement?

- To what extent are partners liable for the acts of their co-partners and for the debts of the firm?
- What are the duties owed by partners to one another?
- How are partnerships terminated, and what happens when they are?
- What are limited partnerships?
- What are limited liability partnerships?
- What are joint ventures?
- What are income trusts?

CHOOSING THE APPROPRIATE FORM OF BUSINESS ORGANIZATION

Almost all businesses in Canada are carried on in at least one of the following forms:[1]

- sole proprietorship,
- partnership, or
- corporation.

Sole proprietorships and partnerships come into existence without government involvement—the actions of the individuals involved establish the business. However, a corporation may only be formed by following the steps outlined in the legislation and registering with the designated government department. The procedure for incorporation was originally expensive and cumbersome, but now a corporation can be formed quickly and for a few hundred dollars. In addition, almost all provinces currently permit a corporation to be created with a single shareholder and director, so that corporations are a viable alternative not only to partnerships but also to sole proprietorships. When an individual or a group of persons contemplate establishing a business, the initial decision is whether or not to incorporate. Professional legal, accounting, and management advice should be sought. Many small businesses decide to incorporate at the outset, whereas others make the decision to do so later, or they remain unincorporated. A number of professions do not permit their members to carry on their practice in the form of a corporation. In those cases, sole proprietorship or partnership is the only option. This chapter addresses the legal environment surrounding unincorporated businesses. Chapter 25 considers the legal issues surrounding incorporation of a business.

SOLE PROPRIETORSHIPS

sole proprietorship an unincorporated business owned by a single individual

As soon as an individual starts doing business, a **sole proprietorship** is created. No formalities are necessary. The business activity is still subject to the same regulations that apply to all forms of business. Laws regarding public health, zoning, and, of course, taxation apply to all businesses, whether sole proprietorships, partnerships, or corporations. A sole proprietor may need a licence to carry on a particular type of business. For example, a municipal licence is normally required before one may start business as an electrician, plumber, restaurateur, or taxi driver. Provincial licensing and registration may be required for a car dealer, insurance broker, or employment agency. The proprietor must keep proper accounts for income tax purposes, but sole

---

[1] Other businesses operate as cooperatives, trusts, and other types of unincorporated associations. Sometimes multiple business forms are used, such as when two corporations form a joint venture or partnership.

proprietor income is reported on the personal income tax form. No separate filing is done. The proprietor must make payroll deductions for employee income tax, employment insurance, and Canada Pension Plan. In hiring staff, she must observe human rights legislation and must comply with health and safety regulations.

In most provinces, if a business operates under a name other than the actual name of the owner, the name must be registered.[2] Chapter 20 discusses trademark issues involved naming any business.

PARTNERSHIPS

Advantages and Disadvantages

A **partnership** may be formed by two or more persons, who may be natural persons (individuals) or legal persons (corporations). There are obvious advantages in carrying on a business venture with others. Working together, members of a group can pool their knowledge and skills, and their physical and financial resources. There are also obvious disadvantages. Disagreements may lead to stalemate; the dishonesty or incompetence of one member may lead to losses suffered by other members; when a group wishes to make important decisions, it may lose valuable time in reaching agreement. None of these problems exists when a person acts solely on her own behalf.

partnership the relationship between two or more persons carrying on a business with a view to profit

The *Partnership Act*

Although partnerships may be established without government approval, their affairs are governed by a well-developed body of laws. This is because, until the 20th century, partnership was the usual way for two or more persons to carry on business. Problems concerning almost every aspect of partnership were litigated through the courts, and a complete set of common law rules was created. There were so many cases that it was difficult to keep track of the broader principles. Therefore, the case law was collected into one statute called the *Partnership Act*,[3] which organized the numerous cases under general principles. Each Canadian common law province has a *Partnership Act* covering the basic rules of operation.[4] With one important exception,[5] the legislation has remained virtually unchanged from its original form, and there have been comparatively few cases on its interpretation, so it reflects the legal rules applicable to today's partnerships.

THE NATURE OF PARTNERSHIP

The Definition of Partnership

"Partnership is the relation which subsists between persons carrying on a business in common with a view of profit."[6] Originally there was just one type of partnership, now known as a general partnership. Two additional specialized forms of partnership—limited partnerships and limited liability partnerships—developed over time and are discussed later in this chapter.

---

[2] See e.g. *Business Names Act*, RSO 1990, c B.17, s 2(2). Saskatchewan requires registration even when an owner operates under her own name: *Business Names Registration Act*, RSS 1978, B-11, s 2(c).

[3] 1890, 53 & 54 Vict, c 39 (UK).

[4] See e.g. *Partnerships Act*, RSO 1990, c P.5; *Partnership Act*, RSBC 1996, c 348; RSNS 1989, c 334.

[5] The introduction of the limited liability partnership, considered later in this chapter.

[6] See *Partnership Act*, RSBC 1996, c 348, s 2; RSNS 1989, c 334, s 4; *Partnerships Act*, RSO 1990, c P.5, s 2. Subsequent references within this chapter to British Columbia, Ontario, and Nova Scotia are to these statutes.

> **CHECKLIST**
>
> ## Elements of a Partnership
>
> There are four basic elements in the definition of "partnership." A partnership is
>
> - a relationship,
> - between persons,
> - carrying on business in common,
> - with a view to profit.

This definition of partnership is extremely important because of the consequences that flow from a finding that a person is a partner. Whether two or more persons are partners depends on all the circumstances of a case.

The Partnership Relationship Partnership is a consent based contractual relationship. Normally, a written partnership agreement is drawn up and signed by the partners. However, persons may be found to be partners although no written or even oral agreement was made.[7] This will happen if they behaved as partners despite no prior agreement.[8] The courts look at the substance of the relationship no matter what the parties may call it.[9]

The Business Nature of Partnership The *Partnership Act* defines partnership as a relationship between persons carrying on a business *for profit*. It does not apply to other associations, such as charitable enterprises, joint trustees of an estate, public boards, or corporations.

The term "business" is an imprecise one. It includes "every trade, occupation, or profession," but it does not include every activity carried on for a profit. For instance, owning property and collecting rent from tenants does not necessarily amount to carrying on a business. The joint ownership of property does not of itself make the owners partners. Similarly, if a group of investors forms a syndicate to hold a portfolio of securities, that arrangement does not amount to carrying on a business unless the investors engage in the trading of shares, rather than merely retaining them for investment income.

> **CASE 24.1 Co-ownership not Partnership**
>
> A group of investors purchased a piece of development property with a view to reselling it at a profit. One of the co-owners, March, signed a listing agreement with a real estate agent (Le Page) without the agreement of his co-owners.
>
> The property was sold, and Le Page sued all the owners for its commission, claiming they were partners and were jointly liable for the contract made by March.
>
> The court held that there was no partnership. The members of the group were not carrying on a business but were merely co-owners of the property. March alone was liable for the commission.[10]

---

[7] Conversely, a written "partnership agreement" will not create a partnership if it is found that no such intention existed: M *Tucci Construction Ltd v Lockwood*, [2000] OJ No 3192, aff'd [2002] OJ No 440 (Ont CA).

[8] See e.g. *Pinteric v People's Bar and Eatery Ltd*, [2001] OJ No 499, where the plaintiff alleged the existence of an oral partnership agreement; the court held that the receipt of "advances" rather than a salary pointed to a partnership relationship.

[9] In *Lansing Building Supply (Ontario) Ltd v Ierullo* (1990), 71 OR (2d) 173, co-developers of land entered into a joint venture agreement that specifically provided that they were not to be considered partners. Nevertheless, the court held that the true nature of their relationship was one of partnership.

[10] *AE Le Page Ltd v Kamex Developments Ltd* (1977), 78 DLR (3d) 223, aff'd [1979] 2 SCR 155.

Although a partnership must be a business relationship, not every business relationship makes the parties to the relationship partners with each other. The Act speaks of "carrying on" a business. Isolated transactions undertaken jointly do not by themselves make the parties partners. For example, if two businesses in Nova Scotia pool an order of goods purchased in Montreal so they can fill one freight car and obtain a lower freight rate, that arrangement alone does not make them partners. However, a partnership may exist for even a single venture, depending on the circumstances.

CASE 24.2 Continuing Activity

Some Canadian investors purchased the interests of the members of a Texas partnership that owned a large apartment building. The value of the building had declined drastically, and the whole purpose of the transaction was to realize the loss, which the Canadian investors hoped to set off against their income tax liability. After the transfer of the partnership interests, the building was immediately sold.

The Supreme Court of Canada held that a tax motivation and a short duration do not by themselves negate the existence of a partnership. However, in this case there was never any intention to carry on a "business" as a continuing activity, and therefore the relationship was not a partnership.[11]

The Profit Motive The words "with a view to profit" typically mean that a sharing of profits is an essential element of partnership.

Normally, the sharing of gross receipts does not create a partnership. For example, if an owner of a theatre were to rent it to a drama group, and one of the terms of the contract was that she would receive 10 percent of the gross receipts, such an arrangement would not make the owner a partner of the group. Similarly, in our example of the two businesses pooling an order to reduce shipping charges, there is a sharing of costs but not of profits.

The receipt of a share of the profits of the business is strong evidence of a partnership, though it is not by itself conclusive. In particular, it does not by itself amount to a partnership if the sharing of profits is part of an arrangement to

- repay a debt owed;
- pay an employee or agent of the business as part of his remuneration;
- pay an annuity to a widow, widower, or child of a deceased partner;
- repay a loan under which the lender is to receive a rate of interest varying with the profits;
- pay the seller of a business an amount for goodwill that varies according to the profits (BC, s 4; Ont, s 3.; NS, s 5).

Apart from the above situations, it is difficult to imagine circumstances in which the only evidence of a partnership would be the fact that a person is sharing in the profits of a business. A person receiving a share of profits has usually contributed property or money to the business. Even though partners often share profits according to a ratio that is not based solely on capital contribution, the courts consider profit-sharing that coincides with the ratio of capital contribution to be strong evidence of partnership.

---

[11] *Backman v Canada* (2001), 196 DLR (4th) 193 (SCC). Since there was no business, there was no business loss for which tax relief could be claimed. See also *Hayter v Canada*, [2010] TCJ No 175—lacked a continuing nature to be a partnership, but it qualified as a joint venture (an adventure in the nature of a trade covered by the *Income Tax Act*). Contrast *Backman* with *Spire Freezers Ltd v Canada* (2001), 196 DLR (4th) 211 (SCC) (a case with a similar tax motive, decided at the same time as the *Backman* case), where the Canadian investors retained some of the assets of a California partnership and were held to be carrying on a business. See also *Stow v Canada*, [2010] TCJ No 322.

Another important factor is whether the person receiving the profits has taken part in the management of the business. Evidence showing that she has taken some active role in the business, particularly in making decisions on important matters, when added to the fact that she has shared in the profits, will usually suffice to establish her as a partner.

The Legal Nature of Partnership

Legal Personality As a matter of law, a corporation has a separate legal identity of its own. The law of partnerships is not the same. The Act defines a partnership as a "relation" between persons. Strictly, a partnership has no independent existence and merely represents the collective rights and duties of all the partners. Logically, this means that whenever a partner dies or retires or a new partner is admitted, the partnership comes to an end and is replaced by a new relationship. For accounting purposes, a partnership is initially treated as a separate entity with its own assets, the ability to create liabilities, and financial statements. However, in the end, all income, losses, assets and liabilities are attributed to and the responsibility of the individual partners.

The Continuing Relationship Between Partners The *Partnership Act* recognizes the concept of a **firm**,[12] which members join or leave. It speaks of a person being admitted as a partner into an existing firm, or retiring from a firm, or being expelled from a firm, and of the composition of a firm changing. So while it provides that the death (or insolvency) of a partner dissolves the partnership, the Act allows partners to agree that the partnership will continue between the survivors (BC, s 36(1); Ont, s 33(1); NS, s 36(1)). Therefore, partnership agreements normally expressly state that upon the death, bankruptcy, or retirement of one of them, the partnership will continue among the others.

firm collective reference to the partners in a partnership

Partnership Property Again, it is clear from the Act that a partnership may have property that is distinct from the property of the individual partners. In particular, real property held by a partnership is treated according to the usual rules governing real property as far as the partnership is concerned, but insofar as the individual partners are concerned, their interest in the real property is considered personal property; that is, they do not own the property itself but rather an interest in that property.

Creditors of the Firm Partnership creditors have first call against partnership assets before the personal creditors of an individual partner. This is so because, until the creditors of the partnership have been paid, it is impossible to identify and distribute the share of an individual partner. If, after these creditors are paid, no assets remain, then the partner has no share for personal creditors to seize.

Another example of the concept of the firm occurs in the rule that a deceased partner's personal creditors have first call against the personal assets of her estate (BC, s 11; Ont, s 10; NS, s 11). If the partnership assets are insufficient to pay off the partnership creditors, they must wait for the personal creditors to be paid out of the personal estate of the deceased partner before they can take what is left in order to satisfy their debt. Under the *Bankruptcy and Insolvency Act*, this rule also applies to the estate of a living partner who becomes bankrupt.[13]

Legal Proceedings For the purposes of processing a court action, a partnership may be identified as if it were an entity. The partnership may bring an action in the name of the firm without naming all the partners as plaintiffs, and an outside party may sue a partnership in its firm name without naming all the partners as defendants.

---

[12] See e.g. BC, s 1; Ont, s 5; NS, s 7.

[13] RSC 1985, c B-3, s 142.

However, as we shall see when we consider the question of the liability of partners, the individual partners will be personally responsible for payment of the judgment.

THE CREATION OF A PARTNERSHIP

The Partnership Agreement

A partnership comes into existence through agreement, express or implied, of the partners. Generally speaking, partners may agree to whatever terms they wish, provided the terms are not illegal and do not offend public policy. A **partnership agreement** may be wholly oral and yet be valid and enforceable.[14] As we know an oral agreement is subject to the lapses of memory of the parties to the agreement, and, if only for certainty, it is important to have a written record of the agreement.

partnership agreement an agreement between persons to create a partnership and (usually) to set out the terms of the relationship

Dissolving a partnership is relatively easy, and many break up after a short time. There are lots of reasons for dissolution; the business may have proven unprofitable or may have been so profitable that the partners have gone on to form a corporation. Still others dissolve because of a conflict of personalities between the partners. A substantial number of profitable partnerships are destroyed by misunderstanding or mistrust. The failure to decide important issues in advance often leads to the kind of misunderstanding and mistrust that creates an irreparable breach between the parties.

The main purpose of a partnership agreement is to set out, as carefully and as clearly as possible, the entire terms of the relationship.

CHECKLIST
Contents of a Partnership Agreement

Normally, a partnership agreement deals with the following matters. Depending on the circumstances, there are likely other matters that should also be covered:

- identity of the partners
- name of the firm
- nature of the business to be carried on
- duration of the relationship
- method of terminating the partnership
- rules for introducing new partners
- consequences of retirement or death of an existing partner
- participation in management and in making major decisions
- contribution of each partner in terms of work and responsibilities
- capital contribution of each partner
- ownership of property used in the business
- sharing of profits and losses
- procedure for resolving disputes

Gaps in the agreement may be filled by the *Partnership Act*, which sets out a number of implied terms that apply in the absence of any provision in the agreement to the contrary. It is normally preferable, however, for the parties to make their own express terms rather than rely on implied terms from the Act.

---

[14] In some provinces the *Statute of Frauds* applies (see Chapter 10). However, once the partnership exists, the statute no longer applies.

Partners should not draft their own agreement. The usual problems of ambiguous words can create the same misunderstandings that generally arise in the law of contracts. In addition, novice partners may be unaware of many of the pitfalls that accumulated experience in business and knowledge of partnership law may avoid. Each partner should have his own legal counsel to help protect his investment and provide independent legal advice.

Registration

No specific formal requirements are necessary to form a general partnership; by contrast, as discussed later in this chapter, limited partnerships and limited liability partnerships require registration. However, almost all provinces require even general partnerships to file a declaration giving essential information about the partnership, such as the names and addresses of each partner and the name under which they intend to carry on business. Declarations must also be filed when there is any change in membership or when a firm is dissolved. The registration requirements do not necessarily apply to all partnerships. For example, in British Columbia and New Brunswick only partnerships engaged in trading, manufacturing, or mining are required to register, and in Ontario a partnership is not required to register if it carries on business under a name that is composed solely of the names of all of the partners.[15]

There are penalties for failure to carry out the requirements of the statute, and they vary from province to province, but non-registration in no way affects the existence of the partnership as such. The purposes of this registration system are obvious. The register is open to the public and makes information about a partnership and particularly about the partners in the firm available to those doing business with it. A plaintiff can find out where to serve each partner with notice of an action if she wishes to do so. It is also helpful to prospective creditors or other suppliers in checking the accuracy of information given by a member of the partnership concerning the membership of the firm.

THE LIABILITY OF A PARTNER

The most important characteristic of a general partnership is that partners are personally liable for the debts of the partnership. A person who is a partner in a *general* partnership becomes personally responsible for the debts and liabilities of the partnership.[16]

Contractual Liability

Agency Principles Contractual obligations of the partnership represent a great risk of liability for a partner: "Every partner is an agent of the firm and his other partners for the purpose of the business of the partnership, and the acts of every partner who does any act for carrying on in the usual way business of the kind carried on by the firm of which he is a member, bind the firm and its partners."[17] That is so unless the authority of the partner has been restricted by an agreement with the other partners, and the third party *knows* of this restriction. Any acts done by a partner within the scope of his apparent authority and relied on by an outsider bind the firm and all the partners. A restriction placed on the authority of a partner has the same effect as a restriction placed on the authority of an agent by his

---

[15] See e.g. *Partnership Act*, RSBC 1996, c 342, s 81; Ontario *Business Names Act*, *supra* note 2, s 2(4).

[16] Limited liability partnership and limited partnership are different.

[17] *See* Ont, s 6; BC, s 7; NS, s 8.

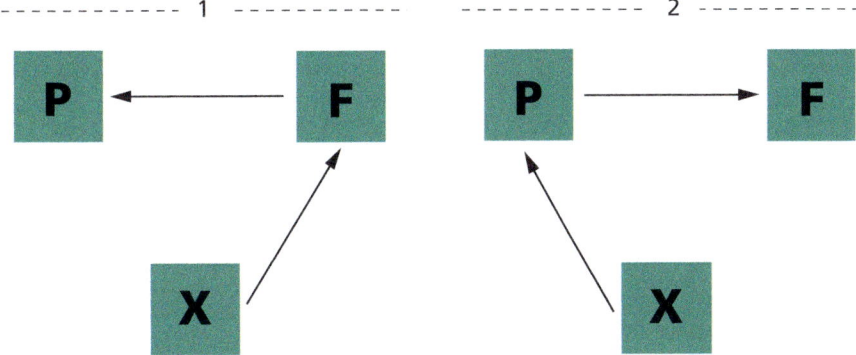

Figure 24.1 Joint Liability

(1) If the outsider (X) sues the firm (F), then any partner (P) is liable to contribute his share to the firm and may be sued by the firm for that share.

(2) If X instead sues P, P is fully liable but is entitled to be indemnified by the firm; that is, P can sue F or his co-partners personally.

principal: It affects only those outsiders who have knowledge of it (BC, s 10; Ont, s 9; NS, s 11). Apparent authority was discussed in Chapter 17, in the context of the law of agency.[18]

Joint Liability "Every partner in a firm is liable jointly with the other partners for all debts and obligations of the firm incurred while he is a partner."[19] The effect of the **joint liability** rule is that each partner is personally liable for the full amount of the firm's debts. When the liabilities of a partnership exceed its assets, a creditor or injured party, having obtained judgment against the partnership and exhausted its assets in trying to satisfy judgment, may look to the personal assets of any partner or partners for payment of the judgment. Therefore, it is important for a person advancing credit to a firm to determine whether it is a partnership and, if so, who are the partners.

joint liability the situation where each of a number of persons is personally liable for the full amount of a debt

Another consequence of this rule is that only one cause of action arises from the obligation. If, by carelessness or ignorance of the facts, a plaintiff brings action against only some of the partners and obtains judgment against them, her rights will be exhausted. If their assets are insufficient to satisfy the judgment and she later discovers there are other partners, she will not be able to sue those others for the deficiency. This risk is eliminated if she sues the defendants in the firm name since that has the effect of suing all the persons who were partners at the relevant time.

If a partner pays the firm's debts in full, he is entitled to be reimbursed by his co-partners for their shares of the debt (BC, s 27(b); Ont, s 24(2); NS, s 27(b)). See Figure 24.1 for an illustration. But if the other partners are insolvent, one partner may be left with payment of the full debt. It is consequently most important to choose one's partners carefully.

Apparent Partners A person is liable only for the obligations of a partnership incurred while he is a member of the firm. "A person who is admitted as a partner into an existing firm does not thereby become liable to the creditors of the firm for anything done before he became a partner," and "a partner who retires from a firm does

---

[18] See *Mercantile Credit Co Ltd v Garrod*, [1962] 3 All ER 1103.

[19] See Ont, s 10, BC, s 1; NS, s 12.

not thereby cease to be liable for partnership debts or obligations incurred before his retirement."[20] The only way he may free himself from his obligations is by novation—that is, by agreement with the partners remaining in the firm and with the firm's creditors.[21]

A person who, not being a partner, represents himself to be, or allows himself to be represented as a partner in a firm, is liable to any person who has given credit to the firm on the faith of that representation (BC, s 16; Ont, s 15; NS, s 17).

CASE 24.3 Appears as Partner

A was a salaried lawyer, employed by another lawyer, S. A was not in partnership with S and did not share in the profits of the practice. However, A's name was on the "firm's" letterhead, and there was a bank account in the firm's name.

The plaintiff hired S to work on a mortgage transaction. S did not register the mortgage and misappropriated the money. He was subsequently disbarred and sent to prison.

A did not perform any work for the plaintiff but had been introduced to its senior officers, apparently as a partner of S.

The court held that A had allowed himself to be represented as a partner and consequently was prima facie liable. However, the plaintiff had enjoyed a long personal relationship with S and had not been induced to deal with the firm by A's holding out. A was therefore not liable.[22]

Although a partner who retires is not supposed to be liable for debts of the firm contracted after he ceased to be a partner, he may be liable if third parties reasonably believe he is still a member of the firm and advance credit to the firm in reliance on his membership. A retiring partner may free himself from this liability by carrying out the requirements of the *Partnership Act* (BC, s 39; Ont, s 36; NS, s 39). An advertisement in the official gazette of the province is adequate notice to persons generally who had not dealt with the firm before the retiring partner left the firm, but all persons who have dealt with the firm before the partner's retirement should receive actual notice of the retirement if the retiring partner is to be fully protected. It is customary, therefore, to send notices to all those persons who have dealt with the firm recently. As well, the retiring partner's name should be removed from the list of partners on all registration.

CHECKLIST

Steps to Be Taken on Retirement from a Partnership

To protect against possible liability for future acts of his partners, a retiring partner should

- ensure that all existing clients of the firm are notified,
- place a notice in the official gazette of the province (and perhaps also in the local newspaper),
- ensure that his name is removed from the register, and
- ensure to the best of his ability that any letterheads are destroyed or altered to remove his name.

---

[20] See Ont, s 18, BC, s 19; NS, s 20.

[21] See Chapter 12 under "Discharge by Agreement" (Substituted Agreement).

[22] *Bet-Mur Investments Ltd v Spring* (1994), 17 BLR (2d) 55, aff'd [1999] OJ No 342 (Ont CA). See also *Brown Economic Assessments Inc v Stevenson*, [2003] SJ No 295, aff'd [2004] S.J. No. 377 (Sask CA).

Figure 24.2 Misapplication of Funds

In situation 1, X entrusts P with money or property to be handed over to the firm (F); instead, P keeps the money or property for himself. In situation 2, X entrusts money or property to the firm, and it is subsequently misappropriated by P.

Tort and Breach of Trust

The liability of a firm and of its partners is not restricted to contracts. The Act makes the firm liable for "any wrongful act or omission of any partner acting in the ordinary course of the business of the firm."[23] Therefore, the firm, including all the partners, is liable for injuries or damage caused by a partner doing the firm's business, such as a defamatory statement made by him in business correspondence or for negligence in dealing with a client's affairs.[24] The principle is similar to that of vicarious liability, discussed in Chapter 4. The firm is also liable for some breaches of fiduciary duty and breaches of trust committed by a partner; for example, for any misapplication by a partner of funds that have been placed in the care of the partner while acting within the scope of his apparent authority or that have been entrusted to the firm.[25] The Act (BC, s 12, 13; Ont, s 12; NS, s 14) specifically describes two situations: see Figure 24.2.

CASE 24.4 Fraud by Partner

A partner in a law firm undertook (privately) the administration of his aunt's estate. The firm's letterhead was used, and funds belonging to the estate passed through the firm's bank accounts.

The partner defrauded the estate and transferred funds to his own account.

In an action against the firm, the firm was found liable, even though the other partners were not aware of the activities in relation to the estate. The partner was acting within the scope of his apparent authority, since the administration of estates is a matter normally undertaken by lawyers.[26]

THE RELATIONSHIP BETWEEN PARTNERS

Partnership is a contractual relationship, and the relations between partners are governed by the terms of their contract. These terms may be found in the partnership agreement, they may be inferred from the conduct of the parties, or they may be

---

[23] See Ont, s 11; BC, s 12; NS, s 13.

[24] *McDonic v Hetherington* (1997), 142 DLR (4th) 648.

[25] See *McDonic Estate (Re)* (1997) 31 OR (3d) 577 (Ont CA.); see also *Strother v 3464920 Canada Inc*, [2007] 2 SCR 177 at paras 113–4.

[26] *Public Trustee v Mortimer* (1985), 16 DLR (4th) 404; see also *Korz v St Pierre* (1988), 43 DLR (4th) 528.

implied from the *Partnership Act*. A partner who acts in a manner that is contrary to the partnership agreement commits a breach of contract and may be liable to compensate the other partners for any damage resulting from the breach.[27]

Implied Terms

The Act implies some terms into the partnership agreement if those matters are not already expressly covered. The key implied terms are summarized below.[28] A partnership agreement may, and frequently does, change these terms either at the time of the original agreement or later by unanimous consent of the partners.[29]

Partnership Property "All property and rights and interests in property originally brought into the partnership stock or acquired, whether by purchase or otherwise, on account of the firm or for the purposes and in the course of the partnership's business are called . . . 'partnership property' and must be held and applied by the partners exclusively for the purposes of the partnership and in accordance with the partnership agreement."[30] Additionally, the Act provides that, unless the contrary intention appears, all property bought with money belonging to the firm is deemed to have been bought on account of the firm and is available only for the use of the firm (BC, s 24; Ont, s 22; NS, s 24).

It is not always clear whether a particular item of property is "brought into the partnership." Property that is used in the business is not necessarily partnership property but may remain the property of the individual partners. Therefore, the partnership agreement should make clear precisely what property considered a contribution to "capital."

ILLUSTRATION 24.1   PROPERTY AS CAPITAL CONTRIBUTIONS

A and B decide to go into equal partnership in a local delivery business. A owns a warehouse, valued at $50 000. B owns two vans, also valued at $50 000. Two years later, the partnership is dissolved. The warehouse is now worth $70 000, and the vans are worth $20 000. How much is each entitled to?

(a) If the warehouse and vans were brought in as partnership property, then the total value of the assets—$90 000—would be divided equally between them, and each would receive $45 000.

(b) If the assets brought into the business remained the individual property of A and B, then A would recover the warehouse ($70 000) and B only the depreciated vans ($20 000).

Either result might be fair, depending upon the original intentions of the parties, but in the absence of a clear agreement, one party might receive a windfall of $25 000 at the expense of the other.

Financial Arrangements   The Act sets some basic presumptions with respect to capital and profits, which apply unless there is another "agreement express or implied between the partners." It should be emphasized that these rules are more often than not varied by agreement.

1. "All the partners are entitled to share equally in the capital and profits of the business and must contribute equally towards the losses, whether of capital or otherwise, sustained by the firm" (BC, s 27(a); Ont, s 24(1); N.S, s 27(a)).

---

[27] See e.g. *Ernst & Young v Stuart* (1997), 144 DLR (4th) 328 (partner leaving firm without giving proper notice and joining competitor).

[28] Quotations are from the Ontario statute; the British Columbia and Nova Scotia versions differ slightly in a few cases.

[29] See BC, s 21; Ont, s 20; NS, s 22.

[30] See Ont, s 21(1); BC, s 23(1); NS, s 23(1).

Partners commonly vary this term: They contribute different proportions of capital and share profits based on other criteria, such as time spent on partnership business or billings.

2. If a partner incurs expenses or personal liabilities "in the ordinary and proper conduct of the business of the firm," or in preserving the business or property of the firm, the firm must indemnify him for these expenses or liabilities (BC, s 27(b); Ont, s 24(2); NS, s 27(b)). If one partner is sued for the firm's debts, he is entitled to a contribution from his fellow partners.[31]

3. A partner is not entitled, before the determination of profits, to interest on the capital subscribed by him (BC, s 27(d); Ont, s 24(4); NS, s 27(d)). In other words, if the agreement provides for the payment of "interest" on a partner's capital, the payment is not regarded as an expense of the firm but rather as an appropriation of profits. But if a partner makes a loan to the firm in addition to what he has agreed to pay in as capital under the partnership agreement, he is entitled to interest at the rate of 5 percent on the value of the excess contribution while it remains with the firm. The rate of interest may be varied by agreement.

4. "No partner is entitled to remuneration for acting in the partnership business."[32] Partnership agreements frequently do provide for periodic payments to partners. Normally, partners are not willing and able to wait until sometime after the end of the firm's accounting year, when the year's profits have been ascertained, before receiving income. It is common, therefore, to provide that a partner may "draw" up to a specified amount each month out of his prospective share of profits. Such an amount will be considered merely an advance on his share of the projected profits, repayable to the firm to the extent that it exceeds his share of the actual profits when they are determined.

CASE 24.5 Employee or Partner?

M was described as a "salaried partner" in a law firm. He was to be paid a fixed salary per year out of profits, plus one-third of the profits of the branch office that he ran.

The firm suffered a substantial loss. M claimed he was still entitled to his fixed salary, which should be paid by the other partners.

M lost. He was a partner, not an employee. His "salary" was a first charge on the profits of the firm. Since there were no profits, his share was nothing.[33]

Conduct of the Business The Act provides the following, unless there is agreement to the contrary:

1. "Every partner may take part in the management of the partnership business."[34] This implied term is often varied. Very large partnerships, such as law or accounting firms, often have two or more classes of partners, and it may be that only the senior partners take part in the management of the firm or partners elect a management committee.

2. "Any difference arising as to ordinary matters connected with the partnership business may be decided by a majority of the partners, but no change may be made in the nature of the partnership business without the consent of all

---

[31] There is an exception for limited liability partnerships, discussed at the end of this chapter.
[32] See Ont, s 24(6); BC, s 27(f); NS, s 27(f).
[33] *Marsh v Stacey* (1963), 103 Sol J 512 (UK).
[34] See Ont, s 24(5); BC, s 27(e); NS, s 27(e).

existing partners."[35] In cases of a serious disagreement, this provision can be troublesome. The minority may insist that the particular decision did not concern an ordinary matter but affected the nature of the partnership business. It is advisable to clearly identify which matters must be decided unanimously.

3. "The partnership books are to be kept at the place of business of the partnership or the principal place if there is more than one and every partner may access, inspect and copy any of them."[36]

Membership Partnership is a personal relationship, a fact that is demonstrated by two provisions of the Act:

1. "No person may be introduced as a partner without the consent of all existing partners."[37] Two common variations occur—where there are senior and junior partners and the consent of only the senior partners is required, and where a partner has reserved the right to have a son or daughter join the firm at a later date.

2. No partner may assign his share in the partnership, either absolutely or by way of mortgage, so as to permit the assignees to take over his duties or "to interfere in the management or administration of the partnership business or affairs, or to require any accounts of the partnership transactions, or to inspect the partnership books." An assignee may, however, "receive the share of profits to which the assigning partner would otherwise be entitled and the assignee must accept the account of profits agreed to by the partners."[38]

An assignee becomes entitled to receive a share of the profits but does not become a partner.[39]

Fiduciary Duties

Three sections of the Act describe the fiduciary duties owed by partners to one another.[40] Partners may not contract out of these duties, meaning the partnership agreement may not alter them.

Information "Partners are bound to render true accounts and full information of all things affecting the partnership to any partner or his legal representatives."[41]

Information regarding the firm's business that is provided to any of the partners must be made available to all of them.[42] The only circumstances under which this term might be varied would be in a partnership having several classes of partners. It is possible that, by express agreement, the most junior group of partners might not have access to all the books and records of the partnership. Even such a reservation, however, would be restricted to a narrow class of information.

Secret Benefits "Every partner must account to the firm for any benefit derived by him without the consent of the other partners from any transaction concerning the

---

[35] See Ont, s 24(8); BC, s 27(h); NS, s 27(h).

[36] See Ont, s 24(9); BC, s 27(i); NS, s 27(i).

[37] See BC, s 27(g); Ont, s 24(7); NS, s 27(g).

[38] See BC, s 34; Ont, s 31; NS, s 34.

[39] The assignee owes no fiduciary duty to the partnership: *Zawadzki v Matthews Group Ltd*, [1999] OJ No 2012 at paras 218–25, aff'd [2001] OJ No 3808 (ONCA).

[40] The BC Act (s. 22(1)) also contains a general rule that a partner shall act with utmost fairness and good faith.

[41] See BC, s 31; Ont, s 28; NS, s 31.

[42] See *Dockrill v Coopers & Lybrand* (1994), 111 DLR (4th) 62.

partnership or from any use by him of the partnership property, name or business connection."[43] A partner may be given permission by his co-partners to use partnership property for his own purposes or to take advantage of an opportunity offered to the firm. But without full disclosure and authorization, any benefit belongs to the firm. A partner in a law firm who teaches a university course part-time would need to seek permission from his firm and assign the compensation to the firm.

CASE 24.6 Full Disclosure

A partner in a firm of chartered accountants was responsible for a major corporate client. The partner was offered a directorship in the corporation. He disclosed this to the firm and paid his director's fees to the firm. However, he failed to disclose that he was also entitled to shares and stock options. When this was discovered, on the dissolution of the partnership, he was held liable to account to the firm for the value of the shares and options.[44]

Duty Not to Compete "Where a partner without the consent of the other partners carries on any business of the same nature as and competing with that of the firm, he must account for and pay over to the firm all profits made by him in that business."[45] These terms are varied occasionally according to the circumstances of the partnership. For example, an individual might be carrying on a retail business in the downtown area and subsequently enter into a partnership to carry on a similar business in a suburban shopping centre. Since the two businesses might well be considered "of the same nature and competing with" each other, the partner owning the downtown business would require, as a term of the partnership agreement, that the partners in the suburban business consent to his continuing the downtown business.

The duty to account for secret profits and the duty not to compete sometimes overlap.

CASE 24.7 Firm Opportunity

Davis and Ouellette formed a partnership to secure certain mining claims. The scheme fell through, but the partnership was never formally dissolved. Ouellette subsequently acquired the opportunity to buy the shares of a corporation that owned some of the claims. He notified Davis that he was terminating the partnership and then purchased the shares on his own behalf.

It was held that when Ouellette acquired the opportunity to buy the shares, he was still a partner. The opportunity belonged to the firm, and he had derived a benefit without the consent of his partner. He was liable to account for the profit he made.[46]

CASE 24.8 Account to the Firm

Olson and Gullo were partners involved in property development and speculation. Gullo acted fraudulently. He bought a piece of land and resold it at a profit of $2.5 million. (Apparently, he also attempted to have Olson killed—which was obviously a breach of his fiduciary duty!) The trial judge awarded the whole profit to Olson. On appeal by Gullo's estate, it was held that he was liable for only half of the profit. It was incorrect to say that this would allow him to profit from his own wrong. As a partner in the firm, half of the profit belonged to him anyway. It was the other half that should go to the plaintiff.[47]

---

[43] See BC, s 32; Ont, s 29; NS, s 32.

[44] *Rochwerg v Truster* (2002), 212 DLR (4th) 498 (ONCA). See also *McKnight v Hutchison* (2002), 28 BLR (3d) 269.

[45] See BC, s 33; Ont, s 30; NS, s 33.

[46] *Davis v Ouellette* (1981), 27 BCLR 162.

[47] *Olson v Gullo* (1994), 113 DLR (4th) 42, leave to appeal refused (1994), 20 BLR (2d) 47 (SCC).

TERMINATION OF PARTNERSHIP

Express Provision

All partnership agreements should address what happens on termination—in particular, on the retirement or death of a partner. What events justify termination? How much notice must a partner give to terminate the arrangement? Will the partnership among the remaining members continue? How is the retiring partner's interest to be valued and paid out? How will the continuing partners buy out the interest of a deceased or retired partner? These are important matters that should be settled in advance.

Implied Statutory Rules

In the absence of express agreement, the *Partnership Act* sets out a number of rules that govern termination.

Termination by Notice or Expiry
"When there is no fixed end date of the partnership, any partner may terminate the partnership at any time by giving notice of his intention to all other partners."[48] The notice so given may be oral or in writing, unless the partnership was originally formed by deed, in which case notice in writing is necessary.

A partnership may be for a fixed term or unlimited duration—that is, so long as the partners wish to continue. Where a partnership was entered into for a fixed term but is continued after the term has expired and without any express new agreement, the rights and duties of the partners remain the same as they were at the expiration of the term (BC, s 30; Ont, s 27; NS, s 30). Without continuing conduct, however, the partnership is dissolved by the expiration of the fixed term. Similarly, if the partnership was entered into for a single venture or undertaking, it expires with the termination of that venture or undertaking.

Termination on Death or Insolvency
Since partnership is a personal relationship, it automatically terminates on the death of a partner, at least so far as the relationship between the deceased and the other partners is concerned. The Act, however, provides that, subject to any contrary agreement, "every partnership is dissolved as regards all the partners by the death or bankruptcy or insolvency of any partner."[49]

This term, perhaps more than any other, is usually changed by the partnership agreement. In a partnership with substantial assets and many members, automatic dissolution of the partnership could be disastrous. Therefore, the partnership agreement usually provides that the partnership will continue in existence even after the death or insolvency of any partner. The surviving partners will buy out the share of a deceased partner according to a pre-set valuation formula and time line, often using life insurance purchased on the life of each partner for that purpose.

Even in a simple partnership between two persons, their agreement should provide for some means of ascertaining the value of the partnership on the death of either of them. The survivor may wish to continue the business as a sole proprietor—or find a new partner—and to buy out the share of the deceased partner.

The problem is primarily financial rather than legal. The arrangements must take into account the ability of the remaining partners to pay for the share of the deceased or insolvent partner, methods for ascertaining the value of that share, and the tax consequences of a particular method.

---

[48] See BC, s 29; Ont, s 26; NS, s 29.
[49] See BC, s 36(1); Ont, s 33(1); NS, s 36(1).

The Act further provides that, if a partner uses his share of the partnership property as security for his personal debts, the other partners are entitled to terminate the relationship (BC, s 36(2); Ont, s 33(2); NS, s 36(2)).[50]

Dissolution by Law

A partnership is automatically dissolved by any event that makes it unlawful for the business of the firm to be carried on or for members of the firm to carry it on in partnership (BC, s 37; Ont, s 34; NS, s 37). This is consistent with the general law of contract concerning illegality.

Even when there is disagreement among the partners concerning dissolution, or where dissolution at a specific time would be contrary to the terms of the partnership agreement, the court may (on an application by one or more partners) order dissolution if:

- a partner is found to be mentally incompetent,
- a partner becomes permanently incapable of performing his part of the agreement,
- a partner is guilty of conduct likely to negatively affect the business,
- a partner breaches the agreement or behaves in a way that makes it unreasonable or impractical for the other partners to carry on the business in partnership with him, or
- it is just and equitable that the partnership be dissolved (BC, s 38; Ont, s 35; NS, s 38)

Effects of Dissolution

When a partnership dissolves, the property of the partnership is first used to pay the debts and liabilities of the firm; any surplus is distributed to the partners, according to their interests (BC, s 42; Ont, s 39; NS, s 42). The Act further provides that, subject to any contrary agreement, in settling accounts between the partners after a dissolution of the partnership, losses (including losses and deficiencies of capital) are to be paid first out of profits, next out of capital, and last, if necessary, by the partners individually in the proportion in which they were entitled to share in the profits. The Act (BC, s 47; Ont, s 44; NS, s 47) also defines the order in which the liabilities of the firm must be met.

CHECKLIST
Sequence of Payments on Dissolution

1. The assets of the firm must be applied in the following sequence:
2. payment of the debts of the firm owed to non-partners
3. repayment of loans made to the firm by partners
4. repayment of the capital contributed by partners
5. sharing any surplus among the partners according to their entitlement to share in profits

The above provisions may only be varied to affect the rights of partners, not non-partners. It could, for example, be agreed that any loss be borne by the wealthier partner, even though he was not entitled to all the profits. What is important to note is that

---

[50] Under the BC Act, where there are three or more partners, this terminates the relationship only as between the partner whose share is charged and the other partners. The relationship between the other partners remains (s. 36(2)).

deficiencies of capital are treated as a loss of the firm; this is in contrast to the situation of shareholders in a corporation.[51]

LIMITED PARTNERSHIPS

The first specialized form of partnership is a limited partnership. It allows a partnership to raise capital from limited partners, without borrowing, just as a corporation does with shareholders. A limited partnership is a specialized vehicle designed to fulfill the needs of particular investors who want to share in the partnership's profits without responsibility for any partnership losses. It is governed by a *Limited Partnership Act* or a set of provisions within the provincial *Partnership Act*.[52]

A limited partnership may carry on business, under certain restricted conditions, without exposing some of its partners to personal liability. Limited partnerships came into existence about the same time that the private limited company (discussed in Chapter 25) came into being. For most business ventures, incorporating a company is a more effective way of raising capital; very little use has been made of limited partnerships.[53]

limited partnership a partnership in which some of the partners limit their liability to the amount of their capital contributions

general partner a partner in a limited partnership whose liability is not limited

limited partner a partner in a limited partnership whose liability is limited to the amount of her capital contribution

There must be two types of partners in a **limited partnership**: one or more **general partners** who have unlimited liability and **limited partners** whose liability is capped at the amount paid into the partnership. A limited partner risks only what she has invested in the business but is not liable to contribute anything further toward the debts or liabilities of the business.

All the Acts prohibit a limited partner from taking an active part in the management or business of the partnership. If she does so, she becomes liable as a general partner. The specific language varies in each of the statutes.[54] A limited partner would be "taking an active part" if she were personally to transact any business for the firm or be employed for that purpose as an agent or as a lawyer. She can examine the records of the firm, inquire into its progress, and advise on its management without incurring the liability of a general partner. The result is that a limited partner who attempts to take part in the management of the firm does so at a considerable personal risk. She may find herself in the dilemma that if she does not interfere, the business may fail completely; yet if she chooses to exercise some control in order to save the business, she will incur unlimited liability. For this reason more than any other, limited partnerships have rarely been used, except for tax-planning purposes.

There are more stringent regulations for registration for this type than for general partnerships. Failure to comply with requirements of detailed essential information also results in the loss of limited liability.

INTERNATIONAL ISSUE
Enron and Limited Partnerships

One of the most high-profile financial scandals in recent U.S. history involved the use of limited partnerships. As with Canadian limited partnerships, the United States requires that at least one general partner be liable for all the debts and liabilities of the operations, and no more than 35 limited partners can belong to the firm.

---

[51] See *Garner v Murray*, [1904] 1 Ch 57, when partners make unequal capital contributions or share losses unequally.

[52] Alberta, British Columbia, Manitoba, and Saskatchewan include the limited partnership provisions in the *Partnership Act*; the other provinces have separate Limited Partnership(s) Acts.

[53] Limited partnerships do have tax advantages in some circumstances.

[54] See e.g. *Partnership Act*, RSBC 1996, c 348, s 64; *Limited Partnerships Act*, RSO 1990, c L.16, s 13; RSNS 1989, c 259, s 17.

Enron Corp. set up many limited partnerships, parking debt in each one. Lenders became limited partners instead of creditors. Andrew Fastow, Enron's CFO and architect of the limited partnership strategy, moved the company away from the use of corporate subsidiaries. In an interview with *CFO Magazine* in 1999, Fastow described the benefits of the limited partnership: "You can get together with one or two investors and craft a particular structure to meet your and their objectives, which is very difficult if you have a public entity [where] you might have to go with shareholder votes and amendments of charters and the like."[55]

Amid much scandal, Enron filed for bankruptcy in late 2001. Of course, the ultimate downfall of Enron did not lie in the use of limited partnerships, but in the way those relationships were accounted for and disclosed to the public. Fastow pleaded guilty to several counts of fraud and was sent to jail. The Enron fiasco triggered a massive overhaul in accounting and corporate governance rules.

One interesting American variety of limited partnership is the public limited partnership. An unlimited number of public investors may become limited partners if the partnership is registered with the Securities and Exchange Commission. Shares in these partnerships are sold through brokerage houses rather than on an exchange.

Questions to Consider

1. How did the layering of limited partnerships on top of a corporation nullify the effect of the general partner's liability?
2. What are the pros and cons of public limited partnerships?

Sources: Ronald Fink, "Beyond Enron," *CFO Magazine*, February 1, 2002, http://ww2.cfo.com/banking-capital-markets/2002/02/beyond-enron; Richard DeGeorge, Chapter 9, "Business Ethics," in *Corporate Governance, Accounting Disclosure and Insider Trading* (Upper Saddle River, NJ: Prentice Hall, 2004); "10 Enron Players: Where They Landed After the Fall," *New York Times*, January 29, 2006, http://www.nytimes.com/2006/01/29/business/businessspecial3/29profiles.html?pagewanted=all&_r=0.

LIMITED LIABILITY PARTNERSHIPS

After remaining virtually unchanged for more than 100 years, Canadian partnership law saw a radical change in 1998 with the introduction in Ontario of another specialized form of partnership: the **limited liability partnership** (LLP).[56] Alberta followed in 1999, and Saskatchewan in 2001.[57] Since then, the LLP has also been introduced in Manitoba, New Brunswick, Nova Scotia, and British Columbia.[58] LLPs are principally used by large accounting and law firms because they cannot incorporate.

As noted, a major disadvantage of a general partnership is the firm's and partner liability for torts committed by another partner in the ordinary course of the business and corresponding joint liability of each partner for the debts and obligations of the firm. An LLP protects a partner from some of this personal liability:

> [A] partner in a limited liability partnership is not liable . . . for debts, liabilities or obligations of the partnership or any partner arising from the negligent acts or omissions that another partner or an employee, agent or representative of the partnership commits in the course of the partnership business while the partnership is a limited liability partnership.[59]

A partner remains liable for his own negligent acts or omissions, and for those of a person who is under the partner's direct supervision or control.[60] It also appears that the firm itself remains liable, so that a non-negligent partner still stands to lose the

limited liability partnership
a partnership in which non-negligent partners are not personally liable for losses caused by the negligence of a partner

---

[55] Ronald Fink, "Beyond Enron," *CFO Magazine*, February 1, 2002, http://ww2.cfo.com/banking-capital-markets/2002/02/beyond-enron.

[56] *Partnerships Statute Law Amendment Act*, 1998, SO 1998, c 2.

[57] *Partnership Act*, RSA 2000, c P-3, ss 81–104: RSS 1978, c P-3 (as amended), ss 78–110.

[58] *Partnership Act*, CCSM c P30, ss 51–88; RSNB 1973, c P-4, ss 46–54; RSNS 1989, c 334, ss 48–71; RSBC 1996, c 348 ss 94–125. The Ontario legislation is far less comprehensive than that of the other provinces.

[59] *Partnerships Act*, RSO 1990, c P.5 (as amended), s 10(2).

[60] *Ibid.*, s 10(3).

entire value of his partnership share. However, an injured party may not look beyond the assets of the firm to the personal assets of the non-negligent partners.[61]

Under the Ontario law, the protection of non-negligent partners appears to extend only to the negligent acts or omissions of a partner—it does not apply to other torts or to breaches of trust, nor does it affect the contractual liability of partners. The Alberta legislation provides broader protection. A member of an LLP is not liable for the "negligence, wrongful acts or omissions, malpractice or misconduct" of a partner, or of an employee or agent of the firm, unless he knew of the act in question and failed to take reasonable steps to prevent its commission, or the act was committed by someone for whom he was directly responsible and he had failed to provide adequate supervision.[62]

The Saskatchewan legislation adopts an entirely different approach: Partners in an LLP are personally liable for any partnership obligation for which they would be liable if the partnership were a corporation of which they were directors.[63] The Manitoba provisions on liability (s. 75) follow those of Alberta quite closely, while New Brunswick (ss. 48, 49) and Nova Scotia adopt both approaches (ss. 57, 58).

Although there are substantial differences in detail, all the provinces require a written agreement that designates the partnership as an LLP. An existing partnership may convert itself into an LLP if all the partners agree. An LLP must register its firm name, and the name must contain (and display) the words "limited liability partnership" or the abbreviation "LLP" or "L.L.P." Those provinces that have adopted the LLP form all permit LLPs from other jurisdictions to register as extra-provincial LLPs.

The most important restriction is that an LLP may carry on business only for the purpose of practising an "eligible profession."[64] In addition, that statute must expressly permit an LLP to practise the profession, and the governing body of the profession must require the partnership to maintain a minimum amount of liability insurance.

The LLP should not be confused with the limited partnership, discussed in the preceding section. In particular,

- in a limited partnership there must be at least one general partner who has unlimited liability;
- limited partners, unlike partners in an LLP, lose their limited liability if they participate in management;
- limited partnerships are not restricted to the professions.

Ethical Issue   To Limit or Not to Limit?

Limited liability partnerships have been allowed in Canada since 1998, though they have been permitted in many states of the United States for even longer. Their use has spread to a number of other countries, especially since the Enron case. Nevertheless, there is still disagreement as to whether becoming "limited," where it is permitted, is necessarily a good move. It involves questions of trust and privacy.

In favour of LLPs, it is argued that

- it obviously makes sense to limit one's personal liability when claims in the millions of dollars are being made against accounting and law firms,
- without LLP status it may be difficult to attract new partners, and

---

[61] Ibid., s 10(4).

[62] RSA 2000, c P-3, s 12.

[63] RSS 1978, c P-3 (as amended), ss 80, 81.

[64] Most provinces define it as a profession governed by statute. Alberta permits LLPs for any profession that allows the formation of professional corporations.

- all the big firms are going limited, so LLP status is a mark of success.
- Arguments against LLP status suggest that
- it is a signal to clients that even the partners do not trust each other,
- the conversion from unlimited to limited status poses some difficult problems and requires unanimity among existing partners,
- disclosure requirements result in a loss of privacy and, perhaps, confidentiality, and
- it is not yet clear just how much legal protection the LLP status provides.

Questions to Consider

1. Which of the above arguments do you find convincing?
2. In what circumstances, if any, would you recommend that an existing partnership "go limited"?

JOINT VENTURES

A joint venture is an agreement between two or more parties (often corporations) to collaborate on the management of a specific project, to each contribute a part of their respective resources (particular assets and expertise), and to share the profits.[65] Sometimes a project requires a greater capital outlay than any one corporation may be prepared to put at risk. A joint venture spreads the risk among the participants. In the oil and gas industry, for example, corporations have found it practical to undertake exploration expenditures jointly to discover and develop oil and gas reserves, as in the Arctic and Atlantic continental shelf explorations.

Legally, a joint venture is contractual. It is just a contractual relationship between the parties for a specific undertaking, and is sometimes referred to as a **contractual joint venture**. However, an alternative method of accomplishing the same end is for the parties to incorporate a separate corporation (a joint subsidiary) for the venture with each participant holding shares in it. This type of arrangement has become known as an **equity joint venture** but is subject to the general rules of corporation law, not contract.

Participants typically regard a contractual joint venture as an extension of their own operations and a project specific collaboration with other parties, rather than as a separate business. While they may look like a partnership, joint ventures are quite different. The venture is for a specific project or series of explorations, and of limited duration, not a continuing activity like a partnership. Nor are they inherently fiduciary relationships as are partnerships.[66] Normally, profits are not retained jointly for investment in other projects but are distributed to each of the participants in proportions set down in the joint venture agreement. The parties may also try to limit their liability by providing that their only contribution will be those things specifically set out in the agreement, that the agreement shall not be construed as a partnership, and that their liability will not be joint and several. They may also try to limit the authority of members to act as agents for one another in the operation of a joint venture and may identify one of themselves (or an independent party) as the "operator" of the joint venture. Whether such an arrangement will be effective to limit the agency of each participating member remains a question of fact to be determined by the court if a dispute arises with an outside third party. Such restrictions

contractual joint venture a joint venture effected by agreement without the creation of any separate legal entity

equity joint venture a corporation formed, and jointly owned, by the parties to a joint venture for the purpose of carrying on the venture

---

[65] *Canlan Investment Corp v Gettling* (1997), 37 BCLR (3d) 140 (BCCA); *Blue Line Hockey Acquisition Co v Orca Bay Hockey Limited Partnership*, [2008] BCJ No 24 at paras 57–77 (BC SC), aff'd 2009 BCCA 34.

[66] A majority of the Supreme Court of Canada held, in *LAC Minerals Ltd v International Corona Resources Ltd* (1989), 61 DLR (4th) 14, that there was no fiduciary duty between parties to a joint venture (though there was a duty not to misuse confidential information). See also *Chitel v Bank of Montreal*, [2002] OJ No 2170; *CadburySchweppes Inc v FBI Foods Ltd*, [1999] 1 SCR 142 at para 30.

may not be effective if it is determined that the venture was, as a matter of fact, a partnership.[67]

INCOME TRUSTS

Trusts are a complicated area of the law, as noted in Chapter 11, and this section will attempt only a basic explanation of their latest business application. Over the past decade, income trusts emerged as a popular Canadian business entity. This was largely due to favourable tax treatment and their unique liability structure. The tax advantage was removed in 2008.[68]

The income trust structure involves the transfer of income-producing assets from the operating company to a trust. The trust is created by an agreement known as a **declaration of trust**, and this document (in conjunction with trust law) governs the trust. The operating company continues to manage the assets under the supervision of the trustees, but all income (less expenses) is the property of the trust. The income is then distributed by the trust to **unitholders** (rather than shareholders) and taxed only once in the hands of the unitholders. When units are offered to the public, the trust is also governed by securities legislation. Tax rules phased in between 2008 and 2011 impose a second layer of taxation and thereby eliminate a trust's major tax advantage over corporations.

As for the liability and governance issues, income trusts are operated by trustees, and their liability has historically been determined under the rules of trust law, not corporate governance law. The Uniform Law Commission of Canada has proposed a model law addressing the structure and governance issues, which recommends that income trusts be treated more like corporations; for example,

- unitholders should have limited liability;
- unitholders should be entitled to elect trustees;
- unitholders should have the same remedies as shareholders; and
- trustees should have the same powers, duties, and liability as directors of a corporation.[69]

So far, only the tax changes have been adopted.

declaration of trust an agreement that establishes a trust and designates the trustees

unitholders beneficiaries of an income trust

Strategies to Manage the Legal Risks

One of the most important legal risk management decisions a business owner and operator will make is to choose the appropriate entity within which to operate the business. This should be done after seeking financial, accounting, and legal advice. Incorporating is a natural choice where the type of business allows it, but it may not be appropriate for short-term, low-risk, and modestly financed ventures. One entity may be converted into another once the business is operating profitably.

For all forms of business, complying with registration requirements is vital. Business names must be registered in all provinces, but this does not give a business

---

[67] *Central Mortgage and Housing Corp v Graham* (1973), 43 DLR (3d) 686; *Lansing Building Supply (Ontario) Ltd v Ierullo, supra* note 9; *LAC Minerals Ltd v International Corona Resources Ltd* (1989), 61 DLR (4th) 14 (each case will turn on its own facts). See also *Chitel v Bank of Montreal*, [2002] OJ No 2170.

[68] Department of Finance, Canada, "Canada's New Government Announces Tax Fairness Plan," press release, October 31, 2008, http://www.fin.gc.ca/n06/06-061-eng.asp.

[69] Uniform Law Commission of Canada, *Uniform Income Trusts Act*, http://www.ulcc.ca/en/uniform-acts-new-order/current-uniform-acts/672-trusts/income-trusts/1444-income-trusts-act.

ownership of the name. Prior to registering the business name, steps as outlined in Chapter 20 should be followed to protect ownership in the intellectual property and trademarks of the business. There may be liability for registering a name that infringes the intellectual property rights of others. Make the appropriate searches before registering.

Written partnership agreements are essential; partners should not rely on the "one size fits all" model set out in the *Partnership Act*. Non-competition agreements and partner buy-out mechanisms are just two examples of things not covered in the legislation. Each partner should seek independent legal advice prior to signing the agreement.

If a need for regular capital infusion is expected, consider the use of a limited partnership so that investors may be sought in the form of limited partners without having to include them in the operation of the business. Accounting and legal partnerships should consider the use of limited liability partnerships to reduce personal liability for torts of other partners. Partners should consider arranging their personal affairs so that family assets are not owned by them and thereby available to satisfy partnership debts.

For specific projects, consider the use of several entities. For example, two corporations may form a partnership for a specific business neither carries on alone. Although the partners will have personal liability, the shareholders of the corporation will be immune from liability. Alternatively, where two limited partnerships form a joint venture, only the general partners in each partnership will face possible liability. It is very common for businesses to layer one entity on top of another.

QUESTIONS FOR REVIEW

1. To what laws are sole proprietorships subject?
2. Is it necessary to have a written agreement in order to create a partnership?
3. What are the advantages and disadvantages of partnerships as opposed to sole proprietorships?
4. What are the basic elements of the partnership relationship?
5. What is the difference between sharing profits and sharing gross receipts?
6. In what circumstances may a person receive a share of the profits of a partnership business without herself being a partner?
7. Why is it important to distinguish between partnership property and the personal property of the individual partners?
8. When is it necessary for a partnership to be registered?
9. What does it mean to say "every partner is an agent of the firm"?
10. What is meant by "apparent authority"?
11. What is "joint liability"?
12. What steps should a partner take to protect herself against ongoing liability when she retires?
13. Can a partner receive a "salary" from the firm? What is the real nature of a partner's salary?
14. What are the three principal fiduciary duties imposed on partners?
15. How is partnership property distributed on the dissolution of a partnership?
16. Is there any difference between a partnership and a joint venture?

17. What are the principal forms that a joint venture may take?
18. What are the principal advantages and disadvantages of being a limited partner?
19. What is a limited liability partnership? How does it differ from a limited partnership?
20. In what ways is the liability of a partner in an LLP limited?
21. What is an income trusts?

CASES AND PROBLEMS

1. Continuing Scenario

    At the end of the first year in business, it appears that Ashley's restaurant has made a profit. She won't know the exact amount until her accountant finishes the financial statements, but he is asking questions about what "type" of business entity she is operating. She knows it is not a corporation because she has not filed any government forms or registrations. But she has promised to share some of the profits with others. To her father, Jim—who guaranteed the poultry supplier account, co-signed her lease, and painted the whole restaurant before opening—Ashley promised she would "pay him back" for all his hard work when the restaurant started making money. Ashley told her mother, who advanced her $50 000 at the start of the business, that there would be a good "return on her investment," and Ashley has already paid her $3000 for use of the money. Ashley asks her lawyer, Brendan, the following questions: Is she in a partnership with her parents? Why or why not? If so what kind of partnership is it, and how will they share the profits? Ashley's parents are old; what would be the consequences to the business if one of them died? What registrations should she have made?

2. Giovanni and Leporello were in partnership together under the registered name "Adventures Unlimited." The partnership was formed for the purpose of providing guided adventure vacations for rich clients. Under a clause in the partnership agreement, it was provided that neither partner may incur expenditures on behalf of the firm in excess of $500 without the approval of the other partner.

    Giovanni purported to enter into a contract—in the name of Adventures Unlimited—with Elvira Sails Ltd. (a corporation engaged in selling and leasing boats) to rent a large cabin cruiser for a period of three months, at a rent of $10 000 per month. He signed the rental agreement in his own name, paid a deposit for $1000 by a cheque drawn on the partnership's bank account, took delivery of the cruiser, and has not been seen since. The cruiser was reportedly last seen in the Virgin Islands.

    What rights (if any) does Elvira Sails have against Leporello?

3. Crawford and McDougall were sisters of relatively advanced years. For some years they had entrusted their financial affairs to Watson, a lawyer, who was a partner in the firm of Heather & Co. Due to some disastrous investments they made on Watson's advice, they lost almost $250 000.

    The loss was discovered when they learned that Watson had been disbarred for misconduct. It was evident that their loss had been caused either by fraud or by negligence on the part of Watson, though it was less clear which.

    The sisters brought an action against Heather & Co, claiming damages for their loss.

    Should they succeed? What particular circumstances might be relevant?

4. Adders LLP is a limited liability partnership, registered in Ontario, practising as chartered accountants. It has 15 partners and over 200 employees. One of its major clients, Norne Inc., is a small but dynamic resource company, incorporated in Ontario.

    Until about two years ago, the Norne account was supervised by Counter, a senior partner. More recently, the corporation's account has been handled by Turner, a young accountant who is considered to be in line for a partnership.

Counter has continued to exercise nominal supervision, discussing the account with Turner from time to time, but increasingly Turner has been left to work by herself.

Shortly after taking over the account, Turner was approached by Plotter, Norne's chief financial officer, who outlined to her a scheme to extract large sums of money from Norne through unauthorized borrowings. Turner would be able to use her position to falsify the accounts and to conceal the transactions. Turner agreed, and over the next 18 months they were able to divert over $5 million from Norne before their scheme was discovered. Turner, Plotter, and the money have all disappeared.

Adders LLP is now being sued by Norne Inc. and also by Driller, an investor resident in British Columbia, who recently purchased a 20 percent share in Norne after examining the accounts prepared by Adders.

Consider the liability of (a) Adders LLP, (b) Counter, and (c) the other partners in the firm.

5. Albinoni, Bonporti, and Corelli were partners. According to the partnership agreement, the following provisions applied:

   (a) **Capital:**

   Albinoni and Bonporti each contributed $20 000; Corelli contributed no capital.

   (b) **Advances:**

   Albinoni advanced $10 000 to the firm by way of a loan, repayable on six months' notice or on dissolution.

   (c) **Profits:**

   Profits were to be shared in the following proportions: Albinoni, 40 percent; Bonporti, 40 percent; Corelli, 20 percent. They were to contribute in the same proportions (40/40/20) to make up any loss or deficiency.

   (d) **Drawings:**

   The partners were entitled to draw, by way of an advance on their prospective shares of profits, up to $60 000 in any year. Since the end of the last accounting period, the following drawings were made: Albinoni, $8000; Bonporti, $7000; Corelli, $15 000.

   The partnership has now been dissolved. At the time of dissolution, the total value of the firm's assets, including undrawn profits, was $100 000. (This does not include the $30 000 already drawn by the partners.)

   Calculate how the surplus, or deficiency, should be shared, if the total liabilities to the firm's external creditors (that is, not including debts owed to partners) are as follows:

   (1) $10 000

   (2) $90 000

   (3) $150 000

Chapter 25
The Nature of a Corporation and Its Formation

- **THE NATURE OF A CORPORATION**
- **METHODS OF INCORPORATION**
- **THE CONSTITUTION OF A CORPORATION**
- **TYPES OF BUSINESS CORPORATIONS**
- **CORPORATE CAPITAL**
- **CORPORATE SECURITIES**
- **STRATEGIES TO MANAGE THE LEGAL RISKS**

This is the first of three chapters dealing with corporations. In it, we discuss some of the most fundamental issues concerning the nature of a corporation.

In this chapter we examine such questions as:

- What is a corporation?
- What are the consequences that flow from incorporation?
- What is meant by "limited liability"?
- How is a corporation formed?
- What are the usual provisions of the corporate charter?
- What is corporate capital?
- What are shares?
- What are the main distinctions between shares and bonds?

THE NATURE OF A CORPORATION

The corporation, or limited company, is the dominant business entity in the world. Not only is it the main form of big business, but it also the most popular form of small business, exceeding sole proprietorships and partnerships.

The Corporation as a Legal Person

A **corporation** is a person in the eyes of the law; it is a **legal person** (an entity recognized by law as having rights and duties of its own). Legal persons are not the same as natural persons. Natural persons are human beings—they automatically have rights and obligations. Their rights and obligations may vary according to age, mental capacity, and other factors,[1] but they are all "persons." By contrast, a legal person is entirely a creation of the state. A legal person has rights and duties under the law, distinct from its owner or creator, but it cannot enforce those rights or carry out its duties except through human agents.

It is a well-established legal principle that once a corporation is created, it is a separate and distinct legal person apart from its creators, owners, and operators.[2]

There are numerous types of corporations: publicly owned corporations created by governments to carry on special activities (for example, the Bank of Canada, Canadian Broadcasting Corporation, Central Mortgage and Housing Corporation, and Canadian National Railway); municipal corporations to run local government; charitable corporations (for example, the Red Cross, Heart and Stroke Foundation, Ford Foundation); educational institutions; cooperatives;[3] and business corporations—the most numerous type of all. We are concerned with business corporations.[4]

corporation a legal person formed by incorporation according to a prescribed legal procedure

legal person an entity recognized at law as having its own legal rights, duties, and responsibilities

Characteristics of Corporations vs. Partnerships

The significance of the separate legal identity of a business corporation is obvious when compared with partnership.

Liability As noted in Chapter 24, each partner in a partnership is normally liable for payment of the debts of the firm, including payment from his personal assets.[5] A corporation is liable for its own debts. A shareholder in a corporation is not required to pay the corporation's debts; shareholders can lose no more than the price paid for the shares. This **limited liability** of shareholders is why business corporations are called "limited" companies, although this is really a misnomer since the corporation itself is liable to the full extent of its assets.[6]

limited liability the liability of shareholders is limited to the amount of their capital contributions

Limited liability is the main advantage of incorporation. However, the benefits of limited liability are sometimes overestimated since, for a small corporation to obtain credit, its directors or shareholders are often required to give personal guarantees or mortgage their own property as collateral security. In addition, when shareholders

---

[1] See Chapter 8.

[2] See DH Bonham and DA Soberman, "The Nature of Corporate Personality," in *Studies in Canadian Company Law*, JS Ziegel, ed, Vol 1, Ch 1 (Toronto: Butterworths, 1967).

[3] There are over 9000 cooperatives, credit unions, and mutuals in Canada and over 750 000 in the world: Measuring the Cooperative Difference Research Network, http://www.cooperativedifference.coop/co-operatives-in-canada.

[4] Business corporations are divided into a number of subcategories.

[5] Exceptions are the limited liability partnership and limited partnership.

[6] In British Columbia, Alberta, and Nova Scotia, it is possible to form an unlimited company in which the shareholders are liable for the company's debts. The main attraction of this form has been to create tax-planning opportunities for U.S. businesses.

become directors—as they usually do in smaller enterprises—they are exposed personal liability from which their limited liability as shareholders does not protect them.

Transfer of Ownership A partner cannot unilaterally end her risk of personal liability—to her partners, to the firm, and to its clients—simply by retiring. She must negotiate her release with both her partners and her creditors and fulfill the notice requirements of the *Partnership Act*. Withdrawal will end the partnership unless a prior agreement says otherwise. Since a shareholder has no liability for corporate debts while he owns shares, he may easily sever all connections with the corporation simply by transferring his shares to another person without disruption to the corporation's ability to carry on business. However, sometimes restrictions are imposed on the transfer of shares by the corporation.

Management A partnership is not suitable for a venture involving a large number of investors. Each partner is an agent of the firm and may enter into contracts on behalf of the firm. By contrast, shareholders have no agency authority to form corporate contracts—only officers of the corporation may do so.

A partnership usually requires unanimity on major business decisions, a requirement that could deadlock a firm with a large number of partners. In a corporation, management is delegated to an elected board of directors that normally reaches decisions by simple majority votes. Major decisions that are referred back to the shareholders do not require unanimity but at most a two-thirds or three-quarters majority, depending on the requirements of the corporation law statutes in the jurisdiction.

Separation of ownership and management and limited liability are the primary advantages of the business corporation. These features enable an investor to invest a specific sum of money and receive a return on it, without either taking any additional risk beyond the sum invested or having to take part in the management of business.

Historically, the major shareholders in a corporation were often its managers as well. Now, separation between those who invest and those who manage is common.[7] The separation is, however, less pronounced in Canada than in the United States because many large Canadian corporations are controlled by a single individual or by members of a family, or are wholly owned subsidiaries of foreign parent corporations.[8]

Duty of Good Faith As noted in Chapter 24, partners owe each other a duty of good faith or fiduciary duty. It would normally be a breach of duty for a partner to carry on another business independently without the consent of her other partners (especially if it were a competing business) or to enter into contracts with the firm on her own behalf. A shareholder owes no such duty to the corporation:[9] He may carry on any independent business himself and may deal freely with the corporation as if he were a stranger.

Continuity In the absence of special provisions in the partnership agreement, the death or bankruptcy of a partner dissolves a partnership. Even when provisions are made in advance to continue the partnership and to buy out the share of the deceased or bankrupt partner, the procedure is often cumbersome and expensive. Not so for corporations.[10] A person's shares may be transferred by gift or by sale, by will or by

---

[7] The classic study of this subject is that by AA Berle and GC Means, *The Modern Corporation and Private Property* (New York: Macmillan, 1932). It is still worth reading.

[8] Randall K Morck, David A Stangeland, and Bernard Yeung, "Inherited Wealth, Corporate Control, and Economic Growth: The Canadian Disease?" in *Concentrated Corporate Ownership*, Randall K Morck, ed (Chicago: National Bureau of Economic Research and University of Chicago Press, 2000).

[9] See *Blacklaws v 470433 Alberta Ltd* (2000), 187 DLR (4th) 614. Directors owe a duty of good faith to their corporation.

[10] It survives even the death of all its shareholders: *Re Noel Tedman Holdings Pty Ltd*, [1967] Qd R 561 (Queensland SC).

statute, or by creditors seizing them—none of these events affects the existence of the corporation. A corporation continues in existence indefinitely unless it is dissolved by order of a court or registrar or by a voluntary resolution of its shareholders.

Taxation Unlike a partnership, a corporation is a taxable entity. Its income is taxed first in the corporation and second as personal income of a shareholder when a dividend is declared. Offsetting this double taxation, corporate tax rates are low; small corporations are taxed at especially low rates, and dividends from Canadian corporations receive preferential tax treatment.[11]

CHECKLIST
Partnerships and Corporate Ownership Contrasted

Characteristic	Partnership	Corporation
Separate legal entity	No	Yes
Personal liability of owners	Yes*	No
Duty of good faith	Yes	No
Agency	Yes	No
Transferability of ownership	No	Yes
Participation of owners in management	Yes*	No
Continuity of business	No	Yes
Taxable entity	No	Yes

*There are exceptions; see Chapter 24.

Consequences of Separate Corporate Personality

Capacity A corporation is created by statute law and has the characteristics that the legislators give it. Originally, corporations were formed for specific purposes and could act only for those purposes expressly stated in their constitution. Any act outside the scope of those objects was *ultra vires*—beyond the powers—of the corporation. Contracts made for an unauthorized purpose were invalid.

The *ultra vires* doctrine, as it applied to corporations, was abolished throughout Canada. Under the federal *Canada Business Corporations Act*, and most of the provincial statutes under which business corporations are formed, a corporation has the capacity and most of the rights, responsibilities, and powers of a natural person.[12]

However, as an "artificial" person, a corporation can act only through its human agents—its directors and officers. For example, human agents must act to form contracts for a corporation.

Separate Existence: *Salomon* The classic case on the existence of the corporation as a separate entity came in 1897 in *Salomon v Salomon & Co Ltd*.[13] It is probably the most widely quoted decision in the whole of corporate law.

---

[11] The small business combined federal (4.5 percent) and provincial (11.5 percent) tax rate in Ontario was approximately 15 percent in 2017 (available on up to $500 000 of business income).

[12] RSC 1985, c C-44, s 15, referred to hereafter as the CBCA. It cannot vote.

[13] [1897] AC 22.

CASE 25.1 One Man Company

Salomon carried on a successful shoe manufacturing business. In 1892, he formed a corporation in which he held almost all the shares (20 001 out of 20 007, the remaining six shares being held by members of his family, in order to meet what was then the statutory requirement of seven shareholders). He then sold his business to the corporation but continued to operate it as the only director and employee. Soon afterward, a downturn in the shoe industry drove the corporation into insolvency, and a trustee was appointed to wind it up. The trustee claimed that the corporation was merely a sham, that Salomon was the true owner of the business and the real debtor, and, as such, he should pay off all debts owed by the corporation. The lower courts supported the trustee's position, but the Appeal Court decided in favour of Salomon. Either the corporation was a true legal entity, or it was not. Since there was no fraud nor intention to deceive, full disclosure of all transactions, and compliance with all statutory regulations, the corporation was properly created and was solely responsible for its own debts.

The *Salomon* case is important because it recognized the separate legal personality of the so-called one-man company at the time when it was becoming a common form of doing business.[14] As a leading writer on the subject has said, "Since the *Salomon* case, the complete separation of the company and its members has never been doubted."[15]

For the most part, the principle of separate legal personality prevails, but in some circumstances, the shareholders' interests may be recognized. In the 1987 *Kosmopoulos* case, the Supreme Court of Canada held that a shareholder, even one who owns all the shares of a corporation, does not own its assets but still has an insurable interest in those assets. If they are destroyed, his shares will lose value, and, consequently, he should be entitled to insure against their destruction.[16]

It remains unclear how far the principle in the *Kosmopoulos* case can be taken and whether it is restricted to insurance claims. Certainly, it does not seem to follow that where an injury is done to a corporation, a shareholder will always have a claim for the consequent reduction in the value of his shares. The fact that the plaintiff is the principal shareholder and directing mind of the corporation that was defrauded does not entitle him to personal compensation for the losses suffered by the corporation.[17] To hold otherwise would enable him to jump to the front of the payment line to the prejudice of other corporate creditors. Where a wrong is done to a corporation, a shareholder has no claim for damages in respect of that wrong merely because he is an owner of that corporation; it is the corporation's cause of action.[18] In Chapter 5, we discussed negligently auditors who were held liable to the audited corporation not to its shareholders.

As stated in section 45 of the *Canada Business Corporations Act*, shareholders are not liable for any act or default of debt of the corporation.

---

[14] CBCA, s 5, allows a corporation to be formed with only one shareholder/director, as do the laws of almost all provinces.

[15] *Gower's Principles of Modern Company Law*, 6th ed, (London: Sweet & Maxwell, 1997) at 79–80.

[16] *Kosmopoulos v Constitution Insurance Co of Canada* (1987), 34 DLR (4th) 208. The concept of insurable interest is discussed in Chapter 16.

[17] *Martin v Goldfarb* (1998), 163 DLR (4th) 639; *Meditrust Healthcare Inc v Shoppers Drug Mart* (2002), 220 DLR (4th) 611; *RLTV Investments Inc v Saskatchewan Telecommunications*, [2009] 9 WWR 15 (Sask CA); *Livent v Deloitte & Touche*, 2017 SCC 63.

[18] *Livent, ibid* (citing *Hercules Management v Ernst Young*, [1997] 2 SCR 165); a separate duty of care must be established before a shareholder loss would be recoverable.

CASE 25.2 Shareholder Liability

K, a Toronto lawyer, incorporated a real estate company, Rockwell, of which he effectively owned almost all the shares. Rockwell became involved in a contractual dispute with another corporation, Newtonbrook, and eventually brought an action against Newtonbrook for specific performance of the contract. Rockwell lost the action, and Newtonbrook was awarded costs of $4800. When Newtonbrook sought to recover the costs, it found that Rockwell's entire assets consisted of $31.85 in its bank account. Newtonbrook's attempt to recover from K personally failed.[19]

Limitations on the Principle of Separate Corporate Existence

When application of the *Salomon* decision leads to unfair results, should the courts refuse to follow it? When should legislation disregard the principle of separate legal identity?

Exceptions to Limited Liability The limited liability of shareholders is not absolute. In practice, shareholders of small private companies are often required to provide security or personal guarantees for loans made to their corporations. The *Canada Business Corporations Act* (CBCA) provides a further exception to the principle: Where shareholders have received an improper distribution of corporate assets—for example, where a dividend has been paid although the corporation had made no profits—they are liable for the corporation's debts to that extent (s. 118(4)).[20] Other statutes, such as the federal *Bankruptcy and Insolvency Act*,[21] require shareholders who have received property from a corporation before it became insolvent to repay the amounts received in certain circumstances.

It is also important to note that the principle of limited liability does not protect persons who happen to be shareholders of corporations from personal liability. For example, a director who behaves negligently or fraudulently while doing company business is not absolved from liability in tort, even though the corporation may also be vicariously liable.[22] And directors who make negligent misrepresentations regarding the affairs of their corporation may be personally liable for any resulting loss.[23] In Chapter 26, we will discuss the other circumstances in which officers and directors are exposed to personal liability.

Other Statutory Provisions There are numerous examples, especially in taxation and labour law, where statutes require the separate personality of corporations to be disregarded. For example, Canadian-controlled private corporations are taxed at a lower rate on the first $500 000 of their annual income; but it is not possible to multiply this concession by forming several distinct corporations, because **associated corporations** are only entitled to a single concession between them.[24] Again, employers

associated corporations corporations that are related either (a) vertically, as where one corporation controls the other (parent–subsidiary), or (b) horizontally, as where both corporations are controlled by the same person (affiliates)

---

[19] *Rockwell Developments Ltd v Newtonbrook Plaza Ltd* (1972), 27 DLR (3d) 651.

[20] There are also several provisions that make directors liable for the debts of their corporation; these are considered in Chapter 27.

[21] RSC 1985, c B-3. See Chapter 29.

[22] See *Berger v Willowdale* (1983), 41 OR (2d) 89, leave to appeal denied [1983] SCCA No 353.

[23] *NBD Bank of Canada v Dofasco Inc* (1999), 181 DLR (4th) 37, leave to appeal denied [2000] SCCA No. 96; contrast *Scotia McLeod Inc v Peoples Jewellers Limited et al* (1995), 26 OR (3d) 481, leave to appeal denied [1996] SCCA No 40. See secondary market liability in Chapters 5, 26, and 27.

[24] *Income Tax Act*, RSC 1985, c 1 (5th Supp), s 125(3). Corporations are associated where one corporation controls the other (parent–subsidiary relationship) or where both corporations are controlled by the same person or group of persons (affiliates) (s. 256).

are not allowed to avoid statutory employment standards by transferring their assets to an associated corporation, thereby leaving the employer unable to meet employee claims for unpaid wages, vacation pay, and other benefits.[25] Nevertheless, the courts and legislature have stopped short of recognizing group liability. It is only in exceptional circumstances that a parent company will be held liable for the debts of its subsidiary or vice versa.

ILLUSTRATION 25.1   Common Ownership

Holdco is the parent company of a major marketing group. It has a number of divisions, each operated by a wholly owned subsidiary corporation. Retailco, its retailing subsidiary, recently became bankrupt, owing $100 million. At the same time, Creditco, the corporation that operates its credit financing division, has profits of $20 million. The assets of Creditco are not available to pay the creditors of Retailco even though they are owned by the same shareholder.

Lifting the Corporate Veil

There have also been cases—although in Canada they are rare—where the courts ignored the separate existence of corporations and acted to "lift the corporate veil" to impose liability on those that control it. It seems that, in order to find an individual within a corporation liable, three conditions must be met:

- The individual must control the corporation.
- That control must have been exercised to commit a fraud, a wrong, or a breach of duty.
- The misconduct must be the cause of the plaintiff's injury.[26]

Rather than equate a controlling shareholder with the corporation she controls, Canadian courts have generally preferred to seek other routes to secure a just result. As we saw in the *Kosmopoulos* case,[27] the Supreme Court of Canada refused to lift the veil and to hold that the corporation and the individual who owned all of its shares were one and the same person but reached the same result by finding that he had an insurable interest in the corporation's property.

INTERNATIONAL ISSUE

Foreign Investment in Canadian Corporations

As will be discussed in Chapters 30 and 31, foreign investment in Canadian corporations is monitored and controlled by Industry Canada, pursuant to the *Investment Canada Act*.[28] In addition, the *Canada Business Corporations Act* (s 105(3)) requires that 25 percent of a Canadian corporation's directors be resident Canadians (as do the Ontario, Alberta, Saskatchewan, and Manitoba statutes).[29] However, there are variations among the provinces. To encourage foreign investment, British Columbia and Nova Scotia have dropped directors' residency requirements.

---

[25] See e.g. *Employment Standards Act*, SO 2000, c 41, s 4, regarding associated businesses being treated as one employer but excluding shareholders from this principle.

[26] *WD Latimer Co Ltd v Dijon Investments Ltd* (1992), 12 OR (3d) 415. Courts are more likely to lift the corporate veil when a shareholder engages in conduct amounting to fraud. See *Gilford Motor Company v Horne*, [1933] Ch. 935 (CA).

[27] *Kosmopoulos*, *supra* note 16.

[28] RSC 1985, c 28 (1st Supp).

[29] See *Business Corporations Act*, RSO 1990, c B-16, s 118(3); RSA 2000, c B-9, s 105(3); RSS 1978, c B-10, s 100(3); *Corporations Act* CCSM c C225, s 100(3).

Another strategy to increase foreign investment (particularly by Americans) is a different type of corporation: the unlimited liability corporation (ULC). As the name suggests, these corporations do not benefit from the protection of limited liability. On windup or dissolution, shareholders in a ULC are personally liable to the ULC's creditors for any unsatisfied debts.[30] So far, Nova Scotia, Alberta, and British Columbia have introduced foreign ULCs in their provincial incorporation legislation.[31] Ontario did not authorize ULCs when it amended its incorporation legislation in 2007. The attraction of ULCs for investors lies in the different tax treatment they receive in the United States. Although ULCs are taxed like any other corporation in Canada, in the United States they are viewed as "flow through" vehicles, and no federal income tax is collected from them. When considering investing in this type of corporation, potential shareholders must weigh the tax benefits against the potential liability involved.

Question to Consider

1. What impact will provincial variation in the availability of ULCs have on foreign investment decisions?

Sources: Maria Severino, "Canadian Unlimited Liability Companies (ULC)—A Viable Vehicle for US Investors Expanding into Canada?" Collins Barrow Chartered Accountants, *Tax Flash*, June 2012, http://www.collinsbarrow.com/uploads/docs/newsletter/national/archive/TaxFlash_May2012.pdf.

METHODS OF INCORPORATION

Early Methods of Incorporation

The oldest method of incorporation in the common law system—dating back to the 16th century—is by **royal charter** granted by the sovereign. Until the 19th century, all corporations were created by charter. Some of these are still in existence—the best known to Canadians being the Hudson's Bay Company, founded in 1670. A few royal charters are still issued today to universities and charitable institutions, but none to business corporations.

royal charter a special licence given by the Crown to form a corporation for the purpose of carrying on a particular activity

At the end of the 18th century, the government began creating corporations by **special Acts of Parliament**, especially for large projects of public interest—railroads, canals, waterworks, and other public utilities. Today, special acts are still used to create such corporations as Bell Canada and Canadian Pacific, and also to create special government corporations such as the Central Mortgage and Housing Corporation, the Canadian Broadcasting Corporation, and Air Canada. Parliament and the provincial legislatures have also passed statutes setting out procedures for the incorporation of particular types of businesses, such as banks and trust and loan companies and cooperatives. Such businesses may be incorporated only under those acts.

special Acts of Parliament legislative acts creating a specific corporation

General Incorporation Statutes

Today, almost all business (for profit) corporations are incorporated under general incorporation statutes. Under a statute of this type, any group of persons that complies with its requirements may form a corporation. In Canada, there is both federal and provincial incorporation legislation. The provincial systems vary from one province to another.

Incorporation Roots: The Memorandum and Letters Patent Systems
In 1862, a system was introduced in England that depended upon Parliament rather than the royal prerogative, and that system was adopted by five provinces. It now remains in force in only one—Nova Scotia.[32] The system requires applicants to register a document that sets out the fundamental terms of their agreement, called a

---

[30] There is some provincial variation in the extent of shareholder liability. Alberta extends shareholder liability beyond liquidation and windup situations. Liability also applies to former shareholders.

[31] See e.g. *Business Corporations Act*, SBC 2002, c 57, s 51.1.

[32] *Companies Act*, RSNS 1989, c 81.

memorandum of association a document setting out the essential terms of an agreement to form a corporation

certificate of incorporation a certificate that a corporation has come into existence

letters patent a document incorporating a corporation, issued by the appropriate authority and constituting the "charter" of the corporation

memorandum of association. If the memorandum and certain other prescribed documents comply with the statute, and the registration fee is paid, the authorized government office issues a **certificate of incorporation**, and the corporation comes into existence. We shall call corporations incorporated in this manner "memorandum corporations."

Other provinces and the federal government adopted a different system that survives today only in Quebec and Prince Edward Island.[33] There, the incorporating document is called the **letters patent**, an offspring of the royal charter but issued under the authority of the Crown's representative in each jurisdiction. Under the letters patent system, a general statute regulates the conditions under which the letters patent may be issued. Although in theory the granting of letters patent is discretionary, in practice, the steps taken by applicants do not differ greatly from those for registering a memorandum under the English system.

The Articles of Incorporation System

In 1970, Ontario passed a substantially different *Business Corporations Act*, creating a new method of incorporation adapted from a system in use in the United States. In 1975, the federal Parliament adopted the same system in its new statute, although many of the provisions of the federal act were quite different from those of the Ontario version. The CBCA became the model for the rest of the provinces. Alberta, Manitoba, New Brunswick, Newfoundland and Labrador, Ontario, Saskatchewan, and British Columbia[34] followed with acts based on the federal scheme, although with local variations. Under the articles of incorporation system, persons who wish to create a corporation sign and deliver the articles of incorporation forms to a government office and are issued "articles" of incorporation as a purely administrative process.

As the articles of incorporation system is now the most widely used one in Canada, our discussion will focus on it.

The Choice of Jurisdiction

The first decision to be made in forming a corporation is whether to incorporate federally or provincially. The CBCA is especially suitable for large businesses that carry on their activities nationwide; but even a small, local, one-person business may incorporate under it.

The activities of a business incorporated under provincial jurisdiction are not restricted to that province. It may carry on business anywhere inside or outside Canada. However, corporations not incorporated within a province—and this includes federally incorporated corporations as well as those incorporated in other provinces—must comply with certain registration requirements in order to operate there.[35] Nevertheless, the act under which it was incorporated governs its internal operating rules for holding shareholder meetings, electing directors, declaring dividends, and other matters that are examined in Chapter 26. The checklist below outlines some of the considerations involved in choosing whether to incorporate under federal or provincial jurisdiction.

---

[33] See *Companies Act*, RSPEI 1988, c C-14.

[34] *Canada Business Corporations Act*, RSC 1985, c C-44; *Ontario Business Corporations Act*, RSO 1990, c B-16; *Alberta Business Corporations Act*, RSA 2000, c B-9; *New Brunswick Corporations Act*, SNB 1981, c B-9.1; *Saskatchewan Corporations Act*, RSS 1977, c B-10; and *Newfoundland Corporations Act*, RSNL 1990, c C-36.

[35] See e.g. the Ontario *Extra-Provincial Corporations Act*, RSO 1990, c E.27. The formalities that must be complied with vary to some extent according to whether the corporation is incorporated federally, elsewhere in Canada, or abroad; for example, only non-Canadian corporations require a licence to do business in Ontario. The *Corporations Information Act*, RSO 1990, c C.39, requires registration of certain information—for example, place of registered office, names of directors, and place within the province where notice may be served.

CHECKLIST

Federal or Provincial Incorporation?

Considerations	Federal	Provincial
Type of business activity	Mandatory for federally regulated activities (s. 91) such as banking	
Location of business activity	All across the country	One province
Registered office	In Canada	In the province
Name selections	Pre-screened	Variation (many leave burden on business)
Name use	Throughout Canada	Within province
Prestige value	Increased prestige	
Initial government fees	Approx. $200	Approx. $350
Directors' Canadian residency	25 percent	0–25 percent*
Annual filings	Multiple separate	Combined

*Saskatchewan, Ontario, Alberta, Manitoba, and Newfoundland and Labrador require 25 percent, and British Columbia, Nova Scotia, PEI, New Brunswick, Northwest Territories, Yukon, Nunavut, and Quebec have eliminated the residency requirement.

THE CONSTITUTION OF A CORPORATION

Articles of Incorporation

Under the articles of incorporation system, a corporation is formed by filing **articles of incorporation** in the prescribed form and paying the required registration fee.[36] The articles of incorporation are often referred to as the "charter" or "constitution" of the corporation and set out essential information about the corporation. In provinces that have not adopted the articles of incorporation system, the corresponding "charter" document is the letters patent or the memorandum of association.

articles of incorporation
founding corporate document, often referred to as the charter or constitution of the corporation

CHECKLIST

Contents of the Articles of Incorporation

- name of the corporation
- place where the registered office is situated
- classes and any maximum number of shares that the corporation is authorized to issue
- if there are two or more classes of shares, the rights and restrictions attached to each class
- any restriction on the transfer of shares
- number of directors
- any restrictions on the business that may be carried on other provisions that the incorporators choose to include

---

[36] The incorporation fee under the CBCA is $250 (reduced to $200 for electronic filing). The corresponding Ontario fee is $360 ($300 for electronic filing).

Occasionally, matters not usually found in a charter will also be included. This may be done in order to give certain "entrenched" rights to minority shareholders. Normally, the charter can be altered only by a special resolution, requiring the approval of a two-thirds majority of the shareholders and the filing of the amended charter. In most circumstances, however, the charter is not the appropriate place for special arrangements among the shareholders. Instead, shareholders enter into a separate shareholders' agreement outside the corporate constitution, setting out how they will exercise their powers. This topic will be discussed further in Chapter 26.

The Corporate Name

As noted above, the articles must include the name of the proposed corporation. The registration of corporate names is closely regulated. The appropriate government office must approve the name and will refuse to register the corporation if it falls within certain prohibited categories (in particular, those that falsely suggest an association with the government or with certain professional bodies, or that are scandalous or obscene) or if it is likely to be confused with the name of some other existing corporation. In order to avoid the inconvenience and delay caused by the rejection of a chosen name, intending incorporators normally first make a "name search" to check that no existing corporation is registered with a similar name and undertake trademark searches. Records of corporations are computerized,[37] which facilitates such checks. Incorporating under a name does not protect the intellectual property rights to the name; see Chapter 20 for the appropriate steps to be followed.

If the name is not important to the incorporators or undetermined, they may use a "number name," where the registry simply assigns a number to the new corporation.[38]

When the business chooses a name after incorporation, it must register the name under the business names legislation discussed in Chapter 24. One of the words "Limited," "Incorporated," or "Corporation" (or their respective short forms) must form part of the name of every corporation (CBCA, s. 10).

Bylaws

bylaws the internal working rules of a corporation

Nature of Bylaws Incorporators generally keep the incorporating documents as short as possible to retain flexibility in the operation of the corporation, but detailed operating rules are needed for its day-to-day affairs. Under both the articles of incorporation and letters patent systems, these operating rules are called **bylaws**.[39] Bylaws are flexible, requiring confirmation by only a simple majority of shareholders, although legislation does identify some matters that must be dealt with by special resolution requiring a two-thirds majority.

Creation of a bylaw is a two-step process involving first the board of directors and then the shareholders., The directors adopt new or amend old bylaws, assigning each a sequential number, but the new or amended bylaws need confirmation at the next general meeting of shareholders in order to remain valid. Bylaws fall into two main categories: general operating rules and specific director authorizations.

---

[37] The name search system is known as NUANS (Newly Upgraded Automated Name Search) system.

[38] CBCA, s 11(2). A number name may be subsequently changed to a "normal" name without the usual formality that is required to amend the articles: CBCA, s 173(3).

[39] For a memorandum corporation, they are called articles of association, which causes confusion. In the memorandum system, articles of association can only be altered by a special resolution of the shareholders, requiring a three-quarters majority.

General Operating Rules Usually, the general operating rules for the business are passed at the first meeting of the shareholders. The first bylaws are often quite long and elaborate, dealing with such matters as the election of directors, their term of office, the place and required notice for meetings of directors, the quorum necessary (that is, the minimum number who must be present) before a meeting of directors can act on behalf of the corporation, the categories of executive officers, provisions for the allotment of shares and for the declaration of dividends, and procedures for holding the annual general meeting and other meetings of shareholders.

CHECKLIST
Provisions Often Included in Typical Bylaws*

- The qualification of a director shall be the holding of at least one share in the capital stock of the corporation.
- A director shall hold office until the third annual general meeting following his appointment.
- Notice of a meeting of directors shall be given in writing to each director not less than seven days before the meeting.
- Three directors shall constitute a quorum for the transaction of any business, except as otherwise provided in these bylaws.
- Questions arising at any meeting of directors shall, except as herein provided, be decided by a majority of votes: In the event of an equality of votes, the Chair of the meeting shall have a second or casting vote.
- Any contract entered into by the corporation that involves the expenditure or the incurring of a liability in excess of $10 000 must be approved by a majority of all the directors.
- Written notice of not less than 28 days, in the case of an annual general meeting, and 21 days, in the case of other shareholder meetings, shall be given to all shareholders entitled to vote at the meeting.
- A quorum is present at a general meeting of shareholders if no fewer than 10 shareholders, together holding a majority of the shares entitled to vote at the meeting, are present in person or by proxy.
- Shares in the corporation shall be allotted by resolution of the board of directors, approved by not less than two-thirds of all directors, on such terms, for such consideration, and to such persons as the directors determine.
- The directors may, at any time, by resolution approved by not less than two-thirds of all directors, declare a dividend or an interim dividend and pay the same out of the funds of the corporation available for that purpose.

*These are not mandatory requirements.

Authorization to Directors Most statutes no longer require a bylaw to be passed in order to confer any particular power on the directors (unless the corporation's own constitution does).[40] Certain matters, such as the sale of substantially all of a corporation's property or the amalgamation with another corporation, are required to be approved by special resolution of the shareholders, and although directors now normally have the power to borrow money on the security of the corporation's assets without special authorization, it is common for them to ask the shareholders to confirm a major loan transaction, because creditors may insist upon such confirmation. Shareholder resolutions of this type are still often referred to as "bylaws."

---

[40] See CBCA, s 16(1).

TYPES OF BUSINESS CORPORATIONS

Public and Private Corporations

Initially, British legislators believed that limited companies would be used primarily for large undertakings having many shareholders as investors (that is, public corporations). Consequently, the regulations focused on protection of the general public through disclosure and publication obligations. Eventually separate regulations were created for the formation of **private companies**, which were not permitted to offer shares to the public and in which the right to transfer shares had to be restricted in some manner. Those provisions found their way into Canadian incorporation statutes but now remain only in Prince Edward Island and Nova Scotia. The CBCA and most other provincial statutes now permit even a single shareholder to form a corporation and do not maintain a formal distinction between public and private corporations. Instead, a more realistic distinction is made between corporations that issue their shares to the general public[41] and those that do not.

private companies corporations with a restricted number of shareholders prohibited from issuing their shares to the general public

Public Corporations
Incorporation statutes, such as the CBCA, apply to both public and private corporations but draw a number of distinctions between them. The CBCA, for example, imposes various obligations upon what it calls a **distributing corporation** with respect to such matters as proxy solicitation, the number of directors, and the need for an audit committee. These requirements are considered further in Chapter 26. But the most important difference is that distributing corporations are also subject to regulation under the relevant provincial securities acts in those provinces in which their securities are issued or traded. As provincial securities regulators control access to the public market through stock exchanges, securities legislation and the policies of securities regulators play an important role in the way in which Canada's larger corporations are structured and conduct their business and affairs. Securities legislation also describes the steps that must be followed to change a private corporation into a publicly traded or distributing corporation. Those topics are considered in Chapters 26 and 27.

distributing corporation a corporation that issues its securities to the public; also referred to as an issuing corporation, reporting issuer, publicly traded corporation, or public corporation

Private Corporations
Private corporations are typically small- and medium-size business enterprises where the number of participants and owners is small. A private corporation is a true limited company with the same legal significance and corporate independence as the public corporation. In fact, when a public corporation creates a subsidiary, it usually does so by incorporating a private corporation. Many large U.S. and other foreign corporations operate wholly owned subsidiaries in Canada that are private. All the shares are held by the parent corporation, except for a few that may be held by corporate officers. A number of these subsidiaries are huge, rivalling our own large public corporations in size. For example, General Motors of Canada Limited is a private corporation owned by its public U.S. parent, General Motors Company.[42]

The vast majority of corporations are private—over 90 percent in Canada. It is, therefore, rather surprising that so much of the literature of economics, finance, accounting, and management directs its attention to public corporations. Private corporations have been permitted the luxury of operating in an atmosphere of relative privacy, as disclosure and transparency obligations are relatively light. In a private corporation, the owners are usually the managers as well, focusing questions of management and ultimate decision making within a small group. The legal implications of this characteristic of private corporations are examined in Chapter 26.

---

[41] The CBCA describes these as "distributing" corporations. Securities legislation refers to these as issuing corporations or reporting issuers.

[42] For a list of the 50 biggest private corporations in Canada, see *The Globe and Mail*, "Rankings of Canada's 50 Biggest Private Companies," June 19, 2017, https://www.theglobeandmail.com/report-on-business/top-1000/article12832820.

Corporate Groups

The largest businesses, in Canada and internationally, frequently comprise a group of corporations, one or more of which is public, with shares held by the public and listed on one or more stock exchanges, together with a number of subsidiaries that are private in the sense that they are often wholly owned by their parent company. For example, the corporate structure of the Hollinger companies and related entities (formerly controlled by Conrad Black) involved over 60 companies—some public, some private—and were subject to a number of different jurisdictions.[43] Groups of this nature can give rise to extremely complex relationships and to possible conflicts.

Cooperatives

Cooperatives are incorporated entities, owned and operated by their members for their mutual benefit or purpose. Knowledge, skill, expertise, and capital are pooled together to achieve a particular purpose. They are widely used for "not for profit" purposes such as housing and childcare or specific support purposes in industries such as farming, milk, and renewable energy. Business cooperatives are growing in popularity for purposes such as marketing and supply. Cooperatives are incorporated by application of three persons pursuant to special cooperative legislation, either federal or provincial.[44] They operate on cooperative principles,[45] using a democratic voting structure that gives one "member" one vote.

Cooperatives are separate legal entities that protect members from personal liability. Their articles of incorporation must declare their purposes and state that they will carry on business on a cooperative basis. Their names must include the word "cooperative" (or short form), "united," or "pool." The organizational structure is similar to that of a traditional corporation, although membership or investment shares are optional.[46] Directors and officers are subject to the same duties of good faith and honesty as in business corporations.[47]

CASE 25.3 Purpose of Cooperative Legislation

Collins Barrow National Cooperative Incorporated is an association of accounting firms. The Cooperative exists to serve its members and to support their independent professional practices. Each is given a designated geographic area of operation. The Vancouver member felt new rules about geographic areas were unfair and sought relief from "oppression," arguing that the rules violated law formed under the business corporation's legislation. The court agreed that the exiting principles governing oppression formed under the *Canada Business Corporations Act* were applicable to oppression under the *Canada Cooperatives Act*. The purpose of cooperative legislation was to simplify incorporation; to clearly define the rights and responsibilities of members, shareholders (if any), and directors; and to create a legislative scheme in line with that in place for business corporations. The court ordered the Cooperative to change its rules.[48]

Some businesses are not allowed to form cooperatives: banks, insurance companies, and trust and loan companies, for example.

---

[43] See *Catalyst Fund General Partner I Inc v Hollinger Inc*, [2004] OJ No 4722, aff'd [2006] OJ No 944 (Ont CA).

[44] *Canada Cooperatives Act*, SC 1998, c 1 (Coop Act); See e.g. *Co-operative Corporations Act*, RSO 1990, c C.35; *Cooperative Association Act*, SBC 1999, c 28; *Cooperatives Act, 2001*, SA 2001, c C-28.1.

[45] Voluntary membership, democratic control, autonomy, independence, member participation, education, training, concern for community.

[46] *Supra* note 44, Canada, s 9.

[47] *Ibid.*, Canada, s 80.

[48] *Collins Barrow Vancouver v Collins Barrow National Cooperative Inc*, 2016 BCCA 60, affirming 2015 BCSC 510 at paras 102, 108–09.

Professional Corporations

As noted in Chapter 24, many professionals are prohibited from incorporating their practices, either by the rules of the professional body to which they belong or under the statute governing the profession. They have consequently been restricted to practising as sole proprietors or in partnership, with the disadvantage, in the latter case, of being liable for obligations incurred by their co-partners. One response to that problem, which has already been discussed, is the creation of limited liability partnerships (LLPs).

Most provinces now also allow the incorporation of a **professional corporation (PC)**. Under this legislation, members of listed professions may form a PC, provided it is permitted by the rules of the profession itself, and the professional controls the voting shares. Saskatchewan's act reads:

professional corporation (PC) a special type of business corporation that may be formed by members of a profession

> One or more members of an association may incorporate a corporation pursuant to the *Business Corporations Act* for the purpose of carrying on, in the name of the corporation, the business of providing professional services that may lawfully be performed by members of the association.[49]

The words "professional corporation" or the abbreviation "PC" must appear in the name of the corporation,[50] and all members of the corporation must be members of the profession.[51] Regarding liability, the act says:

> The liability of a member of an association to a person who receives services from the member is not affected by the fact that the services were provided by the member as an employee of, or on behalf of, a professional corporation.[52]

In effect, a member of a profession who incorporates (either alone or together with other members) remains personally responsible for her own negligence or misconduct toward clients, although the principle of limited liability does seem to provide protection against the claims of other creditors—for example, landlords of premises or suppliers of equipment. The principal advantage of professional incorporation is not to obtain limited liability but to gain tax advantages that are not available to sole proprietorships and partnerships. Many professionals will benefit from the small business tax rate if they practise as a professional corporation, in contrast to the much higher personal income tax rate applied to sole proprietors or partners.

Ethical Issue Undermining Professional Standards?

Recent legislative changes have introduced the LLP and the professional corporation as alternative vehicles for conducting professional activities, and the concept of multidisciplinary partnerships is also gaining ground. This has led to fears, in some quarters, that professional standards are being undermined. In particular, it is argued that such developments may lead to the destruction of the professional–client relationship. Do you really want to have your teeth pulled by a corporation?

Others would argue that there are adequate safeguards to ensure that professional standards are maintained and that there is no valid reason for denying to professionals the benefits of incorporation that are enjoyed by other businesspersons (and by some professions).

Questions to Consider

1. Are the recent changes discarding the traditions of a century, or are they simply keeping up with the times?
2. Is there any reason why professionals, such as accountants, doctors, and lawyers, should not be allowed to incorporate in the normal way?
3. Do professionals comply with professional standards only to avoid personal liability?

---

[49] *Professional Corporations Act*, SS 2001, c P-27.1, s 4(1).
[50] *Ibid.*, s 4(2).
[51] *Ibid.*, ss 5(2), 6(1). Multidisciplinary PCs are not (yet) permitted.
[52] *Ibid.*, s 15.

Only members of listed professions may form a PC, but not all professions are prohibited from incorporating. For example, engineers and geophysicists are not "listed" and consequently cannot form a PC; however, that is no disadvantage since they are able to establish a "normal" business corporation.

CORPORATE CAPITAL

Equity and Debt

Corporations typically raise money by issuing shares (equity) or by borrowing (debt). A third method—financing the corporation's activities out of retained profits—is really the same as the first, since the shareholders are effectively reinvesting part of their profit. Although borrowing increases the funds that are at the disposal of the corporation's management, it is really misleading to speak of debt capital, since borrowing increases both assets and liabilities. A corporation's true capital is its equity capital or share capital—the investment in the company by its owners.

Share Capital

Every business corporation must have a share capital.[53] The word "capital" has different meanings in different contexts. In letters patent and memorandum jurisdictions, when a corporation is incorporated, its charter places an upper limit on the number or money value of shares it may issue. This limit is called the **authorized capital**. A corporation need not issue all its authorized share capital. The **issued capital** and **paid-up capital** of a corporation are, as their names indicate, the parts of the authorized capital that have been issued and paid for.

In articles of incorporation jurisdictions, a corporation may state the maximum number of shares that can be issued if it so wishes, but it does not have to do so. A corporation must still keep a **stated capital account** disclosing the consideration received for each **share** issued. Shares must be fully paid for at the time of issue.[54] Consequently, there is no difference between issued capital and paid-up capital.

There are several ways of becoming a shareholder:

- by being one of the original applicants for incorporation
- by buying shares issued by a corporation subsequent to its incorporation
- by acquiring (by purchase or gift) previously issued shares from another shareholder

The first two ways involve contracts between the shareholder and the corporation, and the transactions increase the issued capital as shown in the accounts of the corporation. The third way is the result of a transfer to which the corporation is not a party at all and does not affect its accounts.

authorized capital the maximum number (or value) of shares that a corporation is permitted by its charter to issue

issued capital the shares that have been issued by a corporation

paid-up capital the shares that have been issued and fully paid for

stated capital account the amount received by a corporation for the issue of its shares

share a member's proportionate interest in the capital of a corporation

Par Values

Until the early part of the 20th century, all shares had a nominal or **par value**—a fixed value established in the charter like a bank note or a bond. Shares were issued by the corporation at their par value. However, par value provided little indication of a share's real value; once issued, a share rarely had the same market price and par value.

A corporation was prohibited from issuing its shares for less than their par value (that is, at a discount). If a corporation's shares were selling on the market below their

par value a nominal value attached to a share at the time of issue

---

[53] Cooperatives and charitable and non-profit corporations need not have a share capital.

[54] CBCA, s 25(3). Previously, shares could be issued partly paid, with the corporation being able to make a subsequent call for the remainder of the price.

par value, and the corporation required additional capital, investors would not purchase a new issue at par. In order to make an issue of shares, the corporation would be compelled to reduce the par value of the shares to a more realistic figure and to reduce its capital accordingly by obtaining an amendment to its charter, causing delay and expense.

The United States introduced **no par value shares**—that is, shares that represent a specific proportion of the issued capital of the corporation rather than a fixed sum of money. The advantages of no par value shares, and in particular the fact that they may be issued from time to time at prices that correspond to their current market value, resulted in their adoption by all the jurisdictions in the United States; soon afterward, they were permitted in Canada. The articles of incorporation system has abolished par value shares entirely.

no par value shares shares that have no nominal value attached

---

ILLUSTRATION 25.2   Changing Market Value

Pliable Plastics Inc. is incorporated under the articles of incorporation system. Its articles contain no restriction on the total number of shares that may be issued, and its shares have no par value. Initially, it issued 50 000 shares at $100 each, giving it a stated capital of $5 000 000. The directors wish to raise a further $3 000 000.

If the current market price of the shares has fallen to $60, they can raise $3 000 000 by issuing 50 000 new shares at that price. On the other hand, if the market price has risen to $120, they will need to issue only 25 000.

---

preferred shares shares carrying preferential rights to receive a dividend and/or to be redeemed on the dissolution of the corporation for a fixed price

Until the introduction of the articles of incorporation system, **preferred shares** were almost always issued with a par value. They paid a preferred dividend expressed as a percentage of the par value, and the corporation could redeem them at par value. For example, a share might have a par value of $100 (and be redeemable at that price) and pay a dividend of 8 percent (that is, $8 per share). With the abolition of par values, preferred shares are now stated to have a redemption price ($100), with a preferred dividend expressed simply as a sum of money ($8).

CORPORATE SECURITIES

The Distinction Between Shares and Bonds

bond a document evidencing a debt owed by a corporation

common share a share carrying no preferential right

A corporation may borrow money in a number of ways, but when it borrows substantial sums on a long-term basis, it normally does so by issuing a **bond**. The classic distinction between shares and bonds (or "debentures," as they are sometimes called) is that the holder of a share is a member of and owner of an interest in the corporation. The holder of a bond is a creditor. In the business world, there is no such clear-cut distinction. In the language of modern business, the true equity owner of a corporation, and the person who takes the greatest risk, is the **common share** holder. From this end of the spectrum, we proceed by degrees to the person who is a mortgagee or secured bondholder, who takes the least risk. In between, we may have the holders of preferred shares. Today, most large corporations have, in addition to an issue of common shares, one or more classes of bonds or debentures and probably also a class of preferred shares.

When deciding whether to invest in the shares or the bonds of a corporation, an individual usually does not make a conscious choice between becoming a member (that is, an equity owner) and becoming a creditor. She regards herself in both instances as an investor. Her investment decisions are determined primarily by economic considerations. Bonds provide a fixed and guaranteed return (provided the corporation remains solvent), in the form of regular interest payments and the right to be redeemed in full at their maturity date. Common shares carry no guarantee that their holders will receive anything, either in the form of dividends or on dissolution, but their holders participate in any "growth" of the corporation. Preferred shareholders land in between. They are entitled to receive dividends and to have their shares redeemed on the dissolution of the corporation, before payments are made to the holders of the common shares, but those rights are often restricted to a fixed dividend and a fixed amount payable on redemption.

The line between shareholder and bondholder is nonetheless a distinct and important one in its legal consequences for a corporation. First of all, since bondholders are creditors, interest paid to them is a debt of the corporation. It must be paid whether or not the corporation has earned profits for the year. Shareholders are not creditors and receive dividends only when the directors declare them. One consequence, especially important for taxation, is that interest payments are normally an expense of doing business and are deducted before taxable income is calculated; dividends, on the other hand, are payable out of after-tax profits. Second, bonds are usually secured by a mortgage or charge on the property of the corporation (see the discussion in Chapter 28 under "Floating Charges"). If a corporation becomes insolvent, its secured bondholders are entitled to be repaid not only before the shareholders but also before the general creditors. They are secured creditors, and the trustee acting for them can sell the corporation's assets to satisfy the debt owed to them.

Rights of Security Holders

Bondholders Bondholders do not normally have a direct voice in the management of the corporation unless it is in breach of the terms of the trust deed or indenture under which the securities were created. Only when a corporation gets into financial difficulty or is in breach of the trust deed may the trustee step in and take part in management on behalf of the bondholders. It is true, however, that bondholders do exert an indirect form of control over management in the restrictive clauses commonly written into bond indentures, which may place a ceiling on the further long-term borrowing of the corporation, on the amount of dividends it may pay, and even, in smaller corporations, on the salaries it pays to its officers.

Common Shareholders By contrast, common shareholders have, in theory at least, a strong voice in the management of the corporation. As we shall see in Chapter 26, common shareholders elect the board of directors and approve major changes in the corporation's activities. Otherwise, however, their rights are limited. They have no entitlement to a dividend and can receive one only after bondholders and preferred shareholders have been paid. On the liquidation of the corporation, their entitlement is to share what is left after the claims of creditors and preferred shareholders have been satisfied.

Preferred Shareholders Preferred shareholders are in an intermediate category. Usually, they are entitled to be paid a fixed dividend before any dividend is paid to the common shareholders, and they are entitled to be paid the fixed redemption price of their shares on liquidation of the corporation before any surplus is distributed to the common shareholders. Frequently, they have no right to vote unless the payment of dividends to them is in arrears. In this respect they are more like creditors than investors. However, payment of preferred dividends is not a contractual commitment of a corporation as bond interest is; a preferred shareholder must enforce her rights as an individual and is not dependent upon a trustee taking action, as a bondholder normally is.

Class Rights Where a corporation issues more than one class of shares—for example, common shares and preferred shares—the precise rights of each class must

pre-emptive right the right of a holder of shares to protect his percentage ownership in the company by buying the same percentage in any new issue of shares

cumulative right the right of a preferred shareholder to be paid arrears from previous years before any dividend is paid on the common shares

participating right the right of a preferred shareholder to participate in surplus profits or assets of the corporation in addition to the amount of the preferred dividend or redemption price

be set out in its constitution (articles).[55] The various combinations of rights and privileges that may attach to a class of shares are extensive and may relate not only to dividend rights and rights of redemption but also to voting rights, to rights to appoint directors, and sometimes to the right to convert a security of one class into a security of another class. A **pre-emptive right**, that is, the right to buy the same percentage ownership in any new issue of shares, is discussed in Chapter 26.

Two questions with respect to preferred shareholders' rights to dividends are particularly important. The first is whether it is a **cumulative right**: If the full preferred dividend is not paid in one year, do the arrears accumulate so that they must be paid in a subsequent year or on winding up the corporation, before the common shareholders are entitled to anything? The second is whether on winding up, it is a **participating right**: if, after the preferred shareholders have been fully paid, do they still participate in any remaining surplus along with the common shareholders? These questions make it important to clearly define class rights.

CHECKLIST

Priority of Payment on Liquidation of a Corporation

On liquidation of a corporation, its assets must be distributed in the following sequence. (Note that bondholders are creditors—and usually they are secured creditors.)

1. secured creditors
2. unsecured creditors
3. preferred shareholders
4. common shareholders

The Transfer of Corporate Securities

Share and bond certificates are a type of personal property known as negotiable instruments subject to different rules of transfer and ownership from those that apply to sales of goods. Articles of incorporation statutes may expressly designate share certificates as a type of negotiable instrument.[56] When bonds and shares are treated as negotiable instruments, an innocent holder for value may acquire a better title than his predecessor had, as, for example, when he purchases valid bonds or share certificates

CASE 25.4 Forged Share Certificates

One of the largest fraud schemes in Canadian history involved the creation of fake share certificates of a small trust company, Vanguard Trust. A former director, lawyer Julius Melnitzer, had access to the company's corporate seal and created five certificates totalling 900 000 shares. He used the fake shares as security to borrow $5.6 million from five major Canadian banks. When the banks got suspicious, he tricked a printing company into helping him forge shares of other companies by saying they were for use as evidence in a case he was defending. Eventually the National Bank obtained an expert opinion, and the fraud was discovered. Melnitzer pleaded guilty and was fined $20 000 000, sentenced to nine years in prison, and disbarred.[57]

---

[55] See CBCA, s 6(1)(c).

[56] Unless there are restrictions on transfer noted on the certificate: CBCA, s 48(3).

[57] *R v Melnitzer*, [1992] OJ No 1363; *Canadian Imperial Bank of Commerce v Melnitzer (Trustee)*, [1993] OJ No 3021, aff'd [1997] OJ No 3021; see also Department of Justice website, "A Typology of Profit Driven Crimes—Bank Fraud," http://www.justice.gc.ca/eng/rp-pr/csj-sjc/crime/rr02_3/p3.html.

that have been stolen. Only those with notice of a defect are subject to it. The innocent holder of a forged (fake) negotiable instrument, as we have seen, obtains no title.

Few shareholders of public corporations receive physical share certificates. Investors trade shares using securities accounts held with intermediaries such as brokers, dealers, and banks. Share purchases are credited to the account as financial assets; rather than holding the security itself, the investor holds a "security entitlement" that gives him the right to the benefits of the share and to direct its transfer. Most provinces have securities transfer legislation defining the rights and obligations of securities intermediaries and securities entitlement holders, establishing the rules for transfer of securities and security entitlements, and protecting innocent purchasers of security entitlements from unknown adverse claims.[58]

Restrictions on Share Transfer In public corporations, shares are almost always freely transferable; if not, the shares will not be accepted for listing on a stock exchange; in fact, when securities intermediaries transfer security entitlements, they warrant that there are no restrictions on share transfer. In contrast, private corporations almost always restrict the transfer of shares; otherwise, it would be difficult for them to remain private.

Restrictions on share transfer must be described in the corporation's constitution[59] and can take almost any form. Restrictions must also be noted on the share certificate; otherwise, they are not binding on a purchaser who has no notice of the restriction.[60] The most common restriction is to require the consent of the board of directors to any transfer, but there are others, such as giving the right of first refusal to existing shareholders or directors before a shareholder can sell to an outsider, or giving a major shareholder the right of veto. Requiring the consent of directors gives them the discretion to approve or reject a proposed member of the corporation, much as partners determine whether they will admit a new partner.

Strategies to Manage the Legal Risks

Planning before incorporating can save time and money in the long run. The first decision is whether to incorporate under the federal or provincial jurisdiction. Provincial incorporation may seem easier and cheaper initially, but if the future plans for the business involve operating in multiple provinces and possibly internationally, federal incorporation may be a better fit.

The share structure of the corporation also needs careful consideration. It should anticipate the short-term and long-term needs of the company. Ownership can be divided among classes of shares so that preferred shares are available to raise capital and common shares may hold the power to vote. Class rights can vary to differentiate between financing and control. Odd numbers are necessary so that majority votes can be obtained.

Ensuring that the name is an available trademark, not in use by another business, is vital. Search not only corporation registries and business name registrations but registered trademark databanks as well. All are publicly available. It is often easier to incorporate a numbered company and then register the business names separately, once the intellectual property rights have been secured. One corporation may operate several businesses under different business names as long as all are properly registered.

---

[58] See e.g. *Securities Transfer Act*, SO 2006, c 8.
[59] See CBCA, s 6(1)(d).
[60] CBCA, s 49(8). See *Bank Leu AG v Gaming Lottery Corp* (2003), 231 DLR (4th) 251.

All corporations start as private corporations that may subsequently be taken public through the steps outlined in the securities legislation. If "going public" is expected, incorporating documents—that is, articles of incorporation and bylaws—should comply with the higher standards of corporate governance discussed in Chapter 26.

Finally, corporations are legal persons and may own shares in other corporations. This permits a business to use multiple corporations, in both private and public forms, in order to operate high-risk activities in separate corporations and protect the existence of the entire business. Subject to some exceptions, assets of one corporation are not available to satisfy the debts of others. Try not to think of business entities such as partnerships, joint ventures, or private and public corporations only as alternatives to each other. They can be employed together to meet the specific needs of the business.

QUESTIONS FOR REVIEW

1. What is meant by a "legal person"?
2. What is meant by "limited liability"? Whose liability is limited?
3. What are the main differences between partnerships and corporations?
4. What were the principal arguments made by the creditors in the *Salomon* case in attempting to make Salomon personally liable?
5. In what ways may two or more corporations be said to be "associated"?
6. What is meant by "lifting the corporate veil"?
7. How does the articles of incorporation system of forming a corporation differ from (a) the letters patent system and (b) the memorandum and articles system?
8. What information must be set out in articles of incorporation?
9. Why must care be taken in selecting a corporate name? What is a "number name"?
10. What is the main function of a corporation's bylaws?
11. What are the principal characteristics of closely held corporations?
12. What are the main advantages of forming a professional corporation?
13. What is the function of a corporation's stated capital account?
14. What special rights are normally carried by preferred shares?
15. What are the usual rights of bondholders?
16. What factors influence an investor's choice between shares and bonds?
17. In what sequence should a corporation's assets be distributed on liquidation of the corporation?
18. In what circumstances are restrictions on the transfer of shares binding on purchasers of the shares?
19. What are the differences between a group of corporations and a cooperative?

CASES AND PROBLEMS

1. Continuing Scenario

    Ashley decided to incorporate her restaurant business. Her lawyer, Brendan, is advising her about the steps involved and the structure of her corporation. So far, Ashley has two restaurants located within 25 kilometres of each other—the first was called "Ashley's Restaurant" and the second she named "Ashley's Too." Ashley's mother invested $50 000 in the business at the start, but Ashley does not want her mother to be involved in business decisions. Ashley promised her mother a good return on her investment: Ashley wants to stay in complete control of the business. Ashley also promised each of her chefs that there will be profit sharing opportunities after five years with the restaurants. How should Brendan answer the following questions? Give reasons for your answers. How many corporations should she incorporate? Should incorporation occur under federal or provincial legislation? Does Ashley have to decide on a name now? What classes of shares should be issued with what rights and restrictions?

2. Oakdale Motors Inc. is a corporation, incorporated under the *Canada Business Corporations Act*, engaged in the selling, repairing, and servicing of automobiles. All of its shares are owned by Faulkner, who is also the sole director. Faulkner acts as the general manager of the corporation and supervises its day-to-day operations.

    Last winter, Hill visited the premises of Oakdale Motors to look at a used car she saw advertised. The area outside the sales office was extremely slippery, being covered by ice that was, in turn, covered by a thin layer of snow that had fallen overnight. Faulkner was working at the Oakdale premises that day and knew of the dangerous state of the premises but had made no effort to have the danger removed.

    Hill slipped on the ice, fell, and broke her leg. The injury was a serious one and has left her with a permanent disability.

    She has learned that Oakdale Motors Inc. is in severe financial difficulties and is likely to be made bankrupt. However, Faulkner appears to be quite wealthy.

    Would Hill have any claim against Faulkner?

3. Macbeth, the owner of 20 hectares located on the outskirts of Niagara Falls, decided to sell, and on January 2 signed an exclusive listing agreement with Ross, a real estate broker. Macbeth agreed to pay Ross a commission of 5 percent on the sale of the property, which he listed at $350 000.

    On January 19, Ross filed articles of incorporation for a new corporation, Burnam Woods Properties Ltd., of which he was the sole shareholder. He appointed his friend Lennox as general manager.

    Several weeks later, Ross introduced Macbeth to Lennox as general manager of Burnam Woods but said nothing to suggest that he, Ross, had any interest in the corporation. Within a few days, Lennox submitted an offer on behalf of the corporation to purchase Macbeth's property for $240 000. Macbeth rejected the offer but made a counter-offer to sell at $290 000. Burnam Woods accepted the counter-offer, and the deal was closed on March 15, when Macbeth paid Ross his commission of $14 500.

    Shortly afterward, Burnam Woods entered into negotiations with another corporation, Castle Hall Developments Ltd., and sold the 20 hectares to it for $450 000, realizing a quick profit of $160 000.

    On April 24 following, Macbeth learned of the resale by Burnam Woods and also learned about Ross's share ownership in the Burnam Woods company. Macbeth immediately sued Ross and Burnam Woods jointly for recovery of the real estate commission of $14 500 and for the $160 000 profit realized on the second sale by Burnam Woods Properties Ltd. to Castle Hall Developments Ltd.

    Examine the validity of Macbeth's claim, and offer an opinion about its chances for success.

4. Stick and Twist are lawyers who have practised in partnership for a number of years. With the introduction of legislation permitting the formation of professional corporations in their province, they decided to convert their partnership into a PC.

    The new corporation, "Stick and Twist Lawyers PC," was formed with a share capital of $1000, with Stick and Twist each holding one share. They are the sole directors. The corporation has very few tangible assets, since its office is rented, as is much of its office equipment.

Twist "disappeared" a few months ago, and Stick has discovered that

(a) a client is claiming $200 000 from the corporation in respect of money she had entrusted to Twist for the purchase of a condominium; and

(b) the landlord is claiming $12 000 in respect of rent owing on the premises. Twist had assured Stick that the rent had been paid.

To what extent are (1) the corporation and (2) Stick liable?

5. Pliable Plastics Inc. issued 50 000 common shares at $100 each. Some years later, in order to raise additional capital, it issued 20 000 Class "A" preferred shares, also at $100 each. The preferred shares were stated to have a redemption price of $100 and were entitled to receive a first dividend of $8 per share. The following year, to raise further funds, the corporation made an issue of bonds, in the sum of $2 000 000, secured by a floating charge on all of its assets.

Soon afterward, Pliable Plastics found itself in serious financial difficulties. Although it had substantial assets, these were not readily realizable, and it was unable to pay its debts as they fell due. The directors resolved to sell off the corporation's assets and to wind up the corporation.

The sale of the assets realized $7 000 000, and, after paying off its creditors (other than the bondholders), the corporation was left with $5 500 000. How much will each common share receive?

Chapter 26
Corporate Governance: The Internal Affairs of Corporations

- **WHAT IS CORPORATE GOVERNANCE?**
- **CORPORATE GOVERNANCE OF PUBLICLY TRADED CORPORATIONS**
- **THE STRUCTURE OF THE MODERN BUSINESS CORPORATION**
- **DIRECTORS**
- **OFFICERS**
- **DUTIES OF DIRECTORS AND OFFICERS**
- **SHAREHOLDERS**
- **THE PROTECTION OF MINORITY SHAREHOLDERS**
- **SHAREHOLDER AGREEMENTS**
- **STRATEGIES TO MANAGE THE LEGAL RISKS**

This chapter and Chapter 27 address corporate governance. They discuss the internal and external affairs and the business of a corporation.

In this chapter we examine such questions as:

- How is a corporation organized and managed?
- What is the function of the board of directors?
- How are the directors appointed and removed?
- Who is an officer?
- What are the duties of directors and officers?
- What are the consequences of a breach of duty by a director or an officer?
- What defences are available to directors and officers?
- What are the rights and duties of shareholders?
- How are the rights of minority shareholders protected?

WHAT IS CORPORATE GOVERNANCE?

corporate governance the rules governing the organization and management of the business and affairs of a corporation in order to meet its internal objectives and external responsibilities

Corporate governance refers to the organization and management of the business and affairs of a corporation in order to meet its internal objectives and external responsibilities. Where do we find the rules of corporate governance? As discussed in Chapter 25, the incorporating documents—the articles of incorporation and the bylaws—create the management structure within the corporation and establish the corporation's own set of corporate governance standards. In addition, each incorporating jurisdiction—Canada and each province—has corporation legislation that must be followed. This legislation establishes the legal standards of corporate governance.

The *Canada Business Corporations Act* (CBCA)[1] and the corresponding provincial statutes differentiate between "business" and "affairs." Section 102 gives directors the responsibility for managing, or supervising "the management of, the *business* and *affairs* of a corporation." The difference is:

(a) the *affairs* are the internal relationships and arrangements among those responsible for running a corporation—the directors and officers—and its main beneficiaries, the shareholders, which we discuss in this chapter; and

(b) the *business* involves the external relations between a corporation and those who deal with it as a business enterprise—its customers, suppliers, creditors, and employees—as well as government regulators and society as a whole (discussed in Chapter 27).

The shareholders in a publicly traded corporation seem to fall into both categories. An invitation to the public to invest in a corporation is directed toward those who may not yet be part of its internal relations, but if the members of the public accept an offer to buy shares, they become involved in its "affairs." These potential public shareholders are protected by special provincial securities regulations imposed on only those companies issuing shares to the public, and so securities regulation is discussed in both Chapters 26 and 27. This chapter covers the basic legal rules of corporate governance and the liability arising from their breach. The rules discussed in this chapter apply to both privately and publicly held corporations and are contained in federal and provincial legislation. Breach of the rules may trigger civil, regulatory, or even criminal liability or a combination of all three.

CORPORATE GOVERNANCE OF PUBLICLY TRADED CORPORATIONS

publicly traded corporations corporations that issue shares to the public, also known as public corporations, widely held corporations, reporting issuers, and issuing corporations

Corporate scandals such as those involving Enron and WorldCom led securities regulators to tighten the rules of corporate governance for **publicly traded corporations** (this chapter will also use the CBCA term *distributing corporation*). First, the United States passed the *Sarbanes-Oxley Act of 2002* (SOX), and next, the Securities and Exchange Commission introduced new rules, policies, and recommendations for the internal operations of public companies.[2] Canadian securities regulators adopted some

---

[1] RSC 1985, c C-44 (CBCA). The Act was substantially amended by Bill S-11, SC 2001, c 14. Unless otherwise stated, statutory references in this chapter are to the CBCA as amended. Provincial legislation: *Business Corporations Act*, SBC 2002, c 57; *Business Corporations Act*, RSA 2000, c B-9; *Business Corporations Act*, RSS 1978, c B-10; *Corporations Act*, CCSM c C225; *Business Corporations Act* (OBCA) RSO 1990, c B-16; *Companies Act*, RSNS 1989, c 81; *Companies Act*, RSNB 1973, c C-13; *Companies Act*, RSPEI 1988, c C-14; *Corporations Act*, RSNL 1990, c C-36. Most provincial legislation is similar to the federal legislation. Relevant major departures will be noted.

[2] 15 USC s 7201 *et seq.*

of the SOX standards.[3] This means that publicly traded companies are required to meet the standards in both the CBCA (or the relevant provincial incorporating legislation) and the provincial securities legislation. Together, these rules and recommendations increase the protection available to the public stakeholders—public shareholders, creditors, employees, and lenders. The general themes and principles underlying the legislation are independence of decision makers, transparency, disclosure, accountability, and organizational checks and balances.[4] Some of the recommendations are:

- A majority of directors should be independent.
- The CEO should not also hold the position of chair of the board.
- The corporation should establish separate, independent committees of the board to address executive compensation and nomination of board members.
- The corporation should adopt and publish a "code of ethics."
- The board should perform regular self-assessments.

Many privately held corporations choose to comply with the higher standard of corporate governance in order to meet their ethical responsibilities and in preparation for any future **public offering**. Where relevant, this chapter will identify the heightened requirements for public companies.

public offering selling shares to the public, which must be done in compliance with provincial securities regulations

THE STRUCTURE OF THE MODERN BUSINESS CORPORATION

Business corporations vary in size and composition. Modern legislation tries to accommodate these differences. However, there are certain essential elements that are the same for all corporations.

Three basic groups are common to all corporations: the shareholders, the **board of directors** (generally referred to as "the board"), and the **officers**. In small private corporations, such as family companies, often most or even all of the shareholders are also directors and officers. Even if the distinction between shareholders and directors may sometimes become blurred in practice—for example, if they get together to discuss business and do not specify whether the meeting is a directors' meeting or a shareholders' meeting—the distinction remains important legally.

In a large corporation, by contrast, the board of directors may have as many as 15 or 20 members who are elected by shareholders. Generally in such cases, the board will appoint or hire a chief executive officer (CEO, also often called the president or managing director) or a smaller committee of directors (the management committee or executive committee) to direct the affairs and business of the corporation and to supervise its other officers and employees. CEOs are most often full-time employees of the company who, together with other officers, manage the corporation. It is this team, not the board, that is known collectively as "the management." The management refers only important policy matters to the full board of directors. In turn, the board of directors usually calls no more than the required annual meeting of shareholders, at which time it reports to them on the state of the corporation's business and affairs and holds elections to determine the board of directors for the coming year.

board of directors the governing body of a corporation, responsible for the management of its business and affairs

officers high-ranking management employees of a corporation as defined in the bylaws or appointed by the directors, such as the president, vice-president, controller, chief executive officer, chief financial officer, general counsel, and general manager

---

[3] National Policy Instrument 58-201 Corporate Governance Guidelines. Each province has its own legislation and Securities Commission; the 13 provincial and territorial regulators cooperate on most regulation through the Canadian Securities Administrators (CSA). The result is nationally consistent instruments, guidelines, and policies that are adopted under the same numbering system. Instruments are mandatory requirements, and policies and guidelines are only recommendations.

[4] Richard DeGeorge, Chapter 9, "Corporate Governance, Accounting Disclosure and Insider Trading," in *Business Ethics*, 7th ed (Upper Saddle River, NJ: Prentice Hall, 2009).

audit committee a group of directors responsible for overseeing the corporate audit and the preparation of financial statements; the committee has wider responsibilities in a distributing corporation

compensation committee committee responsible for setting director and officer pay

nominating committee committee responsible for proposing and recruiting new directors

Public or distributing corporations are required to have an **audit committee**, whose members include at least three directors. Originally, the audit committee's task was only to review the financial statements of the corporation before they were submitted to the full board for approval.[5] Recent provincial securities regulations expand the responsibilities of the committee and require all audit committee members to be independent directors; the auditor must be retained by and report to the audit committee rather than the board or corporate management.[6] A **compensation committee**, responsible for setting director and officer compensation, and a **nominating committee**, responsible for finding new directors, are also recommended but not mandatory.[7] Figure 26.1 illustrates the general structure of a corporation.

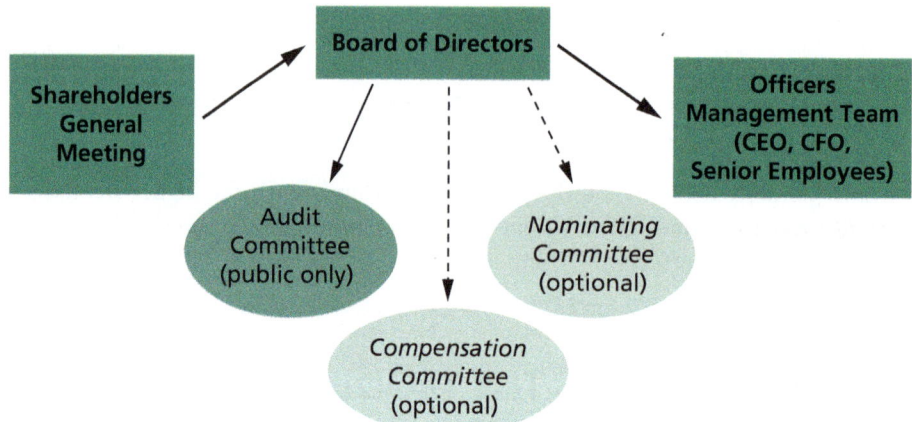

Figure 26.1   Corporate Structure
Power originates with the general meeting of shareholders. The shareholders elect a board of directors to manage the corporation. The directors, in turn, appoint or hire a chief executive officer, who is the highest-ranking employee in charge of the day-to-day running of the corporation. Various committees are given tasks by and report to the board.

INTERNATIONAL ISSUE

Sarbanes-Oxley Act of 2002

The U.S. *Sarbanes-Oxley Act of 2002* (SOX) set higher standards for the internal organization of publicly traded companies. These standards exceed the Canadian regulations and include mandatory codes of ethics and compensation committees, expanded disclosure requirements, and CEO and CFO compensation clawbacks. Compliance does not come cheap; American businesses are complaining about the high cost of implementing SOX standards.

SOX also influenced the Canadian standards for corporate governance because its reach extends beyond American geographic borders and applies to many Canadian corporations. Canadian corporations trading on an American stock exchange must comply with SOX, as must Canadian subsidiaries of U.S. parent corporations. The difficulty in complying with multiple different corporate governance regimes was one of the reasons a proposed overhaul of Canadian corporate governance rules was abandoned in 2009. The abandoned proposal would have moved Canada to a more principle-based regime and away from the rules-based systems currently operating in both Canada and the United States.

Question to Consider

1. Should public corporate governance rules be those of the incorporating jurisdiction or those of the jurisdiction where the shares are sold? Or both?

Sources: L. McCallum and P. Puri, *Canadian Companies' Guide to the Sarbanes-Oxley Act* (Toronto: Butterworths, 2004); Kevin Drawback, "Reform Backlash Gathers Momentum: Restriction on Class-action Suits Part of a Trend," *National Post*, February 21, 2005; Canadian Securities Administrators' Staff Notice 58-3-5—Status Report on the Proposed Changes to the Corporate Governance Regime, November 13, 2009.

---

[5] CBCA, s 171. Any other corporation (that is not public or distributing) may have an audit committee, but it is not required s 163.

[6] National Instrument No. 52-110, ss 2.3, 3.1. This instrument also creates an expanded definition of "independent" that means free of "any direct or indirect material relationship." Previously, only the majority of the directors on this committee had to be independent, and this remains the requirement of the CBCA.

[7] National Policy No. 58-201; Multilateral Instrument 58-101.

DIRECTORS

The Role of the Directors

Directors manage or supervise the management of the business and affairs of the corporation. In addition to the general power of management, the Act confers a number of specific powers on directors. Following are the most important powers:

(a) to issue shares—Subject to the corporation's constitution, the directors may issue shares at such times, to such persons, and for such consideration as they may determine (s. 25).

(b) to declare dividends—The directors determine whether or to what extent profits should be distributed to the shareholders or retained in the corporation.

(c) to adopt bylaws governing the day-to-day affairs of the corporation—The directors may adopt new bylaws or amend existing ones. Although they must be submitted for approval at the next meeting of shareholders, the bylaws remain effective until then (s. 103).

(d) to call meetings of shareholders (s. 133)—The directors must call an annual general meeting each year, but they may call additional meetings whenever they wish.

(e) to delegate responsibilities (except those outlined in (a) to (d)) and appoint officers (s. 115 and 121)—Officers do not have to be directors.

CHECKLIST

Powers of Directors

In relation to the internal affairs of the corporation, these are the most important powers given to the directors:

- to issue shares,
- to declare dividends,
- to adopt bylaws,
- to call meetings of shareholders, and
- to delegate responsibilities and appoint officers.

A corporation is required to have one or more directors.[8] A distributing (public) corporation must have a minimum of three directors, at least two of whom must be independent; that is, they must not be officers or employees of the corporation (s. 102(2)). Provincial securities regulations define "independent" more broadly as "no direct or indirect material relationship with the corporation."

When a corporation has more than one director, decisions of the board of directors are normally made by majority vote, unless the corporate constitution requires a higher special majority or unanimity. Usually, the bylaws make provision for the holding of meetings of the board, the election of a chairperson, rules on voting, quorums, and like matters. When making decisions, directors are not obligated to follow the instructions of shareholders.

---

[8] Even a corporation with only a single shareholder must have one or more directors, though there is no reason why the shareholder should not also be the sole director. The articles of incorporation are required to state the number (or the minimum and maximum number) of directors that the corporation is to have (CBCA s 6(1)(e)).

CASE 26.1 Director's Duty to the Corporation

The majority shareholder of a corporation wanted the corporation to sell its main asset. At his request the directors called a general meeting of shareholders, which passed a resolution (over the opposition of some of the minority shareholders) instructing the board of directors to go ahead with the sale.

The board refused to do so, believing the sale was not in the best interests of the corporation. The majority shareholder sued, claiming that the board was bound to carry out the instructions of the general meeting of shareholders.

The court disagreed, ruling that it is the directors who manage the business of a corporation, and until such time as they are replaced, they must act as they think best for the corporation and are not bound to follow instructions from the shareholders.[9]

One very important effect of this rule is that the shareholders cannot compel the directors to declare a dividend unless there is an express requirement in the corporation's constitution that a dividend be paid in particular circumstances.

Appointment and Removal of Directors

A director of a corporation must be a minimum of 18 years of age, be of sound mind, and not have declared bankruptcy (s. 105). In addition, at least 25 percent of the directors of a corporation must be resident Canadians.[10] Unless required by the articles of incorporation, a director need not hold shares in the corporation.

A corporation's first directors are appointed at the time of incorporation and hold office until the first meeting of shareholders, which must be held not less than 18 months after the corporation comes into existence (s. 133). Subsequently, directors are elected, re-elected, or replaced on a regular basis. Normally this occurs at the annual general meeting of the corporation, but elections may be held at any time at a special meeting called for that purpose. Casual vacancies on the board—for example, where a director dies or becomes seriously ill—may normally be filled by the remaining directors.

Directors are elected by ordinary resolution of the shareholders (s. 106(3)); that is, a simple majority vote is sufficient, and usually each share entitles a shareholder to one vote per director position.[11] The result is that one shareholder holding anything more than 50 percent of the total shares is able to elect the entire board of directors. The articles of incorporation may specify an alternative voting structure,[12] that directors be elected by a system of **cumulative voting**—a form of proportional representation designed to ensure that any substantial minority of shareholders will be represented on the board. The system would allow a shareholder to cast all his votes for one director position.[13]

cumulative voting a method of electing directors by a form of proportional representation

If shareholders are dissatisfied with current directors, a special meeting may be called to vote on the removal of a director before the expiration of the term.[14] Except where cumulative voting is allowed, an ordinary resolution (simple majority) is sufficient for the removal of any director, and the articles may not prescribe a greater majority.

---

[9] *Automatic Self-Cleansing Filter Syndicate Co Ltd v Cuninghame*, [1906] 2 Ch. 34 (UKCA).

[10] CBCA, s 105(3).

[11] The Alberta and Saskatchewan statutes allow directors to be appointed by a class of shareholders, or by creditors or employees, if the articles so provide: *Business Corporations Act*, RSA 2000, c B-9, s 106(9); RSS c B-10, s 101(8).

[12] CBCA, s 140(1).

[13] In New Brunswick cumulative voting is mandatory: *Business Corporations Act*, RSNB c 9.1, s 65.

[14] CBCA ss 109, 143; to call such a meeting, shareholders must have at least 5 percent of the outstanding shares of the corporation.

OFFICERS

As noted, officers are responsible for the day-to-day "hands on" management of the corporation. Officers derive their power from the directors. The CBCA defines an officer as "someone appointed by the directors" with functions similar to "a president, vice-president, secretary, treasurer etc." (s. 2(1))[15] It is for the directors to define and designate responsibilities of each officer (s. 121), and this is usually done in the bylaws. The only statutory requirement is that the officer be of "full capacity." Officers may be removed by the directors. In most corporations, officers exercise tremendous power, and as will be discussed in the next section, they are subject to the same duties as directors. The responsibilities of officers of public (distributing) corporations are attracting more attention from provincial regulators, which now require CEOs and CFOs to certify contents of a corporation's audited financial statements and annual reports.[16]

CHECKLIST
Corporate Governance Legislative Overview

Requirements	Private Corporations	Public Corporations (Distributing)	
	CBCA	CBCA	Provincial Securities Regulation*
Minimum directors	1 (s. 102(2))	3 (s. 102(2))	3
Independent directors	Not required	2 (minimum) (s. 102(2))	*Majority (recommended)*
Chair of board			*Independent (recommended)*
Financial statements	Unaudited (optional) (s. 163(1))	Audited (s. 162)	Audited by public accountant, and certified by CEO/CFO
Annual general meeting of shareholders	Yes (s. 133(1))	Yes (s. 133(1))	Yes
Audit committee	Optional (s. 171)	Required: 3 director minimum, majority independent (s. 171)	Required: All members to be financially literate independent directors
Compensation committee	No	No	*Recommended: Disclose alternative method*
Nominating committee	No (s. 137 (4))	No (s. 137 (4))	*Recommended*
Disclosure of corporate governance practices	No	No	Required
Code of ethics	No	No	*Recommended*

*"Securities regulation" refers to the provincial securities regulators rules, recommendations, and guidelines as set out in the National Instruments and Policies created by the Canadian Securities Administrators and adopted by each province's Securities Commission. See, for example, *Securities Act*, RSO 1990, c S-5, s 121.3. Information drawn from NI-52-110, ss 2.1, 3.1; NI-58-101F1; NP-58-201, ss 3.1, 3.2, 3.10, 3.15.

---

[15] CBCA, s 2(1).

[16] National Instrument 52-109 Certification of Disclosure in Issuers Annual and Interim Filings.

> ### Ethical Issue Who Is "Independent"?
>
> When Bill Gates was appointed to Berkshire Hathaway Inc.'s board of directors in 2004, he was designated by the board as an independent director. His only pre-existing relationship with the corporation was as a shareholder. Still, critics complain about the designation, citing his long friendship with chair Warren Buffett and Mr. Buffett's gifts to the Bill & Melinda Gates Foundation.[17]
>
> What does "independent" mean? The commonly understood meaning of the word is that an independent party is free of any conflicting interests or ties. The CBCA definition designates only employees and officers of the corporation as being non-independent (s.102(2)). The provincial securities regulation definition excludes anyone with a "direct or indirect material relationship with the corporation," and it leaves the determination of what amounts to a "material relationship" for the directors themselves to decide with some minor direction.[18]
>
> The regulation suggests that a material relationship is one that could "reasonably interfere with the exercise of independent judgment." It goes on to suggest that examples include employees, officers, and their immediate family members. But what about friends, distant relatives, or competitors?
>
> **Questions to Consider**
>
> 1. Should a director be free of any potential conflict of interest to be considered independent?
> 2. Is it appropriate to let the board of directors determine its own members' independence?
> 3. How can a nominating committee or a code of ethics help with this issue?
>
> Sources: National Instrument 52-110, s 1.4; Belle Kaura, "The Corporate Governance Conundrum: Re-inventing the Board of Directors and Board Committees" in P Puri and J Larson, eds, *Corporate Governance and Securities Regulation in the 21st Century* (Toronto: Butterworths, 2004).

DUTIES OF DIRECTORS AND OFFICERS

Section 122 of the CBCA describes the statutory duties of directors and officers:

1. Every director and officer of a corporation in exercising their powers and discharging their duties shall

   (a) act honestly and in good faith with a view to the best interests of the corporation; and

   (b) exercise the care, diligence and skill that a reasonably prudent person would exercise in comparable circumstances.

2. Every director and officer of a corporation shall comply with this Act, the regulations, articles, bylaws and any unanimous shareholder agreement.

To fully understand these responsibilities we must consider what duties are owed and also to whom the duties are owed.

What Duties Are Owed?

Section 122(1)(a): Fiduciary Duties
The CBCA requires that directors and officers "act *honestly* and in *good faith* with a view to the best interests of the corporation" (s. 122(1)(a)) (italics added). This is a fiduciary duty, a duty with which we are already familiar. It imposes on directors and officers a high standard of conduct involving loyalty, integrity, and trust.[19] This duty addresses the motives, considerations, and factors that influence decision making apart from the decision itself. We will discuss particular examples of common conflicts of interest in the section called

---

[17] Francine McKenna, "Corporate Governance At Berkshire Hathaway: Maybe It's Not All That" *Forbes*, April 11, 2011, https://www.forbes.com/sites/francinemckenna/2011/04/11/corporate-governance-at-berkshire-hathaway-maybe-its-not-all-that/2/#44553a7a6c63.

[18] NI 58-101, s 1.2, citing NI 52-110, s 1.4.

[19] It may also extend to senior employees. See *MacMillan-Bloedel Ltd v Binstead* (1983), 22 BLR 255.

"Specific Conduct." All of the examples involve, in one way or another, situations where there is a conflict (at least potentially) between a director's personal interest and that of the corporation. However, it is important to understand that section 122(1)(a) imposes a general duty on directors and officers to avoid any conflict of interest with their corporation and to act in the corporation's best interests, not the shareholders'.

Section 122(1)(b): Duty of Care, Diligence, and Skill

Section 122(1)(b) of the CBCA requires directors and officers to exercise the care, diligence, and skill that a reasonably prudent person would exercise in comparable circumstances. A director or officer owes a duty not to be negligent in carrying out her duties. This is an objective standard; behaviour must be comparable to the average director in the same circumstances. There are no precise standards for a professional class of directors.[20] Standards are higher for directors of public corporations; they must be financially literate if they sit on the audit committee, and public directors are recommended to participate in continuing education to enhance their skills as directors and their understanding of the corporation's business.[21] Many corporations have codes of ethics and conduct that set standards of behaviour for directors and employees.

Directors are not expected to give continuous attention to the affairs of the corporation, and unless there are suspicious circumstances, directors are entitled to rely on information received from the officers of the corporation.[22] However, they should read and challenge material provided to them and may not willfully close their eyes to mistakes and misconduct. If they acquiesce in such matters, they may be liable in damages to the corporation for any losses that result.

To Whom Are Directors' and Officers' Duties Owed?

To the Corporation

Section 122 has been interpreted by the courts to mean that the duties of directors and officers are owed, first and foremost, to the corporation as a whole. The interests of "the corporation" are normally taken to mean the interests of the corporate legal entity, present and future. Directors and officers may—and should—consider the short-term and long-term interests of the corporation and not merely the present interests or wishes of the shareholders or other stakeholders. But do directors and officers owe duties to anyone other than the corporation? How should they balance competing stakeholder interests?

To the Shareholders and Other Stakeholders

Although directors are elected and can be removed by a majority of the shareholders, it would be wrong to conclude that their first duty is to those shareholders who have elected them—as was demonstrated in Case 26.1. The fiduciary duty of a director is owed to the corporation as a whole.

However, this does not mean that shareholders or other stakeholders are irrelevant. Modern corporate governance theory recognizes that the conduct of a corporation's business affects not only shareholders but many other sectors of the public as well. If a large corporation is badly managed, the well-being of many people and even the national interest may be seriously affected. Creditors of a bankrupt corporation go unpaid. Employees may lose their jobs, as may other members of the

---

[20] National Instrument 52-110: Financial literacy means the individual "has the ability to read and understand a set of financial statements" (s. 1.6).

[21] *Ibid.*; see also NP 58-201, ss 3.6, 3.7.

[22] *Dovey v Corey*, [1901] AC 477.

community where the corporation carries on business. A corporation that produces defective products may injure consumers, and one that does not take effective measures to prevent pollution may cause severe damage to the environment. Consequently, creditors, employees, and the public in general have a stake in good corporate management.

Therefore, corporate governance law recognizes that directors and officers must act in the best interests of the corporation viewed as a good corporate citizen,[23] meaning there is an obligation to consider the interests of other stakeholders. The corporation's interests remain paramount. Directors must fulfill these duties as they manage the affairs of the corporation, or they will be personally liable. The courts have drawn a distinction between duties owed to the corporation only and those owed to stakeholders.

The *Peoples v Wise* Distinction

In *Peoples v Wise*, the Supreme Court of Canada considered the directors' and officers' duties in section 122 and drew a clear distinction between the fiduciary duty in (a) and the duty of skill and care in (b).[24]

CASE 26.2 Separate Duties

Wise Stores Inc. (Wise) bought Peoples Department Stores Inc. (Peoples). The three sons of the Wise founder (Wise brothers) were the majority shareholders, officers, and directors of Wise. After the purchase they also became the sole directors of Peoples. The integration of the two operations did not go smoothly, especially in the area of inventory control and bookkeeping. The Wise brothers reviewed the inventory problems and accepted the recommendation of the vice-president of administration and finance. They implemented a joint inventory procurement policy that divided purchasing responsibilities between the two operations. Peoples would make purchases from North America, and Wise would make all other international purchases. Within a year of implementation, the inventory system was in total chaos; suppliers went unpaid. Eventually both Wise and Peoples declared bankruptcy, and Peoples' bankruptcy trustee sued the Wise brothers personally, claiming they breached the duties owed to Peoples' creditors.

The Supreme Court of Canada held that there was no fiduciary duty owing to the creditors or other stakeholders, stating "At all times directors and officers owe their fiduciary obligation to only the corporation. The interests of the corporation are not to be confused with the interests of the creditors or those of any other stakeholders."[25] However, the Court also held that the duty of skill and care was not limited to the corporation: "the identity of the beneficiary of the duty of care is much more open-ended, and it appears obvious that it must include creditors."[26]

On the facts, the Court held that the Wise brothers met the required objective standard of skill and care by acting prudently and on a reasonably informed basis. The creditors were denied a remedy.

In *Peoples v Wise*, the Supreme Court extended the director's duty of skill and care (s. 122(1)(b)) to other stakeholders, including shareholders, creditors, and employees. In refusing to extend the fiduciary duty (s. 122(1)(a)) the same way, the Court acknowledged the broad protection afforded to these groups under other statutory provisions. Some of that legislation is discussed later in this chapter, in Chapter 27, and in Chapter 3. Corporate directors must manage their corporations in conformity with these duties, failing which they may incur personal liability.

---

[23] *BCE Inc, Re*, 2008 SCC 69 at para 66.

[24] *Peoples Department Stores Inc v Wise* (2004), 244 DLR (4th) 564 at 582. In Alberta, a director who is appointed by a particular class of shareholders (or by creditors of employees) may give special (but not exclusive) consideration to the interests of that class: RSA 2000, c B-9, s 122(4). There may be special circumstances in which directors owe a fiduciary duty to others—for example, to clients of the firm; see *Air Canada v M & L Travel Ltd* (1993), 108 DLR (4th) 592; *BCE Inc, supra* note 23. It is clear, then, that the fiduciary duty is owed only to the corporation and not the shareholders (except in rare circumstances); see also *Vlastiak v Valastiak*, [2010] BCJ No 233 (BCAA) (an example of a rare case where a fiduciary duty was owed to the only other shareholder).

[25] *Peoples, ibid* at paras 43–4.

[26] *Ibid* at para 57.

In *Peoples v Wise*, the Court also noted that it is often in the best interests of the corporation to consider the interests of others.[27] A corporation that promotes good labour relations by considering the welfare of its employees, enjoys good customer and community relations, and is perceived as socially responsible and responsive to environmental concerns is likely to prosper better in the longer term than one that does not. A corporation's management rightly devotes considerable attention to its public image and relations. The argument may even be made that directors owe a duty to the corporation to do so.[28]

The situation is different in Ontario. In 2007, possibly in response to the *Peoples* decision, the Ontario *Business Corporations Act* was amended to make it clear that both the fiduciary duty and the duty of skill and care are owed *only* to the corporation.[29]

Defences to Breach of Duty

Directors and officers are personally liable for a breach of duty. If the corporation goes bankrupt, disgruntled shareholders, employees, and creditors often accuse officers and directors of breach of duty or "mismanagement." How can directors and officers protect themselves? What defences are available? What risk-management strategies should be in place? Both legislation and the common law provide some relief.

The CBCA includes the following defences and risk-management strategies:[30]

(a) Reasonable diligence, also known as the **due diligence defence**: By establishing that the required degree of care was taken, directors and officers can defend themselves against claims of breach of the articles, bylaws, and the Act (s. 123(4)).

(b) Good faith reliance: Good faith reliance on audited financial statements or expert reports is a defence to breach of fiduciary duty or duty of skill and care (s. 123(5)). Therefore, obtaining expert reports prior to key decisions is a good risk-management strategy.

(c) Corporate indemnity: An agreement with the corporation to reimburse a director or officer for any costs associated with liability for breach of duty is enforceable provided that the director acted honestly, reasonably, and in good faith (s. 124). Naturally, the effectiveness of this risk-management strategy depends on the financial health of the corporation.

(d) Directors' and officers' liability insurance: A corporation may purchase directors' liability insurance on behalf of its board (s. 124(6)). These policies have many exclusions, including bad faith and fraud, and are very expensive.

due diligence defence establishing that an acceptable standard of care and skill was exercised by a director or officer

The key common law defence available to directors and officers is known as the **business judgment rule**. Under this rule, courts will grant business experts the benefit of the doubt and not easily criticize a business decision.[31] Judges recognize that they are not business experts and that even sound decisions may ultimately be unsuccessful. Therefore, courts focus on the process used to arrive at the decision; as long as directors and officers exercise an appropriate degree of prudence and diligence while making the decision, the court will hold that the duty of skill and care is met. As was noted in *Peoples*, establishing and following good corporate governance rules

business judgment rule courts will defer to the business decisions of directors and officers provided they are arrived at using an appropriate degree of prudence and diligence

---

[27] *Ibid* at para 42.

[28] *Re Olympia & York Enterprises Ltd and Hiram Walker Resources Ltd* (1986), 59 OR (2d) 254 at 271 (Ont Div Ct).

[29] Ontario *Business Corporations Act*, RSO 1990, c B-16, s 134(1).

[30] There is some provincial variation: Ontario's reasonable diligence and good faith defence extends to interim financial reports and reports or advice of an officer or employee (OBCA s 135(4)).

[31] *BCE Inc*, *supra* note 23 at paras 96–100.

can protect directors and officers from allegations that they have breached their duty of care.[32]

The business judgment rule has its limits. It will not protect a director from liability for a failure to comply with specific legal obligations such as mandatory disclosure under securities legislation.[33]

Strict Liability

Directors may also be subject to strict liability, even though no breach of duty occurred. The CBCA and corresponding provincial statutes make directors liable to their corporation when they vote at meetings of the board on specified matters that cause financial losses to the corporation, such as the improper redemption of shares or the payment of a dividend in circumstances that leave the corporation unable to meet its liabilities (s. 118(2)). In addition, if the corporation becomes insolvent, the directors are personally liable to all employees of the corporation for unpaid wages while they were directors, up to the amount of six months' wages (s. 119).[34] Directors may also be liable for failure to comply with other statutes. For example, if the corporation is insolvent, the federal government may collect from the directors the income tax that the corporation was required to withhold from the wages and salaries of employees.[35] Even volunteer directors of a non-profit corporation have been held liable under this provision.[36]

Specific Conduct Involving Conflicts of Interest

Contracts with the Corporation
Perhaps the most important fiduciary obligation is the duty to disclose any interest that the director may have in contracts made with the corporation. Examples include when a director negotiates the sale of her own property to the corporation or the purchase of property from the corporation. It may arise indirectly; for example, a director may be a shareholder in another corporation that is selling to or buying from her corporation. The problem occurs frequently among related corporations, where a director of one corporation is a shareholder and perhaps a director of a second corporation.

ILLUSTRATION 26.1 Shares in Multiple Corporations

Brown holds a large number of shares in World Electric and in Universal Shipbuilding, and is a director of each of these corporations. Universal Shipbuilding requires expensive turbo-generator sets for two large ships under construction. World Electric is one of several manufacturers of turbo-generators.

Brown is faced with an obvious conflict of interest: Can she encourage or even support a contract between the two corporations? On one side, it is in Brown's interest to see Universal Shipbuilding obtain the equipment at the lowest possible price. On the other side, it is in her interest to see World Electric get the contract and obtain the highest possible price.

---

[32] *Peoples, supra* note 24 at para 64.

[33] *Kerr v Danier Leather Inc*, 2007 SCC 44 at para 55.

[34] Section 119 uses the word "debts," though it limits the amount to six months' wages. It is, however, not necessary to establish that the debt claimed is for "wages," provided it was incurred for services performed. The section 123(4) defence of reasonable diligence applies to both section 118 and section 119. In *Proulx v Sahelian Goldfields Inc* (2001), 204 DLR (4th) 670, the Ontario Court of Appeal (considering s 131 of the *Ontario Act*) held that vacation pay owing constituted a debt, whether or not it should be regarded as "wages," and was within the section.

[35] *Income Tax Act*, RSC 1985, c 1 (5th Supp), s 227.1.

[36] *MNR v Corsano* (1999), [1999] FCJ No 401 (FCCA).

Section 120 of the CBCA describes the appropriate course of actions; a director who has an interest in a contract must disclose this fact at a meeting of the board of directors that considers the contract and must not participate or vote on the matter. If, after learning of the interest, the remaining members of the board still wish to go through with the contract, they may enter into a binding contract. If the remaining directors are not enough to form a quorum, the contract should be ratified at a general meeting of the shareholders. Failure by a director to disclose an interest gives that director's corporation the right to rescind the contract upon learning of the interest.

One type of contract in which a director clearly has a personal interest is the contract providing for her own remuneration, so it is perhaps surprising that the CBCA simply provides that directors may fix the remuneration of the directors, officers, and employees of the corporation (s. 125). There is an obvious risk that the directors will be excessively generous to each other or to their CEO.[37] Securities regulations require public (distributing) corporations to disclose executive compensation and to develop independent methods of establishing executive compensation, and the creation of compensation committees is recommended.

Interception of Corporate Opportunity A different situation arises when a director learns of a corporate opportunity and keeps it for herself. It could be buying property, investing in another company, or selling assets. It is a director's duty to give the corporation the chance of first refusal before acting for herself. If she does not, she has intercepted an opportunity belonging to the corporation and has committed a breach of duty. If a director has received a mandate to act as agent for the corporation to purchase a specific piece of property or a particular type of property, she is under the same duty as that placed upon any agent to acquire property for her principal. If she buys the property for herself, she has breached her duty. The property is deemed to be held in trust for the corporation, as is any profit made.

CASE 26.3 Part of Director's Mandate

R was a director of a large corporation that was in the process of expanding its chain of retail grocery stores. A major part of his duties was to travel around the country looking for suitable independent stores for the corporation to purchase. R entered into an arrangement with a friend to buy those stores that seemed especially good bargains and to resell them to the corporation, concealing the fact of his ownership. When this was later discovered, the corporation brought proceedings against him.

The court held that R was under a duty to acquire the stores for the corporation and therefore was held to have done so as its agent.[38]

Whenever information is received in her capacity as a director of the corporation, it is her duty to give the corporation first chance of acquiring an interest in the venture or property. If the corporation decides not to acquire the property, the director is probably free to do so. But she makes a dangerous decision if she assumes that the corporation would not want the property anyway and then acquires it for herself without consulting the corporation. In practice, it is sometimes difficult for a court to decide whether, in the circumstances, the information came to the director personally or in her role as a director of the corporation. But once the court decides that the opportunity belonged to the corporation, the result is quite clear: Purchasing on her own behalf is a breach of duty.

---

[37] See *UPM-Kymmene Corp v UPM-Kymmene Miramichi Inc* (2002), 214 DLR (4th) 496, where a court set aside a board approved a "compensation agreement" for the chairman that included a "signing bonus" of 25 million shares.

[38] *Canada Safeway Ltd v Thompson*, [1951] 3 DLR 295. Note that in reselling the stores to the corporation, the director was also in breach of his duty to disclose his interest. The corporation could have chosen instead to rescind the contracts. See also *Slate Ventures Inc v Hurley* (1997), 37 BLR (2d) 138.

CASE 26.4 First Right of Refusal

C was a director of a corporation involved in exploration and natural resource development. C was approached by a prospector, who asked if the corporation would be interested in acquiring certain claims. He reported this at a meeting of the board of directors. A majority of the board considered that the corporation was already overcommitted financially and decided against taking up the offer.

When the prospector approached C again, C decided to take up the claims for himself. He later left the corporation, after a disagreement. The corporation learned of his acquisition of the claims and brought proceedings against him.

The court held that, once the corporation had rejected the opportunity, it no longer belonged to the corporation, and C was free to take advantage of it.[39]

Competing with the Corporation Another application of the conflict of interest principle is the rule that a director may not carry on a business competing with that of her corporation, except with the permission of the corporation. The corporation is entitled to claim all the profit made by the director and to obtain an injunction prohibiting the director from any future competition.

CASE 26.5 Consulting on the Side

O'Malley was a director of Canaero, a corporation specializing in aerial surveying. He was hired to work on a project for the corporation in Guyana, during which he learned a lot about the terrain and made some useful contacts. He subsequently resigned from Canaero, formed his own corporation, and successfully tendered for a surveying contract with the government of Guyana.

O'Malley was held to be in breach of his fiduciary duty to Canaero and accountable to them for his profit on the contract.[40]

Related Party Transactions Large businesses often operate through a group of related corporations. Those corporations deal with each other on a regular basis. Frequently, they share some of the same directors. The potential for conflicts of interest is obvious. Almost inevitably, some intergroup contracts or arrangements will be more beneficial to one party than to the other. The situation becomes especially perilous where the two or more corporations concerned do not have the same shareholders or creditors.

The likelihood of impropriety (or at least of perceptions of impropriety) is further increased where the corporate group is effectively controlled by a single individual or family—a situation that is quite common in Canada.

CASE 26.6 Corporations Controlled by the Same Shareholders

Hollinger Inc., a corporation in which 12 percent of its voting shares were held by the public and the remaining shares were owned by Conrad Black and his associates, made a loan of $1.1 million to Ravelston Corp., all of whose shares were owned or controlled by Black. Minority shareholders in Hollinger alleged that the loan had not been properly approved.[41] In related proceedings it was alleged that improper payments totalling $32 million were made from one Hollinger corporation to another corporation and its directors. The court appointed an inspector to investigate.[42]

---

[39] *Peso Silver Mines Ltd v Cropper* (1966), 56 DLR (2d) 117 (SCC). In contrast, where a majority of the directors (and shareholders) of a corporation purported to pass a resolution rejecting a contractual opportunity offered to the corporation and then took it for themselves, that was held to be a breach of their duties. The resolution was not adopted in good faith: *Cook v Deeks*, [1916] AC 554.

[40] *Canadian Aero Service Ltd v O'Malley* (1973), 40 DLR (3d) 371 (SCC).

[41] *Catalyst Fund General Partner I Inc v Hollinger Inc*, [2004] OJ No 4722, aff'd [2006] OJ No 944 (ONCA).

[42] *Ibid*. In U.S. criminal proceedings initiated by the American Securities and Exchange Commission, Black was convicted of fraud and obstruction of justice arising from redirection of sale proceeds from Hollinger corporations to directors through artificial non-competition agreements (some convictions were reversed on appeal).

Insider Trading

Insider trading is one type of conduct for which courts were slow to impose liability, so the legislatures intervened. Insider trading legislation creates all three types of liability: civil liability, regulatory liability, and criminal liability.

Insider trading occurs when a director or officer of a corporation, or some other person (for example, a shareholder or employee of the corporation), buys or sells the corporation's shares or other securities, using confidential inside information in order to make a profit or avoid a loss.

insider trading the use of confidential information relating to a corporation in dealing in its securities

ILLUSTRATION 26.2 Insider Trading in Various Forms

(a) The directors of a small family company are approached by a large public corporation that offers to buy all the shares of the family company at a price considerably above that at which the shares had previously been valued. The next day, one of the directors is approached by her uncle, who is a shareholder and who offers to sell some of his shares to her. Without disclosing the proposed takeover, she buys the shares at a price well below that of the offer.

(b) The directors of a mining corporation receive a confidential report from their surveyor that very valuable mineral deposits have just been discovered. One of the directors immediately instructs her broker to buy as many of the corporation's shares as possible on the stock exchange, before the good news is released and forces up the price.

(c) The directors of a corporation learn that their major customer has just declared bankruptcy, owing the corporation a large sum of money. Default on the account by their customer is likely to result in the corporation showing a substantial loss in the forthcoming half-yearly accounts. One of the directors promptly sells her shares just before the news becomes public and the shares drop in value.

In each of the hypothetical cases in Illustration 26.2, a director used confidential information that came to her in her capacity as a director for her own benefit.

Legislation sets strict disclosure requirements whenever a director or other insider trades in the securities of her own corporation, and has made insider trading a criminal offence, punishable by fines or imprisonment or both. Under the Ontario *Securities Act*, for example, fines of up to $5 million and prison terms of up to five years may be imposed.[43] There is a possible penalty of 10 years' imprisonment under the *Criminal Code*.[44] Despite the heavy penalties, however, the incidents s of insider trading seems to be increasing, both in Canada and in the United States.

The above provisions apply principally to corporations whose securities are publicly traded as a way of promoting public confidence in the markets. However, section 131 of the CBCA provides that, even in the case of a *private corporation*, an insider who purchases or sells a security of the corporation with knowledge of specific, confidential, price-sensitive information is liable

(a) to compensate the seller or purchaser (as the case may be) for any loss suffered as a result of the transaction, and

(b) to account to the corporation for any benefit or advantage obtained.[45]

For the purposes of the legislation, "insider" includes a director or officer, an employee, any shareholder who holds more than a prescribed percentage of the corporation's securities, and a "tippee"—that is, a person who knowingly receives confidential information from an insider.

---

[43] *Securities Act*, RSO 1990, c S.5, s 122(1). An offender may also be required to pay back three times the amount of any profit made. In *R v Harper* (2003), 232 DLR (4th) 738, a fine of almost $4 million was imposed, though it was reduced to $2 million on appeal.

[44] *Criminal Code*, RSC 1985, c C-46, s 382.1, as amended by SC 2004, c 3. In Canada, most inside traders receive fines and are banned from the securities industry and public boards.

[45] CBCA, s 131.

CHECKLIST

Directors' Personal Liability

A director faces the following types of personal liability for breach of his duties:

Type of Personal Liability	Available Remedy
(a) Civil liability	
(i) to the corporation	
■ breach of fiduciary duty, s 122(1)(a)	■ damages for losses arising from breach
■ specific conduct involving conflicts of interest, s 120	■ accounting of amounts paid for improper dividends or share redemption
■ breach of duty of skill, diligence, and care, s 122(1)(b)	■ rescission of contract involving conflict of interest ■ constructive trust of property ■ accounting of profits ■ injunction to restrain breach of duty
(ii) to others	
■ breach of duty of skill, diligence, and care, s 122(1)(b) ■ strict liability for six months' unpaid wages ■ strict liability for unpaid taxes ■ liability for insider trading damages	■ damages for losses arising from the liability
(b) Regulatory and criminal liability	
■ insider trading	■ fines and imprisonment (*Criminal Code*)
■ other statutory offences discussed in Chapter 27	■ fines and imprisonment (*Securities Act*)

SHAREHOLDERS

The Role of Shareholders

Shareholders play little or no part in management. They have some rights, the most important being the right to vote at shareholder meetings, but generally, once the shareholders have elected a board of directors, they have no further power to participate in management. If they do not like the way the directors are running the corporation's business and affairs, they cannot interfere. Legally, their main course of action is to dismiss the directors and elect new ones in their place.[46]

---

[46] If dissatisfied shareholders hold a sufficient proportion of the shares, they need not wait until the next meeting called by the directors; they may requisition a meeting (s. 143) to elect a new board. See section called "The Protection of Minority Shareholders"; in some situations there may be other court remedies available.

Publicly Traded Corporations   In large, publicly traded corporations, shareholdings may be widely distributed, with no single shareholder or group holding more than 5 percent of the voting stock. Less frequently, one entity may control a majority of shares. Both situations make changing management difficult. Management may respond to calls for change with a piece of practical advice to investors: "If you don't like the management, sell!" In other words, "Do not get into costly corporate struggles. Cut your losses by getting out and reinvesting in a corporation more to your liking." All that may be changing with the recent attempts to strengthen corporate governance through independent directors and the wide use of the oppression remedy (discussed below). However, shareholders do not have direct power over the management of the corporation.

Private Corporations   In private corporations, shareholders' problems are radically different. There is no easily accessible way to sell shares in a private company if a shareholder wants to sell. The usual problem is a serious disagreement among the principal shareholders, who are frequently also directors and senior employees of the corporation. In the absence of careful contractual arrangements providing safeguards, a minority shareholder may find himself "locked in" and "frozen out" at the same time.

The minority shareholder is "locked in" in the sense that he probably cannot sell his shares except at a fraction of what he believes they should be worth. There are two reasons for this. First, in most private corporations the transfer of shares is restricted, usually requiring the consent of the board of directors. They may be unwilling to agree to the transfer of his shares except to someone of their own choosing. Second, even if the minority shareholder is free to sell the shares, he will have great difficulty in finding a buyer who would consider acquiring a minority position in a private corporation.

The minority shareholder may be "frozen out" in the following manner. First, the majority directors may fire him from his job with the corporation or, at the very least, refuse to renew his employment contract when it expires. Second, they may remove him from the board of directors or elect someone else in his place at the next election. Third, they may increase salaries to themselves, so that the corporation itself earns no apparent profit. Even if a profit is shown, it may be retained by the corporation, since dividends are payable only at the discretion of the board of directors. Therefore, a minority shareholder may find himself deprived of his salary-earning position, his directorship, and his prospect of any dividends on his investment.

In these circumstances the majority shareholders may not have broken any law, and no remedy existed at common law. However, a number of statutory provisions provide relief for minority shareholders, discussed, under "The Protection of Minority Shareholders" later in this chapter.

Rights Attached to Shares

Shareholder rights come from two principal sources—the rights attached to their shares by the articles of the corporation and the rights conferred on them by the relevant corporate legislation.

The corporate constitution sets out the rights attached to each class of shares. For example, the CBCA requires that the articles state the classes of shares that may be issued and, if there are to be two or more classes of shares, the rights, privileges, restrictions, and conditions attaching to each class (ss. 6(1)(c) and 24(4)). If there is only one class of shares, the rights of the shareholders include the rights

- to vote at any meeting of shareholders,
- to receive any dividend that is declared, and
- to receive the remaining property of the corporation (after payment of its debts) on dissolution (s. 24(3)).

Additional rights may be attached to shares, and if there are different classes of shares, rights may be granted to some shares and not others; but the three basic rights must exist and be exercisable by one or other class of shares.

Meetings and Voting

Notice and Attendance at Meetings
Shareholders need a forum to voice their objections about the management. The forum provided under all statutes is the **general meeting of shareholders**. The corporation may hold other meetings of shareholders in the course of the year, but it is required by statute to hold at least one **annual general meeting**.[47] Shareholders are entitled to advance notice of all general meetings and are entitled to receive copies of the financial statements before the annual general meeting. They may attend the meetings, question the directors, and criticize the management of the corporation.[48]

The Right to Requisition Meetings
All the provinces provide in their statutes that the shareholders themselves may call a meeting. However, these provisions require a relatively large proportion of the shareholders to petition for the meeting, a requirement that is virtually impossible to meet in big corporations where even a large number of shareholders may hold only a small percentage of the total shares.[49] The right to requisition a **special meeting** is therefore of limited use in large corporations but is especially valuable in the smaller, private companies.

The Right to Vote
The right to attend meetings and to criticize management is reinforced with the right to vote. The shareholders pass (or defeat) resolutions—an **ordinary resolution**, which is passed by a simple majority of votes cast, and a **special resolution**, which requires a two-thirds majority.[50] The CBCA sets out a number of matters that must be approved by the shareholders in either an ordinary or a special resolution, the most important being

(a) the approval of alterations to the articles of incorporation—special resolution (s. 173),
(b) the approval of certain other fundamental changes, such as amalgamation with another corporation (s. 183) or the sale of all, or substantially all, of the corporation's property—special resolution (s. 189),
(c) the approval of any amendments made by the directors to the bylaws—ordinary resolution (s. 103),
(d) the election of the auditor—ordinary resolution (s. 162), and
(e) the election or removal of directors—ordinary resolution (ss. 106, 109).

Except for the items described in (a) and (b), the most important matter voted upon by the shareholders is the election of directors.

Class Voting Rights
Not all shareholders necessarily have the right to vote. A corporation's shares may be divided into different classes, with different voting rights. Common shares almost always carry the right to vote; preferred shares often carry a right to vote only in specified circumstances, such as when preferred dividends are in arrears. The founders of a corporation may create several classes of shares and weigh the voting heavily in favour of a small group of shares held by themselves. For

---

general meeting of shareholders a formal meeting of shareholders at which they are able to vote on matters concerning the corporation

annual general meeting the general meeting of shareholders that is required by law to be held each year to transact certain specified business

special meeting any general meeting of shareholders other than the annual general meeting

ordinary resolution a resolution adopted by the general meeting and passed by a simple majority

special resolution a resolution of the general meeting required to be passed by a special (usually two-thirds) majority

---

[47] CBCA, s 133.
[48] CBCA, ss 132(4), (5).
[49] CBCA, s 143.
[50] CBCA, s 2. In Nova Scotia, a special resolution requires a three-quarters majority.

example, they could give Class "A" shares 100 votes per share and Class "B," issued to a broader group of shareholders, only one vote per share. This is most popular for private corporations because it would be virtually impossible for a publicly traded corporation to have such a share structure today. Securities commissions, stock exchanges, and underwriters would probably refuse such an issue, and without their concurrence a public offering is impossible. Virtually all common stock offered on the public market today carries one vote per share. Within a particular class, however, all shares must enjoy the same rights (s. 24).

Class rights, which may relate not only to voting but also to other matters such as rights to have priority in payment of dividends or to receive the surplus on liquidation of the corporation, must be set out in the articles of incorporation. Consequently, they may only be varied by special resolution of the shareholders. In addition, altering the rights of a particular class requires approval by the votes of two-thirds of that class and of any other class that may be adversely affected (s. 176).

class rights special rights attached to a particular class of shares

Proxies In most publicly traded corporations, only a small proportion of shareholders actually attend general meetings. All corporation statutes permit a shareholder to nominate a **proxy** to attend a general meeting and to cast that shareholder's votes at the meeting as instructed. This is done by signing a form naming the proxy and sending it to the corporation before the meeting. Most jurisdictions now go further and require all corporations, except the smallest private ones, to send a **proxy form**, the contents of which are prescribed in detail, to all shareholders at the same time as notice of a meeting is given.

proxy a person appointed to attend a general meeting of shareholders and to cast the votes of the shareholder appointing him

proxy form a form required to be circulated to shareholders before a general meeting, inviting them to appoint a proxy if they so wish

In the event of a proxy fight between two groups of shareholders—usually the board of directors and a dissenting group—each group solicits all the shareholders by mail in order to persuade them to give their proxy forms to the group making the solicitation. The dissenting group may go to the corporation's head office to obtain lists of all the shareholders from the share register in order to make their solicitations. Here the board of directors has a great advantage. As a matter of practice, they include proxy forms, naming an existing director as the proposed proxy, with the mailed notice of the annual general meeting.[51]

Financial Rights

Shareholders expect to receive a return on their investment in one or both of two forms—earnings distributed regularly in the form of dividends, and growth that can be realized by selling the shares or on dissolution of the corporation. Holders of common shares may be satisfied with smaller dividends if there is capital appreciation in the corporation's assets or if a significant part of the profits is retained within the business and has the effect of increasing the value of the shares. Preferred shares often do not participate in growth, and their holders are primarily concerned with receiving dividends.

Dividends A fundamental right attached to shares is the right to receive any **dividend** that is declared by the corporation. The declaration of dividends is entirely within the discretion of the board of directors. Common shareholders normally have no right to be paid a dividend, even when the corporation makes large profits.

dividend a distribution to shareholders of a share of the profits of the corporation

There can be no discrimination, however, in the payment of dividends among shareholders of the same class. Each shareholder is entitled to such dividends as are declared in proportion to the number of shares of that class held. In addition,

---

[51] This advantage is partly offset by disclosure requirements and by compelling management to provide shareholders with a means to nominate a different proxy (CBCA, s 150).

directors are bound to pay dividends in the order of preference assigned to the classes of shareholders. They may not pay the common shareholders a dividend without first paying the whole of any preferred dividends owing to preference shareholders.

Distribution of Surplus   On the dissolution of a corporation, provided it has assets remaining after paying off all its creditors, shareholders are entitled to a proportionate share of the remaining net assets. The distribution of these net assets among the various classes of shareholders must also be made in accordance with the respective priorities of each class.

Preemptive Rights   One of the more important powers given to the board of directors is the power to issue shares. The issue of new shares involves two possible risks for existing shareholders. First, the issue of shares to some other person will necessarily reduce the proportion of the total number of shares that a shareholder holds. Second, there is the risk of "stock watering"; if new shares are issued for a price that is less than the value of the existing shares, the value of the existing shares will be diluted.

ILLUSTRATION 26.3   Impact of New Share Issue

A owns 34 of the total of 100 shares issued by XYZ Inc. The assets of XYZ Inc. are worth approximately $1 million. The directors wish to raise additional capital and resolve to issue 20 new shares to T, at a price of $5000 per share. As a result, A will now own only 28.3 percent of the total shares and can no longer block the adoption of a special resolution. A's shares, previously worth $10 000 each, will be worth only $9167.

Canadian courts do not recognize a general principle giving all shareholders a preemptive right. This right must be expressly attached to a share when the corporation creates the class of shares in the articles of incorporation (s. 28). Without a preemptive right, directors have the right to issue authorized share capital of the corporation at their discretion, but they must issue shares only for the purpose of raising capital or for purposes that are in the best interest of the corporation. If they have a good faith intention of raising capital, they may distribute the shares to whomever they wish, upon payment of a fair price. But if directors issue shares not for the benefit of the corporation but instead to affect voting control, the issue may be declared void. For example, if directors were to issue shares to themselves for the purpose of outvoting shareholders who, up to that point, had a majority of the issued shares, the extra share issue could be set aside by the court.

CASE 26.7   No Good Faith Intention

Bonisteel was a director of Collis Leather Co. and the owner of 458 of 1208 issued shares. He found another shareholder willing to sell him 150 shares. The purchase would have given Bonisteel control of the corporation. In order to block Bonisteel, the directors resolved to issue 292 new shares, and each director was asked how many shares he wished to subscribe for. Most of the new shares were taken up by directors other than Bonisteel, with the result that he would be left with less than 50 percent of the total shares. Bonisteel brought an action to restrain the directors from issuing the new shares.

The court held that the share issue would be invalid. The corporation was not in need of additional funds, and it was improper to issue new shares solely for the purpose of altering the balance of control.[52]

---

[52] *Bonisteel v Collis Leather Co Ltd* (1919), 45 OR 195.

CASE 26.8 Good Faith Intention

Afton was a "junior" mining company, incorporated in British Columbia; it was looking for a "major" company to help finance a large drilling program. Teck, a large resource corporation, made an offer to buy a controlling block of Afton's shares. The directors of Afton, led by its chief engineer, Millar, rejected the offer and preferred to enter into an arrangement with Canex, the subsidiary of another Canadian corporation, even though Canex was not prepared to match the Teck offer. Following the rejection, Teck started buying Afton shares on the stock exchange, and soon announced that it had acquired more than 50 percent of the issued shares. The Afton directors then entered into a long-term contract with Canex, which involved issuing a large block of new shares to Canex. This arrangement reduced the Teck holding to less than 50 percent.

The share issue was challenged by Teck but upheld by the court. The Afton directors had entered into the arrangement with Canex and had issued the new shares because they genuinely believed that the interests of Afton would be better served as a "partner" of Canex than as a subsidiary of Teck.[53]

Although not required to do so, most corporations give shareholders a pre-emptive right. When a corporation proposes to issue further shares, it may first issue subscription rights or share rights to all existing shareholders, giving each shareholder one right for each share held. The shareholder then has an option to purchase a new share at a specified price for a specified number of subscription rights. For example, a shareholder owning 50 shares may receive 50 rights entitling him to buy 10 shares (one share for every five rights) at a specified price per share. Subscription rights are normally made transferable, and if the market value of the existing shares significantly exceeds the specified price for the new shares, the rights themselves will have a market value; they may be sold to anyone who wishes to purchase them and exercise the option.

The Right to Information

Disclosure is one of the fundamental principles of modern corporate governance. Prompt disclosure of relevant information enables investors to evaluate the effectiveness of management, and publicity may be an effective deterrent to high-handed behaviour or misconduct in management.

The Financial Statements Annual **financial statements** must be presented to the shareholders prior to the annual general meeting. All corporation acts require that basic information be part of the financial statements, though the detailed requirements vary. Generally, the basic items required are

- the income statement, showing the results of operations for the financial year;
- the balance sheet, showing the corporation's assets as of the financial year-end (including details of changes in share capital during the year);
- a statement of changes in financial position, analyzing changes in working capital;
- a statement of retained earnings showing changes during the year, including the declaration of dividends; and
- a statement of contributed surplus.

The annual financial statements should be in comparative form, showing corresponding data for the preceding financial year. In addition, some statutes require that shareholders be sent comparative interim quarterly financial statements. Public companies must

financial statements annual accounts that are required to be presented to the shareholders at the annual general meeting

---

[53] *Teck Corp v Millar* (1973), 33 DLR (3d) 288. See also *Icahn Partners LP v Lionsgate Entertainment Corp*, [2010] BCJ No 2130 at paras 128–54 (BCSC), aff'd 2011 BCCA 228.

produce audited financial statements, and securities regulations require that CEOs and CFOs of public (distributing) companies also certify that the statements fairly reflect the financial condition of the corporation.[54]

Documents of Record
A corporation must maintain certain documents of record at its head office, for inspection by a shareholder during usual business hours. These **documents of record** include

- minutes of shareholders' meetings;
- a register of all transfers of shares, including the date and other particulars of each transfer;
- a copy of the corporation's charter, a copy of all bylaws (or articles) and special resolutions, and a register of shareholders; and
- a register of the directors.

documents of record documents that a corporation is required to keep and make available to shareholders

These documents are useful to a minority group of shareholders attempting to collect evidence to support a claim of misconduct or ineffectiveness on the part of the directors. Access to the share register permits a dissentient group to obtain the names and addresses of all other shareholders so that they may communicate with them, explain their complaints, and attempt to enlist shareholders' support.

Another document of record is the collection of minutes from directors' meetings. Unlike the other documents of record, however, directors alone, not the shareholders, have a right of access to it.[55]

The Auditor
To protect the company from errors and wrongdoing of its management and to provide the shareholders with information to assess management,[56] the acts provide for the appointment of an independent auditor by the shareholders. Private companies may dispense with this requirement, but only if the shareholders unanimously agree to do so. The auditor must be an independent person who is not employed by the corporation.[57] In order to confirm the accuracy of the financial statements, the auditor examines all the records and books of accounts of the corporation. The auditor provides an opinion on whether the statements fairly present the financial position of the corporation in accordance with generally accepted accounting principles.[58] Both the auditor's report and the financial statements must be sent to all shareholders before the corporation's annual general meeting; the period usually specified is at least 21 days before the meeting. These items are included in the corporation's **annual report** to shareholders to help shareholders decide whether to retain or oust the current directors.

annual report the report on the business and affairs of the corporation, which the directors are required to present at the annual general meeting

Only the auditor and the directors have the right to examine the books of account; shareholders as such do not have access to them. If a shareholder suspects that something is wrong, he may communicate his information to the auditor or the audit committee, but the auditor has no duty to undertake a special examination at the request of a shareholder; the auditor's duty is owed to the corporation itself rather than the shareholders.[59] As a last resort, a shareholder may apply to a court for the appointment of an inspector.

---

[54] NI 52-109.

[55] CBCA, ss 20, 21.

[56] *Livent v Deloitt & Touche*, 2017 SCC 63 at paras 58–62.

[57] The auditor's contract is with the corporation, not with the shareholders: see *Roman Corp v Peat Marwick Thorne* (1992), 8 BLR (2d) 43; see *Hercules Managements Ltd v Ernst & Young* (1997), 146 DLR (4th) 577 (SCC) (as to auditor's duty).

[58] See CPA *Canada Public Sector Accounting Handbook* (Chartered Professional Accountants) for a complete statement of the form and content of the auditor's report.

[59] *Hercules, supra* note 57.

In a public (distributing) corporation, the audit must be completed by an auditor registered with the Canadian Public Accountability Board. The audit committee, made up of independent directors, supervises the auditor and must create a process to receive anonymous complaints and reports of irregularities in the financial affairs of the corporation, often referred to as whistle-blower protection.[60]

CASE 26.9   Auditor's Duty Owed to Corporation Not to Shareholder

Livent's auditors, Deloitte & Touche, negligently performed Livent's audit, and the resulting false statements allowed Livent to go deeper and deeper into debt until it was forced into receivership. When Livent's receiver sued Deloitte, the auditor defended it, saying that the company's losses were really those of the shareholders and creditors, to whom it owed no duty. The Supreme Court of Canada agreed that Deloitte owed its auditor's duty to Livent, not its shareholders, but held that the receiver was properly acting on behalf of the company, and the losses were Livent's. How the company distributed the money after it received it was not relevant to Deloitte's duty.[61]

Appointment of Inspector   Case 26.6 provides an example of the typical situation where an inspector is appointed. All the jurisdictions, with the exception of Prince Edward Island, have statutory provisions enabling shareholders to apply to the courts to appoint an **inspector** to investigate the affairs of the corporation and to audit its books. The statutes give inspectors sweeping powers of inquiry, and the remedy can be a very effective one. The CBCA and most of the provincial acts based on it permit a single shareholder to apply, and they expressly state that the applicant is not required to give security for costs (s. 229). A concerned shareholder may choose from two options. He may request the director—a government official appointed to supervise the affairs of corporations—to apply to the court to order an investigation, or he may apply directly to the court himself. In either event, it is necessary to make out an initial case—that is, produce sufficient evidence of the probability of serious mismanagement to warrant further investigation.

inspector a person appointed by the court to investigate the affairs of a corporation

Duties of Shareholders

Directors of corporations are under strict duties of good faith. They use their own assessment of what is in the best interests of the corporation, and they are not bound to follow the instructions of the shareholders. However, when there is a controlling shareholder (or group of shareholders)—with the power to call a general meeting, dismiss directors, and appoint new ones in their place—it is usually the controlling shareholder who determines corporate policy, and the directors often act as a "rubber stamp." In such circumstances do shareholders—and especially controlling shareholders—owe any duty to their corporation?

Unlike some U.S. courts, Canadian courts have consistently held that a majority shareholder owes no positive duty to act for either the welfare of the corporation itself or the welfare of his fellow shareholders.[62] His obligation ends when he has paid the full purchase price for his shares. He has no obligation to attend meetings or to return proxy forms, and he is free to exercise his vote in whatever way he pleases and for whatever purposes he desires. His share is an item of property that he is free to use as he pleases, even if that is against the interests of the corporation or of his fellow

---

[60] National Instruments 52–108 (amendments proposed in 2013) and 52–110.

[61] *Livent, supra* note 56.

[62] See *Brant Investments Ltd v Keeprite Inc* (1991), 3 OR (3d) 289.

shareholders. However, if the shareholder is also a director of the corporation, he must comply with all his director's duties to act honestly and in good faith with a view to the best interests of the corporation (s. 122), but when he votes as a shareholder, he is entitled to consider his own personal interests.[63]

THE PROTECTION OF MINORITY SHAREHOLDERS

Majority Rule

A shareholder is free to cast her vote as she chooses, and the courts will not substitute their judgment for hers provided that her actions are based upon business considerations. Therefore, a controlling group of shareholders—through its ability to determine the composition of the board of directors, to approve their actions, or to decline to do anything about their misdeeds, and even (if they have a two-thirds majority) to amend the corporation's constitution—could ensure that the affairs of the corporation were managed entirely for their own benefit and to the detriment of the minority. As in the dilemma of the "frozen-out" shareholder, these things can happen without any law being broken.

ILLUSTRATION 26.4 Substantial Change

A, B, C, and D are equal shareholders and directors of a corporation, Trattoria Ltd. The articles of incorporation restrict the business of the corporation to the operation of one or more restaurants. Contrary to D's wishes, A, B, and C decide to sell the restaurant to a property developer and to invest the proceeds in a casino business. They use their votes to pass two special resolutions: (1) approving the sale of the restaurant (substantially the only asset of the corporation) and (2) amending the articles to remove the restriction on the business that may be carried on by the corporation.

In this example, the majority has acted within its rights. Nevertheless, D may be upset because the reason he became a shareholder in the corporation has changed.

ILLUSTRATION 26.5 Damage to the Company

Sixty percent of Figaro Ltd.'s shares are held by Almaviva Inc., a large public corporation, and 40 percent are held by its original founder, Susanna. Almaviva uses its majority voting power to appoint three of its own directors to be directors of Figaro. The new directors approve a sale of an important piece of Figaro's property to Bartolo Ltd., a corporation wholly owned by Almaviva. The sale is at a gross undervalue.

Here, the directors of Figaro may have breached their duty and are in a conflict of interest. The corporation, Figaro, may be injured if the value of its assets has been reduced, but the loss falls entirely on its minority shareholder, Susanna, since the majority shareholder, Almaviva, gains more as shareholder of the purchaser, Bartolo (100 percent of the undervalue), than it loses as shareholder of the vendor, Figaro (60 percent of the undervalue). Consequently, Almaviva, as controlling shareholder of Figaro, will not complain about any breach of duty by its directors.

ILLUSTRATION 26.6 Family Business

The shares in Jenufa Ltd. are held in equal proportions by A, her husband, B, and his two sons by a previous marriage, C and D, all of whom had until recently been directors. After A and B's acrimonious divorce, B, C, and D use their majority voting power to remove A from the board. Subsequently, instead of distributing the profits as dividends, they decide to reinvest them in a fund to provide for the long-term capital needs of the corporation. They also refuse to consent to A transferring her shares to any third party.

In this example, A is locked in and frozen out. But the corporation has not been injured, and unless it can be shown that B, C, and D acted in bad faith, there may have been nothing improper in their actions.

---

[63] *North-West Transportation v Beatty* (1887), 12 App Cas 589.

Under common law principles of corporate law, the aggrieved minority shareholders in the above illustrations received little or no help from the courts. However, special statutory remedies have greatly improved the situation of the minority. The following are the most important minority shareholder remedies.

The Appraisal Remedy

In some situations, where the majority shareholders make fundamental changes to the corporation, section 190 offers a procedure whereby a dissenting shareholder need not go along with the change. He may elect instead to have his shares bought out by the corporation. If a price cannot be agreed, the court will fix a fair price. However, this **appraisal remedy** is limited to specific actions by the majority, the most important of which are:

- changing any restriction on the issue, transfer, or ownership of shares;
- changing any restriction on the business that the corporation may carry on;
- amalgamating or merging with another corporation;
- selling, leasing, or exchanging substantially all the assets of the corporation; and
- "going private" or "squeezing out" transactions.

appraisal remedy the right to have one's shares bought by the corporation at a fair price

The remedy is of most use in private corporations, where no ready public market exists for minority shareholdings, since a dissenter in a public corporation would normally just sell his shares on the stock exchange. However, the procedure is a complicated one, and the dissenter must comply with every step prescribed by the Act in order to take advantage of it. If, instead, the shareholder can show that his interests have been "unfairly disregarded," he is more likely to resort to the oppression remedy discussed below.[64]

The Derivative Action

When a corporation has suffered an injury, as in Illustration 26.5, Case 26.9 or, for example, where directors have made a secret profit for themselves by exploiting a "corporate opportunity," the corporation may sue the wrongdoer to recover its losses.

Ordinarily, an action on behalf of the corporation must be started by its directors—it is part of the management function. However, if the directors are the wrongdoers, they are not likely to commence an action against themselves. The common law recognized the right of a minority shareholder to start an action on behalf of the corporation, frequently called a **derivative action**—but it was procedurally difficult.

The modern statutory derivative action (s. 239) overcomes most of the procedural barriers. It permits a shareholder, or other person recognized by the court, to obtain leave from the court to bring an action in the name and on behalf of the corporation. To do so he need only establish that the directors refuse to bring the action themselves, that he is acting in good faith, and that it appears to be in the interests of the corporation or its shareholders that the action be commenced. If he establishes these things, then the court may make an order to commence the action. The acts prohibit the court from requiring the shareholder to give security for costs. At any time, a court may order the corporation to pay to the complainant costs, including legal fees and disbursements (ss. 242(4) and 240(d)). The court may also direct "that any amount payable by a defendant in the action shall be paid, in whole or in part, directly to former and present shareholders of the corporation . . . instead of to the corporation" (s. 240(c)). In Illustration 26.5 above, Susanna could receive direct compensation for her loss, rather than being compensated only indirectly through an increase in the assets of the corporation.

derivative action proceedings brought by one or more shareholders in the name of the corporation in respect of a wrong done to the corporation

---

[64] See e.g. *Wilfred v Dare*, 2017 ONSC 1633 (dissenter seeking buyout using oppression).

The Supreme Court of Canada specifically endorsed the use of derivative action for shareholders bringing actions against negligent corporate auditors.[65] Although the statutory derivative action has substantially improved the position of minority shareholders, the remedy has been somewhat overshadowed by the oppression remedy, discussed below.

Winding Up

Minority partners have better protection than most minority shareholders. They are entitled to an accounting of profits and to receive their share of them regularly. In the event of a total breakdown in relations, they can normally insist on a dissolution and sale of the assets and receipt of a proportionate part of the proceeds. Since the other partners cannot continue to use the partnership assets for their sole benefit, they must either face dissolution or come to a reasonable settlement. Not so in a private corporation. In the absence of a separate agreement among the shareholders, a minority shareholder has none of the rights of a partner.

Corporation statutes have, however, followed partnership law in one important respect. They give the courts discretion to make an order **winding up** a corporation where it is "just and equitable" to do so.[66] It is a drastic remedy, and the courts have been reluctant to use it if the corporation is successful or large. Typically, the remedy is used when the corporation is a small family business or an "incorporated partnership," where there is deadlock, where relations between the participants have broken down, or where a "partner" has been frozen out. In these cases, the remedy is quite effective, since the mere threat of its use may persuade the majority to reach a compromise.

winding up the dissolution (or liquidation) of a corporation

CASE 26.10 Deadlock

G Corp. was a joint venture corporation with two shareholders—J, who owned 52 percent of the shares, and P, who owned the remaining 48 percent. The relationship between J and P broke down, and P applied for an order directing the winding up of the corporation and its sale as a going concern. J responded by offering to purchase P's shares, but P rejected the offer and instead made a counter-offer. No agreement was reached.

The court found that the circumstances justified winding up the corporation, since the parties had lost confidence in each other, but since each party would prefer to continue the business alone, it ordered a "buy/sell shotgun" solution.[67]

Oppression Remedy

oppression remedy a statutory procedure allowing individual shareholders to seek a personal remedy if they have been unfairly treated

The **oppression remedy** is by far the broadest and most flexible remedy available to shareholders because:

- It is available to more than just shareholders; section 238 of the CBCA describes a "complainant" as any person the court approves. Courts will approve persons with a legitimate interest, including creditors.
- It is not necessary to prove wrongdoing; complainants need only show that their interests or reasonable expectations have been treated unfairly or oppressively disregarded by the behaviour of the corporation or its directors.
- Courts are empowered to make any order they consider just and appropriate to remedy the situation.

The oppression remedy is typically used when a minority shareholder is frozen out, as in Illustration 26.6,[68] but it has also been applied in cases of deadlock or

---

[65] *Livent*, supra note 56.
[66] CBCA, s 214(1)(b)(ii).
[67] *Patheon Inc v Global Pharm Inc*, [2000] OJ No 2532.
[68] *Re Ferguson and Imax Systems Corp* (1983), 150 DLR (3d) 718; *Daniels v Fielder* (1989), 52 DLR (4th) 424.

breakdown in the relations between shareholders or directors;[69] in a few cases, the oppression remedy has been used where a wrong has been done to the corporation and a minority shareholder has suffered in consequence, even though a derivative action would seem to be more appropriate in such circumstances. It is possible that Susanna, in Illustration 26.5, might seek an oppression remedy rather than bring a derivative action.[70] It is also commonly used by creditors, as in Case 26.11.

To justify the making of an order under section 241, a complainant[71] must prove two things:

1. First, that the complainant's expectations about how their interests would be managed are reasonable. A court will decide on reasonableness by looking at factors such as

    - general commercial behaviour,
    - the nature of the corporation,
    - the relationship between the complainant and the defendant,
    - past practice,
    - representations and agreements,
    - conflicting interests of other stakeholders, and
    - evasive steps the complainant could have taken.

2. If the complainant's expectations were reasonable, the complainant must then show that the conduct in question "oppressively or unfairly disregards or prejudices the interests." The focus here is on unfair conduct and prejudicial consequences.[72]

However, the courts have emphasized that the conduct need not be wrongful or in bad faith, though this will be a factor to take into account in the remedy.[73]

CASE 26.11 Supreme Court on Oppression

The board of directors of BCE Inc. approved a plan of arrangement involving the sale of all of its shares to a group of purchasers by way of a leveraged buyout with a share price 40 percent above existing market value. The buyout would convert the public company back to a private one. The board believed the sale was in the best interests of the company and shareholders. The shareholders agreed, voting 97.93 percent in favour of the plan. However, a major group of creditors (debenture holders) opposed the idea and applied to the court for an oppression remedy to block the sale. Their complaint was that the trading value of their debentures would drop by approximately 20 percent. The Supreme Court of Canada refused the oppression remedy, saying the reasonableness of expectations must be evaluated in the context of the particular situation. Here, the debenture holders did not prove they had a reasonable expectation that BCE would protect the investment grade or trading value of their debentures. A plan may be in the best interests of a corporation and benefit some stakeholders at the expense of others. The Court held that the directors fulfilled their duty by considering the interests of debenture holders and thereafter deciding that fulfillment of contractual obligations was the only promise that could be made.[74]

---

[69] *Eiserman v Ara Farms* (1989), 52 DLR (4th) 498; *Tilley v Hails* (1992), 7 OR (3d) 257.

[70] See e.g. *Journet v Superchef Food Industries Ltd* (1984), 29 BLR 206. However, it seems that the plaintiff must still show that he has been affected in a way different from that of other shareholders: *NPV Management Ltd v Anthony* (2003), 231 DLR (4th) 681; *Pasnak v Chura*, [2004] BCJ No 790.

[71] In some circumstances a creditor has been held to be a proper "complainant" for the purposes of the section: *Piller Sausages & Delicatessen Ltd v Cobb International Corp*, [2003] OJ No 2647; *Dylex Ltd v Anderson* (2003), 63 OR (3d) 659.

[72] *BCE Inc*, supra note 23 at paras 68, 72, 89, 95.

[73] *Brant Investments Ltd v Keeprite Inc*, supra note 62; *Westfair Food Ltd v Watt* (1991), 79 DLR (4th) 48 (leave to appeal refused).

[74] *BCE Inc*, supra note 23. See *Mennillo v Intramodal Inc*, 2016 SCC 51; *Waxman v Waxman*, [2004] OJ No 1765 (leave to appeal refused) (involving protracted family dispute).

Obviously, stakeholder interests and expectations may conflict and cannot all be met. Directors do not owe a duty to satisfy individual stakeholders. As already stated, the paramount consideration must be the best interests of the corporation as a whole.

Section 241(3) allows the court to make any order it thinks fit. One remedy granted has been to require the majority to buy out the minority interest at a fair price, but a wide range of other orders are possible.[75] Judges may customize a solution that suits the particular needs of the corporation and even order a director to personally compensate the oppressed if the director:

- personally benefited,
- breached a duty or misused power, or
- corporate compensation would prejudice other security holders.[76]

Because of its great flexibility and the absence of technical obstacles, the oppression remedy is quickly becoming the most widely used shareholder remedy in Canada.

CASE 26.12 Custom Designed Remedy

In proceedings related to the improper loan described in Case 26.6, Catalyst, a Hollinger non-voting minority shareholder, sought an oppression remedy removing eight of the 10 Hollinger directors. Conrad Black resigned prior to the hearing. The trial judge ordered the removal of every Hollinger director who was also associated with Ravelston, except Peter White. Although White's conduct was found to be oppressive, he was allowed to remain on the board "at the pleasure" of the remaining independent Hollinger directors. The trial judge felt that White's continued service as an officer and director of Hollinger was in the best interests of the corporation "at least on a transitional basis."

Approximately six months later, at the request of the independent Hollinger directors, the judge ordered White's permanent removal. White appealed both orders, arguing that the trial judge had stripped the shareholders of their right to select directors and changed the nature of his director's duties when the independent directors were given the power to remove him.

The Ontario Court of Appeal upheld both of the orders, declaring that section 241 gives the court the power to "directly interfere with the corporate governance of a corporation and the rights and obligations of directors, officers and shareholders."[77]

SHAREHOLDER AGREEMENTS

Advantages

Although the oppression remedy has greatly increased the protection given to minority shareholders, it still depends on the court exercising its discretion in their favour. A shareholder is still in a less secure position than is a partner.

This uncertainty is a factor to be considered if a small group of equal partners propose to transform their business into a corporation. It may make good business sense to incorporate because of the nature of the business, its growth, and its tax position. Yet each of the partners, if aware of the dangers of being a minority shareholder at odds with the others, might well hesitate to give up the protection of partnership law.

Fortunately, it is possible to approximate the protection available to partners with two agreements. The solution is an agreement among the shareholders that is outside

---

[75] In some cases the court has allowed the minority petitioner to buy out the majority oppressor: see *Tilley v Hails*, *supra* note 69.

[76] *Wilson v Alharayeri*, 2017 SCC 39.

[77] *Catalyst Fund General Partner I Inc v Hollinger Inc*, *supra* note 41 at para 50.

the constitution of the corporation. This process is not simple because, as we have seen, directors owe their primary duty to the corporation. They must not compromise their duty to act in the best interests of the corporation. Subject to an important exception to be discussed below, any agreement among shareholders must be restricted to their role as shareholders and must not infringe on their role as directors.[78] This danger can be avoided in a well drafted **shareholder agreement**. Each agreement must be tailored to the needs of the individual business. Two key elements are normally included in a shareholder agreement.

shareholder agreement an agreement between two or more shareholders that is distinct from the corporation's charter and bylaws

Right to Participate in Management
The shareholders promise to elect each other to the board of directors at each annual meeting and not to nominate or vote for any other person. They may also promise not to vote for any major change in the corporation's capital structure or in the nature of its business except by unanimous agreement.

Right to a Fair Price for a Share Interest
The shareholders may agree to a regular method of valuation of their shares. They may agree not to sell their shares to an outsider without giving the right of first refusal proportionately to the remaining shareholders. If one of them commits a major breach of the shareholder agreement and remains unwilling to remedy it, he can be required to sell his interest to the others at the appraised value. In addition, if any shareholder is wrongfully expelled or dismissed by the others, she may require them to buy out her interest at the appraised value. This provision may also state that in the event of a dispute about appraisal, a named person, usually the auditor, will arbitrate and assess the value of the interest.

Unanimous Shareholder Agreements

The CBCA and most provincial statutes formally recognize the **unanimous shareholder agreement** and permit these to govern relationships among shareholders in a private corporation in much the same manner as in a partnership. The CBCA states that "an agreement among all the shareholders . . . that restricts in whole or in part the powers of the directors to manage the business and affairs of the corporation is valid" (s. 146(2)) and that the shareholders who are given the power to manage "have all the rights, powers, duties and liabilities of a director . . . and the directors are thereby relieved of their rights, powers, duties and liabilities to the same extent" (s. 146(5)).

unanimous shareholder agreement a shareholder agreement to which all shareholders are parties

The Act also states that "a purchaser or transferee of shares subject to a unanimous shareholder agreement is deemed to be a party to the agreement" (s. 146(3)). Thus, on the sale of a share interest in a private corporation that is subject to such an agreement, the transferee not only receives an assignment of rights as a shareholder but is also bound to carry out the duties of the transferor. A unanimous shareholder agreement must be "noted conspicuously" on the face of a share certificate in order to bind subsequent transferees (s. 49(8)).

These provisions modify the common law rule that no agreement may limit the discretion of directors. However, only unanimous agreements have special status under the acts. The CBCA makes frequent reference to unanimous shareholder agreements and treats them almost as if they were part of the corporate constitution, rather like bylaws. In doing so, it has provided the opportunity to develop a new, flexible device for business planning in private corporations.

---

[78] *Motherwell v Schoof*, [1949] 4 DLR 812.

Strategies to Manage the Legal Risks

As discussed above, shareholders of private corporations can protect themselves from the abuse of the majority shareholder and unfair behaviour of the corporation or its management by using unanimous shareholder agreements. These agreements will preserve the shareholders' percentage interest in the company, maintain the decision-making power as part of management, and create liquidity through a prearranged sale formula. Unfortunately, this is not a viable option for public shareholders, and they will be left with only the statutory remedies created for minority interests. Shares should be issued with preemptive rights that allow the shareholder the first opportunity to buy up new issues.

The legal risks for directors and officers of a company are different from those of private and public shareholders. Directors and officers of a corporation risk personal liability if they fail to comply with the statutory and corporation specific governance rules. Therefore, when acting in these positions, certain steps should be followed:

- Ensure the corporation maintains directors' liability insurance.
- Familiarize oneself with the duties of a director and the operation of the business.
- Participate in continuing education.
- Develop a code of conduct relating to ethics and conflicts of interests.
- Design corporate governance structures that ensure independence and transparency, including independent directors, audit committees, nominating committees, and compensation committees—especially if the private corporation intends to go public.
- Follow the processes in place for proper decision making by reading materials in advance, attending and participating in meetings, and investigating; this will allow the use of the business judgment rule defence if complaints are made.
- Seek out and rely on expert opinions when high value changes are proposed.
- Make prompt public disclosure of key changes to reduce the possibility of insider trading.
- Declare even possible conflicts of interests, and seek shareholder approval in borderline circumstances.
- Arrange personal affairs to reduce the exposure of personal assets.

Obviously there are many legal and financial issues about which directors and officers need to consult lawyers and accountants. Form these relationships early so that ongoing advice may be obtained easily and quickly.

QUESTIONS FOR REVIEW

1. What is the distinction between the business and the affairs of a corporation?
2. Where are the rules of corporate governance found?
3. What are the principal powers given to the board of directors of a corporation incorporated under the CBCA?
4. How are directors appointed? How may they be removed?

5. To whom are directors' and officers' duties owed? What about the board of an Ontario corporation?
6. What defences are available to a director accused of breach of duty?
7. When a director enters into a contract with her own corporation, what precautions should be taken to ensure the validity of the contract?
8. What is meant by intercepting a corporate opportunity?
9. In what circumstances might a director have a conflict of interest?
10. What is insider trading?
11. Who is an "insider"?
12. What is meant when one says that a minority shareholder is (a) "locked in" and (b) "frozen out"?
13. What are the principal rights attached to shares in a corporation?
14. What is the difference between an ordinary resolution and a special resolution?
15. What are class rights?
16. What is a proxy? How are proxies appointed?
17. Do shareholders have any right to receive a dividend if the corporation is profitable?
18. What are "pre-emptive rights" in relation to a corporation's shares?
19. Are there any restrictions on the directors' powers to issue new shares?
20. What information must be provided in a corporation's annual financial statements?
21. What is the role of a corporation's auditor? To whom is the auditor's duty owed?
22. What are a corporation's "documents of record"?
23. Do shareholders owe any duty to their corporation?
24. Describe the relationship between shareholders and the company's auditors.
25. Explain the "appraisal remedy" and the "derivative action."
26. What are the principal differences between the "just and equitable" winding-up procedure and the oppression remedy?
27. What matters are commonly dealt with in shareholder agreements? Why?

CASES AND PROBLEMS

1. Continuing Scenario

   Ashley incorporated her restaurant business under the *Canada Business Corporations Act*, and the articles of incorporation named three directors to the board. Ashley is one, her father, Jim, is another, and her accountant, Kristen, is the third. During the last directors' meeting, Ashley suggested it was time for a third restaurant location. Currently, she has one location in downtown Toronto and another in the west end near a congested shopping area. She would like to place a new one in the busy tourist area of Niagara Falls. Kristen volunteers to investigate possible restaurant sites, as she was raised in Niagara Falls. At the next meeting, Kristen presents a report on the Niagara Falls tourist district, identifying three possible sites available for lease. Two are in view of the falls, but Kristen recommends the more expensive location without a view because it is better for parking. Ashley and Jim defer to Kristen's expertise without making any independent investigation; Jim arrived late to the meeting without even reading the report. They instruct her to make the deal. When the lease is signed, Kristen sends a copy to Ashley's lawyer, Brendan. It shows the landlord as 123456 Ontario Limited. Brendan completes a corporate search of the company and is surprised to discover that Kristen is also a director of the landlord company. Further investigation reveals that the rent being charged is well above the typical rent for equivalent premises. What advice should Brendan give Ashley about Kristen and the Niagara Falls lease? Explain the legal principles involved.

2. Ten years ago, Davidson and Farmer formed a corporation to develop a fishing lodge that they bought (in the name of the corporation). They each owned 50 shares in the corporation. There were no other shareholders, and Davidson and Farmer were the only directors.

They worked hard to develop the business, which became quite successful. No dividends were ever paid by the corporation, but Davidson and Farmer had paid themselves generous salaries for their work as directors.

Last year, Davidson died. In his will he left his entire estate to his sister, Eriksen. Before her marriage, Eriksen had occasionally worked at the lodge (for a salary) but recently had not been involved in the business.

Shortly after Davidson's death, Farmer (as the sole surviving director) appointed his niece, Greenberg, as a director to fill the vacancy on the board. Next, Farmer and Greenberg passed a resolution issuing one share in the corporation to Greenberg for a consideration of $10 000 (which was estimated to be approximately 1 percent of the value of the business).

In response to requests from Eriksen, Farmer has agreed to register the transfer of Davidson's shares to her but has made it clear that he will not agree to her becoming a director and that he intends to continue running the business together with Greenberg.

Does Eriksen have any remedy?

3. Until three years ago, Slater was the sole shareholder and director of Lockley Quarries Ltd., a small corporation that owned a quarry and produced trimmed limestone blocks. Then an opportunity arose to purchase a second quarry at a very good price. Slater did not have sufficient funds and persuaded Mason to come into business with him and to help finance the purchase of the new quarry. As a result, Mason became a 40 percent shareholder and a director of Lockley Quarries. Slater and Mason got on well together, and the business prospered.

A few months ago, Slater was approached by an old friend, Chalker, who proposed that they—Chalker and Slater—purchase and operate a gravel pit that had come on the market. Slater agreed, and a new corporation was formed to acquire the gravel pit, with Chalker and Slater as equal shareholders and directors.

Mason has learned of the dealings between Slater and Chalker. He considers that he should have been given the opportunity to participate in the new gravel pit venture. Do you agree? Does Mason have any remedy against Slater?

4. Normin Inc. is a large mining corporation, incorporated under the CBCA, the shares of which are publicly traded and are listed on the Toronto Stock Exchange. It has recently been conducting extensive exploration on land acquired in the Canadian Arctic.

Late in the afternoon of March 31, Normin's chief executive officer, Baffin, received a fax from the mineralogist in charge of the explorations. The fax, headed "Highly Confidential," informed Baffin that a giant deposit of tin had been discovered. It appeared that it would be fairly easy to extract and would be extremely profitable.

Baffin at once informed as many of the directors and senior officers as he could contact. After some discussion they agreed to prepare a press release the next morning. However, the following occurred on the evening of March 31:

(a) One of the directors, Banks, telephoned his broker, Charles, and without giving any reason, instructed Charles to buy as many Normin shares on his account as he could, provided the price did not exceed $30 per share. The following morning, Normin shares opened on the exchange at $28.75. Charles bought 10 000 shares for Banks, at prices between $28.75 and $29.50.

(b) Another director, Melville, contacted her brother, Parry, and offered to buy his shares in Normin. Parry had acquired the shares some years before but had since lost interest in the investment and had several times asked Melville if she would like to buy them. Melville offered to pay $29 per share, and Parry accepted and transferred his 15 000 shares to his sister.

(c) Hudson, a senior executive of Normin, told his bridge partner, Frobisher, that she should tell no one and buy Normin shares as soon as possible. Frobisher bought 2000 shares on the exchange the following morning, at $29.25 per share.

At midday on April 1, the press release was published, giving details of the find. Trading on the exchange became brisk, and by the end of the day the price of Normin shares had reached $47.50.

Discuss the possible liability of any of the individuals mentioned, and the remedies, if any, that Parry and other shareholders who sold their shares before midday on April 1 might have.

5. For many years Sergei (a widower) owned and ran a large farm, initially by himself and later with the help of his four children. Eight years ago, on the advice of his accountant and his lawyer, he decided to transfer the farm to a corporation and, with a view to keeping the farm in the family (and to saving taxes), to make his children shareholders in the corporation.

A corporation, Eisenstein Farms Inc., was formed with two classes of shares. As consideration for the transfer of the farm to the corporation, Sergei received 1000 Class "A" preferred shares, with each share carrying one vote. The four children—Galina, Ivan, Oleg, and Tanya—each received 100 Class "B" common shares, also carrying one vote per share, for which they paid $10 per share. Two of the children—Galina and Ivan—had left home and no longer took an active part in running the farm. The other two—Oleg and Tanya—continued to live with their father and work on the farm, and were made directors and employees of the corporation along with Sergei. No dividends were paid by the corporation in respect of the common shares (Sergei received dividends on his preferred shares), but Sergei, Oleg, and Tanya all received salaries.

Soon things soured. Oleg married, and neither Sergei nor Tanya got on with his wife. They complained that he was neglecting the farm and spending most of his time helping his wife with her business. (Oleg denied this.) After many arguments, Oleg threatened to resign from the board of directors and to quit his employment with the corporation. Sergei and Tanya immediately accepted his "resignation." The situation deteriorated further. Oleg is no longer receiving any remuneration from the corporation, either as a director or employee, has been excluded from directors' meetings, and has been given no information about the corporation's business or affairs.

Oleg considers that he has been treated unfairly. Is there any remedy? Why?

6. Aldeburgh Inc. is a corporation incorporated under the CBCA. It has never issued shares to the public. It owns a large piece of land and a number of vacation cottages fronting on a lake some distance north of Queensville, Ontario. The property has produced relatively little income in the past.

Until recently, Aldeburgh had four shareholders—Balstrode, Crabbe, Orford, and Swallow—who each owned 25 percent of the issued shares. Balstrode, Crabbe, and Orford are the directors of the corporation. Swallow is retired and has taken little interest in the business.

A few months ago, the three directors received a tip from Grimes (a friend of theirs and a prominent local politician) that a large corporation, Maltings Developments Inc., was proposing to establish a major recreational complex along the lake and was almost certain to get permission for the development. When the news became public, he suggested, the price of land in the area would soar.

Balstrode, Crabbe, and Orford held a directors' meeting and resolved that Aldeburgh should try to buy up as much property in the area as possible. They did not tell Swallow the good news. Aldeburgh borrowed as much money as it was able to and bought a number of lots.

During the same period, the following events occurred:

(a) Balstrode approached Swallow and persuaded Swallow to sell her his shares. She said nothing about the proposed development.

(b) Crabbe personally bought one lot for herself (without disclosing the fact to anyone), which she was later able to resell to Maltings at a large profit.

(c) Orford bought one lot (in the name of a numbered company) that she resold to Aldeburgh at a quick profit, without disclosing that she was the beneficial owner.

(d) Grimes bought several lots himself, which he later sold to Maltings at a large profit.

Soon afterward, Maltings offered to buy all the land owned by Aldeburgh or, alternatively, to buy all its shares. An agreement was reached to sell the shares, with the result that all the Aldeburgh shares are now owned by Maltings, and the shareholders of Aldeburgh all made large profits on the sale of their shares.

Maltings has now discovered the secret activities of Balstrode, Crabbe, Orford, and Grimes. Swallow has learned about the profit that Balstrode made on the resale of his shares.

Who is liable for what? To whom? On what grounds? How can liability be enforced?

Chapter 27
Corporate Governance: External Responsibilities

- **LIABILITY ARISING FROM BUSINESS RESPONSIBILITIES**
- **PROTECTION OF CREDITORS**
- **PROTECTION OF EMPLOYEES**
- **PROTECTION OF CONSUMERS AND COMPETITORS**
- **PROTECTION OF INVESTORS**
- **PROTECTION OF THE PUBLIC INTEREST**
- **CIVIL LIABILITY OF CORPORATIONS**
- **CRIMINAL LIABILITY OF CORPORATIONS**
- **CRIMINAL LIABILITY OF DIRECTORS AND OFFICERS**
- **LIABILITY FOR ENVIRONMENTAL OFFENCES**
- **STRATEGIES TO MANAGE THE LEGAL RISKS**

This chapter examines the relationship between the corporation and the outside world—its customers, creditors, employees, competitors, potential investors, and the general public. The corporation is an artificial person that is responsible for its own actions. Still, it acts only through its directors, officers, and agents, and so requires multiple layers of accountability.

In this chapter we examine such questions as:

- How does legislation protect creditors, investors, and other persons who deal with, or are affected by, corporations?
- To what extent is a corporation liable for the acts of its directors, officers, and agents?
- How do corporations enter into contracts?
- Can a corporation be negligent?
- Can a corporation commit a crime?
- To what extent may directors, officers, or agents be held personally liable for acts done, or not done, in the name of a corporation?
- What liability is imposed on corporate officers under environmental legislation?

LIABILITY ARISING FROM BUSINESS RESPONSIBILITIES

stakeholders groups affected by the business activities of a corporation

The business activities of a corporation affect many external groups or **stakeholders**. These stakeholders include the corporation's creditors, employees, consumers, competitors, potential public investors, and the public at large. Legislation imposes liability on the corporation as well as others, including directors, officers, and auditors, to protect these stakeholders. The circle of liability includes outside experts working on behalf of the corporation, such as accountants, underwriters, and lawyers.

Types of Liability

Some of the protective requirements are proactive, such as requiring disclosure of information or licensing of professionals; these are designed to prevent problems before they occur. Other legislative measures are reactive, such as imprisoning for insider trading; these are designed to punish bad behaviour and deter others.

Breach of a legislative requirement may attract civil, regulatory, and even criminal liability. Stakeholders are empowered to enforce some of these standards through civil causes of action. Chapter 26 focused primarily on breaches of duty that create civil causes of action. This chapter expands on the civil causes of action available to stakeholder groups and considers the criminal and regulatory offences created to punish corporations, directors and officers, and others when wrongdoing occurs.

Criminal offences address the most serious types of misconduct and result in the most serious form of punishment: imprisonment. These offences are most often (but not always) found in the *Criminal Code*.[1]

As discussed first in Chapter 1, subordinate legislation may assign a specialized government agency or tribunal, such as the securities commission, tasks such as designing and implementing programs, monitoring conduct, or investigating and punishing misconduct. As part of this responsibility, it implements rules known as regulations to establish the standard of acceptable conduct. These regulations often assign a penalty for failure to comply. The rules and penalties are known as **regulatory offences**. Regulatory offences resemble traditional criminal law because, in order to protect the public interest, they punish those who ignore the rules; however, the penalties are usually less serious. Therefore, the approaches to proving regulatory and criminal offences are similar but not identical.[2]

regulatory offences less serious offences created by government regulation through specialized legislation, agencies, and tribunals

The Requirement of *Mens Rea*

For most offences, the prosecution must prove beyond a reasonable doubt not only that the accused actually did commit the act described in the offence but also that he had the intention to do it—that is, the "intent." The prosecution must establish that the accused had *mens rea* (a guilty mind)—that is, a guilty intention or guilty knowledge. For example, a person who possesses stolen goods has not committed an offence if he did not know they were stolen.

Presumption of Intent For regulatory offences, the courts and statutes tend to reduce the need for *mens rea*. It may be enough to show that if any ordinary person would or should have realized his conduct was an offence, the wrongdoer will be

---

[1] The federal government is given legislative jurisdiction over criminal law and the *Criminal Code*, RSC 1985, c C-46; this comprehensive Act contains most criminal offences. Other statutes may create offences dealing with the specific topic of that legislation.

[2] Some statutory regulations also create civil liability so that a wrongdoer may have to compensate a party harmed by its breach.

convicted. For instance, if a person drove his car at 80 km/h through a crowded shopping area, he would very likely be convicted of the regulatory offence of careless driving, even if he did not intend to harm anyone.

For these strict liability offences, there is a presumption that the accused, in committing the wrongful act, had the requisite *mens rea*. However, the accused can overcome the presumption by persuading the court that he acted with reasonable care in the circumstances.

Absolute Liability No *mens rea* is necessary for a conviction of an absolute liability offence. The prosecution only has to prove that the accused committed the wrongful act—for example, a driver does not need to know she is exceeding the speed limit. Absolute liability offences are typically confined to statutes dealing with public health and safety.

CHECKLIST
Classification of Offences

The Supreme Court of Canada has classified offences into three categories, depending on the seriousness of the penalty and the language of the statute. They are summarized as follows:[3]

- **mens rea offences**, where the prosecution must prove a guilty mind such as intent, knowledge, or recklessness
- **offences of strict liability**, where completing the prohibited act raises a presumption that an offence has been committed, yet the accused to avoid liability by proving he took all reasonable care (due diligence)
- **offences of absolute liability**, where no mental intent is required; simply doing the act makes one guilty of the offence

mens rea offences offences where the prosecution must establish a "guilty mind" on the part of the defendant

offences of strict liability offences where there is a presumption of guilt unless the defendant can show that she took reasonable care

offences of absolute liability offences where the absence of fault is no defence

This third class remains a very limited one. The Supreme Court of Canada has held that an absolute liability offence may be unconstitutional when conviction could lead to imprisonment.[4]

This chapter examines situations where each type of liability (civil, regulatory, and criminal) and various types of offences (*mens rea*, strict liability, and absolute liability) are used to protect stakeholders.

PROTECTION OF CREDITORS

Implications of Limited Liability

When an unincorporated business becomes insolvent, the creditors are entitled to whatever assets are available. If a deficiency remains, they may look to the personal assets of the owner: the sole proprietor or partners. In a corporation, however, a creditor's rights are limited to only the assets owned by the corporation itself. If those assets are inadequate, the creditor normally has no further remedy against the owners: the

---

[3] See *R v City of Sault Ste Marie* (1978), 85 DLR (3d) 161 (SCC); *R v Kanda* (2008) 88 OR (3d) 732, ONCA 22 (CanLII).

[4] *Re BC Motor Vehicle Act*, [1985] 2 SCR 486; *R v Transport Robert (1973) Ltée* (2003), 234 DLR (4th) 546. See also *R v Wilson*, 2014 ONCA 212 (holding the adult seat belt offence is only strict liability not absolute).

shareholders.[5] For this reason, legislatures and courts have established rules to assure creditors that the corporation's assets will not be wasted. As noted in Chapter 26, if the assets are wasted, a creditor may have a claim against the directors and officers personally for breach of their duty of skill and care.

Preservation of Capital

Except for financial institutions such as banks and insurance companies, there are no minimum issued capital requirements for corporations.[6] Legally, a corporation may carry on business with a share capital of $1. Of course, it would be difficult to obtain credit with only a nominal equity investment. Therefore, corporations raise capital by selling shares to shareholders, and this value helps a lender assess the creditworthiness of the corporation.

It is difficult to devise legal rules that will protect creditors from the risk of extending credit to a corporation that becomes unable to pay. Laws tend to focus on ensuring that a corporation's stated capital (money raised from the sale of shares) is not improperly reduced by preferring the rights of shareholders over those of creditors.

On the winding up of a corporation, its creditors are entitled to have the assets applied in satisfaction of their claims before any capital is returned to the shareholders. Sometimes there is not enough money to pay all creditors and return capital to the shareholders. The *Canada Business Corporations Act* (CBCA) (and those provincial statutes modelled on it) set out rules to protect creditors. The rules are divided into two types: rules that prohibit any payment by the corporation to its shareholders that renders the corporation's liquid assets insufficient to pay the existing claims of creditors; and rules that restrict the return of capital to shareholders even when the corporation might still be left with sufficient liquid assets to pay its creditors. Any improper payment of dividends or return of capital will trigger personal liability of the directors.

The Solvency Test
Shareholders usually receive money from the corporation by way of dividends or, in certain circumstances, through redemption or repurchase by the corporation of its own shares. If payments by the corporation in either of these instances are made when the corporation is insolvent, or would have the effect of making the corporation insolvent, the directors may be held personally liable to the corporation for the deficiency.[7]

The effectiveness of this rule depends upon the definition of **insolvency** that is used. Two criteria are applied: A corporation is deemed insolvent if the realizable value of its assets has become less than its total liabilities or if it is unable to pay its debts as they become due.[8]

insolvency having liabilities in excess of the realizable value of one's assets or being unable to pay one's debts as they fall due

---

[5] There are a few limited exceptions to this principle: see the discussion under "Exceptions to Limited Liability" in Chapter 25. As discussed in Chapter 26, creditors may claim against directors and officers personally if the insolvency arises from breach of their duty of skill (except in Ontario). See *Peoples v Wise*, [2004] 3 SCR 461; Ontario *Business Corporations Act*, RSO 1990, c B.16, s 134.

[6] As to banks, see *Bank Act*, SC 1991, c 46, ss 59–35. Rules regulate three forms of capital: Type one includes common and preferred shares, and these must be subordinate to depositors and general creditors and have fully discretionary non-cumulative dividends without maturity dates or incentives to redeem. Common shares must have preemptive rights. See Christopher C Nicholls, "The Regulation of Financial Institutions: A Reflective but Selective Retrospective" (2011), 50 Can Bus LJ 129–55.

[7] See e.g. *Canada Business Corporations Act*, RSC 1985, c C-44 [CBCA], ss 42, 118(2)(c).

[8] The federal *Bankruptcy and Insolvency Act*, RSC 1985, c B-3, s 101 adds an "after the fact" test that permits a trustee in bankruptcy to apply for a court inquiry in respect of dividends paid within 12 months preceding bankruptcy to determine whether the dividend rendered the corporation insolvent, and that authorizes the court to give judgment to the trustee against the directors, jointly and severally, in the amount of such dividend.

The Maintenance of Capital Test In theory, the money paid into the corporation by shareholders should be preserved as far as possible within the corporation as a capital fund, available for absorbing business losses so that creditors (and in some cases, preferred shareholders) may be paid in full. The maintenance of capital test therefore goes beyond the solvency test. It applies in the following circumstances.

(i) Dividends The CBCA (s. 42) provides that a corporation may not pay a dividend if there are reasonable grounds for believing that (a) the corporation is, or would be after the payment, unable to pay its liabilities as they become due (the solvency test), and (b) the realizable value of the corporation's assets would thereby be less than the aggregate of its liabilities and its stated capital of all classes (maintenance of capital test). In other words, after the dividend has been paid, the corporation's net assets must not be less than the amount of its stated capital. The effect of this rule is that dividends may only be paid out of profits. A corporation's net assets will only exceed its stated capital if either it has undistributed profits or its assets have increased in value.

(ii) Return of Capital A corporation may return a part of its capital to its shareholders either by making a pro rata payment to each shareholder—in which case the effect is essentially the same as the payment of a dividend—or by buying back the shares of some of its shareholders. A return of capital, like the payment of a dividend when there are no profits or capital gain out of which to pay it, reduces the funds available to meet the claims of creditors and, if the corporation should subsequently become insolvent, would give a preferred repayment to shareholders before the creditors' claims are met.

> **ILLUSTRATION 27.1 Preferring Shareholders over Creditors**
>
> A corporation originally issued shares for a total of $5 million. For several years it made a profit, in the sense that its revenues exceeded its expenditures. However, its capital assets have depreciated in value. It now has net assets of exactly $5 million. Despite having a trading profit, it cannot pay a dividend. Payment of a dividend in these circumstances will expose the directors to personal civil liability.

The CBCA provides that a corporation may repay capital to its shareholders provided that it will be able to satisfy the solvency and maintenance of capital tests.[9] This rule is reasonable since shareholders may have contributed substantially more capital than the corporation really needs. So long as creditors are protected, there is no reason to insist that excess capital remain in the corporation.

Corporations may also redeem or purchase their own shares for a number of specified reasons, subject to solvency requirements to protect creditors.[10]

Loans to Shareholders, Directors, and Employees Although the CBCA does not prohibit the corporation from lending money to shareholders, directors, or officers, there are income rules that include the loan as income to the borrower.[11] The concern behind considering restricting such loans, especially those that are interest-free, is that they might amount to an indirect return of capital and might deprive the corporation of liquidity. Recent focus on ethics in corporate governance has revived this concern.

---

[9] CBCA, *supra* note 7, s 38. To do so requires a special resolution.

[10] *Ibid.*, ss 30–7. Reducing the stated capital recognizes that the corporation's net assets have decreased in value. As such, it is not objectionable (ss. 38(1)(c) and (3)).

[11] There are exceptions for corporations in the business of lending money, for loans repaid within one year, and for employee home or share purchases. See Canada Revenue Agency Bulletin IT421R2; *Income Tax Act*, RSC 1985, c 1, 5th Supp, ss 15, 246.

PROTECTION OF EMPLOYEES

Chapter 18 deals with employee/employer relationships in detail and so here we make only brief mention of some employee protections. In Chapter 26, we discussed the personal liability of directors for up to six months' wages of employees. Employee safety is protected through occupation health and safety legislation, which requires ongoing monitoring and creates regulatory offences for unsafe workplaces. Injured employees are covered by no-fault insurance through workplace safety legislation. Human rights legislation and tribunals create civil liability and regulatory offences to promote non-discriminatory work environments.

PROTECTION OF CONSUMERS AND COMPETITORS

Businesses compete with each other for customers so the protection of these two stakeholder groups naturally fits together. Their protection involves multiple provincial and federal statutes. Consumer protection is a matter of provincial jurisdiction, and all provinces have legislation limiting unfair business practices and creating regulatory offences and civil causes of action. The federal *Competition Act* addresses unfair conduct among competitors and improper marketing and advertising strategies. The *Competition Act* creates both regulatory and criminal offences. Chapter 3, "Government Regulation of Business," deals with the competitive business environment in detail.

PROTECTION OF INVESTORS

Securities Legislation

Canadian securities regulation is a matter within provincial jurisdiction. Each Canadian province has a *Securities Act*, under which a government board is created, known in most of the provinces as the **securities commission**. The securities commission operates as the regulating, licensing, and enforcing agency responsible for compliance that the requirements of the Act. The 13 provincial and territorial securities commissions support creation of standardized regulation, policy, and administration through a single organization known as the Canadian Securities Administrators and the creation and adoption of "National Policies" and "National Instruments."[12]

securities commission the statutory authority appointed to supervise the issue of securities to the general public, the operation of the securities industry, and the stock exchange

INTERNATIONAL ISSUE
One Federal Securities Regulator

International criticism of Canada's "patchwork" approach to securities regulation[13] is one motivation for change to Canadian securities regulation. Initial reforms proposed the 13 provincial securities commissions be replaced by a single federal regulator. Advantages include consistency, efficiency, lack of duplication, cost effectiveness, and ability to speak with one voice to international markets.

The 2008 chaos in world financial markets led then federal Finance Minister Jim Flaherty to announce that "it was time to move toward a single securities regulator . . . [that] reflects regional interests, yet can quickly respond with a single voice to market developments."[14] Not all provinces supported the consolidation. Alberta and Quebec oppose a national securities regulator, and both the Alberta and Quebec Courts of Appeal

---

[12] Many of the National Rules and Policies have a common number identification system.

[13] International Monetary Fund, *Canada: Financial System Stability Assessment – Update*, IMF Country Report No.08/59, Feb 2008.

[14] Eoin Callan and Barbara Shecter, "Crisis Used to Push for Single Regulator," *National Post*, October 30, 2009 at 1, reporting speech by Jim Flaherty on October 29, 2008.

held that the proposed federal legislation would be an unconstitutional intrusion into an area long recognized as within provincial jurisdiction.[15] The constitutional question was argued before the Supreme Court of Canada, and the Supreme Court held that the federal government lacked the constitutional authority to impose a single regulator; provincial agreement and cooperation was required.[16] A cooperative capital market regulator remains under consideration among the federal government and four interested provinces.

Questions to Consider

1. Should a single securities regulator be a legal issue, a financial issue, or a national security issue?
2. Which federal and provincial constitutional powers are relevant to this reform?
3. How could this reform improve Canada's position when dealing with international financial issues?

Sources: Eoin Callan and Barbara Shecter, "Crisis Used to Push for Single Regulator," *National Post*, October 30, 2009 at 1, reporting speech by Jim Flaherty on October 29, 2008; Ian B Lee, "Balancing and Its Alternatives: Jurisprudential Choice, Federal Securities Legislation and the Trade and Commerce Power" (2011) 50 Can. Bus. LJ 95–128; David Johnston, Kathleen Rockwell & Cristie Ford, "National and Coordinated Approaches to Securities Regulation" in David Johnston, Kathleen Rockwell and Cristie Ford, *Canadian Securities Regulation*, 5th ed (Markham: LexisNexis, 2014) at 631.

Objectives of Securities Legislation Provincial securities legislation delegates control over the public offering of shares to provincial securities commissions.[17] The goals of the legislation are to ensure the integrity, fairness, and efficiency of the market and promote investor confidence in it.[18] To accomplish these goals, securities commissions have three key areas of responsibility:

- the securities industry
- the corporations offering their shares to the public
- the stock exchanges within the provinces (for example, the Toronto Stock Exchange in Ontario)[19]

Canadian securities legislation employs several devices to achieve the objectives described above. They include

1. registering or licensing those engaged in various aspects of the securities business,
2. requiring the issuer of securities to the public to file a prospectus with the securities commission,
3. regulating continuous disclosure by public corporations, and
4. as discussed in Chapter 26, setting standards of corporate governance for public corporations.

The Securities Industry

Licensing Registering people engaged in the securities industry is an important device for ensuring ethical conduct. Licensing is done on an annual basis, and each securities commission has authority under its provincial statute to revoke, suspend, or refuse to renew the licence of anyone when, in its opinion, such action is in the public interest. Operating without a licence is a criminal offence. Depending on the jurisdiction, a licence may be required of persons engaged in a wide variety of activities. Those affected include brokers (who buy and sell securities as agents), investment dealers (who buy and sell

---

[15] *Reference Re Securities Act (Canada), Quebec (Procureure generale) v Canada (Procureure general)*, 2011 ABCA 77, 2011 QCCA 591.

[16] *Reference Re Securities Act*, 2011 SCC 66.

[17] See e.g. *Securities Act*, RSO 1990, c S-5; RSBC 1996, c 418; RSA 2000, c S-4; RSQ c V-1.1.

[18] Ontario *Securities Act, ibid*, s 1.1.

[19] *Ibid.*, ss 21–21.11. It is beyond the scope of this chapter to review the detailed regulations governing stock exchanges.

securities as principals), broker dealers (who may act as either principal or agent in the promotion of companies), securities issuers (companies issuing their securities directly to the public without the intermediate services of investment dealers), salespeople employed by any of these businesses, and investment counsel and securities advisers.

Self-regulating organizations such as the Investment Industry Regulatory Organization of Canada (IIROC) and the Mutual Fund Dealers Association of Canada (MFDA) work with their members to meet requirements of the securities commission and discipline members for violation of rules related to business conduct, financial operations, and trading practices. Under the Universal Market Integrity Rules, the IIROC has the power to suspend, fine, and revoke licences.[20]

The Public Corporation: Public Offering

Corporate Governance Before any company may make a public offering, the internal structure of the company must meet the high standards of corporate governance required by the securities regulations. As discussed in Chapter 26, the internal structure requirements include a larger board of directors than private companies, audit committees, mandatory independent compensation-setting, and audited financial statements, among other things. The specific requirements are based on the following fundamental principles:

- Independence: Decision-makers should be free of conflicts.
- Transparency: Decisions should be made through an open process.
- Disclosure: Information should be available to the public.
- Accountability: Decision-makers should be responsible for their conduct.
- Checks and balances: Internal structures should bring irregularities to light.

Prospectus No corporation, partnership, or other form of business organization may issue securities to the public unless a **prospectus** has been filed with and approved by the securities commission of the province or territory in which the securities are to be sold. Prospectus requirements are an attempt to ensure that prospective investors have the relevant facts about a corporation before deciding to invest in it. In most instances, an investor is entitled to a copy of the prospectus before buying securities and may rescind the purchase contract if she does not receive the prospectus.

The contents of a prospectus are prescribed by statute or in regulations and are too detailed to describe here. It is sufficient to note that the prospectus must include the following items (among others):

- a full description of the securities to be offered (either shares or bonds), with a statement of their voting rights, preference, conversion privileges, and rights on liquidation
- the nature of the business carried on
- the names, addresses, and occupations of the directors
- the proposed use of the proceeds from the issue of securities
- details of any share options to be given by the corporation[21]
- the remuneration of the underwriter
- the dividend record of the corporation

prospectus the document that a corporation is required to produce and file with securities commission when inviting the public to subscribe for its securities

---

[20] http://www.iiroc.ca/industry/rulebook/Pages/UMIR-Marketplace-Rules.aspx.

[21] A share (or stock) option is a right to subscribe for shares in the corporation at a fixed price within a specified time, given by a corporation as consideration for the payment of money, the rendering of services (often the services of directors), or any other valuable consideration. The option becomes valuable at any time before expiry that the market price exceeds the option price.

- the particulars of property and services to be paid for out of the proceeds of the issue
- recent audited financial statements
- a certificate of accuracy signed by the CEO, CFO, the promoter, and two directors

The prospectus must contain full, true, and plain disclosure of all material facts. Failure to do this is a strict liability regulatory offence, punishable by a fine of up to $5 million and/or five years in prison. Knowingly falsifying a prospectus is a criminal offence.[22] It also attracts civil liability on behalf of the corporation and personal liability for the directors, officers, underwriters, and any person that signed the prospectus.[23] There are some exceptions to the requirement of a prospectus for **non-public investors**.[24] In such cases a less detailed document known as an offering memorandum may be required. Equity crowdfunding is also subject to regulatory restrictions.

non-public investors investors that are not members of the general public, including accredited investors such as banks, insurance companies, and municipal corporations or friends and family

Continuing Disclosure Control by the securities commission extends not only to issues of new securities but also to trading in already outstanding securities. Public corporations must make annual and quarterly filings[25] with the securities commissions, disclosing financial and other material information, including

- audited financial information with management's discussion and analysis;[26]
- notice of any change in auditor;
- notice of any change in corporate structure and intercorporate relationships;
- descriptions of internal corporate governance practices, including details of directors' identities and independence, compensation setting and nomination processes, existence of a code of ethics, and ongoing assessment of governance effectiveness;[27]
- notice of material changes relating to the business, operations, or capital of an issuer that would reasonably be expected to affect the share price; and[28]
- acquisitions of other businesses.

CEOs and CFOs must certify the accuracy of all information contained in the annual filing. The Canadian Securities Administrators operate the System of Electronic Disclosure for Analysis and Retrieval (SEDAR) that gives the public electronic access to the filings of public companies.

Other provisions contained in the legislation:

- Make the proxy a more effective means of registering shareholders' opinions.[29]
- Require publication of insiders' transactions involving their corporation's shares[30] (as noted in Chapter 26).

---

[22] Ontario *Securities Act*, *supra* note 17, s 122(1)(b); *Criminal Code*, *supra* note 1, s 400.

[23] Ontario *Securities Act*, *ibid*, s 130. In 2007, the Supreme Court of Canada declined to impose civil liability under the Ontario *Securities Act* with respect to a forecast contained in a prospectus: *Kerr v Danier Leather Inc*, 2007 SCC 44.

[24] Alternate disclosure and filings are required for friends and family, accredited investors, venture capitalists, crowdfunders, and those under the offering memorandum exemption: see National Instruments 45-106 and 45-108.

[25] This filing is called the Annual Information Filing (AIF), and its contents are prescribed by National Instrument 51-102.

[26] Ontario *Securities Act*, *supra* note 17, ss 75–83.

[27] National Instrument 58-101, Disclosure of Corporate Governance Practices.

[28] The Supreme Court of Canada considered the distinction between material change and material fact in a 2007 decision: *Kerr*, *supra* note 23.

[29] Ontario *Securities Act*, *supra* note 17, ss 84–8(1).

[30] *Ibid.*, ss 106–9.

- Authorize civil actions against insiders.
- Make insider trading a regulatory and criminal offence.[31]

The Canadian Securities Administrators operate the SEDI, the System of Electronic Disclosure by Insiders, where insiders may submit their reports online, and the public may view the reports.

The Public Accounting Industry Reliable financial information is at the heart of investor protection. In 2004, the Canadian Securities Administrators imposed requirements for accountants engaged in public accounting or auditing. National Instrument 52-108 created the Canadian Public Accountability Board (CPAB), responsible for setting new standards for public accountants, overseeing their work, and promoting quality independent auditing. The CPAB carries out regular inspections of audit firms as a means of quality control and has disciplinary power. Only those public accountants recognized by and in good standing with the CPAB may provide an auditor's report for the purposes of the securities commission.

Secondary Market Liability Civil liability for inaccurate information extends beyond the information relating to the initial public offering to ongoing release of information during secondary trades in securities. The word *secondary* refers to the "resale" of existing shares between investors as distinct from initial purchases from the corporation. Securities legislation[32] creates a civil cause of action for any person who trades in a corporation's shares while inaccurate public information remains uncorrected. This statutory cause of action is in addition to any other common law negligence or negligent misrepresentation tort.[33] The corporation, its directors, officers, and influential insiders may all be held personally liable for damages suffered by a shareholder or former shareholder. Independent experts such as lawyers, accountants, or financial analysts may also be liable if their reports contain misrepresentations. The plaintiff need not prove that she relied on the misrepresentation, just that it remained uncorrected at the time of the transaction. Eliminating the reliance element makes this cause of action ideal for multiple plaintiffs in a class action.[34] A due diligence defence is available, and damage awards are capped.

Takeovers and Reorganizations Another important objective of securities legislation is to give shareholders who have received a **takeover bid** for their shares sufficient information and time to assess the merits of the bid.[35] Takeover provisions include a requirement for disclosure of the number of shares in the offeree corporation held by the offeror corporation and its officers, and details of recent trading in those shares. In addition, the directors of an offeree corporation are required to issue a **directors' circular** to the shareholders setting out, among other things, their own intentions with respect to the takeover offer and details of any arrangements made with the offeror corporation concerning their continuance in office or compensation for loss of office. However, this legislation does not apply to all corporations; in particular, takeovers of small private corporations are not regulated.

Both corporate and securities legislation contain detailed and complex rules dealing with mergers, with various types of corporate reorganization, and with winding up. No

takeover bid an offer by one corporation to acquire all or a substantial part of the shares of another corporation

directors' circular a document required to be issued to shareholders by the board of directors when a takeover of a widely held corporation is proposed

---

[31] *Ibid.*, ss 76, 122(1)(c), 134.

[32] *Ibid.*, s 138.1; Ontario was the first province to create secondary market liability in its securities act. Others provinces quickly followed: BC (s. 140.1); Alta (s. 211.03); Sask (s. 147); Man (s. 174); Que (s. 225.3); NS (s. 146); NB (s. 161.1); Nfld (s. 138.1).

[33] *CIBC v Green*, 2015 SCC 60 at para 128.

[34] *Ibid.* at para 124.

[35] Ontario *Securities Act*, *supra* note 17, ss 89–105.

one should make a decision in one of the above areas without expert assistance. The problems involved usually concern creditors' rights, the effects of taxation, the relevance of competition legislation, and the rights of various classes of shareholders, in addition to the general economic consequences for the corporations and markets involved.

PROTECTION OF THE PUBLIC INTEREST

Protecting the public interest is a difficult challenge that involves balancing the interests of multiple stakeholders. Usually government is responsible for protecting the public, and the interests of the public are diverse. For example, it is in the public interest that people are employed, that employees earn a competitive wage, that business has access to foreign markets, that domestic products are competitive with imports, and that the environment is preserved. It is impossible to establish standards that protect all of the interests of the public, and difficult choices must be made. Government uses regulation to balance the interests of business, stakeholders, and the public at large. The remaining part of this chapter examines civil, regulatory, and criminal liability imposed to protect the public interest without designating a particular stakeholder. By way of example, this chapter will look at the environmental regulatory scheme. The legal requirements should be viewed as a minimum standard of behaviour that management is encouraged to exceed.

Ethical Issue   Corporate Social Responsibility and Executive Compensation

As discussed in Chapter 1, corporate social responsibility (CSR) is a concept that suggests that corporate management should consider not only what is profitable and legal but also what is ethical when making strategic decisions. Corporations should consider the interests of the communities in which they operate and the public as a whole. Corporate social responsibility is gaining momentum and legal recognition. Some commentators suggest that failing to live up to public endorsements of CSR principles will trigger legal liability.[36]

One explanation for this momentum is, again, the Enron debacle, which demonstrated the dangers of corporate greed. Another lies in the collapse of the market in hi-tech stocks, which suggests that the "bottom line" is not necessarily an accurate measure of corporate success and viability. Hopefully, the lesson will finally be learned from the worldwide collapse of the credit and asset-backed paper markets in 2008.

The Canadian Democracy and Corporate Accountability Commission's 2002 report made a series of recommendations, including the following:

- The law should make it clear that social responsibility considerations may be taken into account by corporate management.
- The structure of corporate governance should be modified to include a corporate social responsibility committee of the board of directors.
- Large corporations should be required to publish a "social audit."
- The law should protect employees against adverse action taken against them for "whistle-blowing."
- Canadian corporations should be required to adhere to a core set of human rights standards in their operations overseas.
- Business schools should develop mandatory courses focusing on corporate social responsibility.

Only a few of the above described recommendations were implemented. Many blame the continued primacy of the profit motive on the structure of executive compensation. Traditionally, executive compensation schemes link performance bonuses to the profitability of the company rather than long-term stability or corporate social responsibility. Bonuses are often in the form of stock options, whose values rise with the price of corporate shares. This structure reinforces "bottom-line" decision-making with a view to short-term profit and may even encourage inflated financial reporting.

The US $700 billion Wall Street bailout, approved by Congress in October 2008, addressed executive compensation. Some of the conditions attached to the bailout were limits on executive severance packages and clawbacks of bonuses. Critics argued that no bailout at all would have been the best way to teach a lesson about greed.

---

[36] Drew Hasselback, "Why Corporate Social Responsibility Is Now Part of Due-Diligence," *Financial Post*, July 29, 2015, http://business.financialpost.com/legal-post/why-corporate-social-responsibility-is-now-part-of-due-diligence.

> **Questions to Consider**
> 1. Are these recommendations realistic? Can ethics be legislated?
> 2. Is there really a conflict between the long-term interests of a corporation and a requirement of social responsibility?
> 3. How should executive compensation be structured to encourage socially responsible behaviour?
>
> Sources: Canadian Democracy and Corporate Accountability Report, *The New Balance Sheet: Corporate Profits and Responsibility in the 21st Century*, January 2002; Stephen Gandel, "How Washington's Bailout Will Boost Wall Street Bonuses," *Time*, October 27, 2008, http://www.time.com /time/business/article/0,8599,1853846,00.html?imw=Y.

CIVIL LIABILITY OF CORPORATIONS

Corporations are exposed to civil liability—liability toward a plaintiff, typically to pay damages for harm done through committing a tort, breaking a contract, or breaching a statutory duty. In the early parts of this chapter and in Chapter 26, we focused on civil liability triggered by statute. We complete this discussion by commenting on key issues in tort and contract.

Tort Liability

A corporation acts through its human agents. Where a corporation is held liable in tort, it is almost invariably on account of a negligent or wrongful act committed by an employee, agent, or officer, and its liability is vicarious.[37] As with any defendant, liability depends on the plaintiff's proving each element of the tort. The corporation might be the only defendant liable if each element of the tort is committed by different employees. As noted in Chapter 2, class actions have levelled the playing field between business and the small stakeholder. Business can no longer ignore minor consequences of its actions.

Contractual Liability

Generally speaking, a corporation is liable for the contracts made by its agents in the ordinary course of business under the rules of agency (discussed in Chapter 17). Agents of a corporation acting within their actual or apparent authority[38] bind the corporation to contracts made with third parties.

The bylaws and other internal corporate documents will define agency powers and the proper process for contract ratification. Still, the courts have held contracts to be enforceable even when the proper rules were not followed. In the absence of notice of an irregularity or of suspicious circumstances, everything that appears normal may be relied upon by an outsider, and the contract will bind the corporation.[39] This principle is known as the **indoor management rule**[40] and is really just an application of the apparent authority principle in agency law. An innocent third party may rely upon the regularity of a corporate act, just as he may rely upon the apparent authority of an agent, if it is reasonable for him to do so in the circumstances.

indoor management rule the principle that a person dealing with a corporation is entitled to assume that its internal procedural rules have been followed unless it is apparent that such is not the case

---

[37] Vicarious liability is discussed in Chapter 4. It is possible for a corporate employer to have primary liability in tort, without the employee being personally liable: see *Edgeworth Construction Ltd v ND Lee & Associates* (1993), 107 DLR (4th) 169.

[38] Where a director or officer acts within the scope of her usual, or apparent, authority, even though she has no actual authority to do so, the corporation will be bound unless the third party knew (or ought to have known) of the lack of authority.

[39] *Royal British Bank v Turquand* (1856), 119 ER 886.

[40] See *Canada Business Corporations Act* (CBCA), *supra* note 7, ss 17, 18. Subsequent references in this chapter are to the CBCA unless otherwise stated.

> **ILLUSTRATION 27.2 Exceeding Authority**
>
> W, the chief executive officer of A Ltd., negotiates a contract to buy equipment from B Inc. for $1 million. The bylaws of A Ltd. provide that any contract involving expenditure of more than $50 000 must be approved by the board of its Japanese parent company. That approval has not been obtained. Consequently, W is acting outside the scope of her actual authority. Can B Inc. enforce the contract?
>
> The answer is yes unless B Inc. knew of the restriction in the bylaws and that the approval of the parent board had not been obtained.

As noted in Chapter 26, certain corporate documents must be filed in a government office and are available to the public for examination. Even so, the public is not deemed to have notice of the contents of those documents. Section 17 of the *Canada Business Corporations Act* (CBCA) provides:

> No person is affected by or is deemed to have notice or knowledge of the content of a document concerning a corporation by reason only that the document has been filed by the Director or is available for inspection at an office of the corporation.[41]

A contracting third party who actually has read or knows the contents of a restriction will be bound by it, but this is merely the common law rule of agency—a third party who knows of a restriction on the authority of an agent cannot rely upon an apparent authority that ignores this restriction. For large or important contracts, one should not take the indoor management rule for granted. Third parties usually hire corporate lawyers to review the corporation's documents of record and ensure that all necessary authorizations have been obtained.

Pre-Incorporation Contracts

As noted in Chapter 17, at common law, a corporation could not ratify a **pre-incorporation contract**—that is, a contract made on its behalf before it came into existence. If a "contract" was made in the name of a corporation even one day before it came into existence, it was of no effect, and a new contract would have to be negotiated once the corporation was formed. Further, the individual who purported to contract on behalf of the corporation normally could not be held to the contract either, since the intention was to contract with the corporation.[42]

The CBCA and the provincial incorporation statutes changed this by providing that a person who enters into, or purports to enter into, a written contract in the name of or on behalf of a corporation before it comes into existence is personally bound by the contract and is entitled to its benefits.[43] In addition, a corporation may, within a reasonable time after it comes into existence, adopt a written pre-incorporation contract. In that event, the corporation is bound by the contract and is entitled to its benefits, and the person who acts in the name of the corporation ceases to be personally liable.[44]

pre-incorporation contract
a purported contract made in the name of a corporation before it comes into existence

---

[41] RSC 1985, c C-44, s 17.

[42] See *Delta Construction Co Ltd v Lidstone* (1979), 96 DLR (3d) 457. The individual may be liable for breach of warranty of authority; this is discussed in Chapter 17. Contrast *Kelner v Baxter* (1866), LR2 CP 174, where the court found that there was an intention that the individual contractor be bound.

[43] CBCA, s 14(1).

[44] *Ibid.*, s 14(2). There are some variations from province to province. For example, Ontario does not restrict the rule to written contracts. In the case of a corporation incorporated under the CBCA, the effect of an oral pre-incorporation contract would be decided under the common law rules; see *Kettle v Borris* (2000), 10 BLR (3d) 122.

The clear intention is that, whether or not the contract is adopted, it will be enforceable by the other party. To prevent unfair manipulation by a corporation and a contractor, the Act (s. 14(3)) gives the court power to apportion liability between the corporation and the contractor in any manner it thinks fit.

A promoter acting on behalf of a corporation before it comes into existence may avoid personal liability and waive any benefits under the contract when the contract includes an express term that the promoter will not be bound by the agreement.[45] Figure 27.1 illustrates some of the possible relationships involved in pre-incorporation contracts.

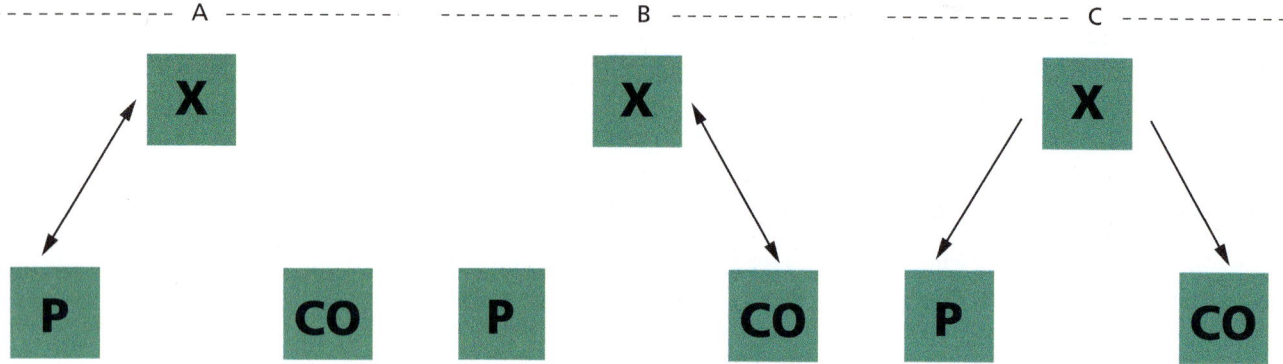

Figure 27.1   Pre-incorporation Contracts

In situation A, the promoter, P, has entered into a contract with a third party, X, in the name of corporation CO, before it has come into existence. The effect is to create a contract between P and X. In situation B, the corporation has since been formed and has adopted the contract. There is now a contract between CO and X, and P is no longer a party to it. In situation C, the court has, on an application by X, apportioned liability, and both P and CO are liable.

CRIMINAL LIABILITY OF CORPORATIONS

A corporation can be charged with, and convicted of, an offence under the *Criminal Code* in the same way as a natural person.[46] For example, in one of the leading Canadian cases on corporate criminal liability, a number of corporations were convicted of conspiracy in rigging bids for a construction contract.[47]

The Nature of Corporate Criminal Liability

How Can Corporations Commit Crimes?
The characteristics of corporations present special problems for criminal liability:

(a) Most criminal offences require the Crown to prove both that the accused actually committed the act and that there was some level of mental intent—but a corporation has neither a physical body with which to carry out the act nor a "mind" of its own capable of forming an intent.

(b) If convicted, a guilty person's punishment is often imprisonment—but a corporation cannot be imprisoned.

---

[45] CBCA, s. 14(4). To be effective, there must be an express exclusion of liability; see *Szecket v Huang* (1998), 168 DLR (4th) 402; *1394918 Ontario Ltd v 1310210 Ontario Inc* (2002), 57 OR (3d) 607.

[46] Corporations have been convicted of manslaughter in some common law jurisdictions. A U.S. pharmaceutical company and the Canadian Red Cross faced criminal charges arising from the Canadian tainted blood scandal; *R v Armour Pharmaceutical Company* (2006) 205 CCC (3d) 97.

[47] *R v Canadian Dredge & Dock Co Ltd* (1985), 19 DLR (4th) 314 (SCC); see also *R v Curragh Inc*, [1997] 1 SCR 537 (Westray Mining Disaster).

The consequences of (b) are that, if convicted, a corporation will be fined or ordered to refrain from certain conduct or, in rare cases, dissolved—all relatively painless forms of punishment. Charges may also be laid personally against directors and senior officers of a corporation, a topic considered later.

With regard to (a), it may be impossible to convict at all if the offence requires intent or **mens rea**. Regulatory offences, which are most often strict or absolute liability, are much more popular vehicles to address corporate conduct. However, the public interest demands that serious corporate misconduct attract criminal consequences, and so the courts and legislature (through the *Criminal Code*) have created rules that attribute individual acts and intent to the corporation.

mens rea mental intent necessary to commit a criminal offence

The "Directing Mind" Principle

The earliest test used to establish corporate criminal liability was the "directing mind" principle. It held that corporate *mens rea* existed if a guilty mind could be found in an "active director" or the "directing mind or will" at "the centre of the personality of the corporation."[48] This meant a person with policy making authority rather than just supervisory or implementation responsibilities.

What if the wrongful act is committed not by a senior officer or director but by a person lower down in the hierarchy? Canadian courts tended to find an act committed by an employee who has significant responsibilities, such as the head of an important department or a branch, to be an act of the corporation itself.[49] But the courts would not hold the act of a low-level employee, for example, a clerk who cheated a customer, to be the act of the corporation.[50] The difference between the two was not always easy to see.

The *Criminal Code*'s Test

Amendments to the *Criminal Code* have clarified the situation and increased corporate exposure to criminal liability,[51] with these important changes:

- First, the physical act and mental intent of any offence are not required to be found in the same person. Corporate criminal liability can be established in multiple employees with different responsibilities.
- Second, the physical act may be committed by virtually any employee or contractor or an aggregate of them.
- Third, corporate *mens rea* may be found not only in those with policy making authority but also in a **senior officer** or employee with operational responsibilities.[52]

senior officer a representative who plays an important role in establishing an organization's policies or is responsible for managing an important aspect of its activities, including the directors, the CEO, and the CFO of a corporation

The type of intent required by the offence will determine the rule:

1. In the case of an offence that requires the prosecution to prove negligence (for example, criminal negligence causing death), an organization is a party to the offence if (a) one of its representatives, acting within the scope of his authority, is a party to the offence, and (b) the senior officer responsible for that aspect of the organization's activities departs markedly from the standard of care that could reasonably be expected to prevent the representative from being a party to the offence.

---

[48] *Lennard's Carrying Co Ltd v Asiatic Petroleum Co Ltd*, [1915] AC 705.

[49] *R v Waterloo Mercury Sales Ltd* (1974), 49 DLR (3d) 131.

[50] *R v Safety-Kleen Canada Inc* (1997), 145 DLR (4th) 276. The corporation was found guilty of another strict liability, regulatory offence.

[51] *Criminal Code*, *supra* note 1, ss 2, 22.1, 22.2. A broader range of organizations are now exposed to criminal liability, including partnerships, trade unions, and municipalities (s. 2).

[52] *Ibid.*, s 2 (as amended).

2. In the case of an offence that requires the prosecution to prove intent (other than negligence), an organization is a party to the offence if one of its senior officers (a) acting within the scope of her authority and with the intent, at least in part, to benefit the organization, is a party to the offence, or (b) with the required intent directs the work of other representatives of the organization so that they commit the specified act or omission, or (c) knowing that a representative of the organization is about to be a party to the offence, does not take all reasonable measures to stop them.

Criminal Code Offences

As already noted, an organization may be charged with any offence, but the *Criminal Code* contains some offences that are particularly applicable to corporate conduct:

- Fraud (s. 380) and fraud affecting the public markets (s. 380(2)).
- Market manipulation—false market activity or manipulating share prices (s. 382).
- Distributing false prospectuses, statements, or accounts (s. 400).
- Criminal negligence causing bodily harm—any duty imposed by common law or statute may form the basis of this offence (s. 219). Section 217.1 specifically imposes a duty on those who direct (or supervise) work to protect workers and the public.[53]
- Whistle-blower retaliation—includes threatening, disciplining, demoting, or firing a whistle-blower or potential whistle-blower (s. 425.1).

Sentencing

Criminal sentences should denounce the conduct, protect the public, deter the offender and others, repair the harm done, rehabilitate the offender, encourage assumption of responsibility by the offender, and promote public confidence (s. 718). Sentencing a corporation is a challenge: It cannot be imprisoned, and a fine is a punishment ultimately borne by the shareholders. Small businesses may simply start up in a new corporation. The *Criminal Code* addresses corporate penalties in the following ways:

- Criminal fines cannot be deducted as a cost of doing business.
- Specific aggravating and mitigating factors for organizations include degree of planning, public costs, depletion of corporate assets, other regulatory offences, and convictions of corporate representatives (s. 718.21).
- Probation for corporations may involve the development of policies and procedures and supervision of management by a court-appointed compliance officer (s. 732.1).

CASE 27.1 Sentencing a Corporation with Little Ability to Pay

A construction company pled guilty for criminal negligence causing death after four construction workers fell to their deaths. It admitted that the construction site supervisor failed to take reasonable care by (1) directing and or permitting six workers to work on equipment that he knew or should have known was unsafe, (2) directing and/or permitting six workers to board the swing stage knowing that only two lifelines were available, and (3) permitting persons under the influence of a drug to work on the project. On sentencing, the Court of Appeal decided that a $200 000 fine was too low. Criminal fines should be bigger than those imposed under regulatory convictions, and an organization's ability to pay is not a prerequisite. The economic viability of a corporation is only a factor to consider. It is not a condition precedent to the imposition of a fine, nor does it necessarily dictate the amount of the fine. The fine was increased to $750 000.[54]

---

[53] See e.g. *R v Metron Construction Corporation*, 2013 ONCA 541.

[54] *Ibid* at paras 15, 108, 121.

CRIMINAL LIABILITY OF DIRECTORS AND OFFICERS

As noted in Chapter 25, limited liability does not protect directors from liability for torts or breaches of fiduciary duty they personally commit. In principle, directors, like employees, are liable for torts they commit in the course of performing their duties, even though the corporation may also be vicariously liable.[55]

Directors (and officers) may also be held criminally liable for offences committed by them for the benefit of the corporation or by the corporation while under their supervision.

CASE 27.2   Fraud for the Survival of the Corporation

While directors and officers, Drabinsky and Gottlieb "were so devoted to the continuation of Livent Inc. that they directed the falsification of the financial statements in order to continue the flow of money to the company."[56] The fraudulent culture was fully understood by the employees at Livent and facilitated new investment money. The fraud eventually drove the company into bankruptcy. Gotlieb and Drabinsky were both convicted of fraud and sentenced to four and five years in prison, respectively.[57]

Directors and officers are held criminally liable because holding only the corporations liable is not a strong enough deterrent to ensure effective enforcement of regulatory schemes. A large corporation with sufficient assets might consider the penalty merely a "licence"; it pays the fine and carries on with its activities. The corporation's manager may pass the costs on to the consumer through higher prices or to the corporation's shareholders through lower dividends. At the other extreme, a corporation may be merely a "shell" with virtually no assets to pay its fine; those who control the enterprise walk away from it and start up a similar activity using a new corporation.

Effective deterrence requires that individuals responsible for the offence be punished directly. Directors and senior officers should be criminally liable for offences committed by their corporation. As has been said, "the threat of jail sends a clear message to corporate executives that they are not immune to criminal sanctions . . . . Incarceration is one cost of business that you can't pass to the consumer."[58]

Still it is difficult to prosecute individuals. In complex organizations, where responsibility is shared among a number of persons, identifying with any certainty who is responsible and who can—and should—be convicted may not be clear. To make it easier, some legislation

- has express provisions making senior officers and directors liable,
- requires CEOs and CFOs to certify annual filings, and
- expands the grounds for individual liability.

---

[55] The fact that they are acting in the corporation's interest does not by itself protect them from personal liability; see *ADGA Systems International Ltd v Valcom Ltd* (1999), 43 OR (3d) 101. See R Flannigan, "The Personal Tort Liability of Directors" (2002) 81 Can Bar Rev 247.

[56] *R v Drabinsky*, 2011 ONCA 582 at paras 25, 27.

[57] *Ibid* at paras 30, 35–7, 189. Interestingly the conduct of Gotlieb and Drabinsky was not attributed to Livent in its lawsuit against the auditors: *Livent v Deloitte & Touche*, 2017 SCC 63.

[58] See Nelson Smith, "No Longer Just a Cost of Doing Business . . ." (1992) 53 *La L. Rev* 119 at 126.

LIABILITY FOR ENVIRONMENTAL OFFENCES

Liability for environmental offences provides a good example of legislation that expands the grounds for corporate and director liability. Environmental protection involves air, water, and land pollution; preservation of natural resources; acceptable use, transportation, and disposal of waste, toxins, and dangerous goods; and assessment of the environmental impact of any activity. These topics are regulated by municipal, provincial, and federal governments. The *Canadian Environmental Protection Act, 1999*, and most of the corresponding provincial statutes create strict liability offences for corporations and their directors and officers when the Act or its regulations are breached. For these offences, establishing due diligence is the only defence.[59] It is beyond the scope of this chapter to review the voluminous federal and provincial legislation[60] on this topic; instead, we will discuss basic principles common to many environmental offences.

What Standard of Skill and Care Must Be Met?

The challenge for the accused is to meet what is generally acknowledged to be a steadily rising standard of care. The enterprise must demonstrate that it has an effective system to prevent offences, must monitor the results of the system, and must improve the system if problems occur. A corporation cannot escape liability simply by delegating responsibility to an employee. Any employee's actions may be treated as those of the corporation itself. If not, the corporation will have failed to put in place an effective system of control.

Each enterprise whose activities may pose a risk must show that it reviews its current monitoring system frequently and makes reasonable efforts to remain current on technological change in the field.

The Expertise Required of Directors and Senior Officers

Should a higher standard of care and skill be imposed if directors or senior officers have expertise in the area where a hazardous activity is carried on? Suppose a senior officer is an engineer with long experience in the field. Would she be expected to take precautions against a risk that an accountant would unlikely be aware of? A common sense view would say yes. There is some support for this view in a case where the accused corporation allowed diesel fuel to escape into fishing waters.[61] The court seemed to expect greater diligence from the corporation's experienced senior officers:

> The accused was required to possess, and did possess sufficient expertise to be aware of the potential risk to the environment posed by a fuel system in northern mining camps . . . . [T]he accused had the opportunity and knowledge in the field, through their employees Mr. Morganti with thirty two months' field experience and Mr. Goddard with twenty five years' experience, to influence the offending conduct on the site.[62]

---

[59] See e.g. *R v MacMillan Bloedel Ltd* (2002), 220 DLR (4th) 173. A statutory civil cause of action for damages is also created.

[60] Examples: Federal Legislation: *Canadian Environmental Protection Act, 1999* (CEPA 1999) and *Canadian Environmental Assessment Act, 2012* (CEAA 2012); British Columbia: *Environmental Management Act, 2003, Environmental Assessment Act, 2002, Waste Management Act, 1996, Water Act, 1996*; Alberta: *Environmental Protection and Enhancement Act, 2000, Natural Resources Conservation Board Act, 2000, Climate Change and Emissions Management Act, 2003, Water Act, 2000*; Ontario: *Environmental Protection Act, 1990, Environmental Bill of Rights, 1993, Environmental Assessment Act, 1990, Waste Diversion Act, 2002, Ontario Water Resources Act, 1990*.

[61] *R v Placer Developments Ltd* (1983), 13 CELR 42 (YT Terr Ct).

[62] *Ibid* at 49.

On the other hand, the court suggested that even if the accused firm did not possess that expertise, it would still be liable for the offence:

> Anyone choosing to become involved in activities posing danger to the public or to the environment assumes an obligation to take whatever measures may be necessary to prevent harm.... Unless equipped with appropriate professional skills, no one ought to undertake any activity involving a danger to the public.... Mining in the north requires not only an expert knowledge of mining, but equally important, an expert appreciation of the special problems caused by remote operations in northern environments.[63]

It seems the accused corporation was caught in one of two ways. Either it failed to employ the expertise it ought to have known that it needed in order to manage the hazardous activity, or if it did employ the necessary expertise, then the expert failed to properly use the professional care and skill. Perhaps an unskilled employee who had been sent to the site would not be found personally liable because he could not have been expected to anticipate the risk, but the employer enterprise would then be caught by its failure to send an employee with the necessary skills to carry out the task.

Who Should Be Found Liable?

Those in Charge of an Activity
Apart from the liability of a business itself, any person who actually commits an offence is personally liable, even when he was acting within the scope of his authorized activities. Regulations sometimes make senior officers and directors liable because they are considered to be in charge of an activity, even though they have not participated directly in the offence. Two different phrases are employed. The first makes liable those who "cause or permit" a hazardous substance to be discharged;[64] the second makes liable "any officer, director or agent ... who directed, authorized, assented to, acquiesced in, or participated in the commission of an offence."[65]

So, who are these persons? In order to "permit" or "acquiesce in" an activity such as disposing of hazardous materials, one must have a significant role in controlling those who actually carry it out. Permitting or acquiescing has no meaning if the person charged is merely one who learned about the activity but could do nothing to affect it. The prosecution must first persuade a court that a person charged had effective powers and responsibility. A senior officer and director who is personally in charge of a hazardous procedure (that is, she is the person to whom those performing the activity report on a regular basis) presents a clear case of effective control and responsibility for the activity.

The Difficulty of Determining Responsibility
What about an independent or "outside" director—a person who was elected to the board because of his experience in financial services and who faithfully attends board meetings twice a year? He reads all the material sent to him and asks probing and useful questions at meetings. However, when it comes to environmental concerns, he relies on the reports and assurances given by the senior officer, the "inside" director, who is in charge. Should the independent director also be considered to share in control? Did he "permit" or "acquiesce in" an offence that occurred under the supervision of the inside director?

Normally an innocent and reasonably diligent independent director would not be held personally liable for the offence. Typically, the charges brought under Canadian

---

[63] *Ibid* at 52.

[64] See e.g. *Fisheries Act*, RSC 1985, c F-14, s 36(3).

[65] CEPA 1999, *supra* note 60, s 280.

legislation have been against "inside" directors. However, in many situations there is not a clear-cut division between insider and outsider: For instance, did the outsider receive any reports that disclosed questionable practices to a reasonable person in his position? Were answers to his questions evasive?

Not all insiders are "in control" of an operation, or directly involved in it, simply because they are directors and senior officers within the enterprise. It will depend upon the degree of involvement of the specific director in the particular circumstances of each case.

CASE 27.3 Proving Due Diligence

A corporation's premises contained a large, toxic, chemical waste storage site with many decaying, rusting, and uncovered containers; soil samples revealed concentrations of various dangerous chemicals. The prosecution charged the corporation with permitting the discharge of liquid industrial waste that could impair the quality of the groundwater and contaminate the environment. Charges were also laid against three directors.

All the defendants argued that they had shown due diligence in carrying out their duties. Ormston, J., found that the corporation—Bata Industries—guilty because it did not establish a proper system to prevent the escape of toxic substances and did not take reasonable steps to ensure the effective operation of even its faulty system.[66]

The court provided a useful summary of the questions that should be asked to assess a director's defence of "due diligence" in his particular circumstances:

(a) Did the board of directors establish a pollution-prevention "system"—that is, was there supervision or inspection?
(b) Did each director ensure that the corporate officers had been instructed to set up a system sufficient within the terms and practices of the industry of ensuring compliance with environmental laws, to ensure that the officers report back periodically to the board?
(c) The directors are responsible for reviewing the environmental compliance reports provided by the officers, but are they justified in placing reasonable reliance on reports?
(d) The directors should substantiate that the officers are promptly addressing environmental concerns brought to their attention by government agencies or other concerned parties including shareholders.
(e) The directors should be aware of the standards of their industry and other industries that deal with similar environmental pollutants or risks.
(f) The directors should immediately and personally react when they have notice that the system has failed.

Of the directors, Mr. Bata was found to be "the director with the least personal contact with the plant" where the offence occurred. His responsibilities were at other plants and "he attended on-site . . . once or twice a year to review the operation and performance goals." Although Mr. Bata did not personally review the operation when he was on site,

> He responded to the matters brought to his attention promptly and appropriately. He had placed an experienced director on site and was entitled in the circumstances to assume that . . . [the on-site director] was addressing the environmental concerns . . . . He was entitled to rely upon his system . . . unless he became aware the system was defective.[67]

Accordingly, Mr. Bata was acquitted.

Another director, Mr. Marchant, was found to have more responsibility than Mr. Bata but less than a third director, who was held to be "on site." Mr. Marchant came to the facility once a month and toured the plant. The court found that the problem was brought to his "personal attention" and that he had personal knowledge and took no steps

> [D]ue diligence requires him to exercise a degree of supervision and control that demonstrate that he was exhorting those whom he may be normally expected to influence or control to an accepted standard of behaviour.

Mr. Marchant was found guilty and ordered to pay a fine. At trial, Bata was ordered not to pay the fine on behalf of the convicted director. The Court of Appeal set aside the prohibition on indemnification by the company. It agreed that the court had the power to make such an order but disagreed that the circumstances justified it.[68]

---

[66] *R v Bata Industries Ltd* (1992), 9 OR (3d) 329 at 362. Sentences were appealed and fines reduced [1993] OJ No 1679.

[67] *Ibid* at 364.

[68] *R v Bata Industries Ltd*, [1995] OJ No 2691 at para 30 (ONCA).

What Should the Punishment Be?

Generally, corporations are fined according to the seriousness of the breach and the harm caused. Directors and officers receive somewhat smaller fines, but in extreme cases, they may be sentenced to prison terms.[69]

CASE 27.4 Severity of the Sentence

A corporation, Varnicolor Chemical Ltd., reprocessed and disposed of industrial wastes. Waste materials escaped from its toxic disposal site into the groundwater and moved toward a river that was used as a source of drinking water for downriver communities. The corporation took no action to clean up the spill; rather, it was the Ministry of the Environment that did so at an estimated cost of $2.5 million. Both the corporation and one of its directors, Mr. Argenton, were charged with offences.[70]

Mr. Argenton was "the only officer and director to take an active part in the operations and actual management of . . . [Varnicolor]. He was clearly, at all relevant times, the sole directing mind of the company." Accordingly, his actions were the actions of the corporation. Mr. Argenton pleaded guilty. Charges against the corporation were stayed. The court discussed the principles for sentencing Mr. Argenton, including protecting the public, deterring and rehabilitating offenders, promoting compliance with the law, and expressing public disapproval.

It summarized the factors that should affect the severity of a sentence as follows:

- *The nature of the environment affected:* Meaning both the sensitivity of the environment affected and the gravity of the risk. In this case, the drinking water of residents in the area would be contaminated.
- *The extent of the damage actually inflicted:* Here, there was a high cost of clean-up.
- *The deliberateness of the offence:* In considering this factor, the court stated:

"Not only was Mr. Argenton involved on site in the operations of the company, but he was as well involved in the negotiations which preceded the issuance of the certificate of approval by the Ministry . . . for the Varnicolor site . . . . Therefore, as a result of this active involvement and in depth knowledge of the business operations, it is clear that Mr. Argenton was uniquely in a position to be aware . . . of . . . the requirements of the Ministry. Mr. Argenton has indicated that he found these requirements to be unclear and ambiguous; however, it was at all times open to . . . [him] to seek clarification . . . . There is no indication . . . that he made any attempts to do so. In a number of respects, Mr. Argenton acted in defiance of the requirements . . . . Such violations are in effect a breach of trust on the part of the person to whom such a certificate has been granted and, as such, jail terms are an appropriate penalty to ensure compliance with the law by both the person being sentenced and society in general."

- *The attitude of the defendant:* Mr. Argenton did not voluntarily report the escape of toxic waste, nor did he show a cooperative attitude.
- *Attempts to comply with the regulations:* There was no evidence of a clean-up at the site by Varnicolor or by Mr. Argenton, and the corporation had become inactive.

The maximum sentence under the *Environmental Protection Act* was 12 months. The court found that the conduct of the defendant amounted to a serious breach of the Act and sentenced him to eight months in jail.

The Business Consequences

Combing the discussion of civil and regulatory environmental liability in Chapter 3 with the contents of this chapter, it is clear that protecting the environment is a high priority. In response, legislatures have created extensive regulatory schemes. Meeting the standards under these schemes imposes substantial costs on many businesses, especially on resource industries and manufacturing and transportation enterprises. The most important challenge is to meet the requirements effectively and efficiently.

---

[69] See *R v Romaniuk* (1993), 112 Sask R 129 (QB) (a fine ($76 000) and a jail sentence (30 days)).

[70] *R v Varnicolor Chemical Ltd*, [1992] OJ No 1978.

INTERNATIONAL ISSUE
International Environmental Regulation

Environmental protection is a global challenge because pollutants move invisibly across national boundaries. Unfortunately, standards vary by jurisdiction, but a number of strategies are being employed to establish universal standards of environmental protection. The *Canadian Environmental Protection Act, 1999*, attempts to extend its reach beyond Canadian borders by addressing international air and water pollution (Part 7, Division 6). The Minister is empowered to regulate polluters and collect clean-up costs. Section 166(4) recognizes the jurisdictional limits of this power:

> If the air pollution referred to in paragraph (1)(a) is in a country where Canada does not have substantially the same rights with respect to the prevention, control or correction of air pollution as that country has under this Division, the Minister shall decide whether to act under subsections (2) and (3) or to take no action at all.

Governments try to create uniform standards around the world by entering into conventions and treaties, such as the Kyoto Protocol. The Kyoto Protocol (an amendment to the United Nations Framework Convention on Climate Change, ratified by Canada in 2002) required greenhouse gas emissions to be reduced by 6 percent (from 1990 levels) by 2012. After failing to reach past targets, Canada announced that it would not accept new targets beyond 2012. The United States is a signatory of Kyoto but never ratified it.

The International Organization for Standardization, a non-governmental organization, has also created an environmental standards program. It established a voluntary certification standard for environmental management systems (ISO 14001). Participating organizations complete environmental audits of their business processes and design customized systems for effective environmental management.

The United Nations Global Compact designates 10 guiding principles of corporate social responsibility, three of which relate to environmental issues:

- to encourage the development of environmentally friendly technologies
- to support the precautionary principle (prove activity does no harm)
- to promote greater environmental responsibility

Organizations voluntarily agree to comply with the principles and publicly report their progress. Canadian participants in the Global Compact include Bell Canada Enterprises, Enbridge, Hydro-Québec, Talisman Energy Inc., and Petro-Canada.

Question to Consider

1. What measures are most likely to achieve uniform global environmental protection?

Sources: Doug Struck, "Canada Altars Course on Kyoto," *Washington Post*, May 3, 2006; "ISO 14000—Environmental Management Standards," International Organization for Standardization, https://www.iso.org/iso-14001-environmental-management.html; "Essential Background," United Nations Framework Convention on Climate Change, http://unfccc.int/essential_background/items/6031.php; United Nations Global Compact website, http://www.unglobalcompact.org; Mike De Souza, "Canada Wants New Climate Deal by 2015: Environment Minister," *Ottawa Citizen*, December 8, 2011.

Strategies to Manage the Legal Risks

For many businesses, regulatory compliance is a full-time job. Meeting securities reporting and disclosure obligations requires knowledge of and familiarity with the many layers of regulations that apply to public companies generally and to specific industries. The best approach is to hire a compliance officer who will put a system in place, meet day-to-day obligations, monitor compliance, confirm accuracy of filings, and respond early to irregularities.

Disclosure requirements exist so that outside stakeholders can protect themselves by making informed decisions. Creditors, shareholders, and potential investors should use the information available to them.

Environmental accidents can result in insurmountable financial obstacles for a business. Steps should be taken to avoid a catastrophe. First, businesses need to review their practices to learn whether any of their activities create a concern about health, safety, or the breach of environmental regulations. They must keep up-to-date with current technology and best practices adopted across their industry. They are expected to take every reasonable precaution to meet the latest standards.

Second, once they are informed about the risks, they should review their insurance coverage with a view to obtaining the maximum risk protection that is available and affordable. The cost of insurance coverage leads to the third stage. If, after obtaining the best advice for implementing safety systems and obtaining insurance, a particular business activity ceases to be competitive, then it becomes necessary to decide whether to continue that branch of operations.

Third, directors and officers cannot turn a blind eye to operational details or suspicious behaviour. Concerns should be expressed and investigated. Directors should educate themselves about the business's activities and risks so that informed decisions are made and personal liability is limited.

QUESTIONS FOR REVIEW

1. What is meant by the "indoor management rule"?
2. Is a person dealing with a corporation expected to know the contents of the corporation's articles of incorporation or its bylaws?
3. Can a corporation adopt a pre-incorporation contract? What is the effect of its purporting to do so?
4. What are the possible legal consequences when a false statement is made in a prospectus?
5. Are there any restrictions on a corporation paying dividends to its shareholders?
6. Why are there restrictions against a corporation returning capital to its shareholders?
7. What are the principal objectives of securities legislation?
8. What is a prospectus? Offering memorandum?
9. What liability is triggered by a false or misleading prospectus?
10. What is the difference between strict liability and absolute liability?
11. Can a corporation be convicted of a criminal offence? How?
12. Does the principle of limited liability protect a director from criminal liability in the course of performing her duties?
13. What standard of care and skill is expected of corporate directors in relation to environmental offences?
14. Who may perform an audit for a public corporation?

CASES AND PROBLEMS

1. Continuing Scenario

   Adam is the new chef at Ashley's restaurant, and his specialty is mozza sticks, deep fried in vats of peanut oil. At the end of each week, Adam dumps the vats of old oil in the back parking lot and fills the pots again. Erin, the dishwasher, has watched Adam dump the oil for months and is sure this is not the proper way to dispose of used oil, so she calls the Ministry of Environment (MOE) hotline and asks some questions about disposal of cooking oil. After the call, the MOE arrives to investigate and issues a "stop order" prohibiting any further dumping of oil and orders Ashley, personally, as director of the company, to "clean up" the soil under the parking lot. The estimated cost of clean-up is $25 000. Ashley is upset and fires Erin for "going behind her back" to the MOE. What advice will Ashley's lawyer, Brendan, give about her personal liability for the clean-up and firing Erin?

2. About a year ago, MacIntosh, a qualified accountant with substantial business experience, met Kellerman, the owner of a number of business ventures. Kellerman persuaded MacIntosh to invest a substantial proportion of her savings in his

ventures, in return for which it was agreed that she would become a shareholder and director of Kellerman's corporation, "AJP Enterprises Inc." In the course of their discussions, MacIntosh was shown books of accounts and other records that appeared to relate to AJP Enterprises.

MacIntosh transferred $50 000 into a bank account in the name of AJP Enterprises Inc. In return, Kellerman gave her a document assigning to her one-half of his shares in that corporation.

Soon afterward, MacIntosh negotiated an arrangement with an advertising agency, Occidental Broadcasts Ltd., to provide radio and television advertising for the AJP business in return for monthly payments of $2000. Occidental was paid (out of the AJP Enterprises bank account) for the first three months but has not been paid since, although the company continued to provide advertising services for a further five months.

When Occidental eventually demanded payment of a further $10 000, MacIntosh discovered that

(a) the AJP Enterprises bank account contained only $1.73,
(b) Kellerman had disappeared, and
(c) there was no record of any corporation by the name of "AJP Enterprises Inc." or any similar name having been incorporated in any jurisdiction in Canada.

Can MacIntosh be held personally liable for the $10 000 claimed by Occidental?

3. Rainbow Sails Ltd. is a corporation incorporated under the CBCA. It has three shareholders, Brown, Green, and White, who are also the directors of the corporation. White acts as CEO, though he has never been formally appointed to that position.

The company's articles and bylaws include the following provisions (among others):

- The business of the corporation is restricted to the manufacture, buying, and selling of sailboats, and under no circumstances is the corporation to engage in the manufacture, buying, or selling of mechanically powered boats or other craft.

- Any contract or proposed contract involving an expenditure in excess of $5000 must be approved unanimously by the board of directors.

Some months ago, White sold, on behalf of Rainbow, a new sailboat they had manufactured to a customer, Mermaid Marinas Inc. White agreed to accept from Mermaid a small motorboat in part exchange. Although White had no difficulty reselling the motorboat, Brown and Green were angry when they learned of the transaction since they both had an aversion to power boats. They warned White not to enter into any other similar transactions; otherwise, they would deprive him of his powers as CEO.

Some weeks later, Mermaid's sales manager asked White if Rainbow would be interested in buying a floatplane that Mermaid no longer had much use for. White thought the plane was an excellent bargain and agreed to pay $15 000 for it. White took delivery of the plane, and the next day he crashed it.

Brown and Green refuse to countersign any cheque to Mermaid, and Mermaid is now threatening to sue for the price of the plane.

Is Rainbow liable to pay for the plane? If so, does Rainbow have any right of action against White personally?

4. Queensville Quality Cars Ltd. is a large automobile dealership specializing in the sale of both new and used cars and light trucks. Until recently its used-car division was managed by Murphy, who was in charge of a dozen salespersons and mechanics. Murphy was not a director of the corporation.

Following several complaints from customers, alleging, among other things, that the odometers on used cars appeared to have been altered, the managing director of the corporation, Patel, sent written instructions to all division heads (including Murphy) warning them that tampering with odometers is a serious offence and that any officer or employee of the corporation found doing so would face instant dismissal.

Ignoring the warning, Murphy instructed one of his mechanics, Ferreira, to change the odometer on a "traded in" car. Ferreira did so, the car was resold, and the purchaser subsequently complained about the condition of the car.

When questioned, Ferreira admitted to having changed the odometer and was dismissed. At about the same time, Murphy disappeared, taking with him a substantial amount of cash belonging to the corporation. Patel reported both the theft and the tampering with odometers to the police.

Should Queensville Quality Cars Ltd. be convicted of the *Criminal Code* offence of altering an odometer?

5. Gigantic Forestry Inc. has multiple pulp and paper mills in various locations across the country, including one in Grizzly River in British Columbia. It has a government permit to discharge up to 18 200 kg of suspended solids per day into the river. The main suspended solids consist of a lime mud, ash, wood bark, clay, sand, and pulp fibre. Gigantic was charged with exceeding the permitted levels of discharge and pleaded guilty. There had been a previous conviction 18 months earlier, with a fine of $50 000 against the corporation. Two directors, described below, were also charged.

On February 27, Gigantic discharged suspended solids at a level significantly in excess of its permit. The spill resulted from a mechanical failure causing an overflow of lime mud from the storage tank into an emergency spill pond. The pond, being near to capacity when the emergency occurred, overflowed to the river. The suspended solid emission was 35 483 kg per day, almost double the permitted level.

Aggravating factors are as follows: (1) Gigantic had a "response manual" to deal with spills but with no specific guidelines in place to deal with this type of event. The general approach followed was a complete shutdown of production until machinery was repaired. (2) The emergency spill pond had not been cleaned for five or six days. (3) The high-level alarm in the storage tank was not working that evening.

Even with the shutdown of the mud system, mud continued to flow from the mud washer to the storage tank. The shift supervisor instituted procedures to minimize the flow of mud from the mud washer. Unfortunately, unknown to the shift supervisor, mud continued to escape from the pond into the sewer. This was the first time the pond had overflowed to the sewer.

Blinkov is a director and president of Gigantic. He resides in Vancouver, where the corporation has its head office, and visits the Grizzly River site several times a year but spends most of his workdays in Vancouver or visiting the other 11 mills. His assistant, Crowe, is in charge of environmental control systems at all 12 mills and regularly prepares detailed reports on each plant for Blinkov to review. Charbonneau is a director and manager of the Grizzly River mill. She spends most of each day at the mill. The supervisors report to her at least once each month and are instructed to report any problems immediately. She had not personally examined the storage tank or emergency spill pond for several months before the spill. When the night shift supervisor telephoned Charbonneau about the spill, she said she would examine the situation the following morning.

The court fined Gigantic $200 000. Should either or both directors, Blinkov and Charbonneau, be found guilty? Why?

Part 7 Creditors and Debtors

Chapter 28
Secured Transactions

- THE MEANING OF "SECURITY"
- CREATING A SECURITY INTEREST IN PERSONAL PROPERTY
- PERSONAL PROPERTY SECURITY LEGISLATION
- EFFECT OF SECURITY INTERESTS ON PURCHASERS
- SECURITY INTERESTS IN INTANGIBLE PROPERTY
- EFFECT OF SECURITY INTERESTS ON OTHER CREDITORS
- SECURITY FOR BANK LOANS
- STRATEGIES TO MANAGE THE LEGAL RISKS

Almost all businesses operate on credit to some extent. Most businesses owe debts, and most have accounts receivable (debts owed to them by others). An important distinction is drawn—in law and in business practice—between secured and unsecured credit.

In this chapter we examine such questions as:

- What is meant by "security"?
- What is the nature of a conditional sale as compared to a lease?
- How are security interests created?
- What is a floating charge?
- How do the *Personal Property Security Acts* operate to protect secured creditors?
- How are secured creditors' rights enforced?
- How do secured interests affect the rights of third parties?
- What additional protection is given to banks as secured creditors?

THE MEANING OF "SECURITY"

In daily life, we associate the word "security" with safety and reduced risk. The same is true of secured debts—they are considered safer than unsecured debts because they have additional ways to collect the debt beyond the debtor's willingness or promise to pay. Various legal devices give a secured creditor additional assurance that debts owing will be repaid. Most of these devices are agreed to in the contract that creates the debt. They are often called consensual security **interests** and typically give a creditor **collateral security**—that is, a right to take possession of and to sell specified assets of the debtor in satisfaction of the debt. Security agreements can be very broad and may cover all existing and future property owned by a debtor. This chapter deals with security interests taken in tangible and intangible **personal property**. Security in land was dealt with in Chapter 23. Confusion can arise because corporate shares, bonds, and other investment vehicles are also referred to as securities; this is intangible property that may be used to secure a debt.

There are also security interests that arise automatically as a consequence of a transaction, not because the parties to a credit transaction have bargained for them but because of rules of the common law or in statutes. They may be described as non-consensual security interests. We examined examples of such interests as rights of lien and resale available to unpaid sellers of goods and repair services in earlier chapters[1] and will examine other interests in Chapter 29. In this chapter, our main concern is with consensual security interests.

interest some form of right to or in an asset

collateral security an interest in property of a debtor that gives a creditor the right to seize and sell it in the event of non-payment of the debt

personal property chattel paper, documents of title, goods, instruments, intangibles, money, and investment property; includes fixtures but does not include building materials that have been affixed to real property

Security Practices

Suppliers often do not require collateral security when extending credit to regular customers. Unsecured transactions are simpler and cheaper to record, their risk is relatively small because trade credit is usually short-term, and suppliers will not want to offend customers by demanding security. If a supplier loses only a small proportion of its sales revenue by defaults in payment, it may be better to accept the loss than incur additional administrative costs and perhaps lose sales by requiring security for each sale and then seizing secured assets if default occurs.

Collateral security is not a good substitute for selecting a "quality" debtor. However, security reduces risk of non-payment and makes sense in large transactions and in consumer sales. It gives a creditor priority over other creditors in the event of a debtor's bankruptcy.

In consumer transactions, security devices operate primarily as a form of incentive to pay the money owing and avoid repossession of the article purchased. The right of repossession is most likely to be used for only expensive durable goods. Even then, the resale value will often be less than the amount owing. It is common for goods in the hands of a defaulting debtor to deteriorate considerably before repossession.

Rights of a Secured Creditor

An **unsecured creditor**—that is, a general creditor with no security interest in any of the debtor's assets—may ultimately acquire an interest like a security interest through a court action to collect an overdue debt. When a creditor obtains judgment for the amount of the debt, and the debtor fails to pay, the creditor can obtain an execution order or writ authorizing the seizure and sale of certain of the debtor's assets.[2] By contrast, a secured creditor does not need a judgment or an execution order but can

unsecured creditor a creditor who has no security interest in any of the debtor's property

---

[1] See e.g. Chapters 14 and 15.
[2] See "Methods of Enforcing Judgment" in Chapter 13.

priority a first, or prior, right to be repaid out of the debtor's assets

proceed on its own to enforce its rights over the secured asset. In this sense, a security interest provides a creditor with a quick self-help remedy. An unsecured judgment creditor generally has no right to seize any assets already subject to a security interest of another creditor. The secured creditor has **priority** over unsecured creditor.

However, even when a debt is stated to be payable "on demand," the debtor must normally be given time to raise the funds to repay the debt before an asset is seized. If the creditor seizes property without giving reasonable notice, it may be liable in damages.[3]

CASE 28.1 Notice

Murano operated a retail store financed in part by a loan from the Bank of Montreal. The bank became concerned about the financial affairs of the store and wrote to Murano, indicating its intention to liquidate if adequate arrangements were not made within the next six weeks. In fact, the bank took no further steps for three months, at which time the parties met to discuss a request by Murano for a new financing arrangement. The bank agreed to consider the request, but one week later, without giving notice, it appointed a receiver and took possession of the store. It also informed Murano's other creditors of its actions.

Murano lost his entire business, including another store that was not included in the bank's financing arrangement. The court held that the bank had failed to give reasonable notice and that the bank was in breach of duty to its client in disclosing information to other creditors. The bank was liable for Murano's damages.[4]

Security agreements frequently require a debtor to waive any right to notice. After a creditor takes possession, statutes generally require the creditor to give notice to the debtor of the time and place at which the goods are to be sold.[5] Unfortunately for the creditor, when a debtor's financial position deteriorates to the point that the creditor decides to act, secured assets in the possession of the debtor are likely to have disappeared, to have lost value, or are subject to competing creditors' security claims.

CREATING A SECURITY INTEREST IN PERSONAL PROPERTY

security interest an interest in personal property (including goods or intangibles) that secures payment or performance of an obligation

security agreement agreement that creates a security interest, including chattel mortgages, conditional sales contracts, and pledges

A **security interest** is created by an agreement between a lender and borrower that secures a debt against personal property controlled by the debtor. There are many forms a security agreement can take, but the result is the same: A security interest is created. The rules relating to the creation and priority of security interests are largely governed by provincial personal property security legislation of each province,[6] although the common law principles of contract law also apply. The specific form a **security agreement** takes remains important because the terms of these agreements will affect the creditor's rights, obligations, and remedies.[7]

---

[3] *Ronald Elwyn Lister Ltd v Dunlop Canada Ltd* (1982), 135 DLR (3d) 1. At least 10 days' notice must be given before enforcing security in the property of an insolvent debtor; see Chapter 29.

[4] *Murano v Bank of Montreal* (1998), 163 DLR (4th) 21. In *Royal Bank of Canada v W Got & Associates Electric Ltd* (1999), 178 DLR (4th) 385; where the bank failed to give notice before foreclosing on a loan, the bank was held to be in breach of contract and to have committed the tort of conversion. The Supreme Court of Canada allowed punitive damages.

[5] See e.g. *Personal Property Security Act* (PPSA): RSO 1990, c P.10, s 63(4); CCSM c P35, s 59(6); SS 1993, c P-6.2, s 59(6).

[6] All types of security agreements are dealt with under one comprehensive statute known as the *Personal Property Security Act*. See e.g. PPSA, s 75 (1) (BC).

[7] *iTrade Finance Inc v Bank of Montreal* 2011 SCC 26; the Supreme Court went behind the label of a pledge to determine that the substance of a pledge of shares. It was intended to be a security interest. See also *Bank of Montreal v Innovation Credit Union*, [2010] 3 SCR 3.

Familiar Security Agreements

Several types of security agreements have already been considered in previous chapters, particularly the following.

Mortgages Although this chapter deals with collateral security in the form of personal property rather than real property, the concept of priority in relation to land mortgages and to other creditors' claims explained in Chapter 23 remains relevant.

Leases Leases of equipment were examined as an example of bailment in Chapter 15, and leases of land as an interest in real property in Chapter 22. As discussed in Chapter 15, leases may also serve as a type of security device, where items of personal property are acquired on credit.

Consignments The distinction between a consignment of goods and a sale of goods was discussed in Chapter 14. A consignment may also amount to an indirect type of secured credit. Retailers may not have sufficient capital to carry all the inventory they need and may bring in a stock of goods shipped on consignment by a manufacturer or wholesaler. The merchandise remains the property of the manufacturer or wholesaler, who effectively provides financing in the form of goods rather than money.

Other Credit Devices Earlier chapters also dealt with assignments of book debts (Chapter 11) and with pledges (Chapter 15), both of which can be considered methods of securing credit. A third-party guarantee (considered in Chapter 16) is slightly different because the "security" consists of a promise by an additional person, rather than a legal interest in an item of property.

Additional Security Agreements

Other popular forms of security agreements are conditional sale contracts, chattel mortgages, and floating charges.[8]

Conditional Sales A conditional sale is similar to a purchase lease. In a lease, the lessee pays to use the item for a specified period and at the end of that period can elect to buy it, applying rent already paid toward the purchase price. In a conditional sale, the sale is agreed to but the transfer of title to the buyer is delayed until the buyer completes the scheduled installment payments. In the meantime, the buyer has possession of the goods, and the seller retains the title to them as security for the full payment of the purchase price. Both a lessee and a conditional buyer are bailees of the goods.[9]

A conditional sale contract gives the secured party (vendor) a right to take the goods if the debtor defaults, and it gives the secured party priority in the goods over the interests of third parties, especially other creditors.

As a creditor, the conditional seller has the ordinary contractual remedy of suing the debtor for the unpaid balance of the debt. In addition, a conditional seller invariably makes it a term of the agreement that he may retake possession of the goods on default by the buyer. **Repossession** does not affect the ownership of the goods since the seller has retained title from the outset.

A conditional seller is not entitled to use force in recovering the goods. In some provinces a seller is not entitled to repossess goods except by court process. However, in most provinces a conditional seller may repossess the goods upon default and later sue the buyer for any deficiency arising because the amount still owed by the buyer exceeds

repossession the act of taking back possession of property that is in the possession of a defaulting debtor

---

[8] Chattel mortgages, conditional sales contracts, floating charges, pledges, and assignments of book debts are all security agreements covered under the PPSA. See e.g. s 75(2) (BC).

[9] A conditional sale contract often places the conditional buyer under a higher duty by making her responsible for damage to the article whether caused by her or not.

the amount realized on resale of the goods.[10] Consumer protection legislation in some provinces provides that a term in the conditional sale contract allowing the conditional seller to repossess and resell the goods on default is unenforceable once the conditional buyer has paid a certain proportion (for example, two-thirds) of the purchase price.[11]

The rights of a conditional buyer also vary considerably from one province to another. Some provinces permit a conditional buyer to **redeem** within specified periods upon payment of the installments in arrears plus interest and any costs incurred by the seller in repossessing.[12] Other provinces require a conditional buyer who has defaulted to pay the whole unpaid balance of the price—not merely the amounts in arrears—when an **acceleration clause** is included in the conditional sale contract.[13] In most jurisdictions a conditional buyer has a statutory right to receive any surplus realized by a conditional seller that repossesses and resells the goods for more than the amount owed by the buyer plus costs of reselling.[14]

Many vendors who sell goods on the installment plan do not finance the credit transactions themselves. Instead, they sell or assign their conditional sale agreements to finance companies that collect the installments and administer the contracts. Conditional sale contracts also play an important role in financing wholesale purchasers. A retailer or dealer may finance its purchases of stock-in-trade from a manufacturer by buying them from the manufacturer under a conditional sale contract. As a conditional seller, the manufacturer acquires an asset in the form of an account receivable, which it almost invariably assigns to a finance company. As an assignee, the finance company stands in the position of the manufacturing company, with title in the goods withheld from the dealer or merchant (the conditional buyer) until the account is paid in full.

Chattel Mortgages

A **chattel mortgage** is a transfer of an interest in personal property by the mortgagor (borrower) to the mortgagee (lender) as security for a debt, with a condition that if the debt is repaid by a specified date, the interest in the property reverts to the mortgagor.

There are two basic ways a chattel mortgage is created. In the first, the vendor of an article of property "takes back" a mortgage on the property sold. Title is transferred to the buyer with possession and immediately charged with the debt to the vendor. In the second case, the owner of an article mortgages it to a non-vendor lender—usually a bank or financial institution—as security for a loan. That loan may be used either to pay for the article that is being mortgaged or to purchase an entirely different article. A chattel mortgage is often used in the sale of a business as a going concern where all of the office equipment, machinery, or vehicles are included in the sale transaction.

Another common use of the chattel mortgage occurs in the sale of a building with equipment, such as a furnished office building or apartment building. Frequently the price includes both real property and equipment in the building. Not only may the vendor take back a real estate mortgage for the unpaid balance of the purchase price, but he may also take back a concurrent chattel mortgage on all moveable equipment. The chattel mortgage (so long as it is duly registered) avoids any question about whether certain equipment is a fixture; a real estate mortgage would cover only fixtures, but with a concurrent chattel mortgage covering furniture and equipment, the question becomes irrelevant.

---

redeem reclaim the goods and continue with the conditional sale

acceleration clause a provision whereby the full outstanding amount of a debt becomes immediately payable if the debtor defaults in making any installment payment

chattel mortgage a mortgage of personal property

---

[10] See e.g. PPSA, SNS 1995–6, c 13, s 61(6); s 63(5)(f) (Ont); s 60(5) (BC).

[11] See e.g. *Consumer Protection Act, 2002*, SO 2002, c 30, Sch A, s 25; PPSA, s 58(3) (BC). However, a court may still grant the right to repossess and resell on special application by the conditional seller.

[12] See e.g. PPSA, s 62(1) (MB and SK).

[13] See e.g. PPSA, s 66(2)(a) (ON).

[14] See e.g. PPSA, s 64 (ON).

More commonly, chattel mortgages are used as security for loans made by financial institutions. In particular, banks use chattel mortgages as a device for securing credit in the field of consumer financing.

When a borrower finances the purchase of goods with a chattel mortgage, the effect may not seem much different from buying the goods under a conditional sale contract. However, in a conditional sale, the actual goods purchased comprise the collateral. In a chattel mortgage, the debtor may give security in the form of other personal property and even in property acquired after the chattel mortgage has been executed.

A chattel mortgage that includes **after-acquired property** is a very flexible device. It may cover inventories that fluctuate during its term, as some goods are bought and added to inventory while others are sold and subtracted from inventory. The mortgage does not transfer title to specific goods to the creditor, and buyers acquire good title to goods sold by the debtor in the ordinary course of business. The creditor's security interest remains as a suspended priority against general creditors. If the debtor defaults, the secured creditor may then seize whatever property is covered by the chattel mortgage and sell it to satisfy the debt. A chattel mortgage may also cover goods not yet in a deliverable state, such as goods in production and growing crops.

after-acquired property property acquired by the debtor after the debt has been incurred

Contractual remedies for a chattel mortgagee are the same as those of a conditional seller; they are determined by the language of the "contract" and the provisions of the security legislation discussed in the next section. As a creditor, he may sue on the mortgagor's promise to pay the debt, and he may take possession of the mortgaged goods upon default by the mortgagor. A chattel mortgagee invariably reserves the right upon default to resell the goods to a third party. In exercising this right of sale, he must act reasonably and fairly to obtain a good price for them. If not, he may be liable to the mortgagor for the deficiency below the goods' fair market price. If on selling at a fair price, the mortgagee obtains less than the debt outstanding, he may sue the mortgagor for the deficiency, but if there is any surplus, he must return that surplus to the mortgagor.

Floating Charges

It is common for a corporation to borrow money by issuing bonds to the public, using its assets as security. Each certificate issued to a bondholder is evidence of an interest in a **trust deed**—an elaborate form of mortgage on the lands and buildings of the company. The parties to a trust deed are the borrowing corporation (as mortgagor) and a trustee for the bondholders (as mortgagee). Generally, a trust company acts as trustee for the bondholders.

trust deed a document evidencing a mortgage on the property of a corporation

Bonds issued by Canadian corporations frequently provide additional security over and above the mortgage of real property through the creation of a **floating charge**. A floating charge adds those remaining corporate assets not already mortgaged or pledged to the security. When a trust deed includes a provision for a floating charge, the trustee also has access to business assets, including chattels and choses in action, ahead of the unsecured creditors of the corporation.

floating charge a form of mortgage on all the assets of a corporation other than those already specifically charged

A floating charge nicely complements a mortgage of real property because it provides security over the whole of the assets as a working unit. If the corporation defaults in the payment of its bond obligations, the trustee may then more easily place the corporation in the hands of a receiver and manager who can operate it in the interest of the bondholders.

Corporations sometimes issue bonds secured by a floating charge alone and without a mortgage of specific assets. Such a bond is commonly called a **debenture**. The interests that are secured by floating charges also fall within the general scope of personal property security legislation (discussed in the next section), as do other security devices.

debenture an alternative term to describe a corporate bond

> ### CHECKLIST
> ### Agreements Creating Personal Property Security Interests
>
> Personal property security interests may take any of the following forms:
> - conditional sales
> - chattel mortgages
> - floating charges
> - chattel leases
> - consignments
> - pledges
> - assignments of accounts receivable

PERSONAL PROPERTY SECURITY LEGISLATION

Jurisdiction and Application

Every province and territory has a *Personal Property Security Act* (PPSA) in substantially the same form.[15] This legislation applies "to every transaction . . . that in substance creates a security interest";[16] it governs not only conditional sale contracts, chattel mortgages, and assignments of book debts, but also floating charges, pledges, leases and consignments intended as security, and other less common forms. These forms of security are collectively referred to as security agreements.

The PPSA consolidates all the rules into one statute and supports electronic public registry for recording interests.[17] A few concerns remain. Although the provinces are working to reduce the minor variations among the Acts, some inconsistencies still exist.[18] Additionally, conflicts can arise between the relevant provincial legislation and

> ### CASE 28.2 Conflicting Laws
>
> Xtra, a corporation with its head office in Ontario, leased 75 truck trailers to TCT, a corporation located in Alberta. The trailers were used throughout the country. When TCT went bankrupt, Xtra claimed its truck trailers back. GMAC opposed the claim because it had a security interest over all the assets of TCT. GMAC's security interest was registered in Alberta. Xtra's lease was not registered. The question was which province's laws should apply: Alberta's or Ontario's?
>
> At the time, Ontario law did not require the registration of a "true lease," whereas the Alberta PPSA did. The Ontario PPSA determined conflict of laws for goods expected to be used in more than one jurisdiction by "where the debtor was located" at the time the security interest attaches.[19] As the debtor's main place of business was in Alberta, the law of Alberta applied, the leases should have been registered, and GMAC's claim prevailed.[20]

---

[15] See e.g. *Personal Property Security Act*, RSO 1990, c P-10.

[16] Security interest is a defined term under each of the Acts: PPSA, s 1 (BC, ON, AB, MB). *Bank of Montreal v Innovation Credit Union*, 2010 SCC 47 at para 18.

[17] Ronald CC Cuming et al, "Secured Transactions Law in Canada—Significant Achievements, Unfinished Business and Ongoing Challenges" (2011) 50 *Can Bus LJ* 156 at 158.

[18] One inconsistency relates to which motor vehicles require serial numbers to be included in the registration. Ontario's requirement only applies to consumer vehicles, whereas Saskatchewan's requirements apply to many more vehicles and beyond consumer goods; see s 2(1)(o) (SK).

[19] Ontario's conflict of law rules vary by collateral type: PPSA, *supra* note 15, ss 5, 7.

[20] *GMAC Commercial Credit Corp v TCT Logistics Inc* (2004), 238 DLR (4th) 487. See also *Gimli Auto Ltd v BDO Dunwoody Ltd* (1998), 160 DLR (4th) 373.

federal laws, such as the *Bank Act*. Finally, the Act does not apply to non-consensual security interests, nor does it apply to interests in real property.

The very nature of personal property means that it is moveable and may cross jurisdictional boundaries. Each Act contains conflict-of-law provisions that determine which province's law applies in various circumstances.

Conflict of law rules vary depending upon the type of personal property. The law of the jurisdiction where the property is located will apply for tangible property, but the law of the jurisdiction where the debtor is located applies for intangible, mobile, or investment property (not in possession of the lender).[21]

Purpose of PPSA Legislation

When parties create a security interest, they create a debtor–creditor relationship that may take priority over the interests of others. The PPSA legislation establishes a uniform public system that deals with all types of security interests and priority questions not only between debtor and creditor but also between competing creditors. The Acts are complex and technical. This chapter provides a general description of how the legislation works.

The Acts recognize that all security devices have the same purpose—to secure repayment by the debtor. Each province's legislation:

- defines and standardizes the remedies a secured party has against a defaulting debtor,
- creates one system of registration to record and give notice of all secured interests, and
- sets priorities between a secured party on the one hand, and third party purchasers, other secured parties, and general creditors on the other.

The legislation does not prohibit businesses from using their standard contract forms to create security interests or from continuing to refer to them by such traditional labels as "conditional sale contracts" or "chattel mortgages." The legislation does not distinguish between the particular forms of security interest—all are considered security agreements. Interests are entered in the registry through the registration of a common form of **financing statement**. Just as in land registry systems, anyone may search the public system and discover the interests recorded there.

financing statement the document summarizing the details of a security interest that is filed in order to protect that interest

The Acts recognize that both leases and consignments of goods can be used as forms of security. However, as we saw in Chapters 14 and 15, these arrangements are frequently used quite apart from any intention to create a security interest. Most provinces have adopted an approach that effectively avoids the difficulty of distinguishing between the two purposes. A consignment or a lease that secures payment or performance of an obligation is within the scope of the Act.[22] Additionally, the Act applies to commercial consignments and to leases for a term in excess of one year, whether or not they are intended to create a security interest.[23]

Assets subsequently acquired by a debtor can be added to a security interest already in existence, and chattel mortgages may cover after-acquired property such as inventories. This is practical in the business setting because goods in inventory are always changing. However, in consumer transactions, the security interest of sellers or

---

[21] *Ibid.*; Ontario created very specific definitions of "location of debtor" in 2016, which may now conflict with the definitions in other provincial legislation.

[22] See e.g. s 1(1) (BC); s 4(1)(b) (NS); s 2 (ON).

[23] *Ibid.*, s 3(c) (BC); s 3(2) (NB); s 4(2) (NS).

> ### CASE 28.3 Application to Leases
>
> Telecom Leasing leased a car to the B.C. Telephone Company, which in turn leased the car to one of its employees, Giffen, who subsequently became bankrupt. The lease was for a term of more than one year and gave the lessee the option of purchasing the vehicle. Telecom failed to register a financing statement under the (BC) PPSA.
>
> All agreed that the lease was a genuine lease rather than a security arrangement. Nevertheless, the lessor's interest was required to be registered (perfected under the PPSA), and since it had not been, Telecom had no right to retake possession of the vehicle. Giffen's trustee in bankruptcy had priority.[24]

creditors is confined to the exact goods financed and does not extend to any other after-acquired assets of the consumer.

Where the property charged as collateral is disposed of by the debtor, the Acts provide that the security interest attaches to the proceeds.[25]

> ### CASE 28.4 Property Subject to Security Interest
>
> Cardinali bought a boat from a marina under a conditional sale agreement. The marina assigned the contract to a financing company. The boat was defective, and the marina gave Cardinali a new boat in its place. When Cardinali subsequently defaulted in his payments, the finance company repossessed the boat, sold it, and sued Cardinali for the deficiency.
>
> The trial judge found that the new boat represented proceeds of the disposal of the first boat and that the finance company had a security interest in it. The Appeal Court held that the new boat had not been exchanged for the first boat and consequently did not represent proceeds of disposal.[26]

Key Components of the *Personal Property Security Act*

The Act functions around three key components:

- creation of a security interest
- **attachment** of the security interest
- **perfection** of the security interest

attachment the moment in time when a debtor's property becomes subject to a security interest

perfection the moment in time when a creditor's security interest becomes protected

The security interest is created when the creditor and debtor enter into some form of security agreement that gives the creditor an interest in the debtor's personal property to secure repayment of a debt or satisfaction of an obligation.

Attachment Attachment occurs upon performance of the security agreement by both debtor and creditor. A security interest cannot attach to an asset until the debtor has acquired a right to it. Nor does a security interest attach until the creditor has performed his part of the bargain by giving the value promised to the debtor.

Perfection Perfection protects and establishes the priority of the security interest, and there are three ways to do it:

- The secured party takes physical possession of the asset(s)—as in a pledge—ending any false impression of ownership given by the debtor's possession.[27]

---

[24] *Re Giffen*, [1998] 1 SCR 91; see also *Fast Labour Solutions (Edmonton) Limited v Kramer's Technical Services Inc*, 2016 ABCA 266.

[25] See e.g. RSA 2000, c P-7, s 28(1); s 28(1) (NB); s 25(1)(b) (ON). A secured creditor will be able to trace the proceeds into the debtor's bank account: *Massey-Ferguson Industries Ltd v Bank of Montreal* (1983), 4 DLR (4th) 96, varied (1985) 21 DLR (4th) 640 (ON). A priority dispute could develop if another creditor has a security interest in the bank account funds: *iTrade Finance Inc*, *supra* note 7.

[26] *General Motors Acceptance Corp of Canada v Cardinali* (2000), 185 DLR (4th) 141. However, the court found in favour of the finance company on the grounds that the purchaser had agreed to an alteration of the original contract.

[27] See e.g. s 22 (ON). Perfection of an interest in a share with a physical certificate may be done by delivery of the certificate (s. 22(2) (ON)).

- The secured party takes control of an asset that is investment property. Few share certificates ever physically change hands in today's investment world; virtual control over the transfer of an investment will perfect a security interest in it.[28]
- Most often, a secured party registers a financing statement in the PPSA system. The financing statement gives details of the security interest and notice of the creditor's interest. Registration is done online.[29]

A perfected security interest is one that has all three components: creation, attachment, and perfection, as illustrated in Figure 28.1.

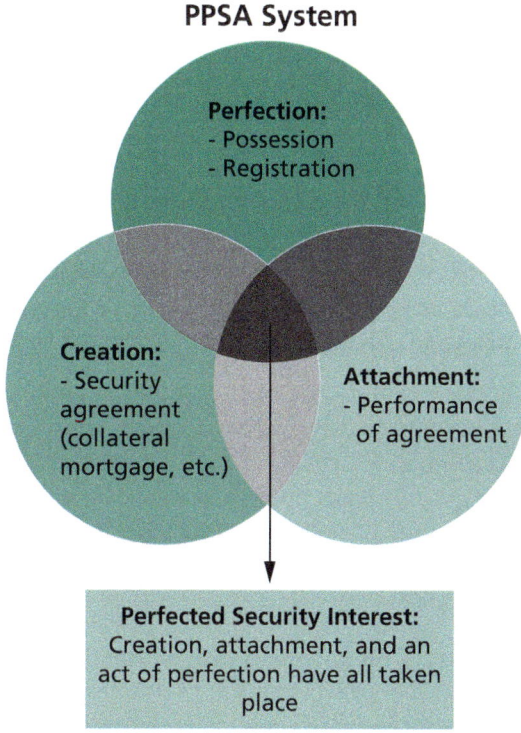

Figure 28.1   The PPSA System

Registration

As described above, each PPSA establishes a centralized online registration system within each province for recording and perfecting security interests. Potential creditors search the system before lending. PPSA searches are completed on a province-by-province basis.

The registration system operates like the land titles system except that the search is usually made against the name of a particular debtor, whereas under the land titles system it is made against a described parcel of land.[30] Where goods have a serial number, this number may be searched as well. The provincial government maintains a compensation fund to reimburse losses caused by incorrectly processed information, and the system provides a guaranteed certificate of search.

---

[28] See e.g. ss 1(2), 22.1, 30.1(ON). See also *Securities Transfer Act, 2006*, SO 2006, c 8, ss 23–26.

[29] See e.g. s 1(1) defining financing statement and s 43 as to registration (BC).

[30] A search against the V.I.N. of any vehicle that may be subject to a security interest; see *Re Lambert* (1994), 119 DLR (4th) 93. This provides additional protection in cases where the debtor's name is incorrectly spelled.

Priority and Competing Interests

unperfected security interest a security interest that is not attached or perfected

perfected security interest a security interest that has attached and is perfected by possession, control, or registration

Completing all three components (creation, attachment, and perfection) protects the security from claims by **unperfected security interest** holders. Subject to some exceptions, the order in time of perfection will determine priority among multiple **perfected security interests**.

ILLUSTRATION 28.1 Perfecting

X Co. borrows money from Y Bank to buy a truck. X Co. gives Y Bank a chattel mortgage on the truck and takes delivery of it. The security interest is created by the loan contract and chattel mortgage. The interest attaches when Y Bank hands over the money to X Co., and X Co. uses it to obtain delivery of the truck from the dealer. Two of the three PPSA requirements are met. The interest will be perfected as soon as Y Bank registers a financing statement.

Generally, the legislation assigns priority to the creditor that first perfects her interest. In practice, this usually means that priority goes to the first to register. A creditor who first creates and attaches her interest might nevertheless lose her priority if she delays perfecting that interest, and a subsequent creditor perfects first. The subsequent creditor might be aware of the unperfected security interest of the first creditor; even so, by registering first, that interest is perfected and obtains priority.

CASE 28.5 First to Register

BMP Corp. sold the assets of its doughnut business to a numbered corporation and took back a chattel mortgage. The mortgage was guaranteed by a Mr. Trafford, whose wife was the sole shareholder of the numbered corporation. Due to an oversight, the financing statement was not registered. Subsequently, Mrs. Trafford registered a financing statement regarding loans she made to the numbered company. She had actual notice of the guarantee given by her husband and of BMP's security interest. When BMP discovered the oversight, it registered its financing statement and brought an application for an order setting aside Mrs. Trafford's financing statement or postponing her interest.

The court held that, notwithstanding her knowledge of the chattel mortgage, Mrs. Trafford's interest had priority.[31]

Perfection or attachment need not occur in any particular order. For example, some lenders register the financing statement (the act of perfection) before the loan money is advanced to the debtor (the act of attachment). Once the loan attaches, perfection dates back to the time of registration.

There are some exceptions to the registration priority rule. If a creditor registers his security interest in after-acquired property, and later a subsequent creditor finances new assets for the same debtor, the new assets become after-acquired property of the debtor and are subject to the original security interest. If the subsequent creditor must stand behind the existing interest in after acquired property, he will not want to finance new acquisitions.

purchase-money security interest (PMSI) the interest that arises when assets purchased by a debtor are charged as security for a loan made to enable acquisition of those specific assets

In recognition of this problem, the Acts give special priority to a **purchase-money security interest (PMSI)** over existing perfected security interests. A PMSI arises when a seller (for example, a conditional seller) reserves a security interest in the actual goods sold to the debtor, or when a lender (for example, a chattel mortgagee) finances a debtor's acquisition of the asset that is used as collateral. The rule ensures financing is available for new asset purchases.

---

[31] *BMP & Daughters Investment Corp v 941242 Ontario Ltd* (1993), 7 BLR (2d) 270.

Business inventories can also give rise to priority disputes. Fortunately, in practice, a business usually has a single source of financing for its inventories, eliminating the need to establish priorities. In financing other business assets, however, competition is likely when one secured creditor claims a charge on after-acquired assets or gives a floating charge over all its assets and then the debtor acquires new equipment under a conditional sale contract. In these circumstances, the legislation gives priority to the PMSI of the conditional seller.[32]

Control has priority over registration for the special category of assets known as investment property, discussed later in this chapter.[33]

EFFECT OF SECURITY INTERESTS ON PURCHASERS

Separation of Possession and Ownership

Security interests typically allow the debtor to have possession of property even when she does not have formal legal ownership of it. Since possession of goods usually creates an appearance of ownership to a third party, the effect may be to mislead an innocent third person. A debtor left in possession of goods may appear to own assets that she, in fact, does not own. The principal safeguard for purchasers now lies in the PPSA requirement that a security interest in goods left in the possession of a debtor must be perfected by registration. Innocent third parties may now search the PPSA databank and discover outstanding registered interests.

Effect of Registration

A properly registered security interest is generally effective to give priority against third parties, except for specified classes of good faith transferees.[34]

Registration is effective indefinitely or for the time period specified in the financing statement, in which case it must be renewed before its expiration in order to maintain its priority.

ILLUSTRATION 28.2 Notice of Security Interest

Peng Ltd. purchases a truck from Federchuk's Ltd. under a conditional sale agreement. Peng makes a down payment and agrees to pay the balance plus finance charges in 18 equal monthly installments. Two months later Peng sells the truck to Tse Ltd. without disclosing the existence of the conditional sale contract. Can Federchuk's gain possession of the truck from Tse despite the fact that it is an innocent purchaser?

In Illustration 28.2, Federchuk's would be able to recover the truck from Tse if it had properly registered its security interest before Peng resold the machine to Tse, since it could have discovered the security interest before making the purchase by making the appropriate search. Tse is not in a stronger position because of her ignorance. Federchuk's claim takes priority because it was perfected before the purported sale to Tse. The same effect would be achieved if, instead of buying on credit by means of a conditional sale, Peng had borrowed the money from a bank, given a chattel mortgage as security, and used the proceeds of the loan to buy the truck.

---

[32] Provided that interest has been perfected; see *Canadian Imperial Bank of Commerce v Otto Timm Enterprises Ltd* (1995), 130 DLR (4th) 91.

[33] *Supra* note 28.

[34] See e.g. s 9(1) (ON); other exceptions exist for employment and pension benefits (s. 30(7)).

Exceptions for Good Faith Buyers

Exceptions to the rights of secured creditors are made for two types of good faith buyers. First, some provinces exempt good faith purchases of small value goods (under $1000) from the PPSA priority rules.[35] This is done because these goods rarely have serial numbers and would be difficult to search effectively. As well, purchase decisions are usually made quickly without the time to do a PPSA search.

The second exception is made for goods sold or leased in the ordinary course of business. When retail purchasers enter a retail outlet, they are entitled to presume that the retailer has ownership of the goods and can sell them free from any security interest. Imagine having to complete a PPSA search before buying a sofa from a furniture store. Still, in the reality of today's business financing, the furniture store has probably financed its entire inventory, which means the sofa is subject to a registered security interest in favour of the finance company. The PPSA provides that when a business secures its inventory either to the original supplier or a finance company, and then sells the products in the ordinary course of business, a retail buyer acquires a good title to the goods.[36] If the dealer fails to meet its obligations, the manufacturer or a finance company holding a registered security interest cannot seize the goods from the retail buyer.

The above rule does not protect buyers of goods from someone who is not a regular seller of those goods. A secured party or his assignee can lawfully seize the goods purchased in a private sale. The buyer's only remedy is to sue the seller for breach of an implied promise to convey good title. Unfortunately, a seller's warranty in a private sale is likely to be of little value.

Registration Practice

If a secured creditor (or his assignee) chooses not to register, his interest continues as an unperfected security interest, and he simply takes a risk that a third party may acquire interests that prevail over his own. Why might a creditor choose not to register? The answer turns on the nature of the creditor's business. Suppose a creditor's business is primarily one of selling relatively low-value goods to many different customers. She may not find it worthwhile to trace goods wrongfully disposed of by a debtor and then to sue in order to recover them from an innocent purchaser. Instead, she may decide to save the trouble and expense of registering the security interest in the first place. In practice, disputes do not often arise between a secured creditor and a subsequent transferee of goods, and, except for more expensive durable goods, retail conditional sellers (or finance companies as their assignees) may decide not to register conditional sale contracts.

On the other hand, sales by a manufacturer or wholesaler often involve taking a security interest in assets of a business that has other creditors as well. For instance, a truck manufacturer may sell a fleet of vehicles under a conditional sale agreement to a large retail business. The retail business purchases stock-in-trade from suppliers who also provide credit. If the business becomes insolvent, a dispute may arise over the truck manufacturer's claim to repossess the vehicles and deprive the other creditors of an important asset in the bankruptcy proceedings. Risk of this kind of dispute provides the main incentive for registration, since registration of a security interest is essential for a creditor to maintain priority against other creditors.[37]

---

[35] See e.g. s 30 (BC), ss 3, 4 (SK); Ontario does not have this exception.
[36] See e.g. s 28(1) (ON).
[37] See e.g. s 20 (AB, BC, ON and SK).

Maintaining Perfection

The creditor must update its registration when changes occur or risk losing its perfected status. In addition to renewing registrations before any expiry date, creditors must update registrations when a debtor's name changes, the location of the debtor or collateral changes, the asset is sold, or changes are made to the terms of the loan.[38]

SECURITY INTERESTS IN INTANGIBLE PROPERTY

Assignment of Book Debts

Businesses often give a conditional **assignment of book debts** or accounts receivable to a bank or other creditor to secure continuing indebtedness such as a line of credit. As noted in Chapter 11, an assignment of this kind is conditional in two respects. First, the amount of the accounts receivable used as security fluctuates with the state of accounts between the borrowing business (assignor) and its customers. Second, the assignment is only triggered by default. As long as the borrowing business keeps its loan in good standing, the security arrangement does not materialize in an actual assignment, with notice to the borrowing business's customers.

assignment of book debts security interest in the debtor's accounts receivable

Under the PPSA, an assignment is ineffective against creditors of an assignor and against subsequent assignees of the book debts unless it is properly registered.[39] The object is to assure prospective creditors of a business that, unless there is registered public notice to the contrary, the assets of the business in the form of accounts receivable will be available to meet their claims. Registration provides public notice that those accounts are not available to satisfy debts. Defences available to the account debtor against the business will be equally effective against the secured creditor.[40]

Investment Property

Financial assets and investment property receive special treatment under the PPSA. Investment property includes shares or bonds (with or without physical certificates), securities accounts (where a dealer, broker, or bank holds financial assets in an investment account on behalf of the investor), futures contracts, and futures accounts. Typically, these assets are held by an intermediary (bank, broker, or dealer) and not by the investor himself, so customized rules for attaching and perfecting a PPSA security interest are required. In addition to possession and registration, a creditor's security interest in investment property may be perfected by "control."[41] The creditor may establish control by changing the name on the intermediary's account to the creditor's or, more often, by entering into a control agreement with the investor and the securities account intermediary under which the investor transfers her power to instruct the intermediary to the creditor. Control is the best way to perfect interests in this type of intangible property because interests perfected by control get priority even over registration when there are competing claims.[42] More than one creditor may have control over financial assets, and if so, priority goes to the one who first obtained control.[43]

---

[38] See e.g. ss 5, 48 (ON) (as to transfer of collateral with or without prior knowledge).

[39] Registration is the only way to perfect an interest in accounts receivable. See e.g. ss. 22, 23 (ON).

[40] See s 40 (ON).

[41] See e.g. s 22.1 (ON), s 24.1(BC); *Securities Transfer Act, 2006, supra* note 28, ss 23–28.

[42] See e.g. s 30.1 (ON).

[43] *Ibid*.

EFFECT OF SECURITY INTERESTS ON OTHER CREDITORS

Conflicting Priorities

Debtors often have multiple creditors who compete with each other for priority over the debtor's assets, especially when a liquidation of all the assets of a debtor is insufficient to pay the full claims of all creditors. Despite the PPSA's single registration system covering most forms of security interest, there can be problems in interprovincial situations, and there are some personal property security interests remaining outside the scope of the PPSA.[44]

Arrears of rent claims are an example. A landlord of premises sometimes distrains for arrears of rent and claims fixtures that are subject to a security interest that has been registered under the PPSA.[45] Repairer's liens are another example that could conflict with a conditional seller of a vehicle with a perfected security interest under the PPSA.[46] Some acts include priority provisions; for example British Columbia's PPSA states that it has priority over other statutes but not the consumer protection legislation.[47] Conflicting claims to PPSA priority frequently arise in bankruptcy proceedings[48] and with respect to pensions.[49] Conflicts exist between provincial PPSA laws and the federal *Bank Act*.[50]

CHECKLIST

Priority Rules Under the PPSA

(a) First to perfect has priority.

(b) When all competing interests have been perfected by registration, first to register has priority.

(c) The first security interest perfected by registration may lose priority to

   (i) a security interest perfected by possession prior to the other interest's registration,

   (ii) a security interest in investment property perfected by control,

   (iii) a purchase-money security interest,

   (iv) a statutory lien or trust (landlord/tenant, repairer's lien, bankruptcy, pension),

   (v) a good faith purchaser of small valued goods or goods in the ordinary course of business, or

   (vi) a subsequent registered interest if the first registration expires (in some provinces registrations expire and must be renewed to maintain priority).

---

[44] See e.g. *GMS Securities & Appraisals Ltd v Rich-Wood Kitchens Ltd* (1995), 121 DLR (4th) 278, involving conflict between the (Ontario) *Mortgages Act*, the *Registry Act*, and the PPSA.

[45] *859587 Ontario Ltd v Starmark Property Management Ltd* (1999), 42 BLR (2d) 16.

[46] See *Canadian Imperial Bank of Commerce v Kawartha Feed Mills Inc* (1998), 41 OR (3d) 124; *General Electric Capital Canada Inc v Interlink Freight Systems Inc* (1998), 42 OR (3d) 348; not followed in *Riordan Leasing Inc v Veer Transportation Services Inc* (2002), 61 OR (3d) 536.

[47] Sections 73, 74 (BC).

[48] See e.g. *Royal Bank of Canada v Sparrow Electric Corp* (1997), 143 DLR (4th) 385, trustee in bankruptcy was faced with claims under the Alberta PPSA, the federal *Bank Act*, and the *Income Tax Act*.

[49] See e.g. s 30(7) (ON); *Grant Forest Products Inc v The Toronto-Dominion Bank*, 2015 ONCA 570.

[50] *Bank of Montreal v Innovation Credit Union.*, 2010 SCC 47; *Royal Bank of Canada v Radius Credit Union Ltd*, 2010 SCC 28.

INTERNATIONAL ISSUE
Mobile Equipment

Large mobile equipment presents a financing challenge. Lenders involved in financing the purchase of things like aircraft equipment often take an interest in the equipment as security for the loan, knowing the equipment will often be in foreign jurisdictions. Creditors need reassurance that their security will be protected and have priority over other interests even when the equipment is far from home.

In 2001, 53 member states of the United Nations International Institute for the Unification of Private Law (UNIDROIT) adopted the Convention on International Interests in Mobile Equipment (the Cape Town Convention), which addressed the creation, perfection, and priority of security in large mobile equipment.[51] The convention proposed a system similar to the domestic PPSA system with the creation of an "international interest" and a searchable electronic registration system. Priority is determined on a "first in time" registration basis. Creditors with priority in the international system are entitled to repossess the secured equipment even when it is in a foreign (member) jurisdiction. The convention came into force on March 1, 2006, after ratification by eight countries. Canada, the United States, the United Kingdom, France, and Germany have ratified the convention and are introducing domestic legislation to implement its terms with respect to aircraft equipment.[52] The international priority regime overrides PPSA rules, so provinces across Canada are adopting corresponding legislation.[53] The international registry is supervised by the International Civil Aviation Organization.

Questions to Consider

1. An international interest would override the domestic rules of priority for PPSA and bankruptcy. What is the rationale for this position?
2. How do you think this convention will affect lending decisions and terms?
3. What is the incentive for a developing nation to adopt the convention?

Sources: Sean D Murphy, *United States Practice in International Law*, Vol. 2, (Cambridge: Cambridge University Press, 2005) at 383–90; "Cape Town Convention on Financing of High-Value, Mobile Equipment" (2004) 94(4) *American Journal of International Law* 852–4; http://www.unidroit.org/english/conventions/mobile-equipment/mobile-equipment.pdf.

SECURITY FOR BANK LOANS

Loans under the *Bank Act*

The right to lend to primary producers against the security of their products is a distinctive feature of Canadian banking practice. The production of raw materials dominated the early Canadian economy. Typically, the producers—usually small-scale farmers—required short-term financial assistance to help defray costs through the growing season. Appropriate financing is a short-term loan that must be repaid from the proceeds of sale of the goods whose production the loan is financing. The *Bank Act* creates a completely separate system for the types of assets that may serve as security and the types of borrowers who may qualify for this type of bank loan.

Section 427 of the current federal *Bank Act*[54] empowers Canadian chartered banks to lend to the special types of borrower, including:

- wholesale or retail purchasers or shippers of, or dealers in, (i) products of agriculture, the forest, the quarry and mine, the sea, lakes, and rivers; and (ii) wares and merchandise whether manufactured or not
- manufacturers

---

[51] UNIDROIT, Convention on International Interests in Mobile Equipment, November 16, 2001, http://www.unidroit.org/instruments/security-interests/cape-town-convention.

[52] *International Interests in Mobile Equipment (Aircraft Equipment) Act*, SC 2005, c 3. The Convention was extended beyond aircraft equipment to include railway and space assets.

[53] See e.g. *International Interests in Mobile Aircraft Equipment Act*, SA 2006, c I-6.5 (proclaimed in force April 1, 2013).

[54] *Bank Act*, SC 1991, c 46.

- aquaculturalists
- farmers
- fishermen

The types of security that banks are authorized to take vary with the type of borrower and have become quite diverse. At the retail and wholesale levels, a bank may take primary produce or manufactured items of inventory held in stock pending resale. Manufacturers may borrow under the section on the security of inventories of raw materials, work-in-process, and finished goods. When lending to farmers, a bank may accept as security crops growing or produced on the farm, livestock, or agricultural equipment. The section permits advances to a farmer for the purchase of seed, fertilizer, or pesticides with future crops serving as security for the loan; the purchase of feed with the livestock as security; the purchase of agricultural equipment, with the equipment itself as security; and repairs, improvements, and additions to farm buildings on the security of agricultural equipment. Fishermen may obtain loans on the security of fishing vessels, equipment, supplies, or products of the sea.

Rights of a Lending Bank

The security taken by a bank is neither a pledge nor a chattel mortgage. The borrower does not physically transfer the assets to the bank as security, and the bank does not acquire title to the property as security as the debtor must be free to sell them.

A borrower under section 427 signs an agreement containing the following promises:[55]

- to keep the property insured and free from claims
- to account to the bank for the proceeds of sales
- to give the bank a right to take possession in the event of default or neglect
- to grant a power of attorney to the bank
- to consent to the sale of the security without notice or advertisement if the borrower defaults

While the loan is in good standing, the borrower must apply the money realized from the sale of the goods toward a reduction of the loan. As a further assurance that the proceeds from sales are applied against the loan, a bank frequently takes a conditional assignment of the borrower's accounts receivable. If the borrower defaults, and the bank takes possession of the goods in the borrower's hands and sells them, the bank is entitled to retain out of the proceeds whatever amount will repay the balance owing on the loan plus costs.[56] Any surplus belongs to the borrower, and any deficiency represents a debt still due.

To protect its security against a borrower's unsecured creditors and subsequent purchasers or mortgagees in good faith, notice of *Bank Act* security is filed with the Bank of Canada.[57] Filing a notice gives the bank priority over other persons dealing with the borrower.[58] In order to protect the value of the security itself, a bank may also require borrowers other than farmers or fishermen to submit at frequent intervals a statement showing the current value and location of the goods comprising the security.

---

[55] *Ibid.*, s 427.

[56] Employees of the borrower take priority over the bank to the extent of three months' arrears of wages. *Ibid.*, s 427(7).

[57] *Ibid.*, ss 427(4), (5).

[58] See *Royal Bank of Canada v Lions Gate Fisheries Ltd* (1991), 76 DLR (4th) 289.

Other Forms of Collateral Security for Bank Loans

In addition to or instead of security under section 427, a bank may require any of the following types of security as a condition for granting credit:

- an assignment of a warehouse receipt, representing title to goods while held in storage, or of an order bill of lading representing title to goods while in the course of transit
- a pledge of shares or bonds, accompanied by a power of attorney signed by the borrower, authorizing the bank to sell them as the borrower's agent if need be
- a pledge of drafts drawn by the borrower against his customers
- an assignment of book debts
- an assignment of the cash surrender value of a life insurance policy
- a chattel mortgage
- a real estate mortgage[59]
- a guarantee by a third party

In addition to holding collateral security provided by the borrower, the bank may exercise a right of lien on other personal property belonging to the borrower in the bank's possession.[60] A bank may apply against a loan any draft that the borrowing business has left with it for collection.[61] It may apply in settlement of the loan any bank deposit balances kept with it by the borrowing business if it has not previously earmarked these balances for some particular purpose.[62] A bank lien does not extend to property left with the bank for safekeeping.[63] When a bank is acting as a securities administrator (administering an investor's securities account), it is entitled to a security interest in the financial assets of the account for unpaid balances; these rights are governed not by the *Bank Act* but by special PPSA rules of attachment and perfection in conjunction with *Securities Transfer Acts*.[64]

Conflicts Between the *Bank Act* and *Personal Property Security Acts*

As described above, banks may utilize a wide range of security devices. They can take advantage of the provisions of section 427 of the *Bank Act*, or they can use the more common forms of security governed by the PPSA. The range of options available has led to conflicting claims between banks and other creditors. The *Bank Act* applies to a narrower list of assets, which means banks make use of both systems.

The provisions of the *Bank Act*, as federal legislation, set the rules for establishing priority when conflicts arise, not the provincial PPSA acts.[65] Section 426 (7) gives priority to security registered under the *Bank Act* system over any after-acquired rights in the security and over any prior existing unperfected interests of which the bank had

---

[59] Normally, a mortgage loan is limited to 80 percent of the value of the property; further restrictions apply to loans made on the security of residential (as opposed to commercial) property: *Bank Act*, *supra* note 54, s 418(1).

[60] *Re Williams* (1903), 7 OLR 156.

[61] *Merchants Bank v Thompson* (1912), 26 OLR 183.

[62] *Riddell v Bank of Upper Canada* (1859), 18 UCQB 139.

[63] *Leese v Martin* (1873), LR 17 Eq 224. Rights may vary depending upon terms of the securities administrator contract.

[64] See e.g. PPSA, ss 12.1, 19.1, 24.1 (BC).

[65] *Bank of Montreal v Innovation Credit Union*, 2010 SCC 47 at paras 16, 27–29, 34.

no knowledge. Therefore, the only PPSA interests that could have priority over a registered *Bank Act* security are those that are perfected before the *Bank Act* registration.[66]

> ### Ethical Issue   Is the Law Too Favourable Toward Secured Creditors?
>
> What about the interests of other stakeholders? According to one commentator, "Nowhere in the world is there a system for the regulation of secured financing that is more accommodating to secured creditors than the Canadian PPSAs."[67] It has been estimated that, in most insolvencies, at least 90 percent of the debtor's assets go to satisfy the claims of secured creditors—mainly the banks—leaving little or nothing for unsecured creditors such as suppliers, contractors, and employees.
>
> Recent high-profile bankruptcies highlighted the problem. Often, employees have been left with unpaid wages and have lost their accrued pension benefits while the banks walk away with all the assets.[68] What is perhaps even worse are those cases where the secured creditors are the owners of the business themselves. In 2004, a pulp plant closed down in a small New Brunswick mill town. About 400 people lost their jobs when the owners of the pulp mill decided to close the plant and declare bankruptcy. Most employees also lost their pensions. Many of them had worked at the plant for over 20 years. The primary secured creditor, with claims exceeding $34 million, was the New York corporation that owned all the company's shares.
>
> **Questions to Consider**
>
> 1. Are secured creditors given too much protection?
> 2. Should the owners of a business be allowed to be its secured creditors?

Strategies to Manage the Legal Risks

Businesses may become creditors as suppliers of goods and services or as financiers of large-scale projects. Obviously the strategy to manage the risks will be different depending upon the amount of money involved. Small amounts owed by many debtors for individually small valued goods may not be worth the time and expense associated with repossession. If this is the case, there is little point in spending the time and money on complying with the PPSA. The creditor may always still sue the debtor on his promise to pay. However, for durable goods of high value, businesses will want to preserve their rights against other creditors and third-party purchasers, and this can only be done if they perfect their interests under the PPSA. Searches of PPSA and *Bank Act* databanks should be completed prior to extending credit. Search not only by debtor name but by serial number whenever possible. Searches should be completed even by consumers whenever they are completing a private sale, such as a used motor vehicle purchase.

Since PPSA priority goes to the first to register, and registration need not wait until attachment, creditors should register immediately upon completion of the agreement. Subsequent attachment will retroactively set the priority date as of registration. Since registration is done by the user online, careful attention to spelling, birth dates, and serial numbers will reduce the possibility of errors that could invalidate the security interest.

Finally, since security interest may lose perfection due to changes in location of debtor or collateral, creditors should monitor changes in names and addresses and train employees to act promptly when information comes to their attention.

---

[66] *Bank Act*, *supra* note 54, ss 425.1, 426(7)(7.1), 428(1)(1.1)(2); see also *Financial System Review Act*, SC 2012, c 5.

[67] R.C.C. Cuming, "Canadian Bankruptcy Law: A Secured Creditor's Heaven" (1994–5) 24 Can. Bus. L.J. 17 at 21. University of Toronto Press.

[68] See e.g. Nortel Retirees and Former Employees Protection Canada (NRPC), http://www.nortelpensioners.ca.

QUESTIONS FOR REVIEW

1. What is meant by "collateral security"?
2. Why might a creditor choose not to take security for a debt?
3. In what way do security devices act as an incentive to repay one's debts?
4. What are the principal types of security interest?
5. Why is a lease of personal property commonly treated as a security interest?
6. What is an "acceleration clause"?
7. Distinguish between a chattel mortgage and a pledge.
8. What is the principal difference between a conditional sale agreement and a chattel mortgage?
9. How can a creditor obtain a security interest in property that the debtor does not yet possess?
10. What is a "floating charge"?
11. How is priority determined in the PPSA system?
12. What is the function of a "financing statement"?
13. What does it mean that a security interest must be "perfected"?
14. What is a "purchase-money security interest," and why is it given special priority?
15. What allowance is made for a consumer buying goods from a seller in the business of selling those goods?
16. What types of loan receive special protection under the *Bank Act*?
17. How is a security interest protected under the *Bank Act*?

CASES AND PROBLEMS

1. Continuing Scenario

    Ashley renovated the "Ashley's Too" kitchen, including a new built-in refrigeration system. She financed the improvements as follows:

    - The restaurant entered into a conditional sales contract with the manufacturer of the refrigerator.
    - Ashley paid for the remaining renovation out of the existing "Ashley's Too" credit line at the bank. When the credit line was opened four years ago, it was secured by a chattel mortgage over all existing and future restaurant equipment.

    Explain how each creditor would obtain maximum protection for its security under the PPSA. Give your opinion on who would have priority if all creditors properly completed all requirements. How would your answer change if Ashley financed the remaining renovation with a separate bank loan secured against her personal investment account held at the same bank?

2. In May 1994, SIS Ltd. leased two large, portable, tent-like structures to Cansaw Services Inc. for a term of 24 months, at a monthly rental of $11 000. In December of the same year, Cansaw negotiated a loan from the Regal Bank and executed a general security agreement, which gave the Bank a security interest in

    > the undertaking of Cansaw and all of Cansaw's present and after-acquired personal property including, without limitation, in all goods, intangibles, money, and securities now owned or hereafter owned or acquired by or on behalf of Cansaw . . . and in all proceeds and renewals thereof, accretions thereto and substitutions therefor . . . , and including, without limitation, all of the following now owned or hereafter owned or acquired by or on behalf of Cansaw: all equipment (other than inventory) of whatever kind and wherever situated, including, without limitation, all machinery, tools, apparatus, plant, furniture, fixtures, and vehicles of whatsoever nature or kind.

The bank registered its security interest under the (Alberta) *Personal Property Security Act* on the same day.

By May 1996, Cansaw's business was in severe financial difficulties. It had not paid rent to SIS for almost six months and owed them $65 000 in arrears. Its debts to the bank now totalled almost $1 million.

On May 3, 1996, the bank delivered a written notice to Cansaw that it was in breach of the financing agreement and gave it one week to remedy its breach. On May 16, 1996, the bank demanded payment of the outstanding debt and delivered a notice of intention to enforce its security (under s 244 of the *Bankruptcy and Insolvency Act*). A few days later, the directors of SIS learned of Cansaw's problems with the bank and gave instructions to a civil enforcement company to enter Cansaw's premises and to dismantle and repossess the structures. At the same time, acting on the advice of its lawyer, SIS registered a security interest in the structures.

The bank demanded that SIS return the structures, claiming that its general security agreement covered the structures and had priority over the claim of SIS. SIS replied that it was the owner of the structures and was entitled to repossess them since Cansaw had defaulted on payment of the rent. Who has the better claim?

3. Clarkson purchased an automobile from Easyprice Autos for $17 000, under a conditional sale agreement. Easyprice assigned the conditional sale contract to CVF Inc., which advanced Clarkson the bulk of the purchase price. CVF immediately registered its security interest under the (Ontario) *Personal Property Security Act*.

    Six months later, Clarkson entered into a second conditional sales contract with Sonmax Corp. for the purchase and installation of stereo equipment in the vehicle at a cost of $3500, including financing charges. CVF was not informed of this second contract. Sonmax promptly registered a lien against the vehicle under the *Repairs and Storage Liens Act*.

    A few months later, when Clarkson fell into arrears with his repayments, Sonmax repossessed the vehicle and gave Clarkson notice of its intention to sell the vehicle to secure repayment of what was owed it. At that point, CVF learned of the action by Sonmax and also claimed the vehicle.

    Which firm has the prior claim?

4. Avila purchased a secondhand Cadillac from Better Buy Motors Ltd. under a conditional sale agreement. She used the car for several months in her work as a sales representative and paid her installments regularly. When she had only two installments left to pay, the car was towed out of her driveway and delivered to Fancy Finance Corp., on instructions of that company. Avila had never heard of Fancy Finance before. It informed her that it had "repossessed" the car under a prior, properly registered chattel mortgage that it held and that the chattel mortgagor had fraudulently sold the car to Better Buy Motors.

    Examine the nature of Avila's rights, and indicate against whom they are available. What factors should be taken into account in assessing her loss?

5. Holmes purchased a refrigerator and stove from Watts Electric Ltd. under a conditional sale agreement. Watts Electric Ltd. discounted the contract with Domestic Finance Co. Neither Watts Electric nor Domestic Finance registered the agreement.

    Several months later, Holmes sold the appliances to Fischer for cash, without disclosing that there was still an unpaid balance owing to Domestic Finance, and left the province. After Holmes defaulted payment, Domestic Finance discovered that Fischer had possession of the appliances and repossessed them. Fischer then sued Domestic Finance for wrongful seizure of the appliances.

    State the arguments for the plaintiff and the defendant. What should the decision be?

6. Oliver purchased a used car from Hardy Motors Ltd. for $5500 and paid $3800 in cash as a down payment on the understanding that he would have 30 days to

pay the balance. The manager of Hardy Motors Ltd. stated that 30-day credit was unusual for this type of purchase and that he would still have to get Oliver's signature on a conditional sale agreement "as a matter of form." Oliver signed the agreement, which included a term that Oliver would pay the balance of the purchase price over 24 months in monthly installments of $89.50 each. The manager told Oliver he would hold the conditional sale agreement for 30 days so Oliver would have that time to raise the balance of the purchase price.

Hardy Motors Ltd. was in financial trouble. In breach of its understanding with Oliver, the company at once discounted (assigned) the conditional sale contract with Vanguard Finance Co. The finance company informed Oliver of the assignment and requested payment to it of the monthly installments specified in the conditional sale agreement. Oliver ignored the notice, and before the expiration of the 30 days, paid the balance of $1700 directly to Hardy Motors Ltd. Soon after, Hardy Motors Ltd. was adjudged bankrupt, and the manager absconded with the cash assets of the business. Vanguard Finance seized the car from Oliver, who then sued the finance company for wrongful seizure, asking for a court order for return of the car to him.

Should Oliver's action succeed?

Chapter 29
Creditors' Rights

- **STATUTORY ARRANGEMENTS FOR THE PROTECTION OF CREDITORS**
- **THE *BANKRUPTCY AND INSOLVENCY ACT***
- **ADMINISTRATION OF A BANKRUPT'S AFFAIRS**
- **OTHER METHODS OF LIQUIDATION AND REORGANIZATION**
- **BUILDERS' LIENS**
- **OTHER STATUTORY PROTECTION OF CREDITORS**
- **LIMITATIONS STATUTES**
- **STRATEGIES TO MANAGE THE LEGAL RISKS**

In this chapter, we examine the ways in which the rights of creditors are protected and enforced. The main focus is on the *Bankruptcy and Insolvency Act*, but consideration is also given to other statutes and, in particular, to the provincial laws regarding builders' liens, also known as mechanics' liens or construction liens in some provinces.

In this chapter we consider such questions as:

- What are the principal objectives of bankruptcy law?
- How does bankruptcy law distinguish between different types of debtors—and why?
- What constitutes an "act of bankruptcy"?
- What principles govern the administration of a bankrupt's assets?
- What is a builders' lien?
- How are the interests of contractors and subcontractors protected?
- What is the effect of limitation periods on creditors' rights?

STATUTORY ARRANGEMENTS FOR THE PROTECTION OF CREDITORS

Most debt debtors are honest and pay their debts promptly if they are able to do so. Consequently, resorting to legal procedures to collect money owed by solvent debtors is comparatively unusual. But, in some cases, a debtor's financial position may become so hopeless that it is unwise or impossible for him to continue to carry on business. A debtor becomes **insolvent** when he is unable to pay his debts as they fall due or when his liabilities exceed his realizable assets. When a debtor finds himself in that condition, at least some of his creditors will go unpaid.

insolvent unable to pay one's debts as they fall due or liabilities exceed realizable assets

A business is typically both a creditor and a debtor. It uses credit to grow the business and extends credit to customers in the ordinary course of doing business. Therefore, it is important to understand the rules of debt collection. A number of statutes have as their main purpose the enforcement of creditors' claims. These acts set out the rights of creditors both against their debtors and against other creditors. In this chapter, we will review the ways in which the *Bankruptcy and Insolvency Act* (BIA), the *Companies' Creditors Arrangement Act*, and the *Builders' Lien Acts* assist in this purpose. Other provincial legislation protects debtors from excessive behaviour by creditors.

THE *BANKRUPTCY AND INSOLVENCY ACT*

Under the *Constitution Act, 1867*, the federal Parliament has jurisdiction over bankruptcy.[1] It passed the *Bankruptcy and Insolvency Act* (BIA) to provide a process for releasing an honest debtor from her obligations once all her assets had been distributed to his creditors.[2]

The *Bankruptcy and Insolvency Act* performs a number of functions:

- It establishes a uniform process for bankruptcy throughout the country as inexpensively as possible.
- It provides for an equitable distribution of the debtor's assets among his various creditors.
- It provides a framework for preserving and reorganizing the debtor's business or affairs by working out an arrangement with the agreement of his creditors to avoid a total liquidation of a debtor's estate, if possible.
- It provides for the release of an honest but unfortunate debtor from his obligations and offers a fresh start free of debts.

Competing Policy Issues

Insolvency involves the balancing of many stakeholder interests: creditors, debtors, consumers, business, government, and the public as a whole. Business confidence and respect for the law are reinforced if creditors are able to recover what is lawfully

---

[1] Other federal insolvency statutes include the *Companies' Creditors Arrangement Act*, RSC 1985, c C-36 and the *Winding-Up and Restructuring Act*, RSC 1985, c W-11. Some provincial legislation also deals with debtor behaviour; see e.g. *Assignments and Preferences Act*, RSO 1990, c A.33; *Execution Act*, RSO 1990, c E.24. When provincial and federal legislation dealing with insolvency conflicts, the federal statute prevails: *British Columbia v Henfrey Samson Belair Ltd* (1989), 59 DLR (4th) 726 (SCC).

[2] *Bankruptcy and Insolvency Act*, RSC 1985, c B-3, as significantly amended by SC 1992, c 27; SC 2005, c 47; and SC 2007, c 36 (in force 2009); *Alberta (Attorney General) v Moloney* 2015 SCC 51 at paras 32–44 (as to purpose of legislation).

owing to them. But their interests may diverge from that of society generally in a number of ways. The chief concern of most creditors is to quickly collect as much as possible of what is owed to them. They may have little interest in whether a debtor's business can be saved and turned around. Bankruptcy law, however, contains provisions whereby creditors may be encouraged, and sometimes compelled, to accept an arrangement designed to save a business and therefore the jobs it provides. Again, a creditor normally wishes to preserve the possibility of recovering in full what she is owed, even if this is not possible in the debtor's present financial circumstances. However, it is in the public interest to allow an honest but unfortunate debtor to be discharged from his debts once he has paid as much as possible and to give him a fresh start.

One of the aims of bankruptcy legislation is to promote an atmosphere of confidence in business relations, and confidence would be undermined if bankruptcy fraud went unpunished. Therefore, the Act contains provisions to punish dishonest debtors and to prevent them from re-engaging in business activities.

There are, of course, limits to what even well-drafted legislation can achieve. In many situations, by the time bankruptcy occurs, the damage done to creditors' claims is irreparable. The best protection for creditors is to be careful in granting credit. To assist prospective creditors by making more information available to them, the Act requires certain information to be filed concerning bankrupt debtors and the directors and officers of bankrupt corporations.

INTERNATIONAL ISSUE
Cross-Border Insolvency

In 1997, the United Nations Commission on International Trade Law adopted a Model Law on Cross-Border Insolvency.[3] It addresses the jurisdictional issues associated with multinational corporations and foreign bankruptcy proceedings. The model law proposes that international cooperation in transborder insolvency be achieved using three strategies:

- authorizing courts to coordinate and cooperate with each other
- restricting the scope of local (domestic) bankruptcy proceedings
- granting local relief to representatives of foreign proceedings.[4]

Canada's 2009 reform of insolvency law incorporates the general concepts advanced by the model law with some modification in form. One interesting variation is the inclusion of a provision that allows a court to refuse to make an order that is not in compliance with Canadian law or if doing so would be contrary to public policy. Also, Canadian courts are not obligated to enforce an order made by a foreign court.[5]

Questions to Consider

1. Why is international cooperation important?
2. What circumstances might be considered contrary to public policy?
3. How do these limitations respect domestic sovereignty?

---

[3] http://www.uncitral.org/uncitral/en/uncitral_texts/insolvency/1997Model.html.

[4] Industry Canada, Office of the Superintendent of Bankruptcy, http://strategis.ic.gc.ca/eic/site/bsf-osb.nsf/eng/br02261.html.

[5] Supra note 2, s 284(2); Macia Jones, "Bill C-12: An Act to amend the Bankruptcy and Insolvency Act, the Companies' Creditors Arrangement Act, the Wage Earner Protection Program Act, and Chapter 47 of the Statutes of Canada 2005," LS-584E, Legislative Summaries, Library of Parliament, December 14, 2007, (clauses 60, 81), http://www.parl.gc.ca/common/bills_ls.asp?lang=E&ls=c12&source=library_prb&Parl=39&Ses=2 (last visited May 30, 2014).

Government Supervision

The BIA (s. 5) creates the position of superintendent of bankruptcy, who keeps a record of all bankruptcy proceedings in Canada and has a general supervisory function over all bankrupt estates. The superintendent is responsible for investigating the character and qualifications of persons applying for licences to act as trustees and has the power to suspend or cancel a trustee's licence. She may issue directives to trustees or receivers regarding the administration of a bankrupt estate, intervene in any court proceeding, and investigate situations where a bankruptcy offence may have been committed (s. 10(1)).

For the purposes of administration, the BIA makes each province and territory a bankruptcy district. Each district may be divided into two or more divisions, according to the size of the province or territory. For each division, an **official receiver** is appointed (or more than one). Official receivers are officers of the court and are required to report to the superintendent all bankruptcies originating in their divisions (s. 12). The superintendent must maintain a public record of all licences issued to trustees and all debtor proposals and bankruptcies (s. 11.1).

official receiver a public official responsible for the supervision of bankruptcy proceedings

The BIA designates the highest trial court in each province or territory as the court to hear bankruptcy proceedings (s. 183). Usually a particular judge or judges of the provincial court are designated to deal with bankruptcy matters, and their courts are commonly referred to as the Bankruptcy Court, though strictly speaking no separate bankruptcy court exists. The courts hear creditors' **petitions** for the bankruptcy of their debtors and determine whether or on what terms certain debtors should be discharged after their affairs have been wound up.

petitions requests to commence bankruptcy proceedings against a defaulting debtor

The actual administration of a debtor's estate is placed in the hands of a licensed **trustee in bankruptcy**, who is normally an accountant and is appointed by the court or, in the case of a voluntary assignment in bankruptcy, by the official receiver. In either case, in appointing the trustee, regard must be paid to the wishes of the creditors, who retain the power to appoint a substitute trustee (s. 14). The creditors also appoint one or more (but not exceeding five) inspectors to instruct and supervise the trustee (s. 116).

trustee in bankruptcy the person appointed to administer the property of a bankrupt

Persons to Whom the Act Applies

Bankrupts and Insolvent Persons
The BIA applies, in general, to debtors who are individuals, partnerships, and corporations—apart from banks, insurance companies, and trust, loan, and railway companies. A **bankrupt** is defined as a person who has made an assignment or against whom a bankruptcy order has been made—that is, a formal legal step must be taken in order to declare a person bankrupt. A distinction is made between debtors who voluntarily declare bankruptcy and those who are petitioned into bankruptcy by their creditors.

bankrupt a person who has made a voluntary assignment in bankruptcy or against whom a bankruptcy order has been made

The BIA applies to insolvent persons as well as to bankrupts. An **insolvent person** is defined, for the purposes of the Act, as a person who is not bankrupt, whose liabilities to creditors amount to at least $1000, and who either

- is unable to meet his obligations as they generally become due,
- has ceased paying his current obligations in the ordinary course of business as they generally become due, or
- has debts due and accruing due, the aggregate of which exceeds the realizable value of his assets (s. 2).

insolvent person a person who is unable to meet (or has ceased to pay) his debts as they become due or whose debts exceed the value of his realizable assets

The BIA distinguishes between two basic types of person: those who are potential candidates for bankruptcy (insolvents), and those who have been declared bankrupt (bankrupts). A person may be insolvent without having been declared bankrupt, and a bankrupt may turn out not to be insolvent.

Consumer Debtors An important distinction is drawn between consumer debtors and other debtors. The Act defines a **consumer debtor** as an insolvent natural person (that is, an individual) whose aggregate debts, excluding any debt secured by the person's principal residence, do not exceed $250 000 (s. 66.11). Consumer bankruptcies represent the vast majority of all bankruptcies (63 406 out of a total of 66 406 in 2015); business bankruptcies fell by 65.1 percent over the 15 years between 1990 and 2010 (3089 in 2015).[6] Consumer bankruptcies rose by 116 percent over the same time period.

The relevance of the distinctions—between insolvent persons and bankrupts, and between business and consumer debtors—will be considered when we discuss the various procedures provided for under the Act.

Corporations The principle of limited liability means the shareholders of a corporation are not liable for its debts. The corporation is liable for its own debts to the full extent of its assets, and it may go bankrupt. Punishment and rehabilitation have little meaning for a bankrupt corporation. A group of individuals may form a corporation with very little capital, and if the corporation becomes bankrupt, they lose very little (unless they have personally guaranteed its debts). To make a fresh start in business, they may simply form a new corporation. However, the worst abuses—for example, where the assets of a corporation are drained by the payment of excessive dividends or by redeeming shares—are governed by provisions that allow such transactions to be reviewed and set aside. If a corporation commits a bankruptcy offence, any director or officer who authorized, participated in, or acquiesced in the offence is liable to punishment for the offence (s. 204).[7] The Court may order the removal of a director if the director is acting inappropriately or impairing the corporation's ability to comply with a proposal. Conversely, a court may protect a director or officer from liability arising from a proposal by granting a charge on the property of the corporation in favour of indemnification of director liability (ss. 64, 64.1). Such indemnification does not cover willful misconduct.

Procedures under the Act

The BIA makes creates three distinct types of procedure, available in different circumstances and each with its own special consequences:

1. a **proposal**—a procedure to avoid bankruptcy/formal liquidation of the debtor's estate, at least temporarily, by allowing the debtor time to attempt to reorganize and save a viable business or, in the case of a consumer debtor, to reorganize her affairs
2. an **assignment**—a voluntary application by a debtor to institute bankruptcy proceedings
3. a **bankruptcy order**—initiated by creditors' petition to have their debtor declared bankrupt by the court.

Proposals There are two types of proposal, commonly referred to as commercial proposals (Division I) and consumer proposals (Division II), the latter being a simplified

---

[6] Statistics are available at the Office of the Superintendent of Bankruptcy, https://www.ic.gc.ca/eic/site/bsf-osb.nsf/eng/h_br01011.html, and "Canadian Bankruptcy Statistics (1980–2013)," BankruptcyCanada.com, http://www.bankruptcycanada.com/bankstats1.htm.

[7] An individual who is a bankrupt is not permitted to be a director of a corporation; see e.g. *Canada Business Corporations Act*, RSC 1985, c C-44, s 105(1)(d).

procedure available to individual consumer debtors. For corporations, an alternative method of avoiding liquidation of the business is provided under the *Companies' Creditors Arrangement Act*. That Act is considered later in this chapter, under the heading "Other Methods of Liquidation and Reorganization."

Commercial Proposals A proposal is an offer made by the debtor to his creditors, providing for the orderly repayment of his debts or of some part of his debts,[8] over a period of time. If the proposal is accepted by a sufficient proportion of the creditors, the court will declare it binding upon all the creditors (except the government), and no other collection efforts may be taken.

A Division I proposal may be made by an insolvent person, a liquidator of an insolvent person's property, or a receiver in relation to an insolvent person. A proposal may also be made by a bankrupt or by the trustee of a bankrupt's estate, provided the estate has not yet been wound up (s. 50(1)).

To make a proposal before bankruptcy, the debtor files a copy of the proposal with the official receiver in the debtor's district. The proposal must be accompanied by a statement showing the debtor's financial position, verified by affidavit of a licensed trustee. An insolvent person can gain additional time by filing a notice of intention with the official receiver, stating his intention to make a proposal (s. 50.4). If the debtor has already been made bankrupt, the proposal and statement of financial position are delivered to the existing trustee. The proposal must be approved by the inspectors (appointed by the creditors to supervise the trustee) before any further action is taken.

Next, the proposal requires approval by a meeting of the creditors. The proposal may be made to secured creditors or to one or more classes of secured creditors as well as to unsecured creditors. Acceptance of a proposal requires the approval of a majority in number, and two-thirds in value, of the unsecured creditors, and a similar proportion of each class of secured creditors (s. 54). Secured creditors not included in the proposal, or whose class has rejected the proposal, keep the protection provided by their security.

If the proposal is accepted by a sufficient proportion of creditors, the next step is for the trustee to apply to the court for approval. Although the court will be reluctant to refuse approval to a proposal that is acceptable to the majority of creditors, it must be satisfied that the terms of the proposal are reasonable and for the benefit of the general body of creditors (s. 59(2)). In particular, it may withhold approval if the proposal fails to provide reasonable security for repayment of at least 50 cents on the dollar to unsecured creditors or if the debtor has committed a bankruptcy offence. If a proposal is rejected by the majority of creditors or by the court, the insolvent debtor is deemed to have made an assignment into bankruptcy (s. 57, 61(2)).

Once approved by the court, the proposal is binding on all unsecured creditors and on all secured creditors of a class that has given its approval. Unless the proposal provides to the contrary, the debtor retains control of his property. However, monies payable under the proposal must be paid to the trustee for distribution to the creditors. If the debtor defaults in the performance of any provision of the proposal, the trustee is required to notify all creditors and the official receiver. Application may then be made, by any creditor or by the trustee, to have the proposal annulled (s. 63(3)). The effect of annulment is that the debtor is deemed to have made an assignment (see below).

Consumer Proposals An insolvent individual who owes no more than $250 000, not including any debt secured by mortgage on a principal residence, may make a proposal

---

[8] Certain debts, notably those to the Crown (government) and to employees, must be paid in full; ss 60(1.1), (1.3).

to her creditors for the reduction of, or extension of time for the payment of, her debts (s. 66.12). A Division II proposal must be prepared with the assistance of an "administrator," a licensed trustee or other person appointed by the superintendent to administer consumer proposals. The administrator is responsible for investigating the debtor's financial affairs and for providing counselling. Procedures are simplified, and a formal meeting of creditors is not required unless requested by creditors representing 25 percent in value of the proven debts. Where no meeting is requested, the proposal is deemed to be accepted by the creditors. A proposal that has been accepted or is deemed to be accepted does not require approval of the court.

An important consequence of filing a consumer proposal is that the debtor also obtains protection against lease terminations, acceleration of installment payments, or having utilities shut off (s. 66.34). Consumers making a proposal must undergo mandatory debt counselling, and there are only limited rights to revive a proposal once a consumer debtor defaults.

Assignments

By making an assignment, an insolvent person voluntarily declares himself bankrupt. A debtor who is no longer able to meet his debts as they fall due may prefer to initiate bankruptcy proceedings himself rather than wait for his creditors to do so. By making an assignment, he puts an end to an unsatisfactory situation and makes an earlier rehabilitation possible. Also, to continue to carry on a business once he knows he is insolvent might well involve him in the commission of a bankruptcy offence and jeopardize his eventual discharge (s. 173(1)(c)).

A debtor makes an assignment by filing a petition with the official receiver, accompanied by a sworn statement listing his property and his debts and creditors (s. 49).[9] When the official receiver files the petition, she appoints a trustee, who becomes responsible for the administration of the debtor's estate and to whom the debtor's property is assigned. From that point on, the debtor ceases to have any right to dispose of or deal with his property.

The estate of a bankrupt who has made an assignment is administered in the same manner as one administered under a receiving order (the procedure will be dealt with in the next section). However, a special simplified form of administration is provided in the case of an individual bankrupt who has made an assignment and whose realizable assets, after deducting the claims of secured creditors, do not exceed $5000 in value (s. 49(6)).

Bankruptcy Orders

A creditor or group of creditors may file a petition with the court in the judicial district where the debtor is located in order to have the debtor declared bankrupt, provided the creditor (or group) is owed not less than $1000 and the debtor has committed an **act of bankruptcy** within the previous six months (s. 43). A secured creditor may initiate a petition but must elect to either give up her security or participate in the bankruptcy only to the extent of any deficiency after deduction of the security's value.

act of bankruptcy a prescribed act of a debtor that must be proved before the debtor may be declared bankrupt

Unlike the rules for making proposals and assignments, there is no requirement that the debtor be insolvent; it is sufficient that he has committed an act of bankruptcy. An act of bankruptcy, discussed below, may be committed by a person who is not insolvent. However, in most cases where a bankruptcy order is made, the debtor is insolvent.

Subject to a few exceptions, a petition may be filed in respect of any debtor, whether an individual, partnership, or corporation. No petition may be made against an individual who is engaged solely in fishing or farming, or against a wage earner who does not earn more than $2500 a year and does not carry on any business on his own account (s. 48).[10]

---

[9] A person who defaults on a proposal may also be deemed to have made an assignment.

[10] Such an individual may, however, make a voluntary assignment. A corporation engaged in farming or fishing may be petitioned.

The burden of proving the facts alleged is on the petitioning creditors, who must comply with all the formalities required by the Act. The petition may be opposed by the debtor, who may dispute the existence of the debt or of an alleged act of bankruptcy. Even where the petitioning creditors succeed in establishing facts that would justify the making of a receiving order, the court has a general discretion to refuse to make the order or to grant a stay of proceedings. For example, it may decline to make an order if it considers that, given a fair chance, the debtor will be able to meet his obligations within a reasonable period. It may also decline to make an order where the debtor has no assets to divide among the creditors and there is no likelihood that he will have assets in the future.

Where a bankruptcy order is made, its effect is to vest the bankrupt's property in the trustee appointed by the court to administer the estate.

Acts of Bankruptcy

Before creditors can obtain a bankruptcy order, they must prove the debtor has committed an act of bankruptcy. The *Bankruptcy and Insolvency Act* defines the conduct that constitutes an act of bankruptcy by a debtor (s. 42) as follows:

- An assignment of assets to a trustee: If a debtor makes an assignment of her property to a trustee for the benefit of her creditors, and the arrangement is not satisfactory to the creditors, they may cite the assignment as an act of bankruptcy and petition to have a bankruptcy order issued. They might choose to do so, for example, when the debtor has transferred her assets to a trustee who is not acceptable to them.

- A fraudulent transfer of assets to a third party other than a trustee: A transfer of property by a debtor in anticipation of bankruptcy in order to withhold assets from distribution to creditors is a fraudulent transfer. Any attempt to deprive creditors of access to assets by transferring them to a third person (including the debtor's spouse or child) is void if the transfer takes place within a specified period prior to bankruptcy.

- A fraudulent preference: Any payment by a debtor that has the effect of settling the claim of one creditor in preference to the outstanding claims of other creditors is a fraudulent preference.

- An attempt by the debtor to abscond, with intent to defraud creditors.

- A failure to redeem goods seized under an execution issued against the debtor.[11] As discussed in Chapter 13, a creditor may sue a debtor, obtain judgment, and seek to satisfy the judgment by having the debtor's assets seized. When a debtor's assets are few, a seizure may well benefit the judgment creditor to the disadvantage of other creditors. Accordingly, if a debtor fails to take steps to prevent the sale of his property under an execution order, he commits an act that entitles his creditors to apply to the court for his bankruptcy. If they do so, all the debtor's property, including the property subject to the execution order, is put in the hands of a licensed trustee for distribution to all the creditors.[12]

---

[11] A debtor commits an act of bankruptcy if he permits an execution to remain unsatisfied for 15 days after seizure by the sheriff, until within five days of the time fixed for sale by the sheriff, or in a variety of other circumstances set out in section 42(1)(e).

[12] It is possible that, instead of petitioning for a bankruptcy order, all the debtor's major creditors may choose to obtain individual judgments and execution orders. In Ontario, the *Creditors Relief Act, 2010*, SO 2010, c C.16, Sch 4 provides for a scheme of distribution of the proceeds of sale among execution creditors.

- The presentation at a meeting of creditors of (a) a statement of assets and liabilities disclosing the debtor's insolvency, or (b) a written admission by the debtor that she is unable to pay her debts.
- An attempt to remove or hide any of his property, with intent to defraud creditors.
- Notice to any of the creditors that the debtor is suspending payment of her debts.
- A default in any proposal that the debtor has previously persuaded the creditors to accept as a means of forestalling bankruptcy proceedings.
- A failure to meet liabilities generally as they become due.

The most common of these acts of bankruptcy are failing to pay debts as they become due and failing to redeem goods seized under an execution.

ADMINISTRATION OF A BANKRUPT'S AFFAIRS

Powers and Duties of the Trustee

Once an assignment or bankruptcy order is made, the trustee takes possession of the assets of the bankrupt debtor and all books and documents relating to his affairs. She becomes in effect a temporary manager of the bankrupt debtor's business, subject to the supervision of inspectors appointed by the creditors. She may carry on the business or, alternatively, sell the assets. She can do such things as employ a lawyer, borrow further money for the business by pledging or mortgaging its remaining free (unsecured) assets, and negotiate with creditors for the acceptance by them of specific assets in lieu of money settlement of their claims. She may even engage the bankrupt debtor himself to assist in the administration of the bankrupt estate. To do these things she must have specific authority from the inspectors (s. 30). The principal duties of a trustee, however, are to recover all property that under bankruptcy law should form part of the debtor's estate and to apply that property in satisfaction of the claims of creditors (ss. 16(3), 25).

Recovery of Property The trustee takes possession of those assets of the debtor that are in the debtor's possession and also seeks to recover any other assets, for example, by collecting debts owed to the debtor. As a general rule, the trustee cannot obtain a better title to property than the debtor himself possessed in that property. Consequently, the trustee's interest is subject to the claims of persons who own property that is in the possession of the debtor or of secured creditors who have interests in that property. The *Personal Property Security Acts* (PPSAs) have an exception to the general principle. If someone has leased personal property to the debtor and has failed to register that interest, the security interest may be ineffective and subordinate to the claim of the trustee.[13] As will be discussed further in later sections, some property (such as household goods) is exempt from seizure by the trustee.

In addition, there may be property that the debtor has disposed of and that by law should form part of her bankrupt estate and be available to satisfy the claims of creditors. For example, money collected for income tax, Canada Pension Plan, or employment insurance payments is deemed to be property held in trust for the government and is not property of the debtor (s. 67(3)). If a debtor has sold or disposed of assets for less than their market value, special rules apply so that a trustee may recover the property (ss. 91–101.2).

---

[13] *Re Giffen*, [1998] 1 SCR 91 considering the BC PPSA s 20(1)(b); not followed in *Re Ouellet*, [2004] 3 SCR 348 and *Lefebvre (Trustee) v Tremblay*, [2004] 3 SCR 326 at para 40 because Quebec lacked a similar provision in its PPSA; See also *Fast Labour Solutions (Edmonton) Limited v Kramer's Technical Services Inc*, 2016 ABCA 266.

Transfers at Undervalue The term **transfer** refers to any sale, gift, trade, or disposition of property or supply of services by the debtor before becoming bankrupt. "Undervalue" means free or for payment that was obviously below fair market value. The intention of the rules is to prevent a person who is insolvent or on the verge of insolvency from prejudicing the claims of his creditors by giving his property away—usually to members of his family or to friends.

In general, any undervalue transfer[14] by a debtor, even to an unsuspecting good faith purchaser, that occurred within a year before her bankruptcy is void, and the property or payment is recoverable by the trustee. In addition, the trustee may attack a transfer of property made as long as five years before the bankruptcy where the transfer was to a non-**arm's length** party—that is, a related or "knowing" purchaser. The trustee must show that at the date of the transfer the debtor was unable to pay her debts in full without the aid of such property, and the transfer was done with the intent to defeat creditors (s. 96).[15]

An undervalue transfer may also be attacked under provincial laws dealing with **fraudulent transfer**;[16] it is not unusual for a trustee in bankruptcy to pursue both kinds of remedies.

transfer a gift, sale, or disposition of property made by a debtor before becoming bankrupt

arm's length a transaction between persons who are not related or associated in any way

fraudulent transfer a transfer of property by a debtor with the intention of putting that property out of the reach of creditors

CASE 29.1 Non-Arm's Length

A husband and wife had jointly owned their home since 1974. In 1978, the husband gave a personal guarantee to a bank in respect of a debt owed by the corporation of which he and his wife were the sole shareholders. In 1990, the husband transferred his half interest in the home to his wife for $1. Shortly thereafter the bank demanded repayment of the debt, and when the husband was unable to meet the guarantee, it appointed a receiver. The husband died insolvent in 1991.

The bank successfully claimed that the transfer of the interest in the home was a fraudulent conveyance and was consequently void under the (Ontario) *Fraudulent Conveyances Act*. The bank was entitled to a 50 percent interest in the property.[17]

CASE 29.2 Fraudulent Transfer

The Chans obtained a judgment against the Stanwoods for an amount exceeding $250 000 and were pressing for immediate payment. In an attempt to avoid the seizure of their family home and other assets, the Stanwoods consulted a lawyer, Davis, who recommended a complex scheme that involved the creation of a corporation with an elaborate share structure and voting rights. The home and assets were transferred to the corporation, but the Stanwoods remained in effective control of the corporation through their power to appoint "friendly" directors.

The Chans commenced proceedings under the (BC) *Fraudulent Conveyances Act* and were successful in having the transfer to the corporation set aside. Their claim for damages against the lawyer who devised the scheme failed. The court held that to advise someone to commit a breach of the Act is not a civil wrong.[18]

---

[14] The rule does not apply to property transferred in a genuine business transaction for good consideration (s. 97); *Re Dowswell* (1999), 178 DLR (4th) 193. Nor does it apply to transfers of property that would otherwise be exempt from execution, such as a RRIF; see, e.g., *Royal Bank of Canada v North American Life Assurance Co* (1996), 132 DLR (4th) 193 (SCC). The trustee may also inquire into dividends paid or stock redemptions or purchases involving a company that goes bankrupt within a year (s. 101).

[15] In practice, it is almost impossible for a trustee to establish the exact financial status of a bankrupt debtor at a time as long as a year or more before the bankruptcy.

[16] See e.g. *Fraudulent Conveyances Act*, RSBC 1996, c 163; RSNL 1990, c F-24; RSO 1990, c F.29; RSA 2000, c F-24; RSS 1978, c F-21.

[17] *Bank of Montreal v Bray* (1997), 36 OR (3d) 99; *Stone v Stone* (2001) 55 OR (3d) 491. See also *XLO Investments Ltd v Hurontario Management Services* (1999), 170 DLR (4th) 381 (ONCA) upholding trial judge's finding of fraudulent conveyance, cost order varied.

[18] *Chan v Stanwood* (2002), 216 DLR (4th) 625 (decided under previous legislation).

The provisions of the provincial legislation differ from those of the *Bankruptcy and Insolvency Act* in a number of respects, and the trustee may rely on the provincial Act to supplement the normal bankruptcy remedies.[19] In particular, it is not necessary to be an established creditor in order to bring proceedings under the *Fraudulent Conveyances Acts* to have a transaction set aside. Decisions have held that a claimant in a tort action (who had not yet obtained a judgment) could challenge a transfer of property to relatives designed to defeat the claim[20] and that a wife could challenge a secret transfer of property by her husband to his children that would have the effect of depriving her of her rights under the *Family Law Act*.[21]

Preferences A solvent debtor is entitled to pay her creditors in any order she pleases. She may choose to pay one creditor before she pays another—that is, to give preference to the claim of the first creditor over the second—perhaps because she depends on the prompt services or delivery of goods from the first creditor. (Another reason is this: If the debtor is a corporation, the directors may have given personal guarantees of one or more of the debts.) By contrast, in bankruptcy the guiding principle is that creditors of the same class should be treated equally.

A debtor on the verge of bankruptcy is not permitted to unfairly favour certain creditors over others. The Act deals with this situation by providing that (a) a payment of money or a transfer of property to a creditor, (b) by an insolvent debtor, (c) within three months preceding bankruptcy, and (d) with a view to giving that creditor preference over other creditors amounts to a **fraudulent preference** and is recoverable (s. 95). The time limit extends to 12 months where the creditor who received the preference is a related person or was not dealing at arm's length. The provisions are intended to nullify transactions that would otherwise defeat the legitimate claims of creditors. They do not invalidate payments made in good faith to creditors who were unaware of the impending bankruptcy or other transfers of property such as the sale of inventory or other business assets in the normal course of business (s. 97).[22]

fraudulent preference the payment of money or transfer of property to a creditor with a view to giving that creditor preference over other creditors

CASE 29.3 Preferred Creditors

Green Gables Manor Inc., a corporation operating a nursing home, made payments of $13 000 to each of its two controlling shareholders and directors. The payments were stated to be in respect of management fees owed to them. It also executed a general security agreement in their favour in respect of outstanding claims. The following day, a receiving order was granted, and Green Gables was declared bankrupt.

The trustee claimed repayment of the sums and a declaration that the security agreement was void. The court found that the two directors were "related" to the corporation for the purposes of the *Bankruptcy and Insolvency Act*, that the transactions represented a "preference," and that they should, accordingly, be set aside.[23]

Exempt Property Not all the bankrupt's property is subject to seizure. For example, RRSPs (registered retirement savings plans) are **exempt** from bankruptcy seizure, save and except for the previous year's contribution. Provincial law may also exempt some property from seizure (ss. 67, 72). Examples include household furnishings and appliances, tools of the bankrupt's trade, some farm property, and insurance policies, though these exemptions vary considerably from one province to another. A maximum

exempt property that is not subject to seizure by the trustee as a result of an exception in a federal or provincial statute

---

[19] *Flightcraft Inc v Parsons* (1999), 175 DLR (4th) 642 (decided under previous legislation).

[20] *Hamm v Metz* (2002), 209 DLR (4th) 385.

[21] *Stone v Stone*, supra note 17. But see *Reisman v Reisman*, 2014 ONCA 109 (reorganization done of tax and estate planning purposes).

[22] *Orion Industries Ltd v Neil's General Contracting Ltd*, 2013 ABCA 330.

[23] *Re Green Gables Manor Inc* (1998), 41 BLR (2d) 299. Contrast *Sheraton Desert Inn Corp v Yeung* (1998), 168 DLR (4th) 126.

amount of equity in the principal residence is reserved for the debtors in some provinces (Alberta, $40,000); in others a minimum amount of equity is required before sale proceeds may be taken (Ontario, $10,000).[24]

Payment of Claims

To rank as a claim against the bankrupt estate and share in distribution of the proceeds, all creditors must "prove" their debts. They do so by submitting declarations to the trustee outlining the details of their accounts with supporting evidence to substantiate the claims. The declaration states whether or not the claim is a secured or preferred claim. A provable claim is a debt or liability with a monetary value, owed to a creditor, which came into existence before the date of bankruptcy. Future and contingent claims are eligible, but uncertain or unquantifiable claims may be denied by the trustee.[25]

Once the trustee has possession of the bankrupt's property, the duty is to use that property to satisfy the proven claims of creditors. That normally involves selling the property and distributing the cash proceeds among the creditors. In appropriate cases the trustee may distribute **liquidating dividends** (payments on account) to the creditors from time to time as required by the inspectors and as realization of the debtor's assets permits. In doing so she must, of course, be careful to take account of the claims of the secured and preferred creditors.

liquidating dividends payments made from time to time by a trustee in bankruptcy to creditors on account of the full amount due to them

Because the assets are almost always insufficient to satisfy all the claims in full, the priority of claims is important. A trustee must act with great care in the administration and liquidation of the debtor's affairs. She may be personally liable to creditors for losses caused them by her failure to pay the claims in the proper order of priority. The determination of priorities can be an extremely difficult matter, especially where the claims of secured creditors are involved. The trustee must determine whether a claim to a secured interest is effectively protected (for example, by registration under the PPSA).[26] Where there are two or more such claims, the trustee must determine their respective priority. That may prove especially difficult where the claims are made under different statutes, such as a provincial PPSA and the federal *Bank Act*.[27]

In such cases, it is normally advisable for the trustee to seek a ruling from the court.

Super Priority
Super priority entitles a creditor to have her claim paid before the claims of any secured creditor. The *Bankruptcy and Insolvency Act* gives specific creditors this status.

super priority entitlement to be paid before secured creditors

Unpaid Sellers An unpaid seller has a right to repossess goods sold and delivered to a bankrupt in the 30 days preceding bankruptcy for use in the bankrupt's business (s. 81.1). The supplier must make a demand within 15 days after bankruptcy, and the goods must still be in the possession of the purchaser, be identifiable, and be in the same condition as when sold. The claim ranks above any other claim to the goods, except that of a bona fide purchaser of the goods for value without notice of the supplier's right. A supplier who repossesses goods cannot subsequently claim against the bankrupt for any deficiency in respect of those goods.

---

[24] *Civil Enforcement Act*, RSA 2000, c C-15, s 88; *Execution Act*, RSO 1990, c E.24, s 2.

[25] BIA, ss 121, 135; *Newfoundland and Labrador v AbitibiBowater Inc*, [2012] 3 SCR 443, 2012 SCC 67 at paras 26, 34 (includes future or contingent claims).

[26] See *Re Giffen*, *supra* note 13 See also *Fast Labour Solutions (Edmonton) Limited v Kramer's Technical Services Inc*, 2016 ABCA 266.

[27] See e.g. *Royal Bank of Canada v Sparrow Electric Corp*, [1997] 1 SCR 411; *Abraham v Canadian Admiral Corp* (1998), 39 OR (3d) 176; *Century Services In. v Canada (Attorney General)*, [2010] 3 SCR 379; *Alberta (Attorney General) v Moloney*, 2015 SCC 51.

Priority is also given to farmers, fishers, and aquaculturalists who have supplied their products to a bankrupt within 15 days of bankruptcy and have not been paid. The claims of such suppliers extend not only to the goods supplied but are also secured by a charge on the entire inventory of the purchaser. This charge ranks above any other claim against that inventory, except that of an unpaid seller of specific goods (s. 81.2).

> ### CASE 29.4 Conditions for Super Priority
>
> Thomson Electronics had supplied goods to Consumers Distributing, for which it had not been paid. Consumers Distributing was declared bankrupt, and Thomson claimed recovery of the goods that it had supplied in the preceding month. The goods were not in the possession of Consumers Distributing but were being stored in a warehouse belonging to Tibbett and Britten Inc., which was also a creditor of Consumers Distributing.
>
> The court held that for section 81.1 to apply, the goods had to be in the actual physical possession of the bankrupt. Thomson's claim to recover the goods failed.[28]

current assets cash or cash equivalent assets such as negotiable instruments, demand deposits, and accounts receivable

Wage Earners The Act gives wage earners super priority for up to six months' unpaid wages (to a maximum of $2000) out of the **current assets** (liquid) of the debtor.[29] The priority extends to wages, commissions, salary, and compensation for services rendered, plus unremitted pension plan deductions. This claim ranks behind the unpaid seller but ahead of secured creditors. There is also a government-backed compensation scheme known as the Wage Earner Protection Program. Employees are entitled to claim up to $3000 (or four weeks) of arrears of wages from the fund.[30]

Interim Financing Creditors Sometimes it is necessary for an insolvent business to obtain credit while it tries to reorganize and survive as a going concern. Naturally, it is difficult to convince a lender to extend credit in such circumstances. A court may prioritize interim financing given during reorganization above any existing secured interest in an asset. The debtor and creditor must obtain permission of the court prior to making the loan. This type of financing is also known as **debtor-in-possession financing** (DIP) (s. 50.6(3)).

debtor-in-possession financing court-sanctioned secured loans advanced during reorganization and given priority over pre-existing secured creditors

Secured Creditors Secured creditors rank behind unpaid sellers, agricultural suppliers, wage earners, and interim financing creditors in payment priority. The Act requires a secured creditor to give at least 10 days' notice to an insolvent person before enforcing her security (s. 244) and contains provisions governing the conduct of a receiver, appointed by a secured creditor, insofar as that conduct relates to the administration of a bankrupt estate (s. 245–7).

Subject to these provisions, however, a secured creditor is entitled to enforce her security (seize the secured property) to obtain payment of what is owing. A secured creditor must pay to the trustee any surplus if the security she holds is worth more than the debt owing to her. When the trustee and secured creditor cannot agree on the value of the security, it may be necessary to sell it and pay the secured claim out of the proceeds (ss. 127–34). The bankrupt estate is entitled to any surplus for the benefit of other creditors. When the value of the security is less than the secured debt, the creditor receives the full value of the security and, in addition, ranks as a general claim along with other unsecured creditors for the deficiency. When the trustee and secured creditor agree on the value of the secured assets without having to sell them, the creditor

---

[28] *Thomson Consumer Electronics Canada, Inc v Consumers Distributing Inc* (1999), 170 DLR (4th) 115.

[29] *Supra* note 2 ss 81.3, 81.4.

[30] *Wage Earner Protection Program Act*, SC 2005, c 47.

may accept the security in settlement of her account, either by paying any excess value to the trustee or by making a claim against the trustee as a general creditor for the deficiency.

Preferred Creditors Out of the assets remaining after payment or settlement of priority and secured claims, the trustee must next pay the **preferred creditors**. Preferred creditors are listed in section 136 of the Act. The following is a summary of preferred claims, in their order of their priority.

preferred creditors unsecured creditors whose claims are given preference over those of other unsecured creditors

1. The reasonable funeral expenses and legal expenses related to the death of a bankrupt debtor.
2. Expenses and fees of the licensed trustee in bankruptcy and her legal costs.
3. A levy to defray the expense of the supervision of the Superintendent in Bankruptcy.
4. Up to six months' arrears of wages and pension deductions of employees of the bankrupt debtor to the extent of $2000 for each employee. This preference is available to satisfy remaining wages owed that were not paid under the super priority over current assets.
5. Spousal or child support arrears (s. 136 (d.1)); any tax refund owing to the debtor is exempt from seizure by the trustee if it is subject to a claim for arrears of spousal or child support.
6. Municipal taxes levied within the two years preceding bankruptcy.
7. Arrears of rent due to the landlord for a period of three months preceding bankruptcy.
8. The costs of the first execution or attachment creditor. (A creditor obtains an execution order against tangibles such as land or goods, and an attachment against choses in action such as accounts receivable or bank deposits.)
9. Indebtedness of the bankrupt under the Canada Pension Plan, the *Employment Insurance Act*, and the *Income Tax Act* for amounts required to be deducted from employees' salaries.
10. Claims for certain injuries sustained by employees not covered by workers' compensation.

General Creditors After settling the priority, secured, and preferred claims, the trustee pays the general creditors rateably to the extent of the funds remaining.

Deferred Creditors The BIA takes the claims of some creditors out of their usual class and delays their payment until after all other creditors. As noted above, non-arm's length creditors are deferred until after all other claims are paid (s. 137(1)). Similarly, silent partner loans (s. 139) and wages and compensation of officers and directors (s. 140) are deferred until after all other creditors are paid.

CHECKLIST

Priority of Payment of Claims

Claims against the property of a bankrupt debtor are paid in the following sequence:

1. Super priority claims
2. Secured creditors
3. Preferred creditors
4. General creditors
5. Deferred creditors

Duties of the Bankrupt Debtor

Following a receiving order or authorized assignment, the debtor must submit himself for examination by the official receiver to explain his conduct, the causes of his bankruptcy, and the disposition of his property. He must provide a sworn statement of his affairs to the trustee, together with a list of the names and addresses of his creditors and the security held by them, attend the first meeting of creditors, and supply the information they require. He must also hand over possession of his property to the trustee, cooperate with the trustee, and "aid to the utmost of his power in the realization of his property and the distribution of the proceeds among his creditors" (s. 158(k)).[31]

Bankruptcy Offences

A bankrupt debtor and any other person who commits an offence listed in the BIA may be to imprisoned for three years and/or face a substantial fine. Offences include failing to perform any of the duties considered above; making a fraudulent disposition of his property before or after bankruptcy; giving untruthful answers to questions put to him at an examination; concealing, destroying, or falsifying books or documents; and obtaining any credit or property by false representations before or after bankruptcy (s. 198). Of course committing a bankruptcy offence will delay any possible discharge.

Discharge of the Bankrupt Debtor

An important object of bankruptcy legislation is to clear an honest but unfortunate debtor of outstanding debts and to leave him free to rehabilitate his financial life. The **discharge** of a bankrupt debtor usually cancels the unpaid portion of his debts remaining after the creditors receive their share of distribution and gives the debtor a clean slate with which to start business again.

discharge a court order whereby a person who has been declared bankrupt ceases to have the status of a bankrupt person

However, discharge does not cancel all debts. As discussed below, student loans are not automatically cancelled, nor are income tax debts over $200 000. Debts arising from a child or spousal support order or the fraud of the bankrupt are not discharged; civil damage awards for intentionally inflicted bodily harm also survive.[32] Discharge is delayed for second-time bankrupts until after 24 or 36 months, depending upon their income.

Ethical Issue   Discrimination Against Students

When a bankrupt person is discharged, the effect is normally to cancel or immediately discharge all her outstanding debts and to give her a fresh start. There are, however, some debts that are not cancelled (s. 178). These include fines, penalties, damages for sexual assault, alimony, and student loans. The Canadian Federation of Students launched an unsuccessful challenge to this rule under the *Charter*.[33] As we have already noted, other debts to the government, such as personal income tax arrears, are also not automatically discharged.[34]

The 2007 amendments to the *Bankruptcy and Insolvency Act* softened but did not eliminate the harsh treatment of student loans. The new rule (s. 176) delays discharge of a student loan until seven years after completion of school (formerly 10 years), and students may apply to further reduce it to five years after completion of their studies for hardship reasons.

Questions to Consider

1. Do students deserve to be lumped together with criminals and "deadbeat" parents, as the *Toronto Star* put it? (April 3, 2004, at C2)
2. Are students (or ex-students) as a class entitled to the protection of the *Charter*?
3. What policy rationale justifies the different treatment of student loans?

---

[31] BIA, *supra* note 2, s 158(k).

[32] BIA, s 178; *Gray (Re)*, 2014 ONCA 236; *Dickerson v 1610396 Ontario Inc*, 2013 ONCA 653 (leave denied).

[33] *Chenier v Canada (Attorney General)*, 2005 CanLII 23125 (Ont Sup Ct).

[34] BIA, s 172.1; see also Stephanie Ven-Ishai et al, "A Retrospective on the Canadian Consumer Bankruptcy System: 40 Years After the Tasse Report" (2011) 50 *Can Bus LJ* 236 at 251–6.

Most debtors (who have completed mandatory counselling) are eligible for automatic discharge unless an objection is filed or tax arrears make up more than 75 percent of the debtor's unsecured debts. The chart below illustrates when an automatic discharge may be obtained under the amended BIA:

Automatic Discharge Availability

Bankruptcy	No Surplus	Surplus	75 Percent of Unsecured Debts are Tax Arrears
First	After 9 months	After 21 months	Hearing required
Second	After 24 months	After 36 months	Hearing required

One of the more important reasons a court may refuse or suspend the debtor's discharge is that his assets have proven to be insufficient to pay the unsecured creditors at least 50 cents on the dollar. He may still obtain a discharge, however, if he can show that he cannot reasonably be held responsible for this circumstance. Other reasons for refusing to give a discharge are the following:

- the bankrupt debtor neglected to keep proper books
- he continued to trade after he knew he was insolvent
- he failed to account satisfactorily for any loss or deficiency of assets
- he caused the bankruptcy by rash speculation or extravagant living
- within three months preceding bankruptcy he gave an undue preference to a creditor
- he was bankrupt or made a proposal to his creditors on a previous occasion
- he is guilty of any bankruptcy offence or has failed to perform his duties

Other related reasons are set out in the Act (s. 173).[35]

CASE 29.5 Actions Contrary to Bankruptcy's Purpose

Seven creditors opposed the discharge of a debtor who had not worked since the bankruptcy and was supported by his wealthy family. He drove a BMW and had monthly expenses of over $4000 all paid by his mother. The court refused to discharge the debtor because he was not willing to work; it was contrary to the rehabilitative purpose of the BIA. The debtor was ordered to pay a further $250 000 to the trustee.[36]

Until obtaining his discharge, a bankrupt debtor is subject to a fine or imprisonment if, without disclosing his status, he obtains credit of $1000 or more for a purpose other than the supply of necessaries for himself and his family, or if he recommences business and fails to disclose to those with whom he deals that he is an undischarged bankrupt (s. 199).

OTHER METHODS OF LIQUIDATION AND REORGANIZATION

Corporate Winding Up

There are other ways, in addition to those under the BIA, to wind up the affairs of a solvent corporation, but it is shareholders rather than the corporation or creditors who initiate the proceedings.

---

[35] In *Bank of Montreal v Giannotti* (2000), 197 DLR (4th) 266, discharge refused for a bankrupt who had been "uncooperative, evasive and untruthful" about his financial affairs.

[36] *Michael Katz (Re)*, 2013 ONSC 7426.

Each province has a separate statute or a section in its corporations act to provide a way to wind up solvent corporations.[37] The legislation may authorize the shareholders to appoint a liquidator (who may be a director, officer, or employee of the corporation) to wind up the affairs of the corporation without recourse to the court; alternatively, it may authorize them to apply to the court for a winding-up order and the appointment of a liquidator.

In addition, under the federal *Winding-up and Restructuring Act*,[38] the shareholders of a solvent, federally incorporated corporation may petition the court to issue a winding-up order. An order may be issued if the capital of the corporation has been impaired to the extent of 25 percent or if a substantial proportion of the shareholders petition for winding up because of a lack of integrity or responsibility on the part of the corporation's management.

A corporation may also surrender its charter, apart from proceedings under either the BIA or a *Winding-up Act*. For example, the *Canada Business Corporations Act* permits dissolution, if a corporation has no property and no liabilities, by special resolution of the shareholders. "Articles of dissolution" are sent to the director of the office that regulates federally incorporated corporations, and she issues a certificate of dissolution.[39] A corporation may wish to dissolve in this way when it has sold all its assets to another corporation and has distributed the proceeds to its shareholders, and when the purchasing corporation has assumed all its liabilities, with the consent of its creditors.

The *Companies' Creditors Arrangement Act*

As discussed, the *Bankruptcy and Insolvency Act* (BIA) provides an alternative to the formal liquidation of a debtor's estate by means of a "proposal." This allows the business to continue operating. For corporations, another method of avoiding liquidation is by entering into a **compromise and arrangement** with the creditors, approved by the court, under the *Companies' Creditors Arrangement Act* (CCAA).[40] The CCAA and the BIA are distinct statutes that provide alternative complementary procedures, with many of their provisions being similar.

compromise and arrangement
an agreement made by a debtor corporation with its creditors whereby arrangements are made for repayment of debts without liquidating the corporation

The CCAA allows a corporation in financial distress to seek court protection and a stay of BIA and creditor collection proceedings while it reorganizes its affairs in a way that may satisfy creditors. If the value of a corporation as a going concern exceeds its break-up value, a reorganization of its debts is usually preferable to the corporation itself, its creditors, and its employees. The mechanism is somewhat similar to that found in Chapter 11 of the U.S. *Bankruptcy Code*.

The purpose of the CCAA is to permit a corporation to restructure its affairs so that it can eliminate some of its debt and resume business in a leaner, more efficient form that will have a greater chance of returning to profitability. During the reorganization, the corporation's creditors are restrained from taking action (either enforcing collection of debts or forcing the debtor into bankruptcy). Creditors must work within the reorganization process. It is often complicated to determine which obligations must be honoured during restructuring and which may be stayed. For example, Nortel's obligation to make termination and severance payments to employees under the Ontario *Employment Standards Act* was stayed by the Ontario Court of Appeal until after CCAA restructuring.[41]

---

[37] See e.g. *Corporations Act*, CCSM c C225, Part XVII; *Business Corporations Act*, RSO 1990, c B.16, Part XVI; *Companies Winding-up Act*, RSNS 1989, c 82.

[38] RSC 1985, c W-11.

[39] RSC 1985, c C-44, s 210.

[40] RSC 1985, c C-36.

[41] *Sproule v Nortel Networks Corp*, 2009 ONCA 833.

A relatively recent development has been the emergence of **vulture funds**—large investors who are prepared to purchase substantial portions of the debtor corporation's debts or its shares at a heavily discounted price, hoping that the reorganization will be successful. This development seems in some ways to be contrary to the true intention of the Act, since these investors are clearly far more concerned with realizing a quick profit on their investment than in securing the rehabilitation of the debtor. However, one advantage is that the process provides a market in which smaller creditors may sell their claims without having to wait for the reorganization to be completed.

There are some differences between the CCAA and the proposal procedures under the BIA. In particular, the CCAA applies only if the total creditor claims exceed $5 million. When a court grants a CCAA stay of bankruptcy and court proceedings (s 11.02), the existing management of the business continues to operate the business under the supervision of a court appointed **monitor** (s 11.7) who watches the management and prepares a report for the court and the Superintendent of Bankruptcy (s 23). The final arrangement must be approved by a two-thirds majority of the creditors.[42] A court may rule on and approve any controversial issues. Under the CCAA, judges have greater discretion and flexibility than under the BIA; courts tend to interpret the two statutes in a compatible and consistent way to discourage forum shopping.[43]

Arrangements may include protecting critical suppliers and interim financiers by granting priority in payment so that they will continue to supply the business during the restructuring phase.[44] As well, the arrangement often includes protection from liability for directors and officers so that they too will continue to manage the business during the restructuring phase. Even with such immunity, disadvantaged groups of creditors often pursue oppression remedies.[45] As part of the CCAA restructuring process, directors may be removed from the board.[46]

vulture funds large investors who purchase the debt or shares of a corporation in the course of its reorganization

monitor a person appointed to supervise the reorganization of a debtor corporation under the *Companies' Creditors Arrangement Act*

BUILDERS' LIENS

A bailee who makes repairs or improvements to goods obtains a possessory lien on the goods for the value of her services. However, when a person or business performs work or supplies materials in the construction of a building or other structure affixed to land, it is physically impossible for him to exercise a possessory lien. Under real property law, goods that are attached permanently to land become fixtures (part of the land). The supplier of the goods is not permitted to separate them from the land. At common law, a supplier had no recourse except to sue for the debt, obtain judgment, and file an execution against the land. Builders' lien legislation provides another solution.

Contractors and Subcontractors In all Canadian jurisdictions, persons who have extended credit in the form of goods and services to improve land have a statutory remedy under provincial **builders' lien** legislation. Although the title and wording of the acts vary from province to province, each act provides substantially the same protection for creditors. Its basic purposes are to give creditors who have provided work and material for the improvement of land an interest in the land as security for

builders' lien an interest that builders and others involved in construction work may have in a building as security for money owed to them for work done (also known as a mechanics' lien or a construction lien)

---

[42] CCAA, s 6; *Grant Forest Products Inc v The Toronto-Dominion Bank*, 2015 ONCA 570 at paras 142–46.

[43] *Century Services Inc v Canada (Attorney General)*, 2010 SCC 60 at paras 47–63.

[44] CCAA, ss 11.2, 11.4.

[45] Janis Sarra, "The Evolution of the *Companies' Creditors Arrangement Act* in Light of Recent Developments" (2011) 50 *Can Bus LJ* 211 at 229–31.

[46] CCCA, ss 11.5, 11.51; similar power exists under the BIA, ss 64, 64.1.

payment and "to prevent multiplicity of actions for small claims, in which the cost would be enormously out of proportion to and in excess of the sums claimed."[47]

The builders' lien acts use a variety of tools: liens, holdbacks, and trusts.

ILLUSTRATION 29.1 Subcontracting

O Co. hires C. Co to build an apartment building on its land for an agreed price. C Co., in turn, subcontracts the specialized tasks of supplying and erecting the structural steel, installing the plumbing and heating systems and electrical wiring, and supplying and installing elevators to various firms specializing in these trades.

Liens In Illustration 29.1, there are two types of contracts: a master contract between O Co., the owner of the property, and the main contractor, C Co., and a series of subcontracts between the main contractor, C Co., and the various specialized trades. In respect to the master contract, O Co. is liable for the whole amount of the contract price as a contractual debt. C Co. also has a builders' lien—that is, an interest in O Co.'s land and building as it is erected—for the total value of work and materials (to the maximum of the contract price) provided by C Co. and its subcontractors. In addition to C Co's lien, even though there is no privity of contract between the subcontractors and suppliers and O Co, the legislation also gives all subcontractors and suppliers the right to lien the land by registering notice on the owner's title.

Holdback The value of these liens is limited to a specified proportion of the price due from the owner, O Co., to the main contractor, C Co., under the master contract. This proportion, called a **holdback**, varies somewhat from province to province but is generally 10–20 percent.[48] Where the value of the work and materials exceeds the holdback, the subcontractors and suppliers have no security in the land for the excess sum. The holdback requirement has a trickle-down effect in that it applies to each contract and subcontract in the chain.

O Co. fully protects itself against liens of the subcontractors and suppliers by retaining the holdback during construction and for a specified period afterward. If C Co. should become insolvent during this period, O Co. would pay the holdback into court for the benefit of the lienholders. The court would then supervise the payment of this money among the lienholders, and neither O Co. nor its land would be subject to their claims.

Trusts In some jurisdictions, all money received by contractors and subcontractors on account of the contract price is deemed to be trust funds held for the benefit of those who have performed work or services or furnished materials and have not been paid yet. The contractor or subcontractor, accordingly, cannot divert those funds to other purposes until all the claims against it are satisfied.[49] Trust rules also apply to funds received by owners from any lender financing the project.

Who Is Protected?

A builders' lien is available only to creditors who participate directly as workers or supply material for use directly in the construction work.[50]

---

holdback an amount that the owner who contracts for construction work may withhold from payments made to the principal contractor to protect against claims from subcontractors and suppliers

---

[47] *McPherson v Gedge* (1883–4), 4 OR 246 at 257.

[48] See e.g. *Builders' Lien Act*, SBC 1997, c 45, s 4(1); *Construction Act*, RSO 1990, c C.30, s 1(1) (10%). (Subsequent references to these particular acts in footnotes will be simply to BC and ON.)

[49] *Ibid.*, Ont, ss 7, 8(1). See *Rudco Insulation Ltd v Toronto Sanitary Inc* (1998), 42 OR (3d) 292.

[50] A land-use consultant engaged by a developer to advise on zoning issues was not entitled to a lien. His work contributed to the project as a whole but did not constitute "work on" any particular improvement: *Kreuchen v Park Savannah Development Ltd* (1999), 171 DLR (4th) 377.

Some provinces bring an architect who prepares the plans for a building within this definition and allow a lien.[51] Some provincial statutes give a lien to a lessor who rents equipment for use on the contract site for the price of the rental of the equipment.[52] On the other hand, a party that sells tools, machinery, or general supplies to a contractor is not entitled to a lien against a building constructed with the use of the tools or machinery it has supplied; the tools and machinery remain the property of the contractor and can be used in other projects as well.[53] Where, however, a supplier delivers the goods directly to the building site, it obtains a lien immediately, whether the materials are eventually used in the structure or not.[54] The reason for this provision is that a supplier who delivers materials to the building site reasonably assumes they will be used there and relies upon the property as security for his claim.

Employees' Rights The bargaining power of wage earners may be unequal to that of the builders and contractors who employ them, and these wage earners may not fully understand the nature of their rights. As a result, the various acts contain provisions that an agreement purporting to waive builders' lien rights is void.[55] However, in some provinces this provision does not apply to employees whose wages exceed a specified amount per day.

Most provinces give wage earners a priority for approximately one month's arrears of wages over all other liens derived through the same contractor or subcontractor.[56] This priority recognizes the fact that wages often provide the sole means of subsistence of wage earners, while suppliers of materials and lessors of equipment probably carry on business with several construction projects at once and usually have larger capital funds to depend on if a single contractor or owner defaults in payment.

Procedures under Builders' Lien Legislation

Registration A builders' lien arises immediately upon the first work being done or materials being used in the improvement of property or (in some provinces) upon the supply of rented equipment for use on a contract site. The lienholder must register it against the title to the land. It may be registered during the performance of the work or services or supply of material or within a specified period of time (usually 45 days) after completion or abandonment of performance. If a lien is not registered within the time specified, it ceases to exist. Following registration, the lienholder must commence a legal action resolve the issue.

Registration in the land registration system provides public notice of a lienholder's claim and establishes the lienholder's priority over unsecured creditors of the owner of the property and over subsequent mortgagees and purchasers of an interest in the property. A lien expires unless the lienholder brings an action to enforce the claim within the prescribed time and registers a certificate stating that the action has been started. Other lien claimants may shelter their claims within the same lawsuit.

Lienholders' Rights A builders' lien does not give a lienholder the right to personally take possession of or to sell land and buildings to realize a claim. In fact, if the lienholder is a subcontractor, and if the owner pays the statutory holdback into court,

---

[51] See e.g. s 14(3) ON; *Chaston Construction Corp v Henderson Land Holdings (Canada) Ltd* (2002), 214 DLR (4th) 405.
[52] Available in Ontario, Alberta, Newfoundland and Labrador, and Saskatchewan: see e.g. ss 1(1), 14(1) ON, *supra* note 48.
[53] *Crowell Bros v Maritime Minerals Ltd*, [1940] 2 DLR 472.
[54] *Supra* note 48, s 15 (ON).
[55] *Ibid.*, s 4(ON).
[56] *Ibid.*, s 37 (BC); s 81 (40 days) (ON).

the lien may be discharged, and the lienholder's rights are limited to its share in this fund. It has no rights against the land and buildings of the owner. Even if an owner fails to pay the statutory holdback into court, the lienholder's claim against the land is limited to the amount the owner should have paid into court. To realize its claim against the land, a lienholder, whether a main contractor or a subcontractor, must first bring an action and obtain a court order appointing a trustee. The trustee then has the power to manage the property and to sell it for the benefit of the lienholder and other creditors.

If eventually the trustee does sell the property, she must pay the proceeds to satisfy, first, the claims for municipal taxes; second, those of mortgagees who have prior registered mortgages; third, lienholders' claims for wages, regardless of the order in which they filed their liens; fourth, all other lienholders' claims, regardless of the order in which they filed their liens; fifth, subsequent mortgagees or other persons who have a secured interest in the land; and, finally, if there are any proceeds left, claims of the general creditors of the owner. After all creditors are paid, any balance remaining belongs to the owner.

Progress Payments During the construction of a building and for the specified statutory period afterward, the owner may safely make progress payments to the contractor for all amounts except the statutory holdback.[57] However, if the owner receives notice from subcontractors or suppliers that liens are outstanding and unlikely to be paid by the contractor, she should cease payments to the contractor at once and ascertain the extent of the liens. If there is some doubt whether the holdback is sufficient to satisfy the claims for liens, she should seek legal advice immediately; as soon as she has knowledge of these claims, she loses the protection of the Act to the extent that she continues to make payments to the contractor. On the other hand, she must not make the error of wrongfully withholding payment due to a solvent contractor because of an unfounded claim for a lien.

Once the statutory period has elapsed and no claims have been registered, the owner may pay the holdback to the contractor and complete her obligations under the contract. Typically, documentation certifying completion is prepared.

Practical Application of Builders' Liens

Mortgage Lenders An owner of land usually finances a construction project by mortgaging the land to a mortgagee who advances the mortgage money as work progresses on the building. Some builders' lien laws require a mortgagee to withhold from the mortgage advances an amount equal to the holdback the owner should withhold from the contractor. Even if the Act does not have such requirements, it is sensible for a mortgagee to hold back. Trust rules apply to these funds as well.

Tenants When a tenant contracts to have a building erected on his landlord's property or, perhaps more commonly, to have improvements made to existing buildings, a builders' lien is not enforceable against the landlord's interest in the property unless the lienholder can establish that the work was undertaken either expressly or impliedly at the request of the landlord.

Contractors Who Own the Land Contractors construct buildings on their own land, especially residential buildings. If bad luck or mismanagement cause insolvency, his "subcontracts" with specialized trades are really main contracts with himself as owner. Accordingly, the land is subject to liability for the total value of the liens, and the holdback provisions do not apply. Often a builder will have obtained mortgage

---

[57] *Ibid.*, s 6(3) (BC); s 22(1) (ON).

money on the land; the mortgagee will have priority over the lienholders for only the money already advanced to the builder before the liens arose.

OTHER STATUTORY PROTECTION OF CREDITORS

Provisions protecting the rights of creditors, or of particular types of creditors, are added to many statutes as incidental to the main aim of the statute.

Business Corporations Acts

As noted in Chapter 26, a corporation's creditors may seek an "oppression remedy," provided in section 241 of the *Canada Business Corporations Act* (CBCA) and the various provincial acts. Although the primary intention behind the oppression remedy was to protect shareholder rights and interests, the CBCA[58] includes, in the definition of a "complainant" who may seek a remedy for oppression, the holder of a "security" of the corporation (which includes a debt obligation) and "any other person who, in the discretion of the court, is a proper person to make an application" under that part of the Act.

The remedy may be granted where the court is satisfied that the actions of a corporation have been oppressive or unfairly prejudicial to the interests of "any security holder, creditor, director, or officer" of the corporation.

In a number of cases, most notably in the Supreme Court of Canada's decision in *BCE Inc v 1976 Bondholders*, it has been held that creditors, both secured and unsecured, have standing to complain of oppression by the managers of their debtor corporation and are entitled to seek any of the wide range of remedies that the court has discretion to order.[59]

To avoid claims of oppression, directors and officers must consider more than just the legal rights of creditors—they have a duty to consider the reasonable expectations of creditors before deciding on a course of action.[60] Usual commercial practice and past behaviour of management play a significant role in forming the reasonable expectations of creditors, and any departure from these should be done cautiously with due regard for the prejudicial effect on the creditor's interests.[61]

CASE 29.6 Oppression

SCI Systems advanced money to GTL Co. in return for a promissory note for $800 000. GTL defaulted when the note became due, and SCI obtained a default judgment against GTL. GTL still failed to pay, claiming it was unable to do so. SCI discovered that, shortly before the note became due, GTL paid dividends amounting to $850 000 to its three directors, who were also its sole shareholders, and also transferred to them other assets worth $250 000.

In an oppression action under the (Ontario) *Business Corporations Act*, the court held that the conduct of the directors had resulted in protecting the company from its payment obligation to SCI Systems. The acts of GTL Co.'s directors were oppressive to SCI, and the directors were personally liable for the full amount of the judgment.[62]

---

[58] RSC 1985, c C-44, ss 238, 241.

[59] *BCE Inc v 1976 Bondholders*, 2008 SCC 69. See also *Levy-Russell Ltd v Shieldings Inc*, [1998] OJ No 3932; *First Edmonton Place Ltd v 315888 Alberta Ltd*, [1988] AJ No 511 (Alta. Q.B.), aff'd [1989] AJ No 1021 (AB). Section 241(3) of the *Canadian Business Corporations Act* empowers a court to make an order as it thinks fit upon a finding of oppression.

[60] *BCE Inc, supra* note 59 at paras 101–2.

[61] *Ibid* at paras 73–94.

[62] *SCI Systems, Inc v Gornitzki Thompson & Little Co* (1997), 147 DLR (4th) 300 varied only as to amount [1998] OJ No. 2299. The applicant also relied on the provisions of the *Fraudulent Conveyances Act*, RSO 1990, c F.29, and the *Assignments and Preferences Act*, RSO 1990, c A.33, but having found oppression, the court considered it unnecessary to deal with that issue. See also *Far East Food Products Ltd v 1104742 Ontario Ltd*, [2009] OJ No 1153.

Although the courts have occasionally warned that debt actions should not be routinely turned into oppression actions,[63] the practice of using the oppression remedy as a means of enforcing creditors' rights is common. This trend is perhaps unfortunate, since it seems that the oppression remedy can be used to allow one creditor to gain an advantage over other creditors with competing claims, creditors who are not parties to the action and whose interests are not required to be considered by the court. It also adds yet another form of action to the already bewildering confusion of potentially conflicting creditors' remedies. In *BCE Inc v 1976 Bondholders*, the Supreme Court denied the bondholders' claim of oppression arising from the directors' decision to accept a buyout offer to privatize the company. The transaction was in the best interests of the company and necessary to remain financially viable, and conflicting stakeholder interests could not all be met.[64]

LIMITATIONS STATUTES

We noted in Chapter 12 a person with a cause of action against someone who owes a debt or who is in breach of contract must begin that action within a prescribed period or lose the right to sue. In most provinces the usual limitation period is two years.[65] A plaintiff must start court proceedings within two years of the breach of non-payment or lose the right to sue. Time limits to start a lawsuit protect debtors on the grounds that a creditor who fails to pursue a claim leaves the debtor in a state of uncertainty that should not to continue permanently, and because, as the years pass, it becomes more difficult to produce the evidence concerning the facts of the case.

The limitation period runs from the time that the claim is "discoverable." A right of action does not arise until there has been a breach or default. In a contract for the sale of goods on credit, the seller's right of action does not arise until the price becomes due and the buyer fails to pay. A trade account receivable often comprises a number of charges for goods or services invoiced at different times in the past and since paid in part. A customer (debtor) is entitled to specify the particular purchases against which a payment on account is to be applied, but in the absence of such instructions, the supplier (creditor) is entitled to treat each payment as discharging the oldest outstanding purchases and so keep the debt current.

The limitation period for an action for breach of contract starts over again if the debtor makes a part payment or delivers a written promise to pay. However, if the debtor makes a new promise to pay the debt, he is bound by that promise and may be sued upon it.

A debtor need not make an express promise to pay; his promise to pay may be implied from the circumstances of the part payment. Normally, a presumption of a new promise to pay arises from the mere fact of making a part payment or from a written acknowledgment of the debt, without other evidence to contradict the presumption.

Each province has a general limitations statute governing limitation periods for a number of different classes of actions, and limitation periods are often also prescribed in other statutes. The limitation periods vary considerably. For this reason, when considering starting an action or defending one under the provisions of a statute, a lawyer first checks to see if a limitation period might affect the rights of the parties.

---

[63] See *Royal Trust Corp of Canada v Hordo* (1993), 10 BLR (2d) 86. A creditor does not have an automatic right to bring an action for an oppression remedy. The remedy is discretionary and should probably not be granted where ordinary bankruptcy proceedings provide a satisfactory resolution: see *CC Petroleum Ltd v Allen* (2003), 36 BLR (3d) 244.

[64] *BCE Inc, supra* note 59 at paras 61, 110–4.

[65] See e.g. *Limitations Act*, RSA 2000, c L-12, s 3; *Limitation Act*, RSBC 1996, c 266, s 3; *Limitations Act*, SO 2002, c 24, s 4. In some provinces, the period for actions in contract is still six years; for example, *Limitation of Actions Act*, RSNS 1989, c 258, s 2(1)(e).

Strategies to Manage the Legal Risks

Businesses are both debtors and creditors. From a creditor perspective, the best strategy is to be careful when granting credit. Take advantage of the available public records of credit history, proposals, and bankruptcies. Search not only the corporate name of the debtor but also its directors and officers to determine if the current company is merely a fresh start after a bankrupt business. Ask for the personal guarantee of the principal where credit history is weak or unavailable. Take security in the goods provided; this will raise the priority of the debt in an eventual bankruptcy. Set up a control system to monitor lien periods for building supplies and limitation periods for all debts so the collection actions are commenced within the necessary legal time periods. If dealing with an insolvent debtor, seek super priority before extending further credit or continuing to supply.

From a debtor's perspective, consider carefully before personally guaranteeing the debts of the business; monitor accounts receivable so payments are made on time, and check credit history regularly to ensure that it properly reflects the position of the business. Take evasive action early by communicating with creditors and considering proposals or CCAA arrangements before bankruptcy is the only solution. Be careful not to mislead creditors as to the financial credibility of the company, as this is a bankruptcy offence, and resulting debts are not discharged. Directors and officers may be personally liable if they do this.

Directors and officers of an insolvent corporation that is undertaking a BIA proposal or a restructuring under the CCAA should seek indemnification from liability either through director's liability insurance or a court-ordered preferred charge against the assets of the corporation. Such a charge ranks ahead of secured creditors. Of course, directors and officers must still act with due diligence in the best interests of the corporation as gross negligence or willful misconduct will not be indemnified.

When considering proposals under the BIA, arrangements under the CCAA or restructuring plans under business corporations legislation, directors and officers should be aware of their obligations to consider not only the legal rights of creditors but their reasonable expectations. Claims of oppression will follow any decision that unduly or unfairly prejudices the rights of a creditor. Due consideration of all interests and expectations balanced against the best interests of the corporation are management's best defence.

QUESTIONS FOR REVIEW

1. What objectives does the *Bankruptcy and Insolvency Act* seek to achieve?
2. What are the functions of the Superintendent of Bankruptcy, the Official Receiver, and the Trustee in Bankruptcy?
3. Distinguish between a bankrupt and an insolvent person.
4. How is a "consumer debtor" defined?
5. What is the difference between an assignment and a bankruptcy order?
6. What is the effect, in bankruptcy law, of a proposal?
7. Distinguish between an act of bankruptcy and a bankruptcy offence.
8. Distinguish between an arm's length and non-arm's length transaction preference.
9. What is a "transfer under value"?
10. What special right does an unpaid seller of goods have when the buyer is bankrupt?

11. What is a "preferred creditor"? What are the principal categories of preferred claims?
12. How does a bankrupt become "discharged"?
13. What is the aim of the *Companies' Creditors Arrangement Act*?
14. What is the purpose of a "holdback" under builders' lien legislation?
15. Whose interests are protected by a builders' lien?
16. How do the business corporations statutes protect creditors of corporations?

CASES AND PROBLEMS

1. Continuing Scenario

    Most of Ashley's customers pay their accounts on a per visit basis. Credit is extended to only a few regular customers and some food services businesses that carry her bakery line. Bunch-A-Lunch is a lunch-truck sole proprietorship that carries Ashley's baked goods and is billed monthly. Its account has been in arrears for six months when Ashley receives a letter from a trustee in bankruptcy for Jason Bunch, the sole proprietor of Bunch-A-Lunch. The letter announces that Jason has made an assignment into bankruptcy and lists Ashley's restaurant among his creditors. A prove claim form is enclosed. Upon further investigation, Ashley discovers that the bank has a PPSA security interest registered in the lunch truck; that Steven, the part-time driver who fills in for Jason, has not been paid in two months; and that the business has only been in operation for two years. This is a surprise to Ashley because Jason said that the business was 10 years old on the customer account application form he filled out for Ashley a year ago. What should Brendan, Ashley's lawyer, tell her about the bankruptcy process, where her claim would rank among other creditors, and whether her debt could survive the bankruptcy?

2. Leung was in serious financial difficulties. She owed $150 000 to Desert Rose Inc., in respect of a business venture. She also owed $100 000 to Kwan. She entered into an agreement with Kwan whereby she sold her house to Kwan for $500 000, which was approximately its fair market value. The debt of $100 000 was set off against the purchase price, and it was further agreed that Kwan would lease the house back to Leung for a period of two years at a rent of $30 000 a year. That sum of $60 000 was also set against the purchase price. The balance of $340 000 was paid on completion of the transfer and was mostly used by Leung to pay off debts to her other creditors.

    When Desert Rose sought to collect the debt owed to it, Leung was unable to pay. Does Desert Rose have grounds for impugning the transaction between Leung and Kwan?

3. On April 1, Greenfingers Garden Centre Ltd. was declared bankrupt as a result of a petition entered by the Agricultural Bank Ltd. The Bank was owed $250 000 by Greenfingers and had registered a security interest pursuant to a general security agreement that covered all of Greenfingers's inventory and other business assets.

    On the preceding March 1, Snow White Ornaments Inc. had supplied Greenfingers with 120 garden gnomes, to the value of $2500. On March 12, Bauer, a farmer, supplied a number of fruit trees to Greenfingers for $1000. And on March 15, Spreaders Inc. supplied Greenfingers with a quantity of bags of fertilizer for $800. None of them has been paid. Some of the trees and fertilizer, and almost all the gnomes, remain unsold.

    What claims do the respective creditors have?

4. Buckhouse Inc. is the owner of a large office building in the downtown area of a major Canadian city. It entered into a 10-year lease, at a monthly rental of $8000, with Justitia Ltd. As an inducement to enter into the lease, Buckhouse granted Justitia an 18-month rent-free period, a leasehold improvement allowance of $100 000, and a cash payment of $150 000.

Justitia Ltd. is a corporation formed by two lawyers, Straight and Narrow, as a management company for their law practice. Straight and Narrow are the sole shareholders and directors of Justitia.

The law practice occupied the premises for a period of 21 months, though Straight and Narrow never entered into a written lease with Justitia Ltd. At the end of that period, with rent having been paid for only three months, they moved out of the building and found other premises.

Justitia has ceased to pay rent to Buckhouse and, apart from the lease, has no assets. The inducement payment of $150 000 was paid out as a dividend to Straight and Narrow.

Does Buckhouse have any claim against Straight and Narrow?

5. The N.S.F. Manufacturing Co. Ltd. was adjudged bankrupt on a petition of its creditors, and the trustee in bankruptcy realized the following amounts from the sale of its business assets:

Cash in bank	$ 1 000
Accounts receivable	52 000
Inventories	25 000
Land and buildings	74 000
	$152 000

The liabilities of the business were as follows at the time of the receiving order:

Bank loan secured under section 427 of the *Bank Act*	$ 40 000
Trade accounts payable	65 000
Municipal taxes payable	5 000
Wages payable (five months at $3000 per month for one employee)	15 000
First mortgage on land and buildings	50 000
Second mortgage on land and buildings	25 000
	$200 000

The expenses of liquidation were $5000. The trustee's fee was $3000.

How many cents on the dollar should the general creditors receive? Show the order in which the trustee in bankruptcy made payments to the various types of creditors. Assume that all secured creditors had taken the necessary steps to protect their security.

6. Yorkville Construction Inc. was the main contractor on a large construction project on land owned by Mayfair Properties Ltd. Yorkville engaged Rodwell Ltd. to provide piping insulation services for the project. Yorkville received a series of payments from Mayfair under the contract and used all the monies to pay its general overhead expenses, including advertising and promotion expenses, bank charges, insurance, lease payments on its vehicles, office rent, and utilities. It did not pay Rodwell for its work. Yorkville became insolvent.

Does Rodwell have any claim against (a) Mayfair or (b) the directors of Yorkville?

Part 8 The Modern Legal Environment for Business

Chapter 30
International Business Transactions

- **CANADIAN BUSINESS IN A GLOBAL ECONOMY**
- **LAW AND INTERNATIONAL BUSINESS**
- **FOREIGN TRADE**
- **FOREIGN INVESTMENT**
- **THE RESOLUTION OF INTERNATIONAL BUSINESS DISPUTES**
- **STRATEGIES TO MANAGE THE LEGAL RISKS**

As previous chapters have identified, both law and business administration in Canada often involve international issues. Increasingly, the world is becoming a single giant marketplace in which businesses from different countries compete against and sometimes cooperate with each other. This chapter provides an overview of the legal framework within which international business is conducted, discussing various aspects of foreign trade, foreign investment, and the resolution of international business disputes.

In this chapter we examine such questions as:

- What are the common features of export contracts?
- How are export contracts interpreted and enforced?
- How do governments regulate international trade?
- How is international trade affected and promoted by the World Trade Organization (WTO) and international treaties?
- What are the legal forms available to foreign investors?
- How do governments regulate foreign investment?
- In what ways does international law apply to investment?
- How are international business obligations enforced by the courts?
- What is the role of international commercial arbitration?
- How are international trade disputes resolved?

CANADIAN BUSINESS IN A GLOBAL ECONOMY

The international dimension of Canadian business is very important. Canadian exports amount to approximately 30 percent the nation's gross domestic product.[1] Canada ranks among the top 15 of the world's trading nations and is a major exporter of both goods and services. In 2017, its total exports amounted to $662.6 billion, and imports to $711.9 billion. To put these figures in perspective, one of the world's largest exporters, the United States, exports approximately three times as much merchandise as Canada, and Japan not even double.

Canada's largest trading partner is the United States, which takes over 70 percent of our exports and provides over 50 percent of our imports. In turn, Canada is one of the largest trading partners of the United States. The United States exports more to Canada than to any other trading partner except the European Union and imports more from Canada than from anywhere else except the European Union, China, and Mexico.[2] Canada also has substantial trading relations with China, the United Kingdom, Germany, Korea, Japan, the Netherlands, France, and Mexico.

Traditionally, Canada's strength was as an exporter of raw materials and minerals—Canada remains among the world's largest exporters in these categories—as well as resource-based products, but we have become an important exporter of manufactured goods, chemicals, and transport and telecommunications equipment.

As one of the world's major industrialized economies, Canada ranks among the top 10 countries as both an exporter and importer of investment capital. Foreign direct investment (FDI) is not only important as a source of funding but also as a transfer of know-how and job creation. Recent uncertainty surrounding North American free trade and oil development has caused a drop in FDI. In 2017 foreign companies sold more foreign business than they bought.[3]

LAW AND INTERNATIONAL BUSINESS

Historically, establishing international business operations was a progression for an existing business. First, a business marketed its products to the local community. Eventually it expanded, creating substantial regional or national presence. At some stage, it found its first customer in another country, and its operations became international. This is the **foreign trade** stage.

As a business's foreign markets grew, a **foreign presence** was developed by appointing an agent in the other country or establishing a representative office there. Gradually, its activities might expand from simply seeking customers and providing information to supplying spare parts, repairs, and maintenance services. Eventually, the firm would commence other activities abroad, such as processing its products, labelling, packaging, or assembling components. Finally, the operations would develop into full-scale manufacturing, and a branch or subsidiary might be established. In this typical progression, the business graduated from foreign trade to **foreign investment** and became, by definition, a multinational enterprise.

foreign trade the buying and selling of goods and services between parties from different countries

foreign presence placing representatives of a business in foreign markets

foreign investment conducting operations in a foreign market

---

[1] Exports were 31 percent of GDP in 2016 and 30.9 percent in 2017. Global Affairs Canada, http://w05.international.gc.ca/Commerce_International/Canada_Indicator-Indicateur.aspx?lang=eng. Other statistics in this section are drawn from the aforesaid source and the World Trade Organization's Canadian trade profiles, http://stat.wto.org/CountryProfile/WSDBCountryPFView.aspx?Language=E&Country=US.

[2] According to the WTO, China supplied 21.4 percent of the total imports to the United States in 2016, the European Union supplied 18.9 percent of total U.S. imports, Mexico supplied 13.2 percent, and Canada was a close fourth at 12.6 percent. The United States sent 18.3 percent of its exports to Canada, the second most to any country; first was the European Union, which received 18.7 percent.

[3] Theophilos Argitis, "Foreign Direct Investment Plunges to Lowest in 8 Years," *Bloomberg News*, March 1, 2018, https://business.financialpost.com/news/economy/foreign-direct-investment-in-canada-plunges-on-oil-exodus-1.

Two developments have altered the typical progression. First, the ecommerce revolution has allowed many new businesses to attract domestic and international customers at the same time. Launching a business online may mean that the very first customers of a new business could be international, accelerating the new business to the foreign trade stage. Second, access to cheap labour abroad has meant that many new ventures start with imported parts or even manufacture products abroad from the inception of the business. Therefore, in the current business environment, familiarity with international business issues is a necessity for even start-up businesses.

Foreign trade and foreign investment create a wide variety of legal relationships and involve law from multiple jurisdictions. There are contractual relationships of many different types—sale of goods and services, carriage of goods, bailment, insurance, agency, and employment. Questions arise regarding the law of negotiable instruments, intellectual property, partnerships and corporations, secured transactions, and creditors' remedies. International business transactions, by definition, involve parties in two or more different countries. Which country's law will apply to a transaction? This is a question of private law—the law that governs transactions between private parties such as a seller and a buyer of goods.

Virtually every government regulates foreign trade and investment to some extent, controlling access to its market. Therefore, international business also involves legal relationships between private persons or entities and governments. This raises questions of public law involving the foreign and domestic governments. Canada, like most developed nations, requires some domestic business behaviour abroad to conform to minimum domestic standards. For example, as discussed in Chapter 3, Canada's *Corruption of Foreign Public Officials Act* prohibits bribery of foreign government officials even when the practice is not prohibited by the foreign country.[4]

Finally, in an effort to open international markets for their businesses, governments often make bilateral agreements or multilateral agreements (such as the General Agreement on Tariffs and Trade (GATT), the North American Free Trade Agreement (NAFTA), NAFTA's successor the United States-Mexico-Canada Agreement (USMCA) currently being ratified and the International Convention for the Protection of Industrial Property). As a result, issues of **public international law**, involving relations between states, also arise. Signing a treaty imposes a duty on a government to pass domestic legislation to implement the terms of the treaty. All proposed international treaties are debated in Parliament before Canada formally ratifies a **treaty**.[5] The USMCA is currently moving through this ratification process.

Various **non-governmental organizations** (NGOs) and super-governmental organizations (SGOs) work to establish common standards and laws around the world. Member countries of SGOs send government representatives to lobby for their positions and negotiate on their country's behalf. Examples include the World Trade Organization (WTO), the United Nations Commission on International Trade Law, and the Organisation for Economic Co-operation and Development (OECD). Some standards are introduced as codes of conduct, guiding principles, and suggested contractual language, with the hope that private business will voluntarily adopt them. Other times, treaties are negotiated or suggested legislative models are produced to influence governments as they implement domestic legislation. These organizations play a major role in the development of international business law.

public international law law involving relations between states

treaty an international agreement concluded between states in written form and governed by international law

non-governmental organizations voluntary, non-profit associations of private entities working to influence policy, raise awareness, and effect change, such as the International Chamber of Commerce

---

[4] SC 1998, c 34, s 3.

[5] Global Affairs Canada, Policy on Tabling of Treaties in Parliament, http://www.treaty-accord.gc.ca/procedures.aspx.

FOREIGN TRADE

Export/Import Contracts

Export/import contracts are either contracts for the international sale of goods or contracts for the supply of services abroad. Goods or services may be supplied in one of three main ways:

- The supplier may deliver directly to the customer in the other country.
- Delivery may be made through the supplier's own marketing organization established in the other country.
- The customer may accept delivery in the supplier's home country and himself arrange to ship the goods home.

The following discussion concentrates on the most common type of export transaction—contracts for the international sale of goods.

The Contract of Sale Much of the law of contract described earlier in this text applies equally to export contracts as it does to contracts with domestic parties. However, contracts with an international element present special problems due to the involvement of a customer in, and therefore the law of, another country.

Usually, the international sale of goods involves a number of parties and consists of several distinct though related contracts. In addition to the basic agreement for the sale of the goods, the parties normally arrange for the transportation of the goods, for their insurance during shipment, and, frequently, for the financing of the transaction. Carriers, insurers, banks, or finance houses may be involved as well as the buyer and seller. Since export transactions require special expertise, the parties commonly appoint specialist brokers, **export houses or freight forwarders**, as agents to make the arrangements for shipment, insurance, and financing.

export houses or freight forwarders specialist firms that make the arrangements for shipment, insurance, and financing in export sales

The Proper Law of the Contract This phrases identifies which of the two or more countries' laws govern the contract or any dispute arising under it. Why does it matter?

ILLUSTRATION 30.1 Multi-Country Transaction

A Canadian manufacturer sells goods to a Hungarian customer. The goods are to be shipped by a German airline, insured by a British insurance company, and financed by a Swiss bank.

Several contracts make up the entire transaction in Illustration 30.1, and each one might be governed by a different country's law. The laws of the different countries may not be the same with respect to the rights of unpaid vendors or carriers or implied terms of quality or fitness.

To determine which law applies—that is, the **proper law of the contract**—it is necessary to refer to a body of principles known as the **conflict of laws or private international law**. Canadian courts, and the courts of most other countries, hold that the proper law of the contract is the law that the parties intended to govern their relationship. The clearest method of establishing the proper law is for the parties themselves to name it in their contract.[6] A contract might state that it is subject to the law of Ontario or Michigan. The choice of law need not be that of the location of one of the parties or be related to the place where the contract is to be performed—sometimes the parties choose a "neutral" law.

proper law of the contract the law of the country or jurisdiction by which the terms of a contract or disputes under it are to be interpreted and decided

conflict of laws or private international law the principles of law that apply to determine which country's laws govern a dispute involving private parties

---

[6] *Vita Food Products Inc v Unus Shipping Co Ltd*, [1939] AC 277.

If the contract does not expressly identify the proper law, a court will attempt to determine the intention of the parties first by considering the contract as a whole in light of the surrounding circumstances.[7] For example, if the contract states that any dispute is to be submitted to arbitration in a particular country, or that the courts of a particular country shall have jurisdiction, then it is probable that they also intended the law of that country to govern the contract.[8] An intention may also be inferred from the use of particular legal terminology or the form of the document. Where the court cannot draw such an inference, it will apply the system of law that it considers to be most closely connected with the contract. In making this determination, it will consider all the circumstances and pay special attention to such factors as the place where the contract was made, the place where it is to be performed, the subject matter of the contract, and the place of business of the parties.[9]

Contractual Terms Theoretically terms or expressions in import/export contracts may have different meanings in different legal systems or to parties from different countries. In practice, the problem is not as severe as it might seem. Over time widely accepted standard terminology has evolved. The meaning of short forms, such as "FOB" and "CIF" discussed next, became largely standardized through continuous use. Eventually, use of a set of standard terms (known as **Incoterms**) adopted by the International Chamber of Commerce became standard commercial practice. The original Incoterms were first published in 1936, and the current version date is 2010.[10]

> **Incoterms** a set of standard contractual terms adopted by the International Chamber of Commerce

Another important development has been the publication and widespread adoption of standard form contracts, published by various trade associations and by international bodies such as the International Chamber of Commerce or the United Nations Economic Commission for Europe. SGOs, such as the International Institute for the Unification of Private Law (**UNIDROIT**), the United Nations Commission on International Trade Law (**UNCITRAL**), and the Organisation for Economic Co-operation and Development (**OECD**) have encouraged the harmonization of national commercial laws or the adoption of uniform laws. For example, the 1980 Vienna Convention on Contracts for the International Sale of Goods, implemented in Canada in 1991,[11] standardized sale-of-goods terms and practices resulting in an international standard of interpretation. Canadian ecommerce legislation, discussed in Chapter 31, follows the template of the UNCITRAL model law. The process of harmonization is an ongoing one, continually evolving in order to support globalization.

> **UNIDROIT** International Institute for the Unification of Private Law, founded by the League of Nations in 1926 to harmonize laws; currently has 63 member states, including Canada

> **UNCITRAL** United Nations Commission on International Trade Law established by the United Nations General Assembly in 1966 to further harmonization and unification in international trade through conventions, model laws, and guidelines

> **OECD** Organisation for Economic Co-operation and Development, established in 1961, has 34 member countries, including Canada, and promotes world trade and sustainable economic growth by setting standards for best practice

The Documentation An export sale normally requires at least four documents:

- the contract of sale
- the bill of lading
- the insurance policy or certificate
- the invoice

---

[7] *Lilydale Cooperative Limited v Meyn Canada Inc*, 2015 ONCA 281 at para 9. *Consolidated Bathurst Export Limited v Mutual Boiler and Machinery Insurance Company*, [1980] 1 SCR 888; *Herman v Alberta (Public Trustee)*, 2002 ABQB 255.

[8] *Hamlyn & Co v Talisker Distillery*, [1894] AC 202.

[9] *Imperial Life Assurance Co of Canada v Colmenares*, [1967] SCR 443 at 448. See also *Pope & Talbot Ltd (Re)*, [2009] BCJ No 2248 at paras 29–41.

[10] See http://www.iccwbo.org/incoterms.

[11] *International Sale of Goods Contracts Convention Act*, SC 1991, c 13. It has also been adopted by several of the provinces; see e.g. *International Sale of Goods Act*, SNS 1988, c 13; RSO 1990, c I.10.

We already discussed the contract of sale and bills of lading in Chapter 14 and insurance in Chapter 16. A bill of lading is an acknowledgment by the carrier that the goods have been delivered for shipment. It operates as a document of title to the goods, facilitating the financing of the transaction. The insurance policy, similarly, is evidence that the goods are insured against loss or damage during transit and is usually necessary in order to obtain financing.

These tangible forms of documentation have been replaced by computerized communications. NGOs such as the Comité Maritime International[12] have devised uniform sets of rules dealing with electronic data exchange for international maritime business transactions.

Shipment and Insurance Terms describing transportation arrangements are an essential element of an export contract as transportation presents a significant risk of damage. Usually, the goods will be insured against loss or damage during transit, and either the buyer or the seller assumes responsibility for arranging insurance depending on the travel arrangements. The contract price reflects whether it is the seller or the buyer who arranges and pays for shipment and insurance, and up to which stage of the journey. The parties may agree that the buyer will collect the goods from the seller's factory and make its own arrangements for transportation, or that the seller will deliver the goods to the buyer's premises in the other country, or that each will be responsible for some stage of the transportation. The specific arrangements for shipment may determine the point at which title to the goods, or the risk of loss, passes from the seller to the buyer.

Standard terms have evolved to describe the more common types of arrangements for shipment. Examples of these terms (with the corresponding Incoterm abbreviations) are as follows:

- EXW (ex works): The buyer picks up the goods from the seller's factory gate.
- FOB (free on board): The seller delivers the goods onto the buyer's carrier; if the carrier must load the freight then the FCA (free to carrier) and FAS (free alongside ship) acronyms apply, where the seller's duty is, respectively, to deliver to the first carrier (for example, where the goods are collected by the carrier and loaded into a container for shipment to a cargo terminal) and to deliver to a specified pier or warehouse at the port of shipment.
- CIF (cost, insurance, and freight): Seller must arrange the carrier shipment, and the buyer picks up the goods at the port of destination.[13]
- DDP (delivery duty paid): The seller delivers the goods to the buyer's location and pays all duty along the way.

The terms broadly correspond to the stages of shipment and the extent of the obligations undertaken by the seller. Figure 30.1 illustrates the primary four contract types.

Container shipping revolutionized the carriage of goods and triggered new legal terms, such as "full container load" (FCL) and "less than a full container load" (LCL). Where the consignment comprises a full container load, shipment may be made door to door in a sealed container. If there is less than a full container load, the goods are consolidated with the goods of other exporters in a "groupage container" and are loaded and separated at a container freight station.

---

[12] A non-governmental international non-profit organization devoted to the harmonization of maritime law: http://www.comitemaritime.org.

[13] Under a CFR (cost and freight) contract, the seller pays carriage, but the buyer arranges its own insurance.

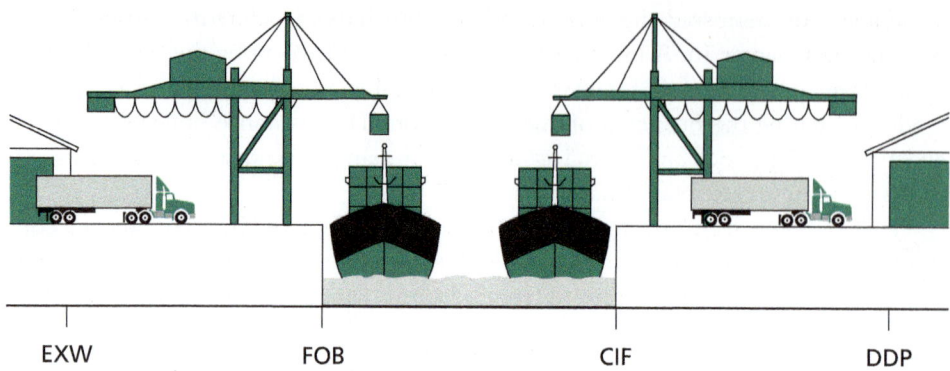

Figure 30.1   Export Contracts

Payment   A key element in any contract of sale is the payment of the price. In an international contract, the currency used to define the price and to make payment should be named. The price may be defined in one currency but paid in some other currency. Generally, a seller does not mind in which currency the price is paid, so long as that currency is freely convertible. However, the price should be stated in a stable currency, especially if there is to be a substantial time lag between contract and payment; if the buyer's country imposes **exchange controls** or does not permit its currency to be freely converted—as is often the case in developing countries—the seller should also require actual payment to be made in a "hard" currency. An exporter or importer may also "hedge" against the risk of currency fluctuations by using a method of **foreign exchange risk management**, such as borrowing in foreign currency or taking an option to buy or sell foreign currency.

exchange controls   restrictions on the conversion or export of currency

foreign exchange risk management   methods of reducing the risk involved in currency fluctuations

Financing   The time between the goods leaving the seller and reaching the buyer tends to be longer in international rather than domestic sales, and the amounts involved in international sales tend to be larger. A seller would like to receive payment as soon as its goods leave the factory or warehouse, whereas the buyer would prefer to postpone payment until the goods have been safely delivered. Accommodating both priorities normally requires the services of a banker.

Historically, the bill of exchange (see Chapter 19) was the most important method of payment in export sales. In recent years, other methods of financing have been adopted, the most important of which are the *collection arrangement* and the *letter of credit*. Under a **collection arrangement**, the seller employs the services of its bank to collect payment by depositing the documents with the bank and receiving credit for the price (less the bank's charges). By contrast, a buyer obtains a **letter of credit** from its bank and uses it to pay the seller.[14] More recently, banks and finance houses have developed other highly flexible methods of financing, such as non-recourse finance, factoring, and financial leasing, methods that require more detailed explanation and are beyond the scope of this text.

collection arrangement   an arrangement whereby the seller employs the services of its bank to collect payment by depositing the documents with the bank and receiving credit for the price

letter of credit   a document that the buyer of goods obtains from the bank and uses to pay the seller

countertrade   a form of barter, under which a seller agrees to accept payment in goods produced or procured by the buyer

Countertrade   In its simplest form, **countertrade** is a form of barter. A seller agrees to accept, instead of money, payment in goods produced or procured by the buyer. Another increasingly common arrangement is for a corporation that sells machinery to a firm in a developing country to agree to accept part of that firm's production as the price; thus it might sell modern cutting and sewing equipment and receive finished clothing in return. The forms of countertrade are virtually unlimited, but countertrade involves greater risks than do simple sales, since the "seller" will have

---

[14] An alternative method is for the buyer to obtain a banker's guarantee.

to find a way of disposing of the goods acquired in exchange. Further, parties should not assume that a good is exempt from government regulation: Certain products will be banned and import duties may attach to others.[15]

Export and Import of Services Trade in services can take a number of forms. A buyer may come to a seller, as where a foreign tourist stays in a hotel or attends a concert in Canada. Transactions of this nature generally do not involve any element of foreign law. Or a seller might go to a buyer, as where a Canadian bank or insurance company opens a branch in another country to serve customers there. It is also possible for services to be transmitted to customers in other countries. Data, legal or financial advice, or technological expertise may be supplied to customers in other countries. Property in one country may be insured by an insurance company in another country. Banks may lend money to foreign clients. The value of Canadian service trade is much smaller than its trade in goods, reaching only $85.6 billion in exports and $105 billion in imports in 2017.[16]

Much of what has been said in relation to the international sale of goods applies equally to the provision of services—for example, the importance of determining the proper law of the contract and the problems of payment. Of particular importance in contracts involving the transfer of technology are the local rules governing the protection of intellectual property. A Canadian corporation that licenses a patent or a trademark or supplies "know-how" to an enterprise in another country will first want to ensure that its rights are protected by the laws of that country and that its trade secrets do not become public knowledge.

Intellectual Property Most developing nations are not members of the World Intellectual Property Organization discussed in Chapter 20 and do not integrate their intellectual property rules or standards with the developed world. Protection must be sought in the target country. China, for example, has a first-to-register system for trademarks,[17] and failure to register will mean loss of ability to protect a brand. There are also usually special rules for foreign companies seeking to register. Naturally, a business will want to convert its name, logo, or brand to a Chinese version that has meaning to the targeted consumer. As in Canada, copyrights do not have to be registered in China, but completing the optional registration process is recommended. Registration is not a guarantee of protection. Sometimes a developing nation lacks an effective or independent legal system, so enforcing a properly registered trademark against a resident may still be unsuccessful.[18] For added protection, import and export contracts should confirm the ownership of existing intellectual property; designate ownership of any new products, designs, etc., that are generated under the contract; and call for the safeguarding, return, and non-disclosure of any confidential information, including product specifications, designs, or moulds, at the end of the contract.[19] The effectiveness of foreign intellectual property protection should be a consideration when entering a foreign market or designating the proper law of a contract.

---

[15] UNCITRAL *Legal Guide on International Countertrade Transactions*, United Nations, NY, 1993.

[16] *Supra* note 1.

[17] Canadian Intellectual Property Office, "Protecting Your Intellectual Property in China," https://www.ic.gc.ca/eic/site/cipointernet-internetopic.nsf/eng/wr04329.html; U.S. China Business Council, Best Practices: Intellectual Property Protection in China, https://www.uschina.org/reports/best-practices-intellectual-property-protection-china.

[18] *Ibid.*; Craig Wong, "Investing in China Tricky Business at Best of Times, Experts Say," *The Record*, June 11, 2011 at C3; Voler Behr, "Development of a New Legal System in the People's Republic of China" (2006–07) 67 La. L. Rev. 1161.

[19] See e.g. *Ann of Green Gables Licensing Authority Inc v Avonlea Traditions Inc*, [2000] OJ No 740 (contractual term as to ownership of copyright influenced outcome).

Government Regulation of International Trade

Since foreign trade first began, governments have tried to regulate it by controlling exports and imports and imposing customs duties. Trade relations are a matter of national importance, and although many countries, such as Canada and most of its major trading partners, are generally committed to the principle of free trade, they still maintain barriers that a would-be exporter must overcome. Governments want a reasonable positive **balance of trade** with other countries. Consequently, the tendency is to encourage exports and discourage imports that compete with local business.

balance of trade offset of value of exports against value of imports

Export Promotion Governments provide a variety of services to their own producers in order to assist them to compete in the global market. An important function of Canadian foreign affairs staff is to collect commercial information and disseminate it to Canadian business. More tangible support—mostly in the form of insurance, guarantees, and financial services—is provided by Export Development Canada,[20] a Crown corporation credit agency owned by the Government of Canada whose purpose is to facilitate and develop Canada's export trade. Government support is especially important with respect to exports to less-developed countries, by providing loan guarantees, insurance, bonding services, and long-term credit. International aid programs may also provide indirect assistance to exporters. Still, these promotional efforts must not violate trade treaties that guarantee equal treatment to domestic and foreign producers.

Export Controls Although the general policy of most countries is to encourage exports, restrictions upon exports remain common. Export controls in Canada date back to the *Export Act* of 1897,[21] which regulated the export of a number of commodities, notably lumber. The federal government introduced further controls for reasons of national security during the First World War and created a more comprehensive system following the Second World War and the commencement of the Cold War in 1947 under the *Export and Import Permits Act*.[22] The Act introduced a system of licensing for exports of certain listed products and for most exports to listed countries. Among the listed products are armaments, munitions, and other strategic materials. Listed countries were mostly confined to members of the then communist bloc. Further regulations and other statutes have added to the lists both of products and of countries. Restrictions have been imposed on the export of certain types of cultural property and of some energy and agricultural products, and from time to time countries such as South Africa, Iran, Libya, and Iraq have joined the list of proscribed countries. Canada is also a member of the Wassenaar Arrangement, under which 40 countries set restrictions on exports of high-tech products to communist and some other countries (Wassenaar Arrangement on Export Controls for Conventional Arms, Dual Use Goods and Technologies).[23] Finally, the *Special Economic Measures Act*[24] contains a general power to make orders and regulations restricting or prohibiting the exportation by Canadians of goods, whether from Canada or anywhere else in the world, to designated foreign states or to persons in such states.

An added problem, which has probably affected Canada more than any other country, has been the extraterritorial application of U.S. legislation. Such legislation is intended to prevent the re-export (from Canada and other countries) of products

---

[20] EDC is governed by the *Export Development Act*, RSC 1985, c E-20. It reports to the federal government through the Minister of International Trade, SI/93-108.

[21] SC 1897, c 17: now RSC 1985, c E-18.

[22] SC 1947, c 17; now RSC 1985, c E-19.

[23] http://www.wassenaar.org.

[24] SC 1992, c 17 (see s. 4).

originating in the United States to countries such as Cuba and also prohibits dealings with those countries by foreign subsidiaries of U.S. corporations. The so-called Helms-Burton law[25] carries the process still further, potentially rendering Canadian (and other) firms with investments in Cuba liable to penalties in U.S. courts. In response, the federal government amended the *Foreign Extraterritorial Measures Act*, rendering judgments under the Helms-Burton law unenforceable in Canada.[26] In 2015, the U.S. restored diplomatic relations with Cuba but the trade embargo remains.

Import Duties

Customs duties on imports have been in existence almost as long as international trade itself. Originally these duties provided an important source of revenue for many countries but growth of other sources of government revenue, especially income tax, and the worldwide movement to tariff reduction have steadily reduced the fiscal importance of import duties. Now their most important function is to protect domestic products against competition from cheaper imports.

Two statutes contain most of Canada's import duty legislation—the *Customs Act*[27] and the *Customs Tariff*.[28] The first deals with the administration of the system by the Canada Revenue Agency and provides the basis for regulations that classify products and determine their dutiable value and country of origin. The Customs Tariff sets out the rates of duty (tariff) imposed on each category of products.

The setting of tariffs is no longer determined unilaterally by domestic governments but is largely guided by international treaties, such as GATT, NAFTA, and NAFTA's successor USMCA (still pending all three government's ratification) discussed next. For goods imported into Canada, various preferences are granted, notably for products coming from Commonwealth, Caribbean, and less-developed countries, and from our North American trading partners, Mexico and the United States. Determining the "legal" origin of goods becomes very important, since goods may be manufactured in one country from raw material or components originating in another country and may ultimately be destined for a third country.[29]

Import Restrictions

Countries often impose restrictions on imports. Sometimes the restrictions are overt, such as duties; in other instances, they are less visible. Treaties restricting the use of import duties have made **non-tariff barriers** more significant as obstacles to international trade. By Canadian law, some goods (for example, narcotics) may not be imported at all; other goods may be imported only under licence and subject to particular conditions.

non-tariff barriers national rules, other than import duties, that restrict or prevent the importation of goods

Generally, Canada adopts a relatively liberal policy toward imports from other countries and adheres to the principles established by the GATT. Nevertheless, Canada does impose import **quotas**, or quantity restrictions, on certain products,[30] particularly textiles and agricultural products. A wide variety of other statutes impose restrictions on imports in order to protect public health, public safety, and the environment, and for other reasons of public policy. Other countries impose their own restrictions, and a Canadian manufacturer wishing to export its products must always check to ensure that the products will be allowed to enter the other country.

quotas restrictions on the quantities of goods that may be imported

---

[25] *The Cuban Liberty and Democratic Solidarity Act of 1996*, 22 USC s 6021–91.

[26] *Foreign Extra-Territorial Measures Act*, RSC 1985, c F-29, s 7.1.

[27] RSC 1985, c 1 (2nd Supp).

[28] SC 1997, c 36.

[29] The dispute between Canada and the United States regarding the origin of Honda cars manufactured in Canada, using components made in Japan and sold in the United States, is a good example. See Frederic P. Cantin and Andreas F. Lowenfeld, "Rules of Origin, The Canada–U.S. FTA, and the Honda Case" (1993) 87(3) *American Journal of International Law* 375–90.

[30] See *Export and Import Permits Act*, RSC 1985, c E-19. Other restrictions are contained in the *Customs Act*, supra note 27 and the *Special Import Measures Act*, RSC 1985, c S-15.

Frequently, national rules on the marketing of products are just as important as restrictions on importation. There is little point exporting products to a country if they cannot legally be resold there. National health and safety standards and labelling requirements must be complied with, and they are sometimes formulated in such a way that, although ostensibly applicable to domestic and imported products alike, in practice they discriminate against imports. For example, most food products sold in Canada must be labelled in both French and English and described in metric units.

Dumping and Subsidies The desire to promote exports, by producers themselves and by their governments, sometimes leads to two types of practices that are generally regarded as unfair or unethical—dumping and export subsidies. **Dumping** occurs when a firm sells goods abroad at prices lower than those at which similar goods sell in the domestic market. In effect, the firm uses the profits on its domestic sales to subsidize its exports and undercut its competitors. An **export subsidy** occurs when the government of a country provides special benefits, financial or otherwise, to its producers in order to assist them to export. Benefits may take a wide variety of forms, such as reduced freight charges, income tax rebates, or unusually favourable credit terms or guarantees.

Dumping and export subsidies, by reducing the price of imported goods, confer a benefit on the consumers of the importing country. Not surprisingly, however, such practices are resented by domestic manufacturers of competing products. Where domestic competition exists, and it appears that material injury has been or is likely to be caused to domestic producers of similar goods, importing countries often impose countermeasures to nullify the benefits of foreign subsidies. Countermeasures take the form of **anti-dumping duties and countervailing duties**, designed to increase the cost of imports by the amount of the margin of dumping or of the export subsidy. In Canada, such duties are imposed under the *Special Import Measures Act*.[31] Many Canadian exporters have encountered difficulties with the corresponding measures imposed by the United States.[32] Later in this chapter we will consider the impact of the WTO, NAFTA and USMCA on export subsidies and the softwood lumber trade dispute.

dumping selling products abroad at prices below those charged on domestic sales

export subsidy the granting by governments of financial assistance to promote exports

anti-dumping duties and countervailing duties special duties imposed on imported products to counter the advantage obtained from dumping or export subsidies

The International Law of Trade

In theory, national governments are free to adopt whatever measures they choose to regulate imports into, and exports from, their own territories. Of course, other countries may retaliate. If Country A imposes restrictions on imports from Country B, it can hardly expect Country B to accept Country A's exports freely. The international law of trade is primarily based on the principle of reciprocity, an approach generally followed in negotiating agreements between countries, sometimes bilaterally and sometimes on a multilateral basis. Canada is a party to many trade agreements that provide reciprocal access to domestic markets; the two most important are the General Agreement on Tariffs and Trade (GATT) and the North American Free Trade Agreement (NAFTA), which is currently being renegotiated and is expected to be replaced by the United States-Mexico-Canada Agreement (USMCA) sometime in 2019.

The GATT and the World Trade Organization (WTO)

The GATT is the principal document that formulates the rules for international trade around the world. It came into force on January 1, 1948, with nine original members,

---

[31] *Supra* note 30, s 3.

[32] See e.g. *IPSCO Inc & IPSCO Steel Inc v United States & Lone Star Steel Co* (1990) 899 F2d 1192 (U.S. Court of Appeals), and commentary by McConnell (1991), 70 *Can. Bar Rev* 180.

one of which was Canada. It grew under supervision of the World Trade Organization (WTO) to its 2016 membership of 164 countries, including Russia, admitted in 2012, and Afghanistan, admitted in 2016.

The GATT was negotiated after the Second World War. Despite its title, the GATT was far more than just an "agreement." It had an administrative arm, its own secretariat (in Geneva), a council of members, and the capacity to establish tribunals (or panels) to adjudicate disputes between member countries. Over the years its scope was extended and its rules augmented by new agreements reached in a series of conferences or "rounds." The Uruguay Round commenced in 1986 and finally concluded in December 1993 with the creation of a new administrative organization, the WTO, which formally came into existence on January 1, 1995, to facilitate negotiation of new agreements and resolve disputes under existing agreements. The WTO supersedes the GATT as an organization. The actual GATT agreement, however, remains in effect as the foundation of the trade rules, together with the various amendments and "side agreements" entered into overtime.

Probably the most serious shortcoming of the GATT was that it applied only to the international trade in *goods*, and even then it did not apply to most agricultural products or to textiles. The Uruguay Round extended GATT arrangements to include trade in some farm products, textiles, and some services, and to the protection of intellectual property rights. It also extended its application to include **trade-related investment measures** (TRIMs) and considerably strengthened the mechanisms available for the settlement of disputes. In 1997, further agreements were negotiated in relation to financial services, information technology, and telecommunications services. However, disagreements among WTO members still remain with respect to a number of sectors, in particular, agricultural products, cultural products, transportation services, electronic commerce, and environmental and labour standards.

trade-related investment measures national measures regulating investment that have an impact upon international trade

In addition to providing a forum for negotiations and for the resolution of trade disputes, the most important functions of the GATT and WTO have been the harmonization of customs rules and the progressive reduction of customs duties. In addition, the GATT sets out a code of rules governing international trade and such matters as the transportation of goods, customs procedures, and valuation.

Non-discrimination is the fundamental principle that underlies the WTO. This principle, in turn, has two elements: First, goods originating from one contracting state should not be treated more or less favourably than goods from another state—that is, all should receive **most-favoured-nation (MFN) treatment**;[33] second, goods from other member states should, once the appropriate tariff has been paid, be treated no less favourably than corresponding domestic goods—that is, they should receive **national treatment**. In accordance with these basic principles, the WTO generally prohibits quotas and other forms of non-tariff barriers, export subsidies, and, except under strict conditions, the imposition of anti-dumping duties and countervailing duties.

most-favoured-nation (MFN) treatment the principle that goods imported from one country should not be treated less favourably than those imported from any other country

national treatment the principle that goods from another country should not be treated less favourably than domestic goods

The GATT and WTO have had a two-way impact upon Canadian law and the laws of the other contracting states. First, membership imposes a positive duty to enact laws to implement the obligations agreed to within the framework of the organization. Therefore, Canada has implemented the GATT tariff schedule through the Customs Tariff. Second, there is a negative duty not to apply laws that are contrary to the obligations undertaken as a member. Consequently, insofar as Canada imposes anti-dumping and countervailing duties, it may do so only within the limits prescribed by the GATT. If Canada is found to be in breach of its WTO obligations, it is required to take the necessary steps to amend its legislation in order to comply.

---

[33] By way of exception, reduced rates of duty are applied to many goods coming from less-developed countries.

CASE 30.1 Canadian Non-tariff Barrier Violates the GATT

The United States complained that Canada was in violation of the GATT by prohibiting or restricting the importation into Canada of certain American periodicals and magazines through discriminatory tax treatment of so-called split-run periodicals and by applying favourable postage rates to certain Canadian periodicals. A WTO panel found that the Canadian measures were incompatible with the GATT. As a result, Canada was required to change its legislation.[34]

CASE 30.2 Subsidy Violates the GATT

In 2002, the United States and New Zealand complained to the WTO that Canada was illegally subsidizing its dairy industry by allowing Canadian processors to buy lower-priced milk to manufacture cheese and other products for export under a scheme known as the Commercial Export Milk Program. A WTO panel concluded that the scheme amounted to an illegal subsidy; as a result, Canada agreed to discontinue the scheme.[35]

CASE 30.3 Import Ban Violates the GATT

Canada filed a complaint against the European Communities' ban on imported seal products. Iceland and Norway joined in the complaint. In 2014 a WTO panel found that the regulations violated the GATT in that it gave imported seal products less favourable treatment than domestic products. The appeal panel also found the special treatment of domestic seal products was unjustified.[36]

North American Free Trade

free trade areas groups of countries within which customs duties are eliminated

One exception to the MFN principle, allowed under WTO rules, permits the creation of regional **free trade areas**, within which customs duties may be eliminated entirely. The most important and best known of such areas is the European Union (EU), a customs and economic union of 28 European states (as of 2018). In 2016 the United Kingdom, an original member of the EU, voted to leave the union in an outcome known as "Brexit." Formal notice of withdrawal was served in 2017,[37] with an exit date of March 29, 2019. Negotiations produced a withdrawal plan in December of 2018; it is unclear whether the British Parliament will approve the plan or what impact the withdrawal will have on the EU and the United Kingdom.

Another regional free trade area was created in 1988 with the signing of the Canada–United States Free Trade Agreement. This agreement, which came into force at the beginning of 1989,[38] provided for the phasing out of tariffs in trade between the two nations over a period of 10 years. Four years later, on December 17, 1992, the leaders of Canada, Mexico, and the United States signed the North American Free Trade Agreement (NAFTA), bringing into existence the world's largest free trade area, with more than 360 million consumers.[39] As with Brexit, there is instability

---

[34] See *United States v Canada: Certain Measures Concerning Periodicals*, WTO panel report WT/DS31/R, March 14, 1997.

[35] WTO panel report WT/DS103/33, May 15, 2003.

[36] WTO panel report WT/DS400, Nov. 25, 2013 and WTO appeal report May 22, 2014.

[37] European Union website, https://europa.eu/european-union/about-eu/countries/member-countries/unitedkingdom_en.

[38] It takes effect in Canada by virtue of the *Canada–United States Free Trade Agreement Implementation Act*, SC 1988, c 65.

[39] The NAFTA is implemented in Canada by the *North American Free Trade Agreement Implementation Act*, SC 1993, c 44, and came into effect on January 1, 1994. The Canada–United States agreement is suspended during the operation of the NAFTA.

surrounding NAFTA in 2018. High-level negotiations targeting amendments and changes to NAFTA were initiated by the United States following the election of President Donald Trump. These negotiations have produced an agreement in principle known as USMCA, that has not received formal legislative ratification in any of the three countries in 2018. Therefore, the following discussion relates to NAFTA as at 2016 and flags some major areas that the new USMCA agreement might change. The USMCA has not been introduced in legislative form to the Canadian parliament at 2018 as is required for ratification of a treaty.

Although the NAFTA invokes similar principles to the WTO, including non-discrimination, national treatment, most favoured nation, and fairness in tariffs, barriers, and subsidies, in many respects it goes considerably further in liberalizing trade and investment:

- Most tariffs on goods among the three countries are eliminated. Interest Prime Minister Trudeau signed the USMCA without insisting on the removal of a U.S. tariff imposed on Canadian steel and aluminium.
- Customs procedures are streamlined and user fees eliminated.
- Agricultural products are covered; import barriers, export subsidies, and domestic support on these products were phased out. Supply management remains but is one of the key issues in the 2018 negotiations. USMCA would give American dairy producers greater access to the Canadian market.
- Special rules apply to energy and natural resources, generally prohibiting export restrictions.
- Services, including financial services, are covered in the agreement, entitling providers to receive national treatment (or MFN treatment, if that is better).
- Government procurement—the purchase of goods and services by governments—is partly opened to foreign competition.
- Country of origin rules are specifically defined as origin impacts tariff classification or regional value content requirements.
- All principal intellectual property rights—copyright, patents, and trademarks—are recognized and protected, and laws are to be harmonized to secure broadly equivalent protection in each country.[40] USMCA would require Canada to expand copyright protection from 50 to 70 years after death of the creator; it would also require lengthening the minimum patent time period for biological medicines.
- NAFTA is not restricted to trade in goods and services; it also contains provisions relating to investment (discussed later in this chapter).

Members may avoid NAFTA requirements if they can fit the activity into one of NAFTA's exceptions, which include the following:

- Cultural industries
- National security
- Taxation
- Health and safety

Canada has eight other FTAs, including one with the member states of the European Free Trade Association (EFTA)[41] and most recently with Honduras in 2014.

---

[40] Canadian laws are not in complete conformity with the United States, yet the *Copyright Modernization Act* discussed in Chapter 20 has moved Canada closer.

[41] Member states of the EFTA are Iceland, Liechtenstein, Norway, and Switzerland. The EFTA is not to be confused with the EU.

Trans-Pacific Partnership

Canada has entered into trade agreements with other countries,[42] most recently with Australia, Japan, Mexico, and eight others, in what is called the Comprehensive and Progressive Agreement for Trans-Pacific Partnership, signed in March 2018.[43] The United States withdrew from the Partnership shortly after President Trump took office in 2017. This agreement allows for enforcement of environmental and labour standards through the agreement's dispute resolution process. Protections for Canada's motor vehicle and cultural industries are retained.

FOREIGN INVESTMENT

Forms of Foreign Investment

A distinction is commonly drawn between portfolio or capital investment and direct investment. Portfolio investment is essentially "passive" investment, normally in government or corporate bonds or stocks, shares, and securities. Foreign direct investment (FDI) occurs as part of active business operations. It can be defined as

> investment made to acquire a lasting interest in an enterprise operating in an economic environment other than that of the investor, with the investor's purpose being to have an effective voice in the management of the enterprise.[44]

It may involve the acquisition of tangible property, such as a factory or hotel, or of all or a substantial part of the shares[45] in an existing corporation in the host country. FDI may also involve the establishment of an entirely new business ("greenfield" investment), and also includes the reinvestment of earnings in the host country.

Normally, FDI is conducted through the establishment of

- a branch,
- a subsidiary, or
- a joint venture.

branch a business carried on by the owner in its own name at a location distinct from its head office

subsidiary a separate corporation owned or controlled by its "parent" corporation

Where it establishes a **branch**, the investor carries on business in the host country in its own name, the foreign branch being an integral part of its global business, with the assets of the branch owned directly by the foreign investor. By contrast, a **subsidiary** is a separate corporation, incorporated in the host country and owning assets there. The parent investor owns the shares in the subsidiary (or a majority of them) but not the assets. The distinction can sometimes be very important. For example, some countries do not allow foreign ownership of land but permit a local corporation to do so, even if a majority of its shares are held by foreigners. One of Canada's largest private corporations is an example: Walmart Canada Corp. is a wholly owned subsidiary of the U.S. parent company, Wal-Mart Stores Inc.[46]

---

[42] Honduras (2014), Panama (2013) Peru (2009), Chile (1997), Costa Rica (2002), and Israel (1997). See Foreign Affairs and International Trade Canada, Negotiations and Agreements, http://www.international.gc.ca/tradeagreementsaccordscommerciaux/agracc/index.aspx.

[43] Australia, Brunei, Canada, Chile, Japan, Malaysia, Mexico, New Zealand, Peru, Singapore, and Vietnam, representing 495 million people and a combined GDP of $13.5 trillion: https://www.canada.ca/en/global-affairs/news/2018/03/statement-by-minister-champagne-on-signing-of-comprehensive-and-progressive-agreement-for-trans-pacific-partnership.html.

[44] United Nations, World Investment Directory 1992 (New York: UNCTC, 1992).

[45] To be classified as direct rather than capital (portfolio) investment, the acquisition must normally be of at least 10 percent of the shares of the host country corporation.

[46] See "Ranking of Canada's Biggest Private Companies," *The Globe and Mail*, June 27, 2013, updated 2017.

A **joint venture** is formed by two or more parties, at least one of which is normally from the host country. It can take the form either of a type of partnership (contractual joint venture) or of a jointly owned subsidiary corporation (equity joint venture). Canadian investors overseas generally prefer the subsidiary or equity joint venture forms, principally for tax reasons, and some host countries permit foreign investment only in those forms.

joint venture a form of business venture between two or more independent enterprises, or a corporation jointly owned by them

Government Regulation of Foreign Investment

A business wanting to operate in another country must, of course, comply with the laws of that country. For example, a foreign corporation that carries on business in Canada through a branch may be required by the laws of the province where the branch is located to obtain a licence and to register certain information.[47] If it wishes to incorporate a subsidiary in Canada, it may be required to have a certain number of directors who are resident Canadians.[48] In the same way, a Canadian business seeking to establish a branch or subsidiary abroad will have to comply with the local laws. Some countries do not permit foreign corporations to conduct business through a branch. Others do not allow foreigners to own a majority of the shares in a domestic corporation, at least in some economic sectors, making a joint venture (with a local partner) the only feasible method of carrying on business.

Foreign investment is desirable because it brings much-needed capital into the economy, creates employment, opens up export markets, and introduces modern technology and management skills. On the other hand, some worry it may cause social and environmental damage, stifle the development of local business, and exert undue political influence. Consequently, countries seek both to attract foreign investment and to control it, by a mixture of incentives and restrictions. Inducements such as tax holidays may be offered, but at the same time foreign investors may be excluded from participating in certain activities (such as finance, communications, and transportation), forbidden to own real estate, or required to meet specific conditions such as creating jobs or utilizing domestic raw materials. Of course, such measures may violate the NAFTA/USMCA or GATT if applied to treaty partners.

Like many other countries, Canada requires that certain types of inward direct investment be reviewed and prior authorization be obtained from the Investment Review Division of Industry Canada.[49] The establishment of a new business is generally not reviewed; it requires only that Industry Canada be notified. The acquisition of "larger," existing Canadian businesses requires authorization[50] and must be "of significant benefit to Canada"; in practice, authorization is almost always granted. NAFTA and WTO members benefit from a much higher threshold value before review is required. In certain cases, the approval of provincial governments and of other bodies may also be required. For example, the 1999 takeover of MacMillan Bloedel by the U.S. company Weyerhaeuser required the approval of the British Columbia and Ontario governments, the Canadian Competition Bureau, the Canadian Ministry for International Trade, and Investment Canada, in addition to court approval and the support of two-thirds of the MacMillan Bloedel shareholders.

---

[47] See, in Ontario, *Corporations Information Act*, RSO 1990, c C-39, and *Extra-Provincial Corporations Act*, RSO 1990, c E.27.

[48] See e.g. *Canada Business Corporations Act*, RSC 1985, c C-44, s 105(3).

[49] *Investment Canada Act*, RSC 1985, c 28 (1st Supp). Investment review responsibilities are assigned to Industry Canada under the direction of the Director of Investments (s. 6).

[50] General review limits are $5 million for direct investment and $50 million for indirect investment; the NAFTA review threshold is tied to Statistics Canada's Nominal Gross Domestic Product and is set at $1 billion for 2017; see Industry Canada, Thresholds for Review, http://www.ic.gc.ca/eic/site/icalic.nsf/eng/h_lk00050.html.

CASE 30.4 Best Interests of Canada?

In 2010, a British–Australian company, BHP Billiton, initiated a $38.6 billion takeover bid of the publicly traded Potash Corporation of Saskatchewan Inc., the world's largest fertilizer company. Approval of the deal was required under the *Investment Canada Act*, and although Industry Canada might have approved the deal with conditions, the government refused approval, saying the takeover was not in the best interests of Canada. As a result, the bid was withdrawn. The BBC reported that the decision was a political one taken because the Harper government was in a minority position, and the Saskatchewan government and the majority of Saskatchewan people opposed the deal.[51]

A restrictive approach to foreign investment is taken in some sectors. All acquisitions or investments to establish a new business in cultural sectors such as book publishing and filmmaking are subject to review, regardless of the amount involved. A variety of federal and, in some cases, provincial statutes restrict foreign ownership of banking, financial, and telecom services and of businesses involved in insurance, transportation, fishing, oil, gas, and uranium. The existence of public monopolies—such as the post office, electricity, and liquor sales—further restricts the potential for foreign investment.

CASE 30.5 Protected Industries

The Ontario Teachers' Pension Fund (OTPF) sought approval for a $51.7 billion purchase and privatization of BCE Inc., the country's largest telecommunications company and Bell Canada's parent. The proposal involved significant foreign investment through three private American equity partners and therefore required the approval of many different agencies, including the Canadian Radio-television and Telecommunications Commission (CRTC, for impact on telecommunications), the Competition Bureau (for market dominance issues), and Industry Canada (for foreign control issues).

Legislation requires that foreign control of telecom companies must not exceed 46.9 percent. The CRTC voiced a concern that future Canadian control of BCE should be protected. On March 27, 2008, the CRTC approved the deal on conditions, including the following corporate governance provisions:

1. The number of directors must be fixed at 13.
2. Six Canadian directors must be nominated by Canadian investors, and non-Canadian investors may nominate only five.
3. The chairperson and CEO must be Canadian and cannot be the same person.
4. A second OTPF delegate must sit on the executive committee.
5. Independent programming committee members must be Canadians not affiliated with the non-Canadian investors.[52]

The deal collapsed in December 2008 when BCE could not obtain an acceptable financial opinion.

Foreign Investment and International Law

Certain types of investment rules clearly have an impact on trade. If, in granting approval to a foreign investment, a host country attaches conditions (usually called **performance requirements**)—for example, that the investor must use local raw materials or components, or that it must export a stipulated percentage of its total production—those conditions will interfere with the investor's freedom to trade. The legality of such trade-related investment measures (TRIMs) was considered by a panel of the GATT, in a complaint referred to it in 1982.[53] The United States, at the request of a number of American corporations that had invested in Canada, complained that

performance requirements
conditions attached by the host country in granting approval to a foreign investment

---

[51] See CBC News, "Clement Denies PotashCorp Deal Influenced by Politics," Dec. 24, 2010, https://www.cbc.ca/news/politics/clement-denies-potashcorp-deal-influenced-by-politics-1.952687; The Star.com "BHP Scraps $39 Billion Potash Bid," Nov. 14, 2010, https://www.thestar.com/news/canada/2010/11/14/bhp_scraps_39_billion_potash_bid.html.

[52] Broadcasting Decision CRTC 2008-69, http://www.crtc.gc.ca/eng/archive/2008/db2008-69.htm; Teresa Tedesco, "BCE Takeover Deal Falls Through," *Financial Post*, December 10, 2008.

[53] *United States v Canada: Administration of the Foreign Investment Review Act*, report of February 7, 1984 (Case No 108, GATT Doc. L/5308).

conditions requiring the investors to buy components and materials from local Canadian sources were in effect imposing restrictions on the importation of similar goods. The panel upheld the complaint, ruling against Canada.

Probably the greatest fear of a potential foreign investor is that its assets might be expropriated by the host country government or nationalized without adequate compensation. **Expropriation** has been one of the more controversial issues in international law. Some industrialized countries would like to see expropriation entirely prohibited, whereas many developing countries consider the power to nationalize to be essential to their economic development. The United Nations supports a state's right to nationalize, expropriate, or transfer ownership of foreign-owned property but declares that appropriate compensation must be paid.[54]

expropriation a state's right to assume ownership of private property within its geographic borders

The 1985 convention establishing the Multilateral Investment Guarantee Agency, under the auspices of the World Bank, provides some protection against the consequences of expropriation, but probably of greater importance are **bilateral investment protection treaties**, many of which have been entered into between capital-importing and capital-exporting countries. These treaties usually provide that foreign investment receive national treatment—that is, it should be treated no less favourably than a comparable domestic enterprise. It is usual to provide that a host country may not expropriate or nationalize the property of an investor from the other country "except for a public purpose, under due process of law, in a non-discriminatory manner," and that any such expropriation "must be accompanied by prompt, adequate, and effective compensation."[55]

bilateral investment protection treaty a treaty entered into between two countries, whereby each country undertakes to protect investors from the other country and to give them certain rights

NAFTA significantly relaxed the general rules of the *Investment Canada Act* for Mexican and U.S. investment in Canada. Performance requirements regarding such matters as exporting or local sourcing of goods or services are not permitted, and as a general principle, investors are entitled to national treatment or to MFN treatment, if

Ethical Issue   Weapons in Space

In January 2008, MacDonald, Dettwiler and Associates Ltd., a British Columbia company involved in satellite technology, announced it would sell its space and satellite division to an American company, Alliance Techsystems, for $1.325 billion. The proposed sale drew immediate reaction because this division includes the "Canadarm" used on the space shuttle. Many Canadians consider the Canadarm a source of national pride. The Canadarm technology was developed by MacDonald, Dettwiler with the help of $430 million in grant money from the Canadian government.

To add to the controversy, Alliance Techsystems supplies arms such as land mines and cluster bombs to the U.S. military. Concern was expressed that the Canadarm, taxpayer-funded technology, might now be used to weaponize space and contravene Canada's position on the Mine Ban Treaty. Pursuant to the *Investment Canada Act*, the proposed sale required Industry Canada approval. On March 14, 2008, the Industry Minister stated that the sale would only be approved if there was a net benefit for Canada. In April 2008, the minister blocked the sale.

Questions to Consider

1. Could it be argued that there was a net benefit to Canada, and should the possible use of the technology to weaponize space have been a factor in Industry Canada's decision?

2. Should government grants include conditions about future use or sale of the developments made using grant money?

Sources: Petti Fong, "Canadarm Sale Sparks Revolt," TheStar.com, January 18, 2008, https://www.thestar.com/news/canada/2008/01/18/canadarm_sale_sparks_revolt.html; Andrew Mayeda et al., "Space Sale of 'No Net Benefit' Says Minister," *The National Post*, April 10, 2008, http://www.nationalpost.com/related/topics/Space+sale+benefit+says+minister/436123/story.html.

---

[54] United Nations *Charter of Economic Rights and Duties of States*, adopted December 12, 1974, GA Res. 3281 (xxix), UN GAOR, 29th Sess Sup No 31 (1974) 50. Canada abstained from voting on this proposition.

[55] See e.g. Art. VI of the "Agreement between the Government of Canada and the Government of the Republic of Poland for the Promotion and Reciprocal Protection of Investments," signed in Warsaw on April 6, 1990 (Canada Treaty Series 1990, No 43) http://www.wipo.int/wipolex/en/details.jsp?id=12278.

that is better.[56] Canadian investment in Mexico and the United States enjoys similar privileges and protection.

THE RESOLUTION OF INTERNATIONAL BUSINESS DISPUTES

Like all other business activities, foreign trade and foreign investment can give rise to disputes. These may be based in private law, as, for example, between parties to an international contract for the sale of goods. Or disputes may be primarily about public or administrative law, between governments on the one hand and importers or investors on the other. In addition, questions of public international law may arise where it is alleged that one state is in breach of its treaty obligations to another. Disputes may be resolved before a national court, an arbitrator, or some form of international tribunal.

Courts

In principle, Canadian courts and those of most other countries are open to the world in the sense that there is no citizenship or residency requirement in order to sue or be sued in them. Still, a lawsuit may not be allowed to proceed in the location where it was started. Courts do not encourage "forum shopping"—that is, allowing a plaintiff to pick the location only because it is likely to view the claim favourably. There must be some connection to the location or the defendant must be present or consent. The level of connection varies by country; the following is a general overview of the Canadian approach.

ILLUSTRATION 30.2 Multiple Possible Jurisdictions

A Canadian manufacturer contracts to sell electrical equipment to a Korean construction company, with delivery to be made at a construction site in Saudi Arabia. The price is stated to be payable in Swiss francs. The manufacturer ships the equipment to Saudi Arabia, but the Korean company refuses to take delivery, claiming that the equipment does not meet the contract specifications.

The Canadian firm wishes to sue for the price; perhaps the Korean party will claim damages. But in which country should the action be brought? In Canada, Korea, Saudi Arabia, Switzerland, or perhaps somewhere entirely different? What if the contract stipulates that it is governed by the laws of New York State?

The question in Illustration 30.2 is one of jurisdiction.

assume jurisdiction hear the action; allow the lawsuit to proceed in the courts of that jurisdiction

Jurisdiction The question of whether a court will hear an action—that is, **assume jurisdiction** over a lawsuit—is decided by Canadian courts in a two-step analysis:

1. First, the court decides whether the location where the lawsuit was started has jurisdiction at all (jurisdiction simpliciter).
2. Second, if jurisdiction exists, the court may be asked by the defendant not to hear the matter and to defer the lawsuit to a more appropriate foreign court (*forum non conveniens*).[57]

To establish jurisdiction in the first analysis if the defendant is not present or has not consented, the plaintiff must prove that the action has a "real and substantial connection" with the country or province in which the action was commenced. The real

---

[56] Sometimes a country imposes restrictions on its own investors that do not apply to foreign investors. In such a case, MFN treatment may be more favourable than national treatment.

[57] *Club Resorts Ltd v Van Breda*, 2012 SCC 17. There are two distinct processes with different tests to be applied.

and substantial connection is established using objective factual connections between the location of the court and the action. The factual connecting factors may vary by province or depending upon the cause of action of the lawsuit. The Supreme Court has identified four connecting factors for tort actions:

- The defendant is resident in the jurisdiction.
- The defendant carries on business in the jurisdiction.
- The jurisdiction is the location where the tort occurred.
- A contract connected with the dispute was made in the jurisdiction.[58]

In a contract action, the location with jurisdiction is sometimes identified by a term of the contract; this contractual choice is almost always followed by the court.[59] When no forum selection clause exists, courts may consider the four factors above and have relied upon the following connecting factors in the past:

- a contract was to be performed there,
- damage from a breach of contract was sustained there,
- the dispute concerned property or goods situated there, or
- the contract stipulated that it should be governed by the laws of the country or province.

British Columbia, Nova Scotia, Saskatchewan, and Yukon have passed legislation contemplating consideration of additional factors.[60]

As in Case 30.6, more than one country or province may have a real and substantial connection to the dispute and therefore jurisdiction over it. If multiple lawsuits proceeded in different jurisdictions, conflicting outcomes could result. Therefore, in the second part of the analysis, a court may decline to exercise its jurisdiction, even though it might have a connection to the dispute, if the defendant proves that there is some other forum that is clearly more appropriate—this is the *forum non conveniens* principle.[61] Under this principle, criteria related to efficiency and fairness are used to pick the most appropriate of the multiple forums, such as:

- the location of parties and witnesses;
- the cost of transferring to another jurisdiction or proceeding;
- the avoidance of multiple proceedings—that is, whether a foreign jurisdiction has already assumed jurisdiction;
- the avoidance of conflicting decisions;
- the ability to enforce any resulting judgment;
- the fair and efficient functioning of the Canadian legal system; and
- the relative strength of the connections of the two parties to each location.[62]

None of the described criteria is decisive on its own.

forum non conveniens refusing to hear a proceeding because another jurisdiction is more appropriate or more closely connected to the matter

---

[58] *Ibid* at para 64. The Supreme Court specifically created tests for tort actions—it is not clear yet whether they also apply to contract or other actions: *Trillium v General Motors*, 2013 ONSC 2289; *Wang v Lin*, 2013 ONCA 33; *Sears Canada Inc v C&S Interior Designs Ltd*, [2012] ABQB 573.

[59] When there are multiple competing jurisdictions, courts have (rarely) ignored contractual choice of forum clauses in exceptional circumstances only: *ZI Pompey Industrie v ECU-Line NV*, [2003] 1 SCR 450; *Momentous.ca Corp v Canadian American Association of Professional Baseball Ltd*, [2012] SCJ No 9.

[60] *Court Jurisdiction and Proceedings Transfer Act*, SBC 2003, c 28, s 56 (in force May 4, 2006); SNS 2003, c 2 (in force June 1, 2008); SS 1997, c C-41.1 (in force March 1, 2004); these Acts are based on the model law produced by the Uniform Law Conference of Canada.

[61] *Club Resorts*, *supra* note 57; *Teck Cominco Metals Ltd v Lloyd's Underwriters*, 2009 SCC 11.

[62] *Club Resorts*, *supra* note 57.

CASE 30.6 Not *Clearly* More Appropriate

Van Breda, an Ontario resident, was seriously injured while vacationing at Club Resort in Cuba. The Club Resort vacation package was booked from the website of an Ontario web-based travel agency called Sport au Soleil. Although the resort was in Cuba, it was managed by a corporation in the Cayman Islands, and the management company hired Ontario professionals and Ontario tour operators, including Sport au Soleil, to advertise, promote, and obtain bookings for the resorts. Van Breda sued Sport au Soleil, Club Resort, and the management company in Ontario for negligence. The Resort claimed that Ontario did not have jurisdiction over the dispute, and even if it did, Cuba was the more appropriate forum. The Supreme Court held that a real and substantial connection in a tort case could be demonstrated if the defendant was resident or carried on business in Ontario, the tort occurred in Ontario, or a contract connected to the action was made in Ontario. The Court found that the travel contract was made through the Ontario-based travel agency and therefore Ontario had jurisdiction. Cuba also had a real and substantial connection to the action as the tort occurred there. Applying fairness and efficiency principles to factors such as travel expense and transport issues for witnesses and the Canadian-based paraplegic plaintiff, the Supreme Court held that the Resort had not shown that Cuba was a clearly more appropriate forum than Ontario.[63]

Canadian courts take a holistic view of "appropriateness," considering all the relevant circumstances, and will only defer if the other location is substantially, obviously, or clearly more appropriate. Even if actions are already under way in multiple jurisdictions, the Canadian approach is still to determine the most appropriate forum and not simply defer to the jurisdiction where the first action was started.[64] Rarely, parallel actions will be allowed to proceed in their respective jurisdictions.

CASE 30.7 Multiple Actions

The mining and smelting business of Teck Cominco Metals Ltd. in British Columbia was alleged to have caused waste to be discharged into the Columbia River, resulting in environmental damage to property in British Columbia and Washington State. A lawsuit was commenced in U.S. District Court. When Teck's insurers, Lloyd's and Lombard, denied coverage, Teck commenced an action in Washington against its own insurers, seeking an order that they must defend the company under the terms of the policy. The insurers commenced actions in British Columbia seeking an order that they did not have to defend the company. Teck brought an application to stay the B.C. proceedings under the *forum non conveniens* provisions of the B.C. legislation. The Supreme Court of Canada refused to stay the B.C. proceedings. Considering all the circumstances, the prior court action in Washington did not oust B.C.'s jurisdiction, and the avoidance of multiple proceedings was just one factor among many to be considered. International jurisdictions should be viewed differently than interprovincial ones: "Blind acceptance of a foreign court's prior assertion of jurisdiction carries with it the risk of declining jurisdiction in favour of jurisdiction that is not more appropriate."[65]

The Supreme Court of Canada has ruled that, where the parties themselves have provided that disputes be referred to a particular forum, that is, in a contractual choice of forum clause, effect should normally, but not always, be given to that agreement.[66] Again, a two-step approach is followed to determine whether a forum selection clause should be enforced:

- First, the party seeking a stay of the action must establish that the clause is valid, clear, and enforceable and that it applies to the cause of action before the court.
- If the first step succeeds, the onus shifts to the plaintiff, who must show a strong reason why the court should not enforce the forum selection clause. A court will consider all the circumstances, including the convenience of the parties, fairness between the parties, and the interests of justice. Public policy may also be a relevant factor at this step.[67]

---

[63] *Ibid*.

[64] *Teck Cominco Metals*, *supra* note 61 at para 30.

[65] *Ibid* at para 30.

[66] *ZI Pompey Industrie v Ecu-Line NV*, *supra* note 59.

[67] *Douez v Facebook, Inc*, 2017 SCC 33.

CASE 30.8 Public Policy

A British Columbia class action claimed that Facebook's non-consensual use of members' pictures violated their privacy contrary to B.C. privacy legislation. Facebook sought a stay of the action citing the choice of forum clause contained in the Terms of Use agreed to by members at registration. It said all disputes must be resolved in California.

The Supreme Court of Canada followed the two-step approach to enforcing the clause. The first step was met. The clause was valid, and the dispute was covered by it. Under the second step, the court refused to enforce the clause for public policy reasons. The clause was in a consumer contract of adhesion with gross inequality of bargaining power, and the dispute was about privacy rights. Privacy is a quasi-constitutional Canadian right that Canadian courts should retain adjudicative authority over.[68]

Standing Although parties need not be residents or citizens of a country in order to have access to its courts, some restrictions may apply. A foreign corporation that has not been licensed or registered in Canada cannot be a plaintiff in Canadian courts. Foreign plaintiffs without assets within the jurisdiction may be required to post **security for costs**. A further problem arises where the defendant is not present or does not have an establishment within the jurisdiction and cannot be served with the writ or originating process. Although courts may give leave to serve the defendant outside the jurisdiction, they are generally reluctant to grant judgments against absent defendants unless there is a very strong connection between the cause of action and the country concerned.

> **security for costs** money deposited into the court in case an unsuccessful foreign plaintiff is ordered to pay the legal costs of the successful defendant

Choice of Law The easiest way to establish the proper law of the contract is by naming the choice of law in a contractual term. Sometimes the result is that the courts of one country apply the law of another. In Illustration 30.2, if the contract had stipulated that the law of New York was to apply, that clause might in itself be adequate reason for a Canadian court to decline jurisdiction to a Canadian plaintiff. Even so, it might be possible for the Korean party to sue a Canadian defendant in a Canadian court for damages for non-performance, in which case the court would determine the rights of the parties according to New York law. Deference will be given to these clauses, but just as with choice of forum clauses, exceptions will be made. For other types of actions, choice of law will be decided using a real and substantial connection analysis.

Enforcement of Foreign Judgments Even if a plaintiff persuades a court to accept jurisdiction in a dispute of an international nature and succeeds in obtaining a judgment against the defendant, the matter does not necessarily end there. The question then arises of whether a foreign judgment may be enforced in Canada, and vice versa. This is another complex legal issue, often without a clear answer and dependent on the circumstances of each case.

Canada has treaties with trading parties agreeing to enforce their judgments, and provinces have passed legislation to enforce each other's judgments.[69] Still, there are limits. A foreign judgment debt will normally only be recognized so long as the foreign court was exercising proper jurisdiction according to the standards of the Canadian courts (the local "forum"): Did the foreign court properly assume jurisdiction over the dispute? As described above, the presence of the defendant, consent, or a "real and

---

[68] *Ibid*.

[69] Only a few provincial reciprocal agreements with other countries have been entered into, the ones with the United Kingdom being the most important; see e.g. *Reciprocal Enforcement of Judgments (U.K.) Act*, RSO1990, c R.6.

substantial connection" between the substance of the action and the country granting the judgment must exist;[70] the judgment must not be obtained by fraud; and the proceedings cannot offend against natural justice or public policy.[71]

> ### CASE 30.9 Absence of Fraud
>
> In 1981, the Beals bought a building lot in Florida for US $8000 from the Saldanhas, who were residents of Ontario. By mistake, the wrong lot was sold, and the Beals built a home on a lot they did not own. The Beals brought an action for damages, for breach of contract, in a Florida court.
>
> The Saldanhas did not defend the action, apparently because they feared that the costs of defending the action, even if they won, would greatly exceed any award against them (which they did not expect would be much more than the $8000 paid for the land). In 1991, a Florida jury awarded triple compensatory damages of $210 000 and additional punitive damages of $50 000. The Beals sought to enforce the judgment in Ontario, by which time, interest and the change in exchange rate meant the value of the judgment had risen to CDN $800 000.
>
> The Ontario trial judge refused to enforce the judgment, holding that the Florida judgment had been obtained by fraud and that it would be contrary to public policy to enforce it in Ontario. On appeal, the Supreme Court of Canada ruled that the Florida judgment should be enforced. Since the land was situated in Florida, Florida had jurisdiction. Although there were some procedural features that would not have been allowed in Ontario, there was no evidence of fraud or a denial of natural justice. International courtesy required that the Florida judgment be respected.[72]

Equitable remedies may not be as easily recognized. When the Supreme Court of Canada issued a global interlocutory injunction requiring Google to de-list certain websites that were alleged to be infringing intellectual property rights,[73] a U.S. District Court granted a stay of the order because it deprived Google of protection available under U.S. federal law.[74]

Commercial Arbitration

Sometimes a forum selection clause in an international contract chooses a private forum rather than the public courts. Arbitration, sometimes referred to as private justice, is an alternative dispute resolution process in which disputing parties select an independent neutral adjudicator to privately decide their dispute. The parties agree in advance to be bound by the decision of the arbitrator, with very limited rights to appeal. Parties design their own process through the selection of the arbitrator, the procedural rules, and the choice of law to be applied in determining the outcome. This control over the process, or **party autonomy** as it is often described, is considered a major benefit of arbitration.

party autonomy the parties' freedom to determine how their dispute will be resolved

The delays, costs, publicity, and uncertainties surrounding international litigation make binding arbitration attractive for resolution of any disputes arising in international commercial transactions. Rather than risk a dispute being heard before the "home" court of one party, parties usually insert an **arbitration clause** into the contract at the time of agreement. The arbitration clause designates the arbitrator, the location or forum, the choice of law to be applied, and the procedural rules to be followed. Sometimes it specifically names an arbitrator, but more commonly it nominates an organization that provides arbitration services such as the International

arbitration clause a term in a commercial contract designating arbitration as the process for resolution of any disputes arising between the parties

---

[70] *Club Resorts Ltd*, *supra* note 61 at para 16; Tanya Montestier, "Still A 'Real and Substantial' Mess: The Law of Jurisdiction in Canada" (2013) 36 *Fordham Int'l LJ* 397 at 457.

[71] *Morguard Investments Ltd v de Savoye* (1990), 76 DLR (4th) 256. That case concerned the recognition by a British Columbia court of an Alberta judgment. However, the principles enunciated by the Supreme Court of Canada have subsequently been applied to judgments by foreign courts: *Beals v Saldanha*, [2003] 3 SCR 416; *Sincies Chiementin SpA (Trustee) v King*, [2010] OJ No 5124, aff'd [2012] OJ No 4562.

[72] *Ibid.*

[73] *Google Inc v Equustek Solutions Inc*, 2017 SCC 34.

[74] See discussion in *Equustek Solutions Inc v Jack*, 2018 BCSC 610.

Chamber of Commerce. There are many private providers of international arbitration services located in all major commercial centres around the world. As part of an international trend, Canadian legislation and courts support a policy in favour of arbitration and generally refuse to assume jurisdiction over commercial disputes covered by a valid arbitration agreement.[75] Some provinces have limited the enforcement of standard form pre-dispute arbitration clauses involving consumers, but business-to-business agreements are routinely enforced, provided the dispute falls within the scope of the clause.[76]

One major advantage of arbitration, as opposed to litigation, is the ability to select an arbitrator with great experience in the specific area of the dispute, a right not available in the public courts. Other advantages are the non-public nature and confidentiality of the proceedings, which are especially important where the dispute concerns trade secrets, and usually costs are lower and decisions are speedier. Most modern commercial arbitration employs standard procedures, such as those adopted in the UNCITRAL model, which are generally better adapted to international disputes than regular court procedures.

Perhaps the greatest advantage of commercial arbitration, as opposed to litigation, lies in the relative ease with which awards may be enforced. Unlike litigation, arbitration is consensual: The parties to the original contract have agreed to submit any dispute to arbitration and to abide by the award. As a result, there is no valid reason for a court to refuse to enforce an arbitration award should one of the parties fail to comply with it. Canada has legislation, at both the federal and provincial levels, that implements the 1958 United Nations Convention on the Recognition and Enforcement of Foreign Arbitral Awards and adopts the 1985 UNCITRAL Model Law on International Commercial Arbitration.[77]

Disputes Involving Governments

Generally, governments cannot be compelled to appear as defendants before the courts of another country or to submit to arbitration. An individual or corporation that wishes to challenge the actions or decisions of a government—for example, the refusal of an import licence or the expropriation of an investment—may normally do so only in the courts of that country.

However, where a member state complainant alleges that a state is in breach of a treaty obligation owed to one or more other states, a number of procedures exist for the resolution of the dispute. Most often the treaty or convention designates a process to be followed for dispute resolution. For example, bilateral investment protection treaties usually provide that the parties agree to submit to binding arbitration any dispute concerning the expropriation of assets or payment of proper compensation, with such arbitration to be conducted by the International Centre for the Settlement of Investment Disputes or according to the UNCITRAL rules.[78] Most important from a Canadian perspective are the procedures provided for in the WTO and NAFTA. Dispute resolution was a key focus of USMCA negotiations.

---

[75] 1985 UNCITRAL Model Law on International Commercial Arbitration, UN doc. A/40/17, Ann. I (June 21, 1985); *Bisaillon v Concordia University*, [2006] 1 SCR 666; *Dell Computer Corp v Unions des consommateurs*, 2007 SCC 34; *Seidel v TELUS Communications*, 2011 SCC 15.

[76] See e.g. *Consumer Protection Act, 2002*, SO 2002, c 30, Sch A, ss 7–8; *Seidel v TELUS*, ibid (interpreting ss 3, 171 and 172 of the *Business Practices and Consumer Protection Act*, SBC 2004, c 2); *Fair Trading Act*, RSA 2000, c F-2, s 16.

[77] *Commercial Arbitration Act*, RSC 1985, c 17 (2nd Supp); *United Nations Foreign Arbitral Awards Convention Act*, RSC 1985, c 16 (2nd Supp); *International Commercial Arbitration Act*, RSBC 1996, c 233; RSO 1990, c I.9.

[78] See *Settlement of International Investment Disputes Act*, SC 2008, c 8. British Columbia, Newfoundland and Labrador, Ontario, and Saskatchewan have similar legislation.

The GATT and WTO From its inception in 1948, the GATT contained a mechanism for the resolution of disputes between states that are parties to the agreement. The mechanism was revised and strengthened when the WTO was created in 1995.

Only states that are contracting parties (members) may raise a complaint against another contracting party. Private persons have no standing as such, though an individual or firm that has been injured by an action of a foreign government in violation of the GATT may request that its own government bring proceedings.

The WTO contains two types of proceedings for the settlement of disputes. There is provision for consultation between the parties and, if necessary, a conciliation procedure—essentially a negotiated diplomatic solution. Alternatively, a contracting state that considers that the proper operation of the rules is being "nullified or impaired" by the actions of another contracting state may request the WTO Council to appoint a panel to adjudicate the dispute. After hearing the submissions of the parties, the panel makes recommendations, which may require an offending state to remove a provision of law or an administrative practice found to be contrary to the rules or, in certain cases, to compensate an injured party. Under the WTO procedures, a panel decision may be appealed to a special appellate panel, and a reasonable time is allowed for implementation of any compliance orders.

The overwhelming majority of disputes submitted to WTO panels involve at least one of four parties—Canada, the European Union, Japan, and the United States. Not surprisingly, considering the volume of trade between the two countries, disputes between Canada and the United States are common. Notable are those by the United States in respect of Canadian countervailing duties on grain corn and in respect of provincial rules on the marketing of alcoholic beverages, and by Canada against the United States in respect of countervailing duties on Canadian pork and on softwood lumber. The Canada–United States disputes concerning the Canadian treatment of "split-run" American magazines, and the subsidies given to the Canadian dairy industry, have already been mentioned (Cases 30.1 and 30.2). Adverse findings of the panel have led to changes in Canadian legislation. Two examples of complaints filed are:

- 2004—Canadian import duties on hormone-treated beef from the EU were held to be no longer legitimate after the EU changed its rules following an earlier adverse panel ruling in which Canada had been a complainant.
- 2013—A WTO appeal panel agreed with Japan that a Canadian renewable energy generation program that paid private solar and wind producers for energy fed back into the public system (that is, homeowner rooftop solar panels) violated Canada's WTO obligations because it required the use of equipment made in Ontario. Canada was ordered to reduce the amount of Ontario equipment required to qualify for the program by March 2014.

Canada files almost twice as many WTO complaints as are filed against it (33 as compared to 17, in 2014); the following are successful examples:

- 2008—A WTO panel held that Chinese import duties on Canadian, EU, and American automotive parts were illegal.
- 2013—A WTO appeal panel held that U.S. country of origin labelling requirements for beef and pork products violated the Technical Barriers to Trade Treaty by treating Canadian meat less favourably than domestic.
- 2014—As noted in Case 30.3, a WTO appeal panel upheld Canada's complaint about the EU's restriction on imported seal products.

NAFTA In its 2016 form NAFTA offers three dispute resolution procedures, depending on the type of dispute operated by the NAFTA Secretariat:

- Chapter 20 is the primary process for disputes between governments about the application and interpretation of NAFTA.
- Chapter 19 is for disputes between governments about anti-dumping and countervailing duties, which was at risk in the of 2018 renegotiations but ultimately retained in USMCA.
- Chapter 11 is for complaints by investors (private business) against the host government. This private investor right is essentially eliminated by USMCA save and except for complaints relating to investment in Mexican oil, gas, power, telecommunication, and infrastructure.

The processes in Chapters 19 and 20 are similar to those of the WTO, though the NAFTA has more effective implementation measures. When a dispute arises under both the NAFTA and the WTO, the complainant may choose under which set of procedures it should be settled.[79]

In the event of a dispute, Chapter 20 of the NAFTA provides for the holding of consultations at the request of either party. Should no mutually satisfactory agreement be reached, the dispute is then referred to a free trade commission. If, in turn, the commission fails to find an acceptable solution, either party may request that the commission appoint an arbitral panel. A panel is composed of five members, two of whom are appointed by each of the parties from lists of experts in trade law or practice, with a chairperson selected by agreement or by lot. The panel hears the submissions of the parties and produces a report, published by the commission. The parties must implement the report within 30 days; if a party fails to do so, an aggrieved party may withdraw benefits in retaliation. A party may appeal a panel decision to an Extraordinary Challenge Committee.

Chapter 19 disputes about the imposition of anti-dumping and countervailing duties occur frequently and are often more important, at least in financial terms, than the general disputes that are dealt with under Chapter 20. In particular, U.S. countervailing duties are widely perceived as constituting the most serious threat to Canadian exports, and this is one reason the United States wanted revisions to Chapter 19 as part of the 2018 negotiations of USMCA.

Currently, each country applies its own anti-dumping and countervail laws, though in the longer term the parties are required to establish common rules on subsidies and on anti-competitive practices such as dumping. Under the NAFTA, the parties are entitled to ensure that the national laws are correctly applied. The nature of a complaint, consequently, is that the country imposing the anti-dumping or countervailing duty has incorrectly or improperly applied its own law. The complaint procedure has already been used on a number of occasions, most controversially in the softwood lumber case.

CASE 30.10 Chapter 19 Complaints Process

The softwood lumber dispute between Canada and the United States continued for over 20 years. In the United States, most forestry land is privately owned, whereas in Canada it is largely owned by the provinces, which grant long-term licences to lumber firms in return for the payment of "stumpage" rates. The United States claims that the Canadian system operates as a subsidy to Canadian lumber producers, who are then able to undercut their American competitors. At the request of the American lumber industry, the United States imposed countervailing duties on Canadian lumber. A Canadian complaint against those duties was upheld by a NAFTA panel in 1992 and confirmed on appeal two years later. Following fresh complaints from U.S. producers, new countervailing duties were imposed in 2002, leading to a fresh round of complaint procedures, both in the WTO and in the NAFTA (under both Chapters 19 and 20).

---

[79] There are a few exceptions, where the NAFTA procedures must be used.

Through decisions in September 2004 and March 2006, NAFTA tribunals again ruled that the countervailing duties were improper and should be refunded. In December 2005, the WTO Appellate division also held that the U.S. countervailing duties were improperly collected, and Canada was entitled to take retaliatory measures. A separate arbitration was scheduled to determine the amount of retaliation. Canadian softwood lumber companies have paid approximately $3.7 billion in countervailing duties. Despite the many adverse trade rulings, the U.S. government did not revoke the duties.

Finally, in April 2006, the United States and the newly elected Canadian government arrived at a negotiated settlement. The agreement revoked the duties, provided for the return of at least 80 percent of the deposits collected since 2002, and ensured seven years of stability in the industry. The agreement was implemented in October 2006, and Export Development Canada began processing refunds. The *Softwood Lumber Products Export Charge Act, 2006* received royal assent on December 14, 2006, by which time 98.9 percent of refunds had been paid to Canadian softwood lumber companies. Unfortunately, the softwood lumber dispute reignited again in 2017 when the United States placed a new 20.8 percent tariff as part of the Trump Administration's efforts to renegotiate the NAFTA.[80]

NAFTA Chapter 11 Chapter 11, which deals with foreign investment, is unique and innovative and will be lost when (and if) USMCA is ratified. It provides a way in which Canadian, Mexican, and U.S. businesses that invest in another NAFTA country may sue the host government directly for infringement of the rights guaranteed by the agreement. NAFTA investor rights primarily protect firms from illegal expropriation by a government, but governments must also treat foreign investors no less favourably than domestic investors (national treatment). Businesses have used, or threatened to use, Chapter 11 to sue governments when their foreign operations have been affected by government policy measures that are "tantamount to expropriation" decisions, when those measures make it effectively impossible for the firm to carry on its normal operations.[81] USMCA will eliminate this process save and except for investments in specific Mexican industries, as noted earlier.

Several Chapter 11 tribunal rulings or actions involved challenges to environmental or health legislation:[82]

- 2005—The Canadian-based company Methanex failed in its claim against the United States, which alleged that the State of California's decision to phase out the use of its gasoline additive, MTBE, cost the company $970 million. Methanex was ordered to pay the United States costs valued at approximately $4 million.[83]

- 2007—Canada successfully defended a $160 million claim brought by UPS that alleged that Canada Post received preferential treatment due to its government ownership, especially from Canadian Border Services.[84]

- 2013—Eli Lilly commenced a $500 million claim against the Government of Canada alleging that the invalidation of two of its Canadian drug patents by the Federal Court violated Canada's NAFTA obligations, saying the negative court decisions amounted to an "expropriation" of exclusive rights.[85]

---

[80] The agreement will refund more than $5 billion to Canadian companies. For a review of the history of the dispute, see the press releases issued by the Minister of International Trade on December 5, 2005; March 17, 2006; April 27, 2006; October 6, 2006; October 30, 2006; and December 14, 2006; available on the Foreign Affairs and International Trade Canada website (https://www.international.gc.ca); BBC News, "US Sets Final Tariffs on Softwood Lumber from Canada," November 2 2017, https://www.bbc.com/news/world-us-canada-41838828.

[81] Most famous actions have been by Canadian softwood lumber manufacturers claiming damages as a consequence of the illegal U.S. countervailing duties.

[82] For an excellent review, see Soloway (2000) 33 CBLJ 92.

[83] *Methanex Corporation v United States of America*, https://www.state.gov/documents/organization/51052.pdf.

[84] *United Parcel Service of America, Inc ("UPS") v Government of Canada*, https://www.italaw.com/cases/1138.

[85] Eli Lilly Notice of Intent, NAFTA–Chapter 11–Investment, Government of Canada, Foreign Affairs, Trade and Development Canada website; see also *Eli Lilly Canada Inc v Novopharm Limited*, 2011 FC 1288, aff'd 2012 FCA 232 (CanlII), leave to SCC denied 2013 CanLII 26762 (SCC).

- 2013—Detroit International Bridge Company, owner of the Ambassador Bridge that connects Detroit and Windsor, filed a statement of claim alleging that the Government of Canada's plan to build a new government-owned bridge between Detroit and Windsor, just 2.3 km from the Ambassador Bridge, undermined the financial feasibility of the Ambassador Bridge (and its planned expansion) by diverting traffic away from it and therefore amounted to discrimination in violation of the NAFTA's national treatment obligation.

The NAFTA's arbitration tribunal proceedings have been criticized by consumer activists on the grounds that they are mostly conducted in private. In Canada, the Canadian Union of Postal Workers and the Council of Canadians launched an unsuccessful legal challenge against the Chapter 11 tribunal process, claiming the secrecy of the proceedings violates the *Canadian Charter of Rights and Freedoms*.[86] If and when USMCA eliminates Chapter 11, investors will have to lobby their respective governments to advance their complaints through the government dispute resolution processes, as is done with WTO disputes.

CHECKLIST
United States-Mexico-Canada Agreement (USMCA)

Major Areas of Change	USMCA
Particular Industries	Canadian dairy opened to US suppliers
	Automobiles factories subject to minimum wage
	Prohibits subsidies the contribute to over fishing
Intellectual Property	Canada required to extend copyright term to 70 years after death
Currency	Restricts currency devaluation management
Dispute Resolution	Eliminates Chapter 11 leaving, only 2 avenues for resolution
Expiration	Adds new fixed term of 16 years for expiration

Strategies to Manage the Legal Risks

First and foremost, Canadian businesses must address international issues early—at the initial stages of commencing business activities. The traditional model of waiting to develop an international presence until after a domestic market is established is no longer applicable in the internet era. Otherwise, a business could lose rights to valuable business assets. Do not assume the laws of foreign jurisdictions are the same as Canada's—very often they are not. Intellectual property rights must be secured in the domestic and foreign customer, supplier, and creditor markets. Contracts should expressly specify intellectual property ownership, proper law of the contract, and choice of forum.

The regulations controlling access to foreign markets are complicated, and navigating them might be difficult for a small business operator. Government agencies are

---

[86] *Council of Canadians v Canada (Attorney General)*, [2006] 277 DLR (4th) 527 (OAC) leave to appeal to SCC denied [2007] SCCA No 48. The NAFTA received parliamentary approval as an international treaty, but this did not incorporate it into domestic law subject to the *Charter*.

available to assist in this area, so contact with Economic Development Canada and the Canadian International Development Agency is beneficial. They may be able to access funding as well as information. Government assistance is also needed to obtain maximum benefits from the international trade agreements.

Canadian regulations also protect penetration of the domestic market, and businesses need to respect the controls on importing as well as the limits on foreign investment. Major restructuring with foreign capital, merging with foreign companies, and dissolving a Canadian subsidiary by a foreign parent all require Industry Canada approval, which is discretionary. On a smaller scale, losing the income tax designation of a Canadian-controlled private corporation will have negative consequences for the taxation on dividends.

International business disputes are a natural consequence of doing business internationally, and so they should be expected. Quick resolution before the business's brand is damaged is a typical business priority, and in this light, arbitration should be considered as an alternative to court proceedings. It is often easier to get agreement to arbitration before any dispute arises (in the original contract between the parties) than after the parties are disagreeing over the dispute. One downside to arbitration is that appeal rights are limited, so outcomes are final.

Sometimes businesses ignore foreign court proceedings against them, especially if they have no assets in the subject jurisdiction. This is a mistake. Provided basic requirements are met, Canadian courts recognize and enforce foreign judgments, and a business will soon find its Canadian assets seized to satisfy the foreign order. Businesses should respond to and participate in every complaint process that is initiated against them.

QUESTIONS FOR REVIEW

1. Distinguish between foreign trade and foreign investment.
2. Distinguish between public international law and private international law.
3. What is meant by the "proper law of the contract"?
4. What are "Incoterms"? Give examples.
5. What documentation is usually involved in an international sale of goods?
6. What is the purpose of foreign exchange risk management?
7. How can services be exported?
8. In what ways do governments attempt to promote exports? Are export subsidies permissible?
9. What is meant by "non-tariff barriers"? Give examples.
10. What is dumping?
11. What are countervailing duties?
12. What is the relationship between the GATT and the WTO?
13. What are TRIMs?
14. Distinguish between most-favoured-nation treatment and national treatment.
15. Distinguish between portfolio (capital) investment and direct investment.
16. Distinguish between (a) a branch, (b) a subsidiary, and (c) a joint venture.
17. What are "performance requirements"?
18. What purposes are normally served by bilateral investment protection treaties?
19. What is "forum shopping"? Why is it considered objectionable?
20. What is meant by *forum non conveniens*?

21. What are the principal advantages of commercial arbitration as opposed to litigation?
22. How are disputes resolved within the WTO? Within the NAFTA?
23. Explain how the softwood lumber dispute demonstrates both the strengths and the weaknesses in the WTO and NAFTA dispute resolution processes.
24. In what way is Chapter 11 of the NAFTA novel and how would the pending USMCA impact Chapter 11?

CASES AND PROBLEMS

1. Continuing Scenario

    Steven is a regular customer at Ashley's Toronto restaurant and loves Ashley's chocolate truffle cake so much that he wants it served at his company's sales convention being held at the Chateau Frontenac (CF) in Quebec City. He instructs the CF's caterer to buy enough cake for the 1000 attendees and get it to Quebec. CF sends an email to Ashley asking for a quote. Ashley replies, saying that that amount of cake will cost $10 000 and will need to be refrigerated during shipping. She tells CF that ABC Trucking Company has the appropriate truck. CF sends Ashley a purchase order for $10 000 worth of cake and instructs her to arrange for ABC to ship the cake to the hotel. Ashley does not notice the acronym DDP typed on the purchase order, and her quote does not include the cost of shipping. Answer the following questions about the cake delivery.

    (a) If the cake is damaged due to the negligence of a crane operator while being loaded onto the refrigeration truck, is this Ashley's problem or the hotel's? Why? What difference would it make if "EKW" had been typed on the order?

    (b) If CF refused to pay for the cake because it was damaged, where should Ashely commence her lawsuit, and why?

    (c) Should the law of Ontario or Quebec apply to this transaction?

    (d) What steps should Ashley take the next time she sends goods out of province?

2. XYZ Ltd., a large Canadian mining corporation, entered into an agreement three years ago with the government of the Republic of Utopia to develop the mining and processing of the rich zinc deposits in that country. A joint venture corporation, Cantopia Ltd., was established (under the law of Utopia), in which XYZ held 49 percent of the shares, and the government of Utopia held the remainder. XYZ invested $25 million in the project, in the form of machinery, technology, and capital to finance the operation of mines and smelters; the Utopian government's contribution to the project took the form of a lease, at nominal rent, of a large tract of land where valuable deposits had been discovered. It was agreed that Cantopia would mine the zinc, process it, and export it through XYZ's worldwide marketing organization. Profits would be shared proportionately, with 49 percent for XYZ and 51 percent for the government of Utopia.

    Recently, following a military coup, the new government of Utopia enacted a law requiring all mining enterprises to sell their total output to the newly established National Resources Corporation, wholly owned by the Utopian government, at prices to be established by a government agency. Under the prices established for zinc, it has become impossible for Cantopia to operate at a profit.

    Are there any steps that XYZ can take to protect its investment?

3. Canadian production of widgets is almost entirely in the hands of three corporations—Altawidge Ltd., Ontwidge Ltd., and Scotiawidge Ltd. All three corporations export a substantial volume of their products to the United States.

    Two years ago, as a result of increased competition from Malaysian widget producers, two of the Canadian corporations—Ontwidge and Scotiawidge—experienced financial difficulties. As a result, the governments of Ontario and Nova Scotia stepped in to help save the widget industry. They provided long-term, low-interest loans to the corporations and granted other benefits, such as research grants and exemption from property taxes. By contrast, Altawidge has received no government support but has been able to compete with its rivals because its operations are more advanced technologically.

Recently, there have been complaints from widget producers in the United States that they have lost a substantial share of the American market to imports from Canada and Malaysia. They allege that widget production in both countries is heavily subsidized. As a result of these complaints, the U.S. Department of Commerce has introduced a countervailing duty of 17 cents for each widget imported from Canada. The effect of the duty is to make Canadian widgets more expensive in the United States than domestically produced widgets.

Altawidge has in turn complained that, whether or not the Nova Scotia and Ontario producers receive an improper subsidy, its own products enjoy no such benefit and should not be subjected to the duty.

Discuss the issues raised, and suggest what steps might be taken to resolve the dispute.

4. Maxrevs Ltd. is a Manitoba corporation; it manufactures small gasoline-powered motors for use in a variety of power tools. It sells its motors directly to tool manufacturers throughout North America and also sells in substantial quantities to wholesale dealers in motor parts and components. One of those dealers supplied a number of Maxrevs motors to Weed Eater manufacturer Snapper Inc., a corporation incorporated in Michigan.

Gonzalez, a resident of Texas, purchased a Snapper Weed Eater and subsequently sustained a severe injury to his leg and hand when the tool malfunctioned. He brought an action in a Texas court against both Snapper and Maxrevs. Although Maxrevs was served with notice of the proceedings, it did not enter an appearance and did not defend the action.

The Texas court found that the connection between the motor and the revolving blade was defective, and held Snapper liable. It also found that Maxrevs had been negligent in failing to provide adequate instructions for installation of its motors in tools of that kind and awarded damages against Maxrevs amounting to US $5 million.

Gonzalez has now filed a claim in the Manitoba court to enforce his judgment against Maxrevs. Is it likely that the Manitoba court will enforce the judgment?

Chapter 31
Electronic Commerce

- **ECOMMERCE**
- **ECOMMERCE AND THE LAW**
- **INTERNATIONAL ASPECTS OF ECOMMERCE**
- **STRATEGIES TO MANAGE THE LEGAL RISKS**

Electronic commerce (Ecommerce) is the most rapidly growing sector of the economy, along with information technology. Increasingly, business is being conducted through the internet and through other electronic means. Applying existing legal rules and principles to the new business environment raises challenging new legal issues.

In this chapter we examine such questions as:

- What is ecommerce?
- How is the law changing to accommodate the challenges of ecommerce?
- How are contracts made on the internet?
- What law governs those contracts?
- How are consumers protected in ecommerce transactions?
- How has the internet affected the law of defamation?
- How do trademark and copyright laws apply to the internet?
- Should government regulate ecommerce?
- Which courts have jurisdiction over internet disputes?
- To what extent is international cooperation necessary in order to regulate ecommerce?

ECOMMERCE

What Is Ecommerce?

electronic commerce (ecommerce) the use of computer networks to facilitate commercial activities, including the production, distribution, sale, and delivery of goods and services

internet the interconnected logical networks that link computers worldwide

intranet closed systems linking specific users internal to a company or group; commonly used for data exchange

Electronic commerce (Ecommerce) is broadly defined as "the delivery of information, products, services, or payments by telephone, computer, or other automated media."[1] More commonly, ecommerce refers to commercial activity that makes use of computer networks, including the **internet** or **intranet** systems.[2]

According to one report, "the Internet has done for electronic commerce what Henry Ford did for the automobile—converted a luxury for the few into a relatively simple and inexpensive device for the many."[3]

Increasing Impact of Ecommerce on Business

Before 1995, ecommerce was almost non-existent. Then firms such as Amazon, Cisco, and Dell began to use the internet extensively for commercial transactions. The worldwide volume of ecommerce grew from $28 billion in 1998 to more than $1 trillion by 2003. Business-to-business (B2B) transactions account for about two-thirds of all ecommerce. They include intranet activities—between branches of the same company or between related companies in a multinational group—and arm's-length transactions with other businesses involving internet supply of services or products, technical support, invoicing, or payment. Business-to-consumer (B2C) transactions most often involve electronic retailing where a consumer accesses a business website to purchase or license tangible or electronic goods or services. By 2018, Canadian retail commerce sales were almost 1.5 billion per month; most Canadian businesses incorporate social media tools into their online presence.[4] In 2016, the value of Canadian electronic fund transfers exceeded cheque values for the first time.[5]

Ecommerce has changed the business world in many ways, including:

- operational business practices,
- cashless society, and
- surrounding business environment.

electronic retailing (etailing) the supply of tangible or electronic goods or services over the internet; the supply of tangible goods involves a conventional mode of delivery, and electronic goods are downloaded directly to the customer's computer

Pre-existing Business Practices
Businesses are adapting all aspects of their operations to the online model. The hard-copy, tangible processes of the past are rapidly being replaced by the instantaneous movement of intangible bits of electronic data. The use of internet and intranet systems is transforming B2B and B2C relationships, as well as relationships with employees, government, and the public. Businesses supply their products to customers through **electronic retailing (etailing)**. They electronically monitor their supply chain, record keeping, and employees, and use

---

[1] "Electronic Commerce and Canada's Tax Administration: A Report to the Minister of National Revenue from the Minister's Advisory Committee on Electronic Commerce," Ottawa, April 1998.

[2] M Fecenko and A Huntley, *Ecommerce Corporate–Commercial Aspects* (Markham, ON: Lexis Nexis, 2003) at 3. The use of the internet raises other legal issues that are not related to ecommerce, as defined here. These are not considered in this chapter. For a comprehensive survey, see M Geist, *Internet Law in Canada*, 3rd ed (North York, ON: Captus Press, 2002).

[3] "The Economic and Social Impacts of Electronic Commerce: Preliminary Findings and Research Agenda" (Paris: OECD, 1998) at 10, http://www.oecd.org.

[4] Data from Statistics Canada "Retail E-commerce Sales", https://www.statcan.gc.ca/eng/start.

[5] Payments Canada, 2017 Canadian Payment Methods and Trends, at 4, https://www.payments.ca/about-us/our-systems-and-rules/retail-system/statistics; As of July 2016, Canada had an estimated 32.12 million internet users, representing 81.19 percent of the population: https://www.statista.com/statistics/243808/number-of-internet-users-in-canada.

electronic transfer of funds to bank, make payments, and collect accounts receivable online. The internet is a natural advertising medium. Even businesses not involved in etailing maintain websites as a form of advertising. An online presence has become a business necessity.

Establishing a Website A business website may be passive, seeking only to provide information to advertise and market its products or services; or it may be active, to interact with others in the exchange of information or completion of sale transactions. Establishing a website involves several contracts. Generally, the business will

- negotiate a website development agreement—Creating a website involves obtaining various development services (content, graphics, software, etc.) and raises intellectual property issues. Both confidentiality and the ownership of the intellectual property should be addressed in the agreement.
- negotiate a website-hosting agreement—once developed, the site must be operated on a web server, usually operated by an internet service provider (ISP).
- negotiate an internet access agreement with the ISP—This agreement includes terms allowing the ISP to discontinue service for any behaviour it finds unacceptable. It will also have an exemption clause protecting the ISP from liability for service interruption and consent for release of private information for specific purposes.
- register a domain name[6] and protect the intellectual property associated with the website—this could involve trademark, copyright, and patents.

Additionally, if the site is active, it must be secure, and encryption services will be required. Privacy of collected information must be protected, and businesses must develop terms and conditions for those using the site.

Cashless Society Canada is among the world's most cashless countries.[7] The 2016 Canadian payment world was divided into two segments—point-of-sale transactions in which payments were made at the merchants' physical or virtual locations (80 percent of volume) and remote transactions that involved financial service providers or financial institutions as intermediaries who moved the funds to the payee (20 percent of volume). Although cash payments made up the highest number of point-of-sale payments (38 percent), followed closely by debit cards (34 percent) and credit cards (27 percent), their total value has shrunk to 13 percent, behind both debit and credit cards.[8]

In the ecommerce marketplace, traditional banks are competing with **ecash**—online payment systems that enable the secure and anonymous transfer of money over the internet or other networks (including ewallets, **payment card networks**, and **social media payment channels**).[9] Ewallets are financial intermediary systems such as PayPal Inc., which store funds outside a financial institution for use online. Payment card networks include debit card systems (such as the Interac Association) that process point-of-sale demands for funds held in a financial institution. eCash facilitates secure, small-value transactions that are not cost-effective when conventional credit cards are

electronic transfer of funds payment made through electronic (intangible) media such as telephone or internet rather than by cash or cheque; payment may take the form of credit card charges, debit of bank accounts, or even ecash, often through the business's website

ecash an online payment system that enables the anonymous transfer of money over the internet

payment card networks an electronic payment system used to accept, transmit, or process transactions made by payment card to transfer funds or information among issuer, user, and merchants

social media payment channels messenger services that connect with existing credit card and bank systems; consumers pre-fund or link bank accounts to new apps of financial service providers

---

[6] It may be necessary to register multiple domain names. See domain names under the heading "Intellectual Property."

[7] Daniel Tencer, "Canada At #1 in Ranking of World's Most Cashless Societies," *Huffington Post*—Business, Oct 12, 2017, http://www.huffingtonpost.ca/2017/10/11/canada-at-1-in-ranking-of-worlds-most-cashless-societies_a_23240067.

[8] *Supra* note 5 at 15, https://www.payments.ca/about-us/our-systems-and-rules/retail-system/statistics.

[9] For background on Canadian payment systems, see Task Force for the Payments Systems Review, "Canadian Payments Landscape—Report," (September 2010), http://paymentsystemreview.ca/indes.php/resources/the-canadian-payment-system/index.html (Executive Summary; 94 percent of Canadians had debit cards by 2013).

used. Payment cards include *pay later* cards (traditional credit cards), *pay now* cards (debit cards), and *pay before* cards (pre-paid cards). The three forms of payment cards move between traditional banks, regulated under the *Bank Act* and the *Loans and Trust Companies Act*, and payment card network systems, regulated under the *Payment Card Networks Act*.[10] Social media payment channels use messenger services to connect with existing credit card and bank systems; consumers pre-fund or link bank accounts to new apps of financial service providers.[11]

As discussed in Chapter 19, payment law established for traditional banking focuses on cheques and negotiable instruments regulated under the *Bills of Exchange Act*. It has been modified to regulate pre-authorized debits, irrevocable payment messages, and immediate fund transfers. The Canadian government regulates electronic payment facilitators with a Code of Conduct for the Credit and Debit Card Industry in Canada.[12] Two of its requirements are that credit and debit functions be on separate cards and that merchants be given 90 days' notice of fee increases. *The Payment Card Networks Act* assigns the responsibility for monitoring and regulating the payment card industry to the Financial Consumer Agency of Canada (FCAC).[13] FCAC also oversees prepaid cards, including the control of activation, maintenance, and dormancy fees.[14] Businesses that intend to issue "gift certificates" need to comply with these regulations.

Surrounding Business Environment The business environment is filled with new industries. Examples include ISPs; network infrastructure support and outsourcing, including data management and security; payments facilitators described above; and countless new online products and services. The global nature of the internet offers businesses access to customers and suppliers from around the world. Ecommerce is one of the major reasons why business has "gone global." Even small, local businesses are able to do business internationally via ecommerce, and the marketplace has expanded exponentially. Unfortunately, the explosion in ecommerce has also attracted abuse. Ecommerce increases concern about public safety, fraud, invasion of privacy, identity theft, money laundering, and tax evasion. Governments have responded with increased regulation, and businesses must protect themselves and their stakeholders with increased security and proactive measures.

Net Neutrality In a net neutral environment, small and large businesses have equal access to services, ecommerce customers, and the market place, which fosters innovation. ISPs, sometimes considered the gatekeepers to the internet, are in a position to give preferential benefit or access to particular users or influence the content being provided over their networks. The *Telecommunications Act*[15] authorizes the Canadian Radio-television and Telecommunications Commission (CRTC) to license and regulate ISPs, and it professes support for net neutrality, but it recently approved differential pricing on speed rate and data usage.[16] One of the assessment criteria is the "impact on Internet openness and innovation." Start-up businesses may be shut out of the marketplace if different speed and pricing models discriminate against them.

---

[10] *Bank Act*, SC 1991, c 46; *Loans and Trust Companies Act*, SC 1991, c 45; *Payment Card Networks Act*, SC 2010, c 12, s 1834.

[11] *Supra* note 5 at 8.

[12] Available on the Department of Finance Canada website: http://www.fin.gc.ca/n10/data/10-049_1-eng.asp.

[13] *Supra* note 10, s 1834.

[14] *Prepaid Payments Products Regulation*, SOR/2013-2009.

[15] SC 1993, c 38.

[16] Government of Canada, Canadian Radio-television and Telecommunications Commission, Telecom Regulatory Policy CRTC 2017-104: Framework for assessing the differential pricing practices of Internet service providers, https://crtc.gc.ca/eng/archive/2017/2017-104.pdf.

The Impact of Ecommerce on the Law

Traditional legal principles involving contract, tort, intellectual property, and international law are being adapted to meet ecommerce challenges. Privacy and consumer protection laws are stretching to cover online risks. Courts, legislatures, and the international community are creating new law in the form of case decisions, legislation, and international treaties.

Cases involving ecommerce issues are coming before the courts, and judges are reinterpreting long-held principles. Pressing issues require the immediate response of government. The federal government has the power to regulate the financial aspects of ecommerce under its banking power, and indeed all uses of the internet within Canada, under its general power to regulate intraprovincial communication.[17] In addition, provincial governments have power to regulate ecommerce under various constitutional categories, including property and civil rights.[18] As a result, both federal and provincial governments have passed legislation addressing ecommerce issues.[19]

A consistent global approach to ecommerce law is considered best, but both courts and legislatures face jurisdictional boundaries. Non-governmental organizations such as the Organisation for Economic Co-operation and Development (OECD), the World Trade Organization (WTO), the United Nations Commission on International Trade Law (UNCITRAL), and the World Intellectual Property Organization (WIPO) work toward standardization through international guidelines, treaties, conventions, and model laws. Member nations are encouraged to adopt domestic legislation consistent with international guidelines. Unfortunately, not all countries follow the international standards, and businesses face jurisdictional variation in ecommerce law.

ECOMMERCE AND THE LAW

Contract Law

Electronic commerce, like any other form of commerce, is principally about making contracts. Traditional contract law principles have been adapted to the ecommerce environment.

Formation of Contracts Key elements in the formation of a contract remain offer and acceptance. When does a contract come into existence in a typical ecommerce transaction?

ILLUSTRATION 31.1   When is An Online Contract Formed?

Elektra visits her favourite online music store, clicks on "Browse," and chooses the classical music category. Following the website's instructions, she selects five songs, each time clicking on "Add this to my shopping basket." She then clicks on "Buy," types in her credit card details, and finally clicks on "Confirm."

Has any contract been made? If so, when? Does the store's website constitute an offer to sell, or is it simply an advertisement or an invitation to treat? Is the offer made when Elektra clicks on "Buy" or on "Confirm"? At what point is her order accepted

---

[17] *Constitution Act, 1867*, s 92(10)(a). Internet usage can constitute "broadcasting" under the *Broadcasting Act*, SC 1991, c 11.

[18] *Constitution Act, 1867*, ibid., ss 92(13), (14).

[19] Initial support for self-regulation of the internet and ecommerce stemmed from its international usage and the belief that any attempt by one country to regulate ecommerce might simply result in business migrating to less restrictive regimes; see Geist, "The Reality of Bytes: Regulating Economic Activity in the Age of the Internet" (1998) 73 *Wash L Rev* 521. Criminal use of the internet was always of greater concern. See the section in this chapter headed "Illegal Activities."

web-wrap agreement a website document setting out contractual terms, the acceptance of which is indicated by clicking on the appropriate icon

click-wrap agreements require the buyer to open the terms page before clicking acceptance of them

browse-wrap agreements provide a link to additional terms and conditions but do not require a buyer to open them before accepting the web-wrap agreement

by the store? Does that acceptance have to be communicated to Elektra before a contract comes into existence?[20]

These are some of the questions that arise in even the simplest type of ecommerce transaction. To answer these questions, courts refer to similar cases where communication has been by mail, phone, or fax. A business should design its website to spell out very clearly the legal consequences of clicking on each icon. It has become common for businesses to use a **web-wrap agreement**, **click-wrap agreement**, or **browse-wrap agreement** that requires the consumer to click on the appropriate box to indicate agreement with the non-negotiable standard terms of sale prepared in advance by the business.[21] These are the online versions of standard form contracts discussed in Chapter 6.

CASE 31.1 Accepting Standard Form Terms

A group of law students in Ontario entered into an online agreement to subscribe to the Microsoft Network. In doing so, they were directed to the "membership rules," and before concluding the agreement, they were required to click on a box indicating that they had read and accepted those membership rules. They subsequently brought an action in Ontario against Microsoft, alleging that Microsoft had taken payments from their credit cards in breach of contract.

One of the terms in the membership rules was that all disputes should be decided under the law of, and by the courts of, the State of Washington. The Ontario court held that the membership rules had been agreed to and formed part of the contracts. Consequently, the Ontario courts had no jurisdiction.[22]

Web-wrap agreements should be designed to ensure that all intended terms and conditions are brought to the attention of potential customers before an offer is submitted. In 2007, the Supreme Court of Canada stated that hyperlinks to "terms and conditions" must be visible, functional, and accessible.[23]

The Law Governing the Contract Determining when the contract is made may also determine where it is made, which in turn may determine the law that governs the transaction.[24]

ILLUSTRATION 31.2 Multiple Legal Jurisdictions

Imagine an online consumer is a resident of British Columbia. The vendor is incorporated in Delaware. The website is operated through a server located in the Cayman Islands. On receiving the buyer's order, the server automatically notifies a warehouse in Alberta the vendor uses to dispatch goods ordered by Canadian customers.

Is the contract governed by the laws of British Columbia, Delaware, the Cayman Islands, or Alberta? This is important because the law of the contract determines such matters as

- any restrictions on contractual capacity,
- the legality of the contract,
- any writing requirements,
- any implied terms,

---

[20] See Chapter 6 under "Transactions Between Parties at a Distance from Each Other."

[21] *Century 21 Canada Limited Partnership v Rogers Communications Inc*, 2011 BCSC 1196 at paras 98–108.

[22] *Rudder v Microsoft Corp*, [1999] OJ No 3778. See also *Kanitz v Rogers Cable Inc* (2002), 58 OR (3d) 299; *Wembley Marketing Ltd v ITEX Corp*, [2008] OJ No 5194. But see *Douez v Facebook* 2017 SCC 33 (consumers may have forum selection clauses applied less strictly than in B2B contexts).

[23] *Dell Computer Corp v Union des consommateurs*, 2007 SCC 34; in *Rogers Wireless Inc v Muroff*, 2007 SCC 35 at para 15, 229, the Supreme Court accepted that internet consumers must have a certain level of computer competence.

[24] The place where a contract is made is one of a number of factors that may determine the law governing the contract. See Chapter 30, under "The Proper Law of the Contract."

- the available remedies for breach of contract, and
- the applicability of consumer protection legislation.

Again, placing a term in the contract will answer the question of which law is intended to govern, although consumer protection legislation in the customer's country may still apply, regardless of such a statement.[25]

Formal Requirements The law that governs a contract may impose certain formal requirements—for example (as noted in Chapter 10), some contracts must be in writing. Are electronic contracts "in writing"? Do electronic signatures constitute legal signatures? The *Personal Information Protection and Electronic Documents Act* (PIPEDA) answers these questions for individual-to-government contracts.[26]

This statute allows for substitution of electronic alternatives where pre-existing legislation requires paper copies, notice, or communication of information or transactions (s. 32), and it recognizes electronic documents and signatures.[27]

In Canada, the private law of contract falls almost exclusively within provincial jurisdiction, so provincial legislation governs B2B and B2C electronic contracts.[28] It adapts contract law to the internet environment by addressing topics such as acceptance by clicking an icon, communication of acceptance, electronic signatures, and writing.

The provincial legislation is based on the *Uniform Electronic Commerce Act*, a model statute prepared by the Uniform Law Conference of Canada in accordance with the principles of the United Nations model law,[29] which states the following:

- Information in electronic form has legal effect or enforceability (s. 5).[30]
- Information in electronic form (with continued permanent availability) satisfies a writing requirement (s. 7).[31]
- A legal signature of a person may be an electronic signature (s. 8).[32]
- An offer or the acceptance or any other part of contract formation may be in an electronic document or done by an electronic action such as touching or clicking on a designated icon or place on a computer screen or otherwise communicating electronically (unless otherwise agreed, s. 20).[33]

Consumer Protection Legislation Consumer protection is primarily an area of provincial jurisdiction, although particular industries may also fall under federal protection, such as banking. In an attempt to offer Canadian consumers uniform online protection and provide international consistency, the federal government—together with the governments of Ontario, Alberta, and Quebec, and representatives of business—developed eight principles entitled "The Canadian Code of Practice for Consumer Protection in Electronic Commerce."[34] The principles incorporate the

---

[25] *Consumer Protection Act, 2002*, SO 2002, c 30, Sch A.

[26] SC 2000, c 5.

[27] *Ibid.*, ss 41, 43 and 46.

[28] See e.g. *Electronic Commerce Act*, SNL 2001, c E-5.2; SNS 2000, c 26; SO 2000, c 17; RSPEI 1988, c E-4.1; *Electronic Commerce and Information Act*, CCSM c E-55; *Electronic Information and Documents Act*, SS 2000, c E-7.22; and *Electronic Transactions Act*, SA 2001, c E-5.5; SBC 2001, c 10; SNB 2001, c E-5.5.

[29] The text of the Uniform Electronic Commerce Act is available from the Uniform Law Conference of Canada website: http://www.ulcc.ca.

[30] For corresponding provisions in the provincial legislation, *supra* note 28, see e.g. s 3 (BC); s 6 (NS); s 4 (ON).

[31] See *ibid.*, s 5 (BC); s 8 (NS); s 5 (ON).

[32] See *ibid.*, s 11 (BC); s 11 (NS); s 11 (ON).

[33] See *ibid.*, s 15 (BC); s 21 (NS); s 19 (ON).

[34] The Canadian Code of Practice for Consumer Protection in Electronic Commerce has three goals: equivalent protection, harmonization, and international consistency. The eight principles will be subject to periodic review and are available at http://cmcweb.ca/epic/site/cmc-cmc.nsf/eng/fe00064.html.

OECD Guidelines for Consumer Protection in the Content of Electronic Contracts.[35] The Canadian code of practice and the OECD guidelines reflect the developing international standards of consumer protection in online contracting.

Federal, provincial, and territorial consumer affairs representatives developed a model for B2C internet consumer protection legislation.[36] Some provinces have adopted consumer protection legislation based on the model law.[37] Protective measures include mandatory disclosure of terms, cancellation rights or cooling-off periods, and printable consumer copies. Consumer protection laws may apply to transactions completed outside their specific jurisdiction. The Ontario legislation applies to all consumers located in Ontario, no matter where the vendor or the goods are based. Alberta's protections apply when either the consumer or vendor is a resident of Alberta or the offer or acceptance is made in Alberta.[38] Quebec consumers are protected from waivers of Quebec authority.[39] An online vendor needs to be familiar with the specifics of the consumer protection laws in relevant jurisdictions.

CHECKLIST

Precautions to Be Taken by Vendors When Contracting Online

When a website is used to sell goods and services, the trader should take the following precautions:

- Become familiar with the ecommerce and consumer protection laws of provinces, countries, or jurisdictions in which it intends to do business.
- Where necessary, customize contract terms for the specific jurisdiction.
- Design the website so that the terms of the contract are brought to the attention of customers before any contract is concluded. Ensure any hyperlinks are visible, easily accessible, and functional.
- State clearly which law and jurisdiction apply to any contracts formed.
- Avoid giving customers too much freedom to amend terms—use yes/no or accept/decline options wherever possible.
- Maintain full backups of all contracts made via webpages.
- Generate and forward a printable customer copy of the contract at the time of purchase.

Torts

The internet raises tort issues relating to damages, jurisdiction, and limitation periods, as well as issues about how and by whom a tort is committed. The two torts most often associated with the internet are defamation and negligent security. Chapter 32 discusses

---

[35] The OECD consumer guidelines cover fair business practices, advertising, and marketing and are available at www.oecd.org/fr/sti/consommateurs/oecdguidelinesforconsumerprotectioninthecontextofelectroniccommerce1999.htm.

[36] Canada's Office of Consumer Affairs, Internet Sales Contract Harmonization Template, available at http://ic.gc.ca/eic/site/oca-bc.nsf/eng/ca01642.html.

[37] *Consumer Protection and Business Practices Act*, SNL 2009, c C-31.1, ss 21V–21AF; *Consumer Protection Act, 2002*, SO 2002, c 30, Sch A, ss 37–40; *Consumer Protection Act*, CCSM c C200, ss 127–35; *Consumer Protection Act*, SS 1996, c C-30.1, ss 75.5–75.91; *Fair Trading Act*, RSA 2000, c F-2, s 42. Details of disclosure, notice, and cancellation protections are usually set out in the regulations rather than the legislation: Alberta Regulation 81/2001 (Internet Sales Regulation) passed pursuant to the *Fair Trading Act*. Particular industries may be subject to additional regulation: Alberta Regulation 246/2005 (Energy Marketing Regulation), Part 3: Internet Marketing Contracts.

[38] Ontario *Consumer Protection Act, 2002*, *supra* note 25, s 2; Alberta Regulation 81/2001, s 2 (*Fair Trading Act*).

[39] Article 3149 CCQ; Quebec law requires websites of firms whose place of business is in the province to be in the French language.

the negligence liability faced by companies whose security protocols and encryption systems do not meet industry standards allowing hackers to steal customer's electronically stored private information. Class actions alleging negligent security aggregate the damages of millions of online victims.[40]

Defamation   Posting defamatory material on a website or message board is publication for the purposes of libel and constitutes "broadcasting" for purposes of libel and slander legislative notice or apology provisions.[41] The internet's ability to instantaneously reach a very large audience increases the size of damage awards.[42]

CASE 31.2   Publishing to the World

Fromm, a director of the Canadian Association of Free Expression Inc. (CAFÉ), posted nine comments on various websites complaining about W., an investigator with the Canadian Human Rights Commission (CHRC). He said W. was "a member of the thought police" and a "high priest of censorship" who abused his position with the CHRC. Fromm's posting triggered insulting responding posts. W. sued both Fromm and CAFÉ, who admitted making the postings as well as sending emails to a large distribution list.

They made no apology or retraction and argued fair comment as a defence. The trial judge found (and the Court of Appeal agreed) that the comments were defamatory and awarded general damages of $20 000 plus aggravated damages of $10 000. Internet libel has global reach and the ability to instantaneously and irrevocably publish to a limitless audience. The fact that the comments were published literally to the world justified the award of aggravated damages.[43]

ISPs are an integral part of the ecommerce system. They have been described as the "gatekeepers" to the internet. Some anonymous internet posters mistakenly believe they are not liable for defamatory comments because ISPs will keep their identities confidential. This is not always true—courts may order ISPs to release identifying information in some situations. Unfortunately for plaintiffs, ISPs may have only limited contact information. Still it can be valuable for service or notice purposes.

CASE 31.3   Anonymous Posting

Brian Burke, former general manager of the Toronto Maple Leafs and Vancouver Canucks, started a defamation lawsuit against anonymous message board posters known only by their posting names. The message board administrators refused to provide the identity and residence of the defendants. The British Columbia court gave Burke permission to serve notice of the lawsuits through the message board's personal message service, which sends notification to users when logging into their accounts.[44]

Are ISPs legally responsible for material placed on the internet through their servers? Can the ISPs be considered to have "published" a libel? Courts generally take the view that ISPs are like a postal service or phone company and should not be responsible

---

[40] Canadian Press, "How to Participate in the Growing Number of Privacy Class Actions in Canada," Sept 21, 2017, http://www.cbc.ca/news/business/class-action-lawsuits-privacy-1.4300338.

[41] *Janssen-Ortho Inc v Amgen Canada Inc*, [2005] OJ No 2265 (dealing with an internet radio broadcast); *Bahlieda v Santa* (2003), 233 DLR (4th) 382 (ONCA). In the context of the Ontario *Libel and Slander Act*, whether posting on the internet was "broadcasting" was a triable issue, and the Act requires written notice of intended legal action; see Chapter 3. See also *Warman v Fromm*, [2007] OJ No 4754, aff'd [2008] OJ No 5043, leave to appeal denied [2009] SCCA No 40; *Breeden v Black*, [2012] SCC 19.

[42] See e.g. *Barrick Gold Corporation v Lopehandia* (2004), 71 OR (3d) 416 (ONCA). Damages were increased from $15 000 to $75 000 based on the "internet factor." Publishing a libel in a limited number of personal emails is likely to be less harmful than posting it on a website: *Ross v Holley*, [2004] OJ No 4643; *Newman v Halstead*, (2006) BCJ No 59. Popularity of blogs and social networks such as Facebook increase the likelihood of large defamation awards: *Newman v Halstead*, [2006] BCSC 65.

[43] *Warman v Fromm*, *supra* note 41. See also *Warman v Grosvenor*, [2008] OJ No 4462.

[44] *Burke v John Doe*, 2013 BCSC 964.

for any material transmitted by them.⁴⁵ ISPs are not considered parties to a tort so long as their activities are restricted to the transmission of information and content neutral.⁴⁶ Similarly, hyperlinks to another website containing defamatory content do not create a presumption that the first site has republished the defamatory content; hyperlinks are compared to footnotes—"they do not make the author of the footnotes a publisher of what the reader finds when the footnote is followed."⁴⁷ However, there could be liability if there is direct evidence of publication (members of the public following the link and reading the content); the defamatory content is commented upon, endorsed, or reproduced on the **linking or hyperlinking** site; or readers are encouraged to follow the link.⁴⁸

> **linking or hyperlinking** an electronic connection of one website to another website; links may be automatic or activated by the user, and the new website may replace the original website or open in its own frame or browser window

Others Ecommerce can produce other tort claims. Sometimes an eproduct may trigger product liability. Some have argued (so far with little success) that manufacturers of violent video games should be held liable for violence done by their customers.⁴⁹ Many ecommerce services depend on the use of sophisticated computer programs, which can malfunction. In one case, an investor was awarded damages against a discount electronic trading broker when faults in the broker's data entry system caused the posting of multiple transaction records in the plaintiff's account and resulted in the plaintiff selling securities he did not own.⁵⁰ In another tort example, a student successfully sued Laurentian University for negligent misrepresentations made on the university website.⁵¹

Intellectual Property

Intellectual property law is covered in Chapter 20. However, ecommerce and the use of the internet create special challenges and opportunities for infringement. For example, although the components of a website may be quite standard or ordinary, the specific organization, presentation, operation, and content of a website are often unique and could attract copyright and trademark protection. How the website operates maybe a patentable business method. In this section, we review intellectual property issues arising in ecommerce.

Trademarks

> **infringement** violation of the rights of the owner of the intellectual property
>
> **trademark** an identifiable feature that is used by a person for the purpose of distinguishing his goods or services from those of others
>
> **passing-off** a common law tort involving the misrepresentation of goods, services, or a business in such a way as to deceive the public into believing that they are the goods, services, or business of some other person

A trademark is an identifiable feature used to distinguish one's goods or services from others; **infringement** is unauthorized use of a **trademark** or use of a confusingly similar mark. Infringement is actionable by the tort of **passing-off** or under the *Trademarks Act*,⁵² even when unintentional. The internet increases the probability of infringements, their seriousness, and the likelihood of detection. In the past two businesses with confusingly similar names could operate in different countries, or in different jurisdictions within the same country, without causing confusion.

Without the internet, each business and their respective customers would likely have been unaware of the other's existence, and there would be little chance of confusion. However, in the internet era, the names would likely appear on any search results and be far more likely to confuse searchers.

---

⁴⁵ *Canadian Association of Internet Providers v SOCAN* (2004), 240 DLR (4th) 193 (SCC). See also *Re Broadcasting Act*, 2012 SCC 4 where ISPs were found not to carry on (in whole or in part) a broadcasting undertaking (subject to the *Broadcasting Act*)—they merely provide end-users with access to broadcasting.

⁴⁶ "Caching" information is "content neutral" and is simply a consequence of the improvement of internet technology and did not give rise to liability: *SOCAN*, *ibid* at para 115.

⁴⁷ *Crookes v Wikimedia Foundation Inc*, 2008 BCSC 1424, aff'd [2009] BCJ No 1832 at paras 18–20, 41, 59, aff'd *Crookes v Newton*, 2011 SCC 47.

⁴⁸ *Ibid* [[2009] BCJ No 1832] at paras 59–72.

⁴⁹ Dylan Reeves, "Tort Liability for Violent Video Games," (2009) 60 *Ala L Rev* 519.

⁵⁰ *Robert v Brokerage Services Inc* (2001), 104 ACWS (3d) 988.

⁵¹ *Olar v Laurentian University* (2007), CarswellOnt 3595, aff'd [2008] OJ No 4623.

⁵² RSC 1985 c T-13; See Chapter 20 about pending revision of trademark legislation.

> **ILLUSTRATION 31.3   Expanded Infringement**
>
> Caitlin, the owner of the Enchanted Florist flower shop serving the greater Toronto area, creates a website to enable her customers to order flowers for delivery. On this website, she posts photographs of her flower arrangements and takes orders over the phone from regular customers with account numbers. A month later, Caitlin receives notice that shops in Halifax and Victoria—also named the Enchanted Florist—are claiming that she is infringing their trademarks.[53]

Trademark infringement on the internet is not always accidental; sometimes the goal is to take advantage of the public's familiarity with the existing trademark.

> **CASE 31.4   Deliberate Infringement**
>
> Bell Actimedia Inc. produced online telephone and business directories in Canada, using the trademarks "Yellow Pages" and "Pages Jaunes." It learned that Globe Communications, a Quebec partnership, had a website with the address www.lespagesjaunes.com and was advertising itself as the "business directory of the French-speaking world."
>
> Bell owned several internet sites, including www.yellowpages.ca, www.canadayellowpages.com, www.pagesjaunes.ca, and www.pagesjaunescanada.com, and sought an injunction to restrain Globe from using its "Pages Jaunes" trademark, alleging passing-off and unfair competition. The Court granted the injunction because Bell established that there was confusion and Bell would suffer irreparable harm if an injunction was not granted.[54]
>
> In another case, trademark infringement damages were awarded against two corporations, and personal fines against their directors, for continued infringement of the "Yellow Pages" mark (as well as of the "walking fingers" logo) after an injunction was issued.[55]

The confusion must arise from the trademark and not from other generic content.

> **CASE 31.5   Right to the Mark**
>
> The Software Guy was established in 2002 as an online retailer of business application software. In 2003 another firm, the Software King, started up a similar business, with a remarkably similar webpage. The two domain names were also very similar: www.thesoftwareguy.com and www.thesoftwareking.com. The proprietors of the two businesses had previously discussed setting up business together. Software Guy sought an injunction to restrain Software King from using that name and from using text from its website.
>
> The court dismissed the application. The names were confusingly similar because of the word "software," which is a generic term to which the applicant had no exclusive right. As to the website, it seemed obviously pirated, even reproducing a grammatical error. However, there was a strong suggestion that the applicant had itself pirated the design from elsewhere. It was not the creator and had no copyright in the design.[56]

Unauthorized linking of websites may be trademark infringement if it suggests affiliation, endorsement, or sponsorship. Infringement is most likely when the link is opened in its own frame within a single browser window so that both websites are visible at the same time.

> **CASE 31.6   Linking Content**
>
> Showmax Inc. intended to open a big-screen movie theatre. Its website contained an unauthorized link to a picture of an IMAX theatre from the IMAX website. The Federal Court found that the linkage incorrectly conveyed the impression that the two businesses were associated.[57]

---

[53] GM Kalow, "From the Internet to Court: Exercising Jurisdiction Over World Wide Web Communications" (1997) 65 *Fordham L Rev* 2241.

[54] *Bell Actimedia Inc v Puzo* (1999), 166 FTR 202.

[55] *Tele-Direct (Publications) Inc v Canadian Business Online Inc* (1998), 85 CPR (3d) 332, varied [2000] FCJ No 2.

[56] *Software Guy Brokers Ltd v Hardy*, [2004] BCJ No 95.

[57] *IMAX Corp v Showmax Inc* (2000), 5 CPR (4th) 81 (FCTD). It was also argued that linking infringed copyright. See also and Huntley, *supra* note 2 at 177.

domain name the registered internet address of a website

generic words in wide public use that cannot be trademarked alone

Domain Names Trademark infringement sometimes results from confusingly similar internet addresses, or domain names.[58] A **domain name** has two or more parts, separated by dots. The part on the left is the most specific. The part on the right is the most general and is referred to as the "top-level domain." Historically, top-level domains were "**generic**" (gTLDs), such as commercial (.com), educational (.edu), organizational (.org), or "national," such as Canada (.ca). Generic names are assigned by authorized registrars whose activities are supervised by the Internet Corporation for Assigned Names and Numbers (ICANN), a non-profit body established in 2000. National names are assigned by national authorities. In Canada, the ".ca" domain is controlled by the Canadian Internet Registration Authority (CIRA).

In 2011, ICANN announced that it would "deregulate" gTLDs—any word in any language can follow the dot (for a significantly higher price than generic suffixes). New top-level domains called strings are being released all the time (for example, coffee, land), producing lots of new registrants who will issue names for their string. ICANN continues to supervise the expanded group of registrants, including Staples and Homesense.[59]

It is common for a business's domain name to include an existing trademark. Consequently, the use of an exclusive domain name may amount to the infringement of another's trademark. Businesses should register their domain names as trademarks, and the Canadian Intellectual Property Office is accepting such registrations, provided the generic or national portion (.com, .ca, etc.) is disclaimed. Examples of trademarked domain names are TSN.ca and GLOBALTV. COM.[60] **Hashtags** that include trademarks should be similarly treated.

hashtags topical phrases used to link similar content in social media channels

Canadian business corporations typically register in multiple gTLDs (.com, .ca, .eu). Registering a domain name in gTLD costs very little, so multiple registrations prevent imposters from buying the name and diverting traffic away from the business. Traffic to a site may determine its advertising value, and this might motivate imposters to choose domain names very similar to existing high traffic sites in hopes of diverting web traffic.[61]

CASE 31.7 Likely Confusion

In 1995, ITV Technologies Inc., a British Columbia web-services provider, registered the domain name www.itv.net. WIC Television Ltd., an Edmonton-based television broadcaster since 1974, owned a number of stations throughout Canada. WIC owned several registered trademarks using the letters "ITV" and had registered a website with the domain name itv.ca. In 1996, WIC contacted ITV and asked it to stop using the ITV domain name.

ITV launched a pre-emptive strike and brought an action for an order expunging (removing) WIC's "ITV" trademarks, on the grounds that they were not registrable. WIC counter-claimed, alleging infringement of its trademarks and seeking an injunction.

After a nine-year court battle, both sides eventually lost.[62] There was nothing unlawful about WIC's marks, which were well-known and distinctive in Alberta, and there was no reason for them to be expunged. Conversely, there was no evidence, or likelihood, of confusion between the products of the two companies, so the mark was not infringed.

In Case 31.7, the infringement of the trademark appears innocent, at least initially, with no intention to "steal" business. In other instances, there is an intention to derive a benefit from the use of another's well-known trademark and to divert business away

---

[58] See Rebecca Gole, "Playing the Name Game: A Glimpse at the Future of the Internet Domain Name System" (1999) 51 *Fed. Com LJ* 403. See also Marc Watkins, "Government Regulation of the Dot-ca Domain Name Space" (2005) 2(1) *U Ottawa L & Tech J* 145.

[59] See http://newgtlds.icann.org/en/program-status/delegated-strings.

[60] TSN.ca was registered by the Sports Network Inc. (TMA551540). The generic portions were disclaimed because they lack distinctiveness. GLOBALTV.COM was registered by Canwest Global Communications Corp. in 2000 (TMA540987), owned by Corus Media Global Inc. (2018).

[61] In one trademark validity case, the court considered evidence of the number of website hits and advertising expenses: *Candrug Health Solutions Inc v Thorkelson*, [2007] FCJ No 586 at para 16, rev'd [2008] FCJ 426.

[62] *ITV Technologies, Inc v WIC Television Ltd* (2003), 239 FTR 203, aff'd [2005] FCJ No 438 (FCA).

from the owner of the mark to a competing business.[63] This type of passing-off succeeds because internet users, when trying to locate a well-known firm, may guess about the address by trying the trade name plus ".com" or complete a keyword search and click on the first item. In a form of internet advertising, businesses bid on keywords to tie their website's domain name to early search results. **Keyword bidding** may be trademark infringement if the keyword that is bid upon is another business's trademark.[64] Placing a trademark in the invisible **metadata** used by search engines to compile search results is not necessarily infringement unless the searcher is confused by the initial search results.[65]

Other forms of domain name infringement may not involve a competitor. One of the earliest forms was **cybersquatting**, where a person registers a domain name that includes a well-known trademark or brand name, and then offers to sell the domain name to the owner of the mark for a high price. If sued, the infringer will have to relinquish the domain name and to pay court costs.[66] However, cybersquatters rely on the fact that the trademark owner may find it less expensive and more convenient simply to buy the domain name from the registrant.

Other infringers may be protesters or criminals:

- An anti-abortion activist registered the domain name www.plannedparenthood.com in order to promote opposing views.[67]
- Trademarked domain names are used for misleading email rather than website purposes in an effort to disguise an email that may be phishing for personal information.[68]
- An injunction and damages were granted against an individual using a domain name to redirect unsuspecting people to a website containing adult content.[69]

In these cases, the intent is not to benefit from another's trademark but to damage it, for example, with registrations of (trademark) sucks.com. Sometimes these protest site registrations are held to be confusingly similar to the trademark and therefore infringing in a way that damages goodwill.[70] Other decisions have found them not confusing at all; it is obvious from the negative meaning of the word "sucks" that the two sites are not connected, and free speech rights protect the operation of a protest site.[71]

keyword bidding paying to have your website revealed in search results of a keyword

metadata embedded coding in webpages that summarizes information about data

cybersquatting the registration of a domain name containing the trademark of another person, with the intention of selling the domain name to the owner of the mark

---

[63] See also *Peinet Inc v O'Brien* (1995), 61 CPR (3d) 334; *Molson Breweries v Kuettner* (1999), 94 ACWS (3d) 550; *Saskatchewan Star Phoenix Group Inc v Noton*, [2001] SJ No 275.

[64] *Vancouver Community College v Vancouver Career College (Burnaby) Inc*, 2017 BCCA 41 at para 55 (confusion assessed at first impression).

[65] *Red Label Vacations Inc (Redtag.ca) v 411 Travel Buys Limited (411 Travel Buys Limited)*, 2015 FCA 290. See Fecenko and Huntley, *supra* note 2 at 175.

[66] See e.g. *Panavision International Inc v Toeppen* (1996), US Dist LEXIS 19698. The United States has legislation on cybersquatting: *Anticybersquatting Consumer Protection Act*, 15 USC § 1125. In the United Kingdom see *British Telecommunications, plc v One in a Million Ltd*, [1998] EWJ No 954 (CA).

[67] *Planned Parenthood v Bucci* (1997), US Dist LEXIS 3338. Other examples are discussed in the article by Gole, *supra* note 58.

[68] *Fluor Corporations v Fluor Curling*, CDRP Dispute No 0281.

[69] *Law Society of British Columbia v Canada Domain Name Exchange Corp* (2004), 243 DLR (4th) 746, aff'd (2005), 259 DLR (4th) 171 (BCCA).

[70] See *Trade-marks Act*, *supra* note 52, s 21; See e.g. WIPO Decision No D2005-0168 (*Air France v Virtual Dates, Inc*). The United States has legislation protecting against trademark dilution: *Trademark Dilution Revision Act of 2006*, 15 USC § 114.

[71] See e.g. *British Columbia Automobile Assn v Office and Professional Employees' International Union, Local 378*, [2001] BCJ No 151 (copying a website design was found to be copyright infringement); WIPO Decision No D2000-1104 (*Wal-Mart Stores, Inc v wallmartcanadasucks.com and Kenneth J Harvey*).

CASE 31.8 Injunction

A travel retailer had a website, located at www.itravel2000.com, and had registered the name "itravel" under the Ontario *Business Names Act*. It applied to the CIRA to register the .ca domain name but was informed that the name had already been registered. The registrant was an individual who had no connection with the travel business and had acquired the name with the sole purpose of selling it to the highest bidder.

On application by the travel retailer, an injunction was granted, preventing the defendant from using or selling the name.[72] If the CIRA complaints process had been used, a transfer of the domain name to the travel retailer could have been ordered.[73]

---

alternative dispute resolution
the use of private procedures such as arbitration and mediation to resolve disputes

Courts resolve infringement cases by granting damages and injunctions. Transfer of the domain name may be sought, in the case of generic names, through ICANN's **alternative dispute resolution** process, and the CIRA has a similar process for names within the ".ca" domain.[74] The World Intellectual Property Office operates an arbitration and mediation service.

CASE 31.9 Alternative Dispute Resolution

Bill Cosby owned all the trademarks associated with the television show *Fat Albert and the Cosby Kids*, which was the basis for the December 2004 feature film entitled *Fat Albert*. Six months prior to the movie's release, Sterling Davenport registered the domain name fatalbert.org. After release of the movie, Davenport linked the domain name to a website selling sexually explicit products. Davenport had over 500 domain names, often using celebrity names.

Bill Cosby filed an email complaint with the World Intellectual Property Office Arbitration and Mediation Center. Davenport never responded to the complaint, and the arbitrator found that the domain name was confusingly similar to the Cosby trademark, that Davenport registered the domain name in order to trade on Cosby's fame, and that both Davenport's registration and use of the domain name were done in bad faith. The arbitrator ordered that the domain name be transferred to Bill Cosby.[75]

---

work an original published or unpublished literary, dramatic, musical, or artistic creation, including the title

Copyright The *Copyright Act* gives the creator of a **work** the exclusive right to copy, produce, or distribute that work during the life of the author and for the 50 years thereafter. This monopoly applies to the publication, copying, and reproduction of materials on the internet or in email, in instant messaging, digitally, or in telecommunications. Anyone who copies, distributes, or uses a work without the owner's permission infringes the copyright and is liable for damages. The internet makes infringement of copyright, whether deliberate or unintentional, very easy.[76] The legal risk of infringement affects every business with a website or an employee with internet access.

In Canada, copyright law and policy are balanced between users' and owners' rights. No one set of rights is dominant. The *Copyright Act* contains the rules for use,

---

[72] *itravel2000.com Inc v Fagan* (2001), 197 DLR (4th) 760.

[73] See e.g. CIRA Dispute No 00239/13—americangirl.ca, http://www.cira.ca/legal/cdrp/dispute-resolution-decisions.

[74] Details of the ICANN uniform domain-name dispute-resolution policy can be obtained from the ICANN website at http://www.icann.org/en/help/dndr/udrp/policy. For the CIRA dispute-resolution policy, see http://www.cira.ca/assets/Documents/Legal/Dispute/CDRPpolicy.pdf.

[75] WIPO Decision No D2005-076, (*William H Cosby, Jr v Sterling Davenport*), www.wipo.int/amc/en/domains/decisions/-html/2005/d2005-0756.html.

[76] See Charlotte Waelde and Hector MacQueen, "Entertainment to Education: The Scope of Copyright" (2004) 3 IPQ 259–83. Caching is not copyright infringement: SOCAN, *supra* note 45. Section 41.27 of the *Copyright Act* offers protection for search engines. Infringement may depend on whether the link is user-activated, automatic, or "deep." For further discussion, see Geist, *supra* note 2, and IMAX, *supra* note 57.

infringement, and **royalty** collection for copyrighted material. The act is "technologically neutral"—copying in any form (print, telecommunication, or internet) is covered, and royalties should not differ according to the medium used to deliver the work to the end user.[77] Many internet users incorrectly believe that when material is posted on a website, the author or owner consents to its being copied or reproduced. With some exceptions for "fair dealing,"[78] material posted on a website, and the site's design and visual appearance, cannot be copied or adopted without infringing the creator's copyright. The appearance of a website is recognized as an artistic work, and merely linking websites may also infringe copyright because it associates the work with someone other than the creator. Businesses should clearly state the acceptable terms of use of material placed on their websites. Although not strictly required in Canada, it is prudent to give notice of copyright ownership by using the "©" symbol.

royalty fee paid to the copyright owner for permission to copy the work

CASE 31.10 Virtually Identical Content

Sotramex, a firm specializing in cleaning up mining and forestry sites, prepared a technical description (written by one of its employees) to appear on the website of the International Centre for the Advancement of Environmental Technologies. A year or so later, Sorenviq, a competitor in the reforestation market, posted virtually identical content on its own website without acknowledging the true authorship.

The court found that the author's copyright had been infringed and ordered Sorenviq to remove the text from its website and pay $10 000 damages plus $5000 exemplary damages.[79]

The *Copyright Act* exempts some technical and private personal use copies from liability (s. 29.22). Format shifting (moving material already purchased from one device to another), time shifting (recording material to be viewed later), and backing up computer programs are all allowed. Private use reproduction of musical works, performances, and sound recording is also allowed (ss. 30.6, 80). The "YouTube exception" allows the use of copyrighted material to generate new content for non-commercial use (s. 29.22).[80]

Some businesses whose main activity involves the supply of technological copyrightable works, such as software developers and music producers, have seen their industries transformed by internet copying. Reproduction and communication to the public are supposed to be the exclusive rights of the copyright owner. How are owners compensated if personal users copy for free?

First, the personal use exception for sound recordings does not apply if the copying is done for sale, rental, distribution, communication to the public, or performance in public (s. 80(2)). Second, copyright owners are compensated through tariffs levied on the manufacturers of audio (non-digital) recording devices (s. 82)[81] and businesses that distribute or facilitate the transmission of online material (s. 70.13). The business incorporates the tariffs into the final price of its product.

The tariff model "taxes" infringing behaviour of *businesses* facilitating copying of works, sound recordings, or performances (ss. 19, 70.1, 80). Individual creators assign the rights in their works to a "collective society." In turn, the society issues licences

---

[77] *Entertainment Software Association v SOCAN*, 2012 SCC 34 at para 9.

[78] The concept of "fair dealing" is discussed in Chapter 20 and includes research, private study, and news reporting: *Copyright Act*, RSC 1985, c C-42, ss 28–9 as amended.

[79] *Sotramex Inc v Sorenviq Inc*, [1998] AQ No 2241.

[80] The nickname is developing because YouTube users often post their own video works merged with existing copyrighted sound recordings.

[81] The levy on the sale of each blank CD was 29 cents; since CD sales have dropped below minimum levels, this levy will end.

over the entire inventory for a fee.[82] It distributes the fees collected to the creators, after payment of the society's costs. The licence fee can be set by agreement with licensees or, more typically, by a tariff approved by the Copyright Board (s. 70.15). The collective society's application to the Copyright Board will identify specific activity and businesses to be subject to the tariff. Those businesses receive notice and may oppose the imposition of the tariff. The Society of Composers, Authors and Music Publishers of Canada (SOCAN) is one collective; there are many others.[83]

A collective society can only request a fee or tariff for what would otherwise amount to an infringement of copyright. The fairness of the private use exception depends on revenue being generated by a fee or tariff at the distribution level. Balancing all the competing interests is a challenge. For example, microSD memory cards are exempt from the audio recording levy because they are so widely used as components in many manufactured goods (for example, smartphones) that the cost increases resulting from a tariff would negatively impact "ecommerce businesses and Canada's participation in the digital economy."[84] Many of the cases discussed in Chapter 20 are appeals of Copyright Board rulings on whether or not a tariff is appropriate in the circumstances. For internet tariffs, the analysis often focuses on whether the targeted activity is "communication to the public" and if so, whether infringement is excused by one of the fair dealing exceptions.[85]

ILLUSTRATION 31.4 Tariff Requests

(a) The Supreme Court of Canada denied SOCAN's request for a tariff on ISPs arising from transmission of copyrighted music. ISPs were merely intermediaries who provided the means of telecommunication; they were not communicators.[86]

(b) When SOCAN applied for a tariff on cell phone service providers who were allowing subscribers to download copyrighted music as ringtones, the Federal Court of Appeal held that the cell phone providers were "communicating a musical work to the public," and a tariff was justified.[87] Ringtones were offered to the public even though they were individually copied.

(c) The Supreme Court denied SOCAN's request for a tariff on cell phone service providers who were offering prospective purchasers short free music previews. The behaviour was "communicating to the public" but was exempt under the fair dealing exception as consumer research—it actually promoted the purchase of music to the benefit of SOCAN.[88]

(d) SOCAN's request for a new tariff on online music providers for the individual streaming and downloading of music by its customers was allowed only for streaming. Downloading was not communicating (it was copying or reproducing and therefore already covered by an existing tariff equally applicable to any physical sale of music). Streaming was considered communication (a form of performance) not caught by any existing tariff.[89] "To the public" is not limited to mass or bulk communication but can arise from multiple individual transmissions of the same work that are user initiated.

---

[82] *Copyright Act, supra* note 78, ss 2, 19, 70.1, 70.12.

[83] Canadian Private Copying Collective (CPCC) is an umbrella organization whose members include the collectives such as SOCAN, http://www.cpcc.ca/en/the-cpcc It is responsible for the collection of the audio equipment levy. This levy was held not to apply to the sale of iPods or any digital recording devices because s 82 only applies to audio equipment. *Apple Canada Inc v Canadian Private Copying Collective*, [2008] FCJ No 5 (FCA).

[84] *MicroSD Cards Exclusion Regulation (Copyright Act)* SOR/2012-226, PC 2012-1370 Canada Gazette, Oct. 18, 2012.

[85] *Copyright Act, supra* note 78, ss 3(1)(f), 80, 83.

[86] *Canadian Association of Internet Providers v SOCAN, supra* note 45.

[87] *Canadian Wireless Telecommunications Association, Bell Mobility Inc, and Telus Communications Company v SOCAN*, [2008] FCJ No 21, leave to SCC denied.

[88] *SOCAN v Bell Canada*, 2012 SCC 366.

[89] *Rogers Communications Inc v SOCAN*, 2012 SCC 35; *Entertainment Software Associations v SOCAN*, 2012 SCC 34.

Together, the foregoing SOCAN decisions support internet users' rights over the interests of collective societies and copyright owners.[90] The protection of owners' rights was emphasized in legislative amendments. Subject to a few exceptions, the legislation supports the owners' use of self-help measures such as **technical protection measures (TPMs)** and a **digital rights management system (DRMS)** to block unauthorized copying of their works.[91] Section 41.1 prohibits the circumvention of TPMs; the manufacture, import, or sale of technology for the purpose of circumvention; and the offering of services to assist in circumvention. Remedies for violation vary depending on whether circumvention was intentional or knowing and whether the circumventer is a library, museum, or educational institution. In these latter cases, the only remedy available is an injunction (s. 41.2). Tampering with a DRMS is also forbidden (s. 41.22). The Act adds these activities to the existing criminal offences for copyright infringement with fines up to $1 000 000 and/or imprisonment for five years.

ISPs must also assist copyright owners in policing the internet for infringers. ISPs have the responsibility of notifying subscribers about allegations of infringements; however, ISPs do not have to cut off the services of allegedly infringing subscribers, as is required in the United States (ss. 41.25–41.27).[92]

The TPM, DRMT, and ISP measures were adopted to bring Canada into closer conformity with the World Intellectual Property Organization (WIPO) Internet Treaties, WIPO Copyright Treaty (WCT), and WIPO Performances and Phonograms Treaty (WPPT). These treaties call for domestic legislation to create legal remedies for circumvention of TPMs or DRMS, impose obligations on ISPs, and entrench a copyright holder's exclusive rights to make work available on the internet.[93] Canadian copyright laws are not as owner-rights' friendly as the WIPO treaties. Canada is passed the *Combating Counterfeit Products Act*[94] in compliance with the international Anti-Counterfeiting Trade Agreement.

Patents In Canada, the federal *Patent Act* defines a patentable invention as any "new and useful art, process, machine, manufacture or composition of matter, or any new and useful improvement in any art, process, machine, manufacture or composition of matter" (s. 2). In granting a patent to Amazon's one-click buy software, the Federal Court of Appeal said that "patentable subject matter must be something with physical existence, or something that manifests a discernible effect or change."[95] This case opened the door for patenting software and computer-implemented inventions.

A mere scientific principle or abstract theorem is not patentable (s. 27(8)), but a practical application of a scientific principle, mathematical formula, or theorem is patentable if it is essential to the resolution of a real issue. Still, computer-implemented inventions will not be patentable just because they do something more efficiently than could be done with mere pen and paper—the computer element must be essential to the solution of the problem. This is often the challenge for data analytic software that could be processed manually, just slower. The output of the process cannot be simply

technical protection measures (TPMs) access locks or use locks for electronic material. An access lock requires a password to access the work; a use lock blocks particular uses of the work such as copying

digital rights management system (DRMS) a system collecting data about the licensing, payment for, and authenticity of a work

---

[90] Daniel Gervais, *The Internet Taxi: Collective Management of Copyright and the Making Available Right*, after Pentalogy, in The Copyright Pentalogy—How the Supreme Court of Canada Shook the Foundations of Canadian Copyright Law, Micahel Geist, ed (University of Ottawa Press, 2013).

[91] These measures are not without their critics. See CM Correa, "Fair Use in the Digital Era," UNESCO INFOethics 2000, http://unesdoc.unesco.org/images/0012/001233/123352m.pdf. For a discussion of other self-help efforts such as hacking, data poisoning, and defamation attacks launched against offenders, see Jennifer A Chandler, "Technological Self-Help and Equality in Cyberspace" (2010) 56(1) *McGill LJ* 39.

[92] See *Digital Millennium Copyright Act, 1998*. Nathan Irving, "Copyright Law for the Digital World: An Evaluation of Reform Proposals" (2010) 10 *Asper Rev Int'l Bus & Trade L* 1141.

[93] The United States implemented the WIPO treaty provisions in 1998, *supra* note 91, and the European Union Copyright Directive, passed May 22, 2001, adopts WIPO treaty provisions.

[94] SC 2014, c 32.

[95] *Canada (Attorney General) v Amazon.com, Inc*, 2011 FCA 328.

information or numerical data, which is abstract; it must be connected to an effect or change. For example, a database in isolation is not patentable because it is just a collection of information organized so it can be stored, searched, and retrieved easily. The Patent Office considers a database to be disembodied and not patentable subject matter unless it is essential to the subject matter of a larger invention. Deciding when the computer is essential to the invention is the challenge for patent examiners.

Privacy

Concern is growing over the fact that organizations—government and business—have accumulated vast amounts of electronic information about private individuals that might be used for purposes not contemplated by the individual who originally supplied it. Electronic commerce greatly increases the amount of information made available, and being in computerized form, that information is easily edited and transmitted. Data about data (known as metadata) can easily be sold to marketers and others. Failure to properly safeguard private information may expose a business to tort liability.

The *Personal Information Protection and Electronic Documents Act* (PIPEDA), which has already been referred to in the context of contract law and will be discussed in greater detail in Chapter 32, imposes restrictions on the use and misuse of personal information. The Act applies to every organization that collects, uses, or discloses personal information in the course of commercial activity. Organizations are required to develop and publish privacy policies. Probably its most important feature is the requirement to obtain an individual's consent to use or disclose information collected. In addition, individuals will have the right to inspect their personal information held by a company and to have it corrected. To mitigate damage from identity theft, PIPEDA requires businesses to report privacy breaches to the Office of the Privacy Commission and notify affected individuals and relevant third parties.[96] When a province has adopted its own privacy legislation, affected organizations may be exempt from the application of PIPEDA.[97]

Ethical Issue   Employee Technology Use

The internet is part of everyday business activity, and the majority of employees have access to the internet at work. In their personal lives, employees use the internet as a form of social networking and expression. Social networking sites allow members to chat; post biographical information, pictures, and personal opinions; and share all of this information with fellow members. Business is struggling with the level of acceptable personal internet use in the workplace. Employers are concerned about issues such as wasted time, viruses, security, confidentiality, harassment, and infringing or illegal activity, including downloading copyrighted material, gambling, and accessing pornography. Employers may be found vicariously liable for such behaviour.

A 2007 survey of employers conducted on behalf of the American Management Association reported that 66 percent of employers monitor employee internet activities, 43 percent retain and review employee email, and 30 percent have fired an employee for misuse of the internet.

Many employers have developed codes of conduct for technology use, but there is no uniform position on the use of social networking sites. Some employers have banned their use entirely, whereas others allow unlimited access. PIPEDA permits federal works, undertakings, and businesses to collect, use, and disclose personal information, without the knowledge or consent of an individual, to establish, manage, or terminate their employment relationships with the individual (s 7.3).

---

[96] *Digital Privacy Act*, SC 2015, c 32 (in force as of November 1, 2018).

[97] *Personal Information Protection Act*, SA 2003, c P-6.5; *Personal Information Protection Act*, SBC 2003, c 63; *An Act Respecting the Protection of Personal Information in the Private Sector*, RSQ, c P-39.1.

Questions to Consider

1. Should employees access social networking sites while at work?
2. Should employers be entitled to monitor employee internet use?
3. When making employment decisions, should employers (or potential employers) make use of information available on potential employees' personal or social networking sites?
4. Should an employer have a say in what employees post after hours on personal sites?

Sources: American Management Association and the ePolicy Institute, 2007 Electronic Monitoring & Surveillance Survey, http://www.amanet.org/training/articles/the-latest-on-workplace-monitoring-and-surveillance.aspx; Virginia Galt, "Firms Develop Codes of Conduct to Curb Porn Surfing on Internet," *The Globe and Mail*, July 19, 2004, B4; Virginia Galt, "Keyword for Workplace Messaging? Caution," *The Globe and Mail*, October 7, 2006, B14; Dianne Stafford, "Employers Limiting Use of Internet by Staff," *National Post*, February 28, 2007, WK 7; Shelley McGill and Mark Baetz, "Technology Use Codes of Conduct: Is It a Choice Between Shaping the Organizational Culture and Effective Legal Enforcement?" (2012) 15(2) *Empl. Rights & Empl. Policy J* 101.

Should people be protected from electronic junk mail, or "spam"? Arguably, spam constitutes an invasion of privacy and might be actionable under the common law of trespass. Spam can be a well-intentioned marketing campaign or an unscrupulous attempt to sabotage or steal from the recipient. Spam has become a major worldwide concern. In 2017, spam accounted for 58.02 percent of global email traffic and has spread to text messaging and social networking.[98] Time is wasted, hard-drive space is used, computers can be paralyzed, and money is spent on special programs designed to block spam.

CASE 31.11 Controlling Spam

A firm brought an action against its ISP, seeking restoration of its internet service after the ISP discontinued the service. The ISP disconnected service after complaints that the plaintiff firm had been sending out up to 200 000 unsolicited messages each day to promote the sale of its furniture. The court ruled that spam is a breach of "netiquette"—the internet's unwritten rules of conduct—and refused to order restoration. It is normal for ISP contracts to include a "netiquette clause," so that the dissemination of spam would constitute a breach of the contract with the ISP.[99]

Canada's federal Anti-Spam Legislation (CASL)[100] prohibits sending (or permitting the sending of) a commercial electronic message to an electronic address without the consent of the recipient (s. 6). The CRTC is in charge of a regulatory regime to enforce the prohibition, complete with offences. The definitions of "electronic message" and "address" are sufficiently broad to capture emails, text messaging, tweeting, and webcam messaging, as well as voice mails. Even when permission is granted, the message must identify the sender with contact information and set out the mechanism to unsubscribe from further communications. Fines of up to $10 000 000 per violation may be imposed. Directors and officers are personally liable for their companies' infractions unless they can show due diligence. Employers are vicariously liable for violations committed by employees in the scope of their employment. Internet service providers are not liable as long as their involvement is restricted to supply of telecommunication services.

Businesses that rely on electronic communications as part of their marketing or advertising plan will have to adjust their mailing lists to fit within the business relationship exception. Consent is implied if

---

[98] Kaspersky Internet Security Centre, http://www.usa.kaspersky.com.
[99] *1267623 Ontario Inc v Nexx Online Inc* (1999), 45 OR (3d) 40.
[100] *An Act to promote the efficiency and adaptability of the Canadian economy by regulating certain activities that discourage reliance on electronic means of carrying out commercial activities and to amend the Canadian Radio-television and Telecommunications Commission Act, the Competition Act, the Personal Information Protection and Electronic Documents Act, and the Telecommunications Act*, SC 2010, c 23.

- the business transacted with the recipient within the last two years,
- the business and recipient were parties to a written contract that expired within the last two years, or
- the business received an inquiry from the recipient in the last six months (s. 10(10)).

Consent is also implied if a person conspicuously publishes his electronic address without stating she does not want to receive unsolicited commercial electronic messages. Businesses should add this disclaimer to all employee emails.

An important sacrifice to privacy is incorporated into CASL. For the purposes of investigating compliance and violations, ISPs may turn over information to authorities, including personal information (s. 56). Spam violations may be investigated by the Privacy Commissioner or the Commissioner of Competition (where they amount to deceptive business practices, discussed in Chapter 3), and these organizations may share personal information in pursuit of their common goals.

Other Illegal Activities

Spam is just one of the potentially damaging activities undertaken on the internet that is now prohibited by federal legislation. Identity theft and "phishing," the practices of using fraudulent emails and fake websites to induce recipients into disclosing personal financial data, are offences caught by CASL's prohibition of unsolicited emails. Spyware can secretly collect data and mount virus attacks; malware can disable computers, destroy files, and cause millions of dollars of damage. CASL restricts these practices by prohibiting the installation of computer programs into the receiver's computer without the express consent of the recipient (s. 8). Some forms of hacking, such as "man in the middle" schemes, are banned by CASL's prohibition of redirecting electronic messages without express consent. All of these behaviours are offences subject to major fines, and directors and officers may face personal liability. The *Criminal Code* punishes unauthorized use of computers and fraudulent activities. Deceptive or misleading emails may also be violations of the *Competition Act*.

Many illegal activities originate in other countries. The CRTC, the Privacy Commissioner, and the Commissioner of Competition are expressly authorized to share the results of their investigations, including personal information, with foreign organizations pursuing the same goals.

Pornography is one of the most infamous sectors of ecommerce in financial terms. The internet provides an easy method of distribution and one that makes detection and prosecution extremely difficult. Another activity that, if not illegal, is often strictly regulated by governments is gambling. Again, the internet provides a means of circumventing local laws by establishing offshore "virtual casinos" and betting offices. In 1998, a British company established what was claimed to be the first worldwide online betting service at www.sportingbet.com, based in the tax-haven island of Alderney. The principal attraction of offshore, online gambling—to both bookmakers and punters—is that it enables the taxes that governments often impose on gambling to be avoided, increasing profits and pay-outs.

Perhaps the greatest concern that governments have with respect to ecommerce is tax evasion. Tax administrators have concerns, including evasion of sales taxes, income tax, and customs duties, as well as the difficulty of following an "audit trail" in online and ecash transactions.[101]

---

[101] Canada Revenue Agency GST/HST Technical Information Bulletin B-090 explains the agency's position on GST and electronic commerce: https://www.cra-arc.gc.ca/E/pub/gm/b-090/b-090-e.pdf.

INTERNATIONAL ASPECTS OF ECOMMERCE

The international nature of the internet is one of the greatest challenges for ecommerce. Businesses are uncertain about which laws apply to their contracts and other activities and which courts have jurisdiction to resolve their disputes. Governments are unsure if they should attempt to regulate ecommerce and even less sure whether such attempts would be effective. For example, if Canadian businesses are subjected to stricter privacy regulation than their American competitors, they may lose out in the race to develop ecommerce. However, the European Union's privacy legislation bans foreign firms from conducting ebusiness in most of Europe unless those firms are subject to equally strict privacy rules at home. Therefore, Canada must draft legislation that is sufficiently strict to satisfy the Europeans, without losing out in the American market.

Jurisdiction

Chapter 30 discussed the principles applied by courts to determine whether they have **jurisdiction** to hear a dispute with international aspects. It is usually easy to establish jurisdiction if the defendant lives in the jurisdiction or agrees to it. Jurisdiction over international commercial contract disputes is often decided based upon a choice of forum clause in the contract. However, if a forum selection clause is contained in a web-wrap consumer contract it may not be so simple.

jurisdiction the right of a court to hear and resolve a dispute

CASE 31.12 Consumer Contract Forum Selection Clauses

Ms. Douez sued Facebook in British Columbia over the use of her name and profile in a "sponsored story." Facebook opposed the lawsuit, saying Douez agreed in Facebook's terms and conditions that all lawsuits would be brought in Santa Clara County, California. The Supreme Court of Canada refused to enforce the term because consumer contracts are more vulnerable to unequal bargaining power, and privacy rights are quasi-constitutional. Given these public policy factors, the Court felt Canada should retain jurisdiction.[102]

If the defendant lives elsewhere, and no agreement exists, the court will assume jurisdiction over a case only when there is a "real and substantial connection" with the dispute or its parties. However, even when the court has jurisdiction, it may decide not to hear the dispute when there is a *clearly* more appropriate foreign jurisdiction that should deal with the lawsuit; this is the rule of *"forum non conveniens."*[103] These principles are complex even when applied to conventional business transactions that cross provincial, state, or national borders. Jurisdictional issues in the context of online transactions present an even greater challenge because internet communication is not geographically dependent, and websites reach a global market.[104]

Lawsuits without an enforceable agreement require a determination of real and substantial connection.[105] This connection is found by looking at a number of established factors, including whether the tort is "committed" in the province or whether the defendant "carries on business" in the province. These connections are difficult to evaluate in the online context.

---

[102] *Douez v Facebook, Inc*, 2017 SCC 33.

[103] *Van Breda v Club Resorts*, [2012] SCC 17.

[104] Ogilvy Renault, "Jurisdiction and the Internet: Are Traditional Rules Enough?" The study is reproduced by Uniform Law Conference of Canada at http://www.ulcc.ca.

[105] *Van Breda v Club Resorts, supra* note 103.

Sometimes, determining where the business operates is not even possible, since its web address does not necessarily indicate its physical location. This difficulty has led some provinces to assert jurisdiction over all its residents' consumer disputes.[106] That solution is not ideal. To do business internationally, a business would have to comply with the consumer laws of many different jurisdictions, some of which might regard a simple disclaimer of liability as ineffective. Also, a judgment against a foreign supplier might be useless if the supplier has no assets in the customer's country or if the judgment is not recognized in the business's country.

American courts[107] developed a **level-of-interactivity test** (also called an *active-versus-passive test*) to determine where an online business is being carried on; it identifies three levels of business activity:

1. where the out-of-state defendant is carrying on substantial business (actually and virtually) within the jurisdiction
2. where the defendant maintains an interactive site
3. where the defendant's site provides purely passive advertising

For level 1, there is jurisdiction where the business is being carried on; in level 3, there is no jurisdiction; level 2 remains an uncertain "grey area."[108] Some Canadian courts have used this level-of-interactivity test.[109] In 2012, the Supreme Court of Canada stated that carrying on business requires some kind of actual, not merely virtual, presence in the jurisdiction.

> **level-of-interactivity test** a review of the features of a website to determine if it is active or passive; only active sites will be considered connected to the jurisdiction (also called the *active-versus-passive test*)

CASE 31.13   More Than a Virtual Presence

Van Breda, an Ontario resident, was seriously injured while vacationing at Club Resort in Cuba. The Club Resort vacation package was booked from the website of an Ontario web-based travel agency called Sport au Soleil. Although the resort was in Cuba, it was managed by a corporation in the Cayman Islands, and the management company hired Ontario professionals and Ontario tour operators, including Sport au Soleil, to advertise, promote, and obtain bookings for the resorts. Van Breda sued Sport au Soleil, Club Resort, and the management company in Ontario. The resort claimed that Cuba should have jurisdiction over the dispute. The Supreme Court held that carrying on business in the jurisdiction was one factor that could show a real and substantial connection to the jurisdiction but it required more than virtual presence or active advertising. The Court did not define what level of etrade was necessary to be "carrying on business" in the jurisdiction. In the end it found that Ontario had a real and substantial connection to this action because the travel contract was made through the Ontario-based travel agency.[110]

Internet defamation actions demonstrate the difficulty with determining where an online tort is "committed." Typically, defamation is committed where the defamatory statement is published—that is, where it is made available to be seen, heard, read, *downloaded*, or republished. But a defamatory statement posted on the internet could

---

[106] *Supra* note 37.

[107] *Zippo Manufacturing Co v Zippo Dot Com, Inc* (1997), 952 F Supp 1119 (WD Pa).

[108] *Ibid.* In *Zippo*, the California corporation was doing substantial business in Pennsylvania, and the Pennsylvania courts were entitled to exercise jurisdiction. Contrast *Cybersell Inc (Arizona) v Cybersell Inc (Florida)* (1997), U.S. App LEXIS 33871, where the Florida-incorporated defendant was found to be engaging solely in "passive" advertising in Arizona, and the Arizona court declined jurisdiction.

[109] *Braintech Inc v Kostiuk* (1999), 171 DLR (4th) 46. See also *Pro-C Ltd v Computer City Inc* (2000), 7 CPR (4th) 193, rev'd [2001] OJ No 3600; *Wiebe v Bouchard*, [2005] BCJ No 73; *Desjean v Intermix Media, Inc* (2006), 57 CPR (4th) 314, aff'd [2007] FCJ No 1523 (FCA). In *Easthaven Ltd v Nutrisystem.com Inc* (2001), 202 DLR (4th) 560, the Court declined jurisdiction in a dispute between a Barbados corporation and a Delaware corporation, where the only connection with Ontario was that the domain name was registered by an Ontario corporation.

[110] *Van Breda v Village Resorts Ltd.*, [2010] OJ No 402, aff'd 2012 SCC 17 at para 87, 114. See also *Charron Estate v Bel Air Travel Group Ltd*, [2010] SCCA 114. The cases revise the factors relevant to determining the most convenient forum as set out in *Muscutt v Courcelles* (2002), 60 OR (3d) 20 (ONCA).

be read everywhere.[111] That would seem to suggest that a plaintiff alleging libel might sue anywhere in the world, choosing a jurisdiction where the law of defamation is most favourable and where damages are likely to be highest, acting as a *libel tourist*.

CASE 31.14 Defamation

Bangoura had been employed by the United Nations and had worked in a number of African countries. After he retired, he settled in Ontario and became a Canadian citizen. The *Washington Post* published a story on its website alleging that Bangoura had been removed from his position with the UN Drug Control Programme because of a scandal that had occurred in Kenya.

Bangoura commenced a libel action against the *Post* in the Ontario Superior Court. The *Post* brought a motion to have the claim set aside on the grounds that the Ontario court did not have jurisdiction. Initially, the court ruled that, even though the libel was published in Washington, D.C., injury was suffered by the plaintiff in Ontario, and the Ontario court could assume jurisdiction.[112] Reversing the trial court, the Court of Appeal held that the Washington court had jurisdiction; it was unreasonable to expect the newspaper to foresee that Bangoura would be a resident of Ontario three years later.[113]

Selecting the "clearly most appropriate" forum among multiple possibilities is done based on the values of fairness and efficiency. In the next case, the Supreme Court suggests that it is fair to pick the location where the most serious injury to reputation is suffered. Normally, that will be where the plaintiff lives, for that is where her reputation is harmed. Some level of foreseeability must be applied to this test; otherwise a defendant could again be sued anywhere.

CASE 31.15 Foreseeable Harm

Conrad Black started a defamation lawsuit in Ontario against 10 members of a special committee who prepared a report on his activities as director and chairman of Hollinger International, a publicly traded U.S. company. Only one of the defendants resided in Ontario. The report was very critical of Black's behaviour and of payments received by him. It was posted on the company's website, and electronic press releases were sent to Ontario newspapers. The defendants challenged Ontario's jurisdiction. The Supreme Court held that Ontario had jurisdiction because the tort was committed in Ontario—the report was downloaded and republished by the Ontario newspapers. Repetition or republication constitutes new publication—the defendants anticipated republication when they sent the press releases. Ontario was the most appropriate forum because the most substantial harm to reputation occurred in Ontario. Black was a longtime resident of Ontario, his family resides in Ontario, and he made his newspaper reputation in Ontario. It was foreseeable to the defendants that damage would occur in Ontario as evidenced by press releases directed to Ontario media.[114]

Some provinces, including British Columbia, have adopted legislation that lists the relevant factors and process for consideration in first establishing that the province has jurisdiction and then selecting the most appropriate location from all other provinces, states, or countries with jurisdiction.[115]

---

[111] See Gosnell, "Jurisdiction on the Net: Defining Place in Cyberspace" (1998), 29 *Can Bus LJ* 345. Without evidence that someone in the jurisdiction downloaded or read the statement, the tort was not committed in the jurisdiction: *Crookes v Yahoo*, 2007 BCSC 1325, aff'd [2008] BCJ No 834.

[112] *Bangoura v Washington Post* (2004), 235 DLR (4th) 564. Although enforcement of an Ontario judgment might be a problem, Pitt, J., pointed out that a defamation action is often more about character vindication than about money. See also *Burke v NYP Holdings Inc* (2005), 48 BCLR (4th) 363 (BCSC).

[113] *Bangoura v Washington Post* (2005), 258 DLR (4th) 341; the Supreme Court of Canada refused leave to appeal.

[114] *Breedan v Black*, 2012 SCC 19.

[115] *Court Jurisdiction and Proceedings Transfer Act*, SBC 2003, c 28.

INTERNATIONAL ISSUE
Global Remedy

Equustek Solutions Inc., sued its former distributor, Datalink Technologies Gateways LLC ("Datalink"), because Datalink was using confidential information to manufacture and sell Equustek's online products under Datalink's name. Datalink ignored a British Columbia injunction ordering Datalink to stop carrying on business through any website and freezing Datalink's worldwide assets. Datalink continued to sell the product, so Equustek asked Google to de-index the website from any search results. Google partially complied by de-indexing on "google.ca" only. Other Datalink sites remained accessible, so Equusteck obtained a court ordered injunction de-listing Datalink's websites in search results generated by any of Google's worldwide search engines. The Supreme Court upheld the injunctions, saying, "Without the injunctive relief, it was clear that Google would continue to facilitate the ongoing harm"[116] and that a Canadian court had the jurisdiction to grant an injunction with global reach "where it is necessary to ensure the injunction's effectiveness."[117]

Google took the dispute back to the United States, where a California court granted Google a temporary injunction blocking the enforceability of the Supreme Court of Canada's order, saying that Google is a "neutral intermediary" protected by the *U.S. Communications Decency Act 1996*. It also said that "By forcing intermediaries to remove links to third-party material, the Canadian order undermines the policy goals of Section 230 and threatens free speech on the global internet."[118] This dispute is not over.

Questions to Consider

1. How do the principles of free speech and net neutrality impact these decisions?
2. In the era of online businesses and global marketing, is it realistic to limit a court order to geographic borders?
3. How can the results in the Canadian *Google* case be reconciled with the result in the *Facebook* case in Case 31.12.

Non-Governmental Organizations

Non-governmental organizations play an important role in building international harmony where conflicting laws exist. They work to build consensus among different governments; create model laws that governments can adopt in their own countries; and establish guidelines and codes of conduct for international behaviour.

The Organisation for Economic Co-operation and Development (OECD) is one such non-governmental organization. It has developed guidelines for domestic legislation in consumer protection, multinational corporate governance, bribery, and taxation.[119] The United Nations Committee on International Trade Law (UNCITRAL) produced model laws on international commercial arbitration, and enforcement of foreign arbitral awards that have been adopted by many countries.[120] The 2005 United Nations Convention on the Use of Electronic Communication in International Contracts addresses contract formation and jurisdiction issues. And, as has been noted, the WIPO has multiple treaties addressing intellectual property law. Governments may choose to adopt these international standards completely, partially, or not at all. Although we are still a long way from international harmony in the regulation of ecommerce, progress is being made.

---

[116] *Google Inc v Equustek Solutions Inc*, 2017 SCC 34 at para 35.

[117] *Ibid* at para 38.

[118] *Google LLC v Equustek Solutions Inc et al*, USDC, Northern District of California, San Jose Division, Case No 5:17-cv-04207-EJD.

[119] OECD guidelines for regulation of multinational corporations are available at https://www.oecd.org.

[120] See Chapter 30; the United Nations created UNCITRAL to harmonize international trade law around the world.

Strategies to Manage the Legal Risks

Many of the legal risks associated with ecommerce can be avoided with a well-designed website and detailed contractual terms and conditions. Websites should be original, claim ownership in content, prohibit copying, and resist linking sites. Alternatively, disclaimers denying responsibility for linked content or third-party postings should be clearly displayed. Contract law enforces typical terms and conditions incorporated into a contract through an online click-wrap agreement. Therefore, including choice of law and forum provisions in addition to ADR clauses will reduce the jurisdictional problems for international disputes. Terms relating to ownership of intellectual property, restricted right to use or copy, and confidentiality will reduce intellectual property disputes. Exemption clauses and liquidated damage clauses will contain the size of damage awards—a necessary step because internet damages are often larger than those suffered in the physical world.

An online intellectual property strategy must address counterfeiting of electronic products as well as unauthorized use of marketing, communication, and business systems. Trademarks should be searched in all available databases, both domestically and internationally, before investment or promotion begins. Corresponding positive and negative domain names should be secured in popular generic top-level domains. Applying for the suffix should be considered. Patent protection of business methods should be obtained and copyright claimed in online visual, literary, and graphic work. As well as protecting the business's own IP, steps should be taken to ensure that employees do not infringe others' rights. A code of conduct for technology use can be a valuable tool. Particular attention should be paid to the new Canadian anti-spam legislation, as it restricts some traditional marketing practices, particularly the use of unsolicited emails. Consequences of violation can be quite severe, including personal liability for directors and officers.

QUESTIONS FOR REVIEW

1. What contracts are normally involved in establishing a business website?
2. What is a click-wrap agreement?
3. How has legislation addressed the formation of contracts made over the internet?
4. Why is it important to ascertain which legal system governs a contract?
5. Are internet service providers exposed to liability when users infringe copyright? Or violate anti-spam legislation?
6. What is ecash?
7. How can a domain name infringe some other person's trademark?
8. What are the legal consequences of violating Canada's anti-spam legislation?
9. What is the level-of-interactivity test?
10. What factors influence jurisdiction over an internet libel case?
11. How does Canada protect an individual's privacy in ecommerce transactions?
12. Why are non-governmental organizations important to ecommerce?
13. In what ways does the internet facilitate illegal activities?

CASES AND PROBLEMS

1. Continuing Scenario

    Jack was disappointed with his dining experience at Ashley's restaurant. He was in town for a conference and made a reservation at Ashley's. When he arrived, he was advised that the guest dress code prohibited jeans; Jack protested that he had not been told this at the time of booking, so he was allowed to dine but was seated at an out-of-the-way table by the kitchen door. His meal was fine, but he remained angry about his table location after he returned home to Chicago. Jack decided to warn other diners, so he logged on to an Ontario restaurant review website and registered under the name "foodie257." Jack gave a very negative review. He scored the food, service, and atmosphere as 1 out of a possible 10 points. In the comment section, he said, "Ashley was rude and unprofessional," mistakenly believing Ashley herself had acted as hostess and assigned his table. His review went on to say she had no skill in the restaurant business, and her business would surely fail. He encouraged others to spread the word. Finally, he clicked the icon that said, "Share this review with friends" and sent it to all his social network friends. One of Ashley's regular diners saw the review and told her about it. She was very upset and worried that other diners would see it.

    What obstacles will Ashley face if she tries to take legal action arising from this review?

2. On Saturday at 10:00 p.m., Jane (a resident of Manitoba) ordered a computer online from SMART Computers for $49 plus tax and delivery charges. Jane entered her credit card information and her email address, and clicked "BUY NOW." At 10:04 p.m., she received an email confirmation of her purchase showing a total credit card charge of $75. Jane placed the order after she was told by a friend that the SMART website mistakenly priced the computer at $49 instead of $449. Although SMART blocked the order page when it discovered the error on Friday, Jane successfully bypassed the block and also the webpages disclosing the terms and conditions of the sale. The order page indicated that the purchase was subject to terms and conditions, but there was no hyperlink to the terms. SMART refused to supply the computer, indicating that the computer was not available for $49. Jane started a breach-of-contract action in Manitoba. The terms and conditions stated that supply of the computer was subject to availability and that all disputes must be settled in the courts of Michigan in the United States.

    Consider the principles of offer, acceptance, consideration, and intention, and determine if there is a valid contract. If so, do the terms and conditions form part of the sale contract? What information will be important in order to determine the status of the contract and the terms and conditions?

3. Altanet Inc. is incorporated in Alberta and carries on the business of providing internet access and related services to its clients. In March 2007, it registered the domain name altanet.ca. One of its employees, O'Connor, developed a new technique for designing webpages for clients. He tried to persuade Altanet's management to adopt the technique, and when they decided not to, he resigned from the corporation and decided to go into business on his own. In May 2007, he established a corporation, Rocky Netservices Inc., and registered the domain name alta.net.

    When Altanet's managers discovered the existence of the Rocky website, they wrote to O'Connor, alleging that he was attempting to pass his business off as that of Altanet in order to lure its clients away, and they demanded that he cease to use the domain name. O'Connor replied that the two domain names were different and equally legitimate, that no similarity existed between the names of the two corporations, and that Altanet had no cause to complain about his using the new webpage technique since it had declined to adopt it when given the opportunity.

    How should the ownership issues of domain name and website design be resolved?

4. Midas Prospecting Inc. is a corporation incorporated in British Columbia that is engaged in mineral exploration. Goldfinger, its CEO, lives in Vancouver.

From time to time, Goldfinger likes to search the internet for references to his company. One day, using his favourite search engine, Gargle, he discovered a story written by Sleaze, a university professor from New Zealand, published on the website of a little-known Australian journal that deals with environmental issues. The story, entitled "The Poisoners of Paraguay," alleged that Midas had discharged tonnes of cyanide into a river in Paraguay and that Goldfinger had managed to suppress the news by bribing that country's Minister of the Environment. Although there is evidence that some such event might have taken place, the story was clearly incorrect since neither Midas nor any other corporation with which it is associated has ever carried on operations in Paraguay.

The journal offered to publish a full retraction, and the offer was accepted by Goldfinger. Sleaze, however, insists that his story is substantially true and refuses to apologize.

Midas and Goldfinger have commenced an action for defamation in British Columbia against Sleaze and against Gargle (which is based in California), which they claim published the libel by providing the link to the story.

Consider (a) whether the B.C. court has jurisdiction to try the action and (b) whether the claim against Gargle has any validity.

Chapter 32
Privacy

- **PRIVACY**
- **GOVERNMENT REGULATION OF PRIVACY**
- **CIVIL LIABILITY**
- **CRIMINAL LIABILITY**
- **CODES OF CONDUCT**
- **STRATEGIES TO MANAGE THE LEGAL RISKS**

In the age of technology, individual privacy is more and more difficult to protect. Privacy law regulates everyday business activities through a maze of overlapping federal and provincial privacy legislation that imposes civil, regulatory, and even criminal liability on businesses that fail to comply.

In this chapter we examine such questions as:

- What aspects of a person's life are considered private?
- Is privacy a human right?
- What level of privacy should individuals expect?
- What provincial and federal regulatory regimes exist to supervise public sector activities?
- What legislation governs private sector personal information management?
- What laws govern privacy in the workplace?
- What concerns exist for personal information that is transferred to another country?
- How has tort law responded to invasion of privacy?
- How does criminal law address privacy issues?

PRIVACY

What Is Privacy?

Early scholars described privacy as "the right to be left alone" and considered it essential to a person's "autonomy, liberty, and integrity."[1] Modern **privacy** has three key dimensions: personal privacy, territorial or spatial privacy, and privacy of personal information.[2] **Personal privacy** involves issues of bodily integrity, including surveillance, search, and seizure. **Territorial privacy** covers the protection of one's home, business, and other personal spaces (even laptops).[3] **Privacy of personal information** involves protection of the trail of information left behind as we live our daily lives and has three elements: secrecy, control, and anonymity.[4] Protection of personal information covers information about an individual and depends upon the nature of the information and the purpose for which it was made and obtained.[5] It extends beyond what is typically considered "personal and confidential." Relatively ordinary information can be used to identify us or reveal our personal habits, opinions, behaviours, beliefs, or characteristics. Controlling your personal information is "intimately connected" to your individual autonomy, dignity, and privacy.[6]

Participation in normal society means complete privacy is impossible. Privacy law and, to some extent, individuals themselves determine how much privacy they will sacrifice. For example, how much private information is revealed on a personal website is entirely the individual's choice. Some people post pictures and blog about personal relationships, whereas others would never dream of such disclosure. On the other hand, residents are required by law to file a tax return containing very personal information. Privacy law attempts to balance freedom of expression with the individual's right to privacy. Privacy expectations are constantly changing, so this chapter attempts only a general overview of the law.

privacy has three key dimensions: personal privacy, territorial or spatial privacy, and privacy of personal information

personal privacy the respect of bodily integrity free from unreasonable surveillance, search, and seizure

territorial privacy lack of intrusion in one's home, business, and other personal spaces

privacy of personal information the protection of the trail of information left behind as we go about our daily lives involving secrecy, control, and anonymity

CASE 32.1 Imbalance

The Alberta Privacy Commissioner received complaints from people who were videoed and photographed crossing the picket line during a 305-day legal strike. Notices of surveillance were posted at the picket line. At first, it was held that the collection, use, and disclosure of the images violated Alberta's privacy legislation and should stop, but when the matter rose to the Supreme Court of Canada, the privacy protection was found to be too broad and unreasonably suppressed the union's right to freedom of expression. Alberta had to revise its privacy legislation.[7]

Privacy as a Human Right

In 1984, the Supreme Court of Canada declared that the right to privacy was a fundamental human right protected by section 8 of the *Charter of Rights and Freedoms*.[8]

---

[1] Alysia Davies, "Invading the Mind: The Right to Privacy and the Definition of Terrorism in Canada" (2006) 3(1) U Ottawa Law & Tech J 249, 261.

[2] *R v Dyment*, [1988] 2 SCR 417 discussing three aspects of privacy; see also *R v Tessling*, [2004] 3 SCR 432; *R v Gamboc*, [2010] SCJ No 55; *R v Spencer*, 2014 SCC 43 at para 35 (although not mutually exclusive). Privacy involves "concepts of intimacy, identity, dignity and integrity of the individual": *Canada (Information Commissioner) v Canada (Transportation Accident Investigation & Safety Board)*, 2006 FCA 157 (CA), leave denied [2006] SCCA No 259.

[3] *R v Cole* 2012 SCC 53 at paras 1–3.

[4] *R v Spencer*, *supra* note 2 at para 38.

[5] Teresa Scassa et al, "Privacy by the Wayside: The New Information Superhighway, Data Privacy and the Development of Intelligent Transportation Systems" (2011) 11 74 Sask L Rev 117 at paras 36, 46–51.

[6] *Alberta (Information and Privacy Commissioner) v United Food and Commercial Workers, Local 401*, 2013 SCC 62 at para 19.

[7] *Ibid.*; Letter of Jill Clayton, Information and Privacy Commissioner of Alberta, December 20, 2013, available at https://www.oipc.ab.ca/media/387459/letter_pipa_ufcw_dec2013.pdf.

[8] *Hunter v Southam Inc*, [1984] 2 SCR 145; section 8 of the *Charter* protects against unreasonable search and seizure by government. Informational privacy depends on the nature of the information and the purpose for which it is made—it is not confined to only personal and confidential information: *R v Gamboc*, *supra* note 2; *Alberta v United Food*, *supra* note 6.

reasonable expectation of privacy the subjective and objective assessment of reasonable privacy expectations in a given situation

right to be forgotten the right to have one's personal information removed from public circulation

However, it also held that the right to privacy was not absolute; individuals were only entitled to as much privacy as could reasonably be expected in the circumstance. This standard of protection, commonly referred to as the **reasonable expectation of privacy**, requires a subjective and objective assessment of privacy expectations in each situation.[9] The existence of a "**right to be forgotten**" remains unsettled.[10]

Section 7 of the *Charter*, dealing with life, liberty, and security of person, is also constitutional authority for a right to privacy: "privacy is at the heart of liberty."[11] The combined effect of sections 7 and 8 is to limit the government's ability to interfere with an individual's privacy rights. Government invasion of privacy is acceptable only when no reasonable expectation of privacy exists or when, despite a reasonable expectation, the invasion itself is reasonable and the principles of **natural justice** are respected. The federal government and most provinces have enacted privacy legislation to protect individual privacy during public sector activities.[12]

natural justice procedural fairness or due process

Federal and provincial human rights legislation prohibits private sector discrimination and harassment based on race, gender, religion, age, marital status, sexual orientation, ethnic origin, and disability.[13] Although privacy issues are not specifically addressed in the human rights legislation, the collection or use of personal information relating to a prohibited ground may lead to discriminatory or harassing behaviour. As a result, human rights and privacy complaints often arise out of the same circumstances.

Privacy and Technology

data shadows electronic records of the internet activity of a user

biometrics technological analysis of physical characteristics, such as fingerprints

cloud computing a server-focused computing system in which all processing and storage is done at the server level, and users access the system over the internet from anywhere through a variety of devices

Technological advancements such as **data shadows**, digital cameras, **biometrics**, digital storage devices, and **cloud computing** pose serious threats to privacy.[14] The technological ability to create, collect, store, transmit, and alter personal information has transformed privacy risks. Also expanded is the ability to track movements, surveil subjects, and reveal findings to an expansive audience. Text messages are not always considered private.[15] Personal information may be used for obviously criminal purposes, such as identity theft, or subtler activities such as targeted marketing or employment decisions. As early commentary colourfully describes, the "computer is to privacy what the machine gun was to the horse cavalry."[16]

In addition to making invasion of privacy much easier, technology has made protection of privacy much more difficult. Data flow freely across geographic borders.

---

[9] *R v Marakah*, 2017 SCC 59 at paras 10–12, the subjective expectation of privacy must be objectively reasonable in the circumstances.

[10] Right to be forgotten refers to the right to have one's personal information removed from circulation (that is, the website of the poster) once the purpose for collection is gone; Globe24h.com 2017 FC 114; Google Spain SL, Google Inc. Agencia Espanola de Proteccoin de Datos, Mario Costeja Gonzalez (2014) C-131/12 (CJEU).

[11] *R v Dyment*, *supra* note 2 at 427–8.

[12] See e.g. *Privacy Act*, RSC 1985, c P-21; *Freedom of Information and Protection of Privacy Act*, RSO 1990, c F-31.

[13] *Canadian Human Rights Act*, RSC 1985, c H-6; *Alberta Human Rights Act*, RSA 2000, c A-25.5; British Columbia *Human Rights Code*, RSBC 1996, c 210; Manitoba *Human Rights Code*, CCSM c H-175; *Human Rights Act*, RSNB 2011, c 171; Nova Scotia *Human Rights Act*, RSNS 1989, c 214; Ontario *Human Rights Code*, RSO 1990, c H-19; Prince Edward Island *Human Rights Act*, RSPEI 1988, c H-12; *Saskatchewan Human Rights Code, 2018*, SS 2018, c S-24.2 Newfoundland *Human Rights Code, 2010*, SNL 2010, c H-13.1.

[14] Scassa et al, *supra* note 5; *R v Spencer*, *supra* note 2 at para 46.

[15] *R v Marakah*, 2017 SCC 59 at para 5; *R v Jones*, 2017 SCC 60.

[16] Dan Savantesson and Roger Clarke, "Privacy and Consumer Risks in Cloud Computing," (2010) 26(4) *Computer L & Security Rev* 391; McIsaac, Shields, and Klein, *The Law of Privacy in Canada* (Toronto: Thomson Carswell, 2007) at 1–4.2.

The creator, host, and user of a website could all be in different jurisdictions. Canadian laws protecting electronic personal information may be ineffective if the website, its server, and/or its creator are located in different countries.

> **CASE 32.2 Cross-Border Breaches**
>
> Lawson's personal information was being used without her consent by Accusearch Inc., an American company in the business of selling background checks and other tracing services. Lawson filed a complaint with the Canadian Privacy Commissioner, who declined to investigate, stating that she lacked jurisdiction to investigate an American company. The Federal Court held that the Privacy Commissioner was wrong; she did have jurisdiction to investigate. The complainant was Canadian, the source of the information was Canadian, the request for the background check originated in Canada, and the website displayed a Canadian presence with a ".ca" domain name. The court acknowledged that the non-resident status of the operator of the website might limit the success of the investigation, but this should not be confused with lack of jurisdiction.[17]

The Supreme Court of Canada also takes an expansive view of jurisdiction when privacy rights are involved.

> **CASE 32.3 Choice of Forum Clause Unenforceable**
>
> A class action against Facebook alleged that it allowed the unauthorized use of names and pictures of members to advertise products to other members in violation of British Columbia's privacy law. Facebook opposed the B.C. class action because Facebook's terms and conditions required all disputes to be resolved in California. The Supreme Court of Canada refused to enforce the California choice because Canadian courts have a greater interest in lawsuits involving the quasi-constitutional privacy rights of Canadians.[18]

Privacy and Business

Businesses constantly create, collect, use, store, and transfer personal information about their employees, customers, consumers, suppliers, and competitors. Technology expands an employer's ability to monitor employee conduct and customer behaviour through video surveillance, email and telephone monitoring, and key-card access systems. All of this means that privacy is a major private sector issue. The *Personal Information Protection and Electronic Documents Act*[19] (PIPEDA) is the primary piece of federal legislation regulating privacy issues in the private sector. Common law and criminal laws also expose businesses to liability for invasion of privacy.

> **INTERNATIONAL ISSUE**
>
> **Outsourcing, Cloud Computing, and Transborder Data Flow**
>
> Outsourcing specialized operational tasks is common. When outsourcing involves the transfer of personal information, issues of security and privacy are raised. Customers may consent to the collection of personal data without realizing their information could be shared with another business located outside Canada and subject to different disclosure and protection rules. The location and nationality of the custodian may be more important than the actual location of the data in questions of government-forced disclosure.[20] In recognition of international privacy concerns, the Organisation

---

[17] *Lawson v Accusearch Inc*, 2007 FC 125 (FC); the Court agreed that PIPEDA did not have extraterritorial effect.

[18] *Douez v Facebook, Inc*, 2017 SCC 33.

[19] SC 2000, c 5, as amended.

[20] *eBay Canada Ltd v MNR*, 2008 FCA 348; but see *Microsoft v United States*, No 14-2985 (2d Cir 2016) (quashing a warrant to produce emails stored in Ireland).

for Economic Co-operation and Development (OECD) created guidelines to enhance privacy protection during transborder data exchanges. Guideline 10 states that personal data should not be used or disclosed without the consent of the owner or authority of law.

Canadian outsourcing to the United States became more controversial after the USA PATRIOT Act was passed.[21] It allows U.S. law-enforcement officials to obtain personal records or information from any source in the United States without the data owner knowing. As a result, there have been several Canadian challenges of personal data outsourcing to the United States. In *BCGEU v British Columbia (Minister of Health)*, union members argued that the Ministry of Health was violating patients' rights to privacy under section 7 of the *Charter* by outsourcing physician billing data that contained personal patient information to a private U.S. company.[22] The B.C. Supreme Court disagreed, holding that as long as the contractual arrangement authorized under the *Canada Health Act* ensured that a reasonable expectation of privacy was protected, the practice was acceptable. Decisions depend on the specific terms of the outsourcing agreement and prior regulatory approval of the terms. Now British Columbia, Nova Scotia, and Alberta have legislation that restricts public (not private) sector transborder outsourcing.[23]

When considering sending sensitive information across the border or outsourcing to American firms, businesses should

- undertake a security analysis of the American company prior to contracting;
- inform the affected customer/data owner;
- include specific confidentiality, security, and reporting provisions in the outsourcing agreement;
- seek regulatory approval of the agreement, if available; and
- regularly audit the privacy practices of the outsourcing company.

Increased privacy risks are likely as transnational cloud computing replaces user-owned software, desk, and laptops as the primary custodians of personal information. Spending on cloud-based computing is projected to consume 60–70 percent of all business IT infrastructure spending by 2020.[24]

Questions to Consider

1. If Canadian data is at greater risk of disclosure when transferred to the United States, why not ban all public and private outsourcing to the United States?
2. Are there certain types of information that should remain within Canadian borders?
3. How can personal information be protected when stored on a transnational cloud server?

Sources: Donna L Davis, "Case Comment: Tracking Cross-border Data Flows: A Comment on *Lawson v Accusearch Inc*" (2007) 6(2) *Canadian J of L & Tech* 119; "Frequently Asked Questions: USA PATRIOT Act Comprehensive Assessment Results," Treasury Board of Canada Secretariat, March 28, 2006, https://www.tbs-sct.gc.ca/pubs_pol/gospubs/TBM_128/usapa/faq_e.asp.

GOVERNMENT REGULATION OF PRIVACY

Privacy legislation has quasi-constitution status.[25] Federal and provincial privacy statutes set general privacy standards applicable to most public and private sector activities. Separate legislation targets specific conduct such as telemarketing. Other statutes focus on particular industries such as healthcare or credit reporting. It would be impossible to provide an exhaustive review of all privacy legislation here. Instead, we focus on the general legislation addressing privacy of personal information and specific conduct involving creation and collection, intentional or accidental disclosure, and theft.

---

[21] *Uniting and Strengthening America by Providing Appropriate Tools Required to Intercept and Obstruct Terrorism (USA PATRIOT) Act of 2001* (renewed through 2019 save and except for an amendment that prohibits the NSA from mass phone data collection).

[22] *BCGEU v British Columbia (Minister of Health Services)*, 2005 BCSC 446 (SC), aff'd [2007] BCJ No 650 (BCCA). See also Office of the Privacy Commissioner of Canada, Case Summary, #2007-365; Scassa et al, *supra* note 5 at para 66.

[23] See *Freedom of Information and Protection of Privacy Act* (FIPPA), RSBC 1996, c 165, s 30.1 (creating an offence to store, access, or disclose personal information outside Canada); Nova Scotia passed similar legislation: *Personal Information International Disclosure Act*, SNS 2006, c 3. See also *Freedom of Information and Protection of Privacy Act*, RSA 2000, c F-25, ss 92(3),(4).

[24] IDC FutureScape: Worldwide Cloud 2016 Predictions—Mastering the Raw Material of Digital Transformation, http://cofinaeventos.pt/portugaldigitalawards/wp-content/uploads/sites/37/2016/05/IDC-FutureScape-Worldwide-Cloud-2016-Predictions.pdf.

[25] *Doue v Facebook*, *supra* note 18 at para 59.

Regulation of Privacy in the Public Sector

Government activities are subject to both federal and provincial legislation. The federal legislation governs the conduct of the federal government, its agencies, and public institutions. Similarly, provincial legislation regulates the provincial government, agencies, and public institutions.

As noted, the *Charter of Rights and Freedoms* establishes constitutional protection of privacy, and it, along with the *Criminal Code*, protects individual privacy during law-enforcement activities of government.

The collection, use, and disclosure of personal information by federal **government institutions** are regulated by the *Privacy Act*.[26] The definition of personal information covers information about an identified individual recorded in any form. The Act includes a non-exhaustive list of examples such as information about a person's educational, financial, medical, criminal, or employment history, and the personal opinions about the individual expressed by another person (s. 3).

The **purpose of collection** must relate directly to an operating program or activity of the institution (s. 4), and information should be obtained directly from the individual (s. 5(1)) after disclosure of the purpose (s. 5(2)). An institution need not comply with section 5 if to do so might compromise the purpose of collection or the accuracy of the information (s. 5(3)). **Consent** of the individual is only required in order to use the information for a purpose other than the one for which it was collected (s. 7).

government institutions government departments and agencies listed in Schedule 1 of the *Privacy Act*

purpose of collection a need for collecting personal information that must be related directly to an operating program or activity of the institution

consent approval of the person to whom the collected information relates

CASE 32.4 Sharing Without Consent

Bernard, an employee, who was not a member of the union but part of the bargaining unit represented by the union, objected to the federal government employer releasing his home contact information to the union as required under the collective agreement. The Supreme Court of Canada held that the union had a duty to keep all members of the bargaining unit informed, (even non-union members) and that required contacting them—this was a legitimate need. The employer collected the information for the purpose of the administration of the employment relationship, and sharing it with the union was consistent with this purpose. Therefore, sharing it without employee permission was allowed under section 7 of the *Privacy Act*.[27]

The *Privacy Act* regulates the disclosure of recorded personal information under its control (that is, under its administrative management). Society expects government to be open and transparent, so institutions have discretion to disclose information without the consent of the individual (s. 8),[28] including

- for the purpose it was collected,
- for any purpose in accordance with a statute,
- in compliance with a subpoena or court order,
- in legal proceedings involving the government,
- to a regulatory investigative body,
- for research or statistical purposes,
- when the head of the institution believes that disclosure is in the public interest and the benefit clearly outweighs the invasion of privacy (with notice to the *Privacy Commissioner*),[29] and
- to provincial or foreign governments investigating illegal activity.

---

[26] RSC 1985, c P-21.

[27] *Bernard v Canada (Attorney General)*, 2014 SCC 13.

[28] *Merck Frosst Canada Ltd v Canada (Health)*, 2012 SCC 3 at paras 6, 23, 71, 80.

[29] Public access to government records may be requested under the *Access to Information Act*, RSC 1985, c A-1. This statute allows the head of an institution to refuse public access to any record of personal information (s. 19). The privacy of personal information was given priority over the right of access: *H J Heinz Co of Canada Ltd v Canada (Attorney General)*, [2006] 1 SCR 441.

retain keep information available for subsequent access by the individual

Individuals are entitled to access their information held by government and to have inaccuracies corrected (s. 12). The institution must **retain** personal information for at least two years after its last use so that the individual has time to access it (s. 4).[30] However, the right of access is complicated in the public sector, given the overriding responsibilities associated with law enforcement, national security, and public confidence. Therefore, there are a number of exceptions to the right of access to personal information. Access may be refused if the information is

- contained in designated exempt data banks (s. 18),
- obtained in confidence from another government (domestic or international) (s. 19),
- injurious to federal–provincial relations (s. 20),
- injurious to international affairs (s. 21),
- prepared for or injurious to law enforcement or policing (s. 22),
- obtained by the Privacy Commissioner (s. 22.1),
- obtained as part of the *Public Servants Disclosure Protection Act* (s. 22.2),
- about someone other than the individual (s. 26),
- a threat to safety (s. 25),
- subject to solicitor–client privilege, or
- medical in nature and access would not be in the best interests of the individual (s. 28).

Compliance with the requirements of the *Privacy Act* is monitored by the Privacy Commissioner, who has the power to investigate and initiate complaints; compel written, oral, or documentary evidence; and assess whether or not the complaint is well founded.[31] After completion of a private investigation, a report of the findings, together with any corrective recommendations, is given to the head of the government institution under review and the complainant. Reports relating to a denial of access to personal information are reviewable by the Federal Court (s. 41).

Government Transparency and Accountability

The Privacy Commissioner has identified some deficiencies in the current *Privacy Act* that reduce the transparency and accountability of the federal government. The following changes have been recommended:[32]

- Require a necessity or "needs" test before collecting personal information.
- Expand the review powers of the Federal Court to include all privacy complaints, not just those involving a denial of access.
- Make breach reporting mandatory.
- Allow the Privacy Commissioner to make orders rather than just recommendations.
- Strengthen the provisions governing the disclosure of personal information by the Canadian government to foreign states.[33]

---

[30] *Privacy Regulations*, SOR/83-508, s 4.

[31] Two policies give guidance on compliance: the Policy on Privacy Protection (2008) and the Directive on Privacy Impact Assessment (2010); see Treasury Board of Canada Secretariat website (Policies), http://www.tbs-sct.gc.ca/pol/doc-eng.aspx?id=18308&section=text.

[32] Review of the *Privacy Act*—Revised Recommendations (November, 2016), https://www.priv.gc.ca/en/privacy-topics/privacy-laws-in-canada/the-privacy-act/pa_r/pa_ref_rec_161101; pending amendments to the *Access to Information Act* addressed some of these issues: See Bill C-58, First Session, Forty-second Parliament, 64-65-66 Elizabeth II, 2015-2016-2017.

[33] Office of the Privacy Commissioner of Canada, "Privacy Act Reform," http://www.priv.gc.ca/parl/pa_r_e.asp.

The importance of the last recommendation is highlighted by the findings of the Commission of Inquiry into the Actions of Canadian Officials in Relation to Maher Arar.[34] Justice O'Connor found that it was very likely that American authorities detained and deported Arar to Syria (where he was subsequently tortured) because of inaccurate information supplied to them by the RCMP. The *Privacy Act* expressly authorizes government institutions to share information with foreign governments investigating illegal behaviour.[35]

Ethical Issue: Government Transparency and Accountability

The U.S. National Security Agency's mission (NSA) includes tracking suspected terrorists to uncover terrorist plots against the United States. Edward J. Snowden, an NSA contractor, collected documents describing the NSA's wide scale surveillance, interception, and collection of electronic written and oral communications, facial images, and fingerprints of unsuspected Americans and foreigners located inside and outside the United States. The release of some documents to the press and publication of the NSA's practices by the *Guardian* and subsequently the *New York Times* shocked the world both as to the extent of NSA's invasion of privacy and the lengths to which governments would go to keep the practices secret. The U.K. government pressured the *Guardian* newspaper to destroy computer hard drives, and reporters and family were detained and questioned under terrorism laws. The *Guardian* enlisted the *New York Times* as a "safe haven" archive for the documents and partner in publication, believing it was beyond the reach of government suppression. Edward Snowden was charged with espionage by the U.S. government; he fled the country, eventually receiving asylum in Russia after his U.S. passport was revoked.

Questions to Consider

1. Under what circumstances should a government be permitted to use covert surveillance to collect and generate personal information about its citizens without prior legal grounds?
2. Should the standards be different for surveillance of non-citizens or those located outside the country?
3. Why are transparency and accountability important in government?
4. Was Snowden's collection and selective release of documents right?

Sources: James Risen and Laura Poitras, "N.S.A. Collecting Millions of Faces From Web Images," *The New York Times*, Sunday, June 1, 2014, 1; Ryan Lizza, "The Political Scene: State of Deception, Why Won't the President Rein in the Intelligence Community," *The New Yorker*, December 16, 2013; CBC News Video, "Guardian Alleges Pressure by British Agents," http://www.cbc.ca/player/Embedded-Only/News/ID/2401978333/; "Inside the Mind of Edward Snowden," NBC News, http://www.nbcnews.com/feature/edward-snowden-interview.

CHECKLIST

Privacy Act

Government institutions dealing with personal information should

- only collect information that directly relates to the operation of a government program or activity,
- collect information directly from the individual,
- keep information secure and up to date,
- use or disclose information only for the purpose for which it was collected (with some exceptions),
- obtain consent for any other use,
- allow access to information by the individual (subject to broad exceptions), and
- respond to complaints of individuals and recommendations of the Privacy Commissioner.

---

[34] *Commission of Inquiry into the Actions of Canadian Officials in Relation to Maher Arar (Arar Commission): Report of Events Relating to Maher Arar* (Ottawa: Canadian Government Publishing, 2006).

[35] Section 8(2)(f). See also *Mutual Legal Assistance in Criminal Matters Act*, RSC 1985 (4th Supp), c 30.

Provincial Variation

Provincial legislation addresses public sector handling of personal information and access to information held by provincial agencies. Most provinces combine these topics into one "Freedom of Information and Protection of Privacy" (FIPPA) statute.[36] Some designate a provincial information and privacy commissioner (British Columbia, Alberta, Ontario, New Brunswick), whereas others leave supervision in the hands of the provincial ombudsman (Manitoba). Some other important distinctions from the federal legislation are as follows:

- British Columbia and Alberta: The Privacy Commissioner can make binding orders and comment on the privacy implications of proposed legislation.
- Ontario and Saskatchewan: Separate legislation covers municipal governments.
- Ontario: The provincial Crown can be held liable for damages arising from negligent disclosure of a record.
- In addition, some provincial public sectors are regulated by specialized legislation.

Municipalities As noted, Saskatchewan and Ontario have separate privacy legislation covering municipal governments, boards, and agencies.[37] The form and substance of the municipal statutes mirror the FIPPA protection and access standards. Supervision of compliance is also managed by the provincial privacy commissioners.

The Saskatchewan *Local Authority Freedom of Information and Protection of Privacy Act* applies to boards of education, universities, colleges, and hospitals. The right of access under this Act has priority over confidentiality provisions. In Ontario, universities, colleges, boards of education, and hospitals fall under the provincial, not municipal, legislation.

Healthcare Healthcare is an area of provincial jurisdiction involving both public sector and private sector stakeholders. For example, most hospitals are government institutions (already covered by FIPPA), whereas pharmacies and medical labs would be considered private sector commercial activities (subject to private sector legislation, as will be discussed later). Some (but not all) hospice, counselling, and support services are private sector, not-for-profit organizations. All have access to very sensitive **personal health information** about individuals. Therefore, specific provincial legislation focusing on healthcare providers and custodians of health information exists to address the highly sensitive nature of this information. New Brunswick, Alberta, Manitoba, Saskatchewan, and Ontario have adopted legislation specifically addressing the protection of health information across all sectors of the healthcare industry (**PHIPA**).[38] Non-compliance with personal health legislation can result in fines ranging from $50 000 in Manitoba to $500 000 for corporations in Saskatchewan.

---

personal health information
information relating to the physical or mental health of an identifiable individual that is used or obtained primarily for the purpose of providing healthcare

PHIPA *Personal Health Information Protection Act* (in Alberta and Saskatchewan, simply HIPA)

---

[36] British Columbia *Freedom of Information and Protection of Privacy Act*, *supra* note 23; Alberta *Freedom of Information and Protection of Privacy Act*, RSA 2000, c F-25; Saskatchewan *Freedom of Information and Protection of Privacy Act*, SS 1990-1, c F-22.01; Manitoba *Freedom of Information and Protection of Privacy Act*, CCSM c F175; Ontario *Freedom of Information and Protection of Privacy Act*, RSO 1990, c F.31; Nova Scotia *Freedom of Information and Protection of Privacy Act*, SNS 1993, c 5; Newfoundland *Access to Information and Protection of Privacy Act*, SNL 2015, c A-1.2 Prince Edward Island *Freedom of Information and Protection of Privacy Act*, RSPEI 1988, c F-15.01; *Right to Information and* New Brunswick *Protection of Privacy Act*, SNB 2009, c R-10.6.

[37] Saskatchewan *Local Authority Freedom of Information and Protection of Privacy Act*, SS 1990-91, c L-27.1; *Municipal Freedom of Information and Protection of Privacy Act*, RSO 1990, c M-56.

[38] *Personal Health Information Act*, CCSM c P-33.5; *Health Information Act*, RSA 2000, c H-5; *Health Information Protection Act*, SS 1999, c H-0.021; *Personal Health Information Protection Act*, SO 2004, c 3, Sch A; *Personal Health Information Privacy and Access Act*, SNB 2009, c P-7.05. In other provinces, the privacy of health information is addressed through the standard federal and provincial public or private sector privacy statutes.

Organizations continue to be subject to general privacy legislation for non-health personal information such as financial or employment records. Classifying the type of information can be difficult.

Many individuals participating in the healthcare sector are licensed professionals bound by provincial legislation and also professional codes of ethics requiring confidentiality. Doctors, nurses, and pharmacists are just a few examples. Breach of confidentiality by these professionals triggers investigation and discipline by the professional licensing body.

CASE 32.5 Exception to Unauthorized Release

An Ontario court approved the release of a nurse's occupational health records by the employer hospital. The records were released to the College of Nurses without her consent and used in an investigation of the nurse. The hospital identified the primary purpose of the record as employment. The court characterized the records as personal health information entitled to the protection of PHIPA. However, a PHIPA exception exists for release of information to a regulatory body.[39]

Naturally, both the legislation and professional standards allow non-consensual collection, use, and disclosure of personal health information when it is necessary for the effective delivery of health services or public safety. Individuals must be notified of disclosure.

Education Education also falls under provincial jurisdiction and involves public and private sector participants. Privacy issues in this sector are regulated by multiple statutes:

- Public schools (elementary and secondary), boards, universities, and colleges are covered by the provincial Freedom of Information and Protection of Privacy Act(s) (FIPPA).
- Private schools (as private sector commercial activities) are covered by PIPEDA.
- In Manitoba, school boards, universities, and colleges are subject to the *Personal Health Information Act*.[40]
- Both public and private schools (and boards) are subject to provincial education act(s) that regulate the use and disclosure of students' records.[41]

Ethical Issue Privacy Versus Security: The Virginia Tech Shooting

Seung Hui Cho, a student at Virginia Polytechnic Institute (Virginia Tech), walked into the West-Amber Johnston Hall co-ed residence at 7:15 a.m. on April 16, 2007, and started shooting. Two hours later, after returning to his apartment to rearm, Cho entered the Norris Hall Engineering building, chained the doors shut, and continued his shooting spree. When it was all over, 33 people, including Cho, were dead, and 23 others were injured.

Obviously, the primary responsibility for the shootings lies with Cho, but victims' families questioned the conduct of the school administrators when it was revealed that Cho struggled with mental illness his whole life. Problems surfaced in elementary and high school; school administrators became involved, and Cho received treatment that seemed to help. However, his medical history was not passed on to Virginia Tech when Cho enrolled in postsecondary education. Cho purchased his guns legally from a registered firearms dealer who was also unaware of Cho's mental condition. At Virginia Tech, some students and faculty expressed concern about Cho's violent writings, but no action was taken.

Questions to Consider

1. Who is served by keeping medical information private?
2. Does keeping medical information secret further stigmatize the illness, or does it prevent discrimination?

Source: Marc Fisher, Richard Brusca, and Colin Ram, "A Failure to Communicate: Did Privacy Laws Contribute to the Virginia Tech Tragedy?" (2010) 17 *Wash. & Lee J CR & Soc Jus*t 141.

---

[39] *Hooper v College of Nurses of Ontario*, 2006 CanLII 22656 (ON SCDC).

[40] Manitoba, *supra* note 38, s 1.1.

[41] See e.g. Ontario *Education Act*, RSO 1990, c E-2, s 266.

Regulation of Privacy in the Private Sector

Private sector privacy is a matter of both federal and provincial legislative jurisdiction. Federal jurisdiction stems from the general power over trade and commerce and the interprovincial and international nature of data flow, as well as major privacy concerns in key federally controlled industries such as banking and telecommunications.[42] Provincial authority to regulate privacy falls in the property and civil rights power. Therefore, some provinces have their own comprehensive private sector privacy legislation separate from federal legislation.

PIPEDA The *Personal Information Protection and Electronic Documents Act* (PIPEDA) is the comprehensive private sector federal legislation controlling the collection, **use**, and **disclosure** of personal information during a **commercial activity** (s. 4(1)(a)).[43] It applies to all persons, corporations, individuals, organizations, associations, partnerships, and trade unions operating in Canada that are not already covered by the *Privacy Act*. However, if a province has adopted substantially similar legislation, businesses covered by the provincial legislation will be exempt from compliance with PIPEDA. As discussed below, some provinces have taken this step.

use (of personal information) any access, change, or destruction of data within the organization

disclosure (of personal information) transfer of data to third parties outside the organization

commercial activity any general or particular activity performed or stated in the objectives of an organization, that has a commercial aspect

Enforcement The federal Privacy Commissioner monitors compliance with PIPEDA. The Privacy Commission receives and investigates complaints and reports findings. The Commissioner lacks the power to make orders and functions more like an ombudsman;[44] however, any report may be reviewed by the Federal Court, and appropriate orders made (ss. 14–16). In addition, the Commissioner may undertake research, educational initiatives, and audit organizations to determine their level of PIPEDA compliance. The Act creates offences for destruction of requested information (s. 8(8)), whistle-blower retaliation (s. 27.1), and obstruction of an investigation or audit (s. 28).

CASE 32.6 Production and Solicitor–Client Privilege

A dismissed employee requested access to her employment file and complained to the Privacy Commissioner when the employer refused to make full disclosure. The Privacy Commissioner requested access to some documents for which solicitor–client privilege was claimed. Section 12.1 of PIPEDA gives the Commissioner power to order production in the same manner as a court. The employer appealed, and the Supreme Court of Canada held that solicitor–client privilege is a fundamental part of the Canadian justice system, and PIPEDA (s. 12.1) does not confer a right of access to solicitor–client documents.[45] In 2016 the Supreme Court of Canada took a similar view of the production powers of the Alberta Privacy Commissioner under Alberta's FIPPA language.[46] Although the *Privacy Act* is in the process of being amended to expand the Commissioner's power to compel privileged documents, no similar amendment is proposed for PIPEDA.[47]

---

personal information recorded and unrecorded information about an identifiable individual, including that supplied by the individual and created by the organization

individual natural person, not a corporation

Requirements PIPEDA regulates the handling of **personal information** about an identifiable **individual** whether recorded or not, excluding the name, title, business address, or telephone number of an employee. Personal information includes information

---

[42] Limits of trade and commerce assessed using five questions: *General Motors of Canada Ltd v City National Leasing* (1989), 58 DLR (4th) 255 (SCC). The *Telecommunications Act* empowers the CRTC to protect the privacy of persons. The *Bank Act* does not address privacy; PIPEDA applies to banks.

[43] The legislation was initiated to satisfy data protection requirements of European Union (EU Data Protection Directive). The 1996 Model Code for the Protection of Personal Information developed by the Standards Council of Canada served as the model for PIPEDA.

[44] Stronger enforcement power is recommended: Office of the Privacy Commissioner of Canada, 2016–17 Annual Report to Parliament, https://www.priv.gc.ca/en/opc-actions-and-decisions/ar_index/201617/ar_201617.

[45] *Canada (Privacy Commissioner) v Blood Tribe Department of Health*, 2008 SCC 44.

[46] *Alberta (Privacy Commissioner) v University of Calgary*, 2016 SCC 53 (differing language but still not clear enough to override solicitor–client privilege).

[47] Bill C-58, *supra* note 32.

supplied to the organization, such as birth dates, health history and marital status, and information created by the organization, such as employee salary, identification numbers, and performance evaluations. The requirements of the legislation follow the 10 guiding principles of the Canadian Standards Association Model Code.[48]

Principle 1: Accountability (Clause 4.1)

- *Policies and procedures*—Organizations shall create, implement, and publicize internal policies and procedures that will assist in complying with PIPEDA.
- *Complaints process*—The policies must include a simple and accessible process for responding to and investigating complaints.
- *Compliance monitor*—Every organization shall identify a person to be responsible for compliance with the Act.
- *Data transfers*—The organization is responsible for data transferred to third parties and must ensure their protection using contractual or other methods.

CASE 32.7 Deficient Internal Policies and Procedures

Sensitive medical information was disclosed on a debtor's credit report. The Privacy Commissioner's investigation revealed that the credit agency obtained the health information from the loan application submitted to the debtor's financial institution. The employee who filled out the loan application said the financial institution's standard practice was to record "Disability" in the employment field of the document, and she did not know that everything on the application would be revealed to the credit reporting agency. The Commissioner found that the employee was not properly trained, and the standard practice was a violation of PIPEDA. The financial institution agreed to revise its policies for handling information and improve training of employees.[49]

CASE 32.8 Data Transfers and Subcontracting

A bank customer complained to the Privacy Commissioner after a market research firm contacted her to participate in a survey using information from the bank's database. The bank hired the market research firm to survey on its behalf, and the firm subcontracted the telephone calling to a third party. The bank had a confidentiality agreement with the market research firm, but no agreement existed with the third party. The Privacy Commissioner found that the bank's confidentiality agreement "was deficient in that it made no provision for sub-contracting." The bank was in violation of the accountability principle.[50]

Principle 2: Identifying Purpose (Clause 4.2)

- *Collection*—An organization may only collect information that is necessary for an expressly identified purpose.
- *Communication*—The purpose of collection should be communicated to the data owner at time of collection but must be communicated before use.
- *Reasonableness*—The purpose must be one that a reasonable person would consider appropriate in the circumstances (s. 5(3)).

---

[48] Model Code for the Protection of Personal Information, CAN/CSA Q830-96 forms part of PIPEDA as a schedule: SC 2000, c 5, Sch 1. Section 5 requires mandatory compliance with all obligations in the Schedule using the word "shall." When the word "should" is used, the statement is a recommendation.

[49] Office of the Privacy Commissioner of Canada, PIPEDA Case Summary #2015-017, https://www.priv.gc.ca/en/opc-actions-and-decisions/investigations/investigations-into-businesses/2015/pipeda-2015-017.

[50] Office of the Privacy Commissioner of Canada, PIPEDA Case Summary #2002-35, https://www.priv.gc.ca/en/opc-actions-and-decisions/investigations/investigations-into-businesses/2002/pipeda-2002-035.

CASE 32.9 Reasonableness of Purpose

Canadian Pacific Railway installed six video surveillance cameras in its maintenance facility, focusing on entrances and exits. The railway posted signs warning of the security system and identifying the purpose of the cameras as protection against "theft, vandalism, unauthorized personnel, and incidents related." An employee alleged that the cameras were being used to track punctuality of employees and were a violation of PIPEDA. The Privacy Commissioner agreed that the use of the cameras was unreasonable (violating section 5(3)). The Federal Court overruled the Commissioner and found the use of cameras reasonable for the identified purpose.[51]

In Case 32.9, the Court applied a four-part test to determine reasonableness:

(a) Is the measure demonstrably necessary to meet a specific need?
(b) Is it likely to be effective in meeting that need?
(c) Is the loss of privacy proportional to the benefit gained?
(d) Is there a less privacy-invasive way of achieving the same end?

CASE 32.10 Invasiveness of Biometrics

The Privacy Commissioner investigated complaints about biometric data collected from students writing GMAT, MCAT and LSAT. Palm-vein scanning of GMAT students and finger printing of MCAT and LSAT students were intended to reduce cheating by catching proxy text writers, impersonators, and other fraud. Both GMAT and MCAT organizers presented strong evidence of a real and demonstrable problem of this type of fraud where the biometric was actually used to identify fraudsters who had previously taken the test under other names. One U.S. GMAT writer was imprisoned for fraud arising from writing the GMAT over 300 times. The Commissioner approved the use of biometrics by GMAT and MCAT providers. However, the LSAT administrators could not describe a single case when the fingerprints were necessary. Therefore the loss of privacy was greater than the benefit gained; the LSAT provider was asked to revert to the less intrusive practice of collecting photos of test writers.[52]

Principle 3: Consent (Clause 4.3)

- *Collection, use, and disclosure* require the knowledge and consent of the data owner.
- *Meaningful consent* requires the organization to explain the purpose of the collection, use, or disclosure in understandable language prior to obtaining consent, and once given, consent may be withdrawn.
- *Exceptions*—Section 7 describes situations when collection, use, or disclosure of data is acceptable without knowledge or consent.
- *Reasonableness* (s. 5(3)) may cure a lack of consent, but consent will not cure unreasonableness.

CASE 32.11 Proposed Use and Disclosure

A credit bureau collected social insurance numbers from the data owners' banks. The data were to be used for identification purposes. The Privacy Commissioner held that this indirect collection was acceptable if the credit bureau received contractual confirmation from the banks that they had received all necessary consents from the data owners. Reliance upon the banks' consents was reasonable in the circumstances because a large volume of data was being processed on a daily basis.[53] The opposite conclusion was reached in Case 32.7 because the financial institution's customer consent did not cover disclosure of disability status as part of the information shared, and therefore disclosure violated PIPEDA.

---

[51] *Eastmond v Canadian Pacific Railway*, 2004 FC 852 at para 127.

[52] Office of the Privacy Commissioner of Canada, PIPEDA Case Summary #2010-007, https://www.priv.gc.ca/en/opc-actions-and-decisions/investigations/investigations-into-businesses/2010/pipeda-2010-007.

[53] Office of the Privacy Commissioner of Canada, PIPEDA Case #2003-194, https://www.priv.gc.ca/en/opc-actions-and-decisions/investigations/investigations-into-businesses/2003/pipeda-2003-194.

Consent requirements vary, given the circumstances and sensitivity of the information. Consent may be oral or written, express or implied. Implied consent is reserved for less-sensitive information that a reasonable person would expect to be disclosed in the circumstances.[54] **Opt-out consent**, a form of implied consent, is allowed in only some situations and not those involving medical information.[55]

opt-out consent data-owner consent is implied from a failure to refuse consent

CASE 32.12 Use of Email Address Without Consent

Email addresses imported by Facebook members to send Facebook invitations to non-users were subsequently used by Facebook to send friend suggestions. The use of the non-member email address to identify friends was a mechanical exercise done without consent. The Privacy Commissioner found that Facebook breached PIPEDA because it "failed to obtain the knowledge and consent of non-user's prior to the use of their e-mail addresses to generate friend suggestions (contrary to Principle 4.3)."[56] Facebook now provides clear notice to non-users that their email addresses may be used to generate friend suggestions and offers non-users an easy opt-out process.

Five factors make opt-out consent acceptable in a particular circumstance:

- The personal information is non-sensitive in nature and context.
- The context in which information is shared is narrow with well-defined limits to the use or disclosure.
- The organization's purposes are limited, well-defined, and stated in a clear and understandable manner.
- Individuals are informed of the proposed use or disclosure and able to opt out at the earliest opportunity.
- The organization establishes a convenient procedure for opting out of or withdrawing consent to secondary purposes, with the opt-out taking effect immediately and prior to any use or disclosure of personal information for the proposed new purposes.[57]

CHECKLIST
Some Exceptions to the Need for Consent

Section 7(1): Collection of information **without** consent must be

(a) in the interests of the owner and in a circumstance when consent cannot be obtained in a timely manner;

(b) for the purpose of investigating a breach of law where consent would likely compromise accuracy or availability;

(c) for journalistic, literary, or artistic purposes;

(d) of publicly available information and specified in regulations; or

(e) in compliance with a legal obligation to disclose.

---

[54] *Royal Bank of Canada v Trang*, 2016 SCC 50 at paras 42–44.

[55] *Townsend v Sun Life Financial*, 2012 FC 550 at para 25.

[56] Office of the Privacy Commissioner of Canada, PIPEDA Case Summary #2012-002, para 50, https://www.priv.gc.ca/en/opc-actions-and-decisions/investigations/investigations-into-businesses/2012/pipeda-2012-002.

[57] *Ibid* at para 47.

Section 7(2): Use of information <u>without</u> consent must be

(a) for the purpose of investigating a breach of law (committed or about to be committed);
(b) in an emergency that threatens the life, health, or security of an individual;
(c) for statistical or scholarly research or study;
 (c.1) of information publicly available and specified in regulations; or
(d) of information collected under section 7(1)(a)(b) or (c).

Section 7(3): Disclosure <u>without</u> consent must be

(a) to a lawyer for the organization;
(b) for the purpose of collecting a debt owed by the individual to the organization;
(c) required by a subpoena, warrant, or rules of a court;
(d) made to a government agency for national security or law-enforcement purposes;
(e) during an emergency that threatens the life, health, or security of an individual;
(f) for statistical or scholarly research or study;
(g) made to a historic conservationist for the above purpose;
(h) made 100 years after the record was created or 20 years after the death of the data owner,
 (h.1) of information publicly available and specified in regulations;
 (h.2) made by an investigative body arising from an investigation of breach of law; or
(i) required by law.

Section 7.3 Employment Relationship

(a) organizations may collect, use or disclose personal information without consent when necessary to establish, manage or terminate the individual's employment relation.

Principle 4: Limiting Collection (Clause 4.4)

- *Identified purpose*—Only information necessary to fulfill the purpose may be collected.
- Collection must use *fair and lawful means* without deception.

Principle 5: Limiting Use, Disclosure, and Retention (Clause 4.5)

- *Use and disclosure*—Information shall be used or disclosed only for the identified purpose and with the consent of the data owner.
- *Retention*—Information may be kept for only as long as is necessary for the identified purpose.
- *Destruction*—The organization shall have policies and guidelines governing the safe and secure destruction of the information.

CASE 32.13 Secure Destruction When Purpose Fulfilled

A movie theatre chain offered accessibility equipment to assist persons with disabilities when viewing movies. The names, addresses, and phone numbers of people using accessibility equipment were recorded on a sheet of paper held at the counter. The identified purpose was to allow follow-up with the patron if the equipment was returned damaged or not at all. The company believed this collection discouraged damage and theft.

The Privacy Commissioner's investigation found that the collection was reasonable for the identified purpose; however, practices varied among specific theatres, and there were no policies with respect to safeguarding, retaining, or destroying the information. The breach of the retention and destruction requirements was remedied by implementing a policy of releasing the original record of the information to the patron when the equipment was returned in good repair.[58]

---

[58] Office of the Privacy Commissioner of Canada, PIPEDA Case #2005-304, https://www.priv.gc.ca/en/opc-actions-and-decisions/investigations/investigations-into-businesses/2005/pipeda-2005-304.

Principle 6: Accuracy (Clause 4.6)

- Information must be *complete, accurate, and current*.

Since organizations should not collect more information than required for their purpose, they cannot unnecessarily update personal information. This appears to conflict with the need for accuracy and currency. One solution is to clearly display a currency date for the information.

Principle 7: Safeguards (Clause 4.7)

- *Security shall be appropriate* for the type of information and shall include physical, organizational, and technological measures.
- *Measures must protect* against theft, loss, unauthorized access, copying, or alteration.
- *Employee confidentiality* is one necessary component.

If there is a security breach PIPEDA requires three notifications: the Privacy Commissioner, the affected individual, and other organizations that could reduce the risk of harm.[59] In the case of hacked credit card information, this means notification of the Privacy Commissioner, the holder of the card, and the issuing credit card company. Notification is only necessary if there is a real risk of significant harm that includes bodily harm, humiliation, damage to reputation or relationships, loss of employment, business or professional opportunities, financial loss, identity theft, negative effects on the credit record, and damage to or loss of property.

CASE 32.14 No Notification of Breach

CIBC's privacy safeguards were found to be inadequate because loan applications containing personal information about applicants were mistakenly faxed to unintended recipients in the United States and Quebec for several years. The misdirected faxes continued even after the bank was repeatedly notified by the recipients. Eventually, one of the unintended recipients contacted the media. The interim efforts of the bank were deemed insufficient by the Privacy Commissioner because they did not involve retrieval of the customer data, confirmation of destruction, or notification of affected customers.[60]

Principle 8: Openness (Clause 4.8)

- *Availability*—Information about policies and practices shall be available to the public.
- *Disclosure*—Information about who has access to personal information shall be available to the public.

Openness is limited by the safeguard principle. Organizations are not required to publicize any parts of policies or practices that would compromise the effectiveness of the security.[61]

Principle 9: Access (Clause 4.9)

- *Accuracy*—A data subject shall have access to the recorded personal information and shall be able to dispute the accuracy of the record.

---

[59] Breach notification: *Digital Privacy Act, 2015*, SC 2015, c 32, s 10 (10.1, 10.2, 10.3) came in to force on November 1, 2018.

[60] Office of the Privacy Commissioner of Canada, 2005 Incident Summary #2: https://www.priv.gc.ca/en/opc-actions-and-decisions/investigations/investigations-into-businesses/incidents/2005/050418_01.

[61] Safeguarding personal information, https://www.priv.gc.ca/en/privacy-topics/safeguarding-personal-information.

- *Correction*—The data subject is entitled to have the record corrected once the inaccuracy or incompleteness is established.

Despite this principle, individuals are not entitled to access information that is subject to solicitor–client privilege, doctor–patient confidentiality, or other legal proprietary interests. The safeguard principle requires that the organization confirm that the individual requesting the information is entitled to access. Organizations are not entitled to charge for access unless prior notice is given, and even then, the cost should be minimal.

Principle 10: Challenging Compliance (Clause 4.10)

- *Complaints process*—Each organization must have an internal process to handle complaints.

In order to satisfy the Privacy Commissioner during any subsequent investigation or audit, a record of the internal investigation process and outcome should be maintained. Modifications made to privacy policies should be documented in order to establish responsiveness to concerns of the public.

Provincial Variation British Columbia, Alberta, Manitoba (once proclaimed), and Quebec have provincial legislation acknowledged to be "substantially similar" to the federal statute.[62] Therefore, private sector protection of personal information in these provinces is governed by the provincial statutes (not PIPEDA), with two key exceptions. First, federal agencies, works, and undertakings within the province still need to comply with PIPEDA. Second, extra-provincial transfer of the personal information continues to be governed by the federal legislation.

The provincial statutes broaden privacy protection to include less-structured groups and not-for-profit activities[63] and expand the authority of the provincial privacy commissioners to include order-making powers. Manitoba's legislation includes a civil cause of action for damages.[64] Protection is extended to employees working in businesses within provincial constitutional jurisdiction, as discussed below. However, extending privacy protection too broadly has its risks—in Case 32.1, the Supreme Court of Canada declared the Alberta *Protection of Personal Information Act* unconstitutional for violating the *Charter*'s protection of freedom of expression.

Specific Stakeholders

Employers and Employees Privacy in the workplace involves balancing employees' reasonable expectations of privacy with the relevant business and property interests of the employer. Legislative protection varies depending on the nature of the employment relationship. Personal information of public sector employees is protected by the *Privacy Act* or its provincial equivalent. Private sector employee information is protected by PIPEDA if the employment is with a business within federal jurisdiction or crosses provincial boundaries. For employees of businesses within provincial jurisdiction, only British Columbia, Alberta, Manitoba, and Quebec (as described above) have legislation protecting their data. In other provinces, protection must be found in the employment contract, the collective agreement, or the common law.[65]

---

[62] *Personal Information Protection Act*, SBC 2003, c 63; *Personal Information Protection Act*, SA 2003, c P-6.5; *Personal Information Protection and Identity Theft Prevention Act*, CCSM c P33.7 (not proclaimed in force at 2018); *Act Respecting the Protection of Personal Information in the Private Sector*, RSQ, c P-39.1.

[63] *Re Surrey Creep Catcher*, 2017 BCIPC 38 (CanLII).

[64] *Supra* note 62 (Manitoba) (not proclaimed in force at 2018), s 34(4).

[65] *International Association of Bridge, Structural, Ornamental and Reinforcing Iron Workers and Its Local 736 v ES Fox Ltd*, 2006 CanLII 468 (ON LRB) at para 14, aff'd 2006 CanLII 6007; *McKesson Canada v Teamsters Chemical Energy and Allied Workers Union, Local 424*, 136 LAC (4th) 102; *Rodgers v Calvert* (2004), 49 BLR (3d) 53.

Countless privacy issues arise in the workplace. One of the most controversial is surveillance of employees by employers. Surveillance can take many forms: electronic, video, or observational tracking, and it can be **covert**, **disclosed**, or **consensual**. Video surveillance of employees in the workplace is a controversial practice and will only be considered reasonable if it meets the Federal Court's four criteria described in relation to Case 32.9. Other forms of surveillance may still be too invasive, especially when surveillance is covert.

covert surveillance the employee is unaware of surveillance and has not consented to it

disclosed surveillance the employee is given advance notice of surveillance but does not consent to it

consensual surveillance the employee is aware of and consents to the surveillance

Case 32.15 suggests that employer surveillance practices should reflect that surveillance

- is a last resort,
- should be undertaken only after all other methods of collecting information have been unsuccessful, and
- should be limited to the least intrusive form possible.

CASE 32.15 Covert Surveillance

After receiving a *Health and Safety* complaint about the "messy" condition of the washroom, the employer began secretly monitoring washroom visits. A log was kept by staff recording who used the washroom, when, and the condition in which it was left. Within three days, it was determined that the washroom only needed attention after visits by one employee, and the monitoring ceased. The offender was interviewed, issued a disciplinary letter, and warned that continued conduct would result in dismissal.

The Privacy Commissioner found that the covert surveillance was unreasonable in the circumstances (in violation of section 5(3)). Washrooms are places where a high expectation of privacy exists. The employer could not rely on the section 7 exceptions to the need for consent for an unreasonable invasion. The employer did not exhaust less-invasive measures first.[66]

Monitoring employee email and internet use involves not only privacy but also property issues. The hardware, software, and network used in the workplace are company property, and communications using an employer's network could be considered communications from the employer. It is unlikely that any reasonable expectation of privacy exists when using a company asset.[67] The expectation of privacy is reduced if the employer gives notice of the monitoring to the employee.[68] Common forms of notice include codes of conduct, privacy policies, and collective agreements.

CASE 32.16 Email Misuse

Imperial Oil's dismissal of an employee for personal use of company email was upheld. The contents of the employee's emails could be considered sexist and racist and, therefore, violated the harassment policy of the employer. The employee was aware of Imperial Oil's technology-use policy, prohibiting personal use of the company's email system.[69]

---

[66] Office of the Privacy Commissioner of Canada, PIPEDA Case Summary #2007 – 379, https://www.priv.gc.ca/en/opc-actions-and-decisions/investigations/investigations-into-businesses/2007/pipeda-2007-379.

[67] *Milson v Corporate Computers Inc*, [2003] WWR 250 paras 40–1; *Camosun College v CUPE*, [1999] BCCAAA No 490 (dismissal based on the contents of an email sent using the employer's system). See also *Johnson v Bell Canada*, 2008 FC 1086, supp'l reasons [2009] FCJ No 1066, where personal emails about an employee saved in Bell's computer system were not subject to disclosure under PIPEDA because they were not business related. *R v Cole*, *supra* note 3 the expectation of privacy is reduced by workplace policies and notices but not eliminated with respect to further disclosure to police.

[68] *Briar et al v Treasury Board* (2003), PSRB 3, http://www.fpslreb-crtespf.gc.ca/Decisions/summaries/31092_e.asp (system gave notice of monitoring at log-in). Covert monitoring requires reasonable cause. See Alberta Office of the Information and Privacy Commissioner, Parkland Regional Library, Review Number 2005-3016, https://www.oipc.ab.ca/decisions/orders.aspx?postback=1&year=2005&legislationType=FOIP&page=2.

[69] *Bhamre Employment Insurance Claim Appeal*, (September 23, 1998) CUB42012A. See also *Poliquin v Devon Canada Corporation*, 2009 ABCA 216.

Consumers Protection of personal information is only one area of concern for consumers and potential consumers. Spam and telemarketing have become a major intrusion on territorial privacy. Consumers are bombarded in their homes with unwanted emails and solicitation calls disguised as market surveys and free giveaways. Legislative attempts to curb these invasions include amendments to the federal *Telecommunications Act* that allowed the Canadian Radio-television and Telecommunications Commission (CRTC) to create a National Do Not Call List (DNCL).[70] Any telemarketers contacting consumers whose names are on the DNCL may be subject to fines of up to $15 000 per offending call. It is the obligation of the telemarketer to regularly check the list. Registered charities, political parties, and businesses with a pre-existing relationship with the consumer are exempt from the DNCL rules.

Other telemarketing controls implemented by the CRTC's require that:

- calls and faxes be confined to designated time periods such as 9:00 a.m. to 9:30 p.m. on weekdays,
- consumer do not call requests, when made during a telemarketing call, must be processed without further contact, and
- upon request, a telemarketer must provide a toll-free number for an employee of the telemarketer or client.[71]

Second, Canadian Anti-Spam legislation (CASL)[72] prohibits unsolicited commercial electronic messages. The definition of "electronic" is so broad that it also covers telemarketing. As discussed in Chapter 31, CASL also makes installing a computer program without prior permission an offence. CASL is designed to combat spyware and phishing, tactics often used to steal personal information about the computer user. Legitimate businesses must adjust their marketing practices to fit within the CASL exceptions discussed below. Information collected in the course of a PIPEDA or CASL investigation may be shared between authorities.

Specific Businesses Some private sector businesses are subject to specific privacy regulation, such as the following:

- Private investigators and security guards have privacy and confidentiality obligations.[73]
- Credit reporting agencies' disclosure of information is controlled by provincial consumer-protection legislation.[74]
- Airline and airline reservation system operators may be ordered to share passenger information with various government agencies in the interest of national security under the *Aeronautics Act*.[75]

In sum, privacy issues are heavily regulated in both the private and public sectors. Businesses should familiarize themselves with the legislation that affects their industry before they develop privacy policies.

---

[70] SC 1993, c 38, s 41.1. Some provinces also regulate the conduct of telemarketers. See, for example, British Columbia *Business Practices and Consumer Protection Act*, Telemarketer Regulation 83/05.

[71] Canadian Radio-television and Telecommunications Commission, "Fact Sheet: New and Revised Unsolicited Telecommunications Rules," https://www.crtc.gc.ca/eng/trules-regest.htm.

[72] *An Act to promote the efficiency and adaptability of the Canadian economy by regulating certain activities that discourage reliance on electronic means of carrying out commercial activities and to amend the Canadian Radio-television and Telecommunications Commission Act, the Competition Act, the Personal Information Protection and Electronic Documents Act, and the Telecommunications Act*, SC 2010, c 23.

[73] See e.g. Ontario *Private Security and Investigative Services Act 2005*, SO 2005, c 34, O Reg 363/07.

[74] See e.g. British Columbia *Business Practices and Consumer Protection Act*, SBC 2004, c 2, Part 6.

[75] RSC 1985, c A-2, s 4.81.

CHECKLIST
Summary of Key Privacy Legislation

Legislation	Public Sector	Private Sector
Federal	• Charter of Rights and Freedoms	• Personal Information Protection and Electronic Documents Act (PIPEDA)
	• Criminal Code	• Telecommunications Act
	• Privacy Act	• Canadian Anti-Spam Legislation
Provincial	• Freedom of Information and Protection of Privacy (Acts)	• Personal Information Protection and Protection of Privacy (Acts) (B.C., Alta.,Man Que.)
	• Municipal Freedom of Information and Protection of Privacy (Sask., Ont.)	• Education (Acts) (Alta., Man., Sask., and Ont.)
	• Education (Acts)	
	• Health Information Protection (N.B., Alta., Man., Sask., and Ont.)	

CIVIL LIABILITY

Failure to meet privacy obligations can result in civil liability through contract, tort, or statute. Outsourcing contracts usually include security obligations and confidentiality terms. In addition, employment contracts now typically include confidentiality agreements. Consumer-protection laws imply privacy obligations into consumer agreements. Damages arising from any failure to comply with these terms may be recovered in a breach-of-contract action.

Tort Liability

Common Law Invasion of Privacy Historically, the right to privacy was protected through property-based torts such as trespass, nuisance, and defamation. For example, the Alberta Supreme Court found that harassing collection calls so invaded the privacy of the debtor that an action in private nuisance was successful.[76] At present, the provinces disagree about whether an independent common law tort of invasion of privacy exists, separate from any property interest or statutory duties. Ontario has two privacy torts: *intrusion on seclusion* addresses improper access, and *public disclosure of embarrassing private facts* focuses on disclosure.[77]

CASE 32.17 Intrusion on Seclusion

A bank employee used her work computer to look up the personal banking records of her common-law spouse's former wife. The former wife sued for invasion of privacy, and the bank employee defended, saying there was no such tort. The Court of Appeal decided it was time to recognize the tort of intrusion on seclusion separate from any legislation.

The tort occurs when the reckless or intentional conduct of the defendant invades the private affairs or concerns of the plaintiff without legal justification, and a reasonable person would find the invasion "highly offensive causing distress, humiliation or anguish."[78] Importantly, proof of economic harm is not required.

---

[76] *Motherwell v Motherwell* (1976), 73 DLR (3d) 62 (Alta CA).

[77] *Jones v Tsige* 2012 ONCA 32; followed by *Hopkins v Kay*, 2014 ONSC 321; considered in Nova Scotia: *Trout Point Lodge Ltd v Handshoe*, 2012 NSSC 245 at paras 55–65; *Condon v Canada*, 2014 FC 250; *Jane Doe 464533 v ND*, 2016 ONSC 541 (CanLII),

[78] *Jones, ibid* at para 71.

Courts in British Columbia and Alberta have taken the opposite position; in 2009, the British Columbia Court of Appeal denied a claim for damages arising from common law tort of invasion of privacy,[79] saying "there is no common law claim for breach of privacy." The claim must be brought under the privacy legislation.[80]

Statutory Cause of Action Some provinces have statutory causes of action. British Columbia, Manitoba, Saskatchewan, and Newfoundland and Labrador each have statutory causes of action for **willful invasion of privacy**.[81] The legislation includes a list of considerations to be taken into account when determining liability, including the nature of the action, the effect of the action, the relationship between the parties, the conduct of the parties, and any apology. In Manitoba, these factors are used to assess damages. Some situations are exempt from liability, including those where there is consent or the invasion is lawfully authorized or part of a lawful right of defence. Some provinces exempt news-gathering activities undertaken in the public interest. Manitoba also has a cause of action specifically designed to deal with non-consensual sharing of intimate images.[82]

willful invasion of privacy a person knew or should have known that her actions would invade the privacy of another

Tort: Negligence

Protecting personal information is part of complying with privacy legislation and involves security measures. Inadequate security invites internal or external unauthorized access to private information. The tort of negligence imposes liability when a duty of care is owed, the standard of care is not met, and damage is caused as a result. PIPEDA imposes a duty on businesses to protect personal information. If security measures are inadequate when compared to the reasonable efforts undertaken by other similar businesses, then liability will follow. This tort imposes liability on the custodian of the information, even when someone else actually accesses or misuses the information. Theft and unauthorized access are expected risks that must be secured against. In some circumstances, even breach of fiduciary duty could impose liability for improper use or disclosure of personal information.

CASE 32.18 Paying for Inadequate Security

TJX, the parent company of Winners and HomeSense stores, experienced a huge personal information security breach affecting approximately 45 million debit and credit cards (including Canadian customers). Using an unauthorized wireless connection, an intruder accessed credit card information, driver's licence data, and provincial identification numbers. The Privacy Commissioner found that PIPEDA was breached because[83]

- TJX collected driver's licence data and provincial identification numbers unnecessarily;
- indefinite retention of the information unreasonably increased the risks to the customer, and
- technical protection measures in place (locks, swipe cards, employee training, and codes of conduct) were below industry standard, including
- "weak" (wired equivalent) encryption protocol and inadequate monitoring, and
- below industry standard Wi-Fi protection.

---

[79] *Mohl v University of British Columbia*, 2009 BCCA 249. See as to Alberta: *Martin v General Teamsters*, 2011 ABQB 412; *Bank of Montreal v Cochrane*, [2010] AJ No 1210.

[80] *Mohl, ibid* at para 13.

[81] *Privacy Act*, RSBC 1996, c 373, s 1; *Privacy Act*, CCSM c P125, s 2; *Privacy Act*, RSS 1978, c P-24, s 2; *Privacy Act*, RSNL 1990, c P-22, s 3.

[82] *Intimate Image Protection Act*, CCSM c I87, s 11.

[83] Office of the Privacy Commissioner of Canada and Office of the Information and Privacy Commissioner of Alberta, Report of an Investigation Into the Security, Collection and Retention of Personal Information: TJX Companies Inc./Winners Merchant International L.P., Sept. 25, 2007, http://www.priv.gc.ca/cf-dc/2007/tjx_rep_070925_e.asp.

> Consumer class actions alleging negligent security were settled by giving each consumer a modest sum, identity theft insurance, and credit report monitoring.[84] Banks also sued for costs associated with issuing new credit cards.
>
> Alternatively, when hackers breached Uber's cybersecurity obtaining personal data of 57 million customers and drivers, Uber did not report the breach to the Privacy Commissioner; instead it paid the hackers' ransom request of $100 000 to delete the data and remain silent about the incident. This cheaper (yet illegal) response is chosen by more and more companies.[85]

Security measures should include physical barriers, such as locks on doors; organization controls, including limiting those entitled to access material; and technological measures, including current encryption techniques.[86]

CRIMINAL LIABILITY

Criminal liability is another way of dealing with privacy violations resulting in identity theft. General *Criminal Code* offences such as fraud (s. 383) and impersonation (s. 402) are effective measures to deal with the perpetrators of identity theft. Unauthorized intruders may be charged with unauthorized use of a computer (s. 342.1), theft of telecommunications (s. 326), mischief in relation to data (s. 430(1.1)), or improper transfer of identity documents (s. 56.1).

Sections 402.1 and 402.2 of the *Criminal Code* create specific offences for identity theft and identity fraud. Digital forms of identity information such as images, electronic signatures, and voice prints are included along with personal information such as names, addresses, credit card numbers, social insurance numbers, etc. Use, possession, sale, and transmission of the identity information are among the prohibited activities. Criminal harassment (s. 264) can apply to offensive websites publicizing degrading personal content.[87]

Part VI of the *Criminal Code* deals with invasion of privacy through the offence of willful interception of private communications (s. 184). Private communications may be intercepted with the consent of either party involved or with court authorization. What is considered a private communication is central to the offence, and this involves the concept of reasonable expectation. Most often these provisions are used in consideration of admissibility of criminal evidence and authorization of law-enforcement interception.

CODES OF CONDUCT

The principles underlying the federal *Privacy Act* were drawn from the Organisation for Economic Co-operation and Development guidelines. One motivation for PIPEDA was to meet the standards set by the European Directive on Protection of Data. Although Canada was not legally required to comply, the desire to do business with the European Union encouraged action.

Similar logic applies to voluntary codes of conduct developed by industry associations and international organizations. In order to be respected and competitive within

---

[84] Robert Westervelt, "TJX Should Have Had Stronger Wi-Fi Encryption, Say Canadian Officials," SearchSecurity.com, Sept. 25, 2007, http://searchsecurity.techtarget.com/news/1273889/TJX-should-have-had-stronger-Wi-Fi-encryption-say-Canadian-officials.

[85] Peter Holley, "Uber Paid Off Its Hackers and They're Not Alone" *The Washington Post*, Nov. 23, 2017, https://www.pressreader.com/usa/the-washington-post/20171123/281809989203451.

[86] Scassa et al, *supra* note 5 at para 86.

[87] *R v Sim*, 2017 ONCA 856.

their industries, businesses comply with standards that may be more rigorous than those required by law. The Canadian Association of Internet Providers has a privacy code developed around the Canadian Standards Association's model code. The Canadian Bankers Association Privacy Code governs more than 50 domestic and foreign banks operating in Canada. The Insurance Bureau of Canada has a model personal information code available for use by its 120 member companies. The Canadian Marketing Association requires members to follow its code of seven privacy principles.[88]

Some professional associations govern the privacy practices of their members through professional codes of conduct or ethics. Violations trigger investigation and possible discipline by the self-regulating body. For example, the Health Information Privacy Code of the Canadian Medical Association covers most of the physicians in Canada.

Strategies to Manage the Legal Risks

Privacy is a complicated legal area involving provincial and federal legislation, voluntary codes of conduct, and potential civil or criminal liability. In order to develop effective and legally compliant privacy policies, a business should

- identify a person responsible for privacy within the organization;
- become familiar with the privacy legislation, industry standards, and codes of conduct applicable to its activities;
- complete an audit of the company's activities to determine
  - what personal information is collected, used, disclosed, and retained and for what purposes,
  - what privacy risks exist, and
  - what security measures and policies are currently in place;
- assess each type of information, practice, and risk based on
  - degree of sensitivity,
  - relevance to purpose,
  - invasiveness, and
  - seriousness of potential damage;
- develop and implement privacy policies and codes of conduct that comply with the legislation, meet or exceed industry standards, and reduce the likelihood of breach;
- develop a response protocol for privacy breaches that includes incident reporting, immediate containment of the breach, preservation of evidence, and notification of the affected individuals, police, or privacy commissioner (where relevant);
- educate and train employees; and
- communicate policies to relevant stakeholders, including customers, suppliers, and the public.

Finally, regular review and updating of policies and procedures is vital in our ever-changing technological environment.

---

[88] The codes referred to in this section are available at Industry Canada website (Office of Consumer Affairs) or through the individual association websites.

QUESTIONS FOR REVIEW

1. What are the three key components of modern privacy?
2. What is the constitutional basis for declaring the right to privacy a human right?
3. What is the standard of protection that the *Charter* gives to privacy?
4. What federal legislation protects privacy in the public sector, and how is compliance monitored?
5. What federal legislation protects personal information held in the private sector, and what does this statute require businesses to do?
6. What test does a court apply to determine if a privacy-invasive activity is reasonable?
7. Does a common law tort of invasion of privacy exist in Canada?
8. How does inadequate security expose business to civil and possibly criminal liability?
9. What steps should be followed by a business considering outsourcing data processing to an American company?
10. How does the requirement of "consent" for collection, use, and disclosure of personal information differ in the public and private sectors?
11. What protection is available for employee personal information?

CASES AND PROBLEMS

1. Continuing Scenario

    Ashley's restaurant always has a line-up of walk-in customers on Fridays and Saturdays. Approximately 50 percent of the tables are reserved. To discourage "no-shows" and maximize profit, Ashley has a policy that requires the hostess to obtain a credit card number (plus expiry date) and a phone number with each reservation. This information is entered into the online reservation calendar beside the time slot. If the party does not appear, a $50 "no-show" charge is applied to their credit card.

    Bill is standing beside the hostess station waiting for a table when Erin calls to make a reservation. The hostess opens the reservation system on the computer and enters the required information. Bill watches as the name, phone number, and credit card details are displayed on the screen. A few hours later Erin's credit card is declined when she tries to buy gas because Bill fraudulently charged approximately $14 000 of merchandise to her account between the time she made the reservation and the time she bought gas. Discuss any potential liability for Ashley's restaurant.

2. KDP Limited operates a pool-servicing business in Vancouver with eight service vans on the road. Each van has two employees. It seems that fewer and fewer service calls are being completed each day, and the manager is concerned about productivity. The employees say it is the increased traffic in the city; it just takes longer to get to and from each call. It also seems that gas expenses are rising. The cost of gas is high, and the vans are on average eight years old. The manager wonders whether more fuel-efficient vehicles should be leased.

    Before making such a big investment, the manager decides to collect work-productivity information. He wonders if the vans are making unauthorized stops or not taking the most efficient routes to service calls. GPS units are installed in each van to track the start and stop times, speed, locations, routes taken, and mileage. The units cannot be turned off by the driver.

    After secretly tracking each van for one week, it is discovered that Jim and Jeff, the employees operating van 3, are spending each afternoon at Jim's parents' backyard pool. They are dismissed. Jeff files a complaint with the Privacy Commissioner.

What should the Privacy Commissioner consider when investigating this complaint? Would your answer be different if the business were located in Toronto?

3. Primtel Ltd., a wireless telephone company, produced a telephone directory that included all the telephone numbers of its subscribers except numbers that were "unlisted." The directory was initially available to only other subscribers. When Primtel decided make the directory public on the company's website, it advised customers with an attachment to their monthly bill. They advised those customers not wishing to appear in the directory to contact the company and arrange for "unlisted" status. Primtel charged an additional $2 per month for unlisted service.

   Mary declined the unlisted option when the directory was subscribers only, but this was long before it was made public. She did not notice the bill attachment. After receiving several annoying phone calls from a former boyfriend, she discovered that her phone number was available online. She complained to the Privacy Commissioner.

   What are the relevant rules relating to consent, and how should the Privacy Commissioner decide this case?

4. Ticketmarketer is a company that sells tickets online for concerts, plays, and sporting events. Payment is made by credit card, but purchasers are asked to provide their home address, phone number, and email. The company uses this information for verification of identity when tickets are picked up at the venue.

   Joan is a marketing manager at Ticketmarketer and has started tracking what type of event each customer attends. She then uses the information for promotional purposes: Once repeat customers' preferences are identified, they receive advance notification of similar events by email.

   Is there any privacy concern about this practice? If so, how should Joan revise the plan to become privacy compliant?

Glossary

Aboriginal peoples Canadian Indian, Inuit, and Métis peoples

absolute privilege complete immunity from liability for defamation

abuse of dominant position taking an unfair advantage of possessing a monopoly or dominant position in the marketplace

acceleration clause upon default in a payment the entire principal sum accrued interest comes due immediately

acceleration clause a provision whereby the full outstanding amount of a debt becomes immediately payable if the debtor defaults in making any installment payment

acceptance any conduct by the buyer in relation to the goods that amounts to recognition of an existing contract of sale

acceptor the drawee who consents to the bill of exchange by signing it together with the word "accepted" and the date

accommodation bill bill of exchange that contains an anomalous endorsement

accord and satisfaction a compromise between contracting parties to substitute a new contractual obligation and release a party from the existing one

act of bankruptcy a prescribed act of a debtor that must be proved before the debtor may be declared bankrupt

act of God the raging of the natural elements

action lawsuit

action for impeachment an action challenging the validity of a patent

actual authority the authority given expressly or impliedly to the agent by the principal

additional rent a tenant's proportionate share of maintenance costs, utilities, and taxes

administrative law law about actions and operations of government administrators and administrative tribunals

administrator the personal representative of a person who dies intestate

admissible evidence evidence that is acceptable to the court

adjudicate hear parties and deliver a decision with reasons

adverse possession the exclusive possession of land by someone who openly uses it like an owner and ignores the claims of other persons, including the owner

advocate a barrister in Quebec

after-acquired property property acquired by the debtor after the debt has been incurred

age of majority the age at which a person is recognized as an adult according to the law of his or her province

agency agreement the agreement between principal and agent whereby the agent undertakes to act on behalf of the principal

agent a person acting for another person in contractual relations with third parties

agreements in restraint agreements that restrict competition, also known as non-competition agreements, non-solicitation agreements, or restrictive covenants when they are included in a larger contract

agreement to sell a contract of sale in which the transfer of ownership in the goods is deferred to some future time

alternative dispute resolution the use of private procedures such as arbitration and mediation to resolve disputes

amortization period length of time it should take to repay an entire debt with the specified payment schedule

annual general meeting the general meeting of shareholders that is required by law to be held each year to transact certain specified business

annual report the report on the business and affairs of the corporation, which the directors are required to present at the annual general meeting

anomalous endorsement an endorsement that is added as a guarantee to make it easier for the drawer to obtain credit on the bill

anti-dumping duties and countervailing duties special duties imposed on imported products to counter the advantage obtained from dumping or export subsidies

anticipatory breach an express repudiation that occurs before the time agreed for performance

apparent authority the authority that a third party is entitled to assume the agent possesses

appearance notice of an intention to defend an action

appellant the party who petitions for an appeal

appraisal remedy the right to have one's shares bought by the corporation at a fair price

appropriated designated as the subject matter of the contract

arbitration a form of ADR where a dispute is referred to an arbitrator who adjudicates the matter, and the parties agree to be bound by the arbitrator's decision, although there may be a right to appeal to the courts

arbitration agreements contracts that require all disputes to be resolved in arbitration, not in the court

arbitration clause a term in a commercial contract designating arbitration as the process for resolution of any disputes arising between the parties

arbitration procedure the procedure in a rights dispute that binds the parties to accept the interpretation of the collective agreement by an arbitrator

arm's length a transaction between persons who are not related or associated in any way

articles of incorporation founding corporate document, often referred to as the charter or constitution of the corporation

assault the threat of violence to a person

assign transfer to another person outside the contract

assignee a third party to whom rights under a contract have been assigned

assignment the transfer by a party of its unperformed rights under a contract to a third party

assignment into bankruptcy a voluntary declaration of bankruptcy by the debtor

assignment of book debts security interest in the debtor's accounts receivable

assignor a party that assigns its rights under a contract to a third party

associated corporations corporations that are related either (a) vertically, as where one corporation controls the other (parent–subsidiary), or (b) horizontally, as where both corporations are controlled by the same person (affiliates)

assume jurisdiction hear the action; allow the lawsuit to proceed in the courts of that jurisdiction

assumption agreement a contract between the mortgagee and the new purchaser in which the new purchaser agrees to comply with all the requirements in the original mortgage

assumption of the mortgage a subsequent purchaser takes over the responsibility of paying off the vendor's existing mortgage

attachment the moment in time when a debtor's property becomes subject to a security interest

attorney a lawyer in the United States, encompassing the roles of both barrister and solicitor

audit committee a group of directors responsible for overseeing the corporate audit and the preparation of financial statements; the committee has wider responsibilities in a distributing corporation

authorized capital the maximum number (or value) of shares that a corporation is permitted by its charter to issue

bailee party accepting possession of goods from a bailor

bailment possession of personal property without ownership

bailments for value contractual bailment

bailor owner or transferor of the goods

bait-and-switch advertising advertising a product at a bargain price but not supplying it in reasonable quantities

balance of probabilities more likely than not

balance of trade offset of value of exports against value of imports

bankrupt a person who has made a voluntary assignment in bankruptcy or against whom a bankruptcy order has been made

bankruptcy order a court order made in proceedings instituted by creditors, whereby a debtor is declared bankrupt

bargain each party pays a price for the promise of the other

bargaining agent a union that has the exclusive right to bargain with the employer on behalf of the bargaining unit

bargaining unit a specified group of employees eligible to join the union

barrister a lawyer in England who accepts cases from solicitors and presents them in court and also acts as consultant in complex legal issues

basic law a constitution that lists the founding legal principles accepted by the citizens of a country and that they regard as legitimate and binding

battery unlawful physical contact with a person

bearer form a negotiable instrument that does not name a specific payee

beneficial contracts of service contracts of employment or apprenticeship found to be for a minor's benefit

beneficial owner a person who, although not the legal owner, may compel the trustee to provide benefits to him

beneficiary a person who is entitled to the benefits of a trust or the person entitled to receive insurance monies

bid-rigging agreeing not to submit a bid or agreeing in advance what bids will be submitted in response to a call for bids or tenders

bilateral contract a contract where offeror and offeree trade promises and both are bound to perform later

bilateral investment protection treaty a treaty entered into between two countries, whereby each country undertakes to protect investors from the other country and to give them certain rights

bill of exchange a written order by one party to another party to pay a specified sum of money to a named party or to the bearer of the document

bill of lading a document signed by a carrier acknowledging that specified goods have been received by it for shipment

biometrics technological analysis of physical characteristics, such as fingerprints

board of directors the governing body of a corporation, responsible for the management of its business and affairs

bond a document evidencing a debt owed by a corporation

branch a business carried on by the owner in its own name at a location distinct from its head office

breach of contract a cause of action where a party to the contract claims that the other party has not fulfilled its promises

browse-wrap agreements provide a link to additional terms and conditions but do not require a buyer to open them before accepting the web-wrap agreement

builders' lien an interest that builders and others involved in construction work may have in a building as security for money owed to them for work done (also known as a mechanics' lien or a construction lien)

building-scheme covenant a restrictive covenant that regulates land use over an entire neighbourhood or shopping centre

burden the requirement that, unless a party can establish facts and law to prove its case, it will lose

burden of proof the responsibility to provide evidence

business judgment rule courts will defer to the business decisions of directors and officers provided they are arrived at using an appropriate degree of prudence and diligence

bylaws the internal working rules of a corporation

calculation period stages at which accrued interest is added to principal

caveat emptor let the buyer beware

canon law law created by the Church, which had its own jurisdiction and courts in matters pertaining to itself, family law, and wills

capital adequacy sufficient assets as compared to liabilities

case law a collection of individual cases decided by the courts that develop and shape legal principles

causation connection between the injury and the breach of the standard of care

cause of action an event or set of events that gives rise to legal liability

caveat emptor let the buyer beware

certificate of incorporation a certificate that a corporation has come into existence

certificate of title summary of registered interests in a property, showing the owner and any mortgages, easements, or other interests held by others, which may be relied upon by the public

certification an acknowledgment by an administrative tribunal that a particular union commands sufficient membership to justify its role as exclusive bargaining agent for the employees

certification an undertaking by the bank to pay the amount of the cheque to its holder when later presented for payment

certification mark a special type of trademark used to identify goods or services that conform to a particular standard

chain of title the series of grants over the title search period that can be traced to the current owner (vendor)

charge a lien or encumbrance on land

chargee mortgagee

chargor mortgagor

chattel moveable personal property or goods; not land

chattel mortgage a mortgage of personal property

cheque a bill of exchange drawn against a bank and payable on demand

cheque truncation the physical movement of cheques is replaced by the electronic transfer of digital information

choses in action rights to intangible property such as patents, stocks, and contracts that may be enforced in the courts

choses in action rights to intangible property such as unperformed contracts

choses in possession rights to tangible property that may be possessed physically

circumstantial evidence principle an initial case of negligence may be established by drawing reasonable inferences from the circumstances surrounding the product manufacture and failure

civil law the system of law involving a comprehensive legislated code, derived from Roman law that developed in continental Europe and greatly influenced by the Code Napoléon of 1804

civil liability responsibility arising from a breach of a private law, enforced through a lawsuit initiated by the injured victim

claim a statement of the features claimed to be new and in respect of which the applicant claims an exclusive right

class action an action in which an individual represents a group of possible plaintiffs, and the judgment decides the matter for all members of the class

class rights special rights attached to a particular class of shares

click-wrap agreements require the buyer to open the terms page before clicking acceptance of them

closed mortgage a mortgage that does not permit early repayment of the debt without a substantial penalty

cloud computing a server-focused computing system in which all processing and storage is done at the server level, and users access the system over the internet from anywhere through a variety of devices

code of conduct a common standard of behaviour that may take the form of a values statement or a prescribed set of rules often used by a professional organization setting out the duties and appropriate standards of behaviour to be observed by its members

codified existing common law rules collected and put in statute form

codify summarize in a statute the existing common law rules governing a particular area of activity

coercion improperly forced payment under protest

collateral agreement a separate agreement between the parties made at the same time as, but not included in, the written document

collateral security an interest in property of a debtor that gives a creditor the right to seize and sell it in the event of non-payment of the debt

collection arrangement an arrangement whereby the seller employs the services of its bank to collect payment by depositing the documents with the bank and receiving credit for the price

collective bargaining establishing conditions of employment through negotiation between an employer and the collective bargaining agent for its employees

collective rights society a society to which authors of musical and dramatic works assign performing and communication rights and that grants licences and collects fees

commercial activity any general or particular activity performed or stated in the objectives of an organization, that has a commercial aspect

commercial tenancies a lease of premises used for a business or non-residential purpose

commission agent one who sells on behalf of a principal to third parties and receives compensation through commissions

common area expense unit owner's proportionate share of the costs of operating the corporation and maintaining the common elements

common carrier a business that holds itself out to the public as a transporter of goods for reward

common elements structures and areas external to a condominium unit, including communal facilities

common law the case-based system of law originating in England and covering most of the English-speaking world—based on the recorded reasons given by courts for their decisions

common law precedents developed over time from the decisions of many cases

common mistake a situation in which both parties believe the same misunderstanding or mistake about the contract

common share a share carrying no preferential right

comparative value equal pay for work of equal value

compensation committee committee responsible for setting director and officer pay

compliance officer an employee who monitors regulatory and legislative requirements applicable to the business and ensures that the business complies

comprehensive land claims claims involving land not covered by treaty nor part of a reserve

compromise and arrangement an agreement made by a debtor corporation with its creditors whereby arrangements are made for repayment of debts without liquidating the corporation

compulsory licence a licence granted to a person to work a patent without the consent of the owner of the patent

conciliation procedure bargaining with the help of a conciliation officer or board

concurrent powers overlapping powers of both levels of government to regulate the same activities

condominium corporation a corporation—whose members are the condominium owners—that is responsible for managing the property as a whole

condominium unit a unit in a multiple-unit development that is owned in fee simple without surface land

condition a major or essential term of the contract, the breach of which may relieve the injured party from further performance

condition precedent any set of circumstances or events that the parties stipulate must be satisfied or must happen before their contract takes effect

condition precedent a future act or event that must happen before the obligation to perform the promises arises

condition subsequent a future event that brings a promisor's liability to an end if it happens

conditions essential terms of a contract

conflict of interest a duty is owed to a client whose interests conflict with the interests of the professional, another client, or another person to whom a duty is owed

conflict of laws or private international law the principles of law that apply to determine which country's laws govern a dispute involving private parties

conspiracies agreements or arrangements between competitors to lessen competition

consent approval of the person to whom the collected information relates

consensual surveillance the employee is aware of and consents to the surveillance

consequential damages secondary losses incurred by the non-breaching party that were foreseeable at the time of contracting

consideration the price for which the promise of the other is bought

consignment the transfer of only possession of goods from one business to another for the purpose of offering for sale

contra proferentem preference for the interpretation of a term that favours the non-drafting party

constructive dismissal a substantial change to an employee's job that amounts to termination of the existing employment

constructive trust a trust relationship imposed by the court to prevent a party from being unjustly enriched by keeping property that should benefit another

construing interpreting

consumer an individual (not an organization) purchasing a product or service for personal, family, household, non-business purposes

consumer debtor an individual who is insolvent but whose aggregate debts do not exceed $250 000

consumers individuals who purchase goods and services from a business for their personal use and enjoyment

contempt of court a finding by a court that a person has willfully refused to obey a court order and therefore will be punished

contingency fee a fee paid for a lawyer's services only if the client is successful; there is no charge if the client is unsuccessful

contra proferentem a rule of contract interpretation that prefers the interpretation of a clause that is least favourable to the party that drafted the clause

contract a set of promises that the law will enforce

contractual joint venture a joint venture effected by agreement without the creation of any separate legal entity

contributory negligence a partial defence to a negligence action when the plaintiff's or another defendant's conduct also contributed to the injury

cooling-off period a time during which a consumer may cancel (rescind) a contract without any reason; length of the time period is set in provincial legislation

cooling-off period a time during which the employer cannot declare a lockout nor can the union begin a strike

corporate governance the rules governing the organization and management of the business and affairs of a corporation in order to meet its internal objectives and external responsibilities

corporate social responsibility a concept that suggests business decision makers consider ethical issues—including the interests of customers, employees, creditors, the public, and other stakeholders—in addition to legal and financial concerns

corporation a legal person formed by incorporation according to a prescribed legal procedure

costs funds ordered by the court to be paid a party toward the expenses of the other party

counsel lawyer representing a plaintiff or defendant

counterclaim a claim by the defendant arising from the same facts as the original action by the plaintiff to be tried along with that action

countertrade a form of barter, under which a seller agrees to accept payment in goods produced or procured by the buyer

courts of chancery a system of courts under the king's chancellor and vice-chancellors developed from the hearing of petitions to the king—courts of equity

covenant a term, clause, or promise contained in a contract or lease

coverage maximum amount payable for an insured risk

covert surveillance the employee is unaware of surveillance and has not consented to it

criminal liability responsibility arising from commission of an offence against the government or society as a whole

criminal offences most serious offences that require proof of mental intent with penalties imposed by the courts

covenant of quiet enjoyment a landlord's promise that nothing will interfere or disturb the tenant's possession and use of the premises

covenantor one who makes a covenant

Crown grant the first transfer of an estate in time from the government to a new owner

cumulative right the right of a preferred shareholder to be paid arrears from previous years before any dividend is paid on the common shares

cumulative voting a method of electing directors by a form of proportional representation

current assets cash or cash equivalent assets such as negotiable instruments, demand deposits, and accounts receivable

cybersquatting the registration of a domain name containing the trademark of another person, with the intention of selling the domain name to the owner of the mark

damages a sum of money awarded as compensation for loss or injury

data shadows electronic records of the internet activity of a user

debenture an alternative term to describe a corporate bond

debtor-in-possession financing court-sanctioned secured loans advanced during reorganization and given priority over pre-existing secured creditors

deceit an intentional tort imposing liability when damage is caused by a false statement made with the intention of misleading another person

declaration of trust an agreement that establishes a trust and designates the trustees

deductible clause a clause requiring the insured to bear the loss up to a stated amount

deed a document under seal, which today is usually a small, red, gummed wafer

deed of conveyance a document under seal that transfers an interest in land from the owner to another party

defamation making an untrue statement that causes injury to the reputation of another person

delivery physically handing over a negotiable instrument to the next holder

demand draft a bill of exchange payable immediately upon presentation without any days of grace

dependent agent an agent who acts exclusively, or mostly, for a single principal

dependent contractor contractors with a level of exclusivity and permanence that makes them economically dependent on one client

demotion transferring an employee to a job with less responsibility and/or income potential

deposit a sum of money paid by the buyer to the seller, to be forfeited if the buyer does not perform her part of the contract

derivative action proceedings brought by one or more shareholders in the name of the corporation in respect of a wrong done to the corporation

detrimental reliance the worsening of one's situation after acting upon false information

devices medical apparatus and test kits such as pregnancy tests

digital rights management technology (DRMT) a system collecting data about the licensing, payment, use, and authenticity of a work

digital rights management system (DRMS) a system collecting data about the licensing, payment for, and authenticity of a work

direct regulation controls the characteristics of the product or service, such as pricing, profit margin, production level

direct sales contract a contract formed at a place other than the business's place of business

directors' circular a document required to be issued to shareholders by the board of directors when a takeover of a widely held corporation is proposed

disbarred expelled from the law society and deprived of the privilege of practising law

discharge a court order whereby a person who has been declared bankrupt ceases to have the status of a bankrupt person

discharge a contract cancel or end the obligations of a contract; make an agreement or contract inoperative

discharge statement mortgagee's calculation payment necessary to obtain a discharge of the mortgage

disclaimer an express statement to the effect that the person making it takes no responsibility for its accuracy

disclosed surveillance the employee is given advance notice of surveillance but does not consent to it

disclosure (of personal information) transfer of data to third parties outside the organization

discriminatory pricing where a seller makes a practice of discriminating between purchasers with respect to the price charged for goods or services

dishonor the failure by the party primarily liable to pay the instrument according to its terms

dismissal for cause dismissal without notice or further obligation by the employer when the employee's conduct amounts to breach of contract

distinguish identify a factual difference that renders a precedent inapplicable to the case before the court

distinguishing guise the configuration of goods or their containers, or a distinctive mode of wrapping or packaging

distress the right of the landlord to seize assets of the tenant found on the premises and sell them to realize arrears of rent

distributing corporation a corporation that issues its securities to the public; also referred to as an issuing corporation, reporting issuer, publicly traded corporation, or public corporation

dividend a distribution to shareholders of a share of the profits of the corporation

doctrine of frustration the law excuses a party from performance when unforeseeable circumstances beyond the control of the parties make performance impossible, pointless, or radically different from that contemplated by the parties

document under seal a covenant recorded in a document containing a wax seal, showing that the covenantor adopted the document as his act and deed

documents of record documents that a corporation is required to keep and make available to shareholders

domain name the registered internet address of a website

domestic bank a bank incorporated in Canada in compliance with the *Bank Act*; publicly owned and traded on a Canadian stock exchange

dominant tenement the piece of land that benefits from an easement

double aspects laws that have an aspect that falls within provincial power and another aspect that falls under federal power

down payment a sum of money paid by the buyer as an initial part of the purchase price

dower a widow's right to a life interest in one-third of the real property held by her husband in fee simple before his death

drawee the party who is required to make payment on the bill of exchange

drawer the party who draws up the bill of exchange

drawing party the contracting party that prepared the agreement or the particular clause

dual offence an offence under the *Competition Act* that may be either a criminal or a regulatory offence, depending upon the seriousness of the conduct

due diligence defence establishing that an acceptable standard of care and skill was exercised by a director or officer

dumping selling products abroad at prices below those charged on domestic sales

duress actual or threatened violence or imprisonment as a means of coercing a party to enter into a contract

duty of care a relationship so close that one could reasonably foresee causing harm to the other

duty to account the duty of a person who commits a breach of trust to hand over any profits derived from the breach

duty to warn manufacturer's responsibility to make users aware of the risks associated with the use or misuse of the product

earnest a token sum or article given to seal a bargain—now a rare practice

easement a right enjoyed by one landowner over the land of another for a special purpose but not for occupation of the land

ecash an online payment system that enables the anonymous transfer of money over the internet

ediscovery examination of electronic records and documents relevant to the dispute

electronic commerce (ecommerce) the use of computer networks to facilitate commercial activities, including the production, distribution, sale, and delivery of goods and services

electronic retailing (etailing) the supply of tangible or electronic goods or services over the internet; the supply of tangible goods involves a conventional mode of delivery, and electronic goods are downloaded directly to the customer's computer

electronic transfer of funds payment made through electronic (intangible) media such as telephone or internet rather than by cash or cheque; payment may take the form of credit card charges, debit of bank accounts, or even ecash, often through the business's website

endorse sign one's name on a negotiable instrument

endorsement written evidence of a change in the terms of a policy

endorsement the named payee's signature on a negotiable instrument transferring the right to payment to the new holder

endorsement in blank payee signs name only

entirety clause a term in a contract stating that the whole agreement is contained in the written documents, and there are no other terms, conditions, representations, or warranties

enurement clause a clause in a contract that extends the rights and benefits to those inheriting from a party, succeeding the party, or taking an assignment from a party

estates in time the right to exclusive possession of the land for a period of time

estopped prevented

equitable assignment an assignment other than a statutory assignment

equitable remedies new remedies created by the courts of equity to address situations where money damages did not solve the problem

equitable relief a discretionary remedy first developed by the courts of equity to undo an injustice

equity rules developed by the courts of equity as exceptions to existing rules of common law

equity joint venture a corporation formed, and jointly owned, by the parties to a joint venture for the purpose of carrying on the venture

equity of redemption the right of the mortgagor to redeem mortgaged land on payment of the debt in full

examination for discovery process allowing either party to examine the other in order to narrow the issues

exchange controls restrictions on the conversion or export of currency

exclusive dealing when a supplier of goods makes it a condition that the buyer should deal only or primarily in the supplier's products

exclusive use clause a landlord's promise not to rent adjoining premises to any other entity in the same or competing business as the tenant

execution order an order that gives the sheriff authority to levy execution

executor the personal representative of a deceased person named in his or her will

executor or administrator legal representative of the estate of a dead person

exemplary damages money over and above losses to punish bad behaviour

export subsidy the granting by governments of financial assistance to promote exports

exempt property that is not subject to seizure by the trustee as a result of an exception in a federal or provincial statute

exemption clause a clause in a contract that exempts or limits the liability of a party or third parties

exercise an option accept the offer contained in an option

expectation damages an amount awarded for breach of contract, based on expected benefits or profits

expert opinions opinions given by a person who purports to have specialized knowledge of a subject

export houses or freight forwarders specialist firms that make the arrangements for shipment, insurance, and financing in export sales

express repudiation one of the contracting parties communicates to the other that it does not intend to perform as promised

expropriation a private owner is forced by stature to transfer its land to a government body that needs it

expropriation a state's right to assume ownership of private property within its geographic borders

extinguish the title end the title of the owner and the owner's right to regain possession

fair comment publication of a researched and reasonably held opinion that is honestly believed to be true

false arrest causing a person to be arrested without reasonable cause

false imprisonment unlawfully restraining or confining another person

fault unjustifiable injurious conduct that intentionally or carelessly disregards the interests of others

federal paramountcy the principle that a federal law prevails over a conflicting provincial law

federal paramountcy rule when valid federal and provincial laws conflict with each other, the federal law overrides the provincial one

fee simple the interest in land closest to complete ownership

feudal law a system of land ownership rooted in sovereign ownership: land was handed down to lords who gave possession of parcels of land to lesser "royals" in exchange for military service and loyalty

fiduciary duty a duty imposed on a person who stands in a special relation of trust and loyalty to another

finance lease an arrangement where a third person provides credit financing, becomes the owner of the property, and leases it to the lessee

financial statements annual accounts that are required to be presented to the shareholders at the annual general meeting

financing statement the document summarizing the details of a security interest that is filed in order to protect that interest

FINTRAC Financial Transactions and Report Analysis Centre of Canada

firm collective reference to the partners in a partnership

First Nation Canadian Indigenous people who are not Métis or Inuit

fixed stored in a permanent or lasting form

fixed term a contract of employment with defined start and end dates

fixtures all things permanently attached to land are deemed part of the land

floating charge a form of mortgage on all the assets of a corporation other than those already specifically charged

foreclosure an order by a court ending the mortgagor's right to redeem within a fixed time

foreign bank a bank incorporated in a country other than Canada according to that country's banking laws

foreign exchange risk management methods of reducing the risk involved in currency fluctuations

foreign investment conducting operations in a foreign market

foreign presence placing representatives of a business in foreign markets

foreign trade the buying and selling of goods and services between parties from different countries

forfeiture to lose or give back to the landlord the balance of the term of a lease

format shifting transferring purchased material, such as music, from one of the owner's devices to another

foreseeability predictability

foreseeability reasonableness of the plaintiff's injury

forum non conveniens refusing to hear a proceeding because another jurisdiction is more appropriate or more closely connected to the matter

franchise agreement an agreement under which a franchisor grants to the franchisee a right to market the franchisor's products

fraudulent misrepresentation deceit

fraudulent preference the payment of money or transfer of property to a creditor with a view to giving that creditor preference over other creditors

fraudulent transfer a transfer of property by a debtor with the intention of putting that property out of the reach of creditors

free trade areas groups of countries within which customs duties are eliminated

freehold estate an interest in land that is indeterminate in time

fungible goods goods that may be replaced with different but identical goods

future goods goods that have not yet been produced

garnishee order an order requiring the debtor's employer to retain a portion of the debtor's wages each payday and surrender the sum to the creditor

general creditor a creditor that has no security other than the debtor's promise to pay

general damages money to compensate for injuries that cannot be precisely expressed in monetary terms

general meeting of shareholders a formal meeting of shareholders at which they are able to vote on matters concerning the corporation

general partner a partner in a limited partnership whose liability is not limited

generic word or feature that is commonly used and not distinguishing

generic words in wide public use that cannot be trademarked alone

goods personal property, excluding both money and choses in action

goodwill positive association that attracts customers toward the owner's wares or services rather than those of its competitor

government institutions government departments and agencies listed in Schedule 1 of the *Privacy Act*

gratuitous bailment a bailment where one party provides no consideration, or where there is no intention to create a contractual relationship

gratuitous promise a promise made without bargaining for or accepting anything in return

grey marketing acquiring authentic goods through legal channels, then importing or exporting them for sale in another country without the trademark owner's permission

grievances disputes arising under the collective agreement

guarantee a promise to perform the obligation of another person if that person defaults

guarantor one who agrees to pay the debts of another person if that person defaults

guardian a person appointed to manage the affairs of a minor in the place of his or her parents

hashtags topical phrases used to link similar content in social media channels

hearsay words attributed by a witness to a person who is not before the court

hire-purchase an agreement to lease an item of property with an option for the lessee to purchase it at the end of the stipulated term

holdback an amount that the owner who contracts for construction work may withhold from payments made to the principal contractor to protect against claims from subcontractors and suppliers

holder a party who acquires a negotiable instrument from the transferor

holder in due course a party who is not the original payee that acquires the cheque from that payee or a subsequent holder and is unaware of any defects

holding out representing by words or conduct that a person is one's agent or has a particular authority

human rights recognized entitlements encompassing traditional freedoms associated with civil liberty and basic human necessities

illegal offends the public good or violates a statute

implied term a term not expressly included by the parties in their agreement but which, as reasonable people, they would have included had they thought about it

implied term as to description it is implied that goods sold by description will conform to the description

implied term as to title it is implied that the seller has a right to sell the goods

implied term of fitness it is implied that the goods are of a type that is suitable for the purpose for which they are bought

implied term of merchantable quality it is implied that the goods are in reasonable condition and free from defects that would make them unsuitable for use

implied term that goods correspond with sample the actual goods supplied will correspond to that sample in type and quality

immediate parties the holder of an instrument and the party alleged to be liable on it who have had direct dealings with each other

Incoterms a set of standard contractual terms adopted by the International Chamber of Commerce

indefinite hiring a contract of employment for an undetermined length of time, with no expectation of termination or described end date

indemnity a promise by a third party to be primarily liable to pay the debt

indemnity or compensation a money award given as a supplement to rescission for loss sustained in performing a contract

independent agent an agent who carries on an independent business and acts for a number of principals

independent contractor contractors that is not exclusive, permanent, and economically dependent on one client

identification endorsement a third party confirms the identity of the endorser

indeterminate liability inability to determine the size, time, or possible plaintiffs so that the magnitude of liability cannot be reasonably predicted

Indian bands groups of Indian persons for whose benefit land or money are held by the Crown as described in the *Indian Act*

Indigenous people international global term referring to a variety of Aboriginal groups

individual natural person, not a corporation

indoor management rule the principle that a person dealing with a corporation is entitled to assume that its internal procedural rules have been followed unless it is apparent that such is not the case

inducing breach of contract intentionally causing one party to breach her contract with another

infringement violation of the rights of the owner of the intellectual property

inherent vice a latent defect or dangerous condition of goods

in-house counsel a lawyer who provides legal services to a business as a full-time employee of the business

injunction a court order restraining a person from doing, or continuing to do, a particular act

injurious reliance loss or harm suffered by a promisee who, to his detriment, relied reasonably on a gratuitous promise

innkeeper a person or firm that maintains an establishment offering lodging to any member of the public

insider trading the use of confidential information relating to a corporation in dealing in its securities

inspector a person appointed by the court to investigate the affairs of a corporation

interest some form of right to or in an asset

internet the interconnected logical networks that link computers worldwide

intranet closed systems linking specific users internal to a company or group; commonly used for data exchange

invitee a person permitted by an occupier to enter premises for business purposes

insolvency having liabilities in excess of the realizable value of one's assets or being unable to pay one's debts as they fall due

insolvent unable to pay one's debts as they fall due or liabilities exceed realizable assets

insolvent person a person who is unable to meet (or has ceased to pay) his debts as they become due or whose debts exceed the value of his realizable assets

insurable interest genuine risk of loss that may be suffered from damage to the thing insured

insurance adjuster a person who appraises property losses

insurance agent an agent or employee of an insurance company

insurance broker an independent business that arranges insurance coverage for its clients

insurance policy the document describing the terms of a contract of insurance

interest dispute an employer and the union disagree about the particular terms to be included in the collective agreement

interests less than estates interests in land that do not give the right to exclusive possession

interlocutory injunction a temporary injunction preventing immediate harm from being done before the full trial of the matter

intestate when a person dies without leaving a will

intestate succession government rules that determine who gets the property of someone who dies without a will

invitee a person permitted by an occupier to enter premises for business purposes

inviting tenders seeking offers from suppliers

irregularity on the face something appears unusual on the document itself

issued capital the shares that have been issued by a corporation

issuing commencing the lawsuit by filing a copy of the statement of claim with the court office

job description a description of the responsibilities of a position, including objectives, qualifications, and supervisor

joint liability the situation where each of a number of persons is personally liable for the full amount of a debt

joint tenants concurrent holders, each of whom has a right of survivorship

joint venture a form of business venture between two or more independent enterprises, or a corporation jointly owned by them

judgment creditor a party who has obtained a court judgment for a sum of money

judgment debtor a party who has been ordered by the court to pay a sum of money

judicial review a court's review of the legality of administrative acts and decisions

jurisdiction the province, state, or country whose laws apply to a particular situation

jurisdiction the right of a court to hear and resolve a dispute

jurisdictional dispute two or more unions compete for the right to represent a particular group of employees

keyword bidding paying to have your website revealed in search results of a keyword

labour relations board an administrative tribunal regulating labour relations

land comprises the surface, all that is under the surface, including the minerals and oil, and most everything above and attached to the surface, including buildings and trees

land titles system a system of land registration where the land titles office records outstanding interests in the land and certifies them as being correct

lapse the termination of an offer when the offeree fails to accept it within a specified time, or if no time is specified, then within a reasonable time

latent defect defect not readily apparent to an ordinary purchaser during an ordinary inspection

lease (1) an agreement where the owner of property allows another person to have possession and use of the property for a specific period in return for the payment of rent and (2) the agreement between landlord and tenant creating the leasehold interest

leaseback a financial arrangement enabling a business to buy a building and sell it to a financial institution that, in turn, gives a long-term lease of the property back to the business

leasehold an interest in land for a definite period of time

legal aid a system where the government pays for many legal services provided to low-income litigants

legal audit a review of each area, action, and interaction of the business to identify potential legal liability and legal compliance risks

legal capacity competence to bind oneself legally

legal liability responsibility for the consequences of breaking the law

legal person an entity recognized at law as having its own legal rights, duties, and responsibilities

legal risk business activities, conduct, events, or scenarios that could expose a business to some type of legal liability

legal risk management plan a plan developed by a business that identifies potential legal liability and provides preventive and remedial strategies

legal title an interest in land recognized by the common law

lessee the person who takes possession of the leased property; when applied to land the lessee is a tenant, the person to whom an interest in a leasehold estate is granted

lessor the owner of the leased property; when applied to land, known as a landlord being a grantor

let the loss fall where it lies the court will enforce the contract up to the moment of discharge—obligations due before the frustrating event remain; obligations arising after the frustrating event are discharged

letter of credit a document that the buyer of goods obtains from the bank and uses to pay the seller

letters patent a document incorporating a corporation, issued by the appropriate authority and constituting the "charter" of the corporation

level-of-interactivity test a review of the features of a website to determine if it is active or passive; only active sites will be considered connected to the jurisdiction (also called the *active-versus-passive test*)

levy execution to seize and sell a debtor's chattels or arrange for a sale of his lands

libel written defamation

licence a right to use another's land for the benefit of a person

licensee a visitor (other than an invitee) who enters premises with the consent of the occupier

lien a right of a person in possession of property to retain that property until payment

life estate an estate in land that lasts for the life of one person

life tenant a holder of a life estate

limitation period the time period within which a right of action must be pursued or it is lost forever

limited liability the liability of shareholders is limited to the amount of their capital contributions

limited liability partnership a partnership in which non-negligent partners are not personally liable for losses caused by the negligence of a partner

limited partner a partner in a limited partnership whose liability is limited to the amount of her capital contribution

limited partnership a partnership in which some of the partners limit their liability to the amount of their capital contributions

linking or hyperlinking an electronic connection of one website to another website; links may be automatic or activated by the user, and the new website may replace the original website or open in its own frame or browser window

liquidated damages an amount agreed on to be paid in damages by a party to a contract if it should commit a breach

liquidating dividends payments made from time to time by a trustee in bankruptcy to creditors on account of the full amount due to them

liquidity how quickly and easily an asset is convertible into cash

listing agreement contract between the vendor and his real estate agent creating the obligation to pay commission

major breach a breach of the whole contract or of an essential term so that the purpose of the contract is defeated

maker the party who signs and delivers a promissory note

malicious prosecution causing a person to be prosecuted for a crime without an honest belief that the crime was committed

mandatory injunction an order requiring a person to do a particular act

market allocation divide sales, territories, customers, or markets for the production or supply of the product or service

market restriction where a supplier makes it a condition that the buyer markets the product only within a designated area

material could reasonably be expected to influence or induce the decision of a party to enter into a contract

maturity date the end of the term when debt must be repaid

mediation a form of ADR where a neutral third party who is acceptable to both sides acts as a mediator, assisting the parties to reach a settlement

memorandum of association a document setting out the essential terms of an agreement to form a corporation

mens rea mental intent necessary to commit a criminal offence

mens rea offences offences where the prosecution must establish a "guilty mind" on the part of the defendant

merchant law rules and trade practices developed by merchants in medieval trade guilds and administered by their own courts

merger the amalgamation of two or more businesses into a single business entity

metadata embedded coding in webpages that summarizes information about data

minor breach a breach of a non-essential term of a contract or of an essential term in a minor respect

minor or infant a person who has not attained the age of majority according to the law of his or her province

miscarriage an injury caused by the tort of another person

mitigate duty to act reasonably and quickly to minimize the extent of damage suffered

mitigation action by the injured party to reduce the extent of loss caused by the other party's breach

model laws recommended templates for domestic laws that are developed by advisory organizations such as law reform commissions

money laundering transfer of proceeds of crime to conceal their origin

monitor a person appointed to supervise the reorganization of a debtor corporation under the *Companies' Creditors Arrangement Act*

month-to-month tenancy a periodic tenancy that renews itself monthly

moral cause moral duty of promisor to perform his promise

moral rights the non-transferable rights of an author or creator to prevent a work from being distorted or misused

mortgage a loan contract that gives the lender an interest in the borrower's land as security for a debt

mortgage commitment document in which parties to a mortgage initially agree to borrow and lend

mortgagee a lender who accepts an interest in land as security for a loan

mortgagor a borrower who gives his lender an interest in his land as security for repayment of a debt

most-favoured-nation (MFN) treatment the principle that goods imported from one country should not be treated less favourably than those imported from any other country

mutual mistake a situation in which both parties believe a mistake exists in the contract but their understandings of the mistake are different

national treatment the principle that goods from another country should not be treated less favourably than domestic goods

natural justice procedural fairness or due process

necessaries essential goods and services

negative covenant a promise not to do something

negative option billing a practice of adding services and sending bills without request and relying upon the customer to cancel if they don't wish the service

negligence carelessly causing injury to the person or property of another

negligent misrepresentation an unintentional tort imposing liability when an incorrect statement is made without due care for its accuracy, and injury is caused

negotiable instrument a written contract containing a promise, express or implied, to pay a specific sum of money to a designated person or to "bearer"

negotiability the transfer of payment rights in a negotiable instrument

negotiation the process of assigning a negotiable instrument

new trial a case sent back by the appeal court for retrial by the lower court

no par value shares shares that have no nominal value attached

no-fault insurance a system of compulsory insurance that eliminates fault as a basis for compensation

nominating committee committee responsible for proposing and recruiting new directors

non est factum "it is not my doing"

non-competition agreements agreements that restrict a person's right to carry on a business that competes with that of the other party or to work for a business that competes

non-governmental organizations voluntary, non-profit associations of private entities working to influence policy, raise awareness, and effect change, such as the International Chamber of Commerce

non-public investors investors that are not members of the general public, including accredited investors such as banks, insurance companies, and municipal corporations or friends and family

non-solicitation agreements agreements that prevent a person from contacting the other party's customers, employees, or suppliers with a view to moving their business or employment

non-tariff barriers national rules, other than import duties, that restrict or prevent the importation of goods

notice to quit notice of an intention to bring the tenancy to an end

notary a solicitor in Quebec

notice advance warning that the employment relationship will end

novation the parties to a contract agree to terminate it and substitute a new contract

occupier's liability a negligence tort imposing liability on occupants of land for harm suffered by visitors to the property

OECD Organisation for Economic Co-operation and Development, established in 1961, has 34 member countries, including Canada, and promotes world trade and sustainable economic growth by setting standards for best practice

offences of absolute liability offences where the absence of fault is no defence

offences of strict liability offences where there is a presumption of guilt unless the defendant can show that she took reasonable care

offer a description of a promise one party is willing to make, subject to the agreement of the other party

offeree the person to whom the offer is made

offeror the person making the offer

officers high-ranking management employees of a corporation as defined in the bylaws or appointed by the directors, such as the president, vice-president, controller, chief executive officer, chief financial officer, general counsel, and general manager

official receiver a public official responsible for the supervision of bankruptcy proceedings

open mortgage a mortgage permitting repayment of the debt at any time without notice or bonus

operating lease a lease under which there is no intention to transfer ownership

opportunity cost the lost chance of making a similar contract with a different promisor

oppression remedy a statutory procedure allowing individual shareholders to seek a personal remedy if they have been unfairly treated

opt-out consent data-owner consent is implied from a failure to refuse consent

option a contract to keep an offer open for a specified time in return for a sum of money

order instrument an instrument that names the person to be paid

ordinary resolution a resolution adopted by the general meeting and passed by a simple majority

output restrictions fix, maintain, control, prevent, lessen, or eliminate the production or supply of the product or service

outside counsel self-employed lawyers who work alone, in small partnerships, or in large national firms, and bill the business for services rendered

overholding tenant a tenant who remains on the premises without a new agreement with the landlord after the term of the lease expires

overrule declare an existing precedent no longer binding or effective

paid-up capital the shares that have been issued and fully paid for

par value a nominal value attached to a share at the time of issue

paralegal a non-lawyer who provides some form of legal service to the public

parallel pricing the practice, among competing firms, of adopting similar pricing strategies

parol evidence rule a rule preventing a party to a written contract from later using parol evidence to add to, subtract from, or modify the final written contract

part payment something tendered by the buyer and accepted by the seller after formation of the contract, to be deducted from the price

part performance performance undertaken in reliance on an oral contract relating to an interest in land and accepted by the courts as evidence of the contract without writing

partial discharge a discharge of a definite portion of the mortgaged lands

partial payment endorsement the date and amount of a part payment to be deducted from outstanding balance of the instrument

participating right the right of a preferred shareholder to participate in surplus profits or assets of the corporation in addition to the amount of the preferred dividend or redemption price

partnership the relationship between two or more persons carrying on a business with a view to profit

partnership agreement an agreement between persons to create a partnership and (usually) to set out the terms of the relationship

party and party costs a court order that shifts some of the winning party's costs to the losing side according to a published scale of fees

party autonomy the parties' freedom to determine how their dispute will be resolved

passing-off a common law tort involving the misrepresentation of goods, services, or a business in such a way as to deceive the public into believing that they are the goods, services, or business of some other person

past consideration a gratuitous benefit previously conferred upon a promisor

patent agent a registered agent who pursues applications for patents on behalf of individual inventors

patent defect a defect discoverable by a purchaser during an ordinary inspection

pawnbroker a business that loans money on the security of pawned goods

payee the party named to receive payment on the bill of exchange

payment card networks an electronic payment system used to accept, transmit, or process transactions made by payment card to transfer funds or information among issuer, user, and merchants

payment cards credit or debit or gift cards

payment in lieu of notice payment of the amount of compensation the employee would have earned during the reasonable notice period

penalty clause a term specifying an exorbitant amount for breach of contract, intended to frighten a party into performance

perfected security interest a security interest that has attached and is perfected by possession, control, or registration

perfection the moment in time when a creditor's security interest becomes protected

performance requirements conditions attached by the host country in granting approval to a foreign investment

periodic tenancy a leasehold interest that renews itself automatically on the last day of the term for a further term of the same duration

personal health information information relating to the physical or mental health of an identifiable individual that is used or obtained primarily for the purpose of providing healthcare

personal information recorded and unrecorded information about an identifiable individual, including that supplied by the individual and created by the organization

personal insurance insurance against death, injury, or ill health of an individual

personal privacy the respect of bodily integrity free from unreasonable surveillance, search, and seizure

personal property chattel paper, documents of title, goods, instruments, intangibles, money, and investment property; includes fixtures but does not include building materials that have been affixed to real property

petitions requests to commence bankruptcy proceedings against a defaulting debtor

PHIPA *Personal Health Information Protection Act* (in Alberta and Saskatchewan, simply HIPA)

pith and substance the true character of a law determined by examining its purpose and legal effect on those subject to it

plaintiff the party that commences a private (civil) legal action against another party

pleadings documents filed by each party to an action providing information it intends to prove in court

pledge or pawn a bailment of personal property as security for repayment of a loan where possession passes to the bailee

postdate date a cheque later than the time when it is delivered to the payee

power of attorney a type of agency agreement authorizing the agent to sign documents on behalf of the principal

power of sale a right upon default to sell mortgaged land

predatory pricing where a seller temporarily reduces prices to an unreasonably low level with the aim of driving competitors out of business

pre-emptive right the right of a holder of shares to protect his percentage ownership in the company by buying the same percentage in any new issue of shares

preferred creditors unsecured creditors whose claims are given preference over those of other unsecured creditors

preferred shares shares carrying preferential rights to receive a dividend and/or to be redeemed on the dissolution of the corporation for a fixed price

pre-incorporation contract a purported contract made in the name of a corporation before it comes into existence

premium the price paid by the insured to purchase insurance coverage

prescription the creation of an easement over adjoining land through exercising a right continuously and openly

presents produces the instrument to the drawee bank, promisor, or maker for payment

price fixing fix, maintain, increase, or control the price of a product or service

principal the person on whose behalf the agent acts

principled exception allows third parties to rely upon a contractual exemption clause when the parties to the contract intended to include them and their activities come within the scope of the contract and the exemption clause

priority a first, or prior, right to be repaid out of the debtor's assets

priority of registration priority of interests in real property is determined based on the order of registration in the public system

private companies corporations with a restricted number of shareholders prohibited from issuing their shares to the general public

privacy has three key dimensions: personal privacy, territorial or spatial privacy, and privacy of personal information

privacy of personal information the protection of the trail of information left behind as we go about our daily lives involving secrecy, control, and anonymity

private law law that regulates the relations between private persons and groups of private persons

private nuisance substantial and unreasonable interference with an occupier's use and enjoyment of land

privilege the right of a professional to refuse to divulge information obtained in confidence from a client

privity of contract the relationship that exists between parties to a contract

privity of estate the relationship between tenant and landlord created by their respective interests in the land that passes to a transferee of the interest

probate the process of administering and settling the estate of a deceased person

procedural law rules that deal with how substantive rights and duties may be enforced

product defamation making false and damaging statements about the products of another person

product liability a negligence tort imposing liability on manufacturers for harm caused by defective products

professional corporation (PC) a special type of business corporation that may be formed by members of a profession

progressive discipline imposing increasingly serious consequences for each event of improper employee behaviour beginning with a warning and ending with dismissal

promise a party who has the right to performance according to the terms of the contract

promisor a party who is under an obligation to perform a promise according to the terms of the contract

promissory estoppel or equitable estoppel the court's exercise of its equitable jurisdiction to estop a promisor from claiming that she was not bound by her gratuitous promise where reliance on that promise caused injury to the promisee

promissory note a written promise to pay a specified sum of money to another party at a fixed or determinable future time or on demand

proper law of the contract the law of the country or jurisdiction by which the terms of a contract or disputes under it are to be interpreted and decided

property (1) everything that is the subject of ownership or (2) the legal interest in a thing

property condition disclosure statement written statement of vendor's current actual knowledge of the property's condition

property insurance insurance against damage to property

proposal a procedure whereby a debtor, by agreement with the creditors, repays all or a portion of his debts over time without being made bankrupt

prospectus the document that a corporation is required to produce and file with securities commission when inviting the public to subscribe for its securities

protected geographical indications word or feature that connects a wine, spirit, or food product to a geographic location

proximity closeness and directness of the relationship of the subject parties

proxy a person appointed to attend a general meeting of shareholders and to cast the votes of the shareholder appointing him

proxy form a form required to be circulated to shareholders before a general meeting, inviting them to appoint a proxy if they so wish

public international law law involving relations between states

public law law that regulates the conduct of government and the relations between government and private persons

public liability insurance insurance to cover damage to others caused by the business, also known as third-party liability

public offering selling shares to the public, which must be done in compliance with provincial securities regulations

public nuisance unreasonable interference with the lawful use of public amenities or the public interest

public policy economic, social, and political considerations or objectives that are believed to be beneficial to society as a whole

publicly traded corporations corporations that issue shares to the public, also known as public corporations, widely held corporations, reporting issuers, and issuing corporations

punitive damages damages awarded with the intention of punishing a wrongdoer

purchase lease a lease whereby ownership is intended to change hands at the end of the lease term

purchase-money security interest (PMSI) the interest that arises when assets purchased by a debtor are charged as security for a loan made to enable acquisition of those specific assets

purpose of collection a need for collecting personal information that must be related directly to an operating program or activity of the institution

qualified privilege immunity from liability for defamation provided a statement was made in good faith

quantum meruit the fair amount a person deserves to be paid for benefit conferred

quasi-contract an obligation that may arise not as a result of contractual relations but because one party has received an unfair benefit at the expense of the other

quiet possession a warranty that there will be no interference with the lessee's possession or use of the asset

quotas restrictions on the quantities of goods that may be imported

ratification subsequent adoption by the proposed principal of a contract made by an agent acting without authority

ratifies acknowledges and promises to perform

real action an action to repossess an interest in land that had been interfered with

reasonable expectation of privacy the subjective and objective assessment of reasonable privacy expectations in a given situation

reasonable notice the acceptable length of advance notice of termination considering the length and character of employment, the age of the employee, and the availability of similar employment, given the education, training, and experience of the employee

rebut overcome

receiving order a court order to commence bankruptcy proceedings

recognition dispute an employer refuses to recognize the union as the employees' bargaining agent

rectification correction of a written document to reflect accurately the contract made by the parties

redeem have the land reconveyed to the mortgagor

redeem reclaim the goods and continue with the conditional sale

regulation detailed legal rules enacted under the authority of an existing government statute typically by an administrative agency

regulations administrative rules implemented by government as a result of authorization given in a statute

regulatory offences less serious offences created by government regulation through specialized legislation, agencies, and tribunals

regulatory or quasi-criminal liability responsibility arising from breaches of less serious rules of public law, often enforced through specialized regulatory tribunals set up by the government for specific purposes

relationship of master and servant the contractual relationship between an employer and an employee

reliance acting in a certain way because one believed the information received

reliance damages costs of expenditures and wasted effort reasonably made in preparation for performance

remainder the balance of a fee simple that goes to a third person at the end of a life estate

remainderman a person who holds the reversion or remainder in a fee simple

remote unrelated or far removed from the conduct

remote parties parties to an instrument who have not had direct dealings with one another

repossession the act of taking back possession of property that is in the possession of a defaulting debtor

representative action an action brought by one or more persons on behalf of a group having the same interest

repudiate reject or declare an intention not to be bound by

requisitions questions concerning claims against a seller's title to property

res judicata a case that has already been decided by a court and cannot be brought before a court again

rescind set aside; undo or revoke a contract and return the parties as nearly as possible to their original positions

rescission setting aside or rescinding a contract in order to restore the parties as nearly as possible to their pre-contract positions

reserve fund money set aside for future major projects and emergencies

reserve judgment postpone giving a decision after the hearing ends

residential tenancies a lease of premises used as living accommodation

residual powers powers that fall within federal jurisdiction because they are not expressly allocated to the provinces by the Constitution

restitution an order to restore property wrongfully taken

restitution a requirement that an "enriched" defendant must restore or return the benefit to the donor *in specie* or by money

restrictive covenant a covenant requiring the holder of the land to refrain from certain conduct or certain use of the land

restrictive endorsement limits transferability

respondent the party who defends on an appeal

responsible communication on matters of public interest a statement that is published in the public interest and is done responsibly

restrictive covenant a term in restraint of trade, that is, a promise not to carry on a competing business activity

resulting trust a trust relationship recognized when the conduct of the parties demonstrates the intention to hold property for the benefit of the other

retail electronic payments low-value everyday transactions conducted through a variety of different payment methods, such as debit, credit cards and etransfers

retail sales sales of consumer goods by retail businesses, in the ordinary course of their business, to private individuals

retain keep information available for subsequent access by the individual

retainer the contract between a lawyer and client that describes the work that will be done and the fee that will be charged

reverse mortgage a form of mortgage under which no repayment is due until the mortgagor sells or dies

reversion the balance of a fee simple reserved to the grantor and her heirs at the end of a life estate

rider additional provisions attached to a standard policy of insurance

right of re-entry a landlord's remedy of evicting the tenant for failure to pay rent or breach of another major covenant

right of subrogation the right to assume the insured's "legal" rights against the wrongdoer after the paying compensation for all the insured's damages

right of survivorship the right of a surviving tenant to the interest of a deceased joint tenant

right-of-way an easement that gives the holder a right to pass back and forth over the land of another in order to get to and from her own land

right to be forgotten the right to have one's personal information removed from public circulation

rights dispute an employer and the union differ in their interpretation or application of terms in an existing collective agreement

Roman law the system of law codified by the Eastern Roman Emperor Justinian in the 6th century

royal charter a special licence given by the Crown to form a corporation for the purpose of carrying on a particular activity

royalty fee paid to the copyright owner for permission to copy the work

royalty payments fees paid for permission to use another person's copyrighted material

rule of law established legal principles that treat all persons equally and that government itself obeys

rules of civil procedure the provincial regulations that set out the steps in a private lawsuit, including forms, fees, and timelines

run with the land bind subsequent land owners

sale-and-leaseback a transaction in which the owner of property sells it and immediately leases it back from the new owner

secured creditor a creditor that has collateral security in the form of a recognized claim against specified assets of the debtor

security agreement agreement that creates a security interest, including chattel mortgages, conditional sales contracts, and pledges

security for costs money deposited into the court in case an unsuccessful foreign plaintiff is ordered to pay the legal costs of the successful defendant

security interest an interest in personal property (including goods or intangibles) that secures payment or performance of an obligation

security lease a purchase lease in which the lessor provides the credit

securities commission the statutory authority appointed to supervise the issue of securities to the general public, the operation of the securities industry, and the stock exchange

self-induced frustration a party willfully disables itself from performing a contract in order to claim that the contract has been frustrated

senior officer a representative who plays an important role in establishing an organization's policies or is responsible for managing an important aspect of its activities, including the directors, the CEO, and the CFO of a corporation

servient tenement the land subject to the easement

serving providing a copy of the issued claim to each defendant

set aside rescind; undo or revoke a contract and return the parties as nearly as possible to their original positions

set off the right of a promisor to deduct an existing debt owed to him by the promisee

settlement when one of the parties agrees to pay a sum of money or perform an act in return for a waiver by the other party of all rights claimed in the lawsuit

severance a procedure that turns a joint tenancy into a tenancy in common

severed removed from the contract

share a member's proportionate interest in the capital of a corporation

shareholder agreement an agreement between two or more shareholders that is distinct from the corporation's charter and bylaws

sight draft a bill of exchange payable "at sight"—three days of grace are allowed after presentation

slander spoken defamation

social media payment channels messenger services that connect with existing credit card and bank systems; consumers pre-fund or link bank accounts to new apps of financial service providers

social regulation sets standards about how the product or service is made or delivered, such as health, safety, and environmental standards

sole proprietorship an unincorporated business owned by a single individual

solicitor an "office" lawyer in England who interviews clients, carries on legal aspects of business and family affairs, and prepares cases for trial

solicitor–client fee payment for the time and expenses of a lawyer when representing the client

solicitor–client privilege a client's right to have all communications with his or her lawyer kept confidential

special Acts of Parliament legislative acts creating a specific corporation

special damages money to compensate for quantifiable injuries

special endorsement payee names next person to be payee

special meeting any general meeting of shareholders other than the annual general meeting

special resolution a resolution of the general meeting required to be passed by a special (usually two-thirds) majority

specific goods goods in existence, identified and agreed upon as the subject matter of the sale

specific land claims claims involving treaty or reserve lands

specific performance an order requiring a defendant to do a contracted-for act, usually to complete a transaction

specification the description of the invention, its use, operation, or manufacture

stakeholder a person or organization that manages a betting arrangement for a fee and redistributes winnings

stakeholders groups affected by the business activities of a corporation

standard form contract an offer prepared in advance by the offeror, including terms favourable to the offeror that cannot be changed by the offeree but must be accepted as is or rejected in their entirety, also known as a contract of adhesion

standard of care the level of care that a person must take in the circumstances

standing the right to bring a lawsuit

standing offer an offer that may be accepted as needed from time to time

stare decisis to stand by a previous decision

stated capital account the amount received by a corporation for the issue of its shares

statement of adjustments a document setting out all the items—both credits and debits—that must be adjusted between the parties to arrive at the correct amount to be paid on closing

statement of claim document that starts a lawsuit containing a description of the facts and law that give rise to legal liability

statement of defence a reply to a statement of claim, admitting facts not in dispute, denying other facts, and setting out facts in support of the defence

statute barred an action that may no longer be brought before a court because the party wishing to sue has delayed beyond the limitation period in the statute

statutes pieces of legislation passed by government

statutory assignment an assignment that complies with statutory provisions enabling the assignee to sue the other party without joining the assignor to the action

statutory damages damages a plaintiff may request instead of proving actual loss

statutory interpretation determining the meaning of words in a statute by considering the legislative intent, purpose, and object of the statute, as well as the definition and entire context of the language

stop payment an instruction from the drawer of a cheque to the bank not to pay the cheque

strict grammatical or plain-meaning of the words the ordinary, grammatical, or dictionary meaning

strict liability liability that is imposed based upon causation regardless of fault

sub-bailee a person who receives a bailment of property from a bailee

subject to the equities The assignee takes title subject to any rights the promisor has against the assignor

subject to the equities subject to any rights or defences the promisor had against the original assignor

subordinate legislation law created by administrative agencies whose authority is granted by statute in order to carry out the purposes of the legislation

subrogation where one person becomes entitled to the rights and cause of action of another

subsidiary an entity controlled by another entity

subsidiary a separate corporation owned or controlled by its "parent" corporation

subsidiary promise an implied promise that the offeror will not revoke once the offeree begins performance in good faith and continues to perform

substantial performance performance that does not comply in some minor way with the requirements of the contract

substantive law the rights and duties that each person has in society

sui generis a unique collective right stemming from Indigenous peoples' prior occupation and connection with the land

super priority entitlement to be paid before secured creditors

super-governmental organizations non-profit associations of governments from around the world working to find common approaches to international issues, such as the World Trade Organization or the United Nations

surface rights lease grant from owner of land to allow access to minerals

surrender abandonment of the premises by the tenant during the term of the lease

surrounding contextual circumstances the factual matrix in which the contract is formed including the purpose of the contract and the intent of the parties

survey detailed drawing or map of the real property showing all the boundaries of the land and the location of all fixtures, encroachments, or overhangs

system of courts the organization of courts into a hierarchy that designates the responsibilities of the court and determines the importance of the precedent; the standard system has three levels: trial, appeal, and final appeal

systemic discrimination discrimination that is pervasive throughout an employer's workforce

systemically important banks large domestic banks that OSFI identifies as having a major impact on the Canadian financial system

takeover bid an offer by one corporation to acquire all or a substantial part of the shares of another corporation

technical protection measures (TPMs) access locks or use locks for electronic material. An access lock requires a password to access the work; a use lock blocks particular uses of the work such as copying

telemarketing the use of telephone communications for promoting the supply of a product or for promoting a business interest

tenant's fixtures trade fixtures or any other fixtures attached for the convenience of the tenant or for the better enjoyment of the object

tenants in common concurrent holders of equal undivided shares in an estate

tender of performance an attempt by one party to perform according to the terms of the contract

term the duration of the policy

term an interest in land for a definite period of time

term the time period during which an interest rate is fixed and principal lent

term certain a tenancy that expires on a specific day

term insurance personal insurance that provides coverage for a limited period only

territorial privacy lack of intrusion in one's home, business, and other personal spaces

third party a person who is not one of the parties to a contract but is affected by it

third-party liability liability to some other person who stands outside a contractual relationship

tied selling when a supplier makes it a condition that, to obtain one type of product, the buyer must also deal in other products of the supplier

time draft a bill of exchange payable within a stipulated period after the date stated on the instrument or after presentation

title holding ownership of a thing

title fraud fraudulent transfer or mortgaging of land by a non-owner

title insurance a policy of insurance that compensates the policy holder for defects in a title

tort a wrongful act causing harm to the person or property of another

trade-related investment measures national measures regulating investment that have an impact upon international trade

trade fixture an object attached to the premises for the purpose of carrying on a trade or business

trade union an organization of employees formed for purposes that include the regulation of relations between employees and employers

trademark an identifiable feature or combination of features that is used by a person for the purpose of distinguishing his goods or services from those of others

trademark an identifiable feature that is used by a person for the purpose of distinguishing his goods or services from those of others

transfer under the land titles system, the equivalent of a grant; not required to be made under seal

transfer a gift, sale, or disposition of property made by a debtor before becoming bankrupt

treaty an international agreement concluded between states in written form and governed by international law

treaties sacred agreements between the Crown and Indigenous peoples with a solemn, special, public nature that rank above personal contracts but below international treaties

trespass unlawful entering, or remaining, on the land of another without permission

trespasser one who enters without consent or lawful right on the lands of another or who, having entered lawfully, refuses to leave when ordered to do so by the owner

trust an arrangement that transfers property to a person who administers it for the benefit of another person

trust agreement the document that conveys property to a trustee to be used for the benefit of a third-party beneficiary

trust deed a document evidencing a mortgage on the property of a corporation

trustee a person or company who administers a trust

trustee in bankruptcy the person appointed to administer the property of a bankrupt

ultra vires beyond the powers and therefore void

unanimous shareholder agreement a shareholder agreement to which all shareholders are parties

unascertained goods goods that have not been set aside and agreed upon as the subject of a sale

UNCITRAL United Nations Commission on International Trade Law established by the United Nations General Assembly in 1966 to further harmonization and unification in international trade through conventions, model laws, and guidelines

unconscionable contracts contracts where there is unequal bargaining power between the parties, and the powerful party gets an extremely advantageous deal

unconscionable terms terms agreed to by parties of unequal bargaining power that give an unfair advantage to the powerful party over the weaker party

undisclosed principal a contracting party who, unknown to the other party, is represented by an agent

undue influence the domination of one party over the mind of another to such a degree as to deprive the weaker party of the will to make an independent decision

unenforceable no court assistance or remedy is available to parties of the contract

unenforceable contract a contract that still exists for other purposes but neither party may obtain a remedy under it through court action

unjust enrichment an unfair benefit

UNIDROIT International Institute for the Unification of Private Law, founded by the League of Nations in 1926 to harmonize laws; currently has 63 member states, including Canada

unilateral contract a contract in which the offer is accepted by performing an act or series of acts required by the terms of the offer

unilateral mistake a situation in which only one of the parties believes there is a mistake in the contract

unincorporated collectivity a group of persons that in most cases is not recognized by the courts and that may not sue or be sued

unitholders beneficiaries of an income trust

unlawful interference with economic relations attempting by threats or other unlawful means to induce one person to discontinue business relations with another

unlawful means conduct triggering civil liability under common law

unperfected security interest a security interest that is not attached or perfected

unsecured creditor a creditor who has no security interest in any of the debtor's property

use (of personal information) any access, change, or destruction of data within the organization

utmost good faith a duty of disclosure owed when a special relationship of trust exists between the parties

utmost good faith to act with fairness and integrity

vicarious liability strict liability of an employer to compensate for torts committed by an employee during the course of his or her employment

vicarious performance a third party performs contractual obligations on behalf of the promisor who remains responsible for proper performance

void never formed in law

void a contract that never existed and passed no rights

voidable the contract exists until set aside by a court; rights may pass to third parties before it is set aside

voidable contract a contract that may be rendered non-binding at the option of one of the parties

voluntary assumption of risk a defence to a negligence action when the plaintiff was aware of the risk and continued with the activity anyway

vulture funds large investors who purchase the debt or shares of a corporation in the course of its reorganization

wager an agreement between two persons in which each has some probability of winning or losing

waiver an agreement not to proceed with the performance of an existing contract

warranty a lesser or non-essential term that, when breached, does not relieve the injured party from performance

warranty of authority a person falsely represents that she has authority to contract on behalf of the principal

waste damage to the premises that reduces its value

web-wrap agreement a website document setting out contractual terms, the acceptance of which is indicated by clicking on the appropriate icon

willful invasion of privacy a person knew or should have known that her actions would invade the privacy of another

winding up the dissolution (or liquidation) of a corporation

without recourse no ability to claim against the endorser

work an original published or unpublished literary, dramatic, musical, or artistic creation, including the title

workers' compensation a scheme in which employers contribute to a fund used to compensate workers injured in industrial accidents regardless of how the accident was caused

World Intellectual Property Organization a specialized agency of the United Nations dedicated to harmonizing intellectual property laws and regimes worldwide

writ an ancient form required in order to take a grievance to court

wrongful detention the refusal by the seller to deliver goods whose title has passed to the buyer

Index

Note: Locators followed by 'n' and 'f' refer to notes and figures respectively.

A

Aboriginal peoples, 169–170, 485–486
aboriginal rights, 485–488
aboriginal title, 485–488
absolute liability, 647
absolute privilege, 81
abuse of dominant position, 57, 58–59
acceleration clauses, 319, 537, 674
acceptance, 135–136, 216
acceptors, 427, 435
accommodation bill, 433
accord and satisfaction, 256
accountability, 652
action for impeachment, 474
action for the price, 313
actions, 35
active legislation, 25–26, 52
act of God, 259, 335
acts of bankruptcy, 698–700
actual authority, 373–374
actual delivery, 430
additional rent, 517
adjudicate, 42
administrative law
 defined, 52
 and government, 25
administrative rulings, 12
administrators, 209, 247
admissible evidence, 37
adverse economic conditions, 403
adverse possession, 500, 502–503
advertising, 13, 52, 63–65, 201
Advertising Standards Canada (ASC), 65
advocates, 8
affairs, 612
affirmative action, 16
after-acquired property, 675
agency. *see also* agents
 by agreement, 370
 breach of warranty of authority, 380
 defined, 369
 duty of care, 371
 duty to comply with agency
  agreement, 371
 effect of, 310
 and employment contracts, 394–395
 legal risk management, 388–389
 listing agreements, 372–373
 power of attorney, 370
 relationship, creation of, 369–371
 relationship, termination of, 381
 writing requirement, 370
agency agreements, 369
agency principles, 570–571

agents. *see also* agency
 authority of, 373–377
 checklist, 376
 defined, 369
 duties of agent and principal, 371–372
 good faith, 371–372
 holding out, 375
 liability of principal and agent,
  377–380
 personal performance, 371
 ratification, 375–377
 rights of principal and agent, 377–380
 usual authority, 374–375
age of majority, 164
agreements in restraint, 178–182
agreement to sell, 300
AIDS, 475
alternative dispute resolution (ADR),
 41–44, 762
amortization period, 537
analytical approach, 281–283
annual general meetings, 628
annual reports, 632
anomalous endorsement, 433
anticipatory breach, 277
anti-dumping duties, 728
apparent authority, 374–375
apparent partners, 571–572
appeals, 29, 37. *see also* Court of Appeal;
 Supreme Court
appearance, 36
appellant, 29
appraisal remedy, 635
appropriated, 311
arbitration, 42, 319–320, 414, 415,
 740–741
arbitration agreements, 175
arbitration clause, 740
arbitration procedures, 415
arm's length, 701
arrears of taxes, 503
art, 471
articles of incorporation, 596–597
artistic works, 464
assault, 79
assign, 239, 241
assignees, 240, 244–246
assignment
 assignee's title, 244–246
 and bankruptcy, 247, 696, 698
 of book debts, 683
 checklist, 250
 of copyright, 465–466
 and credit, 320–321

and credit cards, 246
on death, 247
defences of promisor, 249
defined, 240
equitable assignment, 241–242
equity, role of, 241
exceptions to, 249
form of action, 249
importance of, 240–241
of insurance, 360
legal risk management, 251
of mortgages, 547
nature of, 239–240
negotiable instruments, 247–250
notice from multiple assignees, 244
notice to promisor, 243–244, 247, 248
by operation of law, 247
of partnership, 576
of part of bad debt, 241–242
right to set off, 245–246
statutory assignment, 243
of tenancy, 513
of trademarks, 457–458
assignors, 240
associated corporations, 593
associations, 168–169
assumed risk, 411
assume jurisdiction, 736
assumption agreements, 544
assumption of the mortgage, 543
attachments, 678
attorneys, 8
auctioneers, 369
audit committees, 614
auditors, 632–633
authority
 actual, 373–374
 agent's, 376
 apparent, 374–375
 misuse of, 53
authorization to directors, 599
authorized capital, 603

B

bad debt, 241–42
bad faith, 403
bailees, 328, 330–333
bailment
 damages, 332
 defined, 328
 innkeepers, 336–337
 leasing, 337–338
 liability, 329, 330
 liens, 332

nature of, 328–329
pawns, 337
pledges, 337
quantum meruit, 332
remedies, 332
repairs and work on a chattel, 334
right of sale, 333
rights, 332
standard of care, 331
storage and safekeeping, 333–334
sub-bailment, 329
transportation, 334–335
types of, 333–337
bailments for value, 331
bailors, 328
bait-and-switch advertising, 64
balance of probabilities, 36
balance of trade, 726
bank loans, 685–688
bank notes, 432
bankrupt, 247
bankruptcy. *see also* Bankruptcy and Insolvency Act (BIA)
acts of bankruptcy, 698–700
administration of bankrupt's affairs, 700–707
assignment, 247, 696, 698
bankruptcy orders, 696, 698–699
bankrupt debtors, 167, 267–268, 695–696, 706
builders' liens, 709–713
bylaws, 598–599
capacity of, 591–592
characteristics of, 589–591
checklist, 599
civil liability, 656–658
claims, payment of, 703–705
constitution of, 597–599
continuity, 590–591
corporate capital, 603–604
corporate groups, 601
corporate structure, 613–614
criminal liability, 658–661
debt, 603
defined, 589
discharge of bankrupt debtor, 267–268, 706–707
dissolution of, 636, 648, 707–709
duty of good faith, 590
employment law, 593–594
equity, 603
executive compensation, 655
exempt property, 702–703
general incorporation statutes, 595–596
general operating rules, 599
interim financing creditors, 704
jurisdiction, choice of, 596–597
as a legal person, 589
legal risk management, 607–608
legislation, 593, 612, 713–714
liability, 589–591, 656–667

lifting the corporate veil, 594
limitations statutes, 714
limited liability, 589, 593
management of, 590
memorandum and letters patent systems, 595–596
methods of incorporation, 595–597
name of, 598
nature of, 589–595
offences, 706
vs. partnerships, 589–591
par values, 603–604
preferences, 702
priority of payment on liquidation, 606
private corporations, 600, 627
professional corporations (PC), 602–603
proposals, 696–698
public corporations, 600, 652–655
publicly traded corporations, 612–613, 627
recovery of property, 700
registration of, 598
and repossession, 312
restrictions on share transfers, 607
rights of security holders, 605–606
securities, 604–608
separate corporate personality, consequences of, 591–593
separate corporate personality, limitations on, 593–594
share capital, 603
social responsibility, 655
taxation, 591, 593
of tenant, 520–521
transfer of ownership, 590
transfer of securities, 606–607
transfers at undervalue, 701–702
trustees, 700–703
types of, 600–603
unlimited liability corporation, 595
wage earners, 704
winding up, 636, 648, 707–708
Bankruptcy and Insolvency Act (BIA)
acts of bankruptcy, 698–700
competing policy issues, 693–694
compromise and arrangement, 708
discharge of bankrupt debtor, 267–268
dissolution of corporation, 708–709
functions of, 693
government supervision, 695
persons to whom the Act applies, 695–696
procedures under the Act, 696–699
student loans, 706
transfers at undervalue, 701–702
bankruptcy orders, 696, 698–699
bankrupts, 695
banks
definition, 423
regulation, 423–424

bargaining agents, 413
bargaining units, 413
bargains, 146
barristers, 7
barter, 299
basic law, 11
battery, 79
BCE, 734
bearer form, 432
behaviour, 4
beneficial contracts of service, 164–165
beneficial owners, 236
beneficiaries, 236, 350
betting debts, 172–173
bid-rigging, 57
bilateral contracts, 137
bilateral investment protection treaties, 735
bills of exchange, 425, 426–427
bills of lading, 311
binding codes of conduct, 11
biometrics, 405, 778
board of directors, 613
bondholders, 604, 605
bonds, 604
branches, 732
breach of a term, 314
breach of contract
anticipatory breach, 277
conditions, 276
damages. *see* damages
defined, 137
duty of honesty in performance, 280
equitable remedies, 291–293
exemption clauses, 281–283
express repudiation, 276–277
failure of performance, 279–281
how breach may occur, 276
implications of, 275–276
impossibility of performance, 278
inducing, 82
injunctions, 292
judgments, 293
loss from, 284–285
major and minor breaches, 276
overperformance, 280–281
remedies, 283, 291–293
repudiation, 276–277
rescission, 292–293
specific performance, 291–292
substantial performance, 280
warranties, 276
breach of duty, 621–622
breach of trust, 573
breach of warranty of authority, 380
bribery, 71
British system of courts, 29–30
Broadcasting Act, 25
broadcasts, 463
browse-wrap agreements, 754
builders' liens, 709–713
building-scheme covenants, 493–494

Index **819**

burden, 15
burden of proof, 200
business. *see also* corporations
   vs. affairs, 612
   Charter's protection, 51–52
   competition. *see* competition
   consumer protection. *see* consumer
   electronic commerce. *see* electronic commerce
   environmental protection, 68–72
   and ethics, 10
   government regulation, 48–54
   and intentional torts, 82–83
   international business. *see* international business
   jurisdiction over, 48–51
   labelling, product safety, and performance standards, 65–67
   and the law, 5, 52–53
   legal framework for, 48
   and the legal profession, 9
   licensing, 67
   meaning of, 566
   occupier's liability, 94–95
   organizational forms of, 564
   patentable, 470–472
   and privacy, 779–780, 786–792, 794
   product liability, 90–92
   protection legislation contracts, 168
   sales tactics, 316–318
business corporations acts, 713–714
business names, 450
"but for" test, 87
bylaws, 598–599

C

calculation period, 537
Canada Consumer Product Safety Act (CCPSA), 62, 64, 65, 66
Canada Food Inspection Agency, 66
Canada Labour Code, 405
Canada's Anti-Spam Legislation (CASL), 767
Canadian business in global economy, 719
Canadian court system, 30–32
Canadian Environmental Assessment Act (CEAA), 70
Canadian Environmental Protection Act (CEPA), 68
Canadian Intellectual Property Office (CIPO), 448, 760
Canadian Public Accountability Board (CPAB), 654
Canadian Radio-television and Telecommunications Commission, 318
Canadian Securities Administrators, 653
Canadian Standards Association Model Code, 787–792
Canadian Tire, 83
canon law, 27

capacity to contract, 164
capital, 603–604, 648–649
capital adequacy, 423
capital lease, 339
carriers, 334
case law, 12, 27–29
cashless society, 751–752
cash on delivery (COD), 309
causation, 87
causes of action, 35
caveat emptor, 554
caveat emptor, 199, 302
certainty *vs.* flexibility, 24
certificates of incorporation, 596
certificates of title, 501
certification, 413, 428–429
certification marks, 449
CETA, 470, 475
chain of title, 501
Chapter 11, 744–745
chargees, 539
charges, 539
chargors, 539
charitable donations, 146
Charter of Rights and Freedoms, 14–17, 407, 410, 777–778
chattel leasing, 338–340. *see also* leasing
chattel mortgages, 674–675
chattels, 300, 334, 338
checks and balances, 652
cheques, 425, 428–430, 440
cheque truncation, 429
chief executive officer (CEO), 613
choice of law, 739
choses in action, 240, 300, 426
choses in possession, 240
CIF, 309, 722
circumstantial evidence principle, 92
civil law, 22–24
civil liability, 4, 795–797
civil liberties. *see* human rights
civil litigation, 33–41. *see also* litigation
civil rights. *see* human rights
claims, 473
class actions, 34–35
class rights, 605–606, 629
clauses, special, 221
clean hands, 291
click-wrap agreements, 754
closed mortgages, 543
closing, 556–557
cloud computing, 778–780
COD, 309
codes of conduct, 10, 11, 116, 797–798
codified, 299
codify, 25
coercion, 202
collateral agreements, 223
collateral security, 671, 687
collection arrangement, 724
collective agreements, 413–414, 415–416
collective bargaining, 413–414

collective rights society, 465
collective society, 763
commercial activity, 786
commercial arbitration, 740–741
commercial tenancies, 509
commission agents, 369
common carriers, 334
common elements, 498
common law
   case law, 27
   certainty *vs.* flexibility, 24
   change, accommodation of, 24
   and contracts, 176–177
   defined, 23, 27n, 28, 176
   employment law, 396
   and liens, 332
   privacy, 795
   theory of precedent, 24
   trademarks, 450–452
   workers' compensation, 411–412
common mistakes, 189, 191
common shareholders, 605
common shares, 604
communication of acceptance, 132–133
communication of an offer, 126–127
communication signals, 463–464
comparative value, 408
compensation, 197
compensation committees, 614
competition
   conspiracies, 55–57
   of directors with corporation, 624
   duty not to compete, 577
   mergers, 60
   monopolizing, 57–59
   and patents, 475
   protection of competitors, 650
   restraint of trade, 178–182
   restricting, 59
   and torts, 82
Competition Act, 54–57, 317
Competition Bureau, 55, 64
competition tribunal, 55, 57, 64
compliance officers, 9
composition of matter, 470
compromise and arrangement, 708
compulsory licences, 475
compulsory sale, 499–500
computer software, 463
conciliation procedures, 415
concurrent powers, 13
conditional sales, 673–674
condition precedent, 224, 258
conditions, 276, 302
condition subsequent, 258–259
condominium corporation, 498
condominiums, 497–498
confidential information, 477–478
confidentiality clauses, 178
conflicting testimony, 220–221
conflict of duty, 117–118
conflict of interest, 104

conflict of laws, 721
conflicts of interest, 622–624
consensual surveillance, 793
consent, 79, 114, 781, 788
consequential damages, 287–288
considerations
   adequacy of, 147–148
   defined, 146
   and existing legal duty, 148–150
   in franchise agreements, 382–383
   and guarantees, 212, 362
   past consideration, 148
   and privity of contract, 233
consignments, 300, 673
consistency of law, 23–24
conspiracies, 55–57
Constitution, Canadian
   challenging, 18
   Charter of Rights and Freedoms, 14–17, 407, 410, 777–778
   and federalism, 12–13
constitutions, 11, 597–599
constructive delivery, 430
constructive discrimination, 408
constructive dismissal, 391
constructive trusts, 236
construing, 208
consumer bills, 440
consumer debtors, 696
consumer negotiable instruments, 249
consumer protection, 201
consumer protection legislation
   arbitration, 319–320
   checklist, 68, 322
   contracts, 217–218
   electronic commerce, 755–756
   legislated terms, 318–319
   misleading advertising, 63–65
   necessity of, 61–62
   pressure selling, 316–317
   severance, 320
   telemarketing, 317–318
   types of, 62–67
   unsolicited goods, 317
consumer remedies, 321
consumers
   business sales tactics, 316–318
   defined, 61, 217, 316
   legislation protecting. see consumer protection legislation
   and privacy, 794
   protection of, 650
container shipping, 723
contempt of court, 28, 294
contingency fees, 39–40
continuing disclosure, 653–654
contract formation
   Aboriginal peoples, 169–170
   acceptance of, 132–134, 135–136
   affected by statutes, 171–176
   beneficial contracts of service, 164–165

bilateral, 137
and common law, 176–177
considerations, 146
contract law, role of, 125
corporations, 167–168
diminished contractual capacity, 167
electronic commerce, 753–754
equitable estoppel, 151–154
essential elements of, 164
gratuitous promises, 146–147, 150
gratuitous reduction of a debt, 150–151
indirectly affecting minor, 166
injurious reliance, 153–154
insurance, 173
intention to create legal relations, 157–158
international jurisdiction, 139
internet contracts, 139
jurisdiction, 136–137
labour unions, associations, organizations, 168–169
legality, role of, 170–171
limited capacity to contract, 164–170
minor's liability, 166–167
minors or infants, 164–167
moment of formation, 133–134
necessaries, 164–165
and public policy, 177
request for goods or services, 155–156
restraint of trade, 178–182
revocation, 130, 136
seals, 155–156
stock exchange transactions, 173
and tenders, 133–134
third parties, 150
unilateral contracts, 137–138
without liability for minor, 165–166
contractors, 709–710, 712–713
contracts
   affected by statutes, 171–176
   agency contracts. see agency
   and bailment, 329
   bilateral, 137
   breach of. see breach of contract
   collateral agreements, 223
   condition precedents, 224
   consumer contracts, 199, 316, 318–321
   consumer protection legislation. see consumer protection legislation
   contracts of guarantee. see guarantees
   defined, 125
   discharge of. see discharge of contracts
   electronic commerce, 753–756
   employment contracts. see employment contracts
   essential terms, 212–213
   export/import contracts, 721–725
   formation of. see contract formation
   forms of, 208
   franchising. see franchising
   guarantees, 210, 213

illegal contracts, 170
insurance, 221
   of insurance, 198
   insurance contracts. see insurance
internet contracts, 139
interpretation of express terms. see contractual interpretation
land, 210–211
lease contracts. see leasing
legal risk management, 140, 158–159, 182–183, 203, 251, 268, 295
and liability, 396
mortgages. see mortgages
offers. see offers
oral, 211, 214, 223
parol evidence rule, 221–224
partnership agreement, 569–570
pre-incorporation contracts, 657–658
prior written contracts, 214
privity of contract. see privity of contract
recovery for goods and services, 214
recovery of money, 213–214
for sale of corporate securities, 199
for sale of goods and services. see contracts of sale
setting aside. see setting aside a contract
signatures, 213
special, 221
standard form, 221
standard form contracts, 197, 316
vs. torts, 196–197
unenforceable, 213
unilateral contracts, 137–138
voidable contracts, 166, 189–191
void vs. illegal, 170–171
written records, 208
contracts of adhesion, 127
contracts of bailment. see bailment
contracts of sale. see also Sale of Goods Act
   arbitration, 319–320
   breach of a term, 314
   business sales tactics, 316–318
   caveat emptor, 302
   conditions and warranties, 302
   consumer contracts, 316
   delivery, 309
   description, 303–304
   direct sales contracts, 316
   exemption clauses, 307–308, 319
   explained, 299–300
   export/import, 721
   financing arrangements and cost of credit, 320–321
   goods, 300–301
   implied terms, 302–307
   legal risk management, 322
   legislated terms, 318–319
   misrepresentation, 199
   payment, 309

contracts of sale (continued)
  remedies of the buyer, 315
  remedies of the seller, 311–314
  repossession, 312, 319
  risk of loss before delivery, 309–310
  sale by sample, 304
  seller's liability, 314–315
  seller's title, 303
  services, 301
  severance, 320
  statutory protection for the buyer, 302–307
  suitability and quality, 304–306
  terms in, 302–307
  title to goods, 310–311
  writing requirement, 215–216
  wrongful detention, 314
contractual interpretation
  conflicting testimony, 220–221
  credibility, 220–221
  general approach, 220
  goal of courts, 219
  implied terms, 224–226
  legal principles, 219–220
  parol evidence rule, 221–224
  reasonable expectations, 226
  special clauses, 221
  special contracts, 221
  words, special usage of, 220
contractual joint ventures, 583
contractual liability, 570–572, 656–657
contractual relationship, 102
contractual rights, 240
contra proferentem, 221, 356
contributory negligence, 89
cooling-off period, 199, 317, 415
cooperative housing, 498–499
co-ownership, 491
copyright
  artistic works, 464
  assignment, 465–466
  communication signals, 463–464
  computer software, 463
  digital rights management technology, 459
  dramatic works, 463
  duration of, 464–465
  electronic commerce, 762–765
  fair dealing, 467–468
  and industrial designs, 476–477
  infringement of, 466–469
  international treaties, 458–459
  licensing, 465–466
  limits to, 462
  literary works, 462–463
  moral rights, 461–462
  musical works, 464
  nature of, 459–462
  notice of infringement, 467
  ownership of, 465
  owner's rights, 459–461
  vs. patent, 469
  performers' performances, 464
  permitted uses, 467–468
  protection of, 464–466
  reform, 459
  registration of, 464
  remedies for infringement, 468–469
  statutory origin, 458
  telecommunications, 463–464
  works in which copyright exists, 462–464
Copyright Board, 465
corporate capital, 603–604
corporate governance, 612
  absolute liability, 647
  affairs *vs.* business, 612
  annual reports, 632
  appraisal remedy, 635
  audit committees, 614
  auditors, 632–633
  board of directors, 613
  capital, preservation of, 648–649
  checklist, 617
  civil liability, 656–658
  compensation committees, 614
  competitors, protection of, 650
  consumers, protection of, 650
  corporate structure, 613–614
  creditors, protection of, 647–649
  criminal liability, 658–661
  criminal offences, 646
  defined, 612
  derivative action, 635–636
  documents of record, 632
  employees, protection of, 650
  environmental offences, liability for, 662–667
  financial statements, 631–632
  inspector, appointment of, 633
  investors, protection of, 650–655
  legal risk management, 640, 666–667
  legislation, 612, 613, 617, 621–622
  liability, 646–647, 656–658
  limited liability, 647–648
  majority rule, 634–635
  meetings, 628–629
  mens rea, 646–647, 659
  minority shareholders, 634–638
  nominating committees, 614
  officers, 613, 617–618
  oppression remedy, 636–638
  public accounting industry, 654
  public interest, protection of, 655–656
  publicly traded corporations, 612–613
  public offerings, 652–655
  regulatory offences, 646
  reorganizations, 654–655
  securities industry, 651–652
  shareholder agreements, 638–640
  takeovers, 654–655
  voting, 628–629
  winding up, 636
corporate groups, 601
corporate opportunity, 623, 635
corporate securities, 199, 604–608. *see also* shares
corporate social responsibility, 10, 65, 655
corporations. *see also* corporate governance
  and agency, 369
  articles of incorporation, 596–597
  articles of incorporation system, 596
  associated corporations, 593
  authorization to directors, 599
  bankruptcy, 696
  social responsibility, 10, 65
cost, insurance, freight (CIF), 309, 722
cost of performance, 290–291
costs, 37–38, 739
counsel, 35
counterclaims, 36
counter-offers, 131
countertrade, 724–725
countervailing duties, 728
Court of Appeal, 29–30, 32
courts
  administrative tribunal decision, 26
  delays in, 41
  and legislation, 12–14
  merger of, 28–29
  procedural law, 22, 33–44
  role of, 12
  system of courts. *see* system of courts
courts of chancery, 27
courts of first instance, 29, 31–32
covenantors, 155
covenants
  breach of, 493
  building-scheme covenants, 493–494
  defined, 155
  and interests in land, 493–494
  landlord and tenant, 512–517, 529
  in leases, 517
  restrictive, 178, 383–384, 493
coverage, 349
covert surveillance, 793
credibility, 220–221
credit cards, 246, 440, 751–752
credit, cost of, 320–321
creditors
  in bankruptcy, 696–697
  contractors and subcontractors, 709–710, 712–713
  deferred creditors, 705
  general creditors, 705
  interim financing creditors, 704
  legal risk management, 715
  partnership creditors, 568
  preferred creditors, 705
  protection of, 647–649, 693, 713–714
  secured creditors, 546, 671–672, 704–705
  unsecured creditors, 671–672
creditors' claims, 503

credit sales, 137
Criminal Code, 659–660
criminal liability, 4, 658–661, 797
criminal negligence causing bodily harm, 660
criminal offences, 55, 646, 660
cumulative rights, 606
cumulative voting, 617
currency, 250
current assets, 704
custom, 225
cybersquatting, 761

D

damages, 87–89
  in bailment, 332
  consequential damages, 287–288
  in contracts of sale, 315
  cost of performance vs economic loss, 290–291
  defined, 96, 283
  expectation damages, 286–287, 315
  general damages, 97, 288
  and leased property, 518–519
  liquidated damages, 285–286
  loss from the breach, 284–285
  lost holidays, 290
  measurement of, 285–286, 289–291
  mental anguish, 289–290
  mitigation of, 285
  moral damages, 403, 404
  nominal, 286
  for non-acceptance, 312–313
  penalty clause, 286
  prerequisites for, 284–285
  punitive damages, 96, 288–289
  purpose of, 283–284
  quantum meruit, 332
  reliance damages, 288
  restitution, 97
  special damages, 97
  statutory damages, 469
  types of, 286–289
  wrongful dismissal, 289–290, 403–406
data shadows, 778
DDP, 723
death
  and assignment, 247
  and corporations, 590
  and interests in land, 499
debentures, 604, 675
debit cards, 440, 751–752
debtor-in-possession financing, 704
debtors
  bankrupt debtors, 267–268, 695–696, 706
  judgment debtors, 293
  principal debtors, 361
debts
  assignment of. *see* assignment
  vs. bailments, 328
  betting debts, 172–173
  and corporations, 603
  secured debts. *see* security
deceit, 108
declarations of trust, 584
deductible clauses, 351
deeds, 156
deeds of conveyance, 499
defamation, 81, 757–758
defences
  to breach of duty, 621–622
  defamation, 81
  defect of title defences, 439
  due diligence defence, 621
  forgery, 432
  guarantees, 363–364
  injurious reliance, 154
  negligence, 89
  negotiable instruments, 438–439
  personal defences, 438–439
  of promisors, 137
  real, 439
deferred creditors, 705
delays, 41
delivery, 309, 432
delivery duty paid (DDP), 723
demand drafts, 427
demotion, 400
dependent agents, 369
deposits, 314
deregulation, 48
derivative action, 635–636
description, 303–304
detrimental reliance, 115
devices, 63
digital rights management system (DRMS), 765
digital rights management technology (DRMT), 459
diminished contractual capacity, 167
"directing mind" principle, 659–660
directors
  appointment of, 616
  board of directors, 613
  breach of duty, 621–622
  conflicts of interest, 622–624
  corporation, duties to, 619–621
  criminal liability, 661
  defences to breach of duty, 621–622
  duties of, 618–626
  duty of care, diligence, and skill, 619
  environmental liability, 662–663
  fiduciary duties, 618–619
  independent, 618
  insider trading, 625–626
  legal risk management, 640
  liability, 626, 661
  loans to, 649
  Peoples v. Wise distinction, 620–621
  personal liability, 626
  powers of, 615
  removal of, 616
  role of, 615–616
  vs. shareholders, 613
  shareholders and stakeholders, duties to, 619–620
  shares, issuing, 630
directors' circular, 654
direct regulation, 48
direct sales contracts, 316
disability, 401, 406–407
disbarred, 8
discharge of bankrupt debtor, 706–707
discharge of contracts
  accord and satisfaction, 256
  act of God, 259
  by agreement, 255–259
  by breach of contract, 275
  condition precedent, 258
  condition subsequent, 258–259
  contract's own dissolution, 257–259
  defined, 255
  expiration of limitation period, 268
  by frustration, 260–267
  guarantees, 363
  novation, 256
  by operation of law, 267–268
  option to terminate, 259
  by performance, 255
  substituted agreement, 256–257
  tender of performance, 255
  waiver, 255–256
discipline, 117
disclaimer, 108
disclosed surveillance, 793
disclosure, 357, 364, 652, 653–654, 786
discovery of cause, 402
discrimination, 706
discriminatory pricing, 58
dishonour, 435, 437
dismissal for cause, 400
dismissal without notice, 400–403
disobedience, 401
dispute resolution, 41–44, 45, 384, 762. *see also* international dispute resolution
disputes involving governments, 741–745
dissolution. *see also* termination
  of contract, 257–259
  of corporations, 707–709
  of partnerships, 579
distinguish, 24
distinguishing guises, 449
distress, 519–520, 529
distributing corporations, 600, 612
distributing false prospectuses, statements, or accounts, 660
distribution practices, 58
dividends, 629–630, 649
doctrine of frustration, 260–263
documents, in import/export, 722–723
documents of record, 632
documents under seal, 156
domain names, 760–762
domestic banks, 423

dominant tenements, 492
double aspects, 50
dowers, 497
down payments, 314
drafts, 426–427
dramatic works, 463
drawee banks, 428
drawees, 426, 435
drawers, 426, 435
drawing parties, 282
dual offences, 64
due diligence defence, 621
dumping, 728
duration, 341
duress, 202
duty of care, 84–85, 109–112, 371, 619
duty of good faith, 590
duty of honesty in performance, 280
duty of skill, 619
duty to account, 107
duty to warn, 93

E

earnest, 216
easements, 491–493
easements by prescription, 492–493
ecash, 751
echeques. *see* electronic cheques
ecommerce. *see* electronic commerce
economic loss, 290–291
economics of civil litigation, 38–39
ediscovery, 36
education, 785
egg shell doctrine, 88
electronic cheques, 429–430
electronic commerce
    business, impact on, 750–752
    cashless society, 751–752
    consumer protection legislation, 755–756
    contract law, 753–756
    copyright, 762–765
    defined, 750
    existing business practices, 750–751
    formal contract requirements, 755
    illegal activities, 768
    intellectual property, 758–766
    international aspects of, 769–773
    and international business, 723
    jurisdiction, 769–772
    law, governing various aspects, 754–768
    law, impact on, 753
    legal risk management, 773
    non-governmental organizations, 772–773
    patents, 765–766
    precautions to be taken by vendors, 756
    privacy, 766–768
    spam, 767–768
    surrounding business environment, 752
    torts, 756–758
    trademarks, 761
    website, 751
electronic registration, 502
electronic retailing (etailing), 750
electronic signatures, 213
electronic transfer of funds, 751
electronic transmission, 212
employee privacy, 405–406
employee recruitment, 83
employee rights, 407–410, 711
employees
    vs. agency, 394–395
    vs. independent contractors, 395
    loans to, 649
    and privacy, 792–793
    and relationship to employer, 394–395
    and technology use, 766–767
employee safety, 650
employers, 394–395, 792–793
employment
    employee privacy, 405–406
    international standards, 412
    job descriptions, 401
    relationship of employer and employee, 394–395
    relationship of master and servant, 394
    termination, 398–401
employment contracts
    adverse economic conditions, 403
    agency, 394–395
    damages, 403–404
    discovery of cause, 402
    dismissal without notice, 400–403
    dismissal, wrongful, 403–406
    disobedience, 401
    fixed term, 398
    illness, 401
    implied term of reasonable notice, 398
    incompetence, 401
    independent contractors, 395
    legislation, 399
    liability, 396
    misconduct, 400–401
    mitigation, 404
    progressive discipline, 402
    reasonable notice, 398, 399
    reinstatement, 404–405
    termination, 398–401
employment equity, 409
employment insurance, 411
employment law
    common law, 396
    and corporations, 593–594
    development of, 394, 406
    employee rights, 407–410
    employee welfare legislation, 406–412
    employment equity, 409
    employment insurance, 411
    federal and provincial jurisdiction, 406
    mandatory retirement, 410
    occupational health, 412
    pay equity, 408–409
    systemic discrimination, 409
    workers' compensation, 411–412
    working conditions, 410–411
employment résumés, 197–198
endorse, 248
endorsement, 432, 433–434
endorsement in blank, 433
endorsements, 350
endorser, 434–435
endorsers, 435–436
England
    common law, 23, 27
    hire-purchase, 338
    incorporation system, 595–596
    leases, 510
    legal profession, 7
    privity of contract, 239
    Statute of Frauds, 208, 215
    system of courts, 29–30
Enron, 105, 580–581
entirety clause, 203
enurement clause, 237
environmental impact assessment review, 70
environmental offences
    business consequences of, 665
    international regulation, 666
    liability for, 663–664
    punishment for, 665
    standard of skill and care, 662–663
environmental protection, 68–72
equality rights, 16
equitable assignment, 241–242, 243
equitable estoppel, 151–154
equitable relief, 189
equitable remedies, 28, 291–293, 315
equity
    and corporations, 603
    defined, 28
    development of principle of, 27
    role of in assignments, 241
equity joint ventures, 583
equity of redemption, 538
errors in recording an agreement, 191–192
essential terms, 212–213
estates in time, 484, 489–491
estopped, 152
estoppel, 151–154
etailing, 750
ethics
    access to justice, 44
    advertising, 65
    bad faith, 358
    business ethics, 10
    clotheslines, 493
    confidentiality clauses and public policy, 178
    consumer leases, 344
    consumer protection legislation, 218

corporate social responsibility and executive compensation, 655
credit cards, 246
digital transactions, 442
directors, independent, 618
discrimination, 528
drugs for AIDS, 475
employee privacy, 405–406
employee recruitment, 83
employee technology use, 766–767
employment résumé, 197–198
Enron, 105
exemption clauses, 308
good faith performance, 278–279
government transparency and accountability, 783
insurance broker compensation, 373
and the law, 2–3
limited liability partnerships, 582–583
money laundering and solicitor–client privilege, 551
negotiation in good faith, 134
online pharmacies, 276
privacy *versus* security, 785
professional standards, 602
promises, 148
secured creditors, 688
self induced frustration, 263–264
student loans, 706
weapons in space, 735
European Free Trade Association, 731n
European Union, 730
eviction, 529
evidence, 36
examination for discovery, 36
exchange controls, 724
exclusive dealing, 58
exclusive possession, 509–510
exclusive use clause, 514
execution orders, 294
executive, 25
executive compensation, 655
executors, 209, 247
exemplary damages, 321
exempt, 702
exemption clauses
   analytical approach, 281–283
   defined, 221, 235, 281
   ethics, 308
   principled exception, 238
   public policy and public interest, 283
   purpose of, 281
   in Sale of Goods Act, 307–308, 319
   unconscionable terms, 282
exempt property, 702–703
exercise an option, 131
existing legal duty, 148–150
expectation damages, 286–287, 315
expert opinions, 197
expiration date, 268
export and import of services, 725
export controls, 726–727

Export Development Canada, 726
export houses, 721
export/import contracts, 721–725
export promotion, 726
export subsidies, 728
express provisions, 578
express repudiation, 276–277
express terms, interpretation of, 219–221
expropriation, 500, 735
extinguish the title extinguish the title, 500
EXW, 723
ex works (EXW), 723

F

fair comment, 81
fair dealing, 387, 467–468
fair-market-value (FMV) leases, 341
fairness, 357
false arrest, 81
false imprisonment, 80–81
fault, 76–77
FCL, 723
Federal Courts, 32, 53
Federal Courts of Appeal, 32
federalism, 12–13
federal paramountcy, 14
federal paramountcy rule, 50
federal powers, 49
federal securities regulator, 650–651
fee simple, 489
feudal law, 27
fiduciary duties, 103–104, 576–577, 618–619
fiduciary relationship, 102
finance leases, 339
financial statements, 631–632
Financial Transactions and Report Analysis Centre of Canada (FINTRAC), 424
financing, 320–321, 724
financing statements, 677
firms, 568
first in time, 501
First Nation, 169
fitness for occupancy, 514
fixed, 463
fixed term, 398
fixtures, 484, 524–525
flexibility *vs.* certainty, 24
floating charges, 675
FOB, 309, 722
foreclosure, 538, 539
foreign bank, 423
foreign direct investment, 732
foreign exchange risk management, 724
foreign investment, 594–595, 719, 732–736
foreign presence, 719
foreign trade
   defined, 719
   dumping, 728

export controls, 726–727
export/import contracts, 721–725
export promotion, 726
GATT and WTO, 728–730. *see also* GATT; WTO
government regulation, 726–728
import duties, 727
import restrictions, 727–728
international law, 728
North American free trade, 730–731
subsidies, 728
trans-pacific partnership, 732
foreseeability, 85, 88, 110
forfeiture, 519, 522
forgery, 432, 436
format shifting, 460
form *vs.* substance, 208
forum non conveniens, 737
franchise agreements, 382–384
franchising
   checklist, 385
   conduct of the business, 383
   considerations, 382–383
   dispute resolution, 384, 387
   fair dealing, 387
   franchise agreements, 382
   intellectual property rights, 384
   legal relationships, 385–386
   legal risk management, 388–389
   legislation, 386–387
   mandatory franchisor disclosure, 386–387
   models, 386
   nature of, 381–382
   no waiver, 387
   restrictive covenants, 383–384
   right to associate, 387
   termination of the franchise, 383
   and trademarks, 457–458
franchisors, 382
franshisees, 382–383
fraud, 502, 550–551, 660
fraudulent misrepresentation, 108, 380
fraudulent preference, 702
fraudulent transfers, 701
freedom of association, 51
freedom of expression, 51, 52
freedoms, 16
freehold estates, 489–490
free on board (FOB), 309, 722
free trade areas, 730
freight forwarders, 721
frozen out, 627
frustration
   checklist, 264
   discharge by, 260–267
   doctrine of, 260–263
   effect of, 264–267
   landlord and tenant, 529
   let the loss fall where it lies, 265
   release of further performance, 264–265

Index **825**

frustration *(continued)*
  requirements of, 264
  and sale of goods, 265–267
  self-induced frustration, 263
  statutory reform, 265
full container load (FCL), 723
fungible goods, 333
future goods, 311

G

gambling, 172, 173–174, 768
gaming, 172
garnishee orders, 294
gas leases, 494–495
GATT, 720, 727–730, 742
General Agreement on Tariffs and Trade (GATT), 720, 727–730, 742
general creditors, 546, 705
general damages, 97, 288
general incorporation statutes, 595–596
generally accepted accounting principles (GAAP), 113
general meetings of shareholders, 628
general operating rules, 599
general partners, 580
global economy, 719
good faith, 357–358, 371–372, 590, 633, 682
good faith performance, 278–279
goods. *see also* contracts of sale; Sale of Goods Act
  defined, 300
  fungible goods, 333
  future goods, 311
  vs. services, 301
  specific goods, 311
  title to, 310–311
  unascertained goods, 311
  unsolicited goods, 317
  writing requirement, 215–216
goodwill, 450
government
  institutions, 781
  transparency and accountability, 782–783
government regulation
  of business. *see* business
  challenging, 48–54
  checklist, 54
  defined, 48
  of foreign investment, 733–734
  of foreign trade, 726–728
  judicial review of, 53
  of privacy, 780–795
gratuitous bailments, 328
gratuitous promises, 146–147, 148, 150
gratuitous reduction of a debt, 150–151
grievances, 413
guarantees
  considerations, 362
  continuing guarantees, 362
  defences, 363–364
  defined, 210, 360
  discharge of, 363
  vs. indemnity, 361
  legal risk management, 364
  liability on, 361f
  nature of, 360–362
  rights of guarantors, 363–364
  and Statute of Frauds, 210
  subrogation, 364
  writing requirement, 212, 364
guarantors, 200, 364
guardians, 164

H

Hamilton hockey, 259–260
hashtags, 760
healthcare, 784–785
hearsay, 37
Hedley Byrne, 109
Helms-Burton law, 727
hire-purchase, 338
holdbacks, 710
holder, 248
holder in due course, 428, 437–439
holding out, 375
hostile workplace, 408
human rights, 14, 407–408, 777–778. *see also* Charter of Rights and Freedoms
hyperlinking, 758

I

identification endorsement, 434
identity theft, 768
illegal, 170
illegal contracts, 170–171
illness, 401
immediate parties, 439
implied term as to description, 303
implied term as to title, 303
implied term of fitness, 305
implied term of merchantable quality, 306
implied terms
  in contracts of sale, 302–307
  defined, 224
  as method of interpretation, 224–226
  of partnership agreement, 574–576
implied term that goods correspond with sample, 304
import duties, 727
import/export contracts, 721–725
import restrictions, 727–728
impossibility of performance, 278
income trusts, 584–585
incompetence, 401
incorporation methods, 595–597
Incoterms, 722
indefinite hiring, 398
indemnity, 197, 210, 361
independence, 652
independent agent, 369
independent contractors, 395
indeterminate liability, 110, 111
Indian bands, 169
Indigenous people, 170
individuals, 786
indoor management rule, 656
inducing breach of contract, 82
industrial designs, 476–477
infants, 164–167
information, right to, 631–633
informed consent, 114
infringement, 758
ingenuity, 472
inherently dangerous products, 92–93
inherent vice, 335
in-house counsel, 9
injunctions, 97, 292, 520, 521
injurious reliance, 153–154
innkeepers, 336–337
insider trading, 625–626
insolvency, 312, 648, 693–694. *see also* Bankruptcy and Insolvency Act (BIA)
insolvent, 693
insolvent persons, 695–696
inspectors, 633
insurable interest, 173, 354–355
insurance. *see also* insurance contracts
  beneficiaries, 350
  broker compensation, 373
  comprehensive, 352
  on condominiums, 498
  deductible clauses, 351
  employment insurance, 411
  ethics, 373
  in import/export, 723
  interpretation rules, 221
  and leasing, 341, 516
  legal risk management, 349, 364
  against liability, 352
  life insurance, 355
  against loss or damage, 351–352
  medical malpractice insurance, 353
  personal insurance, 350
  premiums, 349
  property insurance, 350, 355
  public liability insurance, 352
  regulation of business, 350–351
  terminology, 349–350
  term insurance, 350
  title insurance, 503–504
  and torts, 90
  types of, 351–352
insurance adjusters, 350
insurance agents, 350
insurance brokers, 350
insurance contracts. *see also* insurance
  affected by statutes, 173
  assignment, 360
  bad faith, 358
  disclosure, 357
  fairness, 357

formation of, 355
good faith, 364–365
insurable interest, 354–355
interpreting terms of, 356
legality of objects, 353–354
and liability for negligence, 174
and misrepresentation, 198
and privity of contract, 237
recovery, 359–360
renewals, 355
special aspects, 353–360
subrogation, 359
wrongful act of the insured, 353–354
insurance policy, 349
intangible property, 240, 426, 683
intellectual property
confidential information, 477–478
copyright. *see* copyright
domain names, 760–762
electronic commerce, 758–766
forms of, 448
in franchising, 384
industrial designs, 476–477
international, 725, 731
know-how, 477–478
nature of, 448–449
protection of, 448–449
trade secrets, 477–478
intent, 646–647
intentional torts, 79–83, 108
intention to create legal relations, 157–158
interest disputes, 415
interest rates, 201
interests in land
aboriginal rights, 485–488
aboriginal title, 485–488
adverse possession, 500, 502–503
arrears of taxes, 503
assignment, 547
compulsory sale, 499–500
condominiums, 497–498
cooperative housing, 498–499
co-ownership, 491
covenants, 493–494
creditors' claims, 503
crown grants, 484–485
death of owner, 499
estates in time, 489–491
exclusive possession, 509–510
expropriation, 500
fee simple estates, 489
freehold estates, 489–490
gift, 499–500
interests less than estates, 491–495
joint tenancy, 491
leasehold estates, 490–491, 499, 509
licenses, 495
life estates, 489–490
matrimonial home rights, 497
mortgagees, 538
nature of, 484–488

oil, gas, and mineral leases, 494–495
remedies for breach of covenant, 493
sale, 499–500
severance, 491
tenancy in common, 491
tenant in possession, 503
transfer, 547–548
transfer of, 499–500
types of, 495f
interests less than estates, 489, 491–495
interlocutory injunctions, 292
Intermediate Appellate Courts, 32
international business. *see also* foreign trade
Canadian business in global economy, 719
dispute resolution. *see* international dispute resolution
foreign investment, 732–736
foreign trade. *see* foreign trade
and law, 5, 719–720, 728, 734–736
legal risk management, 745–746
International Chamber of Commerce, 722
International Convention for the Protection of Industrial Property, 453
international dispute resolution
choice of law, 739
commercial arbitration, 740–741
courts, 736–740
disputes involving governments, 741–745
enforcement of foreign judgments, 739–740
jurisdiction, 736–738
International Institute for the Unification of Private Law (UNIDROIT), 722
international issues
bribery, 71
Canada–U.S. tension re copyright, 460
Canadian business in global economy, 719
copyright, 458–459
electronic commerce, 769–773
electronic transfers of funds, 441–443
Enron, 580–581
environmental regulation, 666
foreign franchisors, 388
foreign investment in Canadian corporations, 594–595
foreign judgments, 294
Hamilton hockey, 259–260
injurious reliance, 154
insolvency, 693–694
intellectual property, 458–459
international standards, 412
internet gambling, 173–174
jurisdiction and internet contracts, 139
limited partnerships, 580–581

medical malpractice insurance, 353
mobile equipment, 685
mortgage crisis, 542
non-bank financial institutions, 425
non-governmental organizations, 772–773
outsourcing, cloud computing, and transborder data flow, 779–780
patents, 469–470
payday loans, 201–202
privity of contract, 239
rent control, 529
sale of goods, 315
Sarbanes-Oxley Act, 614
security interests, 685
solicitor–client privilege, 118
spam, 767–768
Statute of Frauds, 215
strict liability or negligence, 97
and technological change, 478–480
tobacco litigation, 93–94
transport of goods, 336
International Organization for Standardization, 666
internet
contracts on, 139
defined, 750
and ecommerce, 750
electronic commerce. *see* electronic commerce
employee use of, 766–767
gambling, 173–174, 768
illegal activities, 768
internet gambling, 768
internet service providers (ISPs), 467, 765
interpretation of express terms, 219–221
intervention of equity, 291
intestate, 247
intestate succession, 499
intranet, 750
inventions, 470–472
investment property, 683
investors, 650–655
invitees, 94
inviting tenders, 133
irregularity on the face, 439
ISPs, 751–752, 757, 765
issued capital, 603
issuing, 35

J

job descriptions, 401
joint liability, 571
joint tenancy, 491
joint ventures, 583–584, 733
judge-made law. *see* case law
judges, 19–20
judgment creditors, 293
judgment debtors, 293
judgments, 37, 293, 294
judicial review, 53

jurisdiction
   and contracts, 136–137, 139
   and corporations, 596–597
   defined, 136
   and electronic commerce, 769–772
   in employee welfare legislation, 406
   federal/provincial powers, 49
   for international disputes, 736–738
   for trademark infringement, 457
   for trademarks, 457
jurisdictional disputes, 414
justice, 3

K
keyword bidding, 761
know-how, 477–478
Kyoto Protocol, 666

L
labelling, 65–67
labour disputes, 414–416
labour law
   collective agreements, 413–414, 415–416
   labour disputes, 414–416
labour relations board, 413
labour unions, 417
   capacity to contract, 168–169
   collective bargaining. *see* collective bargaining
   and contracts, 168–169
   legal status of, 416–417
land. *see also* interests in land
   condominiums, 497–498
   contracts, 210–211
   defined, 484
   government regulation, 495–499
   leasehold estates, 499
   matrimonial home rights, 497
   use and development, 495–497
land law
   and privity of contract, 237
   Statute of Frauds, 210–211
landlord and tenant. *see also* tenancy
   assignment, 513
   bankruptcy of tenant, 520–521
   checklist, 517
   classes of tenancies, 511–512
   covenants, 512–517, 529
   damages, 518–519, 521
   definite or ascertainable period, 510
   discrimination, 528
   distress, 519–520, 529
   eviction, 519, 529
   exclusive possession, 509–510
   fitness for occupancy, 514
   forfeiture, 522
   injunctions, 520, 521
   insurance, 516–517
   landlord's mortgagee, 526
   leasebacks, 527
   leasehold estates, 490–491, 499, 509

lease registration, 526
legislation, 52, 211, 528–529
month-to-month tenancy, 511
nature of relationship, 509–510
notice to quit, 522–523, 529
oral leases, 525
periodic tenancy, 511, 522
privity of contract, 526
privity of estate, 526
provision of services, 517
quiet enjoyment, 515–516
recovery of rent, 518–519
remedies of tenant, 521
remedies of the landlord, 518–521
renewal, 523–524
rent, 512
repairs, 515
residential tenancies, 528–531
restrictions on use of premises, 514
sale of landlord's interest, 526–527
subletting, 513–514
surrender, 522
taxes, 517
tenancy at sufferance, 511–512
tenancy at will, 511
tenant in possession after expiration of fixed term, 523
term certain, 511
termination of tenancy, 522–525, 529
terms for notice, 523
waste, 515
land titles system, 501–502, 539
land use and development, 495–497
lapses, 129–130
latent defects, 554
law. *see also* legislation; specific types of law
   administrative law, 25
   and behaviour, 4
   and business, 5
   case law, 27–29
   choice of law, 739
   classifying, 22
   contract law. *see* contracts
   defined, 2
   electronic commerce, 753–768
   and ethics, 2–3
   government made law, 25–27
   and international business, 719–720, 728, 734–736
   vs. justice, 3
   and morals, 2–3
   need for, 2
   private international law, 721
   private law, 2
   public law, 2
   role of, 2
   rule of, 2
   sources of, 11–12, 22, 25–29
   tort law. *see* torts
lawsuits, 33–41
LCL, 723

learned intermediary, 93
leasebacks, 527
leasehold estates, 490–491, 499, 509
leases, 517, 673. *see also* landlord and tenant; leasing
   defined, 338, 509
   oil, gas, and mineral leases, 494–495
   oral leases, 525
   registration of, 526
   statutes, 211
lease-to-buy (LTB) leases, 341
lease-to-own, 339*n*
leasing
   as bailment, 337–338
   chattel leases, 338–340
   checklist, 342
   consent to assignment, 341
   costs payable by the lessee, 341
   duration, 341
   early termination—minimum payment, 342
   ethics, 344
   fair-market-value (FMV) leases, 341
   finance leases, 339
   implied terms, 342–343
   insurance, 341
   leasehold estates, 490–491, 499, 509
   lease-to-buy (LTB) leases, 341
   lease-to-own, 339*n*
   legal risk management, 344
   lessees, 343–344
   lessors, 343
   operating leases, 338
   purchase options, 341
   purchases leases, 338–339
   real estate, 490
   reasons for, 340
   rights of the parties, 343–344
   sale-and-leaseback, 340
   security leases, 339
   sub-bailment, 341
   terms in, 340–343
   true leases, 338
legal advice, importance of, 201
legal aid, 38
legal audit, 6
legal capacity, 164
legal duty, 148–150
legal liability, 4
legal personality, 568
legal persons, 589
legal principles of interpretation, 219–220
legal proceedings, 568–569
legal profession, 7–9
legal rights, 16
legal risk, 6
legal risk management
   agency, 388–389
   assignment, 251
   breach of contract, 295
   capacity to contract, 182–183

checklist, 7
contract formation, 140, 158–159
contracts, assignment, 251
contracts, capacity to contract, 182–183
contracts of sales, 322
corporate governance, 640, 666–667
corporations, 607–608
creditors, 715
directors, 640
discharge of contracts, 268
dispute settlement, 45
electronic commerce, 773
employment relationships, 417
franchising, 388–389
government regulation, 71–72
guarantees, 364
insolvency, 712
insurance, 349
insurance contracts, 364
intellectual property, 479–480
interests in land, 504
international business, 745–746
landlord and tenant, 530–531
leasing, 344
legal audit, 6
legal profession, use of, 7–8
legal risk management plans, 6–7
mortgages, 557–558
negotiable instruments, 443
partnerships, 584–585
privacy, 798
professional liability, 119
real estate transaction, 557–558
security interests, 688
setting aside a contract, 203
shareholders, 639
strategies for, 7
torts, 98
writing requirement, 227
legal risk management plans, 6–7
legal systems, 22–24
legal title, 538
legislated terms, 318–319
legislation. *see also* law; statutes
   active legislation, 25–26
   Bank Act, 685–688
   builders' liens, 710–713
   business corporations acts, 713–714
   Canada Labour Code, 405
   Canada's Anti-Spam Legislation (CASL), 794
   Competition Act, 54–57, 317
   condominiums, 497
   consumer protection legislation, 68, 217–218, 316, 320
   copyright, 458
   Copyright Act, 762
   corporate governance, 612, 617, 621–622
   corporations, 595–596
   and the courts, 12–14
   Criminal Code, 659–660

described, 25
ecommerce, 753–754
employee welfare legislation, 406–412
foreign trade, 726–728
framework of, 25
on franchising, 386–387
government made law, 25–27
Helms-Burton law, 727
on insurance, 350–351
land use and development, 495–497
on leasehold estates, 499
on liens, 333
on matrimonial home rights, 497
non-bank financial institutions, 424
Partnership Act, 568, 569
passive, 25
Personal Health Information Protection Act, 784
Personal Information Protection and Electronic Documents Act (PIPEDA), 791
Personal Property Security Act (PPSA), 684
personal property security legislation, 672–676, 676–681, 687–688
privacy, 766–768, 777–782, 794
Privacy Act, 783
rights of lending bank, 686
Sarbanes-Oxley Act, 612
securities legislation, 650–651
as source of law, 11–12, 25–27
special Acts of Parliament, 595
subordinate legislation, 25, 26
tenant protection, 528–529
Trade-marks Act, 449, 452
writing requirement, 208–209
lessees, 338, 343–344, 490
lessors, 338, 343–344, 490
less than a full container load (LCL), 723
letter of credit, 724
letters patent, 596
let the loss fall where it lies, 265
level-of-interactivity test, 770
levy execution, 294, 503
liability
   absolute liability, 647
   on agency contract, 379f
   agency principles, 570–571
   in bailment, 329, 330, 335
   basis for, 76–78
   breach of trust, 573
   civil liability, 4, 656–658, 795–797
   in contract, 396
   contractual liability, 106f, 656–657
   of corporate directors, 626
   of corporations, 589–590, 646–647, 656–658
   criminal liability, 4, 658–661, 797
   of employers, 395–397
   environmental offences, 662–667
   on guarantees, 361f
   indeterminate liability, 111

   insurance, 352
   joint liability, 571
   and leased property, 516
   legal liability, 4
   of manufacturers, 234
   mens rea, 646–647, 659
   and negotiable instruments, 430
   of partners, 570–573
   of principal and agent, 377–380
   and privacy, 794–797
   product liability, 90–92
   professional liability. *see* professional liability
   public policy and, 77–78
   quasi-criminal liability, 4
   regulatory liability, 4
   secondary market liability, 654
   of sellers of goods, 234, 314
   statutory liability, 106–107
   strict liability, 76, 77, 97, 621–622
   third-party liability, 106, 349
   torts, 105–106, 396–397, 573, 656
   vicarious liability, 78
libel, 81
licences
   vs. bailments, 328
   of land interest, 492
licensees, 94
licensing
   of businesses, 67
   of intellectual property, 457–458, 465
   and interests in land, 495
   in securities industry, 651–652
liens, 311–312, 332, 539, 709–713
life estates, 489–490
life insurance, 355
life tenants, 489
lifting the corporate veil, 594
limitation period, 500
limitation periods, 437
Limitations Act, 268
limitations statutes, 714
limited liability, 589, 593, 647–648, 661
limited liability partnerships, 581–583
limited partners, 580
limited partnerships, 580–581
linking, 758
liquidated damages, 285–286
liquidating dividends, 703
liquidation, 707–709
liquidity, 423
listing agreements, 372–373, 552
literary works, 462–463
litigation
   appeals, 37
   class actions, 34–35
   contingency fees, 39–40
   costs of, 37–38
   economics of, 38–39
   judgment, 37
   pre-trial procedure, 35–36
   settlement out of court, 40–41

litigation (continued)
   standing to sue, 34
   trial procedure, 36–37
litigation lawyers, 8
loans, 67, 201–202, 649, 685–688, 706
locked in, 627
lock outs, 411, 413–415
"loser pays" rule, 38
lost holidays, 290
lotteries, 172

M

machine, 471
maintenance of capital test, 649
major breach, 276
majority rule, 634–635
makers, 427–428, 435
malicious prosecution, 81
mandatory injunctions, 97
mandatory retirement, 410
manufacture, 471
market allocation, 56
market manipulation, 660
market restrictions, 58
material misrepresentations, 196
matrimonial home rights, 497
maturity date, 537
mediation, 42
medical malpractice insurance, 353
memorandum of association, 595–596
mens rea, 646–647, 659
mental anguish, 289–290
merchant law, 27
mercury contamination, 68
mergers, 60
metadata, 761
mineral leases, 494–495
minor breach, 276
minority shareholders, 634–638
minors, 164–167, 369
misapplication of funds, 573f
miscarriages, 210
misconduct, 400–401
misrepresentation
   in agent contracts, 380
   consequences of, 197–199
   contract vs. tort, 196–197
   errors in recording an agreement, 191–192
   fraudulent, 108
   negligent, 108, 109–115, 380
   by omission, 113–114, 198–199
   setting aside a contract, 196–199
   by silence, 198–199
mistakes
   about contract terms, 191–193
   about identity of party to a contract, 194–195
   about meanings of words, 192–193
   about nature of signed document, 196
   narrow meaning of, 189
   words used inadvertently, 191

misunderstandings about meanings of words, 192–193
mitigate, 89
mitigation, 285, 404, 518–519
model laws, 5
money laundering, 424, 551
monitors, 709
monopolizing, 57–59
month-to-month tenancy, 511
moral causes, 148
moral damages, 403, 404
moral rights, 461–462
morals, 2–3
mortgage commitments, 537
mortgage crisis, 542
mortgagees, 537, 539–540, 545
mortgages, 673
   assignment, 547
   assumption agreements, 544
   chattel mortgages, 674–675
   closed mortgages, 543
   as contracts, 537
   default by purchases, 543–544
   defined, 537
   discharge of, 547–548
   financial arrangements, 543–544
   foreclosure, 538, 539
   as interest in land, 538
   land titles system, 539
   legal risk management, 557–558
   and liens, 712
   mortgage fraud, 550–551
   mortgage law, essence of, 537–539
   open mortgages, 548
   partial discharge of, 548
   prepayment, 548
   provincial variations, 549
   registration, 539
   remedies of mortgagee, 540–542
   reverse mortgages, 549–550
   rights mortgagor, 540, 549
   rights of mortgagee, 538–540, 549
   sale by court, 541
   sale by mortgagee, 541–542
   sale by mortgagor, 543–544
   second mortgages, 544–546
   subsequent after second, 545–546
   transfer of mortgagee's interest in land, 547–548
   typical real estate transaction, 551–558
mortgagors, 537, 539–540, 549
most-favoured-nation (MFN) treatment, 729
motives, 148
multi-disciplinary partnerships, 118–119
Multilateral Investment Guarantee Agency, 735
municipalities, 784
musical works, 464
mutual mistakes, 193

N

NAFTA, 720, 730–731, 735, 743–745
name search system, 598n
National Do Not Call List, 318, 794
National Mobility Agreement, 8
National Money Mart, 40
national treatment, 729
natural justice, 778
necessaries, 164–165
negative covenants, 292
negative option billing, 132
negligence
   causation of damage, 87–88
   checklist, 96
   contributory negligence, 89
   damage to the plaintiff, 87
   defences to, 89
   defined, 84
   duty of care, 84–85
   elements of, 84–89
   elements of negligence action, 84
   international approaches, 97
   negligent misrepresentation, 109–115
   occupier's liability, 94–95
   and privacy, 796–797
   remoteness of damage, 88–89
   standard of care, 86, 89, 91–92
negligent misrepresentation, 108, 380
   accuracy of the statement, 112
   checklist, 109
   duty of care, 109–112
   elements of, 109
   omissions, 113–114
   reliance and detriment, 114–115
   standard of care for professionals, 112–114
negotiability, 248–250, 430–432
negotiable instruments
   acceptors, 427, 435
   vs. assignability, 249
   bank notes, 432
   bearer form, 432
   bills of exchange, 426–427
   checklist, 430, 431, 434, 439
   cheques, 425, 428–430, 440
   commercial importance of negotiability, 249–250
   consequences when not negotiable, 432
   consumer bills, 440
   currency, 250
   defences, 249, 438–439
   defined, 247
   delivery only, 432
   drawees, 426, 435
   drawers, 435
   electronic transfers of funds, 441–443
   endorsement, 433–434
   endorser, 434–435
   endorsers, 435–436
   form of action, 249
   holder in due course, 437–439

liability of parties, 434–436
limitation periods, 437
makers, 427, 435
methods of negotiation, 432
nature and uses of, 247–248, 426–430
negotiability, 430–432
notes, 440
notice to promisor, 248
origin of, 425
partial payment, 434
personal defences, 438–439
as personal property, 426
prerequisites for liability, 430
promissory notes, 427–428, 432
real defences, 439
types of, 426
negotiation, 248, 430, 432
net neutrality, 752
new trial, 29
no-fault insurance, 78
nominal damages, 286
nominating committees, 614
non-bank financial institutions, 424–425
non-competition agreements, 178
non est factum, 196
non-governmental organizations, 5, 720, 772–773
non-public investors, 653
non-solicitation agreements, 178
non-tariff barriers, 727
no par value shares, 604
North American Free Trade Agreement (NAFTA), 720, 730–731, 735, 743–745
notaries, 8
notes, 440
notice of revocation, 130
notice of terms, 128–129
notice to quit, 522–523, 529
novation, 256–257
novelty, 472
NUANS (Newly Upgraded Automated Name Search) system, 598*n*
nuisance, 79–80
number names, 598

O

occupational health, 412
occupier, 80
occupier's liability, 94–95, 514
OECD, 722, 753, 772
offences, classification of, 647
offerees, 125
offerors, 125
offers. *see also* contracts
 acceptance of, 132–134, 135–136
 checklist, 135
 communication of, 126–127
 counter-offers, 131
 defined, 125
 lapses of, 129–130
 notice of terms, 128–129
 options, 130–131

promise for an act, 137–138
promise for a promise, 137
rejection of, 131
revocation of, 130, 136
standing offers, 134
uncertainty in wording, 139
written offers, 127–129
offer to purchase, 552–553
officers, 613, 618–626, 660, 661
official receivers, 695
oil leases, 494–495
omissions, 113–114, 198–199
online pharmacies, 276
Ontario Securities Commission, 52
Ontario Teachers' Pension Fund, 734
open mortgages, 548
operating leases, 338
operation of law, 247, 267–268
opportunity cost, 286
oppression remedy, 636–638
options, 130–131
option to terminate, 259
opt-out consent, 789
oral contracts, 211, 214, 221, 569
oral leases, 525
order-in-council, 25*n*
order instrument, 432
ordinary fortitude, 88
ordinary resolutions, 628
Organisation for Economic Co-operation and Development (OECD), 71, 412, 722, 753, 772
organizations, 168–169
output restriction, 56
outside counsel, 9
outsourcing, 779–780
overholding tenants, 511
overperformance, 280–281
overrule, 24
ownership, 301–302, 590, 681

P

paid-up capital, 603
paralegals, 8
parallel pricing, 56
parol evidence rule, 221–224
partial discharge, 548
partial payment endorsement, 434
participating rights, 606
parties at a distance from each other, 135–136
Partnership Act, 565, 568, 569
partnership agreement, 569–570
partnership property, 568, 574
partnerships
 advantages, 565
 apparent partners, 571–572
 assignment, 576
 breach of trust, 573
 business nature of, 566–567
 conduct of the business, 575–576
 contractual liability, 570–572

 vs. corporations, 589–591
 creation of, 569–570
 defined, 565
 disadvantages, 565
 dissolution by law, 579
 duty not to compete, 577
 elements of, 566
 express provisions, 578
 fiduciary duties, 576–577
 financial arrangements, 574–575
 implied statutory rules, 578–579
 implied terms, 574–576
 income trusts, 584–585
 information, 576
 joint ventures, 583–584
 legal nature of, 568–569
 legal proceedings, 568–569
 legal risk management, 584–585
 legislation, 565
 liability of partners, 570–573
 limited liability partnerships, 581–583
 limited partnerships, 580–581
 membership, 576
 nature of, 565–569
 partnership property, 574
 profit motive, 567
 registration, 570
 relationship of, 566, 568, 573–577
 retirement from, 572
 secret benefits, 576–577
 termination, 578–580
 torts, 573
 writing requirement, 566, 569
part payment, 216
part performance, 211–212
party and party costs, 38
party autonomy, 740
par values, 603–604
passing-off, 83, 450–452, 758
passive legislation, 25
past consideration, 148
patent agents, 473
patent defects, 554
patents, 765–766
 abuse of patent rights, 474–475
 business methods, 470–471
 challenging, 474
 competition law, 475
 compulsory licences, 475
 vs. copyright, 469
 for copyright infringement, 469
 enforcing, 473–474
 ethics, 475
 ingenuity, 472
 international treaties, 469–470
 legislation, 469
 nature of, 470
 novelty, 472
 obtaining, 473
 patentable inventions, 470–472
 and the public interest, 474–475
 utility, 472

pawnbrokers, 337
pawns, 337
payday loans, 67, 201–202
payees, 426
pay equity, 408–409
payment, 309, 724
payment card networks, 751
payment in lieu of notice, 499
penalty clauses, 286
perfected security interest, 680–681
perfection, 678–679
performance
    and agency, 371
    duty of honesty, 280
    failure of, 279–281
    impossibility of, 278
    overperformance, 280–281
    specific performance, 291–292
    substantial performance, 280
performance requirements, 734
performances, 464
performance standards, 65–67
performers' performances, 464
periodic tenancy, 511, 522
personal defences, 438–439
personal health information, 784–785
Personal Health Information Protection Act, 784
personal information, 786
Personal Information Protection and Electronic Documents Act (PIPEDA), 405–406, 755, 766, 786–787, 791
personal insurance, 350
personal performance, 371
personal privacy, 777
personal property, 300, 671–676
Personal Property Security Act (PPSA), 684
petitions, 695
pharmacies, online, 276
PHIPA, 784
phishing, 768
PIPEDA, 405–406, 755, 766, 786–787, 791
pith and substance, 13
plain meaning of words, 219
plaintiff, 35
pleadings, 36
pledges, 337
policy concerns, 85
positive and unconditional acceptance, 132
possession
    delivering, of real estate, 557
    of goods, 310–311
    vs. ownership, 301–302
    vs. ownership, 681
postal rule, 135
postdated cheques, 429
power of attorney, 370
power of sale, 541

predatory pricing, 58
predictability of law, 23–24
pre-emptive rights, 606, 630–631
preferences, 702
preferred creditors, 705
preferred shareholders, 606
pre-incorporation contracts, 657–658
premiums, 349
prescriptions, 492–493
presentment, 430
presents, 436
pressure selling, 316–317
presumption of intent, 646–647
pre-trial procedure, 35–36
previously recognized relationship categories, 111
price fixing, 56
principals, 369, 372–373, 377–380
principled exception, 238
priority, 672, 684–685
priority of registration, 501
prior written contracts, 214
privacy
    access, 791–792
    accountability, 787
    accuracy, 791
    aspects of, 777
    and business, 779–780, 794
    Canadian Standards Association Model Code, 787–792
    challenging compliance, 792
    civil liability, 795–797
    codes of conduct, 797–798
    common law, 795
    consent, 781, 788–789
    of consumers, 794
    criminal liability, 797
    defined, 777
    in education, 785
    and electronic commerce, 766–768
    employees and employers, 405–406, 792–793
    government regulation of, 780–795
    government transparency and accountability, 782–783
    in healthcare, 784–785
    as human right, 777–778
    identifying purpose, 787–788
    invasion of privacy, 795
    legal risk management, 798
    legislation, 795
    limiting collection, 790
    limiting use, disclosure and retention, 790
    and municipalities, 784
    negligence, 796–797
    openness, 791
    of personal information, 777
    Privacy Act, 783
    in private sector, 786–792
    provincial variations, 784–785, 792
    in public sector, 781–782

    reasonable expectation of, 778
    safeguards, 791
    vs. security, 785
    specific stakeholders, 792–795
    statutory cause of action, 796
    and technology, 778–779
    torts, 795–796
privacy of personal information, 777
private companies, 600
private corporations, 627
private international law, 721
private law, 2, 720
private nuisance, 80
private sector, 786–792
privilege, 81, 118
privity of contract
    assignment. see assignment
    checklist, 240
    and consideration, 233
    defined, 233
    exceptions to, 236–238
    exemption clause, 235, 238
    express language in, 237–238
    insurance, 237
    international approaches, 239
    land contracts, 237
    principled exception, 238
    scope of contractual rights and duties, 233
    third parties, 233, 234–235
    tort liability, 234–235
    vs. tort rights and duties, 234
    trusts, 236–237
    undisclosed principal, 237
    vicarious performance, 234–235
privity of estate, 526
probate, 491
Probate Courts, 31
procedural irregularity, 53
procedural law, 22, 33–44
procedural unfairness, 53
process, 471
product defamation, 83
product liability, 90–92
product safety, 65–67
professional corporations, 602–603
professional liability
    cause of action, choosing, 107
    challenges, 102
    conflict of duty, 117–118
    contracts, 102
    duty of care, 109–112
    fiduciary duty, 103–104
    multi-disciplinary partnerships, 118–119
    professional organizations, role of, 115–118
    relationships, 102
    standard of care, 112–113
    tort liability, 105–106
professional organizations, 115–118
professional standards, 602

profit motive, 567
progressive discipline, 402
progress payments, 712
promise, 137
promisee, 137
promises
  betting debts, 172–173
  ethics, 148
  gratuitous promises, 146–147, 150
  guarantees, 210, 212
  of negotiable instruments, 426
  promise for an act, 137–138
  promise for a promise, 137
promisors, 137, 240, 243–244, 248–249, 428
promissory estoppel, 152, 154
promissory notes, 427–428, 432, 440
proof
  burden of, 200
  standard of, 36
proper law of the contract, 721–722
property
  defined, 484
  personal *vs.* real, 300
  real property, 484
  recovery of, 700
  tangible *vs.* intangible, 240, 300
property insurance, 350, 355
property rights, 240
proposals, 696–698
prospectus, 199, 652–653
protected geographical indications, 454
provincial court system, 31–32
Provincial Division, 31
provincial powers, 49
provision of services, 517
proxies, 629
proximity, 85, 110
proxy forms, 629
public accounting industry, 654
public corporations, 600, 652–655
public interest, 283, 655–656
public international law, 720
public law, 2, 720
public liability insurance, 352
publicly traded corporations, 612–613, 627
public nuisance, 79–80
public offerings, 613, 652–655
public policy
  and confidentiality clauses, 178
  and contracts, 170, 177
  defined, 77, 170
  and exemption clauses, 283
  and liability, 77–78
  statutes affecting, 172–173
punitive damages, 96, 288–289
purchase-money security interest (PMSI), 680
purchase options, 341
purchases leases, 338–339
purpose of collection, 781

Q

qualified privilege, 81
quantum meruit, 155, 293, 332
quasi-contracts, 280
quasi-criminal liability, 4
quiet enjoyment, 515–516
quiet possession, 342
quotas, 727

R

ratification, 375–377
ratify, 167
real action, 484
real defences, 439
real estate
  meaning of, 484
  typical real estate transaction, 551–558
reasonable expectation of privacy, 778
reasonable expectations, 226
reasonable notice, 398, 399
reasonable quality, 306
reasonable restraint, 181
reasonable scope, 180
reasonable time, 129–130, 437
rebut, 178
received, 136
receiving orders, 247
recognition disputes, 414
recovery, 359–360
recovery for goods and services, 214
recovery of money, 213–214
recovery of rent, 518–519
rectification, 192
redeem, 538, 674
registered agreements, 57
registered trademarks, 449, 452–456
registration
  of builders' liens, 711
  of corporate names, 598
  of domain names, 760
  of mortgages, 539
  of partnership, 570
  of security interests, 679, 681, 682
registration of interests in land
  claims not registered on title, 502–503
  electronic registration, 502
  first in time, 501
  land titles system, 501–502
  registry system, 501
  title insurance, 503–504
regulations, 12, 50
regulatory liability, 4
regulatory offences, 55, 646
reinstatement, 404–405
related party transactions, 624
relationship of master and servant, 394
reliance, 114–115
reliance damages, 288
remainder, 489
remainderman, 489
remedies
  aboriginal land claim, 488
  action for the price, 313
  appraisal remedy, 635
  in bailment, 332
  for breach of contract, 283, 291–293
  for breach of covenant, 493
  of the buyer, 315
  checklist, 293
  in contracts of sale, 311–314
  for corporate directors' liability, 626
  damages. *see* damages
  equitable remedies, 291–293, 315
  injunctions, 292
  of the landlord, 518–521
  liens, 311–312
  of mortgagee, 540–542
  oppression remedy, 636–638
  quantum meruit, 293
  repossession, 312, 319
  resale, 312
  rescission, 292–293
  retention of deposit, 313–314
  of the seller, 311–314, 319
  specific performance, 291–292
  of the tenant, 521
  in torts, 96–97
remote, 88
remote parties, 439
renewal, 523–524
renewals, 355
rent, 341, 512, 517–519, 529. *see also* landlord and tenant; leasing; tenancy
reorganizations, 654–655, 707–709
repossession, 312, 319, 673
representative action, 168
repudiate, 164
repudiation, 276–277, 314
request for goods or services, 155–156
requisitions, 553
resale, 312
rescind, 189
rescission, 190, 292–293, 315
reserve judgment, 37
residential leases, 211
residential tenancies, 509, 519, 528–531
residual policy considerations, 110–112
residual powers, 13
res judicata, 35
respondent, 29
responsible communication on matters of public interest, 82
restitution, 97, 281
restraint of trade, 178–182
restrictive covenant, 178
restrictive covenants, 178, 383–384, 493
restrictive endorsement, 433
resulting trusts, 236
résumés, 197–198
retail sales, 302
retain, 782
retainers, 9
retention of deposit, 313–314

reverse discrimination, 16
reverse mortgages, 549–550
reversion, 489
revocation, 130, 136
riders, 350
right of re-entry, 519
right of sale, 333
right of subrogation, 359
right of survivorship, 491
right-of-way, 492
rights. *see also* Charter of Rights and Freedoms
   agents, 377–380
   bailment, 333
   civil rights. *see* human rights
   contractual rights, 240
   cumulative rights, 606
   employee rights, 407–410, 711
   equality rights, 16
   guarantees, 363–364
   human rights, 14, 407–408, 777–778
   intellectual property rights, 384
   leasing, 343–344
   legal rights, 16
   lienholders' rights, 711–712
   participating rights, 606
   pre-emptive rights, 606
   of security holders, 605–606
   of strikers, 415
rights disputes, 414
right to associate, 387
right to be forgotten, 778
risk, 89
risk of loss before delivery, 309–310
Roman law, 22–23
royal charters, 595
royalties, 763
royalty payments, 460
rule of law, 2
rules of civil procedure, 33. *see also* civil law
run with the land, 493

S
safekeeping, 333–334
sale-and-leaseback, 340
sale by court, 541
sale by mortgagee, 541–542
sale by mortgagor, 543–544
sale by sample, 304
sale of goods, 199, 265–267, 315
Sale of Goods Act
   action for the price, 313
   application of, 299
   breach of a term, 314
   conditions, 302
   contracts of sale. *see* contracts of sale
   description, 303–304
   exemption clauses, 307–308, 319
   frustration situation, 265–267
   goods, 300–301
   history of, 299
   implied terms, 302–307
   ownership, 301–302
   passing of title, 311
   performance of contract, 315
   possession, 301–302
   quality, 304–306
   requirements of, 215–217
   sale by sample, 304
   seller's title, 303
   statutory protection for the buyer, 302–307
   suitability, 304–306
   terms in contracts, 302–310, 318–321
   title to goods, 310–311
   warranties, 302
   writing requirement, 215–216
sale or return, 311
sales. *see also* Sale of Goods Act
   vs. bailments, 328
   contracts of sale. *see* contracts of sale
sales tactics, 316–318
Sarbanes-Oxley Act, 612, 614
seals, 155–156
secondary market liability, 654
secured creditors, 546, 671–672
securities, 604–608
Securities and Exchange Commission, 612
securities commission, 650
securities industry, 651–652
securities legislation, 650–651
security. *see also* security interests
   for bank loans, 685–688
   collateral security, 671, 687
   meaning of, 671–672
   security practices, 671
security agreements
   conditional sales, 673–674
   consignments, 673
   credit devices, 673
   defined, 672
   floating charges, 675
   leases. *see* leases
   mortgages. *see* mortgages
   personal property security interests, 676
security entitlement, 607
security for costs, 739
security holders, 605–606
security interests, 671–672. *see also* security
   assignment of book debts, 683
   attachment, 678
   competing interests, 680–681
   creation of, 678
   effects on other creditors, 684–685
   effects on purchasers, 681–683
   ethics, 688
   exceptions for good faith buyers, 682
   in intangible property, 683
   investment property, 683
   legal risk management, 688
   legislation, 672–676, 676–681, 687–688
   non-consensual security interests, 671
   perfection, 678–679
   Personal Property Security Act (PPSA), 684
   possession *vs.* ownership, 681
   priority, 680–681, 684–685
   registration, 679, 681, 682
   security interest in personal property, 672–676
security leases, 339
self-imposed codes of conduct, 11
self-induced frustration, 263
seller's title, 303
senior officers, 659, 662–663
sentencing, 660
services, export and import of, 725
servient tenements, 492
serving, 35
set off, 245
setting aside a contract
   consumer protection, 201
   defined, 190
   duress, 202
   legal advice, importance of, 201
   misrepresentation, 196–199
   mistakes, 189–196
   undue influence, 199–201
   void and voidable contracts, 189–191
settlement out of court, 40–41
severance, 320, 491
severed, 170
sexual harassment, 408
sexual orientation, 19
sex worker industry, 20
share capital, 603
shareholders
   annual reports, 632
   appraisal remedy, 635
   auditors, 632–633
   class rights, 629
   common shareholders, 605
   derivative action, 635–636
   vs. directors, 613
   directors' duties to, 619–620
   dividends, 629–630
   documents of record, 632
   duties of, 633–634
   financial rights, 629–631
   financial statements, 631–632
   information, right to, 631–633
   inspector, appointment of, 633
   legal risk management, 639
   loans to, 649
   majority rule, 634–635
   meetings, 628–629
   minority shareholders, 634–638
   oppression remedy, 636–638
   pre-emptive rights, 630–631
   preferred shareholders, 606
   in private corporations, 627

proxies, 629
rights of, 605–606, 627–634
rights of second mortgagee, 639
role of, 626–627
shareholder agreements, 639
surplus, distribution of, 630
voting, 628–629
winding up, 636
shares
  vs. bonds, 605
  class rights, 605–606
  common shares, 604
  defined, 604
  dividends, 629–630
  no par value shares, 604
  par values, 603–604
  preferred shares, 604
shark fins, 50
shipment, 723
sight drafts, 427
signatures, 213
silence, 132, 198–199
slander, 81
Small Claims Court, 31
social media payment channels, 751
social regulation, 48
social responsibility, 655
Society for Composers and Music Publishers (SOCAN), 466
Society of Composers, Authors and Music Publishers of Canada (SOCAN), 764
sole proprietorships, 564–565
solicitor–client fees, 38
solicitor–client privilege, 8, 551
solicitors, 7
solvency test, 648
spam, 767–768
special Acts of Parliament, 595
special damages, 97
special endorsement, 433
special meetings, 628
special resolutions, 628
specifications, 473
specific goods, 311
specific land claims, 485
specific performance, 28, 291, 315
spouses, 200, 497n
stakeholders, 172, 646–647
standard form contracts, 127, 197, 221, 316
standard of care
  and bailment, 331
  defined, 86
  for professionals, 112–113
  proving breach of, 91–92
  and public policy, 172–173
  and torts, 86, 91–92, 112–113
standing, 34, 739
standing offers, 134
stare decisis, 24
stated capital account, 603

statement of adjustments, 555
statement of claim, 36
statements of defence, 36
statute barred, 268
Statute of Frauds
  consequences, 213–214
  contracts covered by, 209–212
  guarantees, 210
  history of, 209
  international trends, 215
  land, 210–211
  part performance, 211–212
  and Sale of Goods Acts, 218
  written memorandum, 212–213, 215
statutes. *see also* legislation
  agreement legal by statute, 173–174
  agreements illegal by statute, 174–175
  challenging, 18
  contracts affected by statute, 171–176
  defined, 11
  Freedom of Information and Protection of Privacy (FIPPA) statute, 785
  general incorporation statutes, 595–596
  interpretation, 26–27
  of limitation, 714
  wording of, 171
statutory assignment, 243
statutory damages, 469
statutory easements, 492
statutory interpretation, 26–27
statutory liability, 106–107
statutory reform, 265
stockbrokers, 369
stock exchange, 173
stop payments, 429
storage, 333–334
strict grammatical words, 219
strict liability, 76, 77, 97, 621–622
strikes, 411
student loans, 706
sub-bailees, 329
sub-bailment, 329, 341
subcontractors, 709–710
subject to the equities, 244, 431
subletting, 513–514
subordinate legislation, 25, 26
subrogation, 90, 359, 364
subsidiaries, 732
subsidiary, 423
subsidiary promises, 138
subsidies, 728
substance *vs.* form, 208
substantial performance, 280
substantive law, 22
substituted agreement, 256–257
Sui generis, 485
suing, 33–41
suitability and quality, 304–306
sum certain, 431
super-governmental organizations, 5, 720

Superior Trial Courts, 31
super priority, 703–704
Supreme Court, 14–15, 30, 32
surplus, distribution of, 630
surrender, 518, 522
Surrogate Courts, 31
surrounding contextual circumstances, 219
surveillance, 793
surveys, 502–503
systemically important banks, 423
systemic discrimination, 409
system of courts
  in Canada, 30–32
  Court of Appeal, 29–30
  courts of first instance, 29
  defined, 27
  in England, 29–30
  trial courts, 29
  in the U.S., 33
System of Electronic Disclosure by Insiders (SEDI), 654
System of Electronic Disclosure for Analysis and Retrieval (SEDAR), 653

T

takeover bid, 654
takeovers, 654
tangible personal property, 240, 241, 300
tariffs, 727–728
Tax Court of Canada, 32
taxes
  in arrears, 503
  and corporations, 591, 593
  on leased property, 517
technical protection measures (TPMs), 765
technological change, 478–480
technological protection measures (TPM), 459
technology, and privacy, 778–779
telecommunications, 463–464
telemarketing, 317–318
tenancy
  bankruptcy of tenant, 520–521
  classes of, 511–512
  commercial tenancies, 509
  eviction, 519, 529
  fixtures, 525
  forfeiture, 522
  injunctions, 520, 521
  landlord's mortgagee, 526
  leasebacks, 527
  legislation, 528–529
  month-to-month tenancy, 511
  notice to quit, 522–523, 529
  periodic tenancy, 511, 522
  privity of contract, 526
  privity of estate, 526
  quiet enjoyment, 515–516
  registration of, 526

tenancy *(continued)*
  remedies of tenant, 521
  renewal, 523–524
  residential tenancies, 509
  restrictions on use of premises, 514
  subletting, 513–514
  at sufferance, 511–512
  surrender, 522
  tenancy in common, 491
  tenant in possession after expiration of fixed term, 523
  term certain, 511
  termination of lease, 521
  termination of tenancy, 522–525, 529
  terms for notice, 523
  at will, 511
tenants, 489, 712
tenant's fixtures, 525
tender of performance, 255
tenders, inviting, 133
term, 509, 537
term certain, 511
termination
  of agency relationship, 383
  on death or insolvency, 578–579
  dismissal without notice, 400–403
  dissolution by law, 579
  of employment contract, 398–401
  express provisions, 578
  of a franchise, 383
  implied statutory rules, 578–579
  by notice or expiry, 578
  option to terminate, 259
  and partnership, 578–579
  of partnerships, 578–580
  wrongful dismissal, 403–406
term insurance, 350
term of policy, 349
territorial privacy, 777
terrorism, 425
testimony, conflicting, 220–221
theory of precedent, 24
thin skull doctrine, 88
third parties
  checklist, 240
  defined, 233
  and privity of contract, 233
  and trusts, 236–237
third-party liability, 106
threshold amounts, 216
tied selling, 58
time drafts, 427, 427f
title
  defined, 484
  to goods, 310–311
  passing of, 311
  verifying, 554–555
title fraud, 502
title insurance, 503–504
tobacco, 52, 93–94
tort liability

fraudulent misrepresentation, 108
negligent misrepresentation, 108
in professional liability, 105–106
tort of negligent misrepresentation, 102
torts
  agent's liability, 380
  and bailment, 330
  and business, 82–83
  causation of damage, 84–89
  and common law, 176
  vs. contracts, 196–197
  damage to the plaintiff, 87
  deceit, 108
  defined, 76
  duty of care, 84–85
  electronic commerce, 756–758
  fault, 76–77
  and insurance, 90
  intentional torts, 79–83, 108
  law, development of, 76
  liability, 76–78, 396–397, 573, 656
  negligence, 796–797
  occupier's liability, 94–95
  passing-off, 450–452
  privacy, invasion of, 795–796
  and privity of contract, 234–235
  product liability, 90–92
  professional liability. *see* professional liability
  remedies, 96–97
  remoteness of damage, 88–89
  standard of care, 86, 87, 89, 91
  tort liability. *see* tort liability
  trademarks, 450–452
  unintentional torts, 84–89
total costs of litigation, 38
trade fixtures, 525
trademarks
  assignment, 457–458
  business names, 450
  defined, 449
  and electronic commerce, 758–759, 761
  and franchising, 457–458
  and industrial designs, 476–477
  infringement actions, 456–457
  jurisdiction, 457
  legislation, 449, 453
  licensing, 457–458
  the mark, 453–455
  nature of, 449
  opposition proceedings, 455–456
  ownership and use, 455
  protection of, 450–452
  registration, 452–456
  remedies, 457
  unauthorized use, 456
Trade-marks Act, 449, 452
trade-related investment measures, 729
trade secrets, 477–478
transborder data flow, 779–780
transfer of ownership, 590

transfers, 499, 555, 606–607, 701–702
trans-pacific partnership, 732
transparency, 652
transportation
  and bailment, 334–335
  in import/export, 723
Travel Assurance Funds, 67
treaties, 484
treaty, 720
trespass, 79
trespassers, 95, 512
trial courts, 29, 31–32
trial procedure, 36–37
true leases, 338
trust agreements, 236
trust deeds, 675
trustees, 236
trustees in bankruptcy, 695, 700–703
trusts, 710
  vs. bailments, 328
  defined, 236
  and privity of contract, 236–237

U

ultra vires, 13, 591
unanimous shareholder agreements, 639
unascertained goods, 311
uncertainty in wording of an offer, 139
UNCITRAL, 722, 753
UNCITRAL model laws, 139, 694, 741, 772
unconscionable contracts, 201
unconscionable terms, 282
undervalue, 701–702
undisclosed principals, 237
undue influence, 199–201
unenforceable, 170
unenforceable contracts, 213
UNIDROIT, 722
unilateral contracts, 137–138
unilateral mistakes, 189, 191
unincorporated collectivity, 34
unintentional torts, 84–89
United Nations Commission on International Trade Law (UNCITRAL), 315, 722
United Nations Commission on International Trade Law (UNCITRAL) model laws, 139, 694, 741, 753, 772
United Nations Conference on Trade and Development (UNCTAD), 336
United Nations Convention on Contracts for the International Sale of Goods (CISG), 215
United Nations Convention on the Use of Electronic Communications in International Contracts, 139, 772
United Nations Framework Convention on Climate Change, 666
United Nations Global Compact, 412, 666

United States
  contingency fees, 39
  privity of contract, 239
  Restatements of Contracts, 278
  Sarbanes-Oxley Act, 612, 614
  system of courts, 33
unitholders, 584
unjust enrichment, 280
unlawful interference with economic relations, 82
unlawful means, 83
unlimited liability corporation, 595
unpaid sellers, 703–704
unperfected security interest, 680–681
unsecured creditors, 671–672
use, 786
USMCA, 720, 727–728, 731, 733, 741, 743–745
usual authority, 374–375
utility, 472
utmost good faith, 198, 357–358, 385

V

vicarious liability, 78
vicarious performance, 234–235
Virginia Tech Shooting, 785
void, 168, 170–171, 189
voidable, 189
voidable contracts, 166, 170–171
void and voidable contracts, 189–191

voluntary assumption of risk, 89
voluntary codes of conduct, 11
vulture funds, 709

W

wage earners, 704
wagers, 172
waiver of conditions, 553–554
waivers, 255–256, 387
warranties, 276, 302, 343
warranty of authority, 380
waste, 515
weapons in space, 735
websites, 751
web-wrap agreements, 754
whistle-blower retaliation, 660
willful invasion of privacy, 796
winding up, 636, 707–708
WIPO, 753, 765
without recourse, 433
words
  special usage of, 220
  used inadvertently, 191
workers' compensation, 78, 411–412
workforce analysis, 409
working conditions, 410–411
workplace safety, 650
works, 762
World Intellectual Property Organization (WIPO), 459, 469, 725, 753, 765

World Trade Organization (WTO), 728–730, 742, 753
writing requirement
  for assignment, 248
  consumer protection legislation, 217–218
  electronic contracts, 754
  electronic transmission, 212
  guarantees, 209–210, 212, 364
  interpretation of express terms, 219–221
  land, 210–211
  leases, 509
  leasing, 344
  legal risk management, 227
  legislation, 208–209
  for memorandum, 212–213
  negotiable instruments, 431
  parol evidence rule, 221–224
  for partnerships, 566, 569
  Sale of Goods Act, 215–216
  signatures, 212
writs, 35
written memorandum, 215
written offers, 127–129
written records, 208
wrongful detention, 314
wrongful dismissal, 289–290, 403–406
wrongful withholding, 314–315
WTO, 728–730, 742, 753